SIXTH CANADIAN EDITION

THE ECONOMICS OF MONEY, BANKING, AND FINANCIAL MARKETS

FREDERIC S. MISHKIN
Columbia University

APOSTOLOS SERLETIS
University of Calgary

PEARSON

Toronto

Editorial Director: Claudine O'Donnell
Acquisitions Editor: Megan Farrell
Marketing Manager: Loula March
Program Manager: Patricia Ciardullo
Project Manager: Richard di Santo
Manager of Content Development: Suzanne Schaan
Developmental Editor: Rebecca Ryoji
Production Services: Cenveo® Publisher Services
Permissions Project Manager: Joanne Tang
Photo Permissions Research: Lumina
Text Permissions Research: Lumina
Art Director: Alex Li
Interior and Cover Designer: Anthony Leung
Cover Image: Thep Urai/Shutterstock

Vice-President, Cross Media and Publishing Services: Gary Bennett

Credits and acknowledgments for material borrowed from other sources and reproduced, with permission, in this textbook appear on the appropriate page within the text.

Original edition published by Pearson Education, Inc., Upper Saddle River, New Jersey, USA. Copyright © 2016 Pearson Education, Inc. This edition is authorized for sale only in Canada.

If you purchased this book outside the United States or Canada, you should be aware that it has been imported without the approval of the publisher or the author.

3   16

Library and Archives Canada Cataloguing in Publication

Mishkin, Frederic S., author
        The economics of money, banking and financial markets / Frederic
S. Mishkin (Columbia University), Apostolos Serletis (University of
Calgary).—Six Canadian edition.

Includes bibliographical references and index.
ISBN 978-0-13-389738-8 (bound)

        1. Finance—Textbooks. 2. Money—Textbooks. 3. Banks and banking—
Textbooks. I. Serletis, Apostolos, 1954-, author II. Title.

HG173.M58 2015   332   C2015-906778-2

ISBN: 978-0-13-389738-8

To Aglaia

BRIEF CONTENTS

PART 1   INTRODUCTION   1

1   Why Study Money, Banking, and Financial Markets?........ 2
2   An Overview of the Financial System 22
3   What Is Money? 50

PART 2   FINANCIAL MARKETS   67

4   The Meaning of Interest Rates 68
5   The Behavior of Interest Rates 89
6   The Risk and Term Structure of Interest Rates............. 120
7   The Stock Market, the Theory of Rational
     Expectations, and the Efficient Market Hypothesis 147

PART 3   FINANCIAL INSTITUTIONS   169

8   An Economic Analysis of Financial Structure 170
9   Financial Crises 194
10   Economic Analysis of Financial Regulation 222
11   Banking Industry: Structure and Competition 245

**PART 4   THE MANAGEMENT OF FINANCIAL
            INSTITUTIONS   282**

12   Banking and the Management of Financial
     Institutions 283
13   Risk Management with Financial Derivatives 312

**PART 5   CENTRAL BANKING AND THE CONDUCT
            OF MONETARY POLICY   341**

14   Central Banks and the Bank of Canada 342
15   The Money Supply Process 365

16   Tools of Monetary Policy.. 390
17   The Conduct of Monetary Policy: Strategy
     and Tactics 430

**PART 6   INTERNATIONAL FINANCE
            AND MONETARY POLICY   459**

18   The Foreign Exchange Market.. 460
19   The International Financial System................................ 484

PART 7   MONETARY THEORY   512

20   Quantity Theory, Inflation, and the Demand
     for Money 513
21   The *IS* Curve 530
22   The Monetary Policy and Aggregate
     Demand Curves 550
23   Aggregate Demand and Supply Analysis 565
24   Monetary Policy Theory 607
25   The Role of Expectations in Monetary Policy................ 634
26   Transmission Mechanisms of Monetary Policy 653

CHAPTERS ON THE WEB

1   Financial Crises in Emerging Market Economies
2   The *ISLM* Model
3   Nonbank Finance

CONTENTS

PART 1 INTRODUCTION 1

CHAPTER 1
Why Study Money, Banking, and Financial Markets? 2
Why Study Financial Markets? 2
  The Bond Market and Interest Rates 3
  The Stock Market 3
Why Study Financial Institutions and Banking? 5
  Structure of the Financial System 5
  Banks and Other Financial Institutions 6
  Financial Innovation 6
  Financial Crises 7
Why Study Money and Monetary Policy? 7
  Money and Business Cycles 7
  Money and Inflation 8
  Money and Interest Rates 10
  Conduct of Monetary Policy 11
  Fiscal Policy and Monetary Policy 11
Why Study International Finance? 12
  The Foreign Exchange Market 12
  The International Financial System 13
How We Will Study Money, Banking, and
Financial Markets 14
  Exploring the Web 14
Concluding Remarks 15

Summary 15 • Key Terms 16 • Questions 16 •
Applied Problems 17 • Data Analysis Problems 17 •
Web Exercises 18 • Web References 18

APPENDIX TO CHAPTER 1
Defining Aggregate Output, Income, the Price Level, and the Inflation Rate 19
Aggregate Output and Income 19
Real Versus Nominal Magnitudes 19
Aggregate Price Level 20
Growth Rates and the Inflation Rate 21

CHAPTER 2
An Overview of the Financial System 22
Function of Financial Markets 22
Structure of Financial Markets 25
  Debt and Equity Markets 25
  Primary and Secondary Markets 25
  Exchanges and Over-the-Counter Markets 26
  Money and Capital Markets 26
Financial Market Instruments 27
  Money Market Instruments 27

Following the Financial News Money Market Rates 28
  Capital Market Instruments 29
Following the Financial News Capital Market Interest Rates 30
Internationalization of Financial Markets 32
  International Bond Market, Eurobonds, and Eurocurrencies 32
Global Are U.S. Capital Markets Losing Their Edge? 33
Following the Financial News Foreign Stock Market Indexes 34
  World Stock Markets 34
Global The Importance of Financial Intermediaries Relative
to Securities Markets: An International Comparison 35
Function of Financial Intermediaries: Indirect Finance 35
  Transaction Costs 36
  Risk Sharing 36
  Asymmetric Information: Adverse Selection and
  Moral Hazard 37
  Economies of Scope and Conflicts of Interest 38
Types of Financial Intermediaries 39
  Depository Institutions 40
  Contractual Savings Institutions 41
  Investment Intermediaries 42
Regulation of the Financial System 43
  Increasing Information Available to Investors 43
  Ensuring the Soundness of Financial Intermediaries 44
  Financial Regulation Abroad 45

Summary 46 • Key Terms 46 • Questions 47 •
Applied Problems 48 • Data Analysis Problems 48 •
Web Exercises 49 • Web References 49

CHAPTER 3
What Is Money? 50
Meaning of Money 50
Functions of Money 51
  Medium of Exchange 51
  Unit of Account 52
FYI Money in a Prisoner-of-War Camp and Modern Prisons 52
  Store of Value 53
Evolution of the Payments System 54
  Commodity Money 54
  Fiat Money 55
  Cheques 55
  Electronic Payment 56
  E-Money 56
FYI Are We Headed for a Cashless Society? 57
APPLICATION Will Bitcoin Become the Money
of the Future? 57

Measuring Money **58**

The Bank of Canada's Monetary Aggregates 58

FYI Where Are All the Dollars? 62

Money as a Weighted Aggregate 62

Summary 64 • Key Terms 64 • Questions 64 •
Applied Problems 66 • Data Analysis Problems 66 •
Web Exercises 66 • Web References 66

PART 2 FINANCIAL MARKETS 67

CHAPTER 4
The Meaning of Interest Rates 68

Measuring Interest Rates **68**

Present Value 69

APPLICATION Simple Present Value 70

APPLICATION How Much Is That Jackpot Worth? 71

Four Types of Credit Market Instruments 71
Yield to Maturity 72

APPLICATION Yield to Maturity on a Simple Loan 72

APPLICATION Yield to Maturity and the Yearly Payment
on a Fixed-Payment Loan 74

APPLICATION Yield to Maturity and Bond Price
for a Coupon Bond 75

APPLICATION Yield to Maturity on a Perpetuity 77

APPLICATION Yield to Maturity on a Discount Bond 78

**The Distinction Between Interest Rates and
Returns** **79**

Maturity and the Volatility of Bond Returns:
Interest-Rate Risk 82
Summary 83

**The Distinction Between Real and Nominal
Interest Rates** **83**

APPLICATION Calculating Real Interest Rates 84

Summary 86 • Key Terms 86 • Questions 86 •
Applied Problems 87 • Data Analysis Problems 88 •
Web Exercises 88 • Web References 88

CHAPTER 4 WEB APPENDIX
Measuring Interest-Rate Risk: Duration
Go to MyEconLab at www.myeconlab.com

CHAPTER 5
The Behaviour of Interest Rates 89

Determinants of Asset Demand **89**

Wealth 90

Expected Returns 90
Risk 90
Liquidity 91
Theory of Portfolio Choice 91

Supply and Demand In the Bond Market **92**

Demand Curve 92
Supply Curve 93
Market Equilibrium 94
Supply and Demand Analysis 95

Changes in Equilibrium Interest Rates **95**

Shifts in the Demand for Bonds 96
Shifts in the Supply of Bonds 99

APPLICATION Changes in the Interest Rate Due to
Expected Inflation: The Fisher Effect 101

APPLICATION Changes in the Interest Rate Due
to a Business Cycle Expansion 103

APPLICATION Explaining Low Japanese Interest Rates 104

**Supply and Demand in the Market for Money:
The Liquidity Preference Framework** **105**

**Changes in Equilibrium Interest Rates in the
Liquidity Preference Framework** **108**

Shifts in the Demand for Money 108
Shifts in the Supply of Money 108

APPLICATION Changes in the Equilibrium Interest
Rate Due to Changes in Income, the Price Level,
or the Money Supply 108

Changes in Income 109
Changes in the Price Level 110
Changes in the Money Supply 110

APPLICATION Money and Interest Rates 111

**Does a Higher Rate of Growth of the Money
Supply Lower Interest Rates?** **113**

Summary 116 • Key Terms 116 • Questions 116 •
Applied Problems 117 • Data Analysis Problems 118 •
Web Exercises 119 • Web References 119

CHAPTER 5 WEB APPENDIX 1
Models of Asset Pricing
Go to MyEconLab at www.myeconlab.com

CHAPTER 5 WEB APPENDIX 2
Applying the Asset Market Approach to a Commodity Market: The Case of Gold
Go to MyEconLab at www.myeconlab.com

CHAPTER 5 WEB APPENDIX 3
LOANABLE FUNDS FRAMEWORK
Go to MyEconLab at www.myeconlab.com

CHAPTER 6
The Risk and Term Structure of Interest Rates 120

Risk Structure of Interest Rates **120**
Default Risk 120

FYI Conflicts of Interest at Credit-Rating Agencies and the Global Financial Crisis   124

APPLICATION The Global Financial Crisis and the BBB-Treasury Spread in the United States 124
Liquidity 125
Income Tax Considerations 125

APPLICATION Tax-Exempt Versus Taxable Bonds 126
Summary 126

Term Structure of Interest Rates **126**

Following the Financial News Yield Curves   128

Expectations Theory 128

APPLICATION Expectations Theory and the Yield Curve 130
Segmented Markets Theory 132
Liquidity Premium and Preferred Habitat Theories 133

APPLICATION Liquidity Premium Theory and the Yield Curve 135
Evidence on the Term Structure 136
Summary 137

FYI The Yield Curve as a Forecasting Tool for Inflation and the Business Cycle   138

APPLICATION Interpreting Yield Curves, 1986–2014 138

APPLICATION Using the Term Structure to Forecast Interest Rates 139

APPLICATION Forward Rate 141

Summary 142 • Key Terms 143 • Questions 143 •
Applied Problems 144 • Data Analysis Problems 145 •
Web Exercises 146 • Web References 146

CHAPTER 7
The Stock Market, the Theory of Rational Expectations, and the Efficient Market Hypothesis 147

Computing the Price of Common Stock **147**
The One-Period Valuation Model 148
The Generalized Dividend Valuation Model 149
The Gordon Growth Model 149

How the Market Sets Stock Prices **150**

APPLICATION Monetary Policy and Stock Prices 152

APPLICATION The Global Financial Crisis and the Stock Market 152

The Theory of Rational Expectations **152**

Formal Statement of the Theory 154
Rationale Behind the Theory 154
Implications of the Theory 155

The Efficient Market Hypothesis: Rational Expectations in Financial Markets **156**
Rationale Behind the Hypothesis 157
Random-Walk Behaviour of Stock Prices 158

Global Should Foreign Exchange Rates Follow a Random Walk?   159

APPLICATION Practical Guide to Investing in the Stock Market 159
How Valuable Are Reports Published by Investment Advisers? 159

FYI Should You Hire an Ape as Your Investment Adviser?   160

Should You Be Skeptical of Hot Tips? 161
Do Stock Prices Always Rise When There is Good News? 161
Efficient Market Prescription for the Investor 161

Why the Efficient Market Hypothesis Does Not Imply that Financial Markets are Efficient **162**

APPLICATION What Do Stock Market Crashes Tell Us About the Efficient Market Hypothesis and the Efficiency of Financial Markets? 163

Behavioural Finance **164**

Summary 165 • Key Terms 165 • Questions 166 •
Applied Problems 167 • Data Analysis Problems 167 •
Web Exercises 167 • Web References 168

CHAPTER 7 WEB APPENDIX
Evidence on the Efficient Market Hypothesis
Go to MyEconLab at www.myeconlab.com

PART 3   FINANCIAL INSTITUTIONS   169

CHAPTER 8
An Economic Analysis of Financial Structure 170

Basic Facts About Financial Structure Throughout the World **170**

Transaction Costs **173**
How Transaction Costs Influence Financial Structure 173
How Financial Intermediaries Reduce Transaction Costs 174

Asymmetric Information: Adverse Selection and Moral Hazard **175**

The Lemons Problem: How Adverse Selection Influences Financial Structure **175**
Lemons in the Stock and Bond Markets 176
Tools to Help Solve Adverse Selection Problems 176

FYI The Enron Implosion   178

How Moral Hazard Affects the Choice Between Debt and Equity Contracts..................................... **181**
Moral Hazard in Equity Contracts:
The Principal–Agent Problem 181
Tools to Help Solve the Principal–Agent Problem 182

How Moral Hazard Influences Financial Structure in Debt Markets **184**
Tools to Help Solve Moral Hazard in Debt Contracts............. 184
Summary 186

APPLICATION Financial Development and Economic Growth 187

FYI The Tyranny of Collateral   188

APPLICATION Is China a Counterexample to the Importance of Financial Development? 189

Summary 190 • Key Terms 191 • Questions 191 • Applied Problems 192 • Data Analysis Problems 193 • Web Exercises 193 • Web References 193

CHAPTER 9
Financial Crises   194
What Is A Financial Crisis?.. **195**
Dynamics of Financial Crises... **195**
Stage One: Initial Phase 195
Stage Two: Banking Crisis 197
Stage Three: Debt Deflation 198

APPLICATION The Mother of All Financial Crises: The Great Depression in the United States........................... 199
Stock Market Crash 199
Bank Panics 199
Continuing Decline in Stock Prices.................................. 200
Debt Deflation 201
International Dimensions... 201

The Global Financial Crisis of 2007–2009 .... **201**
Causes of the 2007–2009 Financial Crisis 201

FYI Collateralized Debt Obligations (CDOs)   202

Effects of the 2007–2009 Financial Crisis......................... 203

FYI Was the Fed to Blame for the Housing Price Bubble?   205

Global The European Sovereign Debt Crisis   207

Height of the 2007–2009 Financial Crisis.......................... 208
Government Intervention and the Recovery......................... 208

Global Worldwide Government Bailouts During the 2007–2009 Financial Crisis   210

Canada and the 2007–2009 Financial Crisis...................... **210**
Subprime Mortgages in Canada 210

FYI Canada's Asset-Backed Commercial Paper Crisis   211

Why was Canada Spared the Worst of the Financial Crisis? 212

Response of Financial Regulation **213**
Macroprudential Versus Microprudential Supervision.. 213
Dodd-Frank Wall Street Reform and Consumer Protection Act of 2010... 214

Too-Big-To-Fail and Future Regulation.............................. **216**
What Can Be Done About the Too-Big-to-Fail Problem?.. 216
Other Issues for Future Regulation 217

Summary 218 • Key Terms 219 • Questions 219 • Data Analysis Problems 220 • Web Exercises 220 • Web References 221

CHAPTER 10
Economic Analysis of Financial Regulation   222
Asymmetric Information and the Government Safety Net **222**
Bank Panics and the Need for Deposit Insurance 222

Global The Spread of Government Deposit Insurance Throughout the World: Is It a Good Thing?   224

Other Forms of the Government Safety Net......................... 224
Moral Hazard and the Government Safety Net...................... 225
Adverse Selection and the Government Safety Net................ 225
"Too Big to Fail" 225
Financial Consolidation and the Government Safety Net... 226

Types of Financial Regulation **226**
Restrictions on Asset Holdings 226
Capital Requirements.. 227
Prompt Corrective Action 228
Financial Supervision: Chartering and Examination 228

Global Where Is the Basel Accord Heading After the Global Financial Crisis?   229

Assessment of Risk Management....................................... 230
Disclosure Requirements 231
Consumer Protection 232
Restrictions on Competition 232

FYI Mark-to-Market Accounting and the Global Financial Crisis   233

Summary... 233

Global International Financial Regulation   234

CDIC Deposit Insurance Coverage **237**
Differential Premiums 237
Opting Out... 238

APPLICATION Evaluating CDIC Deposit Insurance Coverage and Other Proposed Reforms of the Banking Regulatory System 239

Limits on the Scope of Deposit Insurance **239**

Prompt Corrective Action... **239**

Risk-Based Insurance Premiums... **240**

Other CDIC Provisions **240**

Other Proposed Changes in Banking Regulations **241**
Regulatory Consolidation.. 241

Overall Evaluation.. **241**

Summary 241 • Key Terms 242 • Questions 242 •
Applied Problems 243 • Data Analysis Problems 243 •
Web Exercises 244 • Web References 244

CHAPTER 10 WEB APPENDIX 1
The 1980s Canadian Banking Crisis
Go to MyEconLab at www.myeconlab.com

CHAPTER 10 WEB APPENDIX 2
Banking Crises Throughout the World
Go to MyEconLab at www.myeconlab.com

CHAPTER 11
Banking Industry: Structure and Competition   245

**Historical Development of the Canadian
Banking System** **246**

FYI The Dual Banking System in the United States   247

The Free Banking Experiment 247
The Provincial Notes Act, 1866 248
The Dominion Notes Act, 1870 248
The First Bank Act, 1871... 249
The Bank Act, 1881–1913.. 249
The Finance Act, 1914.. 250

**Financial Innovation and the Growth of the
"Shadow Banking System"** **251**
Responses to Changes in Demand Conditions:
Interest-Rate Volatility.. 251
Responses to Changes in Supply Conditions:
Information Technology... 252

Global Will "Clicks" Dominate "Bricks" in the
Banking Industry?   254

Securitization and the Shadow Banking System 255
Avoidance of Existing Regulations.. 257

FYI Bruce Bent and the Money Market
Mutual Fund Panic of 2008   258

Financial Innovation and the Decline of
Traditional Banking.. 259

**Structure of the Canadian Chartered
Banking Industry**.. **261**
Schedule I, Schedule II, and Schedule III Banks 261
Competition and Technology.. 262

Comparison with the United States....................................... **263**

Response on Branching.. 264
Response to Branching Restrictions.. 265

Competition Across All Four Pillars **266**
Convergence... 266
Implications for Financial Consolidation 267
Separation of Banking and Other Financial
Services Industries Throughout the World.............................. 267

FYI The Global Financial Crisis and the Demise of Large,
Free-Standing Investment Banks   268

The Near Banks: Regulation and Structure **268**
Trust Companies.. 268
Loan Companies... 269
Cooperatives: Credit Unions and *Caisses Populaires* 269
Government Savings Institutions 271

International Banking... **271**
Eurocurrencies Market... 271

Global Ironic Birth of the Eurodollar Market   272

Canadian Banking Overseas.. 273
Foreign Banks in Canada 273

The 2001 Bank Act Reform.. **275**
Bank Holding Companies... 275
Permitted Investments 276
Ownership Rules 276
The CP Act and Access to the Payments and
Clearance System... 277
Merger Review Policy... 277
The National Financial Services OmbudService.................... 278
Implications for the Canadian Banking Industry.................... 278

Summary 279 • Key Terms 279 • Questions 280 •
Data Analysis Problems 280 • Web Exercises 281 •
Web References 281

PART 4   THE MANAGEMENT OF FINANCIAL INSTITUTIONS   282

CHAPTER 12
Banking and the Management of Financial Institutions   283

The Bank Balance Sheet **283**
Liabilities... 283
Assets 285

Basic Banking **287**

General Principles of Bank Management............................... **290**
Liquidity Management and the Role of Reserves 290
Asset Management.. 293
Liability Management 294
Capital Adequacy Management... 295

APPLICATION Strategies for Managing Bank Capital 297

APPLICATION How a Capital Crunch Caused a Credit Crunch
During the Global Financial Crisis 298

Managing Credit Risk..**298**
Screening and Monitoring.......................................299
Long-Term Customer Relationships 300
Loan Commitments 301
Collateral and Compensating Balances.....................301
Credit Rationing 302
Managing Interest-Rate Risk..**302**
Gap and Duration Analysis 303

APPLICATION Strategies for Managing Interest-Rate Risk.....304
Off-Balance-Sheet Activities **305**
Loan Sales...305
Generation of Fee Income.......................................305
Trading Activities and Risk Management Techniques 306

Global Barings, Daiwa, Sumitomo, Société Générale, and JP Morgan Chase: Rogue Traders and the Principal–Agent Problem 307

Summary 308 • Key Terms 309 • Questions 309 • Applied Problems 310 • Data Analysis Problems 311 • Web Exercises 311 • Web References 311

CHAPTER 12 WEB APPENDIX 1
Duration Gap Analysis
Go to MyEconLab at www.myeconlab.com

CHAPTER 12 WEB APPENDIX 2
Measuring Bank Performance
Go to MyEconLab at www.myeconlab.com

CHAPTER 13
Risk Management with Financial Derivatives   312

Hedging **312**
Forward Contracts and Markets **313**
Interest-Rate Forward Contracts.................................313

APPLICATION Hedging with Interest-Rate Forward Contracts..313
Pros and Cons of Forward Contracts 314
Financial Futures Contracts and Markets...........................**315**
Interest-Rate Futures Contracts.................................315

APPLICATION Hedging with Interest-Rate Futures 316
Organization of Trading in Financial Futures Markets...........317
The Globalization of Financial Futures Markets....................318
Explaining the Success of Futures Markets 319

APPLICATION Hedging Foreign Exchange Risk...................320
Hedging Foreign Exchange Risk with Forward Contracts 321
Hedging Foreign Exchange Risk with Futures Contracts.......321
Stock Index Futures **322**
Stock Index Futures Contracts.................................322

APPLICATION Hedging with Stock Index Futures 323
Options...**323**

Stock Options..324
Futures Options...327

APPLICATION Hedging with Futures Options 329
Factors Affecting the Prices of Option Premiums 331
Summary 332
Swaps...**332**
Interest-Rate Swap Contracts.................................332

APPLICATION Hedging with Interest-Rate Swaps.................333
Advantages of Interest-Rate Swaps 334
Disadvantages of Interest-Rate Swaps.........................334
Financial Intermediaries in Interest-Rate Swaps 334
Credit Derivatives **335**
Credit Options..335
Credit Swaps...336
Credit-Linked Notes 336

APPLICATION Lessons from the Global Financial Crisis: When Are Financial Derivatives Likely to Be a Worldwide Time Bomb? 336

Summary 338 • Key Terms 338 • Questions 339 • Applied Problems 339 • Data Analysis Problems 340 • Web Exercises 340 • Web References 340

PART 5   CENTRAL BANKING AND THE CONDUCT OF MONETARY POLICY   341

CHAPTER 14
Central Banks and the Bank of Canada   342

Origins of the Bank of Canada...**342**

Global Establishment of Selected Central Banks 343

Formal Structure of the Bank of Canada **343**
The Functions of the Bank of Canada **344**

FYI The Political Environment and the Bank of Canada 344

Currency 345
Funds Management 345
Financial System...345
Monetary Policy..346

FYI Role of the Bank's Research Staff 347

How Independent Is the Bank of Canada? **347**
The Changing Face of the Bank of Canada..........................**349**
From Opaqueness to Accountability and Transparency 351
Should the Bank of Canada Be Independent? **352**
The Case for Independence 352

FYI Economics and Politics 353

The Case Against Independence 353

Central Bank Independence and Macroeconomic
Performance Throughout the World 354

Explaining Central Bank Behaviour 354

Structure and Independence of Foreign Central Banks 355
Federal Reserve System 355

FYI The Special Role of the Federal Reserve Bank of
New York   358

European Central Bank 359
Bank of England 361
Bank of Japan 361
The Trend Toward Greater Independence 362

Summary 362   •   Key Terms 363   •   Questions 363   •
Data Analysis Problems 364   •   Web Exercises 364   •
Web References 364

CHAPTER 15
The Money Supply Process   365

Three Players in the Money Supply Process 365

The Bank of Canada's Balance Sheet 366
Liabilities 366
Assets 367

Control of the Monetary Base 368
Bank of Canada Open Market Operations 368
Shifts from Deposits into Currency 370
Loans to Financial Institutions 370
Other Factors That Affect the Monetary Base 371
Overview of the Bank of Canada's Ability to
Control the Monetary Base 372

Multiple Deposit Creation: A Simple Model 372
Deposit Creation: The Single Bank 372
Deposit Creation: The Banking System 374
Deriving the Formula for Multiple Deposit Creation 376
Critique of the Simple Model 378

Factors That Determine the Money Supply 378
Changes in the Nonborrowed Monetary Base, MB_n 378
Changes in Borrowed Reserves, BR, from the
Bank of Canada 379
Changes in the Desired Reserve Ratio, r_d 379
Changes in Excess Reserves 379
Changes in Currency Holdings 379

Overview of the Money Supply Process 379

The Money Multiplier 380
Deriving the Money Multiplier 380
Intuition Behind the Money Multiplier 382

FYI The 2007–2009 Financial Crisis and the Money
Multiplier in the United States   383

Money Supply Response to Changes in the Factors 383

APPLICATION Quantitative Easing and the Money Supply,
2007–2014 384

Summary 386   •   Key Terms 387   •   Questions 387   •
Applied Problems 388   •   Data Analysis Problems 388   •
Web Exercises 389   •   Web References 389

CHAPTER 15 WEB APPENDIX 1
The Bank of Canada's Balance Sheet and the Monetary Base
Go to MyEconLab at www.myeconlab.com

CHAPTER 15 WEB APPENDIX 2
The M2+ Money Multiplier
Go to MyEconLab at www.myeconlab.com

CHAPTER 15 WEB APPENDIX 3
**The Great Depression Bank Panics, 1930–1933,
and the Money Supply in the United States**
Go to MyEconLab at www.myeconlab.com

CHAPTER 16
Tools of Monetary Policy   390

**The Framework for the Implementation of
Monetary Policy** 390
The Large Value Transfer System (LVTS) 391
Non-LVTS (ACSS) Transactions 392
The Bank of Canada's Policy Rate 392
The Operating Band for the Overnight Interest Rate 393

FYI Monetary Policy Implementation in the
LVTS Environment   394

The Bank of Canada's Standing Facilities 395
The Bank of Canada's Implementation of the
Operating Band for the Overnight Interest Rate 395

**The Market for Settlement Balances and the
Channel/Corridor System for Setting the Overnight
Interest Rate** 396
Demand and Supply in the Market for Reserves 396
Demand Curve 396
Supply Curve 397
Market Equilibrium 398

APPLICATION How the Bank of Canada's Operating
Procedures Limit Fluctuations in the Overnight
Interest Rate 398

The Bank of Canada's Approach to Monetary Policy 399

FYI Price-Level Targeting Versus Inflation-Rate Targeting   399

How Monetary Policy Affects the Economy 400
Nominal Interest Rates and Monetary Policy 402

Conventional Monetary Policy Tools 403
Open Market Operations 404
Settlement Balances Management 406

APPLICATION Monetary Control in the
Channel/Corridor System 409
Bank of Canada Lending 410
Operation of the Standing Lending Facility 410

FYI Emergency Lending Assistance to Troubled Banks   413

Nonconventional Monetary Policy Tools During the Global Financial Crisis **413**
Liquidity Provision 414
Large-Scale Asset Purchases 414

FYI Quantitative Easing in the Channel/Corridor System   416

Quantitative Easing Versus Credit Easing.............. 416
Forward Guidance and the Commitment to
Future Policy Actions.. 418
Summary.. 419
Policy Tools of the Federal Reserve....................... 419
Open Market Operations 421
Discount Lending 422
Monetary Policy Tools of the European
Central Bank... 425

Summary 426 • Key Terms 427 • Questions 427 •
Applied Problems 428 • Data Analysis Problems 429 •
Web Exercises 429 • Web References 429

CHAPTER 17
The Conduct of Monetary Policy: Strategy and Tactics   430

The Price Stability Goal and the Nominal Anchor **430**
The Role of a Nominal Anchor................................ 431
The Time-Inconsistency Problem........................... 431
Other Goals of Monetary Policy.................................... **432**
High Employment and Output Stability 432
Economic Growth.. 433
Stability of Financial Markets................................. 433
Interest-Rate Stability 433
Stability in Foreign Exchange Markets 434
Should Price Stability Be the Primary Goal of Monetary Policy? **434**
Hierarchical Versus Dual Mandates...................... 434
Price Stability as the Primary Long-Run Goal of
Monetary Policy.. 435
Inflation Targeting.. **435**
Inflation Targeting in New Zealand, Canada,
and the United Kingdom 436

Global The European Central Bank's Monetary Policy Strategy   438

Advantages of Inflation Targeting.......................... 439
Disadvantages of Inflation Targeting 440
Lessons for Monetary Policy Strategy from the Global Financial Crisis **442**
Implications for Inflation Targeting....................... 443
Should Central Banks Try to Stop Asset-Price Bubbles?........ **444**
Two Types of Asset-Price Bubbles.......................... 444
The Debate over Whether Central Banks
Should Try to Pop Bubbles..................................... 445
Tactics: Choosing the Policy Instrument **448**
Criteria for Choosing the Policy Instrument.......... 451
Tactics: The Taylor Rule **452**

FYI The Bank of Canada's Use of the Taylor Rule   454
FYI Bank of Canada Watchers   454

Summary 455 • Key Terms 455 • Questions 456 •
Applied Problems 457 • Data Analysis Problems 457 •
Web Exercises 458 • Web References 458

CHAPTER 17 WEB APPENDIX 1
Monetary Targeting
Go to MyEconLab at www.myeconlab.com

CHAPTER 17 WEB APPENDIX 2
A Brief History of Bank of Canada Policymaking
Go to MyEconLab at www.myeconlab.com

PART 6   INTERNATIONAL FINANCE AND MONETARY POLICY   459

CHAPTER 18
The Foreign Exchange Market   460
Foreign Exchange Market.. **460**
What Are Foreign Exchange Rates?........................ 461

Financial News Foreign Exchange Rates   462

Why Are Exchange Rates Important? 462
How Is Foreign Exchange Traded?.......................... 463
Exchange Rates in the Long Run **463**
Law of One Price 463
Theory of Purchasing Power Parity 464
Why the Theory of Purchasing Power Parity Cannot
Fully Explain Exchange Rates 464
Factors That Affect Exchange Rates in the Long Run 465
Exchange Rates in the Short Run: A Supply and Demand Analysis **467**
Supply Curve for Domestic Assets 467
Demand Curve for Domestic Assets 467
Equilibrium in the Foreign Exchange Market........ 468
Explaining Changes in Exchange Rates **469**
Shifts in the Demand for Domestic Assets............. 469
Recap: Factors That Change the Exchange Rate 472

APPLICATION Effects of Changes in Interest Rates
on the Equilibrium Exchange Rate 474

APPLICATION Why Are Exchange Rates So Volatile?........... 476

APPLICATION The Global Financial Crisis
and the U.S. Dollar... 476

Summary 477 • Key Terms 477 • Questions 478 •
Applied Problems 478 • Data Analysis Problems 479 •
Web Exercises 479 • Web References 480

APPENDIX TO CHAPTER 18
The Interest Parity Condition **481**

**Comparing Expected Returns on Domestic
and Foreign Assets**.. **481**

Interest Parity Condition.. **483**

CHAPTER 19
The International Financial System **484**

Intervention in the Foreign Exchange Market...................... **484**
Foreign Exchange Intervention and the Money Supply 484
Unsterilized Intervention 486
Sterilized Intervention 487

Balance of Payments... **488**

Global Why the Large U.S. Current Account Deficit Worries
Economists 488

**Exchange Rate Regimes in the International
Financial System** **489**
Gold Standard 490
The Bretton Woods System 490
How a Fixed Exchange Rate Regime Works 491
Speculative Attacks 492

APPLICATION The Foreign Exchange Crisis of
September 1992.. 493
The Policy Trilemma 494

APPLICATION How Did China Accumulate $4 Trillion
of International Reserves? 496

Global Will the Euro Survive? 497

Monetary Unions.. 497
Managed Float 497

Capital Controls **498**
Controls on Capital Outflows... 498
Controls on Capital Inflows.. 498

The Role of the IMF.. **499**
Should the IMF Act as an International Lender of
Last Resort?.. 499

International Considerations and Monetary Policy **500**
Direct Effects of the Foreign Exchange Market on
Monetary Policy.. 500
Balance-of-Payments Considerations.................................... 501
Exchange Rate Considerations 501

**To Peg or not to Peg: Exchange-Rate Targeting as an
Alternative Monetary Policy Strategy** **501**
Advantages of Exchange-Rate Targeting 502
Disadvantages of Exchange-Rate Targeting........................... 502
When Is Exchange-Rate Targeting Desirable for
Industrialized Countries?.. 504
When Is Exchange-Rate Targeting Desirable for
Emerging Market Countries? 505
Currency Boards... 505

Global Argentina's Currency Board 506

Dollarization.. 507

Summary 507 • Key Terms 508 • Questions 509 •
Applied Problems 510 • Data Analysis Problems 510 •
Web Exercises 511 • Web References 511

PART 7   MONETARY THEORY   512

CHAPTER 20
Quantity Theory, Inflation, and the Demand
for Money **513**

Quantity Theory of Money **513**
Velocity of Money and Equation of Exchange 513
From the Equation of Exchange to the Quantity
Theory of Money 515
Quantity Theory and the Price Level..................................... 515
Quantity Theory and Inflation.. 516

APPLICATION Testing the Quantity Theory
of Money 516

Budget Deficits and Inflation..................................... **519**
Government Budget Constraint 519
Hyperinflation.. 520

APPLICATION The Zimbabwean Hyperinflation.................... 520

Keynesian Theories of Money Demand **521**
Transactions Motive 521
Precautionary Motive 521
Speculative Motive.. 522
Putting the Three Motives Together 522

Portfolio Theories of Money Demand.................................. **523**
Theory of Portfolio Choice and Keynesian
Liquidity Preference.. 523
Other Factors That Affect the Demand for Money................. 523
Summary.. 524

Empirical Evidence for the Demand for Money **524**
Interest Rates and Money Demand.. 525
Stability of Money Demand 525

Summary 526 • Key Terms 526 • Questions 527 •
Applied Problems 528 • Data Analysis Problems 528 •
Web Exercises 529 • Web References 529

CHAPTER 20 WEB APPENDIX 1
The Baumol-Tobin and the Tobin Mean-Variance Models
of the Demand for Money

Go to MyEconLab at **www.myeconlab.com**

CHAPTER 20 WEB APPENDIX 2
Empirical Evidence on the Demand for Money

Go to MyEconLab at **www.myeconlab.com**

CHAPTER 21
The *IS* Curve   530

Planned Expenditure and Aggregate Demand 530
The Components of Aggregate Demand 531
  Consumption Expenditure 531

FYI Meaning of the Word *Investment*   532

  Planned Investment Spending 532
  Net Exports 534
  Government Purchases and Taxes 535
Goods Market Equilibrium 536
  Solving for Goods Market Equilibrium 536
  Deriving the *IS* Curve 537
Understanding the *IS* Curve 537
  What the *IS* Curve Tells Us: Intuition 537
  What the *IS* Curve Tells Us: Numerical Example 537
  Why the Economy Heads Toward Equilibrium 539
Factors that Shift the *IS* Curve 539
  Changes in Government Purchases 539

APPLICATION The Vietnam War Buildup, 1964–1969 540
  Changes in Taxes 541

APPLICATION The Fiscal Stimulus
Package of 2009 543
  Changes in Autonomous Spending 543
  Changes in Financial Frictions 545
  Summary of Factors That Shift the *IS* Curve 545

Summary 545 • Key Terms 546 • Questions 546 •
Applied Problems 547 • Data Analysis Problems 548 •
Web Exercises 549 • Web References 549

CHAPTER 22
The Monetary Policy and Aggregate Demand Curves   550

The Bank of Canada and Monetary Policy 550
The Monetary Policy Curve 551
  The Taylor Principle: Why the Monetary Policy
  Curve Has an Upward Slope 551
  Shifts in the *MP* Curve 553
  Movements Along Versus Shifts in the *MP* Curve 554

APPLICATION Shift in the *MP* Curve: Autonomous
Monetary Easing at the Onset of the
Global Financial Crisis 554
The Aggregate Demand Curve 555
  Deriving the Aggregate Demand Curve
  Graphically 555
  Factors That Shift the Aggregate
  Demand Curve 557

FYI Deriving the Aggregate Demand Curve Algebraically   557

Summary 561 • Key Terms 561 • Questions 562 •
Applied Problems 562 • Data Analysis Problems 563 •
Web Exercises 564 • Web References 564

CHAPTER 23
Aggregate Demand and Supply Analysis   565

Aggregate Demand 565

Following the Financial News Aggregate Output,
Unemployment, and Inflation   566

  Deriving the Aggregate Demand Curve 566
  Factors That Shift the Aggregate
  Demand Curve 567

FYI What Does *Autonomous* Mean?   569

Aggregate Supply 571
  Long-Run Aggregate Supply Curve 571
  Short-Run Aggregate Supply Curve 571
  Price Stickiness and the Short-Run Aggregate
  Supply Curve 573
Shifts in the Aggregate Supply Curves 573
  Shifts in the Long-Run Aggregate Supply Curve 573
  Shifts in the Short-Run Aggregate Supply Curve 574
Equilibrium in Aggregate Demand and Supply
Analysis 578
  Short-Run Equilibrium 578
  How the Short-Run Equilibrium Moves to the
  Long-Run Equilibrium over Time 579
  Self-Correcting Mechanism 581
Changes in Equilibrium: Aggregate Demand
Shocks 581

APPLICATION The Bank of Canada Disinflation,
1981–1985 582

APPLICATION Negative Demand Shocks in the
United States, 2001–2004 584
Changes in Equilibrium: Aggregate Supply
(Inflation) Shocks 584
  Temporary Supply Shocks 584

APPLICATION Negative Supply Shocks, 1973–1975
and 1978–1980 587
  Permanent Supply Shocks and Real Business
  Cycle Theory 587

APPLICATION Positive Supply Shocks,
1995–1999 590
  Conclusions 591
AD/AS Analysis of Foreign Business Cycle
Episodes 591

APPLICATION The United States and the 2007–2009
Financial Crisis 591

APPLICATION The United Kingdom and the
2007–2009 Financial Crisis 593

APPLICATION China and the 2007–2009
Financial Crisis 593

Summary 596 • Key Terms 596 • Questions 597 •
Applied Problems 597 • Data Analysis Problems 598 •
Web Exercises 598 • Web References 598

APPENDIX TO CHAPTER 23
The Phillips Curve and the Short-Run Aggregate Supply Curve   599

The Phillips Curve.. **599**
Phillips Curve Analysis in the 1960s................................... 599

FYI The Phillips Curve Tradeoff and Macroeconomic Policy in the 1960s   601

The Friedman-Phelps Phillips Curve Analysis...................... 601
The Phillips Curve After the 1960s................................... 603
The Modern Phillips Curve... 603
The Modern Phillips Curve with Adaptive
(Backward-Looking) Expectations 604

The Short-Run Aggregate Supply Curve **605**

CHAPTER 23 WEB APPENDIX 1
The Effects of Macroeconomic Shocks on Asset Prices
Go to MyEconLab at www.myeconlab.com

CHAPTER 23 WEB APPENDIX 2
Aggregate Demand and Supply: A Numerical Example
Go to MyEconLab at www.myeconlab.com

CHAPTER 23 WEB APPENDIX 3
The Algebra of the Aggregate Demand and Supply Model
Go to MyEconLab at www.myeconlab.com

CHAPTER 23 WEB APPENDIX 4
The Taylor Principle and Inflation Stability
Go to MyEconLab at www.myeconlab.com

CHAPTER 24
Monetary Policy Theory   607

Response of Monetary Policy to Shocks **607**
Response to an Aggregate Demand Shock 608
Response to a Permanent Supply Shock............................. 610
Response to a Temporary Supply Shock............................. 612
The Bottom Line: The Relationship Between
Stabilizing Inflation and Stabilizing
Economic Activity... 615

How Actively Should Policymakers Try to Stabilize Economic Activity?.. **615**
Lags and Policy Implementation 615

FYI The Activist/Nonactivist Debate Over the Obama Fiscal Stimulus Package in the United States   616

Inflation: Always and Everywhere a Monetary Phenomenon... **617**

Causes of Inflationary Monetary Policy **618**
High Employment Targets and Inflation 618

Monetary Policy at the Zero Lower Bound.......................... **621**
Deriving the Aggregate Demand Curve with the
Zero Lower Bound.. 621
The Disappearance of the Self-Correcting
Mechanism at the Zero Lower Bound................................ 623

APPLICATION Nonconventional Monetary
Policy and Quantitative Easing....................................... 624
Liquidity Provision 625
Asset Purchases and Quantitative Easing........................... 626
Management of Expectations 627

APPLICATION Abenomics and the Shift in
Japanese Monetary Policy in 2013 628

Summary 630 • Key Terms 631 • Questions 631 •
Applied Problems 632 • Data Analysis Problems 632 •
Web Exercises 633 • Web References 633

CHAPTER 25
The Role of Expectations in Monetary Policy   634

Lucas Critique of Policy Evaluation **634**
Econometric Policy Evaluation.. 635

APPLICATION The Term Structure of Interest Ratess 635

Policy Conduct: Rules or Discretion?................................ **636**
Discretion and the Time-Inconsistency Problem 636
Types of Rules... 637
The Case for Rules.. 637

FYI The Political Business Cycle and Richard Nixon   638

The Case for Discretion 638

Global The Demise of Monetary Targeting in
Switzerland   639

Constrained Discretion 639

The Role of Credibility and a Nominal Anchor.................... **640**
Benefits of a Credible Nominal Anchor.............................. 640
Credibility and Aggregate Demand Shocks 640
Credibility and Aggregate Supply Shocks........................... 643

APPLICATION A Tale of Three Oil Price Shocks 644
Credibility and Anti-Inflation Policy 646

Global Ending the Bolivian Hyperinflation: A Successful
Anti-Inflation Program   647

APPLICATION Credibility and the Bank of Canada's
Victory over Inflation 648

Approaches to Establishing Central Bank Credibility **648**
Nominal GDP Targeting.. 649
Appoint "Conservative" Central Bankers 649

Summary 650 • Key Terms 650 • Questions 651 •
Applied Problems 652 • Data Analysis Problems 652 •
Web Exercises 652

CHAPTER 26
Transmission Mechanisms of Monetary Policy   653

Transmission Mechanisms of Monetary Policy 653
   Traditional Interest-Rate Channels 654
   Other Asset Price Channels... 655
   Credit View 658

FYI Consumers' Balance Sheets and the Great Depression   660

   Why Are Credit Channels Likely to Be Important? 661

APPLICATION The Great Recession....................................... 661

Lessons for Monetary Policy.. 662

APPLICATION Applying the Monetary Policy Lessons
to Japan's Two Lost Decades 664

Summary 665 • Key Terms 665 • Questions 665 •
Applied Problems 666 • Data Analysis Problems 666 •
Web Exercises 667 • Web References 667

CHAPTER 26 WEB APPENDIX
Evaluating Empirical Evidence: The Debate Over the
Importance of Money in Economic Fluctuations
Go to MyEconLab at www.myeconlab.com

Glossary G-1

Index... I-1

CONTENTS ON THE WEB

The following chapters are available on the MyEconLab
at www.myeconlab.com.

WEB CHAPTER 1
Financial Crises in Emerging Market
Economies   W1-1

Dynamics of Financial Crises in Emerging Market
Economies.. W1-1
   Stage One: Initial Phase W1-1
   Stage Two: Currency Crisis W1-5
   Stage Three: Full-Fledged Financial Crisis W1-6

APPLICATION Crisis in South Korea, 1997–1998 .... W1-7
   Financial Liberalization and Globalization
   Mismanaged W1-7
   Perversion of the Financial Liberalization
   and Globalization Process: Chaebols and the
   South Korean Crisis W1-9
   Stock Market Decline and Failure of
   Firms Increase Uncertainty W1-10
   Adverse Selection and Moral Hazard Problems Worsen,
   and the Economy Contracts................................... W1-11
   Currency Crisis Ensues.. W1-11

   Final Stage: Currency Crisis Triggers Full-Fledged
   Financial Crisis.. W1-11
   Recovery Commences W1- 12

APPLICATION The Argentine Financial Crisis,
2001–2002.. W1-13
   Severe Fiscal Imbalances....................................... W1-13
   Adverse Selection and Moral Hazard Problems
   Worsen W1-14
   Bank Panic Begins... W1-14
   Currency Crisis Ensues... W1-14
   Currency Crisis Triggers Full-Fledged Financial Crisis..... W1-15
   Recovery Begins.. W1-18

Global When an Advanced Economy Is Like
an Emerging Market Economy: The Icelandic
Financial Crisis of 2008   W1-18

Preventing Emerging Market Financial Crises.................. W1-19
   Beef Up Prudential Regulation and Supervision of Banks. W1-19
   Encourage Disclosure and Market-Based Discipline W1-19
   Limit Currency Mismatch W1-20
   Sequence Financial Liberalization....................... W1-20

Summary W1-20 • Key Terms W1-21 • Questions W1-21

WEB CHAPTER 2
The *ISLM* Model   W2-1

Keynes's Fixed Price Level Assumption
and the *IS* Curve W2-1
   The *LM* Curve.. W2-1
   Equilibrium in the Market for Money:
   The *LM* Curve.. W2-2

***ISLM* Approach to Aggregate Output and Interest Rates W2-4**

Factors That Cause the *LM* Curve to Shift W2-5

Changes in Equilibrium Level of the Interest Rate
and Aggregate Output.. W2-7
   Response to a Change in Monetary Policy W2-7
   Response to a Change in Fiscal Policy W2-8

APPLICATION The Economic Stimulus Act of 2008
in the United States W2-9

Effectiveness of Monetary Versus Fiscal Policy................ W2-11
   Monetary Policy Versus Fiscal Policy:
   The Case of Complete Crowding Out W2-11

APPLICATION Targeting Money Supply Versus
Interest Rates W2-13

***ISLM* Model in the Long Run.. W2-16**

Summary W2-18 • Key Terms W2-19 • Questions and
Applied Problems W2-19 • Web Exercises W2-20 •
Web References W2-20

APPENDIX TO WEB CHAPTER 2
Algebra of the *ISLM* Model   W2-21

Basic Closed-Economy *ISLM* Model W2-21
   IS and *LM* Curves W2-22

Solution of the Model W2-22
Implications W2-22
Open-Economy *ISLM* Model W2-23
Implications W2-24

WEB CHAPTER 3
Nonbank Finance   W3-1

Insurance W3-1
Life Insurance W3-1
Property and Casualty Insurance W3-3
The Competitive Threat from the Banking Industry W3-4
Credit Insurance W3-4

FYI Credit Default Swaps on Greek Sovereign Debt   W3-5

FYI The AIG Blowup   W3-5

FYI The Global Financial Crisis and the Monoline Insurers   W3-6

The New Legislative Framework W3-6

APPLICATION Insurance Management W3-6
Screening W3-7
Risk-Based Premiums W3-7
Restrictive Provisions W3-8
Prevention of Fraud W3-8
Cancellation of Insurance W3-8
Deductibles W3-8
Coinsurance W3-9
Limits on the Amount of Insurance W3-9
Summary W3-9

Pension Funds W3-10
Private Pension Plans W3-11
Public Pension Plans W3-11

FYI Should Public Pension Plans Be Privatized?   W3-12

Personal Pension Plans W3-13
Finance Companies W3-13
Securities Market Operations W3-14
Investment Banking W3-14
Securities Brokers and Dealers W3-15
Organized Exchanges W3-15
Mutual Funds W3-16

FYI Sovereign Wealth Funds: Are They a Danger?   W3-17

Money Market Mutual Funds W3-18
Hedge Funds W3-18

FYI The Long-Term Capital Management Debacle   W3-19

Private Equity and Venture Capital Funds W3-19
Government Financial Intermediation W3-20
Crown Finance Companies W3-20
Government-Sponsored Enterprises in the
United States W3-21

FYI The Global Financial Crisis and the Bailout of
Fannie Mae and Freddie Mac   W3-22

Summary W3-22 • Key Terms W3-23 • Questions W3-24 •
Applied Problems W3-24 • Data Analysis Problems W3-25 •
Web Exercises W3-25 • Web References W3-25

PREFACE

HALLMARKS

Although this text has undergone a major revision, it retains the basic hallmarks that have made it the best-selling textbook on money and banking over the past five editions:

- A unifying, analytic framework that uses a few basic economic principles to organize students' thinking about the structure of financial markets, the foreign exchange markets, financial institution management, and the role of monetary policy in the economy
- A careful, step-by-step development of models (an approach found in the best principles of economics textbooks), which makes it easier for students to learn
- The complete integration of an international perspective throughout the text
- A thoroughly up-to-date treatment of the latest developments in monetary theory
- A special features called "Financial News," included to encourage reading of a financial newspaper
- An applications-oriented perspective with numerous applications and special-topic boxes that increase students' interest by showing them how to apply theory to real-world examples

WHAT'S NEW IN THE SIXTH CANADIAN EDITION

In addition to the expected updating of all data through the end of 2014 whenever possible, there is major new material in every part of the text.

Pearson eText with Mini-Lecture Videos: A New Way of Learning

The Pearson eText in MyEconLab for the sixth Canadian edition is available online from MyEconLab textbook resources. Instructors and students can highlight the text, bookmark, search the glossary, and take notes. More importantly, the enhanced Pearson eText provides a new way of learning that is particularly geared to today's students. Not only will students be able to read the material in the textbook, but by a simple click on an icon they will be able to watch over 80 mini-lecture videos presented by the authors for select figures in the text. For analytic figures, these mini-lectures build up each graph step-by-step and explain the intuition necessary to fully understand the theory behind the graph. For data figures, the mini-lectures highlight the key data points that are of greatest interest. The mini-lectures are an invaluable study tool for students who typically learn better when they see and hear economic analysis rather than read it.

Major Improvements and revisions in Part 3, Financial Institutions

The global financial crisis of 2007–2009 has become a central topic in the teaching of money and banking. We have added the following new material to Part 3 of the text:

- A new FYI box on the tyranny of collateral (Chapter 8)
- A new section on the response of financial regulation to the global financial crisis (Chapter 9)

- A new section exploring what can be done about the too-big-to-fail problem (Chapter 9)
- A new section that provides more detail on securitization and the shadow banking system (Chapter 11)

Nonconventional Monetary Policy and the Zero Lower Bound

Monetary policy entered a brave new world when policymakers had to resort to nonconventional measures when the policy interest rate—the overnight interest rate in Canada or the federal funds rate in the United States—hit a floor of zero, or the so-called "zero lower bound." Because the policy rate cannot be driven lower than zero, under this condition conventional monetary policy becomes infeasible. Nonconventional monetary policy at the zero lower bound, such as quantitative easing, has become a very controversial topic that stimulates a lot of student interest. The sixth Canadian edition contains extensive discussion of this topic, including the following new material:

- A new Application on quantitative easing and the money supply from 2007 to 2014 (Chapter 15)
- An updated section on forward guidance and the commitment to future policy actions (Chapter 16)
- A new section on monetary policy at the zero lower bound that uses the aggregate demand and aggregate supply models to explain how the zero lower bound affects the conduct of monetary policy (Chapter 24)
- A new application on nonconventional monetary policy and quantitative easing (Chapter 24)
- A new application on Abenomics and the shift in Japanese monetary policy in 2013 (Chapter 24)

The Euro Crisis

The Euro crisis has been a continuing drama since 2010, and so this edition includes the following new material:

- A new Global box on the European sovereign debt crisis (Chapter 9)
- A new section on monetary unions (Chapter 19)
- A new Global box on whether the Euro will survive (Chapter 19)

Additional New Material

New developments in the money and banking field have prompted us to add the following new material that we feel is necessary to keep the text current:

- A new Application on whether Bitcoin will become the money of the future (Chapter 3)
- A new section on movements along, versus shifts in the *MP* curve, with a new Application that discusses the movement along the *MP* curve that occurred when the Bank of Canada raised the overnight interest rate target during the years 2004 to 2006 (Chapter 22)
- A new FYI box that describes the meaning of the word *autonomous* (Chapter 23)
- A new section on nominal GDP targeting (Chapter 24)

FLEXIBILITY AND MODULARITY

In using previous editions, adopters, reviewers, and survey respondents have continually praised this text's flexibility and modularity—that is, the option to pick and choose which chapters to cover and in what order to cover them. Flexibility and modularity are especially important in the money and banking course, because there are as many ways to teach this course as there are instructors. To satisfy the diverse needs of instructors, the text achieves flexibility as follows:

- Core chapters provide the basic analysis used throughout the book, while other chapters or sections of chapters can be used or omitted according to instructor preferences. For example, Chapter 2 introduces the financial system and basic concepts such as transaction costs, adverse selection, and moral hazard. After covering Chapter 2, the instructor may decide to give more detailed coverage of financial structure by assigning Chapter 8 or may choose to skip Chapter 8 and take any of a number of different paths through the book.

- The text allows instructors to cover the most important issues in monetary theory even if they do not wish to present a detailed development of the *IS*, *MP*, and *AD* curves (provided in Chapters 21 and 22). Instructors who want to teach a more complete treatment of monetary theory can make use of these chapters.

- Part 6 on monetary theory can easily be taught before Part 4 of the text if the instructor wishes to give students a deeper understanding of the rationale behind monetary policy.

- Chapter 24, on the transmission mechanisms of monetary policy, can be taught at many different points in the course—either with Part 4, when monetary policy is discussed, or with Chapter 21 or Chapter 23, when the concept of aggregate demand is developed. Transmission mechanisms of monetary policy can also be taught as a special topic at the end of the course.

- The international approach of the text, accomplished through marked international sections within chapters as well as separate chapters on the foreign exchange market and the international monetary system, is comprehensive yet flexible. Although many instructors will teach all the international material, others will not. Instructors who wish to put less emphasis on international topics can easily skip Chapter 18 on the foreign exchange market and Chapter 19 on the international financial system and monetary policy. The international sections within chapters are self-contained and can be omitted with little loss of continuity.

To illustrate how this book can be used for courses with varying emphases, several course outlines are suggested for a semester teaching schedule. More detailed information about how the text can be used flexibly in your course is available in the Instructor's Manual.

- *General Money and Banking Course:* Chapters 1–5, 10–12, 16, 17, 23–24, with a choice of 6 of the remaining 14 chapters.
- *General Money and Banking Course with an International Emphasis:* Chapters 1–5, 10–12, 16–19, 23–24, with a choice of 4 of the remaining 12 chapters.
- *Financial Markets and Institutions Course:* Chapters 1–13, with a choice of 7 of the remaining 13 chapters.
- *Monetary Theory and Policy Course:* Chapters 1–5, 14–17, 20–25, with a choice of 4 of the remaining 11 chapters.

PEDAGOGICAL AIDS

Whether teaching theory or its applications, a textbook must be a solid motivational tool. To this end, we have incorporated a wide variety of pedagogical features that will make the material easy to learn:

1. **Previews** at the beginning of each chapter tell students where the chapter is heading, why specific topics are important, and how these topics relate to other topics discussed in the book.
2. **Applications**, numbering over 50, demonstrate how the analysis presented in the book can be used to explain many important real-world situations.
3. **Financial News boxes** introduce students to relevant news articles and data that are reported daily in the press, and teach students how to interpret these data.
4. **Inside the Central Bank boxes** give students a feel for the operation and structure of central banks.
5. **Global boxes** present interesting material with an international focus.
6. **FYI boxes** highlight dramatic historical episodes, interesting ideas, and intriguing facts related to the subject matter.
7. **Summary tables** provide a useful study aid for reviewing material.
8. **Key statements** are important points set in boldface italic type so that students can easily find them for later reference.
9. **Graphs** with captions, numbering more than 120, help students clearly understand the interrelationships among the plotted variables and the principles of analysis.
10. A **Summary** at the end of each chapter lists the main points covered in the chapter.
11. **Key terms** are important words or phrases introduced in the chapter. They are set in boldface when they are defined for the first time, and listed by page number at the end of each chapter.
12. **End-of-chapter questions and applied problems**, numbering more than 600, help students learn the subject matter by applying economic concepts.
13. **Data analysis problems** ask students to apply actual data taken from the CANSIM database or the St. Louis Federal Reserve Bank's FRED database to specific problems, so that they can understand what is happening in the economy.
14. **Web exercises** encourage students to collect information from online sources or to use online resources to enhance their learning experience.
15. **Web sources** report the URL sources of the data used to create the many tables and charts.
16. **Web references** point students to websites that provide information or data that supplement the text material.
17. A **Glossary** at the back of the book provides definitions of all the key terms.

AN EASIER WAY TO TEACH: SUPPLEMENTS
TO ACCOMPANY THE SIXTH CANADIAN EDITION

The Economics of Money, Banking, and Financial Markets, sixth Canadian edition includes the most comprehensive program of supplements of any money, banking, and financial markets textbook. These items are available to qualified domestic adopters.

MyEconLab

MyEconLab is the premier online assessment and tutorial system, pairing rich online content with innovative learning tools. The MyEconLab course for the sixth Canadian edition of *The Economics of Money, Banking, and Financial Markets* includes online versions of end-of-chapter Questions and Applied Problems from the text as well as additional questions for further study, which can be easily assigned and automatically graded.

Students and MyEconLab This online homework and tutorial system puts students in control of their own learning through a suite of study and practice tools correlated with the online, interactive version of the textbook and other media tools. Within MyEconLab's structured environment, students practice what they learn, test their understanding, and then pursue a study plan that MyEconLab generates for them based on their performance on practice tests.

Instructors and MyEconLab MyEconLab provides flexible tools that allow instructors to easily and effectively customize online course materials to suit their needs. Instructors can create and assign tests, quizzes, or homework assignments. MyEconLab saves time by automatically grading all questions and tracking results in an online grade book. MyEconLab can even grade assignments that require students to draw a graph.

After registering for MyEconLab, instructors have access to downloadable supplements such as an instructor's manual, PowerPoint lecture notes, and the test bank. The test bank can also be used within MyEconLab, giving instructors ample material from which they can create assignments.

Additional MyEconLab features include

- *New Mini-Lecture Videos* provide a step-by-step analysis of select data and analytic figures included in the text. The videos can be used in class or viewed by students on their own time.
- *Mishkin Interviewed on the Financial Crisis*. Watch video footage from a recent interview with one of the authors.
- *CANSIM Data*. CANSIM data are available for relevant text questions in the Resources section of MyEconLab.
- *Answers to Questions and Applied Problems*. Check your understanding of Questions and Applied Problems by viewing the solutions on MyEconLab.
- *Mini-Cases*. Online mini-cases are available for select chapters in the text. Each mini-case includes a unique Economics scenario and associated questions that provide real-life context for key chapter concepts.
- *Web Appendices*. Online appendices include additional information to supplement core chapter concepts and theories.
- *A Pearson eText* is available within the online course materials and off-line via iPad and Android apps. The Pearson eText enables instructors and students to highlight, bookmark, and take notes.

Chapters and Appendices on MyEconLab

The online chapters for the sixth Canadian edition of *The Economics of Money, Banking, and Financial Markets* include:

Web Chapter 1:   Financial Crises in Emerging Market Economies
Web Chapter 2:   The *ISLM* Model
Web Chapter 3:   Nonbank Finance

The web appendices include:

Web Appendix to Chapter 4:	Measuring Interest-Rate Risk: Duration
Web Appendix 1 to Chapter 5:	Models of Asset Pricing
Web Appendix 2 to Chapter 5:	Applying the Asset Market Approach to a Commodity Market: The Case of Gold
Web Appendix 3 to Chapter 5:	Loanable Funds Framework
Web Appendix to Chapter 7:	Evidence on the Efficient Market Hypothesis
Web Appendix 1 to Chapter 10:	The 1980s Canadian Banking Crisis
Web Appendix 2 to Chapter 10:	Banking Crises Throughout the World
Web Appendix 1 to Chapter 12:	Duration Gap Analysis
Web Appendix 2 to Chapter 12:	Measuring Bank Performance
Web Appendix 1 to Chapter 15:	The Bank of Canada's Balance Sheet and the Monetary Base
Web Appendix 2 to Chapter 15:	The M2+ Money Multiplier
Web Appendix 3 to Chapter 15:	The Great Depression Bank Panics, 1930–1933, and the Money Supply in the United States
Web Appendix 1 to Chapter 17:	Monetary Targeting
Web Appendix 2 to Chapter 17:	A Brief History of Bank of Canada Policymaking
Web Appendix 1 to Chapter 20:	The Baumol-Tobin and the Tobin Mean-Variance Models of the Demand for Money
Web Appendix 2 to Chapter 20:	Empirical Evidence on the Demand for Money
Web Appendix 1 to Chapter 23:	The Effects of Macroeconomic Shocks on Asset Prices
Web Appendix 2 to Chapter 23:	Aggregate Demand and Supply: A Numerical Example
Web Appendix 3 to Chapter 23:	The Algebra of the Aggregate Demand and Supply Model
Web Appendix 4 to Chapter 23:	The Taylor Principle and Inflation Stability
Web Appendix to Chapter 26:	Evaluating Empirical Evidence: The Debate Over the Importance of Money in Economic Fluctuations

Instructors can either use these web chapters and appendices in class to supplement the material in the textbook, or recommend them to students who want to expand their knowledge of the money and banking field.

For more information and to register, please visit **www.myeconlab.com**.

Additional Instructor Resources

These instructor supplements are available for download from a password-protected section of Pearson Canada's online catalogue (catalogue.pearsoned.ca). Navigate to your book's catalogue page to view a list of those supplements that are available. See your local sales representative for details and access.

1. **Instructor's Manual** Prepared by the authors, the Instructor's Manual provides conventional elements such as sample course outlines, chapter outlines, and answers to questions and problems in the text.

2. **PowerPoint® Slides** A complete set of slides that are specifically designed for the textbook is available electronically.
3. **Computerized TestGen** The computerized test bank allows the instructor to produce exams efficiently. This product consists of multiple-choice and short-answer questions and offers editing capabilities. It is available in Windows and Macintosh versions.
4. **Test Item File in Word** This test bank includes all the questions from the TestGen version in Microsoft Word format.
5. **Image Library** This library contains .gif or .jpg versions of figures from the textbook.
6. **Learning Solutions Managers** Pearson's Learning Solutions Managers work with faculty and campus course designers to ensure that Pearson technology products, assessment tools, and online course materials are tailored to meet your specific needs. This highly qualified team is dedicated to helping schools take full advantage of a wide range of educational resources by assisting in the integration of a variety of instructional materials and media formats. Your local Pearson Education sales representative can provide you with more details on this service program.

ACKNOWLEDGMENTS

This book is the result of efforts by many people. We are extremely grateful to Megan Farrell, Acquisitions Editor; Rebecca Ryoji, Developmental Editor; Patricia Ciardullo, Program Manager; Richard di Santo, Project Manager; and the many others at Pearson Canada who have contributed to the completion of this edition.

We are also grateful to all of the many people who commented on various chapters of the book, made valuable suggestions, and kindly provided us with data.

Although we have done our best to make this edition as complete and error free as possible, as most of you know, perfection is impossible. We would greatly appreciate any suggestions for improvement.

Please send your comments to serletis@ucalgary.ca.

Frederic S. Mishkin
Apostolos Serletis
2016

ABOUT THE AUTHORS

Frederic S. Mishkin is the Alfred Lerner Professor of Banking and Financial Institutions at the Graduate School of Business, Columbia University. He is also a Research Associate at the National Bureau of Economic Research and past president of the Eastern Economics Association. Since receiving his Ph.D. from the Massachusetts Institute of Technology in 1976, he has taught at the University of Chicago, Northwestern University, Princeton University, and Columbia. He has also received an honorary professorship from the People's (Renmin) University of China. From 1994 to 1997, he was Executive Vice President and Director of Research at the Federal Reserve Bank of New York and an associate economist of the Federal Open Market Committee of the Federal Reserve System. From September 2006 to August 2008, he was a member (governor) of the Board of Governors of the Federal Reserve System.

Professor Mishkin's research focuses on monetary policy and its impact on financial markets and the aggregate economy. He is the author of more than 15 books, including *Financial Markets and Institutions*, sixth edition (Addison-Wesley, 2009); *Monetary Policy Strategy* (MIT Press, 2007); *The Next Great Globalization: How Disadvantaged Nations Can Harness Their Financial Systems to Get Rich* (Princeton University Press, 2006); *Inflation Targeting: Lessons from the International Experience* (Princeton University Press, 1999); *Money, Interest Rates, and Inflation* (Edward Elgar, 1993); and *A Rational Expectations Approach to Macroeconometrics: Testing Policy Ineffectiveness and Efficient Markets Models* (University of Chicago Press, 1983). In addition, he has published more than 150 articles in such journals as *American Economic Review*, *Journal of Political Economy*, *Econometrica*, *Quarterly Journal of Economics*, *Journal of Finance*, and *Journal of Monetary Economics*.

Professor Mishkin has served on the editorial board of *American Economic Review* and has been an associate editor at *Journal of Business and Economic Statistics*, the *Journal of Applied Econometrics* and *Journal of Money, Credit and Banking*; he also served as the editor of the Federal Reserve Bank of New York's *Economic Policy Review*. He is currently an associate editor (member of the editorial board) at six academic journals, including *Macroeconomics and Monetary Economics Abstracts*; *Journal of International Money and Finance*; *International Finance*; *Finance India*; *Economic Policy Review*; and *Emerging Markets, Finance and Trade*. He has been a consultant to the Board of Governors of the Federal Reserve System, the World Bank, and the International Monetary Fund, as well as to many central banks throughout the world. He was also a member of the International Advisory Board to the Financial Supervisory Service of South Korea and an adviser to the Institute for Monetary and Economic Research at the Bank of Korea. Professor Mishkin was a Senior Fellow at the Federal Deposit Insurance Corporation's Center for Banking Research and was an academic consultant to and served on the Economic Advisory Panel of the Federal Reserve Bank of New York.

Apostolos Serletis is Professor of Economics and Finance at the University of Calgary. Since receiving his Ph.D. from McMaster University in 1984, he has held visiting appointments at the University of Texas at Austin, the Athens University of Economics and Business, and the Research Department of the Federal Reserve Bank of St. Louis.

Professor Serletis's teaching and research interests focus on monetary and financial economics, macroeconometrics, and nonlinear and complex dynamics. He is the author of eight books, including *Principles of Economics* (Canadian edition) with R. Glenn Hubbard, Anthony Patrick O. Brien, and Jason Childs (Pearson, 2015); *Macroeconomics: A Modern Approach* (Canadian edition) with Robert J. Barro (Nelson, 2010); *The Demand for Money: Theoretical and Empirical Approaches* (Springer, 2007); *Financial Markets and Institutions: Canadian Edition*, with Frederic S. Mishkin and Stanley G. Eakins (Addison-Wesley, 2004); and *The Theory of Monetary Aggregation*, co-edited with William A. Barnett (Elsevier, 2000). In addition, he has published over 150 articles in such journals as *Journal of Economic Literature; Journal of Monetary Economics; Journal of Money, Credit, and Banking; Journal of Econometrics; Journal of Applied Econometrics; Journal of Business and Economic Statistics; Macroeconomic Dynamics; Journal of Banking and Finance; Journal of Economic Dynamics and Control; Economic Inquiry;* and the *Canadian Journal of Economics.*

Professor Serletis is Associate Editor of *Macroeconomic Dynamics, Energy Economics,* and the *Journal of Economic Asymmetries.* He is also a member of the editorial board of the *Journal of Economic Studies.* He is listed in a variety of directories, including *Who's Who in Economics* and *Who's Who in the World.*

PART 1

Introduction

Chapter 1   Why Study Money, Banking, and Financial Markets?

Chapter 2   An Overview of the Financial System

Chapter 3   What Is Money?

Crisis and Response: Global Financial Crisis and Its Aftermath

In August 2007, financial markets began to seize up, and over the next two years the world economy experienced its most severe financial crisis since the Great Depression years of the 1930s. The financial crisis started in the United States and was the result of a credit-driven, asset-price bubble in the U.S. housing market. When that bubble burst, housing prices in the United States plummeted, the stock market crashed, unemployment skyrocketed, and both businesses and households found they couldn't get credit. Not only did the central bank of the United States, the Federal Reserve, respond by sharply lowering interest rates and intervening in credit markets to provide them with massive amounts of liquidity, but governments around the world worked on full-scale banking bailouts and rescue packages adding up to trillions of dollars. However, even with these aggressive actions aimed at stabilizing the financial system and boosting the economy, eight years after the crisis, economies throughout the world are still experiencing problems and the finances of many governments are in tatters.

The global financial crisis and its aftermath demonstrate the importance of banks and financial systems to economic well-being, as well as the major role of money in the economy. Part 1 of this book provides an introduction to the study of money, banking, and financial markets. Chapter 1 outlines a road map of the book and discusses why it is so worthwhile to study money, banking, and financial markets. Chapter 2 provides a general overview of the financial system. Chapter 3 then explains what money is and how it is measured.

1 Why Study Money, Banking, and Financial Markets?

Learning Objectives

After studying this chapter you should be able to

1. Recognize the importance of financial markets in the economy.

2. Describe how financial intermediation and financial innovation affect banking and the economy.

3. Identify the basic links among monetary policy, the business cycle, and economic variables.

4. Explain the importance of exchange rates in a global economy.

PREVIEW

You have just heard on the evening news that the Bank of Canada is raising the overnight interest rate by one-half of a percentage point. What effect might this have on the interest rate of an automobile loan when you finance your purchase of a sleek new sports car? Does it mean that a house will be more or less affordable in the future? Will it make it easier or harder for you to get a job next year?

This book provides answers to these and other questions by examining how financial markets (such as those for bonds, stocks, and foreign exchanges) and financial institutions (banks, insurance companies, mutual funds, and other institutions) work and by exploring the role of money in the economy. Financial markets and institutions affect not only your everyday life but also the flow of billions of dollars of funds throughout our economy, which in turn affects business profits, the production of goods and services, and even the economic well-being of countries other than Canada. What happens to financial markets, financial institutions, and money is of great concern to politicians and can have a major impact on elections. The study of money, banking, and financial markets will reward you with an understanding of many exciting issues. In this chapter we provide a road map of this book by outlining these issues and exploring why they are worth studying.

WHY STUDY FINANCIAL MARKETS?

Financial markets are markets in which funds are transferred from people who have an excess of available funds to people who have a shortage. Financial markets, such as bond and stock markets, are crucial to promoting greater economic efficiency by channeling funds from people who do not have a productive use for them to those who do. Indeed, well-functioning financial markets are a key factor in producing high economic growth, and poorly performing financial markets are one reason that many countries in the world remain desperately poor. Activities in financial markets also have a direct effect on personal wealth, the behaviour of businesses and consumers, and the cyclical performance of the economy. Part 2 of this book focuses on financial markets.

The Bond Market and Interest Rates

A **security** (also called a *financial instrument*) is a claim on the issuer's future income or **assets** (any financial claim or piece of property that is subject to ownership). A **bond** is a debt security that promises to make payments periodically for a specified period of time.[1] The bond market is especially important to economic activity because it enables corporations and governments to borrow to finance their activities, and because it is where interest rates are determined. An **interest rate** is the cost of borrowing or the price paid for the rental of funds (usually expressed as a percentage of the rental of $100 per year). Many types of interest rates are found in the economy—mortgage interest rates, car loan rates, and interest rates on many different types of bonds.

Interest rates are important on a number of levels. On a personal level, high interest rates could deter you from buying a house or a car because the cost of financing would be high. Conversely, high interest rates could encourage you to save because you can earn more interest income by putting aside some of your earnings as savings. On a more general level, interest rates have an impact on the overall health of the economy because they affect not only consumers' willingness to spend or save, but also businesses' investment decisions. High interest rates, for example, may cause a corporation to postpone building a new plant that would provide more jobs.

Because changes in interest rates affect individuals, financial institutions, businesses, and the overall economy, it is important to explain substantial fluctuations in interest rates over the past 35 years. For example, the interest rate on three-month Treasury bills peaked at over 20% in August 1981. This interest rate then fell to less than 3% in 1997, rose to near 5% in the late 1990s, fell to a low of 2% in the early 2000s, rose to above 4% by 2007, and fell to close to 1% from 2008 to 2014.

Because different interest rates have a tendency to move in unison, economists frequently lump interest rates together and refer to "the" interest rate. As Figure 1-1 shows, however, interest rates on different types of bonds can differ substantially. The interest rate on three-month Treasury bills, for example, fluctuates more than other types of interest rates, and is lower on average. The interest rate on long-term corporate bonds is higher on average than other interest rates, and the spread between it and the other rates fluctuates over time.

In Chapter 2 we study the role of bond markets in the economy, and in Chapters 4 through 6 we examine what an interest rate is, how the common movements in interest rates come about, and why the interest rates on different bonds vary.

The Stock Market

A **common stock** (typically just called a **stock**) represents a share of ownership in a corporation. It is a security that is a claim on the earnings and assets of the corporation. Issuing stock and selling it to the public is a way for corporations to raise funds to finance their activities. The stock market, in which claims on the earnings of corporations (shares of stock) are traded, is the most widely followed financial market in almost every country that has one; that's why it is often called simply "the market." A big swing in the prices of shares in the stock market is always a major story on the evening news.

---

[1]The definition of *bond* used throughout this book is the broad one in common use in academic settings, which covers short- and long-term debt instruments. However, some practitioners in financial markets use the word *bond* only to describe specific long-term debt instruments such as corporate bonds or government of Canada bonds.

FIGURE 1-1   Interest Rates on Selected Bonds, 1977–2014

Although different interest rates have a tendency to move in unison, they often differ substantially, and the spreads between them fluctuate.

Note: Shaded areas represent recessions.

Source: Statistics Canada CANSIM series V122531, V122544, and V122518.

People often speculate on where the market is heading and get very excited when they can brag about their latest "big killing," or become depressed when they suffer a big loss. The attention the market receives can probably be best explained by one simple fact: it is a place where people get rich—or poor—very quickly.

As Figure 1-2 indicates, stock prices are extremely volatile. After rising steadily during the 1980s, the market experienced the worst one-day drop in its entire history on October 19, 1987—"Black Monday"—with the S&P/TSX Composite Index (the Toronto Stock Exchange index of stock prices) falling by 11%. From then until 2000, the stock market experienced one of the greatest rises (often referred to as a "bull market") in its history, with the S&P/TSX climbing to a peak of over 11 000. With the collapse of the high-tech bubble in 2000, the stock market again fell sharply, dropping by over 40% by late 2002. It then rose to an all-time high above the 14 000 level in early 2008, only to fall by over 50% of its value to a low of close to 8000 in early 2009. Another bull market then began, with the S&P/TSX reaching new highs of close to 16 000 by early 2014, only to fall again to below 14 000 by late 2014. These considerable fluctuations in stock prices affect the size of people's wealth and, as a result, their willingness to spend.

The stock market is also an important factor in business investment decisions, because the price of shares affects the amount of funds that can be raised by selling newly issued stock to finance investment spending. A higher price for a firm's shares

FIGURE 1-2 **Stock Prices as Measured by the S&P/TSX Composite Index, 1956–2014**
Stock prices are extremely volatile.
Source: Statistics Canada CANSIM series V122620.

means that the firm can raise a larger amount of funds, which it can then use to buy production facilities and equipment. In Chapter 2 we examine the role that the stock market plays in the financial system, and in Chapter 7 we return to the issue of how stock prices behave and respond to information in the marketplace.

WHY STUDY FINANCIAL INSTITUTIONS AND BANKING?

Banks and other financial institutions are what make financial markets work. Without them, financial markets would not be able to move funds from people who save to people who have productive investment opportunities. Thus financial institutions play a crucial role in the economy. Part 3 of this book focuses on financial institutions and the business of banking.

Structure of the Financial System

The financial system is complex, comprising many different types of private sector financial institutions, including banks, insurance companies, mutual funds, finance companies, and investment banks, all of which are heavily regulated by the government. If an individual wanted to make a loan to Bombardier or BlackBerry, for example, he or she would not go directly to the president of the company and offer a loan. Instead, he or she would lend to such a company indirectly through **financial intermediaries**, which are institutions that borrow funds from people who have saved and in turn make loans to people who need funds.

Why are financial intermediaries so crucial to well-functioning financial markets? Why do they extend credit to one party but not to another? Why do they usually write complicated legal documents when they extend loans? Why are they the most heavily regulated businesses in the economy?

We answer these questions in Chapter 8 by developing a coherent framework for analyzing financial structure in Canada and in the rest of the world.

Banks and Other Financial Institutions

Banks are financial institutions that accept deposits and make loans. The term *banks* includes firms such as chartered banks, trust and loan companies, and credit unions and *caisses populaires*. Banks are the financial intermediaries that the average person interacts with most frequently. A person who needs a loan to buy a house or a car usually obtains it from a local bank. Most Canadians keep a large proportion of their financial wealth in banks in the form of chequing accounts, savings accounts, or other types of bank deposits. Because banks are the largest financial intermediaries in our economy, they deserve the most careful study. However, banks are not the only important financial institutions. Indeed, in recent years, other financial institutions, such as insurance companies, finance companies, pension funds, mutual funds, and investment banks, have been growing at the expense of banks, so we need to study them as well.

In Chapter 10, we extend the economic analysis in Chapter 8 to understand why financial regulation takes the form it does and what can go wrong in the regulatory process. In Chapter 11, we look at the banking industry and examine how the competitive environment has changed this industry. We also learn why some financial institutions have been growing at the expense of others. For a further discussion on the differences between banks and nonbank financial institutions and the regulation of nonbank financial institutions in the context of adverse selection and moral hazard problems, see Web chapter 3, "Nonbank Finance," which can be found on MyEconLab.

In Chapter 12, we examine how banks and other financial institutions manage their assets and liabilities to make profits. Because the economic environment for banks and other financial institutions has become increasingly risky, these institutions must find ways to manage risk. How financial institutions manage risk with financial derivatives is the topic of Chapter 13.

Financial Innovation

In Chapter 11, we study **financial innovation**, the development of new financial products and services. We will see why and how financial innovation takes place, with particular emphasis on how the dramatic improvements in information technology have led to new financial products and the ability to deliver financial services electronically through what has become known as **e-finance**. We also study financial innovation because it shows us how creative thinking on the part of financial institutions can lead to higher profits but can also sometimes result in financial disasters. By studying how financial institutions have been creative in the past, we obtain a better grasp of how they may be creative in the future. This knowledge provides us with useful clues about how the financial system may change over time.

Financial Crises

At times, the financial system seizes up and produces financial crises, which are major disruptions in financial markets that are characterized by sharp declines in asset prices and the failures of many financial and nonfinancial firms. Financial crises have been a feature of capitalist economies for hundreds of years, and are typically followed by severe business cycle downturns. Starting in August 2007, the United States economy was hit by the worst financial crisis since the Great Depression. Defaults in subprime residential mortgages led to major losses in financial institutions, producing not only numerous bank failures but also the demise of Bear Stearns and Lehman Brothers, two of the largest investment banks in the United States. The crisis produced the worst economic downturn since the Great Depression, and as a result, it is now referred to as the "Great Recession."

We discuss why these crises occur and why they do so much damage to the economy in Chapter 9.

WHY STUDY MONEY AND MONETARY POLICY?

Money, also referred to as the **money supply**, is defined as anything that is generally accepted as payment for goods or services or in the repayment of debts. Money is linked to changes in economic variables that affect all of us and are important to the health of the economy. The final two parts of the book examine the role of money in the economy.

Money and Business Cycles

During 1981–1982, the total production of goods and services (called **aggregate output**) in the Canadian economy fell and the **unemployment rate** (the percentage of the available labour force unemployed) rose to close to 12%. After 1982, the economy began to expand rapidly, and by 1989, the unemployment rate had declined to 7.5%. In 1990, that eight-year expansion came to an end, with unemployment rising to above 11%. The economy bottomed out in 1991, and the subsequent recovery was the longest in Canadian history, with the unemployment rate falling to around 6% in 2008 before rising to over 8% in early 2009 in the aftermath of the global financial crisis.

Why did the economy undergo such pronounced fluctuations? Evidence suggests that money plays an important role in generating **business cycles**, the upward and downward movement of aggregate output produced in the economy. Business cycles affect all of us in immediate and important ways. When output is rising, for example, it is easier to find a good job; when output is falling, finding a good job might be difficult. Figure 1-3 shows the movements of the rate of money growth from 1968 to 2014, with the shaded areas representing **recessions**, or periods of declining aggregate output. We see that the rate of money growth declined before most recessions, indicating that changes in money growth might be a driving force behind business cycle fluctuations. However, declines in the rate of money growth are often not followed by a recession.

We explore how money and monetary policy might affect aggregate output in Chapters 20 through 26 (Part 7) of this book, where when we study **monetary theory**, the theory that relates the quantity of money and monetary policy to changes in aggregate economic activity and inflation.

FIGURE 1-3   **Money Growth (M2++ (Gross) Annual Rate) and the Business Cycle in Canada, 1968–2014**

Although money growth has declined before almost every recession, not every decline in the rate of money growth is followed by a recession. Shaded areas represent recessions.

Source: Statistics Canada CANSIM series V41552801.

Money and Inflation

The movie you paid $13 to see last week would have set you back only a dollar or two thirty years ago. In fact, for $13, you probably could have had dinner, seen the movie, and bought yourself a big bucket of hot buttered popcorn. As shown in Figure 1-4, which illustrates the movement of average prices in the Canadian economy from 1968 to 2014, the prices of most items are quite a bit higher now than they were then. The average price of goods and services in an economy is called the **aggregate price level** or, more simply, the *price level* (a more precise definition is found in the appendix to this chapter). From 1968 to 2014, the price level has increased more than sixfold. **Inflation**, a continual increase in the price level, affects individuals, businesses, and the government. It is generally regarded as an important problem to be solved and is often at the top of political and policy-making agendas. To solve the inflation problem, we need to know something about its causes.

What explains inflation? As we can see in Figure 1-4, the price level and the money supply generally rise together. These data seem to indicate that a continuing increase in the money supply might be an important factor in causing the continuing increase in the price level that we call inflation. Further evidence that inflation may be tied to continuing increases in the money supply is found in Figure 1-5, which plots the average **inflation rate** (the rate of change of the price level, usually measured as a percentage change per year) for a number of countries over the 10-year period 2003–2013 against the average rate of money growth over the same period. As you can see, a positive association exists between inflation and the growth rate of the money supply: the countries with the highest inflation rates are also the ones with the highest money growth rates. Turkey, Ukraine, and Zambia, for example, experienced high inflation

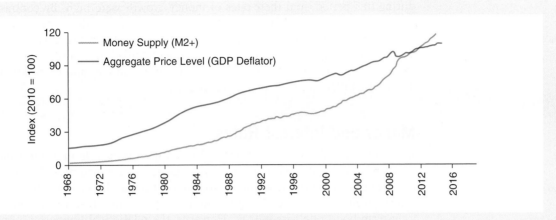

FIGURE 1-4   Aggregate Price Level and the Money Supply in Canada, 1968–2014

From 1968 to 2014, the price level has increased more than sixfold.
Source: Federal Reserve Bank of St. Louis, FRED database: **http://research.stlouisfed.org/fred2/**.

MyEconLab Mini-lecture

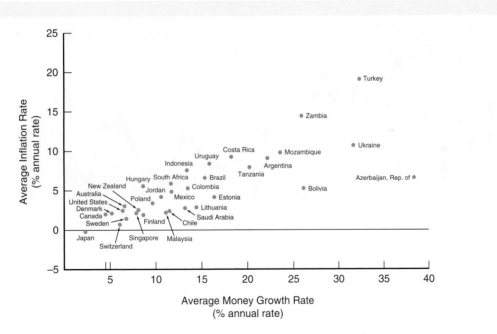

FIGURE 1-5   Average Inflation Rate Versus Average Rate of Money Growth for Selected Countries, 2003–2013

A positive association can be seen between the 10-year averages of inflation and the growth rate of the money supply: the countries with the highest inflation rates are also the ones with the highest money growth rates.
Source: International Financial Statistics. **www.imf.org/external/data.htm**

during this period, and their rates of money growth were high. By contrast, Canada, Sweden, and the United States had low inflation rates over the same period, and their rates of money growth were low. Such evidence led Milton Friedman, a Nobel laureate in economics, to make the famous statement "Inflation is always and everywhere a monetary phenomenon."[2] We look at the quantity of money and monetary policy's role in creating inflation in Chapters 20 and 24.

Money and Interest Rates

In addition to other factors, money plays an important role in interest rate fluctuations, which are of great concern to businesses and consumers. Figure 1-6 shows the changes in the interest rate on long-term Canada bonds and the rate of money growth from 1977 to 2014. As the money growth rate rose in the late 1970s, the long-term bond rate rose with it. However, the relationship between money growth and interest rates has been less clear-cut since 1980. We analyze the relationship between money growth and interest rates when we examine the behaviour of interest rates in Chapter 5.

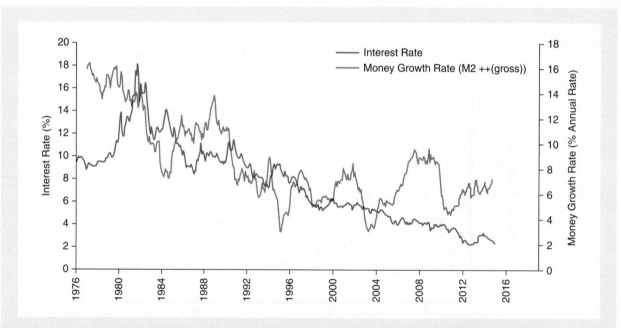

FIGURE 1-6 **Money Growth (M2++ (Gross) Annual Rate) and Interest Rates (Long-Term Government of Canada Bonds), 1976–2014**

As the money growth rate fell in the 1980s and 1990s, the long-term bond rate fell with it. However, the relationship between money growth and interest rates has been less clear-cut since 2000.
Source: Statistics Canada CANSIM series V41552801 and V122544.

[2]Milton Friedman, *Dollars and Deficits* (Upper Saddle River, NJ: Prentice Hall, 1968), 39.

Conduct of Monetary Policy

Because money can affect many economic variables that are important to the well-being of our economy, politicians and policymakers throughout the world care about the conduct of **monetary policy**, the management of money and interest rates. The organization responsible for the conduct of a nation's monetary policy is the **central bank**. Canada's central bank is the **Bank of Canada** (also called simply "**the Bank**"). In Chapters 14 through 17 (Part 5), we study how central banks such as the Bank of Canada can affect interest rates and the quantity of money and interest rates in the economy, and then we look at how monetary policy is actually conducted in Canada and elsewhere.

Fiscal Policy and Monetary Policy

Fiscal policy involves decisions about government spending and taxation. A **budget deficit** is an excess of government expenditures with respect to tax revenues for a particular time period, typically a year, while a **budget surplus** arises when tax revenues exceed government expenditures. The government must finance any budget deficit by borrowing, whereas a budget surplus leads to a lower government debt burden. As Figure 1-7 shows, the budget deficit, relative to the size of the

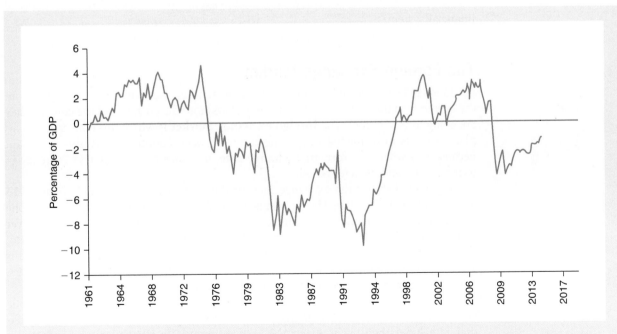

FIGURE 1-7 **Government Budget Surplus or Deficit as a Percentage of Gross Domestic Product, 1961–2014**

The budget deficit, relative to the size of the Canadian economy, has fluctuated a lot over the years, rising to close to 9% of GDP in 1993 and falling subsequently to where there were budget surpluses from 1997 to 2008, only to rise subsequently with budget deficits of over 4% of GDP by 2009.

Source: Statistics Canada CANSIM series V498316, V498326, V498086, V62425528, V62425550, and V62295562.

Canadian economy, peaked in 1992 at 8.7% of national output (as calculated by the **gross domestic product**, or **GDP**, a measure of aggregate output described in the appendix to this chapter). Since then, the budget deficit at first declined and the budget actually went into surplus from 1997 to 2008. In the aftermath of the 2007–2009 global financial crisis the budget has swung back again into deficit, with recent deficits at one point exceeding 4% of GDP and then falling substantially thereafter. What to do about budget deficits has been the subject of bitter battles between Canadian politicians.

You may have read statements online or heard on TV that budget surpluses are a good thing, while deficits are undesirable. In Chapter 20, we examine why deficits might result in a higher rate of money growth, a higher rate of inflation, and higher interest rates.

WHY STUDY INTERNATIONAL FINANCE?

The globalization of financial markets has accelerated at a rapid pace in recent years. Financial markets have become increasingly integrated throughout the world. Canadian companies often borrow in foreign financial markets, and foreign companies borrow in Canadian financial markets. Banks and other financial institutions have become increasingly international, with operations in many countries throughout the world. Part 6 of this book explores the foreign exchange market and the international financial system.

The Foreign Exchange Market

For funds to be transferred from one country to another, they have to be converted from the currency in the country of origin (say, dollars) into the currency of the country they are going to (say, euros). The **foreign exchange market** is where this conversion takes place, so it is instrumental in moving funds between countries. It is also important because it is where the **foreign exchange rate**, the price of one country's currency in terms of another's, is determined.

Figure 1-8 shows the exchange rate for the Canadian dollar from 1971 to 2014 in terms of the U.S. dollar. The exchange rate is defined as the U.S. dollar price of one Canadian dollar. Clearly, the exchange rate has experienced four long swings over this period. The first is a 30.8% depreciation from January 1973 to February 1986; the second is a 26.0% appreciation from February 1986 to January 1992; the third is a 26.7% depreciation from January 1992 to October 2002; and the fourth is a 54% appreciation from October 2002 to December 2011.

What have these fluctuations in the exchange rate meant to the Canadian public and Canadian businesses? A change in the exchange rate has a direct effect on Canadian consumers because it affects the cost of imports. In particular, a weaker dollar leads to more expensive foreign goods, makes vacationing abroad more expensive, and raises the cost of indulging your desire for imported delicacies. When the value of the dollar drops, Canadians decrease their purchases of foreign goods and increase their consumption of domestic goods (such as travel within Canada or Canadian-made wine).

FIGURE 1-8   Exchange Rate for the Canadian Dollar, 1971–2014

The value of the Canadian dollar relative to the United States dollar has fluctuated substantially over the years.
Source: Statistics Canada CANSIM series V37426.

Conversely, a strong dollar means that Canadian goods exported abroad will cost more in foreign countries, and hence foreigners will buy fewer of them. Exports of steel, for example, declined sharply when the dollar strengthened in the late 1980s. A strong dollar benefited Canadian consumers by making foreign goods cheaper, but hurt Canadian businesses leading to job losses when both domestic and foreign sales of those businesses' products declined. The increase in the value of the dollar since 2002 has had a similar effect: it made foreign goods less expensive but made Canadian businesses less competitive. Fluctuations in the foreign exchange markets have major consequences for the Canadian economy.

In Chapter 18, we study how exchange rates are determined in the foreign exchange market, in which Canadian dollars are bought and sold for foreign currencies.

The International Financial System

The tremendous increase in capital flows between countries has heightened the international financial system's impact on domestic economies. Issues we will explore in Chapter 19 include:

- How does a country's decision to fix its exchange rate to that of another nation shape the conduct of its monetary policy?
- What is the impact of capital controls that restrict mobility of capital across national borders on domestic financial systems and the performance of its economy?
- What role should international financial institutions, such as the International Monetary Fund, play in the international financial system?

HOW WE WILL STUDY MONEY, BANKING, AND FINANCIAL MARKETS

This text stresses the "economic way of thinking" by developing a unifying framework to study money, banking, and financial markets. This analytic framework uses a few basic economic concepts to help you organize your thinking about the determination of asset prices, the structure of financial markets, bank management, and the role of money in the economy. It encompasses the following basic concepts:

- A simplified approach to the demand for assets
- The concept of equilibrium
- Basic supply and demand to explain behaviour of financial markets
- The search for profits
- An approach to financial structure based on transaction costs and asymmetric information
- Aggregate supply and demand analysis

The unifying framework used in this book will keep your knowledge from becoming obsolete and make the material more interesting. It will enable you to learn what *really* matters without having to memorize a mass of dull facts that you will forget soon after the final exam. This framework will also provide you with the tools to understand trends in the financial marketplace and in variables such as interest rates, exchange rates, inflation, and aggregate output.

To help you understand and apply the unifying analytic framework, simple models are constructed in which the variables held constant are carefully delineated. Each step in the derivation of the model is clearly and carefully laid out, and the models are then used to explain various phenomena by focusing on changes in one variable at a time, holding all other variables constant.

To reinforce the models' usefulness, this text uses case studies, applications, and special-interest boxes to present evidence that supports or casts doubts on the theories being discussed. This exposure to real-life events and empirical data should dissuade you from thinking that all economists make abstract assumptions and develop theories that have little to do with actual behaviour.

To function better in the real world outside the classroom, you must have the tools with which to follow the financial news that is reported in leading financial publications and on the Web. To help and encourage you to read the financial news, this book contains special boxed inserts titled "Following the Financial News" that provide detailed information and definitions to help you evaluate data that are discussed frequently in the media. This book also contains over 700 end-of-chapter questions and applied problems that ask you to apply the analytic concepts you have learned to real-world issues.

Exploring the Web

The World Wide Web has become an extremely valuable and convenient resource for financial research. This book emphasizes the importance of this tool in several ways.

First, at the end of almost every chapter there are several real-time data analysis problems, which ask you to download the most recent data from the Statistics Canada CANSIM database or the Federal Reserve Bank of St. Louis's FRED database and then use these data to answer interesting questions. Second, there are additional Web exercises at the end of many chapters that prompt you to visit sites related to the chapter and use them to learn more about macroeconomic issues—issues pertaining to the study of economic activity in the overall economy. Web references are also supplied at the end of each chapter; these list the URLs of sites related to the material being discussed. You can visit these sites to further explore a topic you find of particular interest. Note: Website URLs are subject to frequent change. We have tried to select stable sites, but we realize that even government URLs change.

CONCLUDING REMARKS

The study of money, banking, and financial markets is an exciting field that directly affects your life. Interest rates influence earnings on your savings and the payments on loans you may seek on a car or a house, and monetary policy may affect your job prospects and the prices you will pay for goods in the future. Your study of money, banking, and financial markets will introduce you to many of the controversies related to economic policy that are hotly debated in the political arena, and will help you gain a clearer understanding of economic phenomena you hear about in the news media. The knowledge you gain will stay with you and benefit you long after your course is over.

MyEconLab

MyEconLab is an online homework and tutorial system that puts you in control of your own learning with study and practice tools directly correlated to this chapter's content. Visit MyEconLab to access the eText, the Questions and Applied Problems with answers, as well as additional assessment. You will also find web chapters, mini-lectures, appendices, mini-cases, videos, glossary flashcards, news feeds, CANSIM data, and graphing tools.

SUMMARY

1. Activities in financial markets directly affect individuals' wealth, the behaviour of businesses, and the efficiency of our economy. Three financial markets deserve particular attention: the bond market (where interest rates are determined), the stock market (which has a major effect on people's wealth and on firms' investment decisions), and the foreign exchange market (because fluctuations in the foreign exchange rate have major consequences for the Canadian economy).

2. Banks and other financial institutions channel funds from people who might not put them to productive use to people who can do so, and thus play a crucial role in improving the efficiency of the economy. When the financial system seizes up and produces a financial crisis, financial firms fail, which causes severe damage to the economy.

3. Money and monetary policy appear to have a major influence on inflation, business cycles, and interest rates. Because these economic variables are so important to the health of the economy, we need to understand how monetary policy is and should be conducted. We also need to study government fiscal policy because it can be an influential factor in the conduct of monetary policy.

4. This textbook stresses the "economic way of thinking" by developing a unifying analytic framework in which to study money, banking, and financial markets, using a few basic economic principles. This textbook also emphasizes the interaction of theoretical analysis and empirical data.

KEY TERMS

aggregate output, p. 7
aggregate price level, p. 8
assets, p. 3
Bank of Canada, p. 11
Banks, p. 6
bond, p. 3
budget deficit, p. 11
budget surplus, p. 11
business cycles, p. 7
central bank, p. 11
common stock, p. 3

e-finance, p. 6
financial innovation, p. 6
financial intermediaries, p. 5
Financial markets, p. 2
Fiscal policy, p. 11
foreign exchange market, p. 12
foreign exchange rate, p. 12
GDP, p. 12
gross domestic product, p. 12
Inflation, p. 8
inflation rate, p. 8

interest rate, p. 3
monetary policy, p. 11
monetary theory, p. 7
Money, p. 7
money supply, p. 7
recessions, p. 7
security, p. 3
stock, p. 3
the Bank, p. 11
unemployment rate, p. 7

QUESTIONS

All questions are available in MyEconLab *at*
www.myeconlab.com.

1. What is the typical relationship among interest rates on three-month Treasury bills, long-term Canada bonds, and corporate bonds?

2. What effect might a fall in stock prices have on business investment?

3. What effect might a rise in stock prices have on consumers' decisions to spend?

4. Why are financial markets important to the health of the economy?

5. What was the main cause of the global financial crisis that began in 2007?

6. What is the basic activity of banks?

7. What are the other important financial intermediaries in the economy, besides banks?

8. Can you think of any financial innovation in the past 10 years that has affected you personally? Has it made you better off or worse off? Why?

9. Has the inflation rate in Canada increased or decreased in the past few years? What about interest rates?

10. If history repeats itself and we see a decline in the rate of money growth, what might you expect to happen to:
    a. real GDP?
    b. the inflation rate?
    c. interest rates?

11. When interest rates decrease, how might businesses and consumers change their economic behaviour?

12. Is everybody worse off when interest rates rise?

13. Why do managers of financial institutions care so much about the activities of the Bank of Canada?

14. How does the current size of the Canadian budget deficit compare to the historical budget deficit or surplus for the time period since 1960?

15. How would a fall in the value of the pound sterling affect British consumers?

16. How would an increase in the value of the pound sterling affect Canadian businesses?

17. How can changes in foreign exchange rates affect the profitability of financial institutions?

18. According to Figure 1-8, in which years would you have chosen to visit the Canadian Rockies rather than the Grand Canyon in Arizona?

19. When the dollar is worth more in relation to currencies of other countries, are you more likely to buy Canadian-made or foreign-made jeans? Are Canadian companies that manufacture jeans happier when the dollar is strong or when it is weak? What about a Canadian company that is in the business of importing jeans into Canada?

20. Much of the Canadian government debt is held by foreign investors in the form of Canada bonds and currency. How do fluctuations in the dollar exchange rate affect the value of that debt held by foreigners?

APPLIED PROBLEMS

All applied problems are available in MyEconLab *at* **www.myeconlab.com.**

21. The following table lists monthly exchange rates between the U.S. dollar and the Canadian dollar (in $/US$) for 2013 (this is CANSIM series V37426).

January	0.99213
February	1.00984
March	1.02473
April	1.01869
May	1.01985
June	1.03146
July	1.04032
August	1.04086
September	1.03424
October	1.00363
November	1.04923
December	1.06391

a. Which month would have been the best for converting Canadian dollars into U.S. dollars? Which month would have been the worst?

b. Did the Canadian dollar appreciate or depreciate in 2013?

c. What was the percentage appreciation or depreciation of the Canadian dollar in 2013?

d. If you convert the monthly observations into an annual observation (by taking the arithmetic average), how representative will the annual observation be of the exchange rate during 2013?

DATA ANALYSIS PROBLEMS

Download data for these problems from MyEconLab *at* **www.myeconlab.com**.

1. Go to the Statistics Canada CANSIM database and find data on the M2++ (gross) money supply and the 10-year Canada bond rate from June 1982 to November 2014. Add the two series into a single graph. Transform the M2++ money supply variable into the M2++ growth rate by adjusting the *units* for the M2++ money supply to "Percent Change from Year Ago."

a. In general, how have the growth rate of the M2++ money supply and the 10-year Canada bond rate behaved during recessions and during expansionary periods since the year 2000?

b. In general, is there an obvious, stable relationship between money growth and the 10-year interest rate since the year 2000?

c. Compare the money growth rate and the 10-year interest rate for the most recent month available to the rates for January 2000. How do the rates compare?

2. Go to the Bank of Canada Website and find data (from January 1981 to January 2015) on the 3-month treasury bill rate (CANSIM series V122541), the three-month prime corporate paper rate (CANSIM series V122491), the 5-year Canada bond rate (CANSIM series V122540), and the 5-year conventional mortgage rate (CANSIM series V122521).

a. In general, how do these interest rates behave during recessions and during expansionary periods?

b. In general, how do the 3-month rates compare to the 5-year rates? How do the treasury rates compare to the respective commercial paper and mortgage rates?

c. For the most recent available month of data, take the average of the 3-month rates and compare it to the average of the 3-month rates from January 2000. How do the averages compare?

d. For the most recent available month of data, take the average of the 5-year rates and compare it to the average of the 5-year rates from January 2000. How do the averages compare?

WEB EXERCISES

1. In this exercise, we will practice collecting data from the Web and graphing it using Excel. Go to **www.forecasts.org/data/index.htm,** click on "Exchange Rate Data" at the top of the page, and choose the Canada Dollar CAD—Monthly option. This will give you data on the Canadian Dollar per U.S. dollar exchange rate.

   a. Move the data into an Excel spreadsheet.

   b. Using the data from part (a), prepare a graph. Use the Excel Chart Wizard to properly label your axes.

2. In Web Exercise 1, you collected data on and then graphed the Canadian dollar per U.S. dollar exchange rate. This same site reports forecast values of the Canadian dollar per U.S. dollar exchange rate. Go to **www.forecasts.org/data/index.htm**, and click on FFC Home at the top of the page. Click on the "Canadian Dollar to USD" link under Forecasts in the far-left column.

   a. What is the Canadian dollar per U.S. dollar exchange rate forecast to be in six months?

   b. What percentage increase is forecast for the next six months?

WEB REFERENCES

www.bankofcanada.ca/

Daily, weekly, monthly, quarterly, and annual releases and historical data for selected interest rates, foreign exchange rates, and key economic indicators, for Canada.

research.stlouisfed.org/fred2/

The Federal Reserve Economic Data (FRED) database reports historical data for the United States and other countries, including Canada.

www.oanda.com/currency/converter/

This site reports exchange rates for many countries.

www.bankofcanada.ca/rates/related/inflation-calculator/

This calculator lets you compute how the dollar's buying power has changed since 1914.

www.nationaldebtclocks.org/debtclock/canada

National debt clock. This site reports the exact national debt of Canada at each point in time.

stockcharts.com/freecharts/historical/

Historical charts of various stock indexes over differing time periods.

1

Defining Aggregate Output, Income, the Price Level, and the Inflation Rate

Because these terms are used so frequently throughout the text, we need to have a clear understanding of the definitions of *aggregate output, income*, the *price level*, and the *inflation rate*.

AGGREGATE OUTPUT AND INCOME

The most commonly reported measure of aggregate output, the **gross domestic product (GDP)**, is the market value of all final goods and services produced in a country during the course of the year. This measure excludes two sets of items that at first glance you might think it would include. Purchases of goods that have been produced in the past, whether a Rembrandt painting or a house built 20 years ago, are not counted as part of GDP; nor are purchases of stocks or bonds. Neither of these enter into the GDP because these categories do not include goods and services produced during the course of the year. Intermediate goods, which are used up in producing final goods and services, such as the sugar in a candy bar or the energy used to produce steel, are also not counted separately as part of the GDP. Because the value of the final goods already includes the value of the intermediate goods, to count them separately would be to count them twice.

Aggregate income, the total income of *factors of production* (land, labour, and capital) from producing goods and services in the economy during the course of the year, is best thought of as being equal to aggregate output. Because the payments for final goods and services must eventually flow back to the owners of the factors of production as income, income payments must equal payments for final goods and services. For example, if the economy has an aggregate output of $2 trillion, total income payments in the economy (aggregate income) are also $2 trillion.

REAL VERSUS NOMINAL MAGNITUDES

When the total value of final goods and services is calculated using current prices, the resulting GDP measure is referred to as *nominal GDP*. The word *nominal* indicates that values are measured using current prices. If all prices doubled but actual production of goods and services remained the same, nominal GDP would double, even though people would not enjoy the benefits of twice as many goods and services. As a result, nominal variables can be misleading measures of economic well-being.

A more reliable measure of economic production expresses values in terms of prices for an arbitrary base year, currently 2007. GDP measured with constant prices is referred to as *real GDP*, the word *real* indicating that values are measured in terms of fixed prices. Real variables thus measure the quantities of goods and services and do not change because prices have changed, but rather only if actual quantities have changed.

A brief example will make the distinction clearer. Suppose that you have a nominal income of $30 000 in 2017 and that your nominal income was $15 000 in 2007. If all prices doubled between 2007 and 2017, are you better off? The answer is no: although your income has doubled, your $30 000 buys you only the same amount of goods because prices have also doubled. A *real* income measure indicates that your income in terms of the goods it can buy is the same. Measured in 2007 prices, the $30 000 of nominal income in 2017 turns out to be only $15 000 of real income. Because your real income is actually the same in the two years, you are no better or worse off in 2017 than you were in 2007.

Because real variables measure quantities in terms of real goods and services, they are typically of more interest than nominal variables. In this text, discussion of aggregate output or aggregate income always refers to real measures (such as real GDP).

AGGREGATE PRICE LEVEL

In this chapter, we defined the aggregate price level as a measure of average prices in the economy. Three measures of the aggregate price level are commonly encountered in economic data. The first is the *GDP deflator*, which is defined as nominal GDP divided by real GDP. Thus, if 2017 nominal GDP is $10 trillion but 2017 real GDP in 2007 prices is $9 trillion,

$$\text{GDP deflator} = \frac{\$10 \text{ trillion}}{\$9 \text{ trillion}} = 1.11$$

The GDP deflator equation indicates that, on average, prices have risen 11% since 2007. Typically, measures of the price level are presented in the form of a price index, which expresses the price level for the base year (in our example, 2007) as 100. Thus the GDP deflator for 2017 would be 111.

Another popular measure of the aggregate price level (which officials in the Bank of Canada frequently focus on) is the *PCE deflator*, which is similar to the GDP deflator and is defined as nominal personal consumption expenditures (PCE) divided by real PCE.

The measure of the aggregate price level that is most frequently reported in the press is the *consumer price index* (CPI). The CPI is measured by pricing a "basket" of goods and services bought by a typical urban household. If, over the course of the year, the cost of this basket of goods and services rises from $500 to $600, the CPI has risen by 20%. The CPI is also expressed as a price index with the base year equal to 100.

The CPI, the PCE deflator, and the GDP deflator measures of the price level can be used to convert or deflate a nominal magnitude into a real magnitude. This is accomplished by dividing the nominal magnitude by the price index. In our example, in which the GDP deflator for 2017 is 1.11 (expressed as an index value of 111), real GDP for 2017 equals

$$\frac{\$10 \text{ trillion}}{1.11} = \$9 \text{ trillion in 2007 prices}$$

which corresponds to the real GDP figure for 2017 assumed earlier.

GROWTH RATES AND THE INFLATION RATE

The media often talk about the economy's growth rate, and particularly the growth rate of real GDP. A growth rate is defined as the percentage change in a variable, i.e.,

$$\text{growth rate of } x = \frac{x_t - x_{t-1}}{x_{t-1}} \times 100$$

where t indicates today and $t - 1$ a year earlier.

For example, if real GDP grew from \$9 trillion in 2017 to \$9.5 trillion in 2018, then the GDP growth rate for 2018 would be 5.6%:

$$\text{GDP growth rate} = \frac{\$9.5 \text{ trillion} - \$9 \text{ trillion}}{\$9 \text{ trillion}} \times 100 = 5.6\%$$

The inflation rate is defined as the growth rate of the aggregate price level. Thus, if the GDP deflator rose from 111 in 2017 to 113 in 2018, the inflation rate using the GDP deflator would be 1.8%:

$$\text{inflation rate} = \frac{113 - 111}{111} \times 100 = 1.8\%$$

If the growth rate is for a period less than one year, it is usually reported on an annualized basis; that is, it is converted to the growth rate over a year's time, assuming that the growth rate remains constant. For GDP, which is reported quarterly, the annualized growth rate would be approximately four times the percentage change in GDP from the previous quarter. For example, if GDP rose $\frac{1}{2}$% from the first quarter of 2017 to the second quarter of 2017, then the annualized GDP growth rate for the second quarter of 2017 would be reported as 2% $(= 4 \times \frac{1}{2}\%)$. (A more accurate calculation would be 2.02%, because a precise quarterly growth rate should be compounded on a quarterly basis.)

2

An Overview of the Financial System

Learning Objectives

After studying this chapter you should be able to

1. Compare and contrast direct and indirect finance.
2. Identify the structure and components of financial markets.
3. List and describe the different types of financial market instruments.
4. Recognize the international dimensions of financial markets.
5. Summarize the roles of transaction costs, risk sharing, and information costs as they relate to financial intermediaries.
6. List and describe the different types of financial intermediaries.
7. Identify the reasons for, and list the types of financial market regulations.

PREVIEW

Inez the Inventor has designed a low-cost robot that cleans the house (even does the windows!), washes the car, and mows the lawn, but she has no funds to put her wonderful invention into production. Walter the Widower has plenty of savings, which he and his wife accumulated over the years. If Inez and Walter could get together so that Walter could provide funds to Inez, Inez's robot would see the light of day, and the economy would be better off: We would have cleaner houses, shinier cars, and more beautiful lawns.

Financial markets (bond and stock markets) and financial intermediaries (such as banks, insurance companies, and pension funds) serve the basic function of getting people like Inez and Walter together so that funds can move from those who have a surplus of funds (Walter) to those who have a shortage of funds (Inez). More realistically, when Apple invents a better iPod, it may need funds to bring its new product to market. Similarly, when a local government needs to build a road or a school, it may require more funds than local property taxes provide. Well-functioning financial markets and financial intermediaries are crucial to economic health.

To study the effects of financial markets and financial intermediaries on the economy, we need to acquire an understanding of their general structure and operation. In this chapter, we learn about the major financial intermediaries and the instruments that are traded in financial markets, as well as how these markets are regulated.

This chapter presents an overview of the fascinating study of financial markets and institutions. We return to a more detailed treatment of the regulation, structure, and evolution of the financial system in Chapters 8 through 13.

FUNCTION OF FINANCIAL MARKETS

Financial markets perform the essential economic function of channeling funds from households, firms, and governments that have surplus funds by spending less than their income to those that have a shortage of funds because they wish to spend more than their income. This function is shown schematically in Figure 2-1. Those who have saved

MyEconLab Mini-lecture

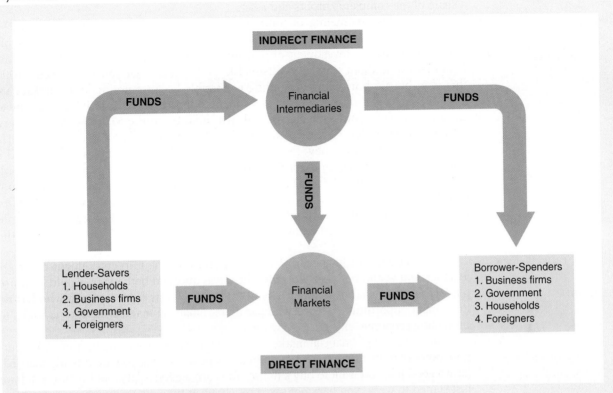

FIGURE 2-1   **Flows of Funds Through the Financial System**

The arrows show that funds flow from lender-savers to borrower-spenders via two routes: *direct finance*, in which borrowers borrow funds directly from financial markets by selling securities, and *indirect finance*, in which a financial intermediary borrows funds from lender-savers and then uses these funds to make loans to borrower-spenders.

and are lending funds, the lender-savers, are at the left, and those who must borrow funds to finance their spending, the borrower-spenders, are at the right. The principal lender-savers are households, but business enterprises and the government (particularly provincial and municipal government), as well as foreigners and their governments, sometimes also find themselves with excess funds and so lend them out. The most important borrower-spenders are businesses and the government (particularly the federal government), but households and foreigners also borrow to finance their purchases of cars, furniture, and houses. The arrows show that funds flow from lender-savers to borrower-spenders via two routes.

In *direct finance* (the route at the bottom of Figure 2-1), borrowers borrow funds directly from lenders in financial markets by selling the lenders *securities* (also called *financial instruments*), which are claims on the borrower's future income or assets. Securities are **assets** for the person who buys them but **liabilities** (IOUs or debts) for the individual or firm that sells (issues) them. For example, if Ford needs to borrow funds to pay for a new factory to manufacture electric cars, it might borrow the funds from savers by selling them a *bond*—a debt security that promises to make periodic payments for a specified period of time, or a *stock*—a security that entitles the owner to a share of the company's profits and assets.

Why is this channeling of funds from savers to spenders so important to the economy? The answer is that the people who save are frequently not the same people who have profitable investment opportunities available to them, the entrepreneurs. Let's first think about this on a personal level. Suppose that you have saved $1000 this year, but no borrowing or lending is possible because no financial markets are available. If you do not have an investment opportunity that will permit you to earn income with your savings, you will just hold on to the $1000 and it will earn no interest. However, Carl the Carpenter has a productive use for your $1000: He can use it to purchase a new tool that will shorten the time it takes him to build a house, thereby earning an extra $200 per year. If you could get in touch with Carl, you could lend him the $1000 at a rental fee (interest) of $100 per year, and both of you would be better off. You would earn $100 per year on your $1000, instead of the zero amount that you would earn otherwise, while Carl would earn $100 more income per year (the $200 extra earnings per year minus the $100 rental fee for the use of the funds).

In the absence of financial markets, you and Carl the Carpenter might never get together. You would both be stuck with the status quo, and both of you would be worse off. Without financial markets, it is hard to transfer funds from a person who has no investment opportunities to one who has them. Financial markets are thus essential to promoting economic efficiency.

The existence of financial markets is beneficial even if someone borrows for a purpose other than increasing production in a business. Say that you are recently married, have a good job, and want to buy a house. You earn a good salary, but because you have just started to work, you have not saved much. Over time, you would have no problem saving enough to buy the house of your dreams, but by then you would be too old to get full enjoyment from it. Without financial markets, you are stuck; you cannot buy the house and must continue to live in your tiny apartment.

If a financial market were set up so that people who had built up savings could lend you the funds to buy the house, you would be more than happy to pay them some interest so that you could own a home while you are still young enough to enjoy it. Then, over time, you would pay back your loan. If this loan could occur, you would be better off, as would the persons who made you the loan. They would now earn some interest, whereas they would not if the financial market did not exist.

Now we can see why financial markets have such an important function in the economy. They allow funds to move from people who lack productive investment opportunities to people who have such opportunities. Financial markets are critical for producing an efficient allocation of **capital** (wealth, either financial or physical, that is employed to produce more wealth), which contributes to higher production and efficiency for the overall economy. Indeed, as we will explore in Chapter 9, when financial markets break down during financial crises, as they did during the recent global financial crisis, severe economic hardship results, which can sometimes lead to dangerous political instability.

Well-functioning financial markets also directly improve the well-being of consumers by allowing them to time their purchases more efficiently. They provide funds to young people to buy what they need (and will eventually be able to afford) without forcing them to wait until they have saved up the entire purchase price. Financial markets that are operating efficiently improve the economic welfare of everyone in the society.

STRUCTURE OF FINANCIAL MARKETS

Now that we understand the basic function of financial markets, let's look at their structure. The following descriptions of several categories of financial markets illustrate essential features of these markets.

Debt and Equity Markets

A firm or an individual can obtain funds in a financial market in two ways. The most common method is through the issuance of a debt instrument, such as a bond or a mortgage, which is a contractual agreement by the borrower to pay the holder of the instrument fixed dollar amounts at regular intervals (interest and principal payments) until a specified date (the maturity date), when a final payment is made. The **maturity** of a debt instrument is the number of years (term) until that instrument's expiration date. A debt instrument is **short-term** if its maturity term is less than a year and **long-term** if its maturity term is ten years or longer. Debt instruments with a maturity term between one and ten years are said to be **intermediate-term**.

The second method of raising funds is through the issuance of **equities**, such as common stock, which are claims to the *net income* (income after expenses and taxes) and the assets of a business. If you own one share of common stock in a company that has issued one million shares, you are entitled to 1 one-millionth of the firm's net income and 1 one-millionth of the firm's assets. Equities often make periodic payments (**dividends**) to their holders and are considered long-term securities because they have no maturity date. In addition, owning stock means that you own a portion of the firm and thus have the right to vote on issues important to the firm and to elect its directors.

The main disadvantage of owning a corporation's equities rather than its debt is that an equity holder is a *residual claimant*; that is, the corporation must pay all its debt holders before it pays its equity holders. The advantage of holding equities is that equity holders benefit directly from any increases in the corporation's profitability or asset value because equities confer ownership rights on the equity holders. Debt holders do not share in this benefit, because their dollar payments are fixed. We examine the pros and cons of debt versus equity instruments in more detail in Chapter 8, which provides an economic analysis of financial structure.

Primary and Secondary Markets

A **primary market** is a financial market in which new issues of a security, such as a bond or a stock, are sold to initial buyers by the corporation or government agency borrowing the funds. A **secondary market** is a financial market in which securities that have been previously issued can be resold.

The primary markets for securities are not well known to the public because the selling of securities to initial buyers often takes place behind closed doors. An important financial institution that assists in the initial sale of securities in the primary market is the **investment bank**. The investment bank does this by **underwriting** securities: It guarantees a price for a corporation's securities and then sells them to the public.

The Toronto Stock Exchange (TSX) and the TSX Venture Exchange, in which previously issued stocks are traded, are the best-known examples of secondary markets, although the bond markets, in which previously-issued bonds of major corporations and the Canadian government are bought and sold, actually have a larger trading volume. Other examples of secondary markets are foreign exchange markets, futures markets, and options markets. Securities brokers and dealers are crucial to a well-functioning secondary market. **Brokers** are agents of investors who match buyers with sellers of securities; **dealers** link buyers and sellers by buying and selling securities at stated prices.

When an individual buys a security in the secondary market, the person who has sold the security receives money in exchange for the security, but the corporation that issued the security acquires no new funds. A corporation acquires new funds only when its securities are first sold in the primary market. Nonetheless, secondary markets serve two important functions. First, they make it easier and quicker to sell these financial instruments to raise cash; that is, they make the financial instruments more **liquid**. The increased liquidity of these instruments then makes them more desirable and thus easier for the issuing firm to sell in the primary market. Second, secondary markets determine the price of the security that the issuing firm sells in the primary market. The investors who buy securities in the primary market will pay the issuing corporation no more than the price they think the secondary market will set for this security. The higher the security's price in the secondary market, the higher the price the issuing firm will receive for a new security in the primary market, and hence the greater the amount of financial capital it can raise. Conditions in the secondary market are therefore the most relevant to corporations issuing securities. For this reason, books like this one, which deal with financial markets, focus on the behaviour of secondary markets rather than that of primary markets.

Exchanges and Over-the-Counter Markets

Secondary markets can be organized in two ways. One method is through **exchanges**, where buyers and sellers of securities (or their agents or brokers) meet in one central location to conduct trades. The Toronto Stock Exchange for stocks and ICE Futures Canada (a subsidiary of Intercontinental Exchange) for commodities (wheat, oats, barley, and other agricultural commodities) are examples of organized exchanges. The Montreal Exchange (ME) is another example of an organized exchange, offering a range of equity, interest rate, and index derivative products.

The other forum for a secondary market is an **over-the-counter (OTC) market**, in which dealers at different locations who have an inventory of securities stand ready to buy and sell securities "over the counter" to anyone who comes to them and is willing to accept their prices. Because over-the-counter dealers are in contact via computers and know the prices set by one another, the OTC market is very competitive and not very different from a market with an organized exchange.

Many common stocks are traded over-the-counter, although a majority of the largest corporations have their shares traded at organized stock exchanges. The Canadian government bond market, by contrast, is set up as an over-the-counter market. Dealers establish a "market" in these securities by standing ready to buy and sell Canadian government bonds. Other over-the-counter markets include those that trade other types of financial instruments, such as negotiable certificates of deposit, federal funds, and foreign exchange instruments.

Money and Capital Markets

Another way of distinguishing between markets is on the basis of the maturity of the securities traded in each market. The **money market** is a financial market in which only short-term debt instruments (generally those with original maturity terms of less than one year) are traded; the **capital market** is the market in which longer-term debt instruments (generally those with original maturity terms of one year or greater) and equity instruments are traded. Money market securities are usually more widely traded than longer-term securities and so tend to be more liquid. In addition, as we will see in Chapter 4, short-term securities have smaller fluctuations in prices than long-term securities, making them safer investments. As a result, corporations and banks actively use the money market to earn interest on surplus funds that they expect to have only temporarily. Capital market securities, such as stocks and long-term bonds, are often held by financial intermediaries such as insurance companies and pension funds, which have little uncertainty about the amount of funds they will have available in the future.

FINANCIAL MARKET INSTRUMENTS

To complete our understanding of how financial markets perform the important role of channeling funds from lender-savers to borrower-spenders, we need to examine the securities (instruments) traded in financial markets. We first focus on the instruments traded in the money market and then turn to those traded in the capital market.

Money Market Instruments

Because of their short terms to maturity, the debt instruments traded in the money market undergo the least price fluctuations and so are the least risky investments. The money market has undergone great changes in the past three decades, with the amounts of some financial instruments growing at a far more rapid rate than others.

The principal money market instruments are listed in Table 2-1, along with the amount at the end of 1980, 1990, 2000, and 2013. The Following the Financial News box discusses the money market interest rates most frequently reported in the media.

TABLE 2-1	Principal Money Market Instruments			
	Amount Outstanding ($ millions)			
Type of Instrument	**1980**	**1990**	**2000**	**2013**
Treasury bills				
Government of Canada	13 709	113 654	76 634	162 184
Provincial governments	905	12 602	17 523	45 782
Municipal governments	113	514	188	455
Short-term paper				
Commercial paper	2555	12 971	24 330	11 510

Source: Statistics Canada Cansim series V37377, V122256, V122257, and V122652.

Following the Financial News   Money Market Rates

The four money market interest rates discussed most frequently in the media are:

Prime rate: The base interest rate on corporate bank loans, an indicator of the cost to businesses borrowing from banks

Overnight interest rate: The interest rate charged on overnight loans in the overnight funds market, a sensitive indicator of the cost to banks of borrowing funds from other banks and the stance of monetary policy

Treasury bill rate: The interest rate on Government of Canada Treasury bills, an indicator of general interest-rate movements

Libor rate: The British Bankers' Association average of interbank rates for dollar deposits in the London market

The data for these interest rates are reported daily in newspapers and on Internet sites such as **www .bankrate.com**.

Government of Canada Treasury Bills   These short-term debt instruments of the Canadian government are issued in 1-, 3-, 6-, and 12-month maturities to finance the federal government. They pay a set amount at maturity with no additional interest payments; however, they effectively pay interest by initially selling at a discount, that is, at a price lower than the set amount paid at maturity. For instance, you might pay $9600 in May 2017 for a one-year Treasury bill that can be redeemed in May 2018 for $10 000.

Treasury bills are the most liquid of all money market instruments because they are the most actively traded. They are also the safest money market instrument because there is a low probability of **default**, a situation in which the party issuing the debt instrument (the federal government, in this case) is unable to make interest payments or pay off the amount owed when the instrument matures. The federal government can always meet its debt obligations because it can raise taxes or issue **currency** (paper money or coins) to pay off its debts. Treasury bills are held mainly by banks, although small amounts are held by households, corporations, and other financial intermediaries.

Certificates of Deposit   A *certificate of deposit* (CD) is a debt instrument sold by a bank to depositors that pays annual interest of a given amount and at maturity pays back the original purchase price. CDs are often negotiable, meaning that they can be traded, and in bearer form (called **bearer deposit notes**), meaning that the buyer's name is not recorded in either the issuer's books or on the security itself. These negotiable CDs are issued in multiples of $100 000 and with maturities of 30 to 365 days, and can be resold in a secondary market, thus offering the purchaser both yield and liquidity.

Chartered banks also issue non-negotiable CDs. That is, these CDs cannot be sold to someone else and cannot be redeemed from the bank before maturity without paying a substantial penalty. Non-negotiable CDs are issued in denominations ranging from $5000 to $100 000, with maturities of one day to five years. They are also known as **term deposit receipts** or **term notes**.

CDs are also an extremely important source of funds for trust and loan companies. These institutions issue CDs under a variety of names; for example: DRs (Deposit Receipts), GTCs (Guaranteed Trust Certificates), GICs (Guaranteed Investment Certificates), and GIRs (Guaranteed Investment Receipts).

Commercial Paper   *Commercial paper* is a short-term debt instrument issued in either Canadian dollars or other currencies by large banks and well-known corporations, such as Bank of Montreal and Bombardier. Because commercial paper is unsecured, only the largest and most creditworthy corporations issue commercial paper. The interest rate the corporation is charged reflects the firm's level of risk. The interest rate on commercial paper is low relative to those on other corporate fixed-income securities and slightly higher than the rates of Government of Canada Treasury bills.

Sales finance companies also issue short-term promissory notes known as **finance paper**. Finance and commercial paper are issued in minimum denominations of $50 000 and in maturities of 30 to 365 days for finance paper and 1 to 365 days for commercial paper. Most finance and commercial paper is issued on a discounted basis. Chapter 11 discusses why the commercial paper market has had such tremendous growth.

Repurchase Agreements   *Repurchase agreements*, or *repos*, are effectively short-term loans (usually with a maturity of less than two weeks) for which Treasury bills serve as *collateral*, an asset that the lender receives if the borrower does not pay back the loan. Repos are made as follows: A large corporation, such as Bombardier, may have some idle funds in its bank account, say $1 million, which it would like to lend for a week. Bombardier uses this excess $1 million to buy Treasury bills from a bank, which agrees to repurchase them the next week at a price slightly above Bombardier's purchase price. The net effect of this agreement is that Bombardier makes a loan of $1 million to the bank and holds $1 million of the bank's Treasury bills until the bank repurchases the bills to pay off the loan. Repurchase agreements are now an important source of bank funds. The most important lenders in this market are large corporations.

Overnight Funds   These instruments are typically overnight loans between banks of their deposits with the Bank of Canada. The *overnight funds* designation is somewhat confusing because these loans are not made by the federal government or by the Bank of Canada but rather by banks to other banks. One reason why a bank might borrow in the overnight funds market is that it might find it does not have enough settlement balances in its deposit accounts at the Bank of Canada. It can then borrow these balances from another bank with excess settlement balances. This market is very sensitive to the credit needs of the banks, so the interest rate on these loans, called the **overnight interest rate**, is a closely watched barometer of the tightness of credit market conditions in the banking system and the stance of monetary policy. When it is high, the overnight interest rate indicates that the banks are strapped for funds; when low, it indicates that banks' credit needs are low.

Capital Market Instruments

Capital market instruments are debt and equity instruments with maturities of greater than one year. They have far wider price fluctuations than money market instruments and are considered to be fairly risky investments. The principal capital market instruments are

Following the Financial News   Capital Market Interest Rates

The four interest rates on capital market instruments discussed most frequently in the media are:

10-year Canada rate: The interest rate on Government of Canada bonds maturing in 10 years

5-year variable-rate mortgage rate: The interest rate on a 5-year, variable-rate residential mortgage

5-year fixed-rate mortgage rate: The interest rate on a 5-year, fixed-rate residential mortgage

New-car loan rate: The interest rate on a four-year, fixed-rate new-car loan

The data for these interest rates are reported daily in newspapers and on Internet sites.

listed in Table 2-2, which shows the amount at the end of 1980, 1990, 2000, and 2013. The Following the Financial News box discusses the capital market interest rates most frequently reported in the media.

Stocks   *Stocks* are equity claims on the net income and assets of a corporation. Aggregate Canadian Market Capitalization was about $500 billion at the end of 2014. The amount of new stock issues in any given year is typically quite small—less than 1% of the total value of shares outstanding. Individuals hold around half of the value of stocks; pension funds, mutual funds, and insurance companies hold the rest.

Mortgages and Mortgage-Backed Securities   **Mortgages** are loans to households or firms to purchase housing, land, or other real structures, where the structure or land serves as collateral for the loans. The mortgage market is the largest debt market in Canada, with the amount of residential mortgages (used to purchase residential housing) outstanding more than tenfold the amount of commercial and farm mortgages. Mortgages are provided by financial institutions such as chartered banks, trust and loan

TABLE 2-2   Principal Capital Market Instruments

Type of Instrument	Amount Outstanding ($ billions)			
	1980	**1990**	**2000**	**2013**
Corporate stocks (market value)	42.9	110.7	242.6	466.2
Residential mortgages	91.9	245.3	431.2	1187.9
Corporate bonds	29.8	72.3	185.1	404.7
Government of Canada securities (marketable)	27.9	124.6	301.9	413.4
Bank commercial loans	58.8	102.6	132.2	212.9
Consumer loans	48.4	101.6	203.1	522.7
Nonresidential and farm mortgages	15.1	56.1	50.2	107.7

Source: Statistics Canada Cansim series V122642, V122746, V122640, V37378

companies, and credit unions and *caisses populaires*. However in recent years, a growing amount of the funds for mortgages have been provided by **mortgage-backed securities**, bond-like debt instruments backed by a bundle of individual mortgages, whose interest and principal payments are collectively paid to the holders of the security. As we will see in Chapter 9, mortgage-backed securities and more complicated variants have become notorious because they played a key role in promoting the recent global financial crisis. Banks and life insurance companies provide the majority of non-residential and farm mortgages. The federal government also plays an active role in the mortgage market via the Canada Mortgage and Housing Corporation (CMHC), which provides funds to the mortgage market by selling bonds and using the proceeds to buy mortgages.

Corporate Bonds   These long-term bonds are issued by corporations with very strong credit ratings. The typical *corporate bond* sends the holder an interest payment twice a year and pays off the face value when the bond matures. Some corporate bonds, called *convertible bonds,* have the additional feature of allowing the holder to convert them into a specified number of shares of stock at any time up to the maturity date. This feature makes these convertible bonds more desirable to prospective purchasers than bonds without it, and it allows the corporation to reduce its interest payments because the bonds can increase in value if the price of the stock appreciates sufficiently. Because the outstanding amount of both convertible and nonconvertible bonds for any given corporation is small, corporate bonds are not nearly as liquid as other securities such as government of Canada bonds.

Although the size of the corporate bond market is substantially smaller than that of the stock market, with the amount of corporate bonds outstanding less than one-third that of stocks, the volume of new corporate bonds issued each year is substantially greater than the volume of new stock issues. Thus the behaviour of the corporate bond market is probably far more important to a firm's financing decisions than is the behaviour of the stock market. The principal buyers of corporate bonds are life insurance companies; pension funds and households are the other large holders.

Government of Canada Bonds   These intermediate-term bonds (those with initial maturities from 1 to 10 years) and long-term bonds (those with initial maturities greater than 10 years) are issued by the federal government to finance the deficits of the federal government. Because they are the most widely traded bonds in Canada, they are the most liquid security traded in the capital market. They are held by the Bank of Canada, banks, households, and foreigners. These debt instruments are issued in either bearer or registered form and in denominations of $1000, $5000, $25 000, $100 000, and $1 million. In the case of **registered bonds**, the name of the owner appears on the bond certificate and is also recorded at the Bank of Canada. Some issues have the additional **call** (or **redemption**) feature of allowing them to be "called" on specified notice (usually 30 to 60 days).

Canada Savings Bonds   These are nonmarketable bonds issued by the Government of Canada and sold each year from early October through to April 1. *Canada Savings Bonds* (CSBs) are floating-rate bonds, available in denominations from $100 to $10 000 and offered exclusively to individuals, estates, and specified trusts. They are issued as registered bonds and can be purchased from financial institutions or through payroll savings plans. CSBs are different from all other bonds issued by the Government of Canada in that they do not rise or fall in value, like other bonds do. They have the valuable option of being redeemable at face value plus accrued interest, at any time prior to maturity, by being presented at any financial institution. In October 1998 the Government of Canada introduced another type of bond that is similar to CSBs—Canada Premium Bonds (CPBs). CPBs offer a slightly higher coupon rate than CSBs offer, but can be redeemed only once a year, on the anniversary of the issue date and during the month after that date.

Provincial and Municipal Government Bonds   Provincial and municipal governments also issue bonds to finance expenditures on schools, roads, and other large programs. The securities issued by provincial governments are referred to as **provincial bonds** or **provincials**, and those issued by municipal governments as **municipal bonds** or **municipals**—the securities issued by the federal government are referred to as **Canadas**. Provincials and municipals are denominated in either domestic currency or foreign currencies, mostly U.S. dollars, Swiss francs, and Japanese yen. Provincial and municipal government bonds are mainly held by trusteed pension plans, social security funds (predominantly the Canada Pension Plan), and foreigners.

Government Agency Securities   These are long-term bonds issued by various government agencies such as the Ontario Municipal Improvement Corporation and the Alberta Municipal Financing Corporation to assist municipalities to finance such items as mortgages, farm loans, or power-generating equipment. The provincial governments guarantee many of these securities. They function much like Canadas, provincials, and municipals and are held by similar parties.

Consumer and Bank Commercial Loans   These loans to consumers and businesses are made principally by banks, but in the case of consumer loans, also by finance companies.

INTERNATIONALIZATION OF FINANCIAL MARKETS

The growing internationalization of financial markets has become an important trend. Before the 1980s, U.S. financial markets were much larger than those outside the United States, but in recent years the dominance of U.S. markets has been weakening. (See the Global box "Are U.S. Capital Markets Losing Their Edge?") The extraordinary growth of foreign financial markets has been the result of both large increases in the pool of savings in foreign countries such as Japan, and the deregulation of foreign financial markets, which has enabled foreign markets to expand their activities. Canadian corporations and banks are now more likely to tap international capital markets to raise needed funds, and Canadian investors often seek investment opportunities abroad. Similarly, foreign corporations and banks raise funds from Canadians, and foreigners have become important investors in Canada. A look at international bond markets and world stock markets will give us a picture of how this globalization of financial markets is taking place.

International Bond Market, Eurobonds, and Eurocurrencies

The traditional instruments in the international bond market are known as **foreign bonds**. Foreign bonds are sold in a foreign country and are denominated in that country's currency. For example, if the German automaker Porsche sells a bond in Canada

Global Are U.S. Capital Markets Losing Their Edge?

Over the past few decades, the United States has lost its international dominance in a number of manufacturing industries, including automobiles and consumer electronics, as other countries became more competitive in global markets. Recent evidence suggests that financial markets now are undergoing a similar trend: Just as Ford and General Motors have lost global market share to Toyota and Honda, U.S. stock and bond markets recently have seen their share of sales of newly-issued corporate securities slip. The London and Hong Kong stock exchanges now handle a larger share of initial public offerings (IPOs) of stock than does the New York Stock Exchange, which had been by far the dominant exchange in terms of IPO value before 2000. Furthermore, the number of stocks listed on U.S. exchanges has been falling, while stock listings abroad have been growing rapidly: Total listings outside the United States are now about ten times greater than those in the United States. Likewise, the portion of new corporate bonds issued worldwide that are initially sold in U.S. capital markets has fallen below the share sold in European debt markets.

Why do corporations that issue new securities to raise capital now conduct more of this business in financial markets in Europe and Asia? Among the factors contributing to this trend are quicker adoption of technological innovation by foreign financial mar-

kets, tighter immigration controls in the United States following the terrorist attacks of 2001, and perceptions that listing on American exchanges will expose foreign securities issuers to greater risks of lawsuits. Many people see burdensome financial regulation as the main cause, however, and point specifically to the Sarbanes-Oxley Act of 2002. The U.S. Congress passed this act after a number of accounting scandals involving U.S. corporations and the accounting firms that audited them came to light. Sarbanes-Oxley aims to strengthen the integrity of the auditing process and the quality of information provided in corporate financial statements. The costs to corporations of complying with the new rules and procedures are high, especially for smaller firms, but largely avoidable if firms choose to issue their securities in financial markets outside the United States. For this reason, there is much support for revising Sarbanes-Oxley to lessen its allegedly harmful effects and induce more securities issuers back to U.S. financial markets. However, evidence is not conclusive to support the view that Sarbanes-Oxley is the main cause of the relative decline of U.S. financial markets and therefore in need of reform.

Discussion of the relative decline of U.S. financial markets and debate about the factors that are contributing to it likely will continue.

denominated in Canadian dollars, it is classified as a foreign bond. Foreign bonds have been an important instrument in the international capital market for centuries. In fact, a large percentage of U.S. railroads built in the nineteenth century were financed by sales of foreign bonds in Britain.

A more recent innovation in the international bond market is the **Eurobond**, a bond denominated in a currency other than that of the country in which it is sold—for example, a bond denominated in Canadian dollars sold in London. Currently, over 80% of the new issues in the international bond market are Eurobonds, and the market for these securities has grown very rapidly. As a result, the Eurobond market is now larger than the U.S. corporate bond market.

A variant of the Eurobond is **Eurocurrencies**, which are foreign currencies deposited in banks outside the home country. The most important of the Eurocurrencies are **Eurodollars**, which are U.S. dollars deposited in foreign banks outside the United States or in foreign branches of U.S. banks. Because these short-term deposits earn interest, they are similar to short-term Eurobonds. Canadian banks borrow Eurodollar

Following the Financial News   Foreign Stock Market Indexes

The most important of these stock market indexes are:

Dow Jones Industrial Average (DJIA): An index of the 30 largest publicly-traded corporations in the United States, maintained by the Dow Jones Corporation

S&P 500: An index of 500 of the largest companies traded in the United States, maintained by Standard & Poor's

NASDAQ Composite: An index for all the stocks that trade on the NASDAQ stock market, where most of the technology stocks in the United States are traded

FTSE 100: An index of the 100 most highly capitalized UK companies listed on the London Stock Exchange

DAX: An index of the 30 largest German companies trading on the Frankfurt Stock Exchange

CAC 40: An index of the 40 largest French companies trading on Euronext Paris

Hang Seng: An index of the largest companies trading on the Hong Kong stock markets

Strait Times: An index of the 30 largest companies trading on the Singapore Exchange

These indexes are reported daily in newspapers and on Internet sites such as **www.finance.yahoo.com**.

deposits from other banks or from their own foreign branches, and Eurodollars are now an important source of funds for Canadian banks.

Note that the currency, the euro, can create some confusion about the terms Eurobond, Eurocurrencies, and Eurodollars. A bond denominated in euros is called a Eurobond *only if it is sold outside the countries that have adopted the euro.* In fact, most Eurobonds are not denominated in euros but are instead denominated in U.S. dollars. Similarly, Eurodollars have nothing to do with euros, but are instead U.S. dollars deposited in banks outside the United States.

World Stock Markets

Until recently, the U.S. stock market was by far the largest in the world, but stock markets in other countries have been growing in importance, with the United States not always number one. The increased interest in foreign stocks has prompted the development in Canada of mutual funds that specialize in trading in foreign stock markets. As the Following the Financial News box indicates, Canadian investors now pay attention not only to the Canadian stock market but also to stock price indexes for foreign stock markets such as the Dow Jones Industrial Average (New York), the Nikkei 300 Average (Tokyo), and the Financial Times Stock Exchange (FTSE) 100-Share Index (London).

The internationalization of financial markets is having profound effects on Canada. Foreigners not only are providing funds to corporations in Canada but are also helping finance the federal government. Without these foreign funds, the Canadian economy would have grown far less rapidly in the past 20 years. The internationalization of financial markets is also leading the way to a more integrated world economy in which flows of goods and technology between countries are more commonplace. In later chapters, we will encounter many examples of the important roles that international factors play in our economy.

Global   The Importance of Financial Intermediaries Relative to Securities Markets: An International Comparison

Patterns of financing corporations differ across countries, but one key fact emerges: Studies of the major developed countries, including Canada, the United States, the United Kingdom, Japan, Italy, Germany, and France, show that when businesses go looking for funds to finance their activities, they usually obtain them indirectly through financial intermediaries and not directly from securities markets.* Even in Canada and the United States, which have the most developed securities markets in the world, loans from financial intermediaries are far more important for corporate finance than securities markets are. The countries that have made the least use of securities markets are Germany and Japan; in these two countries, financing from financial intermediaries has been almost ten times greater than that from securities markets. However, after the deregulation of Japanese securities markets in recent years, the share of corporate financing by financial intermediaries has been declining relative to the use of securities markets.

Although the dominance of financial intermediaries over securities markets is clear in all countries, the relative importance of bond versus stock markets differs widely across countries. In the United States, the bond market is far more important as a source of corporate finance: On average, the amount of new financing raised using bonds is 10 times the amount raised using stocks. By contrast, countries such as France and Italy make more use of equities markets than of the bond market to raise capital.

* See, for example, Colin Mayer, "Financial Systems, Corporate Finance, and Economic Development," in *Asymmetric Information, Corporate Finance, and Investment,* ed. R. Glenn Hubbard (Chicago: University of Chicago Press, 1990), pp. 307–332.

FUNCTION OF FINANCIAL INTERMEDIARIES: INDIRECT FINANCE

As shown previously in Figure 2-1 (p. 23), funds can move from lenders to borrowers by a second route, called *indirect finance* because it involves a financial intermediary that stands between the lender-savers and the borrower-spenders and helps transfer funds from one to the other. A financial intermediary does this by borrowing funds from lender-savers and then using these funds to make loans to borrower-spenders. For example, a bank might acquire funds by issuing a liability to the public in the form of savings deposits (an asset for the public). It might then use the funds to acquire an asset by making a loan to General Motors or by buying a Canada bond in the financial market. The ultimate result is that funds have been transferred from the public (the lender-savers) to General Motors or to the Canadian government (the borrower-spender) with the help of the financial intermediary (the bank).

The process of indirect financing using financial intermediaries, called **financial intermediation**, is the primary route for moving funds from lenders to borrowers. Indeed, although the media focus much of their attention on securities markets, particularly the stock market, financial intermediaries are a far more important source of financing for corporations than securities markets are. This is true not only for Canada but for other industrialized countries as well (see the Global box). Why are financial intermediaries and indirect finance so important in financial markets? To answer this question, we need to understand the roles of transaction costs, risk sharing, and information costs in financial markets.

Transaction Costs

Transaction costs, the time and money spent in carrying out financial transactions, are a major problem for people who have excess funds to lend. As we have seen, Carl the Carpenter needs $1000 for his new tool, and you know that it is an excellent investment opportunity. You have the cash and would like to lend him the money, but to protect your investment, you have to hire a lawyer to write up the loan contract that specifies how much interest Carl will pay you, when he will make these interest payments, and when he will repay you the $1000. Obtaining the contract will cost you $500. When you figure in this transaction cost for making the loan, you realize that you can't earn enough from the deal (you spend $500 to make perhaps $100) and reluctantly tell Carl that he will have to look elsewhere.

This example illustrates that small savers like you or potential borrowers like Carl might be frozen out of financial markets and thus be unable to benefit from them. Can anyone come to the rescue? Financial intermediaries can.

Financial intermediaries can substantially reduce transaction costs because they have developed expertise in lowering them and because their large size allows them to take advantage of **economies of scale**, the reduction in transaction costs per dollar of transactions as the size (scale) of transactions increases. For example, a bank knows how to find a good lawyer to produce an airtight loan contract, and this contract can be used over and over again in its loan transactions, thus lowering the legal cost per transaction. Instead of a loan contract (which may not be all that well written) costing $500, a bank can hire a top-flight lawyer for $5000 to draw up an airtight loan contract that can be used for 2000 loans at a cost of $2.50 per loan. At a cost of $2.50 per loan, it now becomes profitable for the financial intermediary to lend Carl the $1000.

Because financial intermediaries are able to reduce transaction costs substantially, they make it possible for you to provide funds indirectly to people like Carl with productive investment opportunities. In addition, a financial intermediary's low transaction costs mean that it can provide its customers with **liquidity services**, services that make it easier for customers to conduct transactions. For example, banks provide depositors with chequing accounts that enable them to pay their bills easily. In addition, depositors can earn interest on chequing and savings accounts and yet still convert them into goods and services whenever necessary.

Risk Sharing

Another benefit made possible by the low transaction costs of financial institutions is that these institutions can help reduce the exposure of investors to **risk**—that is, uncertainty about the returns investors will earn on assets. Financial intermediaries do this through the process known as **risk sharing**: They create and sell assets with risk characteristics that people are comfortable with, and the intermediaries then use the funds they acquire by selling these assets to purchase other assets that may have far more risk. Low transaction costs allow financial intermediaries to share risk at low cost, enabling them to earn a profit on the spread between the returns they earn on risky assets and the payments they make on the assets they have sold. This process of risk sharing is also sometimes referred to as **asset transformation**, because in a sense, risky assets are turned into safer assets for investors.

Financial intermediaries also promote risk sharing by helping individuals to diversify and thereby lower the amount of risk to which they are exposed. **Diversification** entails investing in a collection (**portfolio**) of assets whose returns do not always move together, with the result that overall risk is lower than for individual assets. (Diversification is just another name for the old adage "You shouldn't put all your eggs in one basket.") Low transaction costs allow financial intermediaries to pool a collection of assets into a new asset and then sell it to individuals.

Asymmetric Information: Adverse Selection and Moral Hazard

The presence of transaction costs in financial markets explains, in part, why financial intermediaries and indirect finance play such an important role in financial markets. An additional reason is that in financial markets, one party often does not know enough about the other party to make accurate decisions. This inequality is called **asymmetric information**. For example, a borrower who takes out a loan usually has better information about the potential returns and risks associated with the investment projects for which the funds are earmarked than the lender does. Lack of information creates problems in the financial system on two fronts: before the transaction is entered into, and afterward.[1]

Adverse selection is the problem created by asymmetric information *before* the transaction occurs. Adverse selection in financial markets occurs when the potential borrowers who are the most likely to produce an undesirable (*adverse*) outcome—the bad credit risks—are the ones who most actively seek out a loan and are thus most likely to be selected. Because adverse selection makes it more likely that loans might be made to bad credit risks, lenders may decide not to make any loans, even though good credit risks exist in the marketplace.

To understand why adverse selection occurs, suppose you have two aunts to whom you might make a loan—Aunt Louise and Aunt Sheila. Aunt Louise is a conservative type who borrows only when she has an investment she is quite sure will pay off. Aunt Sheila, by contrast, is an inveterate gambler who has just come across a get-rich-quick scheme that will make her a millionaire if she can just borrow $1000 to invest in it. Unfortunately, as with most get-rich-quick schemes, the probability is high that the investment won't pay off and that Aunt Sheila will lose the $1000.

Which of your aunts is more likely to call you to ask for a loan? Aunt Sheila, of course, because she has so much to gain if the investment pays off. You, however, would not want to make a loan to her because the probability is high that her investment will turn sour and she will be unable to pay you back.

If you know both your aunts very well—that is, if your information is not asymmetric—you won't have a problem, because you will know that Aunt Sheila is a bad risk and so you will not lend to her. Suppose, though, that you don't know your aunts well. You will be more likely to lend to Aunt Sheila than to Aunt Louise because Aunt Sheila will be hounding you for the loan. Because of the possibility of adverse selection, you might decide not to lend to either of your aunts, even though there are times when Aunt Louise, who is an excellent credit risk, might need a loan for a worthwhile investment.

---

[1] Asymmetric information and the adverse selection and moral hazard concepts are also crucial problems for the insurance industry.

Moral hazard is the problem created by asymmetric information *after* the transaction occurs. Moral hazard in financial markets is the risk (*hazard*) that the borrower might engage in activities that are undesirable (*immoral*) from the lender's point of view, because they make it less likely that the loan will be paid back. Because moral hazard lowers the probability that the loan will be repaid, lenders may decide that they would rather not make a loan.

As an example of moral hazard, suppose that you made a $1000 loan to another relative, Uncle Melvin, who needs the money to purchase a computer so that he can set up a business typing students' term papers. Once you have made the loan, however, Uncle Melvin is more likely to slip off to the track and play the horses than to purchase the computer. If he bets on a 20-to-1 long shot and wins with your money, he is able to pay back your $1000 and live high-off-the-hog with the remaining $19 000. But if he loses, as is likely, you won't get paid back, and all he has lost is his reputation as a reliable, upstanding uncle. Uncle Melvin therefore has an incentive to go to the track because his gains ($19 000) if he bets correctly are much greater than the cost to him (his reputation) if he bets incorrectly. If you knew what Uncle Melvin was up to, you would prevent him from going to the track, and he would not be able to increase the moral hazard. However, because it is hard for you to keep informed about his where-abouts—that is, because information is asymmetric—there is a good chance that Uncle Melvin will go to the track and you will not get paid back. The risk of moral hazard might therefore discourage you from making the $1000 loan to Uncle Melvin, even if you are sure that you will be paid back if he uses it to set up his business.

The problems created by adverse selection and moral hazard are a major impediment to well-functioning financial markets. Again, financial intermediaries can alleviate these problems.

With financial intermediaries in the economy, small savers can provide their funds to the financial markets by lending these funds to a trustworthy intermediary—say, the Honest John Bank—which in turn lends the funds out either by making loans or by buying securities such as stocks or bonds. Successful financial intermediaries have higher earnings on their investments than do small savers, because they are better equipped than individuals to screen out bad credit risks from good ones, thereby reducing losses due to adverse selection. In addition, financial intermediaries have high earnings because they develop expertise in monitoring the parties they lend to, thus reducing losses due to moral hazard. The result is that financial intermediaries can afford to pay lender-savers interest or provide substantial services and still earn a profit.

As we have seen, financial intermediaries play an important role in the economy because they provide liquidity services, promote risk sharing, and solve information problems, thereby allowing small savers and borrowers to benefit from the existence of financial markets. The success of financial intermediaries in performing this role is evidenced by the fact that most Canadians invest their savings with them and obtain loans from them. Financial intermediaries play a key role in improving economic efficiency because they help financial markets channel funds from lender-savers to people with productive investment opportunities. Without a well-functioning set of financial intermediaries, it is very hard for an economy to reach its full potential. We will explore further the role of financial intermediaries in the economy in Part 3.

Economies of Scope and Conflicts of Interest

Another reason why financial intermediaries play such an important part in the economy is that by providing multiple financial services to their customers, such as offering them bank loans or selling their bonds for them, they can also achieve **economies of scope**; that is, they can lower the cost of information production for each service by applying one information resource to many different services. A bank, for example, when making a loan to a corporation, can evaluate how good a credit risk the firm is, which then helps the bank decide whether it would be easy to sell the bonds of this corporation to the public.

Although economies of scope may substantially benefit financial institutions, they also create potential costs in terms of **conflicts of interest**. Conflicts of interest, a type of moral hazard problem, arise when a person or institution has multiple objectives (interests), some of which conflict with each other. Conflicts of interest are especially likely to occur when a financial institution provides multiple services. The potentially competing interests of those services may lead an individual or firm to conceal information or disseminate misleading information. We care about conflicts of interest because a substantial reduction in the quality of information in financial markets increases asymmetric information problems and prevents financial markets from channeling funds into the most productive investment opportunities. Consequently, the financial markets and the economy become less efficient.

TYPES OF FINANCIAL INTERMEDIARIES

We have seen why financial intermediaries have such an important function in the economy. Now we take a look at the principal financial intermediaries and how they perform the intermediation function. Financial intermediaries fall into three categories: depository institutions (banks), contractual savings institutions, and investment intermediaries. Table 2-3 describes the primary liabilities (sources of funds) and assets (uses of funds) of the financial intermediaries in each category. The relative sizes of these intermediaries in Canada are indicated in Table 2-4.

TABLE 2-3	Primary Assets and Liabilities of Financial Intermediaries	
Type of Intermediary	**Primary Liabilities (Sources of Funds)**	**Primary Assets (Uses of Funds)**
Depository institutions (banks)		
Chartered banks	Deposits	Loans, mortgages, government bonds
Trust and loan companies	Deposits	Mortgages
Credit unions and *caisses populaires*	Deposits	Mortgages
Contractual savings institutions		
Life insurance companies	Premiums from policies	Corporate bonds and mortgages
Property and casualty insurance companies	Premiums from policies	Corporate bonds and stocks
Pension funds	Retirement contributions	Corporate bonds and stocks
Investment intermediaries		
Finance companies	Finance paper, stocks, bonds	Consumer and business loans
Mutual funds	Shares	Stocks and bonds
Money market mutual funds	Shares	Money market instruments

TABLE 2-4	Relative Shares of Financial Institutions and Pension Plans Regulated by OSFI (as of October 31, 2014)		

Type of Intermediary	Number	Total assets (in $ millions)	Percent (%)
Chartered Banks			
Domestic	28	4 005 895	66.81
Foreign bank subsidiaries	24	127 207	2.12
Foreign bank branches	29	2722	0.05
Trust Companies	44	145 636	2.43
Loan Companies	19	171 854	2.87
Cooperative Credit Associations	6	23 116	0.39
Life Insurance Companies			
Canadian-incorporated	41	1 180 494	19.69
Foreign branches	33	19 613	0.33
Fraternal Benefit Societies			
Canadian-incorporated	8	6832	0.11
Foreign branches	5	2308	0.04
Property and Casualty Insurance Companies			
Canadian-incorporated	88	108 991	1.82
Foreign branches	76	30 185	0.50
Pension Plans	1234	171 000	2.85
Total		5 995 853	100.00

Source: OSFI web site and OSFI Annual Report 2013–2014.

Depository Institutions

Depository institutions (for simplicity, we refer to these as *banks* throughout this text) are financial intermediaries that accept deposits from individuals and institutions and make loans. The study of money and banking focuses special attention on this group of financial institutions because they are involved in the creation of deposits, an important component of the money supply. These institutions include commercial banks and the so-called near banks: trust and loan companies, credit unions, and *caisses populaires*.

Chartered Banks   These financial intermediaries raise funds primarily by issuing chequable deposits (deposits on which cheques can be written), savings deposits (deposits that are payable on demand but do not allow their owner to write cheques), and term deposits (deposits with fixed terms to maturity). They then use these funds to make commercial, consumer, and mortgage loans to buy Canadian government securities and provincial and municipal bonds. There are 81 chartered banks in Canada, and as a group they are the largest type of financial intermediary with the most diversified portfolios (collections) of assets in this country.

Trust and Loan Companies   These depository institutions obtain funds primarily through chequable and nonchequable savings deposits, term deposits, guaranteed investment certificates, and debentures. In the past, these institutions were constrained in their activities and mostly made mortgage loans for residential housing. Over time, these restrictions have been loosened so that the distinction between these depository institutions and chartered banks has blurred. These intermediaries have become more alike and are now more competitive with each other.

Credit Unions and Caisses Populaires (CUCPs)   Credit unions and *caisses populaires* are very small cooperative lending institutions organized around a particular group: union members, employees of a particular firm, and so forth. They acquire funds from deposits and primarily make mortgage and consumer loans.

Contractual Savings Institutions

Contractual savings institutions, such as insurance companies and pension funds, are financial intermediaries that acquire funds at periodic intervals on a contractual basis. Because they can predict with reasonable accuracy how much they will have to pay out in benefits in the coming years, they do not have to worry as much as depository institutions about losing funds. As a result, the liquidity of assets is not as important a consideration for them as it is for depository institutions, and they tend to invest their funds primarily in long-term securities such as corporate bonds, stocks, and mortgages.

Life Insurance Companies   Life insurance companies, numbering 74 in Canada, insure people against financial hazards following a death, and sell annuities (annual income payments upon retirement). They acquire funds from the premiums that people pay to keep their policies in force and use those funds mainly to buy corporate bonds and mortgages. They also purchase stocks, but are restricted in the amount that they can hold. Currently, with close to $1.2 trillion in assets, they are among the largest of the contractual savings institutions.

Property and Casualty (P&C) Insurance Companies   These companies, numbering 164 in Canada, insure their policyholders against loss from theft, fire, and accidents. They are very much like life insurance companies, receiving funds through premiums for their policies, but they have a greater possibility of loss of funds if major disasters occur. For this reason, they use their funds to buy more liquid assets than life insurance companies do. Their largest holding of assets is government bonds and debentures; they also hold corporate bonds and stocks.

Pension Funds and Government Retirement Funds   Private pension funds and provincial and municipal retirement funds provide retirement income in the form of annuities to employees who are covered by a pension plan. Funds are acquired by contributions from employers and/or from employees who either have a contribution automatically deducted from their paycheques or contribute voluntarily. The largest asset holdings of pension funds are corporate bonds and stocks. The establishment of pension funds has been actively encouraged by the federal government, both through legislation requiring pension plans and through tax incentives to encourage contributions.

Investment Intermediaries

This category of financial intermediary includes finance companies, mutual funds, money market mutual funds, and hedge funds.

Finance Companies   Finance companies raise funds by selling commercial paper (a short-term debt instrument) and by issuing stocks and bonds. They lend these funds to small businesses and to consumers, who use them to purchase such items as furniture, automobiles, and home improvements. Some finance companies are organized by a parent corporation to help sell its product. For example, Ford Motor Credit Company makes loans to consumers who purchase Ford automobiles.

Mutual Funds   These financial intermediaries acquire funds by selling shares to many individuals and then using the proceeds to purchase diversified portfolios of stocks and bonds. Mutual funds allow shareholders to pool their resources so that they can take advantage of lower transaction costs when buying large blocks of stocks or bonds. In addition, mutual funds allow shareholders to hold more diversified portfolios than they otherwise would. Shareholders can sell (redeem) shares at any time, but the value of these shares will be determined by the value of the mutual fund's holdings of securities. Because these fluctuate greatly, the value of mutual fund shares will, too; therefore, investments in mutual funds can be risky.

Money Market Mutual Funds   These financial institutions are similar to mutual funds but also function to some extent as depository institutions because they offer deposit-type accounts. Like most mutual funds, they sell shares to acquire funds that are then used to buy money market instruments that are both safe and very liquid. The interest on these assets is paid out to the shareholders.

Hedge Funds   Hedge funds are a type of mutual fund with special characteristics. Hedge funds are organized as limited partnerships with minimum investments ranging from $100 000 to, more typically, $1 million or more. These limitations mean that hedge funds are subject to much weaker regulation than other mutual funds. Hedge funds invest in many types of assets, with some specializing in stocks, others in bonds, others in foreign currencies, and still others in far more exotic assets.

Investment Banks   Despite its name, an investment bank is not a bank or a financial intermediary in the ordinary sense; that is, it does not take in funds and then lend them out. Instead, an investment bank is a different type of intermediary that helps a corporation issue securities. First it advises the corporation on which type of securities to issue (stocks or bonds); then it helps sell (**underwrite**) the securities by purchasing them from the corporation at a predetermined price and reselling them in the market. Investment banks also act as deal makers, earning enormous fees by helping corporations acquire other companies through mergers or acquisitions.

REGULATION OF THE FINANCIAL SYSTEM

The financial system is among the most heavily regulated sectors of the Canadian economy. The government regulates financial markets for two main reasons: to increase the information available to investors and to ensure the soundness of the financial system. We will examine how these two goals have led to the present regulatory environment. As a study aid, the principal regulatory agencies of the Canadian financial system are listed in Table 2-5.

Increasing Information Available to Investors

Asymmetric information in financial markets means that investors may be subject to adverse selection and moral hazard problems that may hinder the efficient operation of financial markets. Risky firms or outright crooks may be the most eager to sell securities to unwary investors, and the resulting adverse selection problem may keep investors

TABLE 2-5   Principal Regulatory Agencies of the Canadian Financial System

Regulatory Agency	Subject of Regulation	Nature of Regulations
Provincial securities and exchange commissions	Organized exchanges and financial markets	Requires disclosure of information and restricts insider trading
Bank of Canada	Chartered banks, TMLs, and CUCPs	Examines the books of the deposit-taking institutions and coordinates with the federal agencies that are responsible for financial institution regulation: OSFI and CDIC
Office of the Superintendent of Financial Institutions Canada (OSFI)	All federally regulated chartered banks, TMLs, CUCPs, life insurance companies, P&C insurance companies, and pension plans	Sets capital adequacy, accounting, and board-of-directors responsibility standards; conducts bank audits and coordinates with provincial securities commissions
Canada Deposit Insurance Corporation (CDIC)	Chartered banks, TMLs, CUCPs	Provides insurance of up to $100 000 for each depositor at a bank, examines the books of insured banks, and imposes restrictions on assets they can hold
Québec Deposit Insurance Board	TMLs and credit cooperatives in Québec	Similar role to the CDIC
Canadian Life and Health Insurance Compensation Corporation (CompCorp)	Life insurance companies	Compensates policyholders if the issuing life insurance company goes bankrupt
P&C Insurance Compensation Corporation (PACIC)	Property and casualty insurance companies	Compensates policyholders if the issuing P&C insurance company goes bankrupt

out of financial markets. Furthermore, once an investor has bought a security, thereby lending money to a firm, the borrower may have incentives to engage in risky activities or to commit outright fraud. The presence of this moral hazard problem may also keep investors away from financial markets. Government regulation can reduce adverse selection and moral hazard problems in financial markets and enhance the efficiency of the markets by increasing the amount of information available to investors.

Provincial securities commissions, the most significant being the Ontario Securities Commission (OSC), administer provincial Acts requiring corporations issuing securities to disclose certain information about their sales, assets, and earnings to the public and restrict trading by the largest stockholders in the corporation. By requiring disclosure of this information and by discouraging insider trading, which could be used to manipulate securities prices, regulators hope that investors will be better informed and better protected from abuses in financial markets. Indeed, in recent years, the OSC has been particularly active in prosecuting people involved in insider trading in Canada's largest stock exchange, the Toronto Stock Exchange.

Ensuring the Soundness of Financial Intermediaries

Asymmetric information can lead to the widespread collapse of financial intermediaries, referred to as a **financial panic**. Because providers of funds to financial intermediaries may not be able to assess whether the institutions holding their funds are sound, if they have doubts about the overall health of financial intermediaries, they may want to pull their funds out of both sound and unsound institutions. The possible outcome is a financial panic that produces large losses for the public and causes serious damage to the economy. To protect the public and the economy from financial panics, the government has implemented five types of regulations.

Restrictions on Entry   Provincial banking and insurance commissions, the Bank of Canada, and the Office of the Superintendent of Financial Institutions (OSFI), an agency of the federal government, have created tight regulations governing who is allowed to set up a financial intermediary. Individuals or groups that want to establish a financial intermediary, such as a bank or an insurance company, must obtain a charter from the provincial or federal government. Only if they are upstanding corporate citizens with impeccable credentials and a large amount of initial funds will they be given a charter.

Disclosure   Reporting requirements for financial intermediaries are stringent. Their bookkeeping must follow certain strict principles; their books are subject to periodic inspection; and they must make certain information available to the public.

Restrictions on Assets and Activities   Financial intermediaries are restricted in what they are allowed to do and what assets they can hold. Before you put your funds into a chartered bank or some other such institution, you would want to know that your funds are safe and that the financial intermediary will be able to meet its obligations to you. One way of doing this is to restrict the financial intermediary from engaging in certain risky activities. Another way to limit a financial intermediary's behaviour is to restrict it from holding certain risky assets, or at least from holding a greater quantity of these risky assets than is prudent. For example, chartered banks and other depository institutions are not allowed to hold common stock because stock prices experience substantial fluctuations. Insurance companies are allowed to hold common stock, but their holdings cannot exceed a certain fraction of their total assets.

Deposit Insurance   The government can insure people's deposits so that they do not suffer any financial loss if the financial intermediary that holds these deposits fails. The most important government agency that provides this type of insurance is the Canada Deposit Insurance Corporation (CDIC), created by an act of Parliament in 1967. It insures each depositor at a member deposit-taking financial institution up to a loss of $100 000 per account. Except for certain wholesale branches of foreign banks, credit unions, and some provincial institutions, all deposit-taking financial institutions in Canada are members of the CDIC. All CDIC members make contributions into the CDIC fund, which are used to pay off depositors in the case of a bank's failure. The Québec Deposit Insurance Board, an organization similar to the CDIC and set up at the same time as the CDIC, provides insurance for Trust and Mortgage Loan Companies (TMLs) and credit cooperatives in Québec.

Limits on Competition   Politicians have often declared that unbridled competition among financial intermediaries promotes failures that will harm the public. Although the evidence that competition has this effect is extremely weak, provincial and federal governments at times have imposed restrictive regulations. For example, from 1967 to 1980 the entry of foreign banks into the Canadian banking industry was prohibited. Since 1980, however, the incorporation of foreign bank subsidiaries has been regulated, but Canada still ranks low with respect to the degree of competition from foreign banks.

In later chapters we will look more closely at government regulation of financial markets and will see whether it has improved their functioning.

Financial Regulation Abroad

Not surprisingly, given the similarity of the economic systems here and in the United States, Japan, and the nations of Western Europe, financial regulation in those countries is similar to that of Canada's. The provision of information is improved by requiring corporations issuing securities to report details about assets and liabilities, earnings, and sales of stock, and by prohibiting insider trading. The soundness of intermediaries is ensured by licensing, periodic inspection of financial intermediaries' books, and the provision of deposit insurance.

The major differences between financial regulation in Canada and abroad relate to bank regulation. In the past, for example, the United States was the only industrialized country to subject banks to restrictions on branching, which limited banks' size and restricted them to certain geographic regions. These restrictions were abolished by legislation in 1994. U.S. and Canadian banks are also highly restrictive in the range of assets they may hold. Banks in other countries frequently hold shares in commercial firms; in Japan and Germany, those stakes can be sizable.

MyEconLab

MyEconLab is an online homework and tutorial system that puts you in control of your own learning with study and practice tools directly correlated to this chapter's content. Visit MyEconLab to access the eText, the Questions and Applied Problems with answers, as well as additional assessment. You will also find web chapters, mini-lectures, appendices, mini-cases, videos, glossary flashcards, news feeds, CANSIM data, and graphing tools.

SUMMARY

1. The basic function of financial markets is to channel funds from savers who have an excess of funds to spenders who have a shortage of funds. Financial markets can do this either through direct finance, in which borrowers borrow funds directly from lenders by selling them securities, or through indirect finance, which involves a financial intermediary that stands between the lender-savers and the borrower-spenders and helps transfer funds from one to the other. This channeling of funds improves the economic welfare of everyone in society. Because they allow funds to move from people who have no productive investment opportunities to those who do have such opportunities, financial markets contribute to economic efficiency. In addition, channeling of funds directly benefits consumers by allowing them to make purchases when they need them most.

2. Financial markets can be classified as debt and equity markets, primary and secondary markets, exchanges and over-the-counter markets, and money and capital markets.

3. The principal money market instruments (debt instruments with maturities of less than one year) are Treasury bills, certificates of deposit, commercial paper, repurchase agreements, and overnight funds. The principal capital market instruments (debt and equity instruments with maturities greater than one year) are stocks, mortgages, corporate bonds, Canadian government securities, Canada Savings Bonds, government agency securities, provincial and municipal government bonds, and consumer and bank commercial loans.

4. An important trend in recent years is the growing internationalization of financial markets. Eurobonds, which are denominated in a currency other than that of the country in which they are sold, are now the dominant security in the international bond market. Eurodollars, which are dollars deposited in foreign banks, are an important source of funds for Canadian banks.

5. Financial intermediaries are financial institutions that acquire funds by issuing liabilities and, in turn, use those funds to acquire assets by purchasing securities or making loans. Financial intermediaries play an important role in the financial system because they reduce transaction costs, allow risk sharing, and solve problems created by adverse selection and moral hazard. As a result, financial intermediaries allow small savers and borrowers to benefit from the existence of financial markets, thereby increasing the efficiency of the economy. However, the economies of scope that help make financial intermediaries successful can lead to conflicts of interest that make the financial system less efficient.

6. The principal financial intermediaries fall into three categories: (a) banks—chartered banks, trust and loan companies, and credit unions and *caisses populaires*; (b) contractual savings institutions—life insurance companies, property and casualty insurance companies, and pension funds; and (c) investment intermediaries—finance companies, mutual funds, money market mutual funds, and hedge funds.

7. The government regulates financial markets and financial intermediaries for two main reasons: to increase the information available to investors and to ensure the soundness of the financial system. Regulations include requiring disclosure of information to the public, restrictions on who can set up a financial intermediary, restrictions on what assets financial intermediaries can hold, the provision of deposit insurance, and limits on competition.

KEY TERMS

adverse selection, p. 37
asset transformation, p. 37
asymmetric information, p. 37
brokers, p. 26
capital, p. 24
capital market, p. 27
conflicts of interest, p. 39

currency, p. 28
dealers, p. 26
default, p. 28
diversification, p. 37
dividends, p. 25
economies of scale, p. 36
economies of scope, p. 38

equities, p. 25
Eurobond, p. 33
Eurocurrencies, p. 33
Eurodollars, p. 33
exchanges, p. 26
financial intermediation, p. 35
financial panic, p. 44

foreign bonds, p. 32
intermediate-term, p. 25
investment bank, p. 25
liabilities, p. 23
liquid, p. 26
liquidity services, p. 36
long-term, p. 25
maturity, p. 25

money market, p. 26
moral hazard, p. 38
mortgages, p. 30
mortgage-backed securities, p. 31
over-the-counter (OTC) market, p. 26
portfolio, p. 37
primary market, p. 25
risk, p. 36

risk sharing, p. 36
secondary market, p. 25
short-term, p. 25
transaction costs, p. 36
underwrite, p. 42
underwriting, p. 25

QUESTIONS

All questions are available in MyEconLab *at* **www.myeconlab.com**.

1. If I can buy a car today for $5000 and it is worth $10 000 in extra income to me next year because it enables me to get a job as a traveling salesman, should I take out a loan from Larry the Loan Shark at a 90% interest rate if no one else will give me a loan? Will I be better or worse off as a result of taking out this loan? Can you make a case for legalizing loan sharking?

2. Some economists suspect that one of the reasons economies in developing countries grow so slowly is that they do not have well-developed financial markets. Does this argument make sense?

3. Why is a share of Air Canada common stock an asset for its owner and a liability for Air Canada?

4. If you suspect that a company will go bankrupt next year, which would you rather hold, bonds issued by the company or equities issued by the company? Why?

5. "Because corporations do not actually raise any funds in secondary markets, secondary markets are less important to the economy than primary markets are." Is this statement true, false, or uncertain? Explain your answer.

6. Describe who issues each of the following money market instruments:
   a. Treasury bills
   b. Certificates of deposit
   c. Commercial paper
   d. Repurchase agreement
   e. Overnight funds

7. What is the difference between a *mortgage* and a *mortgage-backed security*?

8. The U.S. economy borrowed heavily from the British in the nineteenth century to build a railroad system. Why did this make both countries better off?

9. A significant number of European banks held large amounts of assets as mortgage-backed securities derived from the U.S. housing market, which crashed after 2006. How does this demonstrate both a benefit and a cost to the internationalization of financial markets?

10. How does risk sharing benefit both financial intermediaries and private investors?

11. How can the adverse selection problem explain why you are more likely to make a loan to a family member than to a stranger?

12. One of the factors contributing to the financial crisis of 2007–2009 was the widespread issuance of subprime mortgages. How does this demonstrate adverse selection?

13. Why do loan sharks worry less about moral hazard in connection with their borrowers than some other lenders do?

14. If you are an employer, what kinds of moral hazard problems might you worry about with regard to your employees?

15. If there were no asymmetry in the information that a borrower and a lender had, could a moral hazard problem still exist?

16. "In a world without information costs and transaction costs, financial intermediaries would not exist." Is this statement true, false, or uncertain? Explain your answer.

17. Why might you be willing to make a loan to your neighbour by putting funds in a savings account earning a 5% interest rate at the bank and having the bank lend her the funds at a 10% interest rate, rather than lend her the funds yourself?

18. How do conflicts of interest make the asymmetric information problem worse?

19. How can the provision of several types of financial services by one firm be both beneficial and problematic?

20. If you were going to get a loan to purchase a new car, which financial intermediary would you use: a credit union, a pension fund, or an investment bank?

21. Why would a life insurance company be concerned about the financial stability of major corporations or the health of the housing market?

22. In 2008, as a financial crisis began to unfold in the United States, the Federal Deposit Insurance Corporation (FDIC) raised the limit on insured losses to bank depositors from $100 000 per account to $250 000 per account. How would this help stabilize the financial system?

APPLIED PROBLEMS

All applied problems are available in MyEconLab at **www.myeconlab.com**.

23. Suppose you have just inherited $10 000 and are considering the following options for investing the money to maximize your return:

Option 1: Put the money in an interest-bearing chequing account that earns 2%. The CDIC insures the account against bank failure.

Option 2: Invest the money in a corporate bond with a stated return of 5%, although there is a 10% chance the company could go bankrupt.

Option 3: Loan the money to one of your friend's roommates, Mike, at an agreed-upon interest rate of 8%, even though you believe there is a 7% chance that Mike will leave town without repaying you.

Option 4: Hold the money in cash and earn zero return.

a. If you are risk-neutral (that is, neither seek out nor shy away from risk), which of the four options should you choose to maximize your expected return? (*Hint*: To calculate the *expected return* of an outcome, multiply the probability that an event will occur by the outcome of that event.)

b. Suppose Option 3 is your only possibility. If you could pay your friend $100 to find out extra information about Mike that would indicate with certainty whether he will leave town without paying, would you pay the $100? What does this say about the value of better information regarding risk?

DATA ANALYSIS PROBLEMS

Download data for these problems from MyEconLab at **www.myeconlab.com**.

1. Go to the CANSIM database and find data on the total Canadian dollar assets held by chartered banks in Canada (series V36852). What is the percent increase in growth of assets from January 2000 to December 2014?

2. Go to the CANSIM database and find local credit unions and *caisses populaires* data on total assets (series V122571), cash and deposits (series V53449106), bonds and debentures (series V53450625), and residential mortgages (series V122577). Using these series, calculate both the total amount held and the percentage held in each of the three categories for the most recent quarter available.

WEB EXERCISES

1. One of the single best sources of information about financial institutions is the financial data produced by the Office of the Superintendent of Financial Institutions (OSFI). Go to **www.osfi-bsif.gc.ca**, click on "Banks" and then "Financial Data for Banks," and answer the following questions.

   a. What percentage of assets do domestic chartered banks hold in loans? What percentage of assets is held in mortgage loans?

   b. What percentage of assets do trust companies hold in mortgage loans?

   c. What percentage of assets do cooperatives hold in mortgage loans and in consumer loans?

2. The most famous financial market in the world is the New York Stock Exchange. Go to **www.nyse.com**.

   a. What is the mission of the NYSE?

   b. Firms must pay a fee to list their shares for sale on the NYSE. What would be the fee for a firm with five million common shares outstanding?

WEB REFERENCES

stockcharts.com/charts/historical

Contains historical stock index charts for the Dow Jones Industrial Average, S&P 500, NASDAQ, 30-year Treasury Bond, and gold prices.

www.tmx.com

Toronto Stock Exchange. Find listed companies, quotes, company historical data, real-time market indexes, and more.

www.osfi-bsif.gc.ca

The single best source of information about financial institutions in Canada.

finance.yahoo.com

Major world stock indexes, with charts, news, and components.

3

What Is Money?

Learning Objectives

After studying this chapter you should be able to

1. Describe what money is.
2. List and summarize the functions of money.
3. Identify different types of payment systems.
4. Compare and contrast the M1 and M2 money supplies.

PREVIEW

I f you lived in Canada before the creation of the central bank (the Bank of Canada) in 1935, your money might have consisted primarily of gold and silver coins and paper notes, called banknotes, issued by private banks. Today, you use as money not only coins and paper bills issued by the government, but also debit cards and cheques written on accounts held at banks. Money has taken different forms at different times, but it has *always* been important to people and to the economy.

To understand the effects of money on the economy, we must understand exactly what money is. In this chapter we develop precise definitions by exploring the functions of money, looking at why and how it promotes economic efficiency, tracing how its forms have evolved over time, and examining how money is currently measured.

MEANING OF MONEY

As used in everyday conversation, the word *money* can mean many things, but to economists it has a very specific meaning. To avoid confusion, we must clarify how economists' use of the word *money* differs from conventional usage.

Economists define *money* (also referred to as the *money supply*) as anything that is generally accepted as payment for goods or services or in the repayment of debts. When most people talk about money, they're talking about **currency** (paper money and coins). If, for example, someone comes up to you and says, "Your money or your life," you should quickly hand over all your currency rather than ask, "What exactly do you mean by 'money'?"

To define money merely as currency is much too narrow for economists. Because cheques are also accepted as payment for purchases, chequing account deposits are considered money as well. An even broader definition of money is needed, however, because other items, such as savings deposits, can, in effect, function as money if they can be quickly and easily converted into currency or chequing account deposits. As you can see, no single, precise definition of money or the money supply is possible, even for economists.

To complicate matters further, the word *money* is frequently used synonymously with *wealth*. When people say, "Joe is rich—he has an awful lot of money," they probably mean that Joe not only has a lot of currency and a high balance in his chequing account but also has stocks, bonds, four cars, three houses, and a yacht. Thus while "currency" is too narrow a definition of money, this other popular usage is much too broad. Economists make a distinction between money—in the form of currency, demand deposits, and other items that are used to make purchases—and **wealth**, the total collection of pieces of property that serve to store value. Wealth includes not only money but also other assets such as bonds, common stock, art, land, furniture, cars, and houses.

People also use the word *money* to describe what economists call *income*, as in the sentence "Sheila would be a wonderful catch; she has a good job and earns a lot of money." **Income** is a *flow* of earnings per unit of time. Money, by contrast, is a *stock*: it is a certain amount at a given point in time. If someone tells you that he has an income of $1000, you cannot tell whether he earned a lot or a little without knowing whether this $1000 is earned per year, per month, or even per day. But if someone tells you that she has $1000 in her pocket, you know exactly how much this is.

Keep in mind that when money is discussed in this book, it refers to anything that is generally accepted in payment for goods and services or in the repayment of debts, and is distinct from income and wealth.

FUNCTIONS OF MONEY

Whether money is shells or rocks or gold or paper, it has three primary functions in any economy: as a medium of exchange, as a unit of account, and as a store of value. Of the three functions, its function as a medium of exchange is what distinguishes money from other assets such as stocks, bonds, and houses.

Medium of Exchange

In almost all market transactions in our economy, money in the form of currency or cheques is a **medium of exchange**; it is used to pay for goods and services. The use of money as a medium of exchange promotes economic efficiency by reducing the time spent in exchanging goods and services. To see why, let's look at a *barter economy*, one without money, in which goods and services are exchanged directly for other goods and services.

Take the case of Ellen the Economics Professor, who can do just one thing well: give brilliant economics lectures. In a barter economy, if Ellen wants to eat, she must find a farmer who not only produces the food she likes but also wants to learn economics. As you might expect, this search will be difficult and time-consuming, and Ellen may spend more time looking for such an economics-hungry farmer than she will teaching. It is even possible that she will have to quit lecturing and go into farming herself. Even so, she may still starve to death.

The time spent trying to exchange goods or services is called a *transaction cost*. In a barter economy, transaction costs are high because people have to satisfy a "double coincidence of wants"—they have to find someone who has a good or service they want and who also wants the good or service they have to offer.

Let's see what happens if we introduce money into Ellen the Economics Professor's world. Ellen can teach anyone who is willing to pay money to hear her lecture. She can then go to any farmer (or his representative at the supermarket) and buy the food she needs with the money she has been paid. The problem of the double coincidence of wants is avoided, and Ellen saves a lot of time, which she can spend doing what she does best: teaching.

As this example shows, money promotes economic efficiency by eliminating much of the time spent exchanging goods and services. It also promotes efficiency by allowing people to specialize in what they do best. Money is therefore essential in an economy: it is a lubricant that allows the economy to run more smoothly by lowering transaction costs, thereby encouraging specialization and the division of labour.

The need for money is so strong that almost every society beyond the most primitive has invented it. For a commodity to function effectively as money, it has to meet several criteria: (1) It must be easily standardized, making it simple to ascertain its value; (2) it must be widely accepted; (3) it must be divisible, so that it is easy to "make change;" (4) it must be easy to carry; and (5) it must not deteriorate quickly. Objects that have satisfied these criteria have taken many unusual forms throughout human history, ranging from wampum (strings of beads), used by Native Americans, to tobacco and whiskey, used by the early American colonists, to cigarettes, used in prisoner-of-war camps during World War II. The diverse forms of money that have been developed over the years are as much a testament to the inventiveness of the human race as are the development of tools and language. See, for example, the FYI box Money in a Prisoner-of-War Camp and Modern Prisons.

Unit of Account

The second role of money is to provide a **unit of account**; that is, it is used to measure value in an economy. We measure the value of goods and services in terms of

---

FYI   Money in a Prisoner-of-War Camp and Modern Prisons

An extremely entertaining article on the development of money in a prisoner-of-war camp during World War II is R. A. Radford's "The Economic Organization of a P. O. W. Camp."* He describes his experience with the economy of a German prisoner-of-war camp where cigarettes had become the primary medium of exchange, with most prices expressed in units of cigarettes.

Cigarettes have also been used as currency in prisons in Canada and in other countries in much the same way. Recently, however, with the enactment of a ban on smoking (and therefore the prohibition of the cigarette pack) in federal prisons in the United States, a substitute currency has evolved: pouches of mackerel—in prison lingo, "macks."

In particular, inmates in modern federal prisons in the United States get credits in their commissary accounts from prison jobs, which pay about 40 cents per hour, and use these credits to buy goods such as food and toiletries from the commissary. Prisoners are not allowed to possess cash, but they have developed a substitute medium of exchange by using their commissary account credits to buy macks, which they then use as currency. That is, they use macks to pay for gambling debts and to buy goods and services, such as haircuts and shoeshines, from other prisioners. Macks are a good substitute for the U.S. dollar because they each cost about US $1.

* *Economica* 12 (November 1945): 189–201.

money, just as we measure weight in terms of kilograms or distance in terms of kilometres. To see why this function is important, let's look again at a barter economy, in which money does not perform this function. If the economy has only three goods—say, peaches, economics lectures, and movies—then we need to know only three prices to tell us how to exchange one for another: the price of peaches in terms of economics lectures (that is, how many economics lectures you have to pay for a peach), the price of peaches in terms of movies, and the price of economics lectures in terms of movies. If there were 10 goods, we would need to know 45 prices in order to exchange one good for another; with 100 goods, we would need 4950 prices; and with 1000 goods, 499 500 prices.[1]

Imagine how hard it would be in a barter economy to shop at a supermarket with 1000 different items on its shelves and be faced with deciding whether chicken or fish is a better buy if the price of a kilogram of chicken were quoted as 4 kilograms of butter and the price of a kilogram of fish as 8 kilograms of tomatoes. To make it possible to compare prices, the tag on each item would have to list up to 999 different prices, and the time spent reading them would result in very high transaction costs.

The solution to the problem is to introduce money into the economy and have all prices quoted in terms of units of that money, enabling us to quote the price of economics lectures, peaches, and movies in terms of, say, dollars. If there were only three goods in the economy, this would not be a great advantage over the barter system, because we would still need only three prices to conduct transactions. But for 10 goods we would now need only 10 prices; for 100 goods, 100 prices; and so on. At the 1000-good supermarket, there are now only 1000 prices to be considered, not 499 500!

We can see that using money as a unit of account reduces transaction costs in an economy by reducing the number of prices that need to be considered. The benefits of this function of money grow as the economy becomes more complex.

Store of Value

Money also functions as a **store of value**; it is a repository of purchasing power over time. A store of value is used to save purchasing power from the time income is received until the time it is spent. This function of money is useful because most of us do not want to spend our income immediately upon receiving it, but rather prefer to wait until we have the time or the desire to shop.

Money is not unique as a store of value; any asset—whether money, stocks, bonds, land, houses, art, or jewellery—can be used to store wealth. Many such assets have advantages over money as a store of value: they often pay the owner a higher interest rate than money, experience price appreciation, and deliver services such as providing

---

[1] The formula for telling us the number of prices we need when we have N goods is the same formula that tells us the number of pairs when there are N items. It is

$$\frac{N(N-1)}{2}.$$

In the case of 10 goods, for example, we would need

$$\frac{10(10-1)}{2} = \frac{90}{2} = 45 \text{ prices.}$$

a roof over one's head. If these assets are a more desirable store of value than money, why do people hold money at all?

The answer to this question relates to the important economic concept of **liquidity**, the relative ease and speed with which an asset can be converted into a medium of exchange. Liquidity is highly desirable. Money is the most liquid asset of all because it is the medium of exchange; it does not have to be converted into anything else in order to make purchases. Other assets involve transaction costs when they are converted into money. When you sell your house, for example, you have to pay a brokerage commission (usually 5% to 7% of the sales price), and if you need cash immediately to pay some pressing bills, you might have to settle for a lower price if you want to sell the house quickly. Because money is the most liquid asset, people are willing to hold it even if it is not the most attractive store of value.

How good a store of value money is depends on the price level. A doubling of all prices, for example, means that the value of money has dropped by half; conversely, a halving of all prices means that the value of money has doubled. During a period of inflation, when the price level is increasing rapidly, money loses value rapidly, and people will be more reluctant to hold their wealth in this form. This is especially true during periods of extreme inflation, known as **hyperinflation**, in which the inflation rate exceeds 50% per month.

Hyperinflation occurred in Germany after World War I, with inflation rates sometimes exceeding 1000% per month. By the end of the hyperinflation in 1923, the price level had risen to more than 30 billion times what it had been just two years before. The quantity of money needed to purchase even the most basic items became excessive. There are stories, for example, that near the end of the hyperinflation, a wheelbarrow of cash would be required to pay for a loaf of bread. Money was losing its value so rapidly that workers were paid and then given time off on several occasions during the day to spend their wages before the money became worthless. No one wanted to hold on to money, so the use of money to carry out transactions declined, and barter became more and more dominant. Transaction costs skyrocketed, and as we would expect, output in the economy fell sharply.

EVOLUTION OF THE PAYMENTS SYSTEM

We can obtain a better picture of the functions of money and the forms it has taken over time by looking at the evolution of the **payments system**, the method of conducting transactions in the economy. The payments system has been evolving over centuries, and with it the forms of money. At one point, precious metals such as gold were used as the principal means of payment and were the main form of money. Later, paper assets such as cheques and currency began to be used in the payments system and viewed as money. Where the payments system is heading has an important bearing on how money will be defined in the future.

Commodity Money

To obtain perspective on where the payments system is heading, it is worth exploring how it has evolved. For any object to function as money, it must be universally acceptable; everyone must be willing to take it in payment for goods and services.

An object that clearly has value to everyone is a likely candidate to serve as money, and a natural choice is a precious metal such as gold or silver. Money made up of precious metals or another valuable commodity is called **commodity money**, and from ancient times until several hundred years ago, commodity money functioned as the medium of exchange in all but the most primitive societies. The problem with a payments system based exclusively on precious metals is that such a form of money is very heavy and hard to transport from one place to another. Imagine the holes you'd wear in your pockets if you had to buy things only with coins! Indeed, for a large purchase such as a house, you'd have to rent a truck to transport the money payment.

Fiat Money

The next development in the payments system was *paper currency* (pieces of paper that function as a medium of exchange). Initially, paper currency carried a guarantee that it was convertible into coins or into a quantity of precious metal. However, currency has evolved into **fiat money**, paper currency decreed by governments as legal tender (meaning that legally it must be accepted as payment for debts) but not convertible into coins or precious metals. Paper currency has the advantage of being much lighter than coins or precious metal, but it can be accepted as a medium of exchange only if there is some trust in the authorities who issue it and if printing has reached a sufficiently advanced stage that counterfeiting is extremely difficult. Because paper currency has evolved into a legal arrangement, countries can change the currency they use at will. Indeed, this is what many European countries did when they abandoned their currencies for the euro in 2002.

Major drawbacks of paper currency and coins are that they are easily stolen and can be expensive to transport in large amounts because of their bulk. To combat this problem, another step in the evolution of the payments system occurred with the development of modern banking: the invention of *cheques*.

Cheques

A cheque is an instruction from you to your bank used to transfer money from your account to someone else's account when she deposits the cheque. Cheques allow transactions to take place without the need to carry around large amounts of currency. The introduction of cheques was a major innovation that improved the efficiency of the payments system. Frequently, payments made back and forth cancel each other; without cheques, this would involve the movement of a lot of currency. With cheques, payments that cancel each other can be settled by cancelling the cheques, and no currency need be moved. The use of cheques thus reduces the transportation costs associated with the payments system and improves economic efficiency. Another advantage of cheques is that they can be written for any amount up to the balance in the account, making transactions for large amounts much easier. Cheques are also advantageous in that loss from theft is greatly reduced and because they provide convenient receipts for purchases.

Two problems arise, however, with a payments system based on cheques. First, it takes time to get cheques from one place to another, a particularly serious problem if you are paying someone in a different location who needs to be paid quickly. In addition, if you have a chequing account, you know that it often takes several business days before a bank will allow you to make use of the funds from a cheque you have deposited. If your need for cash is urgent, this feature of paying by cheque can be frustrating. Second, all the paper shuffling required to process cheques is costly.

Electronic Payment

The development of inexpensive computers and the spread of the Internet now make it cheap to pay bills electronically. In the past, you paid a bill by mailing a cheque, but now banks provide websites at which you just log on, make a few clicks, and thereby transmit your payment electronically. Not only do you save the cost of the stamp, but paying bills becomes (almost) a pleasure, requiring little effort. Electronic payment systems provided by banks now even spare you the step of logging on to pay the bill. Instead, recurring bills can be automatically deducted from your bank account. Estimated cost savings when a bill is paid electronically rather than by cheque exceed one dollar per transaction. Electronic payment is thus becoming far more common in Canada.

E-Money

Electronic payment technology can substitute not only for cheques but also for cash, in the form of **electronic money** (or **e-money**)—money that exists only in electronic form. The first form of e-money was the *debit card*. Debit cards, which look like credit cards, enable customers to purchase goods and services by electronically transferring funds directly from their bank accounts to a merchant's account. Debit cards are used in many of the same places that accept credit cards and are now faster to use than cash. At most supermarkets, for example, you can swipe your debit card through the card reader at the checkout station, press a button, and the amount of your purchase is deducted from your bank account. Most banks, as well as companies such as Visa and MasterCard, issue debit cards, and your ATM card typically can function as a debit card.

A more advanced form of e-money is the *stored-value card*. The simplest form of stored-value card is purchased for a preset dollar amount that the consumer pays up front, like a prepaid phone card. The more sophisticated stored-value card is known as a **smart card**. It contains a computer chip that allows it to be loaded with digital cash from the owner's bank account whenever needed. In Asian countries, such as Japan and South Korea, cell phones now have a smart card feature that raises the expression "pay by phone" to a new level. Smart cards can be loaded from ATMs, personal computers with a smart card reader, or specially equipped telephones.

A third form of electronic money, often referred to as **e-cash**, is used on the Internet to purchase goods or services. A consumer gets e-cash by setting up an account with a bank that has links to the Internet and then transferring the e-cash to her PC. When she wants to buy something with e-cash, she surfs to a store on the web and clicks the "buy" option for a particular item, whereupon the e-cash is automatically transferred from her computer to the merchant's computer. The merchant can then have the funds transferred from the consumer's bank account to his own before the goods are shipped.

Given the convenience of e-money, you might think that we would move quickly to a cashless society in which all payments are made electronically. However, this hasn't happened, as discussed in the FYI box Are We Headed for a Cashless Society?

FYI   Are We Headed for a Cashless Society?

Predictions of a cashless society have been around for decades, but they have not come to fruition. For example, *Business Week* predicted in 1975 that electronic means of payment "would soon revolutionize the very concept of money itself," only to reverse its view several years later. In recent years, pilot projects aimed at converting consumers to the use of e-money in the form of smart cards have not been a success. Mondex, which was launched in Great Britain in 1995 and was one of the first widely touted stored-value cards, is now used only on a few British university campuses. In Germany and Belgium, millions of people carry bank cards with computer chips embedded that enable users to access e-money, but very few people actually use that feature. Why has the movement to a cashless society been so slow in coming?

Although e-money might be more convenient and efficient than a payments system based on paper, several factors work against the disappearance of the paper system. First, it is very expensive to set up the computer, card reader, and telecommunications networks necessary to make electronic money the dominant form of payment. Second, electronic means of payment raises security and privacy concerns. We often hear media reports of an unauthorized hacker who has been able to access a computer database and alter the information stored there. Because this is not an uncommon occurrence, unscrupulous persons might be able to access bank accounts in electronic payments systems and steal funds by moving them from someone else's accounts into their own. The prevention of this type of fraud is no easy task, and a whole new field of computer science has developed to cope with such security issues. A further concern is that the use of electronic means of payment leaves an electronic trail that contains a large amount of personal data on buying habits. There are worries that government agencies, employers, and marketers might be able to access these data, thereby enabling them to encroach on our privacy if they choose to do so.

In conclusion, although the use of e-money will surely increase in the future, to paraphrase Mark Twain, "the reports of cash's death are greatly exaggerated."

APPLICATION   Will Bitcoin Become the Money of the Future?

Bitcoin is a new type of electronic money created by software developer Satoshi Nakamoto in 2009. Bitcoin is not controlled by a single entity like a central bank, but rather is created in a decentralized fashion by users who generate new bitcoins when they use their computing power to verify and process Bitcoin transactions, a process referred to as "mining." Some tech enthusiasts have characterized Bitcoin as the money of the future. But does Bitcoin satisfy the three key functions of money that we discussed earlier? That is, does it function as a medium of exchange, a unit of account, and a store of value?

Bitcoin certainly functions well as a medium of exchange. It has two features that make it attractive for conducting transactions. First, the fees for conducting transactions with bitcoins are substantially lower than those associated with credit cards and debit cards. Second, transactions made with bitcoins can be made anonymously, which is very attractive to those who want to preserve their privacy.

Bitcoin, however, does not do well with regard to the other two functions of money—as a unit of account and as a store of value. The price of Bitcoin has been extremely volatile, with its volatility estimated to be over seven times that of the price of gold and over eight times that of stock market indexes such as the S&P 500. For example, in 2011, the price of a Bitcoin fluctuated between 30 cents and $32. It then rose to a peak of $255 on April 10, 2013, only to fall back down to $55 on April 17. On November 30, 2013, the price of a Bitcoin peaked at $1125, but it then fell to close to the $200 level by June of 2015.

The high volatility of the value of the Bitcoin means that it does not function well as a store of value; it is just too risky. Because of this volatility, the Bitcoin has not become a unit of account; almost no one quotes the prices of their products in terms of Bitcoins.

Despite the hype, Bitcoin does not satisfy two of the three key functions of money and thus its use as money is likely to be quite limited. Furthermore, governments are concerned about the use of Bitcoin to conduct drug transactions and money laundering. The Department of Homeland Security in the United States seized Bitcoin assets from the Mt. Gox exchange when the FBI shut down the Silk Road drug website in May of 2013. Countries such as China have outlawed the use of Bitcoin as a currency. There also have been high profile thefts of Bitcoin, with Mt. Gox, one of the largest Bitcoin exchanges, experiencing a theft of almost $500 million worth of Bitcoin in February of 2014, leading Mt. Gox to file for bankruptcy.

Our understanding of the functions of money strongly suggests that Bitcoin will not be the money of the future. However, some of its technology, which enables users to conduct electronic transactions cheaply, may become a feature of future electronic payments systems. ◆

MEASURING MONEY

The definition of money as anything that is generally accepted in payment for goods and services tells us that money is defined by people's behaviour. An asset is considered money only if people believe it will be accepted by others when making payment. As we have seen, many different assets have performed this role over the centuries, ranging from gold to paper currency to chequing accounts. For this reason, a behavioural definition does not tell us which assets in our economy should be considered money. To measure money, we need a precise definition that tells us exactly which assets should be included.

The Bank of Canada's Monetary Aggregates

The Bank of Canada (the Bank), the central banking authority responsible for monetary policy in Canada, has conducted many studies on how to measure money. The problem of measuring money has recently become especially crucial because extensive financial innovation has produced new types of assets that might properly belong in a measure of money.

Since 1980, the Bank of Canada has modified its measures of money several times and has settled on the following measures of the money supply, which are also referred to as **monetary aggregates** (also shown in Table 3-1).

TABLE 3-1 Measures of Monetary Aggregates and Their Components

Asset	M1+	M1++	M2	M2+	M2++	M3
Currency outside banks	✓	✓	✓	✓	✓	✓
Personal deposits at chartered banks			✓	✓	✓	✓
Non-personal demand and notice deposits at chartered banks			✓	✓	✓	✓
Fixed-term deposits			✓	✓	✓	✓
Deposits at trust and mortgage loan companies (TMLs)				✓	✓	
Deposits at credit unions and *caisses populaires* (CUCPs)				✓	✓	
Life insurance company individual annuities				✓	✓	
Personal deposits at government-owned savings institutions				✓	✓	
Money market mutual funds				✓	✓	
Canada Savings Bonds and other retail instruments					✓	
Non-money market mutual funds					✓	
All chequable deposits at chartered banks, TMLs, and CUCPs	✓	✓				
All nonchequable deposits at chartered banks, TMLs, and CUCPs		✓				
Non-personal term deposits at chartered banks						✓
Foreign currency deposits of residents at chartered banks						✓

Note Monetary aggregates exclude interbank deposits and include continuity adjustments. In January 2007, the monetary aggregates were redefined to reflect (i) the elimination of demand deposits and (ii) the inclusion of private-sector float.

The M1+ and M1++ Definitions of The Money Supply   Panel (a) of Figure 3-1 illustrates the narrow definitions of the money supply in Canada. The narrowest definition is called **M1+**. It includes

1. *Currency*, which is all the paper money and coins that are in circulation, where "in circulation" means not held by banks or the government. Surprisingly, there is close to $1500 cash in the hands of each person in Canada and more than US$2000 in the hands of each person in the United States (see the FYI box Where Are All the Dollars?).

2. The value of all chequable deposits at chartered banks, trust and mortgage loans companies (TMLs), and credit unions and *caisses populaires* (CUCPs).

These assets are all extremely liquid because they can be turned into cash quickly at very little cost. A broader definition of the money supply is **M1++**. As panel (a) of Figure 3-1 shows, M1++ includes everything that is in M1+, plus all nonchequable deposits at chartered banks, TMLs, and CUCPs.

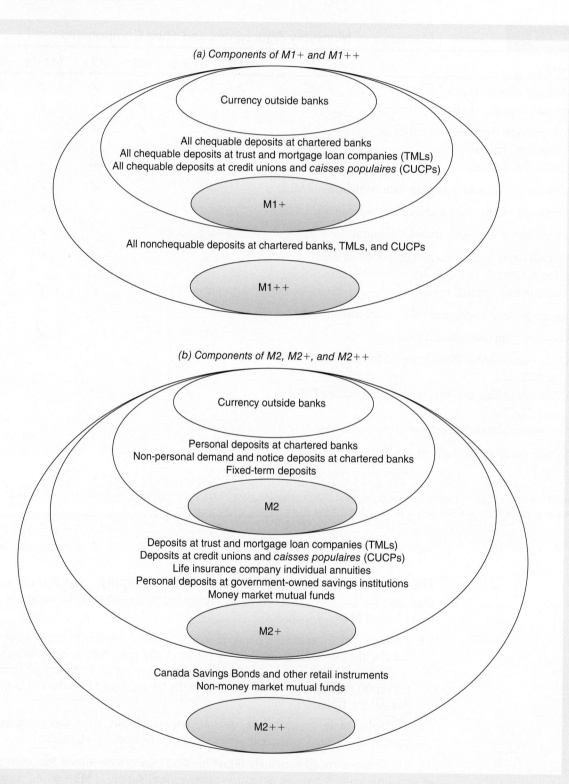

(a) Components of M1+ and M1++

Currency outside banks

All chequable deposits at chartered banks
All chequable deposits at trust and mortgage loan companies (TMLs)
All chequable deposits at credit unions and *caisses populaires* (CUCPs)

M1+

All nonchequable deposits at chartered banks, TMLs, and CUCPs

M1++

(b) Components of M2, M2+, and M2++

Currency outside banks

Personal deposits at chartered banks
Non-personal demand and notice deposits at chartered banks
Fixed-term deposits

M2

Deposits at trust and mortgage loan companies (TMLs)
Deposits at credit unions and *caisses populaires* (CUCPs)
Life insurance company individual annuities
Personal deposits at government-owned savings institutions
Money market mutual funds

M2+

Canada Savings Bonds and other retail instruments
Non-money market mutual funds

M2++

FIGURE 3-1   Definitions of the Money Supply

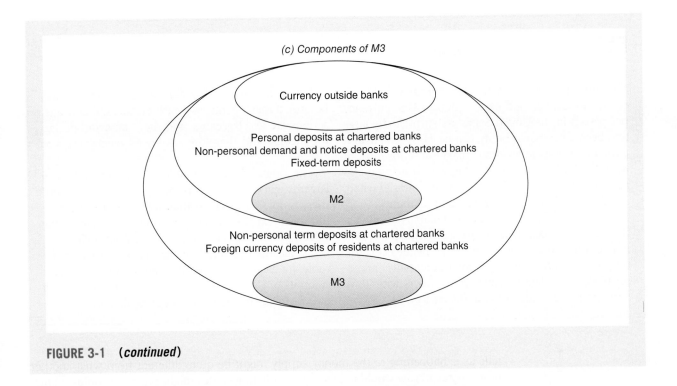

(c) Components of M3

FIGURE 3-1 (*continued*)

The M2, M2+, and M2++ Definitions of The Money Supply As panel (b) of Figure 3-1 shows, the **M2** monetary aggregate includes currency, personal deposits at chartered banks, non-personal demand and notice deposits at chartered banks, and fixed-term deposits. The **M2+** aggregate includes everything that is in M2, plus deposits at TMLs, deposits at CUCPs, life insurance company individual annuities, personal deposits at government-owned savings institutions, and money market mutual funds. The **M2++** is the broadest definition of the money supply in Canada and includes everything that is in M2+, plus Canada Savings Bonds and other retail debt instruments and non-money market mutual funds.

The M3 Definition of The Money Supply Another Definition of the money supply is called M3. As panel (c) of Figure 3-1 shows, M3 includes everything that is in M2, plus non-personal term deposits at chartered banks and foreign currency deposits of residents at chartered banks. The non-personal term deposits are held by provincial and municipal governments, corporations, and institutions, and also include deposits held by one bank with another, known as interbank deposits. The foreign currency deposits are mostly denominated in U.S. dollars.

Notice that the M2 and M3 monetary aggregates do not include deposits with trust and mortgage loan companies and credit unions and *caisses populaires*.

Because we cannot be sure which of the monetary aggregates is the true measure of money, it is logical to wonder if their movements closely parallel one another. If they do, then using one monetary aggregate to predict future economic performance and to conduct policy will be the same as using another, and the fact that we are not sure of the appropriate definition of money for a given policy decision is not too costly. However, if the monetary aggregates do not move together, then what one monetary aggregate

FYI   Where Are All the Dollars?

The almost $2000 of Canadian currency held per person in Canada and over $4000 of U.S. currency per person in the United States are surprisingly large numbers. Currency is bulky, can be easily stolen, and pays no interest, so it doesn't make sense for most of us to hold a lot of it. Do you know anyone who carries $2000 in their pockets? We have a puzzle: where are all these dollars and who is holding them?

One group that holds a lot of dollars is criminals. If you were engaged in illegal activity, you would not conduct your transactions with cheques because they are traceable and therefore a potentially powerful piece of evidence against you. This is why Tony Soprano had so much cash in his backyard.

Some businesses also like to hold a lot of cash because if they operate as a cash business, their transactions are less traceable, and they can avoid declaring income and therefore also avoid paying taxes as a result.

The other group that holds Canadian and (to a larger extent) U.S. dollars is foreigners. In many countries, people do not trust their own currency because they often experience high inflation, which erodes the value of their currency; these people hold dollars as a hedge against this inflation risk. Lack of trust in the ruble, for example, has led Russians to hold enormous amounts of U.S. dollars. In fact, over half the quantity of U.S. dollars in circulation are held abroad.

tells us is happening to the money supply might be quite different from what another monetary aggregate would tell us. The conflicting stories might present a confusing picture that would make it hard for policymakers to decide on the right course of action.

Figure 3-2 plots the growth rates of M2, M1++, and M2++ from 1969 to 2014. The growth rates of these three aggregates do tend to move together. Yet some glaring discrepancies exist in the movements of these aggregates. The average growth rate of money in the 1970s was 14.2% according to M2, 11.9% according to M1++, and 15% according to M2++. The average monetary growth rate in the 2000s was 7.4% according to M2, 10.2% according to M1++, and 6.6% according to M2++. Thus, the different measures of money tell a very different story about the course of monetary policy.

From the data in Figure3-2, you can see that obtaining a single precise, correct measure of money does seem to matter and that it does make a difference which monetary aggregate policymakers and economists choose as the true measure of money.

Money as a Weighted Aggregate

The measures of the money supply listed in Table 3-1 make black-and-white decisions about whether a given asset is money by including it or excluding it. In addition, these measures are simple-sum indices in which all monetary components are assigned a constant and equal (unitary) weight. This index is M in

$$M = x_1 + x_2 + \ldots + x_n$$

where x_i is one of the n monetary components of the monetary aggregate M. This summation index implies that all monetary components contribute equally to the money total and it views all components as dollar-for-dollar perfect substitutes. Such an index, there is no question, represents an index of the stock of nominal monetary wealth, but cannot, in general, represent a valid structural economic variable for the services of the quantity of money.

FIGURE 3-2 **Growth Rates of M2, M1++, and M2++, 1969–2014**

Timing of the rise and fall of growth rates is roughly similar. There are, however, periods when they move in opposite directions, providing conflicting recommendations about the course of monetary policy.

Source: Statistics Canada CANSIM Series V41552796, V37152, V41552801.

Over the years, there has been a steady stream of attempts at properly weighting monetary components within a simple-sum aggregate. Attention has been focused on the gains that can be achieved by a rigorous use of microeconomic theory, aggregation theory, and index number theory. This new approach to monetary aggregation led to the construction of weighted monetary aggregates.[2] These aggregates represent a viable and theoretically appropriate alternative to the simple-sum aggregates. Moreover, recent research indicates that these new measures of money seem to predict inflation and the business cycle somewhat better than more conventional measures do.[3]

[2] William Barnett, Douglas Fisher, and Apostolos Serletis, "Consumer Theory and the Demand for Money," in *Journal of Economic Literature* 30 (1992): 2086–2119, provide a state-of-the-art survey of this literature. See also William Barnett and Apostolos Serletis, *The Theory of Monetary Aggregation* (Amsterdam: North-Holland, 2000), and Apostolos Serletis, *The Demand for Money: Theoretical and Empirical Approaches*, 2nd edition (Springer, 2007).

[3] See, for example, Apostolos Serletis and Periklis Gogas, "Divisia Monetary Aggregates, the Great Ratios, and Classical Money Demand Functions," in *Journal of Money, Credit and Banking* 46 (2014): 229-241.

MyEconLab

MyEconLab is an online homework and tutorial system that puts you in control of your own learning with study and practice tools directly correlated to this chapter's content. Visit MyEconLab to access the eText, the Questions and Applied Problems with answers, as well as additional assessment. You will also find web chapters, mini-lectures, appendices, mini-cases, videos, glossary flashcards, news feeds, CANSIM data, and graphing tools.

SUMMARY

1. To economists, the word *money* has a different meaning than *income* or *wealth*. Money is anything that is generally accepted as payment for goods or services or in the repayment of debts.

2. Money serves three primary functions: as a medium of exchange, as a unit of account, and as a store of value. Money as a medium of exchange avoids the problem of double coincidence of wants that arises in a barter economy, and thus reduces transaction costs, and encourages specialization and the division of labour. Money as a unit of account reduces the number of prices needed in an economy, which also reduces transaction costs. Money also functions as a store of value, but performs this role poorly if it is rapidly losing value due to inflation.

3. The payments system has evolved over time. Until several hundred years ago, the payments system in all but the most primitive societies was based primarily on precious metals. The introduction of paper currency lowered the cost of transporting money. The next major advance was the introduction of cheques, which lowered transaction costs still further. We are currently moving toward an electronic payments system in which paper is eliminated and all transactions are handled by computers. Despite the potential efficiency of such a system, obstacles are slowing the movement to the chequeless society and the development of new forms of electronic money.

4. The Bank of Canada has defined six different measures of the money supply—M1+, M1++, M2, M2+, M2++, and M3. These measures are not equivalent and do not always move together, so they cannot be used interchangeably by policymakers. Obtaining the precise, correct measure of money does seem to matter and has implications for the conduct of monetary policy.

KEY TERMS

commodity money, p. 55
currency, p. 50
e-cash, p. 56
electronic money (e-money), p. 56
fiat money, p. 55
hyperinflation, p. 54
Income, p. 51

liquidity, p. 54
M1++, p. 59
M1+, p. 59
M2++, p. 61
M2+, p. 61
M2, p. 59
medium of exchange, p. 51

monetary aggregates, p. 58
payments system, p. 54
smart card, p. 56
store of value, p. 53
unit of account, p. 52
wealth, p. 51

QUESTIONS

All questions are available in MyEconLab at **www.myeconlab.com**.

1. Why is simply counting currency an inadequate measure of money?

2. In prison, cigarettes are sometimes used among inmates as a form of payment. How is it possible for cigarettes to solve the "double coincidence of wants" problem, even if a prisoner does not smoke?

3. There are three goods produced in an economy by three individuals:

Good	Producer
Apples	Orchard owner
Bananas	Banana grower
Chocolate	Chocolatier

If the orchard owner likes only bananas, the banana grower likes only chocolate, and the chocolatier likes only apples, will any trade between these three persons take place in a barter economy? How will introducing money into the economy benefit these three producers?

4. Why did cavemen not need money?

5. Most of the time it is quite difficult to separate the three functions of money. Money performs its three functions at all times, but sometimes we can stress one in particular. For each of the following situations, identify which function of money is emphasized.

a. Brooke accepts money in exchange for performing her daily tasks at her office, since she knows she can use that money to buy goods and services.

b. Tim wants to calculate the relative value of oranges and apples, and therefore checks the price per kilogram of each of these goods quoted in currency units.

c. Maria is currently pregnant. She expects her expenditures to increase in the future and decides to increase the balance in her savings account.

6. In Brazil, a country that underwent a rapid inflation before 1994, many transactions were conducted in U.S. dollars rather than in reals, the domestic currency. Why?

7. Was money a better store of value in Canada in the 1950s than it was in the 1970s? Why or why not? In which period would you have been more willing to hold money?

8. Why have some economists described money during a hyperinflation as a "hot potato" that is quickly passed from one person to another?

9. Why were people in Canada in the nineteenth century sometimes willing to be paid by cheque rather than with gold, even though they knew that there was a possibility that the cheque might bounce?

10. In ancient Greece, why was gold a more likely candidate for use as money than wine was?

11. If you use an online payment system such as PayPal to purchase goods or services on the Internet, does this affect the M1+ money supply, the M2+ money supply, both, or neither? Explain.

12. Rank the following assets from most liquid to least liquid:

a. Chequing account deposits
b. Houses
c. Currency
d. Automobile
e. Savings deposits
f. Common stock

13. Which of the Bank of Canada's measures of the monetary aggregates—M2+ or M2—is composed of the most liquid assets? Which is the largest measure?

14. It is not unusual to find a business that displays a sign "No personal cheques, please." Based on this observation, comment on the relative degree of liquidity of a chequing account versus currency.

15. For each of the following assets, indicate which of the monetary aggregates (M1+, M2+ and M2++) includes them:

a. Currency
b. Money market mutual funds
c. Canada Savings Bonds
d. Chequable deposits

16. Assume that you are interested in earning some return on idle balances you usually keep in your chequing account and decide to buy some money market mutual funds shares by writing a cheque. Comment on the effect of your action (everything else the same) on M1+ and M2+.

17. In a weighted monetary aggregate, which of the following assets would probably receive the highest weights? Which would receive the lowest weights?

a. Currency
b. Savings account deposits
c. Foreign currency deposits
d. Canada Savings Bonds

18. Suppose that a researcher discovers that a measure of the total amount of debt in the Canadian economy over the past 20 years was a better predictor of inflation and the business cycle than M1+ or M2 was. Does this discovery mean that we should define money as equal to the total amount of debt in the economy?

APPLIED PROBLEMS

All applied problems are available in MyEconLab *at* **www.myeconlab.com.**

19. Look up the M1+, M1++, M2, M2+, M2++, and M3 numbers in the Bank of Canada's Banking and Financial Statistics for the most recent one-year period. Have their growth rates been similar? What implications do their growth rates have for the conduct of monetary policy?

20. Which of the Bank of Canada's measures of the monetary aggregates, M1+, M1++, M2, M2+, M2++, or M3, is composed of the most liquid assets? Which is the largest measure?

DATA ANALYSIS PROBLEMS

Download data for these problems from MyEconLab *at* **www.myeconlab.com.**

1. Go to the CANSIM database and download monthly data from January 1970 to December 2014 on the M2 (gross) monetary aggregate (series V41552796).

   a. What is the average monthly monetary growth rate over the entire period?

   b. Calculate the average monthly monetary growth rate and its standard deviation over each of the last four decades.

   c. Which decade had the lowest money growth rate? The highest?

   d. Which decade had the lowest money growth volatility? The highest?

2. Go to the CANSIM database and find data on M2+ for Canada (series V41552789). Calculate the annual growth rate as $1200*\ln(M_t/M_{t-1})$, from January 2000 to November 2014. What is the average annual monetary growth rate? Its standard deviation?

WEB EXERCISES

1. Go to **www.bankofcanada.ca** and click on "Statistics" and then "Summary of key monetary policy variables."

   a. What has been the growth rate in M1+, M1++, and M2++ over the past 12 months?

   b. From what you know about the state of the economy, does this seem expansionary or restrictive?

2. Go to **www.bankofcanada.ca** and click on "Core Functions" and then on "Monetary Policy." Select one policy on which the Bank of Canada has a written policy. Write a one-paragraph summary of this policy.

WEB REFERENCES

www.bankofcanada.ca/core-functions/monetary-policy/lvts

This site reports on details regarding Canada's payments system.

www.bankofcanada.ca/rates/indicators/key-variables

The Bank of Canada reports the 12-month growth rate of M1+, M1++, and M2++.

www.centerforfinancialstability.org/amfm.php

This site reports data on a number of weighted (Divisia) monetary aggregates for the United States—the narrow aggregates, M1, M2M, MZM, M2, and ALL, as well as the broad aggregates, M4+, M4−, and M3.

Financial Markets

Chapter 4 The Meaning of Interest Rates

Chapter 5 The Behaviour of Interest Rates

Chapter 6 The Risk and Term Structure of Interest Rates

Chapter 7 The Stock Market, the Theory of Rational Expectations, and the Efficient Market Hypothesis

Crisis and Response: Credit Market Turmoil and the Stock Market Crash of October 2008

The financial crisis that started during the summer of 2007 in the United States began snowballing as the value of mortgage-backed securities on financial institutions' balance sheets plummeted. A "flight to quality" drove three-month Treasury bill rates down to almost zero, which had last happened during the Great Depression of the 1930s. Credit spreads—an indicator of risk—shot through the roof, with the U.S. Treasury bill to Eurodollar rate (TED) spread going from around 40 basis points (0.40 percentage points) before the financial crisis started to over 450 basis points in mid-October, the highest value in its history. After earlier sharp declines, the stock market crashed further, with the week beginning on October 6, 2008, showing the worst weekly decline in history.

The recent financial crisis illustrates how volatile financial markets can be. This volatility hit financial consumers directly, leading to difficulty in getting loans, falling property values, declining retirement account portfolios, and putting jobs in jeopardy. How can policy respond to disruptions in financial markets? We begin addressing this question by examining the inner workings of financial markets, particularly interest rate dynamics. Chapter 4 explains what an interest rate is, as well as the relationships among interest rates, bond prices, and returns. Chapter 5 examines how the overall level of interest rates is determined. In Chapter 6, we extend the analysis of the bond market to explain changes in credit spreads and the relationship of long-term to short-term interest rates. Chapter 7 looks at the role of expectations in the stock market and what drives stock prices.

4

The Meaning of Interest Rates

1.39

Learning Objectives

After studying this chapter you should be able to

1. Calculate the present value of future cash flows and the yield to maturity on the four types of credit market instruments.

2. Recognize the distinctions among yield to maturity, current yield, rate of return, and rate of capital gain.

3. Interpret the distinction between real and nominal interest rates.

PREVIEW

Interest rates are among the most closely watched variables in the economy. Their movements are reported almost daily by the news media because they directly affect our everyday lives and have important consequences for the health of the economy. They influence personal decisions such as whether to consume or save, whether to buy a house, and whether to purchase bonds or put funds into a savings account. Interest rates also affect the economic decisions of businesses and households, such as whether to use their funds to invest in new equipment for factories or to save rather than spend their money.

Before we can go on with the study of money, banking, and financial markets, we must understand exactly what the phrase *interest rates* means. In this chapter, we see that a concept known as the *yield to maturity* is the most accurate measure of interest rates; the yield to maturity is what economists mean when they use the term *interest rate*. We'll discuss how the yield to maturity is measured. We'll also see that a bond's interest rate does not necessarily indicate how good an investment the bond is, because what the bond earns (its rate of return) does not necessarily equal its interest rate. Finally, we'll explore the distinction between real interest rates, which are adjusted for inflation, and nominal interest rates, which are not.

Although learning definitions is not always the most exciting of pursuits, it is important to read carefully and understand the concepts presented in this chapter. Not only are they used continually throughout the remainder of this text, but a firm grasp of these terms will give you a clearer understanding of the role that interest rates play in your life as well as in the general economy.

MEASURING INTEREST RATES

Different debt instruments have very different streams of cash payments (known as **cash flows**) to the holder, with very different timing. Thus we first need to understand how we can compare the value of one kind of debt instrument with the value of another before we see how interest rates are measured. To do this, we make use of the concept of *present value*.

Present Value

The concept of **present value** (or **present discounted value**) is based on the commonsense notion that a dollar paid to you one year from now is less valuable than a dollar paid to you today. This notion is true because you can deposit a dollar today in a savings account that earns interest and have more than a dollar in one year. Economists use a more formal definition, as explained in this section.

Let's look at the simplest kind of debt instrument, which we will call a **simple loan**. In this loan, the lender provides the borrower with an amount of funds (called the *principal*) that must be repaid to the lender at the *maturity date*, along with an additional payment for the interest. For example, if you made your friend Jane a simple loan of $100 for one year, you would require her to repay the principal of $100 in one year's time, along with an additional payment for interest—say, $10. In the case of a simple loan like this one, the interest payment divided by the amount of the loan is a natural and sensible way to measure the interest rate. This measure of the so-called *simple interest rate, i*, is

$$i = \frac{\$10}{\$100} = 0.10 = 10\%$$

If you make this $100 loan, at the end of the year you will have $110, which can be rewritten as

$$\$100 \times (1 + 0.10) = \$110$$

If you then lent out the $110 at the same interest rate, at the end of the second year you would have

$$\$110 \times (1 + 0.10) = \$121$$

or, equivalently,

$$\$100 \times (1 + 0.10) \times (1 + 0.10) = \$100 \times (1 + 0.10)^2 = \$121$$

Continuing with the loan again, at the end of the third year you would have

$$\$121 \times (1 + 0.10) = \$100 \times (1 + 0.10)^3 = \$133$$

Generalizing, we can see that at the end of n years, your $100 would turn into

$$\$100 \times (1 + i)^n$$

The amounts you would have at the end of each year by making the $100 loan today can be seen in the following timeline:

This timeline clearly indicates that you are just as happy having $100 today as you will be having $110 a year from now (of course, as long as you are sure that Jane will pay you back). You are also just as happy having $100 today as you will be having $121 two years from now, or $133 three years from now, or $100 \times (1 + 0.10)^n$ dollars

n years from now. The timeline indicates that we can also work backward from future amounts to the present. For example, $133 = \$100 \times (1 + 0.10)^3$ three years from now is worth \$100 today, so

$$\$100 = \frac{\$133}{(1 + 0.10)^3}$$

The process of calculating today's value of dollars received in the future, as we have done above, is called *discounting the future*. We can generalize this process by writing today's (present) value of \$100 as PV and the future cash flow (payment) of \$133 as CF, and then replacing 0.10 (the 10% interest rate) by i. This leads to the following formula:

$$PV = \frac{CF}{(1 + i)^n} \qquad \text{(Equation 1)}$$

Intuitively, Equation 1 tells us that if you are promised \$1 of cash flow, for certain, ten years from now, this dollar would not be as valuable to you as \$1 is today because, if you had the \$1 today, you could invest it and end up with more than \$1 in ten years.

The concept of present value is extremely useful, because it allows us to figure out today's value (price) of a credit (debt) market instrument at a given simple interest rate i by just adding up the individual present values of all the future payments received. This information enables us to compare the values of two or more instruments that have very different timing of their payments.

APPLICATION   Simple Present Value

What is the present value of \$250 to be paid in two years if the interest rate is 15%?

Solution
The present value would be \$189.04. We find this value by using Equation 1,

$$PV = \frac{CF}{(1 + i)^n}$$

where

$$
\begin{aligned}
CF &= \text{cash flow in two years} &&= 250 \\
i &= \text{annual interest rate} &&= 0.15 \\
n &= \text{number of years} &&= 2
\end{aligned}
$$

Thus

$$PV = \frac{\$250}{(1 + 0.15)^2} = \frac{\$250}{1.3225} = \$189.04$$

APPLICATION   **How Much Is That Jackpot Worth?**

Assume that you just hit the $20 million jackpot in a lottery, which promises you a payment of $1 million every year for the next 20 years. You are clearly excited, but have you really won $20 million?

Solution

No, not in the present value sense. In today's dollars, that $20 million is worth a lot less. If we assume an interest rate of 10% as in the earlier examples, the first payment of $1 million is clearly worth $1 million today, but the second payment next year is worth only $1 million$/(1 + 0.10) = \$909\,090$, a lot less than $1 million. The following year, the payment is worth $1 million$/(1 + 0.10)^2 = \$826\,446$ in today's dollars, and so on. When you add up all these amounts, they total $9.4 million. You are still pretty excited (who wouldn't be?), but because you understand the concept of present value, you recognize that you are the victim of false advertising. In present-value terms, you didn't really win $20 million, but instead won less than half that amount. ◆

Four Types of Credit Market Instruments

In terms of the timing of their cash flow payments, there are four basic types of credit market instruments.

1. A simple loan, which we have already discussed, in which the lender provides the borrower with an amount of funds that must be repaid to the lender at the maturity date, along with an additional payment for the interest. Many money market instruments are of this type—for example, commercial loans to businesses.
2. A **fixed-payment loan** (also called a **fully amortized loan**) in which the lender provides the borrower with an amount of funds that the borrower must repay by making the same payment, consisting of part of the principal and interest, every period (such as a month) for a set number of years. For example, if you borrow $1000, a fixed-payment loan might require you to pay $126 every year for 25 years. Installment loans (such as auto loans) and mortgages are frequently of the fixed-payment type.
3. A **coupon bond** pays the owner of the bond a fixed-interest payment (coupon payment) every year until the maturity date, when a specified final amount (**face value** or **par value**) is repaid. (The coupon payment is so named because in the past, the bondholder obtained payment by clipping a coupon off the bond and sending it to the bond issuer, who then sent the payment to the holder. Today, it is no longer necessary to send in coupons to receive payments.) A coupon bond with $1000 face value, for example, might pay you a coupon payment of $100 per year for ten years, and then repay you the face value amount of $1000 at the maturity date. (The face value of a bond is usually in $1000 increments.)

   A coupon bond is identified by four pieces of information: First is the bond's face value; second is the corporation or government agency that issues the bond; third is the maturity date of the bond; and fourth is the bond's **coupon rate**, which is the dollar amount of the yearly coupon payment expressed as a percentage of the face value of the bond. In our example, the coupon bond has a yearly coupon payment of $100 and a face value of $1000. The coupon rate is then $\$100/\$1000 = 0.10$, or 10%. Canada bonds and corporate bonds are examples of coupon bonds.

4. A **discount bond** (also called a **zero-coupon bond**) is bought at a price below its face value (at a discount), and the face value is repaid at the maturity date. Unlike a coupon bond, a discount bond does not make any interest payments; it just pays off the face value. For example, a one-year discount bond with a face value of $1000 might be bought for $900; in a year's time, the owner would be repaid the face value of $1000. Canadian government Treasury bills and long-term zero-coupon bonds are examples of discount bonds.

These four types of instruments make payments at different times: Simple loans and discount bonds make payments only at their maturity dates, whereas fixed-payment loans and coupon bonds make payments periodically until maturity. How can you decide which of these instruments will provide you with the most income? They all seem so different because they make payments at different times. To solve this problem, we use the concept of present value, explained earlier, to provide us with a procedure for measuring interest rates on these different types of instruments.

Yield to Maturity

Of the several common ways of calculating interest rates, the most important is the **yield to maturity**, which is the interest rate that equates the present value of cash flow payments received from a debt instrument with its value today.[1] Because the concept behind the calculation of the yield to maturity makes good economic sense, economists consider it the most accurate measure of interest rates.

To better understand the yield to maturity, we now look at how it is calculated for the four types of credit market instruments. In all of these examples, the key to understanding the calculation of the yield to maturity is realizing that we are equating today's value of the debt instrument with the present value of all of its future cash flow payments.

Simple Loan   Using the concept of present value, the yield to maturity on a simple loan is easy to calculate. For the one-year loan we discussed, today's value is $100, and the payments in one year's time would be $110 (the repayment of $100 plus the interest payment of $10). We can use this information to solve for the yield to maturity i by recognizing that the present value of the future payments must equal today's value of the loan.

APPLICATION   Yield to Maturity on a Simple Loan

If Pete borrows $100 from his sister and next year she wants $110 back from him, what is the yield to maturity on this loan?

Solution
The yield to maturity on the loan is 10%.

$$PV = \frac{CF}{(1 + i)^n}$$

---

[1] In other contexts, the yield to maturity is also called the *internal rate of return*.

where

$$PV = \text{amount borrowed} = \$100$$
$$CF = \text{cash flow in one year} = \$110$$
$$n = \text{number of years} = 1$$

Thus

$$\$100 = \frac{\$110}{(1 + i)}$$

$$(1 + i)\$100 = \$110$$

$$(1 + i) = \frac{\$110}{\$100}$$

$$i = 1.10 - 1 = 0.10 = 10\%$$

Today	Year
0	1

$100 $110

$i = 10\%$

♦

This calculation of the yield to maturity should look familiar because it equals the interest payment of $10 divided by the loan amount of $100; that is, it equals the simple interest rate on the loan. An important point to recognize is that *for simple loans, the simple interest rate equals the yield to maturity*. Hence the same term *i* is used to denote both the yield to maturity and the simple interest rate.

Fixed-Payment Loan   Recall that this type of loan has the same cash flow payment every period throughout the life of the loan. On a fixed-rate mortgage, for example, the borrower makes the same payment to the bank every month until the maturity date, at which time the loan will be completely paid off. To calculate the yield to maturity for a fixed-payment loan, we follow the same strategy that we used for the simple loan—we equate today's value of the loan with its present value. Because the fixed-payment loan involves more than one cash flow payment, the present value of the fixed-payment loan is calculated (using Equation 1) as the sum of the present values of all cash flow payments.

In the case of our earlier example on page 71, the loan is $1000 and the yearly payment is $126 for the next 25 years. The present value (*PV*) is calculated as follows: At the end of one year, there is a $126 payment with a *PV* of $126/(1 + i); at the end of two years, there is another $126 payment with a *PV* of $126/(1 + i)^2; and so on until, at the end of the twenty-fifth year, the last payment of $126 with a *PV* of $126/(1 + i)^{25} is made. Setting today's value of the loan ($1000) equal to the sum of the present values of all the yearly payments gives us

$$\$1000 = \frac{\$126}{1 + i} + \frac{\$126}{(1 + i)^2} + \frac{\$126}{(1 + i)^3} + \cdots + \frac{\$126}{(1 + i)^{25}}$$

More generally, for any fixed-payment loan,

$$LV = \frac{FP}{(1 + i)} + \frac{FP}{(1 + i)^2} + \frac{FP}{(1 + i)^3} + \cdots + \frac{FP}{(1 + i)^n} \qquad \text{(Equation 2)}$$

where

$$LV = \text{loan value}$$
$$FP = \text{fixed yearly payment}$$
$$n = \text{number of years until maturity}$$

For a fixed-payment loan, the loan value, the fixed yearly payment, and the number of years until maturity are known quantities, and only the yield to maturity is not. So we can solve this equation for the yield to maturity i. Because this calculation is not easy, many financial calculators have programs that enable you to find i given the loan's numbers for LV, FP, and n. Consider this example, in the case of a 25-year $1000 loan with yearly payments of $85.81, the yield to maturity that results from solving Equation 2 is 7%. Real estate brokers always have a financial calculator handy that can solve such equations, so that they can immediately tell the prospective house buyer exactly what the yearly (or monthly) payments will be if the house purchase is financed by a mortgage.

APPLICATION Yield to Maturity and the Yearly Payment on a Fixed-Payment Loan

You decide to purchase a new home and need a $100 000 mortgage. You take out a loan from the bank that has an interest rate of 7%. What is the yearly payment to the bank if you wish to pay off the loan in 20 years?

Solution
The yearly payment to the bank is $9439.29.

$$LV = \frac{FP}{(1 + i)} + \frac{FP}{(1 + i)^2} + \frac{FP}{(1 + i)^3} + \cdots + \frac{FP}{(1 + i)^n}$$

where

$$LV = \text{loan value amount} = \$100{,}000$$
$$i = \text{annual interest rate} = 7\%$$
$$n = \text{number of years} = 20$$

Thus

$$\$100\,000 = \frac{FP}{(1 + 0.07)} + \frac{FP}{(1 + 0.07)^2} + \frac{FP}{(1 + 0.07)^3} + \cdots + \frac{FP}{(1 + 0.07)^{20}}$$

To find the monthly payment for the loan using a financial calculator:

$$n = \text{number of years} = 20$$
$$PV = \text{amount of the loan } (LV) = \$100\,000$$
$$FV = \text{amount of the loan after 20 years} = 0$$
$$i = \text{annual interest rate} = 0.07\%$$

Then push the *PMT* button to get the fixed yearly payment $(FP) = \$9439.29.$ ◆

Coupon Bond To calculate the yield to maturity for a coupon bond, follow the same strategy used for the fixed-payment loan: Equate today's value of the bond with its present value. Because coupon bonds also have more than one cash flow payment, the present value of the bond is calculated as the sum of the present values of all the coupon payments plus the present value of the final payment of the face value of the bond.

The present value of a $1000-face-value bond with 10 years to maturity and yearly coupon payments of $100 (a 10% coupon rate) can be calculated as follows: At the end of one year, there is a $100 coupon payment with a *PV* of $100/(1 + i)$; at the end of the second year, there is another $100 coupon payment with a *PV* of $100/(1 + i)^2$; and so on until, at maturity, there is a $100 coupon payment with a *PV* of $100/(1 + i)^{10}$ plus the repayment of the $1000 face value with a *PV* of $1000/(1 + i)^{10}$. Setting today's value of the bond (its current price, denoted by *P*) equal to the sum of the present values of all the cash flow payments for the bond gives

$$P = \frac{\$100}{1 + i} + \frac{\$100}{(1 + i)^2} + \frac{\$100}{(1 + i)^3} + \cdots + \frac{\$100}{(1 + i)^{10}} + \frac{\$1000}{(1 + i)^{10}}$$

More generally, for any coupon bond,[2]

$$P = \frac{C}{1 + i} + \frac{C}{(1 + i)^2} + \frac{C}{(1 + i)^3} + \cdots + \frac{C}{(1 + i)^n} + \frac{F}{(1 + i)^n} \quad \text{(Equation 3)}$$

where
P = price of the coupon bond
C = yearly coupon payment
F = face value of the bond
n = years to maturity date

In Equation 3, the coupon payment, the face value, the years to maturity, and the price of the bond are known quantities, and only the yield to maturity is not. Hence we can solve this equation for the yield to maturity *i*. As in the case of the fixed-payment loan, this calculation is not easy, so business-oriented software and financial calculators have built-in programs that solve the equation for you.

APPLICATION **Yield to Maturity and Bond Price for a Coupon Bond**

Find the price of a 10% coupon bond with a face value of $1000, a 12.25% yield to maturity, and eight years to maturity.

Solution
The price of the bond is $889.20. To solve using a financial calculator:

n = years to maturity = 8
FV = face value of the bond (F) = $1000
i = annual interest rate = 12.25%
PMT = yearly coupon payments (C) = $100

Then push the *PV* button to get the price of the bond = $889.20.

Alternatively, you could solve for the yield to maturity given the bond price by entering $889.20 for *PV* and pushing the *i* button to get a yield to maturity of 12.25%. ◆

---

[2] Most coupon bonds actually make coupon payments on a semiannual basis rather than once a year as we assumed here. The effect on the calculations is very slight and will be ignored here.

Table 4-1 shows the yields to maturity calculated for several bond prices. Three interesting facts emerge:

1. When the coupon bond is priced at its face value, the yield to maturity equals the coupon rate.
2. The price of a coupon bond and the yield to maturity are negatively related; that is, as the yield to maturity rises, the price of the bond falls. As the yield to maturity falls, the price of the bond rises.
3. The yield to maturity is greater than the coupon rate when the bond price is below its face value and is less than the coupon rate when the bond price is above its face value.

These three facts are true for any coupon bond and are really not surprising if you think about the reasoning behind the calculation of the yield to maturity. When you put $1000 in a bank account with an interest rate of 10%, you can take out $100 every year and you will be left with the $1000 at the end of 10 years. This process is similar to buying the $1000 bond with a 10% coupon rate analyzed in Table 4-1, which pays a $100 coupon payment every year and then repays $1000 at the end of 10 years. If the bond is purchased at the par value of $1000, its yield to maturity must equal 10%, which is also equal to the coupon rate of 10%. The same reasoning applied to any coupon bond demonstrates that if the coupon bond is purchased at its par value, the yield to maturity and the coupon rate must be equal.

It is a straightforward process to show that the bond price and the yield to maturity are negatively correlated. As i, the yield to maturity, increases, all denominators in the bond price formula (Equation 3) must necessarily increase, because the rise in i lowers the present value of all future cash flow payments for this bond. Hence a rise in the interest rate, as measured by the yield to maturity, means that the price of the bond must fall. Another way to explain why the bond price falls when the interest rate rises is to consider that a higher interest rate implies that the future coupon payments and final payment are worth less when discounted back to the present; hence the price of the bond must be lower.

The third fact, that the yield to maturity is greater than the coupon rate when the bond price is below its par value, follows directly from facts 1 and 2. When the yield to maturity equals the coupon rate, then the bond price is at the face value; when the yield to maturity rises above the coupon rate, the bond price necessarily falls and so must be below the face value of the bond.

TABLE 4-1	Yields to Maturity on a 10%-Coupon-Rate Bond Maturing in 10 Years (Face Value = $1000)	
Price of Bond ($)		**Yield to Maturity (%)**
1200		7.13
1100		8.48
1000		10.00
900		11.75
800		13.81

One special case of a coupon bond is worth discussing here because its yield to maturity is particularly easy to calculate. This bond is called a **consol** or a **perpetuity**; it is a perpetual bond with no maturity date and no repayment of principal that makes fixed coupon payments of C forever. Consols were first sold by the British Treasury during the Napoleonic Wars and are still traded today; they are quite rare, however, in North American capital markets. The formula in Equation 3 for the price of the consol P_c simplifies to the following:[3]

$$P_c = \frac{C}{i_c}$$ (Equation 4)

where
P_c = price of the perpetuity (consol)
C = yearly payment
i_c = yield to maturity of the perpetuity (consol)

One nice feature of perpetuities is that you can immediately see that as i_c increases, the price of the bond falls. For example, if a perpetuity pays $100 per year forever and the interest rate is 10%, its price will be $1000 = \$100/0.10$. If the interest rate rises to 20%, its price will fall to $500 = \$100/0.20$. We can rewrite this formula as

$$i_c = \frac{C}{P_c}$$ (Equation 5)

APPLICATION   ## Yield to Maturity on a Perpetuity

What is the yield to maturity on a bond that has a price of $2000 and pays $100 of interest annually, forever?

Solution
The yield to maturity is 5%.

$$i_c = \frac{C}{P_c}$$

[3] The bond price formula for a consol is

$$P = \frac{C}{1 + i} + \frac{C}{(1 + i)^2} + \frac{C}{(1 + i)^3} + \ldots$$

which can be written as

$$P = C(x + x^2 + x^3 + \ldots)$$

in which $x = 1/(1 + i)$. The formula for an infinite sum is

$$1 + x + x^2 + x^3 + \ldots = \frac{1}{1 - x} \text{ for } x < 1$$

and so

$$P = C\left(\frac{1}{1 - x} - 1\right) = C\left[\frac{1}{1 - 1/(1 + i)} - 1\right]$$

which by suitable algebraic manipulation becomes

$$P = C\left(\frac{1 + i}{i} - \frac{i}{i}\right) = \frac{C}{i}$$

where

$$C = \text{yearly payment} = \$100$$
$$P_c = \text{price of perpetuity (consol)} = \$2000$$

Thus

$$i_c = \frac{\$100}{\$2000}$$

$$i_c = 0.05 = 5\%$$ ◆

The formula given in Equation 5, which describes the calculation of the yield to maturity for a perpetuity, also provides a useful approximation for the yield to maturity on coupon bonds. When a coupon bond has a long term to maturity (say, 20 years or more), it is very much like a perpetuity, which pays coupon payments forever. This is because the cash flows more than 20 years in the future have such small present discounted values that the value of a long-term coupon bond is very close to the value of a perpetuity with the same coupon rate. Thus i_c in Equation 5 will be very close to the yield to maturity for any long-term bond. For this reason, i_c, the yearly coupon payment divided by the price of the security, has been given the name **current yield** and is frequently used as an approximation to describe interest rates on long-term bonds.

Discount Bond   The yield-to-maturity calculation for a discount bond is similar to that for a simple loan. Let's consider a discount bond such as a one-year Canadian Treasury bill that pays a face value of $1000 in one year's time but today has a price of $900.

APPLICATION   ## Yield to Maturity on a Discount Bond

What is the yield to maturity on a one-year, $1000 Treasury bill with a current price of $900?

Solution
The yield to maturity is 11.1%.
Using the present value formula,

$$PV = \frac{CF}{(1 + i)^n}$$

and recognizing that the present value (*PV*) is the current price of $900, the cash flow in one year is $1000, and the number of years is 1, we can write:

$$\$900 = \frac{\$1000}{1 + i}$$

Solving for *i*, we get

$$(1 + i) \times \$900 = \$1000$$
$$\$900 + \$900i = \$1000$$
$$\$900i = \$1000 - \$900$$
$$i = \frac{\$1000 - \$900}{\$900} = 0.111 = 11.1\%$$ ◆

As we just saw in the preceding application, the yield to maturity for a one-year discount bond equals the increase in price over the year, $1000 − $900, divided by the initial price, $900. Hence, more generally, for any one-year discount bond, the yield to maturity can be written as

$$i = \frac{F - P}{P}$$ (Equation 6)

where $F =$ face value of the discount bond
                 $P =$ current price of the discount bond

An important feature of this equation is that it indicates that, for a discount bond, the yield to maturity is negatively related to the current bond price. This is the same conclusion that we reached for a coupon bond. Equation 6 shows that a rise in the bond price—say, from $900 to $950—means that the bond will have a smaller increase in its price at maturity and so the yield to maturity will fall, from 11.1% to 5.3% in our example. Similarly, a fall in the yield to maturity means that the current price of the discount bond has risen.

Summary   The concept of present value tells you that a dollar in the future is not as valuable to you as a dollar today because you can earn interest on a dollar you have today. Specifically, a dollar received n years from now is worth only $\$1/(1 + i)^n$ today. The present value of a set of future cash flow payments on a debt instrument equals the sum of the present values of each of the future payments. The yield to maturity for an instrument is the interest rate that equates the present value of the future payments on that instrument to its value today. Because the procedure for calculating the yield to maturity is based on sound economic principles, the yield to maturity is the measure that economists think most accurately describes the interest rate.

Our calculations of the yield to maturity for a variety of bonds reveal the important fact that *current bond prices and interest rates are negatively related: **When the interest rate rises, the price of the bond falls, and vice versa**.*

THE DISTINCTION BETWEEN INTEREST RATES AND RETURNS

Many people think that the interest rate on a bond tells them all they need to know about how well off they are as a result of owning it. If Irving the Investor thinks he is well off when he owns a long-term bond yielding a 10% interest rate, and the interest rate then rises to 20%, he will have a rude awakening: As we will shortly see, if he has to sell the bond, Irving will lose his shirt! How well a person does financially by holding a bond or any other security over a particular time period is accurately measured by the security's **return**, or, in more precise terminology, the **rate of return**. We will use the concept of *return* continually throughout this book: Understanding this concept will make the material presented later in the book easier to follow.

For any security, the rate of return is defined as the amount of each payment to the owner plus the change in the security's value, expressed as a fraction of its purchase price. To make this definition clearer, let us see what the return would look like for a $1000-face-value coupon bond with a coupon rate of 10% that is bought for $1000, held for one year, and then sold for $1200. The payments to the owner are the yearly coupon payments of $100, and the change in the bond's value is $1200 − $1000 = $200. Adding these values together and expressing them as a fraction of the purchase price of $1000 gives us the one-year holding-period return for this bond:

$$\frac{\$100 + \$200}{\$1000} = \frac{\$300}{\$1000} = 0.30 = 30\%$$

You may have noticed something quite surprising about the return that we just calculated: It equals 30%, yet as Table 4-1 indicates, initially the yield to maturity was only 10%. This discrepancy demonstrates that **the return on a bond will not necessarily equal the yield to maturity on that bond**. We now see that the distinction between interest rate and return can be important, although for many securities the two may be closely related.

More generally, the return on a bond held from time t to time $t + 1$ can be written as

$$R = \frac{C + P_{t+1} - P_t}{P_t} \qquad \text{(Equation 7)}$$

where
$R =$ return from holding the bond from time t to time $t + 1$
$P_t =$ price of the bond at time t
$P_{t+1} =$ price of the bond at time $t + 1$
$C =$ coupon payment

A convenient way to rewrite the return formula in Equation 7 is to recognize that it can be split into two separate terms:

$$R = \frac{C}{P_t} + \frac{P_{t+1} - P_t}{P_t}$$

The first term is the current yield i_c (the coupon payment over the purchase price):

$$\frac{C}{P_t} = i_c$$

The second term is the **rate of capital gain**, or the change in the bond's price relative to the initial purchase price:

$$\frac{P_{t+1} - P_t}{P_t} = g$$

where g is the rate of capital gain. Equation 7 can then be rewritten as

$$R = i_c + g \qquad \text{(Equation 8)}$$

which shows that the return on a bond is the current yield i_c plus the rate of capital gain g. This rewritten formula illustrates the point we just discovered: Even for a bond for which the current yield i_c is an accurate measure of the yield to maturity, the return can differ substantially from the interest rate. Returns will differ substantially from the interest rate if the price of the bond experiences sizable fluctuations that produce substantial capital gains or losses.

To explore this point even further, let's look at what happens to the returns on bonds of different maturities when interest rates rise. Table 4-2 calculates the one-year returns, using Equation 8 above, on several 10%-coupon-rate bonds, all purchased at par, when interest rates on all these bonds rise from 10% to 20%. Several key findings from this table are generally true of all bonds:

- The only bonds whose returns will equal their initial yields to maturity are those whose times to maturity are the same as their holding periods (see, for example, the last bond in Table 4-2).
- A rise in interest rates is associated with a fall in bond prices, resulting in capital losses on bonds whose terms to maturity are longer than their holding periods.
- The more distant a bond's maturity date, the greater the size of the percentage price change associated with an interest rate change.
- The more distant a bond's maturity date, the lower the rate of return that occurs as a result of an increase in the interest rate.
- Even though a bond may have a substantial initial interest rate, its return can turn out to be negative if interest rates rise.

At first, students are frequently puzzled (as was poor Irving the Investor) that a rise in interest rates can mean that a bond has been a poor investment. The trick to understanding this fact is to recognize Irving has already purchased the bond, so that a rise in the interest rate means that the price of the bond Irving is holding falls and he experiences a capital loss. If this loss is large enough, the bond can be a poor investment indeed. For example, we see in Table 4-2 that the bond that has 30 years to maturity when purchased has a capital loss of 49.7% when the interest rate rises from 10% to 20%. This loss is so large that it exceeds the current yield of 10%, resulting in a negative return (loss) of −39.7%. If Irving does not sell the bond, his capital loss is often referred to as a "paper loss." This is a loss nonetheless because if Irving had not bought this bond and had instead put his money in the bank, he would now be able to buy more bonds at their lower price than he presently owns.

TABLE 4-2	One-Year Returns on Different-Maturity 10%-Coupon-Rate Bonds When Interest Rates Rise from 10% to 20%				
(1) Years to Maturity when Bond is Purchased	(2) Initial Current Yield (%)	(3) Initial Price ($)	(4) Price Next Year* ($)	(5) Rate of Capital Gain (%)	(6) Rate of Return [col (2) + col (5)] (%)
30	10	1000	503	−49.7	−39.7
20	10	1000	516	−48.4	−38.4
10	10	1000	597	−40.3	−30.3
5	10	1000	741	−25.9	−15.9
2	10	1000	917	−8.3	+1.7
1	10	1000	1000	0.0	+10.0

*Calculated with a financial calculator, using Equation 3.

Maturity and the Volatility of Bond Returns: Interest-Rate Risk

The finding that the prices of longer-maturity bonds respond more dramatically to changes in interest rates helps explain an important fact about the behaviour of bond markets: ***Prices and returns for long-term bonds are more volatile than those for shorter-term bonds***. Price changes of +20% and −20% within a year, with corresponding variations in returns, are common for bonds that are more than 20 years away from maturity.

We now see that changes in interest rates make investments in long-term bonds quite risky. Indeed, the risk level associated with an asset's return that results from interest-rate changes is so important that it has been given a special name, **interest-rate risk**.[4] Dealing with interest-rate risk is a major concern of managers of financial institutions and investors, as we will see in later chapters.

Although long-term debt instruments have substantial interest-rate risk, short-term debt instruments do not. Indeed, bonds with a maturity term that is as short as the holding period have no interest-rate risk.[5] We see this for the coupon bond at the bottom of Table 4-2, which has no uncertainty about the rate of return because it equals the yield to maturity, which is known at the time the bond is purchased. The key to understanding why there is no interest-rate risk for *any* bond whose time to maturity matches the holding period is to recognize that (in this case) the price at the end of the holding period is already fixed at the face value. A change in interest rates can then have no effect on the price at the end of the holding period for these bonds, and the return will therefore be equal to the yield to maturity, which is known at the time the bond is purchased.[6]

---

[4] Interest-rate risk can be quantitatively measured using the concept of *duration*. This concept and its calculation are discussed in an appendix to this chapter, which can be found on the MyEconLab.

[5] The statement that there is no interest-rate risk for any bond whose time to maturity matches the holding period is literally true only for discount (zero-coupon) bonds that make no intermediate cash payments before the holding period is over. A coupon bond that makes an intermediate cash payment before the holding period is over requires that this payment be reinvested. Because the interest rate at which this payment can be reinvested is uncertain, some uncertainty also exists about the return on this coupon bond even when the time to maturity equals the holding period. However, the riskiness of the return on a coupon bond from reinvesting the coupon payments is typically quite small, so a coupon bond with a time to maturity equal to its holding period still has very little risk.

[6] In this text we assume that holding periods on all short-term bonds are equal to the term to maturity, and thus the bonds are not subject to interest-rate risk. However, if the term to maturity of the bond is shorter than an investor's holding period, the investor is exposed to a type of interest-rate risk called *reinvestment risk*. Reinvestment risk occurs because the proceeds from the short-term bond need to be reinvested at a future interest rate that is uncertain.

To understand reinvestment risk, suppose that Irving the Investor has a holding period of two years and decides to purchase a $1000, one-year bond at face value and then another one at the end of the first year. If the initial interest rate is 10%, Irving will have $1100 at the end of the first year. If the interest rate rises to 20%, as in Table 4-2, Irving will find that buying $1100 worth of another one-year bond will leave him at the end of the second year with $1100 × (1 + 0.20) = $1320. Thus Irving's two-year return will be ($1320 − $1000)/1000 = 0.32 = 32%, which equals 14.9% at an annual rate. In this case, Irving has earned more by buying the one-year bonds than he would have if he had initially purchased a two-year bond with an interest rate of 10%. Thus, when Irving has a holding period that is longer than the term to maturity of the bonds he purchases, he benefits from a rise in interest rates. Conversely, if interest rates fall to 5%, Irving will have only $1155 at the end of two years: $1100 × (1 + 0.05). His two-year return will be ($1555 − $1000)/1000 = 0.155 = 15.5%, which is 7.2% at an annual rate. With a holding period greater than the term to maturity of the bond, Irving now loses from a decline in interest rates.

We have seen that when the holding period is longer than the term to maturity of a bond, the return is uncertain because the future interest rate when reinvestment occurs is also uncertain—in short, there is reinvestment risk. We also see that if the holding period is longer than the term to maturity of the bond, the investor benefits from a rise in interest rates and is hurt by a fall in interest rates.

Summary

The return on a bond, which tells you how good an investment it has been over the holding period, is equal to the yield to maturity in only one special case—when the holding period and the term to maturity of the bond are identical. Bonds whose terms to maturity are longer than their holding periods are subject to interest-rate risk: Changes in interest rates lead to capital gains and losses that produce substantial differences between the return and the yield to maturity known at the time the bond is purchased. Interest-rate risk is especially important for long-term bonds, on which capital gains and losses can be substantial. This is why long-term bonds are not considered safe assets with a sure return over short holding periods.

THE DISTINCTION BETWEEN REAL AND NOMINAL INTEREST RATES

So far in our discussion of interest rates, we have ignored the effects of inflation on the cost of borrowing. What we have up to this point been calling *the interest rate* makes no allowance for inflation, and it is more precisely referred to as the **nominal interest rate**. We must distinguish the nominal interest rate from the **real interest rate**, which is the interest rate that is adjusted by subtracting expected changes in the price level (inflation) so that it more accurately reflects the true cost of borrowing. This interest rate is more precisely referred to as the *ex ante real interest rate* because it is adjusted for *expected* changes in the price level. The ex ante real interest rate is very important to economic decisions, and typically it is what economists mean when they make reference to the "real" interest rate. The interest rate that is adjusted for *actual* changes in the price level is called the *ex post real interest rate*. It describes how well a lender has done in real terms *after the fact*.

The real interest rate is more accurately defined from the *Fisher equation*, named for Irving Fisher, one of the great monetary economists of the twentieth century. The Fisher equation states that the nominal interest rate i equals the real interest rate r plus the expected rate of inflation π^e:[7]

$$i = r + \pi^e \qquad \text{(Equation 9)}$$

Rearranging terms, we find that the real interest rate equals the nominal interest rate minus the expected inflation rate:

$$r = i - \pi^e \qquad \text{(Equation 10)}$$

To see why this definition makes sense, let's first consider a situation in which you have made a simple one-year loan with a 5% interest rate ($i = 5\%$), and you expect the

---

[7] A more precise formulation of the Fisher equation is

$$i = r + \pi^e + (r \times \pi^e)$$

because

$$1 + i = (1 + r)(1 + \pi^e) = 1 + r + \pi^e + (r \times \pi^e)$$

and subtracting 1 from both sides gives us the first equation. For small values of r and π^e, the term $r \times \pi^e$ is so small that we ignore it, as in the text.

price level to rise by 3% over the course of the year ($\pi^e = 3\%$). As a result of making the loan, at the end of the year you expect to have 2% more in *real terms*—that is, in terms of real goods and services you can buy. In this case, the interest rate you expect to earn in terms of real goods and services is 2%:

$$r = 5\% - 3\% = 2\%$$

as indicated by Equation 10.

APPLICATION   Calculating Real Interest Rates

What is the real interest rate if the nominal interest rate is 8% and the expected inflation rate is 10% over the course of a year?

Solution

The real interest rate is −2%. Although you will be receiving 8% more dollars at the end of the year, you will be paying 10% more for goods. The result is that you will be able to buy 2% fewer goods at the end of the year, and you will be 2% worse off in real terms. Mathematically,

$$r = i - \pi^e$$

where
$$i = \text{nominal interest rate} = 0.08$$
$$\pi^e = \text{expected inflation rate} = 0.10$$

Thus

$$r = 0.08 - 0.10 = -0.02 = -2\% \qquad \blacklozenge$$

As a lender, you are clearly less eager to make a loan in this case, because in terms of real goods and services you have actually earned a negative interest rate of 2%. By contrast, as a borrower, you fare quite well because at the end of the year, the amounts you will have to pay back will be worth 2% less in terms of goods and services—you as the borrower will be ahead by 2% in real terms. **When the real interest rate is low, there are greater incentives to borrow and fewer incentives to lend.**

A similar distinction can be made between nominal returns and real returns. Nominal returns, which do not allow for inflation, are what we have been referring to as simply "returns." When inflation is subtracted from a nominal return, we have the real return, which indicates the amount of extra goods and services that we can purchase as a result of holding the security.

The distinction between real and nominal interest rates is important because the real interest rate, which reflects the real cost of borrowing, is likely to be a better indicator of the incentives to borrow and lend. It appears to be a better guide to how people will respond to what is happening in credit markets. Figure 4-1, which presents estimates from 1953 to 2014 of the real and nominal interest rates on three-month U.S. Treasury bills, shows us that nominal and real rates usually move together but do not always do so. (This is also true for nominal and real interest rates in Canada and the rest of the world.) In particular, when nominal rates were high in the 1970s, real rates were actually extremely low—often negative. By the standard of nominal interest rates, you would have thought that credit market conditions were

FIGURE 4-1   **Real and Nominal Interest Rates (Three-Month Treasury Bill), 1953–2014**

Nominal and real interest rates often do not move together. When nominal rates were high in the 1970s, real rates were actually extremely low—often negative.

Sources: Nominal rates from **www.federalreserve.gov/releases/H15**. The real rate is constructed using the procedure outlined in Frederic S. Mishkin, "The Real Interest Rate: An Empirical Investigation," *Carnegie-Rochester Conference Series on Public Policy* 15 (1981): 151–200. This procedure involves estimating expected inflation as a function of past interest rates, inflation, and time trends, and then subtracting the expected inflation measure from the nominal interest rate.

tight during this period because it was expensive to borrow. However, the estimates of the real rates indicate that you would have been mistaken. In real terms, the cost of borrowing was actually quite low.[8]

[8] Because most interest income in Canada is subject to income taxes, the true earnings in real terms from holding a debt instrument are not reflected by the real interest rate defined by the Fisher equation but rather by the *after-tax real interest rate*, which equals the nominal interest rate *after income tax payments have been subtracted*, minus the expected inflation rate. For a person facing a 30% tax rate, the after-tax interest rate earned on a bond yielding 10% is only 7% because 30% of the interest income must be paid to the Canada Revenue Agency. Thus the after-tax real interest rate on this bond when expected inflation is 5% equals 2% (7% − 5%). More generally, the after-tax real interest rate can be expressed as

$$i(1 - \tau) - \pi^e$$

where $\tau =$ the income tax rate.

This formula for the after-tax real interest rate also provides a better measure of the effective cost of borrowing for many corporations and homeowners in the United States because, in calculating income taxes, they can deduct interest payments on loans from their income (in Canada homeowners are not able to deduct mortgage interest as is the case in the United States). Thus, in the U.S., if you face a 30% tax rate and take out a mortgage loan with a 10% interest rate, you are able to deduct the 10% interest payment and lower your taxes by 30% of this amount. Your after-tax nominal cost of borrowing is then 7% (10% minus 30% of the 10% interest payment), and when the expected inflation rate is 5%, the effective cost of borrowing in real terms is again 2% (7% − 5%).

As the example (and the formula) indicates, after-tax real interest rates are always below the real interest rate defined by the Fisher equation. For a further discussion of measures of after-tax real interest rates, see Frederic S. Mishkin, "The Real Interest Rate: An Empirical Investigation," *Carnegie-Rochester Conference Series on Public Policy* 15 (1981): 151–200.

MyEconLab

MyEconLab is an online homework and tutorial system that puts you in control of your own learning with study and practice tools directly correlated to this chapter's content. Visit MyEconLab to access the eText, the Questions and Applied Problems with answers, as well as additional assessment. You will also find web chapters, mini-lectures, appendices, mini-cases, videos, glossary flashcards, news feeds, CANSIM data, and graphing tools.

SUMMARY

1. The yield to maturity, which is the measure that most accurately reflects the interest rate, is the interest rate that equates the present value of future payments of a debt instrument with the instrument's value today. Application of this principle reveals that bond prices and interest rates are negatively correlated: When the interest rate rises, the price of the bond must fall, and vice versa.

2. The return on a security, which tells you how well you have done by holding the security over a stated period of time, can differ substantially from the interest rate as measured by the yield to maturity. Long-term bond prices experience substantial fluctuations when interest rates change and thus bear interest-rate risk. The resulting capital gains and losses can be large, which is why long-term bonds are not considered safe assets with a sure return.

3. The real interest rate is defined as the nominal interest rate minus the expected rate of inflation. It is both a better measure of the incentives to borrow and lend and a more accurate indicator of the tightness of credit market conditions than is the nominal interest rate.

KEY TERMS

cash flows, p. 68
consol, p. 77
coupon bond, p. 71
coupon rate, p. 71
current yield, p. 78
discount bond, p. 72
face value, p. 71
fixed-payment loan, p. 71

fully amortized loan, p. 71
interest-rate risk, p. 82
nominal interest rate, p. 83
par value, p. 71
perpetuity, p. 77
present discounted value, p. 69
present value, p. 69
rate of capital gain, p. 80

rate of return, p. 79
real interest rate, p. 83
return, p. 79
simple loan, p. 69
yield to maturity, p. 72
zero-coupon bond, p. 72

QUESTIONS

All questions are available in MyEconLab at **www.myeconlab.com.**

1. Would a dollar tomorrow be worth more to you today when the interest rate is 20% or when it is 10%?

2. Write down the formula that is used to calculate the yield to maturity on a 20-year 10% coupon bond with a $1000 face value that sells for $2000.

3. To help pay for university, you have just taken out a $1000 government loan that makes you pay $126 per year for 25 years. However, you don't have to start making these payments until you graduate from university two years from now. Why is the yield to maturity necessarily less than 12%? (This is the yield to maturity on a normal $1000 fixed-payment loan on which you pay $126 per year for 25 years.)

4. Do bondholders fare better when the yield to maturity increases or when it decreases?

5. A financial adviser has just given you the following advice: "Long-term bonds are a great investment because their interest rate is over 20%." Is the financial adviser necessarily right?

6. If mortgage rates rise from 5% to 10% but the expected rate of increase in housing prices rises from 2% to 9%, are people more or less likely to buy houses?

7. When is the current yield a good approximation of the yield to maturity?

8. Why would a government choose to issue a perpetuity, which requires payments forever, instead of a terminal loan, such as a fixed-payment loan, discount bond, or coupon bond?

9. Under what conditions will a discount bond have a negative nominal interest rate? Is it possible for a coupon bond or a perpetuity to have a negative nominal interest rate?

10. True or False: With a discount bond, the return on the bond is equal to the rate of capital gain.

11. If interest rates decline, which would you rather be holding, long-term bonds or short-term bonds? Why? Which type of bond has the greater interest-rate risk?

12. Interest rates were lower in the mid-1980s than in the late 1970s, yet many economists have commented that real interest rates were actually much higher in the mid-1980s than in the late 1970s. Does this make sense? Do you think that these economists are right?

13. Retired persons often have much of their wealth placed in savings accounts and other interest-bearing investments, and complain whenever interest rates are low. Do they have a valid complaint?

APPLIED PROBLEMS

All applied problems are available in MyEconLab at **www.myeconlab.com.**

14. If the interest rate is 10%, what is the present value of a security that pays you $1100 next year, $1210 the year after, and $1331 the year after that?

15. Calculate the present value of a $1000 discount bond with five years to maturity if the yield to maturity is 6%.

16. A lottery claims its grand prize is $10 million, payable over 5 years at $2 000 000 per year. If the first payment is made immediately, what is this grand prize really worth? Use an interest rate of 6%.

17. What is the yield to maturity on a $1000-face-value discount bond maturing in one year that sells for $800?

18. What is the yield to maturity on a simple loan for $1 million that requires a repayment of $2 million in five years' time?

19. Which $1000 bond has the higher yield to maturity, a 20-year bond selling for $800 with a current yield of 15% or a one-year bond selling for $800 with a current yield of 5%?

20. Consider a bond with a 4% annual coupon and a face value of $1000. Complete the following table. What relationships do you observe between years to maturity, yield to maturity, and the current price?

Years to Maturity	Yield to Maturity	Current Price
2	2%	
2	4%	
3	4%	
5	2%	
5	6%	

21. Consider a coupon bond that has a $1000 par value and a coupon rate of 10%. The bond is currently selling for $1044.89 and has two years to maturity. What is the bond's yield to maturity?

22. What is the price of a perpetuity that has a coupon of $50 per year and a yield to maturity of 2.5%? If the yield to maturity doubles, what will happen to the perpetuity's price?

23. Property taxes in a particular district are 4% of the purchase price of a home every year. If you just purchased a $250 000 home, what is the present value of all the future property tax payments? Assume that the house remains worth $250 000 forever, property tax rates never change, and a 6% interest rate is used for discounting.

24. A $1000-face-value bond has a 10% coupon rate, its current price is $960, and its price is expected to increase to $980 next year. Calculate the current yield, the expected rate of capital gain, and the expected rate of return.

25. Assume you just deposited $1000 into a bank account. The current real interest rate is 2%, and inflation is expected to be 6% over the next year. What nominal rate would you require from the bank over the next year? How much money will you have at the end of one year? If you are saving to buy a fancy bicycle that currently sells for $1050, will you have enough money to buy it?

DATA ANALYSIS PROBLEMS

Download data for these problems from MyEconLab *at* **www.myeconlab.com**.

1. Go to the CANSIM database and download monthly data from January 1953 to December 2014 for the three-month T-bill rate (series V122541) and the total consumer price index (series V41690973).

   a. What is the average year-over-year inflation rate, using the formula

   $$\pi_t = 100 \times (P_t - P_{t-12})/P_{t-12}$$

   b. What is the average T-bill rate?

   c. Assume that the expected inflation rate is the same as the actual inflation rate (a restrictive assumption!) and calculate the average real interest rate, r.

2. Go to the CANSIM database and download monthly data (from November 1991 to December 2014) for the interest rate on long-term Canada Real Return Bonds (series V122553). This is a direct measure of the real interest rate.

   a. What is the mean real interest rate over the sample period?

   b. What is its standard deviation? (The standard deviation is the square root of the variance.)

WEB EXERCISES

1. In this chapter, we discussed long-term bonds as if there were only one type, coupon bonds. In fact, investors can also purchase long-term discount bonds. A discount bond is sold at a low price, and the whole return comes in the form of a price appreciation. You can easily compute the current price of a discount bond by using the financial calculator at **www.treasurydirect.gov/indiv/tools/tools_savingsbondcalc.htm**.

   To compute the values for savings bonds, read the instructions on the page and click on "Get Started". Fill in the information (you do not need to fill in the Bond Serial Number field) and click on "Calculate".

WEB REFERENCES

www.bloomberg.com/markets/

Under Rates & Bonds, you can access information on key interest rates, U.S. Treasuries, government bonds, and municipal bonds.

www.teachmefinance.com

A review of the key financial concepts: time value of money, annuities, perpetuities, and so on.

5 The Behaviour of Interest Rates

Learning Objectives

After studying this chapter you should be able to

1. Identify the factors that affect the demand for assets.

2. Draw the demand and supply curves for the bond market, and identify the equilibrium interest rate.

3. List and describe the factors that affect the equilibrium interest rate in the bond market.

4. Describe the connection between the bond market and the money market through the liquidity preference framework.

5. List and describe the factors that affect the money market and the equilibrium interest rate.

6. Identify and illustrate the effects on the interest rate of changes in money growth over time.

PREVIEW

In the early 1950s, nominal interest rates on three-month Treasury bills were about 1% at an annual rate; by 1981, they had reached over 20%. They fell below 2% in 2003, rose to 5% in 2007, and then fell to close to zero in 2008 and for many years afterward. What explains these substantial fluctuations in interest rates? One reason why we study money, banking, and financial markets is to provide some answers to this question.

In this chapter, we examine how the overall level of *nominal* interest rates (which we refer to simply as "interest rates") is determined and which factors influence their behaviour. We learned in Chapter 4 that interest rates are negatively related to the price of bonds, so if we can explain why bond prices change, we can also explain why interest rates fluctuate. We make use of supply and demand analysis for bond markets and markets for money to examine how interest rates change.

To derive a demand curve for assets such as money or bonds, the first step in our analysis, we must first understand what determines the demand for these assets. We do this by examining *portfolio theory*, an economic theory that outlines criteria that are important when deciding how much of an asset to buy. Armed with this theory, we can then go on to derive the demand curve for bonds or money. After deriving supply curves for these assets, we develop the concept of *market equilibrium*, which is defined as the point at which the quantity supplied equals the quantity demanded. Then we use this model to explain changes in equilibrium interest rates.

Because interest rates on different securities tend to move together, in this chapter we will proceed as if there were only one type of security and one interest rate in the entire economy. In the following chapter, we expand our analysis to look at why interest rates on different types of securities differ.

DETERMINANTS OF ASSET DEMAND

Before going on to our supply and demand analysis of the bond market and the market for money, we must first understand what determines the quantity demanded of an asset. Recall that an asset is a piece of property that is a store of value. Items such as money, bonds, stocks, art, land, houses, farm equipment, and manufacturing machinery are all assets. Faced with the question of whether to buy and hold an asset or whether to buy one asset rather than another, an individual must consider the following factors:

1. **Wealth**, the total resources owned by the individual, including all assets
2. **Expected return** (the return expected over the next period) on one asset relative to alternative assets
3. **Risk** (the degree of uncertainty associated with the return) on one asset relative to alternative assets
4. **Liquidity** (the ease and speed with which an asset can be turned into cash) relative to alternative assets

Wealth

When we find that our wealth has increased, we have more resources available with which to purchase assets, and so, not surprisingly, the quantity of assets we demand increases. Therefore, the effect of changes in wealth on the quantity demanded of an asset can be summarized as follows: *Holding everything else constant, an increase in wealth raises the quantity demanded of an asset.*

Expected Returns

In Chapter 4, we saw that the return on an asset (such as a bond) measures how much we gain from holding that asset. When we make a decision to buy an asset, we are influenced by what we expect the return on that asset to be. If a Bell Canada bond, for example, has a return of 15% half the time and 5% the other half, its expected return (which you can think of as the average return) is 10% ($=0.5 \times 15\% + 0.5 \times 5\%$).[1] If the expected return on the Bell bond rises relative to expected returns on alternative assets, then, holding everything else constant, it becomes more desirable to purchase the Bell bond, and the quantity demanded increases. This can occur in either of two ways: (1) when the expected return on the Bell bond rises while the return on an alternative asset—say, stock in Google—remains unchanged or (2) when the return on the alternative asset, the Google stock, falls while the return on the Bell bond remains unchanged. To summarize, *an increase in an asset's expected return relative to that of an alternative asset, holding everything else unchanged, raises the quantity demanded of the asset.*

Risk

The degree of risk or uncertainty of an asset's returns also affects demand for the asset. Consider two assets: stock in Fly-by-Night Airlines and stock in Feet-on-the-Ground Bus Company. Suppose that Fly-by-Night stock has a return of 15% half the time and 5% the other half, making its expected return 10%, while Feet-on-the-Ground stock has a fixed return of 10%. Fly-by-Night stock has uncertainty associated with its returns and so has greater risk than Feet-on-the-Ground stock, whose return is a sure thing.

---

[1] If you are interested in finding out more information on how to calculate expected returns, as well as standard deviations of returns that measure risk, the MyEconLab contains an appendix to this chapter describing models of asset pricing. This appendix also describes how diversification lowers the overall risk of a portfolio and includes a discussion of systematic risk and basic asset pricing models, such as the capital asset pricing model and the arbitrage pricing theory.

A *risk-averse* person prefers stock in Feet-on-the-Ground (the sure thing) to Fly-by-Night stock (the riskier asset), even though the stocks have the same expected return: 10%. By contrast, a person who prefers risk is a *risk preferrer* or *risk lover*. Most people are risk-averse, especially in their financial decisions: Everything else being equal, they prefer to hold the less risky asset. Hence, **holding everything else constant, if an asset's risk rises relative to that of alternative assets, its quantity demanded will fall.**

Liquidity

Another factor that affects the demand for an asset is how quickly it can be converted into cash at low costs—its liquidity. An asset is liquid if the market in which it is traded has depth and breadth, that is, if the market has many buyers and sellers. A house is not a very liquid asset because it may be hard to find a buyer quickly; if a house must be sold to pay off bills, it might have to be sold for a much lower price. And the transaction costs associated with selling a house (broker's commissions, lawyer's fees, and so on) are substantial. A Canadian government Treasury bill, by contrast, is a highly liquid asset. It can be sold in a well-organized market with many buyers, and so it can be sold quickly at low cost. **The more liquid an asset is relative to alternative assets, holding everything else unchanged, the more desirable it is and the greater the quantity demanded will be.**

Theory of Portfolio Choice

All the determining factors we have just discussed can be assembled into the **theory of portfolio choice**, which tells us how much of an asset people will want to hold in their portfolios. It states that, holding all other factors constant:

1. The quantity demanded of an asset is positively related to wealth.
2. The quantity demanded of an asset is positively related to its expected return relative to alternative assets.
3. The quantity demanded of an asset is negatively related to the risk of its returns relative to alternative assets.
4. The quantity demanded of an asset is positively related to its liquidity relative to alternative assets.

These results are summarized in Table 5-1.

SUMMARY TABLE 5-1

Response of the Quantity of an Asset Demanded to Changes in Wealth, Expected Returns, Risk, and Liquidity

Variable	Change in Variable	Change in Quantity Demanded
Wealth	↑	↑
Expected return relative to other assets	↑	↑
Risk relative to other assets	↑	↓
Liquidity relative to other assets	↑	↑

Note: Only increases in the variables are shown. The effects of decreases in the variables on the quantity demanded would be the opposite of those indicated in the rightmost column.

SUPPLY AND DEMAND IN THE BOND MARKET

Our first approach to the analysis of interest-rate determination looks at supply and demand in the bond market so that we can better understand how the prices of bonds are determined. Thanks to our knowledge from Chapter 4 of how interest rates are measured, we know that each bond price is associated with a particular level of the interest rate. Specifically, the negative relationship between bond prices and interest rates means that when a bond's price rises, its interest rate falls, and vice versa.

The first step in our analysis is to obtain a bond **demand curve**, which shows the relationship between the quantity demanded and the price when all other economic variables are held constant (that is, values of other variables are taken as given). You may recall from previous economics courses that the assumption that all other economic variables are held constant is called *ceteris paribus*, which means "other things being equal" in Latin.

Demand Curve

To clarify and simplify our analysis, let's consider the demand for one-year discount bonds, which make no coupon payments but pay the owner the $1000 face value in a year. If the holding period is one year, then, as we saw in Chapter 4, the return on the bonds is known absolutely and is equal to the interest rate as measured by the yield to maturity. This means that the expected return on this bond is equal to the interest rate i, which, using Equation 6 in Chapter 4, is

$$i = R^e = \frac{F - P}{P}$$

where

$$i = \text{interest rate} = \text{yield to maturity}$$
$$R^e = \text{expected return}$$
$$F = \text{face value of the discount bond}$$
$$P = \text{initial purchase price of the discount bond}$$

This formula shows that a particular value of the interest rate corresponds to each bond price. If the bond sells for $950, the interest rate and expected return are

$$\frac{\$1000 - \$950}{\$950} = 0.053 = 5.3\%$$

At this 5.3% interest rate and expected return corresponding to a bond price of $950, let us assume that the quantity of bonds demanded is $100 billion, which is plotted as point A in Figure 5-1.

At a price of $900, the interest rate and expected return are

$$\frac{\$1000 - \$900}{\$900} = 0.111 = 11.1\%$$

Because the expected return is higher, with all other economic variables (such as income, expected returns on other assets, risk, and liquidity) held constant, the quantity demanded of these bonds will be higher, as predicted by portfolio theory. Point B in Figure 5-1 shows that the quantity of bonds demanded at the price of $900 has risen to $200 billion. Continuing with this reasoning, we see that if the bond price is $850 (interest rate and expected return = 17.6%), the quantity of bonds demanded (point C) will be greater than at point B. Similarly, at the even lower prices of $800 (interest rate = 25%)

and \$750 (interest rate = 33.3%), the quantity of bonds demanded will be even higher (points D and E). The curve B^d, which connects these points, is the demand curve for bonds. It has the usual downward slope, indicating that at lower prices of the bond (everything else being equal), the quantity demanded is higher.[2]

Supply Curve

An important assumption behind the demand curve for bonds in Figure 5-1 is that all other economic variables besides the bond's price and interest rate are held constant. We use the same assumption in deriving a **supply curve**, which shows the relationship between the quantity supplied and the price when all other economic variables are held constant.

In Figure 5-1, when the price of the bonds is \$750 (interest rate = 33.3%), point F shows that the quantity of bonds supplied is \$100 billion for the example we are considering. If the price is \$800, the interest rate is the lower rate of 25%. Because at

MyEconLab Mini-lecture

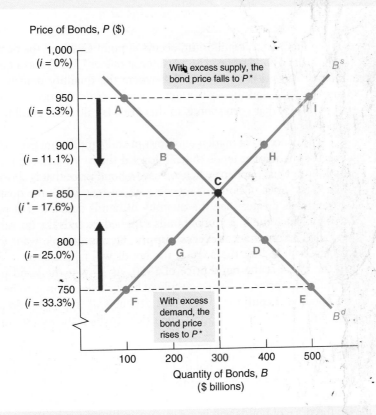

FIGURE 5-1 Supply and Demand for Bonds

Equilibrium in the bond market occurs at point C, the intersection of the demand curve Bd and the bond supply curve Bs. The equilibrium price is P* = \$850, and the equilibrium interest rate is i* = 17.6%.

[2]Although our analysis indicates that the demand curve is downward-sloping, it does not imply that the curve is a straight line. For ease of exposition, however, we will draw demand curves and supply curves as straight.

this interest rate it is now less costly to borrow by issuing bonds, firms will be willing to borrow more through bond issues, and the quantity of bonds supplied is at the higher level of $200 billion (point G). An even higher price of $850, corresponding to a lower interest rate of 17.6%, results in a larger quantity of bonds supplied of $300 billion (point C). Higher prices of $900 and $950 result in even lower interest rates and even greater quantities of bonds supplied (points H and I). The B^s curve, which connects these points, is the supply curve for bonds. It has the usual upward slope found in supply curves, indicating that as the price increases (everything else being equal), the quantity supplied increases.

Market Equilibrium

In economics, **market equilibrium** occurs when the amount that people are willing to buy (*demand*) equals the amount that people are willing to sell (*supply*) at a given price. In the bond market, this is achieved when the quantity of bonds demanded equals the quantity of bonds supplied:

$$B^d = B^s$$

(Equation 1)

In Figure 5-1, equilibrium occurs at point C, where the demand and supply curves intersect at a bond price of $850 (interest rate of 17.6%) and a quantity of bonds of $300 billion. The price of $P^* = \$850$, where the quantity demanded equals the quantity supplied, is called the *equilibrium* or *market-clearing* price. Similarly, the interest rate of $i^* = 17.6\%$ that corresponds to this price is called the equilibrium or market-clearing interest rate.

The concepts of market equilibrium and equilibrium price or interest rate are useful because the market tends to head toward them. We can see this in Figure 5-1 by first looking at what happens when we have a bond price that is above the equilibrium price. When the price of bonds is set too high, at, say, $950, the quantity of bonds supplied at point I is greater than the quantity of bonds demanded at point A. A situation like this, in which the quantity of bonds supplied exceeds the quantity of bonds demanded, is called a condition of **excess supply**. Because people want to sell more bonds than others want to buy, the price of the bonds will fall, as shown by the downward arrow in the figure at the bond price of $950. As long as the bond price remains above the equilibrium price, an excess supply of bonds will continue to be available, and the price of bonds will continue to fall. This decline will stop only when the price has reached the equilibrium price of $850, the price at which the excess supply of bonds has been eliminated.

Now let's look at what happens when the price of bonds is below the equilibrium price. If the price of the bonds is set too low, at, say, $750, the quantity demanded at point E is greater than the quantity supplied at point F. This is called a condition of **excess demand**. People now want to buy more bonds than others are willing to sell, so the price of bonds will be driven up, as illustrated by the upward arrow in the figure at the bond price of $750. Only when the excess demand for bonds is eliminated by the bond price rising to the equilibrium level of $850 is there no further tendency for the price to rise.

We can see that the concept of equilibrium price is a useful one because it indicates where the market will settle. Because each price on the vertical axis of Figure 5-1 corresponds to a particular value of the interest rate, the same diagram also shows that the interest rate will head toward the equilibrium interest rate of 17.6%. When the interest rate is below the equilibrium interest rate, as it is when it is at 5.3%, the price of the bond is above the equilibrium price, and an excess supply of bonds results. The price of the bond then falls, leading to a rise in the interest rate toward the equilibrium level. Similarly, when the interest rate is above the equilibrium level, as it is when it is at 33.3%, an excess demand for bonds occurs, and the bond price rises, driving the interest rate back down to the equilibrium level of 17.6%.

Supply and Demand Analysis

Figure 5-1 is a conventional supply and demand diagram with price on the vertical axis and quantity on the horizontal axis. Because the interest rate that corresponds to each bond price is also marked on the vertical axis, this diagram allows us to read the equilibrium interest rate, giving us a model that describes the determination of interest rates. It is important to recognize that a supply and demand diagram like Figure 5-1 can be drawn for *any* type of bond because the interest rate and price of a bond are *always* negatively related for all kinds of bonds, whether a discount bond or a coupon bond.

An important feature of the analysis here is that supply and demand are always described in terms of *stocks* (amounts at a given point in time) of assets, not in terms of *flows*. The **asset market approach** for understanding behaviour in financial markets—which emphasizes stocks of assets, rather than flows, in determining asset prices—is the dominant methodology used by economists, because correctly conducting analyses in terms of flows is very tricky, especially when we encounter inflation.[3]

CHANGES IN EQUILIBRIUM INTEREST RATES

We will now use the supply and demand framework for bonds to analyze why interest rates change. To avoid confusion, it is important to make the distinction between *movements along* a demand (or supply) curve and *shifts in* a demand (or supply) curve. When quantity demanded (or supplied) changes as a result of a change in the price of the bond (or, equivalently, a change in the interest rate), we have a *movement along* the demand (or supply) curve. The change in the quantity demanded when we move from point A to B to C in Figure 5-1, for example, is a movement along a demand curve. A *shift in* the demand (or supply) curve, by contrast, occurs when the quantity demanded (or supplied) changes *at each given price* (or *interest rate*) of the bond in response to a change in some other factor besides the bond's price or interest rate. When one of these factors changes, causing a shift in the demand or supply curve, there will be a new equilibrium value for the interest rate.

In the following pages, we will look at how the supply and demand curves shift in response to changes in variables, such as expected inflation and wealth, and what effects these changes have on the equilibrium value of interest rates.

---

[3] The asset market approach developed in the text is useful in understanding not only how interest rates behave but also how any asset price is determined. A second appendix to this chapter, which is on the MyEconLab shows how the asset market approach can be applied to understanding the behaviour of commodity markets—in particular, the gold market. The analysis of the bond market that we have developed here has another interpretation that uses a different terminology and framework involving the supply and demand for loanable funds. This loanable funds framework is discussed in a third appendix to this chapter, which is also available on the book's MyEconLab.

Shifts in the Demand for Bonds

The theory of portfolio choice, which we developed at the beginning of the chapter, provides a framework for deciding which factors will cause the demand curve for bonds to shift. These factors include changes in the following four parameters:

1. Wealth
2. Expected returns on bonds relative to alternative assets
3. Risk of bonds relative to alternative assets
4. Liquidity of bonds relative to alternative assets

To see how a change in each of these factors (holding all other factors constant) can shift the demand curve, let's look at some examples. (As a study aid, Table 5-2 summarizes the effects of changes in these factors on the bond demand curve.)

Wealth   When the economy is growing rapidly in a business cycle expansion and wealth is increasing, the quantity of bonds demanded at each bond price (or interest rate) increases, as shown in Figure 5-2. To see how this works, consider point B on the initial demand curve for bonds, B_1^d. With greater wealth, the quantity of bonds demanded at the same price must rise, to point B'. Similarly, for point D, greater wealth causes the quantity demanded at the same bond price to rise to point D'. Continuing with this reasoning for every point on the initial demand curve B_1^d, we can see that the demand curve shifts to the right from B_1^d to B_2^d, as indicated by the arrows.

We can conclude that *in a business cycle expansion with growing wealth, the demand for bonds rises and the demand curve for bonds shifts to the right.* Applying the same reasoning, *in a recession, when income and wealth are falling, the demand for bonds falls, and the demand curve shifts to the left.*

MyEconLab Mini-lecture

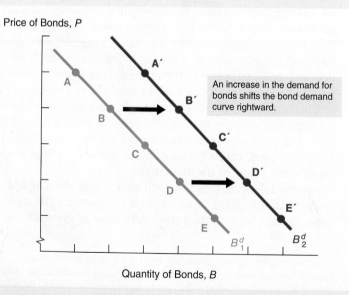

Price of Bonds, *P*

An increase in the demand for bonds shifts the bond demand curve rightward.

Quantity of Bonds, *B*

FIGURE 5-2   Shift in the Demand Curve for Bonds

When the demand for bonds increases, the demand curve shifts to the right as shown.

SUMMARY TABLE 5-2

Factors That Shift the Demand Curve for Bonds

Variable	Change in Variable	Change in Quantity Demanded at Each Bond Price	Shift in Demand Curve
Wealth	↑	↑	P ... B_1^d B_2^d ... B
Expected interest rate	↑	↓	P ... B_2^d B_1^d ... B
Expected inflation	↑	↓	P ... B_2^d B_1^d ... B
Riskiness of bonds relative to other assets	↑	↓	P ... B_2^d B_1^d ... B
Liquidity of bonds relative to other assets	↑	↑	P ... B_1^d B_2^d ... B

Note: Only increases in the variables are shown. The effects of decreases in the variables on demand would be the opposite of those indicated in the remaining columns.

Another factor that affects wealth is the public's propensity to save. If households save more, wealth increases and, as we have seen, the demand for bonds rises and the demand curve for bonds shifts to the right. Conversely, if people save less, wealth and the demand for bonds fall, and the demand curve shifts to the left.

Expected Returns   For a one-year discount bond and a one-year holding period, the expected return and the interest rate are identical, so nothing other than today's interest rate affects the expected return.

For bonds with maturities of greater than one year, the expected return may differ from the interest rate. For example, we saw in Chapter 4, Table 4-2, that a rise in the interest rate on a long-term bond from 10% to 20% would lead to a sharp decline in price and a very large negative return. Hence, if people began to think that interest rates would be higher next year than they had originally anticipated, the expected return today on long-term bonds would fall, and the quantity demanded would fall at each interest rate. *Higher expected future interest rates lower the expected return for long-term bonds, decrease the demand, and shift the demand curve to the left.*

By contrast, an expectation of lower future interest rates would mean that long-term bond prices would be expected to rise more than originally anticipated, and the resulting higher expected return today would raise the quantity demanded at each bond price and interest rate. *Lower expected future interest rates increase the demand for long-term bonds and shift the demand curve to the right* (as in Figure 5-2).

Changes in expected returns on other assets can also shift the demand curve for bonds. If people suddenly become more optimistic about the stock market and begin to expect higher stock prices in the future, both expected capital gains and expected returns on stocks will rise. With the expected return on bonds held constant, the expected return on bonds today relative to stocks will fall, lowering the demand for bonds and shifting the demand curve to the left. *An increase in expected return on alternative assets lowers the demand for bonds and shifts the demand curve to the left.*

A change in expected inflation is likely to alter expected returns on physical assets (also called *real assets*), such as automobiles and houses, which affect the demand for bonds. An increase in expected inflation from, say, 5% to 10% will lead to higher prices on cars and houses in the future and hence higher nominal capital gains. The resulting rise in the expected returns today on these real assets will lead to a fall in the expected return on bonds relative to the expected return on real assets today and thus cause the demand for bonds to fall. Alternatively, we can think of the rise in expected inflation as lowering the real interest rate on bonds, and thus the resulting decline in the relative expected return on bonds will cause the demand for bonds to fall. *An increase in the expected rate of inflation lowers the expected return on bonds, causing their demand to decline and the demand curve to shift to the left.*

Risk   If prices in the bond market become more volatile, the risk associated with bonds increases, and bonds become a less attractive asset. *An increase in the riskiness of bonds causes the demand for bonds to fall and the demand curve to shift to the left.*

Conversely, an increase in the volatility of prices in another asset market, such as the stock market, would make bonds more attractive. *An increase in the riskiness of alternative assets causes the demand for bonds to rise and the demand curve to shift to the right* (as in Figure 5-2).

Liquidity   If more people started trading in the bond market, and as a result it became easier to sell bonds quickly, the increase in their liquidity would cause the quantity of bonds demanded at each interest rate to rise. *Increased liquidity of bonds results in an increased demand for bonds, and the demand curve shifts to the right* (see Figure 5-2). *Similarly, increased liquidity of alternative assets lowers the demand for bonds and shifts the demand curve to the left.* The reduction of brokerage commissions for trading common stocks that occurred when the fixed-rate commission structure was abolished in 1975, for example, increased the liquidity of stocks relative to bonds, and the resulting lower demand for bonds shifted the demand curve to the left.

Shifts in the Supply of Bonds

Certain factors can cause the supply curve for bonds to shift. Among these factors are:

1. Expected profitability of investment opportunities
2. Expected inflation
3. Government budget deficits

We will look at how the supply curve shifts when each of these factors changes (all others remaining constant). (As a study aid, Table 5-3 summarizes the effects of changes in these factors on the bond supply curve.)

SUMMARY TABLE 5-3

Factors that Shift the Supply of Bonds

Variable	Change in Variable	Change in Quantity Supplied at Each Bond Price	Shift in Supply Curve
Profitability of investments	↑	↑	
Expected inflation	↑	↑	
Government deficit	↑	↑	

Note: Only increases in the variables are shown. The effects of decreases in the variables on the supply would be the opposite of those indicated in the remaining columns.

Expected Profitability of Investment Opportunities

When opportunities for profitable plant and equipment investments are plentiful, firms are more willing to borrow to finance these investments. When the economy is growing rapidly, as in a business cycle expansion, investment opportunities that are expected to be profitable abound, and the quantity of bonds supplied at any given bond price increases (see Figure 5-3). *Therefore, in a business cycle expansion, the supply of bonds increases and the supply curve shifts to the right. Likewise, in a recession, when far fewer profitable investment opportunities are expected, the supply of bonds falls and the supply curve shifts to the left.*

Expected Inflation

As we saw in Chapter 4, the real cost of borrowing is most accurately measured by the real interest rate, which equals the (nominal) interest rate minus the expected inflation rate. For a given interest rate (and bond price), when expected inflation increases, the real cost of borrowing falls; hence, the quantity of bonds supplied increases at any given bond price. *An increase in expected inflation causes the supply of bonds to increase and the supply curve to shift to the right* (see Figure 5-3) *and a decrease in expected inflation causes the supply of bonds to decrease and the supply curve to shift to the left.*

Government Budget Deficits

The activities of the government can influence the supply of bonds in several ways. The Canadian government issues bonds to finance government deficits, caused by gaps between the government's expenditures and its revenues. When these deficits are large, the government sells more bonds, and the quantity

MyEconLab Mini-lecture

FIGURE 5-3   Shift in the Supply Curve for Bonds
When the supply of bonds increases, the supply curve shifts to the right.

of bonds supplied at each bond price increases. ***Higher government deficits increase the supply of bonds and shift the supply curve to the right*** (see Figure 5-3). ***On the other hand, government surpluses, as have occurred in recent years, decrease the supply of bonds and shift the supply curve to the left.***

Provincial and municipal governments and other government agencies also issue bonds to finance their expenditures, and this can affect the supply of bonds as well. We will see in later chapters that the conduct of monetary policy involves the purchase and sale of bonds, which in turn influences the supply of bonds.

We now can use our knowledge of how supply and demand curves shift to analyze how the equilibrium interest rate can change. The best way to do this is to pursue several applications that are particularly relevant to our understanding of how monetary policy affects interest rates. In studying these applications, keep two things in mind:

1. When we examine the effect of a variable change, we are assuming that all other variables are unchanged; that is, we are making use of the *ceteris paribus* assumption.
2. The interest rate is negatively related to the bond price, so when the equilibrium bond price rises, the equilibrium interest rate falls. Conversely, if the equilibrium bond price moves downward, the equilibrium interest rate rises.

APPLICATION	# Changes in the Interest Rate Due to Expected Inflation: The Fisher Effect

We have already done most of the work necessary to evaluate how a change in expected inflation affects the nominal interest rate, in that we have already analyzed how a change in expected inflation shifts the supply and demand curves. Figure 5-4 shows the effect on the equilibrium interest rate of an increase in expected inflation.

MyEconLab Mini-lecture

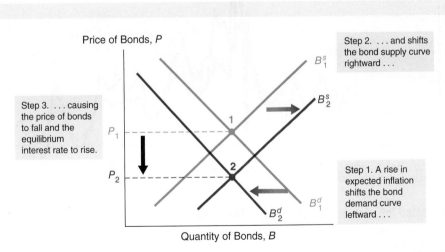

FIGURE 5-4   Response to a Change in Expected Inflation

When expected inflation rises, the supply curve shifts from B_1^s to B_2^s, and the demand curve shifts from B_1^d to B_2^d. The equilibrium moves from point 1 to point 2, causing the equilibrium bond price to fall from P_1 to P_2 and the equilibrium interest rate to rise.

Suppose that expected inflation is initially 5% and the initial supply and demand curves B_1^s and B_1^d intersect at point 1, where the equilibrium bond price is P_1. If expected inflation rises to 10%, the expected return on bonds relative to real assets falls for any given bond price and interest rate. As a result, the demand for bonds falls, and the demand curve shifts to the left from B_1^d to B_2^d. The rise in expected inflation also shifts the supply curve. At any given bond price and interest rate, the real cost of borrowing declines, causing the quantity of bonds supplied to increase and the supply curve to shift to the right, from B_1^s to B_2^s.

When the demand and supply curves shift in response to the change in expected inflation, the equilibrium moves from point 1 to point 2, at the intersection of B_2^d and B_2^s. The equilibrium bond price falls from P_1 to P_2 and, because the bond price is negatively related to the interest rate, this means that the interest rate rises. Note that Figure 5-4 has been drawn so that the equilibrium quantity of bonds remains the same at both point 1 and point 2. However, depending on the size of the shifts in the supply and demand curves, the equilibrium quantity of bonds can either rise or fall when expected inflation rises.

Our supply and demand analysis has led us to an important observation: *When expected inflation rises, interest rates will rise.* This result has been named the **Fisher effect**, after Irving Fisher, the economist who first pointed out the relationship of expected inflation to interest rates. The accuracy of this prediction is shown in Figure 5-5. The interest rate on three-month Treasury bills has usually moved along with the expected inflation rate. Consequently, many economists recommend that inflation must be kept low if we want to keep nominal interest rates low.

MyEconLab Mini-lecture

FIGURE 5-5 **Expected Inflation and Interest Rates (Three-Month Treasury Bills), 1953–2014**

The interest rate on three-month Treasury bills and the expected inflation rate generally move together, as the Fisher effect predicts.

Source: **Federal Reserve Bank of St. Louis FRED database: http://research.stlouisfed.org/fred2/.** Expected inflation calculated using procedures outlined in Frederic S. Mishkin, "The Real Interest Rate: An Empirical Investigation," Carnegie-Rochester Conference Series on Public Policy 15 (1981): 151–200. These procedures involve estimating expected inflation as a function of past interest rates, inflation, and time trends.

APPLICATION   # Changes in the Interest Rate Due to a Business Cycle Expansion

Figure 5-6 analyzes the effects of a business cycle expansion on interest rates. In a business cycle expansion, the amounts of goods and services being produced in the economy increase, so national income rises. When this occurs, businesses are more willing to borrow because they are likely to have many profitable investment opportunities for which they will need financing. Hence, at a given bond price, the quantity of bonds that firms want to sell (that is, the supply of bonds) will increase. This means that during a business cycle expansion, the supply curve for bonds shifts to the right (see Figure 5-6) from B_1^s to B_2^s.

Expansion in the economy also affects the demand for bonds. As the economy expands, wealth is likely to increase, and the theory of portfolio choice tells us that the demand for bonds will rise as well. We see this in Figure 5-6, where the demand curve has shifted to the right, from B_1^d to B_2^d.

Given that both the supply and demand curves have shifted to the right, we know that the new equilibrium reached at the intersection of B_2^d and B_2^s must also move to the right. However, depending on whether the supply curve shifts more than the demand curve or vice versa, the new equilibrium interest rate can either rise or fall.

MyEconLab Mini-lecture

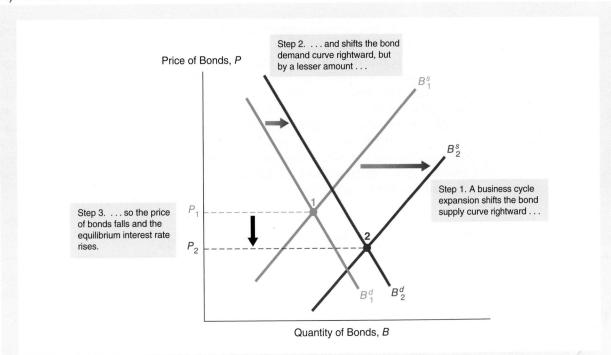

FIGURE 5-6   **Response to a Business Cycle Expansion**

In a business cycle expansion, when income and wealth are rising, the demand curve shifts rightward from B_1^d to B_2^d. If the supply curve shifts to the right more than the demand curve, as in this figure, the equilibrium bond price moves down from P_1 to P_2 and the equilibrium interest rate rises.

FIGURE 5-7 **Business Cycle and Interest Rates (Three-Month Treasury Bills), 1962–2014**

Shaded areas indicate periods of recession. The interest rate tends to rise during business cycle expansions and fall during recessions.

Source: Statistics Canada CANSIM series V122531.

The supply and demand analysis used here gives us an ambiguous answer to the question of what happens to interest rates in a business cycle expansion. Figure 5-6 has been drawn so that the shift in the supply curve is greater than the shift in the demand curve, causing the equilibrium bond price to fall to P_2 and the equilibrium interest rate to rise. The reason the figure has been drawn such that a business cycle expansion and a rise in income lead to a higher interest rate is that this is the outcome we actually see in the data. Figure 5-7 plots the movement of the interest rate on three-month Treasury bills from 1962 to 2014 and indicates when the business cycle went through recessions (shaded areas). As you can see, the interest rate tends to rise during business cycle expansions and fall during recessions, as indicated by the supply and demand diagram in Figure 5-6.

APPLICATION Explaining Low Japanese Interest Rates

In the 1990s and early 2000s, Japanese interest rates became the lowest in the world. Indeed, in November 1998, an extraordinary event occurred: Interest rates on Japanese six-month Treasury bills even turned slightly negative! Why did Japanese interest rates drop to such low levels?

In the late 1990s and early 2000s, Japan experienced a prolonged recession, which was accompanied by deflation (a negative inflation rate). We can use these facts, along with an analysis similar to that used in the preceding applications, to explain the low Japanese interest rates.

Negative inflation caused the demand for bonds to rise because the expected return on real assets fell, thereby raising the relative expected return on bonds and in turn causing the demand curve to shift to the right. Negative inflation also raised the real interest rate and therefore the real cost of borrowing for any given nominal rate, thereby causing the supply of bonds to contract and the supply curve to shift to the left. The outcome was then exactly the opposite of that graphed in Figure 5-4: The rightward shift of the demand curve and leftward shift of the supply curve led to a rise in the bond price and a fall in interest rates.

The business cycle contraction and the resulting lack of profitable investment opportunities in Japan also led to lower interest rates by decreasing the supply of bonds and shifting the supply curve to the left. Although the demand curve also shifted to the left because wealth decreased during the business cycle contraction, the demand curve shifted less than the supply curve, just as we saw in the preceding application. Thus, the bond price rose and interest rates fell (the opposite outcome of that in Figure 5-6).

Usually we think that low interest rates are a good thing because they make it cheaper to borrow. But the Japanese example shows that a fallacy is present in always thinking that lower interest rates are better. In Japan, the low and even negative interest rates were a sign that the country was in real trouble, with falling prices and a contracting economy. Only when the Japanese economy returns to health will interest rates rise back to more normal levels. ◆

SUPPLY AND DEMAND IN THE MARKET FOR MONEY: THE LIQUIDITY PREFERENCE FRAMEWORK

An alternative model for determining the equilibrium interest rate, developed by John Maynard Keynes, is known as the **liquidity preference framework**. This framework determines the equilibrium interest rate in terms of the supply of and demand for money rather than the supply of and demand for bonds. Although the two frameworks look different, the liquidity preference analysis of the market for money is closely related to the supply and demand framework of the bond market.[4]

The starting point of Keynes's analysis is his assumption that people use two main categories of assets to store their wealth: money and bonds. Therefore, total wealth in the economy must equal the total quantity of bonds plus money in the economy, which equals the quantity of bonds supplied (B^s) plus the quantity of money supplied (M^s). The quantity of bonds demanded (B^d) plus the quantity of money demanded (M^d) must also equal the total amount of wealth, because people cannot purchase more assets than their available resources allow. Thus the quantity of bonds and money supplied must equal the quantity of bonds and money demanded:

$$B^s + M^s = B^d + M^d \qquad \text{(Equation 2)}$$

Collecting the bond terms on one side of the equation and the money terms on the other, this equation can be rewritten as

$$B^s - B^d = M^d - M^s \qquad \text{(Equation 3)}$$

[4] Note that the term *market for money* refers to the market for the medium of exchange, money. This market differs from the *money market* referred to by finance practitioners, which, as discussed in Chapter 2, is the financial market in which short-term debt instruments are traded.

Equation 3 tells us that if the market for money is in equilibrium ($M^s = M^d$), then the right-hand side of the equation equals zero, implying that $B^s = B^d$, which in turn means the bond market is also in equilibrium.

Thus we arrive at the same result whether we determine the equilibrium interest rate by equating the supply and demand for bonds or by equating the supply and demand for money. In this sense, the liquidity preference framework, which analyzes the market for money, is equivalent to a framework analyzing supply and demand in the bond market. In practice, the approaches differ because, by assuming there are only two kinds of assets, money and bonds, the liquidity preference approach implicitly ignores any effects on interest rates that arise from changes in the expected returns on real assets such as automobiles and houses. In most instances, however, both frameworks yield the same predictions.

The reason we approach the determination of interest rates using both frameworks is that the bond supply and demand framework is easier to use when analyzing the effects caused by changes in expected inflation, whereas the liquidity preference framework is easier to use when analyzing the effects caused by changes in income, the price level, and the supply of money.

Because the definition of money used by Keynes includes currency (which earns no interest) and chequing account deposits (which in his time typically earned little or no interest), he assumed that money has a zero rate of return. Bonds, the only alternative asset to money in Keynes's framework, have an expected return equal to the interest rate i.[5] As this interest rate rises (holding everything else unchanged), the expected return on money falls relative to the expected return on bonds, causing a fall in the quantity of money demanded, as predicted by the theory of portfolio choice.

We can also see that the quantity of money demanded and the interest rate should be negatively related by using the concept of **opportunity cost**, which is the amount of interest (expected return) sacrificed by not holding the alternative asset—in this case, a bond. As the interest rate on bonds, i, rises, the opportunity cost of holding money rises; thus money is less desirable and the quantity of money demanded falls.

Figure 5-8 shows the quantity of money demanded at a number of interest rates, with all other economic variables, such as income and the price level, held constant. At an interest rate of 25%, point A shows that the quantity of money demanded is $100 billion. If the interest rate is at the lower rate of 20%, the opportunity cost of holding money is lower, and the quantity of money demanded rises to $200 billion, as indicated by the move from point A to point B. If the interest rate is even lower, the quantity of money demanded is even higher, as is indicated by points C, D, and E. The curve M^d connecting these points is the demand curve for money, and it slopes downward.

At this point in our analysis, we will assume that a central bank controls the amount of money supplied at a fixed quantity of $300 billion, so that the supply curve for money M^s in the figure is a vertical line at $300 billion. The equilibrium at which the quantity of money demanded equals the quantity of money supplied occurs at the intersection of the supply and demand curves at point C, where

$$M^d = M^s \qquad \text{(Equation 4)}$$

The resulting equilibrium interest rate is $i^* = 15\%$.

---

[5]Keynes did not actually assume that the expected returns on bonds equaled the interest rate but rather argued that they were closely related. This distinction makes no appreciable difference in our analysis.

MyEconLab Mini-lecture

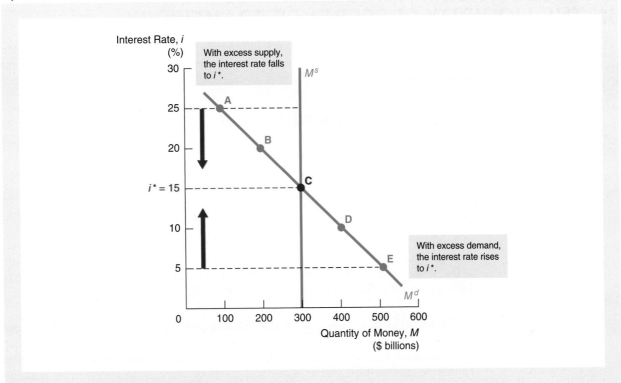

FIGURE 5-8   Equilibrium in the Market for Money

Equilibrium in the market for money occurs at point C, the intersection of the money demand curve M^d and the money supply curve M^s. The equilibrium interest rate is $i^* = 15\%$.

We can again see that there is a tendency to approach this equilibrium rate by first looking at the relationship of money demand and supply when the interest rate is above the equilibrium interest rate. When the interest rate is 25%, the quantity of money demanded at point A is $100 billion, yet the quantity of money supplied is $300 billion. The excess supply of money means that people are holding more money than they desire, so they will try to get rid of their excess money balances by trying to buy bonds. Accordingly, they will bid up the price of bonds. As the bond price rises, the interest rate will fall toward the equilibrium interest rate of 15%. This tendency is shown by the downward arrow drawn at the interest rate of 25%.

Likewise, if the interest rate is 5%, the quantity of money demanded at point E is $500 billion, but the quantity of money supplied is only $300 billion. An excess demand for money now exists because people want to hold more money than they currently have. To try to obtain more money, they will sell their only other asset—bonds—and the price will fall. As the price of bonds falls, the interest rate will rise toward the equilibrium rate of 15%. Only when the interest rate is at its equilibrium value will there be no tendency for it to move further, and so the interest rate will settle at this value.

CHANGES IN EQUILIBRIUM INTEREST RATES IN THE LIQUIDITY PREFERENCE FRAMEWORK

In order to use the liquidity preference framework to analyze how the equilibrium interest rate changes, we must understand what causes the demand and supply curves for money to shift.

Shifts in the Demand for Money

In Keynes's liquidity preference analysis, two factors cause the demand curve for money to shift: income and the price level.

Income Effect   In Keynes's view, there were two reasons why income would affect the demand for money. First, as an economy expands and income rises, wealth increases and people want to hold more money as a store of value. Second, as the economy expands and income rises, people want to carry out more transactions using money as a medium of exchange, and so they also want to hold more money. The conclusion is that *a higher level of income causes the demand for money at each interest rate to increase and the demand curve to shift to the right.*

Price-Level Effect   Keynes took the view that people care about the amount of money they hold in real terms—that is, in terms of the goods and services it can buy. When the price level rises, the same nominal quantity of money is no longer as valuable; it cannot be used to purchase as many real goods or services. To restore their holdings of money in real terms to the former level, people will want to hold a greater nominal quantity of money, so *a rise in the price level causes the demand for money at each interest rate to increase and the demand curve to shift to the right.*

Shifts in the Supply of Money

We will assume that the supply of money is completely controlled by the central bank, which in Canada is the Bank of Canada. (Actually, the process that determines the money supply is substantially more complicated, involving banks, depositors, and borrowers from banks. We will study it in more detail later in the book.) For now, all we need to know is that *an increase in the money supply engineered by the Bank of Canada will shift the supply curve for money to the right.*

APPLICATION   **Changes in the Equilibrium Interest Rate Due to Changes in Income, the Price Level, or the Money Supply**

To see how we can use the liquidity preference framework to analyze the movement of interest rates, we will again look at several applications that will help us evaluate the effect of monetary policy on interest rates. In going through these applications, remember to use the *ceteris paribus* assumption: When examining the effect of a change in one variable, hold all other variables constant. (As a study aid, Table 5-4 summarizes the shifts in the demand and supply curves for money.)

SUMMARY TABLE 5-4

Factors that Shift the Demand for and Supply of Money

Variable	Change in Variable	Change in Money Demand (M^d) or Supply (M^s) at Each Interest Rate	Change in Interest Rate	
Income	↑	M^d↑	↑	
Price level	↑	M^d↑	↑	
Money supply	↑	M^s↑	↓	

Note: Only increases in the variables are shown. The effects of decreases in the variables on demand and supply would be the opposite of those indicated in the remaining columns.

Changes in Income

We have seen that when income is rising during a business cycle expansion, the demand for money also rises, shown in Figure 5-9 by the rightward shift in the demand curve from M_1^d to M_2^d. The new equilibrium is reached at point 2, at the intersection of the M_2^d curve with the money supply curve M^s. As you can see, the equilibrium interest rate rises from i_1 to i_2. The liquidity preference framework thus generates the conclusion that **when income is rising during a business cycle expansion (holding other economic variables constant), interest rates will rise.** This conclusion is unambiguous, unlike the conclusion we reached using the bond demand and supply framework.

MyEconLab Mini-lecture

FIGURE 5-9 **Response to a Change in Income or the Price Level**

In a business cycle expansion, when income is rising, or when the price level rises, the demand curve shifts from M_1^d to M_2^d. The supply curve is fixed at $M^s = \overline{M}$. The equilibrium interest rate rises from i_1 to i_2.

Changes in the Price Level

When the price level rises, the value of money in terms of its purchasing power is lower. To restore their money's purchasing power in real terms to its former level, people will want to hold a greater nominal quantity of money. A higher price level shifts the demand curve for money to the right from M_1^d to M_2^d (see Figure 5-9). The equilibrium moves from point 1 to point 2, where the equilibrium interest rate has risen from i_1 to i_2, illustrating that **when the price level increases, with the supply of money and other economic variables held constant, interest rates will rise.**

Changes in the Money Supply

An increase in the money supply due to expansionary monetary policy by the Bank of Canada will shift the supply curve for money to the right. As shown in Figure 5-10 by the movement of the supply curve from M_1^s to M_2^s, the equilibrium rate moves from point 1 down to point 2, where the M_2^s supply curve intersects with the demand curve M^d and the equilibrium interest rate has fallen from i_1 to i_2. **When the money supply increases (everything else remaining equal), interest rates will decline.**[6]

---

[6]This same result can be generated using the bond supply and demand framework. As we will see in Chapter 14, a central bank increases the money supply primarily by buying bonds and thereby decreasing the supply of bonds available to the public. The resulting shift to the left of the supply curve for bonds leads to an increase in the equilibrium price of bonds and a decline in the equilibrium interest rate.

MyEconLab Mini-lecture

Step 1. An increase in the money supply shifts the money supply curve rightward . . .

Step 2. . . . and the equilibrium interest rate falls.

FIGURE 5-10   Response to a Change in the Money Supply
When the money supply increases, the supply curve shifts from M_1^s to M_2^s and the equilibrium interest rate falls from i_1 to i_2.

APPLICATION   **Money and Interest Rates**

The liquidity preference analysis in Figure 5-10 seems to suggest that an increase in the money supply will lower interest rates. This conclusion has important policy implications because it has frequently caused politicians to call for a more rapid growth of the money supply in an effort to drive down interest rates.

But is it correct to conclude that money and interest rates should be negatively related? Might other important factors have been left out of the liquidity preference analysis in Figure 5-10, factors that would reverse this conclusion? We will provide answers to these questions by applying the supply and demand analysis we used in this chapter to obtain a deeper understanding of the relationship between money and interest rates.

An important criticism of the idea that an increase in the money supply lowers interest rates was raised by Milton Friedman, a Nobel laureate in economics. He acknowledged that the liquidity preference analysis was correct and called the result—that an increase in the money supply (*everything else remaining equal*) lowers interest rates—the *liquidity effect*. However, he viewed the liquidity effect as merely part of the story: An increase in the money supply might not leave "everything else equal" and will have other effects on the economy that may make interest rates rise. If these effects are substantial, it is entirely possible that when the money supply increases, interest rates might also increase.

We have already laid the groundwork for our discussion of these other effects, because we have shown how changes in income, the price level, and expected inflation influence the equilibrium interest rate.

1. *Income Effect.* An increasing money supply can cause national income and wealth to rise. Both the liquidity preference and bond supply and demand frameworks indicate that interest rates will then rise (see Figures 5-6 and 5-9). Thus **the income effect of an increase in the money supply is a rise in interest rates in response to the higher level of income.**

2. *Price-Level Effect.* An increase in the money supply can also cause the overall price level in the economy to rise. The liquidity preference framework predicts that this will lead to a rise in interest rates. Thus **the price-level effect from an increase in the money supply is a rise in interest rates in response to the rise in price level.**

3. *Expected-Inflation Effect.* The higher inflation rate that can result from an increase in the money supply can also affect interest rates by influencing the expected inflation rate. Specifically, an increase in the money supply may lead people to expect a higher price level in the future—and hence the expected inflation rate will be higher. The bond supply and demand framework has shown us that this increase in expected inflation will lead to a higher level of interest rates. Therefore, **the expected-inflation effect of an increase in the money supply is a rise in interest rates in response to the rise in the expected inflation rate.**

At first glance it might appear that the price-level effect and the expected-inflation effect are the same thing. They both indicate that increases in the price level induced by an increase in the money supply will raise interest rates. However, there is a subtle difference between the two, and this is why they are discussed as two separate effects.

Suppose that a one-time increase in the money supply today leads to a rise in prices to a permanently higher level by next year. As the price level rises over the course of this year, the interest rate will rise via the price-level effect. Only at the end of the year, when the price level has risen to its peak, will the price-level effect be at a maximum.

The rising price level will also raise interest rates via the expected-inflation effect, because people will expect that inflation will be higher over the course of the year. However, when the price level stops rising next year, inflation and the expected inflation rate will return to zero. Any rise in interest rates as a result of the earlier rise in expected inflation will then be reversed. We thus see that in contrast to the price-level effect, which reaches its greatest impact next year, the expected-inflation effect will have its smallest impact (zero impact) next year. The basic difference between the two effects, then, is that the price-level effect remains even after prices have stopped rising, whereas the expected-inflation effect disappears.

An important point is that the expected-inflation effect will persist only as long as the price level continues to rise. As we will see in our discussion of monetary theory in subsequent chapters, a one-time increase in the money supply will not produce a continually rising price level; only a higher rate of money supply growth will. Thus, a higher rate of money supply growth is needed if the expected-inflation effect is to persist.

DOES A HIGHER RATE OF GROWTH OF THE MONEY SUPPLY LOWER INTEREST RATES?

We can now put together all the effects we have discussed to help us decide whether our analysis supports the politicians who advocate a greater rate of growth of the money supply when they feel that interest rates are too high. Of all the effects, only the liquidity effect indicates that a higher rate of money growth will cause a decline in interest rates. In contrast, the income, price-level, and expected-inflation effects indicate that interest rates will rise when money growth is higher. Which of these effects is largest, and how quickly does each take effect? The answers are critical in determining whether interest rates will rise or fall when money supply growth is increased.

Generally, the liquidity effect from greater money growth takes effect immediately, because the rising money supply leads to an immediate decline in the equilibrium interest rate. The income and price-level effects take longer to work because time is needed for the increasing money supply to raise the price level and income, which in turn raise interest rates. The expected-inflation effect, which also raises interest rates, can be slow or fast, depending on whether people adjust their expectations of inflation slowly or quickly when the money growth rate is increased.

Three possibilities are outlined in Figure 5-11; each shows how interest rates respond over time to an increased rate of money supply growth, starting at time T. Panel (a) shows a case in which the liquidity effect dominates the other effects so that the interest rate falls from i_1 at time T to a final level of i_2. The liquidity effect operates quickly to lower the interest rate, but as time goes by, the other effects start to reverse some of the decline. Because the liquidity effect is larger than the others, however, the interest rate never rises back to its initial level.

In panel (b), the liquidity effect is smaller than the other effects, with the expected-inflation effect operating slowly because expectations of inflation are slow to adjust upward. Initially, the liquidity effect drives down the interest rate. Then the income, price-level, and expected-inflation effects begin to raise it. Because these effects are dominant, the interest rate eventually rises above its initial level to i_2. In the short run, lower interest rates result from increased money growth, but eventually they end up climbing above the initial level.

In panel (c), the expected-inflation effect dominates and operates rapidly because people quickly raise their expectations of inflation when the rate of money growth increases. The expected-inflation effect begins immediately to overpower the liquidity effect, and the interest rate immediately starts to climb. Over time, as the income and price-level effects start to take hold, the interest rate rises even higher, and the eventual outcome is an interest rate that is substantially higher than the initial interest rate. The result shows clearly that increasing money supply growth is not the answer to reducing interest rates; rather, money growth should be *reduced* to lower interest rates!

An important issue for economic policymakers is deciding which of these three scenarios is closest to reality. If a decline in interest rates is desired, then an increase in money supply growth is called for when the liquidity effect dominates the other effects, as in panel (a). A decrease in money growth is appropriate when the other effects dominate the liquidity effect and expectations of inflation adjust rapidly, as in panel (c). If the other effects dominate the liquidity effect but expectations of inflation are slow to adjust, as in panel (b), then the decision to increase or decrease money growth depends on whether policymakers are more concerned about short-term or long-term issues.

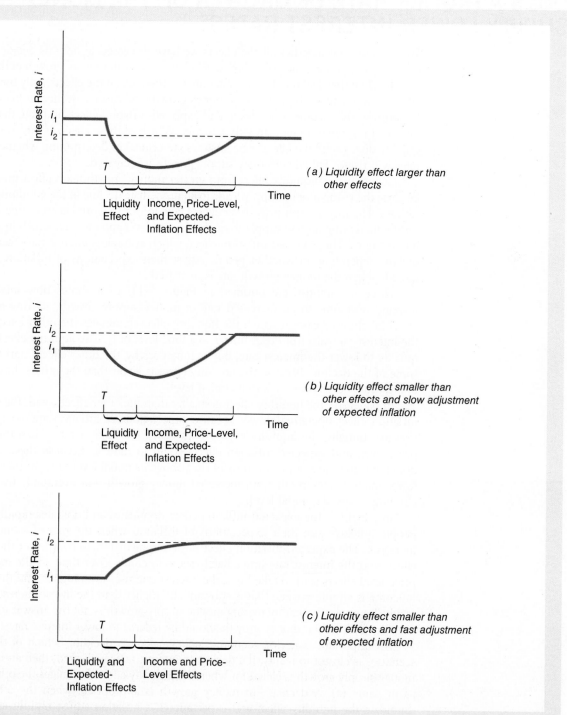

FIGURE 5-11 **Response over Time to an Increase in Money Supply Growth**

Each panel shows how interest rates respond over time to an increased rate of money supply growth, starting at time *T*.

Which scenario is supported by the evidence? The relationship between interest rates and money growth from 1968 to 2014 is plotted in Figure 5-12. When the rate of money supply growth began to climb in the late 1970s, interest rates rose, indicating that the liquidity effect was dominated by the price-level, income, and expected-inflation effects. By the early 1980s, interest rates reached levels unprecedented in the post–World War II period, as did the rate of money supply growth.

The scenario depicted in panel (a) of Figure 5-11 seems doubtful, and the case for lowering interest rates by raising the rate of money growth is much weakened. Looking back at Figure 5-5, which shows the relationship between interest rates and expected inflation, you should not find this too surprising. The rise in the rate of money supply growth in the 1960s and 1970s is matched by a large rise in expected inflation, which would lead us to predict that the expected-inflation effect would be dominant. It is the most plausible explanation for why interest rates rose in the face of higher money growth. However, Figure 5-12 does not really tell us which one of the two scenarios depicted in panels (b) and (c) of Figure 5-11 is more accurate. It depends critically on how fast people's expectations about inflation adjust. Research done using more sophisticated methods than just looking at a graph like Figure 5-12 indicates that increased money growth temporarily lowers short-term interest rates and thus conforms to the scenario in panel (b). ◆

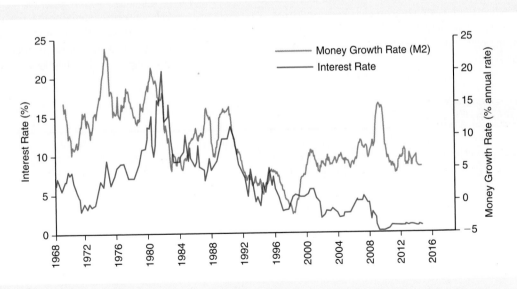

FIGURE 5-12   **Money Growth (M2, Annual Rate) and Interest Rates (Three-Month Treasury Bills), 1968–2014**

When the rate of money supply growth began to climb in the late 1970s, interest rates rose, indicating that the liquidity effect was dominated by the price-level, income, and expected-inflation effects. By the early 1980s, both interest rates and money growth reached levels unprecedented in the post–World War II period.

Source: Statistics Canada CANSIM series V1.22531 and V41552796.

MyEconLab

MyEconLab is an online homework and tutorial system that puts you in control of your own learning with study and practice tools directly correlated to this chapter's content. Visit MyEconLab to access the eText, the Questions and Applied Problems with answers, as well as additional assessment. You will also find web chapters, mini-lectures, appendices, mini-cases, videos, glossary flashcards, news feeds, CANSIM data, and graphing tools.

SUMMARY

1. The theory of portfolio choice tells us that the quantity demanded of an asset is (a) positively related to wealth, (b) positively related to the expected return on the asset relative to alternative assets, (c) negatively related to the riskiness of the asset relative to alternative assets, and (d) positively related to the liquidity of the asset relative to alternative assets.

2. The supply and demand analysis for bonds provides one theory of how interest rates are determined. It predicts that interest rates will change when there is a change in demand caused by changes in income (or wealth), expected returns, risk, or liquidity, or when there is a change in supply caused by changes in the attractiveness of investment opportunities, the real cost of borrowing, or the government budget.

3. An alternative theory of how interest rates are determined is provided by the liquidity preference framework, which analyzes the supply of and demand for money. It shows that interest rates will change when the demand for money changes because of alterations in income or the price level, or when the supply of money changes.

4. There are four possible effects on interest rates of an increase in the money supply: the liquidity effect, the income effect, the price-level effect, and the expected-inflation effect. The liquidity effect indicates that a rise in money supply growth will lead to a decline in interest rates; the other effects work in the opposite direction. The evidence seems to indicate that the income, price-level, and expected-inflation effects dominate the liquidity effect such that an increase in money supply growth leads to higher—rather than lower—interest rates.

KEY TERMS

asset market approach, p. 95
demand curve, p. 92
excess demand, p. 94
excess supply, p. 94
expected return p. 90

Fisher effect, p. 102
liquidity p. 90
liquidity preference framework, p. 105
market equilibrium, p. 94
opportunity cost, p. 106

risk p. 90
supply curve, p. 93
theory of portfolio choice, p. 91
wealth p. 90

QUESTIONS

All questions are available in MyEconLab at **www.myeconlab.com.**

1. Explain why you would be more or less willing to buy a share of BlackBerry stock in the following situations:

   a. Your wealth falls.

   b. You expect the stock to appreciate in value.

   c. The bond market becomes more liquid.

   d. You expect gold to appreciate in value.

   e. Prices in the bond market become more volatile.

2. Explain why you would be more or less willing to buy a house under the following circumstances:

   a. You just inherited $100 000.

   b. Real estate commissions fall from 6% of the sales price to 5% of the sales price.

c. You expect BlackBerry stock to double in value next year.

d. Prices in the stock market become more volatile.

e. You expect housing prices to fall.

3. Explain why you would be more or less willing to buy gold under the following circumstances:

a. Gold again becomes acceptable as a medium of exchange.

b. Prices in the gold market become more volatile.

c. You expect inflation to rise, and gold prices tend to move with the aggregate price level.

d. You expect interest rates to rise.

4. Explain why you would be more or less willing to buy long-term Air Canada bonds under the following circumstances:

a. Trading in these bonds increases, making them easier to sell.

b. You expect a bear market in stocks (stock prices are expected to decline).

c. Brokerage commissions on stocks fall.

d. You expect interest rates to rise.

e. Brokerage commissions on bonds fall.

5. What will happen to the demand for Rembrandt paintings if the stock market undergoes a boom? Why?

6. "The more risk-averse people are, the more likely they are to diversify." Is this statement true, false, or uncertain? Explain your answer.

7. "No one who is risk-averse will ever buy a security that has a lower expected return, more risk, and less liquidity than another security." Is this statement true, false, or uncertain? Explain your answer.

8. What effect will a sudden increase in the volatility of gold prices have on interest rates?

9. How might a sudden increase in people's expectations of future real estate prices affect interest rates?

10. Explain what effect a large federal deficit should have on interest rates.

11. In the aftermath of the global economic crisis that started to take hold in 2008, Canadian government budget deficits increased dramatically, yet interest rates on Canada bonds fell sharply and stayed low for quite some time. Does this make sense? Why or why not?

12. Will there be an effect on interest rates if brokerage commissions on stocks fall? Explain your answer.

13. The governor of the Bank of Canada announces in a press conference that he will fight the higher inflation rate with a new anti-inflation program. Predict what will happen to interest rates if the public believes her.

14. Predict what will happen to interest rates if the public suddenly expects a large increase in stock prices.

15. Predict what will happen to interest rates if prices in the bond market become more volatile.

16. Would fiscal policymakers ever have reason to worry about potentially inflationary conditions? Why or why not?

17. Why should a rise in the price level (but not in expected inflation) cause interest rates to rise when the nominal money supply is fixed?

18. If the next governor of the Bank of Canada has a reputation for advocating an even slower rate of money growth than the current governor does, what will happen to interest rates? Discuss the possible resulting situations.

19. M1 money growth in the United States was about 15% in 2011 and 2012, and 10% in 2013. Over the same time period, the yield on 3-month Treasury bills was close to 0%. Given these high rates of money growth, why did interest rates stay so low, rather than increase? What does this say about the income, price-level, and expected-inflation effects?

APPLIED PROBLEMS

All applied problems are available in MyEconLab *at* **www.myeconlab.com.**

20. Suppose you visit with a financial advisor, and you are considering investing some of your wealth in one

of three investment portfolios: stocks, bonds, or commodities. Your financial advisor provides you with the following table, which gives the probabilities of possible returns from each investment:

a. Which investment should you choose to maximize your expected return: stocks, bonds, or commodities?

b. If you are risk-averse and have to choose between the stock and the bond investments, which should you choose? Why?

Stocks		Bonds		Commodities	
Probability	Return	Probability	Return	Probability	Return
0.25	12%	0.6	10%	0.2	20%
0.25	10%	0.4	7.50%	0.25	12%
0.25	8%			0.25	6%
0.25	6%			0.25	4%
				0.05	0%

21. An important way in which the Bank of Canada decreases the money supply is by selling bonds to the public. Using a supply and demand analysis for bonds, show what effect this action has on interest rates. Is your answer consistent with what you would expect to find with the liquidity preference framework?

22. Using both the liquidity preference framework and the supply and demand for bonds framework, show why interest rates are procyclical (rising when the economy is expanding and falling during recessions).

23. Using both the supply and demand for bonds and liquidity preference frameworks, show how interest rates are affected when the riskiness of bonds rises. Are the results the same in the two frameworks?

24. The demand curve and supply curve for one-year discount bonds with a face value of $1000 are represented by the following equations:

B^d: Price $= -0.6 \times$ Quantity $+ 1140$

B^s: Price $=$ Quantity $+ 700$

a. What is the expected equilibrium price and quantity of bonds in this market?

b. Given your answer to part (a), what is the expected interest rate in this market?

25. The demand curve and supply curve for one-year discount bonds with a face value of $1000 are represented by the following equations:

B^d: Price $= -0.6 \times$ Quantity $+ 1140$

B^s: Price $=$ Quantity $+ 700$

Suppose that, as a result of monetary policy actions, the Bank of Canada sells 80 bonds that it holds. Assume that bond demand and money demand are held constant.

a. How does the Bank of Canada policy affect the bond supply equation?

b. Calculate the effect of the Bank of Canada's action on the equilibrium interest rate in this market.

DATA ANALYSIS PROBLEMS

Download data for these problems from MyEconLab *at* **www.myeconlab.com.**

1. Go to the CANSIM database and download monthly data from 1962:1 to 2014:12 for the three-month T-bill rate (series V122531).

a. What is the average nominal interest rate, i_t?

b. Calculate the change in i_t, $\Delta i_t = i_{t+1} - i_t$. What is the average change? The standard deviation?

2. Go to the St. Louis Federal Reserve FRED database, and find data on the M1 money supply (M1SL) and the 10-year U.S. treasury bond rate. For the M1 money supply indicator, adjust the *units* setting to "Percent Change from Year Ago," and for the 10-year treasury bond, adjust the *frequency* setting to "Quarterly." Download the data into a spreadsheet.

a. Create a scatter plot, with money growth on the horizontal axis and the 10-year treasury rate on the vertical axis, from 2000:Q1 to the most recent quarter of data available. On the scatter plot, graph a fitted (regression) line of the data (there are several ways to do this; however, one particular chart layout has this option built in). Based on the fitted line, are the data consistent with the liquidity effect? Briefly explain.

b. Repeat part (a), but this time compare the contemporaneous money growth rate with the interest rate four quarters later. For example, create a scatter plot comparing money growth from 2000:Q1 with the interest rate from 2001:Q1, and so on, up to the most recent pairwise data available. Compare your results to those obtained in part (a), and interpret the liquidity effect as it relates to the income, price-level, and expected-inflation effects.

c. Repeat part (a) again, except this time compare the contemporaneous money growth rate with the interest rate eight quarters later. For example, create a scatter plot comparing money growth from 2000:Q1 with the interest rate from 2002:Q1, and so on, up to the most recent pairwise data available. Assuming the liquidity and other effects are fully incorporated into the bond market after two years, what do your results imply about the overall effect of money growth on interest rates?

d. Based on your answers to parts (a) through (c), how do the actual data on money growth and interest rates compare to the three scenarios presented in Figure 5.11 of this chapter?

WEB EXERCISES

1. One of the largest single influences on the level of interest rates is inflation. There are a number of sites that report inflation over time. Go to **www.bankofcanada.ca/en/cpi.htm** and review the data. What has the average rate of inflation been since 2000? What year had the lowest level of inflation? What year had the highest level of inflation?

2. Increasing prices erode the purchasing power of the dollar. It is interesting to compute what goods would have cost at some point in the past after adjusting for inflation. Go to **www.bankofcanada.ca/rates/related/inflation-calculator**. What is the

cost today of a car that cost $10,000 the year that you were born?.

3. One of the points made in this chapter is that inflation erodes investment returns. Go to **www.moneychimp.com/articles/econ/inflation_calculator.htm** and review how changes in inflation alter your real return. What happens to the difference between the adjusted value of an investment and its inflation-adjusted value as

a. inflation increases?

b. the investment horizon lengthens?

c. expected returns increase?

WEB REFERENCES

www.bankofcanada.ca/rates

The Bank of Canada reports a number of statistics on its website.

6 The Risk and Term Structure of Interest Rates

PREVIEW

In our supply and demand analysis of interest-rate behaviour in Chapter 5, we examined the determination of just one interest rate. Yet we saw earlier that there are enormous numbers of bonds on which the interest rates can and do differ. In this chapter, we complete the interest-rate picture by examining the relationships of the various interest rates to one another. Understanding why interest rates differ from bond to bond can help businesses, banks, insurance companies, and private investors decide which bonds to purchase as investments and which ones to sell.

We first look at why bonds with the same term to maturity have different interest rates. The relationship among these interest rates is called the **risk structure of interest rates**, although risk and liquidity both play a role in determining the risk structure. A bond's term to maturity also affects its interest rate, and the relationship among interest rates on bonds with different terms to maturity is called the **term structure of interest rates**. In this chapter, we examine the sources and causes of fluctuations in interest rates relative to one another, and look at a number of theories that explain these fluctuations.

RISK STRUCTURE OF INTEREST RATES

Figure 6-1 shows the yields to maturity for several categories of long-term bonds from 1978 to 2014. It shows us two important features of interest-rate behaviour for bonds of the same maturity: Interest rates on different categories of bonds differ from one another in any given year, and the spread (or difference) between the interest rates varies over time. The interest rates on corporate bonds, for example, were higher than those on Canada bonds and provincial bonds. In addition, the spread between the interest rates on corporate bonds and Canada bonds was very large during the 1980–1982 and 1990–1991 recessions as well during the Great Recession that followed the recent global financial crisis. Which factors are responsible for these phenomena?

Default Risk

One attribute of a bond that influences its interest rate is its **risk of default**. Default occurs when the issuer of the bond is unable or unwilling to make interest payments when promised or to pay off the face value when the bond matures. Corporations

FIGURE 6-1   Long-Term Bond Yields, 1978–2014

Interest rates on different categories of bonds differ from one another in any given year, and the spread (or difference) between the interest rates varies over time.

Source: Statistics Canada CANSIM series V122544, V122517, V122518, the latter extended with the Merrill Lynch Canada Corporate Bond Index from Bloomberg.

suffering big losses might be more likely to suspend interest payments on their bonds. The default risk on their bonds would therefore be quite high. By contrast, Canadian government bonds have usually been considered to have no default risk because the federal government can always increase taxes or print money to pay off its obligations. Bonds like these with no default risk are called **default-free bonds**. The spread between interest rates on bonds with default risk and interest rates on default-free bonds, both of the same maturity, is called the **risk premium**. The risk premium indicates how much additional interest people must earn to be willing to hold the risky bond.

Our supply and demand analysis of the bond market in Chapter 5 can be used to explain why a bond with default risk always has a positive risk premium, and why a higher default risk means a larger risk premium.

To examine the effect of default risk on interest rates, let us look at the supply and demand diagrams for the default-free (Canadian government) and corporate long-term bond markets in Figure 6-2. To make the diagrams somewhat easier to read, let's assume that initially, corporate bonds have the same default risk as Canada bonds. In this case, these two bonds have the same attributes (identical risk and maturity); their equilibrium prices and interest rates will initially be equal ($P_1^c = P_1^T$ and $i_1^c = i_1^T$), and the risk premium on corporate bonds ($i_1^c - i_1^T$) will be zero.

If the possibility of a default increases because a corporation begins to suffer large losses, the default risk on corporate bonds will increase, and the expected return on these bonds will decrease. In addition, the corporate bond's return will be more uncertain. The theory of portfolio choice predicts that because the expected return on the corporate bond falls relative to the expected return on the default-free Canada bond

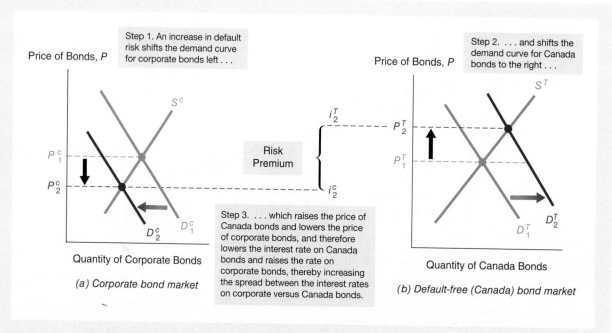

Price of Bonds, *P*

Step 1. An increase in default risk shifts the demand curve for corporate bonds left . . .

Price of Bonds, *P*

Step 2. . . . and shifts the demand curve for Canada bonds to the right . . .

Risk Premium

Step 3. . . . which raises the price of Canada bonds and lowers the price of corporate bonds, and therefore lowers the interest rate on Canada bonds and raises the rate on corporate bonds, thereby increasing the spread between the interest rates on corporate versus Canada bonds.

Quantity of Corporate Bonds

(a) Corporate bond market

Quantity of Canada Bonds

(b) Default-free (Canada) bond market

FIGURE 6-2 **Response to an Increase in Default Risk on Corporate Bonds**

Initially $P_1^c = P_1^T$ and the risk premium is zero. An increase in default risk on corporate bonds shifts the demand curve from D_1^c to D_2^c. Simultaneously, it shifts the demand curve for Canada bonds from D_1^T to D_2^T. The equilibrium price for corporate bonds falls from P_1^c to P_2^c, and the equilibrium interest rate on corporate bonds rises to i_2^c. In the Canada market, the equilibrium bond price rises from P_1^T to P_2^T, and the equilibrium interest rate falls to i_2^T. The brace indicates the difference between i_2^c and i_2^T, the risk premium on corporate bonds. (Note that because P_2^c is lower than P_2^T, i_2^c is greater than i_2^T.)

while its relative riskiness rises, the corporate bond is less desirable (holding everything else equal), and demand for it will fall. Another way of thinking about this is that if you were an investor, you would want to hold (demand) a smaller amount of corporate bonds. The demand curve for corporate bonds in panel (a) of Figure 6-2 then shifts to the left, from D_1^c to D_2^c.

At the same time, the expected return on default-free Canada bonds increases relative to the expected return on corporate bonds, while their relative riskiness declines. The Canada bonds thus become more desirable, and demand rises, as shown in panel (b) by the rightward shift in the demand curve for these bonds from D_1^T to D_2^T.

As we can see in Figure 6-2, the equilibrium price for corporate bonds falls from P_1^c to P_2^c, and since the bond price is negatively related to the interest rate, the equilibrium interest rate on corporate bonds rises to i_2^c. At the same time, however, the equilibrium price for the Canada bonds rises from P_1^T to P_2^T and the equilibrium interest rate falls to i_2^T. The spread between the interest rates on corporate and default-free bonds—that is, the risk premium on corporate bonds—has risen from zero to $i_2^c - i_2^T$. We can now conclude that *a bond with default risk will always have a positive risk premium, and an increase in its default risk will raise the risk premium*.

Because default risk is so important to the size of the risk premium, purchasers of bonds need to know whether a corporation is likely to default on its bonds. This information is provided by **credit-rating agencies**, investment advisory firms that rate the quality of corporate and municipal bonds in terms of the probability of default. Credit-rating agencies have become very controversial in recent years because of the role they played in the global financial crisis of 2007–2009 (see the FYI box Conflicts of Interest at Credit-Rating Agencies and the Global Financial Crisis).

Table 6-1 provides the ratings and their description as defined by the four largest credit-rating agencies in Canada: Dominion Bond Rating Service (DBRS), Moody's Investor Service, Standard & Poor's Corporation (S&P), and Fitch Ratings. Bonds with relatively low risk of default are called *investment-grade* securities and have a rating of

| **TABLE 6-1** | Bond Ratings by DBRS, Moody's, Standard & Poor's, and Fitch |

Rating				
DBRS	**Moody's**	**S&P**	**Fitch**	**Definitions**
AAA	Aaa	AAA	AAA	Prime Maximum Safety
AA high	Aa1	AA+	AA+	High Grade High Quality
AA	Aa2	AA	AA	
AA low	Aa3	AA−	AA−	
A high	A1	A+	A+	Upper Medium Grade
A	A2	A	A	
A low	A3	A−	A−	
BBB high	Baa1	BBB+	BBB+	Lower Medium Grade
BBB	Baa2	BBB	BBB	
BBB low	Baa3	BBB−	BBB−	
BB high	Ba1	BB+	BB+	Noninvestment Grade
BB	Ba2	BB	BB	Speculative
BB low	Ba3	BB−	BB−	
B high	B1	B+	B+	Highly Speculative
B	B2	B	B	
B low	B3	B−	B−	
CCC	Caa1	CCC+	CCC	Substantial Risk
CC	Caa2	CCC	—	In Poor Standing
C	Caa3	CCC−	—	
—	Ca	—	—	Extremely Speculative
—	C	—	—	May Be in Default
—	—	—	DDD	Default
—	—	—	DD	—
D	—	D	D	

Baa (or BBB) and above. Bonds with ratings below Baa (or BBB) have higher default risk and have been aptly dubbed speculative-grade or **junk bonds**. Because these bonds always have higher interest rates than investment-grade securities, they are also referred to as high-yield bonds. Investment-grade securities whose rating has fallen to junk levels are referred to as **fallen angels**.

Next let's look back at Figure 6-1 and see if we can explain the relationship between interest rates on both corporate and Canada bonds. Corporate bonds always have higher interest rates than Canada bonds because they always have some risk of default, whereas Canada bonds do not. Because corporate bonds have a greater default risk than Canada bonds, their risk premium is greater, and the corporate bond rate therefore always exceeds the Canada bond rate. We can use the same analysis to explain the huge jump in the risk premium on corporate bond rates during the 1980–1982, 1990–1991, and 2000 recessions. The recession periods saw a very high rate of business failures and defaults. As we would expect, these factors led to a substantial increase in default risk for bonds issued by vulnerable corporations, and the risk premium for corporate bonds reached unprecedented high levels.

APPLICATION ## The Global Financial Crisis and the BBB-Treasury Spread in the United States

Starting in August 2007, the collapse of the subprime mortgage market in the United States led to large losses among American financial institutions (which will be discussed more extensively in Chapter 9). As a consequence of the subprime collapse and subsequent global financial crisis, many investors began to doubt the financial health of corporations with low credit ratings such as Baa and even the reliability of the ratings themselves. The perceived increase in default risk for Baa bonds made them less desirable at any given interest rate, decreased the quantity demanded, and shifted the demand curve for Baa bonds to the left. As shown in panel (a) of Figure 6-2, the interest rate on Baa bonds should have risen, which is indeed what happened. Interest rates on Baa bonds rose by 280 **basis points** (2.80 percentage points) from 6.63% at the end of July 2007 to 9.43% at the most virulent stage of the global financial crisis in mid-October 2008. But the increase in perceived default risk for Baa bonds in October 2008 made default-free U.S. Treasury bonds relatively more attractive and shifted the demand curve for these securities to the right—an outcome described by some analysts as a "flight to quality." Just as Figure 6-2 suggests they would, interest rates on U.S. Treasury bonds fell by 80 basis points, from 4.78% at the end of July 2007 to 3.98% in mid-October 2008. The spread between interest rates on Baa and Treasury bonds rose by 360 basis points, from 1.85% before the crisis to 5.45% afterward. ◆

Liquidity

Another attribute of a bond that influences its interest rate is its liquidity. As we learned in Chapter 5, a liquid asset is one that can be quickly and cheaply converted into cash if the need arises. The more liquid an asset is, the more desirable it is (holding everything else constant). Canada bonds are the most liquid of all long-term bonds because they are so widely traded that they are the easiest to sell quickly and the cost of selling them is low. Corporate bonds are not as liquid because fewer bonds for any one corporation are traded; thus it can be costly to sell these bonds in an emergency because it may be hard to find buyers quickly.

How does the reduced liquidity of corporate bonds affect their interest rates relative to the interest rate on Canada bonds? We can use supply and demand analysis with the same figure that was used to analyze the effect of default risk, Figure 6-2, to show that the lower liquidity of corporate bonds relative to Canada bonds increases the spread between the interest rates on these two bonds. Let us start the analysis by assuming that initially corporate and Canada bonds are equally liquid and all their other attributes are the same. As shown in Figure 6-2, their equilibrium prices and interest rates will initially be equal: $P_1^c = P_1^T$ and $i_1^c = i_1^T$. If the corporate bond becomes less liquid than the Canada bond because it is less widely traded, then (as the theory of portfolio choice indicates) demand for it will fall, shifting its demand curve from D_1^c to D_2^c, as in panel (a). The Canada bond now becomes relatively more liquid in comparison with the corporate bond, so its demand curve shifts rightward from D_1^T to D_2^T, as in panel (b). The shifts in the curves in Figure 6-2 show that the price of the less liquid corporate bond falls and its interest rate rises, while the price of the more liquid Canada bond rises and its interest rate falls.

The result is that the spread between the interest rates on the two bond types has risen. Therefore, the differences between interest rates on corporate bonds and Canada bonds (that is, the risk premiums) reflect not only the corporate bond's default risk but its liquidity too. This is why a risk premium is more accurately a "risk and liquidity premium," but convention dictates that it be called a *risk premium*.

Income Tax Considerations

In Canada, coupon payments on fixed-income securities are taxed as ordinary income in the year they are received. In some other countries, however, certain government bonds are not taxable. In the United States, for example, interest payments on municipal bonds are exempt from federal income taxes, and these bonds have had lower interest rates than U.S. Treasury bonds for most of the past 70 years. How does taxation affect the interest rate on bonds?

Let us imagine that you have a high enough income to put you in the 40% income tax bracket, where for every extra dollar of income you have to pay 40 cents to the government. If you own a $1000-face-value taxable bond that sells for $1000 and has a coupon payment of $100, you get to keep only $60 of the payment after taxes. Although the bond has a 10% interest rate, you actually earn only 6% after taxes.

APPLICATION ## Tax-Exempt Versus Taxable Bonds

Suppose you had the opportunity to buy either a tax-exempt bond or a taxable bond, both of which have a face value and purchase price of $1000. Assume both bonds have identical risk. The tax-exempt bond has coupon payments of $60 and a coupon rate of 6%. The taxable bond has coupon payments of $80 and an interest rate of 8%. Which bond would you choose to purchase, assuming a 40% tax rate?

Solution

You would choose to purchase the tax-exempt bond because it will earn you $60 in coupon payments and an interest rate after taxes of 6%. In this case, you pay no taxes on the $60 coupon payments and earn 6% after taxes. However, you have to pay taxes on taxable bonds. You will keep only 60% of the $80 coupon payment because the other 40% goes to taxes. Therefore, you receive $48 of the coupon payment and have an interest rate of 4.8% after taxes. Buying the tax-exempt bond would yield you higher earnings. ◆

Suppose, however, that you put your savings into a $1000-face-value tax-exempt bond that sells for $1000 and pays only $80 in coupon payments. Its interest rate is only 8%, but because it is a tax-exempt security, you pay no taxes on the $80 coupon payment, so you earn 8% after taxes. Clearly, you earn more on the tax-exempt bond, so you are willing to hold the bond even though it has a lower interest rate than the taxable bond has. Notice that the tax-exempt status of a bond becomes a significant advantage when income tax rates are very high.

Summary

The risk structure of interest rates (the relationships among interest rates on bonds with the same maturity) is explained by three factors: default risk, liquidity, and the income tax treatment of the bond's interest payments. As a bond's default risk increases, the risk premium on that bond (the spread between its interest rate and the interest rate on a default-free Canadian government bond) rises. The greater liquidity of Canada bonds also explains why their interest rates are lower than interest rates on less liquid bonds. If a bond has a favourable tax treatment, as do municipal bonds in the United States, whose interest payments are exempt from federal income taxes, its interest rate will be lower.

TERM STRUCTURE OF INTEREST RATES

We have seen how risk, liquidity, and tax considerations (collectively embedded in the risk structure) can influence interest rates. Another factor that influences the interest rate on a bond is its term to maturity: bonds with identical risk, liquidity, and tax characteristics may have different interest rates because their times remaining to maturity are different. A plot of the yields on bonds with differing terms to maturity but the same risk, liquidity, and tax considerations is called a **yield curve**, and it describes the term structure of interest rates for particular types of bonds, such as government bonds. The Financial News box shows a yield curve for Government of Canada securities. Yield curves can be classified as upward-sloping, flat, or downward-sloping (the last sort is often referred to as an **inverted yield curve**). When yield curves slope upward, as in the Financial News box, the long-term interest rates are above the short-term interest rates; when yield curves are flat, short- and long-term interest rates are the same; and when yield curves are downward-sloping or inverted, long-term interest rates are below short-term interest rates. Yield curves can also have more complicated shapes in which they first slope up and then down, or vice versa. Why do we usually see upward slopes of the yield curve?

In addition to explaining why yield curves take on different shapes at different times, a good theory of the term structure of interest rates must explain the following three important empirical facts:

1. Interest rates on bonds of different maturities move together over time (see Figure 6-3).
2. When short-term interest rates are low, yield curves are more likely to have an upward slope; when short-term interest rates are high, yield curves are more likely to slope downward and be inverted.
3. Yield curves almost always slope upward, like the yield curves in the Financial News box.

Three theories have been put forward to explain the term structure of interest rates, that is, the relationships among interest rates on bonds of different maturities reflected in yield curve patterns: (1) the expectations theory, (2) the segmented markets theory,

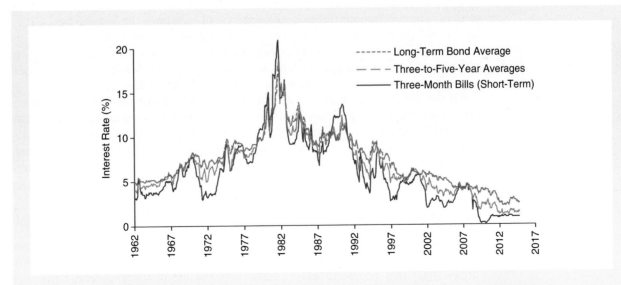

FIGURE 6-3 **Movements over Time of Interest Rates on Government of Canada Bonds with Different Maturities, 1962–2014**

Interest rates on bonds with different maturities move together over time.
Source: Statistics Canada CANSIM series V122531, V122485, and V122487.

Following the Financial News   Yield Curves

Many newspapers and Internet sites such as **www.finance.yahoo.com** publish a daily plot of the yield curve for government securities. An example for November 10, 2014, is presented here. The numbers on the vertical axis indicate the interest rate for the Government of Canada security, with the maturity term given on the horizontal axis, with "m" denoting month and "y" denoting year.

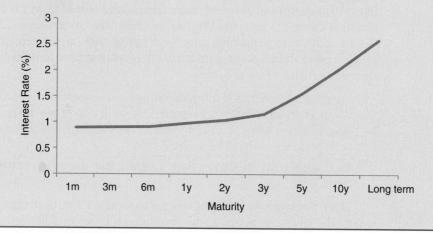

and (3) the liquidity premium theory. Each of these theories is described in the following sections. The expectations theory does a good job of explaining the first two facts on our list, but not the third fact. The segmented markets theory can account for fact 3 but not the other two. Because each theory explains facts that the others cannot, a natural way to seek a better understanding of the term structure is to combine features of both theories, which leads us to the liquidity premium theory, which can explain all three facts.

If the liquidity premium theory does a better job of explaining the facts and is hence the most widely accepted theory, why do we spend time discussing the other two theories? There are two reasons. First, the ideas in these two theories lay the groundwork for the liquidity premium theory. Second, it is useful to see how economists modify theories to improve them when they find that the predicted results are inconsistent with the empirical evidence.

Expectations Theory

The **expectations theory** of the term structure states the following commonsense proposition: the interest rate on a long-term bond will equal an average of short-term interest rates that people expect to occur over the life of the long-term bond. For example, if people expect that short-term interest rates will be 10%, on average, over the coming five years, the expectations theory predicts that the interest rate on bonds with five years to maturity will be 10%, too. If short-term interest rates were expected to rise even higher after this five-year period so that the average short-term interest rate over the coming 20 years is 11%, then the interest rate on 20-year bonds would equal 11% and would be higher than the interest rate on five-year bonds. Thus, the expectations theory predicts that interest rates on bonds of different maturities differ because short-term interest rates are expected to have different values at future dates.

The key assumption behind this theory is that buyers of bonds do not prefer bonds of one maturity over another, so they will not hold any quantity of a bond if its expected return is less than that of another bond with a different maturity. Bonds that have this characteristic are said to be *perfect substitutes*. What this means in practice is that if bonds with different maturities are perfect substitutes, the expected return on these bonds must be equal.

To see how the assumption that bonds with different maturities are perfect substitutes leads to the expectations theory, let us consider the following two investment strategies:

1. Purchase a one-year bond; when it matures in one year, purchase another one-year bond.
2. Purchase a two-year bond and hold it until maturity.

Because both strategies must have the same expected return, the interest rate on the two-year bond must equal the average of the two one-year interest rates. For example, let's say that the current interest rate on the one-year bond is 9%, and you expect the interest rate on the one-year bond next year to be 11%. If you pursue the first strategy of buying the two one-year bonds, the expected return over the two years will average out to be (9% + 11%)/2 = 10% per year. You will be willing to hold both the one- and two-year bonds only if the expected return per year on the two-year bond equals this return. Therefore, the interest rate on the two-year bond must equal 10%, the average interest rate on the two one-year bonds.

We can make this argument more general. For an investment of $1, consider the choice of holding, for two periods, a two-period bond or two one-period bonds. Using the definitions

i_t = today's (time t) interest rate on a one-period bond

i_{t+1}^e = interest rate on a one-period bond expected for next period (time $t + 1$)

i_{2t} = today's (time t) interest rate on the two-period bond

the expected return from investing $1 in the two-period bond and holding it for the two periods can be calculated as

$$(1 + i_{2t})(1 + i_{2t}) - 1 = 1 + 2i_{2t} + (i_{2t})^2 - 1 = 2i_{2t} + (i_{2t})^2$$

After the second period, the $1 investment is worth $(1 + i_{2t})(1 + i_{2t})$. Subtracting the $1 initial investment from this amount and then dividing by the initial $1 investment gives the rate of return calculated in the above equation. Because $(i_{2t})^2$ is extremely small—if $i_{2t} = 10\% = 0.10$, then $(i_{2t})^2 = 0.01$—we can simplify the expected return for holding the two-period bond for the two periods to

$$2i_{2t}$$

With the other strategy, in which one-period bonds are bought, the expected return on the $1 investment over the two periods is

$$(1 + i_t)(1 + i_{t+1}^e) - 1 = 1 + i_t + i_{t+1}^e + i_t(e_{t+1}^e) - 1 = i_t + e_{t+1}^e + i_t(i_{t+1}^e)$$

This calculation is derived by recognizing that after the first period, the $1 investment becomes $1 + i_t$, which is reinvested in the one-period bond for the next period, yielding the amount $(1 + i_t)(1 + i_{t+1}^e)$. Then, subtracting the $1 initial investment from this amount and then dividing by the initial investment of $1 gives the expected return for the strategy of holding one-period bonds for the two periods. Because $i_t(i_{t+1}^e)$ is also extremely small—if $i_t = i_{t+1}^e = 0.10$, then $i_t(i_{t+1}^e) = 0.01$—we can simplify this to

$$i_t + i_{t+1}^e$$

Both bonds will be held only if these expected returns are equal, that is, when

$$2i_{2t} = i_t + i_{t+1}^e$$

Solving for i_{2t} in terms of the one-period rates, we have

$$i_{2t} = \frac{i_t + i_{t+1}^e}{2} \qquad \text{(Equation 1)}$$

which tells us that the two-period rate must equal the average of the two one-period rates. Graphically, this can be shown as

We can conduct the same steps for bonds with a longer maturity allowing us to examine the whole term structure of interest rates. By doing so, we will find that the interest rate of i_{nt} on an n-period bond must equal

$$i_{nt} = \frac{i_t + i_{t+1}^e + i_{t+2}^e + \cdots + i_{t+(n-1)}^e}{n} \qquad \text{(Equation 2)}$$

Equation 2 states that the n-period interest rate equals the average of the one-period interest rates expected to occur over the n-period life of the bond. This is a restatement of the expectations theory in more precise terms.[1]

APPLICATION   Expectations Theory and the Yield Curve

The one-year interest rates over the next five years are expected to be 5%, 6%, 7%, 8%, and 9%. Given this information, what are the interest rates on a two-year bond and a five-year bond? Explain what is happening to the yield curve.

Solution

The interest rate on the two-year bond will be

$$i_{nt} = \frac{i_t + i_{t+1}^e + i_{t+2}^e + \cdots + i_{t+(n-1)}^e}{n}$$

[1]The analysis here has been conducted for discount bonds. Formulas for interest rates on coupon bonds would differ slightly from those used here but would convey the same principle.

where

$$i_t = \text{year 1 interest rate} = 5\%$$
$$i_{t+1}^e = \text{year 2 interest rate} = 6\%$$
$$n = \text{number of years} = 2$$

Thus

$$i_{2t} = \frac{5\% + 6\%}{2} = 5.5\%$$

The interest rate on the five-year bond will be

$$i_{nt} = \frac{i_t + i_{t+1}^e + i_{t+2}^e + \cdots + i_{t+(n-1)}^e}{n}$$

where

$$i_t = \text{year 1 interest rate} = 5\%$$
$$i_{t+1}^e = \text{year 2 interest rate} = 6\%$$
$$i_{t+2}^e = \text{year 3 interest rate} = 7\%$$
$$i_{t+3}^e = \text{year 4 interest rate} = 8\%$$
$$i_{t+4}^e = \text{year 5 interest rate} = 9\%$$
$$n = \text{number of years} = 5$$

Thus

$$i_{5t} = \frac{5\% + 6\% + 7\% + 8\% + 9\%}{5} = 7.0\%$$

By doing similar calculations for the one-, three-, and four-year interest rates, you will be able to verify that one-year to five-year interest rates are 5.0%, 5.5%, 6.0%, 6.5%, and 7.0%, respectively. Thus, we see that the rising trend in expected short-term interest rates produces an upward-sloping yield curve along which interest rates rise as maturity lengthens. ◆

The expectations theory is an elegant theory that explains why the term structure of interest rates (as represented by yield curves) changes at different times. When the yield curve is upward-sloping, the expectations theory suggests that short-term interest rates are expected to rise in the future, as we have seen in our numerical example. In this situation, in which the long-term rate is currently above the short-term rate, the average of future short-term rates is expected to be higher than the current short-term rate, which can occur only if short-term interest rates are expected to rise. This is what we see in our numerical example. When the yield curve is inverted (slopes downward), the average of future short-term interest rates is expected to be below the current short-term rate, implying that short-term interest rates are expected to fall, on average, in the future. Only when the yield curve is flat does the expectations theory suggest that short-term interest rates are not expected to change, on average, in the future.

The expectations theory also explains fact 1: that interest rates on bonds with different maturities move together over time. Historically, short-term interest rates have shown the following trend: If they increase today, they will tend to be higher in the future. Hence a rise in short-term rates will raise people's expectations of future higher short-term rates. Because long-term rates are the average of expected future short-term rates, a rise in short-term rates will also raise long-term rates, causing short- and long-term rates to move together.

The expectations theory also explains fact 2: that yield curves tend to have an upward slope when short-term interest rates are low and a downward slope when short-term rates are high. When short-term rates are low, people generally expect them to rise to some normal level in the future, and the average of future expected short-term rates is high relative to the current short-term rate. Therefore, long-term interest rates will be substantially above current short-term rates, and the yield curve would then have an upward slope. Conversely, if short-term rates are high, people usually expect them to come back down. Long-term rates would then drop below short-term rates because the average of expected future short-term rates would be below current short-term rates and the yield curve would slope downward and become inverted.[2]

The expectations theory is an attractive theory because it provides a simple explanation of the behaviour of the term structure, but unfortunately it has a major shortcoming: it cannot explain fact 3—that yield curves usually slope upward. The typical upward slope of yield curves implies that short-term interest rates are usually expected to rise in the future. In practice, short-term interest rates are just as likely to fall as they are to rise, and so the expectations theory suggests that the typical yield curve should be flat rather than upward-sloping.

Segmented Markets Theory

As the name suggests, the **segmented markets theory** of the term structure sees markets for different-maturity bonds as completely separate and segmented. The interest rate on a bond of a particular maturity is then determined by the supply of and demand for that bond, and is not affected by expected returns on other bonds with other maturities.

The key assumption of the segmented markets theory is that bonds of different maturities are not substitutes at all, and so the expected return from holding a bond of one maturity has no effect on the demand for a bond of another maturity. This theory of the term structure is at the opposite extreme to the expectations theory, which assumes that bonds of different maturities are perfect substitutes.

The argument for why bonds of different maturities are not substitutes is that investors have very strong preferences for bonds of one maturity but not for another, so they will be concerned with the expected returns only for bonds of the maturity they prefer. This might occur because they have a particular holding period in mind, and if they match the maturity of the bond to the desired holding period, they can obtain a certain return with no risk at all.[3] (We have seen in Chapter 4 that if the term to maturity equals

---

[2]The expectations theory explains another important fact about the relationship between short-term and long-term interest rates. As you can see looking back at Figure 6-3, short-term interest rates are more volatile than long-term rates. If interest rates are *mean-reverting*—that is, if they tend to head back down after they are at unusually high levels or go back up when they are at unusually low levels—then an average of these short-term rates must necessarily have lower volatility than the short-term rates themselves. Because the expectations theory suggests that the long-term rate will be an average of future short-term rates, it implies that the long-term rate will have lower volatility than short-term rates will have.

[3]The statement that there is no uncertainty about the return if the term to maturity equals the holding period is literally true only for a discount bond. For a coupon bond with a long holding period, there is some risk because coupon payments must be reinvested before the bond matures. Our analysis here is thus being conducted for discount bonds only. However, the gist of the analysis remains the same for coupon bonds because the amount of this risk from reinvestment is small when coupon bonds have the same term to maturity as the holding period.

the holding period, the return is known for certain because it equals the yield exactly, and there is no interest-rate risk.) For example, people who have a short holding period would prefer to hold short-term bonds. Conversely, if you were putting funds away for your young child to go to university, your desired holding period might be much longer, and you would want to hold longer-term bonds.

In the segmented markets theory, differing yield curve patterns are accounted for by supply and demand differences associated with bonds of different maturities. If, as seems sensible, risk-averse investors have short desired holding periods and generally prefer bonds with shorter maturities that have less interest-rate risk, the segmented markets theory can explain fact 3, which states that yield curves typically slope upward. Because the demand for long-term bonds is typically relatively lower than that for short-term bonds, long-term bonds will have lower prices and higher interest rates, and hence the yield curve will typically slope upward.

Although the segmented markets theory can explain why yield curves usually tend to slope upward, it has a major flaw in that it cannot explain facts 1 and 2. First, because it views the market for bonds of different maturities as completely segmented, there is no reason that a rise in interest rates on a bond of one maturity would affect the interest rate on a bond of another maturity. Therefore, the segmented markets theory cannot explain why interest rates on bonds of different maturities tend to move together (fact 1). Second, because it is not clear how demand and supply for short- versus long-term bonds change with the level of short-term interest rates, the theory also does not explain why yield curves tend to slope upward when short-term interest rates are low and to be inverted when short-term interest rates are high (fact 2).

Because each of our two theories explains empirical facts that the other cannot, a logical step is to combine the theories, which leads us to the liquidity premium theory.

Liquidity Premium and Preferred Habitat Theories

The **liquidity premium theory** of the term structure states that the interest rate on a long-term bond will equal an average of short-term interest rates expected to occur over the life of the long-term bond plus a liquidity premium (also referred to as a *term premium*) that responds to supply and demand conditions for that bond.

The liquidity premium theory's key assumption is that bonds of different maturities are substitutes, which means that the expected return on one bond *does* influence the expected return on a bond of a different maturity. However, the theory allows investors to prefer one bond maturity over another. In other words, bonds of different maturities are assumed to be substitutes but not perfect substitutes. Investors tend to prefer shorter-term bonds because these bonds bear less interest-rate risk. For this reason, investors must be offered a positive liquidity premium to induce them to hold longer-term bonds. Thus, the expectations theory is modified by adding a positive liquidity premium to the equation that describes the relationship between long- and short-term interest rates. The liquidity premium theory is thus written as

$$i_{nt} = \frac{i_t + i_{t+1}^e + i_{t+2}^e + \cdots + i_{t+(n-1)}^e}{n} + l_{nt} \qquad \text{(Equation 3)}$$

where l_{nt} = the liquidity (term) premium for the n-period bond at time t, which is always positive and rises with the term to maturity of the bond, n.

Closely related to the liquidity premium theory is the **preferred habitat theory**, which takes a somewhat less direct approach to modifying the expectations hypothesis but comes to a similar conclusion. It assumes that investors have a preference for bonds of one maturity over another, a particular bond maturity (preferred habitat) in which they prefer to invest. Because they prefer bonds of one maturity over bonds of another, they are willing to buy bonds that do not have the preferred maturity (habitat) only if those bonds earn a somewhat higher expected return. Because investors are likely to prefer the habitat of short-term bonds over that of longer-term bonds, they are willing to hold long-term bonds only if they have higher expected returns. This reasoning leads to the same Equation 3 implied by the liquidity premium theory, with a term premium that typically rises with maturity.

The relationship between the expectations theory and the liquidity premium and preferred habitat theories is shown in Figure 6-4. There, we see that because the liquidity premium is always positive and typically grows as the term to maturity increases, the yield curve implied by the liquidity premium theory is always above the yield curve implied by the expectations theory and generally has a steeper slope. (For simplicity, we are assuming that the expectations theory yield curve is flat.)

MyEconLab Mini-lecture

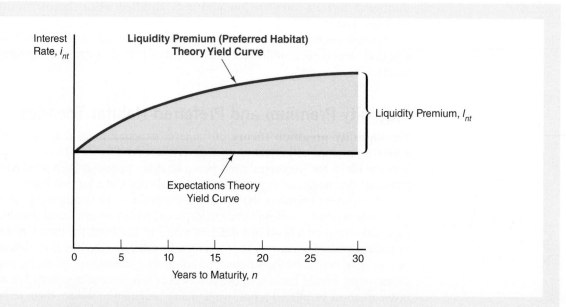

FIGURE 6-4 **The Relationship Between the Liquidity Premium (Preferred Habitat) and Expectations Theories**

Because the liquidity premium is always positive and grows as the term to maturity increases, the yield curve implied by the liquidity premium and preferred habitat theories is always above the yield curve implied by the expectations theory and has a steeper slope. Note that the yield curve implied by the expectations theory is drawn under the scenario of unchanging future one-year interest rates.

APPLICATION

Liquidity Premium Theory and the Yield Curve

Let's suppose that the one-year interest rates over the next five years are expected to be 5%, 6%, 7%, 8%, and 9%, while investors' preferences for holding short-term bonds means that the liquidity premiums for one- to five-year bonds are 0%, 0.25%, 0.5%, 0.75%, and 1.0%, respectively. What is the interest rate on a two-year bond and a five-year bond? Compare these findings with the answer in the previous Application dealing with the pure expectations theory.

Solution
The interest rate on the two-year bond would be

$$i_{nt} = \frac{i_t + i^e_{t+1} + i^e_{t+2} + \cdots + i^e_{t+(n-1)}}{n} + l_{nt}$$

where

$$i_t = \text{year 1 interest rate} = 5\%$$
$$i^e_{t+1} = \text{year 2 interest rate} = 6\%$$
$$l_{2t} = \text{liquidity premium} = 0.25\%$$
$$n = \text{number of years} \quad = 2$$

Thus

$$i_{2t} = \frac{5\% + 6\%}{2} + 0.25\% = 5.75\%$$

The interest rate on the five-year bond would be

$$i_{nt} = \frac{i_t + i^e_{t+1} + i^e_{t+2} + \cdots + i^e_{t+(n-1)}}{n} + l_{nt}$$

where

$$i_t = \text{year 1 interest rate} = 5\%$$
$$i^e_{t+1} = \text{year 2 interest rate} = 6\%$$
$$i^e_{t+2} = \text{year 3 interest rate} = 7\%$$
$$i^e_{t+3} = \text{year 4 interest rate} = 8\%$$
$$i^e_{t+4} = \text{year 5 interest rate} = 9\%$$
$$l_{5t} = \text{liquidity premium} = 1\%$$
$$n = \text{number of years} \quad = 5$$

Thus

$$i_{5t} = \frac{5\% + 6\% + 7\% + 8\% + 9\%}{5} + 1\% = 8.0\%$$

By doing similar calculations for the one-, three-, and four-year interest rates, you should be able to verify that the one-year to five-year interest rates would be as follows: 5.0%, 5.75%, 6.5%, 7.25%, and 8.0%, respectively. Comparing these findings with those from the pure expectations theory, we can see that the liquidity preference theory produces yield curves that slope more steeply upward because of investors' preferences for short-term bonds. ◆

Let's see if the liquidity premium and preferred habitat theories are consistent with all three empirical facts we have discussed. They explain fact 1, that interest rates on different-maturity bonds move together over time: a rise in short-term interest rates indicates that short-term interest rates will, on average, be higher in the future, and the first term in Equation 3 then implies that long-term interest rates will rise along with them.

The liquidity and preferred habitat theories also explain why yield curves tend to have an especially steep upward slope when short-term interest rates are low and to be inverted when short-term rates are high (fact 2). Because investors generally expect short-term interest rates to rise to some normal level when they are low, the average of future expected short-term rates will be high relative to the current short-term rate. With the additional boost of a positive liquidity premium, long-term interest rates will be substantially above current short-term rates, and the yield curve would then have a steep upward slope. Conversely, if short-term rates are high, people usually expect them to come back down. Long-term rates would then drop below short-term rates because the average of expected future short-term rates would be so far below current short-term rates that despite positive liquidity premiums, the yield curve would slope downward.

The liquidity premium and preferred habitat theories explain fact 3, which states that yield curves typically slope upward, by recognizing that the liquidity premium rises with a bond's maturity because of investors' preferences for short-term bonds. Even if short-term interest rates are expected to stay the same on average in the future, long-term interest rates will be above short-term interest rates, and yield curves will typically slope upward.

How can the liquidity premium and preferred habitat theories explain the occasional appearance of inverted yield curves if the liquidity premium is positive? It must be that at times short-term interest rates are expected to fall so much in the future that the average of the expected short-term rates is well below the current short-term rate. Even when the positive liquidity premium is added to this average, the resulting long-term rate will still be below the current short-term interest rate.

As our discussion indicates, a particularly attractive feature of the liquidity premium and preferred habitat theories is that they tell you what the market is predicting about future short-term interest rates just from the slope of the yield curve. A steeply rising yield curve, as in panel (a) of Figure 6-5, indicates that short-term interest rates are expected to rise in the future. A moderately steep yield curve, as in panel (b), indicates that short-term interest rates are not expected to rise or fall much in the future. A flat yield curve, as in panel (c), indicates that short-term rates are expected to fall moderately in the future. Finally, an inverted yield curve, as in panel (d), indicates that short-term interest rates are expected to fall sharply in the future.

Evidence on the Term Structure

In the 1980s, researchers examining the term structure of interest rates questioned whether the slope of the yield curve provides information about movements of future short-term interest rates. They found that the spread between long- and short-term interest rates does not always help predict future short-term interest rates, a finding that may stem from substantial fluctuations in the liquidity (term) premium for long-term bonds. More recent research using more discriminating tests now favours a different view. It shows that the term structure contains quite a bit of information for the very short run (over the next several months) and the long run (over several years) but is

MyEconLab Mini-lecture

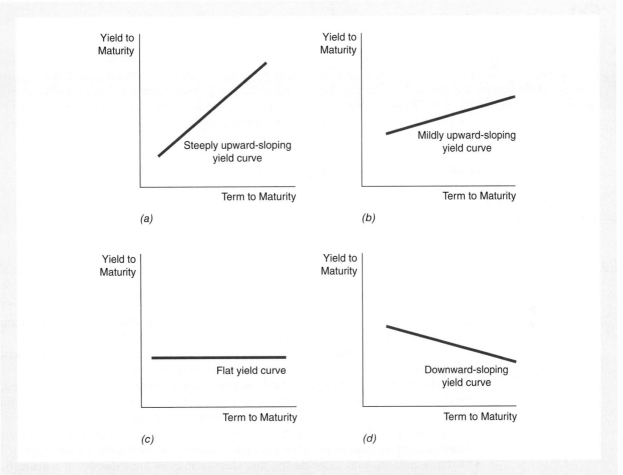

FIGURE 6-5 **Yield Curves and the Market's Expectations of Future Short-Term Interest Rates According to the Liquidity Premium (Preferred Habitat) Theory**

A steeply rising yield curve, as in panel (a), indicates that short-term interest rates are expected to rise in the future. A moderately steep yield curve, as in panel (b), indicates that short-term interest rates are not expected to rise or fall much in the future. A flat yield curve, as in panel (c), indicates that short-term rates are expected to fall moderately in the future. Finally, an inverted yield curve, as in panel (d), indicates that short-term interest rates are expected to fall sharply in the future.

unreliable at predicting movements in interest rates over the intermediate term (the time in between). Research also finds that the yield curve helps forecast future inflation and business cycles (see the FYI box).

Summary

The liquidity premium and preferred habitat theories are the most widely accepted theories of the term structure of interest rates because they explain the major empirical facts about the term structure so well. They combine the features of both the expectations theory and the segmented markets theory by asserting that a long-term interest

---

FYI   The Yield Curve as a Forecasting Tool for Inflation and the Business Cycle

Because the yield curve contains information about future expected interest rates, it should also have the capacity to help forecast inflation and real output fluctuations. To see this, recall from Chapter 5 that rising interest rates are associated with economic booms and falling interest rates with recessions. When the yield curve is either flat or downward sloping, it suggests that future short-term interest rates are expected to fall and, therefore, that the economy is more likely to enter a recession. Indeed, the yield curve is found to be an accurate predictor of the business cycle.

In Chapter 4, we also learned that a nominal interest rate is composed of a real interest rate and expected inflation, implying that the yield curve contains information about the future path of nominal interest rates and future inflation. A steep yield curve predicts a future increase in inflation, while a flat or downward-sloping yield curve forecasts a future decline in inflation.

The ability of the yield curve to forecast business cycles and inflation is one reason why the slope of the yield curve is part of the toolkit of many economic forecasters and is often viewed as a useful indicator of the stance of monetary policy, with a steep yield curve indicating loose policy and a flat or downward-sloping yield curve indicating tight policy.

---

rate will be the sum of a liquidity (term) premium and the average of the short-term interest rates that are expected to occur over the life of the bond.

The liquidity premium and preferred habitat theories explain the following facts: (1) Interest rates on bonds of different maturities tend to move together over time, (2) yield curves usually slope upward, and (3) when short-term interest rates are low, yield curves are more likely to have a steep upward slope, whereas when short-term interest rates are high, yield curves are more likely to be inverted.

The theories also help us predict the movement of short-term interest rates in the future. A steep upward slope of the yield curve means that short-term rates are expected to rise; a mild upward slope means that short-term rates are expected to remain the same; a flat slope means that short-term rates are expected to fall moderately; and an inverted yield curve means that short-term rates are expected to fall sharply.

APPLICATION   Interpreting Yield Curves, 1986–2014

Figure 6-6 illustrates several yield curves that have appeared for Canadian government bonds in recent years. What do these yield curves tell us about the public's expectations of future movements of short-term interest rates?

The inverted yield curve that occurred in January 1990 indicated that short-term interest rates were expected to decline sharply in the future. In order for longer-term interest rates with their positive liquidity premium to be well below the short-term interest rate, short-term interest rates must be expected to decline so sharply that their average is far below the current short-term rate. Indeed, the public's expectations of sharply lower short-term interest rates evident in the yield curve were realized soon after January 1990; by March 1991, three-month Treasury bill rates had declined from over 12% to less than 9%.

The upward-sloping yield curve in November 2014 indicates that short-term interest rates would climb in the future. The long-term interest rate is above the

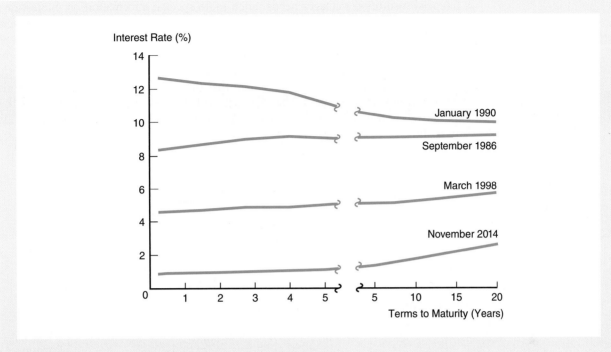

FIGURE 6-6   Yield Curves for Government of Canada Bonds

Yield curves for Government of Canada bonds for different dates from 1986 to 2014.
Source: Statistics Canada CANSIM series V122531, V122532, V122533, V122538, V122539, V122540, V122543, and V122544, and the authors' calculations.

short-term interest rate when short-term interest rates are expected to rise because their average plus the liquidity premium will be above the current short-term rate. The moderately upward-sloping yield curve in September 1986 indicates that short-term interest rates were expected neither to rise nor to fall in the near future. In this case, their average remains the same as the current short-term rate, and the positive liquidity premium for longer-term bonds explains the moderate upward slope of the yield curve.

APPLICATION   Using the Term Structure to Forecast Interest Rates

Interest-rate forecasts are extremely important to managers of financial institutions because future changes in interest rates have a significant impact on the profitability of their institutions. Furthermore, interest-rate forecasts are needed when managers of financial institutions have to set interest rates on loans that are promised to customers in the future. Our discussion of the term structure of interest rates has indicated that the slope of the yield curve provides general information about the market's prediction of the future path of interest rates. For example, a steeply upward-sloping yield curve indicates that short-term interest rates are predicted to rise in the future, and a downward-sloping yield curve indicates that short-term interest rates are predicted to fall. However, a financial institution manager needs much more specific information on interest-rate forecasts than this. Here we show how the manager of a financial institution can generate specific forecasts of interest rates using the term structure.

To see how this is done, let's start the analysis using the approach we took in developing the expectations theory. Recall that because bonds of different maturities are considered perfect substitutes, we assumed that the expected return over two periods from investing $1 in a two-period bond, which is $(1 + i_{2t})(1 + i_{2t}) - 1$, must equal the expected return from investing $1 in one-period bonds, which is $(1 + i_t)(1 + i_{t+1}^e) - 1$. This is shown graphically as follows:

In other words,

$$(1 + i_t)(1 + i_{t+1}^e) - 1 = (1 + i_{2t})(1 + i_{2t}) - 1$$

Through some tedious algebra we can solve for i_{t+1}^e:

$$i_{t+1}^e = \frac{(1 + i_{2t})^2}{1 + i_t} - 1 \qquad \text{(Equation 4)}$$

This measure of i_{t+1}^e is called the **forward rate** because it is the one-period interest rate that the pure expectations theory of the term structure indicates is expected to prevail one period in the future. To differentiate forward rates derived from the term structure from actual interest rates that are observed at time t, we call these observed interest rates **spot rates**.

Going back to the Application, Expectations Theory and the Yield Curve (p. 130), which we used to discuss the expectations theory earlier in this chapter, at time t, the one-year interest rate is 5% and the two-year rate is 5.5%. Plugging these numbers into Equation 4 yields the following estimate of the forward rate one period in the future:

$$i_{t+1}^e = \frac{(1 + 0.055)^2}{1 + 0.05} - 1 = 0.06 = 6\%$$

Not surprisingly, this 6% forward rate is identical to the expected one-year interest rate one year in the future. This is exactly what we should find, as our calculation here is just another way of looking at the pure expectations theory.

We can also compare holding the three-year bond against holding a sequence of one-year bonds, which reveals the following relationship:

$$(1 + i_t)(1 + i_{t+1}^e)(1 + i_{t+2}^e) - 1 = (1 + i_{3t})(1 + i_{3t})(1 + i_{3t}) - 1$$

And plugging in the estimate for i_{t+1}^e derived in Equation 4, we can solve for i_{t+2}^e:

$$i_{t+2}^e = \frac{(1 + i_{3t})^3}{(1 + i_{2t})^2} - 1$$

Continuing with these calculations, we obtain the general solution for the forward rate n periods into the future:

$$i_{t+n}^e = \frac{(1 + i_{n+1t})^{n+1}}{(1 + i_{nt})^n} - 1 \qquad \text{(Equation 5)}$$

Our discussion indicated that the expectations theory is not entirely satisfactory because investors must be compensated with liquidity premiums to induce them to hold longer-term bonds. Hence, we need to modify our analysis, as we did when discussing the liquidity premium theory, by allowing for these liquidity premiums in estimating predictions of future interest rates.

Recall from the discussion of those theories that because investors prefer to hold short-term rather than long-term bonds, the n-period interest rate differs from that indicated by the pure expectations theory by a liquidity premium of ℓ_{nt}. So to allow for liquidity premiums, we need merely subtract ℓ_{nt} from i_{nt} in our formula to derive i_{t+n}^e:

$$i_{t+n}^e = \frac{(1 + i_{n+1t} - \ell_{n+1t})^{n+1}}{(1 + i_{nt} - \ell_{nt})^n} - 1 \qquad \text{(Equation 6)}$$

This measure of i_{t+n}^e is referred to, naturally enough, as the *adjusted forward-rate forecast*.

In the case of i_{t+1}^e, Equation 6 produces the following estimate:

$$i_{t+1}^e = \frac{(1 + i_{2t} - \ell_{2t})^2}{1 + i_t} - 1$$

Using the example from the Application, Liquidity Premium Theory and the Yield Curve on page 135, at time t the ℓ_{2t} liquidity premium is 0.25%, $\ell_{1t} = 0$, the one-year interest rate is 5%, and the two-year interest rate is 5.75%. Plugging these numbers into our equation yields the following adjusted forward-rate forecast for one period in the future:

$$i_{t+1}^e = \frac{(1 + 0.0575 - 0.0025)^2}{1 + 0.05} - 1 = 0.06 = 6\%$$

which is the same as the expected interest rate used in the Application on expectations theory, as it should be.

Our analysis of the term structure thus provides managers of financial institutions with a fairly straightforward procedure for producing interest-rate forecasts. First they need to estimate ℓ_{nt}, the values of the liquidity premiums for various n. Then they need merely apply the formula in Equation 6 to derive the market's forecasts of future interest rates.

APPLICATION   # Forward Rate

A customer asks a bank if it would be willing to commit to making the customer a one-year loan at an interest rate of 8% one year from now. To compensate for the costs of making the loan, the bank needs to charge one percentage point more than the expected interest rate on a Canada bond with the same maturity if it is to make a profit. If the bank manager estimates the liquidity premium to be 0.4%, and the one-year Canada bond rate is 6% and the two-year bond rate is 7%, should the manager be willing to make the commitment?

Solution

The bank manager is unable to make the loan because at an interest rate of 8%, the loan is likely to be unprofitable to the bank.

$$i_{t+n}^e = \frac{(1 + i_{n+1t} - \ell_{n+1t})^{n+1}}{(1 + i_{nt} - \ell_{nt})^n} - 1$$

where

$$i_{n+1t} = \text{two-year bond rate} = 0.07$$
$$\ell_{n+1t} = \text{liquidity premium} = 0.004$$
$$i_{nt} = \text{one-year bond rate} = 0.06$$
$$\ell_{1t} = \text{liquidity premium} = 0$$
$$n = \text{number of years} = 1$$

Thus

$$i_{t+1}^e = \frac{(1 + 0.07 - 0.004)^2}{1 + 0.06} - 1 = 0.072 = 7.2\%$$

The market's forecast of the one-year Canada bond rate one year in the future is therefore 7.2%. Adding the 1% necessary to make a profit on the one-year loan means that the loan is expected to be profitable only if it has an interest rate of 8.2% or higher. ◆

MyEconLab

MyEconLab is an online homework and tutorial system that puts you in control of your own learning with study and practice tools directly correlated to this chapter's content. Visit MyEconLab to access the eText, the Questions and Applied Problems with answers, as well as additional assessment. You will also find web chapters, mini-lectures, appendices, mini-cases, videos, glossary flashcards, news feeds, CANSIM data, and graphing tools.

SUMMARY

1. Bonds with the same maturity will have different interest rates because of three factors: default risk, liquidity, and tax considerations. The greater a bond's default risk, the higher its interest rate relative to other bonds; the greater a bond's liquidity, the lower its interest rate; and bonds with tax-exempt status will have lower interest rates than they otherwise would. The relationship among interest rates on bonds with the same maturity that arises because of these three factors is known as the risk structure of interest rates.

2. Four theories of the term structure provide explanations of how interest rates on bonds with different terms to maturity are related. The expectations theory views long-term interest rates as equalling the average of future short-term interest rates expected to occur over the life of the bond. By contrast, the segmented markets theory treats the determination of interest rates for each bond's maturity as the outcome of supply and demand in that market only. Neither of these theories by itself can explain the fact that interest rates on bonds of different maturities move together over time and that yield curves usually slope upward.

3. The liquidity premium (preferred habitat) theory combines the features of the other two theories, and by so doing is able to explain the facts just mentioned. It views long-term interest rates as equalling the average of future short-term interest rates expected to occur over the life of the bond

plus a liquidity premium. This theory allows us to infer the market's expectations about the movement of future short-term interest rates from the yield curve. A steeply upward-sloping curve indicates that future short-term rates are expected to rise; a mildly upward-sloping curve, that short-term rates are expected to stay the same; a flat curve, that short-term rates are expected to decline slightly; and an inverted yield curve, that a substantial decline in short-term rates is expected in the future.

KEY TERMS

basis points, p. 125
credit-rating agencies, p. 123
default-free bonds, p. 121
expectations theory, p. 128
fallen angels, p. 124
forward rate, p. 140

inverted yield curve, p. 127
junk bonds, p. 124
liquidity premium theory, p. 133
preferred habitat theory, p. 134
risk of default, p. 120
risk premium, p. 121

risk structure of interest rates, p. 120
segmented markets theory, p. 132
spot rates, p. 140
term structure of interest rates, p. 120
yield curve, p. 127

QUESTIONS

All questions are available in MyEconLab at **www.myeconlab.com.**

1. If junk bonds are "junk," why would investors buy them?

2. Which should have the higher risk premium on its interest rates, a corporate bond with a Moody's Baa rating or a corporate bond with a C rating? Why?

3. Why do Canadian Treasury bills have lower interest rates than large-denomination negotiable bank CDs have?

4. In the fall of 2008, AIG, the largest insurance company in the world at the time, was at risk of defaulting due to the severity of the global financial crisis. As a result, the U.S. government stepped in to support AIG with large capital injections and an ownership stake. How would this affect the yield and risk premium on AIG corporate debt, if at all?

5. Risk premiums on corporate bonds are usually *countercyclical* ; that is, they decrease during business cycle expansions and increase during recessions. Why is this so?

6. "If bonds of different maturities are close substitutes, their interest rates are more likely to move together." Is this statement true, false, or uncertain? Explain your answer.

7. The Canadian government offers some of its debt as Real Return Bonds, in which the price of bonds is adjusted for inflation over the life of the debt instrument. Real Return Bonds are traded on a much smaller scale than nominal Canada bonds of equivalent maturity. What can you conclude about the liquidity premium between Real Return Bonds and nominal Canada bonds?

8. Predict what will happen to interest rates on a corporation's bonds if the federal government guarantees today that it will pay creditors if the corporation goes bankrupt in the future. What will happen to the interest rates on Canada bonds?

9. Predict what would happen to the risk premiums on corporate bonds if brokerage commissions were lowered in the corporate bond market.

10. During 2008, the difference in yield (the *yield spread*) between three-month AA-rated financial commercial paper and three-month AA-rated nonfinancial commercial paper steadily increased from its usual level of close to zero, spiking to over a full percentage point at its peak in October 2008. What explains this sudden increase?

11. If the income tax exemption on U.S. municipal bonds were abolished, what would happen to the interest rates on these bonds? What effect would the change have on interest rates on U.S. Treasury securities?

12. Prior to 2008, mortgage lenders in the United States required a house inspection to assess its value, and often used the same one or two inspection companies in the same geographical market. Following the collapse of the housing market in 2008, mortgage lenders required a house inspection, but this was arranged through a third party. How does this illustrate a conflict of interest similar to the role that credit-rating agencies played in the global financial crisis?

13. "Using the expectations theory of the term structure, it is better to invest in one-year bonds, reinvested over two years, than to invest in a two-year bond, if interest rates on one-year bonds are expected to be the same in both years." Is this statement true, false, or uncertain?

14. If bond investors decide that 30-year bonds are no longer as desirable an investment, predict what will happen to the yield curve, assuming (a) the expectations theory of the term structure holds and (b) the segmented markets theory of the term structure holds.

15. Suppose the interest rates on one-, five-, and 10-year Canada bonds are currently 3%, 6%, and 6%, respectively. Investor A chooses to hold only one-year bonds and Investor B is indifferent between holding five- and 10-year bonds. How can you explain the behaviours of Investors A and B?

16. If a yield curve looks like the one shown in the figure below, what is the market predicting about the movement of future short-term interest rates? What might the yield curve indicate about the market's predictions for the inflation rate in the future?

17. If a yield curve looks like the one shown in the figure below, what is the market predicting about the movement of future short-term interest rates? What might the yield curve indicate about the market's predictions for the inflation rate in the future?

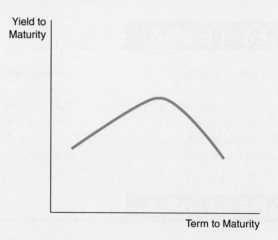

18. If yield curves, on average, were flat, what would this say about the liquidity (term) premiums in the term structure? Would you be more or less willing to accept the expectations theory?

19. If the yield curve suddenly became steeper, how would you revise your predictions of interest rates in the future?

20. If expectations of future short-term interest rates suddenly fell, what would happen to the slope of the yield curve?

21. Suppose that the Bank of Canada made an announcement that it would purchase up to $300 billion of longer-term Canada securities over the following six months. What effect might this policy have on the yield curve?

APPLIED PROBLEMS

All applied problems are available in MyEconLab *at* **www.myeconlab.com.**

22. In 2010 and 2011, the government of Greece risked defaulting on its debt due to a severe budget crisis. Show, using bond market graphs, the effect on the risk premium between Canadian government debt and comparable maturity Greek debt.

23. Assuming that the expectations theory is the correct theory of the term structure, calculate the interest rates in the term structure for maturities of one to five years,

and plot the resulting yield curves for the following paths of one-year interest rates over the next five years:

a. 5%, 7%, 7%, 7%, 7%

b. 5%, 4%, 4%, 4%, 4%

How would your yield curves change if people preferred shorter-term bonds over longer-term bonds?

24. Assuming that the expectations theory is the correct theory of the term structure, calculate the interest rates in the term structure for maturities of one to five years, and plot the resulting yield curves for the following paths of one-year interest rates over the next five years:

a. 5%, 6%, 7%, 6%, 5%

b. 5%, 4%, 3%, 4%, 5%

How would your yield curves change if people preferred shorter-term bonds over longer-term bonds?

25. The table below shows current and expected future one-year interest rates, as well as current interest rates on multi-year bonds. Use the table to calculate the liquidity premium for each multi-year bond.

Year	1-Year Bond Rate	Multi-Year Bond Rate
1	2%	2%
2	3%	3%
3	4%	5%
4	6%	6%
5	7%	8%

DATA ANALYSIS PROBLEMS

Download data for these problems from MyEconLab *at* **www.myeconlab.com**.

1. Go to the CANSIM database and download monthly data from January 1976 to January 2015 on the three-month T-bill rate (series V122531) and the interest rate on long-term Canada bonds (series V122544).

   a. Calculate the mean and standard deviation as well as the maximum and minimum values for each series over the sample period.

   b. When is the spread between the long-term rate and the T-bill rate the highest? The lowest?

2. Go to the CANSIM database and find monthly yield data on the following government securities: one month (series V122529), three month (series V122531), six month (series V122532), one year (series V122533), two year (series V122538), three year (series V122539), five year (series V122540), 10 year (series V122543), and long term (series V122544). Download the last full year of data available into a spreadsheet.

   a. Construct a yield curve by creating a line graph for the most recent month of data available, and for the same month (or as close to the same month as possible) one year prior across all the maturities.

   b. How do the yield curves compare? What does the changing slope say about potential changes in economic conditions?

3. Go to the St. Louis Federal Reserve FRED database, and find U.S. data on Moody's Aaa corporate bond yield (AAA) and Moody's Baa corporate bond yield (BAA). Download the data into a spreadsheet.

   a. Calculate the spread (difference) between the Baa and Aaa corporate bond yields for the most recent month of data available. What does this difference represent?

   b. Calculate the spread again for the same month but one year prior, and compare the result to your answer to part (a). What do your answers say about how the risk premium has changed over the past year?

   c. Identify the month of highest and lowest spreads since the beginning of the year 2000. How do these spreads compare to the most current spread data available? Interpret the results.

WEB EXERCISES

1. Go to **www.bloomberg.com** and click on "Markets" and then "Rates & Bonds" to find information about the yield curve in Australia, Germany, Japan, the United Kingdom, and the United States. What does each of these yield curves tell us about the public's expectations of future movements of short-term interest rates?

2. Figure 6-6 shows a number of yield curves at various points in time. Go to **http://fxtrade.oanda.ca/analysis/economic-indicators/canada/rates/yield-curve** and find the Canadian yield curve. Does the current yield curve fall above or below the most recent one listed in Figure 6-6? Is the current yield curve flatter or steeper than the most recent one reported in Figure 6-6?

WEB REFERENCES

www.bankofcanada.ca/rates/interest-rates/canadian-bonds
The Bank of Canada reports selected bond yields.

http://stockcharts.com/charts/YieldCurve.html
This site lets you look at the dynamic yield curve at any point in time since 1995.

7

The Stock Market, the Theory of Rational Expectations, and the Efficient Market Hypothesis

Learning Objectives

At the end of this chapter you should be able to

1. Calculate the price of common stock.

2. Recognize the impact of new information on stock prices.

3. Compare and contrast adaptive expectations and rational expectations.

4. Explain why arbitrage opportunities imply that the efficient market hypothesis holds.

5. Identify and explain the implications of the efficient market hypothesis for financial markets.

6. Summarize the reasons why behavioural finance suggests that the efficient market hypothesis may not hold.

PREVIEW

Rarely does a day go by that the stock market isn't a major news item. We have witnessed huge swings in the stock market in recent years. The 1990s were an extraordinary decade for stocks: the S&P/TSX Composite in Canada and the Dow Jones and S&P 500 indexes in the United States increased more than 400%, while the tech-based NASDAQ index rose more than 1000%. By early 2002, these indexes had reached record highs. Unfortunately, the good times did not last. Starting in early 2000, the stock market began to decline and many investors lost their shirts. The S&P/TSX crashed, falling by more than 40% through March 2003. After subsequently rising over 120%, the stock market crashed again during the global financial crisis, falling by over 40% from its peak in the fall of 2007. Starting in 2009, the stock market recovered quickly, rising by more than 50% by 2014.

Because so many people invest in the stock market and the prices of stocks affect the ability of people to retire comfortably, the market for stocks is undoubtedly the financial market that receives the most attention and scrutiny. In this chapter, we look first at how this important market works.

We begin by discussing the fundamental theories that underlie the valuation of stocks. These theories are critical to understanding the forces that cause the value of stocks to rise and fall minute by minute and day by day. Once we have learned the methods for stock valuation, we need to explore how expectations about the market affect its behaviour. We do so by examining the *theory of rational expectations*. When this theory is applied to financial markets, the outcome is the *efficient market hypothesis*, which has some general implications for how markets in other securities besides stocks operate. The theory of rational expectations is also central to debates about the conduct of monetary policy, to be discussed in Chapter 23.

COMPUTING THE PRICE OF COMMON STOCK

Common stock is the principal medium through which corporations raise equity capital. **Stockholders**—those who hold stock in a corporation—own an interest in the corporation equal to the percentage of outstanding shares they own. This ownership interest gives them a bundle of rights. The most important are the right to vote and to be a residual claimant of all funds flowing into the firm (known as cash flows), meaning that the stockholder receives whatever remains after all other claims against the firm's assets have been satisfied. Stockholders may receive dividends from the net earnings of the corporation. **Dividends** are payments made periodically, usually every quarter, to stockholders. The board of directors of the firm sets the level of the dividend, usually based on the recommendation of management. In addition, the stockholder has the right to sell the stock.

One basic principle of finance is that the value of any investment is calculated by computing the present value of all cash flows the investment will generate over its life. For example, a commercial building will sell for a price that reflects the net cash flows (rents minus expenses) it is projected to have over its useful life. Similarly, we value common stock as the value in today's dollars of all future cash flows. The cash flows that a stockholder might earn from stock are dividends, the sales price, or both.

To develop the theory of stock valuation, we begin with the simplest possible scenario: You buy the stock, hold it for one period to get a dividend, then sell the stock. We call this the *one-period valuation model*.

The One-Period Valuation Model

Suppose that you have some extra money to invest for one year. After a year, you will need to sell your investment to pay tuition. After watching the Business News Network (BNN) on TV, you decide that you want to buy Royal Bank stock. You call your broker and find that Royal Bank is currently selling for $50 per share and pays $0.16 per year in dividends. The analyst on BNN predicts that the stock will be selling for $60 in one year. Should you buy this stock?

To answer this question, you need to determine whether the current price accurately reflects the analyst's forecast. To value the stock today, you need to find the present discounted value of the expected cash flows (future payments) using the formula in Equation 1 of Chapter 4. In this equation, the discount factor used to discount the cash flows is the required return on investments in equity rather than the interest rate. The cash flows consist of one dividend payment plus a final sales price. When these cash flows are discounted back to the present, the following equation computes the current price of the stock:

$$P_0 = \frac{D_1}{(1 + k_e)} + \frac{P_1}{(1 + k_e)} \qquad \text{(Equation 1)}$$

where
P_0 = the current price of the stock. The zero subscript refers to time period zero, or the present.
D_1 = the dividend paid at the end of year 1
k_e = the required return on equity investments
P_1 = the price at the end of the first period; the predicted sales price of the stock

To see how Equation 1 works, let's compute the price of the Royal Bank stock if, after careful consideration, you decide that you would be satisfied to earn a 12% return on the investment. If you have decided that $k_e = 0.12$, are told that Royal Bank pays $0.16 per year in dividends ($Div_1 = 0.16$), and forecast that the share price of $60 for next year ($P_1 = \$60$), you get the following result from Equation 1:

$$P_0 = \frac{0.16}{1 + 0.12} + \frac{\$60}{1 + 0.12} = \$0.14 + \$53.57 = \$53.71$$

On the basis of your analysis, you find that the present value of all cash flows from the stock is $53.71. Because the stock is currently priced at $50 per share, you would choose to buy it. However, you should be aware that the stock may be selling for less than $53.71, because other investors have placed a greater risk on the cash flows or estimated the cash flows to be less than you did.

The Generalized Dividend Valuation Model

Using the present value concept, we can extend the one-period dividend valuation model to any number of periods: The value of a stock today is the present value of all future cash flows. The only cash flows that an investor will receive are dividends and a final sales price when the stock is ultimately sold in period n. The generalized multi-period formula for stock valuation can be written as

$$P_0 = \frac{D_1}{(1 + k_e)^1} + \frac{D_2}{(1 + k_e)^2} + \cdots + \frac{D_n}{(1 + k_e)^n} + \frac{P_n}{(1 + k_e)^n} \quad \text{(Equation 2)}$$

where
$$P_n = \text{the price of the stock in period } n$$
$$D_i = \text{the dividend paid at the end of year } i$$

If you tried to use Equation 2 to find the value of a share of stock, you would soon realize that you must first estimate the value the stock will have at some point in the future before you can estimate its value today. In other words, you must find P_n before you can find P_0. However, if P_n is far in the future, it will not affect P_0. For example, the present value of a share of stock that sells for $50 seventy-five years from now, using a 12% discount rate, is just one cent [$50/(1.12^{75}) = $0.01]. This reasoning implies that the current value of a share of stock can be calculated as simply the present value of the future dividend stream. The **generalized dividend model** is given in Equation 3. Note that it is the same formula as Equation 2, but without the final sales price:

$$P_0 = \sum_{t=1}^{\infty} \frac{D_t}{(1 + k_e)^t} \quad \text{(Equation 3)}$$

Consider the implications of Equation 3 for a moment. The generalized dividend model states that the price of a stock is determined only by the present value of the dividends and that nothing else matters. Many stocks do not pay dividends, so how is it that these stocks have value? *Buyers of the stock expect that the firm will pay dividends someday.* Most of the time a firm institutes dividends as soon as it has completed the rapid growth phase of its life cycle.

The generalized dividend valuation model requires that we compute the present value of an infinite stream of dividends, a process that could be difficult, to say the least. Therefore, simplified models have been developed to make the calculations easier. One such model is the **Gordon growth model**, which assumes constant dividend growth.

The Gordon Growth Model

Many firms strive to increase their dividends at a constant rate each year. Equation 4 is derived from Equation 3 to reflect this constant growth in dividends:

$$P_0 = \frac{D_0 \times (1 + g)^1}{(1 + k_e)^1} + \frac{D_0 \times (1 + g)^2}{(1 + k_e)^2} + \cdots + \frac{D_0 \times (1 + g)^{\infty}}{(1 + k_e)^{\infty}} \quad \text{(Equation 4)}$$

where
$$D_0 = \text{the most recent dividend paid}$$
$$g = \text{the expected constant growth rate in dividends}$$
$$k_e = \text{the required return on equity investments}$$

Equation 4 can be simplified to obtain Equation 5:[1]

$$P_0 = \frac{D_0 \times (1 + g)}{(k_e - g)} = \frac{D_1}{(k_e - g)} \qquad \text{(Equation 5)}$$

This model is useful for finding the value of a stock, given a few assumptions:

1. *Dividends are assumed to continue growing at a constant rate forever.* Actually, as long as the dividends are expected to grow at a constant rate for an extended period of time, the model should yield reasonable results becuase errors about distant cash flows become small when discounted to the present.
2. *The growth rate is assumed to be less than the required return on equity, k_e.* Myron Gordon, in his development of the model, demonstrated that this is a reasonable assumption. In theory, if the growth rate were faster than the rate demanded by holders of the firm's equity, then in the long run the firm would grow impossibly large.

HOW THE MARKET SETS STOCK PRICES

Suppose you go to an auto auction. The cars are available for inspection before the auction begins, and you find a little Mazda Miata that you like. You test-drive it in the parking lot and notice that it makes a few strange noises, but you decide that you still like the car. You decide that $5000 is a fair price that will allow you to pay some repair bills should the noises turn out to be serious. You see that the auction is ready to begin, so you go in and wait for the Miata to be auctioned.

Suppose another buyer also spots the Miata. She test-drives the car and recognizes that the noises are simply the result of worn brake pads that she can fix herself at a nominal cost. She decides that the car is worth $7000. She also goes in and waits for the Miata to come up for auction.

---

[1]To generate Equation 5 from Equation 4, first multiply both sides of Equation 4 by $(1 + k_e)/(1 + g)$, and then subtract Equation 4 from the result. This yields

$$\frac{P_0 \times (1 + k_e)}{(1 + g)} - P_0 = D_0 - \frac{D_0 \times (1 + g)^\infty}{(1 + k_e)^\infty}$$

Assuming that k_e is greater than g, the term on the far right will approach zero and so can be dropped. Thus, after factoring P_0 out of the left-hand side,

$$P_0 \times \left[\frac{1 + k_e}{1 + g} - 1 \right] = D_0$$

Next, simplify by combining terms:

$$P_0 \times \frac{(1 + k_e) - (1 + g)}{1 + g} = D_0$$

$$P_0 = \frac{D_0 \times (1 + g)}{k_e - g} = \frac{D_1}{k_e - g}$$

Who will buy the car, and for how much? Suppose only the two of you are interested in the Miata. You begin the bidding at $4000. Your competitor ups your bid to $4500. You bid your top price of $5000. She counters with $5100. The price is now higher than you are willing to pay, so you stop bidding. The car is sold to the more informed buyer for $5100.

This simple example raises a number of important points. First, the price is set by the buyer who is willing to pay the highest price. This price is not necessarily the highest price the asset could fetch, but it is incrementally greater than what any other buyer is willing to pay.

Second, the market price will be set by the buyer who can take best advantage of the asset. The buyer who purchased the car knew that she could fix the noise easily and cheaply. As a consequence, she was willing to pay more for the car than you were. The same concept holds for other assets. For example, a piece of property or a building will sell to the buyer who can put the asset to the most productive use.

Finally, the example shows the role played by information in asset pricing. Superior information about an asset can increase its value by reducing its risk. When you consider buying a stock, the future cash flows are subject to many unknowns. The buyer who has the best information about these cash flows will discount them at a lower interest rate than will a buyer who is very uncertain.

Now let's apply these ideas to stock valuation. Suppose you are considering the purchase of stock expected to pay a $2 dividend next year. Market analysts expect the firm to grow at 3% indefinitely. You are *uncertain* about both the constancy of the dividend stream and the accuracy of the estimated growth rate. To compensate yourself for this uncertainty (risk), you require a return of 15%.

Now suppose Jennifer, another investor, has spoken with industry insiders and feels more confident about the projected cash flows. Jennifer requires only a 12% return because her perceived risk is lower than yours. Bud, on the other hand, is dating the CEO of the company. He knows with more certainty what the future of the firm actually looks like, and thus requires only a 10% return.

What value will each investor give to the stock? Applying the Gordon growth model yields the following stock prices:

Investor	Discount Rate	Stock Price
You	15%	$16.67
Jennifer	12%	$22.22
Bud	10%	$28.57

You are willing to pay $16.67 for the stock. Jennifer will pay up to $22.22, and Bud will pay $28.57. The investor with the lowest perceived risk is willing to pay the most for the stock. If there were no other traders but these three, the market price would be between $22.22 and $28.57. If you already held the stock, you would sell it to Bud.

We thus see that the players in the market, bidding against one another, establish the market price. When new information is released about a firm, expectations change, and with them, prices change. New information can cause changes in expectations about the level of future dividends or the risk of those dividends. Because market participants are constantly receiving new information and revising their expectations, it is reasonable that stock prices are constantly changing as well.

APPLICATION   Monetary Policy and Stock Prices

Stock market analysts tend to hang on every word uttered by the governor of the Bank of Canada because they know that an important determinant of stock prices is monetary policy. But how does monetary policy affect stock prices?

The Gordon growth model in Equation 5 explains this relationship. Monetary policy can affect stock prices in two ways. First, when the Bank of Canada lowers interest rates, the return on bonds (an alternative asset to stocks) declines, and investors are likely to accept a lower required rate of return on an investment in equity (k_e). The resulting decline in k_e lowers the denominator in the Gordon growth model (Equation 5), leads to a higher value of P_0, and raises stock prices. Furthermore, a lowering of interest rates is likely to stimulate the economy, so the growth rate in dividends, g, is likely to be somewhat higher. This rise in g also causes the denominator in Equation 5 to decrease, which also leads to a higher P_0 and a rise in stock prices.

As we will see in Chapter 26, the impact of monetary policy on stock prices is one of the key ways in which monetary policy affects the economy.

APPLICATION   The Global Financial Crisis and the Stock Market

The global financial crisis that started in August 2007 led to one of the worst stock market declines in the past 50 years. Our analysis of stock price valuation, again using the Gordon growth model, can help us understand how this event affected stock prices.

The global financial crisis had a major negative impact on the economy, leading to a downward revision of the growth prospects for Canadian companies, thus lowering the dividend growth rate (g) in the Gordon model. In terms of Equation 5, the resulting increase in the denominator would lead to a decline in P_0 and hence a decline in stock prices.

Increased uncertainty about the Canadian economy and the widening credit spreads caused by the subprime crisis also raised the required return on investment in equity. In terms of Equation 5, a higher k_e leads to an increase in the denominator, a decline in P_0, and a general fall in stock prices.

In the early stages of the global financial crisis, the declines in growth prospects and credit spreads were moderate, and so, as the Gordon model predicts, the stock market decline was also moderate. However, when the crisis entered a particularly virulent stage in October 2008, credit spreads shot through the roof, the economy tanked, and as the Gordon model predicts, the stock market crashed. From its peak in October 2007 (high of S&P/TSX of 14 625) to the bottom in February 2009 (S&P/TSX low of 8123) the market lost 45% of its value. ◆

THE THEORY OF RATIONAL EXPECTATIONS

The analysis of stock price evaluation outlined in the previous section depends on people's expectations—especially expectations of cash flows. Indeed, it is difficult to think of any sector of the economy in which expectations are not crucial; this is why it is important to examine how expectations are formed. We do so by outlining the *theory of rational expectations*, currently the most widely used theory to describe the formation of business and consumer expectations.

In the 1950s and 1960s, economists regularly viewed expectations as formed from past experience only. Expectations of inflation, for example, were typically viewed as being an average of past inflation rates. This view of expectation formation, called **adaptive expectations**, suggests that changes in expectations will occur slowly over time, as data for a variable evolve.[2] So, if inflation had formerly been steady at a 5% rate, expectations of future inflation would be 5%, too. If inflation rose to a steady rate of 10%, expectations of future inflation would rise toward 10%, but slowly: In the first year, expected inflation might rise only to 6%; in the second year, to 7%; and so on.

The adaptive expectations hypothesis has been faulted on the grounds that people use more information than just past data on a single variable to form their expectations of that variable. Their expectations of inflation will almost surely be affected by their predictions of future monetary policy, as well as by current and past monetary policy. In addition, people often change their expectations quickly in the light of new information. To address these objections to the validity of adaptive expectations, John Muth developed an alternative theory of expectations, called **rational expectations**, which can be stated as follows: *Expectations will be identical to optimal forecasts (the best guess of the future) using all available information.*[3]

What exactly does this mean? To explain it more clearly, let's use the theory of rational expectations to examine how expectations are formed in a situation that most of us will encounter at some point in our lifetime: our drive to work. Suppose that if Joe Commuter travels when it is not rush hour, his trip takes an average of 30 minutes. Sometimes his trip takes 35 minutes; other times, 25 minutes; but the average, non-rush-hour driving time is 30 minutes. If, however, Joe leaves for work during the rush hour, it takes him, on average, an additional 10 minutes to get to work. Given that he leaves for work during the rush hour, the best guess of his driving time—the **optimal forecast**—is 40 minutes.

If the only information available to Joe before he leaves for work related to his driving time is that he is leaving during the rush hour, what does rational expectations theory allow you to predict about Joe's expectations of his driving time? Since the best guess of his driving time, using all available information, is 40 minutes, Joe's expectation should be the same. Clearly, an expectation of 35 minutes would not be rational, because it is not equal to the optimal forecast, or the best guess of the driving time.

Suppose that the next day, given the same conditions and expectations, it takes Joe 45 minutes to drive to work because he hits an abnormally large number of red lights. The day after that, Joe hits all the lights right and it takes him only 35 minutes to drive to work. Do these variations mean that Joe's 40-minute expectation is irrational? No; an expectation of 40 minutes' driving time is still a rational

---

[2]More specifically, adaptive expectations—say, of inflation—are written as a weighted average of past inflation rates:

$$\pi_t^e = (1 - \lambda) \sum_{j=0}^{\infty} \lambda^j \pi_{t-j}$$

where

$$\pi_t^e = \text{adaptive expectation of inflation at time } t$$
$$\pi_{t-j} = \text{inflation at time } t - j$$
$$\lambda = \text{a constant between the values of 0 and 1}$$

[3]John Muth, "Rational Expectations and the Theory of Price Movements," *Econometrica* 29 (1961): 315–335.

expectation. In both cases, the forecast is off by five minutes, so the expectation has not been perfectly accurate each time. However, the forecast does not have to be perfectly accurate to be rational—it need only be the *best possible* forecast given the available information; that is, it has to be correct *on average*, and the 40-minute expectation meets this requirement. As there is bound to be some randomness in Joe's driving time regardless of driving conditions, an optimal forecast will never be completely accurate.

The example makes the following important point about rational expectations: *Even though a rational expectation equals the optimal forecast using all available information, a prediction based on it may not always be perfectly accurate.*

What if an item of information relevant to predicting driving time is unavailable or ignored? Suppose that on Joe's usual route to work, an accident occurs and causes a two-hour traffic jam. If Joe has no way of ascertaining this information, his rush-hour expectation of 40 minutes' driving time is still rational, because the accident information is not available to him for incorporation into his optimal forecast. However, if there was a radio or TV traffic report about the accident that Joe did not bother to listen to, or heard but ignored, his 40-minute expectation is no longer rational. In light of the availability of this information, Joe's optimal forecast should have been two hours and 40 minutes.

Accordingly, an expectation may fail to be rational for two reasons:

1. People might be aware of all available information but find it takes too much effort to make their expectation the best guess possible.
2. People might be unaware of some available relevant information, so their best guess of the future will not be accurate.

Nonetheless, it is important to recognize that if an additional factor is important but information about it is not available, an expectation that does not take that factor into account can still be rational.

Formal Statement of the Theory

We can state the theory of rational expectations somewhat more formally. If X stands for the variable that is being forecast (in our example, Joe Commuter's driving time), X^e for the expectation of this variable (Joe's expectation of his driving time), and X^{of} for the optimal forecast of X using all available information (the best guess possible of Joe's driving time), the theory of rational expectations then simply states

$$X^e = X^{of} \qquad \text{(Equation 6)}$$

That is, the expectation of X equals the optimal forecast using all available information.

Rationale Behind the Theory

Why do people try to make their expectations match their best possible guess of future results, using all available information? The simplest explanation is that it is costly for people not to do so. Joe Commuter has a strong incentive to make his expectation of the time it takes him to drive to work as accurate as possible. If he underpredicts his driving time, he will often be late to work and risk being fired. If he overpredicts, he will, on average, get to work too early and will have given up sleep or leisure time unnecessarily. Accurate expectations are desirable, and therefore people have a strong incentive to try to make expectations equal to optimal forecasts by using all available information.

The same principle applies to businesses. Suppose an appliance manufacturer—say, General Electric—knows that interest-rate movements are important to the sales of appliances. If GE makes poor forecasts of interest rates, it will earn less profit because it will produce either too many or too few appliances. The incentives are strong for GE to acquire all available information to help it forecast interest rates and make the best possible guess of future interestrate movements.

The incentives for equating expectations with optimal forecasts are especially strong in financial markets. In these markets, people with better forecasts of the future get rich. The application of the theory of rational expectations to financial markets (where it is called the **efficient market hypothesis** or the **theory of efficient capital markets**) is thus particularly useful.

Implications of the Theory

Rational expectations theory leads to two commonsense implications regarding the formation of expectations. These implications are important in the analysis of both the stock market and the aggregate economy:

1. *If there is a change in the way a variable moves, the way in which expectations of this variable are formed will change as well*. This tenet of rational expectations theory can be most easily understood through a concrete example. Suppose interest rates move in such a way that they tend to return to a "normal" level over time. If today's interest rate is high relative to the normal level, an optimal forecast of the interest rate in the future is that it will decline to the normal level. Rational expectations theory would imply that when today's interest rate is high, the expectation is that it will fall in the future.

Suppose now that the way in which the interest rate moves changes so that when the interest rate is high, it stays high. In this case, when today's interest rate is high, the optimal forecast of the future interest rate, and hence the rational expectation, is that it will stay high. Expectations of the future interest rate will no longer indicate that the interest rate will fall. The change in the way the interest-rate variable moves has therefore led to a change in the way that expectations of future interest rates are formed. The rational expectations analysis here is generalizable to expectations of any variable. Hence, when a change occurs in the way any variable moves, the way in which expectations of this variable are formed will change, too.

2. *The forecast errors of expectations will, on average, be zero and cannot be predicted ahead of time*. The forecast error of an expectation is $X - X^e$, the difference between the realization of a variable X and the expectation of the variable. That is, if Joe Commuter's driving time on a particular day is 45 minutes and his expectation of the driving time is 40 minutes, the forecast error is five minutes.

Suppose that in violation of the rational expectations tenet, Joe's forecast error is not, on average, equal to zero; instead, it equals five minutes. The forecast error is now predictable ahead of time because Joe will soon notice that he is, on average, five minutes late for work and can improve his forecast by increasing it by five minutes. Rational expectations theory implies that this is exactly what Joe will do because he will want his forecast to be the best guess possible. When Joe has revised his forecast upward by five minutes, on average, the forecast error will equal zero, so it cannot be predicted ahead of time. Rational expectations theory implies that forecast errors of expectations cannot be predicted.

THE EFFICIENT MARKET HYPOTHESIS: RATIONAL EXPECTATIONS IN FINANCIAL MARKETS

While monetary economists were developing the theory of rational expectations, financial economists were developing a parallel theory of expectations formation for financial markets. It led them to the same conclusion as that of the rational expectations theorists: Expectations in financial markets are equal to optimal forecasts using all available information.[4] Although financial economists, such as Eugene Fama, winner of the 2013 Nobel Prize in economics, gave their theory another name, calling it the *efficient market hypothesis*, in fact their theory is just an application of rational expectations to the pricing of stocks and other securities.

The efficient market hypothesis is based on the assumption that prices of securities in financial markets fully reflect all available information. You may recall from Chapter 4 that the rate of return from holding a security equals the sum of the capital gain on the security (the change in the price), plus any cash payments, divided by the initial purchase price of the security:

$$R = \frac{P_{t+1} - P_t + C}{P_t} \qquad \text{(Equation 7)}$$

where

R = rate of return on the security held from time t to time $t + 1$ (say, the end of 2015 to the end of 2016)

P_{t+1} = price of the security at time $t + 1$, the end of the holding period

P_t = price of the security at time t, the beginning of the holding period

C = cash payment (coupon or dividend payments) made in the period t to $t + 1$

Let's look at the expectation of this return at time t, the beginning of the holding period. Because the current price P_t and the cash payment C are known at the outset, the only variable in the definition of the return that is uncertain is the price next period, P_{t+1}.[5] Denoting expectation of the security's price at the end of the holding period as P_{t+1}^e, the expected return R^e is

$$R^e = \frac{P_{t+1}^e - P_t + C}{P_t}$$

The efficient market hypothesis views expectations of future prices as equal to optimal forecasts using all currently available information. In other words, the market's expectations of future securities prices are rational, so that

$$P_{t+1}^e = P_{t+1}^{of}$$

which in turn implies that the expected return on the security will equal the optimal forecast of the return:

$$R^e = R^{of} \qquad \text{(Equation 8)}$$

---

[4]The development of the efficient market hypothesis was not wholly independent of the development of rational expectations theory in that financial economists were aware of Muth's work.

[5]There are cases in which C might not be known at the beginning of the period, but that does not make a substantial difference to the analysis. We would in that case assume that not only price expectations but also the expectations of C are optimal forecasts using all available information.

Unfortunately, we cannot observe either R^e or P^e_{t+1}, so the rational expectations equations by themselves do not tell us much about how the financial market behaves. However, if we can devise some way to measure the value of R^e, these equations will have important implications for how prices of securities change in financial markets.

The supply and demand analysis of the bond market that we developed in Chapter 5 showed us that the expected return on a security (the interest rate, in the case of the one-year discount bond we examined) will have a tendency to move toward the equilibrium return that equates the quantity demanded to the quantity supplied. Supply and demand analysis enables us to determine the expected return on a security with the following equilibrium condition: The expected return on a security R^e equals the equilibrium return R^*, which equates the quantity of the security demanded to the quantity supplied; that is,

$$R^e = R^* \qquad\qquad \text{(Equation 9)}$$

The academic field of finance explores the factors (risk and liquidity, for example) that influence the equilibrium returns on securities. For our purposes, it is sufficient to know that we can determine the equilibrium return and thus determine the expected return with the equilibrium condition.

We can derive an equation to describe pricing behaviour in an efficient market by using the equilibrium condition to replace R^e with R^* in the rational expectations equation (Equation 8). In this way, we obtain

$$R^{of} = R^* \qquad\qquad \text{(Equation 10)}$$

This equation tells us that *current prices in a financial market will be set so that the optimal forecast of a security's return using all available information equals the security's equilibrium return*. Financial economists state it more simply: In an efficient market, a security's price fully reflects all available information.

Rationale Behind the Hypothesis

To see why the efficient market hypothesis makes sense, we make use of the concept of **arbitrage**, in which market participants (*arbitrageurs*) eliminate **unexploited profit opportunities**, that is, returns on a security that are larger than what is justified by the characteristics of that security. Arbitrage is of two types: *pure arbitrage*, in which the elimination of unexploited profit opportunities involves no risk, and the type of arbitrage we discuss here, in which the arbitrageur takes on some risk when eliminating the unexploited profit opportunities. To see how arbitrage leads to the efficient market hypothesis given a security's risk characteristics, let's look at an example. Suppose the normal return on ExxonMobil common stock is 10% at an annual rate, and its current price P_t is lower than the optimal forecast of tomorrow's price P^{of}_{t+1}, so that the optimal forecast of the return at an annual rate is 50%, which is greater than the equilibrium return of 10%. We are now able to predict that, on average, ExxonMobil's return will be abnormally high, so there is an unexploited profit opportunity. Knowing that, on average, you can earn an abnormally high rate of return on ExxonMobil stock (because $R^{of} > R^*$), you will buy more, which will in turn drive up the stock's current price P_t relative to its expected future price P^{of}_{t+1}, thereby lowering R^{of}. When the current price has risen sufficiently so that R^{of} equals R^* and the efficient market condition (Equation 10) is satisfied, the buying of ExxonMobil stock will stop, and the unexploited profit opportunity will disappear.

Similarly, a security for which the optimal forecast of the return is —5% and the equilibrium return is 10% ($R^{of} < R^*$) would be a poor investment because, on average, the security earns less than the equilibrium return. In such a case, you would sell the security and drive down its current price relative to the expected future price until R^{of} rose to the level of R^* and the efficient market condition was again satisfied. Our discussion can be summarized as follows:

$$R^{of} > R^* \rightarrow P_t\uparrow \rightarrow R^{of}\downarrow$$

$$R^{of} < R^* \rightarrow P_t\downarrow \rightarrow R^{of}\uparrow$$

until

$$R^{of} = R^*$$

Another way to state the efficient market condition is this: ***In an efficient market, all unexploited profit opportunities will be eliminated***.

An extremely important factor in this reasoning is that ***not everyone in a financial market must be well informed about a security or have rational expectations for its price to be driven to the point at which the efficient market condition holds***. Financial markets are structured so that many participants can play. As long as a few people (often referred to as the "smart money") keep their eyes open for unexploited profit opportunities, they will eliminate the profit opportunities that appear, because in doing so they make a profit. The efficient market hypothesis makes sense because it does not require that everyone in a market be cognizant of what is happening to every security.

Random-Walk Behaviour of Stock Prices

The term **random walk** describes the movements of a variable whose future values cannot be predicted (are random) because, given today's value, the value of the variable is just as likely to fall as it is to rise. An important implication of the efficient market hypothesis is that stock prices should approximately follow a random walk; that is, ***future changes in stock prices should, for all practical purposes, be unpredictable***. The random-walk implication of the efficient market hypothesis is the one most commonly mentioned in the press because it is the most readily comprehensible to the public. In fact, when people mention the "random-walk theory of stock prices," they are in reality referring to the efficient market hypothesis.

The case for random-walk stock prices can be demonstrated. Suppose people could predict that the price of Happy Feet Corporation (HFC) stock would rise 1% in the coming week. The predicted rate of capital gains and rate of return on HFC stock would then exceed 50% at an annual rate. Since this is very likely to be far higher than the equilibrium rate of return on HFC stock ($R^{of} > R^*$), the efficient market hypothesis indicates that people would immediately buy this stock and bid up its current price. The action would stop only when the predictable change in the price dropped to near zero, so that $R^{of} = R^*$.

Similarly, if people could predict that the price of HFC stock would fall by 1%, the predicted rate of return would be negative ($R^{of} > R^*$), and people would immediately sell the stock. The current price would fall until the predictable change in the price rose back to near zero, where the efficient market condition again would hold. The efficient market hypothesis suggests that the predictable change in stock prices will be near zero, leading to the conclusion that stock prices will generally follow a

Global   Should Foreign Exchange Rates Follow a Random Walk?

Although the efficient market hypothesis is usually applied to the stock market, it can also be used to show that foreign exchange rates, like stock prices, should generally follow a random walk. To see why this is the case, consider what would happen if investors could predict that a currency would rise in value by 1% in the coming week. By buying this currency, they could earn a greater than 50% return at an annual rate, which is likely to be far above the equilibrium return for holding a currency. As a result, investors would immediately buy the currency and bid up its current price, thereby reducing the expected return. The process would only stop when the predictable change in the exchange rate dropped to near zero so that the optimal forecast of the return no longer differed from the equilibrium return. Likewise, if investors could predict that the currency would fall in value by 1% in the coming week, they would sell it until the predictable change in the exchange rate was again near zero. The efficient market hypothesis therefore implies that future changes in exchange rates should, for all practical purposes, be unpredictable; in other words, exchange rates should follow random walks. Indeed, the random-walk behaviour of exchange rates is exactly what is found in the data.

random walk.[6] As the Global box "Should Foreign Exchange Rates Follow a Random Walk?" indicates, the efficient market hypothesis suggests that foreign exchange rates should also follow a random walk.

APPLICATION   Practical Guide to Investing in the Stock Market

The efficient market hypothesis has numerous applications to the real world.[7] It is especially valuable because it can be applied directly to an issue that concerns many of us: how to get rich (or at least not get poor) by investing in the stock market. A practical guide to investing in the stock market, which we develop here, provides a better understanding of the use and implications of the efficient market hypothesis.

How Valuable Are Reports Published by Investment Advisers?

Suppose you have just read in the Report on Business section of the *Globe and Mail* that investment advisers are predicting a boom in oil stocks because an oil shortage is developing. Should you proceed to withdraw all of your hard-earned savings from the bank and invest them in oil stocks?

---

[6]Note that the random-walk behaviour of stock prices is only an *approximation* derived from the efficient market hypothesis. Random-walk behaviour would hold *exactly* only for a stock for which an unchanged price leads to its having the equilibrium return. Then, when the predictable change in the stock price is exactly zero, $R^{of} = R^*$.

[7] The empirical evidence on the efficient market hypothesis is discussed in an appendix to this chapter, which can be found on the MyEconLab.

The efficient market hypothesis tells us that when purchasing a security, we cannot expect to earn an abnormally high return, or a return greater than the equilibrium return. Information in newspapers and in the published reports of investment advisers is readily available to many market participants and is already reflected in market prices. So acting on this information will not yield abnormally high returns, on average. The empirical evidence for the most part confirms that recommendations from investment advisers cannot help us outperform the general market. Indeed, as the FYI box suggests, human investment advisers in San Francisco do not, on average, even outperform an orangutan!

Probably no other conclusion is met with more skepticism by students than this one when they first hear it. We all know, or have heard of, someone who has been successful in the stock market for a period of many years. We wonder, "How could someone be so consistently successful if he or she did not really know how to predict when returns would be abnormally high?" The following story, reported in the press, illustrates why such anecdotal evidence is not reliable.

A get-rich-quick artist invented a clever scam. Every week, he wrote two letters. In letter A, he would pick team A to win a particular football game; in letter B, he would pick the opponent, team B. He would then separate a mailing list into two groups, and he would send letter A to the people in one group and letter B to the people in the other. The following week he would do the same thing, but this time he would send these letters only to the group who had received the first letters containing the correct prediction. After doing this for 10 games, he had a small cluster of people who had received letters predicting the correct winning team for every game. He then mailed a final letter to this group, declaring that since he was obviously an expert predictor of the outcome of football games (he had picked the winning teams 10 weeks in a row), and since his predictions were profitable for the recipients who bet on the games, he would continue to send his predictions only if he were paid a substantial amount of money. When one of his clients figured out what he was up to, the con man was prosecuted and thrown in jail!

What is the lesson of the story? Even if no forecaster is an accurate predictor of the market, there will always be a group of consistent winners. A person who has done well regularly in the past cannot guarantee that he or she will do well in the future. Note that there will also be a group of persistent losers, but you rarely hear about them because no one brags about a poor forecasting record.

Should You Be Skeptical of Hot Tips?

Suppose your broker phones you with a hot tip to buy stock in the Happy Feet Corporation (HFC) because it has just developed a product that is completely effective in curing athlete's foot. The stock price is sure to go up. Should you follow this advice and buy HFC stock?

The efficient market hypothesis indicates that you should be skeptical of such news. If the stock market is efficient, it has already priced HFC stock so that its expected return will equal the equilibrium return. The hot tip is not particularly valuable and will not enable you to earn an abnormally high return.

You might wonder, though, if the hot tip is based on new information and would give you an edge on the rest of the market. If other market participants have gotten this information before you, the answer again is no. As soon as the information hits the street, the unexploited profit opportunity it creates will be quickly eliminated. The stock's price will already reflect the information, and you should expect to realize only the equilibrium return. But if you are one of the first to gain the new information, it *can* do you some good. Only then can you be one of the lucky ones who, on average, will earn an abnormally high return by helping eliminate the profit opportunity by buying HFC stock.

Do Stock Prices Always Rise When There is Good News?

If you follow the stock market, you might have noticed a puzzling phenomenon: When good news about a corporation, such as a particularly favourable earnings report, is announced, the price of the corporation's stock frequently does not rise. The efficient market hypothesis explains this phenomenon.

Because changes in stock prices are unpredictable, when information is announced that has already been expected by the market, stock prices will remain unchanged. The announcement does not contain any new information that would lead to a change in stock prices. If this were not the case, and the announcement led to a change in stock prices, it would mean that the change was predictable. Because such a scenario is ruled out in an efficient market, **stock prices will respond to announcements only when the information being announced is new and unexpected**. If the news is expected, no stock price response will occur. This is exactly what the evidence shows: Stock prices do reflect publicly available information.

Sometimes an individual stock price declines when good news is announced. Although this seems somewhat peculiar, it is completely consistent with the workings of an efficient market. Suppose that although the announced news is good, it is not as good as expected. HFC's earnings may have risen by 15%, but if the market expected earnings to rise by 20%, the new information is actually unfavourable, and the stock price declines.

Efficient Market Prescription for the Investor

What does the efficient market hypothesis recommend for investing in the stock market? It tells us that hot tips and investment advisers' published recommendations—all of which make use of publicly available information—cannot help an investor outperform the market. Indeed, it indicates that anyone without better information than other market participants cannot expect to beat the market. So what is an investor to do?

The efficient market hypothesis leads to the conclusion that such an investor (and almost all of us fit into this category) should not try to outguess the market by constantly buying and selling securities. This process does nothing but boost the income of brokers, who earn commissions on each trade.[8] Instead, the investor should pursue a "buy and hold" strategy—purchase stocks and hold them for long periods of time. This will lead to the same returns, on average, but the investor's net profits will be higher because fewer brokerage commissions will have to be paid.

A sensible strategy for a small investor, whose costs of managing a portfolio may be high relative to its size, is to buy into a mutual fund rather than to buy individual stocks. Because the efficient market hypothesis indicates that no mutual fund can consistently outperform the market, an investor should not buy into a fund that has high management fees or pays sales commissions to brokers, but rather should purchase a no-load (commission-free) mutual fund that has low management fees.

The evidence indicates that it will not be easy to beat the prescription suggested here, although some anomalies (discussed in Appendix 7.1, Evidence on the Efficient Market Hypothesis, found on this book's MyEconLab) to the efficient market hypothesis suggest that an extremely clever investor (that rules out most of us) may be able to outperform a buy-and-hold strategy. ◆

WHY THE EFFICIENT MARKET HYPOTHESIS DOES NOT IMPLY THAT FINANCIAL MARKETS ARE EFFICIENT

Many financial economists take the efficient market hypothesis one step further in their analysis of financial markets. Not only do they believe that expectations in financial markets are rational—that is, equal to optimal forecasts using all available information—but they also add the condition that prices in financial markets reflect the true fundamental (intrinsic) value of the securities. In other words, all prices are always correct and reflect **market fundamentals** (items that have a direct impact on future income streams of the securities), and so financial markets are efficient.

This stronger view of market efficiency has several important implications in the academic field of finance. First, it implies that in an efficient capital market, one investment is as good as any other because the securities' prices are correct. Second, it implies that a security's price reflects all available information about the intrinsic value of the security. Third, it implies that securities prices can be used by managers of both financial and nonfinancial firms to assess their costs of capital (costs of financing their investments) accurately and hence that securities prices can be used to help these managers make correct decisions about whether a specific investment

---

[8]The investor may also have to pay Revenue Canada capital gains taxes on any profits that are realized when a security is sold—an additional reason why continual buying and selling does not make sense.

is worth making. This stronger version of market efficiency is a basic tenet of much analysis in the finance field.

The efficient market hypothesis may be misnamed, however. It does not imply the stronger view of market efficiency, but rather just that prices in markets like the stock market are unpredictable. Indeed, as the following application suggests, the existence of market crashes and **bubbles**, in which the prices of assets rise well above their fundamental values, casts serious doubt on the stronger view that financial markets are efficient. However, market crashes and bubbles do not necessarily provide strong evidence against the basic tenets of the efficient market hypothesis.

APPLICATION   What Do Stock Market Crashes Tell Us About the Efficient Market Hypothesis and the Efficiency of Financial Markets?

On October 19, 1987, dubbed "Black Monday," the Dow Jones Industrial Average declined by more than 20%, the largest one-day decline in U.S. history. The collapse of the high-tech companies' share prices from their peaks in March 2000 caused the heavily-tech-laden NASDAQ index to fall from about 5000 in March 2000 to about 1500 in 2001 and 2002, a decline of well over 60%. These stock market crashes caused many economists to question the validity of the efficient market hypothesis. These economists do not believe that a rational marketplace could have produced such a massive swing in share prices. To what degree should these stock market crashes make us doubt the validity of the efficient market hypothesis?

Nothing in efficient markets theory rules out large changes in stock prices. A large change in stock prices can result from new information that produces a dramatic decline in optimal forecasts of the future valuation of firms. However, economists are hard pressed to find fundamental changes in the economy that would have caused the Black Monday and tech crashes. One lesson from these crashes is that factors other than market fundamentals probably have an effect on asset prices. Indeed, as we will explore in Chapters 8 and 9, there are good reasons to believe that impediments to the proper functioning of financial markets do exist. Hence these crashes have convinced many economists that the stronger version of market efficiency, which states that asset prices reflect the true fundamental (intrinsic) value of securities, is incorrect. These economists attribute a large role in determination of stock and other asset prices to market psychology and to the institutional structure of the marketplace. However, nothing in this view contradicts the basic reasoning behind rational expectations or the efficient market hypothesis—that market participants eliminate unexploited profit opportunities. Even though stock market prices may not always solely reflect market fundamentals, as long as market crashes are unpredictable, the basic premises of efficient markets theory hold.

However, other economists believe that market crashes and bubbles suggest that unexploited profit opportunities may exist and that the efficient market hypothesis might be fundamentally flawed. The controversy over the efficient market hypothesis continues. ◆

BEHAVIOURAL FINANCE

Doubts about the efficiency of financial markets, triggered by the stock market crash of 1987, led economists such as 2013 Nobel Prize winner Robert Shiller to develop a new field of study called **behavioural finance**. It applies concepts from other social sciences, such as anthropology, sociology, and particularly psychology, to explain the behaviour of securities prices.[9]

As we have seen, the efficient market hypothesis assumes that unexploited profit opportunities are eliminated by "smart money" market participants. But can smart money dominate ordinary investors so that financial markets are efficient? Specifically, the efficient market hypothesis suggests that smart money participants will sell when a stock price goes up irrationally, with the result that the stock price falls back down to a level that is justified by fundamentals. For this to occur, smart money investors must be able to engage in **short sales**; that is, they must borrow stock from brokers and then sell it in the market, with the aim of earning a profit by buying the stock back again ("covering the short") after it has fallen in price. Work by psychologists, however, suggests that people are subject to loss aversion: They are more unhappy when they suffer losses than they are happy when they achieve gains. Short sales can result in losses far in excess of an investor's initial investment if the stock price climbs sharply higher than the price at which the short sale is made (and losses might be unlimited if the stock price climbs to astronomical heights).

Loss aversion can thus explain an important phenomenon: Very little short selling actually takes place. Short selling may also be constrained by rules restricting it, because it seems unsavory for someone to make money from another person's misfortune. The existence of so little short selling can explain why stock prices are sometimes overvalued. That is, the lack of enough short selling means that smart money does not drive stock prices back down to their fundamental value.

Psychologists have also found that people tend to be overconfident in their own judgments. As a result, investors tend to believe that they are smarter than other investors. Because investors are willing to assume that the market typically doesn't get it right, they trade on their beliefs rather than on pure facts. This theory may explain why securities markets have such a large trading volume—something that the efficient market hypothesis does not predict.

Overconfidence and social contagion (fads) provide an explanation for stock market bubbles. When stock prices go up, investors attribute their profits to their intelligence and talk up the stock market. This word-of-mouth enthusiasm and glowing media reports then can produce an environment in which even more investors think stock prices will rise in the future. The result is a positive feedback loop in which prices continue to rise, producing a speculative bubble, which finally crashes when prices get too far out of line with fundamentals.[10]

The field of behavioural finance is a young one, but it holds out hope that we might be able to explain some features of securities markets' behaviour that are not well explained by the efficient market hypothesis.

---

[9]Surveys of this field can be found in Hersh Shefrin, *Beyond Greed and Fear: Understanding of Behavioural Finance and the Psychology of Investing* (Boston: Harvard Business School Press, 2000); Andrei Shleifer, *Inefficient Markets* (Oxford, UK: Oxford University Press, 2000); and Robert J. Shiller, "From Efficient Market Theory to Behavioural Finance," Cowles Foundation Discussion Paper No. 1385 (October 2002).

[10] See Robert J. Shiller, *Irrational Exuberance* (New York: Broadway Books, 2001).

MyEconLab

MyEconLab is an online homework and tutorial system that puts you in control of your own learning with study and practice tools directly correlated to this chapter's content. Visit MyEconLab to access the eText, the Questions and Applied Problems with answers, as well as additional assessment. You will also find web chapters, mini-lectures, appendices, mini-cases, videos, glossary flashcards, news feeds, CANSIM data, and graphing tools.

SUMMARY

1. Stocks are valued as the present value of future dividends. Unfortunately, we do not know very precisely what these dividends will be. This uncertainty introduces a great deal of error into the valuation process. The Gordon growth model is a simplified method of computing stock value that depends on the assumption that the dividends are growing at a constant rate forever. Given our uncertainty regarding future dividends, this assumption is often the best we can do.

2. The interaction among traders in the market is what actually sets prices on a day-to-day basis. The trader who values the security the most (either because of less uncertainty about cash flows or because of greater estimated cash flows) will be willing to pay the most. As new information is released, investors will revise their estimates of the true value of the security and will either buy or sell it, depending on how the market price compares with their estimated valuation. Because small changes in estimated growth rates or required returns result in large changes in price, it is not surprising that the markets are often volatile.

3. The efficient market hypothesis states that current securities prices will fully reflect all available information, because in an efficient market all unexploited profit opportunities are eliminated. The elimination of unexploited profit opportunities necessary for a financial market to be efficient does not require that all market participants be

well informed. The efficient markets hypothesis implies that stock prices generally follow a random walk.

4. The efficient market hypothesis indicates that hot tips and investment advisers' published recommendations cannot help an investor outperform the market. The best prescription for investors is to pursue a buy-and-hold strategy—purchase stocks and hold them for long periods of time. Empirical evidence generally supports these implications of the efficient market hypothesis in the stock market.

5. The existence of market crashes and bubbles has convinced many economists that the stronger version of market efficiency, which states that asset prices reflect the true fundamental (intrinsic) value of securities, is not correct. There is, however, less evidence that these crashes prove that the efficient market hypothesis is wrong. Even if the stock market was driven by factors other than fundamentals, these crashes do not clearly demonstrate that many basic tenets of the efficient market hypothesis are no longer valid, as long as the crashes could not have been predicted.

6. The new field of behavioural finance applies concepts from other social sciences, such as anthropology, sociology, and psychology to our understanding of the behaviour of securities prices. Loss aversion, overconfidence, and social contagion can explain why trading volume is so high, why stock prices become overvalued, and why speculative bubbles occur.

KEY TERMS

adaptive expectations, p. 153
arbitrage, p. 157
behavioural finance, p. 164
bubbles, p. 163
cash flows, p. 148
dividends, p. 148

efficient market hypothesis, p. 155
generalized dividend model, p. 149
Gordon growth model, p. 149
market fundamentals, p. 162
optimal forecast, p. 153
random walk, p. 158

rational expectations, p. 153
residual claimant, p. 148
short sales, p. 164
stockholders, p. 147
theory of efficient capital markets, p. 155
unexploited profit opportunities, p. 157

QUESTIONS

All questions are available in MyEconLab at
www.myeconlab.com.

1. What basic principle of finance can be applied to the valuation of any investment asset?

2. What are the two main sources of cash flows for a stockholder? How reliably can these cash flows be estimated? Compare the problem of estimating stock cash flows to the problem of estimating bond cash flows. Which security would you predict to be more volatile?

3. Some economists think that central banks should try to prick bubbles in the stock market before they get out of hand and cause later damage when they burst. How can monetary policy be used to prick a market bubble? Explain using the Gordon growth model.

4. If monetary policy becomes more transparent about the future course of interest rates, how will stock prices be affected, if at all?

5. "Forecasters' predictions of inflation are notoriously inaccurate, so their expectations of inflation cannot be rational." Is this statement true, false, or uncertain? Explain your answer.

6. "Anytime it is snowing when Joe Commuter gets up in the morning, he misjudges how long it will take him to drive to work. When it is not snowing, his expectations of the driving time are perfectly accurate. Considering that it snows only once every ten years where Joe lives, Joe's expectations are almost always perfectly accurate." Are Joe's expectations rational? Why or why not?

7. If a forecaster spends hours every day studying data to forecast interest rates, but his expectations are not as accurate as predicting that tomorrow's interest rate will be identical to today's interest rate, are his expectations rational?

8. "If stock prices did not follow a random walk, there would be unexploited profit opportunities in the market." Is this statement true, false, or uncertain? Explain your answer.

9. Suppose that increases in the money supply lead to a rise in stock prices. Does this mean that when you see that the money supply has sharply increased in the past week, you should go out and buy stocks? Why or why not?

10. If the public expects a corporation to lose $5 per share this quarter and it actually loses $4, which is still the largest loss in the history of the company, what does the efficient market hypothesis predict will happen to the price of the stock when the $4 loss is announced?

11. If you read in the *Globe and Mail* that the "smart money" on Bay Street expects stock prices to fall, should you follow that lead and sell all your stocks?

12. If your broker has been right in her five previous buy and sell recommendations, should you continue listening to her advice?

13. Can a person with rational expectations expect the price of a share of Google to rise by 10% in the next month?

14. "If most participants in the stock market do not follow what is happening to the monetary aggregates, prices of common stocks will not fully reflect information about them." Is this statement true, false, or uncertain? Explain your answer.

15. "An efficient market is one in which no one ever profits from having better information than the rest of the market participants." Is this statement true, false, or uncertain? Explain your answer.

16. If higher money growth is associated with higher future inflation, and if announced money growth turns out to be extremely high but is still less than the market expected, what do you think will happen to long-term bond prices?

17. "Foreign exchange rates, like stock prices, should follow a random walk." Is this statement true, false, or uncertain? Explain your answer.

18. Can we expect the value of the dollar to rise by 2% next week if our expectations are rational?

19. "Human fear is the source of stock market crashes, so these crashes indicate that expectations in the stock market cannot be rational." Is this statement true, false, or uncertain? Explain your answer.

20. In the late 1990s, as information technology advanced rapidly and the Internet was widely developed, U.S. stock markets soared, peaking in early 2001. Later that year, these markets began to unwind and then crashed, with many commentators identifying the previous few years as a "stock market bubble." How might it be possible for this episode to be a bubble but still adhere to the efficient market hypothesis?

21. Why might the efficient market hypothesis be less likely to hold when fundamentals suggest stocks should be at a lower level?

APPLIED PROBLEMS

All applied problems are available in MyEconLab *at* **www.myeconlab.com.**

22. Compute the price of a share of stock that pays a $1 per year dividend and that you expect to be able to sell in one year for $20, assuming you require a 15% return.

23. After careful analysis, you have determined that a firm's dividends should grow at 7%, on average, in the foreseeable future. The firm's last dividend was $3. Compute the current price of this stock, assuming the required return is 18%.

24. The current price of a stock is $65.88. If dividends are expected to be $1 per share for the next five years, and the required return is 10%, then what should the price of the stock be in 5 years when you plan to sell it? If

the dividend and required return remain the same, and the stock price is expected to increase by $1 five years from now, does the current stock price also increase by $1? Why or why not?

25. A company has just announced a 3-for-1 stock split, effective immediately. Prior to the split, the company had a market value of $5 billion with 100 million shares outstanding. Assuming the split conveys no new information about the company, what are the value of the company, the number of shares outstanding, and the price per share after the split? If the actual market price immediately following the split is $17.00 per share, what does this tell us about market efficiency?

DATA ANALYSIS PROBLEMS

Download data for these problems from MyEconLab *at* **www.myeconlab.com**.

1. Go to the CANSIM database and download monthly data from January 1956 to December 2014 on the S&P TSX Composite Index (series V122620).

  a. Calculate the mean and standard deviation as well as the maximum and minimum values for this series.

  b. Which were the worst and best months in terms of rates of return?

2. Go to the St. Louis Federal Reserve FRED database and find data on the Dow Jones Industrial Average

(DJIA). Assume the DJIA is a stock that pays no dividends. Apply the one-period valuation model, using the data from one year prior up to the most current date available, to determine the required return on equity investment. In other words, assume the most recent stock price of DJIA is known one year prior. What rate of return would be required in order to "buy" a share of DJIA? Suppose that a $100 dividend is paid out instead. How does this change the required rate of return?

WEB EXERCISES

1. Visit **www.forecasts.org/data/index.htm**. Click on Stock Index at the very top of the page. Now choose U.S. Stock Indices—monthly. Review the indexes for the DJIA, the S&P 500, and the NASDAQ composite. Which index appears most

volatile? In which index would you rather have invested in 1985 if the investment had been allowed to compound until now?

2. The Internet is a great source of information on stock prices and stock price movements. Yahoo

Finance is a great source for stock market data. Go to **http://finance.yahoo.com** and click on the DOW ticker in the Market Summary section to view current data on the Dow Jones Industrial Average. Click on the chart to manipulate the different variables. Change the time range and observe the stock trend over various intervals. Have stock prices been going up or down over the past day, week, three months, and year?

3. Eugene Fama and Robert Shiller recently won the Nobel Prize in economics. Go to **http://nobelprize .org/nobel_prizes/economics/** and locate the press release on Eugene Fama and Robert Shiller. What was the Nobel Prize to them awarded for? When was it awarded?

WEB REFERENCES

http://stocks.tradingcharts.com

Access detailed stock quotes, charts, and historical stock data.

http://www.investorhome.com/emh.htm

Learn more about the efficient market hypothesis.

PART 3

Financial Institutions

Chapter 8 An Economic Analysis of Financial Structure
Chapter 9 Financial Crises
Chapter 10 Economic Analysis of Financial Regulation
Chapter 11 Banking Industry: Structure and Competition

Crisis and Response: Trillion-Dollar Bailout Packages

In response to the global financial crisis, governments and central banks around the world departed significantly from their traditional policy tools and introduced new facilities, pouring trillions of dollars into financial institutions. In the United States, for example, the House of Representatives passed the Emergency Economic Stabilization Act on October 3, 2008. This stunning $700 billion bailout package sought to promote recovery from the financial crisis by authorizing the U.S. Treasury to purchase troubled mortgage assets from struggling financial institutions. To calm fears further, the Act raised the federal deposit insurance limit from $100 000 to $250 000.

The initial bill was voted down on September 29, when constituents flooded their representatives with complaints about bailing out the greedy Wall Street executives behind the crisis. The debate in the United States pitted Wall Street against Main Street: bailing out financial institutions was seen as being in opposition to helping struggling homeowners. How could injecting capital into the financial system help those fearful of losing their job or, worse yet, suddenly without work?

The central role of financial institutions in the working of the economy—the focus of Part III—was overlooked. Banks and other financial institutions make financial markets work by moving funds from people who save to people who have productive investment opportunities. That bank branch on Main Street was not going to be able to lend freely to a small business owner or recent university graduate looking to fund a new car purchase until capital once again flowed.

The global financial crisis highlights how the financial system changes over time, be it from financial innovations or hard lessons from crises such as the one at hand. Chapter 8 analyzes financial structure in Canada and in the rest of the world. In Chapter 9, we develop a framework to understand the dynamics of financial crises—and focus in particular on the global crisis of 2007–2009. In Chapter 10, we extend the economic analysis developed in Chapter 8 to understand the motivations for bank regulation and we examine the pitfalls in the regulatory process. Chapter 11 examines the development of the Canadian banking system over time and the growing internationalization of banking. In Chapter 12, we look at the business of nonbank financial institutions.

8 An Economic Analysis of Financial Structure

Learning Objectives

After studying this chapter you should be able to

1. Identify eight basic facts about the global financial system.

2. Summarize how transaction costs affect financial intermediaries.

3. Describe why asymmetric information leads to adverse selection and moral hazard.

4. Recognize adverse selection and summarize the ways in which it can be reduced.

5. Recognize the principal–agent problem arising from moral hazard in equity contracts and summarize the methods for reducing it.

6. Summarize the methods used to reduce moral hazard in debt contracts.

PREVIEW

A healthy and vibrant economy requires a financial system that moves funds from people who save to people who have productive investment opportunities. But how does the financial system make sure that your hard-earned savings get channeled to Paula the Productive Investor rather than to Benny the Bum?

This chapter answers that question by providing an economic analysis of how our financial structure is designed to promote economic efficiency. The analysis focuses on a few simple but powerful economic concepts that enable us to explain features of our financial system, such as why financial contracts are written as they are and why financial intermediaries are more important than securities markets for getting funds to borrowers. The analysis also demonstrates the important link between the financial system and the performance of the aggregate economy, which is the subject of Part 7 of this book.

BASIC FACTS ABOUT FINANCIAL STRUCTURE THROUGHOUT THE WORLD

The financial system is complex in structure and function throughout the world. It includes many different types of institutions: banks, insurance companies, mutual funds, stock and bond markets, and so on—all of which are regulated by governments. The financial system channels trillions of dollars per year from savers to people with productive investment opportunities. If we take a close look at financial structure all over the world, we find eight basic facts, some of which are quite surprising, that we must explain if we are to understand how the financial system works.

The bar chart in Figure 8-1 shows how Canadian businesses financed their activities using external funds (those obtained from outside the business itself) in the period 1970–2000 and compares Canadian data with data for the United States, Germany, and Japan. The conclusions drawn from this period still hold true today. The *Bank Loans* category is made up primarily of loans from depository institutions; *Nonbank Loans* are primarily loans by other financial intermediaries; the *Bonds* category includes marketable debt securities, such as corporate bonds and commercial paper; and *Stock* consists of new issues of equity (stock market shares).

MyEconLab Mini-lecture

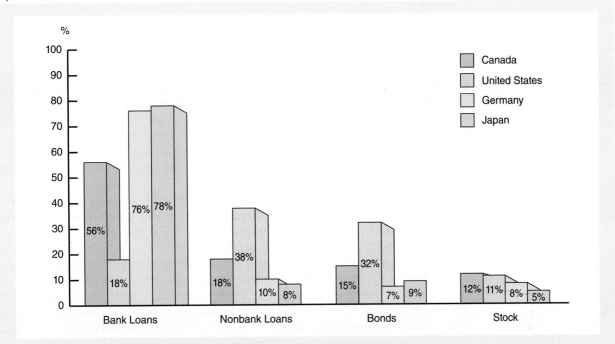

FIGURE 8-1   Sources of External Funds for Nonfinancial Businesses: A Comparison of Canada with the United States, Germany, and Japan

The *Bank Loans* category is made up primarily of loans from depository institutions; the *Nonbank Loans* are primarily loans by other financial intermediaries; the *Bonds* category includes marketable debt securities, such as corporate bonds and commercial paper; and *Stock* consists of new issues of new equity (stock market shares).
Source: Andreas Hackethal and Reinhard H. Schmidt, "Financing Patterns: Measurement Concepts and Empirical Results," Johann Wolfgang Goethe-Universitat Working Paper No. 125, January 2004; and Apostolos Serletis and Karl Pinno, "Corporate Financing in Canada," *Journal of Economic Asymmetries* 3 (2006); 1–20.

Now let's explore the eight facts.

1. ***Stocks are not the most important source of external financing for businesses.*** Because so much attention in the media is focused on the stock market, many people have the impression that stocks are the most important source of financing for Canadian corporations. However, as we can see from the bar chart in Figure 8-1, the stock market accounted for only a small fraction of the external financing of Canadian businesses in the 1970–2000 period: 12%.[1] Similarly low figures apply for the other countries

[1]The 12% figure for the percentage of external financing provided by stocks is based on the flows of external funds to corporations. However, this flow figure is somewhat misleading because when a share of stock is issued, it raises funds permanently, whereas when a bond is issued, it raises funds only temporarily until it is paid back at maturity. To illustrate, suppose a firm raises $1000 by selling a share of stock and another $1000 by selling a $1000 one-year bond. In the case of the stock issue, the firm can hold on to the $1000 it raised by selling the stock. However, in order to hold on to the $1000 it raised through debt, the firm has to issue a new $1000 bond every year. If we look at the flow of funds to corporations over a 30-year period, as shown in Figure 8-1, the firm will have raised $1000 through a stock issue only once in the 30-year period, while it will have raised $1000 through debt 30 times, once in each of the 30 years. Thus, it looks as though debt is 30 times more important than stocks in raising funds, even though our example indicates that the two methods are actually equally important for the firm.

presented in Figure 8-1. Why is the stock market less important than other sources of financing in Canada and other countries?

2. *Issuing marketable debt and equity securities is not the primary way in which businesses finance their operations.* Figure 8-1 shows that bonds are more important source of financing in Canada than stocks are (15% versus 12%). However, stocks and bonds combined (27%), which make up the total share of marketable securities in Canada, still supply less than one-half of the external funds needed by Canadian corporations to finance their activities. The fact that issuing marketable securities is not the most important source of financing is true elsewhere in the world as well. Indeed, as we see in Figure 8-1, other countries (except the United States) have a much smaller share of external financing supplied by marketable securities than does Canada. Why don't businesses use marketable securities more extensively to finance their activities?

3. *Indirect finance, which involves the activities of financial intermediaries, is many times more important than direct finance, in which businesses raise funds directly from lenders in financial markets.* Direct finance involves the sale to households of marketable securities, such as stocks and bonds. The 27% share of stocks and bonds used as a source of external financing for Canadian businesses actually greatly overstates the importance of direct finance in our financial system. In general, only a small fraction of newly issued corporate bonds, commercial paper, and stocks are sold directly to Canadian households. The rest of these securities have been bought primarily by financial intermediaries such as insurance companies, pension funds, and mutual funds. Because in most countries marketable securities are an even less important source of finance than in Canada, direct finance is also far less important than indirect finance in the rest of the world. Why are financial intermediaries and indirect finance so important in financial markets? In recent years, however, indirect finance has been declining in importance. Why is this happening?

4. *Financial intermediaries, particularly banks, are the most important source of external funds used to finance businesses.* As we can see in Figure 8-1, the primary source of external funds for businesses throughout the world is loans made by banks and other nonbank financial intermediaries, such as insurance companies, pension funds, and finance companies (56% in Canada, but more than 70% in Germany and Japan). In other industrialized countries, bank loans are the largest category of sources of external finance (more than 70% in Germany). Thus, the data suggest that banks in these countries have the most important role in financing business activities. In developing countries, banks play an even more important role in the financial system than they do in industrialized countries. What makes banks so important to the workings of the financial system? Although banks remain important, their contributions to external funds for businesses have been declining in recent years. What is driving this decline?

5. *The financial system is among the most heavily regulated sectors of the economy.* The financial system is heavily regulated in Canada and in all other developed countries. Governments regulate financial markets primarily to promote the provision of information and to ensure the soundness (stability) of the financial system. Why are financial markets so extensively regulated throughout the world?

6. *Only large, well-established corporations have easy access to securities markets to finance their activities.* Individuals and smaller businesses that are not well established are less likely to raise funds by issuing marketable securities. Instead, they most often obtain their financing from banks. Why do only large, well-known corporations find it easier to raise funds in securities markets?

7. *Collateral is a prevalent feature of debt contracts for both households and businesses.* **Collateral** is property that is pledged to a lender to guarantee payment in the event that the borrower is unable to make debt payments. Collateralized debt (also known as **secured debt** to contrast it with **unsecured debt**, such as credit card debt, which is not collateralized) is the predominant form of household debt and is widely used in business borrowing as well. The majority of household debt in Canada consists of collateralized loans: Your automobile is collateral for your auto loan, and your house is collateral for your mortgage. Commercial and farm mortgages, for which property is pledged as collateral, make up one-quarter of borrowing by nonfinancial businesses; corporate bonds and other bank loans also often involve pledges of collateral. Why is collateral such an important feature of debt contracts?

8. *Debt contracts typically are extremely complicated legal documents that place substantial restrictions on the behaviour of the borrower.* Many students think of a debt contract as a simple IOU that can be written on a single piece of paper. The reality of debt contracts is far different, however. In all countries, bond or loan contracts typically are long legal documents with provisions (called **restrictive covenants**) that restrict and specify certain activities that the borrower can engage in. Restrictive covenants are not just a feature of debt contracts for businesses; for example, personal automobile loan and home mortgage contracts include covenants that require the borrower to maintain sufficient insurance on the automobile or house purchased with the loan. Why are debt contracts so complex and restrictive?

As you may recall from Chapter 2, an important feature of financial markets is their substantial transaction and information costs. An economic analysis of how these costs affect financial markets will help us understand these eight facts, which will in turn give us a much deeper understanding of how our financial system works. In the next section, we examine the impact of transaction costs on the structure of our financial system. Then we turn to the effects of information costs on financial structure.

TRANSACTION COSTS

Transaction costs are a major problem in financial markets. An example will make this clear.

How Transaction Costs Influence Financial Structure

Say you have $5000 that you would like to invest, and you are thinking about investing in the stock market. Because you have only $5000, you can buy only a small number of shares. Even if you use online trading, your purchase is so small that the brokerage commission for buying the stock you pick will be a large percentage of the purchase price of the shares. If, instead, you decide to buy a bond, the problem becomes even worse; the smallest denomination offered on some bonds that you might want to buy is as large as $10 000, and you do not have that much money to invest. You are disappointed and realize that you will not be able to use financial markets to earn a return on your hard-earned savings. You can take some consolation, however, in the fact that you are not alone in being stymied by high transaction costs. This is a fact of life for many of us: Only about one-half of Canadian households own any securities.

You also face another problem related to transaction costs: Because you have only a relatively small amount of funds available, you can make only a restricted number of investments, because a large number of small transactions would result in very high transaction costs. That is, you have to put all your eggs in one basket, and your inability to diversify will subject you to a lot of risk.

How Financial Intermediaries Reduce Transaction Costs

This example of the problems posed by transaction costs, along with the example outlined in Chapter 2, in which legal costs kept you from making a loan to Carl the Carpenter, illustrate that small savers like you are frozen out of financial markets and are unable to benefit from them. Fortunately, financial intermediaries, an important part of the financial structure, have evolved to reduce transaction costs and allow small savers and borrowers to benefit from financial markets.

Economies of Scale

One solution to the problem of high transaction costs is to bundle the funds of many investors together so that they can take advantage of *economies of scale*, the reduction in transaction costs per dollar of investment as the size (scale) of transactions increases. Bundling investors' funds together reduces transaction costs for each individual investor. Economies of scale exist because the total cost of carrying out a transaction in financial markets increases only a little as the size of the transaction grows. For example, the cost of arranging a purchase of 10 000 shares of stock is not much greater than the cost of arranging a purchase of 50 shares of stock.

The presence of economies of scale in financial markets helps explain the development of financial intermediaries and why financial intermediaries have become such an important part of our financial structure. The clearest example of a financial intermediary that arose because of economies of scale is a mutual fund. A *mutual fund* is a financial intermediary that sells shares to individuals and then invests the proceeds in bonds or stocks. Because it buys large blocks of stocks or bonds, a mutual fund can take advantage of lower transaction costs. These cost savings are then passed on to individual investors after the mutual fund has taken its cut, in the form of management fees for administering their accounts. An additional benefit for individual investors is that a mutual fund is large enough to purchase a widely diversified portfolio of securities. The increased diversification for individual investors reduces their risk, making them better off.

Economies of scale are also important in lowering the costs of resources that financial institutions need to accomplish their tasks, such as computer technology. Once a large mutual fund has invested a lot of money in setting up a telecommunications system, for example, the system can be used for a huge number of transactions at a low cost per transaction.

Expertise

Financial intermediaries are also better able to develop expertise that can be used to lower transaction costs. Their expertise in computer technology, for example, enables them to offer their customers convenient services such as cheque writing privileges on their accounts and toll-free numbers that customers can call for information on how well their investments are doing.

Lower transaction costs enable financial intermediaries to provide their customers with *liquidity services*, which are services that make it easier for customers to conduct transactions. Money market mutual funds, for example, not only pay shareholders relatively high interest rates but also allow them to write cheques for convenient bill paying.

ASYMMETRIC INFORMATION: ADVERSE SELECTION AND MORAL HAZARD

The presence of transaction costs in financial markets partly explains why financial intermediaries and indirect finance play such an important role in financial markets (fact 3). To understand financial structure more fully, however, we turn to the role of information in financial markets.

Asymmetric information—a situation that arises when one party's insufficient knowledge about the other party involved in a transaction makes it impossible for the first party to make accurate decisions when conducting the transaction—is an important aspect of financial markets. For example, managers of a corporation know whether they are honest and usually have better information about how well their business is doing than stockholders do. The presence of asymmetric information leads to adverse selection and moral hazard problems, which were introduced in Chapter 2.

Adverse selection is an asymmetric information problem that occurs *before* a transaction occurs: Potential bad credit risks are the ones who most actively seek out loans. Thus the parties who are most likely to produce an undesirable outcome are also the ones most likely to want to engage in the transaction. For example, big risk takers or outright crooks are often the most eager to take out a loan because they know they are unlikely to pay it back. Because adverse selection increases the chances that a loan might be made to a bad credit risk, lenders might decide not to make any loans, even though good credit risks can be found in the marketplace.

Moral hazard arises *after* the transaction occurs: The lender runs the risk that the borrower will engage in activities that are undesirable from the lender's point of view, because such activites make it less likely that the loan will be paid back. For example, once borrowers have obtained a loan, they may take on big risks (which have possible high returns but also run a greater risk of default) because they are playing with someone else's money. Because moral hazard lowers the probability that the loan will be repaid, lenders may decide that they would rather not make a loan.

The analysis of how asymmetric information problems affect economic behaviour is called **agency theory**. We will apply this theory here to explain why financial structure takes the form it does, thereby explaining the facts outlined at the beginning of the chapter.

THE LEMONS PROBLEM: HOW ADVERSE SELECTION INFLUENCES FINANCIAL STRUCTURE

A particular aspect of the way the adverse selection problem interferes with the efficient functioning of a market was outlined in a famous article by Nobel Prize winner George Akerlof. It is called the "lemons problem" because it resembles the problem created by "lemons," that is, bad cars, in the used-car market.[2] Potential buyers of used cars are

---

[2]George Akerlof, "The Market for 'Lemons': Quality, Uncertainty and the Market Mechanism," *Quarterly Journal of Economics* 84 (1970): 488–500. Two important papers that have applied the lemons problem analysis to financial markets are Stewart Myers and N. S. Majluf, "Corporate Financing and Investment Decisions: When Firms Have Information That Investors Do Not Have," *Journal of Financial Economics* 13 (1984): 187–221; and Bruce Greenwald, Joseph E. Stiglitz, and Andrew Weiss, "Information Imperfections in the Capital Market and Macroeconomic Fluctuations," *American Economic Review* 74 (1984): 194–199.

frequently unable to assess the quality of a car; that is, they can't tell whether a particular used car is one that will run well or a lemon that will continually give them grief. The price that a buyer pays must therefore reflect the *average* quality of the cars in the market, somewhere between the low value of a lemon and the high value of a good car.

The owner of a used car, by contrast, is more likely to know whether the car is a peach or a lemon. If the car is a lemon, the owner is more than happy to sell it at the price the buyer is willing to pay, which, being somewhere between the value of a lemon and that of a good car, is greater than the lemon's value. However, if the car is a peach, that is, a good car, the owner knows that the car is undervalued at the price the buyer is willing to pay, and so the owner may not want to sell it. As a result of this adverse selection problem, fewer good used cars will come to the market. Because the average quality of a used car available in the market will be low, and because very few people want to buy a lemon, there will be few sales. The used-car market will function poorly, if at all.

Lemons in the Stock and Bond Markets

A similar lemons problem arises in securities markets—that is, the debt (bond) and equity (stock) markets. Suppose that our friend Irving the Investor, a potential buyer of securities such as common stock, can't distinguish between good firms with high expected profits and low risk and bad firms with low expected profits and high risk. In this situation, Irving will be willing to pay only a price that reflects the *average* quality of firms issuing securities—a price that lies between the value of securities from bad firms and the value of those from good firms. If the owners or managers of a good firm have better information than Irving and *know* that they have a good firm, then they know that their securities are being undervalued and will not want to sell them to Irving at the price he is willing to pay. The only firms willing to sell Irving securities will be bad firms (because his price is higher than the securities are worth). Our friend Irving is not stupid; he does not want to hold securities in bad firms, and hence he will decide not to purchase any securities in the market. In an outcome similar to that in the used-car market, this securities market will not work very well because few firms will sell securities in it to raise capital.

The analysis is similar if Irving considers purchasing a corporate debt instrument in the bond market rather than an equity share. Irving will buy a bond only if its interest rate is high enough to compensate him for the average default risk of the good and bad firms trying to sell the debt. The knowledgeable owners of a good firm realize that they will be paying a higher interest rate than they should, so they are unlikely to want to borrow in this market. Only the bad firms will be willing to borrow, and because investors like Irving are not eager to buy bonds issued by bad firms, they will probably not buy any bonds at all. Few bonds are likely to sell in this market, so it will not be a good source of financing.

The analysis we have just conducted explains fact 2—why marketable securities are not the primary source of financing for businesses in any country in the world. It also partly explains fact 1—why stocks are not the most important source of financing for Canadian businesses. The presence of the lemons problem keeps securities markets such as the stock and bond markets from being effective in channeling funds from savers to borrowers.

Tools to Help Solve Adverse Selection Problems

In the absence of asymmetric information, the lemons problem goes away. If buyers know as much about the quality of used cars as sellers, so that all involved can tell a good car from a bad one, buyers will be willing to pay full value for good used cars.

Because the owners of good used cars can now get a fair price, they will be willing to sell them in the market. The market will have many transactions and will perform its intended job of channeling good cars to people who want them.

Similarly, if purchasers of securities can distinguish good firms from bad ones, they will pay the full value of securities issued by good firms, and good firms will sell their securities in the market. The securities market will then be able to move funds to the good firms that have the most productive investment opportunities.

Private Production and Sale of Information   The solution to the adverse selection problem in financial markets is to reduce asymmetric information by furnishing the people supplying funds with more details about the individuals or firms seeking to finance their investment activities. One way for saverlenders to get this information is through private companies that collect and produce information distinguishing good firms from bad firms, and then sell it to the saverlenders. In Canada, companies such as Standard and Poor's and the Dominion Bond Rating Service gather information on firms' balance sheet positions and investment activities, publish these data, and sell them to subscribers (individuals, libraries, and financial intermediaries involved in purchasing securities).

The system of private production and sale of information does not completely solve the adverse selection problem in securities markets, however, because of the **free-rider problem**. The free-rider problem occurs when people who do not pay for information take advantage of the information that other people have paid for. The free-rider problem suggests that the private sale of information is only a partial solution to the lemons problem. To see why, suppose you have just purchased information that tells you which firms are good and which are bad. You believe that this purchase is worthwhile because you can make up the cost of acquiring this information, and then some, by purchasing the securities of good firms that are undervalued. However, when our savvy (free-riding) investor Irving sees you buying certain securities, he buys right along with you, even though he has not paid for any information. If many other investors act as Irving does, the increased demand for the undervalued good securities causes their low price to be bid up immediately to reflect the securities' true value. Because of all these free riders, you can no longer buy the securities for less than their true value. Now, because you will not gain any profit from purchasing the information, you realize that you never should have paid for the information in the first place. If other investors come to the same realization, private firms and individuals may not be able to sell enough of this information to make it worth their while to gather and produce it. The weakened ability of private firms to profit from selling information will mean that less information is produced in the marketplace, so adverse selection (the lemons problem) will again start to interfere with the efficient functioning of securities markets.

Government Regulation to Increase Information   The free-rider problem prevents the private market from producing enough information to eliminate all the asymmetric information that leads to adverse selection. Could financial markets benefit from government intervention? The government could, for instance, produce information itself to help investors distinguish good from bad firms and provide it to the public free of charge. This solution, however, would involve the government releasing negative information about firms, a practice that might be politically difficult. A second possibility (and one followed by Canada and most governments throughout the world) is for the government to regulate securities markets in a way that encourages firms to reveal honest information about

FYI   The Enron Implosion

Until 2001, Enron Corporation, a firm that specialized in trading in the energy market, appeared to be spectacularly successful. It controlled a quarter of the energytrading market and was valued as high as $77 billion in August 2000 (just a little over a year before its collapse), making it the seventh-largest corporation in the United States at that time. However, toward the end of 2001, Enron came crashing down. In October 2001, Enron announced a third-quarter loss of $618 million and disclosed accounting "mistakes." The SEC then engaged in a formal investigation of Enron's financial dealings with partnerships led by its former finance chief. It became clear that Enron was engaged in a complex set of transactions by which it was keeping substantial amounts of debt and financial contracts off its balance sheet. These transactions enabled Enron to hide its financial difficulties. Despite securing as much as $1.5 billion in new financing from J. P. Morgan Chase and Citigroup, Enron was forced to declare bankruptcy in December 2001, up to that point the largest bankruptcy declaration in U.S. history.

The Enron collapse illustrates that government regulation can lessen asymmetric information problems but cannot eliminate them. Managers have tremendous incentives to hide their companies' problems, making it hard for investors to know the true value of firms.

The Enron bankruptcy not only increased concerns in financial markets about the quality of accounting information supplied by corporations, but also led to hardship for many of the firm's former employees, who found that their pensions had become worthless. Outrage against the duplicity of executives at Enron was high, and several of them were convicted and sent to jail.

themselves so that investors can determine how good or bad the firms are. In Canada, government regulation exists that requires firms selling securities to have independent **audits**, in which accounting firms certify that the firm adheres to standard accounting principles and discloses information about its sales, assets, and earnings. Similar regulations are found in other countries. However, disclosure requirements do not always work well, as the collapse of Enron and other accounting scandals, such as those at WorldCom and Parmalat (an Italian company) suggest (see the FYI box The Enron Implosion).

The asymmetric information problem of adverse selection in financial markets helps explain why financial markets are among the most heavily regulated sectors of the economy (fact 5). Government regulation aimed at increasing the information available to investors is necessary to reduce the adverse selection problem, which interferes with the efficient functioning of securities (stock and bond) markets.

Although government regulation lessens the adverse selection problem, it does not eliminate it entirely. Even when firms provide information to the public about their sales, assets, or earnings, they still have more information than investors have: Much more is involved in knowing the quality of a firm than statistics alone can provide. Furthermore, poorly performing firms have an incentive to make themselves look like strongly performing firms because this enables them to fetch a higher price for their securities. Poorly performing firms may slant the information they are required to transmit to the public, thus making it harder for investors to accurately assess which firms are successful and which are not.

Financial Intermediation   So far we have seen that both private production of information and government regulation to encourage the transparent provision of information can lessen, but not eliminate, the adverse selection problem in financial markets.

How, then, can the financial structure help promote the flow of funds to people with productive investment opportunities when asymmetric information exists? A clue is provided by the structure of the used-car market.

An important feature of the used-car market is that most used cars are not sold directly by one individual to another. An individual who considers buying a used car might pay for privately produced information by subscribing to a magazine like *Consumer Reports* to find out if a particular make of car has a good repair record. Nevertheless, reading *Consumer Reports* does not solve the adverse selection problem, because even if a particular make of car has a good reputation, the specific car someone is trying to sell could be a lemon. The prospective buyer might also bring the used car to a mechanic for an inspection. But what if the prospective buyer doesn't know a mechanic who can be trusted or the mechanic charges a high fee to evaluate the car?

Because these roadblocks make it hard for individuals to acquire enough information about used cars, most used cars are not sold directly by one individual to another. Instead, they are sold by an intermediary, a used-car dealer who purchases used cars from individuals and resells them to other individuals. Used-car dealers produce information in the market by becoming experts in determining whether a car is a peach or a lemon. Once a dealer knows that a car is good, the dealer can sell it with some form of a guarantee: either an explicit guarantee such as a warranty or an implicit guarantee in which the dealer stands by its reputation for honesty. People are more likely to purchase a used car because of a dealer's guarantee, and the dealer is able to sell the used car at a higher price than the dealer paid for it. Thus the dealer profits from the production of information about automobile quality. If dealers purchase and then resell cars on which they have produced information, they avoid the problem of other people free-riding on the information they produced.

Just as used-car dealers help solve adverse selection problems in the automobile market, financial intermediaries play a similar role in financial markets. A financial intermediary, such as a bank, becomes an expert in producing information about firms so that it can sort out good credit risks from bad ones. It then can acquire funds from depositors and lend them to the good firms. Because the bank is able to lend mostly to good firms, it is able to earn a higher return on its loans than the interest it has to pay to its depositors. The resulting profit that the bank earns gives it the incentive to engage in this information production activity.

An important element of the bank's ability to profit from the information it produces is that it avoids the free-rider problem by primarily making private loans, rather than by purchasing securities that are traded in the open market. Because a private loan is not traded, other investors cannot watch what the bank is doing and bid down the loan's interest rate to the point that the bank receives no compensation for the information it has produced. The bank's role as an intermediary that holds mostly nontraded loans is the key to its success in reducing asymmetric information in financial markets.

Our analysis of adverse selection indicates that financial intermediaries in general— and banks in particular, because they hold a large fraction of nontraded loans—should play a greater role in moving funds to corporations than securities markets do. Our analysis thus explains facts 3 and 4: why indirect finance is so much more important than direct finance and why banks are the most important source of external funds for financing businesses.

Our analysis also explains the greater importance of banks, as opposed to securities markets, in the financial systems of developing countries. As we have seen, better information about the quality of firms lessens asymmetric information problems, making it easier for firms to issue securities. Information about private firms is harder to collect in developing countries than in industrialized countries; therefore, the smaller role played by securities markets leads to a greater role for financial intermediaries such as banks. As a corollary to our analysis, as information about firms becomes easier to acquire, the role of banks should decline. A major development in the past 30 years in Canada has been the significant improvement in information technology. Thus our analysis suggests that the lending role of financial institutions such as banks in Canada should have declined, and this is exactly what has occurred (see Chapter 11).

Our analysis of adverse selection also explains fact 6, which questions why large firms are more likely to obtain funds from securities markets, a direct route, rather than from banks and financial intermediaries, an indirect route. The better known a corporation is, the more information about its activities is available in the marketplace. Thus it is easier for investors to evaluate the quality of the corporation and determine whether it is a good firm or a bad one. Because investors have fewer worries about adverse selection when dealing with well-known corporations, they are more willing to invest directly in their securities. Thus, in accordance with adverse selection, a pecking order for firms that can issue securities should exist. Hence we have an explanation for fact 6: The larger and more established a corporation is, the more likely it will be to issue securities to raise funds.

Collateral and Net Worth

Adverse selection interferes with the functioning of financial markets only if a lender suffers a loss when a borrower is unable to make loan payments and thereby defaults on the loan. *Collateral*, property promised to the lender if the borrower defaults, reduces the consequences of adverse selection because it reduces the lender's losses in the event of a default. If a borrower defaults on a loan, the lender can sell the collateral and use the proceeds to make up for the losses on the loan. For example, if you fail to make your mortgage payments, the lender can take the title to your house, auction it off, and use the receipts to pay off the loan. Lenders are thus more willing to make loans secured by collateral, and borrowers are willing to supply collateral because the reduced risk for the lender makes it more likely that the loan will be made, perhaps even at a better loan rate. The presence of adverse selection in credit markets thus explains why collateral is an important feature of debt contracts (fact 7).

Net worth (also called **equity capital**), the difference between a firm's assets (what it owns or is owed) and its liabilities (what it owes), can perform a similar role to that of collateral. If a firm has a high net worth, then even if it engages in investments that lead to negative profits and so defaults on its debt payments, the lender can take title to the firm's net worth, sell it off, and use the proceeds to recoup some of the losses from the loan. In addition, the higher a firm's net worth, the less likely it is to default, because the firm has a cushion of assets that it can use to pay off its loans. Hence, when firms seeking credit have high net worth, the consequences of adverse selection are less important and lenders are more willing to make loans. This concept lies behind the often-heard lament, "Only the people who don't need money can borrow it!"

Summary

So far we have used the concept of adverse selection to explain seven of the eight facts about financial structure introduced earlier: The first four facts emphasize the importance of financial intermediaries and the relative unimportance of securities markets with regard to the financing of corporations; the fifth, that financial markets are among the most heavily regulated sectors of the economy; the sixth, that only large, well-established corporations tend to have access to securities markets; and the seventh, that collateral is an important feature of debt contracts. In the next section, we will see that the other asymmetric information concept, moral hazard, provides additional reasons for the importance of financial intermediaries and the relative unimportance of securities markets as related to the financing of corporations, the prevalence of government regulation, and the importance of collateral in debt contracts. In addition, the concept of moral hazard can be used to explain our final fact (fact 8): why debt contracts are complicated legal documents that place substantial restrictions on the behaviour of the borrower.

HOW MORAL HAZARD AFFECTS THE CHOICE BETWEEN DEBT AND EQUITY CONTRACTS

Moral hazard is the asymmetric information problem that occurs after a financial transaction takes place, when the seller of a security may have incentives to hide information and engage in activities that are undesirable for the purchaser of the security. Moral hazard has important consequences for whether a firm finds it easier to raise funds with debt than with equity contracts.

Moral Hazard in Equity Contracts: The Principal–Agent Problem

Equity contracts, such as common stock, are claims to a share in the profits and assets of a business. Equity contracts are subject to a particular type of moral hazard called the **principal-agent problem**. When managers own only a small fraction of the firm they work for, the stockholders who own most of the firm's equity (called the *principals*) are not the same people as the managers of the firm. Thus the managers are the *agents* of the owners. This separation of ownership and control involves moral hazard, in that the managers in control (the agents) may act in their own interest rather than in the interest of the stockholder-owners (the principals) because the managers have less incentive to maximize profits than the stockholder-owners do.

To understand the principal–agent problem more fully, suppose that your friend Steve asks you to become a silent partner in his ice cream store. The store set-up requires an initial investment of $10 000, and Steve has only $1000. So you purchase an equity stake (stock shares) for $9000, which entitles you to 90% of the ownership of the firm, while Steve owns only 10%. If Steve works hard to make tasty ice cream, keeps the store clean, smiles at all the customers, and hustles to wait on tables quickly, after all expenses (including Steve's salary) have been paid, the store will make $50 000 in profits per year, of which Steve will receive 10% ($5000) and you will receive 90% ($45 000).

But if Steve doesn't provide quick and friendly service to his customers, uses the $50 000 in income to buy artwork for his office, and even sneaks off to the beach while he should be at the store, the store will not earn any profit. Steve can earn the additional $5000 (his 10% share of the profits) over his salary only if he works hard and forgoes unproductive investments (such as art for his office). Steve might decide that the extra $5000 just isn't enough to make him expend the effort to be a good manager. If Steve feels this way, he does not have enough incentive to be a good manager and will end up with a beautiful office, a good tan, and a store that doesn't show any profits. Because the store won't show any profits, Steve's decision not to act in your interest will cost you $45 000 (your 90% of the profits had he chosen to be a good manager instead).

The moral hazard arising from the principal–agent problem might be even worse if Steve is not totally honest. Because his ice cream store is a cash business, Steve has the incentive to pocket $50 000 in cash and tell you that the profits were zero. He now gets a return of $50 000, and you get nothing.

Further proof that the principal–agent problem created by equity contracts can be severe is provided by past scandals involving corporations such as Enron and Tyco International, in which managers were found to have diverted corporate funds for their own personal use. In addition to pursuing personal benefits, managers might also pursue corporate strategies (such as the acquisition of other firms) that enhance their personal power but do not increase the corporation's profitability.

The principal–agent problem would not arise if the owners of a firm had complete information about what the managers were up to and could prevent wasteful expenditures or fraud. The principal–agent problem, which is an example of moral hazard, arises only because a manager, such as Steve, has more information about his activities than the stockholder does—that is, information is asymmetric. The principal–agent problem also would not occur if Steve alone owned the store, and ownership and control were not separate. If this were the case, Steve's hard work and avoidance of unproductive investments would yield him a profit (and extra income) of $50 000, an amount that would make it worth his while to be a good manager.

Tools to Help Solve the Principal–Agent Problem

Production of Information: Monitoring
You have seen that the principal–agent problem arises because managers have more information about their activities and actual profits than stockholders have. One way for stockholders to reduce this moral hazard problem is for them to engage in a particular type of information production: monitoring the firm's activities by auditing the firm frequently and checking on what management is doing. The problem is that the monitoring process can be expensive in terms of time and money, as reflected in the name economists give it: **costly state verification**. Costly state verification makes the equity contract less desirable and explains in part why equity is not a more important element in our financial structure.

As with adverse selection, the free-rider problem decreases the amount of private information production that would reduce the moral hazard (principal–agent) problem. In this example, the free-rider problem decreases monitoring. If you know that other stockholders are paying to monitor the activities of the company you hold shares in, you can take a free ride on their activities. Then you can use the money you save by not engaging in monitoring to vacation on a Caribbean island. If you can do this, though, so can other stockholders. Perhaps all the stockholders will go to the islands, and no one will spend any resources on monitoring the firm. The moral hazard problem for shares of common stock will then be severe, making it hard for firms to issue them to raise capital (providing an additional explanation for fact 1).

Government Regulation to Increase Information
As with adverse selection, the government has an incentive to try to reduce the moral hazard problem created by asymmetric information, which provides another reason why the financial system is so heavily regulated (fact 5). Governments everywhere have laws to force firms to adhere to standard accounting principles that make profit verification easier. They also pass laws to impose stiff criminal penalties on people who commit the fraud of hiding and stealing

profits. However, these measures can be only partly effective. Catching this kind of fraud is not easy; fraudulent managers have the incentive to make it very hard for government agencies to find or prove fraud.

Financial Intermediation Financial intermediaries have the ability to avoid the free-rider problem in the face of moral hazard, and this is another reason why indirect finance is so important (fact 3). One financial intermediary that helps reduce the moral hazard arising from the principal–agent problem is the **venture capital firm**. Venture capital firms pool the resources of their partners and use the funds to help budding entrepreneurs start new businesses. In exchange for supplying the venture capital, the firm receives an equity share in the new business. Because verification of earnings and profits is so important in eliminating moral hazard, venture capital firms usually insist on having several of their own people participate as members of the managing body— the board of directors—of the new business so that they can keep a close watch on the new firm's activities. When a venture capital firm supplies start-up funds, the equity in the new firm is private—that is, not marketable to anyone *except* the venture capital firm.[3] Thus other investors are unable to take a free ride on the venture capital firm's verification activities. As a result of this arrangement, the venture capital firm is able to garner the full benefits of its verification activities and is given the appropriate incentives to reduce the moral hazard problem. Venture capital firms have been important in the development of the high-tech sector in the United States, which has resulted in job creation, economic growth, and increased international competitiveness.

Debt Contracts Moral hazard arises with an equity contract, which is a claim on profits in all situations, whether the firm is making or losing money. If a contract could be structured so that moral hazard would exist only in certain situations, the need to monitor managers would be reduced, and the contract would be more attractive than the equity contract. The debt contract has exactly these attributes because it is a contractual agreement by the borrower to pay the lender *fixed* dollar amounts at periodic intervals. When a firm has high profits, the lender receives the contractual payments and does not need to know the exact profits of the firm. If the managers are hiding profits or pursuing activities that are personally beneficial but don't increase the firm's profitability, the lender doesn't care, as long as these activities do not interfere with the ability of the firm to make its debt payments on time. Only when the firm cannot meet its debt payments, thereby putting itself in a state of default, does the lender need to verify the state of the firm's profits. Only in this situation do lenders involved in debt contracts need to act more like equity holders; to get their fair share, they now must know how much income the firm has.

The less frequent need to monitor the firm, and thus the lower cost of state verification, helps explain why debt contracts are used more frequently than equity contracts to raise capital. The concept of moral hazard therefore helps explain fact 1, which states that stocks are not the most important source of financing for businesses.[4]

---

[3] Private equity firms, which also engage in private equity investment, solve the free-rider problem in a way that is similar to the method used by venture capital firms. Venture capital firms invest in new businesses and then, when the new company matures, sell shares to the public. In contrast to venture capital firms, which take new companies public, private equity firms take older, public companies and make them private—that is, they purchase all the publicly traded shares and retire them. They then exercise control over the company using methods similar to those used by venture capital firms.

[4] Another factor that encourages the use of debt contracts rather than equity contracts in Canada is our tax code. Debt interest payments are a deductible expense for Canadian firms, whereas dividend payments to equity shareholders are not.

HOW MORAL HAZARD INFLUENCES FINANCIAL STRUCTURE IN DEBT MARKETS

Even with the advantages just described, debt contracts are still subject to moral hazard. Because a debt contract requires the borrowers to pay out a fixed amount and lets them keep any profits above this amount, the borrowers have an incentive to take on investment projects that are riskier than the lenders would like.

For example, suppose you are concerned about the problem of verifying the profits of Steve's ice cream store, and so you decide not to become an equity partner. Instead, you lend Steve the $9000 he needs to set up his business, and you and he sign a debt contract that pays you an interest rate of 10%. As far as you are concerned, this is a surefire investment, because the demand for ice cream is strong and steady in your neighbourhood. However, once you give Steve the funds, he might use them for purposes other than what he proposed to you. Instead of opening up the ice cream store, Steve might use your $9000 loan to invest in chemical research equipment because he thinks he has a 1-in-10 chance of inventing a diet ice cream that tastes every bit as good as the premium brands but has no fat or calories.

Obviously, this is a very risky investment, but if Steve is successful, he will become a multimillionaire. He has a strong incentive to undertake the riskier investment with your money because the gains to him would be so large if he succeeded. You would clearly be very unhappy if Steve used your loan for the riskier investment, because if he were unsuccessful, which is highly likely, you would lose most, if not all, of the money you loaned him. And if he were successful, you wouldn't share in his success—you would still get only a 10% return on the loan because the principal and interest payments are fixed. Because of the potential moral hazard (that Steve might use your money to finance a very risky venture), you would probably not make the loan to Steve, even though an ice cream store in the neighbourhood is a good investment that would provide benefits to everyone.

Tools to Help Solve Moral Hazard in Debt Contracts

Net Worth and Collateral
When borrowers have more at stake because their net worth (the difference between their assets and their liabilities) is high or the collateral they have pledged to the lender is valuable, the risk of moral hazard—the temptation to act in a manner that lenders find objectionable—is greatly reduced because the borrowers themselves have a lot to lose. In other words, if borrowers have more "skin in the game" because they have higher net worth or pledge collateral, they are likely to take less risk at the lender's expense. Let's return to Steve and his ice cream business. Suppose that the cost of setting up either the ice cream store or the research equipment is $100 000 instead of $10 000. Now Steve needs to invest $91 000 (instead of $1000) of his own money in the business, in addition to the $9000 supplied by your loan. If Steve is unsuccessful in inventing the no-calorie, nonfat ice cream, he has a lot to lose—the $91 000 of net worth (the $100 000 in assets minus the $9000 loan from you). He will think twice about undertaking the riskier investment and is more likely to invest in the ice cream store, which is more of a sure thing. Thus, when Steve has more of his own money (net worth) invested in the business, and hence more skin in the game, you are more likely to make him the loan. Similarly, if you have pledged your house as collateral, you are less likely to go to Las Vegas and gamble away your

earnings that month, because you might not be able to make your mortgage payments and therefore might lose your house.

One way of describing the solution that high net worth and collateral provide to the moral hazard problem is to say that it makes the debt contract **incentive-compatible**; that is, it aligns the incentives of the borrower with those of the lender. The greater the borrower's net worth and collateral pledged, then the greater the borrower's incentive to behave in the way that the lender expects and desires, the smaller the moral hazard problem in the debt contract, and the easier it is for the firm or household to borrow. Conversely, when the borrower's net worth and collateral are lower, the moral hazard problem is greater, making it harder to borrow.

Monitoring and Enforcing Restrictive Covenants   As the example of Steve and his ice cream store shows, if you could make sure that Steve doesn't invest in anything riskier than the ice cream store, it would be worth your while to make him the loan. You can ensure that Steve uses your money for the purpose *you* expect by writing provisions (restrictive covenants) into the debt contract that restrict his firm's activities. By monitoring Steve's activities to check whether he is complying with the restrictive covenants and by enforcing the covenants if he is not, you can make sure that he will not take on risks at your expense. Restrictive covenants are directed at reducing moral hazard either by ruling out undesirable behaviour or by encouraging desirable behaviour. There are four types of restrictive covenants that achieve this objective:

1. *Covenants to discourage undesirable behaviour.* Covenants can be designed to lower moral hazard by keeping the borrower from engaging in the undesirable behaviour of undertaking risky investment projects. Some covenants mandate that a loan be used only to finance specific activities, such as the purchase of particular equipment or inventories. Others restrict the borrowing firm from engaging in certain risky business activities, such as purchasing other businesses.

2. *Covenants to encourage desirable behaviour.* Restrictive covenants can encourage the borrower to engage in desirable activities that make it more likely that the loan will be paid off. One such restrictive covenant requires the principal income earners in a household to carry life insurance that will pay off the mortgage in the event of their deaths before the mortgage is discharged. For businesses, restrictive covenants of this type focus on encouraging the borrowing firm to keep its net worth high because higher borrower net worth reduces moral hazard and makes it less likely that the lender will suffer losses. These restrictive covenants typically specify that the borrowing firm must maintain minimum holdings of certain assets relative to the firm's size.

3. *Covenants to keep collateral valuable.* Because collateral is an important protection for the lender, restrictive covenants can encourage the borrower to keep the collateral in good condition and make sure that it stays in the possession of the borrower. This is the type of covenant ordinary people encounter most often. Automobile loan contracts, for example, require the car owner to maintain a minimum amount of collision and theft insurance and prevent the sale of the car unless the loan is paid off. Similarly, the recipient of a home mortgage must have adequate insurance on the home and must pay off the mortgage when the property is sold.

4. *Covenants to provide information.* Restrictive covenants also require a borrowing firm to provide information about its activities periodically, in the form of quarterly

accounting and income reports, thereby making it easier for the lender to monitor the firm and reduce moral hazard. This type of covenant may also stipulate that the lender has the right to audit and inspect the firm's books at any time.

We now see why debt contracts are often complicated legal documents with numerous restrictions on the borrower's behaviour (fact 8): Debt contracts require complicated restrictive covenants in order to lower moral hazard.

Financial Intermediation   Although restrictive covenants help reduce the moral hazard problem, they do not eliminate it completely. It is almost impossible to write covenants that rule out *every* risky activity. Furthermore, borrowers may be clever enough to find loopholes in restrictive covenants that make the covenants ineffective.

Another problem with restrictive covenants is that they must be monitored and enforced. A restrictive covenant is meaningless if the borrower can violate it knowing that the lender won't check up or is unwilling to pay for legal recourse. Because the monitoring and enforcement of restrictive covenants are costly, the free-rider problem arises in the debt securities (bond) market just as it does in the stock market. If you know that other bondholders are monitoring and enforcing the restrictive covenants, you can free-ride on their monitoring and enforcement. But other bondholders can do the same thing, so the likely outcome is that not enough resources will be devoted to monitoring and enforcing the restrictive covenants. Moral hazard therefore continues to be a severe problem for marketable debt.

As we have seen before, financial intermediaries—particularly banks—can avoid the free-rider problem by primarily making *private* loans. Private loans are not traded, so no one else can free-ride on the intermediary's monitoring and enforcement of the restrictive covenants. The intermediary making private loans thus receives the full benefits of monitoring and enforcement, and will work to shrink the moral hazard problem inherent in debt contracts. The concept of moral hazard has provided us with additional reasons why financial intermediaries play a more important role in channeling funds from savers to borrowers than marketable securities do, as described in facts 3 and 4.

Summary

Asymmetric information in financial markets leads to adverse selection and moral hazard problems that interfere with the efficient functioning of those markets. Tools to help solve these problems involve the private production and sale of information, government regulation to increase information in financial markets, the use of collateral and net worth clauses in debt contracts, and the monitoring and enforcement of restrictive covenants. Our analysis suggests that the existence of the free-rider problem for traded securities such as stocks and bonds indicates that financial intermediaries—particularly banks—should play a greater role than securities markets in financing the activities of businesses. Economic analysis of the consequences of adverse selection and moral hazard has helped explain the basic features of our financial system, including the eight facts about our financial structure outlined at the beginning of this chapter.

As a study aid, Table 8-1 summarizes the asymmetric information problems and tools that help solve them. In addition, it notes how these tools and asymmetric information problems explain the eight facts of financial structure described at the beginning of the chapter.

SUMMARY TABLE 8-1

Asymmetric Information Problems and Tools to Solve Them

Asymmetric Information Problem	Tools to Solve It	Explains Fact Number
Adverse selection	Private production and sale of information	1, 2
	Government regulation to increase information	5
	Financial intermediation	3, 4, 6
	Collateral and net worth	7
Moral hazard in equity contracts (principal–agent problem)	Production of information: monitoring	1
	Government regulation to increase information	5
	Financial intermediation	3
	Debt contracts	1
Moral hazard in debt contracts	Collateral and net worth	6, 7
	Monitoring and enforcement of restrictive covenants	8
	Financial intermediation	3, 4

Note: List of facts:

1. Stocks are not the most important source of external financing.
2. Marketable securities are not the primary source of financing.
3. Indirect finance is more important than direct finance.
4. Banks are the most important source of external funds.
5. The financial system is heavily regulated.
6. Only large, well-established firms have access to securities markets.
7. Collateral is prevalent in debt contracts.
8. Debt contracts have numerous restrictive covenants.

APPLICATION   Financial Development and Economic Growth

Recent research has found that an important reason why many developing countries and formerly communist countries like Russia (which are referred to as *transition countries*) experience very low rates of economic growth is that their financial systems are underdeveloped (a situation referred to as *financial repression*).[5] The economic analysis of financial structure helps explain how an underdeveloped financial system leads to a low state of economic development and economic growth.

The financial systems of developing and transition countries face several difficulties that keep them from operating efficiently. As we have seen, two important tools used to help solve adverse selection and moral hazard problems in credit markets are collateral

---

[5]See World Bank, *Finance for Growth: Policy Choices in a Volatile World* (World Bank and Oxford University Press, 2001), and Frederic S. Mishkin, *The Next Great Globalization: How Disadvantaged Nations Can Harness Their Financial Systems to Get Rich* (Princeton University Press, 2006) for a survey of the literature linking economic growth with financial development and a list of additional references.

and restrictive covenants. In many developing countries, the system of property rights (the rule of law, constraints on government expropriation, and the absence of corruption) functions poorly, making it hard for these two tools to function effectively.

As discussed in the FYI box, "The Tyranny of Collateral," the weak systems of property rights common in developing and transition countries impede the use of collateral, making adverse selection problems worse because the lender will need even more information about the quality of the borrower in order to screen out a good loan from a bad one. As a result, it is harder for lenders to channel funds to the borrowers with the most productive investment opportunities, ultimately leading to less productive investment and hence a slower-growing economy.

Similarly, a poorly developed or corrupt legal system makes it extremely difficult for lenders to enforce restrictive covenants. Thus their ability to reduce moral hazard on the part of borrowers is severely limited, and so they are less willing to lend. Again,

---

FYI   The Tyranny of Collateral

To use property, such as land or capital, as collateral, a person must legally own it. Unfortunately, as Hernando De Soto documents in his book *The Mystery of Capital*, it is extremely expensive and time-consuming for the poor in developing countries to make their ownership of property legal. Obtaining legal title to a dwelling on urban land in the Philippines, for example, involved 168 bureaucratic steps and 53 public and private agencies, and the process took anywhere from 13 to 25 years. Obtaining legal title to desert land in Egypt took 77 steps, 31 public and private agencies, and anywhere from five to 14 years. To legally buy government land in Haiti, an ordinary citizen had to go through 176 steps over 19 years. These legal barriers do not mean that the poor do not invest: they still build houses and buy equipment, even if they don't have legal title to these assets. By De Soto's calculations, the "total value of the real estate held but not legally owned by the poor of developing and former communist nations is at least $9.3 trillion (U.S.)."*

Without legal title, however, none of this property can be used as collateral to borrow funds, a requirement for most lenders. Even when people have legal title to their property, the legal system in most developing countries is so inefficient that collateral does not mean much. Typically, creditors must first sue the defaulting debtor for payment, which takes several years, and then, upon obtaining a favourable judgment, the creditor has to sue again to obtain title to the collateral. This process often takes in excess of

five years. By the time the lender acquires the collateral, it is likely to have been neglected or stolen and thus has little value. In addition, governments often block lenders from foreclosing on borrowers in politically powerful sectors of a society, such as agriculture.

When the financial system is unable to use collateral effectively, the adverse selection problem worsens because the lender needs even more information about the quality of the borrower in order to distinguish a good loan from a bad one. Little lending will take place, especially in transactions that involve collateral, such as mortgages. In Peru, for example, the value of mortgage loans relative to the size of the economy is less than 1/20 of that in the United States.

The poor in developing countries have an even harder time obtaining loans because it is too costly for them to get title to their property, and therefore they have no collateral to offer, resulting in what Raghuram Rajan, the governor of India's central bank, and Luigi Zingales of the University of Chicago refer to as the "tyranny of collateral."** Even when poor people have a good idea for a business and are willing to work hard, they cannot get the funds to finance the business, making it difficult for them to escape poverty.

* Hernando De Soto, *The Mystery of Capital: Why Capitalism Triumphs in the West and Fails Everywhere Else* (New York: Basic Books, 2000), 35.
** Raghuram Rajan and Luigi Zingales, *Saving Capitalism from the Capitalists: Unleashing the Power of Financial Markets to Create Wealth and Spread Opportunity* (New York: Crown Business, 2003).

the outcome is less productive investment and a lower growth rate for the economy. The importance of an effective legal system in promoting economic growth suggests that lawyers play a more positive role in the economy than we give them credit for.

Governments in developing and transition countries often use their financial systems to direct credit to themselves or to favoured sectors of the economy by setting interest rates at artificially low levels for certain types of loans, by creating development finance institutions to make specific types of loans, or by directing existing institutions to lend to certain entities. As we have seen, private institutions have an incentive to solve adverse selection and moral hazard problems and to lend to borrowers with the most productive investment opportunities. Governments have less incentive to do so because they are not driven by the profit motive and thus their directed credit programs may not channel funds to sectors that will produce high growth for the economy. The likely outcome is, again, less efficient investment and slower economic growth.

In addition, banks in many developing and transition countries are owned by their governments. Again, because of the absence of the profit motive, these **state-owned banks** have little incentive to allocate their capital to the most productive uses. Not surprisingly, the primary loan customer of these state-owned banks is often the government itself, which does not always use the funds wisely.

We have seen that government regulation can increase the amount of information available in financial markets and thus help them work more efficiently. Many developing and transition countries have an underdeveloped regulatory apparatus that retards the provision of adequate information to the marketplace. For example, these countries often have weak accounting standards, making it very hard to ascertain the quality of a borrower's balance sheet. As a result, asymmetric information problems are more severe, and the financial system is severely hampered in channeling funds to the most productive uses.

The institutional environment of a poor legal system, weak accounting standards, inadequate government regulation, and government intervention through directed credit programs and state ownership of banks all help explain why many countries stay poor while others grow rich.

APPLICATION   Is China a Counterexample to the Importance of Financial Development?

Although China appears to be on its way to becoming an economic powerhouse, its financial development remains in the early stages. The country's legal system is weak, so that financial contracts are difficult to enforce, and accounting standards are lax, making high-quality information about creditors hard to obtain. Regulation of the banking system is still in its formative stages, and the banking sector is dominated by large, state-owned banks. Yet the Chinese economy has enjoyed one of the highest growth rates in the world over the past 20 years. How has China been able to grow so rapidly, given its low level of financial development?

As noted above, China is in an early state of financial development, with a per capita income that is still less than $10 000, one-fifth the per capita income in the United States. With an extremely high savings rate, averaging around 40% over the past two decades, the country has been able to rapidly build up its capital stock and shift a massive pool of underutilized labour from the subsistence-agriculture sector into higher-productivity activities that use capital. Even though available savings have not always been allocated to their most productive uses, the huge increase in capital, combined with the gains in productivity achieved by moving labour out of low-productivity, subsistence agriculture, have been enough to produce high growth.

As China gets richer, however, this strategy is unlikely to continue to work. The former Soviet Union provides a graphic example. In the 1950s and 1960s, the Soviet Union shared many characteristics with modern-day China: high growth fueled by a high savings rate, a massive buildup of capital, and shifts of a large pool of underutilized labour from subsistence agriculture to manufacturing. During this high-growth phase, however, the Soviet Union was unable to develop the institutions needed to allocate capital efficiently. As a result, once the pool of subsistence labourers was used up, the Soviet Union's growth slowed dramatically and it was unable to keep up with Western economies. Today, no one considers the Soviet Union an economic success story, and its inability to develop the institutions necessary to sustain financial development and growth is an important reason for the demise of this superpower.

To move into the next stage of development, China will need to allocate its capital more efficiently, which requires that it improve its financial system. The Chinese leadership is well aware of this challenge; the government has announced that state-owned banks are being put on the path to privatization. In addition, the government is engaged in legal reform aimed at making financial contracts more enforceable. New bankruptcy law is being developed so that lenders will have the ability to take over the assets of firms that default on their loan contracts. Whether the Chinese government will succeed in developing a first-rate financial system, thereby enabling China to join the ranks of developed countries, is a big question mark. ◆

MyEconLab

MyEconLab is an online homework and tutorial system that puts you in control of your own learning with study and practice tools directly correlated to this chapter's content. Visit MyEconLab to access the eText, the Questions and Applied Problems with answers, as well as additional assessment. You will also find web chapters, mini-lectures, appendices, mini-cases, videos, glossary flashcards, news feeds, CANSIM data, and graphing tools.

SUMMARY

1. There are eight basic facts that summarize financial structure throughout the world. The first four emphasize the importance of financial intermediaries and the relative unimportance of securities markets with regard to the financing of corporations; the fifth recognizes that financial markets are among the most heavily regulated sectors of the economy; the sixth states that only large, well-established corporations have access to securities markets; the seventh indicates that collateral is an important feature of debt contracts; and the eighth presents debt contracts as complicated legal documents that place substantial restrictions on the behaviour of the borrower.

2. Transaction costs freeze many small savers and borrowers out of direct involvement with financial markets. Financial intermediaries can take advantage

of economies of scale and are better able to develop expertise, leading to lower transaction costs and thus enabling their savers and borrowers to benefit from the existence of financial markets.

3. Asymmetric information results in two problems: adverse selection, which occurs before the transaction takes place, and moral hazard, which occurs after the transaction has taken place. Adverse selection refers to the fact that bad credit risks are the ones most likely to seek loans, and moral hazard refers to the risk of the borrower engaging in activities that are undesirable from the lender's point of view.

4. Adverse selection interferes with the efficient functioning of financial markets. Tools that help reduce the adverse selection problem include private production and sale of information, government regulation to increase information, financial intermediation, and collateral and net worth. The free-rider problem occurs when people who

do not pay for information take advantage of information that other people have paid for. This problem explains why financial intermediaries, particularly banks, play a more important role in financing the activities of businesses than do securities markets.

5. Moral hazard in equity contracts, known as the principal–agent problem, occurs because managers (the agents) have less incentive to maximize profits than stockholders (the principals) do. The principal–agent problem explains why debt contracts are so much more prevalent in financial markets than equity contracts are. Tools that help reduce the principal–agent problem include monitoring, government regulation to increase information, and financial intermediation.

6. Tools that are used to reduce the moral hazard problem in debt contracts include net worth, monitoring and enforcement of restrictive covenants, and financial intermediaries.

KEY TERMS

agency theory, p. 175
audits, p. 178
collateral, p. 173
costly state verification, p. 182
equity capital, p. 180

free-rider problem, p. 177
incentive-compatible, p. 185
net worth, p. 180
principal-agent problem, p. 181
restrictive covenants, p. 173

secured debt, p. 173
state-owned banks, p. 189
unsecured debt, p. 173
venture capital firm, p. 183

QUESTIONS

All questions are available in MyEconLab at **www.myeconlab.com.**

1. For each of the following countries, identify the single most important (largest) and least important (smallest) source of external funding: Canada; United States; Germany; Japan. Comment on the similarities and differences among the countries' funding sources.

2. How can economies of scale help explain the existence of financial intermediaries?

3. Describe two ways in which financial intermediaries help lower transaction costs in an economy.

4. Why are financial intermediaries willing to engage in information collection activities when investors in financial instruments may be unwilling to do so?

5. Suppose you go to your local bank intending to buy a certificate of deposit with your savings. Explain why you would not offer a loan, at an interest rate that is higher than the rate the bank pays on certificates of deposit (but lower than the rate the bank charges for car loans), to the next individual who enters the bank and applies for a car loan.

6. Wealthy people often worry that others will seek to marry them only for their money. Is this a problem of adverse selection?

7. Do you think the lemons problem would be more severe for stocks traded on the Toronto Stock Exchange or for those traded over-the-counter? Explain.

8. Would you be more willing to lend to a friend if she had put all of her life savings into her business than you would be if she had not done so? Why?

9. What specific procedures do financial intermediaries use to reduce asymmetric information problems in lending?

10. What steps can the government take to reduce asymmetric information problems and help the financial system function more smoothly and efficiently?

11. How can asymmetric information problems lead to a bank panic?

12. In December 2001, Argentina announced it would not honour its sovereign (government-issued) debt. Many investors were left holding Argentinean bonds priced at a fraction of their previous value. A few years later, Argentina announced it would pay back 25% of the face value of its debt. Comment on the effects of information asymmetries on government bond markets. Do you think investors are currently willing to buy bonds issued by the government of Argentina?

13. How does the free-rider problem aggravate adverse selection and moral hazard problems in financial markets?

14. Would moral hazard and adverse selection still arise in financial markets if information were not asymmetric? Explain.

15. How do standardized accounting principles help financial markets work more efficiently?

16. Which firms are most likely to use bank financing rather than issue bonds or stocks to finance their activities? Why?

17. How can the existence of asymmetric information provide a rationale for government regulation of financial markets?

18. "The more collateral there is backing a loan, the less the lender has to worry about adverse selection." Is this statement true, false, or uncertain? Explain your answer.

19. Explain how the separation of ownership and control in Canadian corporations might lead to poor management.

20. Many policymakers in developing countries have proposed the implementation of a system of deposit insurance similar to the system that exists in Canada. Explain why this might create more problems than solutions in the financial system of a developing country.

21. Gustavo is a young doctor who lives in a country with a relatively inefficient legal and financial system. When Gustavo applied for a mortgage, he found that banks usually required collateral for up to 300% of the amount of the loan. Explain why banks might require that much collateral in such a financial system. Comment on the consequences of such a system for economic growth.

APPLIED PROBLEMS

All applied problems are available in MyEconLab *at* **www.myeconlab.com.**

For Problems 22–25, use the fact that the expected value of an event is a probability weighted average, the sum of each possible outcome multiplied by the probability of the event occurring.

22. You are in the market for a used car and decide to visit a used car dealership. You know that the Red Book value of the car you are looking at is between $20 000 and $24 000. If you believe the dealer knows *as much* about the car as you do, how much are you willing to pay? Why? Assume that you care only about the expected value of the car you will buy and that the car values are symmetrically distributed.

23. Refer to Problem 22. Now you believe the dealer knows *more* about the car than you do. How much

are you willing to pay? Why? How can this asymmetric information problem be resolved in a competitive market?

24. You wish to hire Ron to manage your Calgary operations. The profits from the operations depend partially on how hard Ron works, as follows.

	Profit Probabilities	
	Profit = $10 000	Profit = $50 000
Lazy	60%	40%
Hard worker	20%	80%

If Ron is lazy, he will surf the Internet all day, and he views this as a zero-cost opportunity. However,

Ron views working hard as a "personal cost" valued at $1000. What fixed percentage of the profits should you offer Ron? Assume Ron cares only about his expected payment less any "personal cost."

25. You own a house worth $400 000 that is located on a river. If the river floods moderately, the house will be completely destroyed. Moderate flooding happens about once every 50 years. If you build a seawall, the river would have to flood heavily to destroy your house, and such heavy flooding happens only about once every 200 years. What would be the annual premium for a flood insurance policy that offers full insurance? For a policy that pays only 75% of the home value, what are your expected costs with and without a seawall? Do the different policies provide an incentive to be safer (i.e., to build the seawall)?

DATA ANALYSIS PROBLEMS

Download data for these problems from MyEconLab *at* **www.myeconlab.com**.

1. Go to the Bank of Canada's web page at **www.bankofcanada.ca**. Click on the Bank of Canada's latest *Banking and Financial Statistics* and go to Table F10 to find the series for the net new issues of securities by financial and non-financial corporations. Get series V122334 (total bonds) and V122335 (total stocks).

a. Compare the bonds series to the stocks series. Which is a more important source of finance, stocks or bonds?

b. What is the correlation coefficient between the two series? Has the correlation changed in the aftermath of the global financial crisis (after 2008)?

WEB EXERCISES

1. In this chapter, we discuss the lemons problem and its effect on the efficient functioning of a market. This theory was initially developed by George Akerlof. Go to **www.nobel.se/economics/laureates/2001/ public.html**. This site reports that Akerlof, Spence, and Stiglitz were awarded the Nobel Prize in economics in 2001 for their work. Read this report down through the section on George Akerlof. Summarize his research ideas in one page.

WEB REFERENCES

http://nobelprize.org/nobel_prize/economics/laureates/2001/ public.html

A complete discussion of the lemons problem on a site dedicated to Nobel Prize winners.

9 Financial Crises

Learning Objectives

After studying this chapter you should be able to

1. Define the term "financial crisis."

2. Identify the key features of the three stages of a financial crisis.

3. Describe the causes and consequences of the global financial crisis of 2007–2009.

4. Summarize the changes to financial regulation that occurred in response to the global financial crisis of 2007–2009.

5. Identify the gaps in current financial regulation and how those gaps may be addressed with future regulatory changes.

PREVIEW

Financial crises are major disruptions in financial markets characterized by sharp declines in asset prices and firm failures. Beginning in August 2007, defaults in the subprime mortgage market in the United States (by borrowers with weak credit records) sent a shudder through the financial markets, leading to the worst financial crisis since the Great Depression. In Congressional testimony, Alan Greenspan, former chairman of the Fed, described the financial crisis as a "once-in-a-century credit tsunami." Wall Street firms and commercial banks suffered hundreds of billions of dollars of losses. Households and businesses found they had to pay higher rates on their borrowings—and it was much harder to get credit. All over the world, stock markets crashed, with the S&P/TSX market falling by more than 40% from its peak. Many financial firms, including commercial banks, investment banks, and insurance companies, went belly up. A recession began in December of 2007, and by the fall of 2008, the economy was in a tailspin. The recession, which ended in June of 2009, was the most severe since World War II and is now known as the "Great Recession."

Why did this financial crisis occur? Why have financial crises been so prevalent throughout Canadian history, as well as in so many other countries, and what insights do they provide on the most recent crisis? Why are financial crises almost always followed by severe contractions in economic activity, as occurred during the Great Recession? We will examine these questions in this chapter by developing a framework with which to understand the dynamics of financial crises. Building on Chapter 8, we make use of agency theory, the economic analysis of the effects of asymmetric information (adverse selection and moral hazard) on financial markets and the economy in general, to see why financial crises occur and why they have such devastating effects on the economy. We then apply our analysis to explain the course of events that led to a number of past financial crises, including the most recent global financial crisis.[1]

---

[1]Web Chapter 1: Crises in Emerging Market Economies, available on the MyEconLab extends the analysis to financial crises in *emerging market economies*, economies in an early stage of market development that have recently opened up to the flow of goods, services, and capital from the rest of the world.

WHAT IS A FINANCIAL CRISIS?

In Chapter 8, we saw that a well-functioning financial system solves asymmetric information problems (moral hazard and adverse selection) so that capital is allocated to its most productive uses. These asymmetric information problems, which act as a barrier to efficient allocation of capital, are often described by economists as **financial frictions**. When financial frictions increase, financial markets are less capable of channeling funds efficiently from savers to households and firms with productive investment opportunities, with the result that economic activity declines. A **financial crisis** occurs when information flows in financial markets experience a particularly large disruption, with the result that financial frictions increase sharply and financial markets stop functioning. Then, economic activity collapses.

DYNAMICS OF FINANCIAL CRISES

As earth-shaking and headline-grabbing as the most recent financial crisis was, it was only one of a number of financial crises that have hit industrialized countries like Canada and the United States over the years. These experiences have helped economists uncover insights into present-day economic turmoil.

Financial crises in advanced economies have progressed in two and sometimes three stages. To understand how these crises have unfolded, refer to Figure 9-1, which traces the stages and sequence of events in financial crises in advanced economies.

Stage One: Initial Phase

Financial crises can begin in two ways: credit boom and bust, or a general increase in uncertainty caused by failures of major financial institutions.

Credit Boom and Bust   The seeds of a financial crisis are often sown when an economy introduces new types of loans or other financial products, known as **financial innovation**, or when countries engage in **financial liberalization**, the elimination of restrictions on financial markets and institutions. In the long run, financial liberalization promotes financial development and encourages a well-run financial system that allocates capital efficiently. However, financial liberalization has a dark side: In the short run, it can prompt financial institutions to go on a lending spree, called a **credit boom**. Unfortunately, lenders may not have the expertise, or the incentives, to manage risk appropriately in these new lines of business. Even with proper management, credit booms eventually outstrip the ability of institutions—and government regulators—to screen and monitor credit risks, leading to overly risky lending.

As we will learn in Chapter 10, government safety nets, such as deposit insurance, weaken market discipline and increase the moral hazard incentive for banks to take on greater risk than they otherwise would. Because lender-savers know that government-guaranteed insurance protects them from losses, they will supply even undisciplined banks with funds. Without proper monitoring, risk-taking grows unchecked.

Eventually, losses on loans begin to mount, and the value of the loans (on the asset side of the balance sheet) falls relative to liabilities, thereby driving down the net worth (capital) of banks and other financial institutions. With less capital, these financial institutions cut back on their lending to borrower-spenders, a process called **deleveraging**.

MyEconLab Mini-lecture

FIGURE 9-1   **Sequence of Events in Financial Crises in Advanced Economies**

The solid arrows trace the sequence of events during a typical financial crisis; the dotted arrows show the additional set of events that occurs if the crisis develops into a debt deflation. The sections separated by the dashed horizontal lines show the different stages of a financial crisis.

Furthermore, with less capital, banks and other financial institutions become riskier, causing lender-savers and other potential lenders to these institutions to pull out their funds. Fewer funds mean fewer loans to fund productive investments and a credit freeze: The lending boom turns into a lending crash.

When financial institutions stop collecting information and making loans, financial frictions rise, limiting the financial system's ability to address the asymmetric information problems of adverse selection and moral hazard (as shown in the arrow pointing from the first factor, "Deterioration in Financial Institutions' Balance Sheets," in the top row of Figure 9-1). As loans become scarce, borrower-spenders are no longer able to fund their productive investment opportunities and they decrease their spending, causing economic activity to contract.

Asset-Price Boom and Bust Prices of assets such as equity shares and real estate can be driven by investor psychology (dubbed "irrational exuberance" by Alan Greenspan when he was chairman of the Federal Reserve) well above their **fundamental economic values**, that is, their values based on realistic expectations of the assets' future income streams. The rise of asset prices above their fundamental economic values is an **asset-price bubble**. Examples of asset-price bubbles are the tech stock market bubble of the late 1990s and the recent housing price bubble in the United States that we will discuss later in this chapter. Asset-price bubbles are often also driven by credit booms, in which the large increase in credit is used to fund purchases of assets, thereby driving up their price.

When the bubble bursts and asset prices realign with fundamental economic values, stock and real estate prices tumble, companies see their net worth (the difference between their assets and their liabilities) decline, and the value of collateral these companies can pledge drops. Now these companies have less at stake because they have less "skin in the game," and so they are more likely to make risky investments because they have less to lose, the problem of moral hazard. As a result, financial institutions tighten lending standards for borrower-spenders and lending contracts (as shown by the downward arrow pointing from the second factor, "Asset-Price Decline," in the top row of Figure 9-1).

The asset-price bust also causes a decline in the value of financial institutions' assets, thereby causing a decline in the institutions' net worth and hence a deterioration in their balance sheets (shown by the arrow from the second factor to the first factor in the top row of Figure 9-1), which causes them to deleverage, steepening the decline in economic activity.

Increase in Uncertainty Canadian financial crises have usually begun in periods of high uncertainty, such as just after the start of a recession, a crash in the stock market, or the failure of a major financial institution. The failure of major financial institutions (such as Bear Stearns, Lehman Brothers, and AIG in 2008 in the United States) is a particularly important source of heightened uncertainty that features prominently in financial crises. Examples in Canadian history are the Bank of Upper Canada in 1866, the bank panic of 1879, and the Home Bank in 1923. With information hard to come by in a period of high uncertainty, financial frictions increase, reducing lending and economic activity (as shown by the arrow pointing from the last factor, "Increases in Uncertainty," in the top row of Figure 9-1).

Stage Two: Banking Crisis

Deteriorating balance sheets and tougher business conditions lead some financial institutions into insolvency, which happens when their net worth becomes negative. Unable to pay off depositors or other creditors, some banks go out of business. If severe enough, these factors can lead to a bank panic in which multiple banks fail simultaneously. The source of the contagion is asymmetric information. In a panic, depositors, fearing for the safety of their deposits (in the absence of or with limited amounts of deposit insurance) and not knowing the quality of banks' loan portfolios, withdraw their deposits to the point that the banks fail. Uncertainty about the health of the banking system in general can lead to runs on banks, both good and bad, which forces banks to sell off assets quickly to raise the necessary funds. These **fire sales** of assets may cause their prices to decline so much that more banks become insolvent and the resulting contagion can then lead to multiple bank failures and a full-fledged bank panic.

With fewer banks operating, information about the creditworthiness of borrower-spenders disappears. Increasingly severe adverse selection and moral hazard problems in financial markets deepen the financial crisis, causing declines in asset prices and the failure of firms throughout the economy that lack funds for productive investment opportunities. Figure 9-1 represents this progression in the stage two portion. Bank panics were a feature of all Canadian financial crises during the nineteenth and twentieth centuries, occurring in 1866, 1879, 1923, and 1930–1933. Bank panics were also a feature of all U.S. financial crises until World War II, occurring every 20 years or so in 1819, 1837, 1857, 1873, 1884, 1893, 1907, and 1930–33. (The 1933 establishment of federal deposit insurance, which protects depositors from losses, has prevented subsequent bank panics in the United States.)

Eventually, public and private authorities shut down insolvent firms and sell them off or liquidate them. Uncertainty in financial markets declines, the stock market recovers, and balance sheets improve. Financial frictions diminish and the financial crisis subsides. With the financial markets able to operate well again, the stage is set for an economic recovery.

Stage Three: Debt Deflation

If, however, the economic downturn leads to a sharp decline in the price level, the recovery process can be short-circuited. In stage three of Figure 9-1, **debt deflation** occurs when a substantial, unanticipated decline in the price level sets in, leading to a further deterioration in firms' net worth because of the increased burden of indebtedness.

In economies with moderate inflation, which characterizes most advanced countries, many debt contracts with fixed interest rates are typically of fairly long maturity—10 years or more. Because debt payments are contractually fixed in nominal terms, an unanticipated decline in the price level raises the value of borrowing firms' and households' liabilities in real terms (increases the burden of the debt) but does not raise the real value of their assets. The borrowers' net worth in real terms (the difference between assets and liabilities in real terms) thus declines.

To better understand how this decline in net worth occurs, consider what happens if a firm in 2016 has assets of $100 million (in 2016 dollars) and $90 million of long-term liabilities, so that it has $10 million in net worth (the difference between the values of assets and liabilities). If the price level falls by 10% in 2017, the real value of the liabilities would rise to $99 million in 2016 dollars, while the real value of the assets would remain unchanged at $100 million. The result would be that real net worth in 2016 dollars would fall from $10 million to $1 million ($100 million minus $99 million).

The substantial decline in the real net worth of borrowers caused by a sharp drop in the price level creates an increase in adverse selection and moral hazard problems for lenders. Lending and economic activity decline for a long time. The most significant financial crisis that displayed debt deflation was the Great Depression, the worst economic contraction in Canadian history.

APPLICATION   **The Mother of All Financial Crises: The Great Depression in the United States**

With our framework for understanding financial crises in place, we are prepared to analyze how a financial crisis unfolded during the Great Depression and how it led to the worst economic downturn in U.S. history.

Stock Market Crash

In 1928 and 1929, prices doubled in the U.S. stock market. Federal Reserve officials viewed the stock market boom as caused by excessive speculation. To curb it, they pursued a tightening of monetary policy to raise interest rates in an effort to limit the rise in stock prices. The Federal Reserve got more than it bargained for when the stock market crashed in October 1929, falling by 40% by the end of 1929, as shown in Figure 9-2.

Bank Panics

By the middle of 1930, stocks had recovered almost half of their losses and credit market conditions had stabilized. What might have been a normal recession turned into something far worse, however, when severe droughts in the Midwest led to a sharp decline in agricultural production, with the result that farmers could not pay back their bank loans. The resulting defaults on farm mortgages led to large loan losses on bank balance sheets in agricultural regions. The general weakness of the economy, and of

MyEconLab Mini-lecture

FIGURE 9-2   **Stock Prices During the Great Depression Period**

Stock prices in the United States crashed in 1929, falling by 40% by the end of 1929, and then continued to fall to only 10% of their peak value by 1932.

Source: Dow-Jones Industrial Average (DJIA). Global Financial Data: www.globalfinancialdata.com/index_tabs.php?action=detailedinfo&id=1165.

the banks in agricultural regions in particular, prompted substantial withdrawals from banks, building to a full-fledged panic in November and December of 1930, with the stock market falling sharply. For more than two years, the Federal Reserve sat idly by through one bank panic after another, the most severe spate of panics in U.S. history. After what would be the era's final panic in March 1933, President Franklin Delano Roosevelt declared a bank holiday, a temporary closing of all banks. "The only thing we have to fear is fear itself," Roosevelt told the nation. The damage was done, however, and more than one-third of U.S. commercial banks had failed.

Continuing Decline in Stock Prices

Stock prices kept falling. By mid-1932, stocks had declined to 10% of their value at the 1929 peak (as shown in Figure 9-2), and the increase in uncertainty from the unsettled business conditions created by the economic contraction worsened adverse selection and moral hazard problems in financial markets. With a greatly reduced number of financial intermediaries still in business, adverse selection and moral hazard problems intensified even further. Financial markets struggled to channel funds to borrower-spenders with productive investment opportunities. The amount of outstanding commercial loans fell by half from 1929 to 1933, and investment spending collapsed, declining by 90% from its 1929 level.

A manifestation of the rise in financial frictions is that lenders began charging businesses much higher interest rates to protect themselves from credit losses. The resulting rise in the **credit spread**—the difference between the interest rate on loans to households and businesses and the interest rate on completely safe assets that are sure to be paid back, such as U.S. Treasury securities—is shown in Figure 9-3, which displays the

MyEconLab Mini-lecture

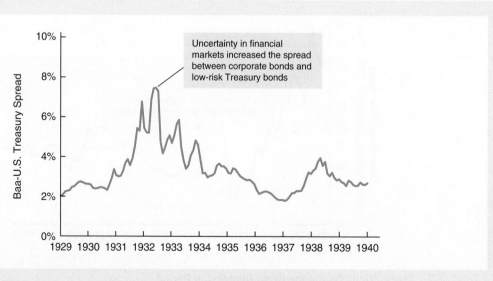

FIGURE 9-3 **Credit Spreads During the Great Depression in the United States**

Credit spreads (the difference between rates on Baa corporate bonds and U.S. Treasury bonds) rose sharply during the Great Depression.

Source: Federal Reserve Bank of St. Louis FRED database: **http://research.stlouisfed.org/fred2/**.

difference between interest rates on corporate bonds with a Baa (medium-quality) credit rating and rates on similar-maturity Treasury bonds. (Note the credit spread is closely related to the risk premium discussed in Chapter 6.)

Debt Deflation

The ongoing deflation that accompanied declining economic activity eventually led to a 25% decline in the U.S. price level. This deflation short-circuited the normal recovery process that occurs in most recessions. The huge decline in prices triggered a debt deflation in which net worth fell because of the increased burden of indebtedness borne by firms and households. The decline in net worth and the resulting increase in adverse selection and moral hazard problems in the credit markets led to a prolonged economic contraction in which unemployment rose to 25% of the labour force. The financial crisis of the Great Depression was the worst ever experienced in the United States, which explains why the economic contraction was also the most severe ever experienced by that nation.

International Dimensions

Although the Great Depression started in the United States, it was not just a U.S. phenomenon. Bank panics in the United States also spread to the rest of the world, including Canada, and the contraction of the U.S. economy sharply decreased the demand for foreign goods. The worldwide depression caused great hardship, with millions upon millions of people out of work, and the resulting discontent led to the rise of fascism and World War II. The consequences of the Great Depression financial crisis were disastrous. ◆

THE GLOBAL FINANCIAL CRISIS OF 2007–2009

For many years, most economists thought that financial crises of the type experienced during the Great Depression were a thing of the past for advanced countries like Canada and the United States. Unfortunately, the financial crisis that engulfed the world in 2007–2009 proved them wrong.

Causes of the 2007–2009 Financial Crisis

We begin our look at the subprime financial crisis in the United States, which was the underlying driving force behind the global financial crisis of 2007–2009. We examine three central factors that caused the U.S. subprime financial crisis: financial innovation in mortgage markets, agency problems in mortgage markets, and the role of asymmetric information in the credit-rating process.

Financial Innovation in the Mortgage Markets   Starting in the early 2000s, advances in information technology made it easier to securitize subprime mortgages, leading to an explosion in subprime mortgage-backed securities. Financial innovation didn't stop there. Financial engineering, the development of new, sophisticated financial instruments, led to **structured credit products** that paid out income streams from a collection of underlying assets, designed to have particular risk characteristics that appealed to investors with differing preferences. The most notorious of these products were collateralized debt obligations (CDOs) (discussed in the FYI box, "Collateralized Debt Obligations).

Agency Problems in the Mortgage Markets   The mortgage brokers who originated the mortgage loans often did not make a strong effort to evaluate whether a borrower could pay off the mortgage, since they planned to quickly sell (distribute) the loans to investors in the form of mortgage-backed securities. This originate-to-distribute business model was exposed to the principal–agent problem of the type discussed in Chapter 8, in which the mortgage brokers acted as agents for investors (the principals) but did not have the investors' best interests at heart. Once the mortgage broker earns his or her fee, why should the broker care if the borrower makes good on his or her payment? The more volume the broker originates, the more money he or she makes.

Not surprisingly, adverse selection became a major problem. Risk-loving real-estate investors lined up to obtain loans to acquire houses that would be very profitable if housing prices went up, knowing they could "walk away" if housing prices went down. The principal–agent problem also created incentives for mortgage brokers to encourage households to take on mortgages they could not afford, or to commit fraud by falsifying information on borrowers' mortgage applications in order to qualify them for mortgages. Compounding this problem was lax regulation of originators, who were

---

FYI   Collateralized Debt Obligations (CDOs)

The creation of a collateralized debt obligation involves a corporate entity called a *special purpose vehicle (SPV)*, which buys a collection of assets such as corporate bonds and loans, commercial real estate bonds, and mortgage-backed securities. The SPV then separates the payment streams (cash flows) from these assets into a number of buckets that are referred to as *tranches*. The highest-rated tranches, called *super senior tranches*, are the ones that are paid off first and so have the least risk. The super senior CDO is a bond that pays out these cash flows to investors, and because it has the least risk, it also has the lowest interest rate. The next bucket of cash flows, known as the *senior tranche*, is paid out next; the senior CDO has a little more risk and pays a higher interest rate. The next tranche of payment streams, the *mezzanine tranche* of the CDO, is paid out after the super senior and senior tranches and so it bears more risk and has an even higher interest rate. The lowest tranche of the CDO is the *equity tranche*; this is the first set of cash flows that are not paid out if the underlying assets go

into default and stop making payments. This tranche has the highest risk and is often not traded.

If all of this sounds complicated, it is. Tranches also included CDO^2s and CDO^3s that sliced and diced risk even further, paying out the cash flows from CDOs to CDO^2s and from CDO^2s to CDO^3s. Although financial engineering carries the potential benefit of creating products and services that match investors' risk appetites, it also has a dark side. Structured products like CDOs, CDO^2s, and CDO^3s can get so complicated that it becomes hard to value the cash flows of the underlying assets for a security or to determine who actually owns these assets. Indeed, in October 2007, Ben Bernanke, then chairman of the Federal Reserve, joked that he "would like to know what those damn things are worth." In other words, the increased complexity of structured products can actually reduce the amount of information in financial markets, thereby worsening asymmetric information in the financial system and increasing the severity of adverse selection and moral hazard problems.

not required to disclose information to borrowers that would have helped them assess whether they could afford the loans.

The agency problems went even deeper. Commercial and investment banks, which were earning large fees by underwriting mortgage-backed securities and structured credit products like CDOs, also had weak incentives to make sure that the ultimate holders of the securities would be paid off. **Financial derivatives**, financial instruments whose payoffs are linked to (i.e., derived from) previously issued securities, also were an important source of excessive risk taking. Large fees from writing a type of financial insurance contract called a **credit default swap**, a financial derivative that provides payments to holders of bonds if they default, also drove units of insurance companies like AIG to write hundreds of billions of dollars' worth of these risky contracts.

Asymmetric Information and Credit-Rating Agencies   Credit-rating agencies, agencies that rate the quality of debt securities in terms of the probability of default, were another contributor to asymmetric information in financial markets. The rating agencies advised clients on how to structure complex financial instruments, like CDOs, while at the same time they were rating these identical products. The rating agencies were thus subject to conflicts of interest because the large fees they earned from advising clients on how to structure products that they themselves were rating meant that they did not have sufficient incentives to make sure their ratings were accurate. The result was wildly inflated ratings that enabled the sale of complex financial products that were far riskier than investors recognized.

Effects of the 2007–2009 Financial Crisis

Consumers and businesses alike suffered as a result of the 2007–2009 financial crisis. The impact of the crisis was most evident in five key areas: the U.S. residential housing market, financial institutions' balance sheets, the shadow banking system, global financial markets, and the headline-grabbing failures of major firms in the financial industry.

Residential Housing Prices: Boom and Bust   The subprime mortgage market took off after the recession ended in the United States in 2001. By 2007, it had become over a trillion-dollar market. The development of the subprime mortgage market was encouraged by economists and politicians alike because it led to a "democratization of credit" and helped raise U.S. homeownership rates to the highest levels in history. The asset-price boom in housing (see Figure 9-4), which took off after the 2000–2001 recession was over, also helped stimulate the growth of the subprime mortgage market. High housing prices meant that subprime borrowers could refinance their houses with even larger loans when their homes appreciated in value. With housing prices rising, subprime borrowers were also unlikely to default because they could always sell their house to pay off the loan, making investors happy because the securities backed by cash flows from subprime mortgages had high returns. The growth of the subprime mortgage market, in turn, increased the demand for houses and so fuelled the boom in housing prices, resulting in a housing price bubble.

Further stimulus for the inflated housing market came from low interest rates on residential mortgages, which were the result of several different forces. First were the huge capital inflows into the United States from countries like China and India.

MyEconLab Mini-lecture

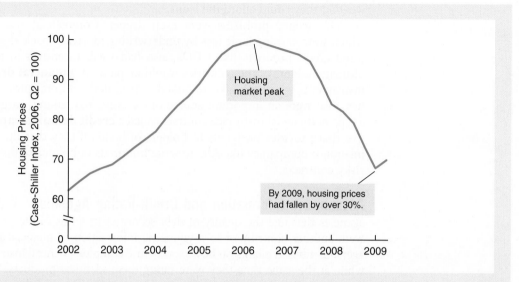

FIGURE 9-4 **Housing Prices in the United States and the Financial Crisis of 2007–2009**

Housing prices in the United States boomed from 2002 to 2006, fuelling the market for subprime mortgages and forming an asset-price bubble. Housing prices began declining in 2006, subsequently falling by more than 30% which led to defaults by subprime mortgage holders.

Source: Case-Shiller U.S. National Composite House Price Index from Federal Reserve Bank of St. Louis FRED database: **http://research.stlouisfed.org/fred2/**.

Second was Congressional legislation that encouraged Fannie Mae and Freddie Mac to purchase trillions of dollars of mortgage-backed securities.[2] Third was Federal Reserve monetary policy that made it easy to lower interest rates. The low cost of financing for housing purchases that resulted from these forces further stimulated the demand for housing, pushing up housing prices. (A highly controversial issue is whether the Federal Reserve was to blame for the housing price bubble, and this is discussed in the FYI box.)

As housing prices rose and profitability for mortgage originators and lenders grew higher, the underwriting standards for subprime mortgages fell lower and lower. High-risk borrowers were able to obtain mortgages, and the amount of the mortgage relative to the value of the house, the loan-to-value ratio (LTV), rose. Borrowers were often able to get piggyback, second, and third mortgages on top of their original 80% loan-to-value mortgage, so that they had to put almost no money down. When asset prices rise too far out of line with fundamentals—in the case of housing, the cost of purchasing a home relative to the cost of renting it, or the cost of houses relative to households' median income—they must come down. Eventually, the housing price bubble burst. With housing prices falling after their peak in 2006 (see Figure 9-4), the rot in the financial system began to reveal itself. The decline in housing prices led many subprime borrowers to find that their mortgages were "underwater"—that is, the value of the house was

[2]For a discussion of the government's role in encouraging the housing boom, which led to a subsequent bust in the housing market, see Thomas Sowell, *The Housing Boom and Bust*, Revised Edition (New York, Basic Books, 2010).

FYI Was the Federal Reserve to Blame for the Housing Price Bubble?

Some economists—most prominently, John Taylor of Stanford University—have argued that the low interest rate policy of the Federal Reserve in the 2003–2006 period caused the housing price bubble.[*] Taylor argues that the low federal funds rate led to low mortgage rates that stimulated housing demand and encouraged the issuance of subprime mortgages, both of which led to rising housing prices and a bubble.

In a speech given in January 2010, then-Federal Reserve Chairman Ben Bernanke countered this argument.[†] He concluded that monetary policy was not to blame for the housing price bubble. First, he said, it is not at all clear that the federal funds rate was too low durng the 2003–2006 period. Rather, the culprits were

the proliferation of new mortgage products that lowered mortgage payments, a relaxation of lending standards that brought more buyers into the housing market, and capital inflows from countries such as China and India. Bernanke's speech was very controversial, and the debate over whether monetary policy was to blame for the housing price bubble continues to this day.

[*]John Taylor, "Housing and Monetary Policy," in Federal Reserve Bank of Kansas City, *Housing, Housing Finance and Monetary Policy* (Kansas City: Federal Reserve Bank of Kansas City, 2007), 463–476.

[†]Ben S. Bernanke, "Monetary Policy and the Housing Bubble," speech given at the annual meeting of the American Economic Association, Atlanta Georgia, January 3, 2010; http://www.federalreserve.gov/newsevents/speech/bernanke20100103a.htm.

---

below the amount of the mortgage. When this happened, struggling homeowners had tremendous incentives to walk away from their homes and just send the keys back to the lender. Defaults on mortgages shot up sharply, eventually leading to foreclosures on millions of mortgages.

Deterioration of Financial Institutions' Balance Sheets

The decline in U.S. housing prices led to rising defaults on mortgages. As a result, the values of mortgage-backed securities and CDOs collapsed, leaving banks and other financial institutions holding those securities with a lower value of assets and thus a lower net worth. With weakened balance sheets, these banks and other financial institutions began to deleverage, selling off assets and restricting the availability of credit to both households and businesses. With no one else able to step in to collect information and make loans, the reduction in bank lending meant that financial frictions increased in financial markets.

Run on the Shadow Banking System

The sharp decline in the values of mortgages and other financial assets triggered a run on the shadow banking system, composed of hedge funds, investment banks, and other nondepository financial firms, which are not as tightly regulated as banks are. Funds from shadow banks flowed through the financial system and for many years supported the issuance of low-interest-rate mortgages and auto loans.

These securities were funded primarily by **repurchase agreements (repos)**, short-term borrowing that, in effect, uses assets like mortgage-backed securities as collateral. Rising concern about the quality of a financial institution's balance sheet led lenders to require larger amounts of collateral, known as **haircuts**. For example, if a borrower took out a $100 million loan in a repo agreement, the borrower might have to post $105 million of mortgage-backed securities as collateral, for a haircut of 5%.

Rising defaults on mortgages caused the values of mortgage-backed securities to fall, which then led to a rise in haircuts. At the start of the crisis, haircuts were close to zero, but eventually they rose to nearly 50%.[3] The result was that financial institutions could borrow only half as much with the same amount of collateral. Thus, to raise funds, financial institutions had to engage in fire sales and sell off their assets very rapidly. Because selling assets quickly requires lowering prices, the fire sales led to a further decline in financial institutions' asset values. This decline lowered the value of collateral further, raising haircuts and thereby forcing financial institutions to scramble even more for liquidity. The result was similar to the run on the banking system that occurred during the Great Depression in the United States, causing massive deleveraging that resulted in a restriction of lending and a decline in economic activity.

The decline in asset prices in the stock market (which fell by over 50% from October 2007 to March 2009, as shown in Figure 9-5) and the more than 30% drop in residential house prices (shown in Figure 9-4), along with the fire sales resulting from the run on the shadow banking system, weakened both firms' and households' balance sheets. This worsening of financial frictions manifested itself in widening credit spreads, causing higher costs of credit for households and businesses and tighter lending standards. The resulting decline in lending meant that both consumption expenditure and investment fell, causing the economy to contract.[4]

MyEconLab Mini-lecture

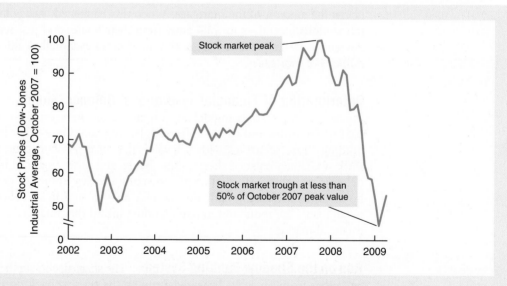

FIGURE 9-5 **Stock Prices in the United States and the Financial Crisis of 2007–2009**

Stock prices in the United States fell by 50% from October 2007 to March 2009.
Source: Dow-Jones Industrial Average (DJIA). Global Financial Data: **www.globalfinancialdata.com/index_tabs.php?action=detailedinfo&id=1165**.

---

[3]See Gary Gorton and Andrew Metrick, "Securitized Banking and the Run on Repo," National Bureau of Economic Research Working Paper No. 15223 (August 2009).

[4]This period was also characterized by a substantial supply shock that occurred when oil and other commodity prices rose sharply until the summer of 2008, but then fell precipitously thereafter. We discuss the aggregate demand and supply analysis of the impact of this supply shock in Chapter 23.

Global Financial Markets   Although the problem originated in the United States, the wake-up call for the financial crisis came from Europe, a sign of how extensive the globalization of financial markets had become. After both Fitch and Standard & Poor's announced ratings downgrades on mortgage-backed securities and CDOs totalling more than $10 billion, on August 7, 2007, a French investment house, BNP Paribas, suspended redemption of shares held in some of its money market funds, which had sustained large losses. The run on the shadow banking system began, only to become worse and worse over time. Despite huge injections of liquidity into the financial system by central banks around the world, banks began to horde cash and were unwilling to lend to each other. The drying up of credit led to the first major bank failure in the United Kingdom in over 100 years when Northern Rock, which had relied on short-term borrowing in the repo market rather than deposits for its funding, collapsed in September 2007. A string of other European financial institutions then failed as well. Particularly hard hit were countries like Greece, Ireland, Portugal, Spain, and Italy. The resulting crisis in markets for government-issued (sovereign) debt in Europe is described in the Global box, The European Sovereign Debt Crisis.

Global   The European Sovereign Debt Crisis

The global financial crisis of 2007–2009 led not only to a worldwide recession but also to a sovereign debt crisis that still threatens to destabilize Europe today. Up until 2007, all of the countries that had adopted the euro found their interest rates converging to very low levels, but with the onset of the global financial crisis, several of these countries were hit very hard by the contraction in economic activity, which reduced tax revenues at the same time that government bailouts of failed financial institutions required additional government outlays. The resulting surge in budget deficits then led to fears that the governments of these hard-hit countries would default on their debt. The result was a surge in interest rates that threatened to spiral out of control.[*]

Greece was the first domino to fall in Europe. In September 2009, with an economy weakened by reduced tax revenues and increased spending demands, the Greek government was projecting a budget deficit for the year of 6% and a debt-to-GDP ratio near 100%. However, when a new government was elected that October, it revealed that the budget situation was far worse than anyone had imagined, because the previous government had provided misleading numbers about both the budget deficit, which was at least double the 6% number, and the amount of government debt, which was 10 percentage points higher than previously reported. Despite austerity measures aimed at dramatically cutting government spending and raising taxes, interest rates on Greek debt soared, eventually rising to nearly 40%, and the debt-to-GDP ratio climbed to 160% of GDP in 2012. Even with bailouts from other European countries and liquidity support from the European Central Bank, Greece was forced to write down the value of its debt held in private hands by more than half, and the country was subject to civil unrest, with massive strikes and the resignation of the prime minister.

The sovereign debt crisis spread from Greece to Ireland, Portugal, Spain, and Italy. The governments of these countries were forced to embrace austerity measures to shore up their public finances while interest rates climbed to double-digit levels. Only with a speech in July 2012 by Mario Draghi, the president of the European Central Bank, in which he stated that the ECB was ready to do "whatever it takes" to save the euro, did the markets begin to calm down. Nonetheless, despite a sharp decline in interest rates in these countries, the countries experienced severe recessions, with unemployment rates rising to double-digit levels and Spain's unemployment rate exceeding 25%. The stresses that the European sovereign debt crisis produced for the euro zone, the countries that have adopted the euro, has raised doubts about whether the euro will survive.

[*] For a discussion of the dynamics of sovereign debt crises and case studies of the European debt crisis, see David Greenlaw, James D. Hamilton, Frederic S. Mishkin, and Peter Hooper, "Crunch Time: Fiscal Crises and the Role of Monetary Policy," *U.S. Monetary Policy Forum* (Chicago: Chicago Booth Initiative on Global Markets, 2013).

Failure of High-Profile Firms   The impact of the financial crisis on firms' balance sheets forced major players in the financial markets to take drastic action. In March 2008, Bear Stearns, the fifth-largest investment bank in the United States, which had invested heavily in subprime-related securities, had a run on its repo funding and was forced to sell itself to J.P. Morgan for less than 5% of its worth of just a year earlier. To broker the deal, the Federal Reserve had to take over $30 billion of Bear Stearns's hard-to-value assets. In July, Fannie Mae and Freddie Mac, the two privately owned, government-sponsored enterprises that together insured over $5 trillion of mortgages or mortgage-backed assets, were propped up by the U.S. Treasury and the Federal Reserve after suffering substantial losses from their holdings of subprime securities. In early September 2008, Fannie Mae and Freddie Mac were put into conservatorship (in effect, run by the government).

On Monday, September 15, 2008, after suffering losses in the subprime market, Lehman Brothers, the fourth-largest investment bank by asset size with over $600 billion in assets and 25 000 employees, filed for bankruptcy, making it the largest bankruptcy filing in U.S. history. The day before, Merrill Lynch, the third-largest investment bank, which had also suffered large losses on its holdings of subprime securities, announced its sale to Bank of America for a price 60% below its value of a year earlier. On Tuesday, September 16, 2008, AIG, an insurance giant with assets of over $1 trillion, suffered an extreme liquidity crisis when its credit rating was downgraded. It had written over $400 billion of insurance contracts (credit default swaps) that had to make payouts on possible losses from subprime mortgage securities. The Federal Reserve then stepped in with an $85 billion loan to keep AIG afloat (with total government loans later increased to $173 billion).

Height of the 2007–2009 Financial Crisis

The financial crisis reached its peak in September 2008 after the U.S. House of Representatives, fearing the wrath of constituents who were angry about the Wall Street bailout, voted down a $700 billion dollar bailout package proposed by the Bush administration. The Emergency Economic Stabilization Act was finally passed nearly a week later. The stock market crash accelerated, with the week beginning October 6, 2008, showing the worst weekly decline in U.S. history. Credit spreads went through the roof over the next three weeks, with the spread between Baa corporate bonds (just above investment grade) and U.S. Treasury bonds going to over 5.5 percentage points (550 basis points), as illustrated by Figure 9-6.

The impaired financial markets and surging interest rates faced by borrower-spenders led to sharp declines in consumer spending and investment. Real GDP declined sharply, falling at a −1.3% annual rate in the third quarter of 2008 and then at a −5.4% and −6.4% annual rate in the next two quarters. The unemployment rate shot up, going over the 10% level in late 2009. The recession that started in December 2007 became the worst economic contraction in the United States since World War II and as a result is now referred to as the "Great Recession."

Government Intervention and the Recovery

Although the recession produced by the global financial crisis was very severe, the economic contraction was far smaller in magnitude than during the Great Depression because of massive interventions by governments to prop up financial markets and stimulate the economy.

The Federal Reserve took extraordinary actions to contain the crisis, actions involving both monetary policy to stimulate the economy and liquidity provision to support orderly

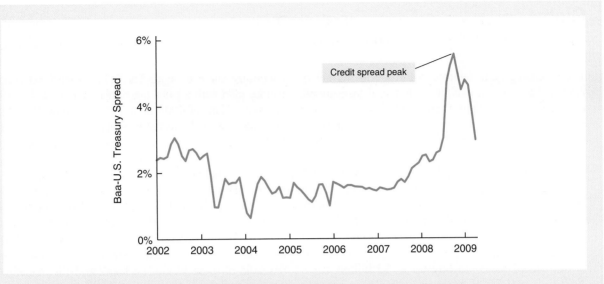

FIGURE 9-6 **Credit Spreads and the 2007–2009 Financial Crisis in the United States**

Credit spreads (the difference between rates on Baa corporate bonds and U.S. Treasury bonds) rose by more than 4 percentage points (400 basis points) during the crisis. Debate over the bailout package and the stock market crash caused credit spreads to peak in December 2008.

Source: Federal Reserve Bank of St. Louis FRED database: **http://research.stlouisfed.org/fred2/**.

functioning of financial markets. In addition, the U.S. government engaged in massive bailouts, with over $150 billion of loans to AIG, and the **Troubled Asset Relief Program (TARP)**, the most important provision of the Bush administration's Emergency Economic Stabilization Act passed in October 2008, which authorized the U.S. Treasury to spend $700 billion, purchasing subprime mortgage assets from troubled financial institutions or to inject capital into these institutions—the route actually followed. In addition, the Act raised the federal deposit insurance limit temporarily from $100 000 to $250 000 in order to limit withdrawals from banks. Shortly thereafter, the FDIC put in place a guarantee for certain debt newly issued by banks, and the U.S. Treasury guaranteed for a year money market mutual fund shares at par value. Similarly, European governments conducted massive bailouts, in excess of $10 trillion, in order to prop up their banking systems (see the Global box, Worldwide Government Bailouts During the 2007–2009 Financial Crisis).

Fiscal policy aimed at stimulating the economy was another key piece of the U.S. government's response to the crisis. In February 2008, the U.S. Congress passed the Bush administration's Economic Stimulus Act of 2008, whereby the government gave out one-time tax rebates totaling $78 billion by sending $600 cheques to individual taxpayers. Shortly after coming to office, the Obama administration proposed the American Recovery and Reinvestment Act of 2009, a much bigger, $787 billion fiscal stimulus package passed by Congress that to this day is highly controversial.

With the government bailouts, the Federal Reserve's extraordinary actions, and the fiscal stimulus, a bull market in stocks got under way starting in March 2009 (see Figure 9-5), and credit spreads began to fall (Figure 9-6). With the recovery of financial markets, the U.S. economy also started to recover, but unfortunately the pace of recovery has been slow.

Global   Worldwide Government Bailouts During the 2007–2009 Financial Crisis

The spreading bank failures in Europe in the fall of 2008 led to massive bailouts of financial institutions: the Netherlands, Belgium, and Luxembourg injected $16 billion to prop up Fortis, a major European bank; the Netherlands injected $13 billion (US) into ING, a banking and insurance giant; Germany provided a $50 billion rescue package for Hypo Real Estate Holdings; and Iceland took over its three largest banks after its banking system collapsed. Ireland's government guaranteed all the deposits of its commercial banks as well as interbank lending, as did Greece. Spain implemented a bailout package similar to the United States' to buy up to 50 billion euros ($70 billion (US)) of assets in its banks in order to

encourage them to lend. The U.K. Treasury set up a bailout plan with a price tag similar to that of the U.S. Treasury's plan, of 400£ billion ($699 billion (US)). It guaranteed 250£ billion of bank liabilities, added 100£ billion to a facility that swaps these assets for government bonds, and allowed the U.K. government to buy up to 50£ billion of equity stakes in British banks. Bailout plans to the tune of over $100 billion (US) in South Korea, $200 billion (US) in Sweden, $400 billion (US) in France, and $500 billion (US) in Germany, all of which guaranteed the debt of their banks as well as the injection of capital into them, then followed. Both the scale of these bailout packages and the degree of international coordination was unprecedented.

CANADA AND THE 2007–2009 FINANCIAL CRISIS

In Canada, the early symptom of the U.S. subprime crisis was the freezing of the asset-backed commercial paper (ABCP) market in August 2007. It caused a sharp decrease in liquidity in short-term Canadian credit markets, including the overnight interbank market and the overnight repurchase market. In order to restore confidence and liquidity in the ABCP market, and to prevent significant write-offs for banks that would have reduced their capital and raised concerns about their solvency, market participants reached an agreement, known as the Montreal Accord, to restructure the frozen ABCP market and minimize the costs to the Canadian taxpayer. (See the FYI box, Canada's Asset-Backed Commercial Paper Crisis for more details.)

Subprime Mortgages in Canada

The subprime mortgage crisis in the United States dominated news headlines, but there is also the Canadian version of subprime mortgages. High-risk, long-term (40-year), zero-down mortgages proliferated in Canada in 2007 and 2008 after the Conservative government opened up the Canadian mortgage market to big U.S. players in its first budget in May of 2006. This created a Canadian version of subprime mortgages. How did Canadian regulators allow the entry into Canada of U.S.-style subprime mortgages?

The Canadian mortgage insurance market is the second largest and one of the most lucrative mortgage insurance markets in the world. For over 50 years, since revisions in the National Housing Act and the Bank Act in 1954 allowed chartered banks to make insured mortgage loans, the business of mortgage insurance was mainly the domain of the Canada Mortgage and Housing Corporation (CMHC). CMHC insured the mortgages of those home buyers that could not make a 25% down payment, charging them an insurance premium, with the federal government backing the CMHC's insurance policies with a 100% federal guarantee.

FYI   Canada's Asset-Backed Commercial Paper Crisis

As we noted in Chapter 2, commercial paper is short-term, unsecured debt issued by corporations, typically for financing accounts receivable and inventories. Asset-backed commercial paper, like traditional commercial paper, is also a short-term security (with a maturity that is typically less than nine months). It is issued by conduits (that is, bankruptcy-remote Special Purpose Vehicles), but instead of being an unsecured promissory note, it is backed by physical assets such as mortgages, trade receivables, credit card receivables, automobile loans and leases, and other types of assets. Because of this backing, the quality of the ABCP depends on the underlying securities and thus ABCP could be very risky. For example, if there are negative developments in the underlying markets, the risk of ABCP will increase and investors will switch out of ABCP and into safer money market instruments such as traditional commercial paper, bankers' acceptances, and Treasury bills. As a result, conduits will not be able to roll over their ABCP and will face a liquidity crunch.

The ABCP market in Canada expanded very rapidly from the 1990s to 2007. By July 31, 2007, the size of the Canadian ABCP market was $115 billion (equal to about 32.5% of the Canadian money market), of which $80 billion was bank-sponsored and $35 billion was non-bank-sponsored. At the same time, the ABCP market in the United States was approximately US$1.2 trillion, equal to about 50% of the U.S. commercial paper market. Bank-sponsored ABCP conduits are invested in "plain vanilla" assets such as residential mortgages and credit card receivables. Non-bank-sponsored ABCP conduits are invested in structured financial assets such as collateralized debt obligations (CDOs) and subprime mortgages. Canadian banks are involved in the distribution of ABCP and also provide liquidity back-stop facilities to non-bank-sponsored ABCP conduits under the so-called general market disruption clause.

In August of 2007, investors in the Canadian ABCP market declined to roll over maturing notes because of concerns about exposure to the U.S. subprime mortgage sector in the underlying assets. As a result, the market was divided into those ABCP conduits that could honour their obligations (bank-sponsored) and those that could not honour their obligations (non-bank-sponsored).

In the case of bank-sponsored ABCP, the Big Six banks took back onto their balance sheets significant amounts of their own sponsored ABCP. Moreover, valuation and fair-value issues led to significant writedowns in the fourth quarter of 2007 and the first quarter of 2008. In the case of non-bank-sponsored ABCP, a number of conduits faced significant liquidity shortages, seeking liquidity funding support from their liquidity providers (banks). However, major liquidity providers denied requests for liquidity support, arguing that the "general market disruption" clause was not met. They interpreted the clause to mean that the majority of the conduits in the entire Canadian ABCP market would need to be unable to roll over before a liquidity provider had to step in. As a result, the Canadian non-bank-sponsored ABCP market froze and investors, including Québec's huge pension fund Caisse de dépôt et placement du Québec, Alberta's ATB Financial, the National Bank of Canada, and about 2000 individual small investors, had their cash frozen in non-bank-sponsored ABCP.

At the time, the Bank of Canada indicated that it would not accept ABCP as collateral for loans to banks and that a solution from participants in the ABCP market was deemed to be appropriate. As a result, major market participants, including non-bank-sponsored ABCP conduits, institutional investors, liquidity providers (ABN AMRO Group, HSBC, Deutsche Bank, Merrill Lynch, Barclays Capital), and the affected trusts, reached an agreement on August 16, 2007, known as the Montreal Accord. Under the Montreal Accord, investors agreed to a standstill period (initially 60 days, to October 16, 2007, extended three times, to February 22, 2008), with the objective of restructuring the frozen ABCP into long-term floating rate notes with maturities matching the maturities of the underlying assets in the conduits. However, the agreement had to be renegotiated again 16 months later, in December 2008, with the participation of the federal government and three provinces (Ontario, Québec, and Alberta), where publicly owned institutions held over $30 billion of frozen non-bank-sponsored ABCP. Small investors (holding less than $1 million of the paper) were fully paid out in cash by the brokerage firms that had sold them the paper, whereas the larger investors were given bonds.

The ABCP crisis in Canada was managed well, although the final cost of the restructuring was in excess of $200 million in fees, with the big investors footing the bill.

For many years, U.S. insurance companies had conducted orchestrated lobbying of Canada's Department of Finance and Office of the Superintendent of Financial Institutions to enter the Canadian mortgage insurance market. In May 2006, the government allowed big U.S. players such as AIG to enter the Canadian mortgage insurance market and also committed to guarantee their business up to $200 billion. In February of 2006, in an attempt to protect its business in anticipation of the entry of the big U.S. insurers, CMHC announced that it would insure 30-year mortgages. Two weeks later, Genworth Mortgage Insurance Co., the Canadian mortgage subsidiary of the U.S. conglomerate General Electric and the only other (private) mortgage insurer in Canada at that time (with an estimated market share of about 30%), announced that it would insure 35-year mortgages. By October of 2006, AIG, CMHC, and Genworth were competing in the Canadian mortgage insurance market by insuring 40-year mortgages.

In response to the subprime meltdown in the United States, the Canadian government banned subprime mortgages in Canada in the summer of 2008. Although there are currently no publicly available figures, it is estimated that more than half of the total new mortgages approved by Canadian financial institutions during this period (worth over $50 billion) were risky, 40-year mortgages, and that 10% of these mortgages (worth over $10 billion) were taken out with zero money down.

More recently, on June 21, 2012, Jim Flaherty, the former finance minister, tightened several regulations for real estate lending, his fourth round of tightening in four years. The most significant regulatory changes were: a maximum amortization period for a mortgage of 25 years, down from 30; refinancing of a home allowed only up to 80% of its value, down from 85%; and homebuyers to demonstrate their housing costs are no more than 39% of their gross household income. In addition, Canada's banking regulator, the Office of the Superintendent of Financial Institutions (OSFI), placed a loan-to-value limit of 65% on borrowing against home equity.

Why was Canada Spared the Worst of the Financial Crisis?

Canadian banks also had their problems during the turbulent financial conditions of the global financial crisis. Their shares fell by almost 50% and some of them experienced huge losses in derivatives trading; for example, CIBC lost $2.1 billion in derivatives trading in 2008. However, while governments in the United States and Europe were working on full-scale banking bailouts and rescue packages (in the trillions of dollars), the Canadian government did not have to bail out any banks. Canada was the only G7 country to experience only a mild recession (even milder than the 1980s and early 1990s recessions), with no bank failures and bailouts of insolvent firms. This is why, in the aftermath of the global financial crisis, Canada has been ranked by the World Economic Forum first among more than 140 countries in terms of banking stability.

One reason that Canada's banks fared better than banks in the United States and other countries is that they are more tightly regulated. For example, depending on its charter, a bank in the United States can be regulated by the Federal Reserve, the Federal Deposit Insurance Corporation, the Office of the Comptroller of the Currency, or state regulators. By contrast, Canada's top banking regulator, the Office of the Superintendent of Financial Institutions (OSFI) oversees all financial firms, including banks, insurance companies, mortgage lenders, and pension funds, among others. Moreover, although Canadian securities markets are regulated by the country's provincial and territorial governments, their regulations are highly harmonized. In addition, bank regulations in Canada are revised every five years, in order to help regulation adapt to emerging risks and innovation.

Another reason is that Canada's big banks have been traditionally more conservative in their lending and acquisition practices in comparison with banks in the United States and major banks around the world. In fact, the Office of the Superintendent of Financial Institutions has been more conservative than banking regulators in the United States and Europe. For example, at the beginning of the global financial crisis, Canada's banks had higher capital requirements, greater leverage restrictions, and fewer off-balance sheet activities than their global peers had. As a result, they had stronger reserves to cushion potential losses. Although this conservative regulatory regime enabled Canadian banks to withstand the financial crisis better than banks in other countries did, it has been argued that it also makes the Canadian banking sector less competitive because of the lower leverage and lower rate of return on capital it earns than other jurisdictions do.

Moreover, the activities of Canada's banks are well diversified and are not limited to traditional retail banking. In particular, the federal government's decision in the late 1980s to allow banks to acquire investment brokers and to engage in the mutual fund and insurance businesses created a more diversified financial services marketplace for Canada's banks. In addition, these arm's-length institutions are subject to the same strict rules and regulations as the banks, unlike investment dealers in the United States that had been subject to very relaxed and minimal regulation from the Securities and Exchange Commission. As a result, shadow banking activity in Canada today accounts for only about 40% of the size of Canada's economy, compared with 95% in the United States.

Finally, Canada's structural and regulatory differences manifest themselves very well in the structure of the Canadian mortgage market. Unlike banks in the United States that sold the bulk of their mortgages to investors, banks in Canada tend to hold a large proportion of their mortgages on their balance sheets; before the global financial crisis, for example, less than a third of Canadian mortgages were securitized, compared with two-thirds in the United States. This practice gives Canadian banks an incentive to make sure that their mortgage loans are good loans. In addition, Canadian law allows banks to go after other assets when a borrower walks away from a mortgage, making it less likely for consumers to do so.

Overall, in the aftermath of the global economic meltdown, Canada's banking system has been viewed as the soundest in the world. In fact, many countries around the world are now considering Canadian-style reforms of their financial markets.

RESPONSE OF FINANCIAL REGULATION

Given the cost to the U.S. economy of the 2007–2009 financial crisis, the size of the bailouts, and the nationalization of so many financial institutions, the system of financial regulation in the United States is currently undergoing dramatic changes.

Macroprudential Versus Microprudential Supervision

Before the global financial crisis, regulatory authorities engaged in **microprudential supervision**, which focuses on the safety and soundness of *individual* financial institutions. Microprudential supervision looks at each individual institution separately and assesses the riskiness of its activities and whether it complies with disclosure requirements. Most importantly, microprudential supervision checks whether a particular institution satisfies capital *ratios* and, if it does not, either engages in prompt corrective action to force the institution to raise its capital ratios or the supervisor closes it down, along the lines we have discussed previously.

A focus on microprudential supervision is not enough to prevent financial crises. The run on the shadow banking system in the United States illustrates how the problems of one financial institution can harm other financial institutions that are otherwise healthy. When the troubled financial institution is forced to engage in fire sales and to sell off assets in order to meet target capital ratios or haircut requirements, this leads to a decline in asset values. The decline in asset values then causes other institutions to engage in fire sales, leading to a rapid deleveraging process and a systemic crisis. In situations like this, even institutions that have high capital ratios and would normally be healthy may find themselves in trouble.

The global financial crisis has therefore made it clear that there is a need for **macroprudential supervision**, which focuses on the safety and soundness of the financial system *in the aggregate*. Rather than focusing on the safety and soundness of individual institutions, macroprudential supervision seeks to mitigate system-wide fire sales and deleveraging by assessing the overall capacity of the financial system to avoid them. In addition, because many institutions that were well capitalized faced liquidity shortages and found that their access to short-term funding was cut off, macroprudential supervision focuses not only on capital adequacy as a whole but also on whether the financial system has sufficient liquidity.

Macroprudential policies can take several forms. The run-up to the global financial crisis included a so-called **leverage cycle**, in which a feedback loop resulted from a boom in issuing credit, which led to higher asset prices, which resulted in higher capital buffers at financial institutions, which supported further lending in the context of unchanging capital requirements, which then raised asset prices further, and so on; in the bust, the value of the capital dropped precipitously, leading to a cut in lending. To short-circuit this leverage cycle, macroprudential policies make capital requirements countercyclical; that is, they are adjusted upward during a boom and downward during a bust. In addition, during the upward swing in the leverage cycle, macroprudential policies might involve forcing financial institutions to tighten credit standards or even direct limits on the growth of credit. In the downward swing, macroprudential supervision might be needed to force the banking system as a whole to raise an aggregate amount of new capital so that banks will not curtail lending in order to reduce the level of their assets and raise capital ratios. To ensure that financial institutions have enough liquidity, macroprudential policies could require that financial institutions have a sufficiently low *net stable funding ratio* (NSFR), which is the percentage of the institution's short-term funding in relation to total funding. Macroprudential policies of the type discussed here are being considered as part of the Basel 3 framework, but have not yet been completely worked out.

Dodd-Frank Wall Street Reform and Consumer Protection Act of 2010

The global financial crisis raised calls for a new regulatory structure that would make a repeat of the crisis less likely. The result was the Dodd-Frank bill in the United States, which was passed in July 2010 after more than a year of discussion. It is the most comprehensive financial reform legislation passed in the United States since the Great Depression. The bill addresses five different categories of regulation, which are discussed next.

Consumer Protection   Dodd-Frank created a new Consumer Financial Protection Bureau that is funded and housed within the Federal Reserve, although it is a completely independent agency. It has the authority to examine and enforce regulations on all businesses with more than $10 billion in assets that are engaged in issuing residential mortgage products, as well as on issuers of other financial products marketed to low-income people. The legislation requires lenders to make sure borrowers can repay residential mortgages by requiring verification of their income, credit history, and job status. It also bans payments to brokers for pushing borrowers into higher-priced loans. It imposes stricter consumer protection laws on national banks and gives state attorneys general the power to enforce certain rules issued by the new bureau. It also permanently increased the level of federal deposit insurance to $250 000.

Resolution Authority   Before the new legislation was passed, the FDIC had the authority to seize failing banks and wind them down, but it did not have such resolution authority over the largest financial institutions—those structured as holding companies. Indeed, the U.S. Treasury and the Federal Reserve argued that one reason they were unable to rescue Lehman Brothers, and instead let it go into bankruptcy, was that they did not have the legal means with which to take over Lehman and break it up. The Dodd-Frank bill now provides the U.S. government with this authority for financial firms that are deemed systemic—that is, firms that pose a risk to the overall health of the financial system because their failure would cause widespread economic damage. It also gives regulators the right to levy fees to recoup any losses on financial institutions with more than $50 billion in assets.

Systemic Risk Regulation   The Dodd-Frank bill created a Financial Stability Oversight Council, chaired by the Treasury secretary, that monitors markets for asset price bubbles and the buildup of systemic risk. In addition, it designates which financial firms are systemically important and so receive the official designation of **systemically important financial institutions (SIFIs)**. These firms are subject to additional regulation by the Federal Reserve, which includes higher capital standards and stricter liquidity requirements, along with the requirement that such firms draw up a "living will," that is, a plan for orderly liquidation if the firm gets into financial difficulties.

Volcker Rule   Under the new legislation, banks in the United States are limited in the extent of their proprietary trading—that is, trading with their own money—and are allowed to own only a small percentage of hedge and private equity funds. These provisions are named after Paul Volcker, a former Chairman of the Board of Governors of the Federal Reserve, who argued that banks should not be allowed to take large trading risks when they receive the benefits of federal deposit insurance.

Derivatives   As will be discussed in Chapter 11, derivatives such as credit default swaps ended up being "weapons of mass destruction" that helped lead to a financial meltdown when AIG had to be rescued after making overly extensive use of them. To prevent this from happening again, the Dodd-Frank bill requires that many standardized derivative products be traded on exchanges and cleared through clearinghouses to reduce the risk of losses if one counterparty in the derivative transaction goes bankrupt. More customized derivative products are subject to higher capital requirements. Banks are banned from some of their derivative-dealing operations, such as those involving riskier swaps. In addition, the bill imposes capital and margin requirements on firms dealing in derivatives and forces them to disclose more information about their activities.

TOO-BIG-TO-FAIL AND FUTURE REGULATION

The Dodd-Frank bill leaves out many of the details of future regulation, and there are doubts as to whether it has dealt sufficiently with the too-big-to-fail problem, which, as we have seen, was an important factor that contributed to the global financial crisis. Here we discuss some possible measures to reduce the too-big-to-fail problem and explore several areas in which regulation might be heading in the future.

What Can Be Done About the Too-Big-to-Fail Problem?

Three approaches to solving the too-big-to-fail problem have been actively debated.

Break Up Large, Systemically Important Financial Institutions
One way to eliminate the too-big-to-fail problem is to make sure that no financial institution is so large that it can bring down the financial system. Then, regulators will no longer see the need to bail out these institutions if they fail, thereby subjecting them to market discipline. One way to shrink overly-large institutions is to force these large SIFIs to break up their different activities into smaller, cohesive companies. Alternatively, regulations could specify that no financial institution can have assets over a specified maximum limit, forcing SIFIs to break up into smaller pieces.

Not surprisingly, both of these approaches have been vehemently opposed by the largest financial institutions in the United States. Although breaking up SIFIs would eliminate the too-big-to-fail problem, if there are synergies available that might enable large institutions to manage risk better or to provide financial services at a lower cost, then breaking up SIFIs might decrease the efficiency of the financial system rather than increase it.

Higher Capital Requirements
Because institutions that are "too big to fail" have incentives to take on excessive risk, another way to reduce their risk taking is to impose higher capital requirements on them. With higher capital, not only will these institutions have a larger buffer with which to withstand losses if they occur, but they will also have more to lose and hence have more "skin in the game," thereby reducing moral hazard and giving them less incentive to take on excessive risk. Another way of describing this approach is to say that higher capital requirements reduce the subsidy to risk-taking for institutions that are too big to fail. In addition, because risk taking by SIFIs is far greater during booms, capital requirements could be increased when credit is expanding rapidly and reduced when credit is contracting. Such measures would cause capital requirements to become more countercyclical and could help restrain the boom-bust credit cycle.

The Swiss central bank has been a leader in this kind of approach: It has the highest capital requirements among advanced countries for its largest banks, and it raises them when credit markets become particularly frothy. Legislation has been proposed in the U.S. Congress to double capital requirements for large financial institutions, legislation that these institutions again vigorously oppose.

Leave It to Dodd-Frank
Another view is that Dodd-Frank has effectively eliminated the too-big-to-fail problem in the United States by making it harder for the Federal Reserve to bail out financial institutions, by imposing stricter regulations on SIFIs, and through application of the Volcker rule. Indeed, the authors of the bill have declared that Dodd-Frank will "end too-big-to-fail as we know it." Although the provisions of Dodd-Frank do take away some of the incentives for excessive risk-taking

by large, systemically important financial institutions, there are doubts that this bill completely removes the too-big-to-fail problem.

Other Issues for Future Regulation

The Dodd-Frank bill leaves out many of the details of future regulation and does not address some important regulatory issues at all. Here we examine four areas in which regulation may be heading in the future.

Compensation in the Financial Services Industry   The high fees and executive compensation that so outraged the public created incentives for the financial industry to create securities that turned out to be much riskier than advertised. Regulators are adopting regulations aimed at modifying compensation in the financial services industry to reduce risk taking. For example, regulators are issuing requirements that bonuses be paid out for a number of years after they have been earned, and only if the firm remains in good health. Such "clawbacks" will encourage employees to reduce the riskiness of their activities so that they are more likely to be paid these bonuses in the future.

Government-Sponsored Enterprises (GSEs)   A major gap in the Dodd-Frank bill is that it does not address privately owned, government-sponsored enterprises, such as Fannie Mae and Freddie Mac. During the global financial crisis, both of these firms got into serious financial trouble and had to be taken over by the government, with massive loans and government guarantees needed to prop them up. To prevent this from occurring again, the government might take any of four routes:

1. Fully privatize GSEs by taking away their government sponsorship, thereby removing the implicit backing for their debt.
2. Completely nationalize them by taking away their private status and making them government agencies.
3. Leave them as privately owned GSEs, but strengthen regulations to restrict the amount of risk they can take and to impose higher capital standards.
4. Leave them as privately owned GSEs, but force them to shrink dramatically so that they no longer expose the taxpayer to huge losses or pose a systemic risk to the financial system when they fail.

Credit-Rating Agencies   Regulations to restrict conflicts of interest at credit-rating agencies and to give them greater incentives to provide reliable ratings have already been strengthened in the aftermath of the global financial crisis, but even more regulation is likely to be imposed. The inaccurate ratings provided by credit-rating agencies helped promote risk taking throughout the financial system and led to investors not having the information they needed to make informed choices about their investments. The reliance on credit ratings in the Basel 2 capital requirements may also have to be rethought, given the poor performance of credit-rating agencies in recent years.

The Danger of Overregulation   As a result of the global financial crisis, the world of financial regulation will never be the same. Although it is clear that more regulation is needed to prevent such a crisis from ever occurring again, the danger is substantial that too much or poorly designed regulation could hamper the efficiency of the financial system. If new regulations choke off financial innovation that can benefit both households and businesses, future economic growth will suffer.

MyEconLab

MyEconLab is an online homework and tutorial system that puts you in control of your own learning with study and practice tools directly correlated to this chapter's content. Visit MyEconLab to access the eText, the Questions and Applied Problems with answers, as well as additional assessment. You will also find web chapters, mini-lectures, appendices, mini-cases, videos, glossary flashcards, news feeds, CANSIM data, and graphing tools.

SUMMARY

1. A financial crisis occurs when a particularly large disruption to information flows occurs in financial markets, with the result that financial frictions increase sharply, thereby rendering financial markets incapable of channeling funds to households and firms with productive investment opportunities, and causing a sharp contraction in economic activity.

2. Financial crises start in advanced countries like Canada and the United States in two ways: credit booms and busts, or a general increase in uncertainty when major financial institutions fail. The result is a substantial increase in adverse selection and moral hazard problems, which leads to a contraction of lending and a decline in economic activity. The worsening business conditions and deterioration in bank balance sheets then trigger the second stage of the crisis, the simultaneous failure of many banking institutions, a banking crisis. The resulting decrease in the number of banks causes a loss of their information capital, leading to a further decline of lending and a spiraling down of the economy. In some instances, the resulting economic downturn leads to a sharp slide in prices, which increases the real liabilities of firms and households and therefore lowers their net worth, leading to a debt deflation. The further decline in borrowers' net worth worsens adverse selection and moral hazard problems, so that lending, investment spending, and aggregate economic activity remain depressed for a long time.

3. The most significant financial crisis in history, which led to the Great Depression, involved several stages: a stock market crash, bank panics, worsening of asymmetric information problems, and finally a debt deflation.

4. The global financial crisis of 2007–2009 was triggered by mismanagement of financial innovations in the United States involving subprime residential mortgages and the bursting of a housing price bubble. The crisis spread globally, with substantial deterioration in banks' and other financial institutions' balance sheets, a run on the shadow banking system, and the failure of many high-profile firms.

5. Financial regulation has undergone many changes in the wake of the global financial crisis. First is the shift from microprudential supervision, which focuses on the safety and soundness of individual institutions, to macroprudential supervision, which focuses on the safety and soundness of the financial system in the aggregate. Second is the most comprehensive financial reform legislation since the Great Depression. It makes provisions in five areas: (1) consumer protection, (2) resolution authority, (3) systemic risk regulation, (4) the Volcker rule in the United States, and (5) derivatives.

6. Future regulation needs to address five issues: (1) the too-big-to-fail problem, which can be at least partially addressed by either breaking up large financial institutions or by imposing higher capital requirements on them; (2) compensation at financial firms to reduce incentives to take on excessive risk; (3) GSEs to make it less likely that they will require government bailouts in the future; (4) credit-rating agencies to improve incentives for these agencies to provide accurate assessments of credit risk; and (5) the dangers of overregulation, which can decrease the efficiency of the financial system.

KEY TERMS

asset-price bubble, p. 197
credit boom, p. 195
credit default swap, p. 203
credit spread, p. 200
debt deflation, p. 198
deleveraging, p. 195
financial crisis, p. 195
financial derivatives, p. 203

financial frictions, p. 195
financial innovation, p. 195
financial liberalization, p. 195
fire sales, p. 198
fundamental economic values, p. 197
haircuts, p. 205
leverage cycle, p. 214
macroprudential supervision, p. 214

microprudential supervision, p. 213
repurchase agreements
  (repos), p. 205
structured credit products, p. 201
systemically important financial
  institutions (SIFIs), p. 215
Troubled Asset Relief Program
  (TARP), p. 209

QUESTIONS

All questions are available in MyEconLab *at*
www.myeconlab.com.

1. How does the concept of asymmetric information help to define a financial crisis?

2. How can the bursting of an asset-price bubble in the stock market help trigger a financial crisis?

3. How does an unanticipated decline in the price level cause a drop in lending?

4. How can a decline in real estate prices cause deleveraging and a decline in lending?

5. How does a deterioration in balance sheets of financial institutions and the simultaneous failures of these institutions cause a decline in economic activity?

6. How does a general increase in uncertainty as a result of the failure of a major financial institution lead to an increase in adverse selection and moral hazard problems?

7. What is a credit spread? Why do credit spreads rise significantly during a financial crisis?

8. What causes bank panics to occur?

9. Why do bank panics worsen asymmetric information problems in credit markets?

10. How can financial innovation lead to financial crises?

11. What role does weak financial regulation and supervision play in causing financial crises?

12. Describe two similarities and two differences between the United States' experiences during the Great Depression and the financial crisis of 2007–2009.

13. What do you think prevented the financial crisis of 2007–2009 from becoming a depression?

14. What technological innovations led to the development of the subprime mortgage market?

15. Why is the originate-to-distribute business model subject to the principal–agent problem?

16. "Financial engineering always leads to a more efficient financial system." Is this statement true, false, or uncertain?

17. How did a decline in housing prices help trigger the subprime financial crisis in the United States that began in 2007?

18. What role did the shadow banking system play in the 2007–2009 financial crisis?

19. Why would haircuts on collateral increase sharply during a financial crisis? How would this lead to fire sales on assets?

20. How did the global financial crisis promote a sovereign debt crisis in Europe?

21. Why is it a good idea for macroprudential policies to require countercyclical capital requirements?

22. How does the process of financial innovation impact the effectiveness of macroprudential regulation?

23. What are the three approaches to limiting the too-big-to-fail problem? Briefly describe the advantages and disadvantages of each of the approaches.

24. Why were consumer protection provisions included in the financial reform legislation in the aftermath of the global financial crisis?

25. What was the Canadian experience during the 2007–2009 financial crisis?

DATA ANALYSIS PROBLEMS

Download data for these problems from MyEconLab at **www.myeconlab.com**.

1. Go to the CANSIM database, and find data on household final consumption expenditure (series V61989012), stock prices (series V122620), and house prices (series V53600423). Download the data into a spreadsheet and convert the monthly stock price and house price series to quarterly frequency. Make sure the data align correctly with the appropriate dates. For all three series, for each quarter, calculate the annualized growth rate from quarter to quarter. To do this, take the current-period data minus the previous-quarter data, and then divide by the previous quarter data. Multiply by 100 to change each result to a percent, and multiply by 4 to annualize the data.

   a. For the three series, calculate the average growth rates over the most recent four quarters of data available. Comment on the relationships among house prices, stock prices, and consumption as they relate to your results.

   b. Repeat part (a) for the four quarters of 2005, and again for the period from 2008:Q3 to 2009:Q2. Comment on the relationships among house prices, stock prices, and consumption as they relate to your results, before and during the crisis.

   c. How do the current household data compare to the data from the period prior to the financial crisis, and during the crisis? Do you think the current data are indicative of a bubble?

2. Go to the St. Louis Federal Reserve FRED database, and find U.S. data on corporate net worth of non-financial businesses (TNWMVBSNNCB), private domestic investment (GPDIC1), and a measure of financial frictions, the St. Louis Fed financial stress index (STLFSI). For all three measures, be sure to convert the *frequency* setting to "Quarterly." Download the data into a spreadsheet, and make sure the data align correctly with the appropriate dates. For corporate net worth and private domestic investment, calculate the annualized growth rates from quarter to quarter. To do this, take the current-period data minus the previous-quarter data, then divide by the previous quarter data. Multiply by 100 to change the results to percentage form, and then multiply by 4 to annualize the data.

   a. Calculate the average growth rates over the most recent four quarters of data available for the corporate net worth and private domestic investment variables. Calculate the difference between the value of the stress index during the most recent quarter and the value of the stress index one year earlier. Comment on the relationships among financial stress, net wealth of corporate businesses, and private domestic investment.

   b. Repeat part (a) for the four quarters of 2005 and for the period from 2008:Q3 to 2009:Q2. Comment on the relationships among financial stress, net wealth of corporate businesses, and private domestic investment before and during the crisis as they relate to your results. Assuming the financial stress measure is indicative of heightened asymmetric information problems, comment on how the crisis-period data relate to the typical dynamics of a financial crisis.

   c. How do the current investment data compare to the data for the period prior to the financial crisis, and during the crisis? Do you think the current data are indicative of a bubble?

WEB EXERCISES

1. This chapter discusses how an understanding of adverse selection and moral hazard can help us better understand financial crises. The greatest financial crisis faced by the United States was the Great Depression of 1929–1933. Go to

www.amatecon.com/greatdepression.html. This site contains a brief discussion of the factors that led to the Great Depression. Write a one-page summary explaining how adverse selection and moral hazard contributed to the Great Depression.

2. Go to the International Monetary Fund's Financial Crisis page at **www.imf.org/external/np/exr/key/finstab .htm**. Report on the three countries that most recently received emergency loans from the IMF in response to a financial crisis. According to the IMF, what caused the crisis in each country?

3. One of the countries hardest hit by the global financial crisis of 2008 was Iceland. Go to **http:// assets.opencrs.com/rpts/RS22988_20081120.pdf** and summarize the causes and events that led to the crisis in Iceland.

WEB REFERENCES

www.amatecon.com/gd/gdtimeline.html

A time line of the Great Depression.

http://freerepublic.com/focus/f-news/2167257/posts

Paper by Carmen Reinhart and Kenneth Rogoff comparing the 2007 subprime crisis to other international crises.

10 Economic Analysis of Financial Regulation

Learning Objectives

At the end of this chapter you should be able to

1. Identify the reasons for and the forms of a government safety net in financial markets.

2. List and summarize the types of financial regulation and how each reduces asymmetric information problems.

PREVIEW

As we have seen in the previous chapters, the financial system is among the most heavily regulated sectors of the economy, and banks are among the most heavily regulated of financial institutions. In this chapter, we develop an economic analysis of why regulation of the financial system takes the form it does.

Unfortunately, the regulatory process may not always work very well, as evidenced by the recent global financial crisis. Here we also use our economic analysis of financial regulation to explain the worldwide crises in banking and to consider how the regulatory system can be reformed to prevent future such disasters.

ASYMMETRIC INFORMATION AND THE GOVERNMENT SAFETY NET

In earlier chapters, we have seen how asymmetric information—the fact that different parties in a financial contract do not have the same information—leads to adverse selection and moral hazard problems, which have an important impact on our financial system. The concepts of asymmetric information, adverse selection, and moral hazard are especially useful in understanding why governments pursue financial regulation.

As we saw in Chapter 8, financial intermediaries, like banks, are particularly well suited to solving adverse selection and moral hazard problems because they make private loans that help avoid the free-rider problem. However, this solution to the free-rider problem creates another asymmetric information problem, because depositors lack information about the quality of these private loans. This asymmetric information problem leads to other problems that interfere with the proper functioning of the financial system.

Bank Panics and the Need for Deposit Insurance

Before the CDIC (Canada Deposit Insurance Corporation) started operations in 1967, a **bank failure** (in which a bank is unable to meet its obligations to pay its depositors and other creditors, and so must go out of business) meant that depositors would have to wait until the bank was liquidated (until its assets had been turned into cash) to get their deposit funds; at that time, they would be paid only a fraction of the value of their deposits. Because they couldn't know if bank managers were taking on too much risk or were outright crooks, depositors would be reluctant to put money in banks, thus making financial institutions less viable. Second, depositors' lack of information about the quality of bank assets can lead to a **bank panic**, in which many banks fail simultaneously. Because the simultaneous failure of many banks leads to a sharp decline in bank lending, bank panics have serious, harmful consequences for the economy.

To understand why bank panics occur, consider the following situation. Deposit insurance does not exist, and an adverse shock hits the economy. As a result of the shock, 5% of banks have such large losses on loans that they become insolvent (have a negative net worth and so are bankrupt). Because of asymmetric information, depositors are unable to tell whether their bank is a "good" bank or one of the 5% that are insolvent. Depositors at bad *and* good banks recognize that they may not get back 100 cents on the dollar for their deposits, and therefore are inclined to withdraw them. Indeed, because banks operate on a "sequential service constraint" (a first-come, first-served basis), depositors have a very strong incentive to be the first to show up at the bank, because if they are last in line, the bank may have paid out all its funds and they will get nothing. The incentive to "run" to the bank to be first is why withdrawals when there is fear about the health of a bank is described as a "bank run." Uncertainty about the health of the banking system in general can lead to runs on both good and bad banks, and the failure of one bank can hasten the failure of others (referred to as the *contagion effect*). If nothing is done to restore the public's confidence, a bank panic can ensue.

A government safety net for depositors can short-circuit runs on banks and bank panics, and by providing protection for the depositor, it can overcome depositors' reluctance to put funds in the banking system. One form of the safety net is deposit insurance, such as that provided by the Canada Deposit Insurance Corporation (CDIC). The CDIC guarantees that current depositors will be paid off in full on the first $100 000 they have deposited in the bank if the bank fails. With fully insured deposits, depositors don't need to run to the bank to make withdrawals—even if they are worried about the bank's health—because their deposits will be worth 100 cents on the dollar no matter what.

The CDIC uses two primary methods to handle a failed bank. In the first, called the *payoff method*, the CDIC allows the bank to fail and pays off deposits up to the $100 000 insurance limit (with funds acquired from the insurance premiums paid by the banks that have bought CDIC insurance). After the bank has been liquidated, the CDIC lines up with other creditors of the bank and is paid its share of the proceeds from the liquidated assets. Typically, when the payoff method is used, account holders with deposits in excess of the $100 000 limit get back more than 90 cents on the dollar, although the process can take several years to complete.

In the second method, called the *purchase and assumption method*, the CDIC reorganizes the bank, typically by finding a willing merger partner who assumes (takes over) all of the failed bank's liabilities so that no depositor or other creditor loses a penny. The CDIC often sweetens the pot for the merger partner by providing it with subsidized loans or by buying some of the failed bank's weaker loans. The net effect of the purchase and assumption method is that the CDIC has guaranteed *all* liabilities and deposits, not just those under the $100 000 limit. The purchase and assumption method is typically more costly for the CDIC than the payoff method, but nevertheless is the CDIC's more common procedure for dealing with a failed bank.

Global The Spread of Government Deposit Insurance Throughout the World: Is It a Good Thing?

Government deposit insurance has taken off throughout the world because of growing concern about the health of banking systems, particularly after the increasing number of banking crises in recent years (documented at the end of this chapter). Has this spread of deposit insurance been a good thing? Has it helped improve the performance of the financial system and prevent banking crises?

The answer seems to be "no" under many circumstances. Research at the World Bank has found that, on average, the adoption of explicit government deposit insurance is associated with less banking sector stability and a higher incidence of banking crises.* Furthermore, on average, deposit insurance seems to retard financial development. However, these negative effects of deposit insurance occur only in countries with weak institutional environments: an absence of rule of law, ineffective regulation and supervision of the financial sector, and high corruption. This is exactly what might be expected because, as we will see later in this chapter, a strong institutional environment is needed to limit the moral hazard incentives for banks to engage in the excessively risky behaviour encouraged by deposit insurance. The problem is that development of a strong institutional environment may be very difficult to achieve in many emerging market countries. We are left with the following conclusion: Adoption of deposit insurance may be exactly the wrong medicine for promoting stability and efficiency of banking systems in emerging market countries.

* See World Bank, Finance for Growth: Policy Choices in a Volatile World (Oxford: World Bank and Oxford University Press, 2001).

In recent years, government deposit insurance has been growing in popularity and has spread to many countries throughout the world. Whether this trend is desirable is discussed in the Global box, The Spread of Government Deposit Insurance Throughout the World: Is It a Good Thing?

Other Forms of the Government Safety Net

Deposit insurance is not the only form of government safety net. In other countries, governments have often stood ready to provide support to domestic banks facing runs even in the absence of explicit deposit insurance. Furthermore, banks are not the only financial intermediaries that can pose a systemic threat to the financial system. When financial institutions are very large or highly interconnected with other financial institutions or markets, their failure has the potential to bring down the entire financial system. This is exactly what happened in the United States with Bear Stearns and Lehman Brothers, two investment banks, and AIG, an insurance company, during the global financial crisis in 2008.

One way governments provide support is through lending from the central bank to troubled institutions, as the Bank of Canada did during the global financial crisis (more on this in Chapter 16). This form of support is often referred to as the "lender of last resort" role of the central bank. In other cases, funds are provided directly to troubled institutions, as was done by the government of Canada through the Canada Mortgage and Housing Corporation (CMHC), by the U.S. Treasury, and by other governments in 2008 during a particularly virulent phase of the global financial crisis. Governments also take over (nationalize) troubled institutions and guarantee that all creditors' loans will be paid in full.

Moral Hazard and the Government Safety Net

Although a government safety net can help protect depositors and other creditors, and prevent, or ameliorate, financial crises, it is a mixed blessing. The most serious drawback of the government safety net stems from moral hazard, the incentives of one party in a transaction to engage in activities detrimental to the other party. Moral hazard is an important concern in insurance arrangements in general because the existence of insurance provides increased incentives for taking risks that might result in an insurance payoff. For example, some drivers who have automobile collision insurance that has a low deductible might be more likely to drive recklessly, because if they get into an accident, the insurance company pays most of the costs for damage and repairs.

Moral hazard is a prominent concern associated with government safety nets. With a safety net, depositors and creditors know that they will not suffer losses if a financial institution fails, so they do not impose the discipline of the marketplace on these financial institutions by withdrawing funds when they suspect that the financial institution is taking on too much risk. Consequently, financial institutions with a government safety net have an incentive to take on greater risks than they otherwise would, because taxpayers will foot the bill if the bank subsequently goes belly up. Financial institutions can place the following bet: "Heads I win, tails the taxpayer loses."

Adverse Selection and the Government Safety Net

A further problem with a government safety net like deposit insurance is adverse selection, the fact that the people who are most likely to produce the adverse outcome the bank is insured against (bank failure) are the same people who most want to take advantage of the insurance. For example, bad drivers are more likely than good drivers to take out automobile collision insurance with a low deductible. Because depositors and creditors protected by a government safety net have little reason to impose discipline on financial institutions, risk-loving entrepreneurs might find the financial industry a particularly attractive one—they know that they will be able to engage in highly risky activities. Even worse, because protected depositors and creditors have so little reason to monitor the financial institution's activities, without government intervention outright crooks might also find finance an attractive industry for their activities because it is easy for them to get away with fraud and embezzlement.

"Too Big to Fail"

The moral hazard created by a government safety net and the desire to prevent financial failures have presented financial regulators with a particular quandary, the **too-big-to-fail problem**, in which regulators are reluctant to close down large financial institutions and impose losses on their depositors and creditors because doing so might precipitate a financial crisis.

One problem with the too-big-to-fail policy is that it increases the moral hazard incentives for big banks. If the CDIC were willing to close a bank using the payoff method, paying depositors only up to the current $100 000 limit, large depositors with more than $100 000 would suffer losses if the bank failed. Thus they would have an incentive to monitor the bank by examining the bank's activities closely and pulling their money out if the bank were taking on too much risk. To prevent such a loss of deposits, the bank would be more likely to engage in less risky activities. However, once large depositors know that a bank is too big to fail, they have no incentive to monitor the bank and pull out their deposits when it takes on too much risk: No matter what the bank does, large depositors will not suffer any losses. The result of the too-big-to-fail policy is that big financial institutions might take on even greater risks, thereby making bank failures more likely.

Similarly, the too-big-to-fail policy increases the moral hazard incentives for non-bank financial institutions that are extended a government safety net. Knowing that the financial institution will get bailed out, creditors have little incentive to monitor the institution and pull their money out when the institution is taking on excessive risk. As a result, large or interconnected financial institutions are more likely to engage in highly risky activities, making a financial crisis more likely.

Indeed, financial institutions in the United States that were considered too big to fail—including Bear Stearns, Lehman Brothers, and AIG—did take on excessive risk in the period leading to the global financial crisis, and their subsequent collapse helped trigger the worst financial crisis since the Great Depression.

Financial Consolidation and the Government Safety Net

Financial consolidation has been proceeding at a rapid pace, leading to both larger and more complex financial organizations. Financial consolidation poses two challenges to financial regulation because of the existence of the government safety net. First, the increased size of financial institutions resulting from financial consolidation increases the too-big-to-fail problem, because there are now more large institutions whose failure would expose the financial system to systemic (system-wide) risk. Thus, more financial institutions are likely to be treated as too big to fail, and the increased moral hazard incentives for these large institutions to take on greater risk increases the fragility of the financial system. Second, financial consolidation of banks with other financial services firms means that the government safety net may be extended to new activities, such as securities underwriting, insurance, or real estate activities, as occurred in the United States during the global financial crisis. This situation increases incentives for greater risk taking in these activities, which can also weaken the fabric of the financial system. Limiting the moral hazard incentives for the larger, more complex financial organizations that have arisen as a result of recent changes in legislation is one of the key issues facing banking regulators in the aftermath of the global financial crisis.

TYPES OF FINANCIAL REGULATION

There are eight basic types of financial regulation aimed at lessening asymmetric information problems and excessive risk taking in the financial system: (1) restrictions on asset holdings, (2) capital requirements, (3) prompt corrective action, (4) chartering and examination, (5) assessment of risk management, (6) disclosure requirements, (7) consumer protection, and (8) restrictions on competition.

1. Restrictions on Asset Holdings

As we have seen, the moral hazard associated with a government safety net encourages excessive risk taking on the part of financial institutions. Financial regulations that restrict asset holdings are directed at minimizing this moral hazard, which can cost the taxpayers dearly.

Even in the absence of a government safety net, financial institutions still have the incentive to take on too much risk. Risky assets may provide the financial institution with higher earnings when they pay off, but if they do not pay off and the institution fails, depositors and creditors are left holding the bag. If depositors and creditors were able to monitor the bank easily by acquiring information on its risk-taking activities, they would be able to withdraw their funds immediately if the institution was taking on too much risk. To prevent such a loss of funds, the institution would be more likely to reduce its risk-taking activities. Unfortunately, acquiring information on an institution's activities to learn how much risk the institution is taking on can be a difficult task. Hence, most depositors and many creditors are incapable of imposing discipline that might prevent financial institutions from engaging in risky activities. A strong rationale for government regulation aimed at reducing risk taking on the part of financial institutions therefore existed even before the establishment of government safety nets like deposit insurance.

Because banks are the financial institutions most prone to panics, they are subjected to strict regulations that restrict their holding of risky assets, such as common stocks. Bank regulations also promote diversification, which reduces risk by limiting the amount of loans given in particular categories or to individual borrowers. With the extension of the government safety net during the global financial crisis, and the calls for regulatory reform in its aftermath, it is likely that nonbank financial institutions may face greater restrictions on their holdings of risky assets in the future. The danger exists, however, that these restrictions may become so onerous that the efficiency of the financial system will be impaired.

2. Capital Requirements

Government-imposed capital requirements are another way of minimizing moral hazard at financial institutions. When a financial institution is forced to hold a large amount of equity capital, the institution has more to lose if it fails and is thus more likely to pursue less risky activities. In addition, as will be illustrated in Chapter 12, capital functions as a cushion when bad shocks occur, making it less likely that a financial institution will fail, thereby directly adding to the safety and soundness of financial institutions.

Capital requirements for banks take two forms. The first type is based on the **leverage ratio**, the amount of capital divided by the bank's total assets. To be classified as well capitalized, a bank's leverage ratio must exceed 5%; a lower leverage ratio, especially one below 3%, triggers increased regulatory restrictions on the bank.

In the past decade, regulators in Canada and the rest of the world have become increasingly worried about banks' holdings of risky assets and about the increase in banks' **off-balance-sheet activities**. Off-balance-sheet activities, which do not appear on bank balance sheets but nevertheless expose banks to risk, involve trading financial instruments and generating income from fees. To help combat the problems of risky assets and off-balance-sheet activities, banking officials from industrialized nations agreed to set up the **Basel Committee on Bank Supervision** (so named because it meets under the auspices of the Bank for International Settlements in Basel, Switzerland), which implemented the **Basel Accord**, which deals with a second type of capital requirement, risk-based capital requirements. The Basel Accord, which requires that banks hold as capital at least 8% of their risk-weighted assets, has been adopted by more than 100 countries, including Canada and the United States. Assets are allocated into four categories, each with a different weight to reflect the degree of credit risk. The first category carries a zero weight and includes items that have little default risk, such as reserves and government securities issued by the Organization for Economic Co-operation and Development (OECD)—industrialized countries. The second category has a 20% weight and includes claims on banks in OECD countries. The third category has a weight of 50% and includes municipal bonds and residential mortgages. The fourth category has the maximum weight of 100% and includes loans to consumers and corporations. Off-balance-sheet activities are treated in a similar manner. They are assigned a credit-equivalent percentage that converts them to on-balance-sheet items to which the appropriate risk weight applies, and there are minimum capital requirements for risks in banks' trading accounts.

Over time, the limitations of the Basel Accord have become apparent, because the regulatory measure of bank risk, as stipulated by the risk weights, can differ substantially from the actual risk the bank faces. This discrepancy has resulted in **regulatory arbitrage**, a practice in which banks keep on their books assets that have the same risk-based capital requirement but are relatively risky, such as a loan to a company with a very low credit rating, while taking off their books low-risk assets, such as a loan to a company with a very high credit rating. The Basel Accord thus might lead to increased risk taking, the opposite of its intent. To address these limitations, the Basel Committee on Bank Supervision came up with a new capital accord, often referred to as Basel 2. However, in the aftermath of the global financial crisis, the committee developed an even newer accord, which the media has dubbed "Basel 3". These accords are described in the Global box, Where Is the Basel Accord Heading After the Global Financial Crisis?

3. Prompt Corrective Action

If the amount of a financial institution's capital falls to low levels, two serious problems result. First, the bank is more likely to fail because it has a smaller capital cushion if it suffers loan losses or other asset write-downs. Second, with less capital, a financial institution has less "skin in the game" and is therefore more likely to take on excessive risks. In other words, the moral hazard problem becomes more severe, making it more likely that the institution will fail and the taxpayer will be left holding the bag. To prevent this, the CDIC adopted prompt corrective action provisions that require the CDIC to intervene earlier and more vigorously when a bank gets into trouble.

4. Financial Supervision: Chartering and Examination

Overseeing who operates financial institutions and how they are operated, referred to as **financial supervision** or **prudential supervision**, is an important method for reducing adverse selection and moral hazard in the financial industry. Because financial institutions can be used by crooks or overambitious entrepreneurs to engage in highly speculative activities, such undesirable people would be eager to run a financial institution. Chartering financial institutions is one method for preventing this adverse selection problem; through chartering, proposals for new institutions are screened to prevent undesirable people from controlling them.

Regular on-site examinations, which allow regulators to monitor whether an institution is complying with capital requirements and restrictions on asset holdings, also function to limit moral hazard. Bank examiners give banks a *CAMELS rating*. The acronym is based on the six areas assessed: capital adequacy, asset quality, management, earnings, liquidity, and sensitivity to market risk. With this information about a bank's activities, regulators can enforce regulations by taking such formal actions as issuing *cease and desist orders* to alter the bank's behaviour, or even closing a bank if its CAMELS rating is too low.

Global   Where Is the Basel Accord Heading After the Global Financial Crisis?

Starting in June 1999, the Basel Committee on Banking Supervision released several proposals to reform the original 1988 Basel Accord. These efforts have culminated in what bank supervisors refer to as Basel 2, which is based on three pillars.

1. Pillar 1 links capital requirements for large, internationally active banks more closely to actual risk of three types: market risk, credit risk, and operational risk. It does so by specifying many more categories of assets, with different risk weights, in its standardized approach. Alternatively, it allows sophisticated banks to pursue an internal ratings-based approach that permits banks to use their own models of credit risk.
2. Pillar 2 focuses on strengthening the supervisory process, particularly in assessing the quality of risk management in banking institutions and evaluating whether these institutions have adequate procedures in place for determining how much capital they need.
3. Pillar 3 focuses on improving market discipline through increased disclosure of details about a bank's credit exposures, its amount of reserves and capital, the officials who control the bank, and the effectiveness of its internal rating system.

Although Basel 2 made great strides toward limiting excessive risk taking by internationally active banking institutions, it greatly increased the complexity of the accord. The document describing the original Basel Accord was 26 pages long, whereas the final draft of Basel 2 exceeded 500 pages. The original timetable called for the completion of the final round of consultation by the end of 2001, with the new rules taking effect by 2004.

However, criticism from banks, trade associations, and national regulators led to several postponements. The final draft of Basel 2 was not published until June 2004, and the "Big Six" internationally active Canadian banks began to implement the new accord at the end of 2007, whereas European banks began to implement it at the start of 2008. U.S. banks submitted plans for compliance with Basel 2 in 2008, but full implementation did not occur until 2009. Only the dozen or so largest U.S. banks are subject to Basel 2; all others will be allowed to use a simplified version of the standards it imposes.

The global financial crisis, however, revealed many limitations of the new accord. First, Basel 2 did not require banks to have sufficient capital to weather the kind of financial disruption that occurred during this period. Second, risk weights in the standardized approach are heavily reliant on credit ratings, which proved to be extremely unreliable in the run-up to the financial crisis. Third, Basel 2 is very procyclical—that is, it demands that banks hold less capital when times are good but more when times are bad, thereby exacerbating credit cycles. Because the probability of default and expected losses on different classes of assets rises during bad times, Basel 2 may require more capital at exactly the time when capital is most short. This has been a particularly serious concern in the aftermath of the global financial crisis. As a result of this crisis, banks' capital balances eroded, leading to a cutback on lending that was a big drag on the economy. Basel 2 made this cutback in lending even worse, doing yet more harm to the economy. Fourth, Basel 2 did not focus sufficiently on the dangers of a possible drying up of liquidity, a problem that brought down financial institutions during the financial crisis.

As a result of these limitations, in 2010 the Basel Committee developed a new accord, Basel 3. It beefs up capital standards not only by raising them substantially but also by improving the quality of the capital, makes capital standards less procyclical by raising capital requirements in good times and lowering them in bad, makes new rules on the use of credit ratings, and requires financial institutions to have more stable funding so that they are better able to withstand liquidity shocks. Measures to achieve these objectives are highly controversial because of concerns that tightening up capital standards might cause banks to restrict their lending, which would make it harder for economies throughout the world to recover from the recent deep recession. Basel 3 is being implemented slowly over time, with the target for full implementation extending out to the end of 2019. Whether Basel 3 will be fully in place by that date, and whether it will be successful in restraining risk taking, is highly uncertain.

Actions taken to reduce moral hazard by restricting banks from taking on too much risk help reduce the adverse selection problem further, because with less opportunity for risk taking, risk-loving entrepreneurs will be less likely to be attracted to the banking industry. Note that the methods used by regulators to cope with adverse selection and moral hazard have their counterparts in private financial markets (see Chapters 8 and 12). Chartering is similar to the screening of potential borrowers; regulations that restrict risky asset holdings are similar to restrictive covenants that prevent borrowing firms from engaging in risky investment activities; capital requirements act like restrictive covenants that require minimum amounts of net worth for borrowing firms; and regular examinations are similar to the monitoring of borrowers by lending institutions.

A chartered bank obtains a charter either by an Act of Parliament or through application to the minister of finance, who has the authority to issue a charter. To obtain a charter, the people planning to organize the bank must submit an application that shows how they plan to operate the bank. In evaluating the application, the regulatory authority looks at whether the bank is likely to be sound by examining the quality of the bank's intended management, the likely earnings of the bank, and the amount of the bank's initial capital. Moreover, the chartering agency typically explores the issue of whether the community needs a new bank. Often a new bank charter would not be granted if existing banks in a community would be hurt by its presence. Today this anticompetitive stance (justified by the desire to prevent bank failures of existing banks) is no longer as strong in the chartering agencies.

Once a bank has been chartered, it is required to file periodic (usually quarterly) *call reports* that reveal the bank's assets and liabilities, income and dividends, ownership, foreign exchange operations, and other details. The bank is also subject to examination by the bank regulatory agencies to ascertain its financial condition at least once a year. To avoid duplication of effort, the three federal agencies work together and usually accept each other's examinations. This means that, typically, chartered banks are examined by the Office of the Superintendent of Financial Institutions, the Canada Deposit Insurance Corporation, and the Bank of Canada.

Bank examinations are conducted by bank examiners, who study a bank's books to see whether it is complying with the rules and regulations that apply to its holdings of assets. If a bank is holding securities or loans that are too risky, the bank examiner can force the bank to get rid of them. If a bank examiner decides that a loan is unlikely to be repaid, the examiner can force the bank to declare the loan worthless (to write off the loan, which reduces the bank's capital). If, after examining the bank, the examiner feels that it does not have sufficient capital or has engaged in dishonest practices, the bank can be declared a "problem bank" and will be subject to more frequent examinations.

5. Assessment of Risk Management

Traditionally, on-site examinations have focused primarily on assessment of the quality of a financial institution's balance sheet at a point in time and whether it complies with capital requirements and restrictions on asset holdings. Although the traditional focus is important for reducing excessive risk taking by financial institutions, it is no longer thought to be adequate in today's world, in which financial innovation has produced new markets and instruments that make it easy for financial institutions and their employees to place huge bets easily and quickly. In this new financial environment, a financial institution that is healthy at a particular point in time can be driven into insolvency extremely rapidly from trading losses, as forcefully demonstrated by the failure of Barings in 1995 (to be discussed in Chapter 12). Thus an examination that focuses only on a financial institution's position at a point in time may not be effective in indicating whether it will, in fact, be taking on excessive risk in the near future.

This change in the financial environment resulted in a major shift in thinking about the prudential supervisory process throughout the world. Bank examiners, for example, are now placing far greater emphasis on evaluating the soundness of a bank's management processes with regard to controlling risk. This shift in thinking is now reflected in a new focus on risk management in the guidelines to examiners on trading and derivatives activities. Now, bank examiners give a separate risk management rating, from 1 to 5, that feeds into the overall management rating as part of the CAMELS system. Four elements of sound risk management are assessed to arrive at the risk management rating: (1) the quality of oversight provided by the board of directors and senior management, (2) the adequacy of policies and limits for all activities that present significant risks, (3) the quality of the risk measurement and monitoring systems, and (4) the adequacy of internal controls to prevent fraud or unauthorized activities on the part of employees.

This shift toward focusing on management processes is also reflected in recent guidelines adopted by the Canadian bank regulatory authorities to deal with interest-rate risk. These guidelines require the bank's board of directors to establish interest-rate risk limits, appoint officials of the bank to manage this risk, and monitor the bank's risk exposure. The guidelines also require that senior management of a bank develop formal risk-management policies and procedures to ensure that the board of directors' risk limits are not violated and to implement internal controls to monitor interest-rate risk and compliance with the board's directives. Particularly important is the implementation of **stress tests**, which calculate losses under fictional dire scenarios and the need for more capital, and **value-at-risk (VaR)** calculations, which measure the size of the loss on a trading portfolio—say, over a two-week period—that might happen 1% of the time. In addition to these guidelines, bank examiners will continue to consider interest-rate risk in deciding the bank's capital requirements.

6. Disclosure Requirements

The free-rider problem described in Chapter 8 indicates that individual depositors and creditors will not have enough incentive to produce private information about the quality of a financial institution's assets. To ensure that better information is available in the marketplace, regulators can require that financial institutions adhere to certain standard accounting principles and disclose a wide range of information that helps the market assess the quality of an institution's portfolio and the amount of its exposure to risk. More public information about the risks incurred by financial institutions and the quality of their portfolios can better enable stockholders, creditors, and depositors to evaluate and monitor financial institutions and so act as a deterrent to excessive risk taking.

Disclosure requirements are a key element of financial regulation. Basel 2 puts a particular emphasis on disclosure requirements, with one of its three pillars focusing on increasing market discipline by mandating increased disclosure by banking institutions of their credit exposure, amount of reserves, and capital. Provincial securities commissions, the most significant being the Ontario Securities Commission (OSC), also impose disclosure requirements on any corporation, including financial institutions, that issue publicly traded securities. In addition, Basel 2 has required financial institutions to provide additional disclosure regarding their off-balance-sheet positions and more information about how they value their portfolios.

Regulation to increase disclosure is needed to limit incentives to take on excessive risk and to upgrade the quality of information in the marketplace so that investors can make informed decisions, thereby improving the ability of financial markets to allocate capital to its most productive uses. The efficiency of markets is assisted by the OSC's disclosure requirements mentioned above, as well as its regulation of brokerage firms, mutual funds, exchanges, and credit-rating agencies to ensure that they produce reliable information and protect investors. Bill 198, introduced by the Ontario government in October 2002 in response to the **Sarbanes-Oxley Act** in the United States, took disclosure of information even further by increasing the incentives to produce accurate audits of corporate income statements and balance sheets and putting in place regulations to limit conflicts of interest in the financial services industry.

Particularly controversial in the wake of the global financial crisis is the move to so-called **mark-to-market accounting**, also called **fair-value accounting**, in which assets are valued on the balance sheet at what they could sell for in the market (see the FYI box, Mark-to-Market Accounting and the Global Financial Crisis).

7. Consumer Protection

The existence of asymmetric information also suggests that consumers may not have enough information to protect themselves fully in financial dealing. Consumer protection regulation has taken several forms. First is "truth in lending," which requires all lenders, not just banks, to provide information to consumers about the cost of borrowing, including the disclosure of a standardized interest rate (called the *annual percentage rate* or *APR*) and the total finance charges on the loan. Legislation also requires creditors, especially credit card issuers, to provide information on the method of assessing finance charges, and requires that billing complaints be handled quickly.

The subprime mortgage crisis in the United States and Canada's own short experiment with subprime lending have illustrated the need for greater consumer protection, because so many borrowers took out loans with terms they did not understand and that were well beyond their means to repay. Most infamous were so-called NINJA loans in the United States, which were issued to borrowers with No Income, No Job, and No Assets. The result was millions of foreclosures, with many people losing their homes. Because weak consumer protection regulation played a prominent role in this crisis, there have been increasing demands to beef up this regulation, not only in Canada and the United States but in other countries as well.

8. Restrictions on Competition

Increased competition can also increase moral hazard incentives for financial institutions to take on more risk. Declining profitability resulting from increased competition could tip the incentives of financial institutions toward assuming greater risk in an effort to maintain former profit levels. Thus governments in many countries have instituted regulations to protect financial institutions from competition. These regulations took different forms in the past, one being preventing nonbank institutions from competing with banks by engaging in banking business.

Although restrictions on competition propped up the health of banks, there were some serious disadvantages: They led to higher charges to consumers and decreased the efficiency of banking institutions, which now did not have to compete as vigorously. Thus, although the existence of asymmetric information provided a rationale for anticompetitive regulations, it did not mean that the regulations would be beneficial to consumers. Indeed, in recent years, the impulse of governments in industrialized countries to restrict competition has been waning.

FYI   Mark-to-Market Accounting and the Global Financial Crisis

The controversy over mark-to-market accounting has made accounting a hot topic. Mark-to-market accounting was made standard practice in the U.S. accounting industry in 1993. U.S. Generally Accepted Accounting Principles (GAAP) established a number of ways for measuring fair value, depending on whether a financial instrument is traded on an active market or in the absence of an active market. Canadian GAAP are similar to U.S. GAAP, as well as to standards in effect in those countries (approximately 110) that have adopted a set of global standards, known as International Financial Reporting Standards (IFRS), developed by the International Accounting Standards Board (IASB).

The rationale behind mark-to-market accounting is that market prices provide the best basis for estimating the true value of assets, and hence capital, in the firm. Before mark-to-market accounting, firms relied on the traditional historical-cost (book value) accounting, in which the value of an asset is set at its initial purchase price. The problem with historical-cost accounting is that fluctuations in the values of assets and liabilities caused by changes in interest rates or default risk are not reflected in the calculation of the firm's equity capital. Yet changes in the market values of assets and liabilities—and hence changes in the market value of equity capital—are what indicate whether a firm is in good shape or, alternatively, is getting into trouble and may therefore be more susceptible to moral hazard.

Mark-to-market accounting, however, is subject to a major flaw. At times, markets stop working, as occurred during the global financial crisis. The price of an asset sold at a time of financial distress does not reflect its fundamental value. That is, the fire-sale liquidation value of an asset can at times be well below the present value of its expected future cash flows.

Many people, particularly bankers, criticized mark-to-market accounting, claiming that it was an important factor driving the recent global financial crisis. They claim that the seizing up of financial markets led to market prices that were well below fundamental values. Mark-to-market accounting requires that the financial firms' assets be marked down in value. This markdown creates a shortfall in capital that leads to a cutback in lending, which causes a further deterioration in asset prices, which in turn causes a further cutback in lending. The resulting adverse feedback loop can then make the financial crisis even worse. Although the criticisms of mark-to-market accounting have some validity, some of the criticism by bankers is self-serving. The criticism was made only when asset values were falling and mark-to-market accounting was painting a bleaker picture of banks' balance sheets, as opposed to when asset prices were booming and mark-to-market accounting made banks' balance sheets look very good.

The criticisms of mark-to-market accounting led the International Accounting Standards Board to form an advisory panel to enhance its guidance on valuing financial instruments in inactive markets in times of crisis. Moreover, in the United States, it led to a Congressional focus on mark-to-market accounting that resulted in a provision in the Emergency Economic Stabilization Act of 2008 that required the SEC, in consultation with the Federal Reserve and the U.S. Treasury, to submit a study of mark-to-market accounting applicable to financial institutions. Who knew that accounting could get even politicians worked up!

Summary

Asymmetric information analysis explains what types of financial regulations are needed to reduce moral hazard and adverse selection problems in the financial system. However, understanding the theory behind regulation does not mean that regulation and supervision of the financial system are easy in practice. Getting regulators and supervisors to do their job properly is difficult for several reasons. First, as we will see in our discussion of financial regulation in Chapter 11, financial institutions, in their search for profits, have strong incentives to avoid existing regulations by loophole mining. Thus, regulation applies to a moving target. Regulators are continually playing cat-and-mouse with financial

Global International Financial Regulation

Because asymmetric information problems in the banking industry are a fact of life throughout the world, financial regulation in other countries is similar to that in Canada. Financial institutions are chartered and supervised by government regulators, just as they are in Canada. Disclosure requirements for financial institutions and corporations issuing securities are similar in other developed countries. Deposit insurance is also a feature of the regulatory systems of most other countries, although its coverage is different across countries. In the United States, for example, the Federal Deposit Insurance Corporation (FDIC) guarantees that depositors will be paid off in full on the first $250 000 they have deposited in a bank if the bank fails. We have also seen that capital requirements are in the process of being standardized across countries in compliance with agreements like the Basel Accord.

Particular problems in financial regulation occur when financial institutions operate in many countries and thus can shift their business readily from one country to another. Financial regulators closely examine the domestic operations of financial institutions in their own country, but they often do not have the knowledge or ability to keep a close watch on operations in other countries, operations run either by domestic institutions' foreign affiliates or by foreign institutions with domestic branches. In addition, when a financial institution operates in many countries, it is not always

clear which national regulatory authority should have primary responsibility for keeping the institution from engaging in overly risky activities.

The difficulties inherent in international financial regulation were highlighted by the collapse of the Bank of Credit and Commerce International (BCCI). BCCI, although it operated in more than 70 countries, including the United States and the United Kingdom, was supervised by Luxembourg, a tiny country unlikely to be up to the task. When massive fraud was discovered, the Bank of England closed BCCI down, but not before depositors and stockholders were exposed to huge losses. Cooperation among regulators in different countries and standardization of regulatory requirements provide potential solutions to the problems of international financial regulation.

The world has moved in this direction through agreements like the Basel Accord and oversight procedures announced by the Basel Committee in July 1992, which require a bank's worldwide operations to be under the scrutiny of a single home-country regulator with enhanced powers to acquire information on the bank's activities. The Basel Committee also ruled that regulators in other countries can restrict the operations of a foreign bank if they believe it lacks effective oversight. Whether agreements of this type will solve the problem of international financial regulation in the future is an open question.

institutions—financial institutions think up clever ways to skirt regulations, which leads regulators to modify their regulatory activities. Regulators continually face new challenges in a dynamically changing financial system, and unless they can respond rapidly, they may not be able to prevent financial institutions from taking on excessive risk. This problem can be exacerbated if regulators and supervisors do not have the resources or expertise necessary to keep up with clever people seeking to circumvent the existing regulations.

Financial regulation and supervision are difficult for two other reasons. In the regulation and supervision game, the devil is in the details. Subtle differences in the details may have unintended consequences; unless regulators get the regulation and supervision just right, they may be unable to prevent excessive risk taking. In addition, regulated firms may lobby politicians to lean on regulators and supervisors to go easy on them or to change regulations altogether.

For all of these reasons, there is no guarantee that regulators and supervisors will be successful in promoting a healthy financial system. These same problems bedevil financial regulators in other countries as well, as the Global box, International Financial

Regulation indicates. Indeed, financial regulation and supervision have not always worked well, leading to banking crises in Canada and throughout the world.[1]

Because so many laws regulating the financial system have been passed in Canada, it is hard to keep track of them all. As a study aid, Table 10-1 lists the major financial legislation in the twentieth century and its key provisions.

TABLE 10-1	Major Financial Legislation in Canada

Bank of Canada Act (1934)
- Created the Bank of Canada following the recommendations of the Macmillan Commission of 1933.

Bank Act of 1936
- Prohibited banks from issuing banknotes
- Imposed reserve requirements on depository institutions to be held with the Bank of Canada

Bank Act of 1954
- Increased reserve requirements on depository institutions
- Allowed chartered banks to offer mortgages issued under the National Housing Act

Canada Deposit Insurance Corporation Act (1967)
- Created the CDIC to insure deposits with all federally chartered banks and near banks

Bank Act of 1967
- Removed the 6% loan interest-rate ceiling
- Restricted foreign competition
- Imposed secondary reserve requirements on depository institutions
- Put chartered banks and near banks on equal footing regarding mortgage lending

Bank Act of 1981
- Created the Canadian Payments Association to operate the national payments system and plan its development
- Lowered reserve requirements on Canadian-dollar deposits
- Increased competition by introducing a less complicated procedure for obtaining a licence to operate as a bank
- Allowed foreign banks to establish subsidiaries in Canada, subject to reciprocal treatment of Canadian banks
- Extended banks' business powers to include financial leasing, factoring, and data processing
- Redesigned corporate clauses to ensure consistency between the Bank Act and the Canada Business Corporations Act
- Provided a simpler incorporation method for new banks (letters patent) while retaining incorporation through a special Act of Parliament

Office of the Superintendent of Financial Institutions Act (1987)
- Created the OSFI to succeed two separate federal regulatory bodies (the Department of Insurance and the Inspector General of Banks) in the supervision of financial institutions

(continued)

[1]Canada suffered a major banking crisis in the 1980s, a crisis that hit the banking industry particularly hard. This crisis is discussed in the first Web appendix to this chapter, "The 1980s Canadian Banking Crisis," which can be found on the book's MyEconLab. A second Web appendix to this chapter, "Banking Crises Throughout the World," discusses banking crises in other countries. The second Web appendix can also be found on the MyEconLab.

TABLE 10-1   (*continued*)

Financial Institutions and Deposit Insurance System Amendment Act (1987)

- Allowed chartered banks to own investment banking subsidiaries, thereby initiating the merging of the four pillars

Savings and Credit Union Act of the Province of Québec (1988)

- Set rules for credit unions, federations, and confederations, with specific reference to the *Mouvement Desjardins* (Desjardins Group)

Bank Act of 1992

- Comprehensive banking law
- Allowed chartered banks to own trust companies
- Allowed trust companies to make commercial loans
- Made provisions for the phasing out of reserve requirements
- Set rules regarding the supervisory role of the Bank of Canada and the OSFI with respect to chartered banks
- Reset the "sunset" clause from 10 years to 5 years to address the changing Canadian financial services marketplace

Cooperative Credit Associations Act (1992)

- Replaced the Cooperative Credit Association Act of 1952–1953 and set rules for federally chartered credit unions
- Followed the same format as the Bank Act

Insurance Companies Act (1992)

- Replaced the Canadian and British Insurance Companies Act and the Foreign Insurance Companies Act, both passed in 1932
- Set rules for life insurance companies and property and casualty (P&C) insurance companies
- Allowed insurance companies to own Schedule II chartered banks
- Followed the same format as the Bank Act

Trust and Loan Companies Act (1992)

- Replaced the Trust Companies Act and the Loan Companies Act, both passed in 1914
- Set rules for federally incorporated Trust and Mortgage Loan Companies (TMLs) and provincially incorporated TMLs reporting to the OSFI
- Required large, formerly closely held TMLs to become 35% widely held
- Followed the same format as the Bank Act

Bank Act of 1997

- Yielded minor changes because the government was waiting for the recommendations of the MacKay Task Force

Bank Act Reform of 2001

- Set new ownership rules
- Established a process for reviewing mergers involving large banks
- Allowed bank financial groups to organize under a holding company structure
- Allowed greater flexibility for bank involvement in the information technology area
- Allowed non-deposit-taking financial institutions access to the payments and clearance systems

Financial System Review Act (FSRA) of March 29, 2012

- Amendments to the Bank Act and other associated statutes

CDIC DEPOSIT INSURANCE COVERAGE

The Canada Deposit Insurance Corporation (CDIC) insures each depositor at member institutions up to a loss of $100 000 per account. All federally incorporated financial institutions and all provincially incorporated trust and mortgage loan companies are members of the CDIC. Insurance companies, credit unions, *caisses populaires*, and investment dealers are not eligible for CDIC membership; the Québec Deposit Insurance Board (QDIB) insures provincially incorporated financial institutions in Québec, and the other provinces have deposit insurance corporations that insure the deposits of credit unions in their jurisdiction, on terms similar to the CDIC's.

The CDIC is allowed to insure only deposits in Canadian currency and payable in Canada; foreign currency deposits, such as accounts in U.S. dollars, are not insured. Moreover, not all deposits and investments offered by CDIC member institutions are insurable. Insurable deposits include savings and chequing accounts, term deposits with a maturity date of less than five years, money orders and drafts, certified drafts and cheques, and traveller's cheques. The CDIC does not insure term deposits with an initial maturity date of more than five years, Treasury bills, bonds and debentures issued by governments and corporations (including the chartered banks), or investments in stocks, mutual funds, and mortgages.

The primary rationale for deposit insurance is protecting depositors from bank insolvency and thus ensuring financial stability. Deposit insurance could also promote competition among financial institutions by removing barriers to entry for new deposit-taking institutions. In the absence of deposit insurance, it is difficult for new banks to attract deposits. Most depositors, for example, are not capable of making appropriate risk calculations to assess the risk of a new bank. Those depositors would tend to place their deposits in banks that are considered too big to fail, thereby producing significant barriers to entry and unfair disadvantages for small new entrants. By insuring deposits at all deposit-taking financial institutions, the CDIC effectively removes barriers to entry for new deposit takers.

Differential Premiums

Until May 1999, CDIC premium revenue was not tied to the risk profile of financial institutions; the premium rate was the same for all deposit-taking institutions, irrespective of their risk profile. For example, in the 1998–1999 fiscal year, the flat-rate insurance premium was 1/6 of 1%, or 0.1667%, meaning that each deposit-taking financial institution paid an insurance premium of close to 17 cents per $100. This was one of the reasons that the Big Six, represented by the Canadian Bankers Association, vigorously opposed the establishment of the CDIC in 1967; it was argued that deposit insurance would be a subsidy to small banks paid by the big banks.

Over the years, the Canadian Bankers Association strongly promoted the reform of the Canadian deposit insurance system. As a result, the CDIC developed the Differential Premiums By-law, which came into effect for the premium year beginning May 1, 1999. The bylaw undergoes regular reviews and has been amended a number of times. The important feature of this legislation is its implicit, prompt corrective action provisions, which require the CDIC to intervene earlier and more vigorously when a bank gets into trouble. CDIC member institutions are classified into four premium groups based on their risk profile. An institution's risk profile is determined using a variety of quantitative and qualitative criteria, including capital adequacy, profitability, asset

TABLE 10-2	Premium Structure and Rates for CDIC Member Institutions in 2014

Category	Premium Rate (as a Percentage of Insured Deposits)
1	1/36 of 1%, or 0.02778
2	1/18 of 1%, or 0.05556
3	1/9 of 1%, or 0.11111
4	2/9 of 1%, or 0.22222

Source: CDIC website: www.cdic.ca.

concentration, income volatility, regulatory ratings, and adherence to CDIC's Standards of Sound Business and Financial Practices, with capital adequacy dominating the criteria, accounting for 20% of the score.

Under the this system, the premium rates for CDIC member institutions are those shown in Table 10-2; they vary from 2 cents to 22 cents per $100. Category 1, classified as "best," is well-capitalized banks that significantly exceed minimum requirements. On the other hand, banks in Category 4, classified as "worst," are significantly (and perhaps critically) undercapitalized and the insurance premium that they pay is 22 basis points, the maximum allowed under the CDIC Act. In addition, for Category 4 banks, the CDIC is required to take prompt corrective actions such as requiring them to submit a capital restoration plan, restrict their asset growth, and seek regulatory approval to open new branches or develop new lines of business. Today, over 90% of CDIC member institutions are classified in Categories 1 or 2, but as in other countries, the premium category and related supervisory information applicable to individual CDIC members are confidential.

Opting Out

Another interesting development is the Opting-Out By-law that came into effect on October 15, 1999. This legislation permits Schedule III banks that primarily accept wholesale deposits (defined as $150 000 or more) to opt out of CDIC membership and therefore to operate without deposit insurance. This legislation, however, includes provisions to protect depositors who hold deposits eligible for CDIC protection. In particular, it requires an opted-out bank to inform all depositors, by posting notices in its branches, that their deposits will not be protected by the CDIC, and not to charge any early withdrawal penalties for depositors who choose to withdraw.

Probably the most important feature of the opting-out legislation is its minimization of CDIC exposure to uninsured deposits. This represents a significant departure from past practices, when the CDIC showed generosity to uninsured depositors. For example, in the Canadian Commercial and Northland Bank failures of the mid-1980s, the CDIC paid 100 cents on the dollar to all depositors, both insured and uninsured. By compensating only the insured depositors rather than all depositors, the opting-out legislation increases the incentives of uninsured depositors to monitor the risk-taking activities of banks, thereby reducing moral hazard risk.

APPLICATION   ## Evaluating CDIC Deposit Insurance Coverage and Other Proposed Reforms of the Banking Regulatory System

The system of risk-based premiums and opting-out rules is a major step in reformulating the financial regulatory system. How will it work to solve the adverse selection and moral hazard problems of the bank regulatory system? Let's use the analysis in the chapter to evaluate the new legislation to answer this question.

LIMITS ON THE SCOPE OF DEPOSIT INSURANCE

CDIC's reductions of the scope of deposit insurance by limiting insurance to insured deposits might have increased the incentives for uninsured depositors to monitor banks and to withdraw funds if the bank were taking on too much risk. Because banks might now fear the loss of deposits when they engage in risky activities, they might have less incentive to take on too much risk.

Although the cited elements of deposit insurance strengthen the incentive of depositors to monitor banks, some critics would take these limitations on the scope of deposit insurance even further. Some suggest that deposit insurance should be eliminated entirely or should be reduced in amount from the current $100 000 limit to, say, $20 000 or $10 000. Another proposed reform would institute a system of **coinsurance** in which only a percentage of a deposit, say, 90%, would be covered by insurance. In this system, the insured depositor would suffer a percentage of the losses along with the deposit insurance agency. Because depositors facing a lower limit on deposit insurance or coinsurance would suffer losses if the bank went broke, they would have an incentive to monitor the bank's activities.

However, other experts do not believe that depositors are capable of monitoring banks and imposing discipline on them. The basic problem with reducing the scope of deposit insurance even further is that banks would be subject to runs—sudden withdrawals by nervous investors. Such runs could by themselves lead to bank failures. In addition to protecting individual depositors, the purpose of deposit insurance is to prevent a large number of bank failures, which would lead to an unstable banking system and an unstable economy. From this perspective, deposit insurance has been a resounding success. Bank panics, in which there are simultaneous failures of many banks and consequent disruption of the financial system, have not occurred since deposit insurance was established.

Eliminating the too-big-to-fail policy altogether would also cause some of the same problems that would occur if deposit insurance were eliminated or reduced: the probability of bank panics would increase. If a bank were allowed to fail, the repercussions in the financial system might be immense. Other banks with a correspondent relationship with the failed bank (those that have deposits at the bank in exchange for services) would suffer large losses and might fail in turn, leading to full-scale panic. In addition, the problem of liquidating the big bank's loan portfolio might create a major disruption in the financial system.

PROMPT CORRECTIVE ACTION

The prompt corrective action provisions of CDIC also substantially reduce incentives for bank risk taking and reduce taxpayer losses. CDIC uses a carrot-and-stick approach to get banks to hold more capital. If they are well capitalized, they receive better ratings and are placed in a better premium rate category (see Table 10-2); if their capital ratio falls, they are subject to more and more onerous regulation. Increased bank capital reduces moral hazard for the bank because the bank now has more to lose if it fails and so is less likely to take on too much risk. In addition, encouraging banks to hold more capital reduces potential losses for the CDIC because increased bank capital is a cushion that makes bank failure less likely.

Prompt corrective action, which requires regulators to intervene early when bank capital begins to fall, is a serious attempt to reduce the principal–agent problem for politicians and regulators. With prompt corrective action provisions, regulators no longer have the option of regulatory forbearance, which, as we have seen, can greatly increase moral hazard incentives for banks.

RISK-BASED INSURANCE PREMIUMS

Under the Differential Premiums By-law, banks deemed to be taking on greater risk, in the form of lower capital or riskier assets, are subjected to higher insurance premiums, as can be seen in Table 10-2. Risk-based insurance premiums consequently reduce the moral hazard incentives for banks to take on higher risk. In addition, the fact that risk-based premiums drop as the bank's capital increases encourages the banks to hold more capital, which has the benefits already mentioned.

One problem with risk-based premiums is that the scheme for determining the amount of risk the bank is taking may not be very accurate. For example, it might be hard for regulators to determine when a bank's loans are risky. Some critics have also pointed out that the classification of banks by such measures as the Basel risk-based capital standard solely reflects credit risk and does not take sufficient account of interest-rate risk. The regulatory authorities, however, are encouraged to modify existing risk-based standards to include interest-rate risk.

OTHER CDIC PROVISIONS

CDIC's requirements that regulators perform frequent bank examinations and member institutions file a Standards report at least once a year are necessary for monitoring banks' compliance with bank capital requirements and asset restrictions. As the Canadian Commercial and Northland Bank debacles illustrate, frequent supervisory examinations of banks are necessary to keep them from taking on too much risk or committing fraud. Similarly, beefing up the ability of the regulators to monitor foreign banks might help dissuade international banks from engaging in these undesirable activities.

The stricter and more burdensome reporting requirements for banks have the advantage of providing more information to regulators to help them monitor bank activities. However, these reporting requirements have been criticized by banks, which claim that the requirements make it harder to lend to small businesses. As a result, the CDIC developed the Modernized Standards By-law, adopted in early 2001, which enables the CDIC to determine the frequency of a member institution's reporting based on its categorization under the Differential Premiums By-law.

The Modernized Standards By-law allows CDIC discretion in examining the performance of problem member institutions. Under this regime, well-capitalized, Category 1 banks will be required to file a Standards report every five years. However, banks in Categories 3 and 4 may be subjected to special examination at any time, the cost of which will be chargeable to the institution. The Modernized Standards By-law, in addition to increasing the regulatory supervision of problem banks, also increases the accountability of the CDIC. Moreover, it decreases the incentives of banks to take on excessive risk and increases their incentives to hold capital.

OTHER PROPOSED CHANGES IN BANKING REGULATIONS

Regulatory Consolidation

The current bank regulatory system in Canada has financial institutions supervised by three federal agencies: the Bank of Canada, the Office of the Superintendent of Financial Institutions, and the Canada Deposit Insurance Corporation. Critics of this system of multiple regulatory agencies with overlapping jurisdictions believe it creates a system that is too complex and too costly because it is rife with duplication. For example, although the CDIC has no direct supervisory role, its Standards of Sound Business and Financial Practices overlap with those of the OSFI.

The MacKay Task Force, named after its chairman Harold MacKay and set up by the government in 1996 to review the financial services sector and propose a framework for its future, considered whether the CDIC and the OSFI should be amalgamated. Although the task force recommended that the regulator (OSFI) and the insurer (CDIC) should not be combined in a single institution, it proposed that the CDIC's mandate be amended to remove the overlap with the OSFI's mandate.

OVERALL EVALUATION

The recent CDIC developments appear to be an important step in the right direction because they increase the incentives for banks to hold capital and decrease their incentives to take on excessive risk. However, more could be done to improve the incentives for banks to limit their risk taking. Yet eliminating deposit insurance and the too-big-to-fail policy altogether may be going too far because these proposals might make the banking system too prone to a banking panic. ◆

MyEconLab

MyEconLab is an online homework and tutorial system that puts you in control of your own learning with study and practice tools directly correlated to this chapter's content. Visit MyEconLab to access the eText, the Questions and Applied Problems with answers, as well as additional assessment. You will also find web chapters, mini-lectures, appendices, mini-cases, videos, glossary flashcards, news feeds, CANSIM data, and graphing tools.

SUMMARY

1. The concepts of asymmetric information, adverse selection, and moral hazard help explain why governments pursue financial regulation.

2. There are eight basic types of financial regulation aimed at lessening asymmetric information problems and excessive risk taking in the financial system: (1) restrictions on assets holdings, (2) capital requirements, (3) prompt corrective action, (4) chartering and examination, (5) assessment of risk management, (6) disclosure requirements, (7) consumer protection, and (8) restrictions on competition.

3. Because of financial innovation, deregulation, and a set of historical accidents, adverse selection and moral hazard problems increased in the 1980s and resulted in huge losses for the Canadian banking industry and for taxpayers.

KEY TERMS

bank failure 222

bank panic 223

Basel Accord 227

Basel Committee on Bank Supervision 227

coinsurance 239

fair-value accounting 232

financial supervision 228

leverage ratio 227

mark-to-market accounting 232

off-balance-sheet activities 227

prudential supervision 228

regulatory arbitrage 228

Sarbanes-Oxley Act 232

stress tests 231

too-big-to-fail problem 225

value-at-risk (VaR) 231

QUESTIONS

All questions are available in MyEconLab at
www.myeconlab.com.

1. Why are deposit insurance and other types of government safety nets important to the health of the economy?

2. If casualty insurance companies provided fire insurance without any restrictions, what kind of adverse selection and moral hazard problems might result?

3. Do you think that eliminating or limiting the amount of deposit insurance would be a good idea? Explain your answer.

4. How could higher deposit insurance premiums for banks with riskier assets benefit the economy?

5. What are the costs and benefits of a too-big-to-fail policy?

6. What types of bank regulations are designed to reduce moral hazard problems? Will they completely eliminate moral hazard problems?

7. Why does imposing bank capital requirements on banks help limit risk taking?

8. At the height of the global financial crisis in October 2008, the U.S. Treasury forced nine of the largest U.S. banks to accept capital injections in exchange for nonvoting ownership stock, even though some of the banks did not need the capital and did not want to participate. What could the rationale have been for doing this?

9. What special problem do off-balance-sheet activities present to bank regulators, and what have they done about it?

10. What are some of the limitations to the Basel and Basel 2 Accords? How does the Basel 3 Accord attempt to address these limitations?

11. How does bank chartering reduce adverse selection problems? Does it always work?

12. Why has the trend in bank supervision moved away from a focus on capital requirements to a focus on risk management?

13. How do disclosure requirements help limit excessive risk taking by banks?

14. Suppose Universal Bank holds $100 million in assets, which are composed of the following:

Desired reserves:	$10 million
Excess reserves:	$ 5 million
Mortgage loans:	$20 million
Corporate bonds:	$15 million
Stocks:	$25 million
Commodities:	$25 million

a. Do you think it is a good idea for Universal Bank to hold stocks, corporate bonds, and commodities as assets? Why or why not?

b. If the housing market suddenly crashed, would Universal Bank be better off with a mark-to-market accounting system or the historical-cost system?

c. If the price of commodities suddenly increased sharply, would Universal Bank be better off with a mark-to-market accounting system or the historical-cost system?

d. What do your answers to (b) and (c) tell you about the tradeoffs between the two accounting systems?

15. Why might more competition in financial markets be bad? Would restrictions on competition be a better idea? Why or why not?

APPLIED PROBLEMS

All applied problems are available in MyEconLab at **www.myeconlab.com.**

16. Consider a failing bank. How much is a deposit of $350 000 worth if the CDIC uses the *payoff method*? The *purchase-and-assumption* method? Which method is more costly to taxpayers?

17. Consider a bank with the following balance sheet:

Assets		Liabilities	
Desired reserves	$ 8 million	Chequable deposits	$100 million
Excess reserves	$ 3 million	Bank capital	$ 6 million
T-bills	$45 million		
Commercial loans	$50 million		

The bank makes a loan commitment for $10 million to a commercial customer. Calculate the bank's capital ratio before and after the agreement. Calculate the bank's risk-weighted assets before and after the agreement.

Problems 18 through 20 relate to a sequence of transactions at Oldhat Financial.

18. Oldhat Financial started its first day of operations with $9 million in capital. A total of $130 million in chequable deposits is received. The bank makes a $25 million commercial loan and another $50 million in mortgages with the following terms: 200 standard 30-year, fixed-rate mortgages with a nominal annual rate of 5.25%, each for $250 000.

Assume that desired reserves are 8%.

a. What does the bank balance sheet look like?

b. How well capitalized is the bank?

c. Calculate the risk-weighted assets and risk-weighted capital ratio after Oldhat's first day.

19. Early the next day the bank invests $50 million of its excess reserves in commercial loans. Later that day, terrible news hits the mortgage markets, and mortgage rates jump to 13%, implying a present value of Oldhat's current mortgage holdings of $124 798 per mortgage. Bank regulators force Oldhat to sell its mortgages to recognize the fair market value. What does Oldhat's balance sheet look like? How do these events affect its capital position?

20. To avoid insolvency, regulators decide to provide the bank with $25 million in bank capital. However, the bad news about the mortgages is featured in the local newspaper, causing a bank run. As a result, $30 million in deposits is withdrawn. Show the effects of the capital injection and bank run on the balance sheet. Was the capital injection enough to stabilize the bank? If the bank regulators decide that the bank needs a capital ratio of 10% to prevent further runs on the bank, how much of an additional capital injection would be required to reach a 10% capital ratio?

DATA ANALYSIS PROBLEMS

Download data for these problems from MyEconLab at **www.myeconlab.com.**

1. Go to the CANSIM database, and find monthly data on total chartered bank assets (series V36883), total liabilities and shareholders' equity (series V36936), and shareholders' equity (series V36960 + V36961 + V36962 + V36964 + V41598372 + V53843372). Download the data from January 2011 through the most recent month available into a spreadsheet and plot the series. For each monthly observation, calculate the bank leverage ratio as the ratio of bank capital to total assets. Create a line graph of the leverage ratio over time. All else being equal, what can you conclude about leverage and moral hazard in Canadian chartered banks over time?

2. Go to the St. Louis Federal Reserve FRED database, and find data on the number of commercial banks in the United States in each of the following categories: average assets less than $100 million (US100NUM), average assets between $100 million and $300 million

(US13NUM), average assets between $300 million and $1 billion (US31NUM), average assets between $1 billion and $15 billion (US115NUM), and average assets greater than $15 billion (USG15NUM). Download the data into a spreadsheet. Calculate the percentage of banks in the smallest (less than $100 million) and largest (greater than $15 billion)

categories, as a percentage of the total number of banks, for the most recent quarter of data available and for 1990.

3. What has happened to the proportion of very large banks? What has happened to the proportion of very small banks? What does this say about the "too-big-to-fail" problem and moral hazard?

WEB EXERCISES

1. Go to **www.cdic.ca** and click on "International Work." Write an essay summarizing how globalization and international financial integration have affected Canada's financial sector safety net.

2. Go to **www.fdic.gov/regulations/laws/important**. This site reports on the most significant pieces of legislation affecting U.S. banks since the 1800s. Summarize the most recently enacted bank regulation listed on this site.

WEB REFERENCES

www.osfi-bsif.gc.ca/Eng/Pages/default.aspx
Search for data on Canadian financial institutions.

www.fdic.gov/bank/historical/bank/index.html
Search for data on U.S. bank failures in any year.

11

Banking Industry: Structure and Competition

Learning Objectives

After studying this chapter you should be able to

1. Recognize the key features of the Canadian banking system and the historical context of the implementation of these features.

2. Explain how financial innovation led to the growth of the shadow banking system.

3. Identify the key structural changes in the chartered banking industry.

4. Summarize the factors that led to consolidation in the chartered banking industry.

5. Assess the reasons for separating banking from other financial services through legislation.

6. Summarize the distinctions between chartered banks and near banks (trust and loan companies and credit unions and *caisses populaires*).

7. Identify the reasons for Canadian banks to operate in foreign countries and for foreign banks to operate in Canada.

PREVIEW

The operations of individual banks (how they acquire, use, and manage funds to make a profit) are roughly similar throughout the world. In all countries, banks are financial intermediaries in the business of earning profits. When you consider the structure and operation of the banking industry as a whole, however, Canada is in a class by itself, with a comparatively concentrated banking industry and small financial institutions. Unlike the United States, where there are over 6500 commercial banks, 1100 savings and loan associations, 400 mutual savings banks, and over 7500 credit unions, Canada has six large commercial banks, commonly called chartered banks, that typically dominate the banking industry.[1]

Is fewer better? Does it mean that the Canadian banking system is more stable and competitive and therefore more economically efficient and sound than banking systems in other countries? What in the Canadian economic and political system explains this small number of banking institutions? In this chapter we try to answer these questions by examining the historical trends in the banking industry and its overall structure.

We start by examining the historical development of the banking system and how financial innovation has increased the competitive environment for the banking industry and is causing fundamental changes in it. We then go on to look at the chartered banking industry in detail and then discuss the near-banking industry, which includes trust and loan companies and credit unions and *caisses populaires*. We spend more time on chartered banks because they are by far the largest depository institutions, accounting for over two-thirds of the deposits in the banking system. In addition to looking at our domestic banking system, we examine the forces behind the growth of international banking to see how it has affected us in Canada.

---

[1]Commercial banks in Canada are called chartered banks because they can be established only by charter granted either in a special act of the federal Parliament or by the federal minister of finance.

HISTORICAL DEVELOPMENT OF THE CANADIAN BANKING SYSTEM

The modern Canadian banking industry began with the creation of the Bank of Montreal in 1817 by nine merchants in Montreal. Initially, the Bank of Montreal was without statutory authority, but a charter was approved by the legislature of Lower Canada and confirmed by royal assent in 1822. Meanwhile, other banks opened for business, and the Canadian banking industry was off and running; the Bank of New Brunswick received royal assent in 1820 and the Chartered Bank of Upper Canada in York (Toronto) in 1821. (As a study aid, Figure 11-1 provides a timeline of the most important dates in the history of Canadian commercial banking before World War II.)

All these banks were authorized to issue notes (redeemable in *specie,* essentially British or American gold or silver coins, on demand), receive deposits, and lend for commercial purposes only; no bank was allowed to lend funds on mortgages, land, or real property. There were, however, some differences between the charters of these banks. For example, the terms of the charter of the Bank of New Brunswick followed the banking tradition of New England. The charter of the Bank of Montreal almost

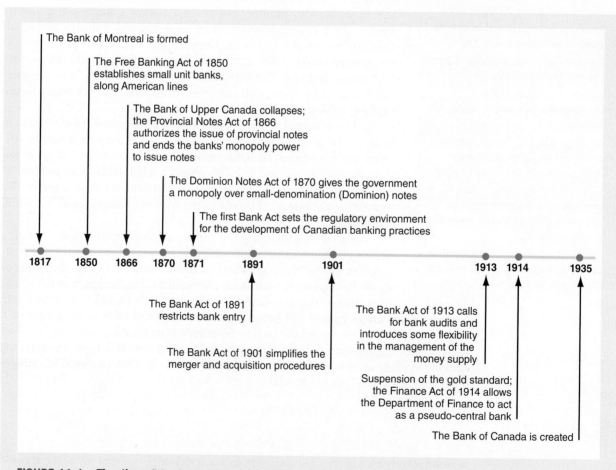

FIGURE 11-1   Timeline of the Early History of Commercial Banking in Canada

---

FYI The Dual Banking System in the United States

The modern commercial banking industry in the United States began when the Bank of North America was chartered in Philadelphia in 1782. A major controversy involving the U.S. banking industry in its early years was whether the federal government or the states should charter banks. The Federalists, particularly Alexander Hamilton, advocated greater centralized control of banking and federal chartering of banks. Their efforts led to the creation in 1791 of the First Bank of the United States.

Until 1863, all commercial banks in the United States were chartered by the banking commission of the state in which each operated. No national currency existed, and banks obtained funds primarily by issuing banknotes (currency circulated by the banks that could be redeemed for gold).

Because banking regulations were extremely lax in many states, banks regularly failed due to fraud or lack of sufficient bank capital; their banknotes became worthless. To eliminate the abuses of the state-chartered banks (called **state banks**), the National Bank Act of 1863 (and subsequent amendments to it) created a new banking system of federally chartered banks (called **national banks**). This legislation was originally intended to dry up sources of funds to state banks by imposing a prohibitive tax on their banknotes while leaving the banknotes of the federally chartered banks untaxed. The state banks cleverly escaped extinction by acquiring funds through deposits.

As a result, today the United States has a **dual banking system** in which banks supervised by the federal government and banks supervised by the states operate side by side.

---

duplicated the terms governing the First Bank of the United States (see the FYI box, The Dual Banking System in the United States), which had elements of both a private and a **central bank**, a government institution that has responsibility for the amount of money and credit supplied in the economy as a whole. Also, the Bank of New Brunswick had to submit regular annual statements to the government and was not allowed to open **branches** (additional offices for the conduct of banking operations), whereas the Bank of Montreal had to provide statements only on request and was allowed to open branches in any part of Upper or Lower Canada.

The Free Banking Experiment

Until 1850, no national currency existed in pre-confederation Canada, and banks obtained funds primarily by issuing *banknotes* (currency circulated by the banks that could be redeemed for gold). No banks failed, but because banking regulations were extremely lax, banks regularly experienced substantial declines in bank capital due to business failures; their banknotes tended to become scarce. The government tried various schemes to guarantee the provision of stable money, including issuing its own notes, but it was significantly influenced by the concept of **free banking**, implemented in New York in 1837. This system, as the name suggests, permitted the organization of a bank by any group that met certain established criteria concerning the amount of equity capital and maintenance of reserves.

The Free Banking Act was passed in Canada in 1850, with the purpose of facilitating the entry of small unit banks along American lines. It allowed the establishment of a bank, without a legislative charter, by any group that met the lax requirements set out in the free banking legislation. Under this legislation, the minimum amount of net worth to organize a bank was $100 000, branching was not allowed, and although the banknotes of the free banks were untaxed, the amount of note issue was limited to the amount of government debt held by the banks. The move to free banking was a step in the right direction, but Canada's experience with free banking was a failure. It did not lead to the establishment of a large number of new banks; only five new banks were established, two of which soon failed, and the other three converted to legislative charters.

The restriction on branching and the issue of banknotes based on government debt, rather than on commercial loans, were blamed for the failure of Canada's free banking experiment. The most important factor, however, was the fact that the option of a legislative charter was still available, unlike the situation in the United States, where the provision of a legislative charter was abolished in those states where free banking was established. In Canada, free banking, with its restrictive provisions, particularly the restriction on branches and the less liberal provision for note issue, proved to be less profitable than banking under legislative charters.

In 1850, there were 15 chartered banks in Canada: eight in Central Canada and seven in what was to become Atlantic Canada. From 1850 until Confederation in 1867, and except for a short period after 1857, the Canadian provinces experienced an economic expansion and 30 new banks were established. However, 11 of these failed or closed their doors for other reasons, leaving 34 chartered banks with a total of 127 branches at the end of 1867.

The Provincial Notes Act, 1866

In the years before Confederation, governments were anxious about the chartered banks' control of note issue. They believed that the best way to protect the public from some of the consequences of bank failures would be to separate the currency of the country from the banking interests. In 1860, Alexander Galt, finance minister of the Province of Canada, proposed the substitution of a government-issued paper currency for banknotes. His proposal, however, was defeated by his critics, especially the chartered banks, for obvious reasons: the substitution of interest-free government debt for interest-free bank debt would have directly reduced their profits.

In the midst of a minor financial crisis in 1866, with the collapse of the Bank of Upper Canada (Canada's first chartered bank failure), the proponents of government-issued paper money finally achieved their objective with the enactment of the Provincial Notes Act. The Act authorized the issue of provincial notes, which, because of their legal reserve status, could be substituted for specie. With the cooperation of the Bank of Montreal, which had become the government's fiscal agent in 1864 by replacing the Bank of Upper Canada, the banks began to hold the new currency, thereby surrendering their power to issue notes.

The Dominion Notes Act, 1870

Canada was created by the Constitution Act (formerly the British North America Act) in 1867. The Act granted the new federal government of Canada exclusive jurisdiction over all matters pertaining to currency and banking, and the first problem to be tackled was the issue of paper money. With the failure in 1867 of the Chartered Bank of Canada (the second chartered bank failure in Canadian history), the Dominion Notes Act was passed in 1870. The Act confirmed the rights of banks to issue banknotes on their own credit, but restricted to large-denomination (over $5) notes, thereby giving the government a monopoly over small-denomination ($1 and $2) notes, the Dominion notes.

Although the Dominion Notes Act of 1870 did not set any reserve requirements, it required banks to hold at least half of their reserves in Dominion notes, thereby giving the government a share of the profits from the issuance of money, which is called **seigniorage**. The Dominion notes themselves were fractionally backed by gold, and in this sense the Dominion Notes Act of 1870 confirmed that Canada would operate under the **gold standard**, meaning that its currency was convertible directly into gold.

Canada operated under the gold standard, keeping its currency backed by and convertible into gold, until World War I. During the years 1870–1935, Dominion notes increased in importance, but they never accounted for a major fraction of currency in circulation. They were superseded, together with the banknotes, by Bank of Canada notes, soon after the creation of the Bank of Canada (Canada's central bank) in 1935.

The First Bank Act, 1871

The first Bank Act came into effect in 1871. It was to be revised every 10 years, in light of experience and changing conditions; this "sunset" clause effectively ensured that governments over the years paid periodic attention to banking reform. The Bank Act set the regulatory environment for Canadian chartered banks and for the future development of Canadian banking practices.

The Act continued the legislative chartering of banks, with each charter running for a 10-year period, then to be reviewed and renewed. New banks had to meet minimum capital requirements: $100 000 paid up before they opened for business against a total of $500 000. The banks' note issue continued to be restricted to large-denomination notes (over $5) and limited to the amount of their paid-up capital plus reserves. There were no reserve requirements, but one-third of a bank's cash reserves were required to be in the form of Dominion notes.

The Act continued the prohibition against mortgage lending and real estate loans, but it reinforced the commercial nature of banking by allowing banks to make loans on the security of most kinds of merchandise. Also, for the greater security of the public, bank shareholders were liable for double the amount of their subscription. Finally, each bank was required to submit a detailed statement to the government on a monthly basis, but there was no provision for government inspection or audit.

The Bank Act, 1881–1913

A depression followed Confederation and lasted from 1873 to 1879. During the depression years, the banks were hard hit and 13 bank failures (four in 1878, five in 1887, and another four in 1890) wiped out the savings of many noteholders. To prevent future losses from such failures, the early decennial revisions of the Bank Act, in 1881, 1891, 1901, and 1913 (postponed since 1911), were intended to provide better protection for the holders of banknotes, but the Act was not substantially changed.

In particular, in the Bank Act revision of 1891, the capital requirement was increased to $250 000 paid up, thereby restricting entry into the industry. The proportion of Dominion notes in bank cash reserves was increased to 40%, and the notes of a failed bank were made a first charge against its assets in the event of liquidation.

Moreover, in the Bank Act revision of 1891, a Bank Circulation Redemption Fund was created, each bank contributing an amount equal to 5% of its average note circulation, to insure noteholders against loss.

In the years between the mid-1890s and the outbreak of World War I, the Canadian economy experienced a phenomenal economic expansion. While bank entry was restrained (due to the increase in capital requirements in the Bank Act of 1891), the Bank Act revision of 1901 simplified the merger and acquisition procedures by requiring only approval of Cabinet; previously, a special Act of Parliament was required for all mergers. As a result of these legislative changes, 13 mergers took place before the end of 1914, compared to only six in the previous 33-year period, and the number of banks declined from 41 in 1890 to 22 in 1914. Over the same period, however, the number of bank branches increased from 426 to over 3000.

Another important legislative change occurred in the 1913 revision of the Bank Act. The Act called for a *bank audit*: annual, independent verification of the financial statements of the banks, with the results distributed to the shareholders and the minister of finance. The objective was to limit the adverse selection and moral hazard problems that had increased over the years and been found to be the cause of a number of bank failures, particularly the failure of the Farmers Bank in 1910.

An additional noteworthy change was the excess circulation provision that introduced some flexibility in the management of the money supply. The economic expansion in the period after the mid-1890s caused banknote issues to reach the ceiling that the Bank Act of 1871 had fixed at the amount of paid-up capital plus reserves. The banks did not increase their capital (and thus their note-issuing capacity), producing a shortage of currency. In order to achieve expansion in the money supply with the growth of economic activity, the Bank Act of 1913 allowed for the issuing of banknotes in excess of a bank's paid-up capital plus reserves.

The Finance Act, 1914

At the end of July 1914, less than a year after the revision of the Bank Act in 1913, World War I looked more and more inescapable. Canada's established banking legislation appeared to be inadequate and the immediate problem was to preserve the stability and liquidity of the financial system. Panic had taken hold, with depositors converting their money into gold for hoarding, and the banks and the government being concerned about their ability to convert money into gold on demand, since their gold reserves were a small fraction of their combined monetary liabilities. In light of these developments, on August 3, 1914, the government suspended the convertibility of Dominion notes and banknotes into gold, thereby ending the gold standard that had emerged over 40 years earlier in 1870. The gold standard was re-established in 1926 and suspended again in 1929, when the Great Depression hit the world.

A major legislative change, following the suspension of the gold standard, was the Finance Act of 1914. Patterned on the episode of 1907, during which banks could obtain cash reserves from the Department of Finance to prevent bank runs (which were triggered by bank failures in the United States), the Finance Act allowed the Department of Finance to act as a **lender of last resort**, that is, to provide Dominion notes to banks (on the pledge of approved securities) when no one else would, thereby preventing bank and financial panics. The Finance Act foreshadowed the increased flexibility in the management of the money supply that was provided by the Bank of Canada in 1935. We will examine in detail the economic forces that led to the creation of the Bank of Canada in Chapter 15.

FINANCIAL INNOVATION AND THE GROWTH OF THE "SHADOW BANKING SYSTEM"

Although banking institutions are still the most important financial institutions in the Canadian economy, in recent years the traditional banking business of making loans that are funded by deposits has been in decline. Some of this business has been replaced by the **shadow banking system**, in which bank lending has been replaced by lending via the securities markets, with the involvement of a number of different financial institutions.

To understand how the banking industry has evolved over time, we must first understand the process of financial innovation, which has transformed the entire financial system. Like other industries, the financial industry is in business to earn profits by selling its products. If a soap company perceives that there is a need in the marketplace for a laundry detergent with fabric softener, it develops a product to fit the need. Similarly, to maximize their profits, financial institutions develop new products to satisfy their own needs as well as those of their customers; in other words, innovation—which can be extremely beneficial to the economy—is driven by the desire to get (or stay) rich. This view of the innovation process leads to the following simple analysis: *a change in the financial environment will stimulate a search by financial institutions for innovations that are likely to be profitable*.

Starting in the 1960s, individuals and financial institutions operating in financial markets were confronted with drastic changes in the economic environment: inflation and interest rates climbed sharply and became harder to predict, a situation that changed demand conditions in financial markets. The rapid advance in computer technology changed supply conditions. In addition, financial regulations became more burdensome. Financial institutions found that many of the old ways of doing business were no longer profitable; the financial services and products they had been offering to the public were not selling. Many financial intermediaries found that they were no longer able to acquire funds with their traditional financial instruments, and without these funds they would soon be out of business. To survive in the new economic environment, financial institutions had to research and develop new products and services that would meet customer needs and prove profitable, a process referred to as **financial engineering**. In their case, necessity was the mother of innovation.

Our discussion of the factors that drive financial innovation suggests that there are three basic types of financial innovation: responses to changes in demand conditions, responses to changes in supply conditions, and avoidance of existing regulations. These three motivations often interact in producing particular financial innovations. Now that we have a framework for understanding why financial institutions produce innovations, let's look at examples of how financial institutions, in their search for profits, have produced financial innovations of the three basic types.

Responses to Changes in Demand Conditions: Interest-Rate Volatility

The most significant change in the economic environment that altered the demand for financial products in recent years has been the dramatic increase in the volatility of interest rates. In the 1950s, the interest rate on three-month Treasury bills fluctuated between 1.0% and 5.5%; in the 1970s, it fluctuated between 3% and 14%; in the 1980s, it ranged from 7% to more than 20%. Large fluctuations in interest rates lead to substantial capital gains or losses and greater uncertainty about returns on investments.

Recall that the risk that is related to the uncertainty about interest-rate movements and returns is called *interest-rate risk,* and high volatility of interest rates, such as we saw in the 1970s and 1980s, leads to a higher level of interest-rate risk.

We would expect the increase in interest-rate risk to increase the demand for financial products and services that could reduce that risk. This change in the economic environment would thus stimulate a search for profitable innovations by financial institutions that meet this new demand and would spur the creation of new financial instruments that help lower interest-rate risk. Two financial innovations that were developed in the 1970s confirm this prediction: adjustable-rate mortgages and financial derivatives.

Adjustable-Rate Mortgages Like other investors, financial institutions find that lending is more attractive if interest-rate risk is lower. They would not want to make a mortgage loan at a 10% interest rate and two months later find that they could obtain 12% in interest on the same mortgage. To reduce interest-rate risk, financial institutions began to issue adjustable-rate mortgages, that is, mortgage loans on which the interest rate changes when a market interest rate (usually the Treasury bill rate) changes. Initially, an adjustable-rate mortgage might have a 5% interest rate. In six months, this interest rate might increase or decrease by the amount of the increase or decrease in, say, the six-month Treasury bill rate, and the mortgage payment would then change. Because adjustable-rate mortgages allow mortgage-issuing institutions to earn higher interest rates on existing mortgages when market rates rise, profits remain high during these periods.

This attractive feature of adjustable-rate mortgages has encouraged mortgage-issuing institutions to issue adjustable-rate mortgages with lower initial interest rates than those on conventional fixed-rate mortgages, making them popular with many households. However, because the mortgage payment on a variable-rate mortgage can increase, many households continue to prefer fixed-rate mortgages. Hence, both types of mortgages are widespread.

Financial Derivatives Given the greater demand for the reduction of interest-rate risk, commodity exchanges such as the Chicago Board of Trade recognized that if they could develop a product that would help investors and financial institutions protect themselves from, or to **hedge**, interest-rate risk, then they could make profits by selling this new instrument. **Futures contracts**, in which the seller agrees to provide a certain standardized commodity to the buyer on a specific future date at an agreed-on price, had been around for a long time. Officials at the Chicago Board of Trade realized that if they created futures contracts in financial instruments, which are called **financial derivatives** because their payoffs are linked to (i.e., derived from) previously issued securities, they could be used to hedge risk. Thus, in 1975, financial derivatives were born.

Responses to Changes in Supply Conditions: Information Technology

The most important source of the changes in supply conditions that stimulate financial innovation has been the improvement in computer and telecommunications technology. This technology, called *information technology,* has had two effects. First, it has lowered the cost of processing financial transactions, making it profitable for financial institutions to create new financial products and services for the public. Second, it has made it easier for investors to acquire information, thereby making it easier for firms to issue securities. The rapid developments in information technology have resulted in many new financial products and services that we examine here.

Bank Credit and Debit Cards   Credit cards have been around since well before World War II. Many individual stores (such as, for example, Sears and the Bay) institutionalized charge accounts by providing customers with credit cards that allowed them to make purchases at these stores without cash. Nationwide credit cards were not established until after World War II, when Diners Club developed one to be used in restaurants. Similar credit card programs were started by American Express and Carte Blanche, but because of the high cost of operating these programs, cards were issued only to selected persons and businesses that could afford expensive purchases.

A firm issuing credit cards earns income from loans it makes to credit card holders and from payments made by stores on credit card purchases (a percentage of the purchase price, say, 5%). A credit card program's costs arise from loan defaults, stolen cards, and the expense involved in processing credit card transactions.

Seeing the success of Diners Club, American Express, and Carte Blanche, bankers wanted to share in the profitable credit card business. Several chartered banks attempted to expand the credit card business to a wider market in the 1950s, but the cost per transaction of running these programs was so high that their early attempts failed.

In the late 1960s, improved computer technology, which lowered the transaction costs for providing credit card services, made it more likely that bank credit card programs would be profitable. The banks tried to enter this business again, and this time their efforts led to the creation of two successful bank credit card programs: Visa and MasterCard. These programs have become phenomenally successful. Indeed, bank credit cards have been so profitable that nonfinancial institutions such as Sears (which launched the Discover card), General Motors, and Walmart have also entered the credit card business. Consumers have benefited because credit cards are more widely accepted than cheques as a method of paying for purchases (particularly abroad), and they allow consumers to take out loans more easily.

The success of bank credit cards has led these institutions to come up with a new financial innovation, *debit cards*. Debit cards often look just like credit cards and can be used to make purchases in an identical fashion. However, in contrast to credit cards, which extend the purchaser a loan that does not have to be paid off immediately, a debit card purchase is immediately deducted from the card holder's bank account. Debit cards depend even more on low costs of processing transactions, because their profits are generated entirely from the fees paid by merchants on debit card purchases at their stores. Debit cards have grown extremely popular in recent years.

Electronic Banking   The wonders of modern computer technology have also enabled banks to lower the cost of bank transactions by having the customer interact with an electronic banking (e-banking) facility rather than with a human being. One important form of an e-banking facility is the **automated teller machine (ATM)**, an electronic machine that allows customers to get cash, make deposits, transfer funds from one account to another, and check balances. ATM machines do not have to be paid overtime and never sleep, and thus are available for use 24 hours a day. Not only does this result in cheaper transactions for the bank, it also provides more convenience for the customer. Because of their low cost, ATMs can be put at locations other than a bank or its branches, further increasing customer convenience. The low cost of ATMs has encouraged banks to install them everywhere. Furthermore, it is now just as easy to get foreign currency from an ATM when you are travelling in Europe as it is to get cash from your local bank.

With the drop in the cost of telecommunications, banks developed another financial innovation, *home banking*. It is now cost-effective for banks to set up an electronic banking facility in which the bank's customer is linked up with the bank's computer and allowed to carry out transactions by using either a telephone or a personal computer. Now a bank's customers can conduct many of their bank transactions without ever leaving the comfort of home. The advantage for the customer is the convenience of home banking, while banks find that the cost of transactions is substantially less than the cost associated with bricks-and-mortar banking. The success of ATMs and home banking has led to another innovation, the **automated banking machine (ABM)**, which combines in one location an ATM, an Internet connection to the bank's website, and a telephone link to customer service.

With the decline in the price of personal computers and their increasing presence in the home, we have seen a further innovation in the home banking area, the creation of a new type of banking institution, the **virtual bank**, a bank that has no physical location but rather exists only in cyberspace. In 1995, Security First Network Bank, based in Atlanta, Georgia, but now owned by Royal Bank of Canada, became the first virtual bank, offering an array of banking services exclusively on the Internet—accepting chequing account and savings deposits, selling certificates of deposit, issuing ATM cards, providing bill-paying facilities, and so on. The virtual bank thus takes home banking one step further, enabling the customer to have a full set of banking services at home, 24 hours a day. In 1996, Bank of America and Wells Fargo entered the virtual banking market, to be followed by many others, with Bank of America now being the largest Internet bank in the United States. Will virtual banking be the predominant form of banking in the future (see the Global box, Will "Clicks" Dominate "Bricks" in the Banking Industry?)?

Global   Will "Clicks" Dominate "Bricks" in the Banking Industry?

With the advent of virtual banks ("clicks") and the convenience they provide, a key question is whether they will become the primary form in which banks do their business, eliminating the need for physical bank branches ("bricks") as the main delivery mechanism for banking services. Indeed, will stand-alone Internet banks be the wave of the future?

The answer seems to be no. Internet-only banks have had disappointing revenue growth and profits. The result is that pure online banking has not been the success that proponents had hoped for. Why has Internet banking been a disappointment?

Internet banking has several strikes against it. First, bank depositors want to know that their savings are secure, so are reluctant to put their money into new institutions without a long track record. Second, customers worry about the security of their online transactions and whether their transactions will truly be kept private. Traditional banks are viewed as being more secure and trustworthy in terms of releasing private information. Third, customers may prefer services provided by physical branches. For example, banking customers seem to prefer purchasing long-term savings products face-to-face. Fourth, Internet banking still has run into technical problems—server crashes, slow connections, mistakes in conducting transactions—that will probably diminish over time as technology improves.

The wave of the future thus does not appear to be pure Internet banks. Instead, it looks as though "clicks and bricks" will be the predominant form of banking, in which online banking is used to complement the services provided by traditional banks. Nonetheless, the delivery of banking services is undergoing massive changes, with more and more banking services delivered over the Internet and the number of physical bank branches likely to decline in the future.

Junk Bonds   Before the advent of computers and advanced telecommunications, it was difficult to acquire information about the financial situation of firms that might want to sell securities. Because of the difficulty in screening out bad from good credit risks, the only firms that were able to sell bonds were very well-established corporations that had high credit ratings.[2] Before the 1980s, only corporations that could issue bonds with ratings of BBB or above could raise funds by selling newly issued bonds. Some firms that had fallen on bad times, so-called *fallen angels,* had previously issued long-term corporate bonds that now had ratings that had fallen below BBB, bonds that were pejoratively dubbed "junk bonds."

With the improvement in information technology in the 1970s, it became easier for investors to acquire financial information about corporations, and thus easier to screen out bad from good credit risks. With easier screening, investors were more willing to buy long-term debt securities from less well-known corporations with lower credit ratings. With this change in supply conditions, we would expect that some smart individual would pioneer the concept of selling new public issues of junk bonds, not for fallen angels but for companies that had not yet achieved investment-grade status. This is exactly what Michael Milken of Drexel Burnham Lambert, an investment-banking firm, started to do in 1977. Junk bonds became an important factor in the corporate bond market. Although there was a sharp slowdown in activity in the junk bond market after Milken was indicted for securities law violations in 1989, the junk bond market heated up again in the 1990s and 2000s.

Commercial Paper Market   Recall that *commercial paper* is a short-term debt security issued by large banks and corporations. The commercial paper market has undergone tremendous growth since 1970, with commercial paper being one of the fastest-growing money market instruments.

Improvements in information technology also help the rapid rise of the commercial paper market. We have seen that improvements in information technology made it easier for investors to screen out bad from good credit risks, thus making it easier for corporations to issue debt securities. Not only did this make it simpler for corporations to issue long-term debt securities, as in the junk bond market, but it also meant that they could raise funds by issuing short-term debt securities, such as commercial paper, with greater ease. Many corporations that used to do their short-term borrowing from banks now frequently raise short-term funds in the commercial paper market instead.

The development of money market mutual funds has been another factor in the rapid growth in the commercial paper market. Because money market mutual funds need to hold liquid, high-quality, short-term assets such as commercial paper, the growth of assets in these funds has created a ready market in commercial paper. The growth of pension and other large funds that invest in commercial paper has also stimulated the growth of this market.

Securitization and the Shadow Banking System

One of the most important financial innovations of the past two decades, arising from improvements in both transaction and information technology, is securitization. **Securitization** is the process of bundling small and otherwise illiquid financial assets (such as residential mortgages, auto loans, and credit card receivables), which have typically been the bread and butter of banking institutions, into marketable capital market securities. Securitization is the fundamental building block of the shadow banking system.

---

[2]The discussion of adverse selection problems in Chapter 8 provides a more detailed analysis of why only well-established firms with high credit ratings were able to sell securities.

How the Shadow Banking System Works In traditional banking, one entity engages in the process of asset transformation—that is, it issues liabilities with one set of desirable characteristics (say, deposits with high liquidity and low risk) to fund the purchase of assets with a different set of characteristics (say, loans with low liquidity and high returns). Securitization, on the other hand, is a process of asset transformation that involves a number of different financial institutions working together. These institutions comprise the shadow banking system. In other words, asset transformation accomplished through securitization and the shadow banking system is not done "under one roof," as is traditional banking.

For example, a mortgage broker (more generally referred to as a *loan originator*) will arrange for a residential mortgage loan to be made by a financial institution that will then service the loan (that is, collect the interest and principal payments). This *servicer* then sells the mortgage to another financial institution, which bundles the mortgage with a large number of other residential mortgages. The *bundler* takes the interest and principal payments on the portfolio of mortgages and "passes them through" (pays them out) to third parties. The bundler goes to a *distributor* (typically an investment bank), which designs a security that divides the portfolio of loans into standardized amounts. The distributor then sells the claims to these interest and principal payments as securities, mostly to other financial intermediaries that are also part of the shadow banking system—for example, a money market mutual fund or a pension fund. Schematically, the securitization process is described by the following sequence:

$$\text{Loan origination} \rightarrow \text{servicing} \rightarrow \text{bundling} \rightarrow \text{distribution}$$

Because the securitization process involves the origination of loans and then finally the distribution of securities, securitization is also characterized as an **originate-to-distribute** business model.

At every step of the securitization process, the loan originator, servicer, bundler, distributor, and purchaser of the security each earns a fee. Each of these five institutions has specialized in a particular element of the financial intermediation process. The shadow banking system, which comprises all of the financial institutions involved in the securitization process, can thus be very profitable if transaction costs and the costs of collecting information are low. Advances in information technology have therefore been critical to the growth of securitization and the shadow banking system. Lower costs of acquiring information make it far easier to sell capital market securities, while lower transaction costs make it cheaper for financial institutions to collect interest and principal payments on bundled loans and then pay them out to the securities holders.

Subprime Mortgage Market A particularly important financial innovation that developed in the 2000s as a result of securitization and the shadow banking system was the **subprime mortgage**, a new class of residential mortgages offered to borrowers with less-than-stellar credit records. Before 2000, only the most credit-worthy (prime) borrowers could obtain residential mortgages. Advances in computer technology and new statistical techniques, known as data mining, led to enhanced, quantitative evaluation of the credit risk for residential mortgages. Households with credit records could now be assigned a numerical credit score that predicted how likely the household would be to default on its loan payments. Because it now became easier to assess the risk associated with a pool of subprime mortgages, it became possible to bundle them into a mortgage-backed security, providing a new source of funding for these mortgages. The result was an explosion of subprime mortgage lending which, as we saw in Chapter 9, was a key factor that led to the global financial crisis of 2007–2009.

Avoidance of Existing Regulations

The process of financial innovation, as we have discussed so far, is much like innovation in other areas of the economy: it occurs in response to changes in demand and supply conditions. However, because the financial industry is more heavily regulated than other industries, government regulation is a much greater spur to innovation in this industry. Government regulation leads to financial innovation by creating incentives for firms to skirt regulations that restrict their ability to earn profits. Edward Kane, an economist at Boston College, describes this process of avoiding regulations as "loophole mining." The economic analysis of innovation suggests that when the economic environment changes such that regulatory constraints are so burdensome that large profits can be made by avoiding them, loophole mining and innovation are more likely to occur.

Two sets of regulations have seriously restricted the ability of banks (especially in the United States) to make profits: reserve requirements that force banks to keep a certain fraction of their deposits as reserves (vault cash and deposits in the Federal Reserve System) and restrictions on the interest rates that can be paid on deposits. For the following reasons, these regulations have been major forces behind financial innovation.

1. *Reserve requirements.* Although in Canada reserve requirements were phased out in the Bank of Canada Act in 1992, banks in the United States are still subject to reserve requirements. The key to understanding why reserve requirements led to financial innovation is to recognize that they act, in effect, as a tax on deposits. Because up until 2008 the Federal Reserve in the United States did not pay interest on reserves, the opportunity cost of holding them was the interest that a bank could otherwise earn by lending the reserves out. For each dollar of deposits, reserve requirements therefore imposed a cost on the bank equal to the interest rate, i, that could be earned if the reserves could be lent out times the fraction of deposits required as reserves, r_r. The cost $i \times r_r$ imposed on the bank was just like a tax on bank deposits of $i \times r_r$ per dollar of deposits.

It is a great tradition to avoid taxes if possible, and banks also play this game. Just as taxpayers look for loopholes to lower their tax bills, banks seek to increase their profits by mining loopholes and by producing financial innovations that allow them to escape the tax on deposits imposed by reserve requirements.

2. *Restrictions on interest paid on deposits.* Canadian banks have never been subject to deposit rate ceilings. In the United States, however, until 1980, legislation prohibited banks in most states from paying interest on chequing account deposits, and through **Regulation Q**, the U.S. Federal Reserve set maximum limits on the interest rate that could be paid on time deposits. To this day, banks in the United States are not allowed to pay interest on corporate chequing accounts. The desire to avoid these **deposit rate ceilings** also led to financial innovations.

If market interest rates rose above the maximum rates that banks paid on time deposits under Regulation Q, depositors withdrew funds from banks to put them into higher-yielding securities. This loss of deposits from the banking system restricted the amount of funds that banks could lend (called **disintermediation**) and thus limited bank profits. Banks had an incentive to get around deposit rate ceilings because by so doing, they could acquire more funds to make loans and earn higher profits.

We can now look at how the desire to avoid restrictions on interest payments and the tax effect of reserve requirements in the United States led to two important financial innovations.

Money Market Mutual Funds   Money market mutual funds issue shares that are redeemable at a fixed price (usually $1) by writing cheques. For example, if you buy 5000 shares for $5000, the money market fund uses these funds to invest in short-term money market securities (Treasury bills, certificates of deposit, commercial paper) that provide you with interest payments. Although money market fund shares effectively function as deposits that earn interest, they are not legally deposits and so are not insured by the CDIC.

In the United States, money market mutual funds also offer chequing privileges, effectively functioning as chequing account deposits that earn interest. For this reason, money market mutual funds in that country have experienced extraordinary growth since 1970, when they first appeared. Currently, their assets are around US$3 trillion. As consumers shift to mutual funds, deposit-taking financial institutions (throughout the world) risk losing a low-cost source of funds.

The first money market mutual fund was created in 1970 by two Wall Street mavericks, Bruce Bent and Henry Brown. In a supreme irony, risky investments by a money market mutual fund founded by Bruce Brent almost brought down the money market mutual fund industry during the subprime financial crisis in 2008 (see the FYI box, Bruce Bent and the Money Market Mutual Fund Panic of 2008).

FYI   Bruce Bent and the Money Market Mutual Fund Panic of 2008

Bruce Bent, one of the originators of money market mutual funds, almost brought down the industry during the subprime financial crisis in the fall of 2008. Mr. Bent told his shareholders in a letter written in July 2008 that the fund was managed on a basis of "unwavering discipline focused on protecting your principal." He also wrote the U.S. Securities and Exchange Commission in September 2007, "When I first created the money market fund back in 1970, it was designed with the tenets of safety and liquidity." He added that these principles had "fallen by the wayside as portfolio managers chased the highest yield and compromised the integrity of the money fund." Alas, Bent did not follow his own advice, and his fund, the Reserve Primary Fund, bought risky assets so that its yield was higher than the industry average.

When Lehman Brothers went into bankruptcy on September 15, 2008, the Reserve Primary Fund, with assets of over $60 billion, was caught holding the bag on $785 million of Lehman's debt, which then had to be marked down to zero. The resulting losses meant that on September 16, Bent's fund could no longer afford to redeem its shares at the par value of $1, a situation known as "breaking the buck." Bent's shareholders began to pull their money out of the fund, causing it to lose 90% of its assets.

The fear that this could happen to other money market mutual funds led to a classic panic in which shareholders began to withdraw their funds at an alarming rate. The whole money market mutual fund industry looked like it could come crashing down. To prevent this, the Federal Reserve and the U.S. Treasury rode to the rescue on September 19, 2008. The Federal Reserve set up a facility to make loans to purchase commercial paper from money market mutual funds so they could meet the demands for redemptions from their investors. The U.S. Treasury then put in a temporary guarantee for all money market mutual fund redemptions and the panic subsided.

Not surprisingly, given the extension of a government safety net to the money market mutual fund industry, there are calls to regulate this industry more heavily. The money market mutual fund industry will never be the same.

Sweep Accounts   Another innovation that enables banks in the United States to avoid the "tax" from reserve requirements is the **sweep account**. In this arrangement, any balances above a certain amount in a corporation's chequing account at the end of a business day are "swept out" of the account and invested in overnight securities that pay interest. Because the "swept out" funds are no longer classified as chequable deposits, they are not subject to reserve requirements and thus are not "taxed." They also have the advantage that they allow banks in effect to pay interest on these chequing accounts, which otherwise is not allowed under existing regulations. Because sweep accounts have become so popular, they have lowered the amount of required reserves to the degree that most banking institutions do not find reserve requirements binding: in other words, they voluntarily hold more reserves than they are required to.

The financial innovations of sweep accounts and money market mutual funds are particularly interesting because they were stimulated not only by the desire to avoid a costly regulation, but also by a change in supply conditions—in this case, information technology. Without low-cost computers to process inexpensively the additional transactions required by these innovations, they would not have been profitable and therefore would not have been developed. Technological factors often combine with other incentives, such as the desire to get around a regulation, to produce innovation.

Financial Innovation and the Decline of Traditional Banking

The traditional financial intermediation role of banking has been to make long-term loans and fund them by issuing short-term deposits, a process of asset transformation commonly referred to as "borrowing short and lending long." Here we examine how financial innovations have created a more competitive environment for the banking industry, causing the industry to change dramatically, with its traditional banking business going into decline.

To understand why traditional banking business has declined in size, we need to look at how the financial innovations described earlier have caused banks to suffer declines in their cost advantages in acquiring funds—that is, on the liabilities side of their balance sheet—while at the same time they have lost income advantages on the assets side of their balance sheet. The simultaneous decline of cost and income advantages has resulted in reduced profitability of traditional banking and an effort by banks to leave this business and engage in new and more profitable activities.

Decline in Cost Advantages in Acquiring Funds (Liabilities)   Until 1980, banks were paying low interest rates on chequable deposits. This worked to the banks' advantage because their major source of funds was chequable deposits. Unfortunately, this cost advantage for banks did not last. The rise in inflation that began in the late 1960s led to higher interest rates, which made investors more sensitive to yield differentials on different assets. The result was the *disintermediation* process, in which people began to take their money out of banks, with their low interest rates on both chequable and time deposits, and began to seek out higher-yielding investments. Also, as we have seen, at the same time, financial innovation led to money market mutual funds, which put the banks at an even further disadvantage because depositors could now obtain chequing-account-like services while earning high interest on their money market mutual fund accounts. One manifestation of these changes in the financial system was that the low-cost source of funds, chequable deposits, declined dramatically in importance for banks.

Decline in Income Advantages on Uses of Funds (Assets) Banks have also been hit by a decline in income advantages on the assets side from the financial innovations we discussed earlier—junk bonds, securitization, and the rise of the commercial paper market. The resulting loss of income advantages for banks relative to these innovations has resulted in a loss of market share and has led to the growth of the shadow banking system, which has made use of these innovations to enable borrowers to bypass the traditional banking system.

We have seen that improvements in information technology have made it easier for firms to issue securities directly to the public. This has meant that instead of going to banks to finance short-term credit needs, many of the banks' best business customers now find it cheaper to go instead to the commercial paper market for funds. In addition, the commercial paper market has allowed finance companies, which depend primarily on commercial paper to acquire funds, to expand their operations at the expense of banks. Finance companies, which lend to many of the same businesses that borrow from banks, have maintained their market share relative to banks.

The emergence of the junk bond market has eaten into banks' loan business. Improvements in information technology have made it easier for corporations to sell their bonds to the public directly, thereby bypassing banks. Although well-established companies started taking this route in the 1970s, now lower-quality corporate borrowers are using banks less often because they have access to the junk bond market.

We have also seen that improvements in computer technology have led to the growth of the shadow banking system and securitization, whereby illiquid financial assets such as bank loans and mortgages are transformed into marketable securities. Computers enable other financial institutions to originate loans because they can now accurately evaluate credit risk with statistical methods. Computers also have lowered transaction costs, making it possible to bundle these loans and sell them as securities. When default risk can be easily evaluated with computers, banks no longer have an advantage in making loans. Without their former advantages, banks have lost loan business to other financial institutions even though the banks themselves are involved in the process of securitization.

Banks' Responses Canadian banks have sought to maintain adequate profit levels by pursuing new off-balance-sheet activities that are more profitable. They have, in effect, embraced the shadow banking system. This strategy, however, has generated concerns about what are proper activities for banks. Nontraditional bank activities can be riskier, and therefore result in excessive risk taking by banks. Indeed, they led to a substantial weakening of bank balance sheets during the subprime financial crisis, as was discussed in Chapter 9.

The decline of banks' traditional business has thus meant that the banking industry has been driven to seek out new lines of business. This search for business opportunities may be beneficial because it may ultimately keep banks vibrant and healthy. Indeed, bank profitability was high up until 2007, and nontraditional, off-balance-sheet activities played an important role in the high bank profits. However, the new directions in banking led to increased risk taking, and thus the decline in traditional banking has required regulators to be more vigilant. Nontraditional bank activities pose new challenges for bank regulators, who, as we saw in Chapter 10 must now be far more concerned about banks' off-balance-sheet activities.

Decline of Traditional Banking in Other Industrialized Countries Forces similar to those in Canada and the United States have led to the decline of traditional banking in other industrialized countries. The loss of banks' monopoly power over depositors has occurred outside Canada and the United States as well. Financial innovation and deregulation are occurring worldwide and have created attractive alternatives for both depositors and borrowers. In Japan, for example, deregulation opened a wide array of new financial instruments to the public, causing a disintermediation process similar to that in Canada and the United States. In European countries, innovations have steadily eroded the barriers that have traditionally protected banks from competition.

In other countries, banks also face increased competition from the expansion of securities markets and the growth of the shadow banking system. Both financial deregulation and fundamental economic forces in other countries have improved the availability of information in securities markets, making it easier and less costly for firms to finance their activities by issuing securities rather than going to banks. Further, even in countries where securities markets have not grown, banks have still lost loan business because their best corporate customers have had increasing access to foreign and offshore capital markets, such as the Eurobond market. In smaller economies, like that of Australia, which still do not have well-developed corporate bond or commercial paper markets, banks have lost loan business to international securities markets.

In addition, the same forces that drove the securitization process in Canada and the United States have been at work in other countries and have undercut the profitability of traditional banking in these countries as well. Canada and the United States have not been unique in seeing their banks face a more difficult competitive environment. Thus, although the decline of traditional banking occurred earlier in North America than in other countries, the same forces have caused a decline in traditional banking abroad.

STRUCTURE OF THE CANADIAN CHARTERED BANKING INDUSTRY

As of October 2014, there were 81 banks in Canada with over 6200 branches and over 280 000 employees. As Table 11-1 indicates, however, the six largest chartered banks, the Royal Bank of Canada, Canadian Imperial Bank of Commerce (CIBC), Bank of Montreal, the Bank of Nova Scotia (Scotiabank), the Toronto-Dominion Bank, and the National Bank of Canada, together hold close to 93% of the assets in the industry.

Schedule I, Schedule II, and Schedule III Banks

The Big Six, together with the Laurentian Bank of Canada, the Canadian Western Bank, and another 28 domestic banks, are Canada's **Schedule I banks**. The remaining 45 banks are **Schedule II banks** (foreign bank subsidiaries, controlled by eligible foreign institutions) and **Schedule III banks** (bank branches of foreign institutions).

Until 1981, foreign banks were not allowed to operate in Canada and there was no distinction between Schedule I and Schedule II banks. The 1981 revisions to the Bank Act focused on introducing more competition into the Canadian financial services industry. Domestic Canadian banks became Schedule I banks and subsidiaries of foreign banks became Schedule II banks.

Schedule I and Schedule II banks have identical powers; the only difference between them is the ownership structure permitted. In particular, according to current ownership policy, all Schedule I banks must be widely held: no individual can own more than 10% of any class of shares. Schedule II banks, however, are exceptions to this rule, if small. In

TABLE 11-1	Canadian Banks (as of August 31, 2014)		
Bank	**Date of establishment**	**Assets ($ millions)**	**Percent (%) of bank assets**
The Big Six			
Royal Bank of Canada	1869	941 325	22.44
Canadian Imperial Bank of Commerce	1961	417 482	9.95
Bank of Montreal	1822	590 897	14.09
The Bank of Nova Scotia	1832	793 327	18.91
The Toronto-Dominion Bank	1955	931 613	22.21
National Bank of Canada	1980	214 862	5.12
Big Six Subtotal		**3 889 506**	**92.73**
Laurentian Bank of Canada	1987	34 725	0.83
Canadian Western Bank	1988	20 480	0.49
8 Domestic Banks Subtotal		**3 944 711**	**94.05**
Other Banks			
Domestic Banks		50 428	1.20
Foreign Banks		199 152	4.75
Total All Banks		**4 194 291**	**100.00**

Source: OSFI web site at **www.osfi-bsif.gc.ca**. Reprinted with permission.

fact, there are three categories of exception. The first exception is that widely held foreign banks can own 100% of a Canadian bank subsidiary. The second exception is that a Schedule II bank may have a significant shareholder (more than 10%) for up to 10 years after chartering, as a transition measure to becoming a Schedule I bank. The third exception, introduced in the 1992 revision of the Bank Act, is that any widely held and regulated Canadian financial institution, other than a bank, may own 100% of a bank. In the case of large Schedule II banks (those with over $5 billion in equity capital), the same widely held ownership rule that applies to Schedule I banks applies.

With the 2001 Bank Act Reform (to be discussed in detail later in this chapter), a foreign bank may enter the Canadian banking industry as either a Schedule II or a Schedule III bank. The difference between Schedule II and Schedule III banks is that a Schedule II bank is a Canadian subsidiary of a foreign bank whereas a Schedule III bank is a foreign bank allowed to branch directly into Canada, under certain restrictions (also to be discussed later in the chapter).

Competition and Technology

Although Canada has a small number of banks relative to other countries, Canadians enjoy one of the most dynamic and competitive financial services industries. Besides chartered banks, there are over 4000 financial institutions providing financial services.

These include trust and loan companies, credit unions and *caisses populaires,* government savings institutions, insurance companies, pension funds, mutual funds, and investment dealers.

New technology and the Internet have also helped in the development of a more competitive and innovative banking system in Canada. They have enabled new entrants to come into the Canadian financial services market and provide innovative services that meet the need of modern consumers.

For example, in November 2012, Scotiabank completed its acquisition of ING Bank of Canada, a former Canadian banking subsidiary of a major Netherlands banking and insurance conglomerate, and changed its name to Tangerine. Tangerine, like Citizens Bank of Canada, a subsidiary of Vancouver City Savings Credit Union (Vancity), are virtual banks (without bricks-and-mortar branches) offering an array of banking services on the Internet. In addition, U.S. credit card banks, such as MBNA and Capital One Financial Corporation, now offer specialized credit card products in Canada, and some of the largest banks in the United States provide loans to Canadian small businesses from the United States.

Moreover, the 2001 changes to bank ownership laws encouraged the establishment of new banks. For example, Canadian Tire established a banking subsidiary (Canadian Tire Bank), as has Loblaws (President's Choice Bank). Western Financial Group, a holding company for a network of insurance agencies, created Bank West (recently renamed to Zag Bank), and the Wheaton Group, a chain of car dealerships, launched a new bank called General Bank of Canada. In addition, a large number of private-sector competitors (for example, General Motors Acceptance Corporation, Ford Credit, GE Capital Group, CIT Group, and Dell Financial Services) participate in Canada's financial services market and offer similar products and services as Canada's banks, including credit cards, residential and commercial mortgages, equipment leasing, and motor vehicle financing.

COMPARISON WITH THE UNITED STATES

The structure of the commercial banking industry in Canada, although similar to that in many other industrialized countries, is radically different from that in the United States. There are approximately 6500 commercial banks in the United States, far more than in any other country in the world. Japan, for example, has fewer than 100 commercial banks—a mere fraction of the number of banks in the United States, even though its economy and population are half the size of the United States—and, as already noted, Canada has 81 banks. Moreover, as Table 11-2 indicates, the United States has an extraordinary number of small banks; 36% of its commercial banks have less than US$100 million in assets, and the 10 largest U.S. banks (listed in Table 11-3) together hold just over 59% of the assets in their industry. Canada's top three banks would be 5th, 6th, and 7th in asset size among the top U.S. banks.

Most industries in the United States have far fewer firms than the commercial banking industry; typically, large firms tend to dominate these industries to a greater extent than in the commercial banking industry. (Consider the computer software industry, which is dominated by Microsoft, or the automobile industry, which is dominated by General Motors, Ford, Daimler-Chrysler, Toyota, and Honda.) Does the large number of banks in the commercial banking industry and the absence of a few dominant firms suggest that commercial banking is more competitive than other industries?

TABLE 11-2		Size Distribution of Insured Commercial Banks, June 30, 2014	
Assets	**Number of Banks**	**Share of Banks (%)**	**Share of Assets Held (%)**
Less than $100 million	1744	30.3	0.7
$100 million–$1 billion	3469	60.3	7.4
$1 billion–$10 billion	451	7.8	8.5
More than $10 billion	93	1.6	83.4
Total	5757	100.00	100.00

Source: www2.fdic.gov/qbp/2014jun/cb4.html.

Response on Branching

The presence of so many commercial banks in the United States actually reflects past regulations that restricted the ability of these financial institutions to open branches (additional offices for the conduct of banking operations). Each state had its own regulations on the type and number of branches that a bank could open. Regulations on both coasts, for example, tended to allow banks to open branches throughout a state; in the middle part of the country, regulations on branching were more restrictive. The McFadden Act of 1927, which was designed to put national banks and state banks on equal footing, effectively prohibited banks from branching across state lines and forced all national banks to conform to the branching regulations of the state in which their headquarters were located.

TABLE 11-3	Ten Largest U.S. Banks, June 30, 2014	
Bank	**Assets ($ millions)**	**Share of All Commercial Bank Assets (%)**
1. J.P. Morgan Chase	1 945 467	14.23
2. Bank of America Corp.	1 433 716	10.49
3. Wells Fargo	1 373 600	10.05
4. Citibank	1 346 747	9.85
5. U.S. Bank	360 478	2.64
6. PNC	310 000	2.27
7. Bank of NY Mellon	296 626	2.17
8. State Street	239 051	1.75
9. Capital One	238 483	1.74
10. TD Bank	217 626	1.59
Total	7 761 794	56.78

Source: www.federalreserve.gov/Releases/Lbr/.

The McFadden Act and state branching regulations constituted strong anticompetitive forces in the U.S. commercial banking industry, allowing many small banks to stay in existence because larger banks were prevented from opening branches nearby. If competition is beneficial to society, why did regulations restricting branching arise in America? The simplest explanation is that the American public has historically been hostile to large banks. States with the most restrictive branching regulations were typically ones in which populist antibank sentiment was strongest in the 19th century. (These states usually had large farming populations whose relations with banks periodically became tempestuous when banks would foreclose on farmers who couldn't pay their debts.) The legacy of 19th-century politics was a banking system with restrictive branching regulations and hence an inordinate number of small banks. However, as we will see later in this chapter, branching restrictions have been eliminated, and the United States has moved toward nationwide banking.

Response to Branching Restrictions

An important feature of the U.S. banking industry is that competition can be repressed by regulation but not completely quashed. As we saw earlier in the chapter, the existence of restrictive regulation stimulates financial innovations that get around these regulations in the banks' search for profits. Regulations restricting branching have stimulated similar economic forces and have promoted the development of two financial innovations: bank holding companies and automated teller machines.

Bank Holding Companies   A holding company is a corporation that owns several different companies. This form of corporate ownership has important advantages for banks. It has allowed them to circumvent restrictive branching regulations, because the holding company can own a controlling interest in several banks even if branching is not permitted. Furthermore, a bank holding company can engage in other activities related to banking, such as the provision of investment advice, data processing and transmission services, leasing, credit card services, and servicing of loans in other states.

The growth of bank holding companies has been dramatic over the past three decades. Today bank holding companies own almost all large banks, and more than 90% of all commercial bank deposits are held in banks owned by holding companies.

Automated Teller Machines   Another financial innovation that resulted from the desire to avoid restrictions on branching is the automated teller machine (ATM). Banks quickly realized that if they did not own or rent the ATM, but instead let it be owned by someone else and paid a fee for each transaction, the ATM would probably not be considered a branch of the bank and thus would not be subject to branching regulations. This is exactly what the regulatory agencies and courts in most states in the United States concluded. Because they enable banks to widen their markets, a number of these shared facilities (such as Cirrus and NYCE) have been established nationwide. Furthermore, even when an ATM is owned by a bank, states typically have special provisions that allow wider establishment of ATMs than is permissible for traditional "bricks and mortar" branches.

As we saw earlier in the chapter, avoiding regulation was not the only reason for the development of the ATM. The advent of cheaper computer and telecommunications technology enabled banks to provide ATMs at low cost, making them a profitable innovation. This example further illustrates that technological factors often combine with incentives such as the desire to avoid restrictive regulations, to produce financial innovation.

COMPETITION ACROSS ALL FOUR PILLARS

Another important feature of the structure of the banking industry in Canada until recently was the separation of the banking and other financial services industries—such as securities, insurance, and real estate. Regulations enforced the separation of institutions according to their core financial service, and only four distinct types of financial services were identified: banking, brokerage, trusts, and insurance. This approach to regulation by institution (versus regulation by function) has been known as the **four-pillar approach**. The separation of the four pillars prohibited chartered banks from engaging in insurance and real estate activities. In turn, it prevented investment banks and insurance companies from engaging in commercial banking activities and thus protected banks from competition.

Convergence

In recent years, however, financial markets have opened up and Canada's traditional four-pillar system has changed. Despite the prohibitions in the legislation, the pursuit of profits and financial innovation stimulated both banks and other financial institutions to bypass the intent of the legislation and encroach on each other's traditional territory. For example, credit unions long offered insurance to their members, and brokerage firms engaged in the traditional banking business of issuing deposit instruments with the development of money market mutual funds and cash management accounts.

Not surprisingly, the regulatory barriers between banking and other financial services markets have been coming down in response to these forces. Before the 1950s, for example, legislation allowed chartered banks to make loans for commercial purposes only and prohibited them from making residential mortgage loans. It was only after the 1967 revision of the Bank Act that banks were allowed to make conventional residential mortgage loans, thereby directly competing with trust and loan companies and credit unions and *caisses populaires*.

In the 1980s, the Bank Act was amended to allow Canadian and foreign financial institutions to own up to 100% of securities firms. Moreover, the 1990s revisions to the Bank Act allowed cross-ownership via subsidiaries between financial institutions. Chartered banks, for example, can either buy independent investment dealers or expand on their own into capital raising, brokerage, and other securities activities. As a result, the Big Six now dominate the investment banking industry through their investment brokerage subsidiaries; they hold about a 70% share in the business. As a result of these legislative changes, Canada's traditional four pillars of financial services—banking, brokerage, trusts, and insurance—have converged into a single financial services marketplace.

Not surprisingly, the advent of the Web and improved computer technology is another factor driving bank consolidation. Economies of scale have increased because large, upfront investments are required to set up information technology platforms for financial institutions. To take advantage of these economies of scale, banks have needed to get bigger, and this development has led to additional consolidation. Information technology has also been increasing **economies of scope**, the ability to use one resource to provide many different products and services. For example, details about the quality and creditworthiness of firms not only inform decisions about whether to make loans to them but also can be useful in determining at what price their shares should trade. Similarly, once you have marketed one financial product to an investor, you probably know how to market another. Business people describe economies of scope by saying that there are "synergies" between different lines of business, and information technology is making these synergies more possible. The result is that consolidation is taking place not only to make financial institutions bigger, but also to increase the combination of products and services they can provide. This consolidation has had two consequences. First, different types of financial intermediaries are encroaching on each other's territory, making them more alike. Second, consolidation has led to the development of large, complex banking organizations.

Implications for Financial Consolidation

As we have seen, recent legislation has stimulated consolidation of the banking industry. The financial consolidation process will speed up even faster in the future, because the way is now open to consolidation in terms not only of the number of banking institutions, but also across financial service activities. Given that information technology is increasing economies of scope, mergers of banks with other financial service firms like that of Citicorp and Travelers in the United States should become increasingly common, and more mega-mergers are likely to be on the way. Banking institutions are becoming not only larger, but also increasingly complex organizations, engaging in the full gamut of financial service activities. The trend toward larger and more complex banking organizations has also been accelerated by the global financial crisis of 2007–2008 (see the FYI box, The Global Financial Crisis and the Demise of Large, Free-Standing Investment Banks).

Separation of Banking and Other Financial Services Industries Throughout the World

In the aftermath of the Great Depression, not many other countries followed the lead of Canada and the United States in separating the banking from other financial services industries. In fact, in the past this separation was the most prominent difference between banking regulation in Canada and the United States and that in other countries. Around the world, there are three basic frameworks for the banking and securities industries.

The first framework is *universal banking,* which exists in Germany, the Netherlands, and Switzerland. It provides no separation at all between the banking and securities industries. In a universal banking system, commercial banks provide a full range of banking, securities, real estate, and insurance services, all within a single legal entity. Banks are allowed to own sizable equity shares in commercial firms, and often they do.

The *British-style universal banking system,* the second framework, is found in the United Kingdom and countries with close ties to it, such as Australia, Canada, and now the United States. The British-style universal bank engages in securities underwriting, but it differs from the German-style universal bank in three ways: separate legal subsidiaries are more common, bank equity holdings of commercial firms are less common, and combinations of banking and insurance firms are less common.

The third framework, found in Japan, features some legal separation of the banking and other financial services industries. A major difference between British-style and

FYI   The Global Financial Crisis and the Demise of Large,
Free-Standing Investment Banks

Although the move toward bringing financial service activities into larger, more complex banking organizations was inevitable after the demise of **Glass-Steagall** (an Act passed in 1933 by the U.S. Congress to legally separate investment banking from commercial banking), no one expected it to occur as rapidly as it did in 2008. Over a six-month period from March to September of 2008, all five of the largest, free-standing investment banks in the United States ceased to exist in their old form. When Bear Stearns, the fifth-largest investment bank, revealed its large losses from investments in subprime mortgage securities, it had to be bailed out by the U.S. Federal Reserve in March 2008; the price it paid was a forced sale to J.P. Morgan for less than one-tenth what it had been worth only a year or so before. The Bear Stearns bailout made it clear that the government safety net had been extended to investment banks. The tradeoff was that investment banks are subject to more regulation, along the lines of commercial banks, in the future.

Next to go was Lehman Brothers, the fourth-largest investment bank in the United States, which declared bankruptcy on September 15, 2008. Only one day before, Merrill Lynch, the third-largest investment bank, which also suffered large losses on its holdings of subprime securities, announced its sale to Bank of America for less than half of its year-earlier price. Within a week, Goldman Sachs and Morgan Stanley, the first- and second-largest investment banks, both of which had smaller exposure to subprime securities, nevertheless saw the writing on the wall. They realized that they would soon become regulated on a similar basis and decided to become bank holding companies so that they could access insured deposits, a more stable funding base.

It was the end of an era. Large, free-standing investment banking firms in the United States are now a thing of the past.

Japanese banking systems is that Japanese banks are allowed to hold substantial equity stakes in commercial firms, whereas British-style universal banks are not. In addition, most American banks use a bank holding company structure, but bank holding companies are illegal in Japan. Although the banking and securities industries are legally separated in Japan under Section 65 of the Japanese Securities Act, commercial banks are increasingly being allowed to engage in securities activities and are thus becoming more like British-style universal banks.

THE NEAR BANKS: REGULATION AND STRUCTURE

Not surprisingly, the regulation and structure of the near banks (trust and loan companies and credit unions and *caisses populaires*) closely parallel the regulation and structure of the chartered banking industry.

Trust Companies

Over the years, the Bank Acts have denied chartered banks the power to function as corporate **trustees** (or fiduciaries). Unlike the situation in the United States, legislators in Canada reasoned that deposit-taking financial institutions might face a conflict of interest if they were to act as both financial fiduciaries and banks. So trust companies were established, under a variety of provincial and federal laws, and specialized in the provision of fiduciary services. As financial fiduciaries, trust companies administer estates, trusts, and agencies (i.e., assets that belong to someone else), for a fee, and under conditions prescribed in a contract.

Over the years, the structure of the trust industry has changed significantly and today trusts offer similar services as those offered by banks (i.e., deposit-taking, loans) as well as fiduciary services. Moreover, over the years the Bank Acts have allowed regulated federal financial institutions (domestic chartered banks and life insurance companies) to own trust companies, thereby providing fiduciary services indirectly through their subsidiaries. As a result, and with the acquisition of Canada Trust (Canada's largest trust company) by the Toronto Dominion Bank in early 2000, trust companies now constitute a relatively small market segment.

Loan Companies

The development of trust companies was paralleled by the growth of loan companies. The concept of loan companies came from the building societies in the United Kingdom (during the early part of the 19th century), whose purpose was to enable members to acquire land, build homes, or develop farms. Today's loan companies take deposits and primarily make residential mortgage loans. They do not act as trustees, unless they are licensed specifically for that purpose. Over the years, the loan companies together with the trust companies formed the second pillar of the traditional financial services industry in Canada. However, as you saw in this chapter, financial innovation, competition, and regulatory evolution have significantly changed the competitive position of financial institutions in recent years.

Trust and loan companies operate under a charter issued by either the federal government or one of the provincial governments. Federally incorporated trust and loan companies come under the federal Trust and Loan Companies Act and are regulated and supervised by OSFI. They must also register in all of the provinces in which they operate and must conform to the regulations of those provinces. In the case of trust companies, the fiduciary component of their business is only subject to provincial legislation, even if the company is federally incorporated. Deposit insurance for trust and loan companies outside Québec is provided by the CDIC (up to $100 000 per account). The Québec Deposit Insurance Board (QDIB) insures deposits for Québec trust and loan companies on terms similar to the CDIC's.

Trust and loan companies are funded almost entirely by chequable and non-chequable savings deposits, term deposits, guaranteed investment certificates, and debentures; together, they account for about 85% of the balance sheet. Their risk asset portfolio is made up mostly by residential mortgages and loans; together they account for about 30% of assets. The low-risk assets are largely deposits with regulated financial institutions.

Cooperatives: Credit Unions and *Caisses Populaires*

Cooperatives are small lending institutions organized around a particular group of individuals with a common bond (union members or employees of a particular firm). Alphonse Desjardins formed Canada's first cooperative bank in 1900 in Québec, and it was based on the cooperative movements in Europe, which among other things, stressed the provision of credit to the "little man." Today, there are two cooperative financial systems in Canada: the *caisses populaires* system in Québec and the credit union system in other parts of the country.

There are about 750 credit unions and *caisses populaires* in Canada, holding combined assets of about $300 billion and serving over 10 million members. They offer products and services ranging from mortgages and car loans to credit lines and automated teller machines. Because their members share a common goal, credit unions and *caisses populaires* are typically quite small; most are about the size of a single bank branch and hold less than $10 million of assets, with the largest being Vancity Savings, with assets over $21 billion. The credit unions and *caisses populaires* are established under provincial legislation and are nonprofit-seeking financial institutions. Unlike the shareholder-owned chartered banks that accept deposits from and lend funds to the general public, the cooperative banks accept deposits (shares) from and lend funds only to their members. Members have voting rights and elect a board of directors, which determines the union's lending and investment policies.

As member-owned, independent financial firms, credit unions and *caisses populaires* constitute an alternative financial system, different from the profit-seeking banking system. They have also developed their own set of institutions, including central banking and deposit insurance arrangements. In particular, each province has a central credit union, owned by the member credit unions, providing financial services to individual credit unions. All central credit unions outside Québec are members of the Credit Union Central of Canada (CUCC), also known as Canadian Central. The Canadian Central serves as the third tier for the credit union movement; it coordinates various functions and provides cheque-clearing services for all provincial central credit unions.

In Québec, *caisses populaires* are assembled under a single federation, the *Fédération des caisses Desjardins du Québec,* which has a similar structure to the provincial central credit unions in the rest of Canada but with considerably broader regulatory responsibilities. The federation dominates retail and corporate financial intermediation in Québec. It owns a major P&C insurance group, *Desjardins General Insurance;* a life and health insurance company, *Desjardins Financial Security;* a venture capital firm, *Desjardins Venture Capital;* and an investment dealer and discount brokerage, *Desjardins Securities and Disnat.* It also owns *Caisse Centrale Desjardins,* which functions as a central bank, as the CUCC does for the rest of Canada.

Credit unions and *caisses populaires* are not directly covered by the CDIC. However, each provincial government has an agency, commonly called a stabilization fund, which has a line of credit with the provincial treasury and provides deposit guarantees for credit unions. Deposits in New Brunswick and Prince Edward Island are insured up to $60 000 per account; in Ontario and British Columbia up to $100 000; in Nova Scotia and Newfoundland and Labrador up to $250 000; and in Alberta, Saskatchewan, and Manitoba there are no limits on the amount of coverage provided. In Québec, the Québec Deposit Insurance Board, the same provincial government agency that insures deposits in other deposit-taking financial institutions in Québec, also provides deposit guarantees for *caisses populaires,* on terms similar to the CDIC's.

The main source of funds of credit unions and *caisses populaires* is deposits—they account for over 70% of liabilities—followed by members' equity (about 8% of liabilities). Their asset portfolio is made up largely by debt securities (47% of the balance sheet), securities issued or guaranteed by federal and/or provincial governments (about 28%), and loans and mortgage loans (close to 17% of the balance sheet). The rest of the balance sheet consists of fixed assets, and shares in central credit unions.

Government Savings Institutions

In addition to the near banks (trust and loan companies and credit unions and *caisses populaires*), there are some government-operated deposit-taking institutions, such as Alberta Treasury Branches (ATB) Financial.

The province of Alberta established Treasury branches back in 1938 in response to Albertans' needs in remote areas. Today, there are 170 branches in 242 communities across the province operating in three target markets: individual financial services, agricultural operations, and independent business. ATB Financial (with assets in excess of $37 billion) is funded almost entirely by demand, notice, and fixed-term deposits, and its risk asset portfolio is made up largely of residential mortgages and personal, commercial, and agricultural loans.

INTERNATIONAL BANKING

Canadian banks have a well-developed presence in the global financial services marketplace, which varies among the individual institutions. From its inception, for example, the Bank of Montreal found some of its best opportunities in international operations and was soon joined by the Canadian Imperial Bank of Commerce and the Bank of Nova Scotia. The spectacular growth in international banking can be explained by three factors.

First is the rapid growth in international trade and multinational (worldwide) corporations that has occurred in recent years. When Canadian firms operate abroad, they need banking services in foreign countries to help finance international trade. For example, they might need a loan in a foreign currency to operate a factory abroad. And when they sell goods abroad, they need to have a bank exchange the foreign currency they have received for their goods into Canadian dollars. Although these firms could use foreign banks to provide them with these international banking services, many of them prefer to do business with the Canadian banks with which they have established long-term relationships and that understand Canadian business customs and practices. As international trade has grown, international banking has grown with it.

Second, Canadian banks have been able to earn substantial profits by being very active in global investment banking, in which they underwrite foreign securities. They also sell insurance abroad, and they derive substantial profits from these investment banking and insurance activities.

Third, Canadian banks have wanted to tap into the large pool of Eurocurrencies—currencies deposited in banks outside the home country. To understand the structure of Canadian banking overseas, let us first look at the Eurocurrencies market, an important source for international banking.

Eurocurrencies Market

The most important of the Eurocurrencies are Eurodollars, which originated after World War II with U.S.-dollar deposits in European banks. They were created when deposits in accounts in the United States were transferred to a bank outside the United States and were kept in the form of U.S. dollars. (For a discussion of the birth of the Eurodollar, see the Global box, Ironic Birth of the Eurodollar Market.) For example, if Rolls-Royce PLC deposits a US$1 million cheque, written on an account at an American bank, in its

Global   **Ironic Birth of the Eurodollar Market**

One of capitalism's great ironies is that the Eurodollar market, one of the most important financial markets used by capitalists, was created by the Soviet Union. In the early 1950s, during the height of the Cold War, the Soviets had accumulated a substantial amount of dollar balances held by banks in the United States. Because the Russians feared that the U.S. government might freeze these assets in the United States, they wanted to move the deposits to Europe, where they would be safe from expropriation. (This fear was not unjustified—consider the U.S. freeze on Iranian assets in 1979 and on Iraqi assets in 1990.) However, they also wanted to keep the deposits in dollars so that they could be used in their international transactions. The solution to the problem was to transfer the deposits to European banks but to keep the deposits denominated in dollars. When the Soviets did this, the Eurodollar was born.

bank in London—specifying that the deposit be payable in U.S. dollars—$1 million in Eurodollars is created.[3] More than 90% of Eurodollar deposits are time deposits, more than half of which are certificates of deposit with maturities of 30 days or more. The Eurodollar market is massive, over US$5 trillion, making it one of the most important financial markets in the world economy.

Although most offshore deposits are denominated in U.S. dollars, some are also denominated in other currencies. Collectively, these offshore deposits are referred to as Eurocurrencies. A Canadian dollar-denominated deposit held in London, for example, is called a Euro Canadian dollar, and a Japanese yen-denominated deposit held in London is called a Euroyen. Why would companies such as Rolls-Royce want to hold Eurocurrencies? First, some currencies are widely used in international trade, so Rolls-Royce might want to hold deposits in these currencies to conduct its international transactions. Second, Eurocurrencies are "offshore" deposits—they are held in countries that will not subject them to regulations such as reserve requirements or restrictions (called *capital controls*) on taking the deposits outside the country.

The main centre of the Eurocurrencies market is London, a major international financial centre for hundreds of years. Eurocurrencies are also held outside Europe in locations that provide offshore status to these deposits—for example, Singapore, the Bahamas, and the Cayman Islands.

The minimum transaction in the Eurocurrencies market is typically $1 million, and approximately 75% of Eurocurrency deposits are held by banks. Plainly, you and I are unlikely to come into direct contact with Eurocurrencies. The Eurocurrencies market is, however, an important source of funds to Canadian banks. Rather than using an intermediary and borrowing all the deposits from foreign banks, Canadian banks decided that they could earn higher profits by opening their own branches abroad to attract these deposits. Consequently, the Eurocurrencies market has been an important stimulus to Canadian banking overseas.

---

[3]Note that the bank in London keeps the $1 million on deposit at the American bank, so the creation of Eurodollars has not caused a reduction in the amount of bank deposits in the United States.

Canadian Banking Overseas

Canadian banks have been present in international financial markets for over 100 years, providing services to Canadians and multinational businesses. The international presence of the Big Six varies among the individual institutions. In particular, the Bank of Montreal, the Canadian Imperial Bank of Commerce, and the Toronto-Dominion Bank have a significant presence in the United States, whereas Scotiabank has established a presence in South America, and the Royal Bank in Europe and Asia.

During the 1970s and early 1980s, a large proportion of the banks' foreign lending was in **sovereign loans**; loans to foreign governments and their agencies in the less developed countries (LDCs), particularly Mexico, Brazil, Venezuela, Argentina, and Chile. Most of this activity in international lending was unregulated, with near disastrous consequences. One example is the international debt crisis, which had its origin in the oil price shocks of the 1970s. In particular, the 1973–1974 increase in the price of oil was a bonanza for some oil-exporting countries like Mexico but a disaster for oil-importing countries like Brazil, which had to either cut their living standards or borrow massively abroad in order to pay their higher oil bills. At the time, real interest rates were very low (in fact negative) and the oil importers couldn't resist the temptation to borrow abroad.

At the same time, the oil exporters were depositing huge sums in banks and as a result the banks were lending not only to the oil-importing countries but also to the oil-exporting countries, because the latter had large oil reserves and seemed like good credit risks. The banks underestimated the **indebtedness** of these countries—the total amount these countries had borrowed from banks—and, as a result, were severely punished in the early 1980s when the recession hit and real interest rates increased significantly. With Argentina, Brazil, Mexico, and Peru threatening to default on their loans, the banks had two choices: to reschedule their loans and make more loans to these countries (to enable them to pay the interest on the debt) or to declare these countries in default and acknowledge large losses on their balance sheets. The banks chose to make more loans, because in many cases the losses would have been large enough to destroy them.

As a result of their lending experience in Latin America, the Big Six have withdrawn from certain countries and focused more of their international activities in the United States. Moreover, the international activities of Canadian banking organizations are now regulated primarily by OSFI.

Foreign Banks in Canada

The growth in international trade not only has encouraged Canadian banks to open offices overseas but also has encouraged foreign banks to establish offices in Canada. Foreign banks have been extremely successful in Canada. Over the past 30 years, since the 1981 revision to the Bank Act, globally prominent foreign banks have set up and expanded banking subsidiaries in Canada. Foreign banks are a highly fragmented group and currently hold about 7% of total Canadian bank assets, with HSBC Bank Canada (a subsidiary of HSBC Holdings PLC) enjoying a national market share of over 2%. It should be noted, however, that these institutions target specific groups, achieving a higher representation within their target groups than their national share would suggest. For example, HSBC, the largest of the Schedule II banks, enjoys a strong presence and success in the Chinese communities of British Columbia and Ontario.

Foreign banks may enter the Canadian financial services industry as either Schedule II or Schedule III banks. As already noted, Schedule II banks don't have to be widely held if small. If, however, their equity capital exceeds $1 billion, then at least 35% of it must be widely held. In the case that their equity capital exceeds $5 billion, then the same widely held ownership rule applies as for Schedule I banks. The major difference between Schedule II and Schedule III banks is that Schedule III banks can branch directly into Canada, following authorization by the minister of finance, whereas Schedule II banks can add branches to their initial branch only with ministerial approval. However, Schedule III banks cannot take retail deposits (i.e., deposits less than $150 000) and, as a result, have the advantage of not being subject to regulations that apply to full-service banks (such as requirements for CDIC insurance). Given that most Schedule II banks do little retail deposit gathering, it is likely that in the future many Schedule II banks will become Schedule III banks.

The internationalization of banking, both by Canadian banks going abroad and by foreign banks entering Canada, has meant that financial markets throughout the world have become more integrated. As a result, there is a growing trend toward international coordination of bank regulation, one example of which is the Basel Accords, discussed in Chapter 10, which were established to standardize minimum bank capital requirements in industrialized countries. Financial market integration has also encouraged bank consolidation abroad, culminating in the creation of the first trillion-dollar bank with the merger of the Industrial Bank of Japan, Dai-Ichi Kangyo Bank, and Fuji Bank, in 2002. Another development has been the importance of foreign banks in international banking. As is shown in Table 11-4, in 2014, the 10 largest banking groups in the world were foreign. The implication of this financial market integration for the operation of our economy is examined further in Chapter 19 when we discuss the international financial system in more detail.

TABLE 11-4	Ten Largest Banks in the World, 2014
Bank	**Assets (U.S. $ millions)**
1. Industrial and Commercial Bank of China, China	3 181 884
2. HSBC Holdings, UK	2 758 447
3. China Construction Bank Corp, China	2 602 536
4. BNP Paribas SA, France	2 589 191
5. The Bank of Tokyo-Mitsubishi UFJ Ltd, Japan	2 508 839
6. JP Morgan-Chase NA, US	2 476 986
7. Agricultural Bank of China, China	2 470 432
8. Bank of China, China	2 435 485
9. Credit Agricole SA, France	2 346 562
10. Barclays PLC, UK	2 266 815

Source: **www.relbanks.com/worlds-top-banks/market-cap**.

THE 2001 BANK ACT REFORM

We have seen that fundamental structural changes make possible new financial products and services, increasing the competitive environment in the financial services industry and changing the financial intermediation role of banking at Internet speed. It is against this backdrop of phenomenal change that the federal government introduced legislation reforming the policy framework of the Canadian financial services sector.[4] This legislation took effect in October of 2001 and is known as **Bank Act reform**.

In what follows we provide an overview of the key elements of the new regulatory environment for financial institutions that has the potential to dramatically change the face of competition in Canada's financial services marketplace. As you will see, the new laws establish the regulatory framework to accelerate changes already taking place throughout the Canadian and world economies and introduce new opportunities for strategic alliances and partnerships, with the objective of fostering more competition and providing more innovative products and services to Canadians.

Bank Holding Companies

Before Bank Act reform, the organizational structure of Canada's bank financial groups was based on the "bank-as-parent" model, where all banking functions and all subsidiaries of the bank are subject to the same regulation. Under the new legislation, bank financial groups have the option of organizing themselves under a holding company.[5] A holding company is a corporation that owns several different companies. For example, under a holding company structure, a bank financial group may have a banking subsidiary, an insurance subsidiary, a securities subsidiary, and another subsidiary for its unregulated businesses.

Most developed countries permit holding company structures, and the growth of holding companies has been dramatic over the past three decades. Today, in the United States, for example, holding companies own almost all large banks, and more than 90% of all commercial bank deposits are held in banks owned by holding companies. The holding company form of corporate ownership has important advantages for bank financial groups in that (1) it allows them to engage in other activities related to banking, such as the provision of investment advice, data processing and transmission services, leasing, and credit card services; (2) a holding company structure allows for lighter regulation throughout the bank financial group because certain activities (those not involving retail deposit taking and insurance) can be undertaken by less regulated, non–bank-affiliated companies held by the holding company parent rather than the regulated operating bank; and (3) the holding company model provides bank financial groups increased flexibility to achieve economies of scale and scope through strategic partnerships, alliances, and joint ventures.

The big advantage of the new regime for establishing holding companies is that financial groups will be able to move parts of their heavily regulated business into

---

[4]Since 1992, the practice of reviewing legislation governing Canada's chartered banks has been extended to reviewing legislation governing all federal financial institutions.

[5]The new legislation introduced a holding company regime for Canada's insurance companies, as well. Under the legislation, insurance holding companies are required to have an investment in at least one life insurance company and are regulated under the Insurance Companies Act. Bank holding companies are regulated under the Bank Act and are required to have an investment in at least one bank.

less-regulated affiliates under a common holding company. The holding company, however, would be a viable option for financial groups if the transition to a holding company would be tax-neutral and without increased costs or regulatory burdens. If, for example, additional taxes or heavier regulation were to arise as a result of a restructuring into a holding company, then the holding company option wouldn't be feasible. For this reason, the new legislation also provides a set of transitional rules to address unintended cost consequences that would be triggered by the transition to a holding company.

Permitted Investments

A second item of the 2001 legislation pertains to the type of investments federally regulated financial institutions are allowed to make. At present, there is a restrictive list of activities beyond banking that banks, for example, can get involved in. The new legislation, however, provides greater flexibility for bank involvement in the information technology area (and, in particular, the Internet and wireless technology). It permits bank financial groups to establish and operate information services entities utilizing recent advances in Internet and wireless banking and voice recognition technologies.

New information technologies are critical to the ability of Canadian banks and insurance companies to provide new financial products and services and adapt to the changing marketplace. Although bank and insurance company involvement in the information technology area is subject to regulation, the new permitted investment regime will enhance the ability of banks and insurance companies to pursue strategic alliances and joint ventures and will further accelerate the technological advances that are already taking place and revolutionize the financial services sector.

Ownership Rules

A third policy measure that can significantly change the face of competition in Canada's financial services marketplace is the new ownership regime that enables investors to take a greater equity interest in widely held bank financial groups, by expanding the definition of "widely held." In particular, the 2001 legislation increased the limit (in place since 1967) a single shareholder can own of a widely held financial institution (either a bank holding company or a bank subsidiary under the holding company) from 10% of any class of shares to 20% of voting shares and 30% of nonvoting shares. The new legislation, however, does not permit a single shareholder to own more than 10% of both a bank holding company and a bank subsidiary under the holding company at the same time. Moreover, acquisitions of more than 10% are subject to approval by the minister of finance based on a "fit and proper person" test.

The new legislation also includes a *three-tiered ownership regime*. Small banks (those with equity capital under $1 billion) don't have to be widely held and can be wholly owned (i.e., have one particular investor own 100% of the shares).

Medium-sized banks (and bank holding companies) with shareholders' equity between $1 billion and $5 billion can be closely held provided that there is a 35% public float (that is, they could have a single shareholder own up to 65% of their shares). Large banks (and bank holding companies), those with shareholders' equity in excess of $5 billion, are required to be widely held.

The new ownership regime, together with other provisions in the legislation, such as the lowering of the capital needed to create a bank from $10 million to $5 million and the allowance of domestic and foreign commercial enterprises (such as department stores and grocery chains) to establish small and medium-sized banks, are fundamentally changing Canada's financial sector.

The CP Act and Access to the Payments and Clearance System

Before the 2001 financial-sector legislation, membership in the Canadian Payments Association (CPA), a nonprofit organization formed in 1980 by an Act of Parliament to operate Canada's payments systems, was limited to the Bank of Canada and the deposit-taking financial institutions—chartered banks, trust and loan companies, and credit unions and *caisses populaires*. The 2001 legislation introduced some important changes for the Canadian Payments Association and also renamed the Canadian Payments Association Act to Canadian Payments Act (CP Act).

In particular, the CP Act extends eligibility for membership in the Canadian Payments Association—and therefore access to Canada's two domestic payments systems, the Large Value Transfer System (LVTS) and the Automated Clearing Settlement System (ACSS), both to be discussed in detail in Chapter 17—to non–deposit-taking financial institutions, such as life insurance companies, securities dealers, and money market mutual funds. This regulatory change will significantly affect Canada's financial services sector, since it will allow these organizations to provide bank-like services, such as chequing accounts and debit cards, without being banks, thereby directly competing with banks, trust and loan companies, and credit unions and *caisses populaires*.

Expanding access to the payments and clearance system, by allowing non–deposit-taking financial institutions to participate will further accelerate the process of the blurring of distinction between deposit-taking and non–deposit-taking financial institutions. As already noted, this process started in 1987, when securities dealers were allowed to own banks, and was reinforced by the 1992 federal financial reforms that permitted cross-ownership of financial institutions.

Merger Review Policy

The government has also issued a statement establishing a process for reviewing mergers involving large banks—banks like the Bank of Montreal and CIBC—with shareholder equity in excess of $5 billion. By doing so, the government acknowledges that mergers are a legitimate business option that should be available to Canadian bank financial groups. The bank merger review process, however, unlike those in other countries such as the United States and the United Kingdom, is political, having Parliament directly involved in it.

Under the new merger review policy, the merger partners are required to submit a public interest impact assessment (PIIA), covering various effects of the merger, such as the impact on the structure and competition of the banking industry, branch closures, and job losses. The merger proposal would then be submitted to the House of Commons Standing Committee on Finance and the Standing Senate Committee on Banking, Trade, and Commerce for consideration and public hearings. Each of these committees will report to the minister of finance, who would make these reports public, together with a report from the Competition Bureau on the competitive aspects of the proposed merger and a report from OSFI on the prudential aspects of the proposed merger. The minister of finance will decide whether the proposed merger will be allowed to proceed.

The government has also indicated that it will not allow mergers between large banks and large demutualized life insurance companies such as Manulife and Sun Life. We would note, however, that in other countries, such as Australia, Germany, the Netherlands, Switzerland, the United Kingdom, and the United States, mergers of banks, insurance companies, and other financial services providers are not prohibited.

The National Financial Services OmbudService

Another significant achievement is the creation of a National Financial Services OmbudService (NFSO), which began operations on July 1, 2002. This service has been created, with the support of the federal and provincial governments, by the banking sector (through the Canadian Bankers Association), the insurance sector (through the Insurance Bureau of Canada and the Canadian Life and Health Association of Canada), and the securities sector (through the Investment Dealers Association of Canada, the Mutual Funds Dealers Association, and the Investment Funds Institute of Canada). The NFSO provides Canadian consumers and small businesses access to dispute-resolution services regarding their dealings with financial institutions.

The creation of the NFSO has been viewed as a first step towards building a national regulatory system and eliminating the overlaps among the many federal, provincial, and territorial departments and agencies that currently regulate the different industries of the Canadian financial services sector.

Implications for the Canadian Banking Industry

A bank holding company structure (as an alternative to the "bank-as-parent" structure), new ownership rules, expanded permitted investments, expanded access to the payments and clearance system, and a transparent merger review policy offer new opportunities for strategic alliances and joint ventures that have the potential to reshape the Canadian financial services marketplace. These developments, together with new information technologies, make possible new financial products and services and a more vibrant and dynamic market for financial services.

As we have seen, the 1991 federal financial reforms have stimulated consolidation of the Canadian banking industry. The financial consolidation process has further been sped up by the 2001 legislation, because the way is now open to both mergers and acquisitions, and strategic alliances, partnerships, and joint ventures. As already noted, bank financial groups will become not only larger, but also increasingly complex organizations, engaging in a full gamut of financial activities.

MyEconLab

MyEconLab is an online homework and tutorial system that puts you in control of your own learning with study and practice tools directly correlated to this chapter's content. Visit MyEconLab to access the eText, the Questions and Applied Problems with answers, as well as additional assessment. You will also find web chapters, mini-lectures, appendices, mini-cases, videos, glossary flashcards, news feeds, CANSIM data, and graphing tools.

SUMMARY

1. The history of banking in Canada has left us with a small number of banks chartered by the federal government. Multiple agencies regulate chartered banks: the Office of the Superintendent of Financial Institutions (OSFI), the Bank of Canada, and the Canada Deposit Insurance Corporation (CDIC).

2. The Big Six (the Royal Bank of Canada, Canadian Imperial Bank of Commerce, Bank of Montreal, Scotiabank, TD Canada Trust, and the National Bank of Canada) together with the *Desjardins* institutions dominate the deposit-taking industry in Canada.

3. In the United States there is a dual banking system, with commercial banks chartered by the states and the federal government. Restrictive state-branching regulations that prohibited branching across state lines led to a large number of small commercial banks in the United States. The large number of commercial banks in the United States reflects the past *lack* of competition, not the presence of vigorous competition.

4. A change in the economic environment will stimulate financial institutions to search for financial innovations: Changes in demand conditions, especially an increase in interest-rate risk; changes in supply conditions, especially improvements in information technology; and the desire to avoid costly regulations have been major driving forces behind financial innovation. Financial innovation has caused banks to suffer declines in cost advantages in acquiring funds and in income advantages on their assets. The resulting squeeze has hurt profitability in banks' traditional line of business and has led to a decline in traditional banking.

5. The regulation and structure of the near banks (trust and loan companies and credit unions and *caisses populaires*) parallel closely the regulation and structure of the chartered banks. Federally incorporated near banks are regulated and supervised by OSFI. They must also register in all the provinces in which they do business and must conform to the regulations of those provinces.

6. With the rapid growth of world trade since 1960, international banking has grown dramatically. Canadian banks engage in international banking activities by opening branches abroad and owning controlling interests in foreign banks. Foreign banks operate in Canada by owning a subsidiary Canadian bank or by operating branches or agency offices in Canada.

7. Until 1981, foreign banks were not allowed to operate in Canada. Today, there are 53 foreign bank subsidiaries and branches, operating as Schedule II and III banks in Canada. They have the same powers as the domestic banks but differ in the ownership structure permitted. That is, all Schedule I banks must be widely held, whereas Schedule II and III banks can be closely held if small.

8. The 2001 Bank Act reform introduced a bank holding company structure, new ownership rules, expanded access to the payments and clearance system, and new opportunities for strategic alliances and joint ventures. These changes are reshaping the financial services marketplace in Canada by making it easier to introduce new financial products and services and increasing the competitive environment in the industry.

KEY TERMS

automated banking machine (ABM), p. 254
automated teller machine (ATM), p. 253
Bank Act reform, p. 275
branches, p. 247
central bank, p. 247
deposit rate ceilings, p. 257
disintermediation, p. 257
dual banking system, p. 247
economies of scope, p. 267
financial derivatives, p. 252

financial engineering, p. 251
four-pillar approach, p. 266
free banking, p. 247
futures contracts, p. 252
Glass-Steagall, p. 268
gold standard, p. 249
hedge, p. 252
indebtedness, p. 273
lender of last resort, p. 250
national banks, p. 247
originate-to-distribute, p. 256
Regulation Q, p. 257

Schedule I banks, p. 261
Schedule II banks, p. 261
Schedule III banks, p. 261
securitization, p. 255
seigniorage, p. 249
shadow banking system, p. 251
sovereign loans, p. 273
state banks, p. 247
subprime mortgage, p. 256
sweep accounts, p. 259
trustees, p. 268
virtual bank, p. 254

QUESTIONS

All questions are available in MyEconLab *at* **www.myeconlab.com.**

1. Describe how the 2001 Bank Act reform attempted to introduce more competition in Canada's financial services marketplace.

2. Which regulatory agency has the primary responsibility for supervising the following categories of financial institutions?
   a. chartered banks
   b. trust and loan companies
   c. credit unions and *caisses populaires*

3. "The commercial banking industry in Canada is less competitive than the commercial banking industry in the United States because in Canada only a few large banks dominate the industry, while in the United States there are around 6500 commercial banks." Is this statement true, false, or uncertain? Explain your answer.

4. How did new technology cause banks' traditional lending activities to decline in balance-sheet importance?

5. Describe and contrast the activities of a Schedule I bank, a Schedule II bank, a trust company, and a credit union.

6. Explain how sovereign loans in the 1970s and early 1980s caused problems for the Big Six banks.

7. Explain how the early development of chartered banks in Canada differed from the development of commercial banks in the United States.

8. What incentives do Canadian regulatory agencies have to encourage the establishment of foreign banks in Canada?

9. Explain how securitization can be used to change illiquid assets into liquid assets.

10. If the bank at which you keep your chequing account is owned by foreigners, should you worry that your deposits are less safe than if the bank were owned by Canadians?

11. What are the essential differences between chartered banks, trust and loan companies, and credit unions and *caisses populaires*?

12. Why have banks been losing cost advantages in acquiring funds in recent years?

13. "If inflation had not risen in the 1960s and 1970s, the banking industry might be healthier today." Is this statement true, false, or uncertain? Explain your answer.

14. Why have banks been losing income advantages on their assets in recent years?

15. "The invention of the computer is the major factor behind the decline of the banking industry." Is this statement true, false, or uncertain? Explain your answer.

DATA ANALYSIS PROBLEMS

Download data for these problems from MyEconLab *at* **www.myeconlab.com**.

1. Go to the Canada Deposit Insurance Corporation website and access the CDIC deposit insurance calculator. Use the calculator to find out if your savings are protected by CDIC in the event that your financial institution fails.

2. Go to the CANSIM database, and find data on the level of money market investment fund assets (series V37245). Download the data into a spreadsheet.
   a. When did assets start entering money market mutual funds? What was the total worth of assets in money market mutual funds at the end of 1977?

   b. For each decade period, calculate the total percentage change in assets from the beginning of the decade to the end of the decade: 1980: M1–1990:M1; 1990:M1–2000:M1; 2000: M1–2010:M1. For each decade period, divide the total percentage change by 10 to get the average yearly percent increase. Which decade had the largest average yearly growth in money market investment funds?

   c. Calculate the growth rate from the most recent month of data available to the same month a year prior. How does this growth rate compare to the highest average yearly growth rate for the decades from part (b)?

WEB EXERCISES

1. Go to the Canadian Bankers Association website at **www.cba.ca** and search for an article called "Automated Banking Machine Market in Canada." Write a short essay on ABM transactions in Canada and bank access points. According to the trends, does the public appear to have more or less access to banking facilities?

2. Despite the regulations that protect banks from failure, some do fail. Go to **www2.fdic.gov/hsob/index.asp**. Select the tab labelled "Failures and Assistance Transactions." How many bank failures occurred in the United States during the most recent complete calendar year? What were the total assets held by the banks that failed? How many U.S. banks failed in 1937?

WEB REFERENCES

www.osfi-bsif.gc.ca

Visit this website to gather statistics on the Canadian banking industry.

www.fdic.gov/index.html

Visit this website to gather statistics on the banking industry in the United States.

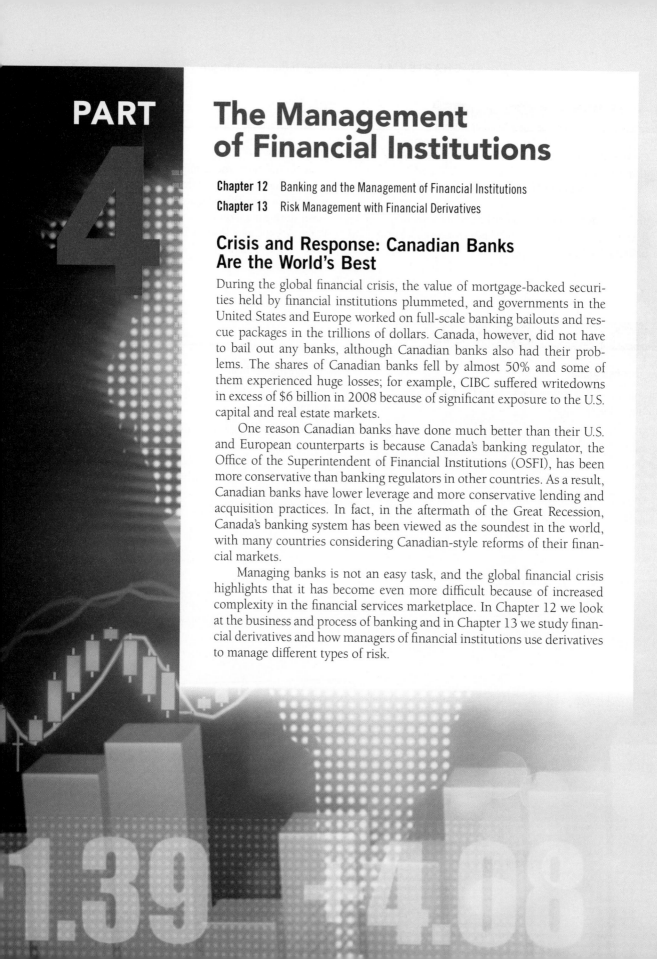

PART 4

The Management of Financial Institutions

Chapter 12 Banking and the Management of Financial Institutions
Chapter 13 Risk Management with Financial Derivatives

Crisis and Response: Canadian Banks Are the World's Best

During the global financial crisis, the value of mortgage-backed securities held by financial institutions plummeted, and governments in the United States and Europe worked on full-scale banking bailouts and rescue packages in the trillions of dollars. Canada, however, did not have to bail out any banks, although Canadian banks also had their problems. The shares of Canadian banks fell by almost 50% and some of them experienced huge losses; for example, CIBC suffered writedowns in excess of $6 billion in 2008 because of significant exposure to the U.S. capital and real estate markets.

One reason Canadian banks have done much better than their U.S. and European counterparts is because Canada's banking regulator, the Office of the Superintendent of Financial Institutions (OSFI), has been more conservative than banking regulators in other countries. As a result, Canadian banks have lower leverage and more conservative lending and acquisition practices. In fact, in the aftermath of the Great Recession, Canada's banking system has been viewed as the soundest in the world, with many countries considering Canadian-style reforms of their financial markets.

Managing banks is not an easy task, and the global financial crisis highlights that it has become even more difficult because of increased complexity in the financial services marketplace. In Chapter 12 we look at the business and process of banking and in Chapter 13 we study financial derivatives and how managers of financial institutions use derivatives to manage different types of risk.

12 Banking and the Management of Financial Institutions

Learning Objectives

After studying this chapter you should be able to

1. Summarize the features of a bank balance sheet.

2. Apply changes to a bank's assets and liabilities on a T-account.

3. Identify the ways in which banks can manage their assets and liabilities to maximize profit.

4. List the ways in which banks deal with credit risk.

5. Apply gap analysis and duration analysis, and identify interest-rate risk.

6. Summarize the types of off-balance-sheet activities.

PREVIEW

Because banking plays such a major role in channeling funds to borrowers with productive investment opportunities, this financial activity is important in ensuring that the financial system and the economy run smoothly and efficiently. In Canada and other countries, banks (depository institutions) provide loans to businesses, help us finance our university educations and our purchases of new cars and homes, and provide us with services such as chequing and savings accounts, debit cards, and ATMs.

In this chapter, we examine how banking is conducted to earn the highest profits possible: how and why banks make loans, how they acquire funds and manage their assets and liabilities (debts), and how they earn income. Although we focus on commercial banks, because commercial banks are the most important financial intermediary, many of the same principles are applicable to other types of financial intermediaries.

THE BANK BALANCE SHEET

To understand how banking works, we start by looking at the bank **balance sheet**, a list of the bank's assets and liabilities. As the name implies, this list balances; that is, it has the characteristic that

$$\text{Total assets} = \text{liabilities} + \text{capital}$$

A bank's balance sheet is also a list of its *sources* of bank funds (liabilities and capital) and *uses* to which the funds are put (assets). Banks obtain funds by borrowing and by issuing other liabilities, such as deposits. They then use these funds to acquire assets such as securities and loans. Banks make profits by earning an interest rate on their holdings of securities and loans that is higher than the expenses on their liabilities. The balance sheet of all banks in Canada, as of August 31, 2014, appears in Table 12-1.

Liabilities

A bank acquires funds by issuing (selling) liabilities such as deposits, which are the *sources of funds* the bank uses. The funds obtained from issuing liabilities are used to purchase income-earning assets.

TABLE 12-1 Balance Sheet of All Banks in Canada (items as a percentage of the total, August 31 2014)

Assets (Uses of Funds)*		Liabilities (Sources of Funds)	
Reserves and cash items	5.38	Demand and notice deposits	33.70
Securities	20.89	Fixed term deposits	31.71
Loans		Advances from the Bank of Canada	0.01
Non-mortgage loans	36.92	Borrowings	28.90
Mortgages	25.45	Bank capital	5.68
Other assets	11.36		
Total	100.00	Total	100.00

*In order of decreasing liquidity
Source: OSFI web site, **www.osfi-bsif.gc.ca**

Demand and Notice Deposits Demand deposits are payable on demand; that is, if a depositor shows up at the bank and requests payment by making a withdrawal, the bank must pay the depositor immediately. Similarly, if a person who receives a cheque written on an account from a bank presents that cheque at the bank, the bank must pay the funds out immediately (or credit them to that person's account). Notice deposits are more important as a source of funds for the banks than are demand deposits. Although notice deposits have a notice requirement in the contractual agreement with the client, the banks rarely enforce this clause, and so in fact most notice deposits are really just like demand deposits in this sense.

Demand deposits and notice deposits are bank accounts that allow the owner to write cheques to third parties. Table 12-1 shows that this category of chequable deposits is an important low-cost source of bank funds, making up close to 34% of bank liabilities. Once, chequable deposits were the most important source of bank funds, but with the appearance of new, more attractive financial instruments, the share of chequable deposits in total bank liabilities has shrunk over time.

A chequable deposit is an asset for the depositor because it is part of his or her wealth. Because the depositor can withdraw funds and the bank is obliged to pay, chequable deposits are a liability for the bank. They are usually the lowest-cost source of bank funds because depositors are willing to forgo some interest in order to have access to a liquid asset that can be used to make purchases. The bank's costs of maintaining chequable deposits include interest payments and the costs incurred in servicing these accounts—processing and storing cancelled cheques, preparing and sending out monthly statements, providing efficient tellers (human or otherwise), maintaining an impressive building and conveniently located branches, and advertising and marketing to entice customers to deposit their funds with a given bank.

Fixed-Term Deposits Fixed-term deposits are the primary source of bank funds (almost 32% of bank liabilities in Table 12-1). Owners cannot write cheques on fixed-term deposits, but the interest rates paid on these deposits are usually higher than those on chequable deposits. There are two main types of fixed-term deposits: savings accounts and time deposits (also called *certificates of deposit*, or *CDs*).

Savings accounts were once the most common type of fixed-term deposit. Funds can be added to or withdrawn from savings accounts at any time. For these accounts, transactions and interest payments are recorded in a monthly statement or in a passbook held by the owners of the account.

Time deposits have a fixed maturity length, ranging from several months to over five years, and assess substantial penalties (the forfeiture of several months' interest) for early withdrawal of funds. Small-denomination time deposits (deposits of less than $100 000) are less liquid for the depositor than passbook savings, earn higher interest rates, and are a more costly source of funds for the banks.

Large-denomination time deposits (CDs) are available in denominations of $100 000 or higher and are typically bought by corporations or other banks. Large-denomination CDs are negotiable; like bonds, they can be resold in a secondary market before they mature. For this reason, negotiable CDs are held by corporations, money market mutual funds, and other financial institutions as alternative assets to Treasury bills and other short-term bonds. Since 1964, when they first appeared in Canada, negotiable CDs have become an important source of bank funds.

Borrowings   Banks obtain funds by borrowing from the Bank of Canada, other banks, and corporations. Borrowings from the Bank of Canada are called **overdraft loans** (also known as **advances**). Banks also borrow reserves overnight in the overnight market from other banks and financial institutions. Banks borrow funds overnight in order to have enough **settlement balances** at the Bank of Canada to facilitate the clearing of cheques and other transfers (these clearing and settlement processes will be discussed in detail in Chapter 16). Other sources of borrowed funds are loan arrangements with corporations (such as repurchase agreements) and borrowings of Eurodollars (deposits denominated in dollars residing in foreign banks or foreign branches of Canadian banks). Borrowings have become a more important source of bank funds over time: in 1960, they made up only a small fraction of bank liabilities; currently, they are close to 29% of bank liabilities.

Bank Capital   The final category on the liabilities side of the balance sheet is bank capital, the bank's net worth, which equals the difference between total assets and liabilities (close to 6% of total bank assets in Table 12-1). Bank capital is raised by selling new equity (stock) or from retained earnings. A bank's capital is its cushion against insolvency, which occurs when a bank has liabilities in excess of assets, meaning that the bank can be forced into liquidation.

Assets

A bank uses the funds that it has acquired by issuing liabilities to purchase income-earning assets. Bank assets are thus naturally referred to as *uses of funds,* and the interest payments earned on them are what enable banks to make profits.

Reserves   All banks hold some of the funds they acquire as deposits in an account at the Bank of Canada, in the form of settlement balances. **Reserves** consist of these settlement balances plus currency that is physically held by banks (called **vault cash** because it is stored in bank vaults overnight). Although Canadian banks are not required to hold reserves in some proportion to their deposits (Canada removed all such legal requirements in June 1994) and there is a requirement of zero settlement balances with the Bank of Canada at the end of each banking day, banks hold some reserves, which we call **desired reserves**.

Banks hold reserves because of their desire to manage their own short-term liquidity requirements and to respond to predictable clearing, over-the-counter, and automated banking machine drains. Moreover, banks hold reserves in order to meet unpredictable and potentially large withdrawals by their liability holders. The risk that net cash withdrawals might be negative is known as **banker's risk**, and from the perspective of this risk, banks hold reserves to meet unpredictable cash and clearing drains. We will refer to the fraction of deposits banks hold in the form of reserves as the **desired reserve ratio**.

Cash Items in Process of Collection

Suppose that a cheque written on an account at another bank is deposited in your bank, and the funds for this cheque have not yet been received (collected) from the other bank. The cheque is classified as a "cash item in process of collection," and it is an asset for your bank because it is a claim on another bank for funds that will be paid within a few days.

Deposits at Other Banks

Many small banks hold deposits in larger banks in exchange for a variety of services, including cheque collection, foreign exchange transactions, and help with securities purchases. This is one aspect of a system called *correspondent banking*.

Collectively, cash items in process of collection and deposits at other banks are referred to as *cash items*. In Table 12-1 they constitute about 5% of total assets, and their importance has been shrinking over time: in 1960, for example, they accounted for over 20% of total assets.

Securities

A bank's holdings of securities are an important income-earning asset: securities (made up entirely of debt instruments for commercial banks, because banks are not allowed to hold stock) account for about 21% of bank assets in Table 12-1. These securities can be classified into three categories: Government of Canada securities, provincial and municipal securities, and other securities. The Government of Canada securities are the most liquid because they can be easily traded and converted into cash with low transaction costs. Because of their high liquidity, short-term Canadian government securities are called **secondary reserves**.

Banks hold provincial and municipal government securities because provincial and municipal governments are more likely to do business with banks that hold their securities. Provincial and municipal government and other securities are both less marketable (less liquid) and riskier than Government of Canada securities, primarily because of default risk: Some possibility exists that the issuer of the securities may not be able to make its interest payments or pay back the face value of the securities when they mature.

Loans

Banks make their profits primarily by issuing loans. In Table 12-1, some 62% of bank assets are in the form of loans, and in recent years they have generally produced more than half of bank revenues. A loan is a liability for the individual or corporation receiving it, but an asset for a bank, because it provides income to the bank. Loans are typically less liquid than other assets because they cannot be turned into cash until the loan matures. If a bank makes a one-year loan, for example, it cannot get its funds back until the loan comes due in one year. Loans also have a higher probability of default than other assets. Because of the lack of liquidity and higher default risk, the bank earns its highest return on loans.

As indicated in Table 12-1, the largest categories of loans for banks are non-mortgage loans (commercial and industrial loans made to businesses, consumer loans, and interbank loans) and mortgages. The balance sheet in Table 12-1 shows that non-mortgage loans exceed mortgage loans (37% versus 25% of bank assets). This is so because a larger portion of the foreign activities of Canadian banks is in corporate loans rather than in mortgages. In fact, the major difference in the balance sheets of the various depository institutions is primarily in the type of loan they specialize in. Trust and loan companies and credit unions and *caisses populaires*, for example, specialize in residential mortgages.

Other Assets   Bankers' acceptances and the physical capital (bank buildings, computers, and other equipment) owned by the banks are included in this category.

BASIC BANKING

Before proceeding to a more detailed study of how a bank manages its assets and liabilities to make the highest profit, you should understand the basic operation of a bank.

In general terms, banks make profits by selling liabilities with one set of characteristics (a particular combination of liquidity, risk, size, and return) and using the proceeds to buy assets with a different set of characteristics. This process is often referred to as **asset transformation**. For example, a savings deposit held by one person can provide the funds that enable the bank to make a mortgage loan to another person. The bank has, in effect, transformed the savings deposit (an asset held by the depositor) into a mortgage loan (an asset held by the bank). Another way of describing this process of asset transformation is to say that the bank "borrows short and lends long" because it makes long-term loans and funds them by issuing short-term deposits.

The process of transforming assets and providing a set of services (cheque clearing, record keeping, credit analysis, and so forth) is like any other production process in a firm. If the bank produces desirable services at low cost and earns substantial income on its assets, it earns profits; if not, the bank suffers losses.

To make our analysis of the operation of a bank more concrete, we use a tool called a **T-account**. A T-account is a simplified balance sheet, with lines in the form of a T, that lists only the changes that occur in balance sheet items starting from some initial balance sheet position. Let's say that Jane Brown has heard that the First National Bank provides excellent service, so she opens a chequing account with a $100 bill. She now has a $100 chequable deposit at the bank, which shows up as a $100 liability on the bank's balance sheet. The bank now puts her $100 bill into its vault so that the bank's assets rise by the $100 increase in vault cash. The T-account for the bank looks like this:

First National Bank			
Assets		**Liabilities**	
Vault cash	+$100	Chequable deposits	+$100

Because vault cash is also part of the bank's reserves, we can rewrite the T-account as follows:

Assets		Liabilities	
Reserves	+$100	Chequable deposits	+$100

Note that Jane Brown's opening of a chequing account leads to *an increase in the bank's reserves equal to the increase in chequable deposits*.

If Jane had opened her account with a $100 cheque written on an account at another bank, say, the Second National Bank, we would get the same result. The initial effect on the T-account of the First National Bank would be as follows:

Assets		Liabilities	
Cash items in process of collection	+$100	Chequable deposits	+$100

Chequable deposits increase by $100 as before, but now the First National Bank is owed $100 by the Second National Bank. This asset for the First National Bank is entered in the T-account as $100 of cash items in process of collection because the First National Bank will now try to collect the funds that it is owed. It could go directly to the Second National Bank and ask for payment of the funds, but if the two banks are in separate provinces, that would be a time-consuming and costly process. Instead, the First National Bank deposits the cheque in its account at the Bank of Canada, and the Bank of Canada collects the funds from the Second National Bank. The net result is that the Bank of Canada transfers $100 of reserves from the Second National Bank to the First National Bank, and the final balance sheet positions of the two banks are as follows:

First National Bank				Second National Bank			
Assets		Liabilities		Assets		Liabilities	
Reserves	+$100	Chequable deposits	+$100	Reserves	−$100	Chequable deposits	−$100

The process initiated by Jane Brown can be summarized as follows: When a cheque written on an account at one bank is deposited in another, the bank receiving the deposit gains reserves equal to the amount of the cheque, while the bank on which the cheque is written sees its reserves fall by the same amount. Therefore, **when a bank receives additional deposits, it gains an equal amount of reserves; when it loses deposits, it loses an equal amount of reserves.**

Now that you understand how banks gain and lose reserves, we can examine how a bank rearranges its balance sheet to make a profit when it experiences a change in its deposits. Let's return to the situation in which the First National Bank has just received the extra $100 of chequable deposits. As you know, the bank wants to keep a certain fraction of its chequable deposits as desired reserves. If the fraction (the desired reserve ratio) is 10%, the First National Bank's desired reserves have increased by $10, and we can rewrite its T-account as follows:

First National Bank			
Assets		**Liabilities**	
Desired reserves	+$10	Chequable deposits	+$100
Excess reserves	+$90		

Let's see how well the bank is doing as a result of the additional chequable deposits. Servicing the extra $100 of chequable deposits is costly, because the bank must keep records, pay tellers, pay for cheque clearing, and so forth. Because reserves earn little interest, the bank is taking a loss! The situation is even worse if the bank makes interest payments on the deposits. To make a profit, the bank must put to productive use all or part of the $90 of excess reserves it has available. One way to do this is to invest in securities. The other is to make loans; as we have seen, loans account for approximately 50% of the total value of bank assets (uses of funds). Because lenders are subject to the asymmetric information problems of adverse selection and moral hazard (discussed in Chapter 8), banks take steps to reduce the incidence and severity of these problems. Bank loan officers evaluate potential borrowers using what are called the "five C's"—character, capacity (ability to repay), collateral, conditions (in the local and national economies), and capital (net worth)—before they agree to lend. (A more detailed discussion of the methods banks use to reduce the risk involved in lending is given later in this chapter.)

Let's assume that the First National Bank chooses not to hold any excess reserves but to make loans instead. The T-account then looks like this:

Assets		**Liabilities**	
Desired reserves	+$10	Chequable deposits	+$100
Loans	+$90		

The bank is now making a profit because it holds short-term liabilities, such as chequable deposits, and uses the proceeds to fund longer-term assets, such as loans with higher interest rates. As mentioned earlier, this process of asset transformation is frequently described by saying that banks are in the business of "borrowing short and lending long." For example, if the loans have an interest rate of 10% per year, the bank earns $9 in income from its loans over the year. If the $100 of chequable deposits is in an account with a 5% interest rate and it costs another $3 per year to service the account, the cost per year of these deposits is $8. The bank's profit on the new deposits is then $1 per year, plus any interest that it earns on desired reserves.

GENERAL PRINCIPLES OF BANK MANAGEMENT

Now that you have some idea of how a bank operates, let's look at how a bank manages its assets and liabilities to earn the highest possible profit. The bank manager has four primary concerns. The first is to make sure that the bank has enough ready cash to pay its depositors when there are **deposit outflows**—that is, when deposits are lost because depositors make withdrawals and demand payment. To keep enough cash on hand, the bank must engage in **liquidity management**, the acquisition of assets that are liquid enough to meet the bank's obligations to depositors. Second, the bank manager must pursue an acceptably low level of risk by acquiring assets that have a low rate of default and by diversifying asset holdings (**asset management**). The manager's third concern is acquiring funds at low cost (**liability management**). Finally, the manager must decide the amount of capital the bank should maintain and then acquire the needed capital (**capital adequacy management**).

To understand bank (and other financial institution) management fully, we must go beyond the general principles of bank asset and liability management described next and look in more detail at how a financial institution manages its assets. The two sections following this one provide an in-depth discussion of how a financial institution manages **credit risk**, the risk arising because borrowers may default, and how it manages **interest-rate risk**, the riskiness of earnings and returns on bank assets caused by interest-rate changes.

Liquidity Management and the Role of Reserves

Let's see how a typical bank, the First National Bank, can deal with deposit outflows that occur when its depositors withdraw cash from chequing or savings accounts or write cheques that are deposited in other banks. In the example that follows, we assume that the bank has ample excess reserves and that the desired reserve ratio is 10% (the bank wants to keep 10% of deposits as reserves). Suppose that the First National Bank's initial balance sheet is as follows:

Assets		Liabilities	
Reserves	$20 million	Deposits	$100 million
Loans	$80 million	Bank capital	$ 10 million
Securities	$10 million		

The bank's desired reserves are 10% of $100 million, or $10 million. Given that it holds $20 million of reserves, the First National Bank has excess reserves of $10 million.

If a deposit outflow of $10 million occurs, the bank's balance sheet becomes

Assets		Liabilities	
Reserves	$10 million	Deposits	$90 million
Loans	$80 million	Bank capital	$10 million
Securities	$10 million		

The bank loses $10 million of deposits **and** $10 million of reserves, but because its desired reserves are now 10% of only $90 million (that is, $9 million), its reserves still exceed this amount by $1 million. In short, *if a bank has ample excess reserves, a deposit outflow does not necessitate changes in other parts of its balance sheet.*

The situation is quite different when a bank holds insufficient excess reserves. Let's assume that instead of initially holding $10 million in excess reserves, the First National Bank makes additional loans of $10 million, so that it holds no excess reserves. Its initial balance sheet would then be

Assets		Liabilities	
Reserves	$10 million	Deposits	$100 million
Loans	$90 million	Bank capital	$ 10 million
Securities	$10 million		

When it suffers the $10 million deposit outflow, its balance sheet becomes

Assets		Liabilities	
Reserves	$ 0	Deposits	$90 million
Loans	$90 million	Bank capital	$10 million
Securities	$10 million		

After $10 million has been withdrawn from deposits and hence reserves, the bank has a problem: Its desired reserves are 10% of $90 million, or $9 million, but it has no reserves! To eliminate this shortfall, the bank has four basic options. One option is to acquire the reserves needed to meet a deposit outflow by borrowing them from other banks in the overnight market, or by borrowing from corporations.[1] If the First National Bank acquires the $9 million shortfall in reserves by borrowing it from other banks or corporations, its balance sheet becomes

Assets		Liabilities	
Reserves	$ 9 million	Deposits	$90 million
Loans	$90 million	Borrowings from other banks or corporations	$ 9 million
Securities	$10 million	Bank capital	$10 million

---

[1]One way in which the First National Bank can borrow from other banks and corporations is by selling negotiable certificates of deposit. This method for obtaining funds is discussed in the section on liability management.

The cost of this activity is the interest rate on these borrowings, such as the overnight interest rate.

A second alternative is for the bank to sell some of its securities to help cover the deposit outflow. For example, it might sell $9 million of its securities and deposit the proceeds with the Bank of Canada, resulting in the following balance sheet:

Assets		Liabilities	
Reserves	$ 9 million	Deposits	$90 million
Loans	$90 million	Bank capital	$10 million
Securities	$ 1 million		

The bank incurs some brokerage and other transaction costs when it sells these securities. The Government of Canada securities that are classified as secondary reserves are very liquid, so the transaction costs of selling them are quite modest. However, the other securities the bank holds are less liquid, and the transaction costs can be appreciably higher.

The bank has a third option for meeting a deposit outflow: It can acquire reserves by borrowing from the Bank of Canada. In our example, the First National Bank could leave its security and loan holdings the same, and borrow $9 million in advances from the Bank of Canada. Its balance sheet would then be

Assets		Liabilities	
Reserves	$ 9 million	Deposits	$90 million
Loans	$90 million	Borrowings from the Bank of Canada	$ 9 million
Securities	$10 million	Bank capital	$10 million

The cost associated with advances from the Bank of Canada is the interest rate that must be paid to the Bank of Canada (called the **bank rate**).

As a last option, a bank can acquire the $9 million of reserves to meet the deposit outflow by reducing its loans by this amount and depositing the $9 million it then receives with the Bank of Canada, thereby increasing its reserves by $9 million. This transaction changes the balance sheet as follows:

Assets		Liabilities	
Reserves	$ 9 million	Deposits	$90 million
Loans	$81 million	Bank capital	$10 million
Securities	$10 million		

The First National Bank is once again in good shape because its $9 million of reserves satisfies the (desired) reserve requirement.

However, this process of reducing its loans is the bank's costliest way of acquiring reserves when a deposit outflow exists. If the First National Bank has numerous short-term loans renewed at fairly short intervals, it can reduce its total amount of loans outstanding fairly quickly by *calling in* loans—that is, by not renewing some loans when they come due. Unfortunately for the bank, this is likely to antagonize the customers whose loans are not being renewed because they have not done anything to deserve such treatment. Indeed, they are likely to take their business elsewhere in the future, which would be a very costly consequence for the bank.

A second method of reducing its loans is for the bank to sell them off to other banks. Again, this is very costly because other banks do not know how risky these loans are and so may not be willing to buy the loans at their full value. (This is an example of the lemons adverse selection problem described in Chapter 8.)

The foregoing discussion explains why banks hold reserves even though loans or securities earn a higher return. When a deposit outflow occurs, reserves enable the bank to escape the costs of (1) borrowing from other banks or corporations, (2) selling securities, (3) borrowing from the Bank of Canada, or (4) calling in or selling off loans. **Reserves are insurance against the costs associated with deposit outflows. The higher the costs associated with deposit outflows, the more reserves a bank will want to hold.**

Just as you and I would be willing to pay an insurance company to insure us against a casualty loss such as the theft of a car, a bank is willing to pay the cost of holding reserves (the opportunity cost—that is, the earnings forgone by not holding income-earning assets such as loans or securities) to insure against losses due to deposit outflows. Because reserves, like insurance, have a cost, banks also take other steps to protect themselves; for example, they might shift their holdings of assets to more liquid securities (secondary reserves).

Asset Management

Now that you understand a bank's need for liquidity, we can examine the basic strategy a bank pursues in managing its assets. To maximize its profits, a bank must simultaneously seek the highest returns possible on loans and securities, reduce risk, and make adequate provisions for liquidity by holding liquid assets. Banks try to accomplish these three goals in four basic ways.

First, banks try to find borrowers who will pay high interest rates and are unlikely to default on their loans. They seek out loan business by advertising their borrowing rates and by approaching corporations directly to solicit loans. It is up to the bank's loan officer to decide if potential borrowers are good credit risks who will make interest and principal payments on time (i.e., banks engage in screening to reduce the adverse selection problem). Typically, banks are conservative in their loan policies; the default rate is usually less than 1%. It is important, however, that banks not be so conservative that they miss out on attractive lending opportunities that earn high interest rates.

Second, banks try to purchase securities with high returns and low risk.

Third, in managing their assets, banks must attempt to lower risk by diversifying. They accomplish this by purchasing many different types of assets (short- and long-term, Government of Canada, and municipal bonds) and approving many types of loans to a variety of customers. Banks that have not sufficiently sought the benefits of diversification often come to regret it later. For example, banks that had overspecialized in making loans to energy companies, real estate developers, or farmers suffered huge losses in the 1980s with the slump in energy, property, and farm prices. Indeed, many of these banks (e.g., the Canadian Commercial Bank and the Northland Bank) went broke because they had "put too many eggs in one basket."

Finally, the bank must manage the liquidity of its assets so that it can meet deposit outflows without bearing huge costs. This means that it will hold liquid securities even if they earn a somewhat lower return than other assets might. The bank must decide, for example, how much it should hold in reserves to avoid the costs associated with a deposit outflow. In addition, it will want to hold Government of Canada securities as secondary reserves so that even if a deposit outflow forces some costs on the bank, these will not be terribly high. Again, it is not wise for a bank to be too conservative. If it avoids all costs associated with deposit outflows by holding only reserves, the bank suffers losses, because reserves earn low interest, while the bank's liabilities are costly to maintain. The bank must balance its desire for liquidity against the benefits of the increased earnings that can be obtained from less liquid assets, such as loans.

Liability Management

Before the 1960s, liability management was a staid affair: For the most part, banks took their liabilities as fixed and spent their time trying to achieve an optimal mix of assets. There were two main reasons for the emphasis on asset management. First, a large part of bank funds were obtained through chequable (demand) deposits that did not pay any interest. Thus banks could not actively compete with one another for these deposits by paying interest on them, and so their amount was effectively a given for an individual bank. Second, because the markets for making overnight loans between banks were not well developed, banks rarely borrowed from other banks to meet their reserve needs.

Starting in the 1960s, however, large banks (called **money centre banks**) in key financial centres such as New York, Chicago, and San Francisco, began to explore ways in which the liabilities on their balance sheets could provide them with reserves and liquidity. This move led to an expansion of overnight loan markets, such as the federal funds market in the United States and the overnight funds market in Canada, and the development of new financial instruments, such as negotiable CDs (first developed in 1961), which enabled money centre banks to acquire funds quickly.[2]

This new flexibility in liability management meant that banks could take a different approach to bank management. They no longer needed to depend on chequable deposits as the primary source of bank funds and as a result no longer treated their sources of funds (liabilities) as given. Instead, they aggressively set target goals for their asset growth and tried to acquire funds (by issuing liabilities) as they were needed.

For example, today, when a money centre bank finds an attractive loan opportunity, it can acquire funds by selling a negotiable CD. Or, if it has a reserve shortfall, it can borrow funds from another bank in the overnight funds market without incurring high transaction costs. The overnight funds market can also be used to finance loans. Because of the increased importance of liability management, most banks now manage both sides of the balance sheet together in an *asset-liability management (ALM) committee.*

The greater emphasis on liability management explains some of the important changes over the past three decades in the composition of banks' balance sheets. While

---

[2]Because small banks are not as well-known as money centre banks and so might be a higher credit risk, they find it harder to raise funds in the negotiable CD market. Hence they do not engage nearly as actively in liability management.

negotiable CDs and bank borrowings have greatly increased in importance as a source of bank funds in recent years, chequable deposits have decreased in importance. New-found flexibility in liability management and the search for higher profits have also stimulated banks to increase the proportion of their assets held in loans, which earn higher income than other assets do.

Capital Adequacy Management

Banks have to make decisions about the amount of capital they need to hold for three reasons. First, bank capital helps prevent *bank failure*, a situation in which the bank cannot satisfy its obligations to pay its depositors and other creditors, and so goes out of business. Second, the amount of capital held affects returns for the owners (equity holders) of the bank. Third, a minimum amount of bank capital (bank capital requirements) is required by regulatory authorities.

How Bank Capital Helps Prevent Bank Failure   Let's consider two banks with identical balance sheets, except that High Capital Bank has a ratio of capital to assets of 10%, while Low Capital Bank has a ratio of 4%.

High Capital Bank				Low Capital Bank			
Assets		**Liabilities**		**Assets**		**Liabilities**	
Reserves	$10 million	Deposits	$90 million	Reserves	$10 million	Deposits	$96 million
Loans	$90 million	Bank capital	$10 million	Loans	$90 million	Bank capital	$ 4 million

Suppose both banks get caught up in the euphoria of the housing market, only to find later that $5 million of their housing loans have become worthless. When these bad loans are written off (valued at zero), the total value of assets declines by $5 million. As a consequence, bank capital, which equals total assets minus liabilities, also declines by $5 million. The balance sheets of the two banks now look like this:

High Capital Bank				Low Capital Bank			
Assets		**Liabilities**		**Assets**		**Liabilities**	
Reserves	$10 million	Deposits	$90 million	Reserves	$10 million	Deposits	$96 million
Loans	$85 million	Bank capital	$ 5 million	Loans	$85 million	Bank capital	−$ 1 million

High Capital Bank takes the $5 million loss in stride because its initial cushion of $10 million in capital means that it still has a positive net worth (bank capital) of $5 million after the loss. Low Capital Bank, however, is in big trouble. The value of its assets has fallen below that of its liabilities, and its net worth is now −$1 million. Because the bank has a negative net worth, it is insolvent: It does not have sufficient assets to pay off all holders of its liabilities. When a bank becomes insolvent, government regulators close the bank, its assets are sold off, and its managers are fired. Because the owners of Low Capital Bank will find their investment wiped out, they clearly would have preferred the bank to have had a large enough cushion of bank capital to absorb the losses, as was the case for High Capital Bank. We therefore see an important rationale for a bank to maintain a sufficient level of capital: *A bank maintains bank capital to lessen the chance that it will become insolvent.*

How the Amount of Bank Capital Affects Returns to Equity Holders

Because owners of a bank must know whether their bank is being managed well, they need good measures of bank profitability. A basic measure of bank profitability is the **return on assets (ROA)**, the net profit after taxes per dollar of assets:

$$ROA = \frac{\text{net profit after taxes}}{\text{assets}}$$

The return on assets provides information on how efficiently a bank is being run because it indicates how much profit is generated, on average, by each dollar of assets.

However, what the bank's owners (equity holders) care about most is how much the bank is earning on their equity investment. This information is provided by the other basic measure of bank profitability, the **return on equity (ROE)**, which is defined as the net profit after taxes per dollar of equity (bank) capital:

$$ROE = \frac{\text{net profit after taxes}}{\text{equity capital}}$$

There is a direct relationship between the return on assets (which measures how efficiently the bank is run) and the return on equity (which measures how well the owners are doing on their investment). This relationship is determined by the **equity multiplier (EM)**, or the amount of assets per dollar of equity capital:

$$EM = \frac{\text{assets}}{\text{equity capital}}$$

To see this, we note that

$$\frac{\text{net profit after taxes}}{\text{equity capital}} = \frac{\text{net profit after taxes}}{\text{assets}} \times \frac{\text{assets}}{\text{equity capital}}$$

which, using our definitions, yields

$$ROE = ROA \times EM \qquad \text{(Equation 1)}$$

The formula in Equation 1 tells us what happens to the return on equity when a bank holds a smaller amount of capital (equity) for a given amount of assets. As we have seen, High Capital Bank initially has $100 million of assets and $10 million of equity, which gives it an equity multiplier of 10 (= $100 million/$10 million). Low Capital Bank, by contrast, has only $4 million of equity, so its equity multiplier is higher, equaling 25 (= $100 million/$4 million). Suppose these banks have been equally well run, so that they both have the same return on assets, 1%. The return on equity for

High Capital Bank equals $1\% \times 10 = 10\%$, whereas the return on equity for Low Capital Bank equals $1\% \times 25 = 25\%$. The equity holders in Low Capital Bank are clearly a lot happier than the equity holders in High Capital Bank because they are earning more than twice as high a return. We now see why the owners of a bank may not want it to hold too much capital. *Given the return on assets, the lower the bank capital, the higher the return for the owners of the bank.*

Trade-off Between Safety and Returns to Equity Holders   We now see that bank capital has both benefits and costs. Bank capital benefits the owners of a bank in that it makes their investment safer by reducing the likelihood of bankruptcy. But bank capital is costly because the higher it is, the lower will be the return on equity for a given return on assets. In determining the optimal amount of bank capital, managers must compare the benefit of maintaining higher capital (increased safety) with the cost of higher capital (the lower return on equity for bank owners).

In more uncertain times, when the possibility of large losses on loans increases, bank managers might want to hold more capital in order to protect the equity holders. Conversely, if the managers have confidence that loan losses won't occur, they might want to reduce the amount of bank capital, have a high equity multiplier, and thereby increase the return on equity.

Bank Capital Requirements   Banks also hold capital because they are required to do so by regulatory authorities. Because of the high costs of holding capital (for the reasons just described), bank managers often want to hold less bank capital relative to assets than is required by the regulatory authorities. In this case, the amount of bank capital is determined by the bank capital requirements. We discussed the details of bank capital requirements and their important role in bank regulation in Chapter 10.

APPLICATION   # Strategies for Managing Bank Capital

Suppose that, as the manager of the First National Bank, you have to make decisions about the appropriate amount of bank capital to hold in your bank. Looking at the balance sheet of the bank, which, like that of High Capital Bank, has a ratio of bank capital to assets of 10% ($10 million of capital and $100 million of assets), you are concerned that the large amount of bank capital is causing the return on equity to be too low. You conclude that the bank has a capital surplus and should increase the equity multiplier to raise the return on equity. What should you do next?

To lower the amount of capital relative to assets and raise the equity multiplier, you can do any of three things: (1) You can reduce the amount of bank capital by buying back some of the bank's stock; (2) you can reduce the bank's capital by paying out higher dividends to its stockholders, thereby reducing the bank's retained earnings; or (3) you can keep bank capital constant but increase the bank's assets by acquiring new funds—say, by issuing CDs—and then seeking out loan business or purchasing more securities with these new funds. Because you think it will enhance your position with the stockholders, you decide to pursue the second alternative and raise the dividend on the First National Bank stock.

Now suppose that the First National Bank is in a situation similar to that of Low Capital Bank and has a ratio of bank capital to assets of 4%. You now worry that the bank is short on capital relative to assets because it does not have a sufficient cushion to prevent bank failure. To raise the amount of capital relative to assets, you now have the following three choices: (1) You can raise capital for the bank by having it issue equity (common stock); (2) you can raise capital by reducing the bank's dividends to shareholders, thereby increasing retained earnings that it can put into its capital account; or (3) you can keep capital at the same level but reduce the bank's assets by making fewer loans or by selling off securities and then using the proceeds to reduce the bank's liabilities. Suppose that raising bank capital is not easy to do at the current time because bank stock is selling at low prices or because shareholders will protest if their dividends are cut. Then you might have to choose the third alternative and shrink the size of the bank.

Our discussion of the strategies for managing bank capital at the First National Bank leads to the following conclusion, which deserves particular emphasis: *A shortfall of bank capital is likely to lead a bank to reduce its assets and therefore is likely to cause a contraction in lending*. In past years, many banks experienced capital shortfalls and had to restrict asset and lending growth. The important consequences of this decision for the credit markets are illustrated by the application that follows.

APPLICATION **How a Capital Crunch Caused a Credit Crunch During the Global Financial Crisis**

The dramatic slowdown in the growth of credit in the wake of the financial crisis that began in 2007 triggered a "credit crunch" during which credit was hard to get. As a result, the performance of the economy in 2008 and 2009 was very poor. What caused the credit crunch?

Our analysis of how a bank manages its capital indicates that the 2008–2009 credit crunch was caused, at least in part, by the capital crunch, in which shortfalls of bank capital led to slower credit growth.

A major boom and bust in the housing market led to huge losses for banks from their holdings of securities backed by residential mortgages. These losses reduced bank capital, which led to capital shortfalls: Banks had to either raise new capital or restrict asset growth by cutting back on lending. Banks did raise some capital, but with the growing weakness of the economy, raising new capital was extremely difficult, so banks also chose to tighten their lending standards and reduce lending. Both of these reactions to capital shortfalls helped produce a weak economy in 2008 and 2009. ◆

MANAGING CREDIT RISK

As noted in our earlier discussion of the general principles of asset management, banks and other financial institutions must make successful loans that are paid back in full (and so subject the institution to little credit risk) if they are to earn high profits. The economic concepts of adverse selection and moral hazard (discussed in Chapters 2 and 8) provide a framework for understanding the principles that financial institutions must follow if they are to reduce credit risk and make successful loans.[3]

---

[3]Other financial intermediaries, such as insurance companies, pension funds, and finance companies, also make private loans, and the credit risk management principles we outline here apply to them as well.

Adverse selection in loan markets occurs because bad credit risks (those most likely to default on their loans) are the ones who usually line up for loans; in other words, those who are most likely to produce an *adverse* outcome are also the most likely to be *selected*. Borrowers with very risky investment projects have much to gain if their projects are successful, so they are the most eager to obtain loans. Clearly, however, they are the least desirable borrowers because of the greater possibility that they will be unable to pay back their loans.

Moral hazard exists in loan markets because borrowers may have incentives to engage in activities that are undesirable from the lender's point of view. In such situations, it is more likely that the lender will be subjected to the *hazard* of default. Once borrowers have obtained a loan, they are more likely to invest in high-risk investment projects—projects that pay high returns to the borrower if successful. The high risk associated with these investments, however, makes it less likely that these borrowers will be able to pay back their loans.

To be profitable, financial institutions must overcome the adverse selection and moral hazard problems that make loan defaults more likely. Financial institutions attempt to solve these problems by using a number of principles for managing credit risk: screening and monitoring, establishment of long-term customer relationships, loan commitments, collateral and compensating balance requirements, and credit rationing.

1. Screening and Monitoring

Asymmetric information is present in loan markets because lenders have less information about the investment opportunities and activities of borrowers than borrowers do. This situation leads banks and other financial institutions to perform two information-producing activities: screening and monitoring. Indeed, Walter Wriston, a former head of Citicorp, one of the largest bank corporations in the United States, was often quoted as stating that the business of banking is the production of information.

Screening   Adverse selection in loan markets requires that lenders screen out the bad credit risks from the good ones, so that loans are profitable to them. To accomplish effective screening, lenders must collect reliable information from prospective borrowers. Effective screening and information collection together form an important principle of credit risk management.

When you apply for a consumer loan (such as a car loan or a mortgage to purchase a house), the first thing you are asked to do is fill out forms that elicit a great deal of information about your personal finances. You are asked about your salary, your bank accounts and other assets (such as cars, insurance policies, and furnishings), and your outstanding loans; your record of loan, credit card, and charge account repayments; and the number of years you've worked and the names of your employers. You also are asked personal questions such as your age, marital status, and number of children. The lender uses this information to evaluate how good a credit risk you are by calculating your credit score, a statistical measure derived from your answers that is used to predict whether you are likely to have trouble making your loan payments. Deciding how good a risk you are cannot be entirely scientific, so the lender must also use judgment. The loan officer, whose job it is to decide whether you should be given the loan, might call your employer or talk to some of the personal references you have supplied. The officer might even make a judgment based on your demeanour or your appearance. (This is why most people dress neatly and conservatively when they go to a bank to apply for a loan.)

The process of screening and collecting information is similar when a financial institution makes a business loan. It collects information about the company's profits and losses (income) along with information about its assets and liabilities. The lender also has to evaluate the likely future success of the business. So, in addition to obtaining information such as sales figures, a loan officer might ask questions about the company's future plans, the purpose of the loan, and competition within the industry. The officer may even visit the company to obtain a firsthand look at its operations. The bottom line is that, whether they are considering making personal loans or business loans, bankers and other financial institutions need to be nosy.

Specialization in Lending

One puzzling feature of bank lending is that a bank often specializes in lending to local firms or to firms in particular industries, such as energy. In one sense, this behaviour seems surprising because it means that the bank is not diversifying its portfolio of loans and thus is exposing itself to more risk. But from another perspective, such specialization makes perfect sense. The adverse selection problem requires that the bank screen out bad credit risks. It is easier for the bank to collect information about local firms and determine their creditworthiness than to collect comparable information on firms that are farther away. Similarly, by concentrating its lending on firms in specific industries, the bank becomes more knowledgeable about these industries and is therefore better able to predict which firms will be able to make timely payments on their debt.

Monitoring and Enforcement of Restrictive Covenants

Once a loan has been made, the borrower has an incentive to engage in risky activities that make it less likely that the loan will be paid off. To reduce this moral hazard, financial institutions must write provisions (restrictive covenants) into loan contracts that restrict borrowers from engaging in risky activities. By monitoring borrowers' activities to see whether they are complying with the restrictive covenants and by enforcing the covenants if they are not, lenders can make sure that borrowers are not taking on risks at their expense. The need for banks and other financial institutions to engage in screening and monitoring explains why they spend so much money on auditing and information-collecting activities.

2. Long-Term Customer Relationships

An additional way for banks and other financial institutions to obtain information about their borrowers is through long-term customer relationships, another important principle of credit risk management.

If a prospective borrower has had a chequing account, a savings account, or a loan with a bank over a long period of time, a loan officer can look at past activity on the accounts and learn quite a bit about the borrower. The balances in the chequing and savings accounts tell the banker how liquid the potential borrower is and at what time of year the borrower has a strong need for cash. A review of the cheques the borrower has written reveals the borrower's suppliers. If the borrower has borrowed previously from the bank, the bank has a record of the loan payments. Thus long-term customer relationships reduce the costs of information collection and make it easier to screen out bad credit risks.

The need for monitoring by lenders adds to the importance of long-term customer relationships. If the borrower has borrowed from the bank before, the bank has already established procedures for monitoring that customer. Therefore, the costs of monitoring long-term customers are lower than the costs of monitoring new customers.

Long-term relationships benefit customers as well as banks. A firm that has had a previous relationship with a bank will find it easier to obtain a loan from the bank at a low interest rate because the bank has an easier time determining if the prospective borrower is a good credit risk and therefore incurs fewer costs in monitoring the borrower.

A long-term customer relationship has another advantage for the bank. No bank can think of every contingency when it writes a restrictive covenant into a loan contract; there will always be risky borrower activities that are not anticipated. However, what if a borrower wants to preserve a long-term relationship with a bank because it will be easier to get future loans from the bank, at low interest rates? The borrower then has the incentive to avoid risky activities that would upset the bank, even if restrictions on these risky activities are not specified in the loan contract. Indeed, if a bank doesn't like what a borrower is doing even when the borrower isn't violating any restrictive covenants, it has some power to discourage the borrower from such activity: The bank can threaten not to give the borrower new loans in the future. Long-term customer relationships therefore enable banks to deal with even unanticipated moral hazard contingencies.

3. Loan Commitments

Banks also create long-term relationships and gather information by issuing **loan commitments** to commercial customers. A loan commitment is a bank's commitment (for a specified future period of time) to provide a firm with loans up to a given amount at an interest rate that is tied to some market interest rate. The majority of commercial and industrial loans are made under the loan commitment arrangement. The advantage for the firm is that it has a source of credit when it needs it. The advantage for the bank is that the loan commitment promotes a long-term relationship, which in turn facilitates information collection. In addition, provisions in the loan commitment agreement require that the firm continually supply the bank with information about the firm's income, asset and liability position, business activities, and so on. A loan commitment arrangement is a powerful method for reducing the bank's costs of screening and information collection.

4. Collateral and Compensating Balances

Collateral requirements for loans are important credit risk management tools. Collateral, which is property promised to the lender as compensation if the borrower defaults, lessens the consequences of adverse selection because it reduces the lender's losses in the case of a loan default. It also reduces moral hazard because the borrower has more to lose from a default. If a borrower defaults on a loan, the lender can sell the collateral and use the proceeds to make up for its losses on the loan. One particular form of collateral required when a bank makes commercial loans is called **compensating balances**: A firm receiving a loan must keep a required minimum amount of funds in a chequing account at the bank. For example, a business getting a $10 million loan may be required to keep compensating balances of at least $1 million in its chequing account at the bank. This $1 million in compensating balances can then be taken by the bank to make up some of the losses on the loan if the borrower defaults.

In addition to serving as collateral, compensating balances increase the likelihood that a loan will be paid off. They do this by helping the bank monitor the borrower and consequently reduce moral hazard. Specifically, by requiring the borrower to use a chequing account at the bank, the bank can observe the firm's cheque payment practices, which may yield a great deal of information about the borrower's financial condition. For example, a sustained drop in the borrower's chequing account balance may signal that the borrower is having financial trouble, or account activity may suggest that the borrower is engaging in risky activities; perhaps a change in suppliers means the borrower is pursuing a new line of business. Any significant change in the borrower's payment procedures is a signal to the bank that it should make inquiries. Compensating balances therefore make it easier for banks to monitor borrowers more effectively and are an important credit risk management tool.

5. Credit Rationing

Another way in which financial institutions deal with adverse selection and moral hazard is through **credit rationing**: refusing to make loans even though borrowers are willing to pay the stated interest rate, or even a higher rate. Credit rationing takes two forms. The first occurs when a lender refuses to make a loan *of any amount* to a borrower, even if the borrower is willing to pay a higher interest rate. The second occurs when a lender is willing to make a loan but restricts the size of the loan to less than what the borrower would like.

Initially, you might be puzzled by the first type of credit rationing. After all, even if the potential borrower is a credit risk, why doesn't the lender just extend the loan, but at a higher interest rate? The answer is that adverse selection prevents this from being a wise course of action. Individuals and firms with the riskiest investment projects are exactly those that are willing to pay the highest interest rates. If a borrower took on a high-risk investment and succeeded, the borrower would become extremely rich. But a lender wouldn't want to make such a loan precisely because the credit risk is high; the likely outcome is that the borrower will *not* succeed and the lender will not be paid back. Charging a higher interest rate just makes adverse selection worse for the lender; that is, it increases the likelihood that the lender is lending to a bad credit risk. The lender would therefore rather not make any loans at a higher interest rate; instead, it would engage in the first type of credit rationing and would turn down loans.

Financial institutions engage in the second type of credit rationing to guard against moral hazard: They grant loans to borrowers, but loans that are not as large as the borrowers want. Such credit rationing is necessary because the larger the loan, the greater the benefits from moral hazard. If a bank gives you a $1000 loan, for example, you are likely to take actions that enable you to pay it back because you don't want to hurt your credit rating for the future. However, if the bank lends you $10 million, you are more likely to fly down to Rio to celebrate. The larger your loan, the greater your incentives to engage in activities that make it less likely that you will repay the loan. Because more borrowers repay their loans if the loan amounts are small, financial institutions ration credit by providing borrowers with smaller loans than they seek.

MANAGING INTEREST-RATE RISK

With the increased volatility of interest rates that occurred in the 1980s, banks and other financial institutions became more concerned about their exposure to interest-rate risk, the riskiness of earnings and returns that is associated with changes in interest rates. To see what interest-rate risk is all about, let's again take a look at the First National Bank, which has the following balance sheet:

First National Bank

Assets		Liabilities	
Rate-sensitive assets	$20 million	Rate-sensitive liabilities	$50 million
Variable-rate and		Variable-rate CDs	
short-term loans		Money market deposit	
Short-term securities		accounts	
Fixed-rate assets	$80 million	Fixed-rate liabilities	$50 million
Reserves		Chequable deposits	
Long-term loans		Savings deposits	
Long-term securities		Long-term CDs	
		Equity capital	

A total of $20 million of First National Bank's assets are rate-sensitive, with interest rates that change frequently (at least once a year), and $80 million of its assets are fixed-rate, with interest rates that remain unchanged for a long period (over a year). On the liabilities side, the First National Bank has $50 million of rate-sensitive liabilities and $50 million of fixed-rate liabilities. Suppose that interest rates rise by 5 percentage points on average, from 10% to 15%. The income on the assets increases by $1 million (= 5% × $20 million of rate-sensitive assets), while the payments on the liabilities increase by $2.5 million (= 5% × $50 million of rate-sensitive liabilities). The First National Bank's profits now decline by $1.5 million (= $1 million − $2.5 million). Conversely, if interest rates fall by 5 percentage points, similar reasoning tells us that the First National Bank's profits increase by $1.5 million. This example illustrates the following point: *If a bank has more rate-sensitive liabilities than assets, a rise in interest rates will reduce bank profits, and a decline in interest rates will raise bank profits.*

Gap and Duration Analysis

The sensitivity of bank profits to changes in interest rates can be measured more directly using **gap analysis**, in which the amount of rate-sensitive liabilities is subtracted from the amount of rate-sensitive assets. In our example, this calculation (called the "gap") is −$30 million (= $20 million − $50 million). By multiplying the gap times the change in the interest rate, we can immediately obtain the effect on bank profits. For example, when interest rates rise by 5 percentage points, the change in profits is 5% × −$30 million, which equals −$1.5 million, as we saw.

The analysis we just conducted is known as *basic gap analysis*, and it can be refined in two ways. Clearly, not all assets and liabilities in the fixed-rate category have the same maturity. One refinement, the *maturity bucket approach*, is to measure the gap for several maturity subintervals, called *maturity buckets*, so that effects of interest-rate changes over a multiyear period can be calculated. The second refinement, called *standardized gap analysis*, accounts for the differing degrees of rate sensitivity among rate-sensitive assets and liabilities.

An alternative method for measuring interest-rate risk, called **duration analysis**, examines the sensitivity of the market value of the bank's total assets and liabilities to changes in interest rates. Duration analysis is based on what is known as Macaulay's concept of *duration*, which measures the average lifetime of a security's stream of payments.[4] Duration is a useful concept because it provides a good approximation of the sensitivity of a security's market value to a change in its interest rate:

percent change in market value of security ≈

−percentage-point change in interest rate × duration in years

where ≈ denotes "approximately equals."

Duration analysis involves using the average (weighted) duration of a financial institution's assets and of its liabilities to see how its net worth responds to a change in interest rates. Going back to our example of the First National Bank, suppose the average duration of the bank's assets is three years (that is, the average lifetime of the stream of payments is three years), whereas the average duration of its liabilities is two years. In addition, the First National Bank has $100 million of assets and, say, $90 million of liabilities, so its bank capital is 10% of assets. With a 5-percentage-point increase in interest rates, the market value of the bank's assets falls by 15% (= −5% × 3 years), a decline of $15 million on the $100 million of assets. However, the market value of the liabilities falls by 10% (= −5% × 2 years), a decline of $9 million on the $90 million of liabilities. The net result is that the net worth (the market value of the assets minus the liabilities) has declined by $6 million, or 6% of the total original asset value. Similarly, a 5-percentage-point decline in interest rates increases the net worth of the First National Bank by 6% of the total asset value.

As our example makes clear, both duration analysis and gap analysis indicate that the First National Bank will suffer if interest rates rise but will gain if they fall. Duration analysis and gap analysis are thus useful tools for a manager of a financial institution who is concerned about its degree of exposure to interest-rate risk.

APPLICATION Strategies for Managing Interest-Rate Risk

Suppose that as manager of the First National Bank, you have done a duration and gap analysis for the bank. Now you need to decide which alternative strategies you should pursue to manage the interest-rate risk.

---

[4]Algebraically, Macaulay's duration, D, is defined as

$$D = \sum_{\tau=1}^{N} \tau \frac{CP_\tau}{(1 + i^\tau)} \bigg/ \sum_{\tau=1}^{N} \frac{CP_\tau}{(1 + i^\tau)}$$

where τ = time until cash payment is made
CP_τ = cash payment (interest plus principal) at time τ
i = interest rate
N = time to maturity of the security

For a more detailed discussion of duration gap analysis using the concept of Macaulay's duration, see the appendix to this chapter on the MyEconLab.

If you firmly believe that interest rates will fall in the future, you may be willing to forego action because you know that the bank has more rate-sensitive liabilities than rate-sensitive assets and so will benefit from the expected interest-rate decline. However, you also realize that the First National Bank is subject to substantial interest-rate risk because there is always a possibility that interest rates will rise rather than fall. What should you do to eliminate this interest-rate risk? One thing you could do is to shorten the duration of the bank's assets to increase their rate sensitivity. Alternatively, you could lengthen the duration of the liabilities. By this adjustment of the bank's assets or liabilities, the bank's income will be less affected by interest-rate swings.

One problem with eliminating the First National Bank's interest-rate risk by altering the balance sheet is that doing so might be very costly in the short run. The bank may be locked into assets and liabilities of particular durations because of where its expertise lies. Fortunately, recently developed financial instruments known as financial derivatives—financial forwards and futures, options, and swaps—can help the bank reduce its interest-rate risk exposure but do not require that the bank rearrange its balance sheet. ◆

OFF-BALANCE-SHEET ACTIVITIES

Although asset and liability management has traditionally been the primary concern of banks, in the more competitive environment of recent years banks have been aggressively seeking out profits by engaging in off-balance-sheet activities.[5] **Off-balance-sheet activities** involve trading financial instruments and generating income from fees and loan sales, activities that affect bank profits but do not appear on bank balance sheets. Indeed, off-balance-sheet activities have been growing in importance for banks: The income from these activities as a percentage of assets has nearly doubled since 1980.

Loan Sales

One type of off-balance-sheet activity that has grown in importance in recent years involves income generated by loan sales. A **loan sale**, also called a *secondary loan participation*, involves a contract that sells all or part of the cash stream from a specific loan and thereby removes the loan so that it is no longer an asset on the bank's balance sheet. Banks earn profits by selling loans for amounts that are slightly greater than the amounts of the original loans. Because the high interest rate on these loans makes them attractive, institutions are willing to buy them, even though the higher price means that they earn a slightly lower interest rate than the original interest rate on the loan, usually on the order of 0.15 percentage point.

Generation of Fee Income

Another type of off-balance-sheet activity involves the generation of income from fees that banks receive for providing specialized services to their customers, such as making foreign exchange trades on a customer's behalf, servicing a mortgage-backed security

---

[5]Managers of financial institutions also need to know how well their banks are doing at any point in time. A second appendix to this chapter discusses how bank performance is measured; it can be found on the MyEconLab.

by collecting interest and principal payments and then paying them out, guarantee-ing debt securities such as banker's acceptances (by which the bank promises to make interest and principal payments if the party issuing the security cannot), and providing backup lines of credit. There are several types of backup lines of credit. We have already mentioned the most important, the loan commitment, under which, for a fee, the bank agrees to provide a loan at the customer's request, up to a given dollar amount, over a specified period of time. Credit lines with "overdraft privileges" are also now available to bank depositors—these bank customers can write cheques in excess of their deposit balances and, in effect, write themselves a loan. Other lines of credit for which banks get fees include standby letters of credit to back up issues of commercial paper and other securities, and credit lines (called *note issuance facilities*, NIFs, and *revolving underwriting facilities*, RUFs) for underwriting Euronotes, which are medium-term Eurobonds.

Off-balance-sheet activities involving guarantees of securities and backup credit lines increase the risk a bank faces. Even though a guaranteed security does not appear on a bank's balance sheet, it still exposes the bank to default risk: If the issuer of the security defaults, the bank is left holding the bag and must pay off the security's owner. Backup credit lines also expose the bank to risk because the bank may be forced to provide loans when it does not have sufficient liquidity or when the borrower is a very poor credit risk.

Trading Activities and Risk Management Techniques

We have already mentioned that banks' attempts to manage interest-rate risk have led them to trading in financial futures, options for debt instruments, and interest-rate swaps. Banks engaged in international banking also conduct transactions in the for-eign exchange market. All transactions in these markets are off-balance-sheet activities because they do not have a direct effect on the bank's balance sheet. Although bank trading in these markets is often directed toward reducing risk or facilitating other bank business, banks also try to outguess the markets and engage in speculation. This specu-lation can be a very risky business and has led to bank insolvencies, the most dramatic being the failure of Barings, a British bank, in 1995.

Trading activities, although often highly profitable, are also highly risky because they make it easy for financial institutions and their employees to make huge bets quickly. The principal–agent problem, discussed in Chapter 8, is an especially severe problem for management of trading activities. Because a trader (the agent) has the opportunity to place large bets, whether she trades in bond markets, foreign exchange markets, or financial derivatives, she has an incentive to take on excessive risks: If her trading strategy leads to large profits, she is likely to receive a high salary and bonuses, but if she takes large losses, the financial institution (the principal) will have to cover them. As the Barings Bank failure of 1995 so forcefully demonstrated, a trader subject to the principal–agent problem can take an institution that is quite healthy and drive it into insolvency very rapidly (see the following Global box).

To reduce the principal–agent problem, managers of financial institutions must set up internal controls to prevent debacles like the one at Barings. Such controls include the complete separation of the people in charge of trading activities from those in charge of the bookkeeping for trades. In addition, managers must set limits on the total amount of traders' transactions and on the institution's risk exposure. Managers must also scrutinize risk assessment procedures using the latest computer technology. One such method involves the value-at-risk approach. In this approach, the institution develops a statistical model with which it can calculate the maximum loss that its portfolio is likely

Global   Barings, Daiwa, Sumitomo, Société Générale, and JP Morgan Chase: Rogue Traders and the Principal–Agent Problem

The demise of Barings, a venerable British bank more than a century old, is a sad morality tale of how the principal–agent problem operating through a rogue trader can take a financial institution that has a healthy balance sheet one month and turn it into an insolvent tragedy the next.

In July 1992, Nick Leeson, Barings's new head clerk at its Singapore branch, began to speculate on the Nikkei, the Japanese version of the Dow Jones stock index. By late 1992, Leeson had suffered losses of $3 million, which he hid from his superiors by stashing the losses in a secret account. He even fooled his superiors into thinking he was generating large profits, thanks to a failure of internal controls at his firm, which allowed him to execute trades on the Singapore exchange *and* oversee the bookkeeping of those trades. (As anyone who runs a cash business, such as a bar, knows, there is always a lower likelihood of fraud if more than one person handles the cash. Similarly, in trading operations, you never mix management of the back room with management of the front room; this principle was grossly violated by Barings management.)

Things didn't get better for Leeson, who by late 1994 had suffered losses exceeding $250 million. In January and February of 1995, Leeson bet the bank. On January 17, 1995, the day of the earthquake in Kobe, Japan, he lost $75 million, and by the end of the week he had lost more than $150 million. When the stock market declined on February 23, leaving him with a further loss of $250 million, he called it quits and fled Singapore. Three days later, he turned himself in at the Frankfurt airport. By the end of his wild ride, Leeson's losses, $1.3 billion in all, ate up Barings's capital and caused the bank to fail. Leeson was subsequently convicted and sent to jail in Singapore for his activities. He was released in 1999 and apologized for his actions.

Our asymmetric information analysis of the principal–agent problem explains Leeson's behaviour and highlights the danger of a management lapse like Barings's. Letting Leeson control both his own trades and the back room increased asymmetric information, because it reduced the principal's (Barings's) knowledge about Leeson's trading activities. This lapse increased the moral hazard incentive for him to take risks at the bank's expense, as he was now less likely to be caught. Furthermore, once he had experienced large losses, he had even greater incentives to take on even higher risk because, if his bets worked out, he could reverse his losses and keep in good standing with the company; whereas if his bets soured, he had little to lose because he was out of a job anyway. Indeed, the bigger his losses, the more he had to gain by bigger bets, which explains the escalation of the amount of his trades as his losses mounted. If Barings's managers had understood the principal–agent problem, they would have been more vigilant at finding out what Leeson was up to, and the bank might still be here today.

Unfortunately, Nick Leeson is no longer a rarity in the rogue traders' billionaires club, made up of those who have lost more than $1 billion. Over eleven years, Toshihide Iguchi, an officer in the New York branch of Daiwa Bank, also had control of both the bond trading operation and the back room bookkeeping activities, and he racked up $1.1 billion in losses over the period. In July 1995, Iguchi disclosed his losses to his superiors, but the management of the bank did not disclose them to its regulators. The result was that Daiwa was slapped with a $340 million fine and the bank was thrown out of the country by U.S. bank regulators.

Yasuo Hamanaka is another member of the billionaires club. In July 1996, he topped Leeson's and Iguchi's record, losing $2.6 billion for his employer, the Sumitomo Corporation, one of Japan's top trading companies. In January 2008, Jerome Kerviel's loss for his bank, Société Générale, set the all-time record for a rogue trader: His unauthorized trades cost the French bank $7.2 billion. In 2012, even the highly successful JP Morgan Chase bank experienced a trading loss of over $2 billion, caused by rogue trader Bruno Iksill, who was colourfully nicknamed "the London Whale."

The moral of these stories is that management of firms engaged in trading activities must reduce the principal–agent problem by closely monitoring their traders' activities, or the rogues' gallery will continue to grow.

to sustain over a given time interval, dubbed the value at risk, or VaR. For example, a bank might estimate that the maximum loss it would be likely to sustain over one day with a probability of 1 in 100 is $1 million; the $1 million figure is the bank's calculated value at risk. Another approach is called "stress testing." In this approach, a manager uses a computer model to project what would happen if a doomsday scenario occurred; that is, she looks at the losses the institution would sustain in the event of an unusual combination of bad events. With the value-at-risk approach and stress testing, a financial institution can assess its risk exposure and take steps to reduce it.

U.S. bank regulators have become concerned about the increased risk that banks are facing from their off-balance-sheet activities and, as we discussed in Chapter 10, are encouraging banks to pay increased attention to risk management. In addition, the Bank for International Settlements is developing additional bank capital requirements based on value-at-risk calculations for a bank's trading activities.

MyEconLab

MyEconLab is an online homework and tutorial system that puts you in control of your own learning with study and practice tools directly correlated to this chapter's content. Visit MyEconLab to access the eText, the Questions and Applied Problems with answers, as well as additional assessment. You will also find web chapters, mini-lectures, appendices, mini-cases, videos, glossary flashcards, news feeds, CANSIM data, and graphing tools.

SUMMARY

1. The balance sheet of a commercial bank can be thought of as a list of the sources and uses of bank funds. A bank's liabilities are its sources of funds, which include chequable deposits, time deposits, advances from the Bank of Canada, borrowings from other banks and corporations, and bank capital. A bank's assets are its uses of funds, which include reserves, cash items in process of collection, deposits at other banks, securities, loans, and other assets (mostly physical capital).

2. Banks make profits through the process of asset transformation: They borrow short (accept short-term deposits) and lend long (make long-term loans). When a bank takes in additional deposits, it gains an equal amount of reserves; when it pays out deposits, it loses an equal amount of reserves.

3. Although more-liquid assets tend to earn lower returns, banks still desire to hold them. Specifically, banks hold excess and secondary reserves because they provide insurance against the costs of a deposit outflow. Banks manage their assets to maximize

profits by seeking the highest returns possible on loans and securities while at the same time trying to lower risk and make adequate provisions for liquidity. Although liability management was once a staid affair, large (money centre) banks now actively seek out sources of funds by issuing liabilities such as negotiable CDs or by actively borrowing from other banks and corporations. Banks manage the amount of capital they hold with the goals of preventing bank failure and meeting bank capital requirements set by the regulatory authorities. However, banks do not want to hold too much capital because by so doing they will lower the returns to equity holders.

4. The concepts of adverse selection and moral hazard explain many credit risk management principles involving loan activities: screening and monitoring, establishment of long-term customer relationships and loan commitments, collateral and compensating balances, and credit rationing.

5. With the increased volatility of interest rates that occurred in the 1980s, financial institutions became

more concerned about their exposure to interest-rate risk. Gap and duration analyses tell a financial institution if it has more rate-sensitive liabilities than assets (in which case a rise in interest rates will reduce profits, and a fall in interest rates will raise profits). Financial institutions manage their interest-rate risk by modifying their balance sheets, but can also use strategies involving financial derivatives.

6. Off-balance-sheet activities consist of trading financial instruments and generating income from fees and loan sales, all of which affect bank profits but are not visible on bank balance sheets. Because these off-balance-sheet activities expose banks to increased risk, bank management must pay particular attention to risk assessment procedures and internal controls to restrict employees from taking on too much risk.

KEY TERMS

advances, p. 285
asset management, p. 290
asset transformation, p. 287
balance sheet, p. 283
banker's risk, p. 286
bank rate, p. 292
capital adequacy management, p. 290
compensating balances, p. 301
credit rationing, p. 302
credit risk, p. 290
deposit outflows, p. 290

desired reserve ratio, p. 286
desired reserves, p. 286
duration analysis, p. 304
equity multiplier (EM), p. 296
gap analysis, p. 303
interest-rate risk, p. 290
liability management, p. 290
liquidity management, p. 290
loan commitments, p. 301
loan sale, p. 305
money centre banks, p. 294

off-balance-sheet activities, p. 305
overdraft loans, p. 285
reserves, p. 285
return on assets (ROA), p. 296
return on equity (ROE), p. 296
secondary reserves, p. 286
settlement balances, p. 285
T-account, p. 287
vault cash, p. 285

QUESTIONS

All questions are available in MyEconLab at **www.myeconlab.com.**

1. Why might a bank be willing to borrow funds from other banks at a higher rate than the rate at which it can borrow from the Bank of Canada?

2. Rank the following bank assets from most to least liquid:

a. Commercial loans

b. Securities

c. Reserves

d. Physical capital

3. The bank you own has the following balance sheet:

Assets		Liabilities	
Reserves	$ 75 million	Deposits	$500 million
Loans	$525 million	Bank capital	$100 million

If the bank suffers a deposit outflow of $50 million with a desired reserve ratio on deposits of 10%, what actions should you take?

4. If a deposit outflow of $50 million occurs, which balance sheet would a bank rather have initially, the balance sheet in Question 3 or the following balance sheet? Why?

Assets		Liabilities	
Reserves	$100 million	Deposits	$500 million
Loans	$500 million	Bank capital	$100 million

5. Why has the development of overnight loan markets made it more likely that banks will hold fewer excess reserves?

6. If the bank you own has no excess reserves and a sound customer comes in asking for a loan, should you automatically turn the customer down, explaining that you don't have any excess reserves to lend out? Why or why not? What options are available that will enable you to provide the funds your customer needs?

7. If a bank finds that its ROE is too low because it has too much bank capital, what can it do to raise its ROE?

8. If a bank is falling short of meeting its capital requirements by $1 million, what three things can it do to rectify the situation?

9. Why do equity holders care more about ROE than about ROA?

10. If a bank doubles the amount of its capital and ROA stays constant, what will happen to ROE?

11. What are the benefits and costs for a bank when it decides to increase the amount of its bank capital?

12. Why is being nosy a desirable trait for a banker?

13. A bank almost always insists that the firms it lends to keep compensating balances at the bank. Why?

14. If the CEO of a bank told you that the bank was so well run that it has never had to call in loans, sell securities, or borrow as a result of a deposit outflow, would you be willing to buy stock in that bank? Why or why not?

15. "Because diversification is a desirable strategy for avoiding risk, it never makes sense for a bank to specialize in making specific types of loans." Is this statement true, false, or uncertain? Explain your answer.

16. If you are a banker and expect interest rates to rise in the future, would you prefer to make short-term loans or long-term loans?

17. "Bank managers should always seek the highest return possible on their assets." Is this statement true, false, or uncertain? Explain your answer.

18. Why has noninterest income been growing as a source of bank operating income?

APPLIED PROBLEMS

All applied problems are available in MyEconLab at **www.myeconlab.com**.

19. Using the T-accounts of the First National Bank and the Second National Bank given in this chapter, describe what happens when Jane Brown writes a $50 cheque on her account at the First National Bank to pay her friend Joe Green, who in turn deposits the cheque in his account at the Second National Bank.

20. What happens to reserves at the First National Bank if one person withdraws $1000 of cash and another person deposits $500 of cash? Use T-accounts to explain your answer.

Questions 21 and 22 relate to the first month's operations of NewBank.

21. NewBank started its first day of operations with $6 million in capital. A total of $100 million in chequable deposits is received. The bank makes a $25 million commercial loan and lends another $25 million in mortgage loans. If desired reserves are 8%, what does the bank balance sheet look like?

22. NewBank decides to invest $45 million in 30-day T-bills. The T-bills are currently trading at $4986.70 (including commissions) for a $5000 face value instrument. How many T-bills does NewBank purchase? What does the balance sheet look like?

23. X-Bank reported an ROE of 15% and an ROA of 1%. How well capitalized is this bank?

24. Suppose you are the manager of a bank whose $100 billion of assets have an average duration of four years and whose $90 billion of liabilities have an average duration of six years. Conduct a duration analysis for the bank, and show what will happen to the net worth of the bank if interest rates rise by 2 percentage points. What actions could you take to reduce the bank's interest-rate risk?

25. Suppose you are the manager of a bank that has $15 million of fixed-rate assets, $30 million of rate-sensitive assets, $25 million of fixed-rate liabilities, and $20 million of rate-sensitive liabilities. Conduct a gap analysis for the bank, and show what will happen to bank profits if interest rates rise by 5 percentage points. What actions could you take to reduce the bank's interest-rate risk?

DATA ANALYSIS PROBLEMS

Download data for these problems from MyEconLab at
www.myeconlab.com.

1. Go to the Office of the Superintendent of Financial Institutions (OSFI) website and find data for all domestic banks on total liabilities, total deposits, and residual of assets less liabilities.

   a. What is the balance sheet interpretation of the residual of assets less liabilities?

   b. For the most recent month of data available, use the three indicators listed above to calculate the total amount of borrowings by banks.

2. Go to the OSFI website and find data for all banks on total assets, reserves, securities held, commercial and industrial loans, mortgage loans, and other assets. Use the most recent month of data available across all indicators.

   a. What is the total amount of loans held by banks? What is this number as a percentage of total bank assets?

WEB EXERCISES

1. It is relatively easy to find up-to-date information on banks because of their extensive reporting requirements. Go to the OSFI website and find balance sheet data on domestic banks as well as on foreign bank subsidiaries.

   a. Have bank loans been increasing or decreasing over the past few years?

   b. Has bank capital been increasing? How does it compare to the figure reported in Table 12-1?

2. Table 12-1 reports the balance sheet of all commercial banks based on aggregate data found on the OSFI website. Compare this table to the balance sheet information reported by CIBC in its latest annual report (found at **www.cibc.com/ca/investor-relations/annual-reports.html**). Does CIBC have more or less of its portfolio in loans than the average Canadian bank?

WEB REFERENCES

www.cibc.com/ca/personal.html
Click on Annual Reports to view the balance sheet.

www.osfi-bsif.gc.ca/eng/Pages/default.aspx
Click on Financial Institutions to find data on banks, trust and loan companies, and cooperative credit and retail associations.

13

Risk Management with Financial Derivatives

1.39 · 1.47

Learning Objectives

After studying this chapter you should be able to

1. Define a hedge, a long position, and a short position.

2. Define a forward contract and summarize its advantages and disadvantages.

3. Summarize the differences between a forward contract and a financial futures contract.

4. Identify the different types of options contracts, and summarize the three conclusions regarding call and put options.

5. Define a swap, and summarize the advantages and disadvantages of interest-rate swaps.

6. Summarize the three types of credit derivatives.

PREVIEW

Starting in the 1970s and increasingly in the 1980s and 1990s, the world became a riskier place for financial institutions. Swings in interest rates widened, and the bond and stock markets went through some episodes of increased volatility. As a result of these developments, managers of financial institutions have become more concerned with reducing the risk their institutions face. Given the greater demand for risk reduction, the process of financial innovation came to the rescue by producing new assets that help financial institution managers manage risk better. These instruments, called **financial derivatives**, have payoffs that are linked to previously issued securities and are extremely useful risk reduction tools.

In this chapter we look at the most important financial derivatives that managers of financial institutions use to reduce risk: forward contracts, financial futures, options, and swaps. We examine not only how markets for each of these financial derivatives work but also how each can be used by financial institutions to manage risk. We also study financial derivatives because they have become an important source of profits for financial institutions, particularly larger banks.

HEDGING

Financial derivatives are effective in reducing risk because they enable financial institutions to **hedge**, that is, engage in a financial transaction that reduces or eliminates risk. When a financial institution has bought an asset, it is said to have taken a **long position**, and this exposes the institution to risk if the returns on the asset are uncertain. Conversely, if it has sold an asset that it has agreed to deliver to another party at a future date, it is said to have taken a **short position**, and this can also expose the institution to risk. Financial derivatives can be used to reduce risk by invoking the following basic principle of hedging: *hedging risk involves engaging in a financial transaction that offsets a long position by taking an additional short position, or offsets a short position by taking an additional long position.* In other words, if a financial institution has bought a security and has therefore taken a long position, it conducts a hedge by contracting to sell that security (take a short position) at some future date. Alternatively, if it has taken a short position by selling a security that it needs to deliver at a future date, then it conducts a hedge by contracting to buy that security (take a long position) at a future date. We first look at how this principle can be applied using forward contracts.

FORWARD CONTRACTS AND MARKETS

Forward contracts are agreements by two parties to engage in a financial transaction at a future (forward) point in time. Here we focus on forward contracts that are linked to debt instruments, called **interest-rate forward contracts**; later in the chapter we discuss forward contracts for foreign currencies.

Interest-Rate Forward Contracts

Interest-rate forward contracts involve the future sale (or purchase) of a debt instrument and have several dimensions: (1) specification of the actual debt instrument that will be delivered at a future date; (2) the amount of the debt instrument to be delivered; (3) the price (or interest rate) on the debt instrument when it is delivered; and (4) the date on which delivery will take place. An example of an interest-rate forward contract might be an agreement for the First Bank to sell to the Rock Solid Insurance Company, one year from today, $5 million face value of the 6s of 2030 Canada bonds (that is, coupon bonds with a 6% coupon rate that mature in 2030) at a price that yields the same interest rate on these bonds as today's rate—say, 6%. Because Rock Solid will buy the securities at a future date, it has taken a long position, while the First Bank, which will sell the securities on that date, has taken a short position.

APPLICATION   ## Hedging with Interest-Rate Forward Contracts

Why would the First Bank want to enter into this forward contract with Rock Solid Insurance Company in the first place?

To understand, suppose that you are the manager of the First Bank and have previously bought $5 million of the 6s of 2030 Canada bonds. The bonds are currently selling at par value, so their yield to maturity is also 6%. Because these are long-term bonds, you recognize that you are exposed to substantial interest-rate risk: If interest rates rise in the future, the price of these bonds will fall, resulting in a substantial capital loss that may cost you your job. How do you hedge this risk?

Knowing the basic principle of hedging, you see that your long position in these bonds can be offset by an equally short position for the same bonds with a forward contract. That is, you need to contract to sell these bonds at a future date at the current par value price. To ensure that this happens, you form an agreement with another party—in this case, Rock Solid Insurance Company—in which you promise to sell to Rock Solid the $5 million of the 6s of 2030 Canada bonds at par one year from today. By entering into this forward contract, you have successfully hedged against interest rate risk. By locking in the future price of the bonds, you have eliminated the price risk that you face from uncertain interest-rate changes.

Why would Rock Solid Insurance Company want to enter into the forward contract with the First Bank? Rock Solid expects to receive premiums of $5 million in one year's time that it will want to invest in the 6s of 2030, but worries that interest rates on these bonds will decline between now and next year. By using the forward contract, it is able to lock in the 6% interest rate on the Canada bonds that will be sold to it by the First Bank. ◆

Pros and Cons of Forward Contracts

The advantage of forward contracts is that they can be as flexible as the parties involved want them to be. This means that an institution like the First Bank may be able to hedge completely the interest-rate risk on the exact security it is holding in its portfolio, just as it did in our example.

However, forward contracts suffer from two problems that severely limit their usefulness. The first is that it may be very hard for an institution like the First Bank to find another party (called a *counterparty*) to make the contract with. There are brokers to facilitate the matching up of parties like the First Bank with the Rock Solid Insurance Company, but few institutions may want to engage in a forward contract specifically for the 6s of 2030. This means that it may prove impossible to find a counterparty when a financial institution like the First Bank wants to make a specific type of forward contract. Furthermore, even if the First Bank finds a counterparty, it may not get as high a price as it wants because there may not be anyone else to make the deal with. A serious problem for the market in interest-rate forward contracts, then, is that it may be difficult to make the financial transaction or that it will have to be made at a disadvantageous price; in the parlance of financial economists, this market suffers from a *lack of liquidity*. (Note that this use of the term *liquidity* when it is applied to a market is somewhat broader than its use when it is applied to an asset. For an asset, liquidity refers to the ease with which the asset can be turned into cash; for a market, liquidity refers to the ease of carrying out financial transactions.)

The second problem with forward contracts is that they are subject to default risk. Suppose that in one year's time, interest rates rise so that the price of the 6s of 2030 falls. The Rock Solid Insurance Company might then decide that it would like to default on the forward contract with the First Bank, because it can now buy the bonds at a lower price. Or perhaps Rock Solid may not have been rock solid after all, and may have gone bust during the year, and is no longer available to complete the terms of the forward contract. Because no outside organization is guaranteeing the contract, the only recourse is for the First Bank to go to the courts to sue Rock Solid, but this process will be costly. Furthermore, if Rock Solid is already bankrupt, the First Bank will suffer a loss; the bank can no longer sell the 6s of 2030 at the price it had agreed with Rock Solid, but instead will have to sell at a price well below that, because the price of these bonds has fallen.

The presence of default risk in forward contracts means that parties to these contracts must check that the counterparty is both financially sound and likely to live up to its contractual obligations. Because this type of investigation is costly, and because all the adverse selection and moral hazard problems discussed in earlier chapters apply, default risk is a major barrier to the use of interest-rate forward contracts. If we consider the dual problems of default risk and lack of liquidity, we see that forward contracts may be of limited usefulness to financial institutions. Although a market does exist for interest-rate forward contracts and mortgage-backed securities, it is not nearly as large as the financial futures market, to which we turn next.

FINANCIAL FUTURES CONTRACTS AND MARKETS

Given the default risk and liquidity problems inherent in the interest-rate forward market, another solution to hedging interest-rate, stock market, and foreign exchange risks was needed. The solution was provided by the Chicago Board of Trade when it began developing financial futures contracts in 1975.

Financial futures are classified as (1) interest-rate futures, (2) stock index futures, and (3) currency futures. In Canada, such contracts are traded on the Montréal Exchange (ME), which maintains active markets in short- and long-term Canada bond futures and stock index futures. In what follows, we discuss interest-rate and stock index futures. Later in the chapter, we also discuss currency futures.

Interest-Rate Futures Contracts

An **interest-rate futures contract** is similar to an interest-rate forward contract in that it specifies that a financial instrument must be delivered by one party to another on a stated future date. However, it differs from an interest-rate forward contract in several ways, and these differences help overcome some of the liquidity and default problems of forward markets.

To understand what interest-rate futures contracts are all about, let's look at one of the most widely traded futures contracts, that for 10-year Canada bonds, which are traded on the Montréal Exchange. The contract value is for $100 000 face value of bonds. Prices are quoted in points, with each point equal to $1000, and the smallest change in price is one hundredth of a point ($10). This contract specifies that the bonds to be delivered must have at least 10 years to maturity at the delivery date. If the Canada bonds delivered to settle the futures contract have a coupon rate different from the (for example) 6% specified in the futures contract, the amount of bonds to be delivered is adjusted to reflect the difference in value between the delivered bonds and the 6% coupon bond. In line with the terminology used for forward contracts, parties who have bought a futures contract and thereby have agreed to buy (take delivery of) the bonds are said to have taken a *long position*, and parties who have sold a futures contract and thereby have agreed to sell (deliver) the bonds have taken a *short position*.

To make our understanding of this contract more concrete, let's consider what happens when you buy or sell one of these Canada bond futures contracts. Let's say that on January 1, you sell one $100 000 March contract at a price of 115 (that is, $115 000). By selling this contract, you agree to deliver $100 000 face value of the long-term Canada bonds to the contract's counterparty at the end of March for $115 000. By buying the contract at a price of 115, the buyer has agreed to pay $115 000 for the $100 000 face value of bonds when you deliver them at the end of March. If interest rates on long-term bonds rise so that when the contract matures at the end of March the price of these bonds has fallen to 110 ($110 000 per $100 000 of face value), the buyer of the contract will have lost $5000 because he or she paid $115 000 for the bonds but can sell them only for the market price of $110 000. But you, the seller of the contract, will have gained $5000 because you can now sell the bonds to the buyer for $115 000 but have to pay only $110 000 for them in the market.

It is even easier to describe what happens to the parties who have purchased futures contracts and those who have sold futures contracts if we recognize the following fact: *at the expiration date of a futures contract, the price of the contract is the same as the price of the underlying asset to be delivered.* To see why this is the case, consider what happens on the expiration date of the March contract at the end of March when the price of the underlying $100 000-face-value Canada bond is 110 ($110 000). If the futures contract is selling below 110, say, at 109, a trader can buy the contract for $109 000, take delivery of the bond, and immediately sell it for $110 000, thereby earning a quick profit of $1000. Because earning this profit involves no risk, it is a great deal that everyone would like to get in on. That means that everyone will try to buy the contract, and as a result, its price will rise. Only when the price rises to 110 will the profit opportunity cease to exist and the buying pressure disappear. Conversely, if the price of the futures contract is above 110, say, at 111, everyone will want to sell the contract. Now the sellers get $111 000 from selling the futures contract but have to pay only $110 000 for the Canada bonds that they must deliver to the buyer of the contract, and the $1000 difference is their profit. Because this profit involves no risk, traders will continue to sell the futures contract until its price falls back down to 110, at which price there are no longer any profits to be made. The elimination of riskless profit opportunities in the futures market is referred to as **arbitrage**, and it guarantees that the price of a futures contract at expiration equals the price of the underlying asset to be delivered.[1]

Armed with our knowledge that a futures contract at expiration equals the price of the underlying asset, we can see even more easily who profits and who loses from such a contract when interest rates change. If interest rates have risen, so that the price of the Canada bond is 110 on the expiration day at the end of March, the March Canada bond futures contract will also have a price of 110. Thus, if you bought the contract for 115 in January, you have suffered a loss of 5 points, or $5000 (5% of $100 000). But if you sold the futures contract at 115 in January, the decline in price to 110 means that you have gained a profit of 5 points, or $5000.

APPLICATION   Hedging with Interest-Rate Futures

The First Bank can also use interest-rate futures to hedge the interest-rate risk on its holdings of $5 million of the 6s of 2030 (Canada bonds with a 6% coupon rate that mature in 2030). To see how, suppose that in March 2016, the 6s of 2030 are the long-term bonds that would be delivered in the Montréal Exchange's Canada bond futures contract expiring one year in the future, in March 2017. Also suppose that the interest rate on these bonds is expected to remain at 6% over the next year, so that both the 6s of 2030 and the futures contract are selling at par (i.e., the $5 million of bonds is selling for $5 million and the $100 000 futures contract is selling for $100 000). The basic principle of hedging indicates that you, as the manager of the First Bank, need to offset the long position in these bonds with a short position, so you have to sell the futures contract. But how many contracts should you sell? The number of contracts required to hedge the interest-rate risk is found by dividing the amount of the asset to be hedged by the dollar value of each contract, as shown in Equation 1.

$$NC = VA/VC \qquad \text{(Equation 1)}$$

where

NC = number of contracts for the hedge
VA = value of the asset
VC = value of each contract

---

[1]In actuality, futures contracts sometimes set conditions for delivery of the underlying assets that cause the price of the contract at expiration to differ slightly from the price of the underlying assets. Because the difference in price is extremely small, we ignore it in this chapter.

Given that the 6s of 2030 are the long-term bonds that would be delivered in the Montréal Exchange's Canada bond futures contract expiring one year in the future and that the interest rate on these bonds is expected to remain at 6% over the next year, so that both the 6s of 2030 and the futures contract are selling at par, how many contracts must the First Bank sell to remove its interest-rate exposure from its $5 million holdings of the 6s of 2030?[2]

Since VA = $5 million and VC = $100 000,

$$NC = \$5 \text{ million}/\$100\,000 = 50$$

You therefore hedge the interest-rate risk by selling 50 of the Canada bond futures contracts. Now suppose that over the next year, an increased threat of inflation causes interest rates to increase to 8%. The value of the 6s of 2030 that the First Bank is holding will then fall to $4 039 640 in March 2017.[3] Thus, the loss from the long position in these bonds is $960 360:

Value in March 2017 @ 8% interest rate	$4 039 640
Value in March 2016 @ 6% interest rate	−$5 000 000
Loss	−$ 960 360

However, the short position in the 50 futures contracts that obligate you to deliver $5 million of the 6s of 2030 in March 2017 has a value equal to $4 039 640, the value of the $5 million of bonds after the interest rate has risen to 8%. Yet when you sold the futures contract, the buyer was obligated to pay you $5 million on the maturity date. Thus the gain from the short position on these contracts is also $960 360:

Amount paid to you in March 2017, agreed in March 2016	$5 000 000
Value of bonds delivered in March 2017 @ 8% interest rate	−$4 039 640
Gain	$ 960 360

Therefore, the net gain for the First Bank is zero, showing that the hedge has been conducted successfully.

The hedge just described is called a **micro hedge** because the financial institution is hedging the interest-rate risk for a specific asset it is holding. A second type of hedge that financial institutions engage in is called a **macro hedge**, in which the hedge is for the institution's entire portfolio. For example, if a bank has more rate-sensitive liabilities than assets, a rise in interest rates will cause the value of the bank's net worth to decline. By selling interest-rate futures contracts that will yield a profit when interest rates rise, the bank can offset the losses on its overall portfolio from an interest-rate rise and thereby hedge its interest-rate risk. ◆

Organization of Trading in Financial Futures Markets

Financial futures contracts are traded on organized exchanges such as the Chicago Board of Trade, the Chicago Mercantile Exchange, the Montréal Exchange, the London International Financial Futures Exchange, and the Marché à Terme International de France. These

---

[2] In the real world, designing a hedge is somewhat more complicated than the example here, because the bond that is most likely to be delivered might not be a 6s of 2030.

[3] The value of the bonds can be calculated using a financial calculator as follows: FV = $5 000 000, PMT = $300 000, I = 8%, N = 14, PV = $4 039 640.

TABLE 13-1	Widely Traded Financial Futures Contracts in the United States

Type of Contract	Contract Size	Open Interest, August 2014
Interest-Rate Contracts		
Treasury bonds	$100 000	984 935
Treasury notes	$100 000	2 753 371
Five-year Treasury notes	$100 000	2 192 905
Two-year Treasury notes	$200 000	1 377 298
Thirty-day Fed funds rate	$5 million	544 115
Eurodollar	$4 million	12 988 737
Stock Index Contracts		
Standard & Poor's 500 Index	$250 × index	164 586
Standard & Poor's MIDCAP 400	$500 × index	835
NASDAQ 100	$100 × index	7001
Nikkei 225 Stock Average	$5 × index	62 676
Currency Contracts		
Yen	12 500 000 yen	226 449
Euro	125 000 euros	413 159
Canadian dollar	100 000 Canadian $	110 965
British pound	100 000 pounds	234 219
Swiss franc	125 000 francs	57 511
Mexican peso	500 000 new pesos	147 059

Source: CME Group: **www.cmegroup.com/market-data/volume-open-interest**; click on CME Group Open Interest Report.

futures exchanges are highly competitive with one another, and each organization tries to design contracts and set rules that will increase the amount of futures trading on its exchange. The exchanges are also regulated to ensure that prices in the market are not being manipulated. Listed in Table 13-1 are the most widely traded financial futures contracts in the United States, along with their contract size and the number of contracts outstanding, called **open interest**, for August 2014.

Given the globalization of other financial markets in recent years, it is not surprising that increased international competition has been occurring in financial futures markets as well.

The Globalization of Financial Futures Markets

Because futures exchanges in the United States were the first to develop financial futures, they dominated the trading of financial futures in the early 1980s. For example, in 1985, all of the top 10 futures contracts were traded on exchanges in the United States. With the rapid growth of financial futures markets and the resulting high profits made by the American exchanges, exchanges in other countries saw a profit opportunity and began to enter the business. By the 1990s, Eurodollar contracts traded on the London International Financial Futures Exchange, Japanese government bond contracts and Euroyen contracts traded on the Tokyo Stock Exchange, French government bond contracts traded on the Marché à Terme International de France (now Euronext), and Nikkei 225 contracts traded on the Osaka Securities Exchange all were among the most widely traded futures contracts in the world.

International competition has spurred knockoffs of the most popular financial futures contracts initially developed in the United States. These contracts, which are traded on financial futures exchanges in other countries, are virtually identical to those traded in the United States and have the advantage that they can be traded when the American exchanges are closed. The movement to 24-hour-a-day trading in financial futures has been further stimulated by the development of the Globex electronic trading platform, which allows traders throughout the world to trade futures even when the exchanges are not officially open. Financial futures trading thus has become completely internationalized, and competition between U.S. and other exchanges is now intense.

Explaining the Success of Futures Markets

Futures contracts were designed to overcome the liquidity problem inherent in forward contracts. They do this in several ways. First, in contrast to forward contracts, the quantities delivered and the delivery dates of futures contracts are standardized, making it more likely that different parties can be matched up in the futures market, thereby increasing the liquidity of the market. In the case of the 10-year Canada bond futures contract, the quantity delivered is $100 000 face value of bonds, and the delivery dates are set to be the last business day of March, June, September, and December. Second, after the futures contract has been bought or sold, it can be traded (bought or sold) again at any time until the delivery date. In contrast, once a forward contract is agreed on, it typically cannot be traded. Third, in a futures contract, not just one specific type of Canada bond is deliverable on the delivery date, as is the case in a forward contract. Instead, any Canada bond that matures in more than 10 years and is not callable for 10 years is eligible for delivery. Allowing continuous trading also increases the liquidity of the futures market, as does the option to deliver a range of Canada bonds rather than one specific bond.

Another reason why futures contracts specify that more than one bond is eligible for delivery is to limit the possibility that someone might corner the market and "squeeze" traders who have sold contracts. To corner the market, someone buys up all the deliverable securities so that investors with a short position cannot obtain from anyone else the securities that they contractually must deliver on the delivery date. As a result, the person who has cornered the market can set exorbitant prices for the securities that investors with a short position must buy to fulfill their obligations under the futures contract. The person who has cornered the market makes a fortune, but investors with a short position take a terrific loss. Clearly, the possibility that corners might occur in the market will discourage people from taking a short position and might therefore decrease the size of the market. By allowing for the delivery of many different securities, the futures contract makes it harder for anyone to corner the market, because a much larger amount of securities would have to be purchased to establish the corner. Corners are a concern to both regulators and the organized exchanges that design futures contracts.

Trading in the futures market has been organized differently from trading in forward markets in order to overcome the default risk problems inherent in forward contracts. In both types of markets, for every contract, there must be a buyer who is taking a long position and a seller who is taking a short position. However, the buyer and seller of a futures contract make their contract not with each other but with the clearinghouse associated with the futures exchange. This setup means that, in contrast to the forward market, the buyer of the futures contract does not need to worry about the financial health or trustworthiness of the seller, and vice versa. As long as the clearinghouse is financially solid, buyers and sellers of futures contracts do not have to worry about default risk.

To make sure that the clearinghouse is financially sound and does not run into financial difficulties that might jeopardize its contracts, buyers or sellers of futures contracts must put an initial deposit, called a **margin requirement**, of perhaps $2000 per Canada bond contract into a margin account kept at their brokerage firm. Futures contracts are then **marked to market** every day. At the end of every trading day, the change in the value of the futures contract is added to or subtracted from the margin account. Suppose that after buying the Canada bond contract at a price of 115 on Wednesday morning, its closing price at the end of the day, the *settlement price*, falls to 114. You now have a loss of 1 point, or $1000, on the contract, and the seller who sold you the contract has a gain of 1 point, or $1000. The $1000 gain is added to the seller's margin account, making a total of $3000 in that account, and the $1000 loss is subtracted from your account, so you now only have $1000 in your account. If the amount in this margin account falls below the maintenance margin requirement (which can be the same as the initial requirement, but is usually a little less), the trader is required to add money to the account. For example, if the maintenance margin requirement is also $2000, you would have to add $1000 to your account to bring it up to $2000. Margin requirements and marking to market make it far less likely that a trader will default on a contract, thus protecting the futures exchange from losses.

A final advantage that futures markets have over forward markets is that most futures contracts do not result in delivery of the underlying asset on the expiration date, whereas forward contracts do. A trader who sold a futures contract is allowed to avoid delivery on the expiration date by making an offsetting purchase of a futures contract. Because the simultaneous holding of the long and short positions means that the trader would in effect be delivering the bonds to itself, under the exchange rules the trader is allowed to cancel both contracts. Allowing traders to cancel their contracts in this way lowers the cost of conducting trades in the futures market relative to the forward market: a futures trader can avoid the costs of physical delivery, something that is not so easy with forward contracts.

APPLICATION   Hedging Foreign Exchange Risk

As we discussed in Chapter 1, foreign exchange rates have been highly volatile in recent years. The large fluctuations in exchange rates subject financial institutions and other businesses to significant foreign exchange risk because such fluctuations generate substantial gains and losses. Luckily for financial institution managers, the financial derivatives discussed in this chapter—forward and financial futures contracts—can be used to hedge foreign exchange risk.

To understand how financial institution managers manage foreign exchange risk, let's suppose that in January, the First Bank's customer Frivolous Luxuries, Inc. is due a payment of 10 million euros in two months for $14 million worth of goods it has just sold in Germany. Frivolous Luxuries is concerned that if the value of the euro falls substantially from its current value of $1.40, the company might suffer a large loss because the 10 million euro payment will no longer be worth $14 million. So Sam, the CEO of

Frivolous Luxuries, calls up his friend Mona, the manager of the First Bank, and asks her to hedge this foreign exchange risk for his company. Let's see how the bank manager does this using forward and financial futures contracts.

Hedging Foreign Exchange Risk with Forward Contracts

Forward markets in foreign exchange have been highly developed by commercial banks and investment banking operations that engage in extensive foreign exchange trading and so are widely used to hedge foreign exchange risk. Mona knows that she can use this market to hedge the foreign exchange risk for Frivolous Luxuries. Such a hedge is quite straightforward for her to execute. Because the payment of euros in two months means that Sam will hold a long position in euros at that time, Mona knows that the basic principle of hedging indicates that she should offset this long position by a short position. Thus, she simply enters a forward contract that obligates her to sell 10 million euros two months from now in exchange for dollars at the current forward rate of $1.40 per euro.[4]

In two months, when her customer receives the 10 million euros, the forward contract ensures that they will be exchanged for dollars at an exchange rate of $1.40 per euro, thus yielding $14 million. No matter what happens to future exchange rates, Frivolous Luxuries will be guaranteed $14 million for the goods it sold in Germany. Mona calls up her friend Sam to let him know that his company is now protected from any foreign exchange movements, and he thanks her for her help.

Hedging Foreign Exchange Risk with Futures Contracts

As an alternative, Mona could have used the currency futures market to hedge the foreign exchange risk. In this case, she will do some research and find that the Chicago Mercantile Exchange has a euro contract with a contract amount of 125 000 euros and a price of $1.40 per euro. To conduct the hedge, Mona must sell euros as with the forward contract, to the tune of $14 million of the March futures. How many of the Chicago Mercantile Exchange March euro contracts must Mona sell in order to hedge the 10 million euro payment due in March?

Using Equation 1 with

$$VA = 10 \text{ million euros}$$
$$VC = 125\ 000 \text{ euros}$$

we have

$$NC = 10 \text{ million}/125\ 000 = 80$$

Thus, Mona conducts the hedge by selling 80 of the CME euro contracts. Given the $1.40 per euro price, the sale of the contract yields 80 × 125 000 euros = $14 million. The futures hedge enables her to lock in the exchange rate for Frivolous Luxuries so that it gets its payment of $14 million.

---

[4] The forward exchange rate will probably differ slightly from the current spot rate of $1.40 per euro because the interest rates in Europe and Canada may not be equal. In that case, as we will see from the interest parity condition in the Chapter 18 Appendix, the future expected exchange rate will not equal the current spot rate, and neither will the forward rate. However, since interest differentials have typically been less than 6% at an annual rate (1% bimonthly), the expected appreciation or depreciation of the euro over a two-month period has always been less than 1%. Thus the forward rate is always close to the current spot rate, and our assumption in the example that the forward rate and the spot rate are the same is a reasonable one.

One advantage of using the futures market is that the contract size of 125 000 euros, worth $175 000, is quite a bit smaller than the minimum size of a forward contract, which is usually $1 million or more. However, in this case, the bank manager is making a large enough transaction that she can use either the forward or the futures market. Her choice depends on whether the transaction costs are lower in one market than in the other. If the First Bank is active in the forward market, that market would probably have the lower transaction costs. If the First Bank rarely deals in foreign exchange forward contracts, Mona might do better by sticking with the futures market.   ◆

STOCK INDEX FUTURES

As we have seen, interest rate futures markets can be useful in hedging interest-rate risk. However, financial institution managers, particularly those who manage mutual funds, pension funds, and insurance companies, also worry about **stock market risk**, the risk that occurs because stock prices fluctuate. Stock index futures were developed in 1982 to meet the need to manage stock market risk, and they have become among the most widely traded of all futures contracts. The futures trading in stock price indexes is now controversial because critics assert that it has led to substantial increases in market volatility.

Stock Index Futures Contracts

To understand stock index futures contracts, let's look at the Standard & Poor's 500 Index futures contract, the most widely traded stock index futures contract in North America. (The S&P 500 Index measures the value of 500 of the most widely traded stocks in the United States.) Stock index futures contracts differ from most other financial futures contracts in that they are settled with a cash delivery rather than with the delivery of a security. Cash settlement gives these contracts the advantage of a high degree of liquidity and also rules out the possibility of anyone cornering the market. In the case of the S&P 500 Index contract, at the final settlement date, the cash delivery due is US$250 times the index, so if the index is at 1000 on the final settlement date, $250 000 would be the amount due. The price quotes for this contract are also quoted in terms of index points, so a change of 1 point represents a change of $250 in the contract's value.

To understand what all this means, let's look at what happens when you buy or sell this futures contract. Suppose that on January 1, you sell one March contract at a price of 1000 (that is, $250 000). By selling the contract, you agree to a delivery amount due of $250 times the S&P 500 Index on the expiration date at the end of March. By buying the contract at a price of 1000, the buyer has agreed to pay $250 000 for the delivery amount due of $250 times the S&P 500 Index at the expiration date at the end of March. If the stock market falls so that the S&P 500 Index declines to 900 on the expiration date, the buyer of the contract will have lost $25 000 because he or she has agreed to pay $250 000 for the contract but has a delivery amount due of $225 000 (900 × $250). But you, the seller of the contract, will have a profit of $25 000 because you agreed to receive a $250 000 purchase price for the contract but have a delivery amount due of only $225 000. Because the amounts payable and due are netted out, only $25 000 will change hands; you, the seller of the contract, will receive $25 000 from the buyer.

APPLICATION   # Hedging with Stock Index Futures

Solution

Financial institution managers can use stock index futures contracts to reduce stock market risk.

Suppose that in March 2016, Mort, the portfolio manager of the Rock Solid Insurance Company, has a portfolio of stocks valued at $100 million that moves percentage-wise one-for-one with the S&P Index. Suppose also that the March 2017 S&P 500 Index contracts are currently selling at a price of 1000. How many of these contracts should Mort sell so that he hedges the stock market risk of this portfolio over the next year?

Because Mort is holding a long position, using the basic principle of hedging, he must offset it by taking a short position in which he sells S&P futures. To calculate the number of contracts he needs to sell, he uses Equation 1.

$$VA = \$100 \text{ million}$$
$$VC = \$250 \times 1000 = \$250\,000$$

Thus

$$NC = \$100 \text{ million}/\$250\,00 = 400$$

Mort's hedge therefore involves selling 400 S&P March 2017 futures contracts.

If the S&P Index falls 10% to 900, the $100 million portfolio will suffer a $10 million loss. At the same time, however, Mort makes a profit of $100 \times \$250 = \$25\,000$ per contract because he agreed to be paid $250 000 for each contract at a price of 1000, but at a price of 900 on the expiration date, he has a delivery amount of only $225 000 (900 × $250). Multiplied by 400 contracts, the $25 000 profit per contract yields a total profit of $10 million. The $10 million profit on the futures contract exactly offsets the loss on Rock Solid's stock portfolio, so Mort has been successful in hedging the stock market risk.

Why would Mort be willing to forgo profits when the stock market rises? One reason is that he might be worried that a bear market was imminent, so he wants to protect Rock Solid's portfolio from the coming decline (and so protect his job). ◆

OPTIONS

Another vehicle for hedging interest-rate, foreign exchange, and stock market risk involves the use of options on assets. **Options** are contracts that give the purchaser the option, or *right*, to buy or sell the underlying asset at a specified price, called the **exercise price** or **strike price**, within a specific period of time (the *term to expiration*). The seller (sometimes called the *writer*) of the option is *obligated* to buy or sell the asset to the purchaser if the owner of the option exercises the right to sell or buy. These option contract features are important enough to be emphasized: the *owner* or buyer of an option does not have to exercise the option; he or she can let the option expire without using it. Hence the owner of an option is not obligated to take any action, but rather has the *right* to exercise the contract if he or she so chooses. The seller of an option, by contrast, has no choice in the matter; he or she *must* buy or sell the asset if the owner exercises the option.

Because the right to buy or sell an asset at a specified price has value, the owner of an option is willing to pay an amount for it called a **premium**. There are two types of option contracts: **American options** can be exercised *at any time up to* the expiration date of the contract, and **European options** can be exercised only *on* the expiration date.

Option contracts are written on a number of financial instruments. Options on individual stocks are called **stock options**, and such options have existed for a long time. Option contracts on financial futures, called **financial futures options** or, more commonly, **futures options**, were developed in 1982 and have become the most widely traded option contracts.

You might wonder why option contracts are more likely to be written on financial futures than on underlying financial instruments such as bonds. As we saw earlier in the chapter, at the expiration date, the price of the futures contract and that of the deliverable debt instrument will be the same because of arbitrage. So it would seem that investors should be indifferent about having the option written on the asset or on the futures contract. However, financial futures contracts have been so well designed that their markets are often more liquid than the markets in the underlying assets. So investors would rather have the option contract written on the more liquid instrument, in this case the futures contract. This explains why the most popular futures options are written on many of the same futures contracts listed in Table 13-1.

In Canada, the regulation of option markets is the responsibility of the Canadian Derivatives Clearing Corporation (CDCC), a firm that is jointly owned by Canada's stock exchanges. The regulation of U.S. option markets is split between the Securities and Exchange Commission (SEC), which regulates stock options, and the Commodity Futures Trading Commission (CFTC), which regulates futures options. Regulation focuses on ensuring that writers of options have enough capital to make good on their contractual obligations and on overseeing traders and exchanges to prevent fraud and ensure that the market is not being manipulated.

Stock Options

To understand option contracts more fully, let's first discuss stock options (options on individual stocks) before we turn to the more complicated futures options (that is, options on financial futures).

Profits and Losses on Calls

Profits and Losses on Calls   A **call option** is a contract that gives the owner the right (but not the obligation) to *buy* a stock (from the option writer) at the exercise price within a specific period of time. Since a call represents an option to buy, the purchase of a call is undertaken if the price of the underlying stock is expected to go up. The buyer of a call is said to be **long in a call** and the writer of a call is said to be **short in a call**. The buyer of a call option will have to pay a premium, called a **call premium**, in order to get the writer to sign the contract and assume the risk.

To illustrate the profitability of a call option, suppose you hold a European call option on an equity security with an exercise price of X (say $100) and a call premium of (say $5), as shown in Figure 13-1. If at the expiration date the price of the underlying asset, S, is less than X, the call will not be exercised, resulting in a loss of the premium. At a price above X, the call will be exercised. In particular, at a price between X and $X + \alpha$, the gain would be insufficient to cover the cost of the premium, while at a price above $X + \alpha$ the call will yield a net profit. In fact, at a price above $X + \alpha$, each $1 rise in the price of the asset will cause the profit of the call option to increase by $1.

The payoff function from writing the call option is the mirror image of the payoff function from buying the call and is represented by the dashed line in Figure 13-1. Note that the writer of the call receives the call premium up front and must stand ready

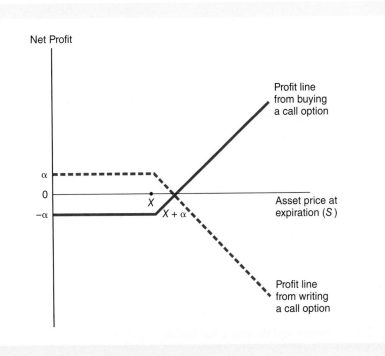

FIGURE 13-1 **Profits from Buying and Writing a Call Option**

to sell the underlying asset to the buyer of the call at the exercise price X, if the buyer exercises the option to buy.

In general, the value of a call option C at expiration with asset price S (at that time) and exercise price X is

$$C = \max(0, S - X)$$

In other words, the value of a call option at maturity (also known as the **intrinsic value**) is the difference between the current asset price and the exercise price, $S - X$, or zero, whichever is greater. If the stock price happens to be greater than the exercise price ($S > X$), the call is said to be **in the money**, and the owner will exercise it for a net profit of $C - \alpha$. If the asset price happens to be less than the exercise price ($S < X$), the call is said to be **out of the money** and will expire worthless. A call with $S = X$ is said to be **at the money** or **trading at par**.

Profit and Losses on Puts   As already noted, a second type of option contract is the put option. A **put option** is a contract that gives the owner the right (but not the obligation) to *sell* an asset (to the option writer) at the specified exercise price within a specific period of time. As a put represents an option to sell rather than buy, it is worth buying a put when the price of the underlying asset is expected to fall. As with calls, the buyer of a put is said to be **long in a put** and the writer of a put is said to be **short in a put**. Also, as with calls, the buyer of a put option will have to pay a premium, called a **put premium**, in order to get the writer to sign the contract and assume the risk.

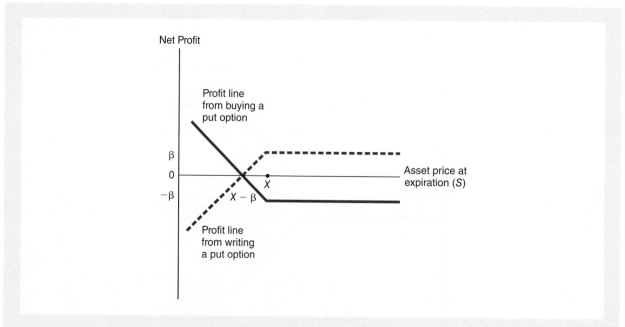

FIGURE 13-2   Profits from Buying and Writing a Put Option

The solid line in Figure 13-2 illustrates the profit line from buying a put with an exercise price of X and a premium of β. At a price of X or higher, the put will not be exercised, resulting in a loss of the premium. At a price below $X - \beta$, the put is sufficiently deep in the money to cover the option premium and yield a net profit. In fact, between $X - \beta$ and X, the put will be exercised, but the gain is insufficient to cover the cost of the premium.

The payoff function from writing a put is the mirror image of that from buying a put and is represented by the dashed line in Figure 13-2. As with writing a call, the writer of a put receives the put premium β up front and must sell the asset underlying the option if the buyer of the put exercises the option to sell.

In general, the value of a put option P at the expiration date with exercise price X and asset price S (at that time) is

$$P = \max(X - S, 0)$$

That is, the value of a put at maturity is the difference between the exercise price of the option and the price of the asset underlying the option, $X - S$, or zero, whichever is greater. If the stock price happens to be greater than the exercise price $(S > X)$, the put is said to be out of the money and will expire worthless. If the asset price happens to be less than the exercise price $(S < X)$, the put is said to be in the money and the owner will exercise it for a net profit of $P - \beta$. If $S = X$, the put is said to be at the money.

Remembering which is a call option and which is a put option is not always easy. To keep them straight, just remember that having a *call* option to *buy* an asset is the same as having the option to *call in* the asset for delivery at a specified price. Having a *put* option to *sell* an asset is the same as having the option to *put up* an asset for the other party to buy.

Futures Options

To understand option contracts on financial futures, let's examine the option on a June Canada bond futures contract. Recall that if you bought this futures contract at a price of 115 (that is, $115 000), you agreed to pay $115 000 for $100 000 face value of long-term Canada bonds when they are delivered to you at the end of June. If you sold this futures contract at a price of 115, you agreed, in exchange for $115 000, to deliver $100 000 face value of the long-term Canada bonds at the end of June. An option contract on the Canada bond futures contract has several key features: (1) it has the same expiration date as the underlying futures contract; (2) it is an American option and so can be exercised at any time before the expiration date; and (3) the premium (price) of the option is quoted in points that are the same as in the futures contract, so each point corresponds to $1000. If, for a premium of $2000, you buy one call option contract on the June Canada bond contract with an exercise price of 115, you have purchased the right to buy (call in) the June Canada bond futures contract for a price of 115 ($115 000 per contract) at any time through the expiration date of this contract at the end of June. Similarly, if you buy for $2000 a put option on the June Canada bond contract with an exercise price of 115, you have the right to sell (put up) the June Canada bond futures contract for a price of 115 ($115 000 per contract) at any time until the end of June.

Futures option contracts are somewhat complicated, so to explore how they work and how they can be used to hedge risk, let's first examine how profits and losses on the call option on the June Canada bond futures contract occur. In February, our old friend Irving the Investor buys, for a $2000 premium, a call option on the $100 000 June Canada bond futures contract with a strike price of 115. (We assume that if Irving exercises the option, it is on the expiration date at the end of June and not before.) On the expiration date at the end of June, suppose that the underlying Canada bond for the futures contract has a price of 110. Recall that on the expiration date, arbitrage forces the price of the futures contract to be the same as the price of the underlying bond, so it too has a price of 110 on the expiration date at the end of June. If Irving exercises the call option and buys the futures contract at an exercise price of 115, he will lose money by buying at 115 and selling at the lower market price of 110. Because Irving is smart, he will not exercise the option, but he will be out the $2000 premium he paid. In such a situation, in which the price of the underlying financial instrument is below the exercise price, a call option is said to be "out of the money." At the price of 110 (less than the exercise price), Irving thus suffers a loss on the option contract of the $2000 premium he paid. This loss is plotted as point A in panel (a) of Figure 13-3.

On the expiration date, if the price of the futures contract is 115, the call option is "at the money," and Irving is indifferent whether he exercises his option to buy the futures contract or not, since exercising the option at 115 when the market price is also at 115 produces no gain or loss. Because he has paid the $2000 premium, at the price of 115 his contract again has a net loss of $2000, plotted as point B.

If the futures contract instead has a price of 120 on the expiration day, the option is "in the money," and Irving benefits from exercising the option: he would buy the futures contract at the exercise price of 115 and then sell it for 120, thereby earning a 5% gain ($5000 profit) on the $100 000 Canada bond futures contract. Because Irving paid a $2000 premium for the option contract, however, his net profit is $3000 ($5000 − $2000). The $3000 profit at a price of 120 is plotted as point C. Similarly, if the price of the futures contract rose to 125, the option contract would yield a net profit of $8000 ($10 000 from exercising the option minus the $2000 premium), plotted as point D. Plotting these points, we get the kinked profit curve for the call option that we see in panel (a).

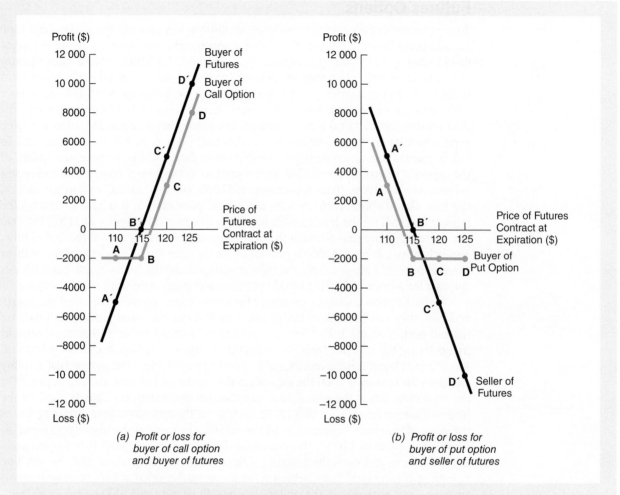

FIGURE 13-3   Profits and Losses on Options Versus Futures Contracts

The futures contract is the $100 000 June Canada bond contract, and the option contracts are written on this futures contract with an exercise price of 115. Panel (a) shows the profits and losses for the buyer of the call option and the buyer of the futures contract, and panel (b) shows the profits and losses for the buyer of the put option and the seller of the futures contract.

Suppose that instead of purchasing the futures *option* contract in February, Irving decides to buy the $100 000 June Canada bond *futures* contract at the price of 115. If the price of the bond on the expiration day at the end of June declines to 110, meaning that the price of the futures contract also falls to 110, Irving suffers a loss of 5 percentage points, or $5000. The loss of $5000 on the futures contract at a price of 110 is plotted as point A′ in panel (a). At a price of 115 on the expiration date, Irving would have a zero profit on the futures contract, plotted as point B′. At a price of 120, Irving would have a profit on the contract of 5 percentage points, or $5000 (point C′), and at a price of 125, the profit would be 10 percentage points, or $10 000 (point D′). Plotting these points, we get the linear (straight-line) profit curve for the futures contract that appears in panel (a).

Now we can see the major difference between a futures contract and an option contract. As the profit curve for the futures contract in panel (a) indicates, the futures contract has a linear profit function: profits grow by an equal dollar amount for every point increase in the price of the underlying asset. By contrast, the kinked profit curve for the option contract is nonlinear, meaning that profits do not always grow by the same amount for a given change in the price of the underlying asset. The reason for this nonlinearity is that the call option protects Irving from having losses that are greater than the amount of the $2000 premium. In contrast, Irving's loss on the futures contract is $5000 if the price on the expiration day falls to 110, and if the price falls even further, Irving's loss will be even greater. This insurance-like feature of option contracts explains why their purchase price is referred to as a premium. Once the underlying asset's price rises above the exercise price, however, Irving's profits grow linearly. Irving has given up something by buying an option rather than a futures contract. As we see in panel (a), when the price of the underlying asset rises above the exercise price, Irving's profits are always less than that on the futures contract by exactly the $2000 premium he paid.

Panel (b) plots the results of the same profit calculations if Irving buys not a call but a put option (an option to sell) with an exercise price of 115 for a premium of $2000 and if he sells the futures contract rather than buying one. In this case, if on the expiration date the Canada bond futures have a price above the 115 exercise price, the put option is "out of the money." Irving would not want to exercise the put option and then have to sell the futures contract he owns as a result of exercising the put option at a price below the market price and lose money. He would not exercise his option, and he would be out only the $2000 premium he paid. Once the price of the futures contract falls below the 115 exercise price, Irving benefits from exercising the put option because he can sell the futures contract at a price of 115 but can buy it at a price below this. In such a situation, in which the price of the underlying asset is below the exercise price, the put option is "in the money," and profits rise linearly as the price of the futures contract falls. The profit function for the put option illustrated in panel (b) of Figure 13-3 is kinked, indicating that Irving is protected from losses greater than the amount of the premium he paid. The profit curve for the sale of the futures contract is just the negative of the profit for the futures contract in panel (a) and is therefore linear.

Panel (b) of Figure 13-3 confirms the conclusion from panel (a) that profits on option contracts are nonlinear but profits on futures contracts are linear.

Two additional differences between futures and option contracts must be mentioned. The first is that the initial investment on the contracts differs. As we saw earlier in the chapter, when a futures contract is purchased, the investor must put up a fixed amount, the margin requirement, into a margin account. But when an option contract is purchased, the initial investment is the premium that must be paid for the contract. The second important difference between the contracts is that with a futures contract, money changes hands daily when the contract is marked to market, whereas with an option contract, money changes hands only when the option is excercised.

APPLICATION   # Hedging with Futures Options

Solution

Earlier in the chapter, we saw how the First Bank could hedge the interest-rate risk on its $5 million holdings of 6s of 2030 by selling $5 million of Canada bond futures (50 contracts). A rise in interest rates and the resulting fall in bond prices and bond futures contracts would lead to profits on the bank's sale of the futures contracts that would exactly offset the losses on the 6s of 2030 the bank is holding.

As suggested in panel (b) of Figure 13-3, an alternative way for the manager to protect against a rise in interest rates and hence a decline in bond prices is to buy $5 million of put options written on the same Canada bond futures. As long as the exercise price is not too far from the current price, as in panel (b), the rise in interest rates and decline in bond prices will lead to profits on the futures and the futures put options, profits that will offset any losses on the $5 million of Canada bonds.

The one problem with using options rather than futures is that the First Bank will have to pay premiums on the options contracts, thereby lowering the bank's profits in order to hedge the interest-rate risk. Why might the bank manager be willing to use options rather than futures to conduct the hedge? The answer is that the option contract, unlike the futures contract, allows the First Bank to gain if interest rates decline and bond prices rise. With the hedge using futures contracts, the First Bank does not gain from increases in bond prices because the profits on the bonds it is holding are offset by the losses from the futures contracts it has sold. However, as panel (b) of Figure 13-3 indicates, the situation when the hedge is conducted with put options is quite different: Once bond prices rise above the exercise price, the bank does not suffer additional losses on the option contracts. At the same time, the value of the Canada bonds the bank is holding will increase, thereby leading to a profit for the bank. Thus, using options rather than futures to conduct the micro hedge allows the bank to protect itself from rises in interest rates but still allows the bank to benefit from interest-rate declines (although the profit is reduced by the amount of the premium).

Similar reasoning indicates that the bank manager might prefer to use options to conduct a macro hedge to immunize the entire bank portfolio from interest-rate risk. Again, the strategy of using options rather than futures has the disadvantage that the First Bank has to pay the premiums on these contracts up front. By contrast, using options allows the bank to keep the gains from a decline in interest rates (which will raise the value of the bank's assets relative to its liabilities) because these gains will not be offset by large losses on the option contracts.

In the case of a macro hedge, there is another reason why the bank might prefer option contracts to futures contracts. Profits and losses on futures contracts can cause accounting problems for banks because such profits and losses are not allowed to be offset by unrealized changes in the value of the rest of the bank's portfolio. Consider the case when interest rates fall. If the First Bank sells futures contracts to conduct the macro hedge, then when interest rates fall and the prices of the Canada bond futures contracts rise, it will have large losses on these contracts. Of course, these losses are offset by unrealized profits in the rest of the bank's portfolio, but the bank is not allowed to offset these losses in its accounting statements. So even though the macro hedge is serving its intended purpose of immunizing the bank's portfolio from interest-rate risk, the bank would experience large accounting losses when interest rates fall. Indeed, bank managers have lost their jobs when perfectly sound hedges with interest-rate futures have led to large accounting losses. Not surprisingly, for this reason bank managers might shrink from using financial futures to conduct macro hedges.

Futures options, however, can come to the rescue of the managers of banks and other financial institutions. Suppose that First Bank conducted the macro hedge by buying put options instead of selling Canada bond futures. Now, if interest rates fall and bond prices rise well above the exercise price, the bank will not suffer large losses on the option contracts because it will just decide not to exercise its options. The bank will not suffer the accounting problems that it would have suffered if it had hedged with financial futures. Because of the accounting advantages of using futures options to conduct macro hedges, option contracts have become important tools for financial institution managers who are looking to hedge interest-rate risk.

Factors Affecting the Prices of Option Premiums

Several interesting facts can be noted about how the premiums on option contracts are priced. First, when the strike (exercise) price for a contract is set at a higher level, the premium for the call option is lower and the premium for the put option is higher. For example, in going from a contract with a strike price of 112 to one with 115, the premium for a call option for the month of March might fall from 1 45/64 to 16/64, and the premium for the March put option might rise from 19/64 to 1 54/64.

Our understanding of the profit function for option contracts illustrated in Figure 13-3 helps explain this fact. As we saw in panel (a), a higher price for the underlying asset (in this case a Canada bond futures contract) relative to the option's exercise price results in higher profits on the call (buy) option. Thus, the lower the strike price, the higher the profits on the call option contract and the greater the premium that investors like Irving are willing to pay. Similarly, we saw in panel (b) that a higher price for the underlying asset relative to the exercise price lowers profits on the put (sell) option, so that a higher strike price increases profits and thus causes the premium to increase.

Second, as the period of time over which the option can be exercised (the term to expiration) gets longer, the premiums for both call and put options rise. For example, at a strike price of 112, the premium on the call option might increase from 1 45/64 in March to 1 50/64 in April and to 2 28/64 in May. Similarly, the premium on a put option might increase from 19/64 in March to 1 43/64 in April and to 2 22/64 in May. The fact that premiums increase with the term to expiration is also explained by the nonlinear profit function for option contracts. As the term to expiration lengthens, there is a greater chance that the price of the underlying asset will be very high or very low by the expiration date. If the price becomes very high and goes well above the exercise price, the call (buy) option will yield a high profit, but if the price becomes very low and goes well below the exercise price, the losses will be small because the owner of the call option will simply decide not to exercise the option. The possibility of greater variability of the underlying asset as the term to expiration lengthens raises profits on average for the call option.

Similar reasoning tells us that the put (sell) option will become more valuable as the term to expiration increases because the possibility of greater price variability of the underlying financial instrument increases as the term to expiration increases. The greater chance of a low price increases the chance that profits on the put option will be very high. But the greater chance of a high price does not produce substantial losses for the put option because the owner will again just decide not to exercise the option.

We can think about this feature of option contracts in another way: Option contracts have an element of "heads, I win; tails, I don't lose too badly." The greater variability of the final price on the expiration date increases the value of both kinds of options. Because a longer term to the expiration date leads to greater variability in the final price on the expiration date, a longer term to expiration raises the value of an option contract.

The reasoning we just developed explains another important fact about option premiums. When the volatility of the price of the underlying instrument is great, the premiums on both call and put options are higher. Higher volatility of price means that, for a given expiration date, there will again be greater variability in the final price on the expiration date. The "heads, I win; tails, I don't lose too badly" property of options implies that the greater variability of possible prices on the expiration date increases average profits for the option and thus increases the premium that investors are willing to pay.

Summary

Our analysis in this application leads us to the following conclusions about the factors that determine the premium on an option contract:

1. The higher the strike price, everything else being equal, the lower the premium on call (buy) options and the higher the premium on put (sell) options.

2. The greater the term to expiration, everything else being equal, the higher the premiums on both call and put options.

3. The greater the volatility of prices of the underlying financial instrument, everything else being equal, the higher the premiums on both call and put options.

The results we have derived here appear in more formal models, such as the Black-Scholes model, that analyze how the premiums on options are priced. You might study such models in finance courses. ◆

SWAPS

In addition to forwards, futures, and options, financial institutions use one other important financial derivative to manage risk. **Swaps** are financial contracts that obligate each party to the contract to exchange (swap) a set of payments (not assets) it owns for another set of payments that are owned by another party. Swaps are of two basic kinds. **Currency swaps** involve the exchange of a set of payments in one currency for a set of payments in another currency. **Interest-rate swaps** involve the exchange of one set of interest payments for another set of interest payments, all denominated in the same currency. We focus on interest-rate swaps.

Interest-Rate Swap Contracts

Interest-rate swaps are an important tool for managing interest-rate risk. They first appeared in the United States in 1982, when, as we have seen, demand increased for financial instruments that could be used to reduce interest-rate risk. The most common type of interest-rate swap (called the *plain vanilla swap*) specifies: (1) the interest rate on the payments that are being exchanged; (2) the type of interest payments (variable or fixed-rate); (3) the amount of **notional principal**, which is the amount on which the interest is being paid; and (4) the time period over which the exchanges will continue to be made. There are many other, more complicated versions of swaps, including forward swaps and swap options (called *swaptions*), but here we will look only at the plain vanilla swap. Figure 13-4 illustrates an interest-rate swap between First Trust and the Friendly Finance Company. First Trust agrees to pay Friendly Finance a fixed rate of 7% on $1 million of notional principal for the next 10 years, and Friendly Finance agrees to pay First Trust the one-year Treasury bill rate plus 1% on $1 million of notional principal for the same period. Thus, as shown in Figure 13-4, every year First Trust would be paying the Friendly Finance Company 7% on $1 million while Friendly Finance would be paying First Trust the one-year T-bill rate plus 1% on $1 million.

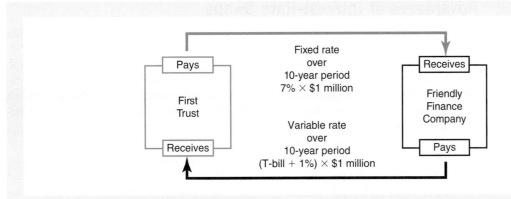

FIGURE 13-4   Interest-Rate Swap Payments

In this swap arrangement, with a notional principal of $1 million and a term of 10 years, First Trust pays a fixed rate of 7% of $1 million to the Friendly Finance Company, which in turn agrees to pay the one-year Treasury bill rate plus 1% of $1 million to First Trust.

APPLICATION   Hedging with Interest-Rate Swaps

You might wonder why these two parties find it advantageous to enter into this swap agreement. The answer is that it may help both of them hedge interest-rate risk.

Suppose that First Trust, which tends to borrow short-term and then lend long-term in the mortgage market, has $1 million less of rate-sensitive assets than it has of rate-sensitive liabilities. As we learned in Chapter 12, this situation means that as interest rates rise, the rise in the cost of funds (liabilities) is greater than the rise in interest payments it receives on its assets, many of which are fixed-rate. The result of rising interest rates is thus a shrinking of First Trust's net interest margin and a decline in its profitability. As we saw in Chapter 12, to avoid this interest-rate risk, the manager of First Trust would like to convert $1 million of its fixed-rate assets into $1 million of rate-sensitive assets, in effect making rate-sensitive assets equal to rate-sensitive liabilities, thereby eliminating the gap. This is exactly what happens when she engages in the interest-rate swap. By taking $1 million of its fixed-rate income and exchanging it for $1 million of rate-sensitive Treasury bill income, she has converted income on $1 million of fixed-rate assets into income on $1 million of rate-sensitive assets. Now when interest rates increase, the rise in rate-sensitive income on its assets exactly matches the rise in the rate-sensitive cost of funds on its liabilities, leaving the net interest margin and bank profitability unchanged.

The manager of the Friendly Finance Company, which issues long-term bonds to raise funds and uses them to make short-term loans, finds that he is in exactly the opposite situation to First Trust: he has $1 million more of rate-sensitive assets than of rate-sensitive liabilities. He is therefore concerned that a fall in interest rates, which will result in a larger drop in income from its assets than the decline in the cost of funds on its liabilities, will cause a decline in profits. By doing the interest-rate swap, the manager eliminates this interest-rate risk because he has converted $1 million of rate-sensitive income into $1 million of fixed-rate income. Now the manager of the Friendly Finance Company finds that when interest rates fall, the decline in rate-sensitive income is smaller and so is matched by the decline in the rate-sensitive cost of funds on its liabilities, leaving profitability unchanged.

Advantages of Interest-Rate Swaps

To eliminate interest-rate risk, both First Trust and the Friendly Finance Company could have rearranged their balance sheets by converting fixed-rate assets into rate-sensitive assets, and vice versa, instead of engaging in an interest-rate swap. However, this strategy would have been costly for both financial institutions for several reasons. The first is that financial institutions incur substantial transaction costs when they rearrange their balance sheets. Second, different financial institutions have informational advantages in making loans to certain customers who may prefer certain maturities. Thus, adjusting the balance sheet to eliminate interest-rate risk may result in a loss of these informational advantages, which the financial institution is unwilling to give up. Interest-rate swaps solve these problems for financial institutions because in effect they allow the institutions to convert fixed-rate assets into rate-sensitive assets without affecting the balance sheet. Large transaction costs are avoided, and the financial institutions can continue to use their informational advantage to make loans to preferred customers.

We have learned that financial institutions can also hedge interest-rate risk with other financial derivatives, such as futures contracts and futures options. Interest-rate swaps have one big advantage over these other derivatives: they can be written for very long horizons, sometimes as long as 20 years, whereas financial futures and futures options typically have much shorter horizons, not much more than a year. If a financial institution needs to hedge interest-rate risk for a long horizon, financial futures and option markets may not do it much good. Instead, it can turn to the swap market.

Disadvantages of Interest-Rate Swaps

Although interest-rate swaps have important advantages that make them very popular with financial institutions, they also have disadvantages that limit their usefulness. Swap markets, like forward markets, can suffer from a lack of liquidity. Let's return to looking at the swap between First Trust and the Friendly Finance Company. As with a forward contract, it might be difficult for First Trust to link up with the Friendly Finance Company to arrange the swap. In addition, even if First Trust is able to find a willing counterparty like the Friendly Finance Company, it might not be able to negotiate a good deal because it has no other institution with which to negotiate.

Swap contracts also are subject to the same default risk that we encountered for forward contracts. If interest rates rise, the Friendly Finance Company would love to get out of the swap contract, because the fixed-rate interest payments it receives are less than it could get in the open market. It might then default on the contract, exposing First Trust to a loss. Alternatively, the Friendly Finance Company could go bust, meaning that the terms of the swap contract would not be fulfilled.

Financial Intermediaries in Interest-Rate Swaps

As we have just seen, financial institutions do have to be aware of the possibility of losses from a default on swaps. As with a forward contract, each party to a swap must have a lot of information about the other party to make sure that the contract is likely to be fulfilled. The need for information about counterparties and the liquidity problems in swap markets could limit the usefulness of these markets. However, when informational and liquidity problems crop up in a market, financial intermediaries come to the rescue. That is exactly what happens in swap markets. Intermediaries such as investment banks and especially large banks have the ability to acquire information cheaply about the creditworthiness and reliability of parties to swap contracts and are also able to match up parties to a swap. Hence, large banks and investment banks have set up swap markets in which they act as intermediaries. ◆

CREDIT DERIVATIVES

In recent years, a new type of derivative to hedge credit risk has arrived on the scene. Like other derivatives, **credit derivatives** offer payoffs on previously issued securities, but only on securities that bear credit risk. In the past 10 years, the markets in credit derivatives have grown at an outstanding pace, and the notional amounts of these derivatives now number in the trillions of dollars. These credit derivatives take several forms.

Credit Options

Credit options work just like the options discussed earlier in the chapter: for a fee, the purchaser gains the right to receive profits that are tied either to the price of an underlying security or to an interest rate. Suppose you buy $1 million of General Motors bonds but worry that a potential slowdown in the sale of SUVs might lead a credit-rating agency to *downgrade* (lower the credit rating on) GM bonds. As we saw in Chapter 6, such a downgrade would cause the price of GM bonds to fall. To protect yourself, you could buy an option for, say, $15 000 to sell the $1 million of bonds at a strike price that is the same as the current price. With this strategy, you would not suffer any losses if the value of the GM bonds declined because you could exercise the option and sell them at the price you paid for them. In addition, you would be able to reap any gains that occurred if GM bonds rose in value.

The second type of credit option ties profits to changes in an interest rate such as a credit spread (the interest rate on the average bond with a particular credit rating minus the interest rate on default-free bonds such as those issued by the Canadian government). Suppose that your company, which has a BBB credit rating, plans to issue $10 million of one-year bonds in three months and expects to have a credit spread of 1 percentage point (i.e., it will pay an interest rate that is 1 percentage point higher than the one-year T-bill rate). You are concerned that the market might start to think that BBB companies in general will become riskier in the coming months. If this were to happen by the time you are ready to issue your bonds in three months, you would have to pay a higher interest rate than the 1 percentage point in excess of the T-bill rate, and your cost of issuing the bonds would increase. To protect yourself against these higher costs, you could buy for, say, $20 000, a credit option on $10 million of BBB bonds that would pay you the difference between the average BBB credit spread in the market minus the 1 percentage point credit spread on $10 million. If the credit spread jumps to 2 percentage points, you would receive $100 000 from the option (= [2% − 1%] × $10 million), which would exactly offset the $100 000 higher interest costs from the 1-percentage-point higher interest rate you would have to pay on your $10 million of bonds.

Credit Swaps

Suppose you manage a bank in Calgary called Oil Drillers' Bank (ODB), which specializes in lending to a particular industry in your local area, oil drilling companies. Another bank, Potato Farmers' Bank (PFB), specializes in lending to potato farmers in Charlottetown. Both ODB and PFB have a problem because their loan portfolios are not sufficiently diversified. To protect ODB against a collapse in the oil market, which would result in defaults on most of its loans made to oil drillers, you could reach an agreement to have the loan payments on, say, $100 million worth of your loans to oil drillers paid to the PFB in exchange for PFB paying you the loan payments on $100 million of its loans to potato farmers. Such a transaction, in which risky payments on loans are swapped for each other, is called a **credit swap**. As a result of this swap, ODB and PFB have increased their diversification and lowered the overall risk of their loan portfolios because some of the loan payments to each bank are now coming from a different type of loan.

Another form of credit swap is, for arcane reasons, called a **credit default swap**, although it functions more like insurance. With a credit default swap, one party who wants to hedge credit risk pays a fixed payment on a regular basis, in return for a contingent payment that is triggered by a credit event such as the bankruptcy of a particular firm or the downgrading of the firm's credit rating by a credit rating agency. For example, you could use a credit default swap to hedge the $1 million of General Motors bonds that you are holding by arranging to pay an annual fee of $1000 in exchange for a payment of $10 000 if the GM bonds' credit rating is lowered. If a credit event happens (such as default on a significant transaction) and GM's bonds are downgraded so that their price falls, you will receive a payment that will offset some of the loss you suffer if you sell the bonds at this lower price.

Credit-Linked Notes

Another type of credit derivative, the **credit-linked note**, is a combination of a bond and a credit option. Just like any corporate bond, the credit-linked note makes periodic coupon (interest) payments and a final payment of the face value of the bond at maturity. If a key financial variable specified in the note changes, however, the issuer of the note has the right (option) to lower the payments on the note. For example, General Motors could issue a credit-linked note that pays a 5% coupon rate, with the specification that if a national index of SUV sales falls by 10%, then GM has the right to lower the coupon rate by 2 percentage points to 3%. In this way, GM can lower its risk because when it is losing money as SUV sales fall, it can offset some of these losses by making smaller payments on its credit-linked notes.

APPLICATION   # Lessons from the Global Financial Crisis: When Are Financial Derivatives Likely to Be a Worldwide Time Bomb?

Although financial derivatives can be useful in hedging risk, the AIG blowup discussed in Chapter 12 illustrates that they can pose a real danger to the financial system. Indeed, Warren Buffett warned about the dangers of financial derivatives by characterizing them as "financial weapons of mass destruction." Particularly scary are the notional amounts of derivatives contracts—more than $700 trillion worldwide. What does the recent global financial crisis tell us about when financial derivatives are likely to be a time bomb that could bring down the world financial system?

Two major concerns surround financial derivatives. The first is that financial derivatives allow financial institutions to increase their leverage; that is, these institutions can in effect hold an amount of the underlying asset that is many times greater than the amount of money they have had to put up. Increasing their leverage enables them to take huge bets, which, if they are wrong, can bring down the institution. This is exactly what AIG did, to its great regret, when it plunged into the credit default swap (CDS) market. Even more of a problem was that AIG's speculation in the CDS market had the potential to bring down the whole financial system. An important lesson from the subprime financial crisis is that having one player take huge positions in a derivatives market is highly dangerous.

A second concern is that banks have holdings of huge notional amounts of financial derivatives, particularly interest-rate and currency swaps, that greatly exceed the amount of bank capital, and so these derivatives expose the banks to serious risk of failure. Banks are indeed major players in the financial derivatives markets, particularly in the interest-rate and currency swaps market, where our earlier analysis has shown that they are the natural market-makers because they can act as intermediaries between two counterparties who would not make the swap without their involvement. However, looking at the notional amount of interest-rate and currency swaps at banks gives a very misleading picture of their risk exposure. Because banks act as intermediaries in the swap markets, they are typically exposed only to credit risk—a default by one of their counterparties. Furthermore, these swaps, unlike loans, do not involve payments of the notional amount but rather the much smaller payments that are based on the notional amounts. For example, in the case of a 7% interest rate, the payment is only $70 000 for a $1 million swap. Estimates of the credit exposure from swap contracts indicate that they are on the order of only 1% of the notional value of the contracts and that credit exposure at banks from derivatives is generally less than a quarter of their total credit exposure from loans. Banks' credit exposures from their derivative positions are thus not out of line with other credit exposures they face. Indeed, during the recent subprime financial crisis, in which the financial system was put under great stress, derivatives exposure at banks was not a serious problem.

In conclusion, recent events indicate that financial derivatives pose serious dangers to the financial system, but some of these dangers have been overplayed. The biggest danger occurs in trading activities of financial institutions, and this is particularly true for credit derivatives, as was illustrated by AIG's activities in the CDS market. As discussed in Chapter 10, regulators have been paying increased attention to this danger and are continuing to develop new disclosure requirements and regulatory guidelines for how derivatives trading should be done. Of particular concern is the need for financial institutions to disclose their exposure in derivatives contracts, so that regulators can make sure that a large institution is not playing too large a role in these markets and does not have too large an exposure to derivatives relative to its capital, as was the case for AIG. Another concern is that derivatives, particularly credit derivatives, need to have a better clearing mechanism so that the failure of one institution does not bring down many others whose net derivatives positions are small, even though they have many offsetting positions. Better clearing could be achieved either by having these derivatives traded in an organized exchange like a futures market, or by having one clearing organization net out trades.

The credit risk exposure posed by interest-rate derivatives, in contrast, seems to be manageable using the standard methods of dealing with credit risk. New regulations for derivatives markets are sure to come in the wake of the global financial crisis. The industry has been given a wake-up call regarding the potential dangers of derivatives products. Now the hope is that any time bomb arising from derivatives can be defused with appropriate efforts on the parts of markets and regulators. ◆

MyEconLab

MyEconLab is an online homework and tutorial system that puts you in control of your own learning with study and practice tools directly correlated to this chapter's content. Visit MyEconLab to access the eText, the Questions and Applied Problems with answers, as well as additional assessment. You will also find web chapters, mini-lectures, appendices, mini-cases, videos, glossary flashcards, news feeds, CANSIM data, and graphing tools.

SUMMARY

1. Interest-rate forward contracts, which are agreements to sell a debt instrument at a future (forward) point in time, can be used to hedge (protect against) interest-rate risk. The advantage of forward contracts is that they are flexible; the disadvantages are that they are subject to default risk and their market is illiquid.

2. A financial futures contract is similar to an interest-rate forward contract in that it specifies that a debt instrument must be delivered by one party to another on a stated future date. However, it has advantages over a forward contract in that it is not subject to default risk and is more liquid. Forward and futures contracts can be used by financial institutions to hedge interest-rate risk.

3. Stock index futures are financial futures whose underlying financial instrument is a stock market index. Stock index futures can be used to hedge stock market risk by reducing systematic risk in portfolios or by locking in stock prices.

4. An option contract gives the purchaser the right to buy (call option) or sell (put option) a security at the exercise (strike) price within a specific period of time. The profit function for options is nonlinear—profits do not always grow by the same amount for a given change in the price of the underlying asset. The nonlinear profit function for options explains why their value (as reflected by the premium paid for them) is negatively related to the exercise price for call options, positively related to the exercise price for put options, positively related to the term to expiration for both call and put options, and positively related to the volatility of the prices of the underlying asset for both call and put options. Financial institutions use futures options to hedge interest-rate risk in a similar fashion to the way they use financial futures and forward contracts. Futures options may be preferred for macro hedges because they suffer from fewer accounting problems than financial futures.

5. Interest-rate swaps involve the exchange of one set of interest payments for another set of interest payments and have default risk and liquidity problems similar to those of forward contracts. As a result, interest-rate swaps often involve intermediaries such as large banks and investment banks that make a market in swaps. Financial institutions find that interest-rate swaps are useful ways to hedge interest-rate risk. Interest-rate swaps have one big advantage over financial futures and options: they can be written for very long horizons.

6. Credit derivatives are a new type of derivative that offer payoffs on previously issued securities that have credit risk. These derivatives—credit options, swaps, and credit-linked notes—can be used to hedge credit risk.

7. There are two major concerns about derivatives: they allow financial institutions to more easily increase their leverage and take big bets (by effectively enabling them to hold a larger amount of the underlying assets than the amount of money put down), and they expose financial institutions to large credit risks because the huge notional amounts of derivative contracts greatly exceed the capital of these institutions. The second danger seems to be overplayed, but the danger from increased leverage using derivatives is very real, as was revealed during the global financial crisis.

KEY TERMS

American options, p. 323
arbitrage, p. 316

at the money, p. 325
call option, p. 324

call premium, p. 324
credit-linked note, p. 336

credit default swap, p. 336
credit derivatives, p. 335
credit options, p. 335
credit swap, p. 336
currency swaps, p. 332
European options, p. 324
exercise price, p. 323
financial derivatives, p. 312
financial futures, p. 315
financial futures options, p. 324
forward contracts, p. 313
futures options, p. 324
hedge, p. 312
interest-rate forward contracts, p. 313

interest-rate futures contract, p. 315
interest-rate swaps, p. 332
in the money, p. 325
intrinsic value, p. 325
long in a call, p. 324
long in a put, p. 325
long position, p. 312
macro hedge, p. 317
margin requirement, p. 320
marked to market, p. 320
micro hedge, p. 317
notional principal, p. 332
open interest, p. 318

options, p. 323
out of the money, p. 325
premium, p. 323
put option, p. 325
put premium, p. 325
short in a call, p. 324
short in a put, p. 325
short position, p. 312
stock market risk, p. 322
stock options, p. 324
strike price, p. 323
swaps, p. 332
trading at par, p. 325

QUESTIONS

All questions are available in MyEconLab *at* **www.myeconlab.com**.

1. Explain why greater volatility or a longer term to maturity leads to a higher premium on both call and put options.

2. Why does a lower strike price imply that a call option will have a higher premium and a put option a lower premium?

APPLIED PROBLEMS

All applied problems are available in MyEconLab *at* **www.myeconlab.com**.

3. If the pension fund you manage expects to have an inflow of $120 million six months from now, what forward contract would you seek to enter into to lock in current interest rates?

4. If the portfolio you manage is holding $25 million of 8s of 2030 Canada bonds with a price of 110, what forward contract would you enter into to hedge the interest-rate risk on these bonds over the coming year?

5. If, on the expiration date, the deliverable Canada bond is selling for 101 but the Canada bond futures contract is selling for 102, what will happen to the futures price? Explain your answer.

6. If you buy a $100 000 June Canada bond contract for 108 and the price of the deliverable Canada bond at the expiration date is 102, what is your profit or loss on the contract?

7. Suppose that the pension you are managing is expecting an inflow of funds of $100 million next year and you want to make sure that you will earn the current interest rate of 8% when you invest the incoming funds in long-term bonds. How would you use the futures market to do this?

8. How would you use the options market to accomplish the same thing as in Problem 9? What are the advantages and disadvantages of using an options contract rather than a futures contract?

9. If you buy a put option on a $100 000 Canada bond futures contract with an exercise price of 95 and the price of the Canada bond is 120 at expiration, is the contract in the money, out of the money, or at the

money? What is your profit or loss on the contract if the premium was $4000?

10. Suppose that you buy a call option on a $100 000 Canada bond futures contract with an exercise price of 110 for a premium of $1500. If on expiration the futures contract has a price of 111, what is your profit or loss on the contract?

11. If the finance company you manage has a gap of +$5 million (rate-sensitive assets greater than rate-sensitive liabilities by $5 million), describe an interest-rate swap that would eliminate the company's income gap.

12. If the bank you manage has a gap of −$42 million, describe an interest-rate swap that would eliminate the bank's income risk from changes in interest rates.

13. If your company has a payment of 200 million euros due one year from now, how would you hedge the foreign exchange risk in this payment with a 125 000 euro futures contract?

14. If your company has to make a 10 million euro payment to a German company three months from now, how would you hedge the foreign exchange risk in this payment with a 125 000 euro futures contract?

15. Suppose that your company will be receiving 30 million euros six months from now and the euro is currently selling for 1.4 Canadian dollars. If you want to hedge the foreign exchange risk in this payment, what kind of forward contract would you want to enter into?

16. A swap agreement calls for Rocky Industries to pay interest annually based on a rate of 2% over the one-year T-bill rate, currently 3%. In return, Rocky Industries receives interest at a rate of 4% on a fixed-rate basis. The notional principal for the swap is $100 000. What is Rocky's net interest for the year after the agreement?

DATA ANALYSIS PROBLEMS

Download data for these problems from MyEconLab at **www.myeconlab.com**.

1. Go to the Bank of Canada's website and find data on the Canadian dollar/euro exchange rate. Suppose that one month ago you entered into a forward contract to sell 10 million euros at the forward rate equivalent to the spot rate one month ago. What exchange rate was specified on the forward contract? (Find the most recent data available, and then use the data from one month prior.) What will be the payment in dollars when the contract is executed? In hindsight, would you have been better off or worse off by not entering into the forward contract?

WEB EXERCISES

1. The following site can be used to demonstrate how the features of an option affect the option's prices. Go to **www.option-price.com/index.php**. What happens to the price of an option under each of the following situations:

a. The strike price increases.

b. Interest rates increase.

c. Volatility increases.

d. The time until the option matures increases.

WEB REFERENCES

www.m-x.ca/accueil_en.php

The website of the Montreal Exchange reports information on all the contracts traded on the exchange.

www.cmegroup.com

The website of the CME Group (Chicago Mercantile Exchange and Chicago Board of Trade) reports information on all the contracts traded on its exchanges.

PART 5

Central Banking and the Conduct of Monetary Policy

Chapter 14   Central Banks and the Bank of Canada

Chapter 15   The Money Supply Process

Chapter 16   Tools of Monetary Policy

Chapter 17   The Conduct of Monetary Policy: Strategy and Tactics

Crisis and Response: The Bank of Canada and the Global Financial Crisis

The onset of the subprime financial crisis in August 2007 was a curve ball for central banks around the world. The global financial crisis, described by former Federal Reserve Chairman Alan Greenspan as a "once-in-a-century credit tsunami," had the potential to devastate the world economy.

The Bank of Canada resolved to come to the rescue of the Canadian economy. Starting in September of 2007, the Bank of Canada enacted monetary policy at a rapid rate by reducing the overnight interest rate. Specifically, the Bank lowered the overnight rate target in December by 25 basis points (0.25 percentage points) from 4.50% to 4.25%, and eventually drove the overnight rate target down to 0.25% by April of 2009.

At the same time, the Bank of Canada implemented large liquidity injections into the credit markets to try to get them lending again. Over the course of the crisis, the Bank broadened its provision of liquidity to the financial system well outside of its traditional lending to depository institutions. The number of new Bank of Canada instruments over the course of the crisis spawned a whole new terminology, including term PRAs, quantitative easing, and credit easing, making the Bank of Canada sound like the military with code-named initiatives and weapons. Like the military, the Bank of Canada was fighting a war, although its weapons were financial rather than guns, tanks, or aircraft.

The recent global financial crisis demonstrated the importance of central banks like the Bank of Canada to the health of a nation's financial system and the economy. Chapter 14 outlines what central banks are trying to achieve, what motivates them, and how they are set up. Chapter 15 describes how the money supply is determined. In Chapter 16, we look at the tools that central banks like the Bank of Canada have at their disposal and how they use them. Chapter 17 extends the discussion of the conduct of monetary policy to focus on the broader picture of central banks' strategies and tactics.

14 Central Banks and the Bank of Canada

Learning Objectives

After studying this chapter you should be able to

1. Recognize the historical context of the development of the Bank of Canada.

2. Describe the key features and functions of the Bank of Canada.

3. Assess the degree of independence of the Bank of Canada.

4. Summarize the arguments for and against the independence of the Bank of Canada.

5. Identify the ways in which the theory of bureaucratic behaviour can help explain central bank actions.

6. Discuss the structure and independence of other major central banks around the world.

PREVIEW

Among the most important players in financial markets throughout the world are central banks, the government authorities in charge of monetary policy. Central banks' actions affect interest rates, the amount of credit available, and the money supply, all of which have direct impacts not only on financial markets but also on aggregate output and inflation. To understand the role that central banks play in financial markets and the overall economy, we need to understand how these organizations work. Who controls central banks and determines their actions? What motivates their behaviour? Who holds the reins of power?

In this chapter, we look at the institutional structure of major central banks, and focus particularly on the Bank of Canada, Canada's central bank, often just called the Bank. We start by examining the elements of the Bank of Canada's institutional structure that determine where the true power within the Bank of Canada lies. By understanding who makes the decisions, we will have a better idea of how they are made. We then examine the reasons behind central bank behaviour and whether it is a good idea to make central banks independent by insulating them from politicians. Finally, we look at the structure and independence of other major central banks, particularly the Federal Reserve System in the United States—the most important central bank in the world—and the European Central Bank. With this context in place, we will be prepared to comprehend the actual conduct of monetary policy described in the following chapters.

ORIGINS OF THE BANK OF CANADA

The devastation of the Great Depression was of fundamental importance in the creation of the Bank of Canada. From 1929 to 1933, Canadian real GDP fell by almost 30% and the unemployment rate increased sevenfold from less than 3% to close to 20%. The Great Depression not only involved the largest decline in the level of economic activity in the history of Canada, but was also followed by an extremely slow recovery. Being such a cataclysmic event, the Great Depression contributed to significant changes in government policy, including fiscal policy, monetary policy, banking policy, and international policy.

Global   Establishment of Selected Central Banks

Canada did not have a central bank for almost the first 70 years after Confederation. By the time the Bank of Canada began operations in 1935, most other countries already had a central bank. In fact, as you can see in the table, Sweden and the United Kingdom created their central banks back in the seventeenth century. These early central banks, however, were initially privately owned and gradually evolved into modern publicly owned central banks.

Country	Year Central Bank Was Established
Sweden	1656
United Kingdom	1694
France	1800
Belgium	1850
Germany	1875
Japan	1882
Italy	1893
Switzerland	1905
United States	1913
Canada	1935

Source: Forrest H. Capie, Terence C. Mills, and Geoffrey E. Wood, "Central Bank Dependence and Inflation Performance: An Exploratory Data Analysis," in *Varieties of Monetary Reform: Lessons and Experiences on the Road to Monetary Union*, ed. Pierre L. Siklos (Dordrecht, The Netherlands: Kluwer Academic Publishers, 1994), 95–132. Reprinted with permission of the publisher.

In particular, as the depth of the Great Depression was blamed on the operation of the monetary system, in 1933 the federal Conservative government established a royal commission to study the problems of the Great Depression. Based on a recommendation of the royal commission, Parliament passed the Bank of Canada Act in 1934 and the newly founded Bank of Canada started operations on March 11, 1935. By this time, most other countries already had a central bank (see the Global box Establishment of Selected Central Banks). Although the primary motivation for the formation of the Bank of Canada was economic (or monetary), other motives within the government included the need for Canada to reflect its growing political independence from Britain and the need to coordinate its international economic policy.

Initially the Bank of Canada was a private institution but was nationalized in 1938, and it is now a national institution with headquarters in Ottawa. The Bank also has regional offices in Toronto (for Ontario), Vancouver (for British Columbia and the Yukon), Calgary (for the Prairies, Northwest Territories, and Nunavut), Montréal (for Quebec), and Halifax (for Atlantic Canada), and in 2002 the Bank also established a post in New York to enhance communication with the world's largest financial community. Unlike a private bank that operates in pursuit of profit, the Bank of Canada is responsible for the country's monetary policy and for the regulation of Canada's deposit-based financial institutions.

FORMAL STRUCTURE OF THE BANK OF CANADA

The overall responsibility for the operation of the Bank of Canada rests with a **Board of Directors**, which consists of 15 members—the governor, the senior deputy governor, the deputy minister of finance, and 12 outside directors. The Board appoints the governor and senior deputy governor with the government's approval, for a renewable term of seven years. The outside directors are appointed by the minister of finance, with Cabinet approval, for a three-year term, and they are required to come from all regions of Canada, representing a variety of occupations with the exception of banking. The governor of the Bank is the chief executive officer and chair of the Board of Directors. Currently, the governor of the Bank of Canada is Stephen Poloz (see the FYI box The Political Environment and the Bank of Canada). Stephen Poloz replaced Mark Carney, (the former Bank of Canada Governor) who accepted an appointment as 120th Governor of the Bank of England to serve a five-year term effective July 1, 2013.

In 1994 the Board of Directors made some changes in the internal organization of the Bank. Most prominently, the Board established a new senior decision-making authority within the Bank called the **Governing Council**. The council is chaired by the governor and is composed of the senior deputy governor and four deputy governors. Since this change, the six members of the Governing Council of the Bank collectively assume responsibility for the Bank's quarterly *Monetary Policy Report*, published in January, April, July, and October. This system of "collective responsibility" ensures that the Bank's governor is not personally identified with the Bank's policy.

THE FUNCTIONS OF THE BANK OF CANADA

In the words of the preamble of the Bank of Canada Act, the functions of the Bank of Canada are

to regulate credit and currency in the best interests of the economic life of the nation, to control and protect the external value of the national monetary unit and to mitigate by its influence fluctuations in the general level of production, trade, prices and employment, so far as may be possible within the scope of monetary action, and generally to promote the economic and financial welfare of Canada.

FYI   The Political Environment and the Bank of Canada

Since the inception of the Bank of Canada there have been eight governors:

1935–1954, Graham Towers
1955–1961, James Coyne
1961–1973, Louis Rasminsky
1973–1987, Gerald Bouey
1987–1994, John Crow
1994–2000, Gordon Thiessen
2001–2007, David Dodge
2008–2013, Mark Carney
2013–   Stephen Poloz

It is interesting to note that during the same period, Canadians went to the polls more than 20 times to elect a federal government. The Bank of Canada is not completely independent from the government. For example, the government can directly influence the Bank by not renewing the governor's appointment when it expires, as the Liberal government did in 1994 when it didn't renew the appointment of John Crow, who was appointed by the Conservative government in 1987.

This is a vague mandate, leaving a lot of room for interpretation. To explore this subject, we discuss four main areas of responsibility of the Bank of Canada as they are mentioned in the Bank's webpage:

- currency
- funds management
- financial system and
- monetary policy

Currency

Before the creation of the Bank of Canada, the federal government and the early banks issued notes designed to circulate as currency. The day it began operations, the Bank replaced the outstanding issue of federal government notes and provision was also made for the gradual removal of notes issued by banks. By 1945 the Bank had a monopoly over note issue. Although the original Bank Act required the Bank to redeem its notes in gold, this provision was never used. In fact, it was removed with the 1967 revision of the Bank Act, thereby providing the Bank with unlimited powers to issue legal tender.

The Bank also conducts ongoing research, working closely with private-sector partnerships and note-issuing authorities in other countries, in order to improve cost-effectiveness, increase the durability of bank notes, and reduce counterfeiting. In its role as provider of paper money, the Bank's overall objective is to preserve the integrity and safety of Canadian currency in the most economical and efficient manner possible.

Funds Management

In its role as the federal government's "fiscal agent", the Bank of Canada provides debt-management services for the federal government such as advising on borrowings, managing new debt offerings, and servicing outstanding debt. Before 1995 these services were provided for all of the federal government's debt. In 1995, however, a special agency of the Department of Finance was created, known as Canada Investment and Savings, to be responsible for the federal government's debt held by individuals, commonly known as retail debt.

Canada Investment and Savings handles Government of Canada securities such as Canada Savings Bonds, Treasury bills, and marketable bonds, and is also responsible for the development of new investment products and marketing initiatives. The Bank of Canada, however, continues to be responsible for all of the government's securities after they are issued, administering millions of bondholder accounts and making payments on behalf of the federal government for interest and debt redemption.

In its role as fiscal agent, the Bank of Canada also manages the government's foreign exchange reserves held by the **Exchange Fund Account** of the Department of Finance. In particular, the Bank assists the Department of Finance in investing these foreign reserves and in borrowing when necessary to maintain an adequate level of reserves. The Bank also engages in international financial transactions, on behalf of the government, in order to influence exchange rates. (We discuss the Bank's foreign exchange interventions more formally in Chapter 19.)

Financial System

The Bank of Canada serves as the lender of last resort if a deposit-taking financial institution faces a liquidity crisis. Because of its unique power to create base money, the Bank can ease the liquidity problems of any financial institution by extending advances, and therefore deter bank runs and panics. **Base money** (also called **monetary base**) consists of the monetary liabilities of the central bank and, as you will see in the next chapter, is an important part of the money supply, because changes in it lead to multiple changes in the money supply. Of course, lender-of-last-resort lending is closely coordinated with the two federal regulatory agencies that are set up specifically to regulate financial institutions—the Office of the Superintendent of Financial Institutions Canada and the Canada Deposit Insurance Corporation.[1] Moreover, such lending is done judiciously, explicitly considering the effects on other financial institutions, the money supply, and government policy.

The Bank of Canada also plays a central role in Canada's national payments system (to be discussed in detail in Chapter 16). This is essentially an electronic system that clears and settles payments and transactions including securities and foreign exchange, currently handling 15 times our gross domestic product per year. Although this system is operated by the Canadian Payments Association, federal legislation that came into force in 1996 gave the Bank explicit responsibility for the regulatory oversight of this system. The Bank's main concern is whether problems that affect one participant in the clearing and settlement system will spread to other participants.

Finally, the Bank of Canada acts as the holder of deposit accounts of the federal government, the directly clearing members of the Canadian Payments Association, international organizations such as the International Monetary Fund, and other central banks. As the federal government's banker, the Bank is also responsible for the government's operating accounts. In this role, as you will see in Chapter 16, the Bank shifts government balances between the government's transactions account with the Bank and the government's non-transactions accounts with the banks, using twice-daily auctions of government term deposits.

Monetary Policy

The Bank of Canada employs such tools as **open market buyback operations** (the purchase and sale of government securities that affect both interest rates and the amount of reserves in the banking system) and, to a lesser extent, the shifting of government balances between it and the directly clearing members of the Canadian Payments Association to implement changes in the money supply. The Bank's ultimate objective is to keep inflation low. The Bank has a staff of professional economists, which provides economic analysis that the Board of Directors uses in making its decisions (see the FYI box Role of the Bank's Research Staff).

The Bank's goal of low inflation is closely related to the goal of steady economic growth, because businesses are more likely to invest in capital equipment to increase productivity and economic growth when inflation is low. Low inflation is also desirable because it protects the purchasing power of pensioners and those on fixed incomes.

Although the Bank determines monetary policy, in the following section you will learn that the ultimate responsibility for policy rests with the government, since it is the government that must answer to Parliament. This system of "joint responsibility" dates back to 1967 when the Bank of Canada Act was amended to give responsibility for monetary policy to the government.

---

[1] The Office of the Superintendent of Financial Institutions Canada was created in 1987 to succeed the Department of Insurance and the Inspector General of Banks, whereas the Canada Deposit Insurance Corporation was created by an act of Parliament in 1967 to insure deposits, currently up to $100 000 per account, of member deposit-taking institutions.

FYI Role of the Bank's Research Staff

The Bank of Canada is the largest employer of economists in Canada. What do all these economists do?

The most important task of the Bank's economists is to follow the incoming data from government agencies and private-sector organizations on the economy and provide guidance to policymakers on where the economy may be heading and what the impact of monetary policy actions on the economy might be. Moreover, the Bank's economists maintain large econometric models (models whose equations are estimated with statistical procedures) that help them produce forecasts of the national economy, and brief the governor and the senior management of the Bank on their forecasts for the Canadian economy.

Because of the increased influence of developments in foreign countries on the Canadian economy, the research staff produces reports on the major foreign economies. They also conduct research on developments in the foreign exchange market because of its growing importance in the monetary policy process and to support the activities of the Bank's foreign exchange desk.

Staff economists also engage in basic research on the effects of monetary policy on output and inflation, developments in the labour markets, international trade, international capital markets, banking and other financial institutions, financial markets, and regional economies, among other topics. This research is published widely in academic journals and in Bank of Canada publications. Bank of Canada publications, such as the *Annual Report* (published in March each year), the *Bank of Canada Review* (published in May and November), the *Financial System Review* (published in June and December), the *Bank of Canada Banking and Financial Statistics* (published monthly), and the *Monetary Policy Report* (published quarterly) are good sources of supplemental material for money and banking students.

Another important activity of the research staff is in the public education area. Staff economists are called on frequently to make presentations to the public.

HOW INDEPENDENT IS THE BANK OF CANADA?

When we look, in the next three chapters, at how the Bank of Canada conducts monetary policy, we will want to know why it decides to take certain policy actions but not others. To understand its actions, we must understand the incentives that motivate the Bank's behaviour. How free is the Bank of Canada from the whims of the government? Do economic, bureaucratic, or political considerations guide it? Is the Bank of Canada truly independent of outside pressures?

Stanley Fischer, who was a professor at MIT and is now the vice-chair of the U.S. Federal Reserve, has defined two different types of independence of central banks: **instrument independence**, the ability of the central bank to set monetary policy instruments, and **goal independence**, the ability of the central bank to set the goals of monetary policy. Unlike the Federal Reserve and the European Central Bank, which have both types of independence and are remarkably free of political pressures that influence other government agencies, the Bank of Canada has instrument independence but not goal independence.

The Bank of Canada's degree of independence has evolved over time, in part because of changing circumstances, and in part because a clear division of authority was not established in the original Bank of Canada Act. Initially, the Bank of Canada was privately owned, with about 12 000 individual shareholders, and so was largely free of political pressures. It was also free of private interference, because of regulations regarding who could hold how much stock in the Bank. The Conservative government in office at the time of the Bank's creation believed that the Bank should possess a large share of the responsibility for the development of monetary policy.

Significant changes in the balance of power occurred with the election of a majority Liberal government in the fall of 1935. The Liberals moved the Bank of Canada in the direction of public ownership, culminating in its complete nationalization by 1938. This was done to further isolate the Bank from the pressures of the private system. However, the nationalization of the Bank of Canada did tilt the balance of authority for monetary policy, back toward the federal Cabinet and Parliament. The Liberals believed that the Bank of Canada should have discretion in internal management and in implementing monetary policy, yet the policies being implemented should be in harmony with the views of the government.

In June 1954, the first governor of the Bank of Canada, Graham Towers, retired after 19 years of service. Graham Towers was replaced by James Coyne (see the FYI box The Political Environment and the Bank of Canada). Like many Canadians at the time, James Coyne was concerned about the level of foreign ownership and the increase in consumer prices during the Korean War. He was convinced that the solution to these problems was a tighter monetary policy stance. A decline in the supply of bank reserves would increase interest rates, thereby raising national savings and reducing Canada's dependence on foreign capital inflows. This tighter monetary policy led to rising unemployment and weak output growth. As a result, the Bank of Canada's policies were criticized in the popular press and by most of the academic community. In fact, 30 economists signed a letter to the minister of finance calling for Coyne's dismissal.[2]

James Coyne, however, did not change his mind. He was convinced that there was no long-term relationship between inflation and unemployment, despite the publication of a famous paper in 1958 by the British economist A. W. Phillips, showing that higher inflation was typically associated with a lower unemployment rate.[3] Although the Phillips hypothesis attracted widespread support in Canada and was replicated with Canadian data, Coyne was anticipating the pathbreaking work by Milton Friedman and Edmund Phelps on the vertical Phillips curve, to be published 10 years later in 1968.[4] But as a former governor of the Bank of Canada, Gordon Thiessen, put it in a recent speech,

> [t]here was one critical area, however, where Coyne and many other policy analysts, both within and outside the Bank, appear to have been misguided. Those who had questioned the effectiveness of monetary policy in earlier years had failed to appreciate that it was likely to be much stronger than fiscal policy under a flexible exchange rate system, especially when capital was highly mobile. The large capital movements triggered by any change in interest rates would put significant pressure on the exchange rate, amplifying the effects of monetary policy while undercutting the effects of any opposing fiscal policy. Coyne did not realize that, for similar reasons, it was unlikely that a tighter monetary policy would ever raise national savings or reduce foreign investment inflows.[5]

[2]See H. S. Gordon, *The Economists Versus the Bank of Canada* (Toronto: The Ryerson Press, 1961): v–vi.

[3]A. W. Phillips, "The Relation Between Unemployment and the Rate of Change of Money Wages in the United Kingdom," *Economica* 24 (1958): 283–299.

[4]Milton Friedman, "The Role of Monetary Policy," *American Economic Review* 58 (1968): 1–17; Edmund Phelps, "Money-Wage Dynamics and Labour Market Equilibrium," *Journal of Political Economy* 76 (1968): 678–711.

[5]Gordon Thiessen, "Can a Bank Change? The Evolution of Monetary Policy at the Bank of Canada 1935–2000," Lecture to the Faculty of Social Science, University of Western Ontario (October 17, 2000). Available online courtesy of the Bank of Canada.

To avoid accepting blame for this state of affairs, the Liberal government in office reversed its previous stand and disavowed its position that the government was responsible for monetary policy. The government was criticized for this reversal and the new hands-off approach to monetary policy. When the government changed hands on June 10, 1957, and Donald Fleming became the federal minister of finance, the stage was set for a confrontation with the governor of the Bank of Canada, James Coyne. After a long and acrimonious debate, the so-called Coyne Affair was resolved in 1961 with the resignation of Governor Coyne.

On July 24, 1961, Louis Rasminsky accepted the position as the third governor of the Bank of Canada on the condition that the relationship between the government and the Bank of Canada be clearly defined. Soon after he assumed office, he issued a public statement containing two main principles reflecting his views on that relationship

> . . . (1) in the ordinary course of events, the Bank has the responsibility for monetary policy, and (2) if the government disapproves of the monetary policy being carried out by the Bank, it has the right and the responsibility to direct the Bank as to the policy which the Bank is to carry out.[6]

A royal commission, whose appointment was partly initiated by the Coyne Affair, accepted Governor Rasminsky's views regarding the relationship between the Bank of Canada and the government. The commission recommended a system of joint responsibility under which the Bank of Canada has considerable autonomy in the conduct of day-to-day monetary policy but the government must accept full responsibility for the policy being followed.

The Bank of Canada Act was amended in 1967 to confirm the joint responsibility system, and this state of affairs regarding monetary policy has generally remained in order to this day. Under this joint responsibility system, the governor of the Bank of Canada and the minister of finance, acting on behalf of the government, consult regularly and, in the event of a serious disagreement over the conduct of monetary policy, the government has the right to override the Bank's decisions. In particular, the minister of finance can issue a directive to the Bank indicating the specific policy changes that the Bank must follow. The directive, however, must be published indicating not only the new policy that the Bank is supposed to undertake but also the period during which it is to apply.

Hence, ultimate responsibility for monetary policy rests with the democratically elected government. However, because of the consequences of issuing a directive, it is unlikely that such a directive would be issued, and none has been issued to date.

THE CHANGING FACE OF THE BANK OF CANADA

The legislation governing the Bank of Canada's responsibility for monetary policy has remained relatively unchanged since the Bank Act of 1967. Over the past decade, however, the Bank has undertaken a broad range of initiatives and made significant institutional changes to the way it operates. The impetus for change came from the interaction of experience and economic theory, the desire to explain and build confidence in the Bank's actions, and (to a smaller extent) from technological change and globalization.

Clarifying objectives is an important starting point for any successful monetary policy framework. The legislation by which the Bank of Canada is governed does not

---

[6]Bank of Canada, *Annual Report*, 1961, p. 3.

facilitate a clear understanding of objectives. For example, the preamble to legislation governing the Bank refers to multiple, and potentially inconsistent, policy objectives. Over the past few decades, however, the performance of the Canadian economy, together with the evolution of economic theory, led to the view that price stability is the most important goal of monetary policy. As John Crow put it, in his January 1988 Hanson Memorial Lecture at the University of Alberta,

> [t]heory and experience—much of this experience not overly cheerful but certainly instructive—both point to a very clear answer. Monetary policy should be conducted so as to achieve a pace of monetary expansion that promotes stability in the value of money. This means pursuing a policy aimed at achieving and maintaining stable prices.[7]

The Hanson lecture was designed to explicitly identify price stability as the objective of Bank of Canada policy. This message was reinforced on February 26, 1991, through a joint announcement by the governor of the Bank and the minister of finance regarding the establishment of formal inflation targets (to be discussed in detail in Chapter 17). Clearly defined targets can be appealed as an institutional way of improving the macroeconomic outcomes of monetary policy.

The effectiveness of such an institutional framework, however, depends on two fundamental requirements: "independence" and "accountability". Although the Bank of Canada has not been given "goal independence"—the goal of price stability has been set jointly by the Bank and the Ministry of Finance—over the last decade the Bank has placed increased emphasis on its responsibility to achieve the goal of price stability and its greater freedom to take whatever action is needed to do so. This freedom is referred to as "operational" (or "instrument") independence and, although it hasn't been explicitly legislated, it exists in practice. Increased operational independence has also raised the standards for accountability. As already noted, for example, the governor of the Bank has delegated the authority for monetary policy decisions to a committee—the six-member internal Governing Council. Moreover, it has become a de facto standard for the governor to appear before a parliamentary committee following the release of the Bank's *Monetary Policy Report*.

The Bank of Canada has also improved its communications activities by moving towards greater transparency in its operations and objectives. In particular, the Bank has noticeably increased the number of its press conferences, press releases, and speeches, and also reorganized its regional offices in 1996–1997, with the objective of improving communication, transparency, and its assessment of economic conditions across Canada. For example, the Bank's regional offices, by maintaining contact with provincial governments, industries, and the general public, present quarterly "grassroots" assessments of current and prospective economic developments to the Bank's Governing Council—information that complements economic projections prepared by the Bank's staff. Finally, the Bank of Canada maintains a comprehensive website (at **www.bankofcanada.ca**) to disseminate information regarding financial statistics, publications, the transmission of monetary policy, and Bank-related material.[8]

---

[7]John Crow, "The Work of Canadian Monetary Policy," The Eric J. Hanson Memorial Lecture, University of Alberta, Edmonton, Alberta. *Bank of Canada Review* (1988): 3–17.

[8]An inside view of how the Bank interacts with the public and the politicians can be found in John Crow, *Making Money: An Insider's Perspective on Finance, Politics, and Canada's Central Bank* (Toronto: John Wiley, 2002).

The direction taken in the recent evolution of the monetary policy framework in Canada has been heavily influenced by the role that the institutional monetary structure plays in influencing the monetary conduct.[9] As the Bank's former governor, Gordon Thiessen, put it in his October 17, 2000, speech to the Faculty of Social Science of the University of Western Ontario,

> [t]he Bank tries to work with markets, rather than against them, to avoid surprising them with unexpected actions. Greater transparency facilitates the policy-transmission process by conditioning market expectations, and helps avoid unnecessary confusion about the reasons for our actions.[10]

From Opaqueness to Accountability and Transparency

The Bank of Canada did not release information regarding its guidelines or resulting consequences during the 1960s and 1970s. As a general rule, the Bank wanted to remain nontransparent, keeping its monetary policy approaches secret. The use of multiple instruments and goals, vague statements about its policies, and moral suasion with banks, resulted in an unnecessary level of secrecy. Due to this instrument and goal opaqueness, the public was not able to question or comprehend the Bank's actions, allowing the accountability of the Bank of Canada to deteriorate.

Over the past decade, however, the Bank of Canada has rejected multiple policy instruments by adopting the overnight interest rate as the centrepiece of its monetary policy implementation and by focusing on an explicit inflation-control target. The goal of the Bank's current monetary policy is to keep the inflation rate within a target range of 1% to 3%, with the midpoint of the inflation target range, 2%, being the most desirable outcome; the 1% to 3% target range for inflation applies until the end of 2016. By announcing a target overnight interest rate, establishing planned dates for policy changes, and implementing the Governing Council for making decisions and disclosing information, the Bank of Canada has moved towards greater accountability and transparency.

The Bank's move toward accountability and transparency was motivated by a number of recent trends in society and the economy. For example, the shift from fixed to flexible exchange rates removed an obstacle to openness. The experience with inflation in the 1970s and the recession in the early 1980s allowed the Bank of Canada to reconsider its analysis of inflation and its costs. In addition, economic comprehension about interest rates, developments about targets and inflation, and greater openness in the government also contributed to the accountability and transparency of the Bank of Canada.[11]

---

[9]For a discussion of similar changes implemented by other central banks around the world, see Graydon Paulin, "The Changing Face of Central Banking in the 1990s," *Bank of Canada Review* (Summer 2000): 3–13.

[10]Gordon Thiessen, "Can a Bank Change? The Evolution of Monetary Policy at the Bank of Canada 1935–2000." Lecture to the Faculty of Social Science, University of Western Ontario (October 17, 2000).

[11]For more details regarding the Bank's recent move toward openness and accountability, see John Chant, "The Bank of Canada: Moving Towards Transparency," *Bank of Canada Review* (Spring 2003): 5–13. Also, regarding Canada's experience with central banking, see Michael D. Bordo and Angela Redish, "70 Years of Central Banking: The Bank of Canada in an International Context, 1935–2005," *Bank of Canada Review* (Winter 2005–2006): 7–14, and David Laidler, "Free Banking and the Bank of Canada," *Bank of Canada Review* (Winter 2005–2006): 15–24.

SHOULD THE BANK OF CANADA BE INDEPENDENT?

As we have seen, the Bank of Canada is probably the most independent government agency in Canada. Every few years, the question arises whether the independence given to the Bank of Canada should be curtailed. Politicians who strongly oppose a Bank policy often want to bring it under their supervision in order to impose a policy more to their liking. Should the Bank of Canada be independent, or would we be better off with a central bank under the control of the government?

The Case for Independence

The strongest argument for an independent Bank of Canada rests on the view that subjecting the Bank to more political pressures would impart an inflationary bias to monetary policy. In the view of many observers, politicians in a democratic society are shortsighted because they are driven by the need to win their next election. With this as the primary goal, they are unlikely to focus on long-run objectives, such as promoting a stable price level. Instead, they will seek short-run solutions to problems, like high unemployment and high interest rates, even if the short-run solutions have undesirable long-run consequences. For example, we saw in Chapter 5 that high money growth might lead initially to a drop in interest rates but might also cause an increase later, as inflation heats up. Would a Bank of Canada under the control of the government be more likely to pursue a policy of excessive money growth when interest rates are high, even though such a policy would eventually lead to inflation and even higher interest rates in the future? The advocates of an independent central bank say yes. They believe that a politically insulated central bank is more likely to be concerned with long-run objectives and thus more likely to defend a sound dollar and a stable price level.

A variation on the preceding argument is that the political process in Canada could lead to a **political business cycle**, in which just before an election, expansionary policies are pursued to lower unemployment and interest rates. After the election, the bad effects of these policies—high inflation and high interest rates—come home to roost, requiring contractionary policies that politicians hope the public will forget before the next election. Although the issue has not been completely settled, research indicates that there is no credible evidence that such a political business cycle exists in Canada (see the FYI box Economics and Politics).

Putting the Bank of Canada under the control of the government is also considered dangerous because the Bank can be used to facilitate government financing of large budget deficits by its purchases of government bonds. Such open market purchases by the Bank of Canada increase the money supply and lead to inflation. Government pressure on the Bank of Canada to "help out" might lead to a more inflationary bias in the economy. An independent Bank of Canada is better able to resist this pressure from the government.

Another argument for central bank independence is that control of monetary policy is too important to leave to politicians, a group that has repeatedly demonstrated a lack of expertise at making hard decisions on issues of great economic importance, such as reducing the budget deficit or reforming the banking system. This argument can also be stated in terms of the principal–agent problem discussed in Chapters 8, 9, and 10. Both the Bank of Canada and politicians are agents of the public (the principals), and both politicians and the Bank of Canada have incentives to act in their own interest rather than in the interest of the public. The argument supporting Bank of Canada independence is that the principal–agent problem is worse for politicians than for the Bank of Canada because politicians have fewer incentives to act in the public interest.

FYI   Economics and Politics

Recent politico-institutional approaches to the theory of economic policy emphasize the incentives of rational and maximizing policymakers in explaining movements in macroeconomic variables. Central to this perspective is the general assumption that policymakers respond to incentives and constraints just like all other economic agents. As a consequence, the actual policies of government give rise to political cycles, which on the basis of the primary motivational force involved are distinguished into opportunistic and partisan cycles.

In opportunistic (or electoral) business cycle models, politicians maximize their popularity or their probability of re-election by following pre-election expansionary fiscal policies in order to please the fiscally knowledgeable voters. As a consequence, their actual policies give rise to **electoral business cycles**, that is, persistent cyclical patterns of key policy and target variables across electoral terms, regardless of the political orientation of the incumbent government. In particular, models of opportunistic cycles predict pre-election high growth and low unemployment, increasing inflation around the election time,

and a post-election contraction, regardless of the political party in power.

In the more accepted partisan cycle models, politicians are ideological; that is, they represent the interests of different pressure groups and, when in office, follow policies that are favourable to their supporting groups. For example, the left-wing parties pursue expansionary policies in order to reduce unemployment, while the right-wing parties tend to induce post-election contractions in economic performance in order to reduce inflation. The outcome, therefore, is **partisan business cycles**, that is, systematic and permanent differences in macroeconomic outcomes that differ by political party.

Work by Apostolos Serletis and Panos Afxentiou of the University of Calgary indicates that there is no credible evidence that such a political business cycle exists in Canada.[12]

---

[12] Apostolos Serletis and Panos C. Afxentiou, "Electoral and Partisan Cycle Regularities in Canada," *Canadian Journal of Economics* 31 (1998): 28–46.

Indeed, some politicians may prefer an independent Bank of Canada because it can be used as a public "whipping boy" to take some of the heat off their backs. It is possible that a politician who in private opposes an inflationary monetary policy will be forced to support such a policy in public for fear of not being re-elected. An independent Bank of Canada can pursue policies that are politically unpopular yet in the public interest.

The Case Against Independence

Proponents of a Bank of Canada under the control of the government argue that it is undemocratic to have monetary policy (which affects almost everyone in the economy) controlled by an elite group responsible to no one. The current lack of accountability of the Bank of Canada has serious consequences: if the Bank performs badly, no provision is in place for replacing members (as there is with politicians). True, the Bank of Canada needs to pursue long-run objectives, but elected government officials vote on long-run issues also (foreign policy, for example). If we push the argument further that policy is always performed better by elite groups like the Bank of Canada, we end up with such conclusions as the Canada Revenue Agency should set tax policies with no oversight from the government. Would you advocate this degree of independence for the Canada Revenue Agency?

The public holds the government responsible for the economic well-being of the country, yet it lacks control over the government agency that may well be the most important actor in determining the health of the economy. In addition, to achieve a cohesive program that will promote economic stability, monetary policy must be coordinated with fiscal policy (the management of government spending and taxation). Only by placing monetary policy under the control of the politicians who also control fiscal policy can these two policies be prevented from working at cross-purposes.

No consensus has yet been reached on whether Bank of Canada independence is a good thing, although public support for independence of the central bank seems to have been growing in both Canada and abroad. As you might expect, people who like the Bank's policies are more likely to support its independence, whereas those who dislike its policies advocate a less independent Bank of Canada.

Central Bank Independence and Macroeconomic Performance Throughout the World

We have seen that advocates of an independent central bank believe that macroeconomic performance will be improved by making the central bank more independent. Empirical evidence seems to support this conjecture: when central banks are ranked from least independent to most independent, inflation performance is found to be the best for countries with the most independent central banks. Although a more independent central bank appears to lead to a lower inflation rate, this is not achieved at the expense of poorer real economic performance. Countries with independent central banks are no more likely to have high unemployment or greater output fluctuations than are those countries with less independent central banks.

EXPLAINING CENTRAL BANK BEHAVIOUR

One view of government bureaucratic behaviour is that bureaucracies serve the public interest (this is called the *public interest view*). Yet some economists have developed a theory of bureaucratic behaviour that emphasizes other factors that influence the operation of bureaucracies. The *theory of bureaucratic behaviour* suggests that the objective of a bureaucracy is to maximize its own welfare, just as a consumer's behaviour is motivated by the desire to maximize personal welfare and a firm's behaviour is motivated by the desire to maximize profits. The welfare of a bureaucracy is related to its power and prestige. Thus this theory suggests that an important factor affecting a central bank's behaviour is its wish to increase its power and prestige.

What predictions does this view of a central bank like the Bank of Canada suggest? One is that the Bank of Canada will fight vigorously to preserve its autonomy, a prediction verified time and time again as the Bank of Canada has continually counterattacked attempts to control its functions. Another prediction is that the Bank of Canada will try to avoid conflict with powerful groups that might threaten to curtail its power and reduce its autonomy. The Bank's behaviour may take several forms. One possible factor explaining why the Bank is sometimes slow to increase interest rates and thus smooth out their fluctuations is that it wishes to avoid a conflict with the government over increases in interest rates.

The theory of bureaucratic behaviour seems applicable to the Bank of Canada's actions, but we must recognize that this view of the Bank of Canada as being solely concerned with its own self-interest is too extreme. Maximizing one's welfare does not rule out altruism. (You might give generously to a charity because it makes you feel good about yourself, but in the process you are helping a worthy cause.) The Bank of Canada is surely concerned with conducting monetary policy that is in the public interest. However, much uncertainty and disagreement often exist over what that monetary policy should be.[13] When it is unclear what policy will best serve the public interest, other motives may influence the Bank's behaviour. In these situations, the theory of bureaucratic behaviour may be a useful guide to predicting what motivates the Bank of Canada and other central banks.

STRUCTURE AND INDEPENDENCE OF FOREIGN CENTRAL BANKS

In contrast to the Bank of Canada, which is a centralized unit owned by the government, central banks in other industrialized countries have a more decentralized structure. Here we examine the structure and degree of independence of four of the most important foreign central banks: the Federal Reserve System of the United States, the European Central Bank, the Bank of England, and the Bank of Japan.

Federal Reserve System

Of all the central banks in the world, the **Federal Reserve System** of the United States (also called simply **the Fed**) probably has the most unusual structure. It includes the following entities: the **Board of Governors of the Federal Reserve System**, the **Federal Reserve Banks**, the **Federal Open Market Committee (FOMC)**, the Federal Advisory Council, and around 2000 member commercial banks. Figure 14-1 outlines the relationships of these entities to one another and to the three policy tools of the Fed—open market operations, the discount rate (the U.S. equivalent of the bank rate in Canada), and reserve requirements.

Board of Governors of the Federal Reserve System   At the head of the Federal Reserve System is the seven-member Board of Governors, headquartered in Washington, D.C. Each governor is appointed by the President of the United States and confirmed by the Senate. To limit the President's control over the Fed and insulate the Fed from other political pressures, the governors can serve one nonrenewable 14-year term plus part of another term, with one governor's term expiring every other January. The chair of the Board of Governors is chosen from among the seven governors and serves a four-year, renewable term. It is expected that once a new chair is chosen, the old chair resigns from the Board of Governors, even if there are many years left to his or her term as a governor.

Federal Reserve Banks   Each of the 12 Federal Reserve districts has one main Federal Reserve bank, which may have branches in other cities in the district. The

---

[13]One example of the uncertainty over how best to conduct monetary policy was discussed in Chapter 3: economists are not sure how to measure money. So even if economists agreed that controlling the quantity of money is the appropriate way to conduct monetary policy (a controversial position, as we will see in later chapters), the Bank of Canada cannot be sure which monetary aggregate it should control.

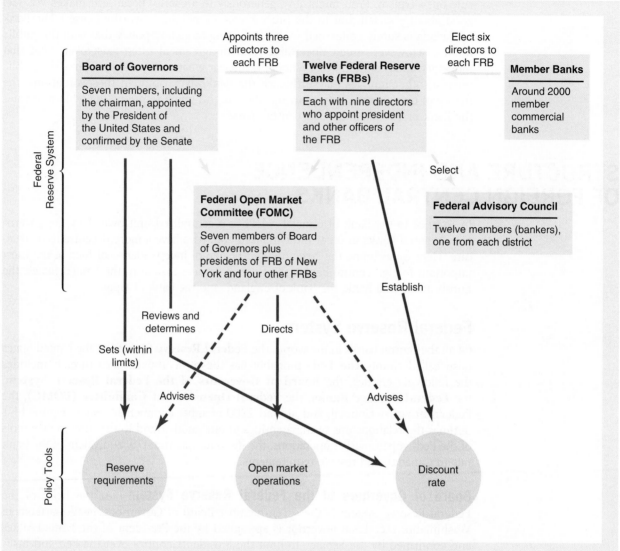

FIGURE 14-1 **Structure and Responsibility for Policy Tools in the Federal Reserve System**

The relationships of the Federal Reserve banks, the Board of Governors of the Federal Reserve System, and the FOMC to the three policy tools of the Fed (open market operations, the discount rate, and reserve requirements). Dashed lines indicate that the FOMC "advises" on the setting of reserve requirements and the discount rate.

locations of these districts, the Federal Reserve banks, and the Federal Reserve Bank branches are shown in Figure 14-2. The three largest Federal Reserve banks in terms of assets are those of New York, Chicago, and San Francisco—combined they hold more than 50% of the assets (discount loans, securities, and other holdings) of the Federal Reserve System. The New York bank, with around one-quarter of the assets, is the most important of the Federal Reserve banks (see the FYI box The Special Role of the Federal Reserve Bank of New York).

MyEconLab Mini-lecture

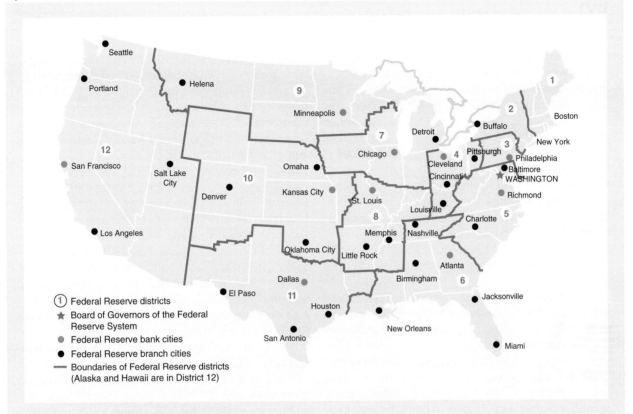

FIGURE 14-2 Federal Reserve System

The locations of the Federal Reserve districts, the Federal Reserve banks, and their branches.
Source: Federal Reserve *Bulletin.*

Federal Open Market Committee (FOMC) The 12 Federal Reserve banks and the Board of Governors are actively involved in decisions concerning the conduct of monetary policy. In particular, all seven governors are voting members of the FOMC, together with the president of the Federal Reserve Bank of New York and presidents of four other Federal Reserve banks. The FOMC usually meets eight times a year (about every six weeks) and makes decisions regarding the conduct of open market operations and the setting of the policy interest rate, the **federal funds rate**, which is the interest rate on overnight loans from one bank to another. Indeed, the FOMC is often referred to as "the Fed" in the press: for example, when the media report that the Fed is meeting, they actually mean that the FOMC is meeting.

How Independent is the Fed? The Federal Reserve appears to be remarkably free of the political pressures that influence other government agencies in the United States. Yet it is still subject to the influence of the president of the United States, since the president appoints members to the Board of Governors. The power of the United States president in appointing members to the Board of Governors is limited, however. Because the term of the chairman of the Board of Governors is not necessarily concurrent with

FYI   The Special Role of the Federal Reserve Bank of New York

The Federal Reserve Bank of New York plays a special role in the Federal Reserve System for several reasons. First, its district contains many of the largest commercial banks in the United States, the safety and soundness of which are paramount to the health of the U.S. financial system. The Federal Reserve Bank of New York conducts examinations of bank holding companies and state-chartered member banks in its district, making it the supervisor of some of the most important financial institutions in the U.S. financial system. Not surprisingly, given this responsibility, the bank supervision group is one of the largest units of the New York Fed and is by far the largest bank supervision group in the Federal Reserve System.

The second reason for the New York Fed's special role is its active involvement in the bond and foreign exchange markets. The New York Fed houses the open market desk, which conducts open market operations—the purchase and sale of bonds—that determine the amount of reserves in the banking system. Because of this involvement in the Treasury securities market, as well as its walking-distance location near the New York Stock Exchange, the officials at the Federal Reserve Bank of New York are in constant contact with the major financial markets in the United States. In addition, the Federal Reserve Bank of New York houses the foreign exchange desk, which conducts foreign exchange interventions on behalf of the Federal Reserve System and the U.S. Treasury. Its

involvement in these financial markets means that the New York Fed is an important source of information on what is happening in U.S. and foreign financial markets, particularly during crisis periods, such as the recent subprime mortgage meltdown, as well as a liaison between officials in the Federal Reserve System and private participants in the markets.

The third reason for the Federal Reserve Bank of New York's prominence is that it is the only Federal Reserve bank to be a member of the Bank for International Settlements (BIS). Thus the president of the New York Fed, along with the chairman of the Board of Governors, represents the Federal Reserve System in its regular monthly meetings with other major central bankers at the BIS. This close contact with foreign central bankers and interaction with foreign exchange markets means that the New York Fed has a special role in international relations, both with other central bankers and with private market participants. Adding to its prominence in international circles is that the New York Fed is the repository for more than US$100 billion of the world's gold, an amount greater than the gold at Fort Knox.

Finally, the president of the Federal Reserve Bank of New York is the only permanent member of the FOMC among the Federal Reserve bank presidents, serving as the vice-chair of the committee. Thus he or she and the chair and vice-chair of the Board of Governors are the three most important officials in the Federal Reserve System.

that of the president of the United States, a president may have to deal with a chairman of the Board of Governors appointed by a previous administration. Alan Greenspan, for example, was appointed chairman in 1987 by President Ronald Reagan and was reappointed to another term by another Republican president, George Bush, in 1992. When Bill Clinton, a Democrat, became president in 1993, Greenspan had several years left to his term. Clinton was put under tremendous pressure to reappoint Greenspan when his term expired and did so in 1996 and again in 2000, even though Greenspan is a Republican.[14] George W. Bush, a Republican, then reappointed Greenspan in 2004.

[14]Similarly, William McChesney Martin Jr., the chairman from 1951 to 1970, was appointed by President Truman (Dem.) but was reappointed by Presidents Eisenhower (Rep.), Kennedy (Dem.), and Nixon (Rep.). Also Paul Volcker, the chairman from 1979 to 1987, was appointed by President Carter (Dem.) but was reappointed by President Reagan (Rep.).

You can see that the Federal Reserve has extraordinary independence for a government agency. Nonetheless, the Fed is not free from political pressures. Indeed, to understand the Fed's behaviour, we must recognize that public support for the actions of the Federal Reserve plays a very important role in its decisions.[15]

European Central Bank

Until recently, the Federal Reserve had no rivals in terms of importance in the central banking world. However, this situation changed in January 1999 with the startup of the European Central Bank (ECB) and European System of Central Banks (ESCB), which now conduct monetary policy for countries that are members of the European Monetary Union. These countries, taken together, have a population that exceeds that of the United States and a GDP comparable to that of the United States. The Maastricht Treaty, which established the ECB and ESCB, patterned these institutions after the Federal Reserve, in that central banks for each country (referred to as *National Central Banks*, or *NCBs*) have a similar role to that of the Federal Reserve Banks. The European Central Bank and the national central banks of the countries that have adopted the euro are referred to as the **Eurosystem**. The Eurosystem excludes the central banks of the European Union countries that have not yet adopted the euro. The Eurosystem should not be confused with the European System of Central Banks, the term used to refer to the European Central Bank and the national central banks of all 27 European Union (EU) member countries—when all EU member countries adopt the euro, the Eurosystem and the European System of Central Banks will become one entity.

The European Central Bank, which is housed in Frankfurt, Germany, has an Executive Board that is similar in structure to the Board of Governors of the Federal Reserve; it is made up of the president, the vice president, and four other members, who are appointed to eight-year, nonrenewable terms. The Governing Council, which comprises the Executive Board and the presidents of the National Central Banks, is similar to the FOMC and makes the decisions on monetary policy. While the presidents of the National Central Banks are appointed by their countries' governments, the members of the Executive Board are appointed by a committee consisting of the heads of state of all the countries that are part of the European Monetary Union.

Differences Between the European System of Central Banks and the Federal Reserve System

In the popular press, the European System of Central Banks is usually referred to as the European Central Bank (ECB), even though it would be more accurate to refer to it as the *Eurosystem*, just as it would be more accurate to refer to the Fed as the Federal Reserve System. Although the structure of the Eurosystem is similar to that of the Federal Reserve System, some important differences distinguish the two. First, the budgets of the Federal Reserve Banks are controlled by the Board of Governors, whereas the National Central Banks control their own budgets *and* the budget of the ECB in Frankfurt. The ECB in the Eurosystem therefore has less power than does the Board of Governors in the Federal Reserve System. Second, the monetary operations of the Eurosystem are conducted by the National Central Banks in each country, so monetary operations are not centralized as they are in the Federal Reserve System. Third, in contrast to the Federal

[15]An inside view of how the Fed interacts with the public and the politicians can be found in Bob Woodward, *Maestro: Greenspan's Fed and the American Boom* (New York: Simon and Schuster, 2000).

Reserve, the ECB is not involved in the supervision and regulation of financial institutions; these tasks are left to the individual countries in the European Monetary Union.

Governing Council   Just as there is a focus on meetings of the FOMC in the United States, there is a similar focus in Europe on meetings of the Governing Council, which gathers monthly at the ECB in Frankfurt to make decisions on monetary policy. Currently, 18 countries are members of the European Monetary Union, and the the heads of the 18 National Central Banks share 15 votes on the Governing Council; each of the six Executive Board members has one vote. In contrast to FOMC meetings, which are attended by staff from both the Board of Governors and the individual Federal Reserve Banks, only the 24 members of the Governing Council attend its meetings, with no staff present.

The Governing Council has decided that although its members have the legal right to vote, no formal vote will actually be taken; instead, the Council operates by consensus. One reason the Governing Council has decided not to take votes is because of worries that the casting of individual votes might lead the heads of National Central Banks to support a monetary policy that would be appropriate for their individual countries, but not necessarily for the countries of the European Monetary Union as a whole. This problem is less severe for the Federal Reserve: Although Federal Reserve Bank presidents do live in different regions of the United States, all have the same nationality and are more likely to take a national view in monetary policy decisions rather than a regional view.

Just as the Federal Reserve releases the FOMC's decision on the setting of the policy interest rate (the federal funds rate) immediately after the meeting is over, the ECB does the same after the conclusion of the monthly Governing Council meeting (by announcing the target for a similar short-term interest rate for interbank loans). In addition, immediately after every monetary policy meeting of the Governing Council, the president and vice president of the ECB hold a press conference in which they take questions from the news media. (A similar press conference is held by the Federal Reserve chair, but it is less frequent, held only four times a year.) The large number of members in the Governing Council presents a particular dilemma. The current size of the Governing Council (24 members) is substantially larger than that of the FOMC (12 voting members). Many commentators have wondered whether the Governing Council is already too unwieldy—a situation that will get considerably worse as more countries join the European Monetary Union. To deal with this potential problem, the Governing Council decided on a complex system of rotation, somewhat like that of the FOMC, in which National Central Banks from the larger countries will vote more often than National Central Banks from the smaller countries.

How Independent is the ECB?   Although the Federal Reserve is a highly independent central bank, the Maastricht Treaty, which established the Eurosystem, has made the latter the most independent central bank in the world. Like the Board of Governors, the members of the Executive Board have long terms (eight years), while heads of National Central Banks are required to have terms at least five years long. Like the Fed, the Eurosystem determines its own budget, and the governments of the member countries are not allowed to issue instructions to the ECB. These elements of the Maastricht Treaty make the ECB highly independent.

The Maastricht Treaty specifies that the overriding, long-term goal of the ECB is price stability, which means that the goal for the Eurosystem is more clearly specified than it is for the Federal Reserve System. However, the Maastricht Treaty does not specify exactly what "price stability" means. The Eurosystem has defined the quantitative goal for monetary policy to be an inflation rate slightly less than 2%, so from this perspective, the ECB is slightly less goal-independent than the Fed. The Eurosystem is, however, much more goal-independent than the Federal Reserve System in another way: the Eurosystem's charter cannot be changed by legislation; it can be changed only by revision of the Maastricht Treaty—a difficult process because *all* signatories to the treaty must agree to accept any proposed change.

Bank of England

Founded in 1694, the Bank of England is the second-oldest central bank (the Riksbank of Sweden is the oldest). The Bank Act of 1946 gave the government statutory authority over the Bank of England. The Court (equivalent to a board of directors) of the Bank of England is made up of the governor and two deputy governors, who are appointed for five-year terms, and 16 non-executive directors, who are appointed for three-year terms.

Until 1997, the Bank of England was the least independent of the central banks examined in this chapter because the decision to raise or lower interest rates resided not within the Bank of England but with the Chancellor of the Exchequer (the equivalent of the Canadian minister of finance). All of this changed when a new Labour government came to power in May 1997 and the Chancellor of the Exchequer, Gordon Brown, made a surprise announcement that the Bank of England would henceforth have the power to set interest rates. However, the Bank was not granted total instrument independence: the government can overrule the Bank and set rates "in extreme economic circumstances" and "for a limited period." Nonetheless, as in Canada, overruling the Bank is likely to be a rare occurrence, because doing so would be highly public and is meant to occur only in highly unusual circumstances and for a limited time.

Because the United Kingdom is not a member of the European Monetary Union, the Bank of England makes its monetary policy decisions independently from the European Central Bank. The power to set interest rates resides with the Monetary Policy Committee, made up of the governor, two deputy governors, two members (normally central bank officials) appointed by the governor after consultation with the chancellor, plus four outside economic experts appointed by the chancellor. (Surprisingly, two of the four outside experts initially appointed to this committee were not British citizens—one was Dutch and the other American—and some later appointments have also not been British citizens, including the current governor, Mark Carney, who is Canadian.) The inflation target for the Bank of England is set by the Chancellor of the Exchequer, so the Bank of England is also less goal-independent than the Fed.

Bank of Japan

The Bank of Japan (Nippon Ginko) was founded in 1882 during the Meiji Restoration. Monetary policy is determined by the Bank's Policy Board, which is composed of the governor, two vice-governors, and six outside members appointed by the cabinet and approved by the parliament, all of whom serve for five-year terms.

Until recently, the Bank of Japan was not formally independent of the government, with the ultimate power residing with the Ministry of Finance. However, the Bank of Japan Law, which took effect in April 1998 and was the first major change in the relative power of the Bank of Japan in 55 years, changed this situation. In addition to stipulating that the objective of monetary policy is to attain price stability, the law granted greater instrument and goal independence to the Bank of Japan. Before this, the government had two voting members on the Policy Board: one from the Ministry of Finance and the other from the Economic Planning Agency. Now the government may send two representatives from these agencies to board meetings, but they no longer have voting rights, although they are allowed to request delays in monetary policy decisions. In addition, the Ministry of Finance lost its authority to oversee many operations of the Bank of Japan, particularly the right to dismiss senior officials. However, the Ministry of Finance continues to have control over the part of the Bank's budget that is unrelated to monetary policy, which might limit its independence to some extent.

The Trend Toward Greater Independence

As our survey of the structure and independence of the major central banks indicates, in recent years we have been seeing a remarkable trend toward increasing independence. It used to be that the Federal Reserve was substantially more independent than almost all other central banks, with the exception of those in Germany and Switzerland. Now the newly established European Central Bank is far more independent than the Fed, and greater independence has been granted to central banks like the Bank of England and the Bank of Japan, putting them more on a par with the Fed, as well as to central banks in such diverse countries as New Zealand, Sweden, and the euro nations. Both theory and experience suggest that more independent central banks produce better monetary policy, thus providing an impetus for this trend.

MyEconLab

MyEconLab is an online homework and tutorial system that puts you in control of your own learning with study and practice tools directly correlated to this chapter's content. Visit MyEconLab to access the eText, the Questions and Applied Problems with answers, as well as additional assessment. You will also find web chapters, mini-lectures, appendices, mini-cases, videos, glossary flashcards, news feeds, CANSIM data, and graphing tools.

SUMMARY

1. The Bank of Canada was created by an act of Parliament in 1934 and began operations on March 11, 1935. Initially it was privately owned but became a Crown corporation in 1938.

2. The overall responsibility for the operation of the Bank of Canada rests with a Board of Directors, consisting of the governor, the senior deputy governor, the deputy minister of finance, and 12 outside directors. The Bank's governor is the chief executive officer and chair of the Board of Directors.

3. Although on paper the Bank of Canada is an arm of the government, in practice the Bank has more independence than the Bank of Canada Act suggests.

4. The Bank of Canada is more independent than most agencies of the Canadian government, but it is still subject to political pressures. The theory of bureaucratic behaviour indicates that one factor driving the Bank's behaviour is its attempt to increase its power and prestige. This view explains many of the Bank's actions, although the agency may also try to act in the public interest.

5. The case for an independent Bank of Canada rests on the view that curtailing the Bank's independence and subjecting it to more political pressures would impart an inflationary bias to monetary policy. An independent Bank of Canada can afford to take the long view and not respond to short-run problems that will result in expansionary monetary policy and a political business cycle. The case against an independent Bank of Canada holds that it is undemocratic to have monetary policy (so important to the public) controlled by an elite group that is not accountable to the public. An independent Bank of Canada also makes the coordination of monetary and fiscal policy difficult.

6. The U.S. Federal Reserve System was created in 1913 to lessen the frequency of bank panics. Because of public hostility to central banks and the centralization of power, the Federal Reserve System was created with many checks and balances to diffuse power.

7. The Federal Reserve System consists of 12 regional Federal Reserve banks, around 2000 member

commercial banks, the Board of Governors of the Federal Reserve System, the Federal Open Market Committee, and the Federal Advisory Council.

8. Although on paper the Federal Reserve appears to be decentralized, in practice it has come to function as a unified central bank controlled by the Board of Governors, especially the board's chair.

9. The European System of Central Banks has a similar structure to that of the Federal Reserve System, with each member country having a National Central Bank, and an Executive Board of the European Central Bank (located in Frankfurt, Germany). The Governing Council, which is made up of the six members of the Executive Board (including the president of the European Central Bank) and the

presidents of the National Central Banks, makes the decisions on monetary policy. The Eurosystem, which was established under the terms of the Maastricht Treaty, is even more independent than the Federal Reserve System because its charter cannot be changed by legislation. Indeed, it is the most independent central bank in the world.

10. There has been a remarkable trend toward increasing independence of central banks throughout the world. Greater independence has been granted to central banks such as the Bank of England and the Bank of Japan in recent years, as well as to other central banks in such diverse countries as New Zealand and Sweden. Both theory and experience suggest that more independent central banks produce better monetary policy.

KEY TERMS

base money, p. 346
Board of Directors, p. 343
Board of Governors of the Federal Reserve System, p. 355
electoral business cycles, p. 353
Eurosystem, p. 359
Exchange Fund Account, p. 345

federal funds rate, p. 357
Federal Open Market Committee (FOMC), p. 355
Federal Reserve Banks, p. 355
Federal Reserve System, p. 355
goal independence, p. 347
Governing Council, p. 344

instrument independence, p. 347
monetary base, p. 346
open market buyback operations, p. 346
partisan business cycles, p. 353
political business cycle, p. 352
the Fed, p. 355

QUESTIONS

All questions are available in MyEconLab at **www.myeconlab.com.**

1. What political realities might explain the creation of the Bank of Canada in 1934?

2. In what ways can the government influence the conduct of monetary policy?

3. Who is responsible for monetary policy in Canada?

4. Do you think that the seven-year renewable term for the governor of the Bank of Canada effectively insulates the Bank from political pressure?

5. How did the "Coyne Affair" motivate the current system of joint responsibility for monetary policy?

6. Over time, which entities have gained power in the conduct of monetary policy in Canada and which have lost power? Why do you think this has happened?

7. "The strongest argument for an independent Bank of Canada rests on the view that subjecting the Bank of Canada to more political pressures would impart an inflationary bias to monetary policy." Is this statement true, false, or uncertain? Explain your answer.

8. The Bank of Canada is the most independent of all Canadian government agencies. What is the main difference between it and other government agencies that explains its greater independence?

9. How can the government directly influence the Bank of Canada?

10. How is the responsibility for monetary policy shared in the Eurosystem?

11. "The theory of bureaucratic behaviour indicates that the Bank of Canada never operates in the public interest."

Is this statement true, false, or uncertain? Explain your answer.

12. Why might eliminating the Bank's independence lead to a more pronounced political business cycle?

13. "The independence of the Bank of Canada leaves it completely unaccountable for its actions." Is this statement true, false, or uncertain? Explain your answer.

14. "The independence of the Bank of Canada has meant that it takes the long view and not the short view." Is this statement true, false, or uncertain? Explain your answer.

15. Why did Canada show little interest in the establishment of a central bank during the first 60 or so years of Confederation?

16. What is the primary tool that the U.S. Congress uses to exercise control over the Fed?

17. Should the Federal Reserve be subject to periodic auditing of its policies, procedures, and finances? Why or why not?

18. The Fed promotes secrecy by not releasing the minutes of FOMC meetings to Congress or the public immediately. Discuss the arguments for and against this policy.

19. Which is more independent, the Federal Reserve or the European Central Bank? Why?

20. Why did the Bank of England up until 1997 have a low degree of independence?

DATA ANALYSIS PROBLEMS

Download data for these problems from MyEconLab at **www.myeconlab.com**.

1. Go to the CANSIM database, and find data on the unemployment rate in New Brunswick (series V2063760), Ontario (series V2063949), and British Columbia (series V2064705). For the most recent month of data available,

determine which province had the highest, and which had the lowest, unemployment rate.

2. Go to the Bank of Canada's website, and find data on the overnight interest rate target. When was the last time the overnight interest rate target was changed? Did the rate increase or decrease?

WEB EXERCISES

1. Go to **www.bankofcanada.ca** and click on "About the Bank." Under "The Board of Directors," click on "See who is on the Board of Directors." Write a short essay about the diversity of the 12 outside directors of the Bank of Canada's Board of Directors.

2. Go to **www.federalreserve.gov/** and click on "About the Fed." Next, click on "The Federal Reserve System" and then on "Structure." According to the Federal Reserve,

what is the most important responsibility of the Board of Governors?

3. Go to the site listed in Web Exercise 2 and click on "Monetary Policy." Then click on "Reports" and go to the "beige book." According to the summary of the most recently published book, is the U.S. economy weakening or strengthening?

WEB REFERENCES

www.bank-banque-canada.ca/
The website for the Bank of Canada.

www.federalreserve.gov/pubs/frseries/frseri.htm
Information on the structure of the Federal Reserve System.

www.ecb.int
The website for the European Central Bank.

www.bankofengland.co.uk/index.htm
The website for the Bank of England.

www.boj.or.jp/en/index.htm
The website for the Bank of Japan.

15

The Money Supply Process

Learning Objectives

After studying this chapter you should be able to

1. List and describe the "three players" that influence the money supply.

2. Classify the factors affecting the Bank of Canada's assets and liabilities.

3. Identify the factors that affect the monetary base and discuss their effects on the Bank of Canada's balance sheet.

4. Explain and illustrate the deposit creation process through T-accounts.

5. List the factors that affect the money supply.

6. Summarize how the "three players" can influence the money supply.

7. Calculate and interpret changes in the money multiplier.

PREVIEW

As we saw in Chapter 5 and will see in later chapters on monetary theory, movements in the money supply affect interest rates and inflation and thus affect us all. Because of its far-reaching effects on economic activity, it is important to understand how the money supply is determined. Who controls it? What causes it to change? How might control of it be improved? In this and subsequent chapters, we answer these questions by providing a detailed description of the *money supply process*, the mechanism that determines the level of the money supply.

Because deposits at banks are by far the largest component of the money supply, learning how these deposits are created is the first step in understanding the money supply process. This chapter provides an overview of how the banking system creates deposits and describes the basic principles of the money supply, concepts that will form the foundation for the material presented in later chapters.

THREE PLAYERS IN THE MONEY SUPPLY PROCESS

The "cast of characters" in the money supply story is as follows:

1. The *central bank*—the government agency that oversees the banking system and is responsible for the conduct of monetary policy; in Canada, the Bank of Canada;

2. *Banks* (depository institutions)—the financial intermediaries that accept deposits from individuals and institutions and make loans: commercial banks, trust and loan companies, and credit unions; AND

3. *Depositors*—individuals and institutions that hold deposits in banks.

Of the three players, the central bank—the Bank of Canada—is the most important. The Bank's conduct of monetary policy involves actions that affect its balance sheet (holdings of assets and liabilities), to which we turn now.[1]

[1]A detailed discussion of the Bank of Canada's balance sheet and the factors that affect the monetary base can be found in Appendix 15.1 to this chapter, which you can find on MyEconLab.

THE BANK OF CANADA'S BALANCE SHEET

The operation of the Bank of Canada and its monetary policy involve actions that affect its balance sheet, or its holdings of assets and liabilities. Here we discuss a simplified balance sheet that includes just four items that are essential to our understanding of the money supply process.

Bank of Canada	
Assets	**Liabilities**
Securities	Currency in circulation
Loans to financial institutions	Reserves

Liabilities

The two liabilities on the balance sheet, currency in circulation and reserves, are often referred to as the *monetary liabilities* of the Bank of Canada. They are an important part of the money supply story, because increases in either or both will lead to an increase in the money supply (everything else being constant). The sum of the Bank's monetary liabilities (currency in circulation and reserves) and the Canadian Mint's monetary liabilities, coins in circulation is called the **monetary base**. When discussing the monetary base, we will focus only on the monetary liabilities of the Bank of Canada, because the monetary liabilities of the Canadian Mint account for a very small fraction of the base.

1. *Notes in circulation.* The Bank of Canada issues notes (those blue, purple, green, red, and brown pieces of paper in your wallet that say "Bank of Canada"). The Bank of Canada notes in circulation is the amount of these notes that is in the hands of the public and the depository institutions. Coins issued by the Canadian Mint are not a liability of the Bank of Canada. The coins and Bank of Canada notes that we use in Canada today are collectively known as *currency*.

   Bank of Canada notes are IOUs from the Bank to the bearer and are also liabilities, but unlike most liabilities, they promise to pay back the bearer solely with Bank of Canada notes; that is, they pay off IOUs with other IOUs. Accordingly, if you bring a $100 bill to the Bank of Canada and demand payment, you will receive two $50s, five $20s, ten $10s, twenty $5 bills, or some other combination of bills that adds to $100.

   People are more willing to accept IOUs from the Bank of Canada than from you or me because Bank of Canada notes are a recognized medium of exchange; that is, they are accepted as a means of payment and so function as *money*. Unfortunately, neither you nor I can convince people that our IOUs are worth anything more than the paper they are written on.[2]

---

[2]The notes item on our balance sheet refers only to notes in circulation—that is, the amount in the hands of the public. Notes that have been printed are not automatically a liability of the Bank. For example, consider the importance of having $1 million of your own IOUs printed up. You give out $100 worth to other people and keep the other $999 900 in your pocket. The $999 900 of IOUs does not make you richer or poorer and does not affect your indebtedness. You care only about the $100 of liabilities from the $100 of circulated IOUs. The same reasoning applies for the Bank of Canada in regard to its notes.

For similar reasons, the currency component of the money supply, no matter how it is defined, includes only currency in circulation. It does not include any additional currency that is not yet in the hands of the public. The fact that currency has been printed but is not circulating means that it is not anyone's asset or liability and thus cannot affect anyone's behaviour. Therefore, it makes sense not to include it in the money supply.

2. *Reserves*. All banks that participate in the Large Value Transfer System (LVTS), to be discussed in detail in Chapter 16, have an account at the Bank of Canada in which they hold deposits (also called **settlement balances**). **Reserves** consist of settlement balances at the Bank of Canada plus currency that is physically held by banks (called *vault cash*, because it is held in bank vaults, cash tills, and automated banking machines). Reserves are assets for the banks but liabilities for the Bank of Canada, because the banks can demand payment on them at any time and the Bank of Canada is required to satisfy its obligation by paying Bank of Canada notes. As you will see, an increase in reserves leads to an increase in the level of deposits and hence in the money supply.

As already noted in Chapter 12, Canadian banks are no longer required to hold reserves. Banks, however, hold reserves in order to manage their own short-term liquidity requirements and to respond to predictable clearing drains and across-the-counter and automated banking machine drains. We call these reserves prudential or **desired reserves**. For example, banks might desire that for every dollar of deposits, a certain fraction (say, 5 cents) must be held as reserves. This fraction (5%) is called the **desired reserve ratio**. Reserves in excess of the desired amounts are called **excess reserves**.

Assets

The two assets on the Bank of Canada's balance sheet are important for two reasons. First, changes in the asset items lead to changes in reserves and the monetary base, and consequently to changes in the money supply. Second, because these assets (government securities and Bank of Canada loans) earn higher interest rates than the liabilities do (currency in circulation, which pays no interest, and reserves), the Bank of Canada makes billions of dollars every year—its assets earn income, and its liabilities cost practically nothing. Although it returns most of its earnings to the federal government, the Bank of Canada does spend some of it on "worthy causes," such as supporting economic research.

1. *Securities*. This category of assets covers the Bank of Canada's holdings of securities issued by the Canadian government and, in unusual circumstances (as discussed in Chapter 16), other securities. As you will see, the primary way the Bank of Canada provides reserves to the banking system is by purchasing securities, thereby increasing its holdings of these assets. An increase in government or other securities held by the Bank of Canada leads to an increase in the money supply.

2. *Loans to financial institutions*. The second way the Bank of Canada can provide reserves to the banking system is by making loans (equivalently, advances) to banks and other financial institutions. The loans taken out by these institutions are referred to as *borrowings from the Bank of Canada* or, alternatively, as *borrowed reserves*. These loans appear as a liability on financial institutions' balance sheets. An increase in loans to financial institutions can also be the source of an increase in the money supply. During normal times, the Bank of Canada makes loans only to banking institutions, and the interest rate charged banks for these loans is called the **bank rate**. (As we will discuss in Chapter 16, during the recent financial crisis, the Bank of Canada made loans to other financial institutions.)

CONTROL OF THE MONETARY BASE

The *monetary base* (also called **high-powered money**) equals currency in circulation *C* plus the total reserves in banking system *R*.[3] The monetary base *MB* can be expressed as

$$MB = C + R$$

The Bank of Canada exercises control over the monetary base through its purchases or sales of securities in the open market, called **open market operations**, and through its extension of loans to banks.

Bank of Canada Open Market Operations

The primary way in which the Bank of Canada causes changes in the monetary base is through its open market operations. A purchase of bonds by the Bank of Canada is called an **open market purchase**, and a sale of bonds by the Bank of Canada is called an **open market sale**. Bank of Canada purchases and sales of bonds are always done through primary dealers, government securities dealers who operate out of private banking institutions.

Open Market Purchases   Suppose the Bank of Canada purchases $100 million of bonds from a primary dealer. To understand the consequences of this transaction, we look at *T-accounts*, which list only the changes that occur in balance sheet items, starting from the initial balance sheet position. When the primary dealer sells the $100 million of bonds to the Bank of Canada, the Bank adds $100 million to the dealer's deposit account at the Bank, so that reserves in the banking system go up by $100 million. The banking system's T-account after this transaction is:

Banking System		
Assets		**Liabilities**
Securities	−$100 m	
Reserves	+$100 m	

The balance sheet shows an increase of $100 million of securities in its assets column, along with an increase of $100 million of reserves in its liabilities column:

Bank of Canada		
Assets		**Liabilities**
Securities	+$100 m	Reserves +$100 m

As you can see, the Bank of Canada's open market purchase of $100 million causes an expansion of reserves in the banking system by an equal amount. Another way of seeing this is to recognize that open market purchases of bonds expand reserves because the central bank pays for the bonds with reserves. Because the monetary base equals

---

[3]Here, currency in circulation includes both Bank of Canada notes and Canadian Mint coins.

currency plus reserves, an open market purchase increases the monetary base by an amount equal to the amount of the purchase.

Open Market Sale   Similar reasoning indicates that if the Bank of Canada conducts an open market sale of $100 million of bonds to a primary dealer, the Bank deducts $100 million from the dealer's deposit account, so the Bank's reserves fall by $100 million. The T-account is now:

Nonbank Public		
Assets		**Liabilities**
Securities	+$100 m	
Currency	−$100 m	

The Bank of Canada, for its part, has reduced its holdings of securities by $100 million and has also lowered its monetary liability by accepting the currency as payment for its bonds, thereby reducing the amount of currency in circulation by $100 million:

Bank of Canada		
Assets		**Liabilities**
Securities	−$100 m	Currency in circulation −$100 m

The effect of the open market sale of $100 million of bonds is to reduce the monetary base by an equal amount, although reserves remain unchanged. Manipulations of T-accounts in cases in which buyers of the bonds are banks or buyers pay for the bonds with cheques written on a chequable deposit account at a local bank lead to the same $100 million reduction in the monetary base, although the reduction occurs because the level of reserves has fallen by $100 million.

The following conclusion can now be drawn from our analysis of open market purchases and sales: *the effect of open market operations on the monetary base is much more certain than the effect on reserves.* Therefore, the Bank of Canada can control the monetary base with open market operations more effectively than it can control reserves.

Open market operations can also be done in other assets besides government bonds and have the same effects on the monetary base we have described here.

Although open market operations are the most important monetary policy tool for most central banks around the world, in 1994 the Bank of Canada stopped conducting open market operations in Government of Canada bills and bonds. Since then, the Bank's most common open market operations involve repurchase transactions, either SPRAs or SRAs. More recently, and in response to the subprime financial crisis, the Bank of Canada introduced term PRAs, which are similar to special PRAs. As we will discuss in detail in Chapter 16, the Bank of Canada is currently conducting repurchase transactions to reinforce its operating target—the midpoint of the operating band for the overnight interest rate—and to address liquidity issues at times of financial instability. The Bank, however, neutralizes the effect on settlement balances of SPRAs and SRAs, so that at the end of the day there is no change in the level of settlement balances in the banking system.

Shifts from Deposits into Currency

Even if the Bank of Canada does not conduct open market operations, a shift from deposits to currency will affect the reserves in the banking system. However, such a shift will have no effect on the monetary base. This tells us that the Bank of Canada has more control over the monetary base than over reserves.

Let's suppose that during the Christmas season, the public wants to hold more currency to buy gifts and so withdraws $100 million in cash. The effect on the T-account of the nonbank public is:

Nonbank Public		
Assets		**Liabilities**
Chequable deposits	−$100 m	
Currency	+$100 m	

The banking system loses $100 million of deposits and hence $100 million of reserves:

Banking System		
Assets		**Liabilities**
Reserves	−$100 m	Chequable deposits	−$100 m

For the Bank of Canada, the public's action means that $100 million of additional currency is circulating in the hands of the public, while reserves in the banking system have fallen by $100 million. The Bank's T-account is:

Bank of Canada		
Assets		**Liabilities**
	Currency in circulation	+$100 m
	Reserves	−$100 m

The net effect on the monetary liabilities of the Bank of Canada is a wash; the monetary base is unaffected by the public's increased desire for cash. But reserves are affected. Random fluctuations of reserves can occur as a result of random shifts into currency and out of deposits, and vice versa. The same is not true for the monetary base, making it a more stable variable.

Loans to Financial Institutions

In this chapter so far, we have seen how changes in the monetary base occur as a result of open market operations. However, the monetary base is also affected when the Bank of Canada makes a loan to a financial institution. When the Bank of Canada makes a $100 million loan to the First National Bank, the bank is credited with $100 million of reserves from the proceeds of the loan. The effects on the balance sheets of the banking system and the Bank of Canada are illustrated by the following T-accounts:

Banking System		Bank of Canada	
Assets	**Liabilities**	**Assets**	**Liabilities**
Reserves +$100 m	Loans +$100 m (borrowings from the Bank of Canada)	Loans +$100 m (borrowings from the Bank of Canada)	Reserves +100 m

The monetary liabilities of the Bank of Canada have now increased by $100 million, and the monetary base, too, has increased by this amount. However, if a bank pays off a loan from the Bank of Canada, thereby reducing its borrowings from the Bank of Canada by $100 million, the T-accounts of the banking system and the Bank of Canada are as follows:

Banking System		Bank of Canada	
Assets	**Liabilities**	**Assets**	**Liabilities**
Reserves −$100 m	Loans −$100 m (borrowings from the Bank of Canada)	Loans −$100 m (borrowings from the Bank of Canada)	Reserves −$100 m

The net effect on the monetary liabilities of the Bank of Canada, and hence on the monetary base, is a reduction of $100 million. We see that the monetary base changes one-for-one with the change in the borrowings from the Bank of Canada.

Other Factors That Affect the Monetary Base

So far in this chapter, it seems as though the Bank of Canada has complete control of the monetary base through its open market operations and loans to financial institutions. However, the world is a little bit more complicated for the Bank of Canada. Two important items that affect the monetary base, but are not controlled by the Bank of Canada, are *float* and *government deposits at the Bank of Canada*. When the Bank of Canada clears cheques for banks, it often credits the amount of the cheque to a bank that has deposited it (increases the bank's reserves) before it debits (decreases the reserves of) the bank on which the cheque is drawn. The resulting temporary net increase in the total amount of reserves in the banking system (and hence in the monetary base) occurring from the Bank of Canada's cheque-clearing process is called **float**. When the government moves deposits from commercial banks to its account at the Bank of Canada, leading to an increase in *government deposits at the Bank of Canada*, it causes a deposit outflow at these banks like that shown in Chapter 12 and thus causes reserves in the banking system and the monetary base to decrease. Thus *float* (affected by random events such as the weather, which influences how quickly cheques are presented for payment) and *government deposits at the Bank of Canada* (determined by the federal government's actions) both affect the monetary base but are not controlled by the Bank of Canada at all. Bank of Canada interventions in the foreign exchange market also affect the monetary base.

Overview of the Bank of Canada's Ability to Control the Monetary Base

Our discussion above indicates that two primary features determine the monetary base: open market operations and lending to financial institutions. Whereas the amount of open market purchases or sales is completely controlled by the Bank of Canada's placing orders with dealers in bond markets, the central bank cannot unilaterally determine, and therefore cannot perfectly predict, the amount of borrowings from the Bank of Canada. The Bank of Canada sets the bank rate (interest rate on loans to banks), and then banks make decisions about whether to borrow. The amount of lending, though influenced by the Bank of Canada's setting of the bank rate, is not completely controlled by the Bank of Canada; banks' decisions play a role, too.

Therefore, we might want to split the monetary base into two components: one that the Bank of Canada can control completely, and another that is less tightly controlled. The less tightly controlled component is the amount of the base that is created by loans from the Bank of Canada. The remainder of the base (called the **nonborrowed monetary base**) is under the Bank of Canada's control, because it results primarily from open market operations.[4] The nonborrowed monetary base is formally defined as the monetary base minus borrowings from the Bank of Canada, which are referred to as **borrowed reserves**:

$$MB_n = MB - BR$$

where
$$MB_n = \text{nonborrowed monetary base}$$
$$MB = \text{monetary base}$$
$$BR = \text{borrowed reserves from the Bank of Canada}$$

Factors not controlled at all by the Bank of Canada (for example, float and government deposits with the Bank of Canada) undergo substantial short-run variations and can be important sources of fluctuations in the monetary base over time periods as short as a week. However, these fluctuations are usually predictable and so can be offset through open market operations. *Although float and government deposits with the Bank of Canada undergo substantial short-run fluctuations, which complicate control of the monetary base, they do not prevent the Bank of Canada from accurately controlling it.*

MULTIPLE DEPOSIT CREATION: A SIMPLE MODEL

With our understanding of how the Bank of Canada controls the monetary base and how banks operate (Chapter 12), we now have the tools necessary to explain how deposits are created. When the Bank of Canada supplies the banking system with $1 of additional reserves, deposits increase by a multiple of this amount—a process called **multiple deposit creation**.

Deposit Creation: The Single Bank

Suppose that the $100 million open market purchase described earlier was conducted with the First National Bank. After the Bank of Canada has bought the $100 million in bonds from the First National Bank, the bank finds that it has an increase in reserves of

[4]Actually, other items on the Bank of Canada's balance sheet (discussed in the appendix on the MyEconLab) affect the magnitude of the nonborrowed monetary base. Because their effects on the nonborrowed base relative to open market operations are both small and predictable, these other items do not present the Bank of Canada with difficulties in controlling the nonborrowed base.

$100 million. To analyze what the bank will do with these additional reserves, assume that the bank does not want to hold excess reserves because it earns little interest on them. We begin the analysis with the following T-account:

First National Bank			
Assets		**Liabilities**	
Securities	−$100 m		
Reserves	+$100 m		

Because the bank has no increase in its chequable deposits, desired reserves remain the same, and the bank finds that its additional $100 million of reserves means that its excess reserves have risen by $100 million. Let's say that the bank decides to make a loan equal in amount to the $100 million rise in excess reserves. When the bank makes the loan, it sets up a chequing account for the borrower and puts the proceeds of the loan into this account. In this way, the bank alters its balance sheet by increasing its liabilities with $100 million of chequable deposits and at the same time increasing its assets with the $100 million loan. The resulting T-account looks like this:

First National Bank			
Assets		**Liabilities**	
Securities	−$100 m	Chequable deposits	+$100 m
Reserves	+$100 m		
Loans	+$100 m		

The bank has created chequable deposits by its act of lending. Because chequable deposits are part of the money supply, the bank's act of lending has, in fact, created money.

In its current balance sheet position, the First National Bank still has excess reserves and so might want to make additional loans. However, these reserves will not stay at the bank for very long. The borrowers took out loans not to leave $100 million sitting idle in a chequing account at the First National Bank but to purchase goods and services from other individuals and corporations. When the borrowers make these purchases by writing cheques, the cheques will be deposited at other banks, and the $100 million of reserves will leave the First National Bank. *As a result, a bank cannot safely make a loan for an amount greater than the excess reserves it has before it makes the loan.*

The final T-account of the First National Bank is:

First National Bank			
Assets		**Liabilities**	
Securities	−$100 m		
Loans	+$100 m		

The increase in reserves of $100 million has been converted into additional loans of $100 at the First National Bank, plus an additional $100 million of deposits that have made their way to other banks. (All the cheques written on accounts at the First

National Bank are deposited in banks rather than converted into cash, because we are assuming that the public does not want to hold any additional currency.) Now let's see what happens to these deposits at the other banks.

Deposit Creation: The Banking System

To simplify the analysis, let's assume that the $100 million of deposits created by First National Bank's loan is deposited at Bank A and that this bank and all other banks hold no excess reserves. Bank A's T-account becomes:

Bank A			
Assets		**Liabilities**	
Reserves	+$100 m	Chequable deposits	+$100 m

If the desired reserve ratio is 10%, this bank will now find itself with a $10 million increase in desired reserves, leaving it $90 million of excess reserves. Because Bank A (like the First National Bank) does not want to hold on to excess reserves, it will make loans for the entire amount. Its loans and chequable deposits will then increase by $90 million, but when the borrowers spend the $90 million of chequable deposits, they and the reserves at Bank A will fall back down by this same amount. The net result is that Bank A's T-account will look like this:

Bank A			
Assets		**Liabilities**	
Reserves	+$10 m	Chequable deposits	+$100 m
Loans	+$90 m		

If the money spent by the borrowers to whom Bank A lent the $90 million is deposited in another bank, such as Bank B, the T-account for Bank B will be:

Bank B			
Assets		**Liabilities**	
Reserves	+$90 m	Chequable deposits	+$90 m

The chequable deposits in the banking system have risen by another $90 million, for a total increase of $190 million ($100 million at Bank A plus $90 million at Bank B). In fact, the distinction between Bank A and Bank B is not necessary to obtain the same result on the overall expansion of deposits. If the borrowers from Bank A write cheques to someone who deposits them at Bank A, the same change in deposits occurs. The T-accounts for Bank B would just apply to Bank A, and its chequable deposits would increase by the total amount of $190 million.

Bank B will want to modify its balance sheet further. It must keep 10% of $90 million ($9 million) as desired reserves and has 90% of $90 million ($81 million) in excess reserves and so can make loans of this amount. Bank B will make loans totaling $81 million to borrowers, who spend the proceeds from the loans. Bank B's T-account will be:

Bank B

Assets		Liabilities	
Reserves	+$ 9 m	Chequable deposits	+$90 m
Loans	+$81 m		

The $81 million spent by the borrowers from Bank B will be deposited in another bank (Bank C). Consequently, from the initial $100 million increase of reserves in the banking system, the total increase of chequable deposits in the system so far is $271 million (= 100 m + 90 m + 81 m).

Following the same reasoning, if all banks make loans for the full amount of their excess reserves, further increments in chequable deposits will continue (at Banks C, D, E, and so on), as depicted in Table 15-1. Therefore, the total increase in deposits from the initial $100 million increase in reserves will be $1000 million: the increase is ten-fold, the reciprocal of the 10% (0.10) desired reserve ratio.

If the banks choose to invest their excess reserves in securities, the result is the same. If Bank A had taken its excess reserves and purchased securities instead of making loans, its T-account would have looked like this:

Bank A

Assets		Liabilities	
Reserves	+$10 m	Chequable deposits	+$100m
Securities	+$90 m		

TABLE 15-1   Creation of Deposits (assuming a 10% desired reserve ratio and a $100 million increase in reserves)

Bank	Increase in Deposits ($ millions)	Increase in Loans ($ millions)	Increase in Reserves ($ millions)
First National	0.00	100.00	0.00
A	100.00	90.00	10.00
B	90.00	81.00	9.00
C	81.00	72.90	8.10
D	72.90	65.61	7.29
E	65.61	59.05	6.56
F	59.05	53.14	5.91
.	.	.	.
.	.	.	.
.	.	.	.
Total for all banks	1000.00	1000.00	100.00

When the bank buys $90 million of securities, it writes $90 million in cheques to the sellers of the securities, who in turn deposit the $90 million at a bank such as Bank B. Bank B's chequable deposits increase by $90 million, and the deposit expansion process is the same as before. **Whether a bank chooses to use its excess reserves to make loans or to purchase securities, the effect on deposit expansion is the same.**

You can now see the difference in deposit creation for the single bank versus the banking system as a whole. Because a single bank can create deposits equal only to the amount of its excess reserves, it cannot by itself generate multiple deposit expansion. A single bank cannot make loans greater in amount than its excess reserves, because the bank will lose these reserves as the deposits created by the loan find their way to other banks. However, the banking system as a whole can generate a multiple expansion of deposits, because when a bank loses its excess reserves, these reserves do not leave the banking system, even though they are lost to the individual bank. So as each bank makes a loan and creates deposits, the reserves find their way to another bank (which may be the original bank), which uses them to make additional loans and create additional deposits. As you have seen, this process continues until the initial increase in reserves results in a multiple increase in deposits.

The multiple increase in deposits generated from an increase in the banking system's reserves is called the **simple deposit multiplier**.[5] In our example, with a 10% desired reserve ratio, the simple deposit multiplier is 10. More generally, the simple deposit multiplier equals the reciprocal of the desired reserve ratio, expressed as a fraction (for example, $10 = 1/0.10$), so the formula for the multiple expansion of deposits can be written as follows:

$$\Delta D = \frac{1}{r_d} \times \Delta R \qquad \text{(Equation 1)}$$

where ΔD = change in total chequable deposits in the banking system
       r_d = desired reserve ratio (0.10 in the example)
      ΔR = change in reserves for the banking system (100 million in the example)

Deriving the Formula for Multiple Deposit Creation

The formula for the multiple creation of deposits can be derived directly using algebra. We obtain the same answer for the relationship between a change in deposits and a change in reserves.

Our assumption that banks do not hold on to any excess reserves means that the total amount of desired reserves for the banking system *DR* will equal the total reserves in the banking system *R*:

$$DR = R$$

The total amount of desired reserves equals the desired reserve ratio r_d times the total amount of chequable deposits *D*:

$$DR = r_d \times D$$

Substituting $r_d D$ in the first equation,

$$r_d \times D = R$$

---

[5]This multiplier should not be confused with the Keynesian multiplier, which is derived through a similar step-by-step analysis. That multiplier relates an increase in income to an increase in investment, whereas the simple deposit multiplier relates an increase in deposits to an increase in reserves.

and dividing both sides of the preceding equation by r_d gives

$$D = \frac{1}{r_d} \times R$$

Taking the change in both sides of this equation and using delta to indicate a change gives

$$\Delta D = \frac{1}{r_d} \times \Delta R$$

which is the same formula for deposit creation found in Equation 1.[6]

This derivation provides us with another way of looking at the multiple creation of deposits, because it forces us to examine the banking system as a whole rather than one bank at a time. For the banking system as a whole, deposit creation (or contraction) will stop only when excess reserves in the banking system are zero; that is, the banking system will be in equilibrium when the total amount of desired reserves equals the total amount of reserves, as seen in the equation $DR = R$. When $r_d \times D$ is substituted for DR, the resulting equation $r_d \times D = R$ tells us how high chequable deposits will have to be for desired reserves to equal total reserves. Accordingly, a given level of reserves in the banking system determines the level of chequable deposits when the banking system is in equilibrium (when $ER = 0$); put another way, the given level of reserves supports a given level of chequable deposits.

In our example, the desired reserve ratio is 10%. If reserves increase by $100 million, chequable deposits must rise by $1000 million for total desired reserves also to increase by $100 million. If the increase in chequable deposits is less than this—say, $900 million—then the increase in desired reserves of $90 million remains below the $100 million increase in reserves, so excess reserves still exist somewhere in the banking system. The banks with the excess reserves will now make additional loans, creating new deposits; this process will continue until all reserves in the system are used up, which occurs when chequable deposits rise by $1000 million.

We can also see this by looking at the T-account of the banking system as a whole (including the First National Bank):

	Banking System		
Assets		**Liabilities**	
Securities	−$ 100 m	Chequable deposits	+$1000 m
Reserves	+$ 100 m		
Loans	+$1000 m		

[6]A formal derivation of this formula follows. Using the reasoning in the text, the change in chequable deposits is $100 ($= \Delta R \times 1$) plus $90 [$= \Delta R \times (1 - r_d)$] plus $81 [$= \Delta R \times (1 - r_d)^2$] and so on, which can be rewritten as

$$\Delta D = \Delta R \times [1 + (1 - r_d) + (1 - r_d)^2 + (1 - r_d)^3 + \cdots]$$

Using the formula for the sum of an infinite series found in footnote 5 in Chapter 4, this can be rewritten as

$$\Delta D = \Delta R \times \frac{1}{1 - (1 - r_d)} = \frac{1}{r_d} \times \Delta R$$

The procedure of eliminating excess reserves by loaning them out means that the banking system (First National Bank and Banks A, B, C, D, and so on) continues to make loans up to the $1000 million amount until deposits have reached the $1000 million level. In this way, $100 million of reserves supports $1000 million (10 times the quantity) of deposits.

Critique of the Simple Model

Our model of multiple deposit creation seems to indicate that the Bank of Canada is able to exercise complete control over the level of chequable deposits by setting the level of reserves. The actual creation of deposits is much less mechanical than the simple model indicates. If proceeds from Bank A's $90 million loan are not deposited but are kept in currency, nothing is deposited in Bank B and the deposit creation process ceases. The total increase in the money supply is now the $90 million increase in currency plus the initial $100 million of deposits created by First National Bank's loans, which were deposited at Bank A, for a total of only $190 million—considerably less than the $1000 million we calculated with the simple model above. Another way of saying this is that currency has no multiple deposit expansion, while deposits do. Thus, if some proceeds from loans are not deposited in banks but instead are used to raise the holdings of currency, less multiple expansion occurs overall, and the money supply will not increase by as much as our simple model of multiple deposit creation tells us.

Another situation ignored in our model is one in which banks do not make loans or buy securities in the full amount of their excess reserves. If Bank A decides to hold on to all $90 million of its excess reserves, no deposits would be made in Bank B, and this would also stop the deposit creation process. The total increase in deposits would be only $100 million, not the $1000 million increase in our example. Hence, if banks choose to hold on to all or some of their excess reserves, the full expansion of deposits predicted by the simple model of multiple deposit creation again does not occur.

Our examples indicate that the Bank of Canada is not the only player whose behaviour influences the level of deposits and therefore the money supply. Depositors' decisions regarding how much currency to hold and banks' decisions regarding the amount of reserves to hold also can cause the money supply to change.

FACTORS THAT DETERMINE THE MONEY SUPPLY

Our critique of the simple model shows how we can expand on it to discuss all the factors that affect the money supply. Let's look at changes in each factor in turn, holding all other factors constant.

Changes in the Nonborrowed Monetary Base, MB_n

As shown earlier in the chapter, the Bank of Canada's open market purchases increase the nonborrowed monetary base, and its open market sales decrease it. Holding all other variables constant, an increase in MB_n arising from an open market purchase raises the amount of the monetary base and reserves, so that multiple deposit creation occurs and the money supply increases. Similarly, an open market sale that reduces MB_n shrinks the amount of the monetary base and reserves, thereby causing a multiple contraction of deposits and a decrease in the money supply. We have the following result: *the money supply is positively related to the nonborrowed monetary base MB_n.*

Changes in Borrowed Reserves, *BR*, from the Bank of Canada

An increase in loans from the Bank of Canada provides additional borrowed reserves and thereby increases the amount of the monetary base and reserves, so that multiple deposit creation occurs and the money supply expands. If banks reduce the level of their loans from the Bank of Canada, all other variables held constant, the monetary base and amount of reserves would fall, and the money supply would decrease. The result is this: ***the money supply is positively related to the level of borrowed reserves, BR, from the Bank of Canada.***

Changes in the Desired Reserve Ratio, r_d

As we have seen, if the desired reserve ratio on chequable deposits increases while all other variables, such as the monetary base, stay the same, multiple deposit expansion is reduced and hence the money supply falls. If, on the other hand, the desired reserve ratio falls, multiple deposit expansion is higher and the money supply rises. We now have the following result: ***the money supply is negatively related to the desired reserve ratio r_d.***

Changes in Excess Reserves

When banks increase their holdings of excess reserves during anxious or crisis times, those reserves are no longer being used to make loans, causing multiple deposit creation to stop dead in its tracks, resulting in less expansion of the money supply. If, on the other hand, banks chose to hold fewer excess reserves, loans and multiple deposit creation would increase and the money supply would rise. ***The money supply is negatively related to the amount of excess reserves.***

Recall from Chapter 12 that the primary benefit to a bank of holding excess reserves is that they provide insurance against losses due to deposit outflows; that is, they enable the bank experiencing deposit outflows to escape the costs of calling in loans, selling securities, borrowing from the Bank of Canada or other corporations, or bank failure. If banks fear that deposit outflows are likely to increase (that is, if expected deposit outflows increase), they will want more insurance against this possibility and excess reserves will rise.

Changes in Currency Holdings

As shown before, chequable deposits undergo multiple expansion, whereas currency does not. Hence, when chequable deposits are converted into currency, holding the monetary base and other variables, such as the amount of excess reserves, constant, a switch is made from a component of the money supply that undergoes multiple expansion to one that does not. The overall level of multiple expansion declines, and the money supply falls. On the other hand, if currency holdings fall, a switch is made into chequable deposits that undergo multiple deposit expansion, so the money supply rises. This analysis suggests the following result: ***the money supply is negatively related to currency holdings.***

OVERVIEW OF THE MONEY SUPPLY PROCESS

We now have a model of the money supply process in which all three of the players—the Bank of Canada, depositors, and banks—directly influence the money supply. As a study aid, Summary Table 15-1 charts the money supply responses to the five factors discussed above and gives a brief synopsis of the reasoning behind them.

SUMMARY TABLE 15-1

Money Supply Response

Player	Variable	Change in Variable	Money Supply Response	Reason
Bank of Canada	Nonborrowed monetary base, MB_n	↑	↑	More *MB* for deposit creation
Banks	Desired reserve ratio, r_d	↑	↓	Less multiple deposit expansion
	Borrowed reserves, *BR*	↑	↑	More *MB* for deposit creation
	Excess reserves	↑	↓	Less loans and deposit creation
Depositors	Currency holdings	↑	↓	Less multiple deposit expansion

Note: Only increases (↑) in the variables are shown. The effects of decreases on the money supply would be the opposite of those indicated in the "Money Supply Response" column.

The variables are grouped by the player who is the primary influence behind the variable. The Bank of Canada, for example, influences the money supply by controlling the first variable. Depositors influence the money supply through their decisions about holdings of currency, while banks influence the money supply with their decisions about borrowings from the Bank of Canada and reserves.

THE MONEY MULTIPLIER

The intuition in the section above is sufficient for you to understand how the money supply process works. For those of you who are more mathematically inclined, we can derive all of the above results using a concept called the **money multiplier**, denoted by *m*, which tells us how much the money supply changes for a given change in the monetary base. The relationship between the money supply *M*, the money multiplier, and the monetary base is described by the following equation:

$$M = m \times MB \qquad \text{(Equation 2)}$$

The money multiplier *m* tells us what multiple of the monetary base is transformed into the money supply. Because the money multiplier is larger than 1, the alternative name for the monetary base, *high-powered money*, is logical: a $1 change in the monetary base typically leads to more than a $1 change in the money supply.

Deriving the Money Multiplier

Let's assume that the desired holdings of currency *C* and excess reserves *ER* grow proportionally with chequable deposits *D*; in other words, we assume that the ratios of these items to chequable deposits are constants in equilibrium, as the braces in the following expressions indicate:

$$c = \{C/D\} \quad = \text{currency ratio}$$
$$e = \{ER/D\} = \text{excess reserves ratio}$$

We will now derive a formula that describes how the currency ratio desired by depositors, the excess reserves ratio set by banks, and the desired reserve ratio desired by banks affect the multiplier m. We begin the derivation of the model of the money supply with the following equation:

$$R = DR + ER$$

which states that the total amount of reserves in the banking system R equals the sum of desired reserves DR and excess reserves ER. (Note that this equation corresponds to the equilibrium condition $DR = R$ earlier in the chapter, where excess reserves were assumed to be zero.)

The total amount of desired reserves equals the desired reserve ratio r_d times the amount of chequable deposits D:

$$DR = r_d \times D$$

Substituting $r_d \times D$ for DR in the first equation yields an equation that links reserves in the banking system to the amount of chequable deposits and excess reserves they can support:

$$R = (r_d \times D) + ER$$

A key point here is that banks set the desired reserve ratio r_d to less than 1. Thus \$1 of reserves can support more than \$1 of deposits, and the multiple expansion of deposits can occur.

Let's see how this works in practice. If excess reserves are held at zero ($ER = 0$), the desired reserve ratio is set at $r_d = 0.10$, and the level of chequable deposits in the banking system is \$800 billion, then the amount of reserves needed to support these deposits is \$80 billion ($= 0.10 \times 800$ billion). The \$80 billion of reserves can support 10 times this amount in chequable deposits because multiple deposit creation will occur.

Because the monetary base MB equals currency C plus reserves R, we can generate an equation that links the amount of the monetary base to the levels of chequable deposits and currency by adding currency to both sides of the equation:

$$MB = R + C = (r_d \times D) + ER + C$$

Notice that this equation reveals the amount of the monetary base needed to support the existing amounts of chequable deposits, currency, and excess reserves.

To derive the money multiplier formula in terms of the currency ratio $c = \{C/D\}$ and the excess reserves ratio $e = \{ER/D\}$, we rewrite the last equation, specifying C as $c \times D$ and ER as $e \times D$:

$$MB = (r_d \times D) + (e \times D) + (c \times D) = (r_d + e + c) \times D$$

We next divide both sides of the equation by the term inside the parentheses to get an expression linking chequable deposits D to the monetary base MB:

$$D = \frac{1}{r_d + e + c} \times MB \qquad \text{(Equation 3)}$$

Using the M1+ definition of the money supply as currency plus chequable deposits ($M = D + C$) and again specifying C as $c \times D$,

$$M = D + (c \times D) = (1 + c) \times D$$

Substituting in this equation the expression for D from Equation 3, we have

$$M = \frac{1 + c}{r_d + e + c} \times MB \qquad \text{(Equation 4)}$$

We have derived an expression in the form of our earlier Equation 2. As you can see, the ratio that multiplies MB is the money multiplier, which tells how much the money supply changes in response to a given change in the monetary base (high-powered money). The money multiplier m is thus

$$m = \frac{1 + c}{r_d + e + c} \qquad \text{(Equation 5)}$$

It is a function of the currency ratio set by depositors c, the excess reserves ratio set by banks e, and the desired reserve ratio also set by banks r_d.

Intuition Behind the Money Multiplier

To get a feel for what the money multiplier means, let's construct a numerical example with realistic numbers for the following variables:

$$r_d = \text{desired reserve ratio} = 0.10$$

$$C = \text{currency in circulation} = \$400 \text{ billion}$$

$$D = \text{chequable deposits} = \$800 \text{ billion}$$

$$ER = \text{excess reserves} = \$0.8 \text{ billion}$$

$$M = \text{money supply (M1+)} = C + D = \$1200 \text{ billion}$$

From these numbers we can calculate the values for the currency ratio c and the excess reserves ratio e:

$$c = \frac{\$400 \text{ billion}}{\$800 \text{ billion}} = 0.5$$

$$e = \frac{\$0.8 \text{ billion}}{\$800 \text{ billion}} = 0.001$$

The resulting value of the money multiplier is

$$m = \frac{1 + 0.5}{0.1 + 0.001 + 0.5} = \frac{1.5}{0.601} = 2.5$$

The money multiplier of 2.5 tells us that, given the desired reserve ratio of 10% on chequable deposits and the behaviour of depositors, as represented by c = 0.5, and banks, as represented by e = 0.001, a $1 increase in the monetary base leads to a $2.50 increase in the money supply (M1+).

An important characteristic of the money multiplier is that it is far less than the simple deposit multiplier of 10 found earlier in the chapter. There are two reasons for this result. First, *although deposits undergo multiple expansion, currency does not.* Thus,

---

FYI   The 2007–2009 Financial Crisis and the Money Multiplier in the United States

In the United States, prior to 2008, the excess reserves ratio e was almost always very close to zero (less than 0.001), and so its impact on the money multiplier (Equation 5) was essentially irrelevant. When e is close to zero, the money multiplier is always greater than 1. However, as we will see in the next chapter, nonconventional monetary policy during the global financial crisis caused excess reserves in the United States to skyrocket to over $2 trillion. Such an extraordinarily large value of e caused the excess reserves factor in the money multiplier equation to become dominant, and so the money multiplier fell to below 1.

---

if some portion of the increase in high-powered money finds its way into currency, this portion does not undergo multiple deposit expansion. In our simple model earlier in the chapter, we did not allow for this possibility, and so the increase in reserves led to the maximum amount of multiple deposit creation. However, in our current model of the money multiplier, the level of currency does rise when the monetary base MB and chequable deposits D increase, because c is greater than zero. As previously stated, any increase in MB that goes into an increase in currency is not multiplied, so only part of the increase in MB is available to support chequable deposits that undergo multiple expansion. The overall level of multiple deposit expansion must be lower, meaning that the increase in M, given an increase in MB, is smaller than indicated by the simple model earlier in the chapter.

Second, since e is positive, ***any increase in the monetary base and deposits leads to higher excess reserves.*** When there is an increase in MB and D, the resulting increase in excess reserves means that the amount of reserves used to support chequable deposits does not increase as much as it otherwise would. Hence the increase in chequable deposits and the money supply are lower, and the money multiplier is smaller.

Money Supply Response to Changes in the Factors

By recognizing that the monetary base is $MB = MB_n + BR$, we can rewrite Equation 2 as

$$M = m \times (MB_n + BR) \qquad \text{(Equation 6)}$$

Now we can show algebraically all the results in Summary Table 15-1, which shows how the money supply responds to the changes in the factors.

As you can see from Equation 6, a rise in MB_n or BR raises the money supply M because the money multiplier m is always greater than zero. We can see that a rise in the desired reserve ratio lowers the money supply by calculating the value of the money multiplier (using Equation 5) in our numerical example when r_d increases from 10% to 15% (leaving all other variables unchanged). The money multiplier then becomes

$$m = \frac{1 + 0.5}{0.15 + 0.001 + 0.5} = \frac{1.5}{0.651} = 2.3$$

which, as we would expect, is less than 2.5.

Similarly, we can see that a rise in currency lowers the money supply by calculating what happens to the money multiplier when c is raised from 0.50 to 0.75. The money multiplier then falls from 2.5 to

$$m = \frac{1 + 0.75}{0.1 + 0.001 + 0.75} = \frac{1.75}{0.851} = 2.06$$

Finally, we can see that a rise in excess reserves lowers the money supply by calculating what happens to the money multiplier when e is raised from 0.001 to 0.005. The money multiplier declines from 2.5 to

$$m = \frac{1 + 0.5}{0.1 + 0.005 + 0.5} = \frac{1.5}{0.605} = 2.48$$

At first glance, this result might seem counterintuitive. After all, a dollar of monetary base that goes into currency increases the money supply by only one dollar, whereas a dollar of monetary base that goes into deposits leads to multiple deposit expansion which increases the money supply by a factor of 10. Thus, it seems as though the shift from currency into deposits should raise the overall amount of multiple expansion and hence the money supply. This reasoning is correct, but it assumes a small change in the amount of excess reserves. Indeed, that is the case during normal times, when the excess reserves ratio is near zero. However, in the current situation in the United States, in which the excess reserves ratio e is abnormally high, when a dollar moves from deposits into currency, the amount of excess reserves falls by a large amount, which releases reserves to support more deposits, causing the money multiplier to rise.[7]

APPLICATION Quantitative Easing and the Money Supply, 2007–2014

When the global financial crisis began in the fall of 2007, the Fed initiated lending programs and large-scale asset-purchase programs in an attempt to bolster the economy. By June 2014, these purchases of securities had led to a quintupling of the Fed's balance sheet and a 377% increase in the monetary base. These lending and asset-purchase programs resulted in a huge expansion of the monetary base and have been given the name "quantitative easing." As our analysis in this chapter indicates, such a massive expansion of the monetary base could potentially lead to a large expansion of the money supply. However, as shown in Figure 15-1, when the monetary base increased by more than 370%, the M1 money supply rose by less than 110%. How can we explain this result using our money supply model?

Figure 15-2 shows the currency ratio c and the excess reserves ratio e for 2007–2014. We see that the currency ratio was relatively steady during this period and

---

[7]All the above results can be derived more generally from the Equation 5 formula for m as follows. When r_d or e increases, the denominator of the money multiplier increases, and therefore the money multiplier must decrease. As long as $r_d + e$ is less than 1 (as is usually the case), an increase in c raises the denominator of the money multiplier proportionally by more than it raises the numerator. The increase in c causes the money multiplier to fall. On the other hand, when $r_d + e$ is greater than 1 (the current situation in the United States), an increase in c raises the numerator of the money multiplier proportionally by more than it raises the denominator, so the money multiplier rises. Recall that the money multiplier in Equation 5 is for the M1+ definition of money. Appendix 15.2 to this chapter on the MyEconLab discusses how the multiplier for M2+ is determined.

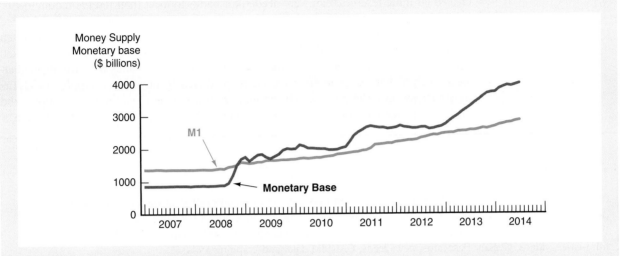

FIGURE 15-1   M1 and the Monetary Base, 2007–2014

The money supply rose by less than 110% despite the increase in the monetary base by over 370%.
Source: Federal Reserve Bank of St. Louis, FRED database: **http://research.stlouisfed.org/fred2/**.

so was not a major source of changes in the money multiplier and the money supply. Instead, we have to look to the extraordinary rise in the excess reserves ratio *e*, which climbed by more than a factor of 1000 during this period.

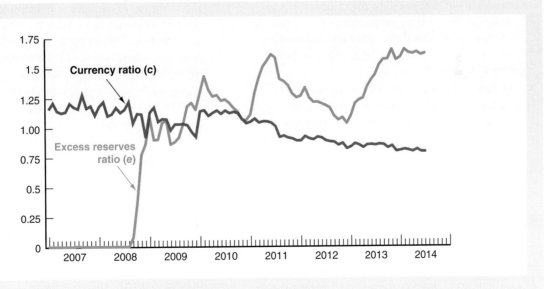

FIGURE 15-2   Excess Reserves Ratio and Currency Ratio, 2007–2014

The currency ratio *c* was relatively steady, whereas the excess reserves ratio *e* rose by a factor of over 1000.
Source: Federal Reserve Bank of St. Louis, FRED database: **http://research.stlouisfed.org/fred2/**.

What explains this substantial increase in the excess reserves ratio e? The Fed's actions created far more reserves than were needed for banks to meet their reserve requirements. Banks were willing to hold the huge increases in excess reserves because, after the Fed began paying interest on these reserves starting in 2008, the interest rate on reserves often exceeded the rate at which the banks could lend them out in the federal funds market. Because excess reserves had a very small or even negative cost, banks were willing to tolerate a much higher excess reserves ratio e. As predicted by our money supply model, the huge increase in e sharply lowered the money multiplier, and so the money supply did not undergo that large of an expansion, despite the huge increase in the monetary base. ◆

MyEconLab

MyEconLab is an online homework and tutorial system that puts you in control of your own learning with study and practice tools directly correlated to this chapter's content. Visit MyEconLab to access the eText, the Questions and Applied Problems with answers, as well as additional assessment. You will also find web chapters, mini-lectures, appendices, mini-cases, videos, glossary flashcards, news feeds, CANSIM data, and graphing tools.

SUMMARY

1. The three players in the money supply process are the central bank, banks (depository institutions), and depositors.

2. Four items in the Bank of Canada's balance sheet are essential to our understanding of the money supply process: the two liability items, currency in circulation and reserves, which together make up the monetary base, and the two asset items, securities and loans to financial institutions.

3. The Bank of Canada controls the monetary base through open market operations and extension of loans to financial institutions and has better control over the monetary base than over reserves. Although float and government deposits with the Bank of Canada undergo substantial short-run fluctuations that complicate control of the monetary base, they do not prevent the Bank of Canada from accurately controlling it.

4. A single bank can make loans up to the amount of its excess reserves, thereby creating an equal amount of deposits. The banking system can create a multiple expansion of deposits, because as each bank makes a loan and creates deposits, the reserves find their way to another bank, which uses them to make loans and create additional deposits. In the simple model of multiple deposit creation in which banks do not hold on to excess reserves and the public holds no currency, the multiple

increase in chequable deposits (simple deposit multiplier) equals the reciprocal of the desired reserve ratio.

5. The simple model of multiple deposit creation has serious deficiencies. Decisions by depositors to increase their holdings of currency or of banks to hold excess reserves will result in a smaller expansion of deposits than the simple model predicts. All three players—the Bank of Canada, banks, and depositors—are important in the determination of the money supply.

6. The money supply is positively related to the nonborrowed monetary base MB_n, which is determined by open market operations, and the level of borrowed reserves (lending) from the Bank of Canada, BR. The money supply is negatively related to the desired reserve ratio, r_d, holdings of currency, and excess reserves. The model of the money supply process takes into account the behaviour of all three players in the money supply process: the Bank of Canada, through open market operations; banks, through their decisions to borrow from the Bank of Canada and hold excess reserves; and depositors, through their decisions about holding of currency.

7. The monetary base is linked to the money supply using the concept of the money multiplier, which tells us how much the money supply changes when the monetary base changes.

KEY TERMS

bank rate, p. 367
borrowed reserves, p. 372
desired reserve ratio, p. 367
desired reserves, p. 367
excess reserves, p. 367
float, p. 371

high-powered money, p. 368
monetary base, p. 366
money multiplier, p. 380
multiple deposit creation, p. 372
nonborrowed monetary base, p. 372
open market operations, p. 368

open market purchase, p. 368
open market sale, p. 368
reserves, p. 367
settlement balances, p. 367
simple deposit multiplier, p. 376

QUESTIONS

All questions are available in MyEconLab *at* **www.myeconlab.com**.

1. Classify each of these transactions as either an asset, a liability, or neither, for each of the "players" in the money supply process—the Bank of Canada, banks, and depositors.

    a. You get a $10 000 loan from the bank to buy an automobile.

    b. You deposit $400 into your chequing account at the local bank.

    c. The Bank of Canada provides an emergency loan to a bank for $1 000 000.

    d. A bank borrows $500 000 in overnight loans from another bank.

    e. You use your debit card to purchase a meal at a restaurant for $100.

2. The First National Bank receives an extra $100 of reserves but decides not to lend out any of these reserves. How much deposit creation takes place for the entire banking system?

3. Suppose that the Bank of Canada buys $1 million of bonds from the First National Bank. If the First National Bank and all other banks use the resulting increase in reserves to purchase securities only and not to make loans, what will happen to chequable deposits?

4. If a bank depositor withdraws $1000 of currency from an account, what happens to reserves, chequable deposits, and the monetary base?

5. If a bank sells $10 million of bonds to the Bank of Canada to pay back $10 million on the loan it owes, what will be the effect on the level of chequable deposits?

6. If you decide to hold $100 less cash than usual and therefore deposit $100 more cash in the bank, what effect will this have on chequable deposits in the

banking system if the rest of the public keeps its holdings of currency constant?

7. "The Bank of Canada can perfectly control the amount of reserves in the system." Is this statement true, false, or uncertain? Explain.

8. "The Bank of Canada can perfectly control the amount of the monetary base, but has less control over the composition of the monetary base." Is this statement true, false, or uncertain? Explain.

9. The Bank of Canada buys $100 million of bonds from the public and there is also a decline in the desired reserve ratio. What will happen to the money supply?

10. Describe how each of the following can affect the money supply: (a) the central bank; (b) banks; and (c) depositors.

11. "The money multiplier is necessarily greater than 1." Is this statement true, false, or uncertain? Explain your answer.

12. What effect might a financial panic have on the money multiplier and the money supply? Why?

13. During the Great Depression years from 1930 to 1933, both the currency ratio c and the excess reserves ratio e rose dramatically in the United States. What effect did these factors have on the money multiplier?

14. In October 2008, the Federal Reserve began paying interest on the amount of excess reserves held by banks. How, if at all, might this affect the multiplier process and the money supply in the United States?

15. The money multiplier declined significantly during the period 1930–1933 and also during the recent financial crisis of 2008–2010. Yet the M1 money supply decreased by 25% in the Depression period but *increased* by more than 20% during the recent financial crisis. What explains the difference in outcomes?

APPLIED PROBLEMS

All applied problems are available in MyEconLab *at* **www.myeconlab.com**.

16. If the Bank of Canada sells $2 million of bonds to the First National Bank, what happens to reserves and the monetary base? Use T-accounts to explain your answer.

17. If the Bank of Canada sells $2 million of bonds to Irving the Investor, who pays for the bonds with a briefcase filled with currency, what happens to reserves and the monetary base? Use T-accounts to explain your answer.

18. If the Bank of Canada lends five banks a total of $100 million but depositors withdraw $50 million and hold it as currency, what happens to reserves and the monetary base? Use T-accounts to explain your answer.

19. Using T-accounts, show what happens to chequable deposits in the banking system when the Bank of Canada lends an additional $1 million to the First National Bank.

20. Using T-accounts, show what happens to chequable deposits in the banking system when the Bank of Canada sells $2 million of bonds to the First National Bank.

21. If the Bank of Canada buys $1 million of bonds from the First National Bank, but an additional 10% of any deposit is held as excess reserves, what is the total increase in chequable deposits? (*Hint:* Use T-accounts to show what happens at each step of the multiple expansion process.)

22. If reserves in the banking system increase by $1 billion as a result of Bank of Canada lending to financial institutions of $1 billion, and chequable deposits increase by $9 billion, why isn't the banking system in equilibrium? What will continue to happen in the banking system until equilibrium is reached? Show the T-account for the banking system in equilibrium.

23. If the Bank of Canada reduces reserves by selling $5 million worth of bonds to the banks, what will the T-account of the banking system look like when the banking system is in equilibrium? What will have happened to the level of chequable deposits?

24. If the Bank of Canada sells $1 million of bonds and banks reduce their borrowings from the Bank of Canada by $1 million, predict what will happen to the money supply.

25. Suppose that currency in circulation is $600 billion, the amount of chequable deposits is $900 billion, excess reserves are $15 billion, and the desired ratio is 10%.

   a. Calculate the money supply, the currency deposit ratio, the excess reserve ratio, and the money multiplier.

   b. Suppose the central bank conducts an unusually large open market purchase of bonds held by banks of $1400 billion due to a sharp contraction in the economy. Assuming the ratios you calculated in part (a) are the same, what do you predict will be the effect on the money supply?

   c. Suppose the central bank conducts the same open market purchase as in part (b), except that banks choose to hold all of these proceeds as excess reserves rather than loan them out, due to fear of a financial crisis. Assuming that currency and deposits remain the same, what happens to the amount of excess reserves, the excess reserve ratio, the money supply, and the money multiplier?

   d. Following the financial crisis in 2008 in the United States, the Federal Reserve began injecting the U.S. banking system with massive amounts of liquidity, and at the same time, very little lending occurred. As a result, the M1 money multiplier was below 1 for most of the time from October 2008 through 2011. How does this relate to your answer to part (c)?

DATA ANALYSIS PROBLEMS

Download data for these problems from MyEconLab *at* **www.myeconlab.com**.

1. Go to the CANSIM webpage and find monthly data from January 1968 to December 2014 on the monetary base (series V37145), M1++ gross (series V37152), and M2++ gross (series V41552801).

   a. What is the average M1++ growth rate? Its variance?
   b. What is the average M2++ growth rate? Its variance?
   c. Which monetary aggregate is more variable?
   d. Calculate the M1++ money multiplier. What is its average value?

e. Calculate the M2++ money multiplier. What is its average value?

f. Compare the two money multipliers.

g. Does it appear that the money multipliers are increasing or decreasing?

2. Go to the St. Louis Federal Reserve FRED database, and find the most current U.S. data available on Currency (CURRNS), Total Checkable Deposits (TCDNS), Total Reserves (RESBALNS), and Required Reserves (RESBALREQ).

a. Calculate the value of the currency deposit ratio c.

b. Use RESBALNS and RESBALREQ to calculate the amount of excess reserves, and then calculate the value of the excess reserve ratio e. Be sure the units of total and required reserves are the same when you do the calculations.

c. Assuming a required reserve ratio r_d of 11%, calculate the value of the money multiplier m.

WEB EXERCISES

1. An important aspect of the supply of money is bank deposits with the Bank of Canada. Go to **www.osfi-bsif. gc.ca** and locate financial data for banks. This site reports the consolidated balance sheet for all banks.

    a. What is the current level of bank deposits with the Bank of Canada?

    b. What is the change in bank deposits with the Bank of Canada since a year ago?

    c. Based on (a) and (b), does it appear that bank reserves with the Bank of Canada are increasing or decreasing?

2. Go to **www.bankofcanada.ca** and click on "Statistics," then "Indicators," and then choose "Summary of Key Monetary Policy Variables."

    a. What is the 12-month growth rate of M1+ (gross), M1++ (gross), and M2++ (gross)?

    b. What is the change in the 12-month growth rate in M1+ (gross), M1++ (gross), and M2++ (gross)?

WEB REFERENCES

www.bankofcanada.ca

This site reports current and historical levels of M1 and M2, as well as other data on the money supply.

www.federalreserve.gov/Releases/h3/

The Federal Reserve website reports data about aggregate reserves and the monetary base. This site also reports on the volume of borrowings from the Fed.

Tools of Monetary Policy

Learning Objectives

After studying this chapter you should be able to

1. Characterize the framework for the implementation of monetary policy in Canada (the LVTS, the target and the operating band for the overnight interest rate, and the Bank of Canada's standing liquidity facilities).

2. Illustrate the market for reserves, and demonstrate how changes in monetary policy can affect the equilibrium overnight interest rate.

3. Summarize how conventional monetary policy tools are implemented and the relative advantages and limitations of each tool.

4. Explain the key monetary policy tools that are used when conventional policy is no longer effective.

5. Identify the distinctions and similarities between the monetary policy tools of the Bank of Canada and those of the Federal Reserve and the European Central Bank.

PREVIEW

In this chapter, we examine the tools of monetary policy used by the Bank of Canada to control the money supply and interest rates. Because the Bank's use of these policy tools has such an important impact on interest rates and economic activity, it is vital to understand how the Bank wields them in practice and how relatively useful each tool is.

In recent years, the Bank of Canada has increasingly focused on the **overnight interest rate** (the interest rate on overnight loans of reserves from one bank to another) as the primary instrument of monetary policy. Since December 2000, the Bank of Canada has announced an overnight rate target eight times throughout the year, an announcement that is watched closely by market participants because it affects interest rates throughout the economy. Thus, to fully understand how the Bank of Canada uses its tools in the conduct of monetary policy, we must understand not only their effects on the money supply but also their direct effect on the overnight interest rate and how they can be used to achieve an overnight interest rate that is close to the target. The chapter therefore begins with the institutional framework within which the Bank of Canada conducts monetary policy, followed by a supply and demand analysis of the market for reserves to explain how the Bank's setting for the three monetary policy tools—open market operations, settlement balances management, and Bank of Canada lending—determine the overnight interest rate. We next go on to look in more detail at each of these tools of monetary policy to see how they are used in practice and to gain a sense of their relative advantages. We then examine the nonconventional tools of monetary policy that the Bank of Canada and other central banks were forced to use during the extraordinary circumstances of the recent financial crisis. The chapter ends with a discussion of the tools of monetary policy used by other central banks besides the Bank of Canada.

THE FRAMEWORK FOR THE IMPLEMENTATION OF MONETARY POLICY

The tools used by the Bank of Canada to implement monetary policy are closely linked to the institutional arrangements regarding the clearing and settlement systems in the Canadian economy. Understanding the tools of monetary policy therefore requires that we know the key features of the framework for the implementation of monetary policy. As you will see, this framework has been designed to encourage deposit-taking financial institutions to deal directly with the market, rather than with the Bank of Canada.[1]

The Large Value Transfer System (LVTS)

The core of the Canadian payments system is the **Large Value Transfer System (LVTS)**, introduced by the Canadian Payments Association on February 4, 1999. The LVTS is an electronic, real-time net settlement network, designed to provide immediate finality and settlement to time-critical transactions. In addition to the Bank of Canada, there are 15 **LVTS participants**.[2] A financial institution can participate directly in the LVTS if it is a member of the Canadian Payments Association, uses the SWIFT telecommunications network, maintains a settlement account at the Bank of Canada, and has agreements regarding borrowing from the Bank of Canada and pledging eligible collateral. All other members of the Canadian Payments Association that are not direct participants in the LVTS are able to arrange LVTS payments through the LVTS participants.

The LVTS has been put in place in order to eliminate **systemic risk**—the risk to the entire payments system due to the inability of one financial institution to fulfill its payment obligations in a timely fashion. In fact, each LVTS payment is subject to real-time risk-control tests to confirm that sufficient collateral is available, and is final and irrevocable in real time. In particular, LVTS participants can make a payment only if they have, in real time (right now), either positive settlement balances in their accounts with the Bank of Canada, posted collateral (such as Government of Canada Treasury bills and bonds), or explicit lines of credit with other participants. As a result, the system will settle at the end of each day even in the face of risk and liquidity problems.

Of course, it is not just Canada that is concerned about systemic risk. Real-time settlement systems were implemented by Sweden in 1986, Germany and Switzerland in 1987, Japan in 1988, Italy in 1989, Belgium and the United Kingdom in 1996, and by France, Hong Kong, and the Netherlands in 1997. Moreover, the central banks of the G-10 countries, through the Bank for International Settlements, have developed minimum standards for the operation of the global payment network for large-value funds transfers.

In Canada's LVTS, participants know in real time their large-value, wholesale transactions (over $50 000). Although these transactions account for less than 1% of the total number of transactions, they account for about 94% of the value of transactions. For example, the LVTS is used to settle over 25 000 payments daily, with a value close to $200 billion. This information eliminates most of the uncertainty from settlement balance prediction—the largest reason for financial institutions not being able to hit their target settlement balances with the Bank of Canada in the pre-LVTS system. Settlement of payment obligations among LVTS participants takes place, at the end of each banking

---

[1]For more details, see Donna Howard, "A Primer on the Implementation of Monetary Policy in the LVTS Environment," *Bank of Canada Review* (Autumn, 1998): 57–66; Kevin Clinton, "Implementation of Monetary Policy in a Regime with Zero Reserve Requirements," Bank of Canada Working Paper: 97–98; and "The Framework for the Implementation of Monetary Policy in the Large Value Transfer System Environment," Bank of Canada Release, March 31, 1999.

[2]These are the Big Six (Bank of Montreal, Bank of Nova Scotia, Canadian Imperial Bank of Commerce, National Bank of Canada, Royal Bank of Canada, and Toronto-Dominion Bank), Alberta Treasury Branches, Bank of America National Association, BNP Paribas, Caisse centrale Desjardins du Québec, Central 1 Credit Union, HSBC Bank Canada, Laurentian Bank of Canada, Manulife Bank of Canada, and State Street Bank and Trust Company.

day, through the transfer of funds in their settlement accounts at the Bank of Canada. The LVTS uses **multilateral netting**, in which only the net credit or debit position of each participant vis-à-vis all other participants is calculated for settlement, thereby reducing the need for a large amount of settlement balances.

Non-LVTS (ACSS) Transactions

Although the LVTS eliminates the uncertainty from daily wholesale settlement balances prediction, there is still a residual stochastic element in settlement balances from non-LVTS paper-based payments items (such as paper cheques, travellers' cheques, gift certificates, and money orders) and small-value electronic payments items (such as pre-authorized debits and fund transfers, direct deposit items, and debit card transactions). Those items are cleared through the Automated Clearing Settlement System (ACSS), an electronic payments system also operated by the Canadian Payments Association, but without the vigorous risk controls of the LVTS. The ACSS aggregates interbank payments and calculates the net amounts to be transferred from and to each participant's settlement account with the Bank of Canada. The Bank completes the settlement the next day (at midday) through the LVTS.

Regarding the smaller value of ACSS settlements, **direct clearers** with positive clearing balances in the ACSS (that is, with net credit positions) receive an interest payment (calculated daily by the Canadian Payments Association, at the Bank of Canada's target overnight interest rate) to cover their cost of crediting their customers' accounts on the business day before receiving funds in settlement. On the other hand, direct clearers with net debit positions in the ACSS make payments (also at the Bank's target overnight interest rate) to offset their benefit of debiting the accounts of their customers on the day before paying funds in settlement. Interest compensation is included in the clearing balances settled at the Bank of Canada using LVTS funds.[3]

The Bank of Canada's Policy Rate

The overnight market in Canada is the key market for finance and monetary policy. This market is very liquid, with a broad range of participants, the most active of which are deposit-taking institutions and their investment dealer affiliates.[4] The interest rate at which participants borrow and lend overnight funds to each other in the money market is called the **overnight interest rate**, i_{or}. This rate is the shortest-term rate available and forms the base of any term structure of interest rates relation.

The Bank of Canada signals its monetary policy stance by announcing a target for the overnight interest rate (the overnight interest rate is known as the **reference rate**). The target for the overnight rate, known as the **policy rate**, is the main tool the Bank uses to conduct monetary policy. This rate refers to collateralized, market-based overnight transactions. The implementation of the stance of monetary policy is more successful when the reference rate is closer to the policy rate; that is, the closer the overnight rate is to the target for the overnight interest rate.

---

[3]There are 11 ACSS direct clearers in addition to the Bank of Canada—the Big Six, Alberta Treasury Branches, La Caisse centrale Desjardins du Québec, Central 1 Credit Union, HSBC Bank Canada, and the Laurentian Bank of Canada. Direct clearers maintain a settlement account at the Bank of Canada and participate directly in the ACSS.

[4]See Eugene Lundrigan and Sari Toll, "The Overnight Market in Canada," *Bank of Canada Review* (Winter 1997–1998): 27–42, for details regarding the evolution of the overnight market.

The Operating Band for the Overnight Interest Rate

The Bank of Canada implements monetary policy by changing the policy rate, in order to influence other short-term interest rates and the exchange rate. In fact, in normal times the Bank's operational objective is to keep the overnight rate within an **operating band** (also known as a *channel* or *corridor*) of 50 basis points (½ of 1%). As Figure 16-1 shows, the upper limit of the operating band defines the bank rate, i_b. *The bank rate is the interest rate the Bank of Canada charges LVTS participants that require an overdraft loan (advance) to cover negative settlement balances on the books of the Bank at the end of the banking day.* The lower limit of the operating band is the rate the Bank pays to LVTS participants with positive settlement balances at the end of the day. The midpoint of the operating band is the Bank of Canada's target for the overnight rate, the operating target of the Bank of Canada's monetary policy. When, for example, the operating band is from 1.5% to 2.0%, the bank rate is 2.0%, the rate the Bank pays on deposits to LVTS participants is 1.5%, and the Bank's target (which is the policy rate referred to earlier) for the overnight interest rate is 1.75%.

Since December 2000, the Bank of Canada has operated under a system of eight "fixed" dates throughout the year for announcing any changes to the target and the operating band for the overnight rate, and has reserved the option of acting between the fixed dates in "extraordinary circumstances." Early in the morning (at 9:00 a.m.) on each of the eight announcement dates, the Bank of Canada announces the target and an operating band of 50 basis points for the overnight interest rate (see the FYI box Monetary Policy Implementation in the LVTS Environment).

A similar channel/corridor system for setting the overnight interest rate is also used by other central banks including the Federal Reserve, the European Central Bank, the Bank of Japan, the Bank of England, the Reserve Bank of Australia, and the Reserve Bank of New Zealand.

FIGURE 16-1   Operating Band for the Overnight Interest Rate

FYI   Monetary Policy Implementation in the LVTS Environment

In the LVTS environment, the Bank of Canada operates under a system of eight fixed dates throughout the year for announcing, via a press release (at 9:00 a.m.), the target and the operating band for the overnight interest rate. The upper limit of the operating band defines the bank rate, i_b, at which the Bank provides overdraft loans to LVTS participants at the end of the day and the lower limit, $i_b - 0.50$, is the rate the Bank pays to LVTS participants with positive settlement balances at the end of the day.

The operating band for the overnight rate, reinforced by the Bank's standing liquidity facilities, and a target level of settlement balances (of roughly $50 million) are currently the framework within which the Bank of Canada implements monetary policy. The midpoint of the operating band, the policy rate, is the operating target of the Bank's monetary policy.

In targeting the midpoint of the operating band, the Bank of Canada will intervene in the overnight market at 11:45 a.m. to conduct open market buyback operations at the target overnight interest rate, if required. In particular, the Bank will use SPRAs if overnight funds are traded above the target for the overnight rate and SRAs if overnight funds are traded below the target for the overnight rate. There will be no Bank of Canada intervention in the overnight market if the overnight rate is around the target rate.

To maintain the desired level of settlement balances, the Bank of Canada must neutralize the net impact of its open market buyback operations and of certain federal government and Bank of Canada flows that potentially affect settlement balances. The neutralization is effected through the shifting (transfer) of federal government deposits (balances) between the government's account at the Bank of Canada and the participants in the auction of government cash balances. The shifting is made through the twice-daily auctions of Receiver General (federal government) balances (the first at 9:15 a.m. and the second at 4:15 p.m.).

The LVTS has a pre-settlement trading period of half an hour, at the end of the banking day (6–6:30 p.m.), to permit participating financial institutions to adjust positions with each other (in the overnight market) at a better return than can be achieved at the Bank of Canada's standing facilities. LVTS participants with settlement imbalances at the end of the banking day use the Bank of Canada's standing facilities to bring their settlement balances to the target level. That is, LVTS participants that require an overdraft loan to cover negative settlement balances on the books of the Bank borrow from the Bank at the bank rate, i_b. LVTS participants with positive settlement balances at the end of the day earn (during normal times) the bank rate less 50 basis points, $i_b - 0.50$.

The Market Timetable

9:00 a.m.	Bank of Canada announces changes (if any) to the target and the operating band for the overnight rate
9:15 a.m.	Auction for (federal) government cash balances
11:45 a.m.	Open market buyback operations (if required)
4:15 p.m.	Auction for (federal) government cash balances
6:00 p.m.	Close of LVTS for client transactions
6:00–6:30 p.m.	Pre-settlement period
8:00 p.m. or earlier	Settlement of LVTS balances at the Bank of Canada

Sources: Donna Howard, "A Primer on the Implementation of Monetary Policy in the LVTS Environment," *Bank of Canada Review* (Autumn 1998): 57–66; and "The Framework for the Implementation of Monetary Policy in the Large Value Transfer System Environment," *Bank of Canada Release*, March 31, 1999. Reprinted with permission.

The Bank of Canada's Standing Facilities

At the end of each banking day, each LVTS participant must bring its settlement balance with the Bank of Canada close to zero. Of course, it can scarcely be expected that LVTS participants will always be successful in ending up with near-zero settlement balances. The Bank of Canada therefore stands ready (with what we call **standing liquidity facilities**) to lend to or borrow from a participant to bring their settlement balances to zero at the end of the banking day. As already noted, participants also know with certainty the rates applicable to positive and negative settlement balances with the Bank of Canada (see the FYI box Monetary Policy Implementation in the LVTS Environment, and Figure 16-1).

To permit participating financial institutions to adjust positions with each other (i.e., reduce the costs of either positive or negative positions), the LVTS has a pre-settlement trading period of half an hour, at the end of the banking day (6–6:30 p.m.). The purpose of the pre-settlement trading period is to allow LVTS participants to reduce their LVTS positions (which resulted during the day from their own transactions and those of their clients) at interest rates better than those at the Bank of Canada's standing liquidity facilities. That is, to provide a window for those participants with excess positions to trade with those in deficit, at a better return than can be achieved at the Bank's facilities, to the advantage of both. In fact, the typical bid–ask spread on overnight funds in the interbank market has been less than 1/8%. This is significantly less than the spread of 50 basis points between the rate charged on overdrafts, i_b, and that paid on deposits by the Bank of Canada, $i_b - 0.50$, after settlement of LVTS multilateral positions.

In general, pre-settlement trading among participants will achieve a zero settlement balance for each participant on wholesale transactions. However, if at the end of the settlement day a participant has a negative balance on the books of the Bank of Canada, the deficit will be financed by a collateralized advance at the bank rate, i_b. Participants with positive settlement balances at the end of the day are paid interest at the bank rate less 50 basis points (i.e., the bottom of the operating band). Hence, as long as the bank rate is set so that the market bid–ask spread is within the operating band, participants will resolve their nonzero settlement balances among themselves rather than through the Bank of Canada's standing facilities. In fact, in a fully competitive market, participants would be expected to trade at the midpoint of the operating band for the overnight interest rate.

Clearly, the LVTS and the Bank of Canada's standing liquidity facilities have been set up in such a way so as to ensure a determinate demand for settlement balances, treating the costs of deficits and surpluses symmetrically. That is, the cost of holding excess settlement balances (an opportunity cost of 25 basis points) equals the cost of holding deficit levels of settlement balances (a premium of 25 basis points for an overdraft loan). These cost incentives are very important as they encourage banks to target zero settlement balances at the Bank of Canada and in doing so to deal directly with the market rather than to rely on the Bank's automatic standing liquidity facilities.

The Bank of Canada's Implementation of the Operating Band for the Overnight Interest Rate

It is through its lending and taking deposits from LVTS participants that the Bank of Canada implements its target band for the overnight interest rate. *If the overnight rate increases toward the upper limit of the operating band, then the Bank will lend at the bank rate to put a ceiling on the overnight rate.* The bank rate is the ceiling on the overnight rate in the money market for LVTS participants, because LVTS participants are unlikely to borrow overnight funds at a higher interest rate, since they can borrow at the bank rate from the Bank of Canada.

If the overnight rate declines toward the lower limit of the operating band, then the Bank will accept deposits from LVTS participants at the bank rate less 50 basis points, to put a floor on the overnight rate. The bank rate less 50 basis points, $i_b - 0.50$, is the floor on the overnight rate because LVTS participants are unlikely to lend overnight funds at a lower rate, since they can leave funds on deposit at this rate at the Bank of Canada.

THE MARKET FOR SETTLEMENT BALANCES AND THE CHANNEL/CORRIDOR SYSTEM FOR SETTING THE OVERNIGHT INTEREST RATE

In Chapter 15, we saw how open market operations (changes in nonborrowed reserves) and Bank of Canada lending (changes in borrowed reserves) affect the balance sheet of the Bank and the amount of reserves. The market for reserves (settlement balances) is where the overnight interest rate is determined, and this is why we turn to a supply and demand analysis of this market to analyze how the tools of monetary policy affect the overnight rate.

Demand and Supply in the Market for Reserves

The analysis of the market for reserves proceeds in a similar fashion to the analysis of the bond market we conducted in Chapter 4 and describes determination of the overnight interest rate in a symmetric channel/corridor system of interest-rate control such as that in Canada, Australia, England, the euro area, and (until spring 2006) New Zealand. First, we derive demand and supply curves for reserves. Then, the market equilibrium in which the quantity of reserves demanded equals the quantity of reserves supplied determines the level of the overnight interest rate, the interest rate charged on the loans of these reserves.

Demand Curve

To derive the demand curve for reserves, we need to ask what happens to the quantity of reserves demanded by banks, holding everything else constant, as the overnight interest rate, i_{or}, changes. Banks in Canada are no longer required to hold reserves determined through government legislation, as is the case with banks in the Federal Reserve system in the United States and the European central bank. Canadian banks, however, hold sufficient cash reserves against their deposit liabilities in order to manage their own short-term liquidity requirements, such as, for example, meeting their depositors' day-to-day demand for cash. We call these reserves *desired reserves*. Desired reserves equal the desired reserve ratio, r_d, times the amount of deposits on which reserves are desired.

Reserves in excess of the desired amounts are called *excess reserves*. Excess reserves are insurance against deposit outflows, and the cost of holding these excess reserves is their opportunity cost, the interest rate that could have been earned on lending these reserves out, minus the interest rate that is earned on these reserves, i_{er}, which in Canada equals the bank rate less 50 basis points, $i_{er} = i_b - 0.50$.

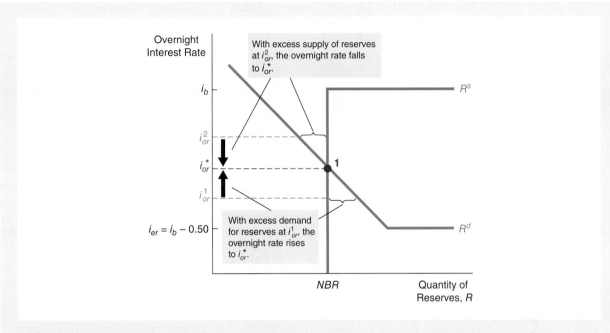

FIGURE 16-2   Equilibrium in the Market for Reserves

When the overnight rate is above the rate paid on excess reserves, i_{er}, then as the overnight rate decreases, the opportunity cost of holding excess reserves falls. Holding everything else constant, including the quantity of desired reserves, the quantity of reserves demanded rises. Consequently, the demand curve for reserves, R_d, slopes downward in Figure 16-2 when the overnight rate is above i_{er}. If, however, the overnight rate begins to fall below the interest rate paid on excess reserves i_{er}, banks do not lend in the overnight market at a lower interest rate. Instead, they just keep on adding to their holdings of excess reserves indefinitely. The result is that the demand curve for reserves, R^d, becomes flat (infinitely elastic) at i_{er} in Figure 16-2.

Supply Curve

The supply of reserves, R^s, can be broken up into two components: the amount of reserves that are supplied by the Bank of Canada's open market operations, called *nonborrowed reserves* (NBR), and the amount of reserves borrowed from the Bank of Canada, called *borrowed reserves* (BR). The primary cost of borrowing from the Bank of Canada is the interest rate charged by the Bank on these loans—the bank rate, i_b, which is set at a fixed amount above the overnight rate target and thus changes when the target changes.

Because borrowing overnight funds from other banks is a substitute for borrowing (taking out advances) from the Bank of Canada, if the overnight interest rate i_{or} is below the bank rate i_b, then banks will not borrow from the Bank of Canada. Borrowed reserves will be zero because borrowing in the overnight funds market is cheaper. Thus, as long as i_{or} remains below i_b, the supply of reserves will just equal the amount of nonborrowed reserves supplied by the Bank of Canada, *NBR*, and so the supply curve will be vertical as shown in Figure 16-2. However, as the overnight rate begins to rise above the bank rate, banks will want to keep borrowing more and more at i_b and then lending out the proceeds in the overnight funds market at the higher rate, i_{or}. The result is that the supply curve becomes flat (infinitely elastic) at i_b, as shown in Figure 16-2.

Market Equilibrium

Market equilibrium occurs where the quantity of reserves demanded equals the quantity supplied, $R^d = R^s$. Equilibrium therefore occurs at the intersection of the demand curve R^d and the supply curve R^s at point 1 in Figure 16-2, with an equilibrium overnight interest rate of i_{or}^*. When the overnight interest rate is above the equilibrium rate at i_{or}^2, more reserves are supplied than are demanded (excess supply), and so the overnight interest rate falls to i_{or}^*, as shown by the downward arrow. When the overnight interest rate is below the equilibrium rate at i_{or}^1, more reserves are demanded than are supplied (excess demand), and so the overnight interest rate rises, as shown by the upward arrow.

APPLICATION

How the Bank of Canada's Operating Procedures Limit Fluctuations in the Overnight Interest Rate

An important advantage of the Bank of Canada's current monetary policy procedures is that they limit fluctuations in the overnight interest rate. We can use our supply and demand analysis of the market for reserves to see why.

Suppose that, initially, the equilibrium overnight interest rate is at the overnight rate target of i_{or}^* in Figure 16-3. If the demand for reserves experiences a large unexpected increase, the demand curve would shift to the right to $R^{d''}$, where it now intersects the supply curve for reserves on the flat portion, where the equilibrium overnight rate i_{or}^2 equals the bank rate, i_b. No matter how far the demand curve shifts to the right, the equilibrium overnight rate i_{or}^2 will just stay at i_b because borrowed reserves will just continue to increase, matching the increase in demand. Similarly, if the demand for reserves experiences a large unexpected decrease, the demand curve shifts to the left to $R^{d'}$, and the supply curve intersects the demand curve on its flat portion, where the equilibrium overnight rate i_{or}^1 equals the interest rate paid on excess reserves, $i_{er} = i_b - 0.50$. No matter how far left the demand curve shifts, the equilibrium overnight interest rate i_{or}^1 will stay at i_{er} because excess reserves will keep on increasing so that the quantity demanded of reserves equals the quantity of nonborrowed reserves supplied.

Our analysis therefore shows that the *Bank of Canada's operating procedures limit the fluctuations of the overnight interest rate so that it remains between $i_{er} = i_b - 0.50$ and i_b*. If the range between i_{er} and i_b is kept narrow enough, then fluctuations around the target rate will be small.

A rightward shift in the demand curve for reserves to $R^{d''}$ will raise the equilibrium overnight rate to a maximum of $i_{or}^2 = i_b$, whereas a leftward shift of the demand curve to $R^{d'}$ will lower the overnight rate to a minimum of $i_{or}^1 = i_{er}(= i_b - 0.50)$. ◆

MyEconLab Mini-lecture

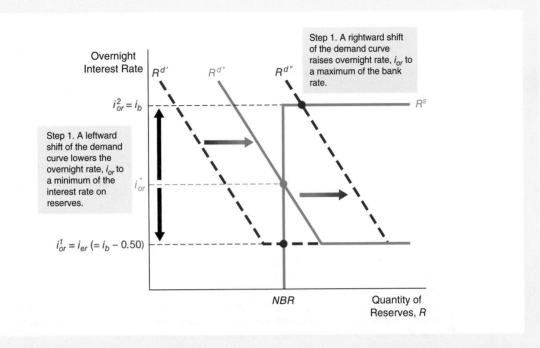

FIGURE 16-3   How the Bank of Canada's Operating Procedures Limit Fluctuations in the Overnight Interest Rate

THE BANK OF CANADA'S APPROACH TO MONETARY POLICY

The goal of the Bank of Canada's current monetary policy is to keep the inflation rate within a target range of 1% to 3%, with the midpoint of the inflation target range, 2%, being the most desirable outcome (see also the FYI box Price-Level Targeting Versus Inflation-Rate Targeting). In setting its inflation targets, the Bank of Canada

---

FYI   Price-Level Targeting Versus Inflation-Rate Targeting

Currently no central bank is targeting the price level, but some central banks (including the Bank of Canada) are considering whether to replace inflation-rate targeting with price-level targeting.

The advantage of price-level targeting is that it reduces the uncertainty about the long-term purchasing power of money. Consider, for example, the Bank of Canada's objective of keeping the (headline) inflation rate between 1% and 3%, with 2% being

the most desirable outcome. This means that over a 30-year period the cumulative inflation rate could be as low as 35% or as high as 143%.

Targeting the price level eliminates that uncertainty. That is, the central bank will make up any lost ground on prices whenever inflation turns out to be less than 2%. Although in theory price-level targeting seems to be superior to inflation-rate targeting, policymakers are reluctant to tinker with the status quo, for now.

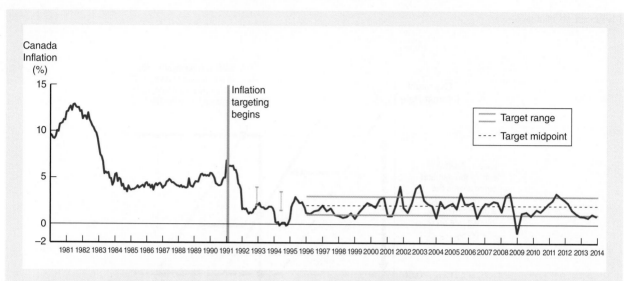

FIGURE 16-4 **Inflation Rates and Inflation Targets for Canada, 1980–2014**

Canada has significantly reduced the rate of inflation and over time has achieved its inflation targets.

Source: Ben S. Bernanke, Thomas Laubach, Frederic S. Mishkin, and Adam S. Poson, Inflation Targeting: Lessons from the International Experience (Princeton: Princeton University Press, 1999); and Federal Reserve Bank of St. Louis, FRED database: **http://research.stlouisfed.org/fred2/**.

uses the rate of change in the consumer price index (CPI), because it is the most commonly used and understood price measure in Canada. Although the Bank's targets are specified in terms of "headline CPI" (all items), the Bank uses "core CPI," which excludes volatile components such as food, energy, and the effect of indirect taxes, as a measure of the headline rate's trend. Also, defining the inflation targets in terms of ranges provides the Bank of Canada sufficient flexibility to deal with supply shocks beyond those already taken care of by the exclusion of volatile components from core inflation.

Figure 16-4 shows what has happened to the Canadian inflation rate since February 26, 1991, after the Bank's governor and the minister of finance jointly announced a series of declining inflation targets, with a band of plus and minus one percentage point around them. In what follows, we examine the tools used by the Bank of Canada to implement monetary policy, leaving a detailed analysis of the Bank's monetary policy for Chapter 18.

How Monetary Policy Affects the Economy

The Bank of Canada affects interest rates and the level of economic activity by changing the target and operating band for the overnight interest rate. As we saw in Chapter 6, interest rates on different assets tend to move together over time. Hence, changes in the target for the overnight interest rate (and thus the bank rate, i_b) influence other rates, such as the prime rate (the interest rate banks charge to their best customers) and the interest rates on bank deposits and mortgages. These changes in interest rates may also lead to changes in the exchange rate. The level of short-term interest rates and the

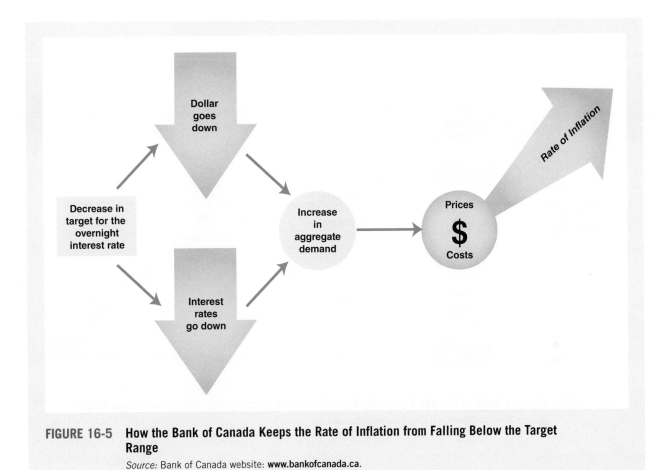

FIGURE 16-5   **How the Bank of Canada Keeps the Rate of Inflation from Falling Below the Target Range**
Source: Bank of Canada website: **www.bankofcanada.ca**.

exchange rate of the Canadian dollar determine the **monetary conditions** in which the economy operates.

The concept of monetary conditions, introduced by the Bank of Canada in its conduct of monetary policy in the early 1990s, focuses on the effect on the economy of both short-term interest rates and the exchange rate. Changes in monetary conditions affect the economy and the Bank's ultimate objective, the inflation rate, only indirectly and are usually felt over a period of several months to several years. This means that the Bank of Canada must always be forward looking in its conduct of monetary policy, anticipating the level of monetary conditions needed today to achieve its ultimate goal of low and stable inflation in the future.

As an example, suppose that the Bank of Canada expects the economy to slow down and wishes to ease monetary conditions. It lowers the target and operating band for the overnight interest rate.[5] As you can see in Figure 16-5, this reduces interest rates and the value of the dollar and leads to an increase in the supply of money, aggregate demand, and the price level, thereby preventing the inflation rate from falling below the target range of 1% to 3%.

---

[5]For example, the Bank might lower the operating band by 25 basis points from 1.5% to 2.0% to 1.25% to 1.75%.

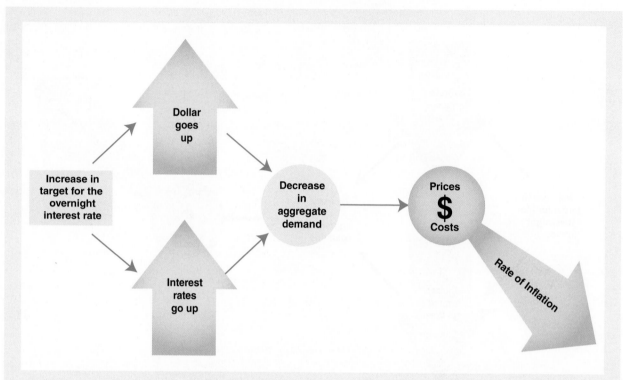

FIGURE 16-6 **How the Bank of Canada Keeps the Rate of Inflation from Moving Above the Target Range**
Source: Bank of Canada website: **www.bankofcanada.ca.**

In the opposite case, if the Bank expects the economy to be exceeding its capacity at some point in the future, it raises the operating band in order to prevent inflationary pressures from building. The consequent increase in interest rates and the value of the dollar lead to a decline in the supply of money, aggregate demand, and the price level, thereby preventing the inflation rate from moving above the Bank's target range of 1% to 3%—see Figure 16-6.

Hence, by changing the target and operating band for the overnight rate, the Bank of Canada sends a signal regarding the direction that it would like interest rates and the money supply to take. A rise in the target and operating band, and thus the bank rate, is a signal that the Bank would like to see higher interest rates and less money in the economy. A fall in the target and operating band is a signal that the Bank would like lower interest rates and more money.

Nominal Interest Rates and Monetary Policy

The Bank of Canada uses the *nominal* overnight interest rate as its operating instrument, but as you will learn in Chapter 24, the effects of monetary policy on economic activity stem from how the *real* interest rate, r, rather than the nominal interest rate, i, affects consumption and investment spending. In fact, the current interest rate targeting approach is based on the belief that it is the real *long-term* interest rate, and not the real short-term interest rate, that affects consumer and business decisions.

How is it that changes in short-term nominal interest rates (such as the Bank of Canada's overnight rate) affect short- and long-term real interest rates? Under the "new Keynesian" assumption of *sticky* prices (that is, under the assumption that prices do not adjust instantaneously to clear the markets), an expansionary monetary policy that lowers the short-term nominal interest rate will also lower the short-term real interest rate, since the aggregate price level adjusts slowly over time and there is not much change in the inflation rate. Moreover, according to the expectations hypothesis of the term structure of interest rates (discussed in detail in Chapter 6), the decline in short-term interest rates will also lead to a decline in long-term interest rates and ultimately to increases in consumer and investment spending.

This transmission mechanism works well even when the short-term nominal interest rate is at or close to zero. With a nominal interest rate of zero, a commitment by the central bank to expansionary monetary policy raises the expected inflation rate, π^e, reduces the real interest rate, r, and leads to a rise in aggregate output. Thus, expansionary monetary policy could stimulate spending even when the short-term nominal interest rate is at zero. In fact, this mechanism is the key element in monetarist discussions of why an expansionary monetary policy could have prevented the sharp decline in output in the United States during the Great Depression, why it would have helped the Japanese economy when nominal interest rates fell to near zero in the late 1990s, and why it could help cope with the recent financial crisis and the global economic meltdown.

However, the collapse of stable relationships in financial markets may be causing the term structure of interest rate relationships on which the Keynesian transmission mechanism depends to loosen. For example, the U.S. Federal Reserve raised the target federal funds rate in 17 consecutive meetings from June 2004 to July 2006, from 1% to 5.25%, but long-term interest rates in the United States and around the world declined for most of this period. It has been argued that the reason long-term interest rates did not respond over this period of monetary tightening was the adoption of an inflation-targeting approach to monetary policy by many countries and increased competition from China and India in labour and product markets that contributed to price stability and put downward pressure on long-term interest rates by reducing inflationary expectations.

Similarly, the recent decline in the federal funds rate to its current range of 0% to 0.25% from 5.25% in August of 2007 has not led to the desired decline in long-term interest rates. Why? Because the turmoil in the financial markets has increased risk premiums, thereby keeping long-term nominal interest rates high. Moreover, with collapsing asset prices (stock and real estate prices), there has been an increase in deflationary expectations, which led to a rise in real interest rates. This has the potential to make monetary policy highly contractionary, despite falling short-term nominal interest rates.

CONVENTIONAL MONETARY POLICY TOOLS

Now that we understand how the overnight interest rate is determined and the Bank of Canada's approach to monetary policy, we can examine how during normal times the Bank of Canada uses the three tools of monetary policy—open market operations, settlement balances management, and Bank of Canada lending—to control the money supply and interest rates. These three tools are referred to as **conventional monetary policy**. We will look at each of them in turn to see how the Bank of Canada wields them in practice and how relatively useful each tool is.

Open Market Operations

Open market operations are an important monetary policy tool for many central banks around the world, because they are the primary determinants of changes in interest rates and the monetary base, the main source of fluctuations in the money supply. Open market purchases expand bank reserves and the monetary base, thereby lowering short-term interest rates and raising the money supply. Open market sales shrink bank reserves and the monetary base, raising short-term interest rates and lowering the money supply.

The Bank of Canada, however, stopped conducting open market operations in Government of Canada Treasury bills and bonds in 1994, and its most common operations since then have been repurchase transactions with **primary dealers**—the Big Six and the major investment dealers that have signed a Purchase and Resale Agreement with the Bank of Canada. In particular, the Bank uses **special Purchase and Resale Agreements (special PRAs or SPRAs)**, commonly referred to as **repos** or **specials**, as a tool to reduce undesired upward pressure on the overnight interest rate, and **Sale and Repurchase Agreements (SRAs)**, commonly referred to as **reverse repos** or **reverses**, as a tool to reduce undesired downward pressure on the overnight rate.

Let's see how the Bank of Canada uses special PRAs and SRAs in order to reinforce the target for the overnight interest rate during the course of a day.

Special PRAs   Assume that the operating band for the overnight interest rate is 1.5% to 2% and that the Bank of Canada is targeting the overnight rate at the midpoint of the band, at 1.75%. If overnight funds are traded at a rate higher than the target rate of 1.75%, then the Bank of Canada enters into special PRAs, typically at 11:45 a.m. at a price that works out to a 1.75% interest rate, the midpoint of the operating band. That is, the Bank purchases Government of Canada Treasury bills or bonds, with an agreement that the seller will repurchase them one business day later (see Figure 16-7 regarding the mechanics of a special PRA).

Since the securities are placed with the Canadian Depository for Securities (CDS), Canada's central securities depository owned and operated by the financial community, the title of the securities changes hands by electronic instruction. The balance sheets of the Bank of Canada and the primary dealers look like this:

Bank of Canada				Primary Dealers			
Assets		Liabilities		Assets		Liabilities	
Government securities	+$100	Settlement balances	+$100	Settlement balances	+$100	SPRAs	+$100

Hence, *special Purchase and Resale Agreements (SPRAs) relieve undesired upward pressure on the overnight interest rate.*

SRAs   If, on the other hand, overnight funds are traded at a rate below the target rate of 1.75%, then the Bank of Canada enters into SRAs, in which the Bank sells government securities and the buyer agrees to sell them back to the Bank one

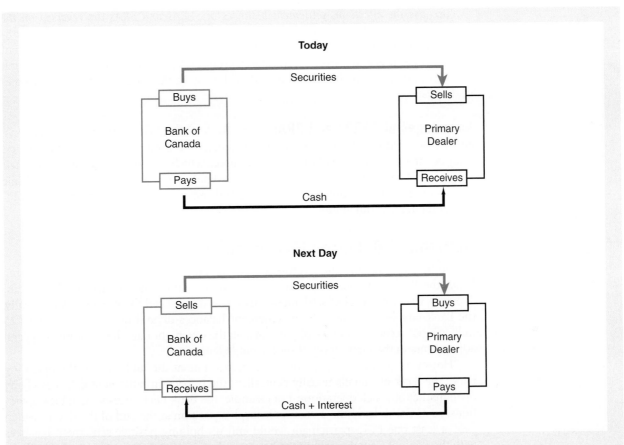

FIGURE 16-7 **The Mechanics of a Special PRA Operation**

Note: In a special PRA (SPRA), the Bank of Canada buys securities from a primary dealer in exchange for cash and the primary dealer agrees to buy the securities back (repurchase them) the next day at the original price plus interest, regardless of what happens in the market. In that arrangement, the primary dealer gets an overnight collateralized loan and the Bank of Canada gets some interest.

business day later. The balance sheets of the Bank of Canada and the direct clearers now look like this:

	Bank of Canada			Primary Dealers		
Assets		**Liabilities**		**Assets**		**Liabilities**
	Settlement balances	−$100		Settlement balances	−$100	
	SRAs	+$100		Government securities	+$100	

Hence, *Sale and Repurchase Agreements (SRAs) alleviate undesired downward pressure on the overnight financing rate.*

Because the effects on settlement balances of SPRAs and SRAs are reversed on the day the agreement matures, SPRAs and SRAs are actually temporary open market operations. Moreover, as you will see in the next section, because the effects on settlement balances of SPRAs and SRAs are typically neutralized by the end of the day by the Bank of Canada, there is no change at the end of the day in the level of settlement balances in the system.

Advantages of SPRAs and SRAs   The Bank of Canada's repurchase transactions, either special PRAs or SRAs, have several advantages over other tools of monetary policy. They occur at the initiative of the Bank of Canada, which has complete control over their volume, and are easily reversed. Moreover, the Bank of Canada can enter into multiple rounds of open market buyback operations and can also conduct these operations outside of the regular timeframe.

Settlement Balances Management

In addition to targeting the overnight interest rate at the midpoint of the operating band, the Bank of Canada also targets the level of settlement balances in the system. Typically, the target level of settlement balances is announced the previous day. Initially, the Bank targeted a daily level of settlement balances of zero or greater (usually $25 million), but recently, because of pressures on the overnight rate, the Bank made several adjustments to the target level of settlement balances.

However, in targeting the overnight interest rate at the midpoint of the operating band, the Bank of Canada usually neutralizes the impact on settlement balances of any open market buyback operations. For example, the Bank neutralizes special PRA operations, so as not to leave the system in a surplus position at the end of the day, in which case at least one LVTS participant would end up holding positive settlement balances with the Bank of Canada earning the bank rate less 50 basis points, $i_b - 0.05$. Similarly, the Bank of Canada neutralizes SRA operations, so as not to leave the system in a deficit position, in which case at least one LVTS participant would end up holding negative settlement balances with the Bank paying the bank rate, i_b.

Moreover, being the federal government's fiscal agent, the Bank of Canada usually neutralizes the net impact on settlement balances of certain federal government payment flows and Bank of Canada transactions.

The neutralization of the effects of open market buyback operations, public-sector flows on the level of settlement balances, and the adjustment of the level of settlement balances are effected through shifts (transfers) of government deposits (balances) between the government's account at the Bank of Canada and the government's accounts at the LVTS participants. In the pre-LVTS system, government deposit transfers between the government's accounts at banks and its account at the Bank of Canada were effected by the Bank of Canada's daily **drawdowns** (transfers of government deposits from the banks to the Bank of Canada) and **redeposits** (transfers of government deposits from the Bank of Canada to the banks). However, with the instantaneous transfers of funds allowed by the LVTS environment, the drawdown/redeposit mechanism is not a practical tool for government deposit shifting. This is so because the Bank of Canada is not able to debit the government's account with a bank on a day with a net disbursement by the government. In the LVTS environment, the Bank of Canada uses twice-daily auctions of federal government (Receiver General) balances, the first at 9:15 a.m. (which are collateralized) and the second at 4:15 p.m. (which are uncollateralized), when all the flows affecting the Bank of Canada's balance sheet are known. This neutralizes the effect of market buyback operations and of public-sector flows, and also adjusts the level of settlement balances.

Receiver General Auctions   To illustrate the process for neutralizing public sector flows using auctions of Receiver General balances, suppose that there is a net government receipt of $100 (i.e., the government's receipts from the public exceed its payments to the public by $100). Net receipts are drawn on the government's deposits at the LVTS participants, creating claims on the LVTS participants in favour of the Bank of Canada and ultimately reducing settlement balances by an amount equal to the government's net receipts. In the absence of any offsetting transactions by the Bank of Canada, through the workings of supply and demand, a decline in settlement balances will normally cause an increase in the overnight interest rate, as many LVTS participants would have to borrow more to meet their settlement obligations.

However, in targeting the overnight interest rate, the Bank of Canada will neutralize the net government receipt by arranging a net increase of $100 in the government deposit auctions to leave the system unchanged. This procedure results in the following balance sheets for the Bank and the LVTS participants:

Bank of Canada			LVTS Participants			
Assets	Liabilities		Assets		Liabilities	
	Government deposits	−100	Settlement balances	+100	Government deposits	+100
	Settlement balances	+100				

Note that government deposits at the Bank of Canada are reduced by $100 and at the same time the settlement balances of the LVTS participants are increased by $100.

If, instead of a net receipt by the government, there were a net disbursement of $100 (i.e., the government's payments to the public exceed its receipts from the public by $100), then the financial system's settlement balances would increase by the same amount. This would prompt a fall in the overnight interest rate, as many LVTS participants would have to borrow less to meet their settlement obligations. The Bank's neutralization process would prevent a decline in the overnight rate by reducing the banking system's settlement balances. This would involve LVTS transfers of $100 (i.e., the difference between the total amount of government balances maturing and the total amount of government balances auctioned) from the government's accounts at the participating institutions to the government's account at the Bank. This procedure results in the following T-accounts:

Bank of Canada			LVTS Participants			
Assets	Liabilities		Assets		Liabilities	
	Government deposits	+100	Settlement balances	−100	Government deposits	−100
	Settlement balances	−100				

In this case government deposits at the Bank of Canada are increased by $100 and at the same time the clearing balances of the participants are reduced by $100.

Swaps with the Exchange Fund Account

When the Bank of Canada transfers government balances, it usually brings onto its balance sheet Exchange Fund Account assets to back its liabilities. It does so by arranging a swap with the Exchange Fund Account, which holds the country's foreign exchange reserves. This involves a spot purchase and a simultaneous forward sale of foreign exchange. To illustrate the operation, assume that the Bank temporarily buys $100 of foreign currency assets from the Exchange Fund Account. It credits the government's account on its own books and the operation results in the following balance sheets for the Bank and the government:

Bank of Canada				Government of Canada		
Assets		**Liabilities**		**Assets**		**Liabilities**
Foreign exchange	+100	Government deposits	+100	Exchange Account Fund	−100	
				Deposits at the Bank of Canada	+100	

We see that government deposit balances at the Bank of Canada increase and these balances can then be transferred to participants to increase settlement balances, as we saw earlier.

Although the spot transaction adds to the government deposits at the Bank of Canada and enables the Bank to auction government balances, the forward contract between the Bank and the Exchange Fund Account does not affect the settlement balances of participating financial institutions. The Bank simply sells foreign exchange to the Exchange Fund Account in the future at a price agreed upon today. The advantage to the Bank of Canada of using swap transactions with the Exchange Fund Account is that it can bring a temporary change in the level of settlement balances or respond to some event that the Bank thinks will have a significant but not long-lived effect.

As we will learn in Chapter 20, the foreign exchange reserves, held in the Exchange Fund Account, can also be used by the Bank of Canada in international financial transactions to prevent undesirable movements in the exchange rate. For example, a Bank of Canada sale of domestic currency and corresponding purchase of foreign assets in the foreign exchange market leads to a gain in international reserves, an increase in the monetary base and the money supply, and a depreciation of the domestic currency. A Bank purchase of domestic currency and corresponding sale of foreign exchange leads to a loss of international reserves, a decline in the monetary base and the money supply, and an appreciation of the domestic currency. We shall discuss such foreign exchange interventions in detail in Chapter 20.

The Target Level of Settlement Balances

In addition to the auctions of Receiver General balances, the Bank of Canada can also adjust the target level of settlement balances if warranted by conditions in the overnight market. That is, the Bank retains the right to adjust the targeted level of settlement balances higher or lower than the typical setting, depending on pressures on the overnight rate.

The Bank of Canada, however, is not always able to completely neutralize special PRA and SRA operations and public sector flows so that the actual level of settlement balances ends up being higher or lower than the target level. However, deviations of the actual level of settlement balances from the target level appear to have insignificant effects on the overnight interest rate the day that they occur, unlike pre-announced changes to the target level of settlement balances, which appear to have a significant effect on the overnight interest rate.

APPLICATION Monetary Control in the Channel/Corridor System

Suppose that the operating band is 1.5% to 2% and the Bank of Canada expects the economy to exceed its capacity in the near future. To prevent inflationary pressures from building, the Bank wishes to tighten monetary policy by raising the target and operating band 25 basis points. In one of the eight fixed days for announcing changes to the target and operating band for the overnight rate, the Bank announces at 9:00 a.m. that it is adjusting the target and operating band up from 1.5% to 2% to 1.75% to 2.25%. From this announcement, LVTS participants know that the bank rate shifts from 2% to 2.25%, the rate on positive settlement balances shifts from 1.5% to 1.75%, and that the Bank of Canada's new target overnight rate, the midpoint of the operating band, shifts from 1.75% to 2%.

Later in the day, at 11:45 a.m., if overnight funds are trading below the target overnight rate (the midpoint of the operating band), the Bank of Canada enters into SRAs to enforce the new target for the overnight rate. That is, it sells government securities to primary dealers, who pay for the securities with settlement balances and agree to sell the securities back to the Bank of Canada on the next business day, at a price that works out to an annual interest rate of 2%—the midpoint of the new operating band. Assuming that the Bank of Canada enters into SRAs in the amount of $100, the T-accounts of the Bank of Canada and the primary dealers will be:

Bank of Canada			Primary Dealers		
Assets	Liabilities		Assets		Liabilities
	Settlement balances	−100	Settlement balances	−100	
	SRAs	+100	Government securities	+100	

The clearing banks find that their settlement balances have declined by $100, and because they had not been holding any excess reserves, their holdings of settlement balances are $100 short. Assuming that no other transactions occur during the day, at 4:15 p.m. the Bank of Canada neutralizes the effect on aggregate settlement balances of its issue of SRAs by auctioning off government deposits. The Bank's neutralization process involves auctioning off $100 of government deposits and paying those LVTS participants taking government deposits with settlement balances, bringing the amount of aggregate settlement balances back to zero. The balance sheets of the Bank of Canada and the LVTS participants now look like this:

	Bank of Canada		LVTS Participants			
Assets	**Liabilities**		**Assets**		**Liabilities**	
	Settlement balances	+100	Settlement balances	+100	Government securities	+100
	Government deposits	−100				

The Bank of Canada's monetary tightening has been effected through the management of settlement balances, during the course of the day, with no change in the aggregate settlement balances of deposit-taking institutions. As already noted, the change in the overnight rate will influence other interest rates and the level of monetary conditions in which the economy operates. ◆

Bank of Canada Lending

The facility at which banks can borrow reserves from the Bank of Canada is called the **standing lending facility**. The easiest way to understand how the Bank of Canada affects the volume of borrowed reserves is by looking at how the standing lending facility operates.

Operation of the Standing Lending Facility

As already noted, the Bank of Canada offers a lending facility, standing ready to lend (upon presentation of suitable collateral) overnight settlement balances to LVTS participants with negative clearing balances at the end of the business day. The lending rate is the bank rate, denoted by i_b in Figure 16-2 (on page 397), and is 25 basis points higher than the target overnight interest rate, so as to penalize participants for not using the overnight interbank market. LVTS participants know with certainty the lending rate applicable to their negative settlement balances with the Bank of Canada.

To see how the standing lending facility works, let's see what happens if there is a large increase in the demand for reserves. This situation is analyzed in Figure 16-8. Suppose that initially the demand and supply curves for reserves intersect at point 1 so that the overnight rate is at its target level, i_{or}^*. Now the increase in reserves shifts the demand curve to R_2^d and the equilibrium moves to point 2. The result is that borrowed reserves increase from zero to BR and the overnight rate rises to i_b and can rise no further. The standing lending facility has put a ceiling on the overnight interest rate of i_b.

Lender of Last Resort　In addition to its use as a standing liquidity facility to reinforce the operating band for the overnight interest rate, Bank of Canada lending is also important in preventing financial panics. In fact, one of the Bank's most important roles is to be the **lender of last resort** in the Canadian economy.[6] It provides emergency lending assistance (against eligible collateral) for a maximum period of six months (which can be extended for periods up to six months as many times as the Bank judges) to solvent (but illiquid) deposit-taking institutions to prevent bank failures from spinning

---

[6]Regarding the policy framework that governs the Bank of Canada's lender-of-last-resort activities, see Daniel Fred and Walter Engert, "The Bank of Canada as Lender of Last Resort," *Bank of Canada Review* (Winter 2004–2005).

FIGURE 16-8   **How the Bank of Canada's Standing Facility Puts a Ceiling on the Overnight Interest Rate**

The rightward shift of the demand curve for reserves from R_1^d to R_2^d moves the equilibrium from point 1 to point 2 where $i_{or} = i_b$ and borrowed reserves increase from zero to *BR*.

further out of control, thereby preventing bank and financial panics. The rate that the Bank normally charges on these loans is the bank rate, although the Bank has discretion to charge a higher rate. In providing emergency lending assistance, the Bank always makes a judgment with respect to the trade-off between morally hazardous behaviour and the costs in terms of financial stability. Last-resort lending is a particularly effective way to provide reserves to the banking system during a banking crisis because reserves are immediately channelled to the banks that need them most.

At first glance, it might appear as though the presence of the CDIC, which insures depositors from losses due to a bank's failure up to a limit of $100 000 per account, would make the lender-of-last-resort function of the Bank of Canada superfluous. (The CDIC is described in detail in Chapter 10.) There are two reasons why this is not the case. First, it is important to recognize that the CDIC's insurance fund amounts to a small fraction of the amount of deposits outstanding. If a large number of bank failures occurred, the CDIC would not be able to cover all the depositors' losses. Indeed, the failures of deposit-based financial institutions in the 1980s and early 1990s in Canada, described in Chapter 10, led to large losses and a shrinkage in the CDIC's insurance fund, which reduced the CDIC's ability to cover depositors' losses. This fact has not weakened the confidence of small depositors in the banking system because the Bank of Canada has been ready to stand behind the banks to provide whatever reserves are needed to prevent bank panics. Second, the large-denomination deposits in the banking system are not guaranteed by the CDIC because they exceed the $100 000 limit. A loss of confidence in the banking system could still lead to runs on banks from the large-denomination depositors, and bank panics could still occur despite the existence of the CDIC.

The importance of the Bank of Canada's role as lender of last resort is, if anything, more important today because of the 2007–2009 global financial crisis and economic downturn. Figure 16-9, which shows Bank of Canada advances to members of the Canadian Payments Association, reveals that the Bank of Canada advanced considerable funds in the recent past to financial institutions facing liquidity crises. Unfortunately, the Bank of Canada's lending policy has not always been successful in preventing financial

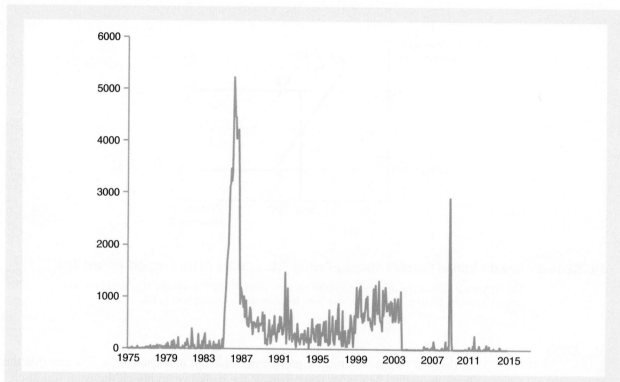

FIGURE 16-9   **Bank of Canada Advances to Members of the Canadian Payments Association, 1975–2014 (in millions of dollars)**

Source: Statistics Canada CANSIM series V36663.

crises. Two examples of the use of the Bank's lending weapon to avoid bank panics are the provisions of huge loans to the Canadian Commercial Bank and the Northland Bank in 1985 (see the FYI box Emergency Lending Assistance to Troubled Banks).

Advantages and Disadvantages of the Bank's Lending Policy

The most important advantage of the Bank of Canada's lending policy is that the Bank can use it to perform its role of lender of last resort and stabilize the financial system in times of stress. Experiences in the 1980s and early 1990s, the Black Monday crash, the terrorist destruction of the World Trade Center, and the recent global financial crisis indicate that this role has become more important in the past couple of decades.

In the past, Bank of Canada advances were used as a tool of monetary policy, with the bank rate changed to affect interest rates and the money supply. However, because the decisions to take out loans are made by banks and are therefore not completely controlled by the Bank of Canada, while open market buyback operations are completely controlled by the Bank of Canada, the use of lending policy to conduct monetary policy has little to recommend it. This is why the Bank of Canada moved to the current channel/corridor system of monetary control in which the bank rate is not used to set the overnight rate, but is only a backup facility to prevent the overnight interest rate from moving outside the operating band.

FYI Emergency Lending Assistance to Troubled Banks

Canadian Commercial and Northland

In 1985, there was public concern over the quality of the assets of two small Alberta-based banks—the Canadian Commercial Bank and the Northland Bank—which had made many bad loans. Larger depositors, whose accounts exceeded the $60 000 limit insured (at that time) by the CDIC, began to withdraw their deposits, and the failure of the banks was imminent. Because the immediate failure of Canadian Commercial and Northland would have had repercussions on other vulnerable banks, the Bank of Canada, under the advice of the Inspector General of Banks (the predecessor of the Office of the Superintendent of Financial Institutions Canada) made extraordinary advances. Total emergency lending assistance amounted to $1.8 billion so that depositors, including the largest, would not suffer any losses.

In doing this, the Bank of Canada was following the precedent established in 1984 by the Federal Reserve's rescue of Continental Illinois National Bank. Continental Illinois had made bad loans (primarily to businesses in the energy industry and to foreign countries), and rumours of financial trouble in early May 1984 caused large depositors to withdraw over US$10 billion of deposits from the bank.

The Federal Deposit Insurance Corporation (FDIC) arranged a rescue effort in July 1984 that culminated in a US$4.5 billion commitment of funds to save the bank. Still, the Fed had to lend Continental Illinois over US$5 billion—making the Bank of Canada's $1.8 billion advances to Canadian Commercial and Northland look like small potatoes! Although Continental Illinois was taken over by the FDIC, the Fed's action prevented further bank failures, and a potential bank panic was averted.

The Bank of Canada, however, was not as successful in preventing a bank crisis in Canada. With the failure of Canadian Commercial and Northland, rumours of financial trouble caused many large depositors to withdraw large deposits from the Bank of British Columbia, Mercantile Bank, and Continental Bank. By the time Mercantile was acquired by the National Bank of Canada, the Bank of British Columbia by the Hongkong Bank of Canada (now HSBC), and Continental by Lloyds Bank of Canada, the Bank of Canada had provided emergency lending assistance of more than $5 billion (see Figure 16-9). The loss of public confidence in the Canadian banking system led to the financial reforms of 1987–1992 and the consolidating of financial institution supervision under the Office of the Superintendent of Financial Institutions Canada.

NONCONVENTIONAL MONETARY POLICY TOOLS DURING THE GLOBAL FINANCIAL CRISIS

In normal times, conventional monetary policy tools, which expand the money supply and lower interest rates, are enough to stabilize the economy. However, when the economy experiences a full-scale financial crisis like the one we recently experienced, conventional monetary policy tools cannot do the job, for two reasons. First, the financial system seizes up to such an extent that it becomes unable to allocate capital to productive uses, and so investment spending and the economy collapse, as discussed in Chapter 9. Second, the negative shock to the economy can lead to the **zero-lower-bound problem**, in which the central bank is unable to lower short-term interest rates further because they have hit a floor of zero, as occurred at the end of 2008. The zero-lower-bound problem occurs because people can always earn more from holding bonds than from holding cash, and therefore nominal interest rates cannot be negative. For both of these reasons, central banks need non–interest-rate tools, known as **nonconventional monetary policy tools**, to stimulate the economy. These nonconventional monetary policy tools take three forms: (1) liquidity provision, (2) asset purchases, and (3) commitment to future monetary policy actions.

Liquidity Provision

Because conventional monetary policy actions were not sufficient to heal the financial markets during the recent financial crisis, central banks around the world implemented unprecedented increases in their lending facilities to provide liquidity to the financial markets. In Canada, according to the Bank of Canada Act, under extreme conditions on a financial market or financial system, the Bank of Canada has the authority to provide liquid funds to any (financial or nonfinancial) Canadian or foreign entities, for the purpose of promoting the stability of the financial system. Such central bank intervention can help prevent financial panics that are not triggered by bank failures. Although there are differences across countries in institutional arrangements for the conduct of monetary policy, most central banks have responded to the recent financial turbulence in a similar fashion, providing liquidity directly to the financial system.

In Canada, during the global financial crisis, the Bank of Canada introduced new facilities to address aggregate system liquidity at times of financial instability. In particular, the Bank introduced **term repos**, known in Canada as **term Purchase and Resale Agreements (term PRAs)**, and term securities lending. Let's see how these new facilities are used in providing liquidity to specific markets as opposed to lending directly to banks.

Term PRAs   Term PRAs are similar to special PRAs (see Figure 16-7) but have a term longer than one business day, typically a term of 28 business days. They are offered to primary dealers and used at times of crisis, when asymmetric information among market participants impairs their ability to buy and sell an asset class or maturity, thereby distorting liquidity premiums in the money market.

For example, against the backdrop of widening spreads and increased volatility in the term interbank market in the second half of 2008, the Bank of Canada announced that it would enter into a series of 28-day PRA transactions, thereby injecting huge amounts of liquidity into the markets. Moreover, the Bank expanded its list of acceptable collateral to include bank-sponsored asset-backed commercial paper and U.S. Treasuries. It also expanded its list of eligible counterparties. In engaging in these trades, the Bank takes securities onto its books in exchange for borrowings from the Bank's standing lending facility.

Term Securities Lending   This mechanism is designed to increase the supply of high-quality securities that could be used for collateral by banks. It can also be used to swap less-liquid securities for more liquid securities that the banks are putting up as collateral. It is also designed to partially offset the temporary increase in assets in the Bank's books associated with the term purchase and resale transactions.

Large-Scale Asset Purchases

A central bank's open market operations normally involve only the purchase of government securities, particularly those that are short-term. However, during the global financial crisis, central banks around the world, including the Federal Reserve, the Bank of Japan, and the Bank of England, started new, large-scale asset purchase programs to lower interest rates for particular types of credit.

For example, in November 2008, the Federal Reserve purchased $1.25 trillion of mortgage-backed securities guaranteed by Fannie Mae and Freddie Mac. Through these purchases, the Federal Reserve hoped to prop up the mortgage-backed securities market and to lower interest rates on residential mortgages to stimulate the housing market. Two years later in November 2010, the Fed announced that it would purchase $600 billion of long-term U.S. Treasury securities at a rate of about $75 billion per month. This large-scale purchase program, which became known as QE2 (which stands for Quantitative Easing 2), was intended to lower long-term interest rates. Although short-term interest rates on Treasury securities hit a floor of zero during the global financial crisis, long-term interest rates did not. Since investment projects have a long life, long-term interest rates are more relevant to investment decisions than short-term rates. The Fed's purchase of long-term Treasuries was an effort to stimulate investment spending and the economy by lowering long-term interest rates. Finally, in September 2012, the Federal Reserve announced a third large-scale asset-purchase program, which became known as QE3, which combined elements of QE1 and QE2. Through QE3, the Fed conducted purchases of $40 billion of mortgage-backed securities and $45 billion of long-term U.S. Treasuries. However, QE3 differed in one major way from the previous QE programs in that its goal was not to increase assets by a fixed dollar amount but instead was open-ended, with the purchase plan set to continue if it appeared that the labour market was unlikely to improve by a substantial margin.

These liquidity-provision and large-scale asset-purchase programs led to an unprecedented quadrupling of the Federal Reserve's balance sheet (shown in Figure 16-10).

MyEconLab Mini-lecture

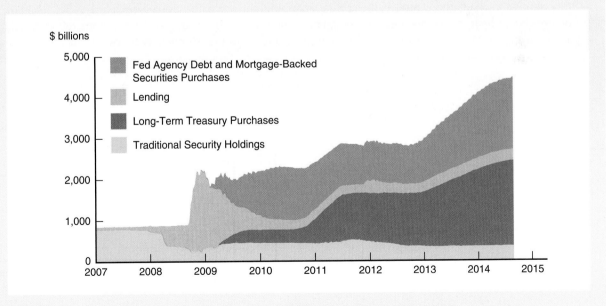

FIGURE 16-10   The Expansion of the Federal Reserve's Balance Sheet, 2007–2014

Quantitative Easing Versus Credit Easing

As we just learned, the programs introduced by the Fed in response to the global financial crisis led to an unprecedented expansion of the Federal Reserve's balance sheet. From before the financial crisis began in September 2007 through 2014, the

---

FYI   Quantitative Easing in the Channel/Corridor System

Consider Figure 16-11, which depicts the symmetric corridor system of Figure 16-2, in which the reserve demand is horizontal at $i_b - 0.50$ and the reserve supply is horizontal at i_b, where both rates are tied to the Bank of Canada's target for the overnight interest rate, i_{or}^*. Initially, the supply curve R_2^s intersects the demand curve R^d in its downward-sloped section at (point 1 and) the target overnight interest rate i_{or}^*.

The central bank can arbitrarily increase the supply of reserves (settlement balances) to undertake expanded asset purchases, shifting its reserve supply schedule from to R_1^s. But if it goes beyond a certain point (designated 2 in Figure 16-11), then the overnight interest rate will not equal the central bank's interest rate target, i_{or}^*, but rather the interest rate paid on excess reserves, i_{er} ($= i_b - 0.50$). Hence, the central bank's ability to arbitrarily choose the quantity of reserves comes at the expense of its ability to enforce its target for the overnight interest rate.

Importantly, however, the central bank can independently choose both the interest rate and the quantity of reserves if it targets the overnight interest rate

at the excess reserves rate, i_{er}. In this case, the central bank could supply any amount of reserves without any consequence for the policy rate, which would remain unchanged at i_{er}, since it is bounded from below at i_{er}.

This is exactly what the Bank of Canada did from April 1, 2009, to June 1, 2010, when it lowered the band for the overnight interest rate from 50 basis points to 25 basis points (from ½% to ¼%) and instead of targeting the overnight rate at the midpoint of the band (as it does during normal times), it started targeting it at the bottom of the operating band. On June 1, 2010, the Bank re-established the normal operating band of 50 basis points for the overnight interest rate and started again targeting the overnight rate at the midpoint of the band.

The central bank's ability to arbitrarily choose the quantity of reserves comes at the expense of its ability to enforce its target for the overnight interest rate. If, however, the central bank targets the overnight interest rate at the rate paid on excess reserves, ($i_{er} = i_b - 0.50$), then it would be able to choose both the overnight interest rate and the quantity of reserves independently.

FIGURE 16-11   Quantitative Easing in the Channel/Corridor System

amount of Federal Reserve assets rose from about $800 billion to over $4 trillion. This expansion of the balance sheet is referred to as **quantitative easing** because, as shown in Chapter 15, it leads to a huge increase in the monetary base—see the FYI box, Quantitative Easing in the Channel/Corridor System, for a better idea of how quantitative easing works. Because such an increase in the monetary base would usually result in an expansion of the money supply, it seems as though such an expansion could be a powerful force in stimulating the economy in the near term and possibly producing inflation down the road.

There are reasons to be very skeptical of this hypothesis. First, as we saw in the final application in Chapter 15, the huge expansion in the Fed's balance sheet and the monetary base did not result in a large increase in the money supply, because most of the increase in the monetary base just flowed into holdings of excess reserves. In fact, as shown in Figure 16-12, bank excess reserves in the United States increased to close to $3 trillion from around $50 billion before the global financial crisis. Second, because the federal funds rate had already fallen to the zero lower bound, the expansion of the balance sheet and the monetary base could not lower short-term interest rates any further and thereby stimulate the economy. Third, an increase in the monetary base does not mean that banks will increase lending, because they can just add to their holdings of excess reserves instead of making loans. Indeed, this appears to be exactly what happened during the global financial crisis, when the huge increase in the monetary base led primarily to a massive rise in excess reserves, and bank lending did not increase. A similar phenomenon seems to have occurred when the Bank of Japan engaged in quantitative easing after Japan's stock and real estate market bubbles burst in the 1990s; yet not only did the Japanese economy fail to recover, but inflation even turned negative.

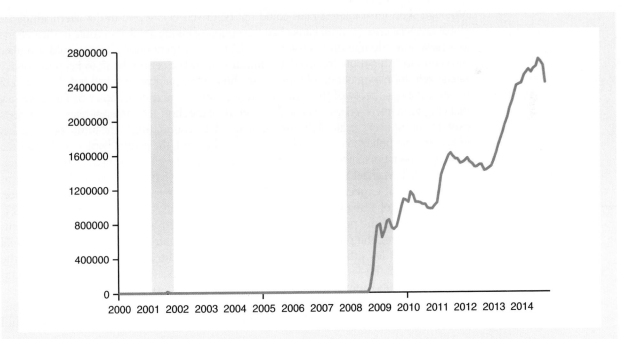

FIGURE 16-12   Excess Reserves of Depository Institutions in the United States (in $ billions)

Source: Federal Reserve Bank of St. Louis FRED database.

Does skepticism about the merits of quantitative easing mean that the Fed's nonconventional monetary policy actions during the financial crisis were ineffective in stimulating the economy? Former Fed Chair Ben Bernanke has argued that the answer is no, because the Fed's policies were directed not at expanding the Fed's balance sheet but rather at **credit easing**—that is, altering the composition of the Fed's balance sheet in order to improve the functioning of particular segments of the credit markets. Indeed, Bernanke was adamant that the Fed's policies should not be characterized as quantitative easing.

Altering the composition of the central bank's balance sheet can stimulate the economy in several ways. First, when the central bank provides liquidity to a particular segment of the credit markets that has seized up, such liquidity can help unfreeze the market and thereby enable it to allocate capital to productive uses, consequently stimulating the economy. Second, when the central bank purchases particular securities, it increases the demand for those securities and, as we saw in Chapter 6, such an action can lower the interest rates on those securities relative to rates on other securities. Thus, even if short-term interest rates have hit a floor of zero, asset purchases can lower interest rates for borrowers in particular credit markets and thereby stimulate spending. For example, purchases of mortgage-backed securities in the United States by the Fed appear to have lowered the interest rates on these securities, which led to a substantial decrease in residential mortgage rates. Purchases of long-term government securities could also lower their interest rates relative to short-term interest rates, and because long-term interest rates are likely to be more relevant to investment decisions, these asset market purchases could boost investment spending. Recent research appears to support this viewpoint.[7]

Forward Guidance and the Commitment to Future Policy Actions

Although short-term interest rates could not be driven below zero in the aftermath of the global financial crisis, central banks had the option of taking a different route in their efforts to achieve lower long-term interest rates, which, as we mentioned above, would stimulate the economy. This route involved a commitment by the central bank to keep the policy rate at zero for a long period of time. To see how this would work, recall our discussion of the expectations theory of the term structure of interest rates in Chapter 6. There we saw that long-term interest rates will equal an average of the short-term interest rates that markets expect to occur over the life of the long-term bond. By committing to the future policy action of keeping the policy rate at zero for an extended period, the central bank could lower the market's expectations of future short-term interest rates, thereby causing the long-term interest rate to fall. Michael Woodford of Columbia University has referred to such a strategy as **management of expectations**, but it is more commonly referred to as **forward guidance**.

The Bank of Canada pursued this forward-guidance strategy when, on April 21, 2009, it lowered the policy rate by 0.25 of a percentage point to 0.25%, and also committed to holding the policy rate at 0.25% until the second quarter of 2010, conditional on the outlook for inflation. Such a commitment by the Bank of Canada to keep the policy rate at 25 basis points for a long period was expected to shape market expectations of future short-term interest rates and lower long-term interest rates.

There are two types of commitments to future policy actions: conditional and unconditional. The commitment by the Bank of Canada to keep the policy rate at 0.25% until

---

[7]See, for example, Joseph Gagnon, Mathew Raskin, Julie Remache, and Brian Sack, "Large Scale Asset Purchases by the Federal Reserve: Did They Work?" *Federal Reserve Bank of New York Economic Policy Review*, Volume 17, Number 1 (May 2011), pp. 41–59.

the second quarter of 2010 was *conditional* because it stated that the decision was predicated on a low inflation rate going forward. If economic circumstances changed, the Bank of Canada was indicating that it might abandon the commitment. Alternatively, the Bank of Canada could have made an *unconditional* commitment by just stating that it would keep the policy rate at 0.25% for an extended period, without indicating that this decision might change depending on the state of the economy. An unconditional commitment is stronger than a conditional commitment because it does not suggest that the commitment will be abandoned and so is likely to have a larger effect on long-term interest rates. Unfortunately, it has the disadvantage that, even if circumstances change in such a way that it would be better to abandon the commitment, the central bank may feel that it cannot go back on its word and therefore cannot abandon the commitment.

Summary

The Bank of Canada and other central banks around the world are switching from the "one tool, one target" mode of operation and are searching for new tools to steer their economies in an environment with interest rates at or near zero. In Canada, the one tool was the overnight interest rate and the target was an inflation rate around 2%. However, with an effective lower bound for the overnight interest rate, a decoupling of long- and short-term interest rates, and the possibility of a deflationary trap (that is, extremely low nominal interest rates and sustained deflation), central banks are now considering new tools to steer their economies.

Monetary Policy Tools of the Federal Reserve and the European Central Bank   Every central bank practices monetary policy somewhat differently and in this section we briefly describe the procedures adopted by the Federal Reserve and the European Central Bank. Understanding monetary policy in the United States and the euro area is very important, because it affects interest rates throughout the world.

Policy Tools of the Federal Reserve

In the United States, according to the Depository Institutions Deregulation and Monetary Control Act of 1980, all depository institutions (including commercial banks, savings and loan associations, mutual savings banks, and credit unions) are subject to the same reserve requirements, which is about 10% of chequable deposits. The percentage set at 10% can be varied between 8% and 14%, at the Fed's discretion. In extraordinary circumstances, the percentage can be raised as high as 18%.

Like the Bank of Canada and most other central banks, the Federal Reserve offers a lending facility, which sets a ceiling on short-term overnight interest rates. In particular, the Fed provides liquidity to the banking system by lending reserves to banks. The Fed's lending of reserves to banks is called **discount window lending** and the interest rate charged banks for these loans is called the **discount rate**, denoted i_d. However, the primary indicator of the stance of monetary policy in the United States is not the discount rate but the **federal funds rate**, i_{ff}, the interest rate on overnight loans of reserves (known as federal funds) that banks trade among themselves. In fact, since February 1994, the Fed announces a federal funds rate target at each FOMC meeting, an announcement that is watched closely by market participants because it affects interest rates throughout the world.

Before 2003, the Fed discouraged banks from borrowing at the discount window, so banks were willing to pay a premium to borrow from other banks in the federal funds market at the federal funds rate. As a result the federal funds rate was usually higher than the discount rate. In 2003, however, the Fed redesigned the architecture of its discount window lending practices and now makes a distinction between *primary credit* discount loans (loans to banks in good condition) and *secondary credit* discount loans (loans to banks that are not in good condition). The interest rate in primary credit discount loans is the discount rate and the Fed now sets the discount rate at 100 basis points (1 percentage point) above its target for the federal funds rate. The secondary credit discount rate is set even higher, at 50 basis points (0.5 percentage points) above the discount rate. Moreover, the Fed stopped discouraging borrowing at the discount window.

For years, the Federal Reserve did not pay interest on reserves. However, during the global financial crisis, legislation was passed and changed the institutional structure within which the Fed carries out monetary policy by authorizing the Fed to pay interest on banks' holdings of reserves.

The Market for Reserves in the United States

The analysis of the market for reserves in the United States proceeds in a similar fashion to the analysis of the market for reserves in Canada depicted in Figure 16-2. The Federal Reserve maintains a two-sided asymmetric corridor system for influencing the federal funds rate as shown in Figure 16-13. The Fed's reserve supply is horizontal at the rate charged by its lending facility, the discount rate i_d, and the bank's reserve demand is horizontal at the interest rate paid by the Fed's deposit facility, i_{er}. Market equilibrium occurs at the intersection of the supply curve R^s and the demand curve R^d at point 1 and a federal funds rate of i_{ff}^*.

Now that we understand how the federal funds rate is determined, we can examine how changes in the tools of monetary policy—open market operations, discount lending, reserve requirements, and the interest rate paid on reserves—affect the market for reserves and the equilibrium federal funds rate in the United States.

MyEconLab Mini-lecture

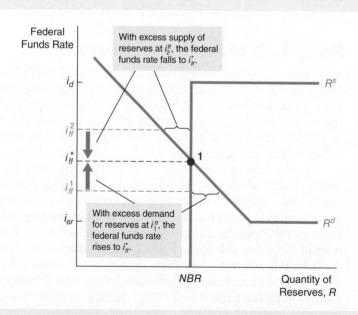

FIGURE 16-13 **Equilibrium in the Market for Reserves in the United States**

Equilibrium occurs at the intersection of the supply curve R^s and the demand curve R^d, at point 1 and an interest rate of i_{ff}^*.

Open Market Operations

The effect of an open market operation depends on whether the supply curve initially intersects the demand curve in its downward-sloped section or in its flat section. Panel (a) of Figure 16-14 shows what happens if the intersection initially occurs on the downward-sloped section of the demand curve. We have already seen that an open market purchase leads to a greater quantity of reserves supplied; this is true at any given federal funds rate because of the higher amount of nonborrowed reserves, which rises from NBR_1 to NBR_2. An open market purchase therefore shifts the supply curve to the right from R_1^s to R_2^s and moves the equilibrium from point 1 to point 2, lowering the federal funds rate from i_{ff}^1 to i_{ff}^2.[8] The same reasoning implies that an open market sale decreases the quantity of nonborrowed reserves supplied, shifts the supply curve to the left, and causes the federal funds rate to rise. Because this is the typical situation—since the Fed usually keeps the federal funds rate target above the interest rate paid on reserves—the conclusion is that an open market purchase causes the federal funds rate to fall, whereas an open market sale causes the federal funds rate to rise.

MyEconLab Mini-lecture

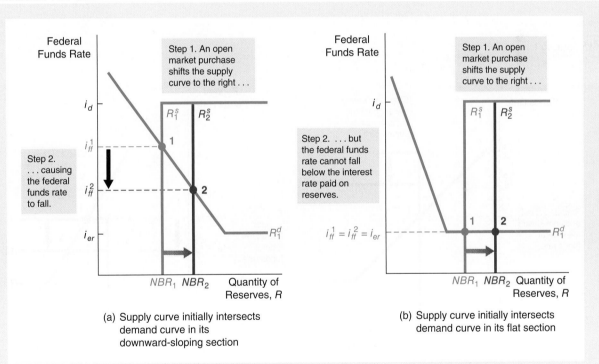

(a) Supply curve initially intersects demand curve in its downward-sloping section

(b) Supply curve initially intersects demand curve in its flat section

FIGURE 16-14 **Response to an Open Market Operation**

In open market purchase increases nonborrowed reserves, and hence the reserves supplied, and shifts the supply curve from R_1^s to R_2^s. In panel (a), the equilibrium moves from point 1 to point 2, lowering the federal funds rate from to i_{ff}^1 to i_{ff}^2. In panel (b), the equilibrium moves from point 1 to point 2, but the federal funds rate remains unchanged, $i_{ff}^1 = i_{ff}^2 = i_{er}$.

---

[8] We come to the same conclusion if we use the money supply framework outlined in Chapter 15, along with the liquidity preference framework outlined in Chapter 5. An open market purchase raises reserves and the money supply, and then the liquidity preference framework shows that interest rates fall as a result.

However, if the supply curve initially intersects the demand curve on its flat section, as in panel (b) of Figure 16-14, open market operations have no effect on the federal funds rate. To see this, let's again look at an open market purchase that raises the quantity of reserves supplied, which shifts the supply curve from R_1^s to R_2^s. However, this time we consider the case in which $i_{ff}^1 = i_{er}$ initially. The shift in the supply curve moves the equilibrium from point 1 to point 2, but the federal funds rate remains unchanged at i_{er} because *the interest rate paid on reserves, i_{er}, sets a floor for the federal funds rate.*

Discount Lending

The effect of a discount rate change depends on whether the demand curve intersects the supply curve in its vertical section or its flat section. Panel (a) of Figure 16-15 shows what happens if the intersection occurs on the vertical section of the supply curve, so that there is no discount lending and borrowed reserves, *BR*, are zero. In this case, when the Fed lowers the discount rate from i_d^1 to i_d^2, the horizontal section of the supply curve falls, as in R_2^s, but the intersection of the supply and demand curves remains at point 1. Thus, in this case, no change occurs in the equilibrium federal funds rate, which remains at i_{ff}^1. Because this is the typical situation—since the Fed now usually keeps the discount rate

MyEconLab Mini-lecture

FIGURE 16-15 Response to a Change in the Discount Rate

In panel (a), when the discount rate is lowered by the Fed from i_d^1 to i_d^2, the horizontal section of the supply curve falls, as in R_2^s, and the equilibrium federal funds rate remains unchanged at i_{ff}^1. In panel (b), when the discount rate is lowered by the Fed from i_d^1 to i_d^2, the horizontal section of the supply curve R_2^s falls, and the equilibrium federal funds rate falls from i_{ff}^1 to i_{ff}^2 as borrowed reserves increase.

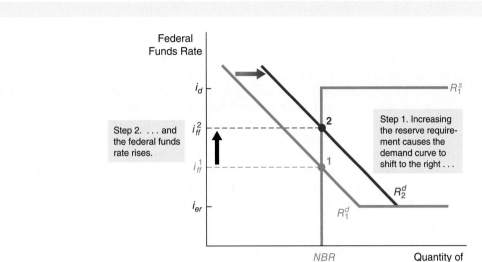

FIGURE 16-16   **Response to a Change in Required Reserves**

When the Fed raises reserve requirements, required reserves increase, which raises the demand for reserves. The demand curve shifts from R_1^d to R_2^d, the equilibrium moves from point 1 to point 2, and the federal fund rate rises from i_{ff}^1 to i_{ff}^2.

above its target for the federal funds rate—the conclusion is that ***most changes in the discount rate have no effect on the federal funds rate.***

However, if the demand curve intersects the supply curve on its flat section, so that there is some discount lending (i.e., $BR > 0$), as in panel (b) of Figure 16-15, changes in the discount rate do affect the federal funds rate. In this case, initially discount lending is positive and the equilibrium federal funds rate equals the discount rate, rate, $i_{ff}^1 = i_d^1$. When the discount rate is lowered by the Fed from i_d^1 to i_d^2, the horizontal section of the supply curve R_2^s falls, moving the equilibrium from point 1 to point 2, and the equilibrium federal funds rate falls from i_{ff}^1 to $i_{ff}^2 (= i_d^2)$, as shown in panel (b). In this case, BR increases from BR_1 to BR_2.

Reserve Requirements   When the required reserve ratio increases, required reserves increase and hence the quantity of reserves demanded increases for any given interest rate. Thus a rise in the required reserve ratio shifts the demand curve to the right from R_1^d to R_2^d in Figure 16-16, moves the equilibrium from point 1 to point 2, and in turn raises the federal funds rate from i_{ff}^1 to i_{ff}^2 The result is that ***when the Fed raises reserve requirements, the federal funds rate rises***.[9]

---

[9] Because an increase in the required reserve ratio means that the same amount of reserves is able to support a smaller amount of deposits, a rise in the required reserve ratio leads to a decline in the money supply. Using the liquidity preference framework from Chapter 5, the fall in the money supply results in a rise in interest rates, yielding the same conclusion given in the text—that raising reserve requirements leads to higher interest rates.

Similarly, a decline in the required reserve ratio lowers the quantity of reserves demanded, shifts the demand curve to the left, and causes the federal funds rate to fall. **When the Fed decreases reserve requirements, the federal funds rate falls**.

Interest on Reserves

The effect of a change in the interest rate paid by the Fed on reserves depends on whether the supply curve intersects the demand curve in its downward-sloping section or its flat section. Panel (a) of Figure 16-17 shows what happens if the intersection occurs at the demand curve's downward-sloping section, where the equilibrium federal funds rate is above the interest rate paid on reserves.

In this case, when the interest rate on reserves is raised from i_{er}^1 to i_{er}^2, the horizontal section of the demand curve rises, as in R_2^d, but the intersection of the supply and demand curves remains at point 1. However, if the supply curve intersects the demand curve on its flat section, where the equilibrium federal funds rate is equal to the interest rate paid on reserves, as in panel (b) of Figure 16-17, a rise in the interest rate on reserves from i_{er}^1 to i_{er}^2 moves the equilibrium to point 2, where the equilibrium federal funds rate rises from $i_{ff}^1 = i_{er}^1$ to $i_{ff}^2 = i_{er}^2$. **When the federal funds rate is at the interest rate paid on reserves, a rise in the interest rate on reserves raises the federal funds rate.**

MyEconLab Mini-lecture

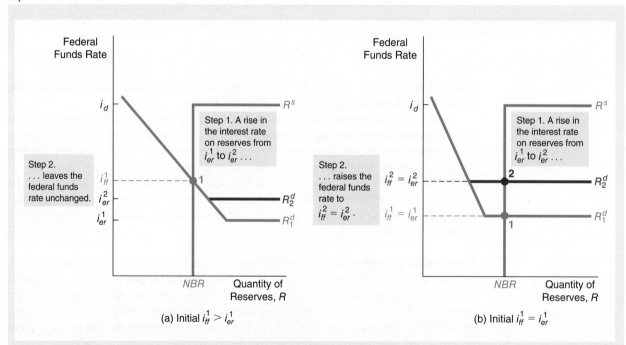

FIGURE 16-17   Response to a Change in the Interest Rate on Reserves

In panel (a), when the equilibrium federal funds rate is above the interest rate paid on reserves, a rise in the interest rate on reserves from i_{er}^1 to i_{er}^2 raises the horizontal section of the demand curve, as in R_1^d, but the equilibrium federal funds rate remains unchanged at i_{ff}^1. In panel (b), when the equilibrium federal funds rate is equal to the interest rate paid on reserves, a rise in the interest rate on reserves from i_{er}^1 to i_{er}^2 raises the equilibrium federal funds rate to $i_{ff}^1 = i_{er}^1$ to $i_{ff}^2 = i_{er}^2$.

Monetary Policy Tools of the European Central Bank

Like the Federal Reserve, the European System of Central Banks (usually referred to as the European Central Bank) signals the stance of its monetary policy by setting a **target financing rate**, which in turn sets a target for the **overnight cash rate**. Like the federal funds rate, the overnight cash rate is the interest rate for very short-term interbank loans. The monetary policy tools used by the European Central Bank are similar to those used by the Federal Reserve and involve open market operations, lending to banks, and reserve requirements.

Open Market Operations   Like the Federal Reserve, the European Central Bank uses open market operations as its primary tool for conducting monetary policy and setting the overnight cash rate at the target financing rate. **Main refinancing operations** are the predominant form of open market operations and are similar to the Fed's repo transactions. They involve weekly **reverse transactions** (purchase or sale of eligible assets under repurchase or credit operations against eligible assets as collateral) that are reversed within two weeks. Credit institutions submit bids, and the European Central Bank decides which bids to accept. Like the Federal Reserve, the European Central Bank accepts the most attractively priced bids and makes purchases or sales up to the point at which the desired amount of reserves is supplied. In contrast to the Federal Reserve, which conducts open market operations in one location at the Federal Reserve Bank of New York, the European Central Bank decentralizes its open market operations by conducting them through the individual national central banks.

A second category of open market operations is the **longer-term refinancing operations**, which are a much smaller source of liquidity for the euro-area banking system and are similar to the Fed's outright purchases or sales of securities. These operations are carried out monthly and typically involve purchases or sales of securities with a maturity of three months. They are not used for signalling the monetary policy stance, but instead are aimed at providing euro-area banks access to longer-term funds.

Lending to Banks   As is the case for the Bank of Canada and the Fed, the next most important tool of monetary policy for the European Central Bank involves lending to banking institutions, which is carried out by the national central banks, just as discount lending in the United States is performed by the individual Federal Reserve Banks. This lending takes place through a standing lending facility called the **marginal lending facility**. Through this facility, banks can borrow (against eligible collateral) overnight loans from the national central banks at the **marginal lending rate**, which is set at 100 basis points above the target financing rate. The marginal lending rate provides a ceiling for the overnight market interest rate in the European Monetary Union, just as the bank rate does in Canada and the discount rate in the United States. As in Canada, the United States, Australia, and New Zealand, the Eurosystem has another standing facility, the **deposit facility**, in which banks are paid a fixed interest rate that is 100 basis points below the target financing rate. The prespecified interest rate on the deposit facility provides a floor for the overnight market interest rate, while the marginal lending rate sets a ceiling. This creates a channel/corridor system as in Canada, New Zealand, and Australia, but with a much wider range of 100 basis points on either side.

Reserve Requirements   Like the Federal Reserve, the European Central Bank imposes reserve requirements such that all deposit-taking institutions are required to hold 2% of the total amount of chequing deposits and other short-term deposits in reserve accounts with national central banks. All institutions that are subject to minimum reserve requirements have access to the European Central Bank's standing lending facilities and participate in open market operations.

MyEconLab

MyEconLab is an online homework and tutorial system that puts you in control of your own learning with study and practice tools directly correlated to this chapter's content. Visit MyEconLab to access the eText, the Questions and Applied Problems with answers, as well as additional assessment. You will also find web chapters, mini-lectures, appendices, mini-cases, videos, glossary flashcards, news feeds, CANSIM data, and graphing tools.

SUMMARY

1. The Bank of Canada views the overnight interest rate as the centrepiece of its monetary policy implementation. At 9:00 a.m. on the fixed action date, the Bank announces an operating band of 50 basis points for the overnight interest rate. The upper limit of the operating band is the bank rate—the rate the Bank charges LVTS participants that require an overdraft loan to cover negative settlement balances. The lower limit is the rate the Bank pays LVTS participants with positive settlement balances.

2. The Bank of Canada targets the value of the overnight interest rate within its operating band, at the midpoint of the band. In doing so, the Bank intervenes in the overnight market using open-market buyback operations at the target rate. If the overnight rate is trading above the target rate, the Bank uses repos in which it purchases Government of Canada securities from primary dealers with an agreement to resell them on the next business day. If the overnight rate is too low relative to the target rate, the Bank uses reverse repos in which it sells Government of Canada securities to primary dealers with an agreement to buy them back on the next day.

3. The Bank uses government deposit shifting to neutralize public-sector flows that affect LVTS participants' settlement balances—this in effect is a cash setting, a cash setting that is typically $25 million. Because its holdings of Government of Canada securities are often

much smaller than its monetary liabilities, the Bank brings onto its balance sheet Exchange Fund Account assets to back its liabilities. These amounts are adjusted daily, depending on factors such as the level of financial institution borrowings and/or deposits.

4. In neutralizing the effects of open market buyback operations and of public-sector flows on the level of settlement balances, and also in adjusting the level of settlement balances, the Bank of Canada uses transfers of government deposits (balances) between the government's account at the Bank of Canada and the government's accounts at the LVTS participants. These transfers are effected by twice-daily auctions of federal government (Receiver General) balances, the first at 9:15 a.m. (which are collateralized) and the second at 4:15 p.m. (which are uncollateralized).

5. In normal times, the Bank of Canada relies mainly on its conventional monetary policy tools—standing liquidity facilities (lending and deposit facilities), settlement balances management, and lender-of-last-resort arrangements. However, conventional monetary policy tools are no longer effective when the zero-lower-bound problem occurs, in which the central bank is unable to lower short-term interest rates because they have hit a floor of zero. In this situation, central banks use nonconventional monetary policy tools, which involve liquidity provision, asset purchases, and commitment to future policy actions. Liquidity provision and asset

purchases lead to an expansion of the central bank balance sheet, which is referred to as *quantitative easing*. Expansion of the central bank balance sheet by itself is unlikely to have a large impact on the economy, but changing the composition of the balance sheet, which is accomplished by liquidity provisions and asset purchases and is referred to as *credit easing*, can have a large impact by improving the functioning of credit markets.

6. A supply and demand analysis of the market for reserves in the United States yields the following results: when the Fed makes an open market purchase or lowers reserve requirements, the federal funds rate drops. When the Fed makes an open market sale or

raises reserve requirements, the federal funds rate rises. Changes in the discount rate and the interest rate paid on reserves may also affect the federal funds rate.

7. The monetary policy tools used by the European Central Bank are similar to those used by the Federal Reserve System and involve open market operations, lending to banks, and reserve requirements. Main financing operations—open market operations in repos that are typically reversed within two weeks—are the primary tool to set the overnight cash rate at the target financing rate. The European Central Bank also operates standing lending facilities, which ensure that the overnight cash rate remains within 100 basis points of the target financing rate.

KEY TERMS

conventional monetary policy, p. 403

credit easing, p. 418

deposit facility, p. 425

direct clearers, p. 392

discount rate, p. 419

discount window lending, p. 419

drawdowns, p. 406

federal funds rate, p. 419

forward guidance, p. 418

Large Value Transfer System (LVTS), p. 391

lender of last resort, p. 410

longer-term refinancing operations, p. 425

LVTS participants, p. 391

main refinancing operations, p. 425

management of expectations, p. 418

marginal lending facility, p. 425

marginal lending rate, p. 425

monetary conditions, p. 401

multilateral netting, p. 392

nonconventional monetary policy tools, p. 414

operating band, p. 393

overnight cash rate, p. 425

overnight interest rate, p. 392

overnight rate, p. 390

policy rate, p. 392

primary dealers, p. 404

quantitative easing, p. 417

redeposits, p. 406

reference rate, p. 392

repos, p. 404

reverse repos, p. 404

reverses, p. 404

reverse transactions, p. 425

Sale and Repurchase Agreements (SRAs), p. 404

special Purchase and Resale Agreements (special PRAs or SPRAs), p. 404

specials, p. 404

standing lending facility, p. 410

standing liquidity facilities, p. 395

systemic risk, p. 391

target financing rate, p. 425

term Purchase and Resale Agreements (term PRAs), p. 414

term repos, p. 414

zero-lower-bound problem, p. 413

QUESTIONS

All questions are available in MyEconLab at **www.myeconlab.com.**

1. If government deposits at the Bank of Canada are predicted to increase, what open market operations could be undertaken to neutralize the effect on settlement balances?

2. During the holiday season, when the public's holdings of currency increase, what open market operations typically occur? Why?

3. If the government has just paid for major computer upgrades and as a result its deposits with the Bank of Canada fall, what open market operations could be undertaken?

4. "In the LVTS environment, government deposit shifting is affected by auctions of government balances." Discuss.

5. Most open market operations are currently repurchase agreements. What does this tell us about the likely volume of open market operations relative to dynamic open market operations?

6. "The only way that the Bank of Canada can affect the level of advances is by adjusting the bank rate." Is this statement true, false, or uncertain? Explain your answer.

7. If the Bank of Canada did not administer the operating band, what do you predict would happen to the money supply if the bank rate were several percentage points below the overnight rate?

8. Discuss how the operating band affects interest rates and the money supply in the economy.

9. "Last-resort lending is no longer needed because the presence of the CDIC eliminates the possibility of bank panics." Is this statement true, false, or uncertain?

10. The benefits of using last-resort lending to prevent bank panics are straightforward. What are the costs?

11. You often read in the newspaper that the Bank of Canada has just lowered the target overnight rate. Does this signal that the Bank is moving to a more expansionary monetary policy? Why or why not?

12. How can the procyclical movement of interest rates (rising during business cycle expansions and falling during business cycle contractions) lead to a procyclical movement in the money supply as a result of the Bank of

Canada's lending policy? Why might this movement of the money supply be undesirable?

13. Explain how SPRAs and SRAs affect the overnight rate.

14. "The channel/corridor system for setting interest rates enables the Bank of Canada to set the overnight rate whatever the demand for reserves, including zero demand." Discuss.

15. Compare the use of open market operations and government deposit shifting to control the money supply, using the following criteria: flexibility, reversibility, effectiveness, and speed of implementation.

16. Following the global financial crisis in 2008, assets on the Federal Reserve's balance sheet increased dramatically, from approximately $800 billion at the end of 2007 to $3 trillion by 2011. Many of the assets held are longer-term securities acquired through various loan programs instituted as a result of the crisis. In this situation, how could reverse repos (matched sale–purchase transactions) help the Fed reduce its assets held in an orderly fashion, while reducing potential inflationary problems in the future?

17. What are the advantages and disadvantages of quantitative easing as an alternative to conventional monetary policy when short-term interest rates are at the zero lower bound?

18. Why is the composition of the central bank's balance sheet a potentially important aspect of monetary policy during an economic crisis?

19. What is the main advantage and the main disadvantage of an unconditional policy commitment?

APPLIED PROBLEMS

All applied problems are available in MyEconLab *at* **www.myeconlab.com**.

20. If a switch occurs from deposits into currency, what happens to the overnight interest rate? Use the supply and demand analysis of the market for reserves to explain your answer.

21. Using the supply and demand analysis of the market for reserves in the United States, indicate what happens to the federal funds rate, borrowed reserves, and nonborrowed reserves, holding everything else constant, under the following situations:

a. The economy is surprisingly strong, leading to an increase in the amount of chequable deposits.

b. Banks expect an unusually large increase in withdrawals from chequing deposit accounts in the future.

c. The Fed raises the target federal funds rate.

d. The Fed raises the interest rate on reserves above the current equilibrium federal funds rate.

e. The Fed reduces reserve requirements.

f. The Fed reduces reserve requirements and then offsets this action by conducting an open market sale of securities.

DATA ANALYSIS PROBLEMS

Download data for these problems from MyEconLab at **www.myeconlab.com**.

1. Go to the CANSIM database, and download daily data, from January 1, 1996 to February 24, 2015, for the bank rate (series V39078) and the target overnight rate (series V39079).

   a. What is the difference between the two series?

   b. Calculate the upper and lower bounds of the operating band and plot the time path of the operating band.

   c. What does the time path of the operating band say about the easiness of monetary policy over this period?

2. Go to the St. Louis Federal Reserve FRED database, and find data on nonborrowed reserves (NONBORRES) and the federal funds rate (FEDFUNDS).

   a. Calculate the percent change in nonborrowed reserves and the percentage point change in the federal funds rate for the most recent month of data available and for the same month a year earlier.

   b. Is your answer to part (a) consistent with what you expect from the market for reserves in the United States? Why or why not?

WEB EXERCISES

1. Go to **www.bankofcanada.ca** and click on "Press." Scroll down and click on the release regarding recent changes in the overnight rate of interest. Summarize the statement in one paragraph. Be sure to note whether the bank rate was increased or decreased. Now review the changes in the operating band for the overnight interest rate in the previous two press releases regarding this issue. Has the stance of monetary policy changed?

2. Refer to Figure 16-1 on page 393. Go to **www.bankofcanada.ca,** click on "Statistics," and then on "Key Interest Rate Lookup." What is the current overnight rate target? What is the overnight rate? Is the difference between them what you would expect it to be?

WEB REFERENCES

www.bankofcanada.ca/monetary-policy-introduction

This site lists key indicators pertaining to Canadian monetary policy.

www.federalreserve.gov/fomc/fundsrate.htm

Historical federal funds rates and discussions about Federal Reserve targets.

17

The Conduct of Monetary Policy: Strategy and Tactics

Learning Objectives

After studying this chapter you should be able to

1. Define and recognize the importance of a nominal anchor.

2. Identify the six potential goals that monetary policymakers may pursue.

3. Summarize the distinctions between hierarchical and dual mandates.

4. Compare and contrast the advantages and disadvantages of inflation targeting.

5. Identify the key changes made over time to the Federal Reserve's monetary policy strategy.

6. List the four lessons learned from the global financial crisis, and discuss what they mean for inflation targeting.

7. Summarize the arguments for and against central bank policy responses to asset-price bubbles.

8. Describe and assess the four criteria for choosing a policy instrument.

9. Interpret and assess the performance of the Taylor rule as a hypothetical policy instrument for setting the federal funds rate.

PREVIEW

Getting monetary policy right is crucial to the health of the economy. Overly expansionary monetary policy leads to high inflation, which decreases the efficiency of the economy and hampers economic growth. Monetary policy that is too tight can produce serious recessions in which output falls and unemployment rises. It can also lead to deflation, a fall in the price level, such as occurred in the United States during the Great Depression and in Japan more recently. As we saw in Chapter 9, deflation can be especially damaging to an economy because it promotes financial instability and can worsen financial crises.

Now that we understand the tools that central banks such as the Bank of Canada use to conduct monetary policy, we can consider how central banks *should* conduct monetary policy. To explore this subject, we start by looking at the goals for monetary policy and then examine one of the most important strategies for the conduct of monetary policy, inflation targeting. We then discuss tactics—that is, the choice and setting of the monetary policy instrument.

THE PRICE STABILITY GOAL AND THE NOMINAL ANCHOR

Over the past few decades, policymakers throughout the world have become increasingly aware of the social and economic costs of inflation and more concerned with maintaining a stable price level as a goal of economic policy. Indeed, **price stability**, which central bankers define as low and stable inflation, is increasingly viewed as the most important goal of monetary policy. Price stability is desirable because a rising price level (inflation) creates uncertainty in the economy, and that uncertainty might hamper economic growth. For example, when the overall level of prices is changing, the information conveyed by the prices of goods and services is harder to interpret, which complicates decision making for consumers, businesses, and governments, thereby leading to a less efficient financial system.

Not only do public opinion surveys indicate that the public is hostile to inflation, but a growing body of evidence also suggests that inflation leads to lower economic growth. The most extreme example of unstable prices is *hyperinflation*, such as Argentina, Brazil, Russia, and Zimbabwe have experienced in the recent past. Hyperinflation has proved to be very damaging to the workings of the economy.

Inflation also makes it difficult to plan for the future. For example, it is more difficult to decide how much to put aside to provide for a child's college education in an inflationary environment. Furthermore, inflation can strain a country's social fabric: conflict might result, because each group in the society may compete with other groups to make sure that its income keeps up with the rising level of prices.

The Role of a Nominal Anchor

Because price stability is so crucial to the long-run health of an economy, a central element in successful monetary policy is the use of a **nominal anchor**, a nominal variable such as the inflation rate or the money supply, which ties down the price level to achieve price stability. For example, if a central bank has an explicit target for the inflation rate, say 2%, and takes steps to achieve this target, then the inflation target becomes a nominal anchor. Adherence to a nominal anchor that keeps the nominal variable within a narrow range promotes price stability by directly promoting low and stable inflation expectations. A more subtle reason for a nominal anchor's importance is that it can limit the **time-inconsistency problem**, in which monetary policy conducted on a discretionary, day-by-day basis leads to poor long-run outcomes.

The Time-Inconsistency Problem

The time-inconsistency problem is something we deal with continually in everyday life. We often have a plan that we know will produce a good outcome in the long run, but when tomorrow comes, we just can't help ourselves and we renege on our plan because doing so has short-run gains. For example, we make a New Year's resolution to go on a diet, but soon thereafter we can't resist having one more bite of that rocky road ice cream—and then another bite, and then another bite—and the weight begins to pile back on. In other words, we find ourselves unable to *consistently* follow a good plan over *time*; the good plan is said to be *time-inconsistent* and will soon be abandoned.

Monetary policymakers also face the time-inconsistency problem. They are always tempted to pursue a discretionary monetary policy that is more expansionary than firms or people expect because such a policy would boost economic output (or lower unemployment) in the short run. The best policy, however, is *not* to pursue expansionary policy, because decisions about wages and prices reflect workers' and firms' expectations about policy; when they see a central bank pursuing expansionary policy, workers and firms will raise their expectations about inflation, driving wages and prices up. The rise in wages and prices will lead to higher inflation, but will not result in higher output on average. (We examine this issue more formally in Chapter 25.)

A central bank will have better inflation performance in the long run if it does not try to surprise people with an unexpectedly expansionary policy, but instead keeps inflation under control. However, even if a central bank recognizes that discretionary policy will lead to a poor outcome (high inflation with no gains in output), it still may not be able to pursue the better policy of inflation control, because politicians are likely to apply pressure on the central bank to try to boost output with overly expansionary monetary policy.

A clue to how we should deal with the time-inconsistency problem comes from how-to books on parenting. Parents know that giving in to a child to keep him from acting up will produce a very spoiled child. Nevertheless, when a child throws a tantrum, many parents give him what he wants just to shut him up. Because parents don't stick to their "do not give in" plan, the child expects that he will get what he wants if he behaves badly, so he will throw tantrums over and over again. Parenting books suggest a solution to the time-inconsistency problem (although they don't call it that): parents should set behaviour rules for their children and stick to them.

A nominal anchor is like a behaviour rule. Just as rules help to prevent the time-inconsistency problem in parenting by helping adults resist pursuing the discretionary policy of giving in, a nominal anchor can help prevent the time-inconsistency problem in monetary policy by providing an expected constraint on discretionary policy.

OTHER GOALS OF MONETARY POLICY

Although price stability is the primary goal of most central banks, five other goals are continually mentioned by central bank officials when they discuss the objectives of monetary policy: (1) high employment and output stability, (2) economic growth, (3) stability of financial markets, (4) interest-rate stability, and (5) stability in foreign exchange markets.

High Employment and Output Stability

High employment is a worthy goal for two main reasons: (1) the alternative situation—high unemployment—causes much human misery and (2) when unemployment is high, the economy has both idle workers and idle resources (closed factories and unused equipment), resulting in a loss of output (lower GDP).

Although it is clear that high employment is desirable, how high should it be? At what point can we say that the economy is at full employment? At first, it might seem that full employment is the point at which no worker is out of a job—that is, when unemployment is zero. But this definition ignores the fact that some unemployment, called *frictional unemployment*, which involves searches by workers and firms to find suitable matchups, is beneficial to the economy. For example, a worker who decides to look for a better job might be unemployed for a while during the job search. Workers often decide to leave work temporarily to pursue other activities (raising a family, travel, returning to school), and when they decide to re-enter the job market, it may take some time for them to find the right job.

Another reason that unemployment is not zero when the economy is at full employment is *structural unemployment*, a mismatch between job requirements and the skills or availability of local workers. Clearly, this kind of unemployment is undesirable. Nonetheless, it is something that monetary policy can do little about.

This goal for high employment is not an unemployment level of zero but a level above zero consistent with full employment at which the demand for labour equals the supply of labour. This level is called the **natural rate of unemployment**.

Although this definition sounds neat and authoritative, it leaves a troublesome question unanswered: What unemployment rate is consistent with full employment? In some cases, it is obvious that the unemployment rate is too high. The unemployment rate in excess of 20% during the Great Depression, for example, was clearly far too high. In the early 1960s, on the other hand, policymakers thought that a reasonable goal was 4%, a level that was probably too low, because it led to accelerating inflation. Current estimates of the natural rate of unemployment place it between 4% and 6%, but even this estimate is subject to much uncertainty and disagreement. It is possible, for example, that appropriate government policy, such as the provision of better information about job vacancies or job training programs, might decrease the natural rate of unemployment.

The high employment goal can be thought of in another way. Because the level of unemployment is tied to the level of economic activity in the economy, a particular level of output is produced at the natural rate of unemployment, which naturally enough is referred to as the **natural rate of output** but is more often referred to as **potential output**.

Trying to achieve the goal of high employment thus means that central banks should try to move the level of output toward the natural rate of output. In other words, they should try to stabilize the level of output around its natural rate.

Economic Growth

The goal of steady economic growth is closely related to the high-employment goal because businesses are more likely to invest in capital equipment to increase productivity and economic growth when unemployment is low. Conversely, if unemployment is high and factories are idle, it does not pay for a firm to invest in additional plants and equipment. Although the two goals are closely related, policies can be specifically aimed at promoting economic growth by directly encouraging firms to invest or by encouraging people to save, which provides more funds for firms to invest. In fact, this approach is the stated purpose of *supply-side economics* policies, which are intended to spur economic growth by providing tax incentives for businesses to invest in facilities and equipment and for taxpayers to save more. Active debate continues over what role monetary policy can play in boosting growth.

Stability of Financial Markets

As our analysis in Chapter 9 showed, financial crises can interfere with the ability of financial markets to channel funds to people with productive investment opportunities and lead to a sharp contraction in economic activity. The promotion of a more stable financial system in which financial crises are avoided is thus an important goal for a central bank. Indeed, as we saw in Chapter 14, the Bank of Canada was created to promote financial stability.

Interest-Rate Stability

Interest-rate stability is desirable because fluctuations in interest rates can create uncertainty in the economy and make it harder to plan for the future. Fluctuations in interest rates that affect consumers' willingness to buy houses, for example, make it more difficult for consumers to decide when to purchase a house and for construction firms to plan how many houses to build. A central bank may also want to reduce upward movements in interest rates for the reasons we discussed in Chapter 14: upward movements in interest rates generate hostility toward central banks and lead to demands that their power be curtailed.

The stability of financial markets is also fostered by interest-rate stability, because fluctuations in interest rates create great uncertainty for financial institutions. An increase in interest rates produces large capital losses on long-term bonds and mortgages, losses that can cause the failure of the financial institutions holding them.

Stability in Foreign Exchange Markets

With the increasing importance of international trade to the Canadian economy, the value of the dollar relative to other currencies has become a major consideration for the Bank of Canada. A rise in the value of the dollar makes Canadian industries less competitive with those abroad, and declines in the value of the dollar stimulate inflation in Canada. In addition, preventing large changes in the value of the dollar makes it easier for firms and individuals purchasing or selling goods abroad to plan ahead. Stabilizing extreme movements in the value of the dollar in foreign exchange markets is thus an important goal of monetary policy. In other countries, which are even more dependent on foreign trade, stability in foreign exchange markets takes on even greater importance.

SHOULD PRICE STABILITY BE THE PRIMARY GOAL OF MONETARY POLICY?

In the long run, no inconsistency exists between the price stability goal and the other goals mentioned earlier. The natural rate of unemployment is not lowered by high inflation, so higher inflation cannot produce lower unemployment or more employment in the long run. In other words, there is no long-run trade-off between inflation and unemployment. In the long run, price stability promotes economic growth as well as financial and interest-rate stability. Although price stability is consistent with the other goals in the long run, in the short run price stability often conflicts with the goals of output stability and interest-rate stability. For example, when the economy is expanding and unemployment is falling, the economy may become overheated, leading to a rise in inflation. To pursue the price stability goal, a central bank would prevent this overheating by raising interest rates, an action that would initially cause output to fall and increase interest-rate instability. How should a central bank resolve this conflict among goals?

Hierarchical Versus Dual Mandates

Because price stability is crucial to the long-run health of the economy, many countries have decided that price stability should be the primary, long-run goal for central banks. For example, the Maastricht Treaty, which created the European Central Bank, states, "The primary objective of the European System of Central Banks (ESCB) shall be to maintain price stability. Without prejudice to the objective of price stability, the ECSB shall support the general economic policies in the Community," which include objectives such as "a high level of employment" and "sustainable and non-inflationary growth." Mandates of this type, which put the goal of price stability first and then state that other goals can be pursued as long as price stability is achieved, are known as **hierarchical mandates**. They are the directives governing the behaviour of such central banks as the Bank of England, the Bank of Canada, and the Reserve Bank of New Zealand, as well as the European Central Bank.

In contrast, the legislation defining the mission of the Federal Reserve states, "The Board of Governors of the Federal Reserve System and the Federal Open Market Committee shall maintain long-run growth of the monetary and credit aggregates commensurate with the economy's long-run potential to increase production, so as to promote effectively the goals of maximum employment, stable prices, and moderate long-term interest rates." Because, as we learned in Chapter 5, long-term interest rates will be very high if inflation is high, this statement in practice is a **dual mandate** to achieve two coequal objectives: price stability and maximum employment (output stability).

Is it better for an economy to operate under a hierarchical mandate or a dual mandate?

Price Stability as the Primary Long-Run Goal of Monetary Policy

Because no inconsistency exists between achieving price stability in the long run and the natural rate of unemployment, these two types of mandates are not very different *if maximum employment is defined as the natural rate of employment*. In practice, however, a substantial difference between these two mandates could exist because the public and politicians may believe that a hierarchical mandate puts too much emphasis on inflation control and not enough on stabilizing output.

Because low and stable inflation rates promote economic growth, central bankers have come to realize that price stability should be the primary, long-run goal of monetary policy. Nevertheless, because output fluctuations should also be a concern of monetary policy, the goal of price stability should be seen as primary only in the long run. Attempts to keep inflation at the same level in the short run, no matter what else is happening in the economy, are likely to lead to excessive output fluctuations.

As long as price stability is a long-run, but not short-run, goal, central banks can focus on reducing output fluctuations by allowing inflation to deviate from the long-run goal for short periods and, therefore, can operate under a dual mandate. However, if a dual mandate leads a central bank to pursue short-run expansionary policies that increase output and employment without worrying about the long-run consequences for inflation, the time-inconsistency problem may recur. Concerns that a dual mandate might lead to overly expansionary policy is a key reason why central bankers often favour hierarchical mandates in which the pursuit of price stability takes precedence. Hierarchical mandates can also be a problem if they lead to a central bank behaving as what the governor of the Bank of England, Mervyn King, has referred to as an "inflation nutter"—that is, a central bank that focuses solely on inflation control, even in the short run, and so undertakes policies that lead to large output fluctuations. The choice of which type of mandate is better for a central bank ultimately depends on the subtleties of how it will work in practice. Either type of mandate is acceptable as long as it operates to make price stability the primary goal in the long run, but not the short run.

INFLATION TARGETING

The recognition that price stability should be the primary long-run goal of monetary policy and that a nominal anchor is a valuable tool in helping to achieve this goal has led to a monetary policy strategy known as inflation targeting. **Inflation targeting** involves several elements: (1) public announcement of medium-term numerical objectives (targets) for inflation; (2) an institutional commitment to price stability as the primary, long-run goal of monetary policy and a commitment to achieve the inflation goal; (3) an information-inclusive approach in which many variables (not just monetary aggregates) are used in making decisions about monetary policy; (4) increased transparency of the monetary policy strategy through communication with the public and the markets about the plans and objectives of monetary policymakers; and (5) increased accountability of the central bank for attaining its inflation objectives. New Zealand was the first country to formally adopt inflation targeting in 1990, followed by Canada in 1991, the United Kingdom in 1992, Sweden and Finland in 1993, and Australia and Spain in 1994. Israel, Chile, and Brazil, among others, have also adopted a form of inflation targeting.[1]

Inflation Targeting in New Zealand, Canada, and the United Kingdom

We begin our look at inflation targeting with New Zealand, because it was the first country to adopt it. We then go on to examine the experiences in Canada and the United Kingdom, which were the next countries to adopt it.

New Zealand   As part of a general reform of the government's role in the economy, the New Zealand parliament passed a new Reserve Bank of New Zealand Act in 1989, which became effective on February 1, 1990. Besides increasing the independence of the central bank, moving it from being one of the least independent to one of the most independent among developed countries, the act committed the Reserve Bank to a sole objective of price stability. The act stipulated that the minister of finance and the governor of the Reserve Bank should negotiate and make public a Policy Targets Agreement—a statement that sets out the targets by which monetary policy performance will be evaluated, specifying numerical target ranges for inflation and the dates by which they are to be reached. An unusual feature of the New Zealand legislation is that the governor of the Reserve Bank is held highly accountable for the success of monetary policy. If the goals set forth in the Policy Targets Agreement are not satisfied, the governor is subject to dismissal.

The first Policy Targets Agreement, signed by the minister of finance and the governor of the Reserve Bank on March 2, 1990, directed the Reserve Bank to achieve an annual inflation rate within a 3–5% range. Subsequent agreements lowered the range to 0–2% until the end of 1996, when the range was changed to 0–3% and later to 1–3% in 2002. As a result of tight monetary policy, the inflation rate was brought down from above 5% to below 2% by the end of 1992 (see Figure 17-1, panel a), but at the cost of a deep recession and a sharp rise in unemployment. Since then, inflation has typically remained within the targeted range, with the exception of brief periods in 1995, 2000, and 2008, when it exceeded the range by a small amount. (Under the Reserve Bank Act, the governor could have been dismissed, but after parliamentary debates he retained his job.) Since 1992, New Zealand's growth rate has generally been high, with some years exceeding 5%, and unemployment has come down significantly.

Canada   On February 26, 1991, a joint announcement by the minister of finance and the governor of the Bank of Canada established formal inflation targets. The target ranges were 2–4% by the end of 1992, 1.5–3.5% by June 1994, and 1–3% by December 1996. After the new government took office in late 1993, the target range was set at 1–3% from December 1995 until December 1998 and has been kept at this level. It was

---

[1]A precursor to the inflation-targeting strategy is monetary targeting. This strategy is discussed in Web Appendix 17.1 to this chapter, "Monetary Targeting," which is available on MyEconLab.

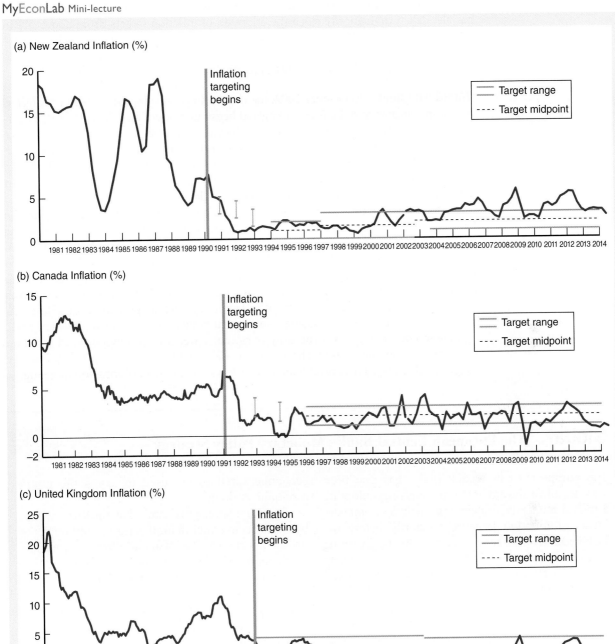

FIGURE 17-1   **Inflation Rates and Inflation Targets for New Zealand, Canada, and the United Kingdom, 1980–2014**

Inflation-targeting countries have significantly reduced the rate of inflation and eventually have achieved their inflation targets.

Source: Data from Ben S. Bernanke, Thomas Laubach, Frederic S. Mishkin, and Adam S. Poson, Inflation Targeting: Lessons from the International Experience (Princeton: Princeton University Press, 1999); and Federal Reserve Bank of St. Louis, FRED database: http://research.stlouisfed.org/fred2/

renewed on November 2011 for another five-year term until 2016. Canadian inflation has also fallen dramatically since the adoption of inflation targets, from above 5% in 1991, to a 0% rate in 1995, and to around 2% subsequently (see Figure 17-1, panel b). As was the case in New Zealand, however, this decline was not without cost: unemployment soared to above 10% from 1991 until 1994, but then declined substantially.[2]

United Kingdom

In October 1992, the United Kingdom adopted an inflation target as its nominal anchor, and the Bank of England began to produce an *Inflation Report*, a quarterly report on the progress being made in achieving that target. The inflation target range was initially set at 1–4% until the next election (spring 1997 at the latest), with the intent that the inflation rate should settle down to the lower half of the range (below 2.5%). In May 1997, the inflation target was set at 2.5% and the Bank of England was given the power to set interest rates henceforth, granting it a more independent role in monetary policy.

Before the adoption of inflation targets, inflation had already been falling in the United Kingdom, with a peak of 9% at the beginning of 1991 and a rate of 4% at the time of adoption (see Figure 17-1, panel c). By the third quarter of 1994, it was at 2.2%, within the intended range. Subsequently, inflation rose, climbing slightly above the 2.5% level by the end of 1995, but then fell and has remained close to the target since then, except for the period from 2008 to 2011. In December 2003, the target was changed to 2.0% for a slightly different measure of inflation. Meanwhile, growth of the U.K. economy was strong until 2008, causing a substantial reduction in the unemployment rate.[3]

These countries are not the only ones that have moved slowly toward inflation targeting. As the Global box The European Central Bank's Monetary Policy Strategy suggests, the European Central Bank also follows a weak form of inflation targeting.

Global   The European Central Bank's Monetary Policy Strategy

The European Central Bank (ECB) has also been slow to move toward inflation targeting, adopting a hybrid monetary strategy that includes some elements of inflation targeting.* Shortly before the ECB became fully operational in 1999, its governing council defined price stability as an inflation rate below 2%. However, in May 2003, the ECB adopted a goal for inflation over the medium term of "below, but close to, 2%." The ECB's strategy has two key "pillars." First, monetary and credit aggregates are assessed for "their implications for future inflation and economic growth." Second, many other economic variables are used to assess the future economic outlook.

The ECB's strategy is somewhat unclear and has been subject to criticism for this reason. Although the "below, but close to, 2%" goal for inflation sounds like an inflation target, the ECB has repeatedly stated that it does not have an inflation target. This central bank seems to have decided to try to "have its cake and eat it, too" by not committing too strongly to an inflation-targeting strategy. The resulting difficulty in assessing the ECB's strategy has the potential to reduce the accountability of the institution.

*For a description of the ECB's monetary policy strategy, go to the ECB's website at www.ecb.int.

---

[2]Inflation targeting in Canada is discussed in more detail in the Brief History of Bank of Canada Policymaking given in Web Appendix 17.2 to this chapter, which is available on MyEconLab.

[3]If you are interested in a more detailed discussion of inflation targeting in these and other countries, see Ben S. Bernanke, Thomas Laubach, Frederic S. Mishkin, and Adam S. Posen, *Inflation Targeting: Lessons from the International Experience* (Princeton: Princeton University Press, 1999).

Advantages of Inflation Targeting

There are a number of benefits associated with inflation targeting: reduction of the time-inconsistency problem, increased transparency, increased accountability, consistency with democratic principles, and improved performance.

Reduction of the Time-Inconsistency Problem Because an explicit numerical inflation target increases the accountability of the central bank, inflation targeting can reduce the likelihood that the central bank will fall into the time-inconsistency trap of trying to expand output and employment in the short run by pursuing overly expansionary monetary policy. A key advantage of inflation targeting is that it can help focus the political debate on what a central bank can do in the long run—that is, control inflation—rather than what it cannot do—that is, permanently increase economic growth and the number of jobs through expansionary monetary policy. Thus inflation targeting can reduce political pressures on the central bank to pursue inflationary monetary policy and thereby reduce the likelihood of the time-inconsistency problem.

Increased Transparency Inflation targeting has the advantage that it is readily understood by the public and is thus highly transparent. Indeed, inflation-targeting regimes place great importance on transparency in policymaking and on regular communication with the public. Inflation-targeting central banks have frequent communications with the government, some mandated by law and some in response to informal inquiries, and their officials take every opportunity to make public speeches on their monetary policy strategy. Although these techniques are also commonly used in countries that have not adopted inflation targeting, inflation-targeting central banks have taken public outreach a step further: Not only do they engage in extended public information campaigns, including the distribution of glossy brochures, but they also publish documents like the Bank of England's *Inflation Report*. These documents are particularly noteworthy because, unlike the usual dull-looking, formal reports of central banks, they make use of fancy graphics, boxes, and other eye-catching design elements to engage the public's interest.

The channels of communication just discussed are used by central banks in inflation-targeting countries to explain the following concepts to the general public, financial market participants, and politicians: (1) the goals and limitations of monetary policy, including the rationale for inflation targets; (2) the numerical values of the inflation targets and how they were determined; (3) how the inflation targets are to be achieved, given current economic conditions; and (4) reasons for any deviations from the targets. These communications have improved private sector planning by reducing uncertainty about monetary policy, interest rates, and inflation; they have promoted public debate of monetary policy, in part by educating the public about what a central bank can and cannot achieve; and they have helped clarify the responsibilities of the central bank and of politicians in the conduct of monetary policy.

Increased Accountability Another key feature of inflation-targeting regimes is the tendency toward increased accountability of the central bank. Indeed, transparency and communication go hand-in-hand with increased accountability. The strongest case of accountability of a central bank in an inflation-targeting regime is in New Zealand, where the government has the right to dismiss the Reserve Bank's governor if the inflation targets are breached, even for one quarter. In other inflation-targeting countries, the central bank's accountability is less formalized. Nevertheless, the transparency of policy associated with inflation targeting has tended to make the central bank highly accountable to the public and the government. Sustained success in the conduct of monetary policy as measured against a pre-announced and well-defined inflation target can be instrumental in building public support for a central bank's independence and for its policies. This building of public support and accountability occurs even in the absence of a rigidly defined and legalistic standard of performance evaluation and punishment.

Consistency with Democratic Principles   Not only is accountability valuable in its own right, but it also makes the institutional framework for the conduct of monetary policy more consistent with democratic principles. The inflation-targeting framework promotes the accountability of the central bank to elected officials, who are given some responsibility for setting the goals of monetary policy and then monitoring the economic outcomes. However, under inflation targeting as it generally has been practised, the central bank has complete control over operational decisions and so can be held accountable for achieving its assigned objectives.

Improved Performance   The performance of inflation-targeting regimes has been quite good. Inflation-targeting countries seem to have significantly reduced both the rate of inflation and inflation expectations beyond what likely would have occurred in the absence of inflation targets. Furthermore, once lowered, inflation in these countries has stayed low; following disinflations, the inflation rate in inflation-targeting countries has not bounced back up during subsequent cyclical expansions of the economy.

Disadvantages of Inflation Targeting

Critics of inflation targeting cite four disadvantages of this monetary policy strategy: (1) delayed signalling, (2) too much rigidity, (3) the potential for increased output fluctuations, and (4) low economic growth. We look at each in turn and examine the validity of these criticisms.

Delayed Signalling   Inflation is not easily controlled by the monetary authorities. Furthermore, because of the long lags in the effects of monetary policy, inflation outcomes are revealed only after a substantial lag. Thus an inflation target does not send immediate signals to the public and the markets about the stance of monetary policy.

Too Much Rigidity   Some economists criticize inflation targeting because they believe it imposes a rigid rule on monetary policymakers and limits their ability to respond to unforeseen circumstances. However, useful policy strategies exist that are "rule-like" in that they involve forward-looking behaviour that limits policymakers from systematically engaging in policies with undesirable long-run consequences. Such policies avoid the time-inconsistency problem and would be best described as "constrained discretion," a term coined by Ben Bernanke and an author of this book.

Indeed, inflation targeting can be described exactly in this way. Inflation targeting, as actually practised, is far from rigid and is better described as "flexible inflation targeting." First, inflation targeting does not prescribe simple and mechanical instructions on how the central bank should conduct monetary policy. Rather, it requires the central bank to use all available information to determine which policy actions are appropriate to achieve the inflation target. Unlike simple policy rules, inflation targeting never requires the central bank to focus solely on one key variable. Second, inflation targeting, as practised, contains a substantial degree of policy discretion. Inflation targets have been modified depending on economic circumstances, as we have seen. Moreover, central banks under inflation-targeting regimes have left themselves considerable scope to respond to output growth and fluctuations through several devices.

Potential for Increased Output Fluctuations

An important criticism of inflation targeting is that a sole focus on inflation may lead to monetary policy that is too tight when inflation is above target and thus may result in larger output fluctuations. Inflation targeting does not, however, require a sole focus on inflation—in fact, experience has shown that inflation targeters display substantial concern about output fluctuations. All the inflation targeters have set their inflation targets above zero.[4] For example, New Zealand, Canada, the United Kingdom, and Sweden currently set the midpoints of their inflation targets at 2%, while Australia sets its midpoint at 2.5%.

The decision by inflation targeters to choose inflation targets above zero reflects the concern of monetary policymakers that particularly low inflation can have substantial negative effects on real economic activity. Deflation (negative inflation, in which the price level actually falls) is especially to be feared because of the possibility that it may promote financial instability and precipitate a severe economic contraction (as discussed in Chapter 9). The deflation in Japan in recent years has been an important factor in the weakening of the Japanese financial system and economy. Inflation-targeting rates above zero make periods of deflation less likely. This is one reason why some economists, both within and outside of Japan, called on the Bank of Japan to adopt an inflation target at levels of 2%, which the Bank of Japan finally did in 2013.

Inflation targeting also does not ignore traditional stabilization goals. Central bankers in inflation-targeting countries continue to express their concern about fluctuations in output and employment, and the ability to accommodate short-run stabilization goals to some degree is built into all inflation-targeting regimes. All inflation-targeting countries have been willing to minimize output declines by gradually lowering medium-term inflation targets toward the long-run goal.

Low Economic Growth

Another common concern about inflation targeting is that it will lead to low growth in output and employment. Although inflation reduction has been associated with below-normal output during disinflationary phases in inflation targeting regimes, once low inflation levels were achieved, output and employment returned to levels at least as high as they were before. A conservative conclusion is that once low inflation is achieved, inflation targeting is not harmful to the real economy. Given the strong economic growth after disinflation in many countries (such as New Zealand) that have adopted inflation targets, a case can be made that inflation targeting promotes real economic growth, in addition to controlling inflation.

---

[4]Consumer price indexes have been found to have an upward bias in the measurement of true inflation, so it is not surprising that inflation targets are chosen to exceed zero. However, the actual targets have been set to exceed the estimates of this measurement bias, indicating that inflation targeters have decided on targets for inflation that exceed zero even after measurement bias is accounted for.

LESSONS FOR MONETARY POLICY STRATEGY FROM THE GLOBAL FINANCIAL CRISIS

Our discussion in previous chapters of the course of events that characterized the global financial crisis suggests four basic lessons for economists and policymakers on how the economy works.[5]

1. *Developments in the financial sector have a far greater impact on economic activity than was earlier realized.* Although before the crisis economists and policymakers generally recognized that financial frictions could play an important role in business cycle fluctuations, as we saw in Chapter 9, the global financial crisis made it abundantly clear that the adverse effects of financial disruptions on economic activity could be far worse than originally anticipated.

2. *The zero lower bound on interest rates can be a serious problem.* As we saw in Chapter 16, the zero lower bound on interest rates has forced central banks to use nonconventional monetary policy tools. Although these nonconventional tools can help stimulate the economy, they are more complicated to use than conventional tools and their impact on the economy is more uncertain, so they may be harder to use effectively.

3. *The cost of cleaning up after a financial crisis is very high.* As we saw in Chapter 9 financial crises are followed by deep recessions. But in addition, recoveries from financial crises are very slow. Carmen Reinhart of the Petersen Institute for International Economics and Vincent Reinhart of the American Enterprise Institute have documented that economic growth is significantly lower during the decade following financial crises, and unemployment rates stay persistently higher for a decade after crisis episodes. In addition, in the aftermath of financial crises, government indebtedness almost always sharply increases and can lead to defaults on government debt, which has become a major concern in Europe in the aftermath of the most recent crisis.[6]

4. *Price and output stability do not ensure financial stability.* Before the recent financial crisis, the common view both in academia and central banks was that achieving price and output stability would promote financial stability. However, the success of central banks in stabilizing inflation and the decreased volatility of business cycle fluctuations before 2007, which became known as the Great Moderation, did not protect the economy from financial instability. Indeed, it may have promoted it. The low volatility of both inflation and output fluctuations may have lulled market participants into thinking less risk was present in the economic system than was really the case, leading them to take excessive risks, which helped promote the global financial crisis.

What implications do these lessons have for monetary policy strategy? We first look at how these lessons might affect our thinking about inflation targeting and then on how central banks should respond to asset-price bubbles.

---

[5] For a more detailed discussion of the lessons of the global financial crisis for monetary policy strategy, see Frederic S. Mishkin, "Monetary Policy Strategy: Lessons from the Crisis," in Marek Jarocinski, Frank Smets, and Christian Thimann, eds., *Monetary Policy Revisited: Lessons from the Crisis*, Sixth ECB Central Banking Conference (Frankfurt, European Central Bank, 2011), 67–118.

[6] See Carmen M. Reinhart and Vincent R. Reinhart, "After the Fall," *Macroeconomic Challenges: The Decade Ahead*, Federal Reserve Bank of Kansas City Economic Symposium, 2010, manuscript available at www.kansascityfed.org; and Carmen M. Reinhart and Kenneth S. Rogoff, *This Time Is Different: Eight Centuries of Financial Folly* (Princeton, NJ: Princeton University Press, 2009).

Implications for Inflation Targeting

Earlier in the chapter, we outlined the arguments for inflation targeting, and none of the lessons listed above contradicts these arguments. Although support for the inflation-targeting strategy is not weakened by the lessons learned from the financial crisis, these lessons do suggest that inflation targeting may need to be more flexible and also may need to be modified on several dimensions. First, we look at what these lessons might mean for the level of the inflation target.

Level of the Inflation Target   As our discussion earlier in the chapter indicated, central banks typically have an inflation target around the 2% level. The seriousness of the zero-lower-bound problem raises the question of whether this target level is too low. A controversial paper written by researchers at the IMF, including its chief economist, suggests that the inflation target might be raised from the 2% to the 4% level.[7] The paper argues that with expectations of inflation anchored to this target, by lowering the nominal interest rate to zero, the real interest rate, $r = i - \pi^e$, could be decreased to as low as $-4\%(= 0 - 4\%)$, rather than $-2\%(= 0 - 2\%)$, associated with the 2% inflation target. Conventional monetary policy, which involves manipulating the nominal policy rate, would then be able to become more expansionary when interest rates fell to a floor of zero than it could with the lower inflation target. In other words, the zero lower bound on the policy rate would be less binding with a higher inflation target.

Although this argument is theoretically sound, and raising the inflation target has benefits, we also have to look at its costs. The benefits of a higher inflation target accrue only when the zero-lower-bound problem occurs. Although this was a major problem during the global financial crisis, such episodes have not been very frequent. If the zero-lower-bound problem is rare, then the benefits of a higher inflation target are not so large because they are available only infrequently. However, the costs of higher inflation in terms of the distortions it produces in the economy, mentioned early in the chapter, are ongoing. Thus, although these costs may not be that large in any given year, they add up over time and may outweigh the intermittent benefits of a higher inflation target when the zero lower bound occurs.

Another problem with a higher inflation target is that the history of inflation suggests that it is more difficult to stabilize the inflation rate at a 4% level than at a 2% level. Once inflation starts to rise above this level, the public is likely to believe that price stability is no longer a credible goal of the central bank. The question then arises, if a 4% level of inflation is okay, then why not 6%, or 8%, and so on? Indeed, this is what seems to have happened in the 1960s, when economists such as Paul Samuelson and Robert Solow of MIT, both eventual recipients of the Nobel Prize, argued that policymakers should be willing to tolerate higher inflation rates in the 4–5% range. But when inflation rose to that level, the policy authorities could not contain it at that level, and it kept on rising to double-digit levels by the early 1980s. Getting inflation back down again was very costly. No central banker wants to go through that cycle again, and this is why central bankers have been so hostile to the IMF researchers' suggestion.

Flexibility of Inflation Targeting   We have seen that inflation targeting as actually practised would be better described as "flexible inflation targeting." However, before the global financial crisis, this flexibility involved allowing some short-run deviations

---

[7]Olivier Blanchard, Giovanni Dell'Ariccia, and Paolo Mauro, "Rethinking Monetary Policy," *Journal of Money, Credit and Banking* 42, Issue Supplement S1 (September 2010): 199–217.

of inflation from the inflation target in order to promote output stability as well as price stability. Two lessons from the crisis—that financial instability can have devastating effects on the economy and that achieving price and output stability does not ensure financial stability—have led to a recognition that central banks need to pay more attention to financial stability, not only in designing inflation-targeting regimes but also in any monetary policy framework. Particularly important in this regard is the issue of how central banks should respond to asset-price bubbles, the topic we discuss next.

SHOULD CENTRAL BANKS TRY TO STOP ASSET-PRICE BUBBLES?

Over the centuries, economies have been subject to periodic **asset-price bubbles**, pronounced increases in asset prices, or "bubbles," that depart from fundamental values and that eventually burst resoundingly. The story of the global financial crisis, discussed in Web Chapter 3, indicates just how costly these bubbles can be. The bursting of the asset-price bubble in the housing market brought down the financial system, leading to an economic downturn, a rise in unemployment, and direct hardship for families who were forced to leave their homes after foreclosures.

The high economic cost of asset-price bubbles raises the following questions: What should central banks do about them? Should they use monetary policy to try to pop the bubbles? Are there regulatory measures they can take to rein in asset-price bubbles? To answer these questions, we need to ask whether there are different kinds of bubbles that require different types of responses.

Two Types of Asset-Price Bubbles

To think about central banks' response to asset-price bubbles, we first need to look at the different types of bubbles and how each might best be addressed. Asset-price bubbles are of two types: one type is driven by credit, and the second type is driven purely by overly optimistic expectations (dubbed "irrational exuberance" by Alan Greenspan).

Credit-Driven Bubbles   When a credit boom begins, an asset-price bubble may begin to form. Easier-to-get credit can be used to purchase particular assets and thereby raise their prices. The rise in asset values, in turn, encourages further lending for these assets, either because it increases the value of collateral, making it easier to borrow, or because it raises the value of capital at financial institutions, which gives them more capacity to lend. The lending for these assets can then further increase demand for them and hence raise their prices even more. This feedback loop—in which a credit boom drives up asset prices, which in turn fuels the credit boom, which drives asset prices even higher, and so on—can generate a bubble in which asset prices rise well above their fundamental values.

Credit-driven bubbles are particularly dangerous, as the recent global financial crisis has demonstrated. When asset prices come back down to earth and the bubble bursts, the collapse in asset prices leads to a reversal of the feedback loop: loans go sour, lenders cut back on the credit supply, the demand for assets declines further, and prices drop even more. These were exactly the dynamics that characterized housing markets during the global financial crisis in the United States. Driven by a credit boom in subprime lending, housing prices rose way above fundamental values; but when housing prices crashed, credit shriveled up and housing prices plummeted.

The resulting losses on subprime loans and securities eroded the balance sheets of financial institutions, causing a decline in credit (deleveraging) and a sharp fall in business and household spending, and therefore in economic activity. During the global financial crisis, the interaction between housing prices and the health of financial institutions following the collapse of the housing price bubble endangered the operation of the financial system as a whole and had dire consequences for the U.S. economy.

Bubbles Driven Solely by Irrational Exuberance   Bubbles that are driven solely by overly optimistic expectations, but that are not associated with a credit boom, pose much less risk to the financial system. For example, the bubble in technology stocks in the late 1990s was not fueled by credit, and the bursting of the tech-stock bubble was not followed by a marked deterioration in financial institutions' balance sheets. The bursting of the tech-stock bubble thus did not have a very severe impact on the economy, and the recession that followed was quite mild. Bubbles driven solely by irrational exuberance are therefore far less dangerous than those driven by credit booms.

The Debate over Whether Central Banks Should Try to Pop Bubbles

Because asset prices are a central element of monetary policy and directly affect its outcomes (the transmission mechanisms of monetary policy are discussed in Chapter 26), monetary policy certainly needs to respond to asset prices in order to obtain good outcomes in terms of inflation and output. Hence, the issue is not whether monetary policy should respond to asset price movements at all, but whether it should respond at a level over and above the level called for in terms of the objectives of stabilizing inflation and employment. Should monetary policy try to pop, or slow, the growth of potential asset-price bubbles to minimize damage to the economy when these bubbles burst? Alternatively, rather than responding directly to possible asset-price bubbles, should the monetary authorities respond only to the asset-price declines that occur after a bubble bursts, to stabilize both output and inflation? These opposing positions have been characterized as *leaning against* asset-price bubbles versus *cleaning up* after the bubbles burst, and so the debate over what to do about asset-price bubbles has been labelled the "lean versus clean" debate.

Whether central banks should try to pop, or prick, bubbles was actively debated before the global financial crisis, with Alan Greenspan arguing against such actions. Greenspan's position held great sway in central banking circles before the crisis. However, the crisis has led economists to reevaluate this viewpoint, and we look at the pro and con arguments below.

Con: Why Central Banks Should Not Try to Prick Asset-Price Bubbles but Should Just Clean Up After They Burst   Alan Greenspan's argument that central banks should not take actions to prick bubbles became known as the "Greenspan doctrine." His position reflected five arguments:

1. Asset-price bubbles are nearly impossible to identify. If central banks or government officials knew that a bubble was in progress, wouldn't market participants know as well? If so, then a bubble would be unlikely to develop, because market participants would know that prices were getting out of line with fundamentals. Unless central bank or government officials are smarter than market participants, an unlikely situation given the savvy of especially talented (and high-earning) market participants,

they will be unlikely to identify when bubbles of this type are occurring. A strong argument, then, exists for not responding to suspected bubbles.

2. Although some economic analysis suggests that raising interest rates can diminish asset price increases, raising interest rates may be very ineffective in restraining bubbles, because market participants expect such high rates of return from buying bubble-driven assets. Furthermore, raising interest rates has often been found to cause a bubble to burst more severely, thereby increasing the damage to the economy. Another way of saying this is that bubbles are departures from normal behaviour, and it is unrealistic to expect that the usual tools of monetary policy will be effective in abnormal conditions.

3. Many different asset prices exist, and at any one time a bubble may be present in only a fraction of asset markets. Monetary policy actions are a very blunt instrument in such a case, as such actions would be likely to affect asset prices in general, rather than the specific assets that are experiencing a bubble.

4. Monetary policy actions to prick bubbles can have harmful effects on the aggregate economy. If interest rates are raised significantly in an effort to curtail a bubble, the economy will slow, people will lose jobs, and inflation might fall below its desirable level. Indeed, as arguments 2 and 3 suggest, the rise in interest rates necessary to prick a bubble may be so high that it can be done only at great cost to workers and the economy. This is not to say that monetary policy should not respond to asset prices per se. The level of asset prices does affect aggregate demand (discussed in Chapter 26) and thus the evolution of the economy. Monetary policy should react to fluctuations in asset prices to the extent that they affect inflation and economic activity.

5. As long as policymakers respond in a timely fashion, by easing monetary policy aggressively after an asset bubble bursts, the harmful effects of a bursting bubble can be kept at a manageable level. Indeed, the Greenspan Fed acted in exactly this way after the stock market crash of 1987 and the bursting of the tech bubble in the stock market in 2000. Aggressive easing after the stock market bubbles burst in 1987 and 2000 was highly successful. The U.S. economy did not enter a recession after the stock market crash of 1987, and the recession that followed the tech bubble burst in 2000 was very mild.

Pro: Why Central Banks Should Try to Pop Bubbles The recent financial crisis clearly demonstrated that the bursting of credit-driven bubbles can be not only extremely costly but also very hard to clean up. Furthermore, credit-driven bubbles can occur even if price and output stability exist in the period leading up to them. Indeed, as we have seen, price and output stability might actually encourage credit-driven bubbles because they lead market participants to underestimate the amount of risk present in the economy. The global financial crisis has therefore provided a much stronger case for leaning against potential bubbles than for just cleaning up after they burst.

However, the distinction between the two types of bubbles, one of which (credit driven) is much more costly to the economy than the other, suggests that the lean versus clean debate may have been miscast. Rather than leaning against potential asset price bubbles, which would include both credit-driven and irrational exuberance-type bubbles, the case is much stronger for leaning against credit *booms*, which would involve leaning against credit-driven asset-price bubbles but not against asset-price bubbles driven by irrational exuberance. **It is much easier to identify credit booms than asset-price bubbles.** When asset-price bubbles are rising rapidly at the same time that credit is booming, the likelihood is greater that asset prices are deviating from fundamentals because laxer credit standards are driving asset prices upward. In this case, central bank or government officials are more likely to identify that a boom is in progress; this was indeed the case during the housing market bubble in the United States, when central banks and government officials were aware that lenders had weakened lending standards and that credit extension in the mortgage markets was rising at abnormally high rates.

The case for leaning against credit-driven bubbles seems strong, but what policies would be most effective in restraining them?

Macroprudential Policies

First, it is important to recognize that the key principle to consider in designing effective policies to lean against credit booms is that such policies must curb excessive risk taking. Only when risk taking is excessive are credit booms likely to develop, and so it is natural to look to prudential regulatory measures to constrain credit booms. Regulatory policy to affect what is happening in credit markets in the aggregate is referred to as macroprudential regulation, and it does seem to be the right tool for reining in credit-driven bubbles.

Financial regulation and supervision, either by central banks or by other government entities, with the usual elements of a well-functioning prudential regulatory and supervisory system, as described in Chapter 10, can prevent the excessive risk taking that can trigger a credit boom, which in turn will lead to an asset-price bubble. These elements include adequate disclosure and capital requirements, prompt corrective action, close monitoring of financial institutions' risk management procedures, and close supervision to enforce compliance with regulations. More generally, regulation should focus on preventing leverage cycles. As the global financial crisis demonstrated, the rise in asset prices that accompanied the credit boom resulted in higher capital buffers at financial institutions, supporting further lending in the context of unchanging capital requirements, which led to higher asset prices, and so on; in the bust, the value of the capital dropped precipitously, leading to a cut in lending. Capital requirements that are countercyclical, that is, adjusted upward during a boom and downward during a bust, might help eliminate the pernicious feedback loops that promote credit-driven bubbles.

A rapid rise in asset prices accompanied by a credit boom provides a signal that market failures or poor financial regulation and supervision might be causing a bubble to form. Central banks and other government regulators can then consider implementing policies to rein in credit growth directly or can implement measures to make sure credit standards are sufficiently high.

Monetary Policy

The fact that the low interest rate policies of the Federal Reserve from 2002 to 2005 were followed by excessive risk taking suggests to many that overly easy monetary policy might promote financial instability, as was discussed in Chapter 9. Although it is far from clear that the Federal Reserve is primarily to blame for the housing bubble in the United States, research does suggest that low interest rates can encourage excessive risk taking, in what has been called the "risk-taking channel of monetary policy." Low interest rates may increase the incentives for asset managers in financial institutions to search for higher yields and hence increase risk taking. Low interest rates may also increase the demand for assets, raising their prices and leading to increased valuation of collateral, which in turn encourages lenders to lend to riskier borrowers.

The risk-taking channel of monetary policy suggests that monetary policy should be used to lean against credit booms. However, many of the Greenspan doctrine's objections to using monetary policy to prick booms are still valid, so wouldn't it be better to use macroprudential supervision to constrain credit booms, leaving monetary policy to focus on price and output stability?

This argument would be quite strong if macroprudential policies were able to do the job. However, there are doubts on this score. Prudential supervision is subject to more political pressure than monetary policy because it affects the bottom line of financial institutions more directly. Thus these institutions have greater incentives to lobby politicians to discourage macroprudential policies that would rein in credit booms, particularly during a credit boom, when they are making the most money. In addition, financial institutions are often very good at finding loopholes to avoid regulation, as we discovered in Chapter 11, and so macroprudential supervision may not be effective. The possibility that macroprudential policies may not be implemented sufficiently well to constrain credit booms suggests that monetary policy may have to be used instead.

An important lesson from the global financial crisis is that central banks and other regulators should not have a laissez-faire attitude and let credit-driven bubbles proceed without any reaction. Figuring out how to do this well, however, is indeed a daunting task.

TACTICS: CHOOSING THE POLICY INSTRUMENT

Now that we are familiar with the alternative strategies for monetary policy, let's look at how monetary policy is conducted on a day-to-day basis. Central banks directly control the tools of monetary policy—open market buyback operations, the bank rate, the interest rate on reserves, quantitative easing, and forward guidance—but knowing the tools and the strategies for implementing a monetary policy does not tell us whether that policy is easy or tight. To ascertain whether a policy is easy or tight, we can observe the **policy instrument** (also called an **operating instrument**), a variable that responds to the central bank's tools and indicates the stance (easy or tight) of monetary policy. A central bank like the Bank of Canada has at its disposal two basic types of policy instruments: reserve aggregates (total reserves, nonborrowed reserves, the monetary base, and the nonborrowed base) and interest rates (the overnight interest rate and other short-term interest rates). (Central banks in small countries can choose another policy instrument, the exchange rate, but we leave this topic to Chapter 19.) The policy instrument might be linked to an **intermediate target**, such as a monetary aggregate like M1+ or a long-term interest rate. Intermediate targets stand between the policy instrument and the goals of monetary policy (e.g., price stability, output growth); they are not as directly affected by the tools of monetary policy but might be more closely linked to the goals of monetary policy. As a study aid, Figure 17-2 shows a schematic of the linkages among the tools of monetary policy, policy instruments, intermediate targets, and the goals of monetary policy.

As an example, suppose the central bank's employment and inflation goals are consistent with a nominal GDP growth rate of 5%. The central bank might believe that the 5% nominal GDP growth rate will be achieved by a 4% growth rate for M1+ (an intermediate target), which will in turn be achieved by a growth rate of 3% for nonborrowed reserves (the policy instrument). Alternatively, the central bank might believe that the best way to achieve its objectives would be to set the overnight interest rate (a policy instrument) at, say, 4%. Can the central bank choose to target both the nonborrowed reserves and the overnight-rate policy instruments at the same time? The answer is no. The application of supply and demand analysis to the market for reserves we developed in Chapter 16 explains why a central bank must choose one or the other.

FIGURE 17-2   **Linkages Among Central Bank Tools, Policy Instruments, Intermediate Targets, and Goals of Monetary Policy**

The tools of the central bank are used to change the policy instruments to achieve the intermediate target and then the goals of monetary policy.

Let's first see why choosing an aggregate target involves losing control of the interest rate. Figure 17-3 contains a supply and demand diagram for the market for reserves. Although the central bank expects the demand curve for reserves to be at R^{d*}, it fluctuates between $R^{d'}$ and $R^{d''}$ because of changes in banks' desire to hold excess reserves. If the central bank has a nonborrowed reserves target of NBR^* (say, because it has a target growth rate of the money supply of 4%), it expects that the overnight

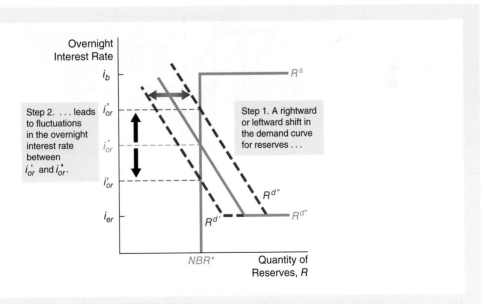

FIGURE 17-3   **Result of Targeting on Nonborrowed Reserves**

Targeting on nonborrowed reserves of NBR^* will lead to fluctuations in the overnight interest rate between $i_{or}^{'}$ and $i_{or}^{''}$ because of fluctuations in the demand for reserves between $R^{d'}$ and $R^{d''}$.

interest rate will be i_{or}^*. However, as the figure indicates, the fluctuations in the reserves demand curve between $R^{d'}$ and $R^{d''}$ will result in a fluctuation in the overnight interest rate between i_{or}' and i_{or}''. Pursuing an aggregate target implies that interest rates will fluctuate.

The supply and demand diagram in Figure 17-4 shows the consequences of an interest-rate target set at i_{or}^*. Again the central bank expects the reserves demand curve to be at R^{d*}, but it fluctuates between $R^{d'}$ and $R^{d''}$ due to unexpected changes in deposits or banks' desire to hold reserves. If the demand curve rises to $R^{d''}$, the overnight interest rate will begin to rise above i_{or}^* and the central bank will engage in open market purchases of bonds until it raises the supply of nonborrowed reserves to NBR'', at which point the equilibrium overnight interest rate is again at i_{or}^*. Conversely, if the demand curve falls to $R^{d'}$ and lowers the overnight interest rate, the central bank would keep making open market sales until nonborrowed reserves fall to NBR'' and the overnight rate returns to i_{or}^*. The central bank's adherence to the interest-rate target thus leads to a fluctuating quantity of nonborrowed reserves and the money supply.

The conclusion from the supply and demand analysis is that interest-rate and reserve (monetary) aggregate targets are incompatible. A central bank can hit one or the other, but not both. Because a choice between them has to be made, we need to examine what criteria should be used to select a policy instrument.

MyEconLab Mini-lecture

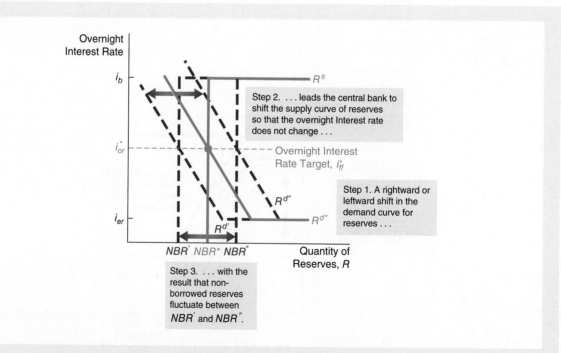

FIGURE 17-4   Result of Targeting on the Overnight Interest Rate

Targeting on the interest rate i_{or}^* will lead to fluctuations in nonborrowed reserves between NBR^* and NBR'' because of fluctuations in the demand for reserves between $R^{d'}$ and $R^{d''}$.

Criteria for Choosing the Policy Instrument

Three criteria apply when choosing a policy instrument: the instrument must be observable and measurable, it must be controllable by the central bank, and it must have a predictable effect on the goals.

Observability and Measurability   Quick observability and accurate measurement of a policy instrument are necessary because it will be useful only if it signals the policy stance rapidly. Reserve aggregates like nonborrowed reserves are straightforward to measure, but some lag in reporting of reserve aggregates (a delay of two weeks) exists. Short-term interest rates, like the overnight interest rate, by contrast, not only are easy to measure but also are observable immediately. Thus, it seems that interest rates are more observable and measurable than are reserves and, therefore, are a better policy instrument.

However, as we learned in Chapter 4, the interest rate that is easiest to measure and observe is the nominal interest rate. It is typically a poor measure of the real cost of borrowing, which indicates with more certainty what will happen to the real GDP. This real cost of borrowing is more accurately measured by the real interest rate—that is, the nominal interest rate adjusted for expected inflation $r = i - \pi^e$. Unfortunately, real interest rates are extremely difficult to measure, because we do not have a direct way to measure expected inflation. Given that both interest rates and aggregates have observability and measurability problems, it is not clear whether one should be preferred to the other as a policy instrument.

Controllability   A central bank must be able to exercise effective control over a variable if it is to function as a useful policy instrument. If the central bank cannot control the policy instrument, knowing that it is off track does little good, because the central bank has no way of getting it back on track.

Because of shifts in and out of currency, even reserve aggregates, such as nonborrowed reserves, are not completely controllable. Conversely, the Bank of Canada can control short-term interest rates, such as the overnight interest rate, very tightly. It might appear, therefore, that short-term interest rates would dominate reserve aggregates on the controllability criterion. However, a central bank cannot set short-term real interest rates because it does not have control over expectations of inflation. Once again, a clear-cut case cannot be made that short-term interest rates are preferable to reserve aggregates as a policy instrument, or vice versa.

Predictable Effect On Goals   The most important characteristic of a policy instrument is that it must have a predictable effect on a goal. If a central bank can accurately and quickly measure the price of tea in China and can completely control its price, what good will that do? The central bank cannot use the price of tea in China to affect unemployment or the price level in its country. Because the ability to affect goals is so critical to the usefulness of any policy instrument, the tightness of the link from reserve or monetary aggregates to goals (output, employment, and inflation) or, alternatively, from interest rates to these goals has been the subject of much research and debate. In recent years, most central banks have concluded that the link between interest rates and goals such as inflation is tighter than the link between reserve aggregates and inflation. For this reason, central banks throughout the world now generally use short-term interest rates as their policy instrument.

TACTICS: THE TAYLOR RULE

As we have seen, the Bank of Canada and most other central banks currently conduct monetary policy by setting a target for short-term interest rates like the overnight interest rate. But how should this target be chosen?

John Taylor of Stanford University has come up with an answer, called the **Taylor rule**. The Taylor rule indicates that the overnight interest rate should be set equal to the inflation rate plus an "equilibrium" real overnight interest rate (the real overnight rate that is consistent with full employment in the long run) plus a weighted average of two gaps: (1) an inflation gap—current inflation minus a target rate, and (2) an output gap—the percentage deviation of real GDP from an estimate of its potential (natural rate) level.[8] This rule can be written as follows:

$$\text{Overnight interest rate target} = \text{inflation rate} + \text{equilibrium real overnight rate}$$
$$+ \frac{1}{2}(\text{inflation gap}) + \frac{1}{2}(\text{output gap})$$

Taylor has assumed that the equilibrium real overnight interest rate is 2% and that an appropriate target for inflation would also be 2%, with equal weights of $\frac{1}{2}$ on the inflation and output gaps. For a numerical example of the Taylor rule, suppose the inflation rate is at 3%, leading to a positive inflation gap of 1% (=3% − 2%), and real GDP is 1% above its potential, resulting in a positive output gap of 1%. Then the Taylor rule suggests that the overnight interest rate should be set at 6 [=3% inflation + 2% equilibrium real overnight rate + $\frac{1}{2}$(1% inflation gap)+ $\frac{1}{2}$(1% output gap)].

An important feature of the Taylor rule is that the coefficient on the inflation gap, $\frac{1}{2}$, is positive. If the inflation rate rises by 1 percentage point, then the overnight interest target is raised by 1.5 percentage points, and so by more than a one-to-one ratio. In other words, a rise in inflation of 1 percentage point leads to a real overnight rate increase of $\frac{1}{2}$ percentage point. The principle that the monetary authorities should raise nominal interest rates by more than the increase in the inflation rate has been named the **Taylor principle**, and it is critical to the success of monetary policy. Suppose that the Taylor principle is not followed and nominal rates rise by *less* than the rise in the inflation rate, so that real interest rates *fall* when inflation rises. Serious instability then results because a rise in inflation leads to an effective easing of monetary policy, which then leads to even higher inflation in the future. Indeed, this was a feature of monetary policy in the 1970s that led to a loss of the nominal anchor and the era of the so-called "Great Inflation," when inflation rates climbed to double-digit levels. Fortunately, since 1979, the Taylor principle has become a feature of monetary policy, with much happier outcomes on both the inflation and the aggregate output fronts.

Some economists take the view that the presence of an output gap in the Taylor rule indicates that the Bank of Canada should care not only about keeping inflation under control but also about minimizing business cycle fluctuations of output around its potential level. Caring about both inflation and output fluctuations is consistent with many statements by Bank of Canada officials that controlling inflation and stabilizing real output are important concerns of the Bank of Canada.

---

[8]The original formulation of the Taylor rule can be found in John B. Taylor, "Discretion Versus Policy Rules in Practice," *Carnegie-Rochester Conference Series on Public Policy* 39 (1993): 195–214. However, a more intuitive discussion with a historical perspective can be found in John B. Taylor, "A Historical Analysis of Monetary Policy Rules," in *Monetary Policy Rules*, ed. John B. Taylor (Chicago: University of Chicago Press, 1999), 319–341.

An alternative interpretation of the presence of the output gap in the Taylor rule is that the output gap is an indicator of future inflation, as stipulated in the **Phillips curve theory**. The Phillips curve theory indicates that changes in inflation are influenced by the state of the economy relative to its productive capacity, as well as by other factors.

This productive capacity can be measured by potential GDP, which is a function of the natural rate of unemployment, the rate of unemployment consistent with full employment. A related concept is the **nonaccelerating inflation rate of unemployment** (NAIRU)—the rate of unemployment at which there is no tendency for inflation to change. Simply put, the theory states that when the unemployment rate is above NAIRU with output below potential, inflation will come down, but if it is below NAIRU with output above potential, inflation will rise. Prior to 1995, the NAIRU was thought to reside around 8%. However, with the decline in unemployment to around the 4% level in the late 1990s, with no increase (and even a slight decrease) in inflation, some critics have questioned the value of the Phillips curve theory. Either they claim that it just doesn't work anymore or, alternatively, they believe that great uncertainty exists about the value of NAIRU. The Phillips curve theory is now highly controversial, and critics question whether it should be used as a guide for the conduct of monetary policy.

As Figure 17-5 shows, the Taylor rule does a pretty good, but not perfect, job of describing the Bank of Canada's setting of the overnight interest rate. Does this mean that the Bank of Canada should fire all its economists and put a computer in charge that simply has to compute the Taylor rule setting for the overnight rate? This would certainly save taxpayers a lot of money. Although the Bank of Canada does not do this, it does make use of the Taylor rule in thinking about how to conduct monetary policy

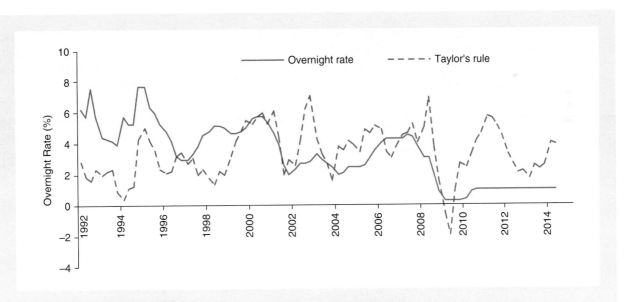

FIGURE 17-5   The Taylor Rule for the Overnight Interest Rate, 1991–2014

The Taylor rule does a pretty good job of describing the Bank of Canada's setting of the overnight interest rate.

Source: Statistics Canada CANSIM series V41690914 and V122514, Bank of Canada historical data, and authors' calculations.

FYI The Bank of Canada's Use of the Taylor Rule

Why hasn't the Bank of Canada put the overnight interest rate on the Taylor rule on autopilot, guided by a computer? There are several reasons why the Bank of Canada hasn't taken this drastic action. First and foremost, no perfect model of the economy exists, so even the best and brightest economists do not know the current inflation rate and output gap with certainty at any given moment. Since the economy is changing all the time, the Taylor rule coefficients are unlikely to stay constant in any event.

Even if we could determine these rates with certainty, monetary policy is by necessity a forward-looking activity because it takes a long time for monetary policy to affect the economy. Good monetary policy requires that the Bank of Canada forecast where inflation and economic activity are going to be in the future, and then adjust the policy instrument accordingly. The Bank of Canada will therefore look at a much wider range of information than just the current inflation rate and output gap in setting

policy, as is done in the Taylor rule. In other words, the conduct of monetary policy is as much an art as it is a science, requiring both careful analytics and human judgment. The Taylor rule leaves out all the art, and so is unlikely to produce the best monetary policy outcomes. For example, financial crises, such as that which occurred from 2007 to 2009, require complex monetary policy actions because changes in credit spreads (the difference between interest rates on securities with credit risk and those without) may alter how the overnight interest rate affects investment decisions, and therefore economic activity.

The bottom line is that putting monetary policy on autopilot with the Taylor rule with fixed coefficients would be a bad idea. The Taylor rule is, however, useful as a guide to monetary policy. If the setting of the policy instrument is very different from what the Taylor rule suggests, policymakers should ask whether they have a good reason for deviating from this rule. If they don't, then they might be making a mistake.

(see the FYI box The Bank of Canada's Use of the Taylor Rule). Given the above reasons, it is no surprise that the Taylor rule does not explain all the movements in the overnight interest rate in Figure 17-5. For this reason, financial institutions hire Bank of Canada watchers, as described in the FYI box, Bank of Canada Watchers.

FYI Bank of Canada Watchers

As we have seen, the most important player in the determination of Canadian interest rates is the Bank of Canada. When the Bank of Canada wants to inject reserves into the system, it conducts open market purchases of bonds, which cause bond prices to increase and their interest rates to fall, at least in the short term. If the Bank withdraws reserves from the system, it sells bonds, thereby depressing their price and raising their interest rates. Knowing what actions the Bank of Canada might be taking can thus help investors and financial institutions to predict the future course of interest rates with greater accuracy. Because, as we have

seen, changes in interest rates have a major impact on investors and financial institutions' profits, they are particularly interested in scrutinizing the Bank of Canada's behaviour. To assist in this task, financial institutions hire Bank of Canada watchers, experts on Bank of Canada behaviour who may have worked in the Bank of Canada and so have an insider's view of Bank of Canada operations. A Bank of Canada watcher who can accurately predict the course of monetary policy is a very valuable commodity, and successful Bank of Canada watchers therefore often earn very high salaries, well into the six-figure range and sometimes even higher.

MyEconLab

MyEconLab is an online homework and tutorial system that puts you in control of your own learning with study and practice tools directly correlated to this chapter's content. Visit MyEconLab to access the eText, the Questions and Applied Problems with answers, as well as additional assessment. You will also find web chapters, mini-lectures, appendices, mini-cases, videos, glossary flashcards, news feeds, CANSIM data, and graphing tools.

SUMMARY

1. The six basic goals of monetary policy are price stability (the primary goal), high employment (output stability), economic growth, stability of financial markets, interest-rate stability, and stability in foreign exchange markets.

2. Having a strong nominal anchor is a key element of a successful monetary policy. A strong nominal anchor helps promote price stability by tying down inflation expectations and limiting the time-inconsistency problem, in which monetary policymakers conduct monetary policy in a discretionary way that focuses on short-run objectives but produces poor long-run outcomes.

3. Inflation targeting has several advantages: (1) By focusing the political debate on long-run inflation, it can reduce the likelihood of the time-inconsistency problem; (2) it is readily understood by the public and is highly transparent; (3) it increases accountability of the central bank; and (4) it appears to ameliorate the effects of inflationary shocks. It does have some disadvantages, however: (1) inflation is not easily controlled by the monetary authorities, so that an inflation target is unable to send immediate signals to both the public and markets; (2) it might impose a rigid rule on policymakers, although this has not been the case in practice; and (3) a sole focus on inflation may lead to larger output fluctuations, or lower economic growth although this also has not been the case in practice.

4. Four lessons can be learned from the global financial crisis: (1) developments in the financial sector have a far greater impact on economic activity than was earlier realized; (2) the zero lower bound on interest rates can be a serious problem; (3) the cost of cleaning up after a financial crisis is very high; and (4) price and output stability do not ensure financial stability.

5. The lessons of the global financial crisis provide support for more flexible inflation targeting, possibly with a higher inflation target.

6. The lessons from the crisis also suggest that monetary policy should lean against credit booms but not asset-price bubbles.

7. Because interest-rate and aggregate policy instruments are incompatible, a central bank must choose between them on the basis of three criteria: measurability, controllability, and the ability to affect goal variables predictably. Central banks now typically use short-term interest rates as their policy instrument.

8. The Taylor rule indicates that the overnight interest rate should be set equal to the inflation rate plus an "equilibrium" real overnight rate plus a weighted average of two gaps: (1) an inflation gap, current inflation minus a target rate, and (2) an output gap, the percentage deviation of real GDP from an estimate of its potential (natural rate) level. The output gap in the Taylor rule could represent an indicator of future inflation, as stipulated in the Phillips curve theory. However, this theory is controversial, because high output relative to potential as measured by low unemployment has not seemed to produce higher inflation in recent years.

KEY TERMS

asset-price bubble, p. 444
dual mandate, p. 435
hierarchical mandates, p. 434
inflation targeting, p. 435

intermediate target, p. 448
natural rate of output, p. 433
natural rate of unemployment, p. 432
nominal anchor, p. 431

nonaccelerating inflation rate
   of unemployment (NAIRU), p. 453
operating instrument, p. 448
Phillips curve theory, p. 453

policy instrument, p. 448
potential output, p. 433

price stability, p. 430
Taylor principle, p. 452

Taylor rule, p. 452
time-inconsistency problem, p. 431

QUESTIONS

All questions are available in MyEconLab at
www.myeconlab.com.

1. What are the benefits of using a nominal anchor for the conduct of monetary policy?

2. What incentives arise for a central bank to fall into the time-inconsistency trap of pursuing overly expansionary monetary policy?

3. Why would it be problematic for a central bank to have a primary goal of maximizing economic growth?

4. "Since financial crises can impart severe damage to the economy, a central bank's primary goal should be to ensure stability in financial markets." Is this statement true, false, or uncertain? Explain.

5. "A central bank with a dual mandate will achieve lower unemployment in the long run than a central bank with a hierarchical mandate in which price stability takes precedence." Is this statement true, false, or uncertain? Explain.

6. Why is a public announcement of numerical inflation rate objectives important to the success of an inflation-targeting central bank?

7. How does inflation targeting help reduce the time-inconsistency of discretionary policy?

8. What methods have inflation-targeting central banks used to increase communication with the public and increase the transparency of monetary policy making?

9. Why might inflation targeting increase support for the independence of the central bank to conduct monetary policy?

10. "Because inflation targeting focuses on achieving the inflation target, it will lead to excessive output fluctuations." Is this statement true, false, or uncertain? Explain.

11. What are the key advantages and disadvantages of the monetary strategy recently used at the Federal Reserve in which the nominal anchor is only implicit?

12. "The zero lower bound on short-term interest rates is not a problem, since the central bank can just use quantitative easing to lower intermediate and longer-term interest rates instead." Is this statement true, false, or uncertain? Explain.

13. If higher inflation is bad, then why might it be advantageous to have a higher inflation target, rather than a lower target closer to zero?

14. Why aren't most central banks more proactive at trying to use monetary policy to eliminate asset-price bubbles?

15. Why would it be better to *lean* against credit-driven bubbles rather than just clean up after them like other types of burst asset bubbles?

16. Under what conditions might a central bank respond to a perceived stock market bubble?

17. Classify each of the following as either a policy instrument or an intermediate target, and explain why.

    a. The 10-year Canada bond rate

    b. The monetary base

    c. M1+

    d. The overnight interest rate

18. "If the demand for reserves did not fluctuate, the Bank of Canada could pursue both a reserves target and an interest-rate target at the same time." Is this statement true, false, or uncertain? Explain.

19. What procedures can the Bank of Canada use to control the overnight interest rate? Why does control of this interest rate imply that the Bank of Canada will lose control of nonborrowed reserves?

20. Compare the monetary base to M1+ on the grounds of controllability and measurability. Which do you prefer as an intermediate target? Why?

21. "Interest rates can be measured more accurately and quickly than reserve aggregates; hence an interest rate is preferred to the reserve aggregates as a policy instrument." Do you agree or disagree? Explain your answer.

22. How can bank behaviour and the Bank of Canada's behaviour cause money supply growth to be procyclical (rising in booms and falling in recessions)?

23. What does the Taylor rule imply that policymakers should do to the overnight interest rate under the following scenarios?

a. Unemployment rises due to a recession.

b. An oil price shock causes the inflation rate to rise by 1% and output to fall by 1%.

c. The economy experiences prolonged increases in productivity growth while actual output growth is unchanged.

d. Potential output declines while actual output remains unchanged.

e. The Bank of Canada revises its inflation target down.

APPLIED PROBLEMS

All applied problems are available in MyEconLab *at* **www.myeconlab.com.**

24. If the Bank of Canada has an interest-rate target, why will an increase in the demand for reserves lead to a rise in the money supply? Use a graph of the market for reserves to explain.

25. Since monetary policy changes through the overnight interest rate occur with a lag, policymakers are usually more concerned with adjusting policy according to changes in the forecasted or expected inflation rate, rather than the current inflation rate. In light of this, suppose that monetary policymakers employ the Taylor rule to set the overnight rate, where the inflation gap is defined as the difference between expected inflation and the target inflation rate. Assume that the weights on both the inflation and the output gaps are ½, the equilibrium real overnight rate is 2%, the inflation rate target is 2%, and the output gap is 1%.

a. If the expected inflation rate is 4%, then at what should the overnight interest rate be set according to the Taylor rule?

b. Suppose half of Bank of Canada economists forecast inflation to be 3%, and half of Bank of Canada economists forecast inflation to be 5%. If the Bank of Canada uses the average of these two forecasts as its measure of expected inflation, then what should the overnight interest rate be according to the Taylor rule?

c. Now suppose half of Bank of Canada economists forecast inflation to be 0%, and half forecast inflation to be 8%. If the Bank of Canada uses the average of these two forecasts as its measure of expected inflation, then what should the overnight interest rate be according to the Taylor rule?

d. Given your answers to (a)–(c) above, do you think it is a good idea for monetary policymakers to use a strict interpretation of the Taylor rule as a basis for setting policy? Why or why not?

DATA ANALYSIS PROBLEMS

Download data for these problems from MyEconLab *at* **www.myeconlab.com.**

1. Go to the Bank of Canada's website, and find data (under "Summary of Key Monetary Policy Variables") on total CPI and core CPI.

a. Calculate the 12-month growth rate for each of total CPI and core CPI in January 2015.

b. How do the inflation rates in a) compare to the inflation target?

2. Go to the Bank of Canada's website, and find quarterly data (under "Indicators of Capacity and Inflation Pressures for Canada") on the output gap and the capacity utilization rate (manufacturing).

a. For the last quarter of 2014, is the output gap positive or negative?

b. Is the capacity utilization rate increasing or decreasing over the two-year period from 2013 to 2014?

c. Compare the output gap and the capacity utilization rate for the most recent quarter available to the values during the global financial crisis, 2007–2009.

3. Go to the St. Louis Federal Reserve FRED database, and find data on the personal consumption expenditure price index (PCECTPI), real GDP (GDPC1), an estimate of potential GDP (GDPPOT), and the federal funds rate (DFF). For the price index, adjust the units setting to "Percent Change From Year Ago" to convert the data to the inflation rate; for the federal funds rate, change the frequency setting to "Quarterly." Download the data into a spreadsheet. Assuming the inflation target is 2%, calculate the inflation gap and the output gap for each quarter, from 2000 until the most recent quarter of data available. Calculate the output gap as the percentage deviation of output from the potential level of output.

a. Use the output and inflation gaps to calculate, for each quarter, the fed funds rate predicted by the Taylor rule. Assume that the weights on inflation stabilization and output stabilization are both $\frac{1}{2}$ (see the formula in the chapter). Compare the current (quarterly average) federal funds rate to the federal funds rate prescribed by the Taylor rule. Does the Taylor rule accurately predict the current rate? Briefly comment.

b. Create a graph that compares the predicted Taylor rule values with the actual quarterly federal funds rate averages. How well, in general, does the Taylor

rule prediction fit the average federal funds rate? Briefly explain.

c. Based on the results from the 2008–2009 period, explain the limitations of the Taylor rule as a formal policy tool. How do these limitations help explain the use of nonconventional monetary policy during this period?

d. Suppose the U.S. Congress changes the Fed's mandate to a hierarchical one in which inflation stabilization takes priority over output stabilization. In this context, recalculate the predicted Taylor rule value for each quarter since 2000, assuming that the weight on inflation stabilization is $\frac{3}{4}$ and the weight on output stabilization is $\frac{1}{4}$. Create a graph showing the Taylor rule prediction calculated in part (a), the prediction using the new "hierarchical" Taylor rule, and the fed funds rate. How, if at all, does changing the mandate change the predicted policy paths? How would the fed funds rate be affected by a hierarchical mandate? Briefly explain.

WEB EXERCISES

1. Go to **www.bankofcanada.ca**, and click on "About the Bank" and then "What We Do."

a. Review the Bank of Canada's main functions.

b. How does the Bank's monetary policy contribute to rising living standards for Canadians?

2. It is possible to access other central bank websites to learn about these banks' structures. One example is the European Central Bank. Go to **www.ecb.int/index.html**.

On the ECB home page, find information about the ECB's strategy for monetary policy.

3. Many countries have central banks that are responsible for their nation's monetary policy. Go to **www.bis.org/cbanks.htm** and select one of the central banks (for example, Norway). Review that bank's website to determine its policies regarding application of monetary policy. How does this bank's policies compare to those of the Bank of Canada?

WEB REFERENCES

www.bankofcanada.ca/about/

The Bank of Canada reports on its primary purposes and functions.

www.economagic.com/

A comprehensive listing of sites that offer a wide variety of economic summary data and graphs.

www.federalreserve.gov/aboutthefed/relatedWebSites.htm

The Federal Reserve provides links to other central bank Web pages.

PART 6

International Finance and Monetary Policy

Chapter 18   The Foreign Exchange Market

Chapter 19   The International Financial System

Crisis and Response: Foreign Exchange Market Turmoil and the IMF

From 2002 until 2008, the Canadian dollar steadily increased in value relative to the U.S. dollar. With the credit markets seizing up in September and October of 2008 after the failure of Lehman Bothers, however, the U.S. dollar appreciated sharply. The same "flight to quality" that led investors to step up their purchases of U.S. Treasury securities also led them to want to hold more U.S. dollars, thereby bidding up the U.S. dollar's value relative to other currencies, including the Canadian dollar and the euro.

This good news for the U.S. dollar was often bad news for other currencies. Many countries in Latin America and Eastern Europe found their currencies in free fall. The International Monetary Fund (IMF) stepped in and set up a new lending facility to make loans to distressed countries with fewer strings attached than had been the case under the IMF's previous lending programs. The IMF started making loans to the tune of billions of dollars. The IMF, which had looked like it was on the sidelines as the global financial crisis spread worldwide, now was moving to front and centre.

The global financial crisis has demonstrated that events that start in the United States have worldwide ramifications and that international financial institutions like the IMF have an important role in responding to make sure that the international financial system continues to work well. Chapter 18 outlines how the foreign exchange market functions and how exchange rates between different countries' currencies are determined. In Chapter 19, we examine how the international financial system operates and how it affects monetary policy.

18 The Foreign Exchange Market

1.39 .48

Learning Objectives

After studying this chapter you should be able to

1. Explain how the foreign exchange market works and why exchange rates are important.

2. Identify the main factors that affect exchange rates in the long run.

3. Draw the demand and supply curves for the foreign exchange market and interpret the equilibrium in the market for foreign exchange.

4. List and illustrate the factors that affect the exchange rate in the short run.

PREVIEW

In the late 1980s and early 1990s, Canadian businesses became less competitive with their counterparts in the United States; subsequently, in the 2000s, their competitiveness increased. Did this swing in competitiveness occur primarily because Canadian management fell down on the job in the late 1980s and early 1990s and then got its act together afterward? Not really. Canadian business became less competitive in the late 1980s and early 1990s because Canadian dollars became worth more in terms of U.S. dollars, making Canadian goods more expensive relative to U.S. goods. By the late 1990s and early 2000s, the value of the Canadian dollar had fallen appreciably from its highs in the late 1980s, making Canadian goods cheaper and Canadian businesses more competitive.

The price of one currency in terms of another (say, euros per Canadian dollar) is called the **exchange rate**. As you can see in Figure 18-1, exchange rates are highly volatile. The exchange rate affects the economy and our daily lives because when the Canadian dollar becomes more valuable relative to foreign currencies, foreign goods become cheaper for Canadians and Canadian goods become more expensive for foreigners. When the Canadian dollar falls in value, foreign goods become more expensive for Canadians and Canadian goods become cheaper for foreigners.

Fluctuations in the exchange rate also affect both inflation and output, and are an important concern to monetary policymakers. When the Canadian dollar falls in value, the higher prices of imported goods feed directly into a higher price level and inflation. A declining Canadian dollar, which makes Canadian goods cheaper for foreigners, increases the demand for Canadian goods and leads to higher production and output.

We begin our study of international finance by examining the **foreign exchange market**, the financial market where exchange rates are determined.

FOREIGN EXCHANGE MARKET

Most countries of the world have their own currencies: Canada has its dollar; the European Monetary Union, its euro; Brazil, its real; and China, its yuan. Trade between countries involves the mutual exchange of different currencies (or, more usually, assets denominated in different currencies). When a Canadian firm buys foreign goods, services, or financial

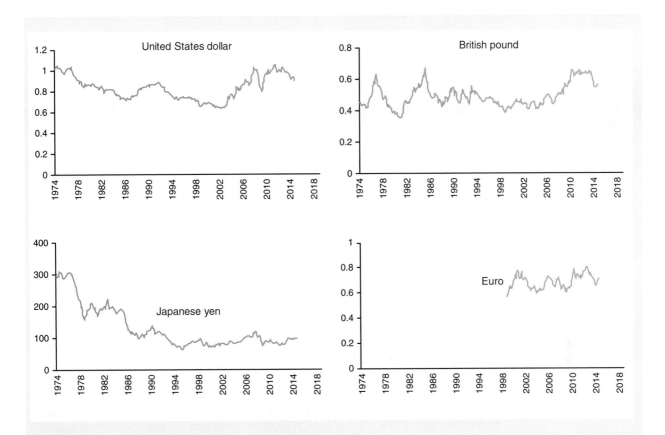

FIGURE 18-1   Canadian Exchange Rates, 1974–2014

Exchange rates are highly volatile. Note that a decline in these plots means a weakening of the Canadian dollar, and an increase indicates a strengthening of the Canadian dollar.

Source: Statistics Canada CANSIM II series V37426, V37430, V37456, and V21570998.

assets, for example, Canadian dollars (typically, assets denominated in Canadian dollars) must be exchanged for foreign currency (assets denominated in the foreign currency).

The trading of currency and assets denominated in particular currencies takes place in the foreign exchange market. Transactions conducted in the foreign exchange market determine the rates at which currencies are exchanged, which in turn determine the cost of purchasing foreign goods and financial assets.

What Are Foreign Exchange Rates?

There are two kinds of exchange rate transactions. The predominant ones, called **spot transactions**, involve the immediate (two-day) exchange of bank deposits. **Forward transactions** involve the exchange of bank deposits at some specified future date. The **spot exchange rate** is the exchange rate for the spot transaction, and the **forward exchange rate** is the exchange rate for the forward transaction.

When a currency increases in value, it experiences **appreciation**; when it falls in value and is worth fewer Canadian dollars, it undergoes **depreciation**. At the beginning of 1999, for example, the euro was valued at 1.76 Canadian dollars; on November 11,

2014, it was valued at 1.41 dollars, as indicated in the Following the Financial News box, Foreign Exchange Rates. The euro *depreciated* by 19.89%: $(1.41 - 1.76)/1.76 = -0.19 = 19\%$. Equivalently, we could say that the Canadian dollar, which went from a value of 0.57 euros per dollar at the beginning of 1999 to a value of 0.71 euros per dollar on November 11, 2014, *appreciated* by 24%: $(0.71 - 0.57)/0.71 = 0.19 = 19\%$.

Why Are Exchange Rates Important?

Exchange rates are important because they affect the relative price of domestic and foreign goods. The dollar price of French goods to a Canadian is determined by the interaction of two factors: the price of French goods in euros and the euro/dollar exchange rate.

Suppose that Wanda the Winetaster, a Canadian, decides to buy a bottle of 1961 (a very good year) Château Lafite Rothschild to complete her wine cellar. If the price of the wine in France is 1000 euros and the exchange rate is $1.32 to the euro, the wine will cost Wanda $1320 (1000 euros × $1.32/euro).[1] Now suppose that Wanda delays her purchase by two months, at which time the euro has appreciated to $1.50 per euro. If the domestic price of the bottle of Lafite Rothschild remains 1000 euros, its dollar cost will have risen from $1320 to $1500.

The same currency appreciation, however, makes the price of foreign goods in that country less expensive. At an exchange rate of $1.32 per euro, a Dell computer priced at $2000 costs Pierre the Programmer 1515 euros; if the exchange rate increases to $1.50 per euro, the computer will cost him only 1333 euros.

A depreciation of the euro lowers the cost of French goods in Canada but raises the cost of Canadian goods in France. If the euro drops in value to $1.20, Wanda's bottle of Lafite Rothschild will cost her only $1200 instead of $1320, and the Dell computer will cost Pierre 1667 euros rather than 1515.

Such reasoning leads to the following conclusion: **when a country's currency appreciates (rises in value relative to other currencies), the country's goods abroad become more expensive and foreign goods in that country become cheaper (holding domestic prices constant in the two countries). Conversely, when a country's currency depreciates, its goods abroad become cheaper and foreign goods in that country become more expensive.**

---

[1]Throughout this book we use the symbol $ for the Canadian dollar. We denote the United States dollar using the symbol US$.

Depreciation of a currency makes it easier for domestic manufacturers to sell their goods abroad and makes foreign goods less competitive in domestic markets. From 2002 to 2013, the appreciating Canadian dollar hurt Canadian industries trying to sell more goods, but helped Canadian consumers because foreign goods were less expensive. The price of French wine and cheese and the cost of vacationing abroad fell as a result of the strong Canadian dollar.

How Is Foreign Exchange Traded?

You cannot go to a centralized location to watch exchange rates being determined; currencies are not traded on exchanges such as the Toronto Stock Exchange. Instead, the foreign exchange market is organized as an over-the-counter market in which several hundred dealers (mostly banks) stand ready to buy and sell assets denominated in foreign currencies. Because these dealers are in constant telephone and computer contact, the market is very competitive; in effect, it functions no differently from a centralized market.

An important point to note is that while banks, companies, and governments talk about buying and selling currencies in foreign exchange markets, they do not take a fistful of dollars and sell them for British pound notes. Rather, most trades involve the buying and selling of assets denominated in different currencies. So when we say that a bank is buying euros in the foreign exchange market, what we actually mean is that the bank is buying *assets denominated in euros*. The volume in this market is colossal, exceeding $4 trillion per day.

Trades in the foreign exchange market consist of transactions in excess of $1 million. The market that determines the exchange rates shown in the Following the Financial News box is not where one would buy foreign currency for a trip abroad. Instead, we buy foreign currency in the retail market from dealers such as Thomas Cook or from banks. Because retail prices are higher than wholesale, when we buy foreign exchange, we obtain fewer units of foreign currency per dollar—that is, we pay a higher price for foreign currency—than the exchange rates quoted in the newspaper.

EXCHANGE RATES IN THE LONG RUN

Like the price of any good or asset in a free market, exchange rates are determined by the interaction of supply and demand. To simplify our analysis of exchange rates in a free market, we divide it into two parts. First, we examine how exchange rates are determined in the long run; then we use our knowledge of the long-run determinants of the exchange rate to help us understand how they are determined in the short run.

Law of One Price

The starting point for understanding how exchange rates are determined is a simple idea called the **law of one price**: if two countries produce an identical good and transportation costs and trade barriers are very low, the price of the good should be the same throughout the world no matter which country produces it. Suppose that Canadian steel costs $100 per tonne and identical Japanese steel costs 10 000 yen per tonne. For the law of one price to hold true, the exchange rate between the yen and the dollar must be 100 yen per dollar ($0.01 per yen) so that one tonne of Canadian steel sells for 10 000 yen in Japan (the price of Japanese steel) and one tonne of Japanese steel sells for $100 in Canada (the price of Canadian steel). If the exchange rate were 200 yen to the dollar, Japanese steel would sell for $50 per tonne in Canada or half the price of Canadian steel, and Canadian steel would sell for 20 000 yen per tonne in Japan, twice the price of

Japanese steel. Because Canadian steel would be more expensive than Japanese steel in both countries and is identical to Japanese steel, the demand for Canadian steel would go to zero. Given a fixed dollar price for Canadian steel, the resulting excess supply of Canadian steel will be eliminated only if the exchange rate falls to 100 yen per dollar, making the price of Canadian steel and Japanese steel the same in both countries.

Theory of Purchasing Power Parity

One of the most prominent theories of how exchange rates are determined is the **theory of purchasing power parity (PPP)**. It states that exchange rates between any two currencies will adjust to reflect changes in the price levels of the two countries. The theory of PPP is simply an application of the law of one price to national price levels rather than to individual prices. Suppose that the yen price of Japanese steel rises 10% (to 11 000 yen) relative to the dollar price of Canadian steel (unchanged at $100). For the law of one price to hold, the exchange rate must rise to 110 yen to the dollar, a 10% appreciation of the dollar. Applying the law of one price to the price levels in the two countries produces the theory of purchasing power parity, which maintains that if the Japanese price level rises 10% relative to the Canadian price level, the dollar will appreciate by 10%.

Another way of thinking about purchasing power parity is through a concept called the **real exchange rate**, the rate at which domestic goods can be exchanged for foreign goods. In effect, it is the price of domestic goods relative to the price of foreign goods denominated in the domestic currency. For example, if a basket of goods in Toronto costs $50, while the cost of the same basket of goods in Tokyo costs $75 because it costs 7500 yen while the exchange rate is at 100 yen per dollar, then the real exchange rate is 0.66 (=50/$75). The real exchange rate is below 1.0, indicating that it is cheaper to buy a basket of goods in Canada than in Japan. It is the real exchange rate that indicates whether a currency is relatively cheap or not. Another way of describing PPP is to say that the real exchange rate is always equal to 1.0, so that the purchasing power of the dollar is the same as the purchasing power of other currencies such as the yen or the euro.

As our Canadian/Japanese example demonstrates, the theory of PPP suggests that if one country's price level rises relative to another's, its currency should depreciate (the other country's currency should appreciate). As you can see in Figure 18-2, this prediction is borne out in the long run. Yet, as the same figure indicates, PPP theory often has little predictive power in the short run. So even though PPP theory provides some guidance to the long-run movement of exchange rates, it is not perfect and in the short run is a particularly poor predictor. What explains PPP theory's failure to predict well?

Why the Theory of Purchasing Power Parity Cannot Fully Explain Exchange Rates

The PPP conclusion that exchange rates are determined solely by changes in relative price levels rests on the assumption that all goods are identical in both countries and that transportation costs and trade barriers are very low. When this assumption is true, the law of one price states that the relative prices of all these goods (that is, the relative price level between the two countries) will determine the exchange rate. The assumption that goods are identical may not be too unreasonable for Canadian and Japanese steel, but is it a reasonable assumption for Canadian and Japanese cars? Is a Toyota the equivalent of a Chevrolet?

Because Toyotas and Chevys are obviously not identical, their prices do not have to be equal. Toyotas might be more expensive relative to Chevys, and both Canadians and Japanese will still purchase Toyotas. Because the law of one price does not hold for all

FIGURE 18-2   Purchasing Power Parity, Canada/United States, 1973–2014

Source: Statistics Canada CANSIM series V37426, and Federal Reserve Bank of St. Louis, FRED database: http://research.stlouisfed.org/fred2/.

goods, a rise in the price of Toyotas relative to Chevys will not necessarily mean that the yen must depreciate by the amount of the relative price increase of Toyotas over Chevys.

Furthermore, PPP theory does not take into account that many goods and services (whose prices are included in a measure of a country's price level) are not traded across borders. Housing, land, and services such as restaurant meals, haircuts, and golf lessons are not traded goods. So even though the prices of these items might rise and lead to a higher price level relative to another country's, the exchange rate would experience little direct effect.

Factors That Affect Exchange Rates in the Long Run

In the long run, four major factors affect the exchange rate: relative price levels, trade barriers, preferences for domestic versus foreign goods, and productivity. We examine how each of these factors affects the exchange rate while holding the others constant.

The basic reasoning proceeds along the following lines: anything that increases the demand for domestically produced goods that are traded relative to foreign-traded goods tends to appreciate the domestic currency because domestic goods will continue to sell well even when the value of the domestic currency is higher. Similarly, anything that increases the demand for foreign goods relative to domestic goods tends to depreciate the domestic currency because domestic goods will continue to sell well only if the value of the domestic currency is lower. In other words, *if a factor increases the demand for domestic goods relative to foreign goods, the domestic currency will appreciate; if a factor decreases the relative demand for domestic goods, the domestic currency will depreciate*.

Relative Price Levels   In line with PPP theory, when prices of Canadian goods rise (holding prices of foreign goods constant), the demand for Canadian goods falls and the dollar tends to depreciate so that Canadian goods can still sell well. By contrast, if prices of Japanese goods rise so that the relative prices of Canadian goods fall, the demand for Canadian goods increases, and the dollar tends to appreciate because Canadian goods will continue to sell well even with a higher value of the domestic currency. *In the long run, a rise in a country's price level (relative to the foreign price level) causes its currency to depreciate, and a fall in the country's relative price level causes its currency to appreciate*.

Trade Barriers   Barriers to free trade such as **tariffs** (taxes on imported goods) and **quotas** (restrictions on the quantity of foreign goods that can be imported) can affect the exchange rate. Suppose that Canada increases its tariff or puts a lower quota on Japanese cars. These increases in trade barriers increase the demand for Canadian cars, and the dollar tends to appreciate because Canadian cars will still sell well even with a higher value of the dollar. *Increasing trade barriers causes a country's currency to appreciate in the long run.*

Preferences for Domestic versus Foreign Goods   If the Japanese develop an appetite for Canadian goods—say, for Bombardier's high-speed trains and Canadian beef and pork—the increased demand for Canadian goods (exports) tends to appreciate the dollar because the Canadian goods will continue to sell well even at a higher value for the dollar. Likewise, if Canadians decide that they prefer Japanese cars to Canadian cars, the increased demand for Japanese goods (imports) tends to depreciate the dollar. *Increased demand for a country's exports causes its currency to appreciate in the long run; conversely, increased demand for imports causes the domestic currency to depreciate.*

Productivity   When productivity in a country rises, it tends to rise in domestic sectors that produce traded goods rather than nontraded goods. Higher productivity is therefore associated with a decline in the price of domestically produced traded goods relative to foreign-traded goods. As a result, the demand for domestically traded goods rises, and the domestic currency tends to appreciate. If, however, a country's productivity lags behind that of other countries, its traded goods become relatively more expensive, and the currency tends to depreciate. In the long run, as a country becomes more productive relative to other countries, its currency appreciates.[2]

Our long-run theory of exchange rate behaviour is summarized in Table 18-1. We use the convention that the exchange rate E is quoted such that an appreciation of the domestic

TABLE 18-1	Factors That Affect Exchange Rates in the Long Run	
Factor	**Change in Factor**	**Response of the Exchange Rate, E***
Domestic price level[†]	↑	↓
Trade barriers	↑	↑
Import demand	↑	↓
Export demand	↑	↑
Productivity[†]	↑	↑

* Units of foreign currency per Canadian dollar: ↑ indicates domestic currency appreciation; ↓, depreciation.
[†] Relative to other countries.

*Note:*Only increases (↑) in the factors are shown; the effects of decreases in the variables on the exchange rate are the opposite of those indicated in the "Response" column.

[2]A country might be so small that a change in productivity or the preferences for domestic or foreign goods would have no effect on prices of these goods relative to foreign goods. In this case changes in productivity or changes in preferences for domestic or foreign goods affect the country's income but will not necessarily affect the value of the currency. In our analysis, we are assuming that these factors can affect relative prices and consequently the exchange rate.

currency corresponds to a rise in the exchange rate. In the case of Canada, this means that we are quoting the exchange rate as units of foreign currency, say, euros, per dollar.[3]

EXCHANGE RATES IN THE SHORT RUN: A SUPPLY AND DEMAND ANALYSIS

We have developed a theory of the long-run behaviour of exchange rates. However, because factors driving long-run changes in exchange rates move slowly over time, if we are to understand why exchange rates exhibit such large changes (sometimes several percentage points) from day to day, we must develop a supply and demand analysis of how current exchange rates (spot exchange rates) are determined in the short run.

The key to understanding the short-run behaviour of exchange rates is to recognize that an exchange rate tells us the price at which domestic assets (those denominated in the domestic currency, which includes domestic bank deposits) trade for foreign assets (those denominated in the foreign currency, which includes foreign bank deposits). Because the exchange rate is the price of one asset in terms of another, the natural way to investigate the short-run determination of exchange rates is to use an asset-market approach that relies heavily on the theory of portfolio choice developed in Chapter 5. As you will see, however, the long-run determinants of the exchange rate we have just outlined also play an important role in the short-run asset-market approach.

In the past, supply and demand approaches to exchange rate determination emphasized the role of import and export demand. The more modern asset-market approach used here emphasizes stocks of assets rather than the flows of exports and imports over short periods, because export and import transactions are quite small relative to the amount of domestic and foreign assets at any given time. For example, foreign exchange transactions in Canada each year are well over 25 times greater than the amount of Canadian exports and imports. Thus over short periods such as a year, decisions to hold domestic or foreign assets play a much greater role in exchange rate determination than the demand for exports and imports does.

Supply Curve for Domestic Assets

We start by discussing the supply curve. In this analysis we treat Canada as the home country, so domestic assets are denominated in Canadian dollars. For simplicity, we use euros to stand for any foreign country's currency, so foreign assets are denominated in euros.

The quantity of dollar assets supplied is primarily the quantity of bank deposits, bonds, and equities in Canada and for all practical purposes we can take this amount as fixed with respect to the exchange rate. The quantity supplied at any exchange rate does not change, so the supply curve, S, is vertical, as shown in Figure 18-3.

Demand Curve for Domestic Assets

The demand curve traces out the quantity demanded at each current exchange rate by holding everything else constant, particularly the expected future value of the exchange

---

[3]Exchange rates can be quoted either as units of foreign currency per domestic currency or alternatively as units of domestic currency per foreign currency. In academic writing, many economists quote exchange rates as units of domestic currency per foreign currency so that an appreciation of the domestic currency is portrayed as a fall in the exchange rate. The opposite convention is used in the text here because it is more intuitive to think of an appreciation of the domestic currency as a rise in the exchange rate.

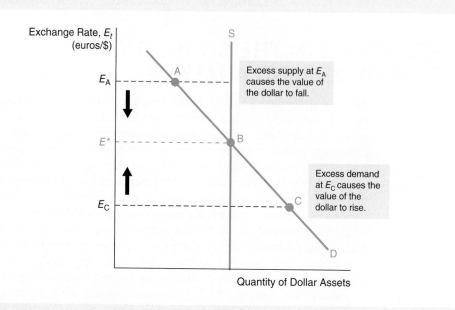

FIGURE 18-3 **Equilibrium in the Foreign Exchange Market**

Equilibrium in the foreign exchange market occurs at point B, the intersection of the demand curve D and the supply curve S at an exchange rate of E*.

rate. We write the current exchange rate (the spot exchange rate) as E_t, and the expected exchange rate for the next period as E_{t+1}^e. As the theory of portfolio choice suggests, the most important determinant of the quantity of domestic (dollar) assets demanded is the relative expected return of domestic assets. Let's see what happens as the current exchange rate, E_t, falls.

Suppose we start at point A in Figure 18-3 where the current exchange rate is at E_A. With the future expected value of the exchange rate held constant at E_{t+1}^e, a lower value of the exchange rate, say, at E*, implies that the dollar is more likely to rise in value, that is appreciate. The greater the expected rise (appreciation) of the dollar, the higher is the relative expected return on dollar (domestic) assets. The theory of portfolio choice then tells us that because dollar assets are now more desirable to hold, the quantity of dollar assets demanded will rise, as is shown by point B in Figure 18-3. If the current exchange rate falls even further to E_C, there is an even higher expected appreciation of the dollar, a higher expected return, and therefore an even greater quantity of dollar assets demanded. This is shown in point C in Figure 18-3. The resulting demand curve, D, which connects these points, is downward-sloping, indicating that at lower current values of the dollar (everything else being equal), the quantity demanded of dollar assets is higher.

Equilibrium in the Foreign Exchange Market

As in the usual supply and demand analysis, the market is in equilibrium when the quantity of dollar assets demanded equals the quantity supplied. In Figure 18-3, equilibrium occurs at point B, the intersection of the demand and supply curves. At point B, the exchange rate is E^*.

Suppose that the exchange rate is at E_A, which is higher than the equilibrium exchange rate of E^*. As we can see in Figure 18-3, the quantity of dollar assets supplied is then greater than the quantity demanded, a condition of excess supply. Given that more people want to sell dollar assets than want to buy them, the value of the dollar will fall. As long as the exchange rate remains above the equilibrium exchange rate, there will continue to be an excess supply of dollar assets, and the dollar will fall in value until it reaches the equilibrium exchange rate of E^*.

Similarly, if the exchange rate is less than the equilibrium exchange rate at E_C, the quantity of dollar assets demanded will exceed the quantity supplied, a condition of excess demand. Given that more people want to buy dollar assets than want to sell them, the value of the dollar will rise until the excess demand disappears and the value of the dollar is again at the equilibrium exchange rate of E^*.

EXPLAINING CHANGES IN EXCHANGE RATES

The supply and demand analysis of the foreign exchange market illustrates how and why exchange rates change.[4] We have simplified this analysis by assuming the amount of dollar assets is fixed: the supply curve is vertical at a given quantity and does not shift. Under this assumption, we need look at only those factors that shift the demand curve for dollar assets to explain how exchange rates change over time.

Shifts in the Demand for Domestic Assets

As we have seen, the quantity of domestic (dollar) assets demanded depends on the relative expected return of dollar assets. To see how the demand curve shifts, we need to determine how the quantity demanded changes, holding the current exchange rate, E_t, constant when other factors change.

For insight into which direction the demand curve shifts, suppose you are an investor who is considering putting funds into domestic (dollar) assets. When a factor changes, decide whether at a given level of the current exchange rate, holding all other variables constant, you would earn a higher or lower expected return on dollar assets versus foreign assets. This decision tells you whether you want to hold more or fewer dollar assets and thus whether the quantity demanded increases or decreases at each level of the exchange rate. Knowing the direction of the change in the quantity demanded at each exchange rate tells you which way the demand curve shifts. In other words, if the relative expected return of dollar assets rises, holding the current exchange rate constant, the demand curve shifts to the right. If the relative expected return falls, the demand curve shifts to the left.

Domestic Interest Rate, i^D

Suppose that dollar assets pay an interest rate of i^D. When the domestic interest rate on dollar assets i^D rises, holding the current exchange rate E_t and everything else constant, the return on dollar assets increases relative to

---

[4]How and why exchange rates change can also be modelled using the *interest parity condition*, an important concept in international finance that shows the relationship between domestic interest rates, foreign interest rates, and the expected appreciation of the domestic currency. The interest parity condition and how it explains the determination of exchange rates is discussed in an appendix to this chapter.

FIGURE 18-4   **Response to an Increase in the Domestic Interest Rate, i^D**

When the domestic interest rate i^D increases, the relative expected return on domestic (dollar) assets increases and the demand curve shifts to the right. The equilibrium exchange rate rises from E_1 to E_2.

foreign assets, so people will want to hold more dollar assets. The quantity of dollar assets demanded increases at every value of the exchange rate, as shown by the rightward shift of the demand curve in Figure 18-4 from D_1 to D_2. The new equilibrium is reached at point 2, the intersection of D_2 and S, and the equilibrium exchange rate rises from E_1 to E_2. *An increase in the domestic interest rate i^D shifts the demand curve for domestic assets, D, to the right and causes the domestic currency to appreciate (E↑).*

Conversely, if i^D falls, the relative expected return on dollar assets falls, the demand curve shifts to the left, and the exchange rate falls. *A decrease in the domestic interest rate i^D shifts the demand curve for domestic assets, D, to the left and causes the domestic currency to depreciate (E↓).*

Foreign Interest Rate, i^F

Suppose that the foreign asset pays an interest rate of i^F. When the foreign interest rate i^F rises, holding the current exchange rate and everything else constant, the return on foreign assets rises relative to dollar assets. Thus the relative expected return on dollar assets falls. Now people want to hold fewer dollar assets, and the quantity demanded decreases at every value of the exchange rate. This scenario is shown by the leftward shift of the demand curve in Figure 18-5 from D_1 to D_2. The new equilibrium is reached at point 2, when the value of the dollar has fallen. Conversely, a decrease in i^F raises the relative expected return on dollar assets, shifts the demand curve to the right, and raises the exchange rate. To summarize, *an increase in the foreign interest rate i^F shifts the demand curve D to the left and causes the domestic currency to depreciate; a fall in the foreign interest rate i^F shifts the demand curve D to the right and causes the domestic currency to appreciate.*

MyEconLab Mini-lecture

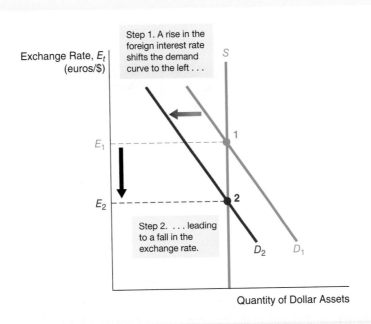

FIGURE 18-5 **Response to an Increase in the Foreign Interest Rate, i^F**

When the foreign interest rate i^F increases, the relative expected return on domestic (dollar) assets falls and the demand curve shifts to the left. The equilibrium exchange rate falls from E_1 to E_2.

Changes in The Expected Future Exchange Rate, E^e_{t+1}   Expectations about the future value of the exchange rate play an important role in shifting the current demand curve, because the demand for domestic assets, like the demand for any durable good, depends on the future resale price. Any factor that causes the expected future exchange rate, E^e_{t+1}, to rise increases the expected appreciation of the dollar. The result is a higher relative expected return on dollar assets, which increases the demand for dollar assets at every exchange rate, thereby shifting the demand curve to the right in Figure 18-6 from D_1 to D_2. The equilibrium exchange rate rises to point 2 at the intersection of the D_2 and S curves. *A rise in the expected future exchange rate, E^e_{t+1}, shifts the demand curve to the right and causes an appreciation of the domestic currency.* Using the same reasoning, *a fall in the expected future exchange rate, E^e_{t+1}, shifts the demand curve to the left and causes a depreciation of the currency*.

Earlier in the chapter we discussed the determinants of the exchange rate in the long run: the relative price level, relative trade barriers, import and export demand, and relative productivity (refer to Table 18-1). These four factors influence the expected future exchange rate. The theory of purchasing power parity suggests that if a higher Canadian price level relative to the foreign price level is expected to persist, the dollar will depreciate in the long run. A higher expected relative Canadian price level should thus have a tendency to lower E^e_{t+1}, lower the relative expected return on dollar assets, shift the demand curve to the left, and lower the current exchange rate.

Similarly, the other long-run determinants of the exchange rate can influence the relative expected return on dollar assets and the current exchange rate. Briefly, the

MyEconLab Mini-lecture

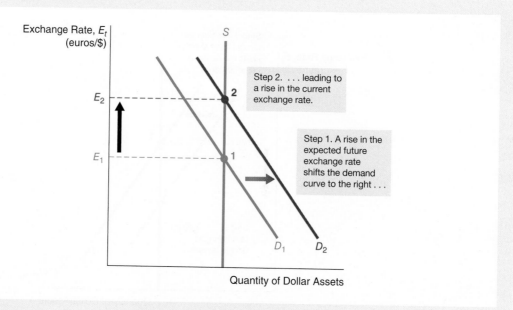

FIGURE 18-6 **Response to an Increase in the Expected Future Exchange Rate, E^e_{t+1}**

When the expected future exchange rate increases, the relative expected return on domestic (dollar) assets rises and the demand curve shifts to the right. The equilibrium exchange rate rises from E_1 to E_2.

following changes, all of which increase the demand for domestic goods relative to foreign goods, will raise E^e_{t+1}: (1) expectations of a fall in the Canadian price level relative to the foreign price level; (2) expectations of higher Canadian trade barriers relative to foreign trade barriers; (3) expectations of lower Canadian import demand; (4) expectations of higher foreign demand for Canadian exports; and (5) expectations of higher Canadian productivity relative to foreign productivity. By increasing E^e_{t+1}, all of these changes increase the relative expected return on dollar assets, shift the demand curve to the right, and cause an appreciation of the domestic currency, the dollar.

Recap: Factors That Change the Exchange Rate

Table 18-2 outlines all the factors that shift the demand curve for domestic assets and thereby cause the exchange rate to change. Shifts in the demand curve occur when one factor changes, holding everything else constant, including the current exchange rate. Again, the theory of asset demand tells us that changes in the relative expected return on dollar assets are the source of shifts in the demand curve.

Let's review what happens when each of the seven factors in Table 18-2 changes. Remember that to understand which direction the demand curve shifts, consider what happens to the relative expected return on dollar assets when the factor changes. If the relative expected return rises, holding the current exchange rate constant, the demand curve shifts to the right. If the relative expected return falls, the demand curve shifts to the left.

TABLE 18-2	Factors That Shift the Demand Curve for Domestic Assets and Affect the Exchange Rate

Factor	Change in Factor	Change in Quantity Demanded of Domestic Assets at Each Exchange Rate	Response of Exchange Rate, E_t	
1. Domestic interest rate, i^D	↑	↑	↑	E_t, S, E_2, E_1, D_1 D_2, Dollar Assets
2. Foreign interest rate, i^F	↑	↓	↓	E_t, S, E_1, E_2, D_2 D_1, Dollar Assets
3. Expected domestic price level*	↑	↓	↓	E_t, S, E_1, E_2, D_2 D_1, Dollar Assets
4. Expected trade barriers*	↑	↑	↑	E_t, S, E_2, E_1, D_1 D_2, Dollar Assets
5. Expected import demand	↑	↓	↓	E_t, S, E_1, E_2, D_2 D_1, Dollar Assets
6. Expected export demand	↑	↑	↑	E_t, S, E_2, E_1, D_1 D_2, Dollar Assets
7. Expected productivity*	↑	↑	↑	E_t, S, E_2, E_1, D_1 D_2, Dollar Assets

*Relative to other countries.

Note: Only increases (↑) in the factors are shown; the effects of decreases in the variables on the exchange rate are the opposite of those indicated in the "Response" column.

1. When the interest rates on domestic assets i^D rise, the expected return on dollar assets rises at each exchange rate and so the quantity demanded increases. The demand curve therefore shifts to the right, and the equilibrium exchange rate rises, as is shown in the first row of Table 18-2.

2. When the foreign interest rate i^F rises, the return on foreign assets rises, so the relative expected return on dollar assets falls. The quantity demanded of dollar assets then falls, the demand curve shifts to the left, and the exchange rate declines, as in the second row of Table 18-2.

3. When the expected price level is higher, our analysis of the long-run determinants of the exchange rate indicates that the value of the dollar will fall in the future. The expected return on dollar assets thus falls, the quantity demanded declines, the demand curve shifts to the left, and the exchange rate falls, as in the third row of Table 18-2.

4. With higher expected trade barriers, the value of the dollar is higher in the long run and the expected return on dollar assets is higher. The quantity demanded of dollar assets thus rises, the demand curve shifts to the right, and the exchange rate rises, as in the fourth row of Table 18-2.

5. When expected import demand rises, we expect the exchange rate to depreciate in the long run, so the expected return on dollar assets falls. The quantity demanded of dollar assets at each value of the current exchange rate therefore falls, the demand curve shifts to the left, and the exchange rate declines, as in the fifth row of Table 18-2.

6. When expected export demand rises, the opposite occurs because the exchange rate is expected to appreciate in the long run. The expected return on dollar assets rises, the demand curve shifts to the right, and the exchange rate rises, as in the sixth row of Table 18-2.

7. With higher expected domestic productivity, the exchange rate is expected to appreciate in the long run, so the expected return on domestic assets rises. The quantity demanded at each exchange rate therefore rises, the demand curve shifts to the right, and the exchange rate rises, as in the seventh row of Table 18-2.

APPLICATION Effects of Changes in Interest Rates on the Equilibrium Exchange Rate

Our analysis has revealed the factors that affect the value of the equilibrium exchange rate. Now we use this analysis to take a closer look at the response of the exchange rate to changes in interest rates and money growth.

Changes in domestic interest rates i^D are often cited as a major factor affecting exchange rates. For example, we see headlines in the financial press like this one: "Dollar Recovers as Interest Rates Edge Upward." But is the view presented in this headline always correct?

Not necessarily, because to analyze the effects of interest-rate changes, we must carefully distinguish the sources of the changes. The Fisher equation (Chapter 4) states that a nominal interest rate such as i^D equals the *real* interest rate plus expected inflation: $i = r + \pi^e$. The Fisher equation thus indicates that the interest rate i^D can change for two reasons: either the real interest rate i_r changes or the expected inflation rate π^e changes. The effect on the exchange rate is quite different, depending on which of these two factors is the source of the change in the nominal interest rate.

Suppose that the domestic real interest rate increases so that the nominal interest rate i^D rises while expected inflation remains unchanged. In this case, it is reasonable to assume that the expected appreciation of the dollar will be unchanged because expected inflation is unchanged. In this case, the increase in i^D increases the relative expected return on dollar assets, increases the quantity of dollar assets demanded at each level of the exchange rate, and shifts the demand curve to the right. We end up with the situation depicted in Figure 18-4, which analyzes an increase in i^D, holding everything else constant. Our model of the foreign exchange market produces the following result: *when domestic real interest rates rise, the domestic currency appreciates*.

When the nominal interest rate rises because of an increase in expected inflation, we get a different result from the one shown in Figure 18-4. The rise in expected domestic inflation leads to a decline in the expected appreciation of the dollar, which is typically thought to be larger than the increase in the domestic interest rate i^D. As a result, at any given exchange rate, the relative expected return on domestic (dollar) assets falls, the demand curve shifts to the left, and the exchange rate falls from E_1 to E_2 as shown in Figure 18-7. Our analysis leads to this conclusion: *when domestic interest rates rise due to an expected increase in inflation, the domestic currency depreciates*.

Because this conclusion is completely different from the one reached when the rise in the domestic interest rate is associated with a higher real interest rate, we must always distinguish between *real* and *nominal* measures when analyzing the effects of interest rates on exchange rates.

MyEconLab Mini-lecture

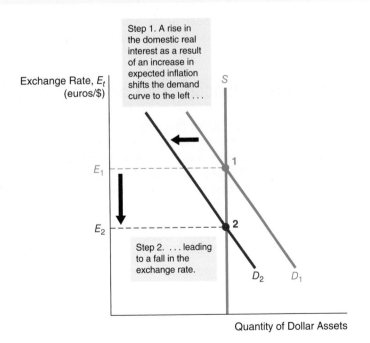

FIGURE 18-7 **Effect of a Rise in the Domestic Interest Rate as a Result of an Increase in Expected Inflation**

Because a rise in domestic expected inflation leads to a decline in expected dollar appreciation that is larger than the increase in the domestic interest rate, the relative expected return on domestic (dollar) assets falls. The demand curve shifts to the left, and the equilibrium exchange rate falls from E_1 to E_2.

APPLICATION   Why Are Exchange Rates So Volatile?

The high volatility of foreign exchange rates surprises many people. Thirty or so years ago, economists generally believed that allowing exchange rates to be determined in the free market would not lead to large fluctuations in their values. Recent experience has proved them wrong. If we return to Figure 18-1, we see that exchange rates over the 1974–2014 period have been very volatile.

The asset-market approach to exchange rate determination that we have outlined in this chapter gives a straightforward explanation of volatile exchange rates. Because expected appreciation of the domestic currency affects the expected return on foreign deposits, expectations about the price level, inflation, trade barriers, productivity, import demand, export demand, and the money supply play important roles in determining the exchange rate. When expectations about any of these variables change, as they do—and often at that—our model indicates that there will be an immediate effect on the expected return on foreign deposits and therefore on the exchange rate. Because expectations on all these variables change with just about every bit of news that appears, it is not surprising that the exchange rate is volatile. Because earlier models of exchange rate behaviour focused on goods markets rather than asset markets, they did not emphasize changing expectations as a source of exchange-rate movements, and so these earlier models could not predict substantial fluctuations in exchange rates. The failure of earlier models to explain volatility is one reason why they are no longer so popular. The more modern approach developed here emphasizes that the foreign exchange market is like any other asset market in which expectations of the future matter. The foreign exchange market, like other asset markets such as the stock market, displays substantial price volatility, and foreign exchange rates are notoriously hard to forecast.

APPLICATION   The Global Financial Crisis and the U.S. Dollar

With the start of the global financial crisis in August 2007, the U.S. dollar began an accelerated decline in value, falling by 9% against the euro, and 6% against a wider basket of currencies until mid-July of 2008. After hitting an all-time low against the euro on July 11, the U.S. dollar suddenly shot upward—by over 20% against the euro and 15% against a wider basket of currencies by the end of October. What is the relationship between the global financial crisis and these large swings in the value of the U.S. dollar?

During 2007, the negative effects of the financial crisis on economic activity were mostly confined to the United States. The Federal Reserve acted aggressively to lower interest rates to counter the contractionary effects, decreasing the federal funds rate target by 325 basis points from September of 2007 to April of 2008. In contrast, other central banks like the ECB did not see the need to lower interest rates, particularly because high energy prices had led to a surge in inflation. The relative expected return on dollar assets thus declined, shifting the demand curve for dollar assets to the left, as in Figure 18-5, leading to a decline in the equilibrium exchange rate. Our analysis of the foreign exchange market thus explains why the early phase of the global financial crisis led to a decline in the value of the dollar.

We now turn to the rise in the value of the U.S. dollar. Starting in the summer of 2008, the effects of the global financial crisis on economic activity began to spread more widely throughout the world. Foreign central banks started to cut interest rates, with the expectation that further rate cuts would follow, as indeed did occur. The expected decline in foreign interest rates then increased the relative expected return of U.S. dollar assets, leading to a rightward shift in the demand curve, and a rise in the value of the U.S. dollar, as shown in Figure 18-4. Another factor driving the U.S. dollar upwards was the "flight to quality," when the global financial crisis reached a particularly virulent stage in September and October of 2008. Both Americans and foreigners wanted to put their money in the safest assets possible: U.S. Treasury securities. The resulting increase in the demand for U.S. dollar assets provided an additional reason for the demand curve for U.S. dollar assets to shift out to the right, thereby helping to produce a sharp appreciation of the U.S. dollar. ◆

MyEconLab

MyEconLab is an online homework and tutorial system that puts you in control of your own learning with study and practice tools directly correlated to this chapter's content. Visit MyEconLab to access the eText, the Questions and Applied Problems with answers, as well as additional assessment. You will also find web chapters, mini-lectures, appendices, mini-cases, videos, glossary flashcards, news feeds, CANSIM data, and graphing tools.

SUMMARY

1. Foreign exchange rates (the price of one country's currency in terms of another's) are important because they affect the price of domestically produced goods sold abroad and the cost of foreign goods bought domestically.

2. The theory of purchasing power parity suggests that long-run changes in the exchange rate between two countries' currencies are determined by changes in the relative price levels in the two countries. Other factors that affect exchange rates in the long run are tariffs and quotas, import demand, export demand, and productivity.

3. In the short run, exchange rates are determined by changes in the relative expected return on domestic

assets, which cause the demand curve to shift. Any factor that changes the relative expected return on domestic assets will lead to changes in the exchange rate. Such factors include changes in the interest rates on domestic and foreign assets as well as changes in any of the factors that affect the long-run exchange rate and hence the expected future exchange rate. Changes in the money supply lead to exchange rate overshooting, causing the exchange rate to change by more in the short run than in the long run.

4. The asset-market approach to exchange rate determination can explain both the volatility of exchange rates and the rise of the dollar in the 1980–1984 period and its subsequent fall.

KEY TERMS

appreciation, p. 461
capital mobility, p. 483
depreciation, p. 461
exchange rate, p. 460
foreign exchange market, p. 460
forward exchange rate, p. 460

forward transaction, p. 461
interest parity condition, p. 481
law of one price, p. 463
quotas, p. 466
real exchange rate, p. 464
spot exchange rate, p. 461

spot transaction, p. 461
tariffs, p. 466
theory of purchasing power
  parity (PPP), p. 464

QUESTIONS

All questions are available in MyEconLab at **www.myeconlab.com**.

1. When the euro appreciates, are you more likely to drink Canadian or French wine?

2. "A country is always worse off when its currency is weak (falls in value)." Is this statement true, false, or uncertain? Explain your answer.

3. When the Canadian dollar depreciates, what happens to exports and imports in Canada?

4. If the Japanese price level rises by 5% relative to the price level in Canada, what does the theory of purchasing power parity predict will happen to the value of the Japanese yen in terms of Canadian dollars?

5. If the demand for a country's exports falls at the same time that tariffs on imports are raised, will the country's currency tend to appreciate or depreciate in the long run?

6. When the Bank of Canada conducts an expansionary monetary policy, what happens to the money supply? How does this affect the supply of dollar assets?

7. From 2009 to 2011, the economies of Australia and Switzerland suffered relatively mild effects from the global financial crisis. At the same time, many countries in the euro area were hit hard with high unemployment and burdened with unsustainably high government debts. How should this affect the euro/Swiss franc and euro/Australian dollar exchange rates?

8. In the mid- to late 1970s, the yen appreciated relative to the U.S. dollar even though Japan's inflation rate was higher than the inflation rate in the United States. How can this be explained by an improvement in the productivity of Japanese industry relative to American industry?

9. Suppose the governor of the Bank of Canada announces a new set of reforms which includes a new anti-inflation program. Assuming the announcement is believed by the public, what will happen to the exchange rate for the Canadian dollar?

10. If the British central bank lowers interest rates to reduce unemployment, what will happen to the value of the pound in the short run and the long run?

11. If the Indian government unexpectedly announces that it will be imposing higher tariffs on foreign goods one year from now, what will happen to the value of the Indian rupee today?

12. If nominal interest rates in Canada rise but real interest rates fall, predict what will happen to the Canadian exchange rate.

13. If Canadian auto companies make a breakthrough in automobile technology and are able to produce a car that gets 50 kilometres to the litre, what will happen to the Canadian exchange rate?

14. If Mexicans go on a spending spree and buy twice as much French perfume, Japanese TVs, English sweaters, Swiss watches, and Italian wine, what will happen to the value of the Mexican peso?

15. Through the summer and fall of 2008 as the global financial crisis began to take hold, international financial institutions and sovereign wealth funds significantly increased their purchases of U.S. Treasury securities as a safe haven investment. How should this affect U.S. dollar exchange rates?

16. In September 2012, the Federal Reserve announced a large-scale asset-purchase program (known as QE3) designed to lower intermediate and longer-term interest rates. What effect should this have had on the U.S. dollar/euro exchange rate?

APPLIED PROBLEMS

All applied problems are available in MyEconLab at **www.myeconlab.com**.

17. A German sports car is selling for 70 000 euros. What is the dollar price in Canada for the German car if the exchange rate is 0.90 euros per dollar?

18. If the Canadian dollar to U.S. dollar exchange rate is 1.28 and the British pound to U.S. dollar exchange rate is 0.62, what must the Canadian dollar to British pound exchange rate be?

19. The New Zealand dollar to U.S. dollar exchange rate is 1.36, and the British pound to U.S. dollar exchange rate

is 0.62. If you find that the British pound to New Zealand dollar were trading at 0.49, what would you do to earn a riskless profit?

20. In 1999, the euro was trading at US $0.90 per euro. If the euro is now trading at US $1.16 per euro, what is the percentage change in the euro's value? Is this an appreciation or depreciation?

21. If the price level recently increased by 20% in England while falling by 5% in Canada, how much must the exchange rate change if PPP holds? Assume that the current exchange rate is 0.55 pounds per dollar.

For Problems 22–24, use a graph of the foreign exchange market for dollars to illustrate the effects in each problem.

22. If expected inflation drops in Europe so that interest rates fall there, what will happen to the exchange rate for the Canadian dollar?

23. If the European central bank decides to pursue a contractionary monetary policy to fight inflation, what will happen to the value of the Canadian dollar?

24. If there is a strike in France, making it harder to buy French goods, what will happen to the value of the Canadian dollar?

DATA ANALYSIS PROBLEMS

Download data for these problems from MyEconLab *at* **www.myeconlab.com**.

1. Go to the CANSIM database and download monthly data from January 1974 to January 2015 (when applicable) on the Canadian-dollar-per-U.S.-dollar exchange rate (series V37426), the Canadian-dollar-per-British-pound exchange rate (series V37430), the Canadian-dollar-per-Japanese-yen exchange rate (series V37456), and the Canadian-dollar-per-euro exchange rate (series V21570998).

Calculate the mean and standard deviation as well as the maximum and minimum values for each series over the sample period.

2. Go to the St. Louis Federal Reserve FRED database, and find data on the daily dollar exchange rates for the euro (DEXUSEU), British pound (DEXUSUK), and Japanese yen (DEXJPUS). Also find data on the daily

three-month London Interbank Offer Rate, or LIBOR, for the United States dollar (USD3MTD156N), euro (EUR3MTD156N), British pound (GBP3MTD156N), and Japanese yen (JPY3MTD156N). LIBOR is a measure of interest rates denominated in each country's respective currency.

a. Calculate the difference between the LIBOR rate in the United States and the LIBOR rates in the three other countries using the data from one year ago and the most recent data available.

b. Based on the changes in interest rate differentials, do you expect the dollar to depreciate or appreciate against the other currencies?

c. Report the percentage change in the exchange rates over the past year. Are the results you predicted in part (b) consistent with the actual exchange rate behaviour?

WEB EXERCISES

1. The Bank of Canada maintains a website that lists the exchange rate between the Canadian dollar and many other currencies. Go to **www.bankofcanada.ca/rates/ exchange/10-year-converter/**. Find the exchange rate between the Canadian dollar and the euro for the past 40 weeks.

a. What has the percentage change in the euro/dollar exchange rate been in the past 40 weeks?

b. What has been the annual percentage change in the euro–dollar exchange rate for each year since the euro's introduction?

2. International travellers and businesspeople frequently need to accurately convert from one currency to another. It is often easy to find the rate needed to convert the Canadian dollar into another currency. It can be more difficult to find exchange rates between two non-Canadian currencies. Go to **www.xe.com/ ucc/full/**. This site lets you convert from any currency into any other currency. How many Lithuanian litas can you currently buy with one Chilean peso?

WEB REFERENCES

www.bankofcanada.ca/rates/exchange/10-year-converter

The Bank of Canada reports current and historical exchange rates for many countries.

http://fx.sauder.ubc.ca

The Pacific Exchange Rate Service at the University of British Columbia's Sauder School of Business provides information on how market conditions are affecting exchange rates and allows easy plotting of exchange rate data.

www.oecd.org/general/searchresults/?q=purchasing%20power%20parities

The purchasing power parities home page includes the PPP program overview, statistics, research, publications, and OECD meetings on PPP.

18

The Interest Parity Condition

All the results in the text can be derived with a concept that is widely used in international finance. The **interest parity condition** shows the relationship between domestic interest rates, foreign interest rates, and the expected appreciation of the domestic currency. To derive this condition, we examine how expected returns on domestic and foreign assets are compared.

COMPARING EXPECTED RETURNS ON DOMESTIC AND FOREIGN ASSETS

As in the chapter, we treat Canada as the home country, so domestic assets are denominated in dollars. For simplicity, we use euros to stand for any foreign country's currency, so foreign assets are denominated in euros. To illustrate further, suppose that dollar assets pay an interest rate of i^D and do not have any possible capital gains, so that they have an expected return payable in dollars of i^D. Similarly, foreign assets have an interest rate of i^F and an expected return payable in the foreign currency, euros, of i^F. To compare the expected returns on dollar assets and foreign assets, investors must convert the returns into the currency unit they use.

First, let us examine how François the Foreigner compares the returns on dollar assets and foreign assets denominated in his currency, the euro. When he considers the expected return on dollar assets in terms of euros, he recognizes that it does not equal i^D; instead, the expected return must be adjusted for any expected appreciation or depreciation of the dollar. If François expects the dollar to appreciate by 3%, for example, the expected return on dollar assets in terms of euros would be 3% higher than i^D because the dollar is expected to become worth 3% more in terms of euros. Thus, if the interest rate on dollar assets is 4%, with an expected 3% appreciation of the dollar, the expected return on dollar assets in terms of euros is 7%: the 4% interest rate plus the 3% expected appreciation of the dollar. Conversely, if the dollar were expected to depreciate by 3% over the year, the expected return on dollar assets in terms of euros would be only 1%: the 4% interest rate minus the 3% expected depreciation of the dollar.

Writing the current exchange rate (the spot exchange rate) as E_t and the expected exchange rate for the next period as E_{t+1}^e, the expected rate of appreciation of the dollar is $(E_{t+1}^e - E_t)/E_t$. Our reasoning indicates that the expected return on dollar assets R^D

in terms of foreign currency can be written as the sum of the interest rate on dollar assets plus the expected appreciation of the dollar.[1]

$$R^D \text{ in terms of euros} = i^D + \frac{E^e_{t+1} - E_t}{E_t}$$

However, François's expected return on foreign assets R^F in terms of euros is just i^F. Thus, in terms of euros, the relative expected return on dollar assets (that is, the difference between the expected return on dollar assets and euro assets) is calculated by subtracting i^F from the expression above to yield

$$\text{Relative } R^D = i^D - i^F + \frac{E^e_{t+1} - E_t}{E_t} \qquad \text{(Equation 1)}$$

As the relative expected return on dollar assets increases, foreigners will want to hold more dollar assets and fewer foreign assets.

Next, let us look at the decision to hold dollar assets versus euro assets from Peter the Canadian's point of view. Following the same reasoning we used to evaluate the decision for François, we know that the expected return on foreign assets R^F in terms of dollars is the interest rate on foreign assets i^F plus the expected appreciation of the foreign currency, equal to minus the expected appreciation of the dollar, $(E^e_{t+1} - E_t)/E_t$

$$R^F \text{ in terms of dollars} = i^F - \frac{E^e_{t+1} - E_t}{E_t}$$

If the interest rate on euro assets is 5%, for example, and the dollar is expected to appreciate by 3%, then the expected return on euro assets in terms of dollars is 2%. Peter earns the 5% interest rate, but he expects to lose 3% because he expects the euro to be worth 3% less in terms of dollars as a result of the dollar's appreciation.

Peter's expected return on the dollar assets R^D in terms of dollars is just i^D. Hence, in terms of dollars, the relative expected return on dollar assets is calculated by subtracting the expression just given from i^D to obtain

$$\text{Relative } R^D = i^D - \left(i^F - \frac{E^e_{t+1} - E_t}{E_t} \right) = i^D - i^F + \frac{E^e_{t+1} - E_t}{E_t}$$

This equation is the same as Equation 1 describing François's relative expected return on dollar assets (calculated in terms of euros). The key point here is that the relative

---

[1] This expression is actually an approximation of the expected return in terms of euros, which can be more precisely calculated by thinking how a foreigner invests in dollar assets. Suppose that François decides to put one euro into dollar assets. First he buys $1/E_t$ of Canadian dollar assets (recall that E_t, the exchange rate between dollar and euro assets, is quoted in euros per dollar), and at the end of the period he is paid $(1 + i^D)(1/E_t)$ in dollars. To convert this amount into the number of euros he expects to receive at the end of the period, he multiplies this quantity by E^e_{t+1}. François's expected return on his initial investment of one euro can thus be written as $(1 + i^D)(E^e_{t+1}/E_t)$ minus his initial investment of one euro:

$$(1 + i^D)\left(\frac{E^e_{t+1}}{E_t}\right) - 1$$

This expression can be rewritten as

$$i^D\left(\frac{E^e_{t+1}}{E_t}\right) + \frac{E^e_{t+1} - E_t}{E_t}$$

which is approximately equal to the expression in the text because, E^e_{t+1}/E_t is typically close to 1. To see this, consider the example in the text in which $i^D = 0.04$; $(E^e_{t+1} - E_t)/E_t = 0.03$, so $E^e_{t+1}/E_t = 1.03$. Then François's expected return on dollar assets is $(0.04 \times 1.03) + 0.03 = 0.0712 = 7.12\%$, rather than the 7% reported in the text.

expected return on dollar assets is the same—whether it is calculated by François in terms of euros or by Peter in terms of dollars. Thus, as the relative expected return on dollar assets increases, both foreigners and domestic residents respond in exactly the same way—both will want to hold more dollar assets and fewer foreign assets.

INTEREST PARITY CONDITION

We currently live in a world in which there is **capital mobility**: foreigners can easily purchase Canadian assets, and Canadians can easily purchase foreign assets. If there are few impediments to capital mobility and we are looking at assets that have similar risk and liquidity—say, foreign and Canadian bank deposits—then it is reasonable to assume that the assets are perfect substitutes (that is, equally desirable). When capital is mobile and when assets are perfect substitutes, if the expected return on dollar assets is above that on foreign assets, both foreigners and Canadians will want to hold only dollar assets and will be unwilling to hold foreign assets. Conversely, if the expected return on foreign assets is higher than on dollar assets, both foreigners and Canadians will not want to hold any dollar assets and will want to hold only foreign assets. For existing supplies of both dollar assets and foreign assets to be held, it must therefore be true that there is no difference in their expected returns; that is, the relative expected return in Equation 1 must equal zero. This condition can be rewritten as

$$i^D = i^F - \frac{E_{t+1}^e - E_t}{E_t} \qquad \text{(Equation 2)}$$

This equation, which is called the interest parity condition, states that the domestic interest rate equals the foreign interest rate minus the expected appreciation of the domestic currency. Equivalently, this condition can be stated in a more intuitive way: the domestic interest rate equals the foreign interest rate plus the expected appreciation of the foreign currency. If the domestic interest rate is higher than the foreign interest rate, there is a positive expected appreciation of the foreign currency, which compensates for the lower foreign interest rate. A domestic interest rate of 5% versus a foreign interest rate of 3% means that the expected appreciation of the foreign currency must be 2% (or, equivalently, that the expected depreciation of the dollar must be 2%).

There are several ways to look at the interest parity condition. First, recognize that interest parity means simply that the expected returns are the same on both dollar assets and foreign assets. To see this, note that the left side of the interest parity condition (Equation 2) is the expected return on dollar assets, while the right side is the expected return on foreign assets, both calculated in terms of a single currency, the Canadian dollar. Given our assumption that domestic and foreign assets are perfect substitutes (equally desirable), the interest parity condition is an equilibrium condition for the foreign exchange market. Only when the exchange rate is such that expected returns on domestic and foreign assets are equal—that is, when interest parity holds—investors will be willing to hold both domestic and foreign assets.

With some algebraic manipulation, we can rewrite the interest parity condition in Equation 2 as

$$E_t = \frac{E_{t+1}^e}{i^F - i^D + 1}$$

This equation produces exactly the same results that we find in the supply and demand analysis in the text: if i^D rises, the denominator falls and so E_t rises. If i^F rises, the denominator rises and so E_t falls. If E_{t+1}^e rises, the numerator rises and so E_t rises.

The International Financial System

Learning Objectives

After studying this chapter you should be able to

1. Use graphs and T-accounts to illustrate the distinctions between the effects of sterilized and unsterilized interventions on foreign exchange markets.

2. Interpret the relationships among the current account, the capital account, and the official reserve transaction balance.

3. Identify the mechanisms for maintaining a fixed exchange rate, and assess the challenges faced by fixed exchange rate regimes.

4. Summarize the advantages and disadvantages of capital controls.

5. Assess the role of the IMF as an international lender of last resort.

6. Identify the ways in which international monetary policy and exchange rate arrangements can affect domestic monetary policy operations.

7. Summarize the advantages and disadvantages of exchange-rate targeting.

PREVIEW

As the Canadian economy and the economies of the rest of the world grow more interdependent, a country's monetary policy can no longer be conducted without taking international considerations into account. In this chapter, we examine how international financial transactions and the structure of the international financial system affect monetary policy. We also examine the evolution of the international financial system during the past half century and consider where it may be headed in the future.

INTERVENTION IN THE FOREIGN EXCHANGE MARKET

In Chapter 18, we analyzed the foreign exchange market as if it were a completely free market that responds to all conventional market pressures. Like many other markets, however, the foreign exchange market is not free of government intervention; central banks regularly engage in international financial transactions, called **foreign exchange interventions**, to influence exchange rates. In our current international environment, exchange rates fluctuate from day to day, but central banks attempt to influence their countries' exchange rates by buying and selling currencies. We can use the exchange rate analysis we developed in Chapter 18 to explain the impact of central bank intervention on the foreign exchange market.

Foreign Exchange Intervention and the Money Supply

The first step in understanding how central bank intervention in the foreign exchange market affects exchange rates is to explore the impact on the monetary base of a central bank sale in the foreign exchange market of some of its holdings of assets denominated in a foreign currency (called **international reserves**). Suppose the Bank of Canada decides to sell $1 billion of its foreign assets in exchange for $1 billion of Canadian currency. The Bank's purchase of dollars has two effects. First, it reduces the Bank of Canada's holdings of international reserves by $1 billion. Second, because the Bank of Canada's purchase of currency removes it from the hands of the public, currency in circulation falls by $1 billion. We can see this in the following T-account for the Bank of Canada:

Bank of Canada			
Assets		**Liabilities**	
Foreign assets (international reserves)	−$1 billion	Currency in circulation	−$1 billion

Because the monetary base is made up of currency in circulation plus reserves, this decline in currency implies that the monetary base has fallen by $1 billion.

If, as is more likely, the persons buying the foreign assets pay for them with cheques written on accounts at domestic banks rather than with currency, then the Bank of Canada deducts the $1 billion from the reserve deposits it holds for these banks. The result is that deposits with the Bank of Canada (reserves) decline by $1 billion, as shown in the following T-account:

Bank of Canada			
Assets		**Liabilities**	
Foreign assets (international reserves)	−$1 billion	Deposits with the Bank of Canada (reserves)	−$1 billion

In this case, the outcome of the Bank of Canada sale of foreign assets and the purchase of dollar deposits is a $1 billion decline in reserves and, as before, a $1 billion decline in the monetary base, because reserves are also a component of the monetary base.

We now see that the outcome for the monetary base is exactly the same when a central bank sells foreign assets to purchase domestic bank deposits or domestic currency. This is why, when we say that a central bank has purchased its domestic currency, we do not have to distinguish between currency and bank deposits denominated in the domestic currency. We have thus reached an important conclusion: *A central bank's purchase of domestic currency and corresponding sale of foreign assets in the foreign exchange market leads to an equal decline in its international reserves and the monetary base.*

We could have reached the same conclusion by a more direct route. A central bank sale of a foreign asset is no different from an open market sale of a government bond. We learned in our exploration of the money supply process that an open market sale leads to an equal decline in the monetary base; therefore, a sale of foreign assets also leads to an equal decline in the monetary base. By similar reasoning, a central bank purchase of foreign assets paid for by selling domestic currency, like an open market purchase, leads to an equal rise in the monetary base. Thus we reach the following conclusion: *A central bank's sale of domestic currency to purchase foreign assets in the foreign exchange market results in an equal rise in its international reserves and the monetary base*.

The intervention we have just described, in which a central bank allows the purchase or sale of domestic currency to have an effect on the monetary base, is called an **unsterilized foreign exchange intervention**. But what if the central bank does not want the purchase or sale of domestic currency to affect the monetary base? All it has to do is counteract the effect of the foreign exchange intervention by conducting an offsetting open market operation in the government bond market. For example, in the case of a $1 billion purchase of dollars by the Bank of Canada and a corresponding $1 billion sale of foreign assets, which, as we have seen, would decrease the monetary base by $1 billion, the Bank of Canada can conduct an open market purchase of $1 billion of government bonds, which will increase the monetary base by $1 billion. The resulting T-account for the foreign exchange intervention and the offsetting open market operation leaves the monetary base unchanged:

Bank of Canada			
Assets		**Liabilities**	
Foreign assets (international reserves)	−$1 billion	Monetary base	0
Government bonds	+$1 billion		

A foreign exchange intervention with an offsetting open market operation that leaves the monetary base unchanged is called a **sterilized foreign exchange intervention**.

Now that we understand that there are two types of foreign exchange interventions—unsterilized and sterilized—let's look at how each affects the exchange rate.

Unsterilized Intervention

Intuition might lead you to suspect that if a central bank wants to raise the value of the domestic currency, it should buy its currency in the foreign exchange market and sell foreign assets. Indeed, this intuition is correct in the case of an unsterilized intervention.

Recall that in an unsterilized intervention, if the Bank of Canada decides to buy dollars and therefore sells foreign assets in exchange for dollar assets, this exchange works just like an open market sale of bonds to decrease the monetary base. Hence the purchase of dollars leads to a decrease in the money supply, which raises the domestic interest rate and increases the relative expected return on dollar assets. As a result, the demand curve shifts to the right from D_1 to D_2, as shown in Figure 19-1, and the exchange rate rises to E_2.[1]

Our analysis leads us to the following conclusion about unsterilized interventions in the foreign exchange market: *An unsterilized intervention in which domestic currency is bought and foreign assets are sold leads to a fall in international reserves, a fall in the money supply, and an appreciation of the domestic currency*.

The reverse result is found for an unsterilized intervention in which domestic currency is sold and foreign assets are purchased. The sale of domestic currency and purchase of foreign assets (which increases international reserves) work like an open market purchase to increase the monetary base and the money supply. The increase in the money supply lowers the interest rate on dollar assets. The resulting decrease in the relative expected return on dollar assets means that people will buy fewer dollar assets, so the demand curve shifts to the left and the exchange rate falls. *An unsterilized intervention in which domestic*

---

[1]An unsterilized intervention in which the Bank of Canada buys dollars decreases the amount of dollar assets slightly because it leads to a decrease in the monetary base while leaving the amount of government bonds in the hands of the public unchanged. The curve depicting the supply of dollar assets thus shifts to the left slightly, which also works toward raising the exchange rate, yielding the same conclusion derived in Figure 19-1. Because the resulting increase in the monetary base is only a minuscule fraction of the total amount of dollar assets outstanding, the supply curve shifts by an imperceptible amount. This is why Figure 19-1 is drawn with the supply curve unchanged.

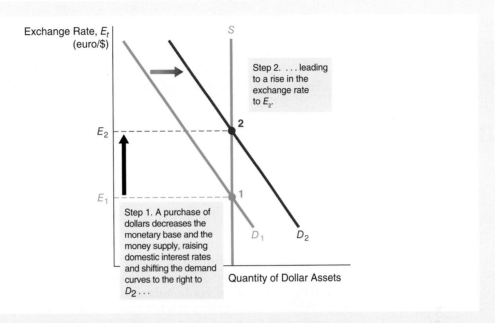

Step 2. ... leading to a rise in the exchange rate to E_2.

Step 1. A purchase of dollars decreases the monetary base and the money supply, raising domestic interest rates and shifting the demand curves to the right to D_2 ...

FIGURE 19-1 **Effect of an Unsterilized Purchase of Dollars and Sale of Foreign Assets**

A purchase of dollars and the consequent open market sale of foreign assets decrease the monetary base and the money supply. The resulting fall in the money supply leads to a rise in domestic interest rates, which raises the relative expected return on dollar assets. The demand curve shifts to the right from D_1 to D_2, and the equilibrium exchange rate rises from E_1 to E_2.

currency is sold and foreign assets are purchased leads to a rise in international reserves, a rise in the money supply, and a depreciation of the domestic currency.

Sterilized Intervention

The key point to remember about a sterilized intervention is that the central bank engages in offsetting open market operations, and so there is no impact on the monetary base and the money supply. In the context of the model of exchange rate determination we have developed here, it is a straightforward task to show that a sterilized intervention has almost *no effect* on the exchange rate. A sterilized intervention leaves the money supply unchanged and thus has no direct way of affecting interest rates.[2] Because the relative expected return on dollar assets is unaffected, the demand curve remains at D_1 in Figure 19-1, and the exchange rate remains unchanged at E_1.

[2]A sterilized intervention changes the amount of foreign securities relative to domestic securities in the hands of the public, called a *portfolio balance effect*. Through this effect, the central bank might be able to influence the interest rate differential between domestic and foreign assets, which in turn affects the relative expected return on domestic assets. Empirical evidence has not revealed this portfolio balance effect to be significant. However, a sterilized intervention *could* indicate what central banks want to happen to the future exchange rate and so might provide a signal about the course of future monetary policy. In this way, a sterilized intervention could lead to a shift in the demand curve for domestic assets and ultimately affect the exchange rate. However, the future change in monetary policy—not the sterilized intervention—is the source of the exchange rate effect. For a further discussion of the signaling and portfolio balance effects and the possible differential effects of sterilized versus unsterilized intervention, see Paul Krugman, Maurice Obstfeld, and Mark Melitz, *International Economics: Theory and Policy*, 9th ed. (Boston: Addison-Wesley, 2012).

At first it might seem puzzling that a central bank purchase or sale of domestic currency that is sterilized does not lead to a change in the exchange rate. A central bank–sterilized purchase of domestic currency cannot raise the exchange rate because, with no effect on the domestic money supply or interest rates, any resulting rise in the exchange rate would lead to an excess supply of dollar assets. With more people willing to sell dollar assets than willing to buy them, the exchange rate would fall back to its initial equilibrium level, where the demand and supply curves intersect.

BALANCE OF PAYMENTS

Because international financial transactions such as foreign exchange interventions have considerable effects on monetary policy, it is worth knowing how these transactions are measured. The **balance of payments** is a bookkeeping system used to record all receipts and payments (both private sector and government) that have a direct bearing on the movement of funds between a nation and foreign countries. Here we examine the key items in the balance of payments, items that you often hear about in the media.

The **current account** shows international transactions that involve currently produced goods and services. The difference between exports and imports, the net receipts from trade, is called the **trade balance**. When imports are greater than exports (by $31.7 billion in 2013), the result is a trade deficit; if exports are greater than imports, the result is a trade surplus.

Additional items included in the current account are the net receipts (cash flows received from abroad minus cash flows sent abroad) from three categories: investment income, service transactions, and unilateral transfers (gifts, pensions, and foreign aid). In 2013, for example, net investment income was minus $26.2 billion for Canada because Canadians received less investment income from abroad than they paid out. Since Canadians made more unilateral transfers to foreign countries than foreigners made to Canada, net unilateral transfers were minus $2.4 billion. The sum of the previous two items plus the trade balance gives the current account balance, which in 2013 showed a deficit of $60.3 billion (−$31.7 − $26.2 − $2.4 = −$60.3). Another important item in the balance of payments is the **capital account**, the net receipts from capital transactions (e.g., purchases of stocks and bonds, bank loans, etc.). In 2013, the capital account was $60.2 billion, indicating that $60.2 billion more capital came into Canada than left Canada.[3] The sum of the current account and the capital account equals the **official reserve transactions balance** (net change in government international reserves), which was minus $0.1 billion in 2013 (−$60.3 + $60.2). When economists refer to a surplus or deficit in the balance of payments, they actually mean a surplus or deficit in the official reserve transactions balance.

Because the balance of payments must balance, the official reserve transactions balance, which equals the current account plus the capital account, gives the net amount of international reserves that must move between governments (as represented by their central banks) in order to finance international transactions; that is,

$$\text{Current account} + \text{capital account} = \text{net change in government international reserves}$$

---

[3]The capital account balance number reported here includes a statistical discrepancy item that represents errors due to unrecorded transactions involving smuggling and other capital flows (−$1.7 billion in 2013). Many experts believe that the statistical discrepancy item, which keeps the balance of payments in balance, is primarily the result of large hidden capital flows, and this is why it is included in the capital account balance.

This equation shows us why the current account receives so much attention from economists and the media. The current account balance tells us whether Canada (private sector and government combined) is increasing or decreasing its claims on foreign wealth. A surplus indicates that Canada is increasing its claims on foreign wealth and thus is increasing its holdings of foreign assets (both good things for Canadians); a deficit (as in 2013) indicates that Canada is reducing its holdings of foreign assets and foreign countries are increasing their claims on Canada.[4]

The large U.S. current account deficit in recent years, which in 2013 was over $400 billion, has raised serious concerns that these large deficits may have negative consequences for the U.S. economy (see the Global box, Why the Large U.S. Current Account Deficit Worries Economists).

Global   Why the Large U.S. Current Account Deficit Worries Economists

The large U.S. current account deficit in recent years, which in 2013 was 2.4% of GDP, worries economists for several reasons. First, it indicates that at current exchange rate values, foreigners' demand for U.S. exports is far less than Americans' demand for imports. As we saw in the previous chapter, low demand for U.S. exports and high U.S. demand for imports may lead to a future decline in the value of the U.S. dollar.

Second, the current account deficit means that foreigners' claims on U.S. assets are growing, and these claims will have to be paid back at some point. Americans are mortgaging their future to foreigners; when the bill comes due, Americans will be poorer. Furthermore, if Americans have a greater preference for dollar assets than foreigners do, the movement of American wealth to foreigners could decrease the demand for U.S. dollar assets over time, also causing the dollar to depreciate.

The hope is that the eventual decline in the U.S. dollar resulting from the large U.S. current account deficit will be a gradual one, occurring over a period of several years. If the decline is precipitous, however, it could potentially disrupt financial markets and hurt the U.S. economy.

EXCHANGE RATE REGIMES IN THE INTERNATIONAL FINANCIAL SYSTEM

Exchange rate regimes in the international financial system are classified into two basic types: fixed and floating. In a **fixed exchange rate regime**, the value of a currency is pegged relative to the value of another currency (called the **anchor currency**) so that the exchange rate is fixed in terms of the anchor currency. In a **floating exchange rate regime**, the value of a currency is allowed to fluctuate against all other currencies. When countries intervene in foreign exchange markets in an attempt to influence their exchange rates by buying and selling foreign assets, the regime is referred to as a **managed float regime** (or a **dirty float**).

In examining past exchange rate regimes, we start with the gold standard of the late nineteenth and early twentieth centuries.

---

[4]The current account balance can also be viewed as showing the amount by which total saving exceeds private sector and government investment in Canada. Total Canadian saving equals the increase in total wealth held by the Canadian private sector and government. Total investment equals the increase in the Canadian capital stock (wealth physically in Canada). The difference between them is the increase in Canadian claims on foreign wealth.

Gold Standard

Before World War I, the world economy operated under the **gold standard**, a fixed exchange rate regime in which the currencies of most countries were convertible directly into gold at fixed rates, so that exchange rates between currencies were also fixed. One Canadian dollar bill, for example, could be exchanged for approximately $\frac{1}{20}$ ounce of gold. Likewise, the British Treasury would exchange $\frac{1}{4}$ ounce of gold for £1. Because a Canadian could convert $20 into 1 ounce of gold, which could be used to buy £4, the exchange rate between the pound and the Canadian dollar was effectively fixed at approximately $5 to the pound. The fixed exchange rates under the gold standard had the important advantage of encouraging world trade by eliminating the uncertainty that occurs when exchange rates fluctuate.

One problem with the gold standard was that monetary policy throughout the world was greatly influenced by the production of gold and gold discoveries. When gold production was low in the 1870s and 1880s, the money supply throughout the world grew slowly and did not keep pace with the growth of the world economy. The result was deflation (falling price levels). Gold discoveries in Alaska and South Africa in the 1890s greatly expanded gold production, causing money supplies to increase rapidly and price levels to rise (inflation) until World War I.

The Bretton Woods System

After World War II, the victors set up a fixed exchange rate system that became known as the **Bretton Woods system**, after the New Hampshire town in which the agreement was negotiated in 1944. The Bretton Woods system remained in effect until 1971.

The Bretton Woods agreement created the **International Monetary Fund (IMF)**, headquartered in Washington, DC, which had 30 original member countries in 1945 and currently has over 180. The IMF was given the task of promoting the growth of world trade by setting rules for the maintenance of fixed exchange rates and by making loans to countries that were experiencing balance-of-payments difficulties. In addition to monitoring the compliance of member countries with its rules, the IMF also took on the job of collecting and standardizing international economic data.

The Bretton Woods agreement also set up the International Bank for Reconstruction and Development, commonly referred to as the **World Bank**. Headquartered in Washington, DC, it provides long-term loans to help developing countries build dams, roads, and other physical capital that will contribute to their economic development. The funds for these loans are obtained primarily by the issuance of World Bank bonds, which are sold in the capital markets of the developed countries. In addition, the General Agreement on Tariffs and Trade (GATT), headquartered in Geneva, Switzerland, was set up to monitor rules for the conduct of trade between countries (tariffs and quotas). The GATT has since evolved into the **World Trade Organization (WTO)**.

Because the United States emerged from World War II as the world's largest economic power, with over half of the world's manufacturing capacity and the greater part of the world's gold, Bretton Woods put in place a system of fixed exchange rates that was based on the convertibility of U.S. dollars into gold (for foreign governments and central banks only) at $35 per ounce. The fixed exchange rates were to be maintained by intervention in the foreign exchange market by central banks in countries besides the United States that bought and sold dollar assets, which these countries held as international reserves. The U.S. dollar, which was used by other countries to denominate the assets that they held as international reserves, was called the **reserve currency**. Thus an important feature of the Bretton Woods system was the establishment of the United

States as the reserve currency country. Even after the breakup of the Bretton Woods system, the U.S. dollar kept its position as the reserve currency in which most international financial transactions are conducted. The fixed exchange rate, which was a feature of the Bretton Woods system, was finally abandoned in 1973. From 1979 to 1990, the European Union instituted among its members its own fixed exchange rate system, called the European Monetary System (EMS). In theory, in the *exchange rate mechanism* (*ERM*) of this system, the exchange rate between any pair of currencies of the participating countries was not supposed to fluctuate outside narrow limits, called the "snake." In practice, all of the countries in the EMS pegged their currencies to the German mark.

How a Fixed Exchange Rate Regime Works

Figure 19-2 uses the supply and demand analysis of the foreign exchange market that we learned in the previous chapter to show how a fixed exchange rate regime works in practice. Panel (a) describes a situation in which the domestic currency is fixed relative to an anchor currency at E_{par}, while the demand curve has shifted left to D_1, perhaps because foreign interest rates have risen, thereby lowering the relative expected return on domestic assets. At E_{par}, the exchange rate is now *overvalued*: The demand curve D_1 intersects the supply curve at an exchange rate E_1 that is lower than the fixed (par) value of the exchange rate E_{par}. To keep the exchange rate at E_{par}, the central bank must intervene in the foreign exchange market and purchase domestic currency by selling foreign assets. This action, like an open market sale, causes both the monetary base and the money supply to decrease, driving up the interest rate on domestic assets, i^D.[5] This increase in the domestic interest rate raises the relative expected return on domestic assets, shifting the demand curve to the right. The central bank will continue to purchase domestic currency until the demand curve reaches D_2 and the equilibrium exchange rate is at E_{par}, at point 2 in panel (a).

We thus conclude that **when the domestic currency is overvalued, the central bank must purchase domestic currency to keep the exchange rate fixed, but as a result it loses international reserves**.

Panel (b) in Figure 19-2 describes the situation in which the demand curve has shifted to the right to D_1 because the relative expected return on domestic assets has risen and hence the exchange rate at E_{par} is *undervalued*: The initial demand curve D_1 intersects the supply curve at exchange rate E_1, which is above E_{par}. In this situation, the central bank must sell domestic currency and purchase foreign assets. This action works like an open market purchase; it increases the money supply and lowers the interest rate on domestic assets i^D. The central bank keeps selling domestic currency and lowering i^D until the demand curve shifts all the way to D_2, where the equilibrium exchange rate is at E_{par}—point 2 in panel (b). Our analysis thus leads us to the following result: **When the domestic currency is undervalued, the central bank must sell domestic currency to keep the exchange rate fixed, but as a result, it gains international reserves**.

Devaluation and Revaluation   As we have seen, if a country's currency is overvalued, its central bank's attempts to keep the currency from depreciating will result in a loss of international reserves. If the country's central bank eventually runs out of international reserves, it cannot keep its currency from depreciating, and a **devaluation**, in which the par exchange rate is reset at a lower level, must occur.

---

[5]Because the exchange rate will continue to be fixed at E_{par}, the expected future exchange rate remains unchanged and so is not addressed in the analysis.

FIGURE 19-2 **Intervention in the Foreign Exchange Market Under a Fixed Exchange Rate Regime**

In panel (a), the exchange rate at E_{par} is overvalued. To keep the exchange rate at E_{par} (point 2), the central bank must purchase domestic currency to shift the demand curve to D_2. In panel (b), the exchange rate at E_{par} is undervalued, so the central bank must sell domestic currency to shift the demand curve to D_2 and keep the exchange rate at E_{par} (point 2).

If, by contrast, a country's currency is undervalued, its central bank's intervention to keep the currency from appreciating leads to a gain of international reserves. As we will see shortly, the central bank might not want to acquire these international reserves, and so it might want to reset the par value of its exchange rate at a higher level (a **revaluation**).

Perfect Capital Mobility If perfect capital mobility exists—that is, if there are no barriers to domestic residents purchasing foreign assets or to foreigners purchasing domestic assets—then a sterilized exchange rate intervention cannot keep the exchange rate at E_{par} because, as we saw earlier in the chapter, the relative expected return on domestic assets is unaffected. For example, if the exchange rate is overvalued, a sterilized purchase of domestic currency will leave the relative expected return and the demand curve unchanged, so pressure for a depreciation of the domestic currency is not removed. If the central bank keeps purchasing its domestic currency but continues to sterilize, it will just keep losing international reserves until it finally runs out of them and is forced to let the value of the currency seek a lower level.

Speculative Attacks

A serious shortcoming of fixed exchange rate systems such as the Bretton Woods system and the European Monetary System is that such systems can lead to foreign exchange crises involving a **speculative attack** on a currency. A speculative attack involves massive sales of a weak currency or purchases of a strong currency that cause a sharp change in the exchange rate. In the following application, we use our model of exchange rate determination to understand how the September 1992 exchange rate crisis that rocked the European Monetary System came about.

APPLICATION   The Foreign Exchange Crisis of September 1992

In the aftermath of German reunification in October 1990, the German central bank, the Bundesbank, faced rising inflationary pressures, with inflation having accelerated from below 3% in 1990 to near 5% by 1992. To get monetary growth under control and to dampen inflation, the Bundesbank raised German interest rates to near double-digit levels. Figure 19-3 shows the consequences of these actions by the Bundesbank in the foreign exchange market for British pounds. Note that in the diagram, the pound is the domestic currency and the German mark (deutsche mark, DM, Germany's currency before the advent of the euro in 1999) is the foreign currency.

The increase in German interest rates i^F lowered the relative expected return on British pound assets and shifted the demand curve to D_2, as shown in Figure 19-3. The intersection of the supply and demand curves at point 2 was now below the lower exchange rate limit at that time (2.778 marks per pound, denoted E_{par}). To increase the

MyEconLab Mini-lecture

FIGURE 19-3   Foreign Exchange Market for British Pounds in 1992

The realization by speculators that the United Kingdom would soon devalue the pound decreased the relative expected return on British pound assets, resulting in a leftward shift of the demand curve from D_2 to D_3. As a result, the British central bank was forced to purchase a large amount of pounds in an effort to raise the interest rate, so that the demand curve would shift back to D_1 and the exchange rate E_{par} would remain at 2.778 German marks per pound.

value of the pound relative to the mark and to restore the mark/pound exchange rate to within the exchange rate mechanism limits, one of two things had to happen. In the first option, the Bank of England would have to pursue a contractionary monetary policy, thereby raising British interest rates sufficiently to shift the demand curve back to D_1, so that the equilibrium would remain at point 1 and the exchange rate would remain at E_{par}. Alternatively, the Bundesbank would have to pursue an expansionary monetary policy, thereby lowering German interest rates. Lower German interest rates would raise the relative expected return on British assets and shift the demand curve back to D_1, so that the exchange rate would remain at E_{par}.

The catch was that the Bundesbank, whose primary goal was to fight inflation, was unwilling to pursue an expansionary monetary policy, and the British, who were facing their worst recession in the postwar period, were unwilling to pursue a contractionary monetary policy to prop up the pound. This impasse became clear when, in response to great pressure from other members of the EMS, the Bundesbank was willing to lower its lending rates by only a token amount on September 14 after a speculative attack was mounted on the currencies of the Scandinavian countries. So, at some point in the near future, the value of the pound would have to decline to point 2. Speculators now knew that depreciation of the pound was imminent. As a result, the relative expected return on the pound fell sharply, shifting the demand curve left to D_3 in Figure 19-3.

As a result of the large leftward shift of the demand curve, a huge excess supply of pound assets now existed at the par exchange rate E_{par}, which caused a massive sell-off of pounds (and purchases of marks) by speculators. The need for the British central bank to intervene to raise the value of the pound now became much greater and required a huge rise in British interest rates. A major intervention effort on the part of the Bank of England, which led to a rise in its lending rate from 10% to 15%, still wasn't enough to save the pound. The British were finally forced to give up on September 16: They pulled out of the ERM indefinitely and allowed the pound to depreciate by 10% against the mark.

Speculative attacks on other currencies forced devaluation of the Spanish peseta by 5% and of the Italian lira by 15%. To defend its currency, the Swedish central bank was forced to raise its daily lending rate to the astronomical level of 500%! By the time the crisis was over, the British, French, Italian, Spanish, and Swedish central banks had intervened to the tune of $100 billion; the Bundesbank alone had laid out $50 billion for foreign exchange intervention. Because foreign exchange crises lead to large changes in central banks' holdings of international reserves and thus significantly affect the official reserve asset items in the balance of payments, these crises are also referred to as **balance-of-payments crises**.

The attempt to prop up the European Monetary System was not cheap for these central banks. It is estimated that they lost $4 to $6 billion as a result of exchange rate intervention during the crisis. What the central banks lost, the speculators gained. A speculative fund run by George Soros ran up $1 billion of profits during the crisis, and Citibank traders reportedly made $200 million. When an exchange rate crisis arises, life certainly can be sweet for exchange rate speculators. ◆

The Policy Trilemma

An important implication of the foregoing analysis is that a country that ties its exchange rate to an anchor currency of a larger country loses control of its monetary policy. If the larger country pursues a more contractionary monetary policy and raises interest rates, this action will lead to lower expected inflation in the larger country, thus causing an appreciation of the larger country's currency and a depreciation of the smaller country's currency. The smaller country, having locked its exchange rate to the anchor currency, will now find its currency overvalued and will therefore have to sell the anchor currency and buy its own to keep its currency from depreciating. The result of this foreign exchange intervention will be a decline in the smaller country's international reserves, a contraction of its monetary base, and a rise in interest rates. Sterilization of this foreign exchange intervention is not an option because this course of action would just lead to a continuing loss of international reserves, until the smaller country was forced to devalue its currency. The smaller country no longer controls its monetary policy because movements in its interest rates are completely determined by movements in the larger country's interest rates.

Our analysis therefore indicates that a country (or a monetary union like the Eurozone) can't pursue the following three policies at the same time: (1) free capital mobility, (2) a fixed exchange rate, and (3) an independent monetary policy. Economists call this result the **policy trilemma** (or, more graphically, the **impossible trinity**). Figure 19-4 illustrates the policy trilemma. A country can choose only two of the three options, which are denoted by the sides of the triangle. In option 1, a country (or monetary union) chooses to have capital mobility and an independent monetary policy, but not a fixed exchange rate. Canada, the Eurozone, and the United States have made this choice. Hong Kong and Belize have chosen option 2, in which there is free capital mobility and the exchange rate is fixed, but the country does not have an independent

MyEconLab Mini-lecture

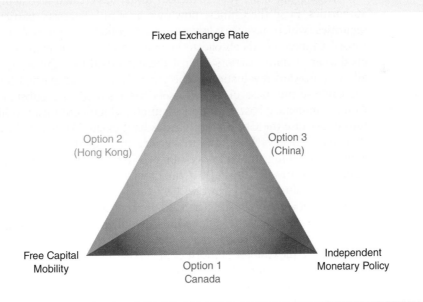

FIGURE 19-4   The Policy Trilemma

A country (or monetary union) cannot pursue the following three policies at the same time: (1) free capital mobility, (2) a fixed exchange rate, and (3) an independent monetary policy. Instead, it must choose two of the three policies denoted by the sides of the triangle.

monetary policy. Other countries, like China, have chosen option 3, in which the country has a fixed exchange rate and pursues an independent monetary policy but does not have free capital mobility because of **capital controls**, or restrictions on the free movement of capital across the borders.

The policy trilemma thus leaves countries with a difficult choice. Do they accept exchange rate volatility (option 1), give up an independent monetary policy (option 2), or restrict capital flows (option 3)?

APPLICATION   How Did China Accumulate $4 Trillion of International Reserves?

By 2014, China had accumulated $4 trillion of international reserves. How did the Chinese get their hands on this vast amount of foreign assets? After all, China is not yet a rich country.

The answer is that in 1994, China pegged its exchange rate to the U.S. dollar at a fixed rate of 12 cents to the yuan (also called the renminbi). China's rapidly growing productivity, accompanied by an inflation rate lower than that of the United States, caused the long-run value of the yuan to increase, leading to a higher relative expected return on yuan assets and a rightward shift of the demand curve for yuan assets. As a result, the Chinese found themselves in the situation depicted in panel (b) of Figure 19-2, in which the yuan is undervalued. To keep the yuan from appreciating above E_{par} to E_1 in the figure, the Chinese central bank has engaged in massive purchases of U.S. dollar assets. Today the Chinese government is one of the largest holders of U.S. government bonds in the world.

The pegging of the yuan to the U.S. dollar has created several problems for Chinese authorities. First, the Chinese now own a lot of U.S. assets, particularly U.S. Treasury securities, which have very low returns. Second, the undervaluation of the yuan has caused Chinese goods abroad to become so cheap that many countries have threatened to erect trade barriers against these goods if the Chinese government does not allow an upward revaluation of the yuan. Third, as we learned earlier in the chapter, the Chinese purchase of dollar assets has resulted in a substantial increase in the Chinese monetary base and money supply, which could lead to high inflation in the future. Because the Chinese authorities have created substantial roadblocks to capital mobility, they have been able to sterilize most of their exchange rate interventions while maintaining the exchange-rate peg. Nevertheless, they still worry about inflationary pressures. In July 2005, China finally made its peg somewhat more flexible by letting the value of the yuan rise 2.1%, and China subsequently allowed the yuan to appreciate at a gradual pace. The Chinese central bank also indicated that it would no longer fix the value of the yuan to the U.S. dollar, but would instead maintain its value relative to a basket of currencies.

Why did the Chinese authorities maintain this exchange-rate peg for so long, despite the associated problems? One answer is that China wanted to keep its export sector humming by keeping the prices of its export goods low. A second answer might be that China wanted to accumulate a large amount of international reserves as a "war chest" that could be sold to buy yuan in the event of a speculative attack against the currency at some future date. Given the pressure from government officials in the United States and Europe on the Chinese government to further revalue its currency, future adjustments to China's exchange rate policy are likely. ◆

Monetary Unions

A variant of a fixed exchange rate regime is a **monetary** (or **currency**) **union**, in which a group of countries decides to adopt a common currency, thereby fixing the countries' exchange rates in relation to each other. One of the earliest monetary unions was formed in 1787, when the 13 American colonies formed the United States of America and gave up their individual currencies for the U.S. dollar. The most recently formed monetary union is the European Monetary Union (EMU), which was formed in January of 1999, when 11 initial member countries adopted a new joint currency, the euro.

The key economic advantage of a monetary union is that it makes trade across borders easier because goods and services in all of the member countries are now priced in the same currency. However, as with any fixed exchange rate regime and free capital mobility, a currency union means that individual countries no longer have their own independent monetary policies with which to address shortfalls of aggregate demand. This disadvantage of a currency union has raised questions about whether the Eurozone will break up, as discussed in the Global box, Will the Euro Survive?

Global   Will the Euro Survive?

The global financial crisis of 2007–2009 led to economic contraction throughout Europe, with the countries in the southern part of the Eurozone hit especially hard. Unemployment in the hard-hit southern countries climbed much faster than in the northern countries, such as Germany. Furthermore, with the contraction of their economies, many of the southern countries began to experience large government budget deficits and sovereign debt crises, as described in Chapter 17, in which investors pulled back from purchasing these countries' bonds, sending interest rates to extremely high levels. The resulting collapse of the southern countries' economies could have been alleviated by easier monetary policy that would have stimulated economic activity, but this option was unavailable to these countries because the European Central Bank had to conduct monetary policy for the Eurozone as a whole, which was not suffering as badly as the individual southern countries.

This "straightjacket" effect of the euro has weakened support for the euro in the southern countries, leading to increased talk of abandoning the euro. Support for the euro has also weakened in the stronger, northern countries, since they have been called upon to provide bailouts to the weaker member countries. Because the stronger countries might wish to abandon their commitment to the euro in order to limit their transfers of funds to the weaker countries, and the weaker countries might wish to abandon their commitment to the euro so that they can boost their economies through more expansionary monetary policy and depreciation of their currencies, there are doubts that the European Monetary Union will survive. However, the euro is still seen by many as an important step in the creation of a more united and powerful Europe, and this political consideration has created strong support for retaining the monetary union.

Managed Float

With the demise of the Bretton Woods system, most exchange rates now change daily in response to market forces, but central banks have not been willing to give up the option of intervening in the foreign exchange market. The ability to prevent large changes in exchange rates makes it easier for firms and individuals purchasing or selling goods abroad to plan for the future. Furthermore, countries with surpluses in their balances of payments frequently do not want to see their currencies appreciate, because it makes their goods more expensive abroad and foreign goods cheaper in the home country. Because an appreciation might hurt sales for domestic businesses and increase unemployment, countries with balance-of-payments surpluses often have sold their currencies in the foreign exchange market and acquired international reserves.

Countries with balance-of-payments deficits do not want to see their currencies lose value because it makes foreign goods more expensive for domestic consumers and can stimulate inflation. To keep the value of the domestic currency high, countries with deficits have often bought their own currencies in the foreign exchange market and given up international reserves.

The current international financial system is a hybrid of a fixed and a flexible exchange rate system. Rates fluctuate in response to market forces but are not determined solely by them. Furthermore, many countries continue to keep the value of their currency fixed against other currencies, as was the case in the European Monetary System before the introduction of the euro and China from 1994 until 2005.

CAPITAL CONTROLS

Emerging market countries are countries that have recently opened up to flows of goods, services, and capital from the rest of the world. Politicians and some economists have advocated that these countries avoid financial instability by restricting capital mobility. Are capital controls a good idea?

Controls on Capital Outflows

Capital outflows can promote financial instability because, when domestic residents and foreigners pull their capital out of a country, the resulting capital outflow forces the country to devalue its currency. Because they want to avoid such instability, politicians in emerging market countries may find capital controls particularly attractive.

Although these controls sound like a good idea, they suffer from several disadvantages. First, empirical evidence indicates that controls on capital outflows are seldom effective during a crisis, because the private sector will find ingenious ways to evade them and will have little difficulty in moving funds out of the country. Second, the evidence suggests that capital flight may actually increase after controls are put into place because confidence in the government is weakened. Third, controls on capital outflows can lead to corruption, since government officials are often paid to look the other way while domestic residents try to move funds abroad. Fourth, controls on capital outflows may lull governments into thinking they do not have to act to reform their financial systems to deal with the crisis, and so opportunities to improve the functioning of the economy are lost.

Controls on Capital Inflows

Although most economists find the arguments against controls on capital outflows persuasive, the idea of controls on capital inflows receives more support. Supporters reason that if speculative capital cannot come in, then it cannot go out suddenly. Thus a potential crisis is averted. Our analysis of financial crises in Chapter 9 provides support for this view by suggesting that capital inflows can lead to credit booms and excessive risk taking on the parts of banks, factors that can help trigger a financial crisis.

However, controls on capital inflows have the undesirable feature that they might block funds that could be used for productive investment opportunities from entering a country. Although controls on capital inflows may limit the amount of fuel supplied to lending booms through capital flows, over time they produce substantial distortions and misallocations of resources as households and businesses try to get around them. Indeed, as with controls on capital outflows, controls on capital inflows can lead to corruption. Serious doubts exist over whether capital controls can be effective in today's environment, in which trade is open and in which the variety of financial instruments makes it easier to get around these controls.

On the other hand, a strong case can be made for improving bank regulation and supervision so that capital inflows are less likely to produce a lending boom that would encourage excessive risk taking by banking institutions. For example, restrictions on the growth of bank borrowing might substantially limit capital inflows. Supervisory controls that focus on the sources of financial fragility, rather than the symptoms, can enhance the efficiency of the financial system rather than hamper it.

THE ROLE OF THE IMF

The International Monetary Fund (IMF) was originally set up under the Bretton Woods system to help countries deal with balance-of-payments problems and stand by the fixed exchange rates by lending to deficit countries. When the Bretton Woods system of fixed exchange rates collapsed in 1971, the IMF took on new roles.

The IMF continues to function as a data collector and continues to provide technical assistance to its member countries. Although the IMF no longer attempts to encourage fixed exchange rates, its role as an international lender has become more important in recent years. This role first came to the fore in the 1980s during the Third World debt crisis, during which the IMF assisted developing countries in repaying their loans. During the financial crises in Mexico from 1994–1995 and in East Asia from 1997–1998, the IMF made huge loans to these and other affected countries to help them recover financially and to prevent the spread of the crises to other countries. Then, starting in 2010, the IMF made large loans to Greece, Ireland, and Portugal to help these countries avoid defaults on their government debt. This role of the IMF, in which it acts as an international lender of last resort and helps countries cope with financial instability, is indeed highly controversial.

Should the IMF Act as an International Lender of Last Resort?

We have seen that when a central bank engages in a lender-of-last-resort operation, as the Federal Reserve did during the recent global financial crisis, such an action can minimize the severity of the financial crisis and sometimes even prevent it from happening. When the IMF acts as an international lender of last resort, this role can have similar benefits, particularly when the central bank of the country it is lending to does not have the capacity to cope with the crisis.

However, when the IMF acts as an international lender of last resort, it can lead to serious moral hazard problems. First, knowing that the IMF is willing to take on this role may encourage governments to be profligate, because they know they are likely to be bailed out by the IMF if things get out of hand. Second, governments use IMF funds to protect depositors and other creditors of banking institutions from losses. This safety net creates the moral hazard problem discussed in Chapter 10, because depositors and other creditors have less incentive to monitor these banking institutions and to withdraw their deposits if the institutions are taking on too much risk.

An international lender of last resort must find ways to limit these two moral hazard problems or it can actually make the situation worse. The international lender of last resort can make it clear that it will extend liquidity only to governments that both put their fiscal houses in order and implement measures to prevent excessive risk taking by financial institutions. Critics of the IMF, however, believe that the IMF has not put enough pressure on the governments to which it lends to contain these two moral hazard problems, and for this reason they believe the IMF should abandon its role as an international lender of last resort. The IMF has also been criticized for imposing so-called austerity programs that force borrowing governments to cut government spending, raise taxes, and raise interest rates. These austerity programs can be highly contractionary (see Chapter 23) and can lead to high unemployment and even political instability.

The debate as to whether the world would be better off with the IMF operating as an international lender of last resort is currently a hot one. Much attention is being focused on efforts to make the IMF more effective in performing this role, and redesign of the IMF is at the centre of proposals for a new international financial architecture that will help reduce international financial instability.

INTERNATIONAL CONSIDERATIONS AND MONETARY POLICY

Our analysis in this chapter so far has suggested several ways in which monetary policy can be affected by international matters. Awareness of these effects can have significant implications for the way in which monetary policy is conducted.

Direct Effects of the Foreign Exchange Market on Monetary Policy

When central banks intervene in the foreign exchange market, they acquire or sell off international reserves, and their monetary base is affected. When a central bank intervenes in the foreign exchange market, it gives up some control of its monetary policy. For example, in the early 1970s, the German central bank faced a dilemma. In attempting to keep the German mark from appreciating too much against the U.S. dollar, the Germans acquired huge quantities of international reserves, leading to a high rate of money growth and lower interest rates that the German central bank considered inflationary.

The Bundesbank could have stopped its intervention in the foreign exchange market, thereby reasserting control over its own monetary policy. Such a strategy has a major drawback when a central bank is under pressure not to allow its currency to appreciate: The lower price of imports and higher price of exports that result from an appreciation of its currency will hurt domestic producers and increase unemployment.

Because the U.S. dollar has been a reserve currency, the U.S. monetary base and money supply have not been greatly affected by developments in the foreign exchange market. As long as foreign central banks, rather than the Fed, intervene to keep the value of the dollar from changing, American holdings of international reserves will remain unaffected. Conducting monetary policy is typically easier when a country's currency is a reserve currency.[6]

---

[6]However, the central bank of a reserve currency country must worry about a shift away from the use of its currency for international reserves.

Balance-of-Payments Considerations

Balance-of-payments considerations were more important under the Bretton Woods system than they are under the current managed float regime. When a nonreserve currency country is running balance-of-payments deficits, it necessarily gives up international reserves. Under the Bretton Woods system, to keep from running out of these reserves, a nonreserve currency country had to implement contractionary monetary policy to strengthen its currency. This is exactly what occurred in the United Kingdom before its devaluation of the pound in 1967. When policy became expansionary, the balance of payments deteriorated, and the British were forced to "slam on the brakes" by implementing a contractionary policy. Once the balance of payments had improved, policy became more expansionary, until the deteriorating balance of payments again forced the British to pursue a contractionary policy. Such on-again, off-again actions became known as a "stop-go" policy, and the domestic instability it created was criticized severely.

Because the United States is a major reserve currency country, it can run large balance-of-payments deficits without losing huge amounts of international reserves. This does not mean, however, that the Federal Reserve is never influenced by developments in the U.S. balance of payments. Current account deficits in the United States suggest that American businesses may be losing some of their ability to compete because the value of the U.S. dollar is too high. In addition, large U.S. balance-of-payments deficits lead to balance-of-payments surpluses in other countries, which can in turn lead to large increases in their holdings of international reserves (this was especially true under the Bretton Woods system). Because such increases put a strain on the international financial system and may stimulate world inflation, the Fed worries about U.S. balance-of-payments and current account deficits. To help shrink these deficits, the Fed might pursue a more contractionary monetary policy.

Exchange Rate Considerations

Unlike balance-of-payments considerations, which have become less important under the current managed float system, exchange rate considerations now play a greater role in the conduct of monetary policy. If a central bank does not want to see its currency fall in value, it may pursue a more contractionary monetary policy to raise the domestic interest rate, thereby strengthening its currency. Similarly, if a country experiences an appreciation in its currency, its domestic industry may suffer from increased foreign competition and may pressure the central bank to ease monetary policy in order to lower the exchange rate.

TO PEG OR NOT TO PEG: EXCHANGE-RATE TARGETING AS AN ALTERNATIVE MONETARY POLICY STRATEGY

In Chapter 17, we discussed several monetary policy strategies that could be used to promote price stability, including inflation targeting. Another strategy that uses a strong nominal anchor to promote price stability is called **exchange-rate targeting** (sometimes referred to as an **exchange-rate peg**).

Targeting the exchange rate is a monetary policy strategy with a long history. It can take the form of fixing the value of the domestic currency to a commodity such as gold, the key feature of the gold standard described earlier in the chapter. More recently, fixed exchange rate regimes have involved fixing the value of the domestic currency to that of a large, low-inflation country like the United States (the *anchor country*). Another alternative is to adopt a *crawling target* or *peg*, in which a currency is allowed to depreciate at a steady rate so that the inflation rate of the pegging country can be higher than that of the anchor country.

Advantages of Exchange-Rate Targeting

Exchange-rate targeting has several advantages. First, the nominal anchor of an exchange-rate target directly contributes to the goal of keeping inflation under control by tying the inflation rate for internationally traded goods to the rate in the anchor country. The exchange-rate target is able to do this because the foreign price of internationally traded goods is set by the world market, whereas the domestic price of these goods is fixed by the exchange-rate target. For example, until 2002, the exchange rate for the Argentine peso was exactly one to the U.S. dollar, so that a bushel of wheat traded internationally at five U.S. dollars had its price set at five Argentine pesos. If the exchange-rate target is credible (i.e., expected to be adhered to), the exchange-rate target has the added benefit of anchoring inflation expectations to the inflation rate in the anchor country.

Second, an exchange-rate target provides an automatic rule for the conduct of monetary policy that helps mitigate the time-inconsistency problem described in Chapter 17. As we saw earlier in the chapter, an exchange-rate target forces a tightening of monetary policy when there is a tendency for the domestic currency to depreciate and a loosening of policy when there is a tendency for the domestic currency to appreciate, so that discretionary monetary policy is less of an option. The central bank will therefore be constrained from falling into the time-inconsistency trap of trying to expand output and employment in the short-run by pursuing overly expansionary monetary policy.

Third, an exchange-rate target has the advantage of simplicity and clarity, which makes it easily understood by the public. A "sound currency" is an easy-to-understand rallying cry for monetary policy. In the past, for example, this aspect of simplicity was important in France, where an appeal to the "franc fort" (strong franc) was often used to justify tight monetary policy.

Given its advantages, it is not surprising that exchange-rate targeting has been used successfully to control inflation in industrialized countries. Both France and the United Kingdom, for example, successfully used exchange-rate targeting to lower inflation by tying the values of their currencies to the German mark. In 1987, when France first pegged its exchange rate to the mark, its inflation rate was 3%, two percentage points above the German inflation rate. By 1992, its inflation rate had fallen to 2%, a level that can be argued is consistent with price stability and that was actually below the German inflation rate. By 1996, the French and German inflation rates had converged to a number slightly below 2%. Similarly, after pegging its currency to the German mark in 1990, the United Kingdom was able to lower its inflation rate from 10% to 3% by 1992, when it was forced to abandon the exchange rate mechanism (ERM).

Exchange-rate targeting has also been an effective means of reducing inflation quickly in emerging market countries. For example, before the devaluation of the Mexican peso in 1994, its exchange-rate target enabled it to bring inflation down from levels above 100% in 1988 to levels below 10% in 1994.

Disadvantages of Exchange-Rate Targeting

Despite the inherent advantages of exchange-rate targeting, several serious criticisms of this strategy can be made. The problem (as we saw earlier in the chapter) is that with capital mobility, the targeting country can no longer pursue its own independent monetary policy and use it to respond to domestic shocks that are independent of those hitting the anchor country. Furthermore, an exchange-rate target means that shocks to the anchor country are directly transmitted to the targeting country, because changes in interest rates in the anchor country lead to corresponding changes in interest rates in the targeting country.

A striking example of these weaknesses occurred when Germany was reunified in 1990. In response to concerns about inflationary pressures arising from reunification and the massive fiscal expansion required to rebuild East Germany, long-term German interest rates rose until February 1991, and short-term rates rose until December 1991. This shock to the anchor country in the exchange rate mechanism (ERM) was transmitted directly to the other countries in the ERM whose currencies were pegged to the mark, and their interest rates rose in tandem with the German rates. Continued adherence to the exchange-rate target slowed economic growth and increased unemployment in countries such as France, which remained in the ERM exchange-rate peg.

A second problem with exchange-rate targets is that they leave countries open to speculative attacks on their currencies. Indeed, one aftermath of German reunification was the foreign exchange crisis of September 1992. As we saw earlier, the tight monetary policy practised in Germany following reunification subjected the countries of the ERM to a negative demand shock that led to declines in economic growth and increases in unemployment. It was certainly feasible for the governments of these countries to keep their exchange rates fixed relative to the mark under these circumstances, but speculators began to question whether these countries' commitment to the exchange-rate peg would eventually weaken. Speculators reasoned that these countries would not tolerate the rise in unemployment that resulted from keeping interest rates high enough to fend off attacks on their currencies.

At this stage, speculators were, in effect, presented with a one-way bet, because the currencies of countries like France, Spain, Sweden, Italy, and the United Kingdom could go in only one direction and depreciate against the mark. Selling these currencies before the likely depreciation occurred gave speculators an attractive profit opportunity with potentially high expected returns. The result was the speculative attack of September 1992. Only in France was the commitment to the fixed exchange rate strong enough that France did not devalue. The governments of the other ERM countries were unwilling to defend their currencies at all costs and eventually allowed their currencies to fall in value.

The different responses of France and the United Kingdom after the September 1992 exchange rate crisis illustrate the potential cost of an exchange-rate target. France, which continued to peg its currency to the mark and thus was unable to use monetary policy to respond to domestic conditions, found that economic growth remained slow after 1992, and unemployment increased. The United Kingdom, on the other hand, which dropped out of the ERM exchange-rate peg and adopted inflation targeting, enjoyed much better economic results: Economic growth was higher, the unemployment rate fell, and yet the inflation rate was not much worse than France's.

In contrast to industrialized countries, emerging market countries (including the transition countries of Eastern Europe) may not lose all that much by giving up an independent monetary policy when they target exchange rates. Because many emerging market countries have not developed the political or monetary institutions that are necessary for the successful use of discretionary monetary policy, they may have little to gain but a lot to lose from an independent monetary policy. Thus they are better off if they adopt, in effect, the monetary policy of a country like the United States through targeting exchange rates than if they pursue their own independent policy. This is one of the reasons so many emerging market countries have adopted exchange-rate targeting.

Nonetheless, exchange-rate targeting is highly dangerous for these countries because it leaves them open to speculative attacks that can have far more serious consequences for their economies than for those of industrialized countries. Indeed, the successful speculative attacks on Mexico in 1994, East Asia in 1997, and Argentina in 2002 plunged their economies into full-scale financial crises that devastated their countries.

An additional disadvantage of an exchange-rate target is that it can weaken the accountability of policymakers, particularly in emerging market countries. Because exchange-rate targeting fixes the exchange rate, it eliminates an important signal that can help constrain monetary policy from becoming too expansionary and thereby limit the time-inconsistency problem. In industrialized countries, particularly in the United States, the bond market provides an important signal about the stance of monetary policy. Overly expansionary monetary policy or strong political pressure to engage in overly expansionary monetary policy produces an inflation scare, in which inflation expectations surge, interest rates rise (because of the Fisher effect, described in Chapter 5), and long-term bond prices decline sharply. Because both central banks and politicians want to avoid this kind of scenario, overly expansionary monetary policy is less likely.

In many countries, particularly emerging market countries, the long-term bond market is essentially nonexistent. Under a floating exchange rate regime, however, if monetary policy is too expansionary, the exchange rate will depreciate. In these countries, the daily fluctuations of the exchange rate can, like the bond market in the United States, provide an early warning signal that monetary policy is too expansionary. Just as the fear of a visible inflation scare in the bond market constrains central bankers from pursuing overly expansionary monetary policy and constrains politicians from putting pressure on the central bank to do so, fear of exchange rate depreciations can make overly expansionary monetary policy, and therefore the time-inconsistency problem, less likely.

The need for signals from the foreign exchange market may be even more acute for emerging market countries because the balance sheets and actions of their central banks are not as transparent as those of industrialized countries. Targeting the exchange rate can make it even harder to ascertain the central bank's policy actions. The public is less able to keep a watch on the central bank and the politicians pressuring it, which makes it easier for monetary policy to become too expansionary.

When Is Exchange-Rate Targeting Desirable for Industrialized Countries?

Given the above disadvantages of exchange-rate targeting, when might it make sense? In industrialized countries, the biggest cost to exchange-rate targeting is the loss of an independent monetary policy to deal with domestic considerations. If an independent, domestic monetary policy can be conducted responsibly, the loss of such a policy can be a serious cost indeed, as the comparison between the post-1992 experiences of France and the United Kingdom indicates. However, not all industrialized countries are capable of conducting their own monetary policies successfully, either because the central bank is not independent or because political pressures on the central bank lead to an inflationary bias in monetary policy. In these cases, giving up independent control of domestic monetary policy may not be such a great loss, while the advantages of having monetary policy determined by a better-performing central bank in the anchor country can be substantial.

Italy provides a good example. It is not a coincidence that the Italian public had the most favourable attitude of all the European countries toward the European Monetary Union. The past record of Italian monetary policy was not good, and the Italian public recognized that a monetary policy controlled by more responsible outsiders had benefits that far outweighed the costs to the country of losing the ability to focus monetary policy on domestic considerations.

A second reason why industrialized countries might find exchange-rate targeting useful is that it encourages integration of the domestic economy with the economies of neighbouring countries. Clearly, this was the rationale for the long-standing pegging of the exchange rate to the deutsche mark by countries such as Austria and the Netherlands, and the more recent exchange-rate pegs that preceded the formation of the European Monetary Union.

In sum, exchange-rate targeting for industrialized countries is probably not the best monetary policy strategy for controlling the overall economy unless (1) domestic monetary and political institutions are not conducive to good monetary policymaking, or (2) an exchange-rate target has other important benefits that have nothing to do with monetary policy.

When Is Exchange-Rate Targeting Desirable for Emerging Market Countries?

In countries with particularly weak political and monetary institutions that have experienced continued bouts of hyperinflation, a characterization that applies to many emerging market (including transition) countries, exchange-rate targeting may be the only way to break inflationary psychology and stabilize the economy. In this situation, exchange-rate targeting is the stabilization policy of last resort. However, if the exchange-rate targeting regimes in emerging market countries are not transparent, they are more likely to break down, often resulting in disastrous financial crises.

Are there exchange rate strategies that will make it less likely that the exchange rate regime will break down in an emerging market country? Two such strategies, currency boards and dollarization, have received increased attention in recent years.

Currency Boards

A **currency board** is an arrangement in which the domestic currency is backed 100% by a foreign currency (say, dollars), and the note-issuing authority, whether it be the central bank or the government, establishes a fixed exchange rate to this foreign currency and stands ready to exchange domestic currency for the foreign currency at this rate whenever the public so requests. A currency board is just a variant of a fixed exchange-rate target in which the commitment to the fixed exchange rate is especially strong because the conduct of monetary policy is, in effect, put on autopilot and taken completely out of the hands of the central bank and the government. In contrast, the typical fixed or pegged exchange rate regime does allow the monetary authorities some discretion in their conduct of monetary policy, because they can still adjust interest rates or print money.

A currency board arrangement thus has important advantages over a monetary policy strategy that just uses an exchange-rate target. First, the money supply can expand only when foreign currency is exchanged for domestic currency at the central bank. Therefore, the increased amount of domestic currency is matched by an equal increase in foreign exchange reserves. The central bank no longer has the ability to print money and thereby cause inflation. Second, the currency board setup involves a stronger commitment by the central bank to the fixed exchange rate and may therefore be effective in bringing inflation down quickly and in decreasing the likelihood of a successful speculative attack against the currency.

Although currency boards solve the transparency and commitment problems inherent in an exchange-rate target regime, they suffer from some of the same shortcomings: the loss of an independent monetary policy, increased exposure of the economy to shocks from the anchor country, and the loss of the central bank's ability to create money and act as a lender of last resort. Other means must therefore be used to cope with potential banking crises. In addition, if a speculative attack on a currency board occurs, the exchange of domestic currency for foreign currency leads to a sharp contraction of the money supply, which can be highly damaging to the economy.

Currency boards have been established in the territory of Hong Kong (1983) and in countries such as Argentina (1991), Estonia (1992), Lithuania (1994), Bulgaria (1997), and Bosnia (1998). Argentina's currency board, which operated from 1991 until 2002 and required the central bank to exchange U.S. dollars for new pesos at a fixed exchange rate of 1 to 1, is one of the most interesting. For more on this subject, see the Global box, Argentina's Currency Board.

Global   Argentina's Currency Board

Argentina has a long history of monetary instability, with inflation rates fluctuating dramatically over the years, sometimes surging to beyond 1000% per year. To end this cycle of inflationary surges, Argentina decided to adopt a currency board in April of 1991. The Argentine currency board worked as follows. Under Argentina's convertibility law, the peso/U.S. dollar exchange rate was fixed at 1 to 1, and a member of the public could go to the Argentine central bank and exchange a peso for a U.S. dollar, or vice versa, at any time.

The early years of Argentina's currency board looked stunningly successful. Inflation, which was running at an 800% annual rate in 1990, fell to less than 5% by the end of 1994, and economic growth was rapid, averaging almost 8% per year from 1991 to 1994. In the aftermath of the Mexican peso crisis, however, concern about the health of the Argentine economy led the public to pull money out of the banks (deposits fell by 18%) and exchange pesos for U.S. dollars, thus causing a contraction of the Argentine money supply. The result was a sharp drop in Argentine economic activity, with real GDP shrinking by more than 5% in 1995 and the unemployment rate jumping above 15%. Only in 1996 did the economy begin to recover.

Because the central bank of Argentina had no control over monetary policy under the currency board system, it was virtually helpless to counteract the contractionary monetary effects stemming from the public's behaviour. Furthermore, because the currency board did not allow the central bank to create pesos and lend them to the banks, it had very little capability to act as a lender of last resort. With help from international agencies such as the IMF, the World Bank, and the Inter-American Development Bank, which lent Argentina more than $5 billion in 1995 to help shore up its banking system, the currency board survived.

In 1998, however, Argentina entered another recession, one that was both severe and very long-lasting. By the end of 2001, unemployment had reached nearly 20%, a level comparable to that experienced in the United States during the Great Depression of the 1930s. The result was civil unrest and the fall of the elected government, as well as a major banking crisis and a default on nearly $150 billion of government debt. Because the Central Bank of Argentina had no control over monetary policy under the currency board system, it was unable to use monetary policy to expand the economy and get Argentina out of its recession. In addition, because the currency board limited the central bank's ability to create pesos and act as a lender of last resort, the central bank was unable to help banks weather the banking crisis. In January 2002, the currency board finally collapsed, the peso depreciated by more than 70%, and inflation shot through the roof. The result was a full-scale financial crisis that led to an extremely severe depression. Clearly, the Argentine public is not as enamored of its currency board as it once was.[*]

---

[*]The Argentine financial crisis is described in detail in Web Chapter 1. "Financial Crises in Emerging Market Economies," which can be found on MyEconLab.

Dollarization

Another solution to the transparency problem and doubts about commitment to the exchange-rate target is **dollarization**, the adoption of a sound currency, like the U.S. dollar, as a country's money. Indeed, dollarization is just another variant of a fixed exchange-rate target, but with an even stronger commitment mechanism than that provided by a currency board. A currency board can be abandoned, allowing a change in the value of the currency, but a change of value is impossible with dollarization: A U.S. dollar bill is always worth one U.S. dollar, whether it is held in the United States or outside it.

Dollarization has been advocated as a monetary policy strategy for emerging market countries: It was discussed actively by Argentine officials in the aftermath of the devaluation of the Brazilian real in January 1999 and was adopted by Ecuador in March 2000. Dollarization's key advantage is that it completely eliminates the possibility of a speculative attack on the domestic currency (because there is no such currency). (Such an attack is still a danger under a currency board arrangement.)

Dollarization is subject to the usual weaknesses of an exchange-rate target (the loss of an independent monetary policy, increased exposure of the economy to shocks from the anchor country, and the inability of the central bank to create money and act as a lender of last resort). Dollarization has one additional weakness not characteristic of currency boards or other exchange-rate target regimes. Because a country adopting dollarization no longer has its own currency, it loses the revenue that a government receives by issuing money, which is called **seigniorage**. Because governments (or their central banks) do not have to pay interest on their domestic currency, they earn revenue (seigniorage) by using this currency to purchase income-earning assets such as bonds. In the case of the Federal Reserve in the United States, this revenue is usually in excess of $30 billion per year. If an emerging market country dollarizes and gives up its currency, it needs to make up this loss of revenue somehow, and this is not always easy for a poor country.

MyEconLab

MyEconLab is an online homework and tutorial system that puts you in control of your own learning with study and practice tools directly correlated to this chapter's content. Visit MyEconLab to access the eText, the Questions and Applied Problems with answers, as well as additional assessment. You will also find web chapters, mini-lectures, appendices, mini-cases, videos, glossary flashcards, news feeds, CANSIM data, and graphing tools.

SUMMARY

1. An unsterilized central bank intervention in which the domestic currency is sold to purchase foreign assets leads to a gain in international reserves, an increase in the money supply, and a depreciation of the domestic currency. Available evidence suggests, however, that sterilized central bank interventions have little long-term effect on the exchange rate.

2. The balance of payments is a bookkeeping system used to record all payments that have a direct bearing on the movement of funds between a country and foreign countries. The official reserve transactions balance is the sum of the current account balance plus the items in the capital account. It indicates the amount of international reserves that must be moved between countries to finance international transactions.

3. Before World War I, the gold standard was predominant. Currencies were convertible into gold, thus fixing exchange rates between them. After World War II, the Bretton Woods system and the IMF were established to promote a fixed exchange rate system in which the U.S. dollar, the reserve currency, was convertible into gold. The Bretton Woods system collapsed in 1971. We now have an international financial system that has elements of a managed float and a fixed exchange rate system. Some exchange rates fluctuate from day to day, even though central banks intervene in the foreign exchange market, while other exchange rates are fixed.

4. Controls on capital outflows receive support because they may prevent domestic residents and foreigners from pulling capital out of a country during a crisis and thereby make devaluation less likely. Controls on capital inflows make sense under the theory that, if speculative capital cannot flow in, then it also cannot go out suddenly. Thus a crisis is averted. However, capital controls suffer from several disadvantages: They are seldom effective, they often lead to corruption, and they may encourage governments to avoid taking the steps that are necessary to reform their financial systems to deal with the crisis.

5. The IMF's role as an international lender of last resort can help lessen the severity of financial crises. However, the IMF's role as an international lender of last resort also creates serious moral hazard problems because it encourages governments to be profligate and also encourages excessive risk taking by financial institutions, making a financial crisis more likely.

6. Three international considerations affect the conduct of monetary policy: direct effects of the foreign exchange market on monetary policy, balance-of-payments considerations, and exchange rate considerations. Inasmuch as the United States has been a reserve currency country in the post–World War II period, U.S. monetary policy has been less affected than that of other countries by developments in the foreign exchange market and its balance of payments. However, in recent years, exchange rate considerations have played a more prominent role in influencing U.S. monetary policy.

7. Exchange-rate targeting has the following advantages as a monetary policy strategy: (1) It directly keeps inflation under control by tying the inflation rate for internationally traded goods to that found in the anchor country to which the targeting country's currency is pegged; (2) it provides an automatic rule for the conduct of monetary policy that helps mitigate the time-inconsistency problem; and (3) it is simple and clear. Exchange-rate targeting also has some serious disadvantages: (1) It results in a loss of independent monetary policy in the pegging country; (2) it leaves the pegging country open to speculative attacks; and (3) it can weaken the accountability of policymakers because the exchange rate signal is lost. Two strategies that make it less likely that the exchange rate regime will break down are currency boards, in which the central bank stands ready to automatically exchange domestic currency for foreign currency at a fixed rate, and dollarization, in which a sound currency like the U.S. dollar is adopted as a country's money.

KEY TERMS

anchor currency, p. 489
balance of payments, p. 488
balance-of-payments crisis, p. 494
Bretton Woods system, p. 490
capital account, p. 489
capital controls, p. 496
currency board, p. 505
current account, p. 488
devaluation, p. 491

dollarization, p. 507
emerging market countries, p. 498
exchange-rate peg, p. 501
exchange-rate targeting, p. 501
fixed exchange rate regime, p. 489
floating exchange rate regime, p. 489
foreign exchange interventions, p. 484
gold standard, p. 490
impossible trinity, p. 495

International Monetary Fund (IMF), p. 490
international reserves, p. 484
managed float regime (dirty float), p. 489
monetary (or currency) union, p.497
official reserve transactions balance, p. 488

policy trilemma, p. 495
reserve currency, p. 490
revaluation, p. 492
seigniorage, p. 507
speculative attack, p. 492

sterilized foreign exchange
intervention, p. 486
trade balance, p. 488
unsterilized foreign exchange
intervention, p. 485

World Bank, p. 490
World Trade Organization
(WTO), p. 490

QUESTIONS

All questions are available in MyEconLab *at* **www.myeconlab.com**.

1. If the Bank of Canada buys dollars in the foreign exchange market but conducts an offsetting open market operation to sterilize the intervention, what will be the impact on international reserves, the money supply, and the exchange rate?

2. If the Bank of Canada buys dollars in the foreign exchange market but does not sterilize the intervention, what will be the impact on international reserves, the money supply, and the exchange rate?

3. For each of the following, identify in which part of the balance-of-payments account the transaction is recorded (current account, capital account, or net change in international reserves) and whether it is a receipt or a payment.

   a. A British subject's purchase of a share of Johnson & Johnson stock

   b. A Canadian's purchase of an airline ticket from Air France

   c. The Swiss government's purchase of Canada bonds

   d. A Japanese citizen's purchase of Canadian wine

   e. $50 million of foreign aid to Honduras

   f. A loan by a Canadian bank to Mexico

   g. A Canadian bank's borrowing of Eurodollars

4. Why does a balance-of-payments deficit for the United States have a different effect on its international reserves than a balance-of-payments deficit does on the Netherlands?

5. How can a large balance-of-payments surplus contribute to a country's inflation rate?

6. Why can balance-of-payments deficits force some countries to implement contractionary monetary policies?

7. Under the gold standard, if Britain became more productive relative to Canada, what would happen to the

money supply in the two countries? Why would the changes in the money supply help preserve a fixed exchange rate between Canada and Britain?

8. What is the exchange rate between dollars and Swiss francs if one dollar is convertible into 1/20 ounce of gold and one Swiss franc is convertible into 1/40 ounce of gold?

9. "Inflation is not possible under the gold standard." Is this statement true, false, or uncertain? Explain your answer.

10. What are some of the disadvantages of China's pegging the yuan to the U.S. dollar?

11. If a country's par exchange rate was undervalued during the Bretton Woods fixed exchange rate regime, what kind of intervention would that country's central bank be forced to undertake, and what effect would the intervention have on the country's international reserves and money supply?

12. "The abandonment of fixed exchange rates after 1973 has led countries to pursue more independent monetary policies." Is this statement true, false, or uncertain? Explain your answer.

13. "If a country wants to keep its exchange rate from changing, it must give up some control over its money supply." Is this statement true, false, or uncertain? Explain your answer.

14. Why is it that in a pure, flexible exchange rate system, the foreign exchange market has no direct effect on the money supply? Does this mean that the foreign exchange market has no effect on monetary policy?

15. Why did the exchange-rate peg lead to difficulties for the countries in the ERM after the German reunification?

16. How can exchange-rate targets lead to a speculative attack on a currency?

17. What are the advantages and disadvantages of having the IMF as an international lender of last resort?

18. How can the long-term bond market help reduce the time-inconsistency problem for monetary policy? Can the foreign exchange market also perform this role?

19. "Balance-of-payments deficits always cause a country to lose international reserves." Is this statement true, false, or uncertain? Explain your answer.

20. How can persistent U.S. balance-of-payments deficits stimulate world inflation?

21. What are the key advantages of exchange-rate targeting as a monetary policy strategy?

22. When is exchange-rate targeting likely to be a sensible strategy for industrialized countries? When is exchange-rate targeting likely to be a sensible strategy for emerging market countries?

23. What are the advantages and disadvantages of currency boards and dollarization over a monetary policy that uses only an exchange-rate target?

APPLIED PROBLEMS

All applied problems are available in MyEconLab *at* **www.myeconlab.com**.

24. Suppose the Bank of Canada purchases $1 000 000 worth of foreign assets.

   a. If the Bank of Canada purchases the foreign assets with $1 000 000 in currency, show the effect of this open market operation, using T-accounts. What happens to the monetary base?

   b. If the Bank of Canada purchases the foreign assets by selling $1 000 000 in T-bills, show the effect of

this open market operation, using T-accounts. What happens to the monetary base?

25. Suppose the Mexican central bank chooses to peg the peso to the U.S. dollar and commits to a fixed peso/dollar exchange rate. Use a graph of the market for peso assets (foreign exchange) to show and explain how the peg must be maintained if a shock in the U.S. economy forces the Federal Reserve to pursue contractionary monetary policy. What does this say about the ability of central banks to address domestic economic problems while maintaining a pegged exchange rate?

DATA ANALYSIS PROBLEMS

Download data for these problems from MyEconLab *at* **www.myeconlab.com**.

1. Visit the Bank of Canada's web site at **www.bankofcanada.ca**. Click on "Statistics" and then "Exchange Rates."

   a. What is the Canadian-dollar effective exchange rate index (CERI)?

   b. How many foreign currencies are included in the index?

   c. Which foreign currency has the highest weight? Which has the lowest?

   d. Go to the CANSIM database and download series V41589522 (this is a daily series for the Canadian-dollar effective exchange rate index). Did the Canadian dollar appreciate or depreciate in 2014?

2. Go to the CANSIM database and find data on the monthly Canadian dollar exchange rate to the U.S. dollar (series V37432), British pound (series V37430), Swiss franc (series V37429), Japanese yen (series V37456), and euro (series V21570998). Download the data into a spreadsheet.

   a. For the most recent five-year period of data available, use the average, max, min, and stdev functions in Excel to calculate the average, highest, and lowest exchange rate values, as well as the standard deviations (this is an absolute measure of the volatility of the exchange rate).

   b. Using the maximum and minimum values of each exchange rate over the last five years, calculate the ratio of the difference between the maximum and minimum values to the average level of the exchange rate (expressed as a percentage by multiplying by 100). This value gives an indication of how tightly the exchange rate moves. Based on your results, which of the exchange rates is more volatile?

   c. Calculate the ratio of the standard deviation to the average exchange rate over the last five years (expressed as a percentage by multiplying by 100). This value gives an indication of how volatile the exchange rate is. Based on your results, which of the exchange rates is more volatile?

WEB EXERCISES

1. The International Monetary Fund stands ready to help nations facing monetary crises. Go to **www.imf.org**. Click on the tab labeled "About the IMF." What is the stated purpose of the IMF? How many nations participate, and when was it established?

WEB REFERENCES

http://research.stlouisfed.org/fred2

This website contains exchange rates, balance of payments data, and trade data for Canada, the United States, and other countries.

www.imf.org/

Find information about the structure and operations of the International Monetary Fund.

PART 7

Monetary Theory

Chapter 20   Quantity Theory, Inflation, and the Demand for Money
Chapter 21   The *IS* Curve
Chapter 22   The Monetary Policy and Aggregate Demand Curves
Chapter 23   Aggregate Demand and Supply Analysis
Chapter 24   Monetary Policy Theory
Chapter 25   The Role of Expectations in Monetary Policy
Chapter 26   Transmission Mechanisms of Monetary Policy

Crisis and Response: The Perfect Storm of 2007–2009

In 2007 and 2008, the Canadian economy was hit by a perfect storm of formidable shocks. By the end of 2007, oil prices had risen from $60 per barrel at the beginning of the year to $100, reaching a peak of over $140 in July 2008. The oil price shock was both contractionary and inflationary, and as a result led to both higher inflation and unemployment—not to mention many unhappy drivers at the gas pumps.

If this supply shock were not bad enough, the global financial crisis hit the economy starting in August 2007 and caused a contraction in both household and business spending. This shock led to a further rise in unemployment, with some weakening of inflationary pressure further down the road.

The result of this perfect storm of adverse shocks was a severe economic contraction, with unemployment rising from the 6% level in 2006 and 2007 to over 8% by the end of 2009. Inflation also accelerated from 2.6% in 2007 to over 5% by the middle of 2008, but with the increase in the unemployment rate and the decline of oil and other commodity prices by the fall of 2008, inflation rapidly came back down again.

Although the Bank of Canada's aggressive monetary policy aimed to address the contractionary forces in the economy, the Government of Canada also took action in a coordinated response to the global financial crisis with the Group of 20 (G-20) countries. Although this policy response helped stimulate household spending, it was overwhelmed by the continued worsening of the financial crisis, and the economy went into a tailspin.

The impact of the perfect storm of adverse shocks highlights the need to understand how monetary and other government policies affect inflation and economic activity. Chapter 20 discusses how the quantity theory of money explains inflation in the long run and presents how theories of the demand for money have evolved. Aggregate supply and demand analysis, the basic framework that will enable us to study the effect of monetary policy on output and inflation, is then developed in Chapters 21–24. In Chapter 25, we expand on aggregate supply and demand analysis in order to understand how monetary policy can be used to stabilize the economy and inflation. Chapter 26 outlines the transmission mechanisms through which monetary policy affects the aggregate economy.

20 Quantity Theory, Inflation, and the Demand for Money

LEARNING OBJECTIVES

After studying this chapter you should be able to

1. Assess the relationship between money growth and inflation in the short run and the long run, as implied by the quantity theory of money.

2. Identify the circumstances under which budget deficits can lead to inflationary monetary policy.

3. Summarize the three motives underlying the liquidity preference theory of money demand.

4. Identify the factors underlying the portfolio choice theory of money demand.

5. Assess and interpret the empirical evidence on the validity of the liquidity preference and portfolio theories of money demand.

PREVIEW

In earlier chapters, we spent a lot of time learning what the money supply is, how it is determined, and what part the Bank of Canada plays in it. Now we are ready to explore the role of the money supply and monetary policy in determining inflation and total production of goods and services (aggregate output) in the economy. The study of the effect of money and monetary policy on the economy is called **monetary theory**, and we examine this branch of economics in the chapters of Part 7.

When economists mention *supply*, the word *demand* is sure to follow, and the discussion of money is no exception. The supply of money is an essential building block in understanding how monetary policy affects the economy, because it suggests the factors that influence the quantity of money in the economy. Not surprisingly, another essential part of monetary theory is the demand for money.

After discussing the quantity theory and its link to the demand for money, we delve more deeply into what determines the demand for money. A central question in monetary theory is whether or to what extent the quantity of money demanded is affected by changes in interest rates. Because this issue is crucial to how we view money's effects on aggregate economic activity, we focus on the role of interest rates in the demand for money.

QUANTITY THEORY OF MONEY

Developed by the classical economists in the nineteenth and early twentieth centuries, the quantity theory of money is a theory of how the nominal value of aggregate income is determined. Because it also tells us how much money is held for a given amount of aggregate income, it is a theory of the demand for money. The most important feature of this theory is that it suggests that interest rates have no effect on the demand for money.

Velocity of Money and Equation of Exchange

The clearest exposition of the classical quantity theory approach is found in the work of the American economist Irving Fisher, in his influential book *The Purchasing Power of Money*, published in 1911. Fisher wanted to examine the link between the total quantity of money M (the money supply) and the total amount of spending on final goods and services produced in the economy $P \times Y$, where P is the price level and Y is aggregate output (income). (Total spending $P \times Y$ is also thought of as aggregate nominal income for the economy or as nominal GDP.) The concept that provides the link between M and $P \times Y$ is called the **velocity of money** (often reduced to *velocity*), the average number of times per year (turnover) that a dollar is spent in buying the total amount of goods and services produced in the economy. Velocity V is defined more precisely as total spending $P \times Y$ divided by the quantity of money M:

$$V = \frac{P \times Y}{M} \qquad \text{(Equation 1)}$$

If, for example, nominal GDP $(P \times Y)$ in a year is \$2 trillion and the quantity of money (M) is \$0.4 trillion, we can calculate velocity to be as follows:

$$V = \frac{\$2 \text{ trillion}}{\$0.4 \text{ trillion}} = 5$$

The value of 5 for velocity means that the average dollar bill is spent five times in purchasing final goods and services in the economy.

By multiplying both sides of this definition by M, we obtain the **equation of exchange**, which relates nominal income to the quantity of money and velocity:

$$M \times V = P \times Y \qquad \text{(Equation 2)}$$

The equation of exchange thus states that the quantity of money multiplied by the number of times that this money is spent in a given year must equal nominal income (the total nominal amount spent on goods and services in that year).[1]

As it stands, Equation 2 is nothing more than an identity—a relationship that is true by definition. It does not tell us, for instance, that when the money supply M changes, nominal income $(P \times Y)$ changes in the same direction; a rise in M, for example, could be offset by a fall in V that leaves $M \times V$ (and therefore $P \times Y$) unchanged. To convert the equation of exchange (an *identity*) into a *theory* of how nominal income is determined requires an understanding of the factors that determine velocity.

Determinants of Velocity Irving Fisher reasoned that velocity is determined by the institutions in an economy that affect the way individuals conduct transactions. If people use charge accounts and credit cards to conduct their transactions, as they can today, and consequently use money less often when making purchases, less money is required to conduct the transactions generated by nominal income (M falls relative to $P \times Y$), and velocity $(P \times Y)/M$ will increase. Conversely, if it is more convenient for purchases to be paid for with cash, cheques, or debit cards (all of which are money), more money is used to conduct the transactions generated by the same level of nominal

---

[1]Fisher actually first formulated the equation of exchange in terms of the nominal value of transactions in the economy PT:

$$MV_T = PT$$

where P = average price per transaction

       T = number of transactions conducted in a year

    $V_T = PT/M$ = transactions velocity of money

Because the nominal value of transactions T is difficult to measure, the quantity theory has been formulated in terms of aggregate output Y as follows: T is assumed to be proportional to Y so that $T = vY$, where v is a constant of proportionality. Substituting vY for T in Fisher's equation of exchange yields $MV_T = vPY$, which can be written as Equation 2 in the text, in which $V = V_T/v$.

income, and velocity will fall. Fisher took the view that the institutional and techno-logical features of the economy would affect velocity only slowly over time, so velocity would normally be reasonably constant in the short run.

Demand for Money   Another way of interpreting Fisher's quantity theory is in terms of the **demand for money**, the quantity of money that people want to hold.

Because the quantity theory of money tells us how much money is held for a given amount of nominal spending, it is, in fact, a theory of the demand for money. To illustrate, let's first divide both sides of the equation of exchange by V to yield the following:

$$M = \frac{1}{V} \times PY$$

When the money market is in equilibrium, money supply equals money demand, so we can replace M in the equation by M^d. In addition, since in the quantity theory of money velocity is assumed to be constant, we can replace $1/V$ with a constant k. Substituting k for $1/V$ and M^d for M, we can rewrite the equation as

$$M^d = k \times PY \qquad \text{(Equation 3)}$$

Equation 3 tells us that because k is constant, the level of transactions generated by a fixed level of nominal income PY determines the quantity of money M^d that people demand. ***Therefore Fisher's theory suggests that the demand for money is purely a function of income, and interest rates have no effect on the demand for money.***[2]

From the Equation of Exchange to the Quantity Theory of Money

Fisher's view that velocity is fairly constant in the short run, so that $V = \overline{V}$, transforms the equation of exchange into the **quantity theory of money**, which states that nominal income (spending) is determined solely by movements in the quantity of money M.

$$P \times Y = M \times \overline{V} \qquad \text{(Equation 4)}$$

The quantity theory equation above indicates that when the quantity of money M doubles, $M \times \overline{V}$ doubles and so must $P \times Y$, the value of nominal income. To illustrate, let's assume that velocity is 5, nominal income (GDP) is initially $2 trillion, and the money supply is $0.4 trillion. If the money supply doubles to $0.8 trillion, the quantity theory of money tells us that nominal income will double to $4 trillion ($=5 \times \$0.8$ trillion).

Quantity Theory and the Price Level

Because the classical economists (including Fisher) thought that wages and prices were completely flexible, they believed that the level of aggregate output Y produced in the economy during normal times would remain at the full-employment level. Hence Y in the equation of exchange could also be treated as reasonably constant in the short run and thus assigned a fixed value of $\overline{Y}$ in Equation 4. Dividing both sides of Equation 4 by $\overline{Y}$, we can then write the price level as follows:

$$P = \frac{M \times \overline{V}}{\overline{Y}} \qquad \text{(Equation 5)}$$

---

[2]While Fisher was developing his quantity theory approach to the demand for money, a group of classical econo-mists in Cambridge, England led by Alfred Marshall and A. C. Pigou, came to similar conclusions, although with slightly different reasoning. They derived Equation 3 by recognizing that two properties of money motivate people to hold it: its utility as a medium of exchange and its utility as a store of wealth.

The quantity of money, as represented by Equation 5, implies that if M doubles, P must also double in the short run because $\overline{V}$ and $\overline{Y}$ are constant. In our example, if aggregate output is $2 trillion, velocity is 5, and the money supply is $0.4 trillion, then the price level equals 1.0.

$$P = \frac{\$0.4 \text{ trillion} \times 5}{\$2 \text{ trillion}} = \frac{\$2 \text{ trillion}}{\$2 \text{ trillion}} = 1.0$$

When the money supply doubles to $0.8 trillion, the price level must also double to 2.0 because

$$P = \frac{\$0.8 \text{ trillion} \times 5}{\$2 \text{ trillion}} = \frac{\$4 \text{ trillion}}{\$2 \text{ trillion}} = 2.0$$

Classical economists relied on the quantity theory of money to explain movements in the price level. In their view, **changes in the quantity of money lead to proportional changes in the price level**.

Quantity Theory and Inflation

We now transform the quantity theory of money into a theory of inflation. You might recall from high school math the mathematical fact that the percentage change ($\%\Delta$) of a product of two variables is approximately equal to the sum of the percentage changes of each of these variables. In other words,

$$\text{Percentage Change in } (x \times y) = (\text{Percentage Change in } x) + (\text{Percentage Change in } y)$$

Using this mathematical fact, we can rewrite the equation of exchange as follows:

$$\%\Delta M + \%\Delta V = \%\Delta P + \%\Delta Y$$

Subtracting $\%\Delta Y$ from both sides of the preceding equation, and recognizing that the inflation rate, π, is the growth rate of the price level, that is, $\%\Delta P$,

$$\pi = \%\Delta P = \%\Delta M + \%\Delta V - \%\Delta Y$$

Since we assume velocity is constant, its growth rate is zero, so the quantity theory of money is also a theory of inflation:

$$\pi = \%\Delta M - \%\Delta Y \qquad \text{(Equation 6)}$$

Because the percentage change in a variable at an annual rate is the same as the growth rate in that variable, this equation can also be stated in words: **the quantity theory of inflation indicates that the inflation rate equals the growth rate of the money supply minus the growth rate of aggregate output**. For example, if the aggregate output is growing at 3% per year and the growth rate of money is 5%, then inflation is 2% ($= 5\% - 3\%$). If the Bank of Canada increases the money growth rate to 10%, then the quantity theory of inflation in Equation 6 indicates that the inflation rate will rise to 7% ($= 10\% - 3\%$).

APPLICATION | ## Testing the Quantity Theory of Money

Now that we have fully outlined the quantity theory of money, let's put it to the test with actual data over the long and short runs.

The Quantity Theory of Money in the Long Run The quantity theory of money provides a long-run theory of inflation because it is based on the assumption that wages and prices are flexible. Panel (a) of Figure 20-1 plots 10-year averages of Canadian inflation rates against the 10-year average rate of Canadian money growth (M2) from 1920

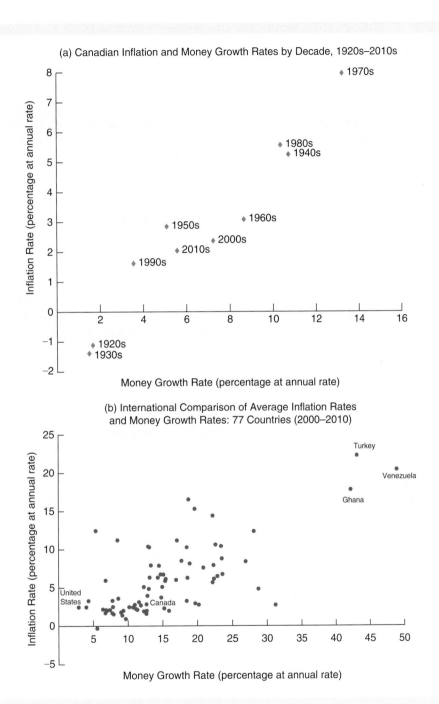

(a) Canadian Inflation and Money Growth Rates by Decade, 1920s–2010s

(b) International Comparison of Average Inflation Rates and Money Growth Rates: 77 Countries (2000–2010)

FIGURE 20-1   Relation Between Inflation and Money Growth

There is a strong positive association between the average money growth rate and the average inflation rate.

Sources: For panel (a), for 1870 to 1960, M.C. Urquhart, "Canadian Economic Growth 1870–1985," Institute for Economic Research, Queens University: Kingston, Ontario, Discussion Paper No. 734; and since 1961, Federal Reserve Bank of St. Louis, FRED database: http://research.stlouisfed.org/fred2/. For panel (b), International Financial Statistics. International Monetary Fund, http://elibrary-data.imf.org/.

through 2014. Because the growth rate of aggregate output Y over 10-year periods does not vary very much, Equation 6 indicates that the 10-year inflation rate should be the 10-year money growth rate minus a constant (the rate of aggregate output growth). Thus a strong positive relationship should exist between inflation and money growth rates—and this relationship is borne out in panel (a) of Figure 20-1. Decades with higher growth rates of the Canadian money supply typically see higher average inflation rates.

Does the quantity theory also explain differing long-run inflation rates across countries? It certainly does. Panel (b) of Figure 20-1 plots the average inflation rate over the 10-year period from 2000 to 2010 against the 10-year money growth rate for 77 countries. Note that countries with high money growth, such as Turkey, Venezuela, and Ghana, tend to have higher inflation.

The Quantity Theory of Money in the Short Run

Does the quantity theory of money provide a good explanation of short-run inflation fluctuations as well? Figure 20-2 provides evidence on the link between money growth and inflation in the short run by plotting the annual Canadian inflation rate (based on the GDP deflator) from 1971 to 2014 against the annual money growth rate (based on M2+). The money supply lags by two years to allow for the time it takes for changes in money growth to affect inflation. Although the correlation between money growth and inflation on an annual basis is positive and strong, there are many years where money growth is high but inflation is low.

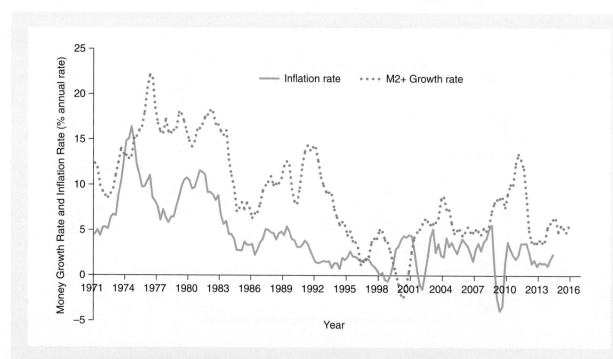

FIGURE 20-2   Annual Canadian Inflation and Money Growth Rates, 1971–2014

Plots of the annual Canadian inflation rate against the annual money (M2+) growth rate from two years earlier (to allow for lagged effects from money growth to inflation) also support a short-run link between inflation and money growth. There are many years, however, where money growth is high yet inflation is low.

Source: Federal Reserve Bank of St. Louis, FRED database: http://research.stlouisfed.org/fred2/.

The conclusion is that *the quantity theory of money is a good theory of inflation in the long run, but not in the short run*. Another way of stating this conclusion is that Milton Friedman's statement that "inflation is always and everywhere a monetary phenomenon" (mentioned in Chapter 1) is accurate in the long run but is not supported by the data for the short run. This insight tells us that the classical assumption that wages and prices are completely flexible may not be a good assumption for short-run fluctuations in inflation and aggregate output. For this reason, we relax this assumption in the following chapters of the book when we develop models of short-run inflation and output fluctuations. ◆

BUDGET DEFICITS AND INFLATION

Budget deficits can be an important source of inflationary monetary policy. To see how this could be the case, we need to look at how a government finances its budget deficits.

Government Budget Constraint

Because the government has to pay its bills just as we do, it has a budget constraint. We can pay for our spending in two ways: raise revenue (by working) or borrow. The government also enjoys these two options: raise revenue by levying taxes or go into debt by issuing government bonds. Unlike us, however, it has a third option: the government can create money and use it to pay for the goods and services it buys.

Methods of financing government spending are described by an expression called the **government budget constraint**, which states the following: the government budget deficit *DEF*, which equals the excess of government spending *G* over tax revenue *T*, must equal the sum of the change in the monetary base ΔMB and the change in government bonds held by the public ΔB. Algebraically, this expression can be written as follows:

$$DEF = G - T = \Delta MB + \Delta B \qquad \text{(Equation 7)}$$

To see what the government budget constraint means in practice, let's look at the case in which the only government purchase is a $100 million supercomputer. If the government convinces the electorate that such a computer is worth paying for, it will probably be able to raise the $100 million in taxes to pay for it, and the budget deficit will equal zero. The government budget constraint then tells us that no issue of money or bonds is needed to pay for the computer, because the budget is balanced. If taxpayers think that the supercomputer is too expensive and refuse to pay taxes for it, the budget constraint indicates that the government must pay for it by selling $100 million of new bonds to the public or by, in effect, printing $100 million of currency to pay for the computer. In either case, the budget constraint is satisfied. The $100 million deficit is balanced by the change in the stock of government bonds held by the public ($\Delta B = \$100$ million) or by the change in the monetary base ($\Delta MB = \$100$ million).

The government budget constraint thus reveals two important facts: *if the government deficit is financed by an increase in bond holdings by the public, there is no effect on the monetary base and hence on the money supply. But if the deficit is not financed by increased bond holdings by the public, the monetary base and the money supply increase*.

There are several ways to understand why a deficit leads to an increase in the monetary base when the public's bond holdings do not increase. The simplest case is when a government's treasury has the legal right to issue currency to finance its deficit. Financing the deficit is then very straightforward: the government just pays for the spending that is in excess of its tax revenues with new currency. Because this increase in currency adds directly to the monetary base, the monetary base rises and the money supply with it through the process of multiple deposit creation described in Chapter 16.

In Canada, however, and in many other countries, the government does not have the right to issue currency to pay for its bills. In this case, the government must finance its deficit by first issuing bonds to the public to acquire the extra funds to pay its bills. Yet if these bonds do not end up in the hands of the public, the only alternative is that they are purchased by the central bank. For the government bonds not to end up in the hands of the public, the central bank must conduct an open market purchase, which, as we saw in Chapter 16, leads to an increase in the monetary base and in the money supply. This method of financing government spending is called **monetizing the debt** because, as indicated by the two-step process described, government debt issued to finance government spending has been removed from the hands of the public and has been replaced by high-powered (base) money. This method of financing, or the more direct method when a government just issues the currency directly, is also, somewhat inaccurately, referred to as **printing money** because high-powered money (the monetary base) is created in the process. The use of the word *printing* is misleading because what is essential to this method of financing government spending is that the monetary base increases when the central bank conducts open market purchases, just as it would if more currency were put in circulation.

We thus see that a budget deficit can lead to an increase in the money supply if it is financed by the creation of high-powered money. However, because the quantity theory of money explains inflation only in the long run, to produce inflation, the budget deficit must be persistent, that is, last for a substantial period of time. This leads to the following conclusion: *financing a persistent deficit by money creation will lead to a sustained inflation*.

Hyperinflation

The analysis here can be used to explain **hyperinflations**, periods of extremely high inflation of more than 50% per month. Many economies—both poor and developed—have experienced hyperinflation over the past century, but Canada has been spared such turmoil. One of the most extreme examples of hyperinflation throughout world history occurred recently in Zimbabwe in the 2000s, and it is discussed in the Application that follows.

APPLICATION   ## The Zimbabwean Hyperinflation

We now use our analysis to explain the Zimbabwean hyperinflation that started in the early 2000s.

After the expropriation of farms, which were redistributed to supporters of Robert Mugabe, the president of the country, agricultural output plummeted and, along with it, tax revenue. The result was that the government's expenditures now massively exceeded revenues. The government could have obtained revenues to cover its expenditures by raising taxes, but given the depressed state of the economy, generating revenue in this way was both hard to do and would have been politically unpopular. Alternatively, the government could have tried to finance its expenditure by borrowing from the public, but given the distrust of the government, this was not an option. There was only one route left: the printing press. The government could pay for its expenditures simply by printing more currency (increasing the money supply) and using it to make payments to individuals and businesses. This is exactly what the Zimbabwean government did and the money supply began to increase rapidly.

As predicted by the quantity theory, the surge in the money supply led to a rapidly rising price level. In February 2007, the Reserve Bank of Zimbabwe, the central bank, outlawed price increases on many commodities. Although this tactic has been tried before by governments in countries experiencing hyperinflations, it has never worked: criminalizing inflation cannot stop inflation when the central bank keeps on printing money. In March 2007, the inflation rate hit a record of over 1500%. By 2008, Zimbabwe's official inflation rate was over 2 million percent (but unofficially over 10 million percent). In July 2008, the Zimbabwean central bank issued a new $100 billion bank note and shortly later issued a $100 trillion dollar bill, the highest denomination dollar note on record. That's a lot of zeros, but don't be too impressed. Although holding one of these bills made you a trillionaire, it could not even buy a bottle of beer. Zimbabwean currency became worth less than toilet paper.

In 2009, the Zimbabwean government allowed the use of foreign currencies like the dollar for all transactions, but the damage had already been done. The hyperinflation wreaked havoc on the economy, and an extremely poor country became even poorer. ◆

KEYNESIAN THEORIES OF MONEY DEMAND

In his famous 1936 book *The General Theory of Employment, Interest and Money*, John Maynard Keynes abandoned the quantity theory view that velocity was a constant and developed a theory of money demand that emphasized the importance of interest rates. In his theory of the demand for money, which he called the **liquidity preference theory**, Keynes presented three motives behind the demand for money: the transactions motive, the precautionary motive, and the speculative motive.

Transactions Motive

In the quantity theory approach, individuals are assumed to hold money because it is a medium of exchange that can be used to carry out everyday transactions. Keynes initially accepted the quantity theory view that the transactions component is proportional to income. Later, he and other economists recognized that new methods for payment, referred to as **payment technology**, could also affect the demand for money. For example, credit cards enable consumers to make even very small purchases without needing to hold money. Electronic payments that can be made from investors' brokerage accounts can also reduce money demand. As payment technology advances, the demand for money will be likely to decline relative to income.

Precautionary Motive

Keynes also recognized that people hold money as a cushion against unexpected wants. Suppose that you have been thinking about buying a new Wii entertainment system and now see that it is on sale at 25% off. If you are holding money as a precaution for just such an occurrence, you can immediately buy it. Keynes argued that the precautionary money balances people want to hold would also be proportional to income.

Speculative Motive

Keynes also believed people choose to hold money as a store of wealth, which he called the *speculative motive*. Because the definition of money in Keynes's analysis includes currency (which earns no interest) and chequing account deposits (which typically earn little interest), he assumed that money earns no interest and hence its opportunity cost relative to holding other assets, such as bonds, is the nominal interest rate on bonds, i. As the interest rate i rises, the opportunity cost of money rises (it is more costly to hold money relative to bonds) and the quantity of money demanded falls.

Putting the Three Motives Together

In putting the three motives for holding money balances together into a demand for money equation, Keynes was careful to distinguish between nominal quantities and real quantities. Money is valued in terms of what it can buy. If, for example, all prices in the economy double (the price level doubles), the same nominal quantity of money will only be able to buy half as many goods. Keynes thus reasoned that people want to hold a certain amount of **real money balances** (the quantity of money in real terms). Combining the three motives for holding money balances into a demand for real money balances led to what Keynes called the liquidity preference function, which is written as follows:

$$\frac{M^d}{P} = L(\underset{-\;\;+}{i,\, Y}) \qquad \text{(Equation 8)}$$

Equation 8 says that the demand for real money balances is negatively related to the nominal interest rate and is positively related to real income.

Later Keynesian economists, such as Nobel Prize winner James Tobin, expanded the analysis and showed that interest rates play a more important role in money demand than even Keynes supposed. They demonstrated that even the transactions and precautionary demand for money would also be negatively related to the interest rate.[3]

An important implication of Keynesian theories of money demand is that velocity is not a constant but will fluctuate with changes in interest rates. To illustrate, we write the liquidity preference function as follows:

$$\frac{P}{M^d} = \frac{1}{L(i, Y)}$$

Multiplying both sides of this equation by Y and recognizing that we can replace M^d by M because they must be equal in money market equilibrium, we solve for velocity:

$$V = \frac{PY}{M} = \frac{Y}{L(i, Y)} \qquad \text{(Equation 9)}$$

We know that the demand for money is negatively related to interest rates; when i goes up, $L(i, Y)$ declines, and therefore velocity rises. Because interest rates have substantial fluctuations, Keynesian theories of the demand for money indicate that velocity has substantial fluctuations as well. Thus Keynesian theories cast doubt on the classical quantity theory view that nominal income is determined primarily by movements in the quantity of money.

[3]Three famous papers that elaborated on Keynes's approach to the demand for money are as follows: William J. Baumol, "The Transactions Demand for Cash: An Inventory Theoretic Approach," *Quarterly Journal of Economics* 66 (1952): 545–556; James Tobin, "The Interest Elasticity of the Transactions Demand for Cash," *Review of Economics and Statistics* 38 (1956): 241–247; and James Tobin, "Liquidity Preference as Behavior Towards Risk," *Review of Economic Studies* 25 (1958): 65–86. For further discussion of the models outlined in these papers, see Web Appendix 20-1 which can be found on MyEconLab.

PORTFOLIO THEORIES OF MONEY DEMAND

Related to Keynes's analysis of the demand for money are so-called portfolio theories of money demand, in which people decide how much of an asset such as money they want to hold as part of their overall portfolio of assets.[4]

Theory of Portfolio Choice and Keynesian Liquidity Preference

In Chapter 5, we developed the theory of portfolio choice, which stated that the demand for an asset is positively related to wealth, expected return relative to other assets, and relative liquidity, whereas it is negatively related to its risk relative to other assets. This theory of portfolio choice can justify the conclusion from the Keynesian liquidity preference function that the demand for real money balances is positively related to income and negatively related to the nominal interest rate.

Because income and wealth tend to move together, when income is higher, wealth is likely to be as well. Hence, higher income means that wealth is higher, and the theory of portfolio choice then indicates that the demand for the money asset will rise and the demand for real money balances will be higher.

As interest rates rise, the expected return for money does not change. However, the return for bonds, an alternative asset, goes up. Thus, although the expected *absolute* return of money did not change, money's expected return *relative* to bonds went down. In other words, as the theory of portfolio choice indicates, higher interest rates make money less desirable, and the demand for real money balances falls.

Other Factors That Affect the Demand for Money

The theory of portfolio choice indicates that other factors besides income and the nominal interest rate can affect the demand for money. We look at each of these in turn.

Wealth   The theory of portfolio choice posits that as wealth increases, investors have more resources to purchase assets, increasing the demand for money. However, when income is held constant, greater wealth has only a small effect on the demand for money. In general, investors will hold only a small amount of money in their investment portfolio, preferring interest-bearing assets with similar risk and liquidity profiles, such as money market mutual funds, that are not included in measures of money such as M1. Currency and chequable deposits are sometimes said to be **dominated assets**, because investors can hold other assets that pay higher returns and yet are perceived to be just as safe.

Risk   It's hard to imagine an asset less risky than money. Currency will always be accepted, unless there's a revolution and the new government does not accept the old government's currency. And bank deposits are safe as long as deposit insurance exists. In the theory of portfolio choice, however, risk is always measured relative to another asset. Thus, if the stock market becomes more volatile, money can become less risky relative to stocks and demand for it will increase. In addition, although money is extremely safe on a nominal basis, its real return (the nominal return minus expected inflation) can become highly variable when inflation becomes more variable. Higher variability in the real return of money lowers demand for money, as people shift into alternative assets

---

[4]This is the approach taken by Milton Friedman in his famous paper "The Quantity Theory of Money: A Restatement," in *Studies in the Quantity Theory of Money*, ed. Milton Friedman (Chicago: University of Chicago Press, 1956), 3–21.

SUMMARY TABLE 20-1

Factors That Determine the Demand for Money

Variable	Change in Variable	Money Demand Response	Reason
Interest rates	↑	↓	Opportunity cost of money rises
Income	↑	↑	Higher transactions
Payment technology	↑	↓	Less need for money in transactions
Wealth	↑	↑	More resources to put into money
Risk of other assets	↑	↑	Money relatively less risky and so more desirable
Inflation risk	↑	↓	Money relatively more risky and so less desirable
Liquidity of other assets	↑	↓	Money relatively less liquid and so less desirable

known as **inflation hedges**, whose real returns are less affected than those of money when inflation varies. Popular inflation hedges include Real Return Bonds (discussed in Chapter 4), gold, and real estate.

Liquidity of other Assets　In recent years, financial innovation has led to the development of new liquid assets, such as money market mutual funds or home equity lines of credit, which allow households to write cheques that are backed by their homes. As these alternative assets become more liquid, the relative liquidity of money falls and so the demand for money falls as well.

Summary

Our analysis of the demand for money using Keynesian and portfolio theories indicates that seven factors affect the demand for money: interest rates, income, payment technology, wealth, riskiness of other assets, inflation risk, and liquidity of other assets. As a study aid, Summary Table 20-1 indicates the response of money demand to changes in each of these factors and gives a brief synopsis of the reasoning behind each response.

EMPIRICAL EVIDENCE FOR THE DEMAND FOR MONEY

Here we examine the empirical evidence for the two key issues that distinguish different theories of money demand and affect their conclusions about whether the quantity of money is the primary determinant of aggregate spending: is the demand for money sensitive to changes in interest rates and is the demand for money function stable over time?[5]

---

[5]If you are interested in a more detailed discussion of the empirical research on the demand for money, you can find it in Web Appendix 20-2 on MyEconLab.

Interest Rates and Money Demand

We have established that if interest rates do not affect the demand for money, velocity is more likely to be constant—or at least predictable—so that the quantity theory view that aggregate spending is determined by the quantity of money is more likely to be true. However, the more sensitive to interest rates the demand for money is, the more unpredictable velocity will be, and the less clear the link between the money supply and aggregate spending will be. Indeed, there is an extreme case of ultrasensitivity of the demand for money to interest rates, called the **liquidity trap**, in which conventional monetary policy has no direct effect on aggregate spending, because a change in the money supply has no effect on interest rates.[6]

The evidence for the interest sensitivity of the demand for money is remarkably consistent. Neither extreme case is supported by the data: in situations in which nominal interest rates have not hit a floor of zero, the demand for money is sensitive to interest rates, and little evidence is present that a liquidity trap has ever existed. However, when nominal interest rates fall to zero, they can go no lower. In this situation, a liquidity trap has occurred because the demand for money is now completely flat. Indeed, exactly this situation has occurred in Canada and the United States in recent years, which is why their central banks have had to resort to nonconventional monetary policy.

Stability of Money Demand

If the money demand function, like the one in Equation 8, is unstable and undergoes substantial, unpredictable shifts, as Keynes believed, then velocity is unpredictable, and the quantity of money may not be tightly linked to aggregate spending, as it is in the quantity theory. The stability of the money demand function is also crucial to whether the Bank of Canada should target interest rates or the money supply. If the money demand function is unstable and so the money supply is not closely linked to aggregate spending, then the level of interest rates the Bank of Canada sets will provide more information about the stance of monetary policy than will the money supply.

Until the early 1970s, evidence strongly supported the stability of the money demand function. However, after 1973, the rapid pace of financial innovation, which changed the items that could be used for money, led to substantial instability in estimated money demand functions. The instability of the money demand function calls into question whether our theories and empirical analyses are adequate. It also has important implications for the conduct of monetary policy, because it casts doubt on the usefulness of the money demand function as a tool to provide guidance to policy makers. In particular, because the money demand function has become unstable, velocity is now harder to predict. Monetary policy makers have found that the money supply does not provide reliable information on the future course of the economy, leading them to think of monetary policy in terms of the setting of interest rates. The instability of money demand has thus led to a downgrading of the focus on money supply in the conduct of monetary policy.

---

[6]If the demand for money is ultrasensitive to interest rates, a tiny change in interest rates produces a very large change in the quantity of money demanded. Hence, in this case, the demand for money is completely flat in the supply and demand diagrams of Chapter 5. Therefore, a change in the money supply that shifts the money supply curve to the right or left results in it intersecting the flat money demand curve at the same unchanged interest rate.

MyEconLab

MyEconLab is an online homework and tutorial system that puts you in control of your own learning with study and practice tools directly correlated to this chapter's content. Visit MyEconLab to access the eText, the Questions and Applied Problems with answers, as well as additional assessment. You will also find web chapters, mini-lectures, appendices, mini-cases, videos, glossary flashcards, news feeds, CANSIM data, and graphing tools.

SUMMARY

1. The quantity theory of money as expressed by the equation of exchange, $M \times V = P \times Y$, indicates that nominal spending is determined solely by movements in the quantity of money. The quantity theory indicates that (1) changes in the quantity of money lead to proportional changes in the price level, because $P = (M \times \overline{V})/\overline{Y}$, and (2) the inflation rate is the growth rate of the money supply minus the growth rate of aggregate output—that is, $\pi = \%\Delta M - \%\Delta Y$. These implications of the quantity theory are borne out in the data in the long run, but not the short run.

2. The government budget constraint indicates that a deficit must be financed by either money creation or the issuing of government bonds. That is, $DEF = G - T = \Delta MB + \Delta B$. Combining this fact with the quantity theory indicates that financing a persistent deficit by money creation will lead to a sustained inflation. This analysis helps explain hyperinflations, in which inflation and money growth go to extremely high levels because of massive budget deficits.

3. John Maynard Keynes suggested three motives for holding money: the transactions motive, the precautionary motive, and the speculative motive. His resulting liquidity preference theory views the transactions and precautionary components of money demand

as proportional to income. However, the speculative component of money demand is viewed as sensitive to interest rates as well as to expectations about the future movements of interest rates. This theory, then, implies that velocity is unstable and cannot be treated as a constant.

4. Portfolio theories of money demand indicate that the demand for money is determined not only by interest rates, income, and payment technology, as in the Keynesian analysis, but also by wealth, riskiness of other assets, inflation risk, and liquidity of other assets.

5. Two main conclusions can be reached from the research on the demand for money: The demand for money is sensitive to interest rates, but little evidence exists that it is or has been ultrasensitive (liquidity trap). Since 1973, money demand has been found to be unstable, with the most likely source of the instability being the rapid pace of financial innovation. Because the money demand function is found to be both unstable and sensitive to interest rates, velocity cannot be viewed as constant and is not easily predictable. This situation has led to a downgrading of the focus on money supply and a greater emphasis on interest rates in the conduct of monetary policy.

KEY TERMS

demand for money, p. 515
dominated assets, p. 523
equation of exchange, p. 514
government budget constraint, p. 519
hyperinflations, p. 520

inflation hedges, p. 524
liquidity preference theory, p. 521
liquidity trap, p. 525
monetary theory, p. 513
monetizing the debt, p. 520

payment technology, p. 521
printing money, p. 520
quantity theory of money, p. 515
real money balances, p. 522
velocity of money, p. 514

QUESTIONS

All questions are available in MyEconLab *at* **www.myeconlab.com**.

1. How would you expect velocity to typically behave over the business cycle?

2. If velocity and aggregate output are reasonably constant (as the classical economists believed), what happens to the price level when the money supply increases from $1 trillion to $4 trillion?

3. If credit cards were made illegal by government legislation, what would happen to velocity? Explain your answer.

4. "If nominal GDP rises, velocity must rise." Is this statement true, false, or uncertain? Explain your answer.

5. Why would a central bank be concerned about persistent long-term budget deficits?

6. "Persistent budget deficits always lead to higher inflation." Is this statement true, false, or uncertain? Explain your answer.

7. Suppose a new "payment technology" allows individuals to make payments using Canada bonds (i.e., Canada bonds are immediately cashed when needed to make a payment and that balance is transferred to the payee). How do you think this payment technology would affect the transaction components of the demand for money?

8. Some payment technologies require infrastructure (e.g., merchants need to have access to credit card swiping machines). In most developing countries, this infrastructure is either nonexistent or very costly. Everything else being the same, would you expect the transaction component of the demand for money to be greater or smaller in a developing country than in a rich country?

9. What three motives for holding money did Keynes consider in his liquidity preference theory of the demand for real money balances? On the basis of these motives, what variables did he think determined the demand for money?

10. In many countries, people hold money as a cushion against unexpected needs arising from a variety of potential scenarios (e.g., banking crises, natural disasters, health problems, unemployment) that are not usually covered by insurance markets. Explain the effect of such behaviour on the precautionary component of the demand for money.

11. In Keynes's analysis of the speculative demand for money, what will happen to money demand if people suddenly decide that the normal level of the interest rate has declined? Why?

12. Why is Keynes's analysis of the speculative demand for money important to his view that velocity will undergo substantial fluctuations and thus cannot be treated as constant?

13. According to the portfolio theories of money demand, what are the four factors that determine money demand? What changes in these factors can increase the demand for money?

14. Explain how the following events will affect the demand for money according to the portfolio theories of money demand:

    a. The economy experiences a business cycle contraction.

    b. Brokerage fees decline, making bond transactions cheaper.

    c. The stock market crashes. (*Hint:* Consider both the increase in stock price volatility following a market crash and the decrease in wealth of shareholders.)

15. Suppose a given country experienced low and stable inflation rates for quite some time, but then inflation picked up and over the past decade has been relatively high and quite unpredictable. Explain how this new inflationary environment would affect the demand for money according to portfolio theories of money demand. What would happen if the government decides to issue inflation-protected securities?

16. Consider the portfolio choice theory of money demand. How do you think the demand for money will be affected during a hyperinflation (i.e., monthly inflation rates in excess of 50%)?

17. Both the portfolio choice and Keynes's theories of the demand for money suggest that as the relative expected return on money falls, demand for it will also fall. Why would the portfolio choice approach predict that money demand is unaffected by changes in interest rates? Why did Keynes think that money demand is affected by changes in interest rates?

18. Why does the Keynesian view of the demand for money suggest that velocity is unpredictable?

19. What evidence is used to assess the stability of the money demand function? What does the evidence suggest about the stability of money demand and how has this affected monetary policy making?

20. Suppose that a plot of the values of the money supply, M, and nominal GDP for a given country over 40 years shows that these two variables are very closely related. In particular, a plot of their ratio (nominal GDP/M) yields very stable and easy-to-predict values. On the basis of this evidence, would you recommend the monetary authorities of this country conduct monetary policy by focusing mostly on the money supply rather than on setting interest rates? Explain why.

APPLIED PROBLEMS

All applied problems are available in MyEconLab at **www.myeconlab.com**.

21. Suppose the money supply M has been growing at 10% per year, and nominal GDP, PY, has been growing at 20% per year. The data are as follows (in billions of dollars):

	2015	2016	2017
M	100	110	121
PY	1000	1200	1440

Calculate the velocity in each year. At what rate is velocity growing?

22. Calculate what happens to nominal GDP if velocity remains constant at 5 and the money supply increases from $200 billion to $300 billion.

23. What happens to nominal GDP if the money supply grows by 20% but velocity declines by 30%?

24. If velocity and aggregate output remain constant at $5 and $1000 billion, respectively, what happens to the price level if the money supply declines from $400 billion to $300 billion?

25. Suppose the liquidity preference function is given by

$$L(i, Y) = \frac{Y}{8} - 1000i$$

Calculate velocity for each period, using the money demand equation, along with the following table of values.

	Period 1	Period 2	Period 3	Period 4	Period 5	Period 6	Period 7
Y (in billions)	12 000	12 500	12 250	12 500	12 800	13 000	13 200
Interest rate	0.05	0.07	0.03	0.05	0.07	0.04	0.06

DATA ANALYSIS PROBLEMS

Download data for these problems from MyEconLab at **www.myeconlab.com**.

1. The formula for computing the velocity of money is Y/(M/P), where Y is real GDP, M is a money supply measure, and P is the price level. Go to the St. Louis FRED database and download quarterly Canadian data from 1981:Q1 to 2013:Q4 on the GDP deflator (series CANGDPDEFQISMEI) and M2+ (series MABMM203CAQ189S). Also download nominal GDP from CANSIM (series V62295562). Compute the velocity of M2+ money in 2013:Q4 and compare it to its level in 1981:Q1. Has it risen or fallen?

2. Use the data from the previous exercise and also download the three-month T-Bill rate (CANSIM series V122531). Run a regression of real money balances on a constant, real GDP, and the nominal interest rate.

   a. Comment on the fit of the regression.

   b. What is the estimated income elasticity of the demand for real money balances? What is the estimated interest rate elasticity?

   c. Are your estimates in (b) statistically significant?

   d. Is your evidence consistent with the Baumol-Tobin model or with the quantity theory of money?

WEB EXERCISES

1. John Maynard Keynes is among the most well-known economic theorists. Go to **http://en.wikipedia.org/wiki/John_Maynard_Keynes** and write a one-page summary of his life and contributions.

WEB REFERENCES

www.usagold.com/gildedopinion/puplava/20020614.html

A summary of how various factors affect the velocity of money.

21

The *IS* Curve

Learning Objectives

After studying this chapter you should be able to

1. List the four components of aggregate demand (or planned expenditure).

2. List and describe the factors that determine the four components of aggregate demand (or planned expenditure).

3. Solve for the goods market equilibrium.

4. Describe why the *IS* curve slopes downward and why the economy heads to a goods market equilibrium.

5. List the factors that shift the *IS* curve and describe how they shift the *IS* curve.

PREVIEW

During the Great Depression of the 1930s, aggregate output fell precipitously, by 30%, with unemployment rising to 30%. Although the recession of 2007–2009 was not as severe, the contraction in economic activity led unemployment to rise to over 8.7%. To understand why these contractions in economic activity occur, economists make use of the concept of *aggregate demand*, the total amount of output demanded in the economy. This concept was developed by John Maynard Keynes in his revolutionary book *The General Theory of Employment, Interest, and Money*, published in 1936, in which he argued that short-run changes in aggregate output, such as the decline in output that occurred during the Great Depression, are determined by changes in aggregate demand. The concept of aggregate demand is a central element in the *aggregate demand–aggregate supply (AD/AS) model*, the basic macroeconomic model used to explain short-run fluctuations in aggregate output.

In this chapter, we develop the first building block in understanding aggregate demand, the *IS curve*, which describes the relationship between real interest rates and aggregate output when the market for goods and services (more simply referred to as the *goods market*) is in equilibrium. We begin by deriving the *IS* curve and then go on to explain what factors cause the *IS* curve to shift. With our understanding of the *IS* curve, we can examine why fluctuations in economic activity occur and how the fiscal stimulus package of 2009 affected the economy. Then, in the next chapter, we make use of the *IS* curve to understand the role played by monetary policy in economic fluctuations.

PLANNED EXPENDITURE AND AGGREGATE DEMAND

We start our analysis by discussing the concept of **planned expenditure**, the total amount that households, businesses, the government, and foreigners want to spend on domestically produced goods and services. In contrast, *actual expenditure* is the amount that these entities actually do spend, which equals the total amount of output produced in the economy. Note that all of the analysis in this chapter refers to expenditure in real terms, that is, in terms of actual physical amounts of goods and services. Keynes viewed **aggregate demand**, the total amount of output demanded in the economy, as being the same as planned expenditure. As we shall see shortly, planned expenditure—and hence aggregate demand—explains the level of aggregate output when the goods market is in equilibrium, that is, when aggregate demand for goods and services is equal to the actual amount of goods and services produced.

The total amount of aggregate demand (planned expenditure) is the sum of four types of spending:

1. **Consumption expenditure** (C), the total demand for consumer goods and services (e.g., hamburgers, iPods, rock concerts, visits to the dentist, etc.)
2. **Planned investment spending** (I), the total planned spending by businesses on new physical capital (e.g., machines, computers, factories), plus planned spending on new homes
3. **Government purchases** (G), the spending by all levels of government on goods and services (e.g., aircraft carriers, salaries of government employees, programs spending, health care, education, red tape), not including transfer payments
4. **Net exports** (NX), the net foreign spending on domestic goods and services, equal to exports minus imports

We represent the total aggregate demand (Y^{ad}) with the following equation:

$$Y^{ad} = C + I + G + NX \qquad \text{(Equation 1)}$$

THE COMPONENTS OF AGGREGATE DEMAND

To understand what determines aggregate demand (total planned expenditure) in the economy, let's look at each of its components in detail.

Consumption Expenditure

What determines how much you spend on consumer goods and services? Your income is likely the most important factor; if your income rises, you most likely will be willing to spend more. Keynes reasoned similarly that consumption expenditure is related to **disposable income** (denoted by Y_D), the total amount of income available for spending, equal to aggregate output Y minus taxes T (Y – T).[1]

Consumption Function   Keynes called the relationship between disposable income Y_D and consumption expenditure C the **consumption function**, and expressed it as follows:

$$C = \overline{C} + mpc \times Y_D \qquad \text{(Equation 2)}$$

or, alternatively,

$$C = \overline{C} + mpc \times (Y - T) \qquad \text{(Equation 3)}$$

The term $\overline{C}$ stands for **autonomous consumption expenditure**, the amount of consumption expenditure that is **exogenous** (independent of variables in the model, such as disposable income). Autonomous consumption is related to consumers' optimism about their future income and household wealth, a factor that induces consumers to increase spending.

---

[1]More precisely, taxes T refers to taxes minus net transfers (government payments to households and businesses that are, in effect, negative taxes). Examples of government transfers include Old Age Security pension payments and Employment Insurance payments.

The term *mpc*, the **marginal propensity to consume**, reflects the change in consumption expenditure that results from an additional dollar of disposable income. Keynes assumed that *mpc* was a constant between the values of 0 and 1. If, for example, a $1.00 increase in disposable income leads to an increase in consumption expenditure of $0.60, then *mpc* = 0.6.

Planned Investment Spending

Investment spending is another key component of total expenditure. There are two types of investment spending: *fixed* and *inventory*. (Note that economists' use of the word *investment* differs from the everyday use of the term, as explained in the FYI box.)

Fixed Investment **Fixed investment** is planned spending by firms on equipment (machines, computers, airplanes) and structures (factories, office buildings, shopping centres), plus planned spending on new residential housing.

Inventory Investment **Inventory investment** is spending by firms on additional holdings of raw materials, parts, and finished goods, calculated as the change in holdings of these items in a given time period—say, a year.

Inventory investment is a much smaller component of investment than fixed investment. We discuss inventory investment in detail at this juncture because it plays an important role in the determination of aggregate output. To illustrate, consider the following scenarios:

1. Suppose that Ford Motor Company has 100 000 cars sitting in its factory lots on December 31, 2016, ready to be shipped to dealers. If each car has a wholesale price of $20 000, Ford has an inventory worth $2 billion. If by December 31, 2017, its inventory of cars has risen to 150 000, with a value of $3 billion, its inventory investment in 2017 is $1 billion—the *change* in the level of its inventory over the course of the year ($3 billion in 2017 minus $2 billion in 2016).

2. Now suppose that by December 31, 2017, Ford's inventory of cars has dropped to 50 000, with a value of $1 billion. Its inventory investment in 2017 is now −$1 billion, the *change* in the level of its inventory over the course of the year ($1 billion in 2017 minus $2 billion in 2016).

3. Ford will have additional inventory investment if the level of raw materials and parts that it is holding to produce these cars increases over the course of the year. If on December 31, 2016, it holds $50 million of steel to be used to produce its cars, and on December 31, 2017, it holds $100 million of steel, it has an additional $50 million of inventory investment in 2017.

An important feature of inventory investment is that some inventory investment can be unplanned (in contrast, fixed investment is always planned). Suppose that the reason Ford finds itself with an additional $1 billion of cars on December 31, 2017, is because it sold $1 billion less of its cars than expected in 2017. This $1 billion of inventory investment in 2017 was unplanned. In this situation, Ford is producing more cars than it can sell, and it will cut production to avoid accumulating unsold goods. The act of adjusting production to eliminate unplanned inventory investment plays a key role in the determination of aggregate output, as we shall see.

Planned Investment Spending and Real Interest Rates   Planned investment spending, a component of aggregate demand Y^{ad}, is equal to planned fixed investment plus the amount of inventory investment *planned* by firms. Keynes considered the level of the real interest rate for investments as a key determinant of planned investment spending.

To understand Keynes's reasoning, we need to recognize that businesses make investments in physical capital (machines and factories) as long as they expect to earn more from the physical capital than the interest cost of a loan to finance the investment will earn. When the real interest rate for investments is high—say, at 10%—few investments in physical capital will earn more than the 10% interest cost of borrowing funds, and so planned investment spending will be low. When the real interest rate for investments is low—say, 1%—many investments in physical capital will earn more than the 1% interest cost of borrowing funds. Therefore, when the real interest rate for investments and hence the cost of borrowing are low, business firms are more likely to undertake investments in physical capital, and planned investment spending increases.

Even if a company has surplus funds and does not need to borrow to undertake an investment in physical capital, its planned investment spending still will be affected by the real interest rate for investments. Instead of investing in physical capital, the company could purchase a corporate bond. If the real interest rate on this security were high—say, 10%—the opportunity cost (forgone interest earnings) of an investment in physical capital would be high. Planned investment spending would then be low, because the firm probably would prefer to purchase the security and earn the high 10% return than to invest in physical capital. As the real interest rate for investments and the opportunity cost of investing fall—say, to 1%—planned investment spending will increase because investments in physical capital are likely to earn greater income for the firm than the measly 1% that would be earned by investing in the security.

Planned Investment and Business Expectations   Keynes also believed that planned investment spending is heavily influenced by business expectations about the future. Businesses that are optimistic about future profit opportunities are willing to spend more, whereas pessimistic businesses cut back their spending. Thus Keynes posited a component of planned investment spending, which he called **autonomous investment**, $\bar{I}$, that is completely exogenous and so is unexplained by variables in his model, such as output or interest rates.

Keynes believed that changes in autonomous spending are dominated by these unstable exogenous fluctuations in planned investment spending, which are influenced by emotional waves of optimism and pessimism—factors he labelled **"animal spirits."** His view was coloured by the collapse in investment spending during the Great Depression, which he saw as the primary reason for the economic contraction.

Investment Function   By combining the two factors that Keynes theorized drive investment, we can derive an investment function that describes how planned investment spending is related to autonomous investment and the real interest rate for investments. We write this function as follows:

$$I = \bar{I} - dr_i \qquad \text{(Equation 4)}$$

where d is a parameter reflecting the responsiveness of investment to the real interest rate for investments, which is denoted by r_i.

However, the real interest rate for investments reflects not only the real interest rate r on short-term, safe, debt instruments, which is controlled by the central bank, but also **financial frictions**, denoted by $\bar{f}$, which are additions to the real cost of borrowing caused by barriers to the efficient functioning of financial markets. (We discussed the origins of these frictions in detail in Chapter 8 as asymmetric information problems under the topics of adverse selection and moral hazard.) Financial frictions make it harder for lenders to ascertain the creditworthiness of a borrower. Lenders need to charge a higher interest rate to protect themselves against the possibility that the borrower may not pay back the loan, which leads to a *credit spread*, the difference between the interest rate on loans to businesses and the interest rate on completely safe assets that are sure to be paid back. Hence financial frictions add to the real interest rate for investments, and we can write:

$$r_i = r + \bar{f} \qquad \text{(Equation 5)}$$

Substituting in Equation 4 the real cost of borrowing from Equation 5 yields:

$$I = \bar{I} - d(r + \bar{f}) \qquad \text{(Equation 6)}$$

Equation 6 states that investment is positively related to business optimism as represented by autonomous investment, and negatively related to the real interest rate and financial frictions.

Net Exports

As with planned investment spending, we can think of net exports as being made up of two components: *autonomous net exports* and the part of net exports that is affected by changes in real interest rates.

Real Interest Rates and Net Exports   Real interest rates influence the amount of net exports through the **exchange rate**. Recall that the exchange rate is the price of one currency, say, the dollar, in terms of another currency, say, the euro.[2] We examined a model that explains the link between the exchange rate and real interest rates in Chapter 18, but here we will only outline the intuition. When Canadian. real interest rates rise, Canadian. dollar assets earn higher returns relative to foreign assets. People then want to hold more dollars, so they bid up the value of a dollar and thereby increase its value relative to the values of other currencies. Thus a rise in Canadian real interest rates leads to a higher value of the dollar.

A rise in the value of the dollar makes Canadian exports more expensive in foreign currencies, so foreigners will buy less of these exports, thereby driving down net exports.

---

[2]If a government pegs the exchange rate to another country's currency, so that the rate is fixed in what is called a *fixed exchange rate regime* (see Chapter 19), then real interest rates do not directly affect net exports as in Equation 5, and $NX = \overline{NX}$. Taking out the response of net exports to the real interest rates does not change the basic analysis of the chapter but does lead to a slightly different equation—Equation 12—described later in the chapter.

A rise in the value of the dollar also makes foreign goods less expensive in terms of dollars, so Canadian imports will rise, also causing a decline in net exports. We therefore see that a rise in the real interest rate, which leads to an increase in the value of the dollar, in turn leads to a decline in net exports.

Autonomous Net Exports   The amount of exports is also affected by the demand by foreigners for domestic goods, while the amount of imports is affected by the demand by domestic residents for foreign goods. For example, if the Chinese have a poor harvest and want to buy more Canadian wheat, Canadian exports will rise. If the Brazilian economy is booming, then Brazilians will have more money to spend on Canadian goods, and Canadian exports will rise. On the other hand, if Canadian consumers discover how good Chilean wine is and want to buy more, then Canadian imports will rise. Thus we can think of net exports as being determined by real interest rates as well as by a component called **autonomous net exports**, $\overline{NX}$, which is the level of net exports that is treated as exogenous (outside the model).[3]

Net Export Function   Putting these two components of net exports together, we can write a net export function:

$$NX = \overline{NX} - xr \qquad \text{(Equation 7)}$$

where x is a parameter that indicates how net exports respond to the real interest rate. This equation tells us that net exports are positively related to autonomous net exports and are negatively related to the level of real interest rates.

Government Purchases and Taxes

Now we bring the government into the picture. The government affects aggregate demand in two ways: through its purchases and through taxes.

Government Purchases   As we saw in the aggregate demand equation, Equation 1, government purchases add directly to aggregate demand. Here we assume that government purchases are exogenous, and we write government purchases as follows:

$$G = \overline{G} \qquad \text{(Equation 8)}$$

Equation 8 states that government purchases are set at a fixed amount $\overline{G}$.

Taxes   The government affects spending through taxes because, as discussed earlier, disposable income is equal to income minus taxes, $Y - T$, and disposable income affects consumption expenditure. Higher taxes T reduce disposable income for a given level of income and hence cause consumption expenditure to fall. The tax laws in a country like

---

[3]Foreign aggregate output is outside the model, and so its effect on net exports is exogenous and hence is a factor that affects autonomous net exports. Canadian domestic output, Y, could also affect net exports because greater domestic disposable income would increase spending on imports and thus would lower net exports. To build this factor into the *IS* curve, we could modify the net export function given in Equation 7 as follows:

$$NX = \overline{NX} - xr - iY$$

where i is the marginal propensity to spend on imports. This change would lead to a modification of Equation 12 later in the chapter, in which the *mpc* term would be replaced by *mpc* − i.

Canada are very complicated, so to keep the model simple, we assume that government taxes are exogenous and are set at a fixed amount $\overline{T}$:[4]

$$T = \overline{T} \qquad \text{(Equation 9)}$$

GOODS MARKET EQUILIBRIUM

Keynes recognized that equilibrium will occur in the economy when the total quantity of output is equal to the total amount of aggregate demand (planned expenditure). That is,

$$Y = Y^{ad} \qquad \text{(Equation 10)}$$

When this equilibrium condition is satisfied, planned spending for goods and services is equal to the amount that is produced. Producers are able to sell all of their output and have no reason to change their production levels because there is no unplanned inventory investment. By examining the factors that affect each component of planned spending, we can understand why aggregate output goes to a certain level.

Solving for Goods Market Equilibrium

With our understanding of the factors that drive the components of aggregate demand, we can see how aggregate output is determined by using Equation 1, the aggregate demand equation, to rewrite the equilibrium condition given in Equation 10 as follows:

$$Y = C + I + G + NX \qquad \text{(Equation 11)}$$

Aggregate Output = Consumption Expenditure + Planned Investment Spending + Government Purchases + Net Exports

Now we can use our consumption, investment, and net export functions in Equations 3, 6, and 7, along with Equations 8 and 9, to determine aggregate output. Substituting all of these equations into the equilibrium condition given by Equation 11 yields the following:

$$Y = \overline{C} + mpc \times (Y - \overline{T}) + \overline{I} - d(r + \overline{f}) + \overline{G} + \overline{NX} - xr$$

Collecting terms, we can rewrite this equation as follows:

$$Y = \overline{C} + \overline{I} - d\overline{f} + \overline{G} + \overline{NX} + mpc \times Y - mpc \times \overline{T} - (d + x)r$$

Subtracting $mpc \times Y$ from both sides of the equation, we have

$$Y - mpc \times Y = Y(1 - mpc) = \overline{C} + \overline{I} - d\overline{f} + \overline{G} + \overline{NX} - mpc \times \overline{T} - (d + x)r$$

---

[4]For simplicity, we assume here that taxes are unrelated to income. However, because taxes increase with income, we can describe taxes more realistically with the following tax function:

$$T = \overline{T} + tY$$

Using this equation instead of Equation 9 in the derivation of Equation 12 later in the chapter would lead to mpc being replaced by $mpc(1 - t)$ in Equation 12.

Then, dividing both sides of the equation by $1 - mpc$, we obtain an equation that gives us a means of determining aggregate output when the goods market is in equilibrium:[5]

$$Y = [\overline{C} + \overline{I} - d\overline{f} + \overline{G} + \overline{NX} - mpc \times \overline{T}] \times \frac{1}{1 - mpc} - \frac{d + x}{1 - mpc} \times r \quad \text{(Equation 12)}$$

Deriving the *IS* Curve

We refer to Equation 12 as the **IS curve**, and it shows the relationship between aggregate output and the real interest rate when the goods market is in equilibrium. Equation 12 is made up of two terms. Since mpc is between 0 and 1, $1/(1 - mpc)$ is positive, so the first term tells us that an increase in autonomous consumption, investment, government purchases, or net exports, or a decrease in taxes or financial frictions, leads to an increase in output at any given real interest rate. In other words, the first term tells us about shifts in the *IS* curve. The second term tells us that an increase in real interest rates results in a decrease in output, which can be shown as a movement along the *IS* curve.

UNDERSTANDING THE *IS* CURVE

To gain a deeper understanding of the *IS* curve, we will proceed in several steps. In this section, we begin by looking at the intuition behind the *IS* curve, and then we discuss a numerical example. Then, in the following section, we outline the factors that shift the *IS* curve.

What the *IS* Curve Tells Us: Intuition

The *IS* curve traces out the points at which the goods market is in equilibrium. For each given level of the real interest rate, the *IS* curve tells us the level of aggregate output that is necessary for the goods market to be in equilibrium. As the real interest rate rises, planned investment spending and net exports fall, which in turn lowers aggregate demand; aggregate output must be lower if it is to equal aggregate demand and satisfy goods market equilibrium. Hence, the *IS* curve is downward-sloping.

What the *IS* Curve Tells Us: Numerical Example

We can analyze the *IS* curve with the following numerical example, which gives specific values for the exogenous variables and the parameters in Equation 12.

$$\overline{C} = \$1.4 \text{ trillion}$$
$$\overline{I} = \$1.2 \text{ trillion}$$
$$\overline{G} = \$3.0 \text{ trillion}$$
$$\overline{T} = \$3.0 \text{ trillion}$$
$$\overline{NX} = \$1.3 \text{ trillion}$$
$$\overline{f} = 1$$
$$mpc = 0.6$$
$$d = 0.3$$
$$x = 0.1$$

[5]Note that the term $1/(1 - mpc)$ that multiplies $\overline{G}$ is known as the *expenditure multiplier*, and the term $-mpc/(1 - mpc)$ that multiplies $\overline{T}$ is called the *tax multiplier*. The tax multiplier is smaller in absolute value than the expenditure multiplier because $mpc < 1$.

Using these values, we can rewrite Equation 12 as follows:

$$Y = [1.4 + 1.2 - 0.3 + 3.0 + 1.3 - 0.6 \times 3.0] \times \frac{1}{1 - 0.6} - \frac{0.3 + 0.1}{1 - 0.6} \times r$$

Plugging these values into Equation 12 yields the equation of the *IS* curve shown in Figure 21-1:

$$Y = \frac{4.8}{0.4} - \frac{0.4}{0.4} \times r = 12 - r \qquad \text{(Equation 13)}$$

At a real interest rate of $r = 3\%$, the equilibrium output Y is equal to \$12 trillion $-$ \$3 trillion $=$ \$9 trillion. We plot this combination of the real interest rate and equilibrium output as point A in Figure 21-1. At a real interest rate of $r = 1\%$, the equilibrium output Y is equal to \$12 trillion $-$ \$1 trillion $=$ \$11 trillion, which we plot as point B. The line connecting these points is the *IS* curve and, as you can see, it is downward-sloping.

MyEconLab Mini-lecture

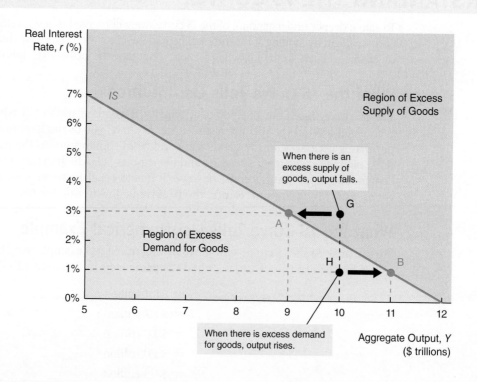

FIGURE 21-1 **The *IS* Curve**

The downward-sloping *IS* curve represents points at which the goods market is in equilibrium—for example, points A and B. Notice that output changes as necessary to return the market to equilibrium. For example, at point G in the orange shaded area, an excess supply of goods exists and firms will cut production, decreasing aggregate output to the equilibrium level at point A. At point H in the blue shaded area, an excess demand for goods exists, so firms will increase production, and aggregate output will increase toward the equilibrium level at point B.

Why the Economy Heads Toward Equilibrium

The concept of equilibrium is useful only if there is a tendency for the economy to settle there. Let's first consider what happens if the economy is located to the right of the *IS* curve (the orange shaded area), where an excess supply of goods exists. In Figure 21-1 at point *G*, actual output is above aggregate demand, and firms are saddled with unsold inventory. To keep from accumulating unsold goods, firms will continue cutting production. As long as production is above the equilibrium level, output will exceed aggregate demand and firms will continue cutting production, sending aggregate output toward the equilibrium level, as indicated by the leftward arrow from point *G* to point *A*. Only when the economy moves to point *A* on the *IS* curve will there be no further tendency for output to change.

What happens if aggregate output is below the equilibrium level of output (the blue shaded area to the left of the *IS* curve), where an excess demand for goods exists? At point *H* in Figure 21-1, actual output is below aggregate demand, so firms will want to increase production because inventories are declining more than they desire, and aggregate output will increase, as shown by the rightward arrow. When the economy has moved to point *B* on the *IS* curve, there will again be no further tendency for output to change.

FACTORS THAT SHIFT THE *IS* CURVE

You have now learned that the *IS* curve describes equilibrium points in the goods market—the combinations of the real interest rate and equilibrium output. The *IS* curve shifts whenever change occurs in autonomous factors (factors independent of aggregate output and the real interest rate). Note that a change in the real interest rate that affects equilibrium aggregate output causes only a *movement along* the *IS* curve. A *shift* in the *IS* curve, by contrast, occurs when equilibrium output changes *at each given real interest rate*.

In Equation 12, we identified six autonomous factors that can shift aggregate demand and hence affect the level of equilibrium output. Although Equation 12 directly tells us how these factors shift the *IS* curve, we will develop some intuition as to how each autonomous factor does so.

Changes in Government Purchases

Let's look at what happens if government purchases rise from $3 trillion to $4 trillion in Figure 21-2. IS_1 represents the same *IS* curve that we developed in Figure 21-1. We determine the equation for IS_2 by substituting the $4 trillion value into Equation 12:

$$Y = [1.4 + 1.2 - 0.3 + 4.0 + 1.3 - 0.6 \times 3.0] \times \frac{1}{1 - 0.6} - \frac{0.3 + 0.1}{1 - 0.6} \times r = \frac{5.8}{0.4} - r$$
$$= 14.5 - r$$

On the basis of these results, at a real interest rate of $r = 3\%$, equilibrium output Y is equal to $14.5 trillion $-$ $3 trillion = $11.5 trillion, which we mark as point C on Figure 21-2. At a real interest rate of $r = 1\%$, equilibrium output has increased to $Y = $14.5 trillion $-$ $1 trillion = $13.5 trillion, which we mark as point D. The increase in government purchases therefore shifts the *IS* curve to the right from IS_1 to IS_2.

Intuitively, we can see why an increase in government purchases leads to a rightward shift of the *IS* curve by recognizing that an increase in government purchases causes aggregate demand to increase at any given real interest rate. Since aggregate

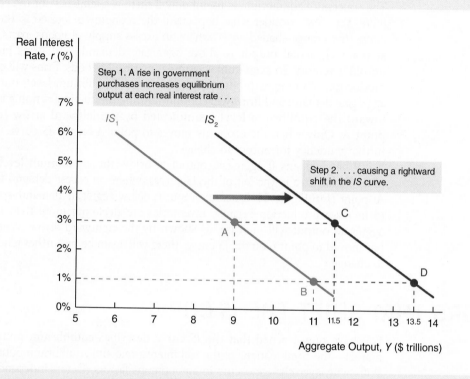

FIGURE 21-2 **Shift in the *IS* Curve from an Increase in Government Purchases**

IS_1 represents the *IS* curve we derived in Figure 21-1. IS_2 reflects a $1.0 trillion increase in government purchases. The increase in government purchases causes aggregate output to rise, shifting the *IS* curve to the right by $2.5 trillion, from IS_1 to IS_2.

output equals aggregate demand when the goods market is in equilibrium, *an increase in government purchases that causes aggregate demand to rise also causes equilibrium output to rise, thereby shifting the IS curve to the right. Conversely, a decrease in government purchases causes aggregate demand to fall at any given real interest rate and leads to a leftward shift of the IS curve.*

APPLICATION   The Vietnam War Buildup, 1964–1969

The United States' involvement in Vietnam began to escalate in the early 1960s. After 1964, the United States was fighting a full-scale war. Beginning in 1965, the resulting increases in military expenditure raised government purchases. When government purchases are rising rapidly, central banks will usually raise real interest rates to keep the economy from overheating. The Vietnam War period, however, was unusual in that the Federal Reserve decided to keep real interest rates constant. Hence, this period provides an excellent example of how policymakers might make use of *IS* curve analysis to inform policy.

The rise in government purchases shifted the *IS* curve to the right, from IS_{1964} to IS_{1969} in Figure 21-3. Because the Federal Reserve decided to keep real interest rates constant

MyEconLab Mini-lecture

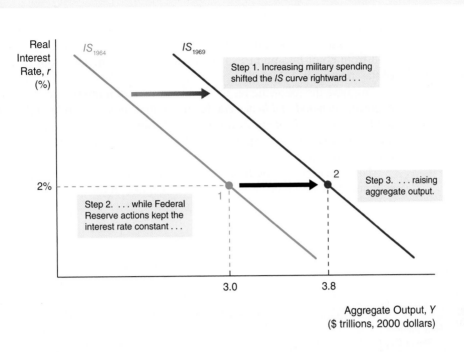

FIGURE 21-3   **Vietnam War Buildup**

Increases in military spending beginning in 1965 caused the *IS* curve to shift from IS_{1964} to IS_{1969}. Because the Federal Reserve decided to keep real interest rates constant at 2% during this period, equilibrium output rose from $3.0 trillion (in 2000 dollars) in 1964 to $3.8 trillion in 1969, setting the stage for an increase in inflation.

at 2% during this period, equilibrium output rose from $3.0 trillion (in 2000 dollars) in 1964 to $3.8 trillion by 1969, with the unemployment rate falling steadily from 5% in 1964 to 3.4% in 1969. However, all was not well for the economy: The combination of an increase in government purchases and a constant real interest rate led to an overheating of the economy that eventually resulted in high inflation. (We will discuss the link between an overheating economy and inflation in the coming chapters.) ◆

Changes in Taxes

Now let's look at Figure 21-4 to see what happens if the government raises taxes from $3 trillion to $4 trillion. IS_1 represents the same *IS* curve that we developed in Figure 21-1. We determine the equation for IS_2 by substituting the $4 trillion value into Equation 12:

$$Y = [1.4 + 1.2 - 0.3 + 3.0 + 1.3 - 0.6 \times 4.0] \times \frac{1}{1 - 0.6} - \frac{0.3 + 0.1}{1 - 0.6} \times r = \frac{4.2}{0.4} - r$$

$$= 10.5 - r$$

At a real interest rate of $r = 3\%$, equilibrium output $Y = \$10.5$ trillion $-\ \$3$ trillion $= \$7.5$ trillion, which we mark as point E in Figure 21-4. At this real interest rate, equilibrium output has decreased from point A to point E, as shown by the leftward arrow. Similarly, at a real interest rate of $r = 1\%$, equilibrium output has decreased to $Y = \$10.5$ trillion $-\ \$1$ trillion $= \$9.5$ trillion, causing a leftward shift from point B to point F. The IS curve shifts to the left, from IS_1 to IS_2, as a result of the increase in taxes.

We have the following result: ***At any given real interest rate, a rise in taxes causes aggregate demand and hence equilibrium output to fall, thereby shifting the IS curve to the left. Conversely, a cut in taxes at any given real interest rate increases disposable income and causes aggregate demand and equilibrium output to rise, shifting the IS curve to the right.***

Policymakers use both tax and government purchase policies to stimulate the economy when it enters a recession, as illustrated in the following Application.

MyEconLab Mini-lecture

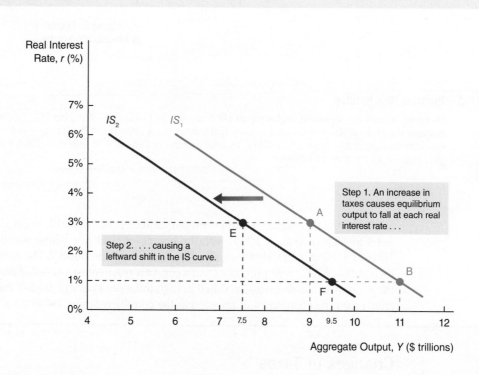

FIGURE 21-4 **Shift in the *IS* Curve from an Increase in Taxes**

IS_1 represents the IS curve we derived in Figure 21-1. IS_2 reflects a $\$1.0$ trillion increase in government tax revenues. The increase in taxes decreases aggregate output levels by $\$1.5$ trillion, shifting the IS curve to the left, from IS_1 to IS_2.

APPLICATION ## The American Fiscal Stimulus Package Experience of 2009

In the fall of 2008, the American economy was in crisis. By the time the new Obama administration took office, the unemployment rate had risen from 4.7% just before the recession began in December 2007 to 7.6% in January 2009. To stimulate the economy, the Obama administration proposed a fiscal stimulus package that, when passed by Congress, included $288 billion in tax cuts for households and businesses and $499 billion in increased federal spending, including transfer payments. What does our *IS* curve analysis suggest should have happened to the economy?

As the analyses in Figure 21-2 and Figure 21-4 indicate, these tax cuts and spending increases should have increased aggregate demand, thereby raising the equilibrium level of aggregate output at any given real interest rate and so shifting the *IS* curve to the right. Unfortunately, things didn't work out quite as the Obama administration had planned. Most of the government purchases did not kick in until after 2010, while the declines in autonomous consumption and investment were much larger than anticipated. The fiscal stimulus was more than offset by the weak consumption and investment caused by an increase in financial frictions and worries about the economy. As a result, aggregate demand ended up contracting rather than rising, and the *IS* curve did not shift to the right as hoped. Despite the good intentions of the fiscal stimulus package, the unemployment rate ended up rising to 10% in 2009. Without the fiscal stimulus package, however, the *IS* curve likely would have shifted even further to the left, resulting in even more unemployment. ◆

Changes in Autonomous Spending

As you can see from Equation 12, autonomous consumption, investment, and net exports—$\overline{C}$, $\overline{I}$, and $\overline{NX}$, respectively—all are multiplied by the term $1/(1 - mpc)$ in the same way as the $\overline{G}$ term is. Thus an increase in any of these variables has the same impact on the *IS* curve as does an increase in government purchases. For this reason, we can lump these variables together as **autonomous spending**: exogenous spending that is unrelated to variables in the model such as output or real interest rates. We look intuitively at how changes in each of these variables affect the *IS* curve in turn.

Autonomous Consumption   Suppose consumers find that their wealth has increased courtesy of a stock market boom, or that they have become increasingly optimistic about their future income prospects because a positive productivity shock to the economy has occurred. Both of these events are autonomous; that is, they are not affected by the level of the real interest rate. *The resulting rise in autonomous consumption would raise aggregate demand and equilibrium output at any given interest rate, shifting the IS curve to the right. Conversely, a decline in autonomous consumption expenditure would cause aggregate demand and equilibrium output to fall, shifting the IS curve to the left.*

Autonomous Investment Spending   Earlier in the chapter, we learned that changes in the real interest rate affect planned investment spending and hence the equilibrium level of output. This change in investment spending merely causes a movement along the *IS* curve, not a shift. An autonomous rise in planned investment spending unrelated to the real interest rate—say, because companies become more confident about investment profitability after the stock market rises—increases aggregate demand. *An increase in autonomous investment spending therefore increases equilibrium output at*

SUMMARY TABLE 21-1

Shifts in the *IS* Curve from Autonomous Changes in $\overline{C}$, $\overline{I}$, $\overline{G}$, $\overline{T}$, $\overline{NX}$, and $\overline{f}$

Variable	Change in Variable	Shift in *IS* Curve	Reason
Autonomous consumption expenditure, $\overline{C}$	↑	r — IS₁ → IS₂ (shift right)	$C\uparrow\ Y\uparrow$
Autonomous investment, $\overline{I}$	↑	r — IS₁ → IS₂ (shift right)	$I\uparrow\ Y\uparrow$
Government spending, $\overline{G}$	↑	r — IS₁ → IS₂ (shift right)	$G\uparrow\ Y\uparrow$
Taxes, $\overline{T}$	↑	r — IS₂ ← IS₁ (shift left)	$T\uparrow \Rightarrow C\downarrow\ Y\downarrow$
Autonomous net exports, $\overline{NX}$	↑	r — IS₁ → IS₂ (shift right)	$NX\uparrow\ Y\uparrow$
Financial frictions, $\overline{f}$	↑	r — IS₂ ← IS₁ (shift left)	$I\downarrow\ Y\downarrow$

Note: Only increases (↑) in the variables are shown; the effects of decreases in the variables on aggregate output would be the opposite of those indicated in the last two columns.

any given interest rate, shifting the IS curve to the right. On the other hand, a decrease in autonomous investment spending causes aggregate demand and equilibrium output to fall, shifting the IS curve to the left.

Autonomous Net Exports An autonomous rise in net exports unrelated to the real interest rate—say, because Canadian-made handbags become more chic than

French-made handbags, or because foreign countries have a boom and thus buy more Canadian goods—causes aggregate demand to rise. *An autonomous increase in net exports thus leads to an increase in equilibrium output at any given interest rate and shifts the IS curve to the right. Conversely, an autonomous fall in net exports causes aggregate demand and equilibrium output to decline, shifting the IS curve to the left.*

Changes in Financial Frictions

An increase in financial frictions, as occurred during the financial crisis of 2007–2009, raises the real interest rate for investments and hence causes investment spending and aggregate demand to fall. *An increase in financial frictions leads to a decline in equilibrium output at any given real interest rate and shifts the IS curve to the left. Conversely, a decrease in financial frictions causes aggregate demand and equilibrium output to rise, shifting the IS curve to the right.*

Summary of Factors That Shift the *IS* Curve

As a study aid, Summary Table 21-1 shows how each factor shifts the *IS* curve and the reason the shift occurs. Now that we have a full understanding of the *IS* curve, we can use this building block to examine the relationship between monetary policy and the aggregate demand curve in the following chapter.

MyEconLab

MyEconLab is an online homework and tutorial system that puts you in control of your own learning with study and practice tools directly correlated to this chapter's content. Visit MyEconLab to access the eText, the Questions and Applied Problems with answers, as well as additional assessment. You will also find web chapters, mini-lectures, appendices, mini-cases, videos, glossary flashcards, news feeds, CANSIM data, and graphing tools.

SUMMARY

1. Planned expenditure, the total amount of goods demanded in the economy, is the same as aggregate demand, which is the sum of four types of spending: consumption expenditure, planned investment spending, government purchases, and net exports. We represent the total aggregate demand (Y^{ad}) with Equation 1: $Y^{ad} = C + I + G + NX$.

2. Consumption expenditure is described by the consumption function, which indicates that consumption expenditure will rise as disposable income increases. Planned expenditure and hence aggregate demand are negatively related to the real interest rate because a rise in the real interest rate reduces both planned investment spending and net exports. An increase in financial frictions raises the real interest rate for investments

and hence lowers investment spending and aggregate demand. The government also affects planned expenditure via spending, which directly changes aggregate demand, or via taxes, which indirectly affect aggregate demand by influencing disposable income and hence consumption expenditure.

3. The level of aggregate output when the goods market is in equilibrium is determined by the condition that aggregate output equals aggregate demand.

4. The *IS* curve traces out the combinations of the real interest rate and aggregate output at which the goods market is in equilibrium. The *IS* curve slopes downward because higher real interest rates lower planned investment spending and net exports and so lower equilibrium output.

5. The *IS* curve shifts to the right when there is a rise in autonomous consumption, a rise in autonomous investment, a rise in government purchases, a rise in autonomous net exports, a fall in taxes, or a decline in financial frictions. Movements of these six factors in the opposite direction will shift the *IS* curve to the left.

KEY TERMS

aggregate demand, p. 530
"animal spirits," p. 533
autonomous consumption
    expenditure, p. 531
autonomous investment, p. 533
autonomous net exports, p. 535
autonomous spending, p. 543
consumption expenditure, p. 531

consumption function, p. 531
disposable income, p. 531
exchange rate, p. 534
exogenous, p. 531
financial frictions, p. 534
fixed investment, p. 532
government purchases, p. 531
inventory investment, p. 532

IS curve, p. 537
marginal propensity
    to consume, p. 532
net exports, p. 531
planned expenditure, p. 530
planned investment
    spending, p. 531

QUESTIONS

All questions are available in MyEconLab *at* **www.myeconlab.com**.

1. "When the stock market rises, investment spending is increasing." Is this statement true, false, or uncertain? Explain your answer.

2. Why is inventory investment counted as part of aggregate spending if it isn't actually sold to the final end user?

3. "Since inventories can be costly to hold, firms' planned inventory investment should be zero, and firms should acquire inventory only through unplanned inventory accumulation." Is this statement true, false, or uncertain? Explain your answer.

4. During and in the aftermath of the financial crisis of 2007–2009, planned investment fell substantially despite significant decreases in the real interest rate. What factors related to the planned investment function could explain this?

5. If households and firms believe the economy will be in a recession in the future, will this necessarily cause a recession, or have any impact on output at all?

6. Why do increases in the real interest rate lead to decreases in net exports, and vice versa?

7. Why does equilibrium output increase as the marginal propensity to consume increases?

8. If firms suddenly become more optimistic about the profitability of investment and planned investment spending rises by $100 billion, while consumers become more pessimistic and autonomous consumer spending falls by $100 billion, what happens to aggregate output?

9. In each of the cases below, what happens to equilibrium output? Briefly explain how it affects the relevant component(s) of planned spending.

    a. The real interest rate rises.

    b. The marginal propensity to consume falls.

    c. Financial frictions increase.

    d. Autonomous consumption decreases.

    e. Both taxes and government spending decrease by the same amount.

    f. The sensitivity of net exports to changes in the real interest rate decreases.

    g. The government provides tax incentives for research and development programs for firms.

10. If an increase in autonomous consumer expenditure is matched by an equal increase in taxes, will aggregate output rise or fall?

11. If a change in the interest rate has no effect on planned investment spending or net exports, what does this imply about the slope of the *IS* curve?

12. Why do companies cut production when they find that their unplanned inventory investment is greater than

zero? If they didn't cut production, what effect would this have on their profits? Why?

13. "Firms will increase production when planned investment is less than (actual) total investment." Is this statement true, false, or uncertain? Explain your answer.

14. In each of the cases below, determine whether the *IS* curve shifts to the right or left, does not shift, or is indeterminate in the direction of shift.

    a. The real interest rate rises.

    b. The marginal propensity to consume declines.

    c. Financial frictions increase.

    d. Autonomous consumption decreases.

    e. Both taxes and government spending decrease by the same amount.

    f. The sensitivity of net exports to changes in the real interest rate decreases.

g. The government provides tax incentives for research and development programs for firms.

15. "The fiscal stimulus package of 2009 caused the *IS* curve to shift to the left, since output decreased and unemployment increased after the policies were implemented." Is this statement true, false, or uncertain? Explain your answer.

16. When the central bank reduces its policy interest rate, how, if at all, is the *IS* curve affected? Briefly explain.

17. Suppose you read that prospects for stronger future economic growth have led the dollar to strengthen and stock prices to increase.

    a. What effect does the strengthened dollar have on the *IS* curve?

    b. What effect does the increase in stock prices have on the *IS* curve?

    c. What is the combined effect of these two events on the *IS* curve?

APPLIED PROBLEMS

All applied problems are available in MyEconLab *at* **www.myeconlab.com.**

18. Calculate the value of the consumption function at each level of income in the table below if autonomous consumption = 300, taxes = 200, and *mpc* = 0.9.

Income Y	Disposable Income YD	Consumption C
0		
100		
200		
300		
400		
500		
600		

19. Assume that autonomous consumption is $1625 billion and disposable income is $11 500 billion. Calculate consumption expenditure if an increase of $1000 in disposable income leads to an increase of $750 in consumption expenditure.

20. Suppose that Dell Corporation has 20 000 computers in its warehouses on December 31, 2016, ready to be shipped to merchants (each computer is valued at $500). By December 31, 2017, Dell Corporation has 25 000 computers ready to be shipped, each valued at $450.

    a. Calculate Dell's inventory on December 31, 2016.

    b. Calculate Dell's inventory investment in 2017.

    c. What happens to inventory spending during the early stages of an economic recession?

21. If the consumption function is $C = 100 + 0.75Y_D$, $I = 200$, government spending is 200, and net exports are zero, what will be the equilibrium level of output? What will happen to aggregate output if government spending rises by 100?

22. If the marginal propensity to consume is 0.75, by how much would government spending have to rise to increase output by $1000 billion? By how much would taxes need to decrease to increase output by $1000 billion?

23. Assuming both taxes and government spending increase by the same amount, derive an expression for the effect on equilibrium output.

24. Consider an economy described by the following data:

$$\overline{C} = \$3.25 \text{ trillion}$$
$$\overline{I} = \$1.3 \text{ trillion}$$
$$\overline{G} = \$3.5 \text{ trillion}$$
$$\overline{T} = \$3.0 \text{ trillion}$$
$$\overline{NX} = -\$1.0 \text{ trillion}$$
$$\overline{f} = 1$$
$$mpc = 0.75$$
$$d = 0.3$$
$$x = 0.1$$

a. Calculate simplified expressions for the consumption function, the investment function, and the net export function.

b. Calculate an expression for the *IS* curve.

c. If the real interest rate is $r = 2$, then what is equilibrium output? If $r = 5$, then what is equilibrium output?

d. Draw a graph of the *IS* curve showing the answers from part (c) above.

e. If government purchases increase to $4.2 trillion, what will happen to equilibrium output at $r = 2$? What will happen to equilibrium output at $r = 5$? Show the effect of the increase in government purchases in your graph from part (d).

25. Consider an economy described by the following data:

$$\overline{C} = \$4 \text{ trillion}$$
$$\overline{I} = \$1.5 \text{ trillion}$$

$$\overline{G} = \$3.0 \text{ trillion}$$
$$\overline{T} = \$3.0 \text{ trillion}$$
$$\overline{NX} = \$1.0 \text{ trillion}$$
$$\overline{f} = 0$$
$$mpc = 0.8$$
$$d = 0.35$$
$$x = 0.15$$

a. Calculate an expression for the *IS* curve.

b. Assume that the central bank controls the interest rate and sets the interest rate at $r = 4$. What is the equilibrium level of output?

c. Suppose that a financial crisis begins, and $\overline{f}$ increases to $\overline{f} = 3$. What will happen to equilibrium output? If the central bank can set the interest rate, then at what level should the interest rate be set to keep output from changing?

d. Suppose the financial crisis causes $\overline{f}$ to increase as indicated in part (c) and also causes planned autonomous investment to decrease to $\overline{I} = \$1.1$ trillion. Will the change in the interest rate implemented by the central bank in part (c) be effective in stabilizing output? If not, what additional monetary or fiscal policy changes could be implemented to stabilize output at the original equilibrium output level given in part (b)?

DATA ANALYSIS PROBLEMS

Download data for these problems from MyEconLab *at* **www.myeconlab.com**.

1. Go to the CANSIM database, find Table 3800067 and find data on household final consumption expenditure (series V61989012), household consumption expenditure on goods (series V61989013), household consumption expenditure on durable goods (series V61989014), household consumption expenditure on semi-durable goods (series V61989015), household consumption expenditure on non-durable goods (series V61989016), and household consumption expenditure on services (series V61989017).

a. What is the annual growth rate of each series?

b. Which series is more volatile?

2. Go to the CANSIM database and find data on Canadian merchandise exports to the United States (V54056222) and Canadian merchandise imports from the United States (V54056194).

a. Move the data into an Excel spreadsheet and calculate the difference between exports and imports. What does this difference represent?

b. Prepare a graph and show the three series, with the exports and imports series on the y_1 axis and the series you calculated in (a) in the y_2 axis. Comment on the values of the series you plotted on the y_2 axis.

WEB EXERCISES

1. Go to **www.eurmacro.unisg.ch/Tutor/ islm.html**. Set the policy instruments to $G = 80$, $t = 0.20$, $c = 0.75$, and $b = 40$. Now increase government spending, G, from 80 to 160. By how much does the *IS* curve shift horizontally to the right? Why is the amount of shift greater than the increase in G? Now increase the marginal propensity to consume, c, from 0.75 to 0.90. In which direction does the *IS* curve shift, and why? By how much does it shift? Now increase the tax rate, t, from 0.20 to 0.28. In which direction does the *IS* curve shift, and why? By how much does it shift?

2. Go to **www.eurmacro.unisg.ch/Tutor/islm.html**. Set the policy instruments to $G = 80$, $t = 0.20$, $c = 0.75$, and $b = 40$. Now increase the sensitivity of investment to the interest rate, b, from 40 to 80. What happens to the slope of the *IS* curve? Why?

WEB REFERENCE

http://research.stlouisfed.org/fred2/

Information about the macroeconomic variables discussed in this chapter.

22 The Monetary Policy and Aggregate Demand Curves

Learning Objectives

After studying this chapter you should be able to

1. Recognize the impact of changes in the nominal overnight interest rate on short-term real interest rates.

2. Define and illustrate the monetary policy (*MP*) curve, and explain shifts in the *MP* curve.

3. Explain why the aggregate demand (*AD*) curve slopes downward, and explain shifts in the *AD* curve.

PREVIEW

In response to the subprime financial crisis in the United States, the Bank of Canada lowered the target overnight interest rate from 4.5% in August 2007 to 0.25% in April 2009. Moreover, for over a year (from April 1, 2009 to June 1, 2010), the Bank of Canada also lowered the operating band for the overnight interest rate from 50 basis points to 25 basis points and instead of targeting the overnight interest rate at the midpoint of the operating band (as it does during normal times), it targeted the overnight rate at the bottom of the operating band, at 0.25%, thus setting an effective lower bound for the overnight interest rate.

To see how a monetary policy action like the one described above affects the economy, we need to analyze how monetary policy affects aggregate demand. We start this chapter by explaining why monetary policymakers set interest rates higher when inflation increases, leading to a positive relationship between real interest rates and inflation that can be illustrated using the *monetary policy (MP) curve*. Then, by combining the *MP* curve with the *IS* curve we developed in the previous chapter, we derive the *aggregate demand curve*, a key element in the aggregate demand/aggregate supply model framework used in the rest of this book to discuss short-run economic fluctuations.

THE BANK OF CANADA AND MONETARY POLICY

Central banks throughout the world use a very short-term interest rate as their primary policy tool. In Canada, the Bank of Canada conducts monetary policy via its setting of the overnight interest rate.

As we saw in Chapter 16, the Bank of Canada controls the overnight interest rate by varying the reserves it provides to the banking system. When it provides more reserves, banks have more money to lend to each other, and this excess liquidity causes the overnight interest rate to fall. When the Bank of Canada drains reserves from the banking system, banks have less to lend, and the lack of liquidity leads to a rise in the overnight interest rate.

The overnight interest rate is a *nominal* interest rate, but as we learned in the previous chapter, it is the *real* interest rate that affects net exports and business spending, thereby determining the level of equilibrium output. How does the Bank of Canada's control of the overnight interest rate enable it to control the real interest rate, through which monetary policy impacts the economy?

Recall from Chapter 4 that the real interest rate, r, is the nominal interest rate, i, minus expected inflation, π^e.

$$r = i - \pi^e$$

Changes in nominal interest rates can change the real interest rate only if actual and expected inflation remain unchanged in the short run. Because prices typically are slow to move—that is, they are *sticky*—changes in monetary policy will not have an immediate effect on inflation and expected inflation. As a result, **when the Bank of Canada lowers the overnight interest rate, real interest rates fall; when the Bank of Canada raises the overnight interest rate, real interest rates rise.**

THE MONETARY POLICY CURVE

We have seen how the Bank of Canada can control real interest rates in the short run. The next step in our analysis is to examine how monetary policy reacts to inflation. The **monetary policy (MP) curve** indicates the relationship between the real interest rate set by the central bank and the inflation rate. We can write the equation of this curve as follows:

$$r = \bar{r} + \lambda\pi \qquad \text{(Equation 1)}$$

where $\bar{r}$ is the autonomous (exogenous) component of the real interest rate set by the monetary policy authorities, which is unrelated to the current level of the inflation rate or any other variable in the model, and λ is the responsiveness of the real interest rate to the inflation rate.

To make our discussion of the monetary policy curve more concrete, Figure 22-1 shows an example of a monetary policy curve MP in which $\bar{r} = 1.0$ and $\lambda = 0.5$:

$$r = 1.0 + 0.5\pi \qquad \text{(Equation 2)}$$

At point A, where inflation is 1%, the Bank of Canada sets the real interest rate at 1.5%; at point B, where inflation is 2%, the Bank sets the real interest rate at 2%; and at point C, where inflation is 3%, the Bank sets the real interest rate at 2.5%. The line going through points A, B, and C is the monetary policy curve MP, and it is upward-sloping, indicating that monetary policymakers raise real interest rates when the inflation rate rises.

The Taylor Principle: Why the Monetary Policy Curve Has an Upward Slope

To see why the MP curve has an upward slope, we need to recognize that central banks seek to keep inflation stable. To stabilize inflation, monetary policymakers tend to follow the **Taylor principle**, named after John Taylor of Stanford University: They raise *nominal* rates by more than any rise in expected inflation so that *real* interest rates will rise when there is a rise in inflation, as illustrated by the MP curve.[1]

To see why monetary policymakers follow the Taylor principle, reacting to rising inflation by raising real interest rates, consider what would happen if monetary policymakers instead allowed the real interest rate to fall when inflation rose. In this case, an increase in inflation would lead to a decline in the real interest rate, which, as we saw in the previous chapter, would increase aggregate output, which would in turn cause inflation to rise

---

[1]Note that the Taylor principle differs from the Taylor rule, described in Chapter 17, in that it does not provide a rule for how monetary policy should react to conditions in the economy, whereas the Taylor rule does.

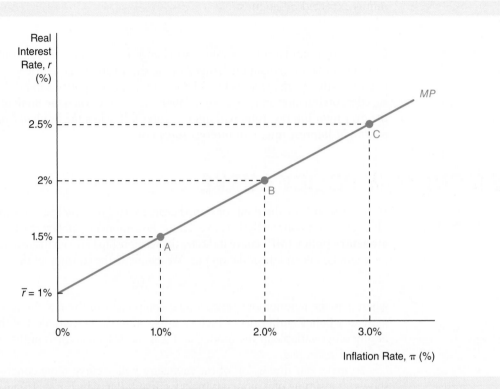

FIGURE 22-1 **The Monetary Policy Curve**

The upward slope of the *MP* curve indicates that the central bank reacts to higher inflation by raising real interest rates, because monetary policy follows the Taylor principle.

further, which would then cause the real interest rate to fall even more, increasing aggregate output again. Schematically, we can write this chain of events as follows:[2]

$$\pi \uparrow \Rightarrow r \downarrow \Rightarrow Y \uparrow \Rightarrow \pi \uparrow \Rightarrow r \downarrow \Rightarrow Y \uparrow \Rightarrow \pi \uparrow$$

Under these conditions, inflation would keep rising and eventually spin out of control. Indeed, this is exactly what happened in the 1970s, when the Bank of Canada did not raise nominal interest rates by as much as inflation rose, so that real interest rates fell. Inflation accelerated to over 10%.[3]

---

[2]The liquidity preference framework developed in Chapter 5 gives another rationale for using the Taylor principle when the path of the money supply curve and inflation expectations are unchanged. A rise in inflation means that the price level will be higher than it otherwise would be, and so the money demand curve shifts to the right, causing both nominal and real interest rates to rise (because inflation expectations are unchanged). Schematically, this can be written as follows:

$$\pi \uparrow \Rightarrow P \uparrow \Rightarrow M^d \text{ to the right} \Rightarrow i \uparrow \Rightarrow r \uparrow$$

[3]In Web Appendix 4 to Chapter 23 we formally demonstrate the instability of inflation when central banks do not follow the Taylor principle.

Shifts in the *MP* Curve

In common parlance, the Bank of Canada is said to "tighten" monetary policy when it raises real interest rates and to "ease" it when it lowers real interest rates. It is important, however, to distinguish between changes in monetary policy that shift the monetary policy curve, which we call *autonomous* changes, and the Taylor principle–driven changes that are reflected in movements along the monetary policy curve, which are called *automatic* adjustments to interest rates.

Central banks may make autonomous changes to monetary policy for various reasons. They may wish to change the inflation rate from its current value. For example, to lower inflation, they could increase $\bar{r}$ by one percentage point and so raise the real interest rate at any given inflation rate, a move that we will refer to as an **autonomous tightening of monetary policy**. This autonomous monetary tightening would shift the monetary policy curve upward by one percentage point, from MP_1 to MP_2 in Figure 22-2,

MyEconLab Mini-lecture

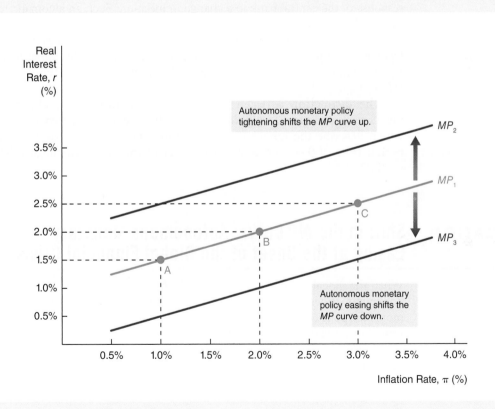

FIGURE 22-2   Shifts in the Monetary Policy Curve

Autonomous changes in monetary policy—for example, when a central bank changes the real interest rate at any given inflation rate—shift the *MP* curve. An autonomous tightening of monetary policy that increases the real interest rate shifts the *MP* curve up to MP_2, whereas an autonomous easing of monetary policy that lowers the real interest rate shifts the *MP* curve down to MP_3.

thereby causing the economy to contract and inflation to fall. Or, the central banks may have other information, unrelated to inflation, suggesting that interest rates must be adjusted to achieve good economic outcomes. For example, if the economy is going into a recession, monetary policymakers will want to lower real interest rates at any given inflation rate, an **autonomous easing of monetary policy**, in order to stimulate the economy and to prevent inflation from falling. This autonomous easing of monetary policy would result in a downward shift of the monetary policy curve by, say, one percentage point, from MP_1 to MP_3 in Figure 22-2.

Movements Along Versus Shifts in the *MP* Curve

A stumbling block for many students studying the aggregate demand/aggregate supply (*AD/AS*) framework is understanding the distinction between *shifts in* the *MP* curve versus *movements along* the *MP* curve. Movements along the *MP* curve—that is, movements from point *A* to *B* to *C* in Figure 22-1—should be viewed as a central bank's normal response (also known as an endogenous response) of raising interest rates when inflation is rising. Thus we can think of a movement along the *MP* curve as an *automatic* response of the central bank to a change in inflation. Such an automatic response does not involve a shift in the *MP* curve.

On the other hand, when the central bank raises interest rates *at a given level of the inflation rate*, this action is not an automatic response to higher inflation but is instead an autonomous tightening of monetary policy that shifts the *MP* curve up, from MP_1 to MP_2 in Figure 22-2.

The distinction between autonomous monetary policy changes and movements along the monetary policy curve is illustrated by the two applications below, which describe the monetary policy actions taken by the Bank of Canada in the period from 2004–2006 and at the onset of the global financial crisis in the fall of 2007.

APPLICATION ## Shift in the *MP* Curve: Autonomous Monetary Easing at the Onset of the Global Financial Crisis

When the global financial crisis started in August 2007, inflation was rising and economic growth was quite strong. Yet the Bank of Canada began an aggressive easing of monetary policy, lowering the overnight interest rate as shown in Figure 22-3. What were the effects on the monetary policy curve?

A movement along the *MP* curve would have suggested that the Bank planned to continue hiking interest rates because inflation was rising, but instead the Bank did the opposite. The Bank of Canada's actions thus shifted the monetary policy curve down, from MP_1 to MP_3, as shown in Figure 22-2. The Bank pursued this autonomous monetary policy easing because the negative shock to the economy caused by the disruption to financial markets (discussed in Chapter 9) indicated that, despite the high inflation rates at the time, the economy was likely to weaken in the near future, and the inflation rate would then fall. Indeed, this is exactly what came to pass, with the economy going into a recession in December 2007 and the inflation rate falling sharply after August 2008.◆

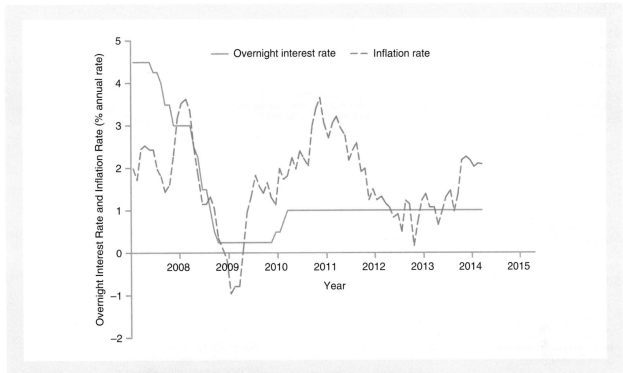

FIGURE 22-3 **The Inflation Rate and the Overnight Interest Rate, 2007–2014**

The Bank of Canada began an aggressive autonomous easing of monetary policy in September 2007, bringing down its policy rate, the overnight interest rate, despite the continuing high inflation.

THE AGGREGATE DEMAND CURVE

We are now ready to derive the relationship between the inflation rate and aggregate output when the goods market is in equilibrium: the **aggregate demand curve**. The *MP* curve that we just developed demonstrates how central banks respond to changes in inflation by changing the interest rate in line with the Taylor principle. The *IS* curve we developed in Chapter 21 showed that changes in real interest rates, in turn, affect equilibrium output. With these two curves, we can now link the quantity of aggregate output demanded with the inflation rate, given the public's expectations of inflation and the stance of monetary policy. The aggregate demand curve is central to the aggregate demand and supply analysis we will develop further in the next chapter, which will enable us to explain short-run fluctuations in both aggregate output and inflation.

Deriving the Aggregate Demand Curve Graphically

Using the hypothetical *MP* curve from Equation 2, we know that when the inflation rate rises from 1% to 2% to 3%, the Bank of Canada reacts by raising the real interest rate from 1.5% to 2% to 2.5%. We plot these points in panel (a) of Figure 22-4 as the *MP* curve. In panel (b), we graph the *IS* curve described in Equation 13 of Chapter 21 ($Y = 12 - r$). As the real interest rate rises from 1.5% to 2% to 2.5%, the equilibrium moves from point

MyEconLab Mini-lecture

FIGURE 22-4
Deriving the *AD* Curve

The *MP* curve in panel (a) shows that as inflation rises from 1.0% to 2.0% to 3.0%, the real interest rate rises from 1.5% to 2.0% to 2.5%. The *IS* curve in panel (b) then shows that higher real interest rates lead to lower planned investment spending and net exports, and hence aggregate output falls from $10.5 trillion to $10.0 trillion to $9.5 trillion. Finally, panel (c) plots the level of equilibrium output corresponding to each of the three inflation rates: the line that connects these points is the *AD* curve, and it is downward-sloping.

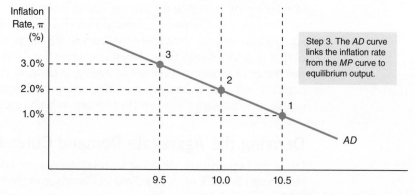

1 to point 2 to point 3, and aggregate output falls from $10.5 trillion to $10 trillion to $9.5 trillion. In other words, as real interest rates rise, investment and net exports decline, leading to a reduction in aggregate demand. Using the information from panels (a) and (b), we can create the curve shown in panel (c). As inflation rises from 1% to 2% to 3%, the equilibrium moves from point 1 to point 2 to point 3 in panel (c), and aggregate output falls from $10.5 trillion to $10 trillion to $9.5 trillion.

The line that connects the three points shown in panel (c) is the aggregate demand curve, *AD*, and it indicates the level of aggregate output corresponding to each of the three real interest rates consistent with equilibrium in the goods market for any given inflation rate. The aggregate demand curve has a downward slope because a higher inflation rate leads the central bank to raise the real interest rate, thereby lowering planned spending and hence lowering the level of equilibrium aggregate output.

By using some algebra (see the FYI box, Deriving the Aggregate Demand Curve Algebraically), the *AD* curve in Figure 22-4 can be written numerically as follows:

$$Y = 11 - 0.5\pi \qquad \text{(Equation 3)}$$

Factors That Shift the Aggregate Demand Curve

Movements along the aggregate demand curve describe how the equilibrium level of aggregate output changes when the inflation rate changes. When factors other than the inflation rate change, however, the aggregate demand curve shifts. We first review the factors that shift the *IS* curve, and then consider the factors that shift the *AD* curve.

Shifts in the *IS* Curve   We saw in the preceding chapter that there are six factors that cause the *IS* curve to shift. It turns out that these same factors will cause the aggregate demand curve to shift as well:

1. Autonomous consumption expenditure
2. Autonomous investment spending
3. Government purchases

FYI   Deriving the Aggregate Demand Curve Algebraically

To derive a numerical *AD* curve, we start by taking the numerical *IS* curve given by Equation 13 in Chapter 21:

$$Y = 12 - r$$

We then use the numerical *MP* curve given in Equation 2, $r = 1.0 + 0.5\pi$, to substitute for *r*, yielding

$$Y = 12 - (1.0 + 0.5\pi)$$
$$= (12 - 1) - 0.5\pi$$
$$= 11 - 0.5\pi$$

which is the same as Equation 3 in the text.

Similarly, we can derive a more general version of the *AD* curve by using the algebraic version of the *IS* curve given by Equation 12 in Chapter 21:

$$Y = [\overline{C} + \overline{I} - d\overline{f} + \overline{G} + \overline{NX} - mpc \times \overline{T}]$$
$$\times \frac{1}{1 - mpc} - \frac{d + x}{1 - mpc} \times r$$

We then substitute for *r* using the algebraic *MP* curve given in Equation 1, $r = \overline{r} + \lambda\pi$, to get the more general equation of the *AD* curve:

$$Y = [\overline{C} + \overline{I} - d\overline{f} + \overline{G} + \overline{NX} - mpc \times \overline{T}]$$
$$\times \frac{1}{1 - mpc} - \frac{d + x}{1 - mpc} \times (\overline{r} + \lambda\pi)$$

4. Taxes
5. Autonomous net exports
6. Financial frictions

We examine how changes in these factors lead to a shift in the aggregate demand curve, as shown in Figure 22-5.

Suppose that inflation is at 2.0%, and so the *MP* curve in panel (a) of Figure 22-5 shows that the real interest rate is at 2.0%. The IS_1 curve in panel (b) then shows that the equilibrium level of output is at $10 trillion at point A_1, which corresponds to an equilibrium level of output of $10 trillion at point A_1 on the AD_1 curve in panel (c). Now suppose there is a rise in, for example, government purchases of $1 trillion. Panel (b) shows that with both the inflation rate and the real interest rate held constant at 2.0%, the equilibrium moves from point A_1 to point A_2, with output rising to $12.5 trillion,[4] and so the *IS* curve shifts to the right from IS_1 to IS_2. The rise in output to $12.5 trillion means that, holding inflation and the real interest rate constant, the equilibrium in panel (c) also moves from point A_1 to point A_2, and so the *AD* curve also shifts to the right, from AD_1 to AD_2.

Figure 22-5 shows that **any factor that shifts the IS curve shifts the aggregate demand curve in the same direction**. Therefore, any factor that shifts the *IS* curve to the right—a rise in autonomous consumption expenditure or planned investment spending encouraged by "animal spirits," a rise in government purchases, an autonomous rise in net exports, a fall in taxes, or a decline in financial frictions—will also shift the aggregate demand curve to the right. Conversely, any factor that shifts the *IS* curve to the left—a fall in autonomous consumption expenditure, a fall in planned investment spending, a fall in government purchases, a fall in net exports, a rise in taxes, or a rise in financial frictions—will shift the aggregate demand curve to the left.

Shifts in the *MP* Curve

We now examine what happens to the aggregate demand curve when the *MP* curve shifts. Suppose the Bank of Canada is worried about the economy overheating and so decides to autonomously tighten monetary policy by raising the real interest rate by one percentage point at any given level of the inflation rate. At an inflation rate of 2.0%, the real interest rate rises from 2.0% to 3.0% in Figure 22-6. The *MP* curve shifts up from MP_1 to MP_2 in panel (a). Panel (b) shows that when the inflation rate is at 2.0%, the higher real interest rate of 3.0% causes the equilibrium to move from point A_1 to point A_2 on the *IS* curve, with output falling from $10 trillion to $9 trillion. The lower output of $9 trillion occurs because the higher real interest leads to a decline in investment and net exports, which lowers aggregate demand. The lower output of $9 trillion then decreases the equilibrium output level from point A_1 to point A_2 in panel (c), and so the *AD* curve shifts to the left, from AD_1 to AD_2.

Our conclusion from Figure 22-6 is that **an autonomous tightening of monetary policy—that is, a rise in the real interest rate at any given inflation rate—shifts the aggregate demand curve to the left. Conversely, an autonomous easing of monetary policy shifts the aggregate demand curve to the right.**

We have now derived and analyzed the aggregate demand curve, an essential element in the aggregate demand and supply framework that we will examine in the next chapter. We will use the aggregate demand curve in this framework to determine both aggregate output and inflation, as well as to examine events that cause these variables to change.

---

[4]As we saw in the numerical example in Chapter 21, a rise in government purchases of $1 trillion leads to a $2.5 trillion increase in equilibrium output at any given real interest rate, and this is why output rises from $10 trillion to $12.5 trillion when the real interest rate is at 2.0%.

MyEconLab Mini-lecture

FIGURE 22-5
Shift in the *AD* Curve from Shifts in the *IS* Curve

At a 2% inflation rate in panel (a), the monetary policy curve indicates that the real interest rate is 2%. An increase in government purchases shifts the *IS* curve to the right in panel (b). At a given inflation rate and real interest rate of 2.0%, equilibrium output rises from $10 trillion to $12.5 trillion, which is shown as a movement from point A_1 to point A_2 in panel (c), shifting the aggregate demand curve to the right from AD_1 to AD_2. Any factor that shifts the *IS* curve shifts the *AD* curve in the same direction.

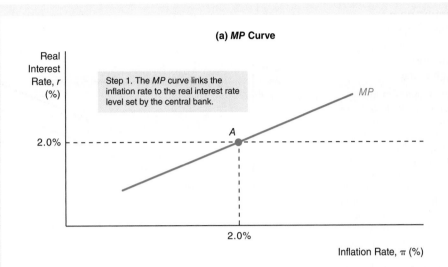

(a) *MP* Curve

Step 1. The *MP* curve links the inflation rate to the real interest rate level set by the central bank.

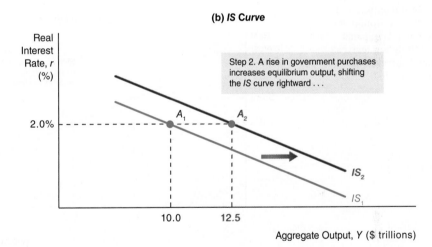

(b) *IS* Curve

Step 2. A rise in government purchases increases equilibrium output, shifting the *IS* curve rightward . . .

(c) Aggregate Demand Curve

Step 3. . . . and shifting the *AD* curve rightward.

FIGURE 22-6
Shift in the *AD* Curve from Autonomous Monetary Policy Tightening

Autonomous monetary tightening that raises real interest rates by one percentage point at any given inflation rate shifts the *MP* curve up, from MP_1 to MP_2 in panel (a). With the inflation rate at 2.0%, the higher 3% interest rate results in a movement from point A_1 to A_2 on the *IS* curve, with output falling from $10 trillion to $9 trillion. This change in equilibrium output leads to movement from point A_1 to point A_2 in panel (c), shifting the aggregate demand curve to the left, from AD_1 to AD_2.

(a) *MP*

Step 1. Autonomous monetary policy tightening increases the real interest rate . . .

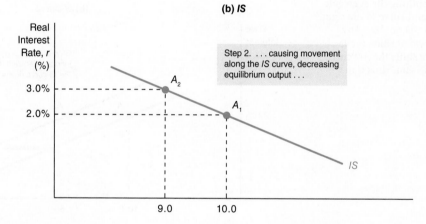

(b) *IS*

Step 2. . . . causing movement along the *IS* curve, decreasing equilibrium output . . .

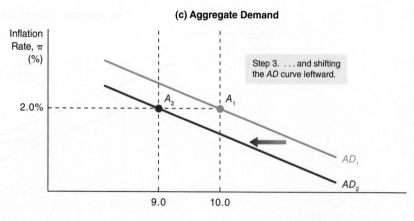

(c) Aggregate Demand

Step 3. . . . and shifting the *AD* curve leftward.

MyEconLab

MyEconLab is an online homework and tutorial system that puts you in control of your own learning with study and practice tools directly correlated to this chapter's content. Visit MyEconLab to access the eText, the Questions and Applied Problems with answers, as well as additional assessment. You will also find web chapters, mini-lectures, appendices, mini-cases, videos, glossary flashcards, news feeds, CANSIM data, and graphing tools.

SUMMARY

1. When the Bank of Canada lowers the overnight interest rate by providing more liquidity to the banking system, real interest rates fall in the short run; when the Bank of Canada raises the overnight interest rate by reducing the amount of liquidity in the banking system, real interest rates rise in the short run.

2. The monetary policy (*MP*) curve shows the relationship between inflation and the real interest rate that arises from monetary authorities' actions. Monetary policy follows the Taylor principle, in which higher inflation results in higher real interest rates, represented by upward movements along the monetary policy curve. An autonomous tightening of monetary policy occurs when monetary policymakers raise the real interest rate at any given inflation rate, resulting in an upward shift of the monetary policy curve. An autonomous easing of monetary policy and a downward shift of the monetary policy curve occur when monetary policymakers lower the real interest rate at any given inflation rate.

3. The aggregate demand curve gives the level of equilibrium aggregate output (which equals the total quantity of output demanded) for any given inflation rate. It slopes downward because a higher inflation rate leads the central bank to raise real interest rates, which leads to a lower level of equilibrium output. The aggregate demand curve will shift in the same direction as the *IS* curve; hence the *AD* curve shifts to the right when government purchases increase, taxes decrease, "animal spirits" encourage consumer and business spending, autonomous net exports increase, or financial frictions decrease. An autonomous tightening of monetary policy—that is, an increase in the real interest rate at any given inflation rate—leads to a decline in aggregate demand, and the aggregate demand curve shifts to the left.

KEY TERMS

aggregate demand curve, p. 555
autonomous easing of monetary policy, p. 554

autonomous tightening of monetary policy, p. 553
monetary policy (*MP*) curve, p. 551

Taylor principle, p. 551

QUESTIONS

All questions are available in MyEconLab *at* **www.myeconlab.com.**

1. When the inflation rate increases, what happens to the overnight interest rate? Operationally, how does the Bank of Canada adjust the overnight interest rate?

2. What is the key assumption underlying the Bank of Canada's ability to control the real interest rate?

3. Why does the *MP* curve necessarily have an upward slope?

4. If $\lambda = 0$, what does this imply about the relationship between the nominal interest rate and the inflation rate?

5. How does an autonomous tightening or easing of monetary policy by the Bank of Canada affect the *MP* curve?

6. How is an autonomous tightening or easing of monetary policy different from a change in the real interest rate caused by a change in the current inflation rate?

7. Suppose that a new Bank of Canada governor is appointed and that his or her approach to monetary policy can be summarized by the following statement: "I care only about increasing employment. Inflation has been at very low levels for quite some time; my priority is to ease monetary policy to promote employment." How would you expect the monetary policy curve to be affected, if at all?

8. "The Bank of Canada decreased the overnight interest rate in late 2007, even though inflation was increasing. This action demonstrated a violation of the Taylor principle." Is this statement true, false, or uncertain? Explain your answer.

9. What factors affect the slope of the aggregate demand curve?

10. "Autonomous monetary policy is more effective at changing output when λ is higher." Is this statement true, false, or uncertain? Explain your answer.

11. If net exports were not sensitive to changes in the real interest rate, would monetary policy be more or less effective in changing output?

12. How does an autonomous tightening or easing of monetary policy by the Bank of Canada affect the aggregate demand curve?

13. For each of the following situations, describe how (if at all) the *IS*, *MP*, and *AD* curves are affected.

a. A decrease in financial frictions

b. An increase in taxes and an autonomous easing of monetary policy

c. An increase in the current inflation rate

d. A decrease in autonomous consumption

e. Firms become more optimistic about the future of the economy.

f. The new Bank of Canada governor begins to care more about fighting inflation.

14. What would be the effect of an increase in Canadian net exports on the aggregate demand curve? Would an increase in net exports affect the monetary policy curve? Explain.

15. Why does the aggregate demand curve shift when "animal spirits" change?

16. If government spending increases and taxes are raised to keep the budget balanced, what happens to the aggregate demand curve?

17. Suppose that government spending is increased at the same time that an autonomous monetary policy tightening occurs. What will happen to the position of the aggregate demand curve?

18. "If $\bar{f}$ increases, then the Bank of Canada can keep output constant by reducing the real interest rate by the same amount as the increase in financial frictions." Is this statement true, false, or uncertain? Explain your answer.

APPLIED PROBLEMS

All applied problems are available in MyEconLab at **www.myeconlab.com**.

19. Assume that the monetary policy curve is given by $r = 1.5 + 0.75\pi$.

a. Calculate the real interest rate when the inflation rate is 2%, 3%, and 4%.

b. Draw a graph of the *MP* curve, labelling the points from part (a).

c. Assume now that the monetary policy curve is given by $r = 2.5 + 0.75\pi$. Does the new monetary policy curve represent an autonomous tightening or loosening of monetary policy?

d. Calculate the real interest rate when the inflation rate is 2%, 3%, and 4%, and draw the new *MP* curve, showing the shift from part (b).

20. Use an *IS* curve and an *MP* curve to derive graphically the *AD* curve.

21. Suppose the monetary policy curve is given by $r = 1.5 + 0.75\pi$, and the *IS* curve is given by $Y = 13 - r$.

a. Calculate an expression for the aggregate demand curve.

b. Calculate the real interest rate and aggregate output when the inflation rate is 2%, 3%, and 4%.

c. Draw graphs of the *IS*, *MP*, and *AD* curves, labelling the points from part (b) on the appropriate graphs.

22. Consider an economy described by the following:

$$\overline{C} = \$4 \text{ trillion}$$
$$\overline{I} = \$1.5 \text{ trillion}$$
$$\overline{G} = \$3.0 \text{ trillion}$$
$$\overline{T} = \$3.0 \text{ trillion}$$
$$\overline{NX} = \$1.0 \text{ trillion}$$
$$\overline{f} = 0$$
$$mpc = 0.8$$
$$d = 0.35$$
$$x = 0.15$$
$$\lambda = 0.5$$
$$\overline{r} = 2$$

a. Derive expressions for the *MP* curve and the *AD* curve.

b. Calculate the real interest rate and aggregate output when $\pi = 2$ and $\pi = 4$.

c. Draw a graph of the *MP* curve and the *AD* curve, labelling the points given in part (b).

23. Consider an economy described by the following:

$$\overline{C} = \$3.25 \text{ trillion}$$
$$\overline{I} = \$1.3 \text{ trillion}$$
$$\overline{G} = \$3.5 \text{ trillion}$$
$$\overline{T} = \$3.0 \text{ trillion}$$
$$\overline{NX} = -\$1.0 \text{ trillion}$$
$$\overline{f} = 1$$
$$mpc = 0.75$$
$$d = 0.3$$
$$x = 0.1$$
$$\lambda = 1$$
$$\overline{r} = 1$$

a. Derive expressions for the *MP* curve and the *AD* curve.

b. Assume that $\pi = 1$. Calculate the real interest rate, the equilibrium level of output, consumption, planned investment, and net exports.

c. Suppose the Bank of Canada increases $\overline{r}$ to $\overline{r} = 2$. Calculate the real interest rate, the equilibrium level of output, consumption, planned investment, and net exports at this new level of $\overline{r}$.

d. Considering that output, consumption, planned investment, and net exports all decreased in part (c), why might the Bank choose to increase $\overline{r}$?

24. Consider the economy described in Applied Problem 23.

a. Derive expressions for the *MP* curve and the *AD* curve.

b. Assume that $\pi = 2$. What are the real interest rate and the equilibrium level of output?

c. Suppose government spending increases to $4 trillion. What happens to equilibrium output?

d. If the Bank of Canada wants to keep output constant, then what monetary policy change should it make?

25. Suppose the *MP* curve is given by $r = 2 + \pi$, and the *IS* curve is given by $Y = 20 - 2r$.

a. Derive an expression for the *AD* curve, and draw a graph labelling points at $\pi = 0$, $\pi = 4$, and $\pi = 8$.

b. Suppose that λ increases to $\lambda = 2$. Derive an expression for the new *AD* curve, and draw the new *AD* curve using the graph from part (a).

c. What does your answer to part (b) imply about the relationship between a central bank's distaste for inflation and the slope of the *AD* curve?

DATA ANALYSIS PROBLEMS

Download data for these problems from MyEconLab *at* **www.myeconlab.com**.

1. A measure of real interest rates can be approximated by the interest rate on inflation-protected long-term Canada bonds, or Real Return Bonds. Go to the CANSIM database and find monthly data from January 1992 to January 2015 on the long-term Real Return Bond (series V122553) and the (all items) Consumer price Index (CPI), a measure of the price index (series V41690914). Convert the price index data to annualized inflation rates by taking the month-to-month percent change in the price index

and multiplying it by 12. Be sure to multiply by 100 so that your results are percentages.

a. Calculate the average inflation rate and the average real interest rate over the most recent 12 months of data available.

b. Calculate the standard deviation of the real interest rate and the annualized inflation rate over the most recent 12 months of data available.

2. Continuing from the previous problem, use the monthly CPI and calculate the percent change from a year ago. Then plot both series on the same graph, using data from 2007 through the most current data available.

WEB EXERCISES

1. Go to **www.bankofcanada.ca/core-functions/ monetary-policy**. Review the Bank of Canada's monetary policy objective. Explain why this objective is consistent with the Taylor principle.

2. Go to **www.federalreserve.gov/pf/pdf/pf_2.pdf**. Review the FOMC's document, "Longer-Run Goals and Monetary Policy Strategy." Explain why these goals are consistent with the Taylor principle.

WEB REFERENCES

Go to **www.bankofcanada.ca/core-functions/monetary-policy**. Review the Bank of Canada's monetary policy objective and the main instruments used to implement it.

www.federalreserve.gov/pf/pf.htm

Describes the purposes and functions of the Federal Reserve System in the United States and its rationale for the conduct of monetary policy.

23 Aggregate Demand and Supply Analysis

Learning Objectives

After studying this chapter you should be able to

1. Summarize and illustrate the aggregate demand curve and the factors that shift it.

2. Illustrate and interpret the short-run and long-run aggregate supply curves.

3. Illustrate and interpret shifts in the short-run and long-run aggregate supply curves.

4. Illustrate and interpret the short-run and long-run equilibriums, and the role of the self-correcting mechanism.

5. Illustrate and interpret the short-run and long-run effects of a shock to aggregate demand.

6. Illustrate and interpret the short-run and long-run effects of temporary and permanent supply shocks.

7. Explain business cycle fluctuations in major economies during the 2007–2009 financial crisis.

PREVIEW

In earlier chapters, we focused considerable attention on monetary policy because it touches our everyday lives by affecting both inflation and the quantity of jobs available. In this chapter, we develop aggregate demand and supply analysis, a basic tool that will enable us to study the effects of monetary policy on output and inflation. *Aggregate demand* is the total amount of output demanded at different inflation rates. *Aggregate supply* is the total amount of output that firms in an economy want to sell at different inflation rates. As was the case in the supply and demand analysis from your earlier economics courses, equilibrium occurs at the intersection of the aggregate demand and aggregate supply curves.

Aggregate demand and supply analysis will enable us to explore how aggregate output and inflation are determined. (The Following the Financial News box indicates where and how often data on aggregate output and the inflation rate are published.) Not only will the analysis help us interpret the past, but it also will help us understand recent episodes in the business cycle, such as the severe recession of 2007–2009, and predict how future events may affect aggregate output and inflation.

AGGREGATE DEMAND

The first building block of aggregate supply and demand analysis is the **aggregate demand curve**, which describes the relationship between the quantity of aggregate output demanded and the inflation rate when all other variables are held constant.

Aggregate demand is made up of four component parts: **consumption expenditure**, the total demand for consumer goods and services; **planned investment spending**,[1]

---

[1]Recall that economists restrict the definition of the word *investment* to mean the purchase of new physical capital, such as a new machine or a new house, which adds to spending on newly produced goods or services. This differs from the everyday use of the term by noneconomists, who use the word *investment* to describe purchases of common stocks or bonds, purchases that do not necessarily involve newly produced goods and services. When economists speak of investment spending, they are referring to purchases that add to aggregate demand.

the total planned spending by business firms on new machines, factories, and other capital goods, plus planned spending on new homes; **government purchases**, spending by all levels of government (federal, provincial, and local) on goods and services (paper clips, computers, computer programming, icebreakers, government employees, and so on); and **net exports**, the net foreign spending on domestic goods and services, equal to exports minus imports. Using the symbols C for consumption expenditure, I for planned investment spending, G for government spending, and NX for net exports, we can write the following expression for aggregate demand Y^{ad}:

$$Y^{ad} = C + I + G + NX \qquad \text{(Equation 1)}$$

Deriving the Aggregate Demand Curve

The first step in deriving the aggregate demand curve is to recognize that when the inflation rate rises ($\pi\uparrow$), the monetary authorities react by raising the real interest rate ($r\uparrow$). They do this to keep inflation from spiralling out of control. Next we can examine the effects of the higher real interest rate on the individual components of aggregate demand. When the real interest rate is higher, the cost of financing purchases of new physical capital becomes higher, making investment less profitable and causing planned investment spending to decline ($I\downarrow$). Because, as shown in Equation 1, planned investment spending is included in aggregate demand, the decline in planned investment spending causes aggregate demand to fall ($Y^{ad}\downarrow$). A higher inflation rate therefore leads to a lower level of the quantity of aggregate output demanded ($\pi\uparrow \Rightarrow Y^{ad}\downarrow$), and so the

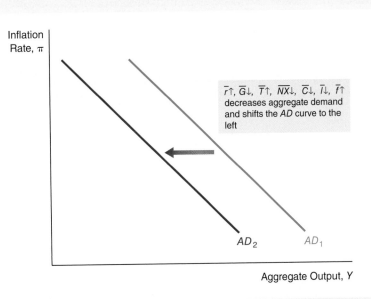

Inflation Rate, π

$\bar{r}\uparrow$, $\bar{G}\downarrow$, $\bar{T}\uparrow$, $\overline{NX}\downarrow$, $\bar{C}\downarrow$, $\bar{I}\downarrow$, $\bar{f}\uparrow$ decreases aggregate demand and shifts the *AD* curve to the left

AD_2 AD_1

Aggregate Output, *Y*

FIGURE 23-1   Leftward Shift in the Aggregate Demand Curve

The aggregate demand curve shifts to the left from AD_1 to AD_2 when there is an autonomous tightening of monetary policy ($\bar{r}\uparrow$), a decrease in government purchases ($\bar{G}\downarrow$), an increase in taxes ($\bar{T}\uparrow$), a decrease in autonomous net exports ($\overline{NX}\downarrow$), a decrease in autonomous consumption expenditure ($\bar{C}\downarrow$), a decrease in autonomous investment ($\bar{I}\downarrow$), or an increase in financial frictions ($\bar{f}\uparrow$).

aggregate demand curve slopes downward, as in Figure 23-1. Schematically, we can write the mechanism just described as follows:[2]

$$\pi\uparrow \Rightarrow r\uparrow \Rightarrow I\downarrow \Rightarrow Y^{ad}\downarrow$$

Factors That Shift the Aggregate Demand Curve

Seven basic factors (often referred to as **demand shocks**) can shift the aggregate demand curve to a new position: (1) autonomous monetary policy, (2) government purchases, (3) taxes, (4) autonomous net exports, (5) autonomous consumption expenditure, (6) autonomous investment, and (7) financial frictions. (The use of the term *autonomous* in the factors listed above sometimes confuses students, and so it is discussed in the FYI box, What Does *Autonomous* Mean?) As we examine each case, we ask what happens to the aggregate demand curve when each of these factors changes while the inflation rate is held constant. As a study aid, Summary Table 23-1 Summarizes the shifts in the aggregate demand curve that occur with changes in each of these seven factors.

1. *Autonomous monetary policy.* We have already noted that when inflation rises, the central bank will raise the real interest rate to keep inflation from spiraling out of control. However, there are central-bank movements in the real interest rate that

[2]If you have already read Chapters 21 and Chapter 22, this discussion of aggregate demand is just a recap of the analysis given in those chapters. Note that an additional mechanism for a downward-sloping aggregate demand curve operates through net exports, as discussed in Chapters 21 and 22.

SUMMARY TABLE 23-1

Factors That Shift the Aggregate Demand Curve

Factor	Change	Shift in Aggregate Demand Curve
Autonomous monetary policy, $\bar{r}$	↑	
Government purchases, $\overline{G}$	↑	
Taxes, $\overline{T}$	↑	
Autonomous net exports, $\overline{NX}$	↑	
Autonomous consumption expenditure, $\overline{C}$	↑	
Autonomous investment, $\bar{I}$	↑	
Financial frictions, $\bar{f}$	↑	

Note: Only increases (↑) in the factors are shown. The effect of decreases in the factors would be the opposite of those indicated in the "Shift" column.

are autonomous, denoted by $\bar{r}$, which are movements unrelated to the variables in the model, such as the current level of the inflation rate. When the Bank of Canada decides to increase this autonomous component of the real interest rate, $\bar{r}$, the higher real interest rate at any given inflation rate leads to a higher cost of financing investment projects, which leads to a decline in investment spending and the quantity of aggregate demand, as demonstrated by the following schematic:

$$\bar{r}\uparrow \Rightarrow I\downarrow \Rightarrow Y^{ad}\downarrow$$

Therefore, aggregate demand falls at any given inflation rate, and the aggregate demand curve shifts to the left as in Figure 23-1.

2. *Government purchases.* An increase in government purchases at any given inflation rate adds directly to aggregate demand expenditure, and hence aggregate demand rises:

$$\bar{G}\uparrow \Rightarrow Y^{ad}\uparrow$$

Aggregate demand, therefore, rises at any given inflation rate, and the aggregate demand curve shifts to the right as in Figure 23-2.

3. *Taxes.* At any given inflation rate, an increase in taxes lowers disposable income, which leads to lower consumption expenditure and aggregate demand, so that aggregate demand falls:

$$\bar{T}\uparrow \Rightarrow C\downarrow \Rightarrow Y^{ad}\downarrow$$

Aggregate demand falls at any given inflation rate, and the aggregate demand curve shifts to the left as in Figure 23-1.

4. *Autonomous net exports.* An autonomous increase in net exports at any given inflation rate adds directly to aggregate demand and so raises aggregate demand:

$$\overline{NX}\uparrow \Rightarrow Y^{ad}\uparrow$$

Aggregate demand rises at any given inflation rate, and the aggregate demand curve shifts to the right as in Figure 23-2.

5. *Autonomous consumption expenditure.* When consumers become more optimistic, autonomous consumption expenditure rises, and so consumers spend more at any given inflation rate. Aggregate demand therefore rises:

$$\bar{C}\uparrow \Rightarrow Y^{ad}\uparrow$$

Aggregate demand rises at any given inflation rate, and the aggregate demand curve shifts to the right as in Figure 23-2.

$\bar{r}\downarrow, \overline{G}\uparrow, \overline{T}\downarrow, \overline{NX}\uparrow, \overline{C}\uparrow, \bar{I}\uparrow, \bar{f}\downarrow$
increases aggregate demand
and shifts the *AD* curve to the
right

AD_1 AD_2

Aggregate Output, *Y*

FIGURE 23-2 **Rightward Shift in the Aggregate Demand Curve**

The aggregate demand curve shifts to the right, from AD_1 to AD_2, when there is an autonomous easing of monetary policy ($\bar{r}\downarrow$), an increase in government purchases ($\overline{G}\uparrow$), a decrease in taxes ($\overline{T}\downarrow$), an increase in autonomous net exports ($\overline{NX}\uparrow$), an increase in autonomous consumption expenditure ($\overline{C}\uparrow$), an increase in autonomous investment ($\bar{I}\uparrow$), or a decrease in financial frictions ($\bar{f}\downarrow$).

6. *Autonomous investment.* When businesses become more optimistic, autonomous investment rises and businesses spend more at any given inflation rate. Planned investment increases and aggregate demand rises:

$$\bar{I}\uparrow \Rightarrow Y^{ad}\uparrow$$

Aggregate demand rises at any given inflation rate, and the aggregate demand curve shifts to the right as in Figure 23-2.

7. *Financial frictions.* The real cost of borrowing reflects not only the real interest rate on default-free debt instruments, *r*, but also financial frictions, denoted by $\bar{f}$, which are additions to the real cost of borrowing caused by asymmetric information problems in financial markets (described in Chapter 8). When financial frictions increase, the real cost of borrowing increases, so that planned investment spending falls at any given inflation rate, and aggregate demand falls:

$$\bar{f}\uparrow \Rightarrow I\downarrow \Rightarrow Y^{ad}\downarrow$$

Aggregate demand falls at any given inflation rate, and the aggregate demand curve shifts to the left as in Figure 23-1.

The conclusion from our analysis is as follows: ***Aggregate demand increases at any given inflation rate, and the aggregate demand curve shifts to the right when there is: (1) an autonomous easing of monetary policy ($\bar{r}\downarrow$), (2) an increase in government purchases ($\overline{G}\uparrow$), (3) a decrease in taxes ($\overline{T}\downarrow$), (4) an increase in autonomous*** *net exports* $(\overline{NX}\uparrow)$, *(5) an increase in autonomous consumption expenditure* $(\overline{C}\uparrow)$, *(6) an increase in autonomous investment* $\overline{I}\uparrow$, *or (7) a decrease in financial frictions* $(\overline{f}\downarrow)$. *Conversely, the aggregate demand curve shifts to the left when any of these factors change in the opposite direction.*

AGGREGATE SUPPLY

To complete our analysis, we need to derive an **aggregate supply curve**, a curve that shows the relationship between the quantity of output supplied and the inflation rate. In the typical supply and demand analysis, we have only one supply curve, but because prices and wages take time to adjust to their long-run levels, the aggregate supply curve differs in the short and long runs. First we examine the long-run aggregate supply curve; then we derive the short-run aggregate supply curve. Finally, we look at how both of these curves shift over time and at how the economy moves from the short run to the long run.

Long-Run Aggregate Supply Curve

The amount of output that can be produced in the economy in the long run is determined by the amount of capital in the economy, the amount of labour supplied at full employment, and the available technology. As discussed in Chapter 17, some unemployment cannot be helped because it is either frictional or structural. Thus, at full employment, unemployment is not at zero but is rather at a level above zero at which the demand for labour equals the supply of labour. This **natural rate of unemployment** is the rate to which the economy gravitates in the long run.[3] Many economists believe that the natural rate of unemployment is currently around 6%.

The level of aggregate output produced at the natural rate of unemployment is called the **natural rate of output** but is more often referred to as **potential output**: It is the level at which the economy settles in the long run for any inflation rate. Suppose potential output is at $1.8 trillion. The long-run aggregate supply curve (*LRAS*) is then vertical at the $1.8 trillion of potential output, denoted by Y^P, as drawn in Figure 23-3.

Short-Run Aggregate Supply Curve

The short-run aggregate supply curve is based on the idea that three factors drive inflation: (1) expectations of inflation, (2) the output gap, and (3) inflation (supply) shocks.

Expected Inflation, π^e Workers and firms care about wages in real terms—that is, in terms of the goods and services that wages can buy. When workers expect a positive inflation rate, they will adjust nominal wages upward one-to-one with the expected inflation rate, so that the real wage rate does not decrease. Thus, holding everything else constant, wage inflation will rise one-to-one with rises in expected inflation. Because wages are the most important cost of producing goods and services, overall inflation will also rise on a one-to-one basis with increases in expected inflation.

---

[3]A more detailed derivation of the short-run aggregate supply curve, based on the Phillips curve (which gives the relationship between unemployment and inflation), can be found in the appendix to this chapter .

MyEconLab Mini-lecture

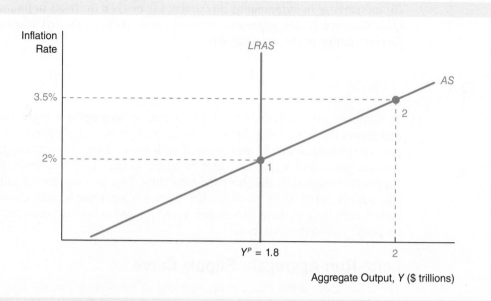

FIGURE 23-3   Long- and Short-Run Aggregate Supply Curves

The amount of aggregate output supplied at any given inflation rate is at potential output in the long run, $1.8 trillion, so that the long-run aggregate supply curve *LRAS* is a vertical line at $Y^P = \$1.8$ trillion. The short-run aggregate supply curve, *AS* (Note that the short-run aggregate supply curve in Figure 23-3 is marked as *AS* ($\pi^e = 2\%$) to indicate it is drawn assuming $\pi^e = 2\%$.), where $\pi^e = 2\%$, is upward-sloping because as *Y* rises relative to Y^P, labour markets get tighter and inflation rises. *AS* intersects *LRAS* at point 1, where current inflation equals expected inflation of 2%.

Output Gap   The **output gap** is defined as the percentage difference between aggregate output and potential output, $Y - Y^P$. When output exceeds its potential level and the output gap is high, there is very little slack in the economy. Workers will demand higher wages, and firms will take the opportunity to raise prices. The end result will be higher inflation. Conversely, when the output gap is negative, there will be a lot of slack in the economy. Thus workers will accept smaller increases in wages, and firms will need to lower prices to sell their goods, resulting in lower inflation.

Inflation (Supply) Shocks   **Supply shocks** occur when there are shocks to the supply of goods and services produced in the economy that translate into **inflation shocks**, that is, shifts in inflation that are independent of the amount of slack in the economy or expected inflation. For example, when the supply of oil is restricted, as has occurred several times when Middle East countries were at war, the resulting rise in the price of oil leads firms to raise prices more to reflect the increased costs of production, thus driving up inflation. Energy inflation shocks can also occur when demand increases—for example, increased demand from developing countries like China such as occurred in 2007–2008—again driving up inflation. Inflation shocks can also come from rises in import prices or from **cost-push shocks** in which workers push for wages that are higher than productivity gains, thereby driving up costs and inflation.

Short-Run Aggregate Supply Curve   Putting all of our analysis together, we can write the following equation for the short-run aggregate supply curve:

$$\pi = \pi^e + \gamma(Y - Y^P) + \rho$$

Inflation = Expected + γ × Output + Price   (Equation 2)
Inflation   Gap   Shock

where

$$\pi = \text{inflation}$$
$$\pi^e = \text{expected inflation}$$
$$Y - Y^P = \text{the output gap}$$
$$\gamma = \text{the sensitivity of inflation to the output gap}$$
$$\rho = \text{the inflation shock}$$

The short-run aggregate supply curve given in Equation 2 tells us that inflation is driven by three factors: (1) expectations of inflation, (2) output gaps, and (3) inflation shocks.

Why the Short-Run Aggregate Supply Curve Is Upward-Sloping   To see why the short-run aggregate supply curve, *AS*, in Figure 23-3 is upward-sloping, let's assume that expected inflation is at 2% and that there are no inflation shocks. When actual output equals potential output at $1.8 trillion, the output gap, $Y - Y^P$, is zero, and so Equation 2 indicates that the inflation rate will equal the expected inflation rate of 2%. The combination of $1.8 trillion of aggregate output and a 2% inflation rate is shown by point 1 on the *AS* curve.

Now suppose that aggregate output rises to $2 trillion. Because there is a positive output gap ($Y = \$2$ trillion $> Y^P = \$1.8$ trillion), Equation 2 indicates that inflation will rise above 2%, say to 3.5%, marked as point 2. The curve connecting points 1 and 2 is the short-run aggregate supply curve, *AS*, and it is upward-sloping. When *Y* rises relative to Y^P and $Y > Y^P$, the labour market is tighter and firms raise their prices at a more rapid rate, causing the inflation rate to rise. Thus the *AS* curve is upward-sloping.

Price Stickiness and the Short-Run Aggregate Supply Curve

If wages and prices are sticky, inflation adjusts slowly over time. The more flexible wages and prices are, the more rapidly they, and inflation, respond to deviations of output from potential output; that is, more flexible wages and prices imply that the absolute value of γ is higher, which in turn implies that the short-run aggregate supply curve is steeper. If wages and prices are completely flexible, then γ becomes so large that the short-run aggregate supply curve becomes vertical and is identical to the long-run aggregate supply curve.

SHIFTS IN THE AGGREGATE SUPPLY CURVES

Now that we have examined the long-run and short-run aggregate supply curves, we can look at why each of these curves shift.

Shifts in the Long-Run Aggregate Supply Curve

The quantity of output supplied in the long run is determined by the three factors that cause potential output to change and thus shift the long-run aggregate supply curve: (1) the total amount of capital in the economy, (2) the total amount of labour supplied in

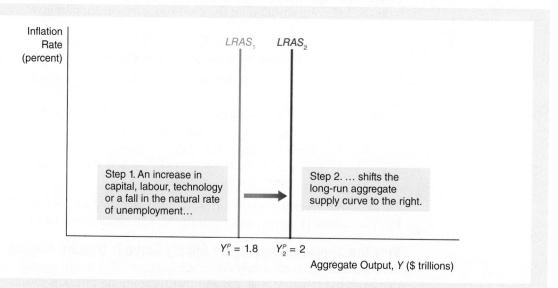

FIGURE 23-4 **Shift in the Long-Run Aggregate Supply Curve**

The long-run aggregate supply curve shifts to the right from $LRAS_1$ to $LRAS_2$ when there is (1) an increase in the total amount of capital in the economy, (2) an increase in the total amount of labour supplied in the economy, (3) an increase in the available technology, or (4) a decline in the natural rate of unemployment. An opposite movement in these variables shifts the $LRAS$ curve to the left.

the economy, and (3) the available technology that puts labour and capital together to produce goods and services. When any of these three factors increases, potential output rises, say, from $Y_1^P = \$1.8$ trillion to $Y_2^P = \$2$ trillion, and the long-run aggregate supply curve shifts to the right, from $LRAS_1$ to $LRAS_2$ in Figure 23-4.

Because all three of these factors typically grow fairly steadily over time, Y^P and the long-run aggregate supply curve will keep shifting to the right at a steady pace. To keep things simple in later diagrams in this and following chapters, when Y^P is growing at a steady rate, we will represent Y^P and the long-run aggregate supply curve as fixed.

Another source of shifts in the long-run aggregate supply curve is changes in the natural rate of unemployment. If the natural rate of unemployment declines, it means that labour is being more heavily utilized, and so potential output will increase. A decline in the natural rate of unemployment thus shifts the long-run aggregate supply curve to the right, from $LRAS_1$ to $LRAS_2$ in Figure 23-4. A rise in the natural rate of unemployment would have the opposite effect, shifting the long-run aggregate supply curve to the left.

The conclusion from our analysis is as follows: *The long-run aggregate supply curve shifts to the right when there is (1) an increase in the total amount of capital in the economy, (2) an increase in the total amount of labour supplied in the economy, (3) an increase in available technology, or (4) a decline in the natural rate of unemployment. An opposite movement in these variables shifts the LRAS curve to the left.*

Shifts in the Short-Run Aggregate Supply Curve

The three terms on the right-hand side of Equation 2 suggest that three factors can shift the short-run aggregate supply curve: (1) expected inflation, (2) a persistent output gap, and (3) inflation shocks.

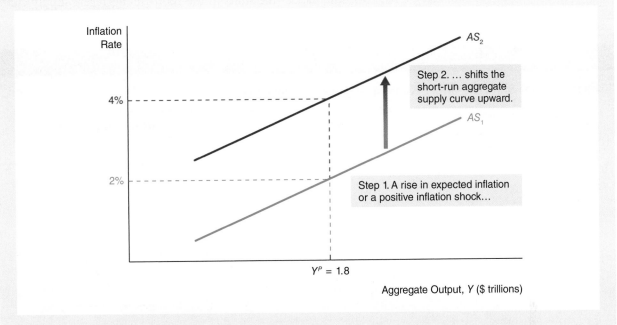

FIGURE 23-5 **Shift in the Short-Run Aggregate Supply Curve from Changes in Expected Inflation and Inflation Shocks**

A rise in expected inflation or a positive inflation shock shifts the short-run aggregate supply curve upward from AS_1 to AS_2. (A decrease in expected inflation or a negative inflation shock would lead to a downward shift of the AS curve.)

Expected Inflation What if a newly appointed governor of the Bank of Canada does not think that inflation is costly and so is willing to tolerate an inflation rate that is two percentage points higher than the current rate? Households and firms will then expect that the Bank of Canada will pursue policies that will let inflation rise by, say, two percentage points in the future, and will want to raise wages and prices by this additional amount. In such a situation, expected inflation will jump by two percentage points, and the short-run aggregate supply curve will shift upward and to the left, from AS_1 to AS_2 in Figure 23-5. *A rise in expected inflation causes the short-run aggregate supply curve to shift upward and to the left. Conversely, a fall in expected inflation causes the short-run aggregate supply curve to shift down and to the right. The larger the change in expected inflation, the larger is the shift.*

Inflation Shock Suppose that energy prices suddenly shoot up because terrorists destroy a number of oil fields. This supply restriction (an unfavourable supply shock) causes the inflation-shock term in Equation 2 to increase, and so the short-run aggregate supply curve shifts up and to the left, from AS_1 to AS_2 in Figure 23-5. A favourable supply shock, which drives down inflation, will have the opposite effect and cause the short-run aggregate supply curve to shift down and to the right. *Unfavourable supply shocks that drive up inflation cause the short-run aggregate supply curve to shift up and to the left, while favourable supply shocks that lower inflation cause* *the short-run aggregate supply curve to shift down and to the right.* As a study aid, Summary Table 23-2 summarizes the shifts in the short-run aggregate supply curve caused by each of these three factors.

SUMMARY TABLE 23-2

Factors That Shift the Short-Run Aggregate Supply Curve

Factor	Change	Shift in Supply Curve
Expected inflation, π^e	↑	π — AS_2 AS_1 — Y
Inflation shock, ρ	↑	π — AS_2 AS_1 — Y
Persistent output gap, $(Y - Y^P)$	↑	π — AS_2 AS_1 — Y

Note: Only increases (↑) in the factors are shown. The effect of decreases in the factors would be the opposite of those indicated in the "Shift" column.

Persistent Output Gap   We have already seen that a higher output gap leads to higher inflation, causing a movement along the short-run aggregate supply curve. We can represent this scenario by the movement from point 1 to point 2 on the initial short-run aggregate supply curve AS_1 in Figure 23-6. A persistent output gap, however, will cause the short-run aggregate supply curve to shift by affecting expected inflation. To see this, consider what happens if the aggregate output stays at $2 trillion, which is greater than the potential output of $Y^P = \$1.8$ trillion, so that the output gap remains persistently positive. At point 2 on the initial short-run aggregate supply curve, AS_1, output has risen to $2 trillion and inflation has risen from 2% to 3.5%. This higher level of inflation will cause expected inflation to rise during the next period, and so the short-run aggregate supply curve for the next period, AS_2, will shift upward. If output remains above potential output at point 3, inflation will rise further, to 5.0%. This higher inflation will then lead to higher expected inflation and, as the vertical arrow indicates, the short-run aggregate supply curve will shift upward to AS_3 during the next period.

When will the short-run aggregate supply curve stop rising? It will stop only when output returns to its potential level and the output gap disappears. At this point,

MyEconLab Mini-lecture

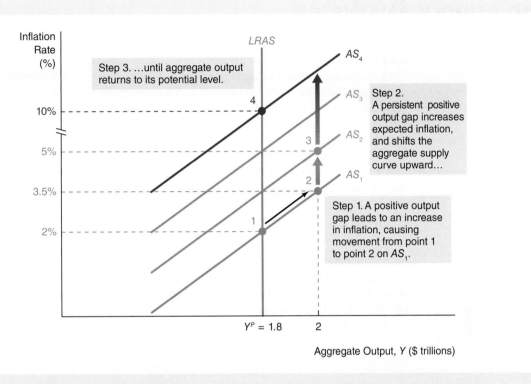

FIGURE 23-6 **Shift in the Short-Run Aggregate Supply Curve from a Persistent Positive Output Gap**

When output is above potential, the economy moves along the AS_1 curve from point 1 to point 2, and inflation rises to 3.5%. If output continues to remain above potential output, where the output gap is positive, the short-run aggregate supply curve will shift upward, to AS_2 and then to AS_3. The short-run aggregate supply curve stops shifting upward when the economy reaches point 4 on the short-run aggregate supply curve AS_4, where the output gap is once again zero.

there is no longer a reason for actual and hence expected inflation to rise. Suppose this happens when inflation is at 10% and aggregate output $Y = \$1.8$ trillion $= Y^P$. Because the output gap is now zero, the aggregate supply curve drawn through point 4, AS_4, has no reason to shift because inflation and expected inflation have stopped rising.

The same reasoning indicates that if aggregate output is kept below potential for a period of time, $Y < Y^P$, then the short-run aggregate supply curve will shift downward and to the right. This downward shift of the aggregate supply curve will stop only when output returns to its potential level and the economy is back on the long-run aggregate supply curve.

Our analysis yields the following conclusion: **When aggregate output is above potential output, so that a persistent positive output gap exists, the short-run aggregate supply curve shifts up and to the left. Conversely, when aggregate output falls below potential output, the short-run aggregate supply curve shifts down and to the right. Only when aggregate output returns to potential output does the short-run aggregate supply curve stop shifting.**

EQUILIBRIUM IN AGGREGATE DEMAND AND SUPPLY ANALYSIS

We can now put the aggregate demand and supply curves together to describe **general equilibrium** in the economy, the point at which all markets are simultaneously in equilibrium and the quantity of aggregate output demanded equals the quantity of aggregate output supplied. We represent general equilibrium graphically as the point at which the aggregate demand curve intersects the aggregate supply curve. However, recall that we have two aggregate supply curves: one for the short run and one for the long run. Consequently, in the context of aggregate supply and demand analysis, there are short-run and long-run equilibriums. In this section, we illustrate equilibrium in the short and long runs. In following sections, we examine aggregate demand and aggregate supply shocks that lead to changes in equilibrium.

Short-Run Equilibrium

Figure 23-7 illustrates a short-run equilibrium in which the quantity of aggregate output demanded equals the quantity of output supplied. In Figure 23-7, the short-run aggregate demand curve AD and the short-run aggregate supply curve AS intersect at point E, with an equilibrium level of aggregate output at $Y^* = \$1.8$ trillion and an equilibrium inflation rate at $\pi^* = 2\%$.

MyEconLab Mini-lecture

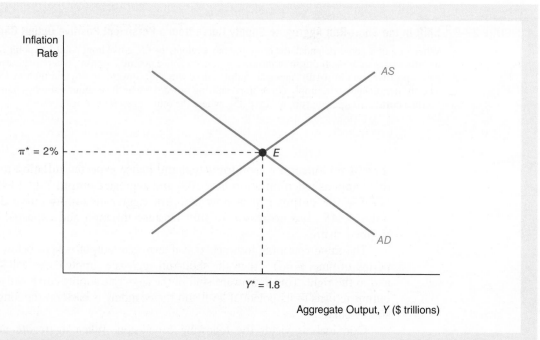

FIGURE 23-7 **Short-Run Equilibrium**

Short-run equilibrium occurs at point E, at the intersection of the aggregate demand curve AD and the short-run aggregate supply curve AS.

How the Short-Run Equilibrium Moves to the Long-Run Equilibrium over Time

In supply and demand analysis, once we find the equilibrium point at which the quantity demanded equals the quantity supplied, additional analysis typically is not needed. In *aggregate* supply and demand analysis, however, that is not the case. Even when the quantity of aggregate output demanded equals the quantity supplied at the intersection of the aggregate demand curve and the short-run aggregate supply curve, if output differs from its potential level ($Y^* \neq Y^P$), the short-run equilibrium will move over time. To understand why, recall that if the current level of inflation changes from its initial level, the short-run aggregate supply curve will shift as wages and prices adjust to a new expected rate of inflation.

We look at how the short-run equilibrium changes over time in response to two situations: when short-run equilibrium output is initially above potential output (the natural rate of output), and when it is initially below potential output.

In panel (a) of Figure 23-8, the initial equilibrium occurs at point 1, the intersection of the aggregate demand curve AD and the initial short-run aggregate supply curve AS_1. The level of equilibrium output, $Y_1 = \$2$ trillion, is greater than the potential output, $Y^P = \$1.8$ trilllion, and there is excessive tightness in the labour market. Hence, the positive output gap at Y_1 drives wages up and causes firms to raise their prices at a more rapid rate. Inflation then rises above the initial inflation rate, π_1. At this higher inflation rate, firms and households adjust their expectations next period, and expected inflation becomes higher. Wages and prices then rise more rapidly, and the aggregate supply curve shifts up and to the left, from AS_1 to AS_2.

The new short-run equilibrium at point 2 is an upward movement along the aggregate demand curve, and output falls to Y_2. However, because aggregate output Y_2 is still above potential output Y^P, inflation again rises above its value last period. Expected inflation rises further, eventually shifting the aggregate supply curve up and to the left to AS_3. The economy reaches long-run equilibrium at point 3 on the vertical long-run aggregate supply curve ($LRAS$), at $Y^P = \$1.8$ trillion. Because output is at potential, there is no further pressure on inflation to rise and thus no further tendency for the aggregate supply curve to shift.

The movements in panel (a) indicate that the economy will not remain at a level of output higher than potential output of $1.8 trillion over time. Specifically, the short-run aggregate supply curve will shift up and to the left, raising the inflation rate and causing the economy (equilibrium) to move upward along the aggregate demand curve until it comes to rest at a point on the long-run aggregate supply curve ($LRAS$) that is at potential output $Y^P = \$1.8$ trillion.

In panel (b), at the initial equilibrium at point 1, output $Y_1 = \$1.6$ trillion is below the level of potential output of $1.8 trillion. Because unemployment is now above its natural rate, there is excess slack in the labour markets. This slack at $Y_1 = \$1.6$ trillion decreases inflation, which decreases expected inflation and shifts the short-run aggregate supply curve in the next period down and to the right, to AS_2.

The equilibrium now moves to point 2, and output rises to Y_2. However, because aggregate output Y_2 is still below potential output Y^P, inflation again declines from its value last period, causing expected inflation to fall. This decline in expected inflation shifts the aggregate supply curve down until it comes to rest at AS_3. The economy (equilibrium) moves downward along the aggregate demand curve until it reaches the long-run equilibrium at point 3, at the intersection of the aggregate demand curve (AD) and the long-run aggregate supply curve ($LRAS$) at $Y^P = \$1.8$ trillion. Here, as in panel (a), the economy comes to rest when output has again returned to its potential level.

MyEconLab Mini-lecture

(a) Initial short-run equilibrium above potential output

Step 2. ... the economy returns to the potential level of output.

Step 1. Excess tightness in the labour market increases expected inflation and shifts the *AS* curve upward until...

(b) Initial short-run equilibrium below potential output

Step 1. Excess slack in the labour market decreases expected inflation and shifts the *AS* curve downward until...

Step 2. ... the economy returns to the potential level of output.

FIGURE 23-8   Adjustment to Long-Run Equilibrium in Aggregate Supply and Demand Analysis

In both panels, the initial short-run equilibrium is at point 1, at the intersection of *AD* and AS_1. In panel (a), initial short-run equilibrium is above potential output, the long-run equilibrium, and so the short-run aggregate supply curve shifts upward until it reaches AS_3, where output returns to Y^P. In panel (b), initial short-run equilibrium is below potential output, and so the short-run aggregate supply curve shifts downward until output returns to Y^P. In both panels, the economy's self-correcting mechanism returns the economy to the level of potential output.

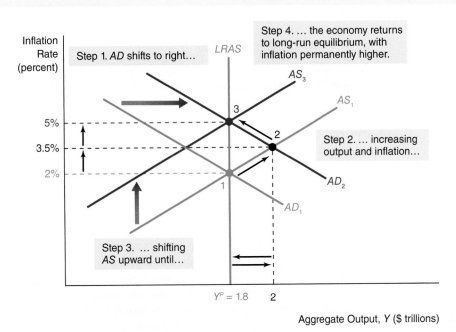

FIGURE 23-9   Positive Demand Shock

A positive demand shock shifts the aggregate demand curve upward from AD_1 to AD_2 and moves the economy from point 1 to point 2, resulting in higher inflation at 3.5% and higher output of $2 trillion. Because output is greater than potential output and therefore expected inflation increases, the short-run aggregate supply curve begins to shift up, eventually reaching AS_3. At point 3, the economy returns to long-run equilibrium, with output at $Y^P = \$1.8$ trillion and the inflation level rising to 5%.

Self-Correcting Mechanism

Notice that in both panels of Figure 23-8, regardless of where output is initially, it returns eventually to potential output, a feature we call the **self-correcting mechanism**. The self-correcting mechanism occurs because the short-run aggregate supply curve shifts up or down to restore the economy to the long-run equilibrium at full employment (aggregate output at potential) over time.

CHANGES IN EQUILIBRIUM: AGGREGATE DEMAND SHOCKS

With an understanding of the distinction between the short-run and long-run equilibriums, we are now ready to analyze what happens when the economy experiences **demand shocks**, shocks that cause the aggregate demand curve to shift. Figure 23-9 depicts the effects of a rightward shift in the aggregate demand curve due to positive demand shocks, which may be caused by the following:

- An autonomous easing of monetary policy ($\bar{r}\downarrow$, a lowering of the real interest rate at any given inflation rate)

- An increase in government purchases ($\overline{G}\uparrow$)
- A decrease in taxes ($\overline{T}\downarrow$)
- An increase in autonomous net exports ($\overline{NX}\uparrow$)
- An increase in autonomous consumption expenditure ($\overline{C}\uparrow$)
- An increase in autonomous investment ($\overline{I}\uparrow$)
- A decrease in financial frictions ($\overline{f}\downarrow$)

Figure 23-9 shows the economy initially in long-run equilibrium at point 1, where the initial aggregate demand curve AD_1 intersects the short-run aggregate supply AS_1 curve at $Y^P = \$1.8$ trillion and the inflation rate is 2%. Suppose that consumers and businesses become more optimistic and that the resulting increases in autonomous consumption and investment create a positive demand shock that shifts the aggregate demand curve to the right to AD_2. The economy moves up the short-run aggregate supply curve AS_1 to point 2, and output and inflation rise to \$2 trillion and 3.5%, respectively. However, the economy will not remain at point 2 in the long run because output at \$2 trillion is above potential output. Expected inflation will rise, and the short-run aggregate supply curve will eventually shift upward to AS_3. The economy (equilibrium) thus will move up the AD_2 curve from point 2 to point 3, which is the point of long-run equilibrium at which inflation equals 5% and output returns to $Y^P = \$1.8$ trillion. *Although the initial short-run effect of the rightward shift in the aggregate demand curve is a rise in both inflation and output, the ultimate long-run effect is a rise in inflation only, because output returns to its initial level at Y^P.*[4]

We now apply the aggregate demand and supply model to demand shocks, as a payoff for our hard work in constructing the model. Throughout the remainder of this chapter, we will apply aggregate supply and demand analysis to a number of business cycle episodes, both in Canada and in foreign countries, over the past 40 years. To simplify our analysis, we will assume in all examples that aggregate output is initially at the level of potential output.

APPLICATION   The Bank of Canada Disinflation, 1981–1985

In the early 1980s, inflation in Canada had spun out of control and the inflation rate exceeded 12%. The Bank of Canada was determined to get inflation down. By early 1981, the Bank of Canada had raised short-term interest rates to over 20%, which led to a sharp increase in real interest rates. The Bank of Canada was indeed successful in bringing inflation down, as panel (b) of Figure 23-10 indicates, with the inflation rate falling from an average of 12.5% in 1981 to an average of 3.9% in 1985. The decline in inflation came at a high cost: in 1981–1982, the economy experienced the worst recession since World War II, with the unemployment rate increasing to over 12% in 1983.

This outcome is exactly what our aggregate demand and supply analysis predicts. The autonomous tightening of monetary policy decreased aggregate demand and shifted the aggregate demand curve to the left from AD_1 to AD_2, as we show in panel (a) of

---

[4]The analysis here assumes that each of these positive demand shocks occurs while everything else is held constant, the usual *ceteris paribus* ("other things being equal") assumption that is standard in supply and demand analysis. Specifically, this means that the central bank is assumed not to be responding to demand shocks. In the next chapter, we relax this assumption and allow monetary policymakers to respond to these shocks. As we will see, if monetary policymakers want to keep inflation caused by a positive demand shock from rising, they will respond by autonomously tightening monetary policy.

(a) Aggregate Demand and Aggregate Supply Analysis

Step 2. . . . lowering output to Y_2 and inflation to π_2 . . .

LRAS

AS_1

AS_3

Step 1. Monetary policy tightening decreases aggregate demand . . .

AD_1

AD_2

Step 3. . . . which decreases expected inflation and shifts aggregate supply downward.

Step 4. Output increases to potential output Y^P and inflation declines further to π_3.

Inflation Rate, π

π_1

π_2

π_3

Y_2 Y^P

Aggregate Output, Y

(b) Unemployment and Inflation, 1981–1985

Year	Unemployment Rate (%)	Inflation (Year to Year) (%)
1981	7.6	12.5
1982	11.0	10.8
1983	11.9	5.8
1984	11.3	4.3
1985	10.5	3.9

FIGURE 23-10   The Bank of Canada Disinflation

Panel (a) shows that the Bank of Canada's actions to decrease inflation were successful but costly: the autonomous monetary policy tightening caused a negative demand shock that decreased aggregate demand and in turn inflation, resulting in soaring unemployment rates. The data in panel (b) support this analysis: note the decline in the inflation rate from 12.5% in 1981 to 3.9% in 1985, while the unemployment rate increased as high as 12% in 1983.
Source: IMF International Financial Statistics and Statistics Canada CANSIM II series V2062815.

Figure 23-10. The economy moved to point 2, indicating that unemployment would rise and inflation would fall. With unemployment above the natural rate and output below potential, the short-run aggregate supply curve shifted downward and to the right to AS_3. The economy moved toward long-run equilibrium at point 3, with inflation continuing to fall, output rising back to potential output, and the unemployment rate moving toward its natural rate level. Figure 23-10 panel (b) shows that by 1985 the unemployment rate had fallen (although not a lot) and the inflation rate was 3.9%, just as our aggregate demand and supply analysis predicts. ◆

The next period we will examine, 2001–2004, again illustrates the effects of negative demand shocks—this time, three at once.

APPLICATION   ## Negative Demand Shocks in the United States, 2001–2004

In 2000, the U.S. economy was expanding when it was hit by a series of negative shocks to aggregate demand.

1. The "tech bubble" burst in March 2000, and the stock market fell sharply.
2. The September 11, 2001, terrorist attacks weakened both consumer and business confidence.
3. The Enron bankruptcy in late 2001 and other corporate accounting scandals in 2002 revealed that corporate financial data were not to be trusted. Interest rates on corporate bonds rose as a result of the increase in financial frictions, making it more expensive for corporations to finance their investments.

All three of these negative demand shocks led to a decline in household and business spending, decreasing aggregate demand and shifting the aggregate demand curve to the left, from AD_1 to AD_2 in panel (a) of Figure 23-11. At point 2, as predicted by our aggregate demand and supply analysis, unemployment rose and inflation fell. Panel (b) of Figure 23-11 shows that the unemployment rate, which had been at 4% in 2000, rose to 6% in 2003, while the annual rate of inflation fell from 3.4% in 2000 to 1.6% in 2002. With unemployment above the natural rate (estimated to be around 5%) and output below potential, the short-run aggregate supply curve shifted downward, to AS_3 in panel (a) of Figure 23-11. The economy moved to point 3, with inflation falling, output rising back to potential output, and the unemployment rate returning to its natural rate level. By 2004, the self-correcting mechanism feature of aggregate demand and supply analysis had begun to come into play, with the unemployment rate dropping back to 5.5% (see Figure 23-11, panel (b)). ◆

CHANGES IN EQUILIBRIUM: AGGREGATE SUPPLY (INFLATION) SHOCKS

Shifts in the aggregate supply curve can be caused by temporary supply (inflation) shocks, in which the long-run aggregate supply curve does not shift, or permanent supply shocks, in which the long-run aggregate supply curve does shift. We will look at these two types of supply shocks in turn.

Temporary Supply Shocks

In our discussion earlier in the chapter of the short-run aggregate supply curve, we showed that inflation will rise independently of tightness in the labour markets or increases in expected inflation caused by temporary supply shocks, such as a decrease in the supply of oil that causes prices to rise. When the temporary shock involves a restriction in supply, we refer to this type of supply shock as a *negative* (or *unfavourable*) *supply shock*, and it results in a rise in commodity prices. Examples of temporary negative supply shocks include a disruption in oil supplies, a rise in import prices when a currency declines in

(a) Aggregate Demand and Aggregate Supply Analysis

(b) Unemployment and Inflation, 2000–2004

Year	Unemployment Rate (%)	Inflation (Year to Year) (%)
2000	4.0	3.4
2001	4.7	2.8
2002	5.8	1.6
2003	6.0	2.3
2004	5.5	2.7

FIGURE 23-11   Negative Demand Shocks, 2001–2004

Panel (a) shows that the negative demand shocks from 2001–2004 decreased consumption expenditure and investment, shifting the aggregate demand curve to the left from AD_1 to AD_2. The economy moved to point 2, where output fell, unemployment rose, and inflation declined. The large negative output gap that occurred when output was less than potential caused the short-run aggregate supply curve to begin falling to AS_3. The economy moved toward point 3, where output would return to potential: Inflation declined further to π_3, and unemployment fell back to its natural rate level of around 5%. The data in panel (b) support this analysis, with inflation declining to around 2% and the unemployment rate dropping back to 5.5% by 2004.
Source: Economic Report of the President.

value, or a cost-push shock from workers pushing for higher wages that outpaces productivity growth, driving up costs and inflation. When the supply shock involves an increase in supply, it is called a *positive* (or *favourable*) *supply shock*. Temporary positive supply shocks include a particularly good harvest or a fall in import prices.

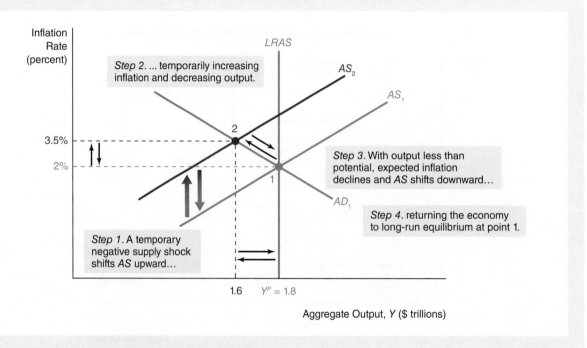

FIGURE 23-12 **Temporary Negative Supply Shock**

A temporary negative supply shock shifts the short-run aggregate supply curve from AS_1 to AS_2, and the economy moves from point 1 to point 2, where inflation increases to 3.5% and output declines to $1.6 trillion. Because output is less than potential, the negative output gap lowers inflation and hence expected inflation. The decline in expected inflation shifts the short-run aggregate supply curve back down, and eventually it returns to AS_1, where the economy is again at the initial long-run equilibrium at point 1.

To see how a temporary supply shock affects the economy, we can use our aggregate supply and demand analysis. We start by assuming that output is at its potential level of $1.8 trillion and inflation is at 2%, at point 1 in Figure 23-12. Suppose that a war in the Middle East causes a temporary negative supply shock. When the negative supply shock hits the economy and oil prices rise, the change in the price shock term ρ indicates that inflation will rise to above 2%, and the short-run aggregate supply curve will shift up and to the left, from AS_1 to AS_2.

The economy then will move up the aggregate demand curve, from point 1 to point 2, where inflation rises to 3.5% but aggregate output *falls* below $1.8 trillion. We use the term **stagflation** (a combination of the words *stagnation* and *inflation*) to describe a situation defined by rising inflation but a falling level of aggregate output, as pictured in Figure 23-12. Because the supply shock is temporary, productive capacity in the economy does not change, and so Y^P and the long-run aggregate supply curve *LRAS* remain stationary at $1.8 trillion. At point 2, output is therefore below its potential level (say, at $1.6 trillion), and so inflation falls. The decline in inflation causes expected inflation to fall and shifts the short-run aggregate supply curve back down to where it was initially, at AS_1. The economy (equilibrium) slides down the aggregate demand curve AD_1 (assuming the aggregate demand curve remains in the same position) and returns to the long-run equilibrium at point 1, where output is again at $1.8 trillion and inflation is again at 2%.

Although a temporary negative supply shock leads to an upward and leftward shift of the short-run aggregate supply curve, which initially raises inflation and lowers output, the ultimate long-run effect is that output and inflation are unchanged.

A favourable (positive) supply shock—say, an excellent harvest of wheat in the Prairie provinces—moves all the curves in Figure 23-12 in the opposite direction and so has the opposite effects. *A temporary positive supply shock shifts the short-run aggregate supply curve downward and to the right, initially leading to a fall in inflation and a rise in output. In the long run, however, output and inflation are unchanged (holding the aggregate demand curve constant).*

We now will once again apply the aggregate demand and supply model, this time to temporary supply shocks. We begin by studying the negative supply shocks of 1973–1975 and 1978–1980. (Recall we assume that aggregate output is initially at its potential level.)

APPLICATION   ## Negative Supply Shocks, 1973–1975 and 1978–1980

In 1973, the Canadian and world economies were hit by a series of negative supply shocks:

1. As a result of the oil embargo stemming from the Arab–Israeli war of 1973, the Organization of Petroleum Exporting Countries (OPEC) engineered a quadrupling of oil prices by restricting oil production.
2. A series of crop failures throughout the world led to a sharp increase in food prices.

The double thrust of these events shifted the short-run aggregate supply curve sharply upward and to the left from AS_1 to AS_2 in panel (a) of Figure 23-13, and the economy moved to point 2. As the aggregate demand and supply diagram in Figure 23-13 predicts, both inflation and unemployment rose as per panel (b) of Figure 23-13.

The 1978–1980 period was almost an exact replay of the 1973–1975 period. By 1978, the economy had just about fully recovered from the 1973–1975 supply shocks, when poor harvests and a doubling of oil prices (as a result of the overthrow of the Shah of Iran) again led to another sharp upward and leftward shift of the short-run aggregate supply curve in 1979. The pattern predicted by Figure 23-13 played itself out again—inflation and unemployment both shot upward. ◆

Permanent Supply Shocks and Real Business Cycle Theory

But what if a supply shock is not temporary? A permanent negative supply shock—such as an increase in ill-advised regulations that cause the economy to become less efficient, thereby reducing supply—would decrease potential output from, say, Y_1^P to Y_2^P and shift the long-run aggregate supply curve to the left, from $LRAS_1$ to $LRAS_2$ in Figure 23-14.

Because the permanent supply shock will lead to higher prices, there will be an immediate rise in inflation—say, to 3% from its previous level of 2%—and so the short-run aggregate supply curve will shift up and to the left, from AS_1 to AS_2. Although output at point 2 has fallen to $1.6 trillion, it is still above $Y_2^P = \$1.4$ trillion. The positive output gap indicates that the aggregate supply curve will shift up and to the left. It will continue to do so until it reaches AS_3, at the intersection of the aggregate demand curve AD and the long-run aggregate supply curve $LRAS_2$. Now, because output is at $Y_2^P = \$1.4$ trillion at point 3, the output gap is zero and, at an inflation rate of 5%, there is no further upward pressure on inflation.

(a) Aggregate Demand and Aggregate Supply Analysis

Step 2. ...increasing inflation and decreasing output.

Step 1. A temporary negative supply shock shifts *AS* upward . . .

(b) Unemployment and Inflation, 1973–1975 and 1978–1980

Year	Unemployment Rate (%)	Inflation (Year to Year) (%)
1973	5.6	9.4
1974	5.3	14.6
1975	6.9	10.3
1978	8.3	6.5
1979	7.4	9.5
1980	7.5	10.9

FIGURE 23-13 **Negative Supply Shocks, 1973–1975 and 1978–1980**

Panel (a) shows that the temporary negative supply shocks in 1973 and 1979 led to an upward shift in the short-run aggregate supply curve from AD_1 to AD_2. The economy moved to point 2, where output fell, and both unemployment and inflation rose. The data in panel (b) support this analysis.
Source: IMF International Financial Statistics and Statistics Canada CANSIM II series V2062815.

One group of economists, led by Nobel Prize winner Edward Prescott of Arizona State University, believes that business cycle fluctuations result from permanent supply shocks alone. Their theory of aggregate economic fluctuations is called **real business cycle theory**. This theory views shocks to tastes (workers' willingness to work, for example) and technology (productivity) as the major driving forces behind short-run fluctuations in the business cycle because these shocks lead to substantial short-run fluctuations in Y^P. By contrast, shifts in the aggregate demand curve, perhaps caused by changes in monetary policy, are not viewed as being particularly important to aggregate output fluctuations. Because real business cycle theory views most business cycle fluctuations as resulting from fluctuations in the level of potential of output, it does not see much need for policies aimed at eliminating high unemployment. Real business cycle theory is highly controversial and is the subject of intensive research.

When we hold the aggregate demand curve constant, we generate the following result, as shown in Figure 23-14: *A permanent negative supply shock initially leads to both a decline in output and a rise in inflation. However, in contrast to a temporary supply shock, in the long run a permanent negative supply shock, which results in a fall in potential output, leads to a permanent decline in output and a permanent rise in inflation.*[5]

The opposite conclusion follows if we consider a positive supply shock—say, from the development of new technology that raises productivity. *A permanent positive supply shock lowers inflation and raises output in both the short run and the long run.*

To this point, we have assumed that potential output Y^P and hence the long-run aggregate supply curve are given. Over time, however, economic growth will cause the potential level of output to increase. If the productive capacity of the economy is growing at a steady rate of 3% per year, for example, every year Y^P will grow by 3% and the long-run aggregate supply curve at Y^P will shift to the right by 3%. To simplify the analysis, when Y^P grows at a steady rate, we represent Y^P and the long-run aggregate supply curve as fixed in the aggregate demand and supply diagrams. Keep in mind,

MyEconLab Mini-lecture

FIGURE 23-14 **Permanent Negative Supply Shock**

A permanent negative supply shock initially leads to a decline in output and a rise in inflation. In the long run, it leads to a permanent decline in output and a permanent rise in inflation, as indicated by point 3, where inflation has risen to 5% and output has fallen to $1.6 trillion.

[5]Our conclusion about the effects of a permanent supply shock assumes that monetary policy is not changing, and so the aggregate demand curve remains unchanged. Monetary policymakers, however, might want to shift the aggregate demand curve in an attempt to keep inflation at the same level. For further discussion, see the following chapter.

however, that the level of aggregate output pictured in these diagrams is actually best thought of as the level of aggregate output relative to its normal rate of growth (trend).

The 1995–1999 period serves as an illustration of permanent positive supply shocks, as indicated in the following application.

APPLICATION   Positive Supply Shocks, 1995–1999

In February 1994, the Bank of Canada began to raise interest rates. It believed the economy would be reaching potential output and the natural rate of unemployment in 1995, and it might become overheated thereafter, with output climbing above potential and inflation rising. As we can see in panel (b) of Figure 23-15, however, the economy continued to grow

(a) Aggregate Demand and Aggregate Supply Analysis

Step 2. …and leads to a permanent rise in output and a permanent decrease in inflation.

Step 1. A permanent positive supply shock shifts *LRAS* rightward and *AS* downward …

(b) Unemployment and Inflation, 1995–1999

Year	Unemployment Rate (%)	Inflation (Year to Year) (%)
1995	9.4	2.0
1996	9.6	2.0
1997	8.5	2.0
1998	8.2	1.0
1999	7.5	2.0

FIGURE 23-15   Positive Supply Shocks, 1995–1999

Panel (a) shows that the positive supply shocks from the rise in productivity from the computer revolution led to a rightward shift in the long-run aggregate supply curve from $LRAS_1$ to $LRAS_2$ and a downward shift in the short-run aggregate supply curve from AS_1 to AS_2. The economy moved to point 2, where aggregate output rose, and unemployment and inflation fell. The data in panel (b) support this analysis: note that the unemployment rate fell from 9.4% in 1995 to 7.5% in 1999, while the inflation rate fell from 2.0% in 1995 to 1.0% in 1998.

rapidly, with the unemployment rate falling to below 8% in 1999. Also, inflation declined to around 1% in 1998, although the Bank of Canada was targeting the inflation rate at 2%.

Can aggregate demand and supply analysis explain what happened? One permanent positive supply shock hit the economy in the late 1990s. In particular, the computer revolution finally began to impact productivity favourably, raising the potential growth rate of the economy (which journalists dubbed the "new economy"). In addition, demographic factors, such as an increase in the relative number of older workers who are less likely to be unemployed, led to a fall in the natural rate of unemployment. These factors led to a rightward shift in the long-run aggregate supply curve to $LRAS_2$ and a downward and rightward shift in the short-run aggregate supply curve from AS_1 to AS_2, as shown in panel (a) of Figure 23-15. Aggregate output rose, and unemployment fell, while inflation also declined. ◆

Conclusions

Aggregate demand and supply analysis leads us to the following conclusions.[6]

1. The economy has a self-correcting mechanism that returns it to potential output and the natural rate of unemployment over time.
2. A shift in the aggregate demand curve—caused by changes in autonomous monetary policy (changes in the real interest rate at any given inflation rate), government purchases, taxes, autonomous net exports, autonomous consumption expenditure, autonomous investment, or financial frictions—affects output only in the short run, and has no effect on output in the long run. Furthermore, the initial change in inflation is lower than the long-run change in inflation when the short-run aggregate supply curve has fully adjusted.
3. A temporary supply shock affects output and inflation only in the short run and has no effect in the long run (holding the aggregate demand curve constant).
4. A permanent supply shock affects output and inflation in both the short and long run.

AD/AS ANALYSIS OF FOREIGN BUSINESS CYCLE EPISODES

Our aggregate demand and supply analysis can help us understand business cycle episodes in foreign countries. Here we look at three such episodes: the experience of the United States with both negative supply and demand shocks during the 2007–2009 global financial crisis, the business cycle experience of the United Kingdom during the 2007–2009 global financial crisis, and the quite different experience of China during the same time period.

APPLICATION   ## The United States and the 2007–2009 Financial Crisis

At the beginning of 2007, high demand for oil in rapidly growing developing countries like China and India, and the slowing of oil production in places like Mexico, Russia, and Nigeria, drove oil prices up sharply. Oil prices rose from around $60 per barrel at the beginning of 2007 to $100 per barrel at the end of 2007 and they reached a peak of over $140 per barrel in July 2008. The rise in oil prices, along with increases

---

[6]Aggregate demand and supply analysis also can be used to understand the effects of macroeconomic shocks on asset prices. This analysis can be found in the first web appendix to this chapter, which can be found on the MyEconLab.

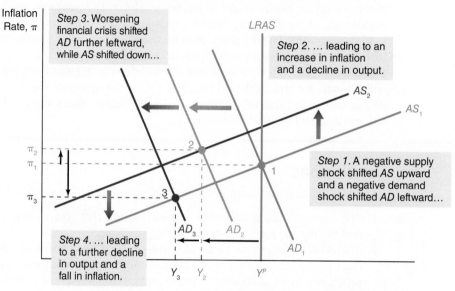

(a) Aggregate Demand and Aggregate Supply Analysis

Inflation Rate, π

Step 3. Worsening financial crisis shifted *AD* further leftward, while *AS* shifted down...

LRAS

Step 2. ... leading to an increase in inflation and a decline in output.

AS_2

AS_1

Step 1. A negative supply shock shifted *AS* upward and a negative demand shock shifted *AD* leftward...

Step 4. ... leading to a further decline in output and a fall in inflation.

π_2
π_1
π_3

AD_3 AD_2 AD_1

Y_3 Y_2 Y^P

Aggregate Output, *Y*

(b) Unemployment and Inflation During the Perfect Storm of 2007–2009

Year	Unemployment Rate (%)	Inflation (Year to Year) (%)
2006	4.6	2.5
2007	4.6	4.1
2008, June	5.5	5.0
2008, Dec.	7.2	0.1
2009, June	9.5	–1.2
2009, Dec.	10.0	2.8

FIGURE 23-16   Negative Supply and Demand Shocks in the United States and the 2007–2009 Crisis

Panel (a) shows that the negative supply shock caused by a rise in the price of oil shifted the short-run aggregate supply curve up, from AS_1 to AS_2, while the negative demand shock caused by the financial crisis led to a sharp contraction in spending, moving the aggregate demand curve from AD_1 to AD_2. The economy thus moved to point 2, leading to a sharp contraction in aggregate output, which fell to Y_2, a rise in unemployment, and a rise in inflation to π_2. The subsequent fall in oil prices shifted the short-run aggregate supply curve back down to AS_1, while the deepening financial crisis shifted the aggregate demand curve to AD_3. As a result, the United States' economy moved to point 3, where inflation fell to π_3 and output to Y_3. The data in panel (b) support this analysis: Note that unemployment rose from 4.6% in 2006 to 5.5% in June 2008, while inflation rose from 2.5% to 5.0% during the same period. In the aftermath of the financial crisis, and with the decline in oil prices, the unemployment rate rose to 10% and inflation fell to 2.8% by the end of 2009.

Source: Economic Report of the President.

in other commodity prices, led to a negative supply shock that shifted the short-run aggregate supply curve sharply upward, from AS_1 to AS_2 in panel (a) of Figure 23-16. To make matters worse, a financial crisis hit the economy starting in August 2007, causing a sharp increase in financial frictions, which led to contraction in both household and business spending (discussed in Chapter 9). This negative demand shock shifted the aggregate demand curve to the left, from AD_1 to AD_2 in panel (a) of Figure 23-16, and moved the economy to point 2. These shocks led to a rise in the unemployment rate, a rise in the inflation rate, and a decline in output, as indicated by point 2. As predicted by our aggregate demand and supply analysis, this perfect storm of negative shocks led to a recession in the United States starting in December 2007, with the unemployment rate rising from 4.6% in 2006 and 2007 to 5.5% by June 2008, and the inflation rate rising from 2.5% in 2006 to 5% in June 2008 (see panel (b) of Figure 23-16).

After July 2008, oil prices fell sharply, shifting short-run aggregate supply back downward to AS_1. However, in the fall of 2008, the financial crisis entered a particularly virulent phase following the bankruptcy of Lehman Brothers, decreasing aggregate demand sharply to AD_3. As a result, the economy moved to point 3, with the unemployment rate rising to 10% and the inflation rate falling to 2.8% by the end of 2009 (see panel (b) of Figure 23-16).

APPLICATION | ## The United Kingdom and the 2007–2009 Financial Crisis

As in the United States, a rise in the price of oil in 2007 led to a negative supply shock in the United Kingdom, which caused the short-run aggregate supply curve to shift upward, from AS_1 to AS_2 in panel (a) of Figure 23-17. The financial crisis initially did not have a large impact on spending, and so the aggregate demand curve did not shift and instead equilibrium moved from point 1 to point 2 on AD_1. Our aggregate demand and supply framework indicates that inflation should have risen, which is exactly what occurred (see the increase in the inflation rate from 2.3% in 2007 to 3.9% in December 2008, shown in panel (b) of Figure 23-17). With output below potential and oil prices falling after July 2008, the short-run aggregate supply curve shifted downward to AS_1. At the same time, the worsening of the financial crisis after Lehman Brothers declared bankruptcy impacted spending worldwide, causing a negative demand shock that shifted the aggregate demand curve to the left to AD_2. The economy now moved to point 3, with a further fall in output, a rise in unemployment, and a fall in inflation. As predicted by aggregate demand and supply analysis, the U.K. unemployment rate rose to 7.8% by the end of 2009, with the inflation rate falling to 2.1%.

APPLICATION | ## China and the 2007–2009 Financial Crisis

The global financial crisis that began in August 2007 at first had very little impact on China.[7] In the fall of 2008, with the collapse of Lehman Brothers and the subsequent escalation of the financial crisis in the United States, things began to change. China's economy had been driven by an extremely strong export market, which up until September of 2008, had been growing at an annual rate of over 20%. Starting in October 2008, Chinese exports collapsed, falling at around a 20% annual rate through August 2009.

The negative demand shock caused by the collapse in exports led to a decline in aggregate demand, shifting the aggregate demand curve to AD_2 and moving the economy

---

[7]Note that China, just like the rest of the world, experienced an increase in energy prices that initially shifted the short-run aggregate supply curve upward. Hence, as in the United Kingdom, in 2007 the Chinese economy experienced a rise in inflation and a slight slowing of growth. These events are not depicted in Figure 23-18 because including them would have made Figure 23-18 too complex.

MyEconLab Mini-lecture

(a) Aggregate Demand and Aggregate Supply Analysis

Step 2. A negative demand shock shifted *AD* leftward, while *AS* shifted down as oil prices fell...

Step 1. A negative supply shock shifted *AS* upward, increasing inflation and reducing output.

Step 3. ... leading to decreased inflation and output.

(b) Unemployment and Inflation, 2006–2009

Year	Unemployment Rate (%)	Inflation (Year to Year) (%)
2006	5.4	2.3
2007	5.3	2.3
2008, June	5.3	3.4
2008, Dec.	6.4	3.9
2009, June	7.8	2.1
2009, Dec.	7.8	2.1

FIGURE 23-17   U.K. Financial Crisis, 2007–2009

Panel (a) shows that a supply shock in 2007 caused by rising oil prices shifted the short-run aggregate supply curve in the United Kingdom up and to the left, from AS_1 to AS_2. The economy moved to point 2. With output below potential and oil prices falling after July 2008, the short-run aggregate supply curve began to shift downward to AS_1. A negative demand shock, caused by an escalation in the global financial crisis after Lehman Brothers declared bankruptcy, shifted the aggregate demand curve to the left to AD_2. The economy now moved to point 3, where output fell to Y_3, unemployment rose, and inflation decreased to π_3. The data in panel (b) support this analysis: Note that the unemployment rate increased from 5.4% in 2006 to 7.8% in December 2009, while the inflation rate rose from 2.3% to 3.9% and then fell to 2.1% over this same time period.

Source: Office of National Statistics, UK. **www.statistics.gov.uk/statbase/tsdtimezone.asp**.

from point 1 to point 2 in panel (a) of Figure 23-18. As predicted by aggregate demand and supply analysis, China's economic growth slowed from over 11% in the first half of 2008 to under 5% in the second half, while inflation declined from 7.9% to 3.9% and became negative thereafter (see panel (b) of Figure 23-18).

Instead of relying solely on the economy's self-correcting mechanism, the Chinese government proposed a massive fiscal stimulus package of $580 billion in 2008, which

MyEconLab Mini-lecture

(a) Aggregate Demand and Aggregate Supply Analysis

(b) Chinese Output Growth and Inflation, 2006–2009

Year	Output Growth (%)	Inflation (Year to Year) (%)
2006	11.8	1.5
2007	12.4	4.8
2008, June	11.2	7.9
2008, Dec.	4.4	3.9
2009, June	11.1	−1.1
2009, Dec.	10.4	−0.3

FIGURE 23-18   China and the Financial Crisis, 2007–2009

Panel (a) shows that the collapse of Chinese exports starting in 2008 led to a negative demand shock that shifted the aggregate demand curve to AD_2, moving the economy to point 2, where output growth fell below potential and inflation declined. A massive fiscal stimulus package and autonomous easing of monetary policy shifted the aggregate demand curve back to AD_1, and the economy very quickly moved back to long-run equilibrium at point 1. The data in panel (b) support this analysis: Note that output growth slowed but then bounced back again, and inflation began to fall at a less rapid rate.

Source: International Monetary Fund. 2010. International Financial Statistics. Country Tables, **www.imf.org/external/data.htm.**

at 12.5% of GDP was three times larger than the U.S. fiscal stimulus package relative to GDP. In addition, the People's Bank of China, the central bank, began taking measures to autonomously ease monetary policy. These decisive actions shifted the aggregate demand curve back to AD_1, and the Chinese economy very quickly moved back to point 1. The Chinese economy thus weathered the financial crisis remarkably well, with output growth rising rapidly in 2009 and inflation becoming positive thereafter. ◆

MyEconLab

MyEconLab is an online homework and tutorial system that puts you in control of your own learning with study and practice tools directly correlated to this chapter's content. Visit MyEconLab to access the eText, the Questions and Applied Problems with answers, as well as additional assessment. You will also find web chapters, mini-lectures, appendices, mini-cases, videos, glossary flashcards, news feeds, CANSIM data, and graphing tools.

SUMMARY

1. The aggregate demand curve indicates the quantity of aggregate output demanded at each inflation rate, and it is downward-sloping. The primary sources of shifts in the aggregate demand curve are (1) autonomous monetary policy, (2) government purchases, (3) taxes, (4) autonomous net exports, (5) autonomous consumption expenditure, (6) autonomous investment, and (7) financial frictions.

2. The long-run aggregate supply curve is vertical at potential output. The long-run aggregate supply curve shifts when technology changes, when there are long-run changes to the amount of labour or capital, or when the natural rate of unemployment changes. The short-run aggregate supply curve slopes upward because inflation rises as output rises relative to potential output. The short-run supply curve shifts when there are changes in expected inflation, inflation shocks, or persistent output gaps.

3. Equilibrium in the short run occurs at the point at which the aggregate demand curve intersects the short-run aggregate supply curve. Although this is the level to which the economy heads temporarily, the self-correcting mechanism leads the economy to settle permanently at the long-run equilibrium, the point at which

the aggregate demand curve intersects the long-run aggregate supply curve and aggregate output is at its potential. Shifts in either the aggregate demand curve or the short-run aggregate supply curve can produce changes in aggregate output and inflation.

4. A positive demand shock shifts the aggregate demand curve to the right and initially leads to a rise in both inflation and output. However, in the long run, such a shock leads only to a rise in inflation, because output returns to its initial level of Y^P.

5. A temporary positive supply shock leads to a downward and rightward shift in the short-run aggregate supply curve, which initially lowers inflation and raises output. However, in the long-run, output and inflation are unchanged. A permanent positive supply shock initially leads to a rise in output and a decline in inflation. However, in contrast to a temporary supply shock, in the long run a permanent positive supply shock, which causes a rise in potential output, leads to a permanent rise in output and a permanent decline in inflation.

6. Aggregate supply and demand analysis can be used to analyze foreign business cycle episodes as well as domestic business cycle episodes.

KEY TERMS

aggregate demand curve, p. 565
aggregate supply curve, p. 571
consumption expenditure, p. 565
cost-push shocks, p. 572
demand shocks, p. 567
general equilibrium, p. 578
government purchases, p. 566

natural rate of output, p. 571
natural rate of unemployment, p. 571
net exports, p. 566
Okun's law, p. 605
output gap, p. 572
planned investment spending, p. 565
potential output, p. 571

inflation shocks, p. 572
real business cycle theory, p. 588
self-correcting mechanism, p. 581
stagflation, p. 586
supply shocks, p. 572

QUESTIONS

All questions are available in MyEconLab *at* **www.myeconlab.com**.

1. Explain why the aggregate demand curve slopes downward and the short-run aggregate supply curve slopes upward.

2. Identify three factors that can shift the aggregate demand curve to the right and three different factors that can shift the aggregate demand curve to the left.

3. "The depreciation of the U.S. dollar from February 2009 to February 2014 had a positive effect on aggregate demand in the United States." Is this statement true, false, or uncertain? Explain your answer.

4. What determines the unemployment rate when output is at potential?

5. As the labour force becomes more productive over time, how is the long-run aggregate supply curve affected?

6. Why are central banks so concerned with inflation expectations?

7. "If prices and wages are perfectly flexible, then $\gamma = 0$ and changes in aggregate demand have a smaller effect on output." Is this statement true, false, or uncertain? Explain your answer.

8. What factors shift the short-run aggregate supply curve? Do any of these factors shift the long-run aggregate supply curve? Why?

9. If large budget deficits cause the public to think there will be higher inflation in the future, what is likely to happen to the short-run aggregate supply curve when budget deficits rise?

10. Internet sites that enable people to post their resumes online reduce the costs of job searches. How do you think the Internet has affected the natural rate of unemployment?

11. When aggregate output is below the natural rate of output, what happens to the inflation rate over time if the aggregate demand curve remains unchanged? Why?

12. Suppose the public believes that a newly announced anti-inflation program will work and so lowers its expectations of future inflation. What will happen to aggregate output and the inflation rate in the short run?

13. If the unemployment rate is above the natural rate of unemployment, holding other factors constant, what will happen to inflation and output?

14. What happens to inflation and output in the short run and the long run when government spending increases?

15. What factors led to decreases in both the unemployment and inflation rates in the 1990s?

16. Are there any "good" supply shocks?

17. Why did the Federal Reserve pursue inherently recessionary policies in the early 1980s?

18. In what ways is the Bank of Canada disinflation considered a success? In what ways is it considered a failure?

19. Why did China fare much better than the United States and the United Kingdom during the 2007–2009 financial crisis?

APPLIED PROBLEMS

All applied problems are available in MyEconLab *at* **www.myeconlab.com**.

20. Using an aggregate demand and supply graph, show and describe the effects in both the short run and the long run of the following:

   a. A temporary negative supply shock.

   b. A permanent negative supply shock.

21. Suppose the government passes legislation that encourages investment in research and the development of

new technologies. Assuming this policy leads to a positive productivity change for the Canadian economy, use aggregate demand and supply analysis to predict the effects on inflation and output. Demonstrate these effects on a graph.

22. Proposals have been made that advocate an increase in the national sales tax. Predict the effects of such an increase on the aggregate supply and demand curves, showing the effects on output and inflation. Use a graph of aggregate supply and demand to demonstrate these effects.

23. Suppose the inflation rate remains relatively constant while output decreases and the unemployment rate increases. Using an aggregate demand and supply graph, show how this scenario is possible.

24. Classify each of the following as a supply shock or a demand shock. Use a graph to show the effects on inflation and output in the short run and in the long run.

    a. Financial frictions increase.

    b. Households and firms become more optimistic about the economy.

    c. Favourable weather produces a record crop of wheat and corn in the Prairie provinces.

    d. Auto workers go on strike for four months.

25. During 2014, some Bank of Canada officials discussed the possibility of increasing interest rates as a way of fighting potential increases in expected inflation. If the public came to expect higher inflation rates in the future, what would be the effect on the short-run aggregate supply curve? Use an aggregate demand and supply graph to illustrate your answer.

DATA ANALYSIS PROBLEMS

Download data for these problems from MyEconLab at **www.myeconlab.com**.

1. Go to the CANSIM database and find monthly data from January 1992 to January 2015 on the total unemployment rate (series V2062815) and the (all items) Consumer Price Index (series V41690914).

    a. What is the average annual inflation rate?

    b. Is the correlation between the annual inflation rate and the unemployment rate negative or positive?

2. Go to the St. Louis Federal Reserve FRED database, and find United States data on real government spending (GCEC1), real GDP (GDPC1), taxes (W006RC1Q027S-BEA), and the personal consumption expenditure price index (PCECTPI), a measure of the price level. Download all of the data into a spreadsheet, and convert the tax data series into real taxes. To do this, for each quarter, divide taxes by the price index and then multiply by 100.

    a. Calculate the level change in real GDP over the four most recent quarters of data available, and the four quarters prior to that.

    b. Calculate the level change in real government spending and real taxes over the four most recent quarters of data available, and the four quarters prior to that.

    c. Are your results consistent with what you would expect? How do your answers to part (b) help explain, if at all, your answer to part (a)? Explain using the *IS* and *AD* curves.

WEB EXERCISES

1. Go to **www.bankofcanada.ca** and follow the link to employment statistics. What has happened to the unemployment rate since the end of the Great Recession in July 2009?

2. As the CPI inflation rate in Canada fell close to 1% at the beginning of 2009, Bank of Canada policymakers were beginning to be concerned about deflation. Go to **www.bankofcanada.ca**, and follow the link to the inflation statistics.

    a. What has happened to the inflation rate since then?

    b. Does deflation still appear to be a threat?

WEB REFERENCES

www.bankofcanada.ca/rates/indicators/key-variables

The home page of the Bank of Canada lists information on key monetary policy variables.

www.research.stlouisfed.org/fred2/

A database of U.S. economic data hosted by the Federal Reserve Bank of St. Louis.

23 The Phillips Curve and the Short-Run Aggregate Supply Curve

This appendix discusses the *Phillips curve*, which describes the relationship of unemployment and inflation and shows how this relationship can be used to derive the short-run aggregate supply curve presented in the chapter.

THE PHILLIPS CURVE

In 1958, New Zealand economist A.W. Phillips published a famous empirical paper that examined the relationship between unemployment and wage growth in the United Kingdom.[1] For the years 1861 to 1957, he found that periods of low unemployment were associated with rapid rises in wages, whereas periods of high unemployment were associated with low growth in wages. Other economists soon discovered that this relationship extended to many other countries. Because inflation is more central to macroeconomic issues than wage growth, these economists studied the relationship between unemployment and inflation. The negative correlation between unemployment and inflation that they found in many countries became known, naturally enough, as the *Phillips curve*.

The idea behind the Phillips curve is quite intuitive. When labour markets are *tight*—that is, the unemployment rate is low—firms may have difficulty hiring qualified workers and may even have a hard time keeping their present employees. Because of the shortage of workers in the labour market, firms will raise wages to attract workers and also raise their prices at a more rapid rate.

Phillips Curve Analysis in the 1960s

Because wage inflation feeds directly into overall inflation, in the 1960s the Phillips curve became extremely popular as a model for inflation fluctuations because it seemed to fit the data so well. Panel (a) of Figure 1 shows a plot of the Canadian inflation rate against the unemployment rate from 1961 (the year that reliable unemployment data are available) to 1969. From this plot, we can see that a very clear negative correlation exists between unemployment and inflation. The Phillips curve for this period seems to

---

[1]A.W. Phillips, "The Relationship Between Unemployment and the Rate of Change of Money Wages in the United Kingdom, 1861–1957," *Economica* 25 (November 1958): 283–299.

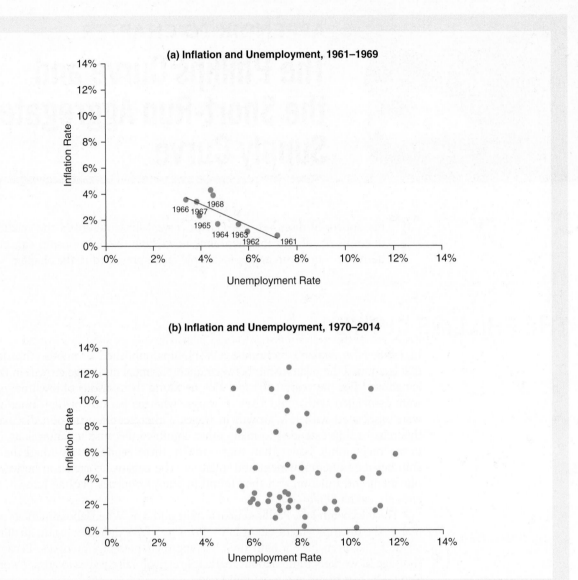

FIGURE 1 **Inflation and Unemployment in Canada, 1961–1969 and 1970–2014**

The plot of inflation against unemployment over the 1961–1969 period in panel (a) shows that a higher inflation rate was generally associated with a lower rate of unemployment. Panel (b) shows that after 1970, the negative correlation between inflation and unemployment disappeared.

Source: Federal Reserve Bank of St. Louis, FRED database: **http://research.stlouisfed.org/fred2**

imply that there is a long-run tradeoff between unemployment and inflation—that is, policymakers can choose policies that will lead to a higher rate of inflation and end up with a lower unemployment rate on a sustained basis. This apparent tradeoff was very influential in policy circles in the 1960s, as we can see in the FYI box, The Phillips Curve Tradeoff and Macroeconomic Policy in the 1960s.

FYI   The Phillips Curve Tradeoff and Macroeconomic Policy in the 1960s

In 1960, Paul Samuelson and Robert Solow published a paper outlining how policymakers could exploit the Phillips curve tradeoff. The policymaker could choose between two competing goals—inflation and unemployment—and decide how high an inflation rate he or she would be willing to accept to attain a lower unemployment rate.[2] Indeed, Samuelson and Solow even stated that policymakers could achieve a "nonperfectionist" goal of a 3% unemployment rate at what they considered to be a tolerable inflation rate of 4–5% per year. This thinking was influential and contributed to the adoption of policies in the mid-1960s to stimulate the economy and bring the unemployment rate down to low levels. At first, these policies seemed to be successful because the subsequent higher inflation rates were accompanied by lower unemployment rates. However, the good times were not to last: From the late 1960s through the 1970s, inflation accelerated yet the unemployment rate remained stubbornly high.

The Friedman-Phelps Phillips Curve Analysis

In 1967 and 1968, Nobel Prize winners Milton Friedman and Edmund Phelps pointed out a severe theoretical flaw in the Phillips curve analysis.[3] Phillips curve analysis was inconsistent with the view that workers and firms care about *real* wages, the amount of real goods and services that wages can purchase, not *nominal* wages. Thus when workers and firms expect the price level to be rising, they will adjust nominal wages upward so that the real wage rate does not decrease. In other words, wages and overall inflation will rise on a one-to-one basis with increases in expected inflation, as well as respond to tightness in the labour market. In addition, the Friedman-Phelps analysis suggested that in the long run the economy would reach the level of unemployment that would occur if all wages and prices were flexible, which they called the *natural rate of unemployment*.[4] The natural rate of unemployment is the full-employment level of unemployment, because some unemployment will still exist even when wages and prices are flexible.

The Friedman-Phelps reasoning suggested a Phillips curve that we can write as follows:

$$\pi = \pi^e - \omega(U - U_n) \qquad \text{(Equation 1)}$$

where π represents inflation, π^e expected inflation, U the unemployment rate, U_n the natural rate of unemployment, and ω the sensitivity of inflation to $U - U_n$. The presence of the π^e term explains why Equation 1 is also referred to as the *expectations-augmented Phillips curve*: It indicates that inflation is negatively related to the difference between the unemployment rate and the natural rate of unemployment $(U - U_n)$, a measure of tightness in the labour markets called the *unemployment gap*.

---

[2]Paul A. Samuelson and Robert M. Solow, "Analytical Aspects of Anti-Inflation Policy," *American Economic Review* 50 (May 1960, Papers and Proceedings): 177–194.

[3]Milton Friedman outlined his criticism of the Phillips curve in his 1967 presidential address to the American Economic Association: Milton Friedman, "The Role of Monetary Policy," *American Economic Review* 58 (1968): 1–17. Phelps's reformulation of the Phillips curve analysis was outlined in Edmund Phelps, "Money-Wage Dynamics and Labor-Market Equilibrium," *Journal of Political Economy* 76 (July/August 1968, Part 2): 687–711.

[4]As we discussed in Chapter 14, there will always be some unemployment—either *frictional unemployment*, unemployment that occurs because workers are searching for jobs, or *structural unemployment*, unemployment that arises from a mismatch of skills with available jobs and is a structural feature of the labour markets. Thus even when wages and prices are fully flexible, the natural rate of unemployment is at a level above zero.

FIGURE 2   The Short- and Long-Run Phillips Curve

The expectations-augmented Phillips curve is downward-sloping because a lower unemployment rate results in a higher inflation rate for any given level of expected inflation. If the economy moves, due to a decline in the unemployment rate, from point 1 to point 2 on PC_1, the inflation rate rises. If unemployment remains at 4%, inflation rises further, shifting the short-run expectations-augmented Phillips curve upward to PC_2 and to point 3. Eventually, when the economy reaches point 4, where $\pi^e = \pi = 10\%$, the expectations-augmented Phillips curve PC_3 stops shifting because unemployment is at the natural rate of unemployment. The line connecting points 1 and 4 is the long-run Phillips curve, *LRPC*, and shows that long-run unemployment is at the natural rate of unemployment for any inflation rate.

The expectations-augmented Phillips curve implies that long-run unemployment will be equal to the natural rate level, as Friedman and Phelps theorized. Recognize that in the long run, expected inflation must gravitate to actual inflation, and Equation 1 therefore indicates that U must be equal to U_n.

The Friedman-Phelps expectations-augmented version of the Phillips curve displays no long-run tradeoff between unemployment and inflation. To show this, Figure 2 presents the expectations-augmented Phillips curve, marked as PC_1, for a given expected inflation rate of 2% and a natural rate of unemployment of 5%. (PC_1 goes through point 1 because Equation 1 indicates that when $\pi = \pi^e = 2\%$, $U = U_n = 5\%$, and the curve's slope is $-\omega$.) Suppose the economy is initially at point 1, where the unemployment rate is at the natural rate level of 5%, but then government policies to stimulate the economy cause the unemployment rate to fall to 4%, a level that is below the natural rate level. The economy then moves along PC_1 to point 2, with inflation rising above 2% to, say, 3.5%. Expected inflation then rises as well, and so the expectations-augmented Phillips curve shifts upward from PC_1 to PC_2. Continued efforts to stimulate the economy and keep the unemployment rate at 4%, below the natural rate level, will cause further increases in the actual and expected inflation rates, causing the expectations-augmented Phillips curve to continue to shift upward.

When will the expectations-augmented Phillips curve stop rising? It will stop only when unemployment is back at the natural rate level, that is, when $U = U_n = 5\%$. Suppose this happens when inflation is at 10%; then expected inflation will also be at 10% because inflation has settled down to that level, with the expectations-augmented Phillips curve at PC_3 in Figure 2. The economy will now move to point 4, where $\pi = \pi^e = 10\%$ and unemployment is at the natural rate $U = U_n = 5\%$. We thus see that in the long run, when the expectations-augmented Phillips curve has stopped shifting, the economy will be at points such as 1 and 4. The line connecting these points is thus the *long-run Phillips curve*, which we mark as *LRPC* in Figure 2.

Figure 2 leads us to three important conclusions:

1. ***There is no long-run tradeoff between unemployment and inflation*** because, as the shown by the vertical long-run Phillips curve, a higher long-run inflation rate is not associated with a lower level of unemployment.
2. ***There is a short-run tradeoff between unemployment and inflation*** because, at a given expected inflation rate, policymakers can attain a lower unemployment rate at the expense of a somewhat higher inflation rate, as indicated by point 2 in Figure 2.
3. ***There are two types of Phillips curves, long-run and short-run***. The expectations-augmented Phillips curves—PC_1, PC_2, and PC_3—are actually short-run Phillips curves: They are drawn for given values of expected inflation and will shift if deviations of unemployment from the natural rate cause inflation and expected inflation to change.

The Phillips Curve After the 1960s

As indicated in Figure 2, the expectations-augmented Phillips curve shows that the negative correlation between unemployment and inflation breaks down when the unemployment rate remains below the natural rate of unemployment for any extended period of time. This prediction of the Friedman and Phelps analysis turned out to be exactly right. Starting in the 1970s, after a period of very low unemployment rates, the negative correlation between unemployment and inflation that was so visible in the 1960s disappeared, as shown in panel (b) of Figure 1. Not surprisingly, given the brilliance of Friedman's and Phelps's work, they were both awarded Nobel Prizes.

The Modern Phillips Curve

Inflation jumped up sharply with the sharp rise in oil prices in 1973 and 1979 (see panel (b) of Figure 1), and Phillips-curve theorists realized that they had to add one more feature to the expectations-augmented Phillips curve. *Supply shocks* are shocks to supply that change the amount of output an economy can produce from the same amount of capital and labour. These supply shocks translate into *inflation shocks*, that is, shifts in inflation that are independent of the tightness of the labour markets or of expected inflation. For example, when the supply of oil was restricted following the war between the Arab states and Israel in 1973, the price of oil more than quadrupled, and firms had to raise prices to reflect their increased costs of production, thus driving up inflation. Adding inflation shocks (ρ) to the expectations-augmented Phillips curve leads to the modern form of the short-run Phillips curve:

$$\pi = \pi^e - \omega(U - U_n) + \rho \qquad \text{(Equation 2)}$$

The modern, short-run Phillips curve implies that wages and prices are sticky. The more flexible wages and prices are, the more they, and inflation, respond to deviations of unemployment from the natural rate. That is, more flexible wages and prices imply that the absolute value of ω is higher, which in turn implies that the short-run Phillips curve is steeper. If wages and prices are completely flexible, then ω becomes so large that the short-run Phillips curve is vertical and identical to the long-run Phillips curve. In this case, there is no long-run or short-run tradeoff between unemployment and inflation.

The Modern Phillips Curve with Adaptive (Backward-Looking) Expectations

To complete our analysis of the Phillips curve, we need to understand how firms and households form expectations about inflation. One simple model assumes that they do so by looking at past inflation:

$$\pi^e = \pi_{-1}$$

where π_{-1} is the inflation rate for the previous period. This form of expectations is known as *adaptive expectations* or **backward-looking expectations** because expectations are formed by looking at the past and therefore change only slowly over time.[5] Substituting π_{-1} for π^e in Equation 2 yields the following short-run Phillips curve:

$$\pi \ = \ \pi - 1 \ - \ \omega(U - U_n) \ + \ \rho$$

Inflation = Expected − ω × Unemployment + Inflation   (Equation 3)
Inflation   Gap   Shock

This form of the Phillips curve has two advantages over the more general formulation given in Equation 2. First, it takes on a very simple mathematical form that is convenient to use. Second, it provides two additional, realistic reasons why inflation might be sticky. One reason is that inflation expectations adjust only slowly as inflation changes over time. Inflation expectations are therefore sticky, which results in some inflation stickiness. Another reason is that the presence of past inflation in the Phillips curve formulation can reflect the fact that some wage and price contracts might be backward-looking, that is, tied to past inflation, and so inflation might not fully adjust to changes in inflation expectations in the short run.

There is, however, one important weakness of the adaptive-expectations form of the Phillips curve given in Equation 3: It takes a very mechanical view of how inflation expectations are formed. More sophisticated analysis of expectations formation has important implications for the conduct of macroeconomic policy and is discussed in Chapter 25. For the time being, we will make use of the simple form of the Phillips curve with adaptive expectations, keeping in mind that the π_{-1} term represents expected inflation.

There is another convenient way of looking at the adaptive-expectations form of the Phillips curve. By subtracting π_{-1} from both sides of Equation 3, we can rewrite it as follows:

$$\Delta\pi = \pi - \pi_{-1} = -\omega(U - U_n) + \rho \qquad \text{(Equation 4)}$$

Written in this form, the Phillips curve indicates that a negative unemployment gap (tight labour market) causes the inflation rate to rise, or *accelerate*. Thus the Equation 4 version of the Phillips curve is often referred to as an **accelerationist Phillips curve**.

---

[5]An alternative, modern form of expectations makes use of the concept *rational expectations*, whereby expectations are formed using all available information and so may react more quickly to new information. We discuss rational expectations and their role in macroeconomic analysis in Chapter 25.

In this formulation, the term U_n has another interpretation. Since inflation stops accelerating (changing) when the unemployment rate is at U_n, we can refer to this term as the *nonaccelerating inflation rate of unemployment* or, more commonly, *NAIRU*.

THE SHORT-RUN AGGREGATE SUPPLY CURVE

To complete our aggregate demand and supply model, we need to use our analysis of the Phillips curve to derive a *short-run aggregate supply curve,* which represents the relationship between the total quantity of output that firms are willing to produce and the inflation rate.

We can translate the modern Phillips curve into a short-run aggregate supply curve by replacing the unemployment gap $(U - U_n)$ with the *output gap*, the difference between output and potential output $(Y - Y^P)$. To do this, we need to make use of a relationship between unemployment and aggregate output that was discovered by the economist Arthur Okun, once the chair of the Council of Economic Advisors in the United States and later an economist with the Brookings Institution.[6] **Okun's law** describes the negative relationship between the unemployment gap and the output gap.

Okun's Law   We show Okun's law in Figure 3, which plots the unemployment gap against the output gap. A tight negative relationship exists between the two variables.

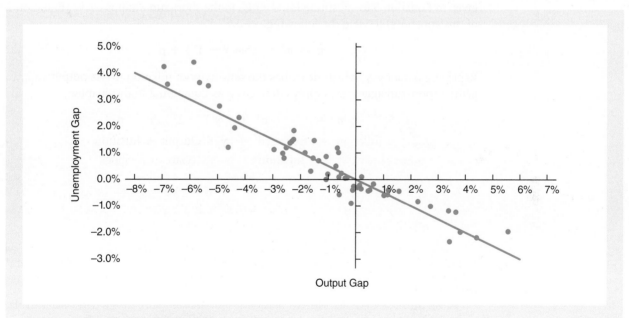

FIGURE 3   Okun's Law, 1960–2014

The plot of the unemployment gap and the output gap in the United States reveals a linear relationship, represented by the solid line with a slope of $-\frac{1}{2}$.

Source: Federal Reserve Bank of St. Louis, FRED database: **http://research.stlouisfed.org/fred2/**.

[6]Arthur M. Okun, "Potential GNP: Its Measurement and Significance," in *Proceeding of the Business and Economics Section: American Statistical Association* (Washington, D.C.: American Statistical Association, 1962), pp. 98–103; reprinted in Arthur M. Okun, *The Political Economy of Prosperity* (Washington, D.C.: Brookings Institution, 1970), pp. 132–145.

When output is above potential, so that the output gap is positive, the unemployment rate is below the natural rate of unemployment; that is, the unemployment gap is negative. The line through the data points in Figure 3 describes this negative relationship, which is given algebraically as follows:[7]

$$U - U_n = -0.5 \times (Y - Y^P) \qquad \text{(Equation 5)}$$

Okun's law thus states that for each percentage point that output is above potential, the unemployment rate is one-half of a percentage point below the natural rate of unemployment. Alternatively, for every percentage point that unemployment is above its natural rate, output is two percentage points below potential output.

Another way of thinking about Okun's law is to realize that a one percentage point increase in output leads to a one-half percentage point decrease in unemployment.[8] Why is the decrease in the unemployment rate only half the increase in the output rate? When output rises, firms do not increase employment commensurately with the increase in output, a phenomenon that is known as *labour hoarding*. Rather, firms work their employees harder, increasing their hours. Furthermore, when the economy is expanding, more people enter the labor force because job prospects are better, and so the unemployment rate does not fall by as much as employment increases.

Deriving the Short-Run Aggregate Supply Curve

We can use Okun's law as given in Equation 5 to substitute for $U - U_n$ in the short-run Phillips curve (Equation 2 of this appendix) to yield the following:

$$\pi = \pi^e + 0.5\omega(Y - Y^P) + \rho$$

Replacing 0.5ω by γ, which describes the sensitivity of inflation to the output gap, we get the short-run aggregate supply curve given as Equation 2 in the chapter:

$$
\begin{array}{ccccc}
\pi & = & \pi^e & + & \gamma(Y - Y^P) & + & \rho \\
\text{Inflation} & = & \text{Expected} & + & \gamma \times \text{Output} & + & \text{Inflation} \\
& & \text{Inflation} & & \text{Gap} & & \text{Shock}
\end{array}
$$

---

[7]The output gap, $Y - Y^P$, in Okun's law is most accurately expressed in percentage terms, so the units of Y and Y^P would be in logarithims. However, to keep the algebra simple in this and later chapters, we will treat Y and Y^P as levels and not logarithms in both the Okun's law equation and the short-run aggregate supply curve developed here.

[8]To see this algebraically, take the differences of Equation 5 and assume that U_n remains constant (a reasonable assumption because the natural rate of unemployment changes only very slowly over time). Then,

$$\%\Delta U = -0.5 \times (\%\Delta Y - \%\Delta Y^P)$$

where $\%\Delta$ indicates a percentage point change. Since potential output grows at a fairly steady rate of around three percent per year, $\%\Delta Y^P = 3\%$, we can also write Okun's law as follows:

$$\%\Delta U = -0.5 \times (\%\Delta Y - 3)$$

or

$$\%\Delta Y = 3 - 2 \times \%\Delta U$$

Hence we can state Okun's law in the following way: for every percentage point rise in output (real GDP), unemployment falls by one-half of a percentage point. Alternatively, for every percentage point rise in unemployment, real GDP falls by two percentage points.

24 Monetary Policy Theory

Learning Objectives

After studying this chapter you should be able to

1. Illustrate and explain the policy choices that monetary policymakers face under the conditions of aggregate demand shocks, temporary supply shocks, and permanent supply shocks.

2. Identify the lags in the policy process, and summarize why they weaken the case for an activist policy approach.

3. Explain why monetary policymakers can target any inflation rate in the long run but cannot target a level of aggregate output in the long run.

4. Identify the sources of inflation and the role of monetary policy in propagating inflation.

5. Explain the unique challenges that monetary policymakers face at the zero lower bound, and illustrate how nonconventional monetary policy can be effective under such conditions.

PREVIEW

Between November 2007 and April 2009, the Bank of Canada lowered the target for its policy interest rate, the overnight interest rate, from 4.5% all the way down to 0.25%, and continued to keep it around 1% for more than five years afterward. Why did the Bank of Canada lower interest rates this aggressively and continue to keep them so low?

Could this monetary policy easing spark undesirable inflation? Many commentators in the media thought so. Starting in the early 1960s, when the inflation rate hovered between 1% and 2%, the economy began to suffer from higher and more variable rates of inflation. By 1974, it reached the double-digit level. After moderating somewhat during the 1976–1978 period, it shot close to 13% in 1981, slowed to around 4% from 1984 to 1988, declined further to less than 2% in the early 1990s, and then climbed to above 4% in 2003. Inflation has become a major concern of politicians and the public, and how best to control it is an issue that frequently dominates the discussion of economic policy.

In this chapter, we will use the aggregate demand/aggregate supply (*AD/AS*) framework developed in Chapter 23 to develop a theory of monetary policy. Specifically, we will examine the role of monetary policy in creating inflation and stabilizing the economy. We apply the theory to four big questions: What are the roots of inflation? Does stabilizing inflation stabilize output? Should policy be *activist*, responding aggressively to fluctuations in economic activity, or passive and *nonactivist*? How can monetary policy work when interest rates hit a floor of zero?

RESPONSE OF MONETARY POLICY TO SHOCKS

As we saw in Chapter 16, the primary goal of central banks is price stability: that is, they try to maintain inflation, π, close to a target level (π^T), referred to as an **inflation target**, that is slightly above zero. Most central banks, like the Bank of Canada, set π^T between 1% and 3%. In other words, central banks pursue price stability through monetary policy that aims to minimize the difference between inflation and the inflation target ($\pi - \pi^T$), a difference economists refer to as the **inflation gap**.

In Chapter 17, we learned that central banks also care about stabilizing economic activity. Because economic activity can be sustained only at potential output, we can describe this objective of monetary policy by saying that monetary policymakers want aggregate output to be close to its potential level, Y^P. Central banks want to minimize the difference between aggregate output and potential output $(Y - Y^P)$, i.e., the *output gap*. In our analysis of aggregate demand and supply in Chapter 23, we examined three categories of economic shocks—demand shocks, temporary supply shocks, and permanent supply shocks—and the effects of each on inflation and output. In this section, we describe a central bank's policy responses, given its objectives, to each of these types of shocks. In the case of both demand shocks and permanent supply shocks, policymakers can simultaneously pursue price stability and stability of economic activity. In the aftermath of a temporary supply shock, however, policymakers can achieve either price stability or economic activity stability, but not both. This tradeoff poses a thorny dilemma, especially for central banks with dual mandates, like the Federal Reserve in the United States.

Response to an Aggregate Demand Shock

We begin by considering the effects of an aggregate demand shock, illustrated in Figure 24-1. The disruption to financial markets that began in August 2007 increased financial frictions and caused both consumer and business spending to fall. In the figure, the economy is initially at point 1, where output is at Y^P and inflation is at π^T. The negative demand shock decreases aggregate demand, shifting AD_1 to the left to AD_2. Policymakers can respond to this shock in two possible ways.

MyEconLab Mini-lecture

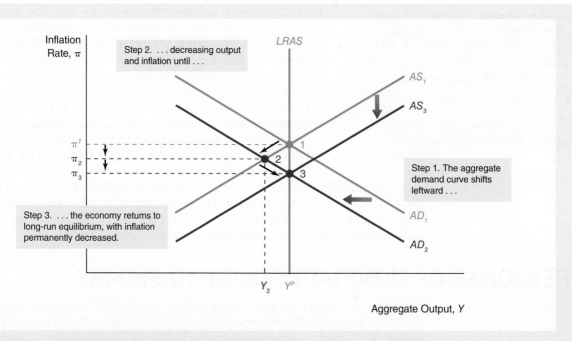

FIGURE 24-1 **Aggregate Demand Shock: No Policy Response**

An aggregate demand shock shifts the aggregate demand curve leftward from AD_1 to AD_2 and moves the economy from point 1 to point 2, where aggregate output falls to Y_2 and inflation falls to π_2. With output below potential, the short-run aggregate supply curve shifts down to AS_3 and the economy moves to point 3, where output is back at Y^P but inflation has fallen to π_3.

No Policy Response   If the central bank does not respond by changing the autonomous component of monetary policy, the aggregate demand curve remains at AD_2, and so the economy moves to the intersection of AS_1 and AD_2. Here, aggregate output falls to Y_2, below potential output Y^P, and inflation falls to π_2, below the inflation target of π^T. With inflation falling and output below potential, expected inflation will decline and the short-run aggregate supply curve will shift down and to the right until it reaches AS_3, and the economy will move to point 3. Output will be back to its potential level and inflation will fall to a lower level of π_3. At first glance, this outcome looks favourable—inflation is lower and output is back at its potential. But aggregate output will remain below potential for some time, and if inflation was initially at its target level, the fall in inflation is undesirable for the reasons outlined in Chapters 9 and 17.

Policy Stabilizes Economic Activity and Inflation in the Short Run
Policymakers can eliminate both the output gap and the inflation gap in the short run by pursuing policies aimed at increasing aggregate demand to its initial level and returning the economy to its preshock state. The central bank does this by autonomously easing monetary policy by cutting the real interest rate at any given inflation rate. This action stimulates investment spending and increases the quantity of aggregate output demanded at any given inflation rate, thereby shifting the AD curve to the right. As a result, the aggregate demand curve shifts from AD_2 back to AD_1 in Figure 24-2, and the economy returns to point 1. (The Federal Reserve in the United States took exactly these steps by lowering the federal funds rate from 5% to $\frac{1}{4}$% to zero over 15 months starting in September 2007.)

MyEconLab Mini-lecture

FIGURE 24-2   Aggregate Demand Shock: Policy Stabilizes Output and Inflation in the Short Run

An aggregate demand shock shifts the aggregate demand curve leftward from AD_1 to AD_2 and moves the economy from point 1 to point 2, where aggregate output falls to Y_2 and inflation falls to π_2. An autonomous easing of monetary policy lowers the real interest rate at any given inflation rate and shifts the AD curve back to AD_1. Aggregate output returns to potential at point 1, and inflation returns to its target level.

Our analysis of this monetary policy response shows that *in the case of aggregate demand shocks, there is no tradeoff between the pursuits of price stability and economic activity stability.* A monetary policy response that focuses on stabilizing inflation is exactly the monetary policy response that will stabilize economic activity. No conflict exists between the dual objectives of stabilizing inflation and stabilizing economic activity, a result that Olivier Blanchard (formerly of MIT but now at the International Monetary Fund) referred to as the **divine coincidence**.

Response to a Permanent Supply Shock

We illustrate a permanent supply shock in Figure 24-3. Again the economy starts out at point 1, where aggregate output is at the natural rate of Y_1^P and inflation is at π^T. Suppose the economy suffers a permanent negative supply shock when an increase in regulations permanently reduces the level of potential output. Potential output falls from Y_1^P to Y_3^P, and the long-run aggregate supply curve shifts leftward from $LRAS_1$ to $LRAS_3$. The permanent supply shock triggers an inflation shock that shifts the short-run aggregate supply curve upward, from AS_1 to AS_2. Two possible policy responses to this permanent supply shock are possible.

MyEconLab Mini-lecture

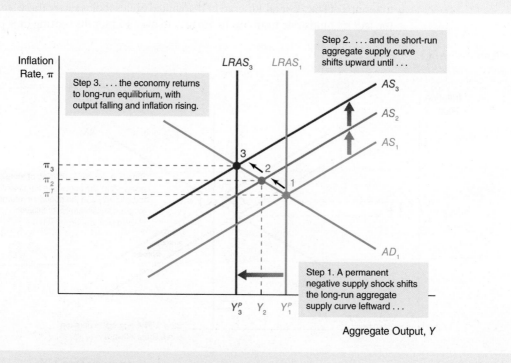

FIGURE 24-3 Permanent Supply Shock: No Policy Response

A permanent negative supply shock decreases potential output from Y_1^P to Y_3^P, and the long-run aggregate supply curve shifts to the left from $LRAS_1$ to $LRAS_3$, while the short-run aggregate supply curve shifts upward from AS_1 to AS_2. The economy moves to point 2, with inflation rising to π_2 and output falling to Y_2. Because aggregate output is still above potential, the short-run aggregate supply curve will keep on shifting until the output gap is zero when it reaches AS_3. The economy moves to point 3, where inflation rises to π_3 and output falls to Y_3^P.

No Policy Response   If policymakers leave autonomous monetary policy unchanged, the economy will move to point 2, with inflation rising to π_2 and output falling to Y_2. Because this level of output is still higher than potential output, Y_3^P, the short-run aggregate supply curve will keep shifting up and to the left until it reaches AS_3, where it intersects AD_1 on $LRAS_3$. The economy moves to point 3, eliminating the output gap but leaving inflation higher at π_3 and output lower at Y_3^P.

Policy Stabilizes Inflation   According to Figure 24-4, monetary authorities can keep inflation at the target inflation rate and thereby stabilize inflation by decreasing aggregate demand. The goal is to shift the aggregate demand curve leftward to AD_3, where it will intersect the long-run aggregate supply curve $LRAS_3$ at the target inflation rate of π^T. To shift the aggregate demand to AD_3, the monetary authorities would autonomously tighten monetary policy by increasing the real interest rate at any given inflation rate, thus causing investment spending to fall, leading to lower aggregate demand at any given inflation rate. The economy thus will go to point 3, where the output gap is zero and inflation is at the target level of π^T.

Here again, keeping the inflation gap at zero leads to a zero output gap, so by stabilizing inflation the policy response has also stabilized economic activity. ***The divine coincidence still holds true when a permanent supply shock occurs: There is no tradeoff between the dual objectives of stabilizing inflation and stabilizing economic activity.***

MyEconLab Mini-lecture

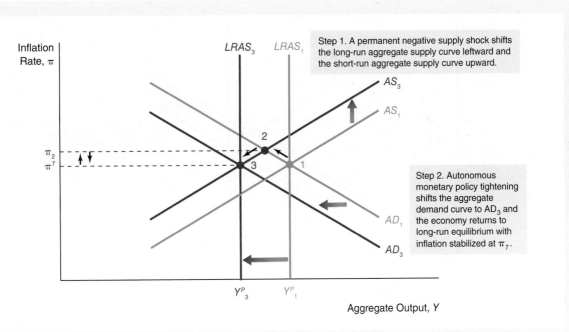

FIGURE 24-4   Permanent Supply Shock: Policy Stabilizes Inflation

A permanent negative supply shock decreases potential output from Y_1^P to Y_3^P, and the long-run aggregate supply curve shifts to the left from $LRAS_1$ to $LRAS_3$, while the short-run aggregate supply curve shifts upward from AS_1 to AS_3. An autonomous tightening of monetary policy shifts the aggregate demand curve to the left to AD_3, thereby keeping the inflation rate at π^T at point 3.

Response to a Temporary Supply Shock

When a supply shock is temporary—for example, when the price of oil surges because of political unrest in the Middle East or because of an act of God such as a devastating drought in the Prairies—the divine coincidence does not always hold. Policymakers face a short-run tradeoff between stabilizing inflation and stabilizing economic activity. To illustrate, we start with the economy at point 1 in Figure 24-5, where aggregate output is at the natural rate Y^P and inflation is at π^T. The negative supply shock—from, say, a rise in the price of oil—shifts the short-run aggregate supply curve up and to the left, from AS_1 to AS_2, but leaves the long-run aggregate supply curve unchanged because the shock is temporary. The economy moves to point 2, with inflation rising to π_2 and output falling to Y_2. Policymakers can respond to the temporary supply shock in three possible ways.

No Policy Response   One potential policy choice is to refrain from making an autonomous change in monetary policy, so that the aggregate demand curve does not shift. Since aggregate output is less than potential output Y^P, eventually the short-run aggregate supply curve will shift back down to the right, returning to AS_1. The economy will return to point 1 in Figure 24-5, and both the output and inflation gaps will close as output and inflation return to their initial levels of Y^P and π^T, respectively.

MyEconLab Mini-lecture

FIGURE 24-5   Response to a Temporary Supply Shock: No Policy Response

A temporary negative supply shock shifts the short-run aggregate supply curve upward from AS_1 to AS_2, moving the economy to point 2, with inflation rising to π_2 and output falling to Y_2. If the autonomous monetary policy remains unchanged, the short-run aggregate supply curve will shift back down and to the right in the long run, eventually returning to AS_1, and the economy will move back to point 1.

Both inflation and economic activity will stabilize over time. While we wait for the long run, however, the economy will undergo a painful period of reduced output and higher inflation rates. To avoid this period of reduced output and high inflation, monetary policymakers might decide to try to stabilize economic activity or inflation in the short run.

Policy Stabilizes Inflation in the Short Run

A second policy choice for monetary authorities is to keep inflation at the target level of π^T in the short run by autonomously tightening monetary policy and raising the real interest rate at any given inflation rate. Doing so will cause investment spending and aggregate demand to fall at each inflation rate, shifting the aggregate demand curve to the left to AD_3 in Figure 24-6. The economy now will move to point 3, where the aggregate demand curve AD_3 intersects the short-run aggregate supply curve AS_2 at an inflation rate of π^T. Because output is below potential at point 3 the short-run aggregate supply curve will shift back down

MyEconLab Mini-lecture

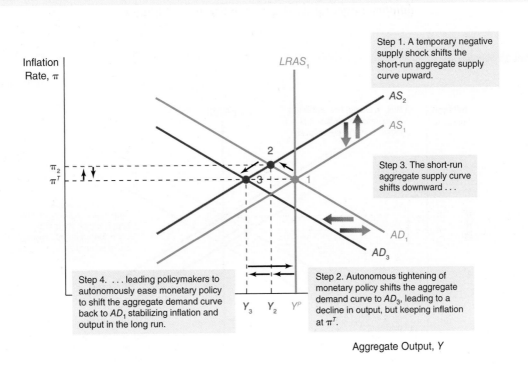

FIGURE 24-6   **Response to a Temporary Supply Shock: Short-Run Inflation Stabilization**

A temporary negative supply shock shifts the short-run aggregate supply curve from AS_1 to AS_2, moving the economy to point 2, with inflation rising to π_2 and output falling to Y_2. Autonomous tightening of monetary policy shifts the aggregate demand curve to the left to AD_3, and the economy moves to point 3, where inflation is at π^T. With output below potential at point 3, the short-run aggregate supply curve shifts back to AS_1. To keep the inflation rate at π^T, the autonomous tightening of monetary policy is reversed, shifting the aggregate demand curve back to AD_1 and the economy back to point 1.

to AS_1. To keep the inflation rate at π^T, the monetary authorities will need to move the short-run aggregate demand curve back to AD_1 by reversing the autonomous tightening, and eventually the economy will return to point 1.

As Figure 24-6 illustrates, stabilizing inflation reduces aggregate output to Y_3 in the short run, and only over time will output return to potential output at Y^P. *Stabilizing inflation in response to a temporary supply shock leads to a larger deviation of aggregate output from potential, so this action does not stabilize economic activity.*

Policy Stabilizes Economic Activity in the Short Run A third policy choice is for monetary policymakers to stabilize economic activity rather than inflation in the short run by increasing aggregate demand. According to Figure 24-7, this policy decision will shift the aggregate demand curve to the right to AD_3, where it intersects the short-run aggregate supply curve AS_2 and the long-run aggregate supply curve *LRAS* at point 3. To achieve this result, policymakers will have to autonomously ease monetary policy by lowering the real interest rate at any given inflation rate. At point 3, the output gap returns to zero, so monetary policy has stabilized economic activity. However, inflation has risen to π_3, which is greater than π^T, and so inflation has *not* been stabilized. *Stabilizing economic activity in response to a temporary supply shock results in a larger deviation of inflation from the inflation target rather than a stabilization of inflation.*

MyEconLab Mini-lecture

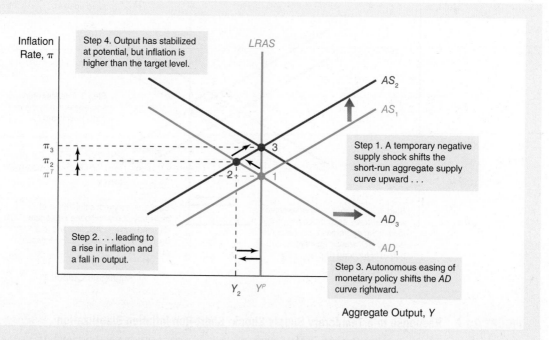

FIGURE 24-7 **Response to a Temporary Supply Shock: Short-Run Output Stabilization**

A temporary negative supply shock shifts the short-run aggregate supply curve from AS_1 to AS_2, moving the economy to point 2, with inflation rising to π_2 and output falling to Y_2. To stabilize output, autonomous monetary policy easing shifts the aggregate demand curve rightward to AD_3. At point 3, the monetary policy action has stabilized economic activity, but inflation at π_3 is greater than the target level π^T.

The Bottom Line: The Relationship Between Stabilizing Inflation and Stabilizing Economic Activity

We can draw the following conclusions from our analysis:

1. *If most shocks to the economy are aggregate demand shocks or permanent aggregate supply shocks, then policy that stabilizes inflation will also stabilize economic activity, even in the short run.*
2. *If temporary supply shocks are the most common type of shock, then a central bank must choose between the two stabilization objectives in the short run.*

HOW ACTIVELY SHOULD POLICYMAKERS TRY TO STABILIZE ECONOMIC ACTIVITY?

All economists have similar policy goals (to promote high employment and price stability), yet they often disagree on the best approach for achieving these goals. Suppose policymakers confront an economy that has high unemployment resulting from a negative demand or supply shock that has reduced aggregate output. **Nonactivists** believe that wages and prices are very flexible and that the self-correcting mechanism works very rapidly. They argue that the short-run aggregate supply curve will shift downward quickly, returning the economy to full employment rapidly. They thus believe that government action to eliminate unemployment is unnecessary. **Activists**, many of whom are followers of Keynes and are thus referred to as **Keynesians**, regard the self-correcting mechanism, which works through wage and price adjustment, as a very slow-working mechanism because of the stickiness of wages and prices. Thus they believe it will take the economy a very long time to reach the long run, agreeing with Keynes's famous adage that "In the long-run, we are all dead." Activists therefore believe that the government should pursue active policies to increase aggregate demand and eliminate high unemployment when it develops.

Lags and Policy Implementation

If policymakers could shift the aggregate demand curve instantaneously, activist policies could be used to move the economy immediately to the full-employment level, as we saw in the previous section. However, several types of lags prevent this immediate shift from occurring, and there are differences in the lengths of these lags for monetary versus fiscal policy.

1. The **data lag** is the time it takes for policymakers to obtain the data that describe what is happening in the economy. Accurate data on GDP, for example, are not available until several months after a given quarter is over.
2. The **recognition lag** is the time it takes for policymakers to feel confident about the signals the data are sending about the future course of the economy. For example, to minimize errors, the government will not declare the economy to be in recession until at least six months after it has determined that a recession has begun.
3. The **legislative lag** represents the time it takes to get legislation passed to implement a particular policy. The legislative lag does not apply to most monetary policy actions, such as the lowering of interest rates. It is, however, important in the implementation of fiscal policy, because it can sometimes take six months to a year to get legislation passed to change taxes or government purchases.

4. The **implementation lag** is the time it takes for policymakers to change policy instruments once they have decided on a new policy. Again, this lag is less important for the conduct of monetary policy, because the Bank of Canada can immediately change its policy interest rate, while it is more important for the implementation of fiscal policy. The implementation of new fiscal policy can take substantial time; for example, getting government agencies to change their spending habits takes time, as does changing tax tables.

5. The **effectiveness lag** is the time it takes for the policy to have a real impact on the economy. The effectiveness lag is both long (often a year long or longer) and variable (that is, substantial uncertainty exists about the length of this lag).

The existence of these lags makes the policymakers' job far more difficult and therefore weakens the case for activism. When unemployment is high, activist policy aimed at shifting the aggregate demand curve rightward to restore the economy to full employment may not produce desirable outcomes. Indeed, if the policy lags described above are very long, then by the time the aggregate demand curve shifts to the right, the self-correcting mechanism may have already returned the economy to full employment. Then, when the activist policy kicks in, it may cause output to rise above potential, leading to a rise in inflation. In situations in which policy lags are longer than the time it takes the self-correcting mechanism to work, a policy of nonactivism may produce better outcomes.

The activist/nonactivist debate came to the fore when the Obama administration advocated a fiscal stimulus package early in its administration in 2009 (see the FYI box, The Activist/Nonactivist Debate Over the Obama Fiscal Stimulus Package in the United States). In Chapter 25, we will return to the issue of just how active policy should be when we look at the role that expectations play in monetary policy.

FYI The Activist/Nonactivist Debate Over the Obama Fiscal Stimulus Package in the United States

When President Obama took office in January 2009, he faced a very serious recession, with unemployment at over 7% and rising rapidly. Although policymakers had been using monetary policy aggressively to stabilize the economy (see Chapters 9 and 16), many activists argued that the government needed to do more by implementing a massive fiscal stimulus package. They argued that without the stimulus package, monetary policy, which had already lowered the federal funds rate to close to zero and so could not lower nominal interest rates further, would be unable to increase aggregate demand to the full-employment level. On the other hand, nonactivists opposed the fiscal stimulus package, arguing that fiscal stimulus would take too long to work because of long implementation lags. They cautioned that if the fiscal stimulus kicked in after the economy had already recovered, the result would be increased volatility in inflation and economic activity.

The economics profession was split over the desirability of fiscal stimulus. Approximately 200 economists who opposed fiscal stimulus in the United States signed a petition published in the *Wall Street Journal* and the *New York Times* on January 28, 2009. An opposing petition, also signed by about 200 economists, was sent to the U.S. Congress on February 8. The Obama administration came down squarely on the side of the activists and proposed the American Recovery and Reinvestment Act of 2009, a $787 billion fiscal stimulus package that was passed by the U.S. Congress on February 13, 2009. Even after the fact, the value of the 2009 stimulus package is still hotly debated, with some believing it helped stabilize the economy and others believing it was not effective.

INFLATION: ALWAYS AND EVERYWHERE A MONETARY PHENOMENON

Milton Friedman is famous for his adage that in the long run, "Inflation is always and everywhere a monetary phenomenon." This adage is supported by our aggregate demand and supply analysis, which asserts that monetary policymakers can target any inflation rate in the long run by shifting the aggregate demand curve through autonomous monetary policy. As an illustration, look at Figure 24-8, where the economy is at point 1, with aggregate output at potential output Y^P and inflation at an initial inflation target of π_1^T.

Suppose the central bank believes that this inflation target is too low and chooses to raise it to π_3^T. The central bank eases monetary policy autonomously by lowering the real interest rate at any given inflation rate, thereby increasing investment spending and aggregate demand. In Figure 24-8, the aggregate demand curve shifts to AD_3. The economy then moves to point 2, at the intersection of AD_3 and AS_1, with inflation rising to π_2. Because aggregate output is above potential output, $Y_2 > Y^P$, the short-run aggregate supply curve shifts up and to the left, eventually stopping at AS_3. The economy moves to point 3, where inflation is at the higher target level of π_3^T and the output gap is back at zero.

MyEconLab Mini-lecture

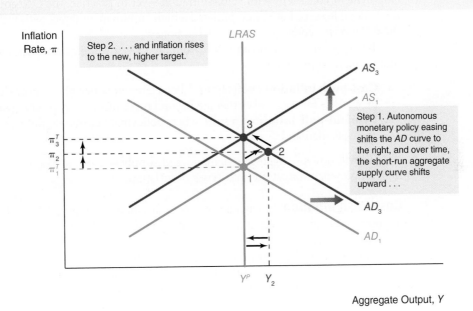

FIGURE 24-8   A Rise in the Inflation Target

To raise the inflation target to π_3^T, the central bank undertakes an autonomous monetary policy easing by lowering the real interest rate at any given inflation rate, thereby shifting the aggregate demand curve rightward to AD_3. The economy then moves to point 2, and the short-run aggregate supply curve shifts up and to the left, eventually stopping at AS_3. The economy then moves to point 3, with the output gap at zero and inflation at π_3^T.

The analysis in Figure 24-8 demonstrates the following key points:

1. *The monetary authorities can target any inflation rate in the long run with autonomous monetary policy adjustments.*
2. *Potential output—and therefore the quantity of aggregate output produced in the long run—is independent of monetary policy.*

CAUSES OF INFLATIONARY MONETARY POLICY

If everyone agrees that high inflation is bad for an economy, why do we see so much of it? Do governments pursue inflationary monetary policies intentionally? We know that monetary authorities can set the inflation rate in the long run, so it must be that in trying to achieve other goals, governments end up with overly expansionary monetary policies and high inflation. In this section, we will examine the government policies that are the most common sources of inflation.

High Employment Targets and Inflation

The primary goal of most governments is high employment, and the pursuit of this goal can bring on high inflation. For example, the U.S. government is committed by law (the Employment Act of 1946 and the Humphrey-Hawkins Act of 1978) to engage in activist policy to promote high employment. Both laws require a commitment to a high level of employment consistent with stable inflation—yet in practice, the U.S. government and the Federal Reserve have often pursued a high employment target with little concern for the inflationary consequences of such a policy.

Two types of inflation can result from an activist stabilization policy aimed at promoting high employment:

1. **Cost-push inflation** results from either a temporary negative supply shock or a push by workers for wage hikes that are beyond those justified by productivity gains.
2. **Demand-pull inflation** results when policymakers pursue policies that increase aggregate demand.

We will now use aggregate demand and supply analysis to examine the effects of a high employment target on both types of inflation.

Cost-Push Inflation   Consider the economy shown in Figure 24-9, which is initially at point 1, the intersection of the aggregate demand curve AD_1 and the short-run aggregate supply curve AS_1. Suppose workers succeed in pushing for higher wages, either because they want to increase their real wages (their wages in terms of the goods and services they can buy) above the level justified by productivity gains or because they expect inflation to increase and therefore want their wages to increase accordingly. This cost-push shock, which acts like a temporary negative supply shock, raises the inflation rate and shifts the short-run aggregate supply curve up and to the left, to AS_2. If the central bank takes no action to change the equilibrium interest rate and the monetary policy curve remains unchanged, the economy will move to point $2'$, at the intersection of the new short-run aggregate supply curve AS_2 and the aggregate demand curve AD_1. Output will decline to Y', below potential output, and the inflation rate will rise to $\pi_{2'}$, leading to an increase in unemployment.

In contrast, activist policymakers with a high employment target would implement policies to increase aggregate demand, such as tax cuts, increases in government purchases,

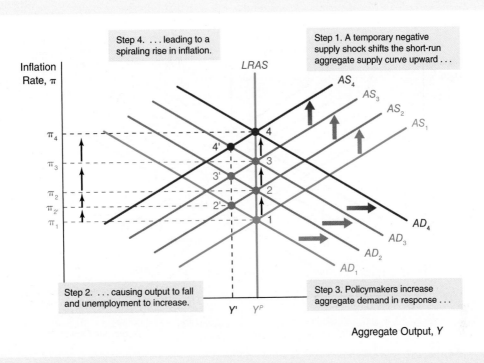

FIGURE 24-9   Cost-Push Inflation

A cost-push shock (which acts like a temporary negative supply shock) shifts the short-run aggregate supply curve up and to the left to AS_2, and the economy moves to point 2′. To keep aggregate output at Y^p and to lower the unemployment rate, policymakers shift the aggregate demand curve to AD_2 so that the economy will return quickly to potential output at point 2 and an inflation rate of π_2. Further upward and leftward shifts of the short-run aggregate supply curve, to AS_3 and beyond, lead the policymakers to continue increasing aggregate demand, leading to a continuing increase in inflation—a cost-push inflation.

or an autonomous easing of monetary policy. These policies would shift the aggregate demand curve in Figure 24-9 to AD_2, quickly returning the economy to potential output at point 2 and increasing the inflation rate to π_2. The workers would fare quite well, earning both higher wages and government protection against excessive unemployment.

The workers' success might encourage them to seek even higher wages. In addition, other workers might now realize that their wages have fallen relative to their fellow workers' wages, leading them to seek wage increases. These actions will lead to another temporary negative supply shock, which will cause the short-run aggregate supply curve in Figure 24-9 to shift up and to the left again, to AS_3. Unemployment will develop again when we move to point 3′, prompting additional activist policies that will shift the aggregate demand curve rightward to AD_3 and return the economy to full employment at a higher inflation rate of π_3. If this process continues, the result will be a continuing increase in inflation—a cost-push inflation.

Demand-Pull Inflation   A goal of high employment can lead to inflationary fiscal and monetary policy in another way. Even at full employment (the natural rate of unemployment), some unemployment is always present because of frictions in the labour market

MyEconLab Mini-lecture

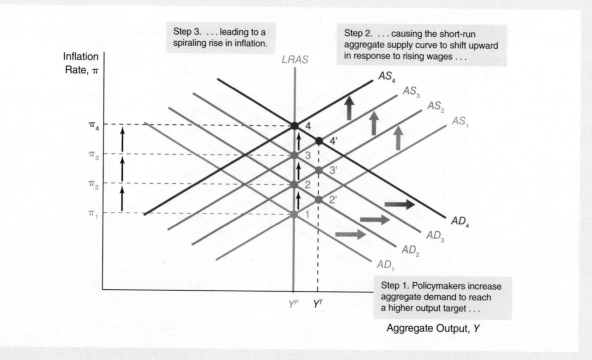

FIGURE 24-10 **Demand-Pull Inflation**

Too low an unemployment target (too high an output target of Y^T) causes the government to increase aggregate demand, shifting the *AD* curve rightward from AD_1 to AD_2 to AD_3 and so on. Because at Y^T the unemployment rate is below the natural rate level, wages will rise and the short-run aggregate supply curve will shift up and leftward, from AS_1 to AS_2 to AS_3 and so on. The result is a continuing rise in inflation known as a demand-pull inflation.

that complicate the matching of unemployed workers with employers. Consequently, the unemployment rate when employment is full is still greater than zero. When policymakers mistakenly underestimate the natural rate of unemployment and so set a target for unemployment that is too low (i.e., less than the natural rate of unemployment), they set the stage for expansionary monetary policy that produces inflation.

Figure 24-10 uses aggregate supply and demand analysis to show how this scenario can unfold. If policymakers set a 4% unemployment target when the natural rate of unemployment is 5%, they are trying to achieve an output target greater than potential output. We mark this target level of output in Figure 24-10 as Y^T. Suppose the economy is initially at point 1: At this point, the economy is at potential output but below the target level of output Y^T. To hit the unemployment target of 4%, policymakers must enact policies, such as expansionary fiscal policy or an autonomous easing of monetary policy, to increase aggregate demand. The aggregate demand curve in Figure 24-10 shifts to the right until it reaches AD_2 and the economy moves to point 2′, where output is at Y^T and policymakers have achieved the 4% unemployment rate goal. But there is more to the story. At Y^T, the 4% unemployment rate is below the natural rate level and output is above potential, causing wages to rise. The short-run aggregate supply curve will now shift up and to the left, eventually reaching AS_2 and moving the economy from point

2′ to point 2, where it is back at potential output but at a higher inflation rate of π_2. Because unemployment is again higher than the target level, policymakers will once more shift the aggregate demand curve rightward to AD_3 in order to hit the output target at point 3′—and the whole process will continue to drive the economy to point 3 and beyond. The overall result is a steadily rising inflation rate.

Pursuing too low an unemployment rate target or, equivalently, too high an output target, thus leads to inflationary monetary or fiscal policy. Policymakers fail on two counts: They have not achieved their unemployment target, and they have caused higher inflation. If the target rate of unemployment is below the natural rate, the process we see in Figure 24-10 will be well under way before the policymakers realize their mistake.

Cost-Push Versus Demand-Pull Inflation   When inflation occurs, how do we know whether it is demand-pull inflation or cost-push inflation? We would normally expect to see demand-pull inflation when unemployment is below the natural rate level, and to see cost-push inflation when unemployment is above the natural rate level. Unfortunately, economists and policymakers still struggle with accurately measuring the natural rate of unemployment. Complicating matters further, a cost-push inflation can be initiated by a demand-pull inflation, blurring the distinction. When a demand-pull inflation produces higher inflation rates, expected inflation will eventually rise and workers will demand higher wages (cost-push inflation) so that their real wages do not fall. Finally, expansionary monetary and fiscal policies produce both kinds of inflation, so we cannot distinguish between the two types of inflation on the basis of their source.

In the United States, the primary reason for inflationary policy has been policymakers' adherence to a high employment target. As we saw in Chapter 18, high inflation can also be caused by persistent government budget deficits that are financed by increases in the monetary base.

MONETARY POLICY AT THE ZERO LOWER BOUND

So far we have assumed that a central bank can continue to lower the real interest rate as inflation falls by lowering its policy rate—say, the overnight interest rate—so that the *MP* curve is always upward-sloping. However, because the overnight interest rate is a nominal interest rate, it can never fall below a value of zero. A negative overnight interest rate would imply that you are willing to earn a lower return by lending in the overnight funds market than you could earn by holding cash, with its zero rate of return. As discussed in Chapter 16, the zero floor on the policy rate is referred to as the *zero lower bound*, and it creates a particular problem for the conduct of monetary policy.

Deriving the Aggregate Demand Curve with the Zero Lower Bound

To understand more deeply the problems created by the zero lower bound with regard to the conduct of monetary policy, let's look at what happens to the aggregate demand curve when a central bank cannot lower its policy rate below zero. Panel (a) of Figure 24-11 shows an *MP* curve that hits the zero lower bound. For our purposes, let's assume that expected inflation moves closely with the actual inflation rate (as it usually does), as indicated on the horizontal axis in panel (a). Let's start at point 3 on the *MP* curve, where inflation is at 3% and the real interest rate is at 2%. Now let's see what happens as inflation falls from 3% to 2%. At this inflation level, the monetary

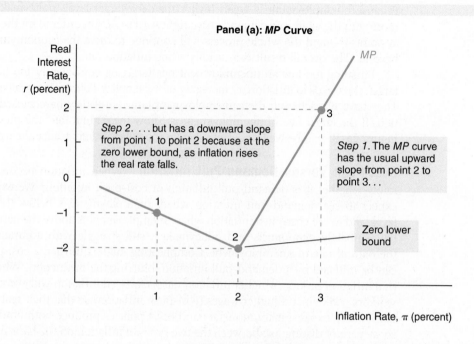

Panel (a): *MP* Curve

Step 2. ...but has a downward slope from point 1 to point 2 because at the zero lower bound, as inflation rises the real rate falls.

Step 1. The *MP* curve has the usual upward slope from point 2 to point 3...

Zero lower bound

Panel (b): Aggregate Demand Curve

Step 3. The *AD* curve has the usual downward slope from point 3 to point 2...

Zero lower bound

Step 4. ...but has an upward slope from point 1 to point 2 because at the zero lower bound, as inflation rises, the real interest rate falls and output increases.

FIGURE 24-11 **Derivation of the Aggregate Demand Curve with a Zero Lower Bound**

In panel (a), the *MP* curve has the usual upward slope in going from point 2 to point 3, but it slopes downward in the segment from point 1 to point 2 because, with the policy rate at the floor of zero, as inflation and expected inflation fall, the real interest rate rises. This produces a kink in the aggregate demand curve as shown in panel (b).

authorities, following the Taylor principle, will want to lower the real interest rate to, say, -2% (point 2 in panel (a)), which will require them to lower the policy rate to zero ($r = 0 - 2\% = -2\%$). At point 2 in panel (a), the zero lower bound has been reached on the *MP* curve. So far, our analysis is identical to the analysis given in Chapter 22, with the MP curve having the usual upward slope.

Now, what happens if the inflation rate falls even further—say, to 1%? The monetary authorities would like to lower the real interest rate by lowering the policy rate again, but they can't because the policy rate has already hit the floor of zero. Indeed, as indicated by point 1 on the *MP* curve, the real interest rate at an inflation rate of 1% has now risen to -1% ($r = 0 - 1\% = -1\%$). Hence, we see that the segment of the *MP* curve that connects point 2 to point 1 is downward-sloping, the opposite of what we found in Chapter 22.

Now let's see what happens to the aggregate demand curve, shown in panel (b) of Figure 24-11. At a 3% inflation rate and a real interest rate of 2% (point 3 on the *MP* curve in panel (a)), the equilibrium level of output is at $1.6 trillion, marked as point 3 on the aggregate demand curve in panel (b). Now, when inflation falls to 2% and the real interest rate is at -2%, as indicated by point 2 on the *MP* curve in panel (a), aggregate output rises to $2 trillion because planned investment spending rises with the lower real interest rate. The inflation rate of 2% and level of output of $2 trillion is marked as point 2 on the *AD* curve in panel (b). This point is also the zero lower bound. The *AD* curve has the usual downward slope from point 3 to point 2.

However, if inflation falls to 1%, point 1 on the *MP* curve indicates that the real interest rate will rise to -1% because, at the zero lower bound, the decrease in both inflation and expected inflation will raise the real interest rate. The rise in the real interest rate will cause aggregate demand to fall, to $1.8 trillion at point 1 on the *AD* curve in panel (b). Therefore, in going from point 1 to point 2, the aggregate demand curve slopes upward rather than downward. The presence of the zero lower bound thus can produce a kinked aggregate demand curve of the type seen in panel (b).

The Disappearance of the Self-Correcting Mechanism at the Zero Lower Bound

Now let's analyze what happens in our aggregate demand and supply diagram when the economy is hit by a large negative shock, such as the shock that occurred during the global financial crisis (see Chapter 9), so that the zero lower bound becomes binding. In this situation, the initial short-run aggregate supply curve intersects the upward-sloping part of the aggregate demand curve at point 1 in Figure 24-12, where aggregate output is below potential output. Because $Y_1 < Y^P$, there is slack in the economy, and so the short-run aggregate supply curve will fall to AS_2 and the economy will move to point 2, at the intersection of the AS_2 and *AD* curves, where inflation and output will have declined to π_2 and Y_2, respectively. Now, Y_2 is even lower than Y_1 relative to Y^P, so the short-run aggregate supply curve will shift down even further, to AS_3, and the economy will move to point 3, where inflation and output have fallen even further, to π_3 and Y_3, respectively.

Our analysis of Figure 24-12 reveals two key results:

- First, the self-correcting mechanism is no longer operational. When the economy is in a situation in which equilibrium output is below potential output and the zero lower bound on the policy rate has been reached, output is not restored to its potential level if policymakers do nothing. Indeed, the opposite occurs—the economy goes into a downward spiral.
- Second, in this situation, the economy goes into a deflationary spiral, characterized by continually falling inflation and output.

MyEconLab Mini-lecture

FIGURE 24-12   **The Absence of the Self-Correcting Mechanism at the Zero Lower Bound**

At the initial equilibrium at point 1, $Y_1 < Y^P$, so the short-run aggregate supply curve shifts down to AS_2 and the economy moves to point 2, where output and inflation have fallen to Y_2 and π_2, respectively. Because Y_2 is even lower than Y_1 relative to Y^P, the short-run aggregate supply curve shifts down even further to AS_2, and the economy moves to point 3, where output and inflation have fallen even further, to Y_3 and π_3, respectively. Both output and inflation therefore experience downward spirals.

The intuition behind these two results is fairly straightforward. When output is below potential and the policy rate has hit the floor of zero, the resulting fall in inflation leads to higher real interest rates, which depress output further, which causes inflation to fall further, and so on. Schematically, this chain of events can be expressed as follows:

$$Y < Y^P \Rightarrow \pi \downarrow \Rightarrow r \uparrow \Rightarrow Y \downarrow \Rightarrow Y < Y^P \Rightarrow \pi \downarrow \Rightarrow r \uparrow \Rightarrow Y \downarrow$$

The final outcome is that both output and inflation go into downward spirals.

APPLICATION   Nonconventional Monetary Policy and Quantitative Easing

At the zero lower bound, conventional expansionary monetary policy is no longer an option because the monetary policy authorities are unable to lower the policy rate. As a result, the central bank has to turn to the nonconventional policies discussed in Chapter 16 to stimulate the economy. Here we will analyze how these different nonconventional policies lead to economic expansion while avoiding the downward spirals in output and inflation that characterized the situation described in Figure 24-12.

Recall that nonconventional monetary policy takes three forms: liquidity provision, asset purchases (quantitative easing), and management of expectations. To see how each of these forms works, recall from Chapter 21 that the real interest rate for investments r_i reflects not only the short-term real interest rate set by the central bank, r, but also an additional term $\bar{f}$, which we referred to previously as financial frictions. This relationship can be written mathematically as follows

$$r_i = r + \bar{f} \qquad \text{(Equation 1)}$$

Each of these nonconventional monetary policy measures helps raise aggregate output and inflation by lowering $\bar{f}$ in the *AD/AS* model. Let's look at each of these measures in turn.

Liquidity Provision

The zero lower bound situation depicted in Figure 24-13 often arises when credit markets seize up and there is a sudden shortage of liquidity, as occurred during

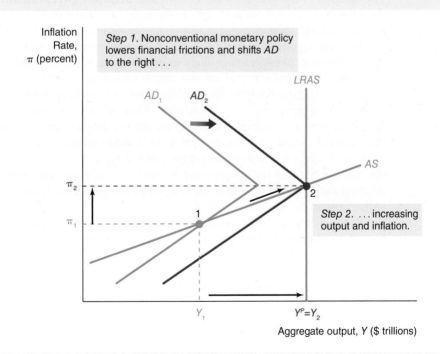

FIGURE 24-13   Response to Nonconventional Monetary Policy

Nonconventional monetary policy, whether it involves liquidity provision, asset purchases, or management of expectations, lowers $\bar{f}$, which in turn lowers the real interest rate for investments at any given inflation rate and shifts the aggregate demand curve to AD_2. The economy moves to point 2, where output and inflation have risen to Y_2 and π_2, respectively.

the recent global financial crisis. The shortage of liquidity results in a sharp rise in financial frictions, which shifts the aggregate demand curve AD_1 in Figure 24-13 to point 1, where it intersects the aggregate supply curve and where the policy rate has hit a floor of zero and output is below potential. A central bank can bring down financial frictions directly by increasing its lending facilities in order to provide more liquidity to impaired markets so that they can return to their normal functions, thereby bringing down the $\bar{f}$ term. As we saw in Chapter 23, this decline in financial frictions lowers the real interest rate for investments, $r_i = r + \bar{f}$, and so increases investment spending and the quantity of aggregate output demanded at any given inflation rate. The aggregate demand curve then shifts to the right to AD_2 and the economy moves to point 2, where both output and inflation have risen. Indeed, if liquidity provisions are sufficiently successful, the economy can move back to its full employment level, where output will return to potential, as indicated by point 2 in the figure.

Asset Purchases and Quantitative Easing

The monetary authorities can also lower the $\bar{f}$ term by lowering credit spreads through the purchase of private assets. When the monetary authorities purchase a private security, such a purchase raises the security's price and therefore lowers its interest rate, thereby lowering the credit spread and hence $\bar{f}$ and the real interest rate for investments. The decline in the real interest rate for investments at any given inflation rate then causes the aggregate demand curve to shift to the right, as shown in Figure 24-13, and raises both output and inflation.

Because investments typically are associated with long-term projects, the real interest rate for investments is likely to be a long-term interest rate and therefore differs from the short-term real interest rate r. Hence the $\bar{f}$ term in Equation 1 can be viewed as reflecting not only financial frictions and credit spreads, but also the spread between long-term and short-term rates. This means that asset purchases of long-term government securities also can lower the real interest rate for investments. When the Bank of Canada purchases long-term Canada bonds, for example, this action raises their price and lowers long-term interest rates. The result is a decline in $\bar{f}$ and the real interest rate for investments at any given inflation rate, and so the aggregate demand curve will shift to the right, to AD_2 in Figure 24-13, thereby raising output and inflation.

When a central bank engages in liquidity provision or asset purchases, its balance sheet necessarily expands. In this regard, from before the financial crisis began in September 2007 through 2014, the value of Federal Reserve assets in the United States rose from about $800 billion to over $4 trillion. Such an expansion of the balance sheet is referred to as *quantitative easing* because it leads to a huge increase in liquidity in the economy, which can be a powerful force in stimulating the economy in the near term and possibly producing inflation down the road.

However, an expansion in the central bank's balance sheet in and of itself may not be enough to stimulate the economy. As we saw in our *AD/AS* analysis of the zero lower bound, unless quantitative easing is able to lower the real interest rate for investments, in what former Fed chair Ben Bernanke referred to as a *credit easing*, there will be no impact on the aggregate demand curve and hence no impact on output and inflation. If the asset purchase program involves only the purchase of short-term government securities, the program is unlikely to affect credit spreads or the spread between long- and short-term interest rates, and so $\bar{f}$ and the real interest rate for investments will remain unchanged. The result will be a minimal impact on the aggregate economy.[1] Indeed, this was the experience in Japan when the Bank of Japan pursued a large-scale asset-purchase program that primarily involved purchases of short-term government bonds. Not only did the economy fail to recover, but inflation even turned negative.

Management of Expectations

Forward guidance, in which the central bank commits to keeping the policy rate low for a long period of time, is another way of lowering long-term interest rates relative to short-term rates and thereby lowering $\bar{f}$ and the real interest rate for investments. Because investors can choose to invest in a long-term bond rather than investing in a sequence of short-term bonds, as we saw in Chapter 6, the interest rate on long-term bonds will be closely related to an average of the short-term interest rates that markets expect to occur over the life of the long-term bond. By committing to the future policy action of keeping the overnight interest rate at zero for an extended period, a central bank can lower the market's expectations of future short-term interest rates, thereby causing the long-term interest rate to fall. The result will be a decline in $\bar{f}$ and the real interest rate for investments, which will shift the aggregate demand curve to the right as in Figure 24-13, raising both output and inflation.

So far, the mechanisms for the efficacy of nonconventional monetary policies have operated through the $\bar{f}$ term and rightward shifts in the aggregate demand curve as in Figure 24-13. However, management of expectations can also operate through shifts in the short-run aggregate supply curve that can be achieved by raising expectations of inflation, as shown in Figure 24-14. Recall from Chapter 23 that a rise in inflation expectations—say, because the central bank commits to doing whatever it takes to raise inflation in the future—will shift the short-run aggregate supply curve up, to AS_2 in Figure 24-14, moving the economy to point 2, where output and inflation rise to Y_2 and π_2, respectively. The intuition behind this result is straightforward: With the policy rate set at zero, the rise in expected inflation will lead to a decline in the real interest rate, which will cause investment spending and aggregate output to rise as the economy slides up the aggregate demand curve from point 1 to point 2, as shown in the figure. One problem with this strategy, however, is that the public must believe that inflation will actually rise in the future. If the central bank's commitment to raising inflation is not credible, then inflation expectations may not rise and this particular type of management of expectations will not work.

---

[1]There are two other reasons that quantitative easing in and of itself will not necessarily be stimulative. First, large expansions in a central bank's balance sheet do not necessarily result in large increases in the money supply. As indicated in the application in Chapter 15, "Quantitative Easing and the Money Supply, 2007–2014," this was exactly the case in the United States from 2007–2014, when huge expansions in the Fed's balance sheet and the monetary base did not result in a large increase in the money supply because most of the increase in the monetary base just flowed into holdings of excess reserves. Second, an increase in the monetary base does not mean that banks will increase lending, because they have the option of just adding to their holdings of excess reserves instead of making loans. This is exactly what happened during the global financial crisis, when a huge increase in the monetary base led primarily to a massive rise in excess reserves, and bank lending did not increase.

FIGURE 24-14 **Response to a Rise in Inflation Expectations**

A rise in inflation expectations causes the short-run aggregate supply curve to shift up to AS_2 and the economy to move to point 2, where output and inflation rise to Y_2 and π_2, respectively.

APPLICATION Abenomics and the Shift in Japanese Monetary Policy in 2013

By 2012, the Japanese economy had been in a funk for well over 10 years, with very low growth, the policy rate stuck at the zero lower bound, and the economy experiencing deflation. With this scenario as his backdrop, Shinzo Abe won the general election for Prime Minister of Japan in December of 2012, and after taking office he promoted a major shift in economic policy aimed at stimulating economic growth, a policy that the media has since dubbed "Abenomics." A key element of Abenomics was a sea change in monetary policy. Abe pressured the Bank of Japan to double its inflation target from 1% to 2% in January of 2013, over the objections of the former Governor of the Bank of Japan, Masaaki Shirakawa, who then resigned in March. After taking over the former governor's position in March of 2013, the new Bank of Japan Governor, Haruhiko Kuroda, announced a major change in the way the Bank of Japan would conduct monetary policy in the future. First, in contrast to the previous governor, who never formally commited to achieving the 1% inflation target, Kuroda committed to achieving the higher 2% inflation objective within two years. Second, he indicated that the Bank of Japan would now engage in a massive asset-purchase (quantitative easing) program that would not only double the size of the Bank of Japan's balance sheet but would also involve the purchase of a very different set of assets. Specifically, rather than purchasing short-term government bonds, the Bank of Japan would now purchase long-term bonds, including private securities such as real estate investment trusts.

We can use our analysis from the previous section to predict how this shift in monetary policy might affect the Japanese economy. First, in contrast to the previous quantitative easing, the Abenomics program sought to lower $\bar{f}$ through the purchase of long-term assets. Specifically, the program would lower $\bar{f}$ by lowering credit spreads through the purchase of private securities and also by lowering long-term interest rates through the purchase of long-term government bonds. As we have seen, with the policy rate at the zero lower bound, a lower $\bar{f}$ would lead to a lower real interest rate for investments, thereby shifting the aggregate demand curve to the right, to AD_2 in Figure 24-15.

Second, the higher inflation target, and even more importantly the stronger commitment by Kuroda to achieving this higher target, should, according to our analysis, raise expected inflation and hence shift the short-run aggregate supply curve to AS_2.

MyEconLab Mini-lecture

FIGURE 24-15   Response to the Shift in Japanese Monetary Policy in 2013

The Bank of Japan's revised asset purchase program lowers $\bar{f}$, which lowers the real interest rate on investments at any given inflation rate and shifts the aggregate demand curve to the right, from AD_1 to AD_2. The rise in inflation expectations causes the short-run aggregate supply curve to shift upward from AS_1 to AS_2. The economy moves to point 2, where output and inflation rise to Y_2 and π_2, respectively.

As we can see in Figure 24-15, the economy would then move to point 2, where both output and inflation would rise.

In other words, the new monetary policy's two-pronged attack would both lower the real interest rate for investments directly through the asset-purchase program and also directly raise inflation expectations, providing another factor that would drive down the real interest rate. Both of these mechanisms would then operate to promote an economic expansion and an exit from the deflationary environment that the Japanese had been experiencing for the past 15 years. This new policy strategy seems to be working, with the Japanese economy growing at a substantial pace in 2013 and 2014 and inflation rising, but the jury is still out. ◆

MyEconLab

MyEconLab is an online homework and tutorial system that puts you in control of your own learning with study and practice tools directly correlated to this chapter's content. Visit MyEconLab to access the eText, the Questions and Applied Problems with answers, as well as additional assessment. You will also find web chapters, mini-lectures, appendices, mini-cases, videos, glossary flashcards, news feeds, CANSIM data, and graphing tools.

SUMMARY

1. For aggregate demand shocks and permanent supply shocks, the price stability and economic activity stability objectives are consistent: Stabilizing inflation stabilizes economic activity, even in the short run. For temporary supply shocks, however, there is a tradeoff between stabilizing inflation and stabilizing economic activity in the short run. In the long run, however, there is no conflict between stabilizing inflation and stabilizing economic activity.

2. Activists regard the self-correcting mechanism, which works through wage and price adjustment, as very slow and hence feel that the government should pursue active, accommodating policy to address high unemployment when it develops. Nonactivists, by contrast, believe that the self-correcting mechanism works quickly and therefore advocate that the government should avoid the implementation of active policies aimed at eliminating unemployment.

3. Milton Friedman's view that in the long run inflation is always and everywhere a monetary phenomenon is borne out by aggregate demand and supply analysis: Such analysis shows that monetary policymakers can target any inflation rate in the long run through autonomous monetary policy, which makes use of the overnight interest rate policy tool to change the level of aggregate demand and thereby adjust the equilibrium inflation rate.

4. Two types of inflation can result from an activist stabilization policy aimed at promoting high employment: cost-push inflation, which is caused by negative supply shocks or a push by workers for wages that are higher than the level justified by productivity gains; and demand-pull inflation, which results when policymakers pursue high output and employment targets through policies that increase aggregate demand.

5. When the policy rate hits the floor of the zero lower bound, the aggregate demand curve becomes upward sloping, which means that the self-correcting mechanism that returns the economy to full employment is no longer operational. At the zero lower bound, in order to boost output and inflation, the monetary authorities must turn to nonconventional policies of three types: liquidity provision, asset purchases (typically referred to as quantitative easing), and management of expectations.

KEY TERMS

activists, p. 615
cost-push inflation, p. 618
data lag, p. 615
demand-pull inflation, p. 618
divine coincidence, p. 610

effectiveness lag, p. 616
implementation lag, p. 616
inflation gap, p. 607
keynesians, p. 615
legislative lag, p. 615

nonactivists, p. 615
recognition lag, p. 615
inflation target, p. 607

QUESTIONS

All questions are available in MyEconLab *at*
www.myeconlab.com.

1. What does it mean when we say that the inflation gap is negative?

2. "If autonomous spending falls, the central bank should lower its inflation target in order to stabilize inflation." Is this statement true, false, or uncertain? Explain your answer.

3. For each of the following shocks, describe how monetary policymakers would respond (if at all) to stabilize economic activity. Assume the economy starts at a long-run equilibrium.

   a. Consumers reduce autonomous consumption.
   b. Financial frictions decrease.
   c. Government spending increases.
   d. Taxes increase.
   e. The domestic currency appreciates.

4. During the global financial crisis, how were central banks around the world able to help offset the sharp increase in financial frictions without the option of lowering interest rates further? Did the plan work?

5. Why does the divine coincidence simplify the job of policymakers?

6. Why do temporary negative supply shocks pose a dilemma for policymakers?

7. In what way is a permanent negative supply shock worse than a temporary negative supply shock?

8. Suppose three economies are hit with the same temporary negative supply shock. In country A, inflation initially rises and output falls; then inflation rises more and output increases. In country B, inflation initially rises and output falls; then both inflation and output fall. In

country C, inflation initially rises and output falls; then inflation falls and output eventually increases. What type of stabilization approach did each country take?

9. "Policymakers would never respond by stabilizing output in response to a temporary positive supply shock." Is this statement true, false, or uncertain? Explain your answer.

10. The fact that it takes a long time for firms to get new plants and equipment up and running is an illustration of what policy problem?

11. If someone told you, "policymakers couldn't vote themselves out of a phone booth," what type of policy lag would that person be referring to?

12. Is stabilization policy more likely to be conducted through monetary policy or through fiscal policy? Why?

13. "If the data and recognition lags could be reduced, activist policy probably would be more beneficial to the economy." Is this statement true, false, or uncertain? Explain your answer.

14. Why do activists believe that the economy's self-correcting mechanism works slowly?

15. If the economy's self-correcting mechanism works slowly, should the government necessarily pursue discretionary policy to eliminate unemployment? Why or why not?

16. Suppose one could measure the welfare gains derived from eliminating output (and unemployment) fluctuations in the economy. Assuming these gains are relatively small for the average individual, how do you think this measurement would affect the activist/nonactivist debate?

17. Given a relatively steep and a relatively flat short-run aggregate supply curve, which curve would support the case for nonactivist policy? Why?

18. "Because government policymakers do not consider inflation desirable, their policies cannot be the source of inflation." Is this statement true, false, or uncertain? Explain your answer.

19. How can monetary authorities target any inflation rate they wish?

20. What will happen if policymakers erroneously believe that the natural rate of unemployment is 7% when it is actually 5% and therefore pursue stabilization policy?

21. How can demand-pull inflation lead to cost-push inflation?

22. How does the policy rate hitting a floor of zero lead to an upward-sloping aggregate demand curve?

23. Why does the self-correcting mechanism stop working when the policy rate hits the zero lower bound?

24. What nonconventional monetary policies shift the aggregate demand curve, and how do they work?

APPLIED PROBLEMS

All applied problems are available in MyEconLab *at* **www.myeconlab.com**.

25. Suppose the government decides to decrease its expenditures as a means of cutting the existing government budget deficit.

   a. Using a graph of aggregate demand and supply, show the effects of such a decision on the economy in the short run. Describe the effects on inflation and output.

   b. What will be the effect on the real interest rate, the inflation rate, and the output level if the Bank of Canada decides to stabilize the inflation rate?

26. Use a graph of aggregate demand and supply to demonstrate how lags in the policy process can result in undesirable fluctuations in output and inflation.

27. As monetary policymakers become more concerned with inflation stabilization, the slope of the aggregate demand curve becomes flatter. How does the resulting change in the slope of the aggregate demand curve

help stabilize inflation when the economy is hit with a temporary negative supply shock? How does this affect output? Use a graph of aggregate demand and supply to demonstrate.

28. Many developing countries suffer from endemic corruption. How does this help explain why these countries' economies typically have high inflation and economic stagnation? Use a graph of aggregate demand and supply to demonstrate.

29. Suppose that $\bar{f}$ is determined by two factors: financial panic and asset purchases.

   a. Using an *MP* curve and an *AS/AD* graph, show how a sufficiently large financial panic can pull the economy below the zero lower bound and into a destabilizing deflationary spiral.

   b. Using an *MP* curve and an *AS/AD* graph, show how a sufficient amount of asset purchases can reverse the effects of the financial panic depicted in part (a).

DATA ANALYSIS PROBLEMS

Download data for these problems from MyEconLab *at* **www.myeconlab.com**.

1. Go to the St. Louis Federal Reserve FRED database, and find quarterly data on the Canadian unemployment rate (aged 15 and over) and the quarterly Canadian Consumer Price Index (all items) since 1961Q1 for both series.

   a. For the most recent four quarters of data available, calculate the average inflation gap using the Bank of Canada's 2% inflation target.

   b. For the most recent four quarters of data available, calculate the average unemployment

gap, using 5.6% as the presumed natural rate of unemployment.

   c. Based on your answers to parts (a) and (b), does the divine coincidence apply to the current economic situation in Canada? Why or why not? What does your answer imply about the sources of shocks that have impacted the current economy? Briefly explain.

2. Go to the St. Louis Federal Reserve FRED database, and find data on the U.S. personal consumption expenditure price index (PCECTPI), the unemployment rate (UNRATE), and an estimate of the natural

rate of unemployment (NROU). For the price index, adjust the *units* setting to "Percent Change From Year Ago." Select the data from 2000 through the most current data available, download the data, and plot all three variables on the same graph. Using your graph, identify periods of demand-pull or cost-push movements in the inflation rate. Briefly explain your reasoning.

WEB EXERCISES

1. It can be an interesting exercise to compare the purchasing power of the dollar over different periods in history. Go to **www.bankofcanada.ca/en/rates.htm** and scroll down to the link to the inflation calculator. Use this calculator to answer the following questions.

   a. If a new house cost $10 000 in 1950, what would it have cost in 2012?

   b. From (a), what is the percent change in the price of the house from 1950 to 2012?
   c. What is the average annual rate of inflation?

WEB REFERENCES

http://research.stlouisfed.org/fred2

The St. Louis Federal Reserve FRED database reports debt levels and gross domestic product, along with many other economic statistics for Canada.

25 The Role of Expectations in Monetary Policy

Learning Objectives

After studying this chapter you should be able to

1. Summarize the Lucas critique.
2. Compare and contrast the use of policy rules versus discretionary policy.
3. Summarize and illustrate the benefits of a credible central bank.
4. Identify the ways in which central banks can establish and maintain credibility.

PREVIEW

After World War II, economists, armed with models like the ones we developed in Chapters 21-24 felt that discretionary policies could reduce the severity of business cycle fluctuations without creating inflation. In the 1960s and 1970s, these economists got their chance to put their policies into practice, but the results were not what they had anticipated. The economic record for that period is not a happy one: Inflation accelerated, with the inflation rate often climbing to above 10%, and unemployment figures deteriorating from those of the 1950s.[1]

In the 1970s and 1980s, economists, including Nobel Prize winners Robert Lucas of the University of Chicago and Thomas Sargent, now at New York University, used the rational expectations theory discussed in Chapter 7 to examine why discretionary policies appear to have performed so poorly. Their analysis cast doubt on whether macroeconomic models can be used to evaluate the potential effects of policy and on whether policy can be effective when the public *expects* that it will be implemented. Because the analysis of Lucas and Sargent has such strong implications for the way in which policy should be conducted, it has been labelled the *rational expectations revolution*.[2]

This chapter examines the analysis behind the rational expectations revolution. We start first with the Lucas critique, which indicates that because expectations are an important part of economic behaviour, it may be quite difficult to predict what the outcome of a discretionary policy will be. We then discuss the effect of rational expectations on the aggregate demand and supply analysis we developed in Chapter 23, and explore how this theoretical breakthrough has shaped current policymaking models and debates.

LUCAS CRITIQUE OF POLICY EVALUATION

Economists have long used **macroeconometric models** to forecast economic activity and to evaluate the potential effects of policy options. In essence, the models are collections of equations that describe statistical relationships among many economic variables. Economists can feed data into such models, which then churn out a forecast or prediction.

---

[1] Some of the deterioration can be attributed to supply shocks in 1973–1975 and 1978–1980.

[2] Other economists who have been active in promoting the rational expectations revolution are Robert Barro of Harvard University, Bennett McCallum of Carnegie-Mellon University, Nobel Prize winner Edward Prescott of Arizona State University, and Neil Wallace of Pennsylvania State University.

In his famous paper "Econometric Policy Evaluation: A Critique," Robert Lucas spurred the rational expectations revolution by presenting a devastating argument against the use of the macroeconometric models used at the time for evaluating policy.[3]

Econometric Policy Evaluation

To understand Lucas's argument, we must first understand how econometric policy evaluation is done. Say, for example, that the Bank of Canada wants to evaluate the potential effects of changes in the overnight interest rate from the existing level of, say, 5%. Using conventional methods, the Bank economists would feed different overnight interest rate options—say, 4% and 6%—into a computer version of a model. The model would then predict how unemployment and inflation would change under the different scenarios. Then, the policymakers would select the policy that the model predicted would have the most desirable outcomes.

Relying on rational expectations theory, Lucas identified faulty reasoning in this approach if the model did not incorporate rational expectations, as was true for the macroeconometric models used by policymakers at the time: When policies change, public expectations shift as well. For example, if the Bank of Canada raises the overnight interest rate to 6%, this action might change the way the public forms expectations about where interest rates will head in the future. Those changing expectations, as we've seen, can have a real effect on economic behaviour and outcomes. Yet econometric models that do not incorporate rational expectations ignore the effects of changing expectations and thus are unreliable for evaluating policy options.

APPLICATION   The Term Structure of Interest Rates

Let's now apply Lucas's argument to a concrete example involving only one equation typically found in econometric models: the term structure equation. The equation relates the long-term interest rate to current and past values of the short-term interest rate. It is one of the most important equations in macroeconometric models because the long-term interest rate, not the short-term rate, is the one believed to have the larger impact on aggregate demand.

In Chapter 6, we learned that the long-term interest rate is related to an average of expected future short-term interest rates. Suppose that in the past, when the short-term rate rose, it quickly fell back down again; that is, any increase was temporary. Because rational expectations theory suggests that any rise in the short-term interest rate is expected to be only temporary, such a rise should have only a minimal effect on the average of expected future short-term rates. Therefore, the rise in the short-term rate should cause the long-term interest rate to rise by only a negligible amount. The term structure relationship as estimated using past data thus indicates that changes in the short-term interest rate will have only a weak effect on the long-term interest rate.

Suppose the Bank of Canada wants to evaluate the effects on the economy of a policy that is likely to raise the short-term interest rate from its existing level of, say, 5%, to a higher level of 6% for the foreseeable future. The term structure equation, which has been estimated using past data, will indicate that just a small change in the long-term interest rate will occur. However, if the public expects that the short-term rate is rising to a permanently higher level, rational expectations theory indicates that people will no longer expect

[3]*Carnegie-Rochester Conference Series on Public Policy* 1 (1976): 19–46.

a rise in the short-term rate to be temporary. Instead, when they see the interest rate rise to 6%, they will expect the average of future short-term interest rates to rise substantially, and so the long-term interest rate will rise greatly, not minimally as suggested by the term structure equation. You can see that using an econometric model to evaluate the likely outcome of the change in Bank of Canada policy can lead to highly misleading information.

The term structure application demonstrates another aspect of the Lucas critique. The effects of a particular policy depend critically on the public's expectations about the policy. If the public expects the rise in the short-term interest rate to be merely temporary, then the response of the long-term interest rate, as we have seen, will be negligible. If, however, the public expects the rise to be more permanent, the response of the long-term rate will be far greater. *The Lucas critique points out not only that conventional econometric models cannot be used for policy evaluation, but also that the public's expectations about a policy will influence the response to that policy.*

The term structure equation discussed here is only one of many equations in the econometric models to which the Lucas critique applies. In fact, Lucas uses examples of consumption and investment equations in his paper. One attractive feature of the term structure example is that it deals with expectations in the financial market, a sector of the economy for which the empirical evidence supporting rational expectations is much stronger. The Lucas critique should also apply, however, to sectors of the economy with regard to which rational expectations theory is more controversial, because the basic principle of the Lucas critique is not that expectations are always rational but rather that the formation of expectations changes when the behaviour of a forecasted variable changes. This less stringent principle is supported by the evidence in sectors of the economy other than financial markets. ◆

POLICY CONDUCT: RULES OR DISCRETION?

The Lucas critique exposed the need for new policy models that reflected the insights of rational expectations theory. Here, we explore the implications of the critique on a long-running debate among economists: whether monetary policymakers should have the flexibility to adapt their policies to a changing situation, or whether they should adopt **rules**, binding plans that specify how policy will respond (or not respond) to particular data such as unemployment and inflation data.

Discretion and the Time-Inconsistency Problem

We say that policymakers operate with **discretion** when they make no commitment to future actions but instead make what they believe in that moment to be the right policy decision for the situation. Complexities are introduced when policymakers are empowered to shape policy "on the fly." The *time-inconsistency problem* discussed in Chapter 17 reveals the potential limitations of discretionary policy. Recall that the time-inconsistency problem is the tendency of policymakers to deviate from good long-run plans when making short-run decisions. Policymakers are always tempted to pursue policies that are more expansionary than firms or people expect because such a policy will boost economic output (and lower unemployment) in the short run. The best policy, however, is *not* to pursue expansionary policy, because decisions about wages and prices reflect workers' and firms' expectations about policy (an implication of the rational expectations revolution). For example, when workers and firms see a central bank pursuing discretionary expansionary policy, they will recognize that this policy is likely to lead to higher inflation in the future. They will therefore raise their expectations of inflation, driving wages and prices up. The rise in wages and prices will lead to higher inflation but may not result in higher output on average.

Policymakers will promote better inflation performance in the long run if they do not try to surprise people with an unexpectedly expansionary policy but instead keep inflation under control. One way of doing this is to abandon discretion and adopt rules to govern policymaking.

Types of Rules

In contrast to discretion, rules are essentially automatic. One famous type of rule, advocated by Milton Friedman and his followers, who are known as **monetarists**, is the **constant-money-growth-rate rule**, whereby policymakers keep the money supply growing at a constant rate regardless of the state of the economy. Other monetarists, such as Bennett McCallum and Alan Meltzer, have proposed variants of this rule that allow the rate of money supply growth to be adjusted for shifts in velocity, nominal income divided by the quantity of money, which has often been found to be unstable in the short run. Rules of this type are deemed nonactivist because they do not "react" to economic conditions. Monetarists advocate rules of this type because they believe that money is the sole source of fluctuations in aggregate demand and that long and variable lags in the effects of monetary policy will lead to greater volatility in economic activity and inflation if policy actively responds to unemployment (as discussed in Chapter 24).

Activist rules, in contrast, specify that monetary policy should react to the level of output as well as to inflation. The most famous rule of this type is the *Taylor rule*, discussed in Chapter 17. It specifies that the Bank of Canada should set its overnight interest rate target by using a formula that considers both the output gap $(Y - Y^P)$ and the inflation gap $(\pi - \pi^T)$.

The Case for Rules

As suggested by our discussion of the time-inconsistency problem, discretionary monetary policy can lead to poor economic outcomes. If monetary policymakers operate with discretion, they will be tempted to pursue overly expansionary monetary policies that will boost employment in the short run but generate higher inflation (but not higher employment) in the long run. A commitment to a policy rule like the Taylor rule or the constant-money-growth-rate rule solves the time-inconsistency problem because policymakers are forced to follow a set plan that does not allow them to exercise discretion and therefore prevents them from exploiting the short-run tradeoff between inflation and employment. With their hands bound by a policy rule, policymakers can achieve desirable long-run outcomes.

Another argument in support of rules posits that policymakers and politicians simply cannot be trusted to make good decisions. Milton Friedman and Anna Schwartz's monumental work, *A Monetary History of the United States*,[4] documents numerous instances in which the Federal Reserve made serious policy errors, with the worst occurring during the Great Depression, when the Fed just stood by and let the banking system and the economy collapse. Proponents of this argument believe that the politicians who make fiscal policy are not to be trusted because they have strong incentives to pursue policies that will help them win the next election. They are therefore more likely

[4]Milton Friedman and Anna Jacobson Schwartz, *A Monetary History of the United States, 1867–1960* (Princeton, NJ: Princeton University Press, 1963).

FYI   The Political Business Cycle and Richard Nixon

You might know that former U.S. President Richard Nixon and his aides took some extraordinary actions to ensure a landslide victory in the 1972 U.S. presidential election, such as breaking into the offices of political rivals at the Watergate Hotel. Less well known are similar actions on the economic front prior to the election. Before the 1972 election, the Nixon administration imposed wage and price controls on the economy, which temporarily lowered the inflation rate. After the election, those same actions contributed to a surge in inflation. Nixon also pursued expansionary fiscal policy by cutting taxes. And it has been rumoured that the chair of the Federal Reserve at the time, Arthur Burns, succumbed to direct pressure from Nixon to maintain low interest rates through election day. The aftermath was ugly. The economy overheated and inflation rose to over 10% by the late 1970s, a rate that was abetted by the negative supply shocks during that period.

The Nixon episode led economists and political scientists to theorize that politicians will take steps to make themselves look good during election years. Specifically, the theory went, they will take steps to stimulate the economy prior to the election, in the hopes of stimulating a boom and low unemployment, outcomes that will increase their electoral chances. Unfortunately, the result of these actions will be higher inflation down the road, which then will require contractionary policies to get inflation under control, leading to a recession in the future. The resulting ups and downs of the economy would be the direct result of political machinations and so could be characterized as a political business cycle. Although the Nixon episode in the United States provided support for the existence of a political business cycle, the research has not led to a definitive answer regarding whether this phenomenon is a general one.[*]

[*]The paper that launched research on the political business cycle was William Nordhaus, "The Political Business Cycle," *Review of Economic Studies* 42 (1975): 169–190.

to focus on increasing employment in the short run without worrying that their actions might lead to higher inflation further down the road. Their advocacy for expansionary policies can lead to a so-called **political business cycle**, in which fiscal and monetary policy are expansionary right before elections, with higher inflation following later. (For an example, see the FYI box, The Political Business Cycle and Richard Nixon.)

The Case for Discretion

Although policy rules have important advantages, they also have serious drawbacks. First, rules can be too rigid because they cannot account for every contingency. For example, almost no one could have predicted that problems in one small part of the financial system, subprime mortgage lending, would lead to the worst financial crisis in over 70 years, with such devastating effects on the world economy. The unprecedented steps taken by central banks around the world to prevent the crisis from causing a depression (described in Chapters 9 and 16) could not have been written into a policy rule ahead of time. The ability to act flexibly through discretion can thus be a key factor in a successful monetary policy.

The second problem with policy rules is that they do not easily incorporate the tool of judgment. Monetary policy is as much an art as it is a science. Monetary policymakers must look at a wide range of information in order to decide on the best course for monetary policy, and some of this information is not easily quantifiable. Judgment is thus an essential element of good monetary policy, and it is very hard to write it into a rule. Only through discretion can monetary policy bring judgment to bear.

Global   The Demise of Monetary Targeting in Switzerland

In 1975, the Swiss National Bank (Switzerland's central bank) adopted monetary targeting in which it announced a growth rate target for the monetary aggregate M1. In 1980, the Swiss switched their growth rate target to an even narrower monetary aggregate, the monetary base. Although monetary targeting had been quite successful in Switzerland for many years, the Swiss economy ran into serious problems with the introduction of a new interbank payment system, the Swiss Interbank Clearing (SIC), and a wide-ranging revision of commercial banks' liquidity requirements in 1988. These structural changes caused a severe drop in banks' desired holdings of deposits at the Swiss National Bank, and these holdings were the major

component of the monetary base. A smaller amount of the monetary base was now needed to conduct transactions, altering the relationship between the monetary base and aggregate spending, and so the 2% target growth rate for the monetary base was suddenly far too expansionary. Inflation subsequently rose to over 5%, well above that of other European countries.

High inflation rates horrified the Swiss, who had always prided themselves on maintaining a low-inflation environment even when the rest of Europe did not. These problems with monetary targeting led the Swiss to abandon it in the 1990s and adopt a much more flexible framework for the conduct of monetary policy.[*]

[*]For a further discussion of monetary targeting in Switzerland, see Chapter 4 of Ben S. Bernanke, Thomas Laubach, Frederic S. Mishkin, and Adam S. Posen, *Inflation Targeting: Lessons from the International Experience* (Princeton, NJ: Princeton University Press, 1999).

Third, no one really knows what the true model of the economy is, and so any policy rule that is based on a particular model will prove to be wrong if the model is flawed. Discretion avoids the straightjacket that would lock in the wrong policy if the model that was used to derive the policy rule proved to be a poor one.

Fourth, even if the model is a good one, any structural changes in the economy will necessitate changes in the coefficients of the model. For example, the Lucas critique points out that the structural shifts caused by changes in policies can lead to changes in the coefficients of macroeconometric models. Another example of structural economic change occurred in the 1980s, when the relationship between monetary aggregates, such as M1+ and M2+, and aggregate spending broke down as a result of financial innovation. Following a rule that assumed a constant growth rate in one of these aggregates would have produced bad outcomes. Indeed, this is what happened in Switzerland in the late 1980s and early 1990s when adherence to a rule that assumed a particular growth rate of monetary aggregates led to a surge in inflation (as discussed in the Global box, The Demise of Monetary Targeting in Switzerland). Discretion enables policymakers to change policy settings when an economy undergoes structural changes.

Constrained Discretion

The tug-of-war between rules and discretion has strongly influenced academic debates about monetary policy for many decades. But either choice may be too rigid. As we have seen, both rules and discretion are subject to problems, and so the dichotomy between rules and discretion may be too simple to capture the realities that macroeconomic policymakers face. Discretion can be a matter of degree. Discretion can be a relatively undisciplined approach that leads to policies that change with the personal views of policymakers or with the direction of political winds, or it might operate within a more clearly articulated framework in which the general objectives and tactics of the policymakers—although not their specific actions—are committed to in advance. Ben Bernanke, former chair of the Federal Reserve, along with one of the authors of this textbook, came up with a name for this type of framework: **constrained discretion**.[5] Constrained discretion imposes a conceptual structure and inherent discipline on policymakers, but without eliminating all flexibility. It combines some of the advantages ascribed to rules with those ascribed to discretion.

THE ROLE OF CREDIBILITY AND A NOMINAL ANCHOR

An important way to constrain discretion, as discussed in Chapter 17, is to commit to a *nominal anchor*, a nominal variable—such as the inflation rate, the money supply, or an exchange rate—that ties down the price level or inflation to achieve price stability. For example, if a central bank has an explicit target for the inflation rate—say, 2%—and takes steps to achieve this target, then the inflation target becomes a nominal anchor. Alternatively, a government could commit to a fixed exchange rate between its currency and a sound currency like the dollar and use this as its nominal anchor. If the commitment to a nominal anchor has **credibility**—that is, it is believed by the public—then it has important benefits.

Benefits of a Credible Nominal Anchor

First, a credible nominal anchor has elements of a behaviour rule. Just as rules help to prevent the time-inconsistency problem in parenting by helping adults resist pursuit of the discretionary policy of giving in, a nominal anchor can help overcome the time-inconsistency problem by providing an expected constraint on discretionary policy. For example, if monetary policymakers commit to a nominal anchor of achieving a specific inflation objective—say, a 2% inflation rate—then they know that they will be subject to public scrutiny and criticism if they miss this objective or pursue policies that are clearly inconsistent with this objective, such as an interest rate target that is too low. Because policymakers wish to avoid embarrassment and possibly legal punishment, they will be less tempted to pursue overly expansionary, discretionary policies in the short run, policies that would be inconsistent with their commitment to the nominal anchor.

Second, a credible commitment to a nominal anchor helps to anchor inflation expectations, which leads to smaller fluctuations in inflation. Such a commitment thus contributes to price stability and also helps stabilize aggregate output. The credibility of a commitment to a nominal anchor is therefore a critical element in enabling monetary policy to achieve both of its objectives, price stability and stabilization of economic activity. In other words, a credible nominal anchor helps make monetary policy more efficient.

We will use the aggregate demand and supply framework to show analytically why a credible nominal anchor helps produce this desirable outcome. First we will look at the effectiveness of stabilization policy when it is responding to an aggregate demand shock, and then we will look at its effectiveness when it is responding to an aggregate supply shock. We will also look at the benefits of credibility for anti-inflation policy.

Credibility and Aggregate Demand Shocks

We now examine the importance of credibility in the short run when positive and negative demand shocks are present.

---

[5]See Ben S. Bernanke and Frederic S. Mishkin, "Inflation Targeting: A New Framework for Monetary Policy?" *Journal of Economic Perspectives* 11 (Spring 1997): 97–116.

Positive Demand Shock   Let's first look at what happens in the short run when a positive aggregate demand shock occurs. For example, suppose businesses suddenly get new information that makes them more optimistic about the future, and so they increase their investment spending. As a result of this positive demand shock, the aggregate demand curve shifts to the right from AD_1 to AD_2, moving the economy from point 1 to point 2 in panel (a) of Figure 25-1. Aggregate output rises to Y_2 and inflation rises above the inflation target of π^T to π_2. As we saw in Chapter 24, the appropriate response, if the monetary authorities wish to stabilize inflation and economic activity, is to tighten monetary policy and shift the short-run aggregate demand curve back down to AD_1 in order to move the economy back to point 1. However, because of the long lags between monetary policy actions and their effects on aggregate demand, it will take some time before the short-run aggregate demand curve shifts back to AD_1.

Now let's look at what happens to the short-run aggregate supply curve. Recall from Chapter 23 that the short-run aggregate supply curve can be expressed as follows:

$$\pi \quad = \quad \pi^e \quad + \quad \gamma(Y - Y^P) \quad + \quad \rho$$

Inflation $=$ Expected Inflation $+ \gamma \times$ Output Gap $+$ Inflation Shock

If the commitment to the nominal anchor is credible, then the public's expected inflation rate π^e will remain unchanged and the short-run aggregate supply curve will remain at AS_1. Inflation therefore will not go higher than π_2, and over time, as the short-run aggregate demand curve shifts back down to AD_1, inflation will fall back down to the inflation target of π^T.

But what if monetary policy is not credible? The public will worry that the monetary authorities are willing to accept a higher inflation rate than π^T and are not willing to drive the short-run aggregate demand curve back to AD_1 quickly. In this case, the weak credibility of the monetary authorities will cause expected inflation π^e to rise and so the short-run aggregate supply curve will rise, shifting from AS_1 to AS_3 and sending the economy to point 3 in the short run, where inflation has risen further to π_3. Even if the monetary authorities tighten monetary policy and return the aggregate demand curve to AD_1, the damage is done: Inflation has risen more than it would have if the central bank had credibility. Our aggregate demand and supply analysis thus yields the following conclusion: ***Monetary policy credibility has the benefit of stabilizing inflation in the short run when faced with positive demand shocks***.

Negative Demand Shock   Panel (b) of Figure 25-1 illustrates a negative demand shock. For example, suppose consumer confidence dips and consumer spending declines. The aggregate demand curve shifts left from AD_1 to AD_2, and the economy moves to point 2 in the short run, where aggregate output has fallen to Y_2, which is below potential output Y^P, and inflation has fallen to π_2, which is below the target level of π^T. To stabilize output and inflation, the central bank will ease monetary policy to move the aggregate demand curve back to AD_1. If the central bank has high credibility, expected inflation will remain unchanged, the short-run aggregate supply curve will remain at AS_1, and the economy will return to point 1, where output is back at its potential level Y^P.

However, what if the central bank's credibility is weak? When the public sees an easing of monetary policy, it might become concerned that the central bank is weakening its commitment to the nominal anchor and intends to pursue inflationary policy in the future. In this situation, inflation expectations might increase, and so the short-run aggregate supply curve will rise to AS_3, sending the economy to

(a) Positive Aggregate Demand Shocks

(b) Negative Aggregate Demand Shocks

FIGURE 25-1 **Credibility and Aggregate Demand Shocks**

In panel (a), the positive aggregate demand shock shifts the aggregate demand curve to the right from AD_1 to AD_2, moving the economy from point 1 to point 2. If monetary policy is not credible, expected inflation will rise and so the short-run aggregate supply curve will rise and shift to the left to AS_3, sending the economy to point 3, where inflation has risen further to π_3. In panel (b), the negative aggregate demand shock shifts the aggregate demand curve left from AD_1 to AD_2, and the economy moves to point 2. If the central bank is not credible, inflation expectations might increase, and the short-run aggregate supply curve will rise and shift to the left to AS_3. Monetary policy easing then will move the economy to point 3, where aggregate output at Y_3 is still below potential output at Y^P.

point 3, where aggregate output will rise only from Y_2 to Y_3, leaving output below potential output Y^P. Weak credibility in the face of a negative demand shock will keep output below potential output for a longer period than would occur if credibility was strong. We have the following additional result: ***Monetary policy credibility has the benefit of stabilizing economic activity in the short run when faced with negative demand shocks.***

Credibility and Aggregate Supply Shocks

Now let's look at what happens in Figure 25-2 if a negative aggregate supply shock occurs. If energy prices increase, the short-run aggregate supply curve will shift up and to the left. How much the aggregate supply curve will shift, however, depends on the amount of credibility the monetary authorities have. If the credibility of the nominal anchor is strong, inflation expectations will not rise, and so the upward and leftward shift of the short-run aggregate supply curve to AS_2 will be small. When the economy moves to point 2 in the short run, the rise in inflation to π_2 will then be minor, and the fall in output to Y_2 will also be minor. If, on the other hand, the

MyEconLab Mini-lecture

FIGURE 25-2   Credibility and Aggregate Supply Shocks

If the credibility of monetary policy is high, the negative aggregate supply shock will shift the short-run aggregate supply curve only to AS_2 and the economy will move to point 2, where the rise in inflation to π_2 will be minor and the fall in output to Y_2 will also be minor. If credibility is weak, then inflation expectations will rise substantially and the upward shift of the short-run aggregate supply curve will be much larger, moving the curve up and to the left to AS_3. The economy will move to point 3, with worse outcomes for both inflation and output—inflation will be higher at π_3 and output will be lower at Y_3.

central bank's commitment to the nominal anchor is perceived as weak, then inflation expectations will rise substantially and the upward and leftward shift of the short-run aggregate supply curve will be much larger, moving the curve up to AS_3. Now the economy will move to point 3 in the short run, with worse outcomes for both inflation and output—inflation will be higher at π_3 and output will be lower at Y_3. We reach the following conclusion: ***Monetary policy credibility has the benefit of producing better outcomes for both inflation and output in the short run when faced with negative supply shocks.***

The theoretical benefits of credibility when the economy is hit by negative supply shocks are confirmed by the data, as illustrated in the following application.

APPLICATION   A Tale of Three Oil Price Shocks

In 1973, 1979, and 2007, the world economy was hit by three major negative supply shocks when the price of oil rose sharply. In the first two episodes the inflation rate in Canada rose sharply, while in the most recent episode it rose much less, as we can see in panel (a) of Figure 25-3. In the case of the first two episodes, monetary policy credibility was extremely weak because the Bank of Canada had been unable to keep inflation under control, which had resulted in high inflation. In contrast, when the third oil price shock hit in 2007–2008, inflation had been low and stable for quite a period of time, so the Bank of Canada had more credibility that it would keep inflation under control. One reason that has been offered to explain why the last oil price shock appears to have had a smaller effect on inflation is that monetary policy has been more credible. Our aggregate demand and supply analysis provides the reasoning behind this view.

In the first two episodes, where the commitment to a nominal anchor and credibility were weak, the oil price shocks would have produced a surge in inflation expectations and a large upward and leftward shift in the short-run aggregate supply curve to AS_3, as seen in Figure 25-2. Thus, the aggregate demand and supply analysis predicts there would be a sharp contraction in economic activity and a sharp rise in inflation. This is exactly what we see in panels (a) and (b) of Figure 25-3, although the unemployment rate series in panel (b) starts in 1976. The economic contractions were very severe, with unemployment rising to almost 13% in the aftermath of the 1979 oil price shock (during the 1981–1982 recession). In addition, inflation shot up to near double-digit levels.

In the 2007–2008 episode, the outcome was quite different. Through greater policy credibility established over many years, inflation expectations remained grounded when the oil price shock occurred. As a result, the short-run aggregate supply curve shifted up and to the left much less, to only AS_2 in Figure 25-2. Our aggregate demand and supply analysis predicts that there would be a much smaller increase in inflation from the negative supply shock and that the contraction in economic activity also would be less. Indeed, this is exactly what transpired until the global financial crisis entered its virulent phase in the fall of 2008. Inflation rose by much less than it had in the previous episodes, and the economy held up fairly well until the financial crisis took a disastrous turn in October 2008. Only then did the economy go into a tailspin, but it is clear that this was not the result of the negative supply shock. Inflation actually fell quite dramatically, indicating that a massive negative demand shock was the source of the sharp contraction in economic activity. ◆

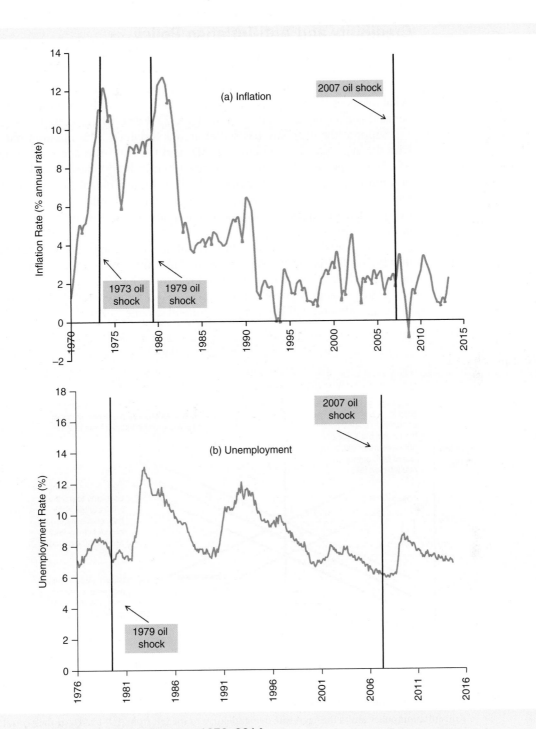

FIGURE 25-3   Inflation and Unemployment, 1970–2014

During the 1973 and 1979 oil shock episodes, inflation was initially high and the Bank of Canada's commitment to a nominal anchor was weak, whereas during the 2007 episode, inflation was initially low and the Bank's credibility was high. As a result, inflation and unemployment rose more in the first two episodes than it did in the last episode, with unemployment rising sharply in the third episode only after the 2007–2009 global financial crisis took a disastrous turn in October 2008.

Credibility and Anti-Inflation Policy

So far we have examined the benefits of credibility when the economy is buffeted by demand and supply shocks. By the end of the 1970s, the high inflation rate (then over 10%) helped shift the primary concern of policymakers to the reduction of inflation. What role does credibility play in the effectiveness of anti-inflation policies? The aggregate demand and supply diagram given in Figure 25-4 will help us answer this question.

Suppose the economy has settled into a sustained 10% inflation rate at point 1, with the aggregate demand curve at AD_1 and the short-run aggregate supply curve at AS_1. Now suppose a new Bank of Canada governor is appointed who decides that inflation must be stopped. He convinces the Governing Council to autonomously tighten monetary policy so that the aggregate demand curve is shifted to the left to AD_4, which in the long run will move the economy to point 4 and slow inflation down to the 2% inflation objective.

If the central bank has very little credibility, then the public will not be convinced that the central bank will stay the course to reduce inflation and therefore they will not revise their inflation expectations down from the 10% level. As a result, the short-run aggregate supply curve will remain at AS_1 and the economy will move to point 2. Although inflation will fall to π_2, output will decline to Y_2.

MyEconLab Mini-lecture

FIGURE 25-4 **Credibility and Anti-Inflation Policy**

Anti-inflation policy shifts the aggregate demand curve to the left from AD_1 to AD_4. If the central bank lacks credibility, the short-run aggregate supply curve remains at AS_1 and the economy moves to point 2, where output falls to Y_2 and inflation falls to π_2. If the central bank has credibility, then expected inflation declines and the short-run aggregate supply curve shifts down to AS_3. The economy moves to point 3, where output has fallen by less, to Y_3, and inflation has fallen by more, to π_3. Eventually the economy moves to point 4, but with credibility, the anti-inflation policy is more effective, lowering inflation faster and at less cost in terms of output.

Now consider what will happen if, instead, the central bank has high credibility and so the public believes that the central bank will do whatever it takes to lower inflation. In this case, expectations of inflation will fall, the short-run aggregate supply curve will fall to AS_3, and the economy will move to point 3. Inflation then will fall even further to π_3, and output will decline by less, to Y_3. Indeed, in the extreme case in which the central bank is perfectly credible, there is even a possibility that inflation expectations will immediately decline to the 2% level and that the short-run aggregate supply curve will shift all the way down to AS_4. In this case, the economy will immediately move to point 4, where inflation has declined to the 2% inflation objective, and yet output will remain at Y^P. In this case, the anti-inflation policy will be costless because it will not require any loss of output. Although this last scenario is unlikely, we have shown the following result to be true: *The greater the credibility of the central bank as an inflation fighter, the more rapid the decline in inflation and the lower the loss of output will be in the attempt to achieve the inflation objective.*

Evidence that credibility plays an important role in successful anti-inflation policies is provided by the dramatic end of the Bolivian hyperinflation in 1985 (see the Global box). But establishing credibility is easier said than done. You might think that an announcement by policymakers at the Bank of Canada that they plan to pursue an anti-inflation policy might do the trick. The public will expect that this policy will be adhered to and will act accordingly. However, this conclusion assumes that the public will believe the policymakers' announcement. Unfortunately, that is not how the real world works.

The history of Bank of Canada policymaking suggests that the Bank of Canada has not always done what it set out to do. In the early 1970s, the Bank of Canada accommodated inflationary shocks by raising the rate of growth of monetary aggregates, thereby forming expectations of rising inflation. When in 1975 the Bank of Canada adopted a

---

Global Ending the Bolivian Hyperinflation: A Successful Anti-Inflation Program

The most remarkable anti-inflation program of recent times was implemented in Bolivia. In the first half of 1985, Bolivia's inflation rate was running at 20 000% and rising. Indeed, the inflation rate was so high that the price of a movie ticket often rose while people waited in line to buy it. In August 1985, Bolivia's new president announced his anti-inflation program, the New Economic Policy. To rein in money growth and establish credibility, the new government took drastic actions to slash the budget deficit by shutting down many state-owned enterprises, eliminating subsidies, freezing public sector salaries, and collecting a new wealth tax. The finance ministry was put on new footing; the budget was balanced on a day-by-day basis.

Without exception, the finance minister would not authorize spending in excess of the amount of tax revenue that had been collected the day before. The Bolivian inflation was stopped in its tracks within one month, and the output loss was minor (less than 5% of GDP).

Certain hyperinflations before World War II were also ended with small losses of output through the implementation of policies similar to Bolivia's,[*] and a more recent anti-inflation program in Israel, which also involved substantial reductions in budget deficits, sharply reduced inflation without any clear loss of output. Without a doubt, credible anti-inflation policies can be highly successful in eliminating inflation.

[*]For an excellent discussion of the end of four hyperinflations in the 1920s, see Thomas Sargent, "The Ends of Four Big Inflations," in *Inflation: Causes and Consequences,* ed. Robert E. Hall (Chicago: University of Chicago Press, 1982), pp. 41–98.

gradual anti-inflation policy, the public had no reason to believe in such a policy. Such episodes reduced the credibility of the Bank of Canada in the eyes of the public and, as Figure 25-4 predicts, the resulting lack of credibility had serious consequences. The reduction of inflation that occurred from 1981 to 1984 was bought at a very high cost; the 1981–1982 recession that helped bring the inflation rate down was one of the most severe recessions in the post–World War II period.

APPLICATION   Credibility and the Bank of Canada's Victory over Inflation

In the period from 1965 through the 1970s, policymakers in Canada had little credibility as inflation fighters—a well-deserved reputation, as they pursued discretionary accommodating policy to achieve high employment. The outcome was not a happy one. Inflation soared to double-digit levels, while the unemployment rate remained high. To wring inflation out of the system, governor of the Bank of Canada Gerald Bouey put the economy through two back-to-back recessions in 1980 and 1981–1982. Only after the 1981–1982 recession—the most severe in the postwar period, with unemployment above the 10% level—did Bouey establish credibility for the Bank of Canada's anti-inflation policy. By the end of 1983, inflation was running at a rate of less than 5%.

From November 1982 to January 1988, the primary objective of the Bank of Canada was price stability in the longer term and inflation containment in the shorter term. This policy, however, was carried out without intermediate targets or a specified path to the longer-term goal. In January 1988, John Crow, then the governor of the Bank of Canada, announced that the Bank would subsequently pursue an objective of price stability. One indication of the Bank of Canada's credibility came in 1991, when the Bank's governor and the minister of finance jointly announced a series of declining inflation targets, with a band of plus and minus one percentage point around them. The targets were 3% by the end of 1992, falling to 2% by the end of 1995, to remain within a range of 1% to 3% thereafter. The 1% to 3% target range for inflation was renewed in November 2011, to apply until the end of 2016.

This has convinced the public and the markets that if inflation reared its head, the Bank of Canada would pursue a nonaccommodating policy of quashing it. Workers and firms have not raised wages and prices, which would have led to both inflation and unemployment. The success of the Bank of Canada's anti-inflation policy has been continuing to date—the inflation rate has been running at a rate of less than 3%. The Bank of Canada's triumph over inflation has been achieved, because it obtained credibility the hard way: it earned it. ◆

APPROACHES TO ESTABLISHING CENTRAL BANK CREDIBILITY

Our analysis has demonstrated that a credible nominal anchor that anchors inflation expectations is a key element in the success of monetary policy. But how do the monetary authorities achieve this credibility? We discussed several approaches in earlier chapters. One approach to credibility, discussed in Chapter 17, is through continued success at keeping inflation under control through concerted policy actions. Another approach that has been growing in popularity in recent years, also discussed in Chapter 17, is *inflation targeting*, which involves the public announcement of a medium-term numerical target for inflation and a commitment to achieving it. Some countries have successfully kept inflation under control by pegging their currency's exchange rate to the currency of an anchor country that already has a strong nominal anchor. We discussed this strategy, sometimes called *exchange-rate targeting*, in Chapter 19. Another way to increase central bank credibility is to give the central bank more independence from the political process, as discussed in Chapter 14. Two additional approaches, not discussed in earlier chapters but discussed below, are nominal GDP targeting and the appointment of "conservative" central bankers.

Nominal GDP Targeting

A variant of inflation targeting that recently has received increased attention is **nominal GDP targeting**, in which the central bank announces an objective of hitting a particular level of nominal GDP growth (recall that nominal GDP is real GDP times the price level). For example, if the inflation objective for the central bank were 2% and potential GDP were expected to grow at an annual rate of 3%, then nominal GDP targeting would mean a commitment by the central bank to keeping nominal GDP growing at 5% per year. Nominal GDP targeting has elements of an inflation targeting regime because the targeted growth rate of nominal GDP is tied to the chosen numerical inflation objective. In addition, nominal GDP targeting implies that the central bank will respond to slowdowns in the real economy even if inflation is not falling. To see this, note that with inflation unchanged, a slowdown in real GDP will result in a slowdown in nominal GDP, and so the monetary authorities will be prompted to pursue more expansionary monetary policy.

A potential advantage of nominal GDP targeting is that it focuses not only on controlling inflation but also explicitly on stabilizing real GDP. Another potential advantage is that with nominal GDP targeting, real GDP growth that is below potential or inflation that is below the inflation objective will encourage more expansionary monetary policy, because actual nominal GDP will fall further below its target. Expectations of this more expansionary policy will help stimulate aggregate demand, which will be particularly useful if the zero-lower-bound problem occurs and the monetary authorities are unable to lower the policy interest rate.

Critics cite two major weaknesses of nominal GDP targeting. First, nominal GDP targeting requires accurate estimates of potential GDP growth, which are not easy to achieve. Second, nominal GDP targeting is more complicated to explain to the public than inflation targeting and thus the public might be confused about the objectives of the central bank. At this time, no central bank has adopted nominal GDP targeting, but this may change in the future.

Appoint "Conservative" Central Bankers

Kenneth Rogoff of Harvard University suggested that another way of establishing central bank credibility is for the government to appoint central bankers who have a strong aversion to inflation.[6] He characterized these central bankers as "conservative," although a better description would be "tough" or "hawkish on inflation."

When the public sees the appointment of a "conservative" central banker, it will expect that he or she will be less tempted to pursue expansionary monetary policy to exploit the short-run tradeoff between inflation and unemployment and will do whatever it takes to keep inflation under control. As a result, inflation expectations and realized inflation are likely to be more stable, with the benefits outlined previously.

---

[6]Kenneth Rogoff, "The Optimal Degree of Commitment to an Intermediary Monetary Target," *Quarterly Journal of Economics* (November 1985): 169–189.

The problem with this approach to solving the credibility problem is that it is not clear that it will continue to work over time. If a central banker has more "conservative" preferences than the public has, won't the public demand the appointment of central bankers who are more in tune with their preferences? After all, in a democratic society, government officials are supposed to represent the will of the people.

MyEconLab

MyEconLab is an online homework and tutorial system that puts you in control of your own learning with study and practice tools directly correlated to this chapter's content. Visit MyEconLab to access the eText, the Questions and Applied Problems with answers, as well as additional assessment. You will also find web chapters, mini-lectures, appendices, mini-cases, videos, glossary flashcards, news feeds, CANSIM data, and graphing tools.

SUMMARY

1. The simple principle (derived from rational expectations theory) that the manner in which expectations are formed changes when the behaviour of forecasted variables changes led to the famous Lucas critique of econometric policy evaluation. Lucas argued that when policy changes, the method of expectations formation changes; hence the relationships in an econometric model will change. An econometric model that has been created on the basis of past data will no longer be a valid model for evaluating the effects of a policy change and may prove to be highly misleading. The Lucas critique also points out that the effects of a particular policy depend critically on the public's expectations of the policy.

2. Advocates of rules for the conduct of monetary policy believe that rules solve the time-inconsistency problem because policymakers are forced to follow a set plan, which eliminates the temptation to deviate from the plan and ensures the achievement of desirable long-run outcomes. Advocates of discretion believe that rules are much too rigid because they cannot predict every contingency and do not allow for the use of judgment. Constrained discretion imposes a conceptual structure and inherent discipline on policymakers, but it does so without eliminating all flexibility, so that it combines some of the advantages ascribed to rules with those ascribed to discretion.

3. An important way for the monetary authorities to constrain discretion is by committing to a credible nominal anchor—a nominal variable, such as the inflation rate, the money supply, or an exchange rate, that ties down the price level or inflation to achieve price stability. A credible nominal anchor helps solve the time-inconsistency problem and helps anchor inflation expectations. Credibility has the benefit of stabilizing both output and inflation fluctuations and also enables anti-inflation policies to lower inflation at a lower cost in terms of lost output.

4. Approaches to establishing credibility include implementing actual policies to keep inflation low, inflation targeting, exchange-rate targeting, and the promotion of central bank independence. Another approach to establishing central bank credibility is the appointment of a "conservative" central banker who is hawkish on controlling inflation.

KEY TERMS

constant-money-growth-rate rule, p. 637
constrained discretion, p. 640
credibility, p. 640
discretion, p. 636
monetarists, p. 637
nominal GDP targeting, p. 649
political business cycle, p. 638
rules, p. 636
macroeconometric models, p. 634

QUESTIONS

All questions are available in MyEconLab *at* **www.myeconlab.com**.

1. What does the Lucas critique state about the limitations of our current understanding of the way in which the economy works?

2. "The Lucas critique by itself casts doubt on the ability of discretionary stabilization policy to be beneficial." Is this statement true, false, or uncertain? Explain your answer.

3. Suppose an econometric model based on past data predicts a small decrease in domestic investment when the Bank of Canada increases the overnight interest rate. Assume the Bank of Canada is considering an increase in the overnight interest rate target to fight inflation and promote a low inflation environment that will encourage investment and economic growth.

   a. Discuss the implications of the econometric model's predictions if individuals interpret the increase in the overnight interest rate target as a sign that the Bank will keep inflation at low levels in the long run.

   b. What would be Lucas's critique of this model?

4. If the public expects the Bank of Canada to pursue a policy that is likely to raise short-term interest rates permanently to 5%, but the Bank does not go through with this policy change, what will happen to long-term interest rates? Explain your answer.

5. In what sense can greater central bank independence make the time-inconsistency problem worse?

6. What are the arguments for and against policy rules?

7. If, in a surprise victory, a new government is elected that the public believes will pursue inflationary policy, predict what might happen to the level of output and inflation even before the new government comes into power.

8. Many economists are worried that a high level of budget deficits may lead to inflationary monetary policies in the future. Could these budget deficits have an effect on the current rate of inflation?

9. In some countries, the government chooses the head of the central bank. The same government can fire the head of the central bank and replace him or her with another director at any time. Explain the implications of such a situation for the conduct of monetary policy. Do you think the central bank will follow a monetary policy rule, or will it engage in discretionary policy?

10. Outline the benefits and costs of sticking to a set of rules in each of the following cases. How does each

of these situations relate to the conduct of economic policy?

   a. Going on a diet

   b. Raising children

11. How does Switzerland's monetary targeting strategy as described in this chapter demonstrate the case against monetary policy rules?

12. How is *constrained discretion* different from *discretion* in monetary policy? How are the outcomes of these policies likely to differ?

13. In general, how does credibility (or lack thereof) affect the aggregate supply curve?

14. As part of its response to the global financial crisis, the Federal Reserve in the United States lowered the federal funds rate target to nearly zero by December 2008 and quadrupled the monetary base between 2008 and 2014, a considerable easing of monetary policy. However, survey-based measures of five- to ten-year inflation expectations remained low throughout most of this period. Comment on the Fed's credibility in fighting inflation.

15. "The more credible the policymakers who pursue an anti-inflation policy, the more successful that policy will be." Is this statement true, false, or uncertain? Explain your answer.

16. Why did the oil price shocks of the 1970s affect the economy differently than the oil price shocks of 2007?

17. Central banks that engage in inflation targeting usually announce the inflation target and time period for which that target will be relevant. In addition, central bank officials are held accountable for their actions (e.g., they could be fired if the target is not reached), and their success or lack thereof is also public information. Explain why transparency is such a fundamental ingredient of inflation targeting.

18. Suppose the statistical office of a country does a poor job in measuring inflation and reports an annualized inflation rate of 4% for a few months, while the true inflation rate has been around 2.5%. What will happen to the central bank's credibility if it is engaged in inflation targeting and its target is 2%, plus or minus 0.5%?

19. What are the purposes of inflation targeting, and how does this monetary policy strategy achieve them?

20. How can the establishment of an exchange-rate target bring credibility to a country with a poor record of inflation stabilization?

21. What traits characterize a "conservative" central banker?

APPLIED PROBLEMS

All applied problems are available in MyEconLab at **www.myeconlab.com**.

22. Suppose the central bank is following a constant-money-growth-rate rule and the economy is hit with a severe economic downturn. Use an aggregate supply and demand graph to show the possible effects on the economy. How does this situation reflect on the credibility of the central bank if it maintains the money growth rule? How does it reflect on the central bank's credibility if it abandons the money growth rule to respond to the downturn?

23. Suppose country A has a central bank with full credibility, and country B has a central bank with no credibility. How does the credibility of each country's central bank affect the speed of adjustment of the aggregate supply curve to policy announcements? How does this result affect output stability? Use an aggregate supply and demand diagram to demonstrate.

24. Suppose two countries have identical aggregate demand curves and potential levels of output, and γ is the same in both countries. Assume that in 2016, both countries are hit with the same negative supply shock. Given the table of values below for inflation in each country, what can you say, if anything, about the credibility of each country's central bank? Explain your answer.

	Country A	Country B
2015	3.0%	3.0%
2016	3.8%	5.5%
2017	3.5%	5.0%
2018	3.2%	4.3%
2019	3.0%	3.8%

25. How does a credible nominal anchor help improve the economic outcomes that result from a positive aggregate demand shock? How does a credible nominal anchor help if a negative aggregate supply shock occurs? Use graphs of aggregate supply and demand to demonstrate.

DATA ANALYSIS PROBLEMS

Download data for these problems from MyEconLab at **www.myeconlab.com**.

1. Go to the Bank of Canada's webpage and find data on the inflation rate (the 12-month growth rate in total CPI).

   a. Calculate the average inflation rate over the last 12 and 24 months of data available. How does it compare to the 2% inflation goal?

   b. What, if anything, does your answer to part (a) imply about Bank of Canada credibility?

2. Go to the St. Louis Federal Reserve FRED database and find data on the GDP deflator (GDPDEF) and the price of a barrel of oil (MCOILWTICO). For the GDP deflator, convert the *units* setting to "Percent Change from Year Ago," and download the data.

   a. Calculate the average percent change in the price of oil over the most recent five years of data available. To do this, calculate the percentage change from the beginning of the period to the end, and divide this number by 5. What is the change in the inflation rate over the same time period?

   b. Calculate the average percent change in the price of oil from October 1986 to October 1990. To do this, calculate the percentage change from the beginning of the period to the end, and divide this number by 4. What is the change in the inflation rate over the same time period?

   c. Based on your answers to parts (a) and (b) above, what can you conclude about credibility of current monetary policy compared to its credibility in the earlier periods?

WEB EXERCISES

1. Robert Lucas won the Nobel Prize in economics. Go to **http://nobelprize.org/nobel_prizes/economics/** and locate the press release on Robert Lucas. What was his Nobel Prize awarded for? When was it awarded?

26

Transmission Mechanisms of Monetary Policy

Learning Objectives

After studying this chapter you should be able to

1. List and summarize the transmission mechanisms through which monetary policy can affect the real economy.

2. Summarize and apply the four lessons outlined in this chapter for the conduct of monetary policy.

PREVIEW

Since 1980, the Canadian economy has been on a roller coaster, with output, unemployment, and inflation undergoing drastic fluctuations. At the start of the 1980s, inflation was running at double-digit levels, and the recession of 1980 was followed by one of the shortest economic expansions on record. After a year, the economy plunged into the 1981–1982 recession, with the unemployment rate climbing to over 10%, and only then did the inflation rate begin to come down to below the 5% level.

For several years following 1984, the Canadian economy enjoyed robust growth, with the inflation rate falling to around 3% and the unemployment rate to around 8% by early 1990. With Iraq's invasion of Kuwait and a rise in oil prices in the second half of 1990, the Canadian economy again plunged into recession. Subsequent growth in the economy was sluggish at first but eventually sped up, lowering the unemployment rate to below 7%. However, with the onset of the global financial crisis, the economy entered a recession in December of 2007, with the unemployment rate rising to over 8.5%. Only in June of 2009 did the economy start to recover, making the recession of 2007–2009 the longest recession since World War II. In light of large fluctuations in aggregate output (reflected in the unemployment rate) and inflation, and the economic instability that accompanies them, policymakers face the following dilemma: What policy or policies, if any, should be implemented to reduce fluctuations in output and inflation in the future?

To answer this question, monetary policymakers must be able to accurately assess the timing and effect of their policies on the economy. To make this assessment, they need to understand the mechanisms through which monetary policy affects the economy. In this chapter, we examine the transmission mechanisms of monetary policy and evaluate the empirical evidence on these mechanisms to better understand the role that monetary policy plays in the economy. We will see that these monetary transmission mechanisms emphasize the link between the financial system (which we studied in the first three parts of this book) and monetary theory, the subject of this part of the book.

TRANSMISSION MECHANISMS OF MONETARY POLICY

In this section, we examine the ways in which monetary policy affects aggregate demand and the economy, which are referred to as **transmission mechanisms of monetary policy**. We start with interest-rate channels because they are the key

653

monetary transmission mechanism of the *AD/AS* model developed in Chapters 21, 22, and 23 and applied to monetary policy in Chapters 24 and 25.

Traditional Interest-Rate Channels

The traditional view of the monetary transmission mechanism can be characterized by the following schematic, which shows the effect of an easing of monetary policy accomplished by lowering the real interest rate:

$$r\downarrow \Rightarrow I\uparrow \Rightarrow Y^{ad}\uparrow \qquad \text{(Equation 1)}$$

This schematic shows that an easing of monetary policy leads to a fall in real interest rates ($r\downarrow$), which in turn lowers the real cost of borrowing, causing a rise in investment spending ($I\uparrow$), thereby leading to an increase in aggregate demand ($Y^{ad}\uparrow$).

Although Keynes originally emphasized this channel as operating through businesses' decisions about investment spending, the search for new monetary transmission mechanisms led economists to recognize that consumers' decisions about housing and **consumer durable expenditure** (spending by consumers on durable items such as automobiles and refrigerators) also are investment decisions. Thus the interest-rate channel of monetary transmission outlined in Equation 1 applies equally to consumer spending, and in this case *I* represents investments in residential housing and consumer durable expenditure.

An important feature of the interest-rate transmission mechanism is its emphasis on the *real* (rather than the nominal) interest rate as the rate that affects consumer and business decisions. In addition, it is often the real *long-term* interest rate (not the real short-term interest rate) that is viewed as having the major impact on spending. How is it that a change in the short-term nominal interest rate induced by a central bank results in a corresponding change in the real interest rate on both short- and long-term bonds? We have already seen that the answer lies in the phenomenon of *sticky prices*—the fact that the aggregate price level adjusts slowly over time, so that expansionary monetary policy, which lowers the short-term nominal interest rate, also lowers the short-term real interest rate. The expectations hypothesis of the term structure described in Chapter 6, which states that the long-term interest rate is an average of expected future short-term interest rates, suggests that a lower real short-term interest rate, as long as it is expected to persist, leads to a fall in the real long-term interest rate. These lower real interest rates then lead to increases in business fixed investment, residential housing investment, inventory investment, and consumer durable expenditure, all of which produce the rise in aggregate demand.

The fact that the real interest rate rather than the nominal rate affects spending suggests an important mechanism through which monetary policy can stimulate the economy, even if nominal interest rates hit a floor of zero during a deflationary episode. With nominal interest rates at a floor of zero, a commitment to future expansionary monetary policy can raise expected inflation (π^e), thereby lowering the real interest rate ($r = i - \pi^e$) even when the nominal interest rate is fixed at zero and stimulating spending through the interest-rate channel:

$$\pi^e\uparrow \Rightarrow r\downarrow \Rightarrow I\uparrow \Rightarrow Y^{ad}\uparrow \qquad \text{(Equation 2)}$$

This mechanism thus indicates that monetary policy can still be effective even when nominal interest rates have already been driven down to zero by the monetary authorities. Indeed, this mechanism explains why during the global financial crisis, the Bank of

Canada and other central banks resorted to the nonconventional monetary policy of committing to keep the their policy rates at zero (or near zero) for an extended period of time. By so doing, the central banks were trying to keep inflation expectations from falling in order to make sure that real interest rates remained low, so as to stimulate the economy. In addition, the commitment to keep interest rates low for an extended period of time would help lower long-term interest rates, which would also induce greater spending.

Some economists, such as John Taylor of Stanford University, take the position that strong empirical evidence exists for substantial interest-rate effects on consumer and investment spending through the real cost of borrowing, making the interest-rate monetary transmission mechanism a strong one. His position is highly controversial, and many researchers, including Ben Bernanke, former chair of the Federal Reserve, and Mark Gertler of New York University, believe that the empirical evidence does not support strong interest-rate effects that operate through the real cost of borrowing.[1] Indeed, these researchers see the empirical failure of traditional interest-rate monetary transmission mechanisms as having provided the stimulus for the search for other transmission mechanisms of monetary policy.

These other transmission mechanisms fall into two basic categories: those operating through asset prices other than interest rates, and those operating through asymmetric information effects on credit markets (the **credit view**). These mechanisms are summarized in the schematic diagram in Figure 26-1.

Other Asset Price Channels

One drawback of the aggregate demand analysis in previous chapters is that it focuses on only one asset price, the interest rate, rather than on many asset prices. In addition to bond prices, two other asset prices receive substantial attention as channels for monetary policy effects: foreign exchange rates and the prices of equities (stocks).

Exchange Rate Effects on Net Exports   With the growing internationalization of economies throughout the world and the advent of flexible exchange rates, more attention has been paid to how monetary policy affects exchange rates, which in turn affect net exports and aggregate demand.

The foreign exchange rate channel also involves interest-rate effects because, as we saw in Chapter 18, when domestic real interest rates fall, domestic dollar assets become less attractive relative to assets denominated in foreign currencies. As a result, the value of dollar assets relative to other currency assets falls, and the dollar depreciates (denoted by $E\downarrow$). The lower value of the domestic currency makes domestic goods cheaper than foreign goods, thereby causing a rise in net exports ($NX\uparrow$) and hence in aggregate demand($Y^{ad}\uparrow$). The schematic for the monetary transmission mechanism that operates through the exchange rate is

$$r\downarrow \Rightarrow E\downarrow \Rightarrow NX\uparrow \Rightarrow Y^{ad}\uparrow \qquad\qquad \text{(Equation 3)}$$

Tobin's q Theory   Nobel Prize winner James Tobin developed a theory, referred to as *Tobin's q theory*, that explains how monetary policy can affect the economy through its effects on the valuation of equities (stock). Tobin defines q as the market value of firms divided by the replacement cost of capital. If q is high, the market price of firms

---

[1]See John Taylor, "The Monetary Transmission Mechanism: An Empirical Framework," *Journal of Economic Perspectives* 9 (Fall 1995): 11–26, and Ben Bernanke and Mark Gertler, "Inside the Black Box: The Credit Channel of Monetary Policy Transmission," *Journal of Economic Perspectives* 9 (Fall 1995): 27–48.

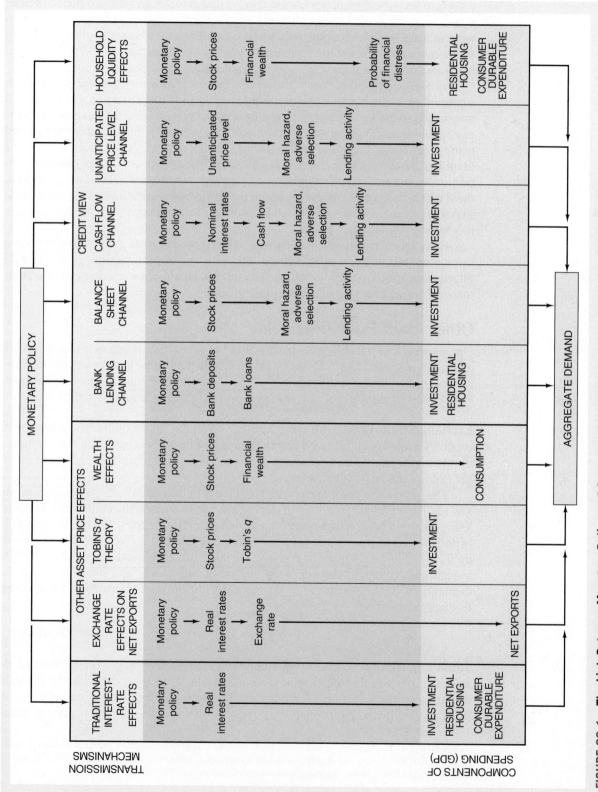

FIGURE 26-1   The Link Between Monetary Policy and Aggregate Demand: Monetary Transmission Mechanisms

This figure shows the different channels through which monetary policy affects aggregate demand.

is high relative to the replacement cost of capital, and new plant and equipment capital is cheap relative to the market value of firms. Companies then can issue stock and get a high price for it relative to the cost of the facilities and equipment they are buying. Investment spending will rise because firms can buy a lot of new investment goods with only a small issue of stock.

Conversely, when q is low, firms will not purchase *new* investment goods because the market value of firms is low relative to the cost of capital. If companies want to acquire capital when q is low, they can buy another firm cheaply and acquire old capital instead. Investment spending, the purchase of new investment goods, will then be very low. Tobin's q theory gives a good explanation for the extremely low rate of investment spending during the Great Depression. In that period, stock prices collapsed, and by 1933, stocks were worth only one-tenth of their value in late 1929; q fell to unprecedentedly low levels.

The crux of this discussion is that a link exists between Tobin's q and investment spending. But how might monetary policy affect stock prices? Quite simply, lower real interest rates on bonds mean that the expected return on this alternative to stocks falls. This makes stocks more attractive relative to bonds, and so demand for them increases, which raises their price.[2] By combining this result with the fact that higher stock prices (P_s) will lead to a higher q and thus higher investment spending I, we can write the following transmission mechanism of monetary policy:

$$r\downarrow \Rightarrow P_s\uparrow \Rightarrow q\uparrow \Rightarrow I\uparrow \Rightarrow Y^{ad}\uparrow \qquad \text{(Equation 4)}$$

Wealth Effects   In their search for new monetary transmission mechanisms, researchers also looked at how consumers' balance sheets might affect their spending decisions. Franco Modigliani was the first to take this tack, using his famous life cycle hypothesis of consumption. **Consumption** is spending by consumers on nondurable goods and services.[3] It differs from *consumer expenditure* in that it does not include spending on consumer durables. The basic premise of Modigliani's theory is that consumers smooth out their consumption over time. Therefore, consumption spending is determined by the lifetime resources of consumers, not just today's income.

An important component of consumers' lifetime resources is their financial wealth, a major part of which is common stocks. When stock prices rise, the value of financial wealth increases, thereby increasing the lifetime resources of consumers, which means that consumption should rise. Considering that, as we have seen, monetary easing can lead to a rise in stock prices, we now have another monetary transmission mechanism:

$$r\downarrow \Rightarrow P_s\uparrow \Rightarrow \text{wealth}\uparrow \Rightarrow \text{consumption}\uparrow \Rightarrow Y^{ad}\uparrow \qquad \text{(Equation 5)}$$

Modigliani's research found this relationship to be an extremely powerful mechanism that adds substantially to the potency of monetary policy.

The wealth and Tobin's q channels allow for a general definition of equity, so they can also be applied to the housing market, where housing is equity. An increase in

---

[2]An alternative way of looking at this transmission mechanism is to use the model discussed in Chapter 7 in which a decrease in the real interest rate lowers the required return on investments in stocks and so increases stock prices. Then the lower yield on stocks reduces the cost of financing investment spending through the issuance of equity. This way of looking at the link between stock prices and investment spending is formally equivalent to Tobin's q theory.

[3]Consumption also includes another small component, the services that a consumer receives from the ownership of housing and consumer durables.

home prices, which raises their prices relative to replacement cost, leads to a rise in Tobin's *q* for housing, thereby stimulating its production. Similarly, housing prices are extremely important components of wealth, so rises in these prices increase wealth, thereby increasing consumption. Monetary expansion, which raises housing prices through the Tobin's *q* and wealth mechanisms described here, thus leads to a rise in aggregate demand.

Credit View

Dissatisfaction with the conventional story that interest-rate effects explain the impact of monetary policy on spending on durable assets has led to a new explanation that is based on the concept of asymmetric information, a problem that leads to financial frictions in financial markets (see Chapter 8). This explanation, referred to as the *credit view*, proposes that two types of monetary transmission channels arise as a result of financial frictions in credit markets: those that operate through effects on bank lending, and those that operate through effects on firms' and households' balance sheets.

Bank Lending Channel
The concept of the bank lending channel is based on the analysis in Chapter 8, which demonstrated that banks play a special role in the financial system because they are especially well suited to solving asymmetric information problems in credit markets. Because of banks' special role, certain borrowers will not have access to the credit markets unless they borrow from banks. As long as there is no perfect substitutability of retail bank deposits with other sources of funds, the bank lending channel of monetary transmission operates as follows: Expansionary monetary policy, which increases bank reserves and bank deposits, raises the quantity of bank loans available. Because many borrowers are dependent on bank loans to finance their activities, this increase in loans causes investment (and possibly consumer) spending to rise. Schematically, the monetary policy effect is written as follows:

$$\text{Bank reserves} \uparrow \Rightarrow \text{bank deposits} \uparrow \Rightarrow \text{bank loans} \uparrow \Rightarrow I \uparrow \Rightarrow Y^{ad} \uparrow \quad \text{(Equation 6)}$$

An important implication of the credit view is that monetary policy will have a greater effect on expenditure by smaller firms, which are more dependent on bank loans, than it will on large firms, which can get funds directly through the stock and bond markets (and not only through banks).

Balance Sheet Channel
Even though the bank lending channel may be declining in importance, it is by no means clear that this is the case for the other credit channel, the balance sheet channel. Like the bank lending channel, the balance sheet channel arises from the presence of financial frictions in credit markets. In Chapter 8, we saw that the lower the net worth of business firms, the more severe the adverse selection and moral hazard problems in lending to these firms become. Lower net worth means that lenders in effect have less collateral for their loans, so their potential losses from adverse selection are higher. A decline in firms' net worth, which raises the adverse selection problem, thus leads to decreased lending to finance investment spending. The lower net worth of businesses also increases the moral hazard problem because it means that owners have a lower equity stake in their firms, giving them more incentive to engage in risky investment projects. When borrowers take on more risky investment projects, it is more likely that lenders will not be paid back, and so a decrease in businesses' net worth leads to a reduction in lending and hence in investment spending.

Monetary policy can affect firms' balance sheets in several ways. Easing of monetary policy, which causes a rise in stock prices ($P_s\uparrow$) along the lines described earlier, raises the net worth of firms and so leads to higher investment spending ($I\uparrow$) and higher aggregate demand ($Y^{ad}\uparrow$) because of the decrease in adverse selection and moral hazard problems. This leads to the following schematic for this particular balance sheet channel of monetary transmission:

$$r\downarrow \Rightarrow P_s\uparrow \Rightarrow \text{firms' net worth}\uparrow \Rightarrow \text{adverse selection}\downarrow, \qquad \text{(Equation 7)}$$
$$\text{moral hazard}\downarrow \Rightarrow \text{lending}\uparrow \Rightarrow I\uparrow \Rightarrow Y^{ad}\uparrow$$

Cash Flow Channel   Another balance sheet channel operates by affecting *cash flow*, the difference between firms' cash receipts and cash expenditures. An easing of monetary policy, which lowers nominal interest rates, also causes an improvement in firms' balance sheets because it raises cash flow. The increase in cash flow increases the liquidity of the firm (or household) and thus makes it easier for lenders to know whether the firm (or household) will be able to pay its bills. The result is that adverse selection and moral hazard problems become less severe, leading to an increase in lending and economic activity. The following schematic describes this alternative balance sheet channel:

$$i\downarrow \Rightarrow \text{firms' cash flow}\uparrow \Rightarrow \text{adverse selection}\downarrow, \qquad \text{(Equation 8)}$$
$$\text{moral hazard}\downarrow \Rightarrow \text{lending}\uparrow \Rightarrow I\uparrow \Rightarrow Y^{ad}\uparrow$$

An important feature of this transmission mechanism is that *nominal* interest rates affect firms' cash flow. Thus this interest-rate mechanism differs from the traditional interest-rate mechanism discussed earlier in which the real interest rate affects investment. Furthermore, the short-term interest rate plays a special role in this transmission mechanism because interest payments on short-term (rather than long-term) debt typically have the greatest impact on the cash flow of households and firms.

A related transmission mechanism involving adverse selection is the credit-rationing phenomenon. Through this mechanism, expansionary monetary policy that lowers interest rates can stimulate aggregate demand. As discussed in Chapter 12, credit rationing occurs when borrowers are denied loans even though they are willing to pay a higher interest rate. The loans are denied because individuals and firms with the riskiest investment projects are exactly the ones who are willing to pay the highest interest rates because, if the high-risk investment succeeds, they will be the primary beneficiaries. Thus higher interest rates increase the adverse selection problem, and lower interest rates reduce it. When expansionary monetary policy lowers interest rates, risk-prone borrowers make up a smaller fraction of those demanding loans, and so lenders are more willing to lend, raising both investment and aggregate demand, along the lines of parts of the schematic given in Equation 8.

Unanticipated Price Level Channel   A third balance sheet channel operates through monetary policy effects on the general price level. Because in industrialized countries debt payments are contractually fixed in nominal terms, an unanticipated rise in the price level lowers the value of firms' liabilities in real terms (decreases the burden of the debt) but should not lower the real value of the firms' assets. An easing of monetary policy, which raises inflation and hence leads to an unanticipated rise in the price level ($P\uparrow$), therefore raises real net worth, which lowers adverse selection and moral hazard problems, thereby leading to a rise in investment spending and aggregate demand, as in the following schematic:

$$r\downarrow \Rightarrow \pi\uparrow \Rightarrow \text{unanticipated } P\uparrow \Rightarrow \text{firms' real net worth}\uparrow$$
$$\Rightarrow \text{adverse selection}\downarrow, \text{moral hazard}\downarrow \Rightarrow \text{lending}\uparrow \Rightarrow I\uparrow \Rightarrow Y^{ad}\uparrow \qquad \text{(Equation 9)}$$

The view that unanticipated movements in the price level affect aggregate demand has a long tradition in economics: It is the key feature in the debt-deflation view of the Great Depression, outlined in Chapter 9.

Household Liquidity Effects Although most literature on the credit channel focuses on spending by businesses, the credit view should apply equally well to consumer spending, particularly spending on consumer durables and housing. Declines in bank lending induced by a monetary contraction should cause corresponding declines in durable and housing purchases by consumers who do not have access to other sources of credit. Similarly, increases in interest rates should cause deteriorations in household balance sheets, because consumers' cash flow is adversely affected.

The balance sheet channel also operates through liquidity effects on consumer durable and housing expenditures. These effects were found to be important factors during the Great Depression (see the FYI box, Consumers' Balance Sheets and the Great Depression). In the liquidity effects view, balance sheet effects work through their impact on consumers' desire to spend rather than on lenders' desire to lend. Because of asymmetric information regarding their quality, consumer durables and housing are very illiquid assets. If, as a result of a severe income shock, consumers needed to sell their consumer durables or housing immediately to raise money, they would expect to suffer a big financial loss because they would not be able to get the full value of these assets in a distress sale. (This is just a manifestation of the lemons problem described in Chapter 8.) In contrast, if consumers held financial assets (such as money in the bank, stocks, or bonds), they could sell them quickly and easily for their full market value and raise the cash. Hence, if consumers expect that they are likely to find themselves in financial distress, they will prefer to hold fewer illiquid consumer durable and housing assets and a greater amount of liquid financial assets.

FYI Consumers' Balance Sheets and the Great Depression

The years between 1929 and 1933 witnessed the worst deterioration in consumers' balance sheets ever seen in the United States. The stock market crash in 1929, which caused an economic slump that lasted until 1933, reduced the value of consumers' wealth by $836 billion (in 2005 dollars), and as expected, consumption dropped sharply (by over $100 billion). Because of the decline in the price level during that period, the level of real debt that consumers owed also increased sharply (by over 20%). Consequently, the value of financial assets relative to the amount of debt declined sharply, increasing the likelihood of financial distress. Not surprisingly, spending on consumer durables and housing fell precipitously: From 1929 to 1933, consumer durable expenditure in the United States declined by over 50%, while expenditure on housing declined by 80%.[*]

[*]For further discussion of the effect of consumers' balance sheets on spending during the Great Depression, see Frederic S. Mishkin, "The Household Balance Sheet and the Great Depression," *Journal of Economic History* 38 (1978): 918–937.

A consumer's balance sheet should be an important influence on his or her estimate of the likelihood of future suffering from financial distress. Specifically, when consumers have a large amount of financial assets relative to their debts, their estimate of the probability of financial distress is low, and they are more willing to purchase consumer durables or housing. When stock prices rise, the value of financial assets increases as well; consumer durable expenditure will also rise because consumers have a more secure financial position and therefore a lower estimate of the likelihood of future financial distress. This leads to another transmission mechanism for monetary policy, one that operates through the link between money and stock prices:

$$r\downarrow \Rightarrow P_s\uparrow \Rightarrow \text{value of households' financial assets}\uparrow$$
$$\Rightarrow \text{likelihood of financial distress}\downarrow \qquad \text{(Equation 10)}$$
$$\Rightarrow \text{consumer durable and housing expenditure}\uparrow \Rightarrow Y^{ad}\uparrow$$

The illiquidity of consumer durable and housing assets provides another reason why a monetary easing, which lowers interest rates and thereby increases cash flow to consumers, leads to a rise in spending on consumer durables and housing. An increase in consumer cash flow decreases the likelihood of financial distress, which increases the desire of consumers to hold durable goods and housing, thus increasing spending on these items and hence increasing aggregate demand. The only difference between this view of cash flow effects and that outlined in Equation 8 is that in this view, it is not the willingness of lenders to lend to consumers that causes expenditure to rise, but the willingness of consumers to spend.

Why Are Credit Channels Likely to Be Important?

There are three reasons to believe that credit channels are important monetary transmission mechanisms. First, a large body of evidence on the behaviour of individual firms supports the view that financial frictions of the type crucial to the operation of credit channels do affect firms' employment and spending decisions. Second, evidence shows that small firms (which are more likely to be credit-constrained) are hurt more by tight monetary policy than large firms are, which are unlikely to be credit-constrained. Third, and maybe most compelling, the asymmetric information view of financial frictions, which is at the core of credit channel analysis, is a theoretical construct that has proved useful in explaining many other important economic phenomena, such as why many of our financial institutions exist, why our financial system has the structure that it has, and why financial crises are so damaging to the economy (topics discussed in Chapters 8 and 14). The best support for a theory is its demonstrated usefulness in a wide range of applications. By this standard, the asymmetric information theory, which supports the existence of credit channels as an important monetary transmission mechanism, has much to recommend it.

APPLICATION   The Great Recession

With the advent of the financial crisis in the summer of 2007, the Bank of Canada and many other central banks around the world began a very aggressive easing of monetary policy. For example, the Federal Reserve dropped the target federal funds rate from $5\frac{1}{4}\%$ to $\frac{1}{4}\%$ to 0% over a 15-month period from September 2007 to December 2008. At first, it appeared that the Fed's actions would keep the growth slowdown mild and prevent a recession. However, the U.S. economy proved to be weaker than the Fed or private forecasters expected, with the most severe recession of the post–World War II period beginning in December 2007. Why did the U.S. economy become so weak despite this unusually rapid reduction in the Fed's policy instrument?

The financial meltdown led to negative effects on the economy from many of the channels we have outlined above. The rising level of subprime mortgage defaults, which led to a decline in the value of mortgage-backed securities and CDOs, led to large losses on the balance sheets of financial institutions. With weaker balance sheets, these financial institutions began to deleverage and cut back on their lending. With no one else available to collect information and make loans, adverse selection and moral hazard problems, and hence financial frictions, increased in credit markets, leading to a slowdown of the economy. Credit spreads also went through the roof with the increase in uncertainty caused by the failure of so many financial markets. The declines in the stock market and housing prices also weakened the economy because they lowered household wealth. The decrease in household wealth led to a drop in Tobin's q, which led to restrained consumer spending and weaker investment spending.

With all these channels operating, it is no surprise that despite the Fed's aggressive lowering of the federal funds rate, the U.S. economy still took a big hit. ◆

LESSONS FOR MONETARY POLICY

What useful lessons regarding the appropriate conduct of monetary policy can we draw from the analysis in this chapter? Four basic lessons can be learned.

1. *It is dangerous to consistently associate an easing or tightening of monetary policy with a fall or rise in short-term nominal interest rates.* Because most central banks use short-term nominal interest rates—typically, the interbank rate—as the key operating instrument in their monetary policies, the danger exists that central banks and the public will focus too much on short-term nominal interest rates as an indicator of the stance of monetary policy. Indeed, it is quite common to see statements that always associate monetary tightenings with a rise in the interbank rate and monetary easings with a decline in the interbank rate. We do not make this mistake in this book because we have been careful to associate monetary easing or tightening with changes in *real* and not *nominal* interest rates.

2. *Other asset prices besides those on short-term debt instruments contain important information about the stance of monetary policy because they are important elements in various monetary policy transmission mechanisms.* As we have seen in this chapter, economists have come a long way in understanding that other asset prices besides interest rates have major effects on aggregate demand. As we saw in Figure 26-1, asset prices such as stock prices, foreign exchange rates, and housing prices play an important role in monetary transmission mechanisms. Furthermore, additional channels, such as those that operate through the exchange rate, Tobin's q, and wealth effects, provide additional evidence that other asset prices play an important role in monetary transmission mechanisms. Although economists strongly disagree among themselves about which channels of monetary transmission are the most important—not surprising, given that economists, particularly those in academia, always enjoy a good debate—they do concur that asset prices other than those on short-term debt instruments play an important role in the effects of monetary policy on the economy.

The view that asset prices other than short-term interest rates matter has important implications for monetary policy. When we try to assess the stance of policy, it is critical that we look at other asset prices in addition to short-term interest rates. For example, if short-term interest rates are low or even zero and yet stock prices are low, housing prices are low, and the value of the domestic currency is high, monetary policy is clearly tight, not easy.

3. Monetary policy can be effective in reviving a weak economy even if short-term interest rates are already near zero. We have recently entered a world in which inflation is not always the norm. Japan, for example, recently experienced a period of deflation during which the price level was actually falling. In the United States, the federal funds rate hit a floor of zero by the end of 2008. One common view is that when a central bank has driven down short-term nominal interest rates to nearly zero, monetary policy can do nothing more to stimulate the economy. The transmission mechanisms of monetary policy described here indicate that this view is false. As indicated in our discussion of the factors that affect the monetary base in Chapter 15, expansionary monetary policy aimed at increasing liquidity in the economy can be conducted through open market purchases, which do not have to be solely in short-term government securities. For example, purchases of private securities, as the Bank of Canada made in 2009, can reduce financial frictions by lowering credit spreads and stimulating investment spending. In addition, a commitment to future expansionary monetary policy helps revive the economy by raising general price-level expectations and by reflating other asset prices, which then stimulate aggregate demand through the channels outlined here. The nonconventional monetary policies we discussed in Chapter 16 are policies of this type. Nonconventional monetary policies can be a potent force in reviving economies that are undergoing deflation and that have short-term interest rates near zero. Indeed, as we saw in Chapter 9 aggressive nonconventional monetary policy during the recent financial crisis helped prevent the Great Recession from turning into a Great Depression and also helped the economy avoid a deflationary episode like the one that occurred during the Great Depression era.

4. Avoiding unanticipated fluctuations in the price level is an important objective of monetary policy, thus providing a rationale for price stability as the primary long-run goal of monetary policy. As we saw in Chapter 17, central banks in recent years have been placing greater emphasis on price stability as the primary long-run goal of monetary policy. Several rationales for this goal have been proposed, including the undesirable effects of uncertainty about the future price level on business decisions and hence on productivity, distortions associated with the interaction of nominal contracts and the tax system with inflation, and increased social conflict stemming from inflation. Our discussion of monetary transmission mechanisms provides an additional reason why price stability is so important. As we have seen, unanticipated movements in the inflation rate can cause unanticipated fluctuations in output, an undesirable outcome. Particularly important in this regard is the knowledge that, as we saw in Chapter 9, price deflation can be an important factor leading to a prolonged financial crisis, as occurred during the Great Depression. An understanding of the monetary transmission mechanisms thus makes it clear that the goal of price stability is desirable because it reduces uncertainty about the future price level. The price stability goal implies that a negative inflation rate is at least as undesirable as too high an inflation rate. Indeed, because of the threat of financial crises, central banks must work very hard to prevent price deflation.

APPLICATION   Applying the Monetary Policy Lessons to Japan's Two Lost Decades

Until 1990, it looked as if Japan might overtake the United States in per capita income. From the early 1990s until 2012, during the years that have become known as the "two lost decades," the Japanese economy stagnated, with deflation and low growth. As a result, Japanese living standards fell further and further behind those of the United States. Many economists take the view that Japanese monetary policy is in part to blame for the poor performance of the Japanese economy during this period. Could Japanese monetary policy have performed better if Japan had applied the four lessons outlined in the previous section?

The first lesson suggests that it is dangerous to think that declines in interest rates always mean that monetary policy has been easing. In the mid-1990s, when short-term interest rates began to decline, falling to nearly zero in the late 1990s and early 2000s, the monetary authorities in Japan took the view that monetary policy was sufficiently expansionary. Now it is widely recognized that this view was incorrect, because the falling and eventually negative inflation rates in Japan meant that real interest rates were actually quite high and that monetary policy was tight, not easy. If the monetary authorities in Japan had followed the advice of the first lesson, they might have pursued a more expansionary monetary policy, which would have helped boost the economy.

The second lesson suggests that monetary policymakers should pay attention to other asset prices, in addition to those on short-term debt instruments, in assessing the stance of monetary policy. At the same time that interest rates were falling in Japan, stock and real estate prices were collapsing, thus providing another indication that Japanese monetary policy was not easy. Knowledge of the second lesson might have led Japanese monetary policymakers to recognize sooner that they needed a more expansionary monetary policy.

The third lesson indicates that monetary policy can still be effective even if short-term interest rates are near zero. Officials at the Bank of Japan frequently claimed that they were helpless to stimulate the economy because short-term interest rates had fallen to nearly zero. By recognizing that monetary policy can be effective even when interest rates are near zero, as suggested by the third lesson, the Japanese monetary authorities could have taken monetary policy actions that would have stimulated aggregate demand by raising other asset prices and inflationary expectations.

The fourth lesson indicates that unanticipated fluctuations in the price level should be avoided. If the Japanese monetary authorities had adhered to this lesson, they might have recognized that allowing deflation to occur could be very damaging to the economy and that such deflation was inconsistent with the goal of price stability.

These four lessons of monetary policy have finally been taken to heart by the Bank of Japan. As we discussed in Chapter 22, monetary policy in Japan has undergone a dramatic shift since 2013, to a highly expansionary, nonconventional monetary policy with a higher inflation target. It is hoped that this shift in policy will lead to better economic outcomes for Japan in future years. ◆

MyEconLab

MyEconLab is an online homework and tutorial system that puts you in control of your own learning with study and practice tools directly correlated to this chapter's content. Visit MyEconLab to access the eText, the Questions and Applied Problems with answers, as well as additional assessment. You will also find web chapters, mini-lectures, appendices, mini-cases, videos, glossary flashcards, news feeds, CANSIM data, and graphing tools.

SUMMARY

1. The transmission mechanisms of monetary policy include traditional interest-rate channels that operate through the real cost of borrowing and affect investment; other asset price channels such as exchange rate effects, Tobin's *q* theory, and wealth effects; and the credit view channels—the bank lending channel, the balance sheet channel, the cash flow channel, the unanticipated price level channel, and household liquidity effects.

2. Four lessons for monetary policy can be drawn from this chapter: (1) It is dangerous to consistently associate monetary policy easing or tightening with a fall or rise in short-term nominal interest rates; (2) other asset prices besides those on short-term debt instruments contain important information about the stance of monetary policy because they are important elements in the monetary policy transmission mechanisms; (3) monetary policy can be effective in reviving a weak economy even if short-term interest rates are already near zero; and (4) avoiding unanticipated fluctuations in the price level is an important objective of monetary policy, thus providing a rationale for price stability as the primary long-run goal of monetary policy.

KEY TERMS

consumer durable expenditure, p. 654

consumption, p. 657

credit view, p. 655

transmission mechanisms of monetary policy, p. 653

QUESTIONS

All questions are available in MyEconLab *at* **www.myeconlab.com**.

1. In 2009, in the wake of the global financial crisis and when interest rates were at their lowest, governments around the world instituted programs designed in part to stimulate new spending on automobiles and major appliances. What does the implementation of these programs imply about views of the health of the interest rate channel during that time?

2. "Considering that consumption accounts for nearly two-thirds of total GDP, this means that the interest rate, wealth, and household liquidity channels are the most important monetary policy channels in Canada" Is this statement true, false, or uncertain? Explain your answer.

3. How can the interest rate channel still function when short term nominal interest rates are at the zero lower bound?

4. Lars Svensson, a former Princeton professor and deputy governor of the Swedish central bank, proclaimed that when an economy is at risk of falling into deflation, central bankers should be "responsibly irresponsible" with monetary expansion policies. What does this mean, and how does it relate to the monetary transmission mechanism?

5. Describe an advantage and a disadvantage of the fact that monetary policy has so many different channels through which it can operate.

6. "If countries fix their exchange rate, the exchange rate channel of monetary policy does not exist." Is this statement true, false, or uncertain? Explain your answer.

7. In the 2007–2009 recession, the value of common stocks in real terms fell by more than 50%. How might this decline in the stock market have affected aggregate demand and thus contributed to the severity of the recession? Be specific about the mechanisms through which the stock market decline affected the economy.

8. "The costs of financing investment are related only to interest rates; therefore, the only way that monetary policy can affect investment spending is through its effects on interest rates." Is this statement true, false, or uncertain? Explain your answer.

9. Predict what will happen to stock prices after a monetary easing. Explain your prediction.

10. From mid-2008 to early 2009, the S&P/TSX declined sharply, while real interest rates were low or falling. What does this scenario suggest should have happened to investment?

11. Nobel Prize winner Franco Modigliani found that the most important transmission mechanisms of monetary policy involve consumer expenditure. Describe how at least two of these mechanisms work.

12. In the late 1990s, the stock market was rising rapidly, the U.S. economy was growing, and the Federal Reserve kept interest rates relatively low. Comment on how this policy stance would affect the economy as it relates to the Tobin q transmission mechanisms.

13. During and after the global financial crisis, the Bank of Canada reduced the overnight interest rate to nearly zero. At the same time, the stock market fell dramatically and housing market values declined. Comment on the effectiveness of monetary policy during this period with regard to the wealth channel.

14. During and after the global financial crisis, the Bank of Canada provided banks with large amounts of liquidity. Banks' excess reserves increased sharply, while credit extended to households and firms decreased sharply. Comment on the effectiveness of the bank lending channel during this time.

15. Why does the credit view imply that monetary policy has a greater effect on small businesses than on large firms?

16. Why might the bank lending channel be less effective today than it once was?

17. One of the classic features of the global financial crisis was the failure of high-profile American investment banks and financial firms such as Lehman Brothers, Bear Stearns, and AIG. These firms experienced sharp contractions in the values of their balance sheets due to risky asset holdings. Comment on how this would affect the U.S. economy as it relates to the balance sheet channel.

18. If adverse selection and moral hazard increase, how does this affect the ability of monetary policy to address economic downturns?

19. How does the Great Depression demonstrate the unanticipated price level channel?

20. How are the wealth effect and the household liquidity effect similar? How are they different?

21. Following the global financial crisis, mortgage rates reached record-low levels in 2011.
    a. What effect should this have had on the economy, according to the household liquidity effect channel?
    b. During the same time, most banks raised their credit standards significantly, making it much more difficult to qualify for home loans and to refinance existing loans. How does this information alter your answer to part (a)?

22. What evidence exists to support the credit view of monetary policy?

23. "A decrease in short-term nominal interest rates necessarily implies a stance of monetary easing." Is this statement true, false, or uncertain? Explain your answer.

24. How does the experience of Japan during the "two lost decades" lend support to the four lessons for monetary policy outlined in this chapter?

APPLIED PROBLEMS

All applied problems are available in MyEconLab *at* **www.myeconlab.com**.

25. Suppose the economy is in recession and the monetary policymakers lower interest rates in an effort to stabilize the economy. Use an aggregate supply and demand diagram to demonstrate the effects of a monetary easing when the transmission mechanisms are functioning normally and when the transmission mechanisms are weak, such as during a deep downturn or when significant financial frictions are present.

DATA ANALYSIS PROBLEMS

Download data for these problems from MyEconLab *at* **www.myeconlab.com**.

1. A "rate cycle" is a period of monetary policy during which the federal funds rate moves from its low point toward its high point, or vice versa, in response to business cycle conditions. Go to the CANSIM database, and find data, from 2000:Q1 to 2014:Q3, on the target overnight interest rate (series V39079),

household final consumption expenditure (series V61989012), household consumption expenditure on durable goods (series V61989014), and household consumption expenditure on services (V61989017). Download the data and convert the daily overnight interest rate series to quarterly frequency.

a. When did the last rate cycle begin and end? (Note: If a rate cycle is currently in progress, use the current period as the end.) Is this rate cycle a contractionary or an expansionary rate cycle?

b. Calculate the percentage change in consumer durable expenditures and consumer expenditures on services over this rate cycle.

c. Based on your answers to parts (a) and (b), how effective was the traditional interest rate channel of monetary policy over this rate cycle?

2. As defined in Exercise 1, a "rate cycle" is a period of monetary policy during which the federal funds rate moves from its low point toward its high point, or vice versa, in response to business cycle conditions.

Go to the St. Louis Federal Reserve FRED database, and find data on the federal funds rate (FEDFUNDS), bank reserves (TOTRESNS), bank deposits (TCDSL), commercial and industrial loans (BUSLOANS), real estate loans (REALLN), real business fixed investment (PNFIC96), and real residential investment (PRFIC96). Use the *frequency* setting to convert the federal funds rate, bank reserves, bank deposits, commercial and industrial loans, and real estate loans data to "quarterly," and download the data.

a. When did the last rate cycle begin and end? (Note: if a rate cycle is currently in progress, use the current period as the end.) Is this rate cycle a contractionary or an expansionary rate cycle?

b. Calculate the percentage change in bank deposits, bank lending, real business fixed investment, and real residential (housing) investment over this rate cycle.

c. Based on your answers to parts (a) and (b), how effective was the bank lending channel of monetary policy over this rate cycle?

WEB EXERCISES

1. Go to **www.econlib.org/library/Enc1/Recessions. html** and review the material on recessions.

a. What is the formal definition of a recession?

b. What are the problems with the definition?

WEB REFERENCES

www.martincapital.com/

Click on "U.S. Financial Data," then on "U.S. Financial Charts," and then on "nominal versus real market rates" to find up-to-the-minute data showing the spread between real rates and nominal rates.

www.conference-board.org/ A site containing extensive data on the factors that define business cycles.

GLOSSARY

activists Economists who regard the self-correcting mechanism through wage and price adjustment as very slow because wages and prices are sticky and so see the need to pursue active policy to eliminate high unemployment when it develops. **615**

adaptive expectations Expectations of a variable based on an average of past values of the variable. **153**

adverse selection The problem created by asymmetric information before a transaction occurs: the people who are the most undesirable from the other party's point of view are the ones who are most likely to want to engage in the financial transaction. **37**

agency theory The analysis of how asymmetric information problems affect economic behaviour. **175**

aggregate demand The total quantity of output demanded in the economy at different price levels. **530**

aggregate demand curve A relationship between the price level and the quantity of aggregate output demanded when the goods and money markets are in equilibrium. **555, 565**

aggregate output The total production of final goods and services in the economy. **7**

aggregate price level The average price of goods and services in an economy. **8**

aggregate supply curve The relationship between the quantity of output supplied and the price level. **571**

American option An option that can be exercised at any time up to the expiration date of the contract. **323**

anchor currency A currency to which other countries' currencies are pegged. **489**

"animal spirits" Waves of optimism and pessimism that affect consumers' and businesses' willingness to spend. **533**

appreciation Increase in a currency's value. **461**

arbitrage Elimination of a riskless profit opportunity in a market. **157, 316**

asset A financial claim or piece of property that is a store of value. **3**

asset management The acquisition of assets that have a low rate of default and diversification of asset holdings to increase profits. **290**

asset market approach An approach to determine asset prices using stocks of assets rather than flows. **95**

asset-price bubbles Increases in asset prices in the stock and real estate markets that are driven well above their fundamental economic values by investor psychology. **197**

asset transformation The process of turning risky assets into safer assets for investors by creating and selling assets with risk characteristics that people are comfortable with and then using the funds acquired by selling these assets to purchase other assets that may have far more risk. **37, 287**

asymmetric information The unequal knowledge that each party to a transaction has about the other party. **37**

at the money (trading at par) option Option whose exercise price is just equal to the current asset price. **325**

audits Certification by accounting firms that a business is adhering to standard business principles. **178**

automated banking machine (ABM) One location that provides an automated teller machine (ATM), an Internet connection to the bank's website, and a telephone link to customer service. **254**

automated teller machine (ATM) An electronic machine that provides banking services 24 hours a day. **253**

autonomous consumption expenditure The amount of consumer expenditure that is independent of disposable income. **531**

autonomous easing of monetary policy Lowering real interest rates at any given inflation rate. **554**

autonomous investment A component of planned investment spending that is completely exogenous and so is unexplained by the variables in a model. **533**

autonomous net exports The level of net exports that is treated as exogenous (outside the model). **535**

autonomous spending Exogenous spending that is unrelated to variables in the model such as output or real interest rate. **543**

autonomous tightening of monetary policy Raising real interest rates at any given inflation rate. **553**

balance of payments A bookkeeping system for recording all payments that have a direct bearing on the movement of funds between a country and foreign countries. **488**

balance-of-payments crisis A foreign exchange crisis stemming from problems in a country's balance of payments. **494**

balance sheet A list of the assets and liabilities of a bank (or firm) that balances: Total assets equal total liabilities plus capital. **283**

Bank Act Reform The legislation that took effect in October of 2001 regarding the policy framework of the Canadian financial services sector. **275**

bank failure A situation in which a bank cannot satisfy its obligations to pay its depositors and other creditors and so goes out of business. **222**

Bank of Canada (the Bank) Canada's central bank. **11**

bank panic The simultaneous failure of many banks, as during a financial crisis. **223**

bank rate The interest rate the Bank of Canada charges to members of the Canadian Payments Association. **292, 367**

banker's risk The risk of not holding enough reserves to make immediate and larger than normal cash payments to liability holders. **286**

banks Financial institutions that accept money deposits and make loans (such as commercial banks, trust and mortgage loan companies, and credit unions and *caisses populaires*). **6**

base money The sum of the Bank of Canada's monetary liabilities (notes outstanding and bank settlement balances) and coins outstanding. Also called *monetary base*. **346**

Basel Accord An agreement that required that banks hold as capital at least 8% of their risk-weighted assets. **227**

Basel Committee on Banking Supervision An international committee of bank supervisors that meets under the auspices of the Bank for International Settlements in Basel, Switzerland. **227**

basis point One one-hundredth of a percentage point. **125**

behavioural finance A subfield of finance that applies concepts from other social sciences such as anthropology, sociology, and, particularly, psychology to understand the behaviour of securities prices. **164**

Board of Directors A board with 15 members (including the governor) that is responsible for the management of the Bank of Canada. **343**

Board of Governors of the Federal Reserve System A board with seven governors (including the chairman) that plays an essential role in decision making within the Federal Reserve System. **355**

bond A debt security that promises to make payments periodically for a specified period of time. **3**

borrowed reserves The loans the central bank makes to deposit-based financial institutions. **371**

branches Additional offices of banks that conduct banking operations. **247**

Bretton Woods system The international monetary system in use from 1945 to 1971 in which exchange rates were fixed and the U.S. dollar was freely convertible into gold (by foreign governments and central banks only). **490**

brokers Agents for investors; they match buyers with sellers. **26**

bubble A situation in which the price of an asset differs from its fundamental market value. **163**

budget deficit The excess of government expenditure over tax revenues. **11**

budget surplus The excess of tax revenues over government expenditures. **11**

business cycles The upward and downward movement of aggregate output produced in the economy. **7**

call option An option contract that provides the right to buy a security at a specified price. **324**

call premium Price of a call option. **324**

capital Wealth, either financial or physical, that is employed to produce more wealth. **24**

capital account An account that describes the flow of capital between a country and other countries. **489**

capital adequacy management A bank's decision about the amount of capital it should maintain and then acquisition of the needed capital. **290**

capital controls Restrictions on the free movement of capital across borders. **496**

capital market A financial market in which longer-term debt (generally with original maturity of greater than one year) and equity instruments are traded. **27**

capital mobility A situation in which foreigners can easily purchase a country's assets and the country's residents can easily purchase foreign assets. **483**

cash flows Cash payments to the holder of a security. **68, 148**

central bank The government agency that oversees the banking system and is responsible for the amount of money and credit supplied in the economy; in Canada, the Bank of Canada. **11, 247**

coinsurance A situation in which only a portion of losses are covered by insurance, so that the insured suffers a percentage of the losses along with the insurance agency. **239**

collateral Property that is pledged to the lender to guarantee payment in the event that the borrower is unable to make debt payments. **173**

commodity money Money made up of precious metals or another valuable commodity. **55**

common stock A security that is a claim on the earnings and assets of a company. **3**

compensating balance A required minimum amount of funds that a firm receiving a loan must keep in a chequing account at the lending bank. **301**

conflicts of interest A manifestation of the moral hazard problem, particularly when a financial institution provides multiple services and the potentially competing interests of those services may lead to a concealment of information or dissemination of misleading information. **39**

consol A perpetual bond with no maturity date and no repayment of principal that periodically makes fixed coupon payments. Also called *perpetuity*. **77**

constant-money-growth-rate rule A policy rule advocated by monetarists whereby the central bank keeps the money supply growing at a constant rate. **637**

constrained discretion A framework in which the general objectives and tactics of policymakers—but not specific actions—are committed to in advance; this imposes a conceptual structure and inherent discipline on policymakers without eliminating all flexibility. **640**

consumer durable expenditure Spending by consumers on durable items such as automobiles and household appliances. **654**

consumption Spending by consumers on nondurable goods and services (including services related to the ownership of homes and consumer durables). **657**

consumption expenditure The total demand for consumer goods and services. **531, 565**

consumption function The relationship between disposable income and consumer expenditure. **531**

cost-push inflation Inflation that occurs because of the push by workers to obtain higher wages. **618**

cost-push shocks Price shocks in which workers push for wages higher than productivity gains, thereby driving up costs and inflation. **572**

costly state verification Monitoring a firm's activities, an expensive process in both time and money. **182**

coupon bond A credit market instrument that pays the owner a fixed interest payment every year until the maturity date, when a specified final amount is repaid. **71**

coupon rate The dollar amount of the yearly coupon payment expressed as a percentage of the face value of a coupon bond. **71**

conventional monetary policy During normal times the Bank of Canada uses the three tools of monetary policy—open market operations, settlement balances management, and Bank of Canada lending—to control the money supply and interest rates. These three tools are referred to as conventional monetary policy. **403**

credibility A commitment to policy actions that is believed by the public. **640**

credit boom A lending spree when financial institutions expand their lending at a rapid pace. **195**

credit default swaps (CDS) Financial insurance contracts that provide payments to holders of bonds if they default. **203**

credit derivatives Derivatives that have payoffs to previously issued securities, but ones that bear credit risk. **335**

credit easing Altering the composition of the central bank's balance sheet in order to improve the functioning of particular segments of the credit markets. **418**

credit-linked note A type of credit derivative that combines a bond and a credit option. **336**

credit options Options in which, for a fee, the purchaser has the right to get profits that are tied either to the price of an underlying risky security or to an interest rate. **335**

credit-rating agencies Investment advisory firms that rate the quality of corporate and government bonds in terms of the probability of default. **123**

credit rationing A lender's refusal to make loans even though borrowers are willing to pay the stated interest rate or even a higher rate or restriction of the size of loans made to less than the full amount sought. **302**

credit risk The risk arising from the possibility that the borrower will default. **290**

credit spread The difference between the interest rate on loans to households and businesses and the interest rate on completely safe assets that are sure to be paid off, such as Canada bonds. **200**

credit swap A transaction in which risky payments on loans are swapped for each other. **336**

credit view Monetary transmission mechanisms operating through asymmetric information effects on credit markets. **655**

currency Paper money (such as bills) and coins. **28, 50**

currency board A monetary regime in which the domestic currency is backed 100% by a foreign currency (say, dollars) and in which the note-issuing authority, whether central bank or the government, establishes a fixed exchange rate to this foreign currency and stands ready to exchange domestic currency at this rate whenever the public requests it. **505**

currency swap The exchange of a set of payments in one currency for a set of payments in another currency. **332**

current account An account that shows international transactions involving currently produced goods and services. **488**

current yield An approximation of the yield to maturity that equals the yearly coupon payment divided by the price of a coupon bond. **78**

data lag The time it takes for policymakers to obtain data indicating what is happening to the economy. **615**

dealers People who link buyers with sellers by buying and selling securities at stated prices. **26**

debt deflation A situation in which a substantial decline in the price level sets in, leading to a further deterioration in firms' net worth because of the increased burden of indebtedness. **198**

default A situation in which the party issuing a debt instrument is unable to make interest payments or pay off the amount owed when the instrument matures. **28**

default-free bonds Bonds with no default risk, such as Canada bonds. **121**

deleveraging When financial institutions cut back on their lending because they have less capital. **195**

demand curve A curve depicting the relationship between quantity demanded and price when all other economic variables are held constant. **92**

demand for money The quantity of money that people want to hold. **515**

demand shocks Shocks that can shift the aggregate demand curve, including changes in the money supply, changes in government expenditure and taxes, changes in net exports, changes in consumer and business spending, and financial frictions. **567**

demand-pull inflation Inflation that results when policymakers pursue policies that shift the aggregate demand curve. **618**

deposit facility The central bank's standing facility in which banks are paid a fixed interest rate that is less than the policy rate; in Canada, 25 basis points below the policy rate. **425**

deposit outflows Losses of deposits when depositors make withdrawals or demand payment. **290**

deposit rate ceiling Restriction on the maximum interest rate payable on deposits. **257**

depreciation Decrease in a currency's value. **461**

desired reserve ratio The fraction of deposits that banks desire to keep as reserves. **286, 367**

desired reserves Reserves that are held to meet the banks' desire that for every dollar of deposits, a certain fraction should be kept as reserves. **286, 367**

devaluation Resetting of the fixed value of a currency at a lower level. **491**

direct clearers Members of the Canadian Payments Association who participate directly in the Automated Clearing Settlement System (ACSS) and maintain a settlement account at the Bank of Canada. **392**

discount bond A credit market instrument that is bought at a price below its face value and whose face value is repaid at the maturity date; it does not make any interest payments. Also called a *zero-coupon bond*. **72**

discount rate The interest rate that the Federal Reserve charges banks on discount loans. **419**

discount window lending The Federal Reserve facility at which discount loans are made to banks. **419**

discretion When policymakers make decisions they believe to be the right policies at the moment for a given situation. **636**

disintermediation A reduction in the flow of funds into the banking system that causes the amount of financial intermediation to decline. **257**

disposable income Total income available for spending, equal to aggregate income minus taxes. **531**

diversification Investing in a collection (portfolio) of assets whose returns do not always move together, with the result that overall risk is lower than for individual assets. **37**

dividends Periodic payments made by equities to shareholders. **25, 148**

divine coincidence Phrase coined by Olivier Blanchard, referring to the situation in which a policy to stabilize inflation is also the right policy to stabilize economic activity—with no conflict between them. **610**

dollarization The adoption of a sound currency, like the U.S. dollar, as a country's money. **507**

dominated assets Assets such as currency and chequable assets which earn lower returns than other assets which are just as safe. **523**

drawdowns Transfers of government deposits from the government's accounts with the direct clearers to the government's account with the Bank of Canada. **406**

dual banking system The system in the United States in which banks supervised by the federal government and banks supervised by the states operate side by side. **247**

dual mandate A central bank mandate that features two co-equal objectives: price stability and maximum employment. **435**

duration analysis A measurement of the sensitivity of the market value of a bank's assets and liabilities to changes in interest rates. **304**

e-cash Electronic money that is used on the Internet to purchase goods or services. **56**

e-finance A new means of delivering financial services electronically. **6**

economies of scale The reduction in transaction costs per dollar of transaction as the size (scale) of transactions increases. **36**

economies of scope The ability to use one resource to provide many different products and services. **267**

effectiveness lag The time it takes for a policy to actually have an impact on the economy. **611**

efficient market hypothesis The application of the theory of rational expectations to financial markets. **146**

electoral business cycles Persistent cyclical patterns of key policy and target variables across electoral terms. **353**

electronic money (e-money) Money that exists only in electronic form and substitutes for cash as well. **56**

emerging market economies Economies in an earlier stage of market development that have recently opened up to the flow of goods, services, and capital from the rest of the world. **199**

equation of exchange The equation $MV = PY$, which relates nominal income to the quantity of money. **514**

equities Claims to share in the net income and assets of a corporation (such as common stock). **25**

equity capital See *net worth*. **180**

equity multiplier (EM) The amount of assets per dollar of equity capital. **296**

Eurobonds Bonds denominated in a currency other than that of the country in which they are sold. **33**

Eurocurrencies A variant of the Eurobond; foreign currencies deposited in banks outside the home country. **33**

Eurodollars U.S. dollars that are deposited in foreign banks outside the United States or in foreign branches of U.S. banks. **33**

European option An option that can be exercised only at the expiration date of the contract. **324**

Eurosystem Refers to the European Central Bank and the national central banks of the countries that have adopted the euro. **359**

excess demand A situation in which quantity demanded is greater than quantity supplied. **94**

excess reserves Reserves in excess of desired reserves. **367**

excess supply A situation in which quantity supplied is greater than quantity demanded. **94**

Exchange Fund Account The fund that holds Canada's official foreign exchange assets. **345**

exchange rate   The price of one currency stated in terms of another currency. 460, 534

exchange-rate peg   Fixing the value of the domestic currency to the value of another currency, so the exchange rate is fixed. 501

exchange-rate targeting   See *exchange-rate peg.* 501

exchanges   Secondary markets in which buyers and sellers of securities (or their agents or brokers) meet in one central location to conduct trades. 26

exercise price (strike price)   The price at which the purchaser of an option has the right to buy or sell the underlying financial instrument. 323

exogenous   Independent of variables in the model. 531

expectations theory   The proposition that the interest rate on a long-term bond will equal the average of the short-term interest rates that people expect to occur over the life of the long-term bond. 128

face value   A specified final amount paid to the owner of a coupon bond at the maturity date. Also called *par value.* 71

fair-value accounting   See *mark-to-market accounting.* 232

fallen angels   Investment-grade securities whose rating has fallen to junk levels. 124

federal funds rate   The interest rate on overnight loans of deposits at the Federal Reserve. 357, 419

Federal Open Market Committee (FOMC)   The committee that makes decisions regarding the conduct of open market operations; composed of the seven members of the Board of Governors of the Federal Reserve System, the president of the Federal Reserve Bank of New York, and the presidents of four other Federal Reserve banks on a rotating basis. 355

Federal Reserve banks   The 12 district banks in the Federal Reserve System. 355

Federal Reserve System (the Fed)   The central banking authority responsible for monetary policy in the United States. 355

fiat money   Paper currency decreed by a government as legal tender but not convertible into coins or precious metal. 55

financial crisis   A major disruption in financial markets that is characterized by sharp declines in asset prices and the failures of many financial and nonfinancial firms. 195

financial derivatives   Instruments that have payoffs that are linked to previously issued securities, used as risk reduction tools. 203, 252

financial engineering   The process of researching and developing new financial products and services that would meet customer needs and prove profitable. 251

financial frictions   Asymmetric information problems that act as a barrier to efficient allocation of capital. 195, 534

financial futures   A futures contract in which the standardized commodity is a particular type of financial instrument. 315

financial futures option   An option in which the underlying instrument is a futures contract. Also called a *futures option.* 324

financial innovation   When an economy introduces new types of financial products. 6, 195

financial intermediaries   Institutions (such as banks, insurance companies, mutual funds, pension funds, and finance companies) that borrow funds from people who have saved and then make loans to others. 5

financial intermediation   The process of indirect finance whereby financial intermediaries link lender-savers and borrower-spenders. 35

financial liberalization   The elimination or restrictions on financial markets. 195

financial markets   Markets in which funds are transferred from people who have a surplus of available funds to people who have a shortage of available funds. 2

financial panic   The widespread collapse of financial markets and intermediaries in an economy. 44

financial supervision (prudential supervision)   Overseeing who operates financial institutions and how they are operated. 228

fire sales   Forced, rapid sales of assets to raise needed funds. 198

fiscal policy   Policy that involves decisions about government spending and taxation. 11

Fisher effect   The outcome that when expected inflation occurs, interest rates will rise; named after economist Irving Fisher. 102

fixed exchange rate regime   A regime in which central banks buy and sell their own currencies to keep their exchange rates fixed at a certain level. 489

fixed investment   Spending by firms on equipment (computers, airplanes) and structures (factories, office buildings) and planned spending on residential housing. 532

fixed-payment loan   A credit market instrument that provides a borrower with an amount of money that is repaid by making a fixed payment periodically (usually monthly) for a set number of years. 71

float   Cash items in process of collection at the Bank of Canada minus deferred-availability cash items. 371

floating exchange rate regime   An exchange rate regime in which the value of currencies are allowed to fluctuate against one another. 489

foreign bonds   Bonds sold in a foreign country and denominated in that country's currency. 32

foreign exchange intervention   An international financial transaction in which a central bank buys or sells currency to influence foreign exchange rates. 484

foreign exchange market   The market in which exchange rates are determined. 12, 460

foreign exchange rate   See *exchange rate.* 12

forward contract   An agreement by two parties to engage in a financial transaction at a future (forward) point in time. 313

forward exchange rate   The exchange rate for a forward transaction. 460

forward guidance   The central bank's intervention in the formation of public expectations about future interest rates through public statements. 418

forward rate   The interest rate predicted by pure expectations theory of the term structure of interest rates to prevail in the future. 140

forward transaction   A transaction that involves the exchange of bank deposits denominated in different currencies at some specified future date. 461

four-pillar approach   Regulation of the banking industry by institution (banking, brokerage, trusts, and insurance), versus regulation by function. 266

free banking   A system that permits the organization of a bank by any group that meets certain established criteria concerning the amount of equity capital and maintenance of reserves. 247

free-rider problem   The problem that occurs when people who do not pay for information take advantage of the information that other people have paid for. 177

fully amortized loan   See *fixed-payment loan.* 71

fundamental economic values   Values of assets based on realistic expectations of their future income streams. 197

futures contract   A contract in which the seller agrees to provide a certain standardized commodity to the buyer on a specific future date at an agreed-on price. 252

futures option   See *financial futures option.* 324

gap analysis   A measurement of the sensitivity of bank profits to changes in interest rates, calculated by subtracting the amount of rate-sensitive liabilities from the amount of rate-sensitive assets. 303

general equilibrium   When all markets are simultaneously in equilibrium at the point where the quantity of aggregate output demanded equals the quantity of aggregate output supplied. 578

generalized dividend model   Calculates that the price of stock is determined only by the present value of the dividends. 149

glass-steagall An Act passed in 1933 by the U.S. Congress to legally separate investment banking from commercial banking. **268**

goal independence The ability of the central bank to set the goals of monetary policy. **347**

gold standard A fixed exchange rate regime under which a currency is directly convertible into gold. **249, 490**

Gordon growth model A simplified model to compute the value of a stock by assuming constant dividend growth. **149**

Governing Council A council with six members (including the governor) that is responsible for the management of the Bank of Canada. **344**

government budget constraint The requirement that the government budget deficit equal the sum of the change in the monetary base and the change in government bonds held by the public. **519**

government purchases Spending by all levels of government (federal, provincial, and local) on goods and services. **531, 566**

gross domestic product (GDP) The value of all final goods and services produced in the economy during the course of a year. **12**

haircuts The excess amount of collateral above the amount of the loan. **205**

hedge To protect oneself against risk. **252, 312**

hierarchical mandate A mandate for the central bank that puts the goal of price stability first, but as long as it is achieved other goals can be pursued. **434**

high-powered money The monetary base. **368**

hyperinflation An extreme inflation in which the inflation rate exceeds 50% per month. **54, 520**

implementation lag The time it takes for policymakers to change policy instruments once they have decided on a new policy. **616**

impossible trinity Another term for the policy trilemma, in which a country cannot pursue the following three policies at the same time: free capital mobility, a fixed exchange rate, and an independent monetary policy. **595**

incentive-compatible Having the incentives of both parties to a contract in alignment. **185**

income The flow of earnings. **51**

indebtedness In describing a country, the total amount it has borrowed from banks. **273**

inflation The condition of a continually rising price level. **8**

inflation gap The difference between inflation and the inflation target. **607**

inflation hedges Alternative assets whose real returns are less affected than that of money when inflation varies. **524**

inflation rate The rate of change of the price level, usually measured as a percentage change per year. **8**

inflation target A central bank target for the inflation rate. **607**

inflation targeting A monetary policy strategy that involves public announcement of a medium-term numerical target for inflation. **435**

instrument independence The ability of the central bank to set monetary policy instruments. **347**

interbank deposits Deposits made at other banks. **296**

interest parity condition The observation that the domestic interest rate equals the foreign interest rate plus the expected appreciation in the foreign currency. **481**

interest rate The cost of borrowing or the price paid for the rental of funds (usually expressed as a percentage per year). **3**

interest-rate forward contract A forward contract that is linked to a debt instrument. **313**

interest-rate futures contract A futures contract that is linked to a debt instrument. It is similar to an interest-rate forward contract. **315**

interest-rate risk The possible reduction in returns associated with changes in interest rates. **82, 290**

interest-rate swap A financial contract that allows one party to exchange (swap) a set of interest payments for another set of interest payments owned by another party. **332**

intermediate target Any of a number of variables, such as monetary aggregates or interest rates, that have a direct effect on employment and the price level and that the Fed seeks to influence. **448**

intermediate-term With reference to a debt instrument, having a maturity of between one and ten years. **25**

International Monetary Fund (IMF) The international organization created by the Bretton Woods agreement whose objective is to promote the growth of world trade by making loans to countries experiencing balance-of-payments difficulties. **490**

international reserves Central bank holdings of assets denominated in foreign currencies. **484**

intrinsic value The value of an option at expiration. **325**

inventory investment Spending by firms on additional holdings of raw materials, parts, and finished goods. **532**

inverted yield curve A yield curve that is downward-sloping. **127**

investment banks Firms that assist in the initial sale of securities in the primary market. **25**

IS curve The relationship that describes the combinations of aggregate output and interest rates for which the total quantity of goods produced equals the total quantity demanded (goods market equilibrium). **537**

junk bonds Bonds with ratings below Baa (or BBB) that have a high default risk. **124**

Keynesian A follower of John Maynard Keynes who believes that movements in the price level and aggregate output are driven by changes not only in the money supply but also in government spending and fiscal policy and who does not regard the economy as inherently stable. **615**

Large Value Transfer System (LVTS) An electronic, net settlement system for the transfer of large-value payments. **391**

law of one price The principle that if two countries produce an identical good, the price of this good should be the same throughout the world no matter which country produces it. **463**

legislative lag The time it takes to pass legislation to implement a particular policy. **615**

lender of last resort Provider of reserves to financial institutions when no one else would provide them to prevent a financial crisis. **250, 410**

leverage cycle A feedback loop from a boom in issuing credit, leading to higher asset prices, resulting in higher capital buffers at financial institutions, which supports further lending, which raises prices further, etc.; in the bust, asset prices fall, leading to a cut in lending, a decline in asset prices, and so on. **214**

leverage ratio A bank's capital divided by its assets. **227**

liabilities IOUs or debts. **23**

liquid Easily converted into cash. **26**

liquidity The relative ease and speed with which an asset can be converted into cash. **54**

liquidity management The decisions made by a bank to maintain sufficient liquid assets to meet the bank's obligations to depositors. **290**

liquidity preference framework A model developed by John Maynard Keynes that predicts the equilibrium interest rate on the basis of the supply of and demand for money. **105**

liquidity preference theory John Maynard Keynes's theory of the demand for money. **521**

liquidity premium theory The theory that the interest rate on a long-term bond will equal an average of short-term interest rates expected to occur over the life of the long-term bond plus a positive term (liquidity) premium. **133**

liquidity services Services financial intermediaries provide to their customers to make it easier for them to conduct their transactions. 36

liquidity trap A case of ultrasensitivity of the demand for money to interest rates in which conventional monetary policy has no direct effect on aggregate spending because a change in the money supply has no effect on the interest rate. 525

loan commitment A bank's commitment (for a specified future period of time) to provide a firm with loans up to a given amount at an interest rate that is tied to some market interest rate. 301

loan sale The sale under a contract (also called a *secondary loan participation*) of all or part of the cash stream from a specific loan, thereby removing the loan from the bank's balance sheet. 305

long in a call Purchase of a call option. 324

long in a put Purchase of a put option. 325

long position A contractual obligation to take delivery of an underlying financial instrument. 312

long-term With reference to a debt instrument, having a maturity of 10 years or more. 25

longer-term refinancing operations A category of open market operations by the European Central Bank that are similar to the U.S. Fed's outright purchases or sales of securities. 425

LVTS participants Members of the Canadian Payments Association (CPA) who participate in the LVTS and maintain a settlement account at the Bank of Canada. 391

M1+ Includes currency, personal chequing accounts, and current accounts, plus other assets that have cheque-writing features—all chequable notice deposits at chartered banks, TMLs, and CUCPs. 59

M1++ M1, plus all nonchequable notice deposits at chartered banks, TMLs, and CUCPs. 59

M2 Adds to M1 money market deposit accounts, money market mutual fund shares, smalldenomination time deposits, savings deposits, overnight repurchase agreements, and overnight Eurodollars. 59

M2+ Includes M2 plus deposits at near banks, life insurance company annuities, and money market mutual funds. 61

M2++ Adds to M2 Canada Savings Bonds and non-money market mutual funds. 61

macro hedge A hedge of interest-rate risk for a financial institution's entire portfolio. 317

macroeconometric models Models to forecast the effects of policy on economic activity that use collections of equations that describe statistical relationships among many economic variables. 634

macroprudential supervision Supervision that focuses on the safety and soundness of the financial system in the aggregate. 214

main refinancing operations Weekly reverse transactions (purchase or sale of eligible assets under repurchase agreements or credit operations against eligible assets as collateral) that are reversed within two weeks and are the primary monetary policy tool of the European Central Bank. 425

managed float regime An exchange rate regime in which countries attempt to influence their exchange rates by buying and selling currencies (also called a *dirty float*). 489

management of expectations Term coined by Michael Woodford that refers to the commitment of the central bank to keeping the federal funds rate at near zero for an extended period in order to cause the long-term interest rate to fall. 418

margin requirement A sum of money that must be kept in an account (the margin account) at a brokerage firm. 320

marginal lending facility The European Central Bank's standing lending facility in which banks can borrow (against eligible collateral) overnight loans from the national central bank at a rate 100 basis points above the target financing rate. 425

marginal lending rate The interest rate charged by the European Central Bank for borrowing at its marginal lending facility. 425

marginal propensity to consume The slope of the consumption function line that measures the change in consumer expenditure resulting from an additional dollar of disposable income. 532

mark-to-market accounting An accounting method in which assets are valued in the balance sheets at what they would sell for in the market. 232

marked to market Repriced and settled in the margin account at the end of every trading day to reflect any change in the value of the future contract. 320

market equilibrium A situation occurring when the quantity that people are willing to buy (demand) equals the quantity that people are willing to sell (supply). 94

market fundamentals Items that have a direct impact on future income streams of a security. 162

maturity Time to the expiration date (maturity date) of a debt instrument. 25

medium of exchange Anything that is used to pay for goods and services. 51

micro hedge A hedge for a specific asset. 317

microprudential supervision Supervision that focuses on the safety and soundness of individual financial institutions. 213

monetarist A follower of Milton Friedman who sees changes in the money supply as the primary source of movements in the price level and aggregate output and who views the economy as inherently stable. 637

monetary aggregates The measures of the money supply used by the central bank (M1, M2, and M3). 58

monetary base See *base money.* 346, 366

monetary conditions Determined by the level of short-term interest rates and the exchange rate of the Canadian dollar. 401

monetary policy The management of the money supply and interest rates. 11

monetary (or currency) union A variant of a fixed exchange rate regime is a monetary (or currency) union , in which a group of countries decides to adopt a common currency, thereby fixing the countries' exchange rates in relation to each other. 497

monetary policy (*MP*) curve The relationship between the real interest rate the central bank sets and the inflation rate. 551

monetary theory The theory that relates changes in the quantity of money to changes in economic activity. 7, 513

monetizing the debt A method of financing government spending whereby the government debt issued to finance government spending is removed from the hands of the public and is replaced with high-powered money instead. Also called *printing money.* 520

money (money supply) Anything that is generally accepted in payment for goods or services or in the repayment of debts. 7

money centre banks Large banks in key financial centres (New York, Chicago, San Francisco). 294

money market A financial market in which only short-term debt instruments (generally those with original maturity of less than one year) are traded. 26

money multiplier A ratio that relates the change in the money supply to a given change in the monetary base. 380

moral hazard The risk that one party to a transaction will engage in behaviour that is undesirable from the other party's point of view. 38

mortgage-backed securities Securities that cheaply bundle and quantify the default risk of the underlying high-risk mortgages. 31

mortgages Loans to households or firms to purchase housing, land, or other real structures, in which the structure or land itself serves as collateral for the loans. 30

multilateral netting The LVTS process by which only the net credit or debit position of each participant vis-à-vis all other participants is calculated for settlement, thereby reducing the need for a large amount of settlement balances. **392**

multiple deposit creation The process whereby, when the central bank supplies the banking system with $1 of additional reserves, deposits increase by a multiple of this amount. **372**

NAIRU (nonaccelerating inflation rate of unemployment) The rate of unemployment when demand for labour equals supply, consequently eliminating the tendency for the inflation rate to change. **458**

national banks Federally chartered banks in the United States. **247**

natural rate of output The level of aggregate output produced at the natural rate of unemployment at which there is no tendency for wages or prices to change. **433**, **571**

natural rate of unemployment The rate of unemployment consistent with full employment at which the demand for labour equals the supply of labour. **432**, **571**

net exports Net foreign spending on domestic goods and services, equal to exports minus imports. **531**, **566**

net worth The difference between a firm's assets (what it owns or is owed) and its liabilities (what it owes). Also called *equity capital*. **180**

nominal anchor A nominal variable such as the inflation rate, an exchange rate, or the money supply that monetary policymakers use to tie down the price level. **431**

nominal gdp targeting A variant of inflation targeting that recently has received increased attention in which the central bank announces an objective of hitting a particular level of nominal GDP growth. **649**

nominal interest rate An interest rate that does not take inflation into account. **83**

nonactivists Economists who believe wages and prices are very flexible, so the self-correcting mechanism is very rapid; they thus do not see the need to pursue policies to return the economy to full employment. **615**

nonborrowed monetary base The monetary base minus discount loans (borrowed reserves). **371**

nonconventional monetary policy tools Non-interest rate tools central banks use to stimulate the economy: liquidity provision, asset purchases, and commitment to future monetary policy actions. **414**

notional principal The amount on which interest is being paid in a swap arrangement. **332**

off-balance-sheet activities Bank activities that involve trading financial instruments and the generation of income from fees and loan sales, all of which affect bank profits but are not visible on bank balance sheets. **227**, **305**

official reserve transactions balance The current account balance plus items in the capital account. **489**

okun's law This law describes the negative relationship between the unemployment gap and the output gap. **605**

open interest The number of contracts outstanding. **318**

open market buyback operations The Bank of Canada's buying or selling of bonds in the open market. **346**

open market operations The central bank's buying or selling of bonds in the open market. **368**

open market purchase A purchase of bonds by the central bank. **368**

open market sale A sale of bonds by the central bank. **368**

operating band The Bank's operational objective is to keep the overnight rate within an operating band of 25 basis points. **393**

operating instrument A variable that is very responsive to the central bank's tools and indicates the stance of monetary policy (also called *a policy instrument*). **448**

opportunity cost The amount of interest (expected return) sacrificed by not holding an alternative asset. **106**

optimal forecast The best guess of the future using all available information. **153**

option A contract that gives the purchaser the option (right) to buy or sell the underlying financial instrument at a specified price, called the exercise price or strike price, within a specific period of time (the term to expiration). **323**

originate-to-distribute model A business model in which the mortgage is originated by a separate party, typically a mortgage broker, and then distributed to an investor as an underlying asset in a security. **256**

out-of-the-money option An option that would not be profitable to exercise. **325**

output gap The difference between aggregate output and potential output. **572**

over-the-counter (OTC) market A secondary market in which dealers at different locations who have an inventory of securities stand ready to buy and sell securities "over the counter" to anyone who comes to them and is willing to accept their prices. **26**

overdraft loans Borrowings from the Bank of Canada. Also called *advances*. **285**

overnight cash rate The interest rate for very-short-term interbank loans in the euro area. **425**

overnight interest rate (reference rate) The interest rate at which participants borrow and lend overnight funds to each other in the money market. **392**

overnight rate The interest rate on overnight (one-day) securities. **390**

par value See *face value*. **71**

partisan business cycles Systematic and permanent differences in macroeconomic outcomes that differ by political party. **353**

payment technology Methods of payment that include credit cards and electronic payments. **521**

payments system The method of conducting transactions in the economy. **54**

perpetuity See *consol*. **77**

Phillips curve theory A theory suggesting that changes in inflation are influenced by the state of the economy relative to its production capacity, as well as to other factors. **453**

planned expenditure The total amount of spending on domestically produced goods and services that households, businesses, the government, and foreigners want to make. **530**

planned investment spending Total planned spending by businesses on new physical capital (e.g., machines, computers, apartment buildings) plus planned spending on new homes. **531**, **565**

policy instrument A variable that is very responsive to the central bank's tools and indicates the stance of monetary policy (also called an *operating instrument*). **448**

policy rate The target for the Bank of Canada's overnight interest rate. **392**

policy trilemma Situation in which a country cannot pursue the following three policies at the same time: free capital mobility, a fixed exchange rate, and an independent monetary policy. **495**

political business cycle A business cycle caused by expansionary policies before an election. **352**, **638**

portfolio A collection or group of assets. **37**

potential output The level of aggregate output produced at the natural rate of unemployment (also called *natural rate of output*). **433**, **571**

preferred habitat theory A theory that is closely related to liquidity premium theory, in which the interest rate on a long-term bond equals an average of short-term interest rates expected to occur over the life of the long-term bond plus a positive term premium. **134**

premium The amount paid for an option contract. **323**

present discounted value See *present value*. **69**

present value Today's value of a payment to be received in the future when the interest rate is i. Also called *present discounted value*. **69**

price shocks   Shifts in inflation that are independent of the amount of slack in the economy or expected inflation. **572**

price stability   Low and stable inflation. **430**

primary dealers   Government securities dealers, operating out of private firms or commercial banks, with whom the central bank's open market desk trades. **404**

primary market   A financial market in which new issues of a security are sold to initial buyers. **25**

principal–agent problem   A moral hazard problem that occurs when the managers in control (the agents) act in their own interest rather than in the interest of the owners (the principals) due to different sets of incentives. **181**

printing money   See *monetizing the debt*. **520**

prudential supervision   See *financial supervision*. **228**

put option   An option contract that provides the right to sell a security at a specified price. **325**

put premium   Price of a put option. **325**

quantity theory of money   The theory that nominal income is determined solely by movements in the quantity of money. **515**

quantitative easing   An expansion of the central bank's balance sheet. **425**

quotas   Restrictions on the quantity of foreign goods that can be imported. **466**

random walk   The unpredictable movements in the price of a security. **158**

rate of capital gain   The change in a security's price relative to the initial purchase price. **80**

rate of return   See *return*. **79**

rational expectations   Expectations that reflect optimal forecasts (the best guess of the future) using all available information. **153**

real business cycle theory   A theory that views real shocks to tastes and technology as the major driving force behind short-run business cycle fluctuations. **588**

real exchange rate   The rate at which domestic goods can be exchanged for foreign goods; i.e., the price of domestic relative to foreign goods denominated in domestic currency. **464**

real interest rate   The interest rate adjusted for expected changes in the price level (inflation) so that it more accurately reflects the true cost of borrowing. **83**

real money balances   The quantity of money in real terms. **522**

real terms   Terms reflecting actual goods and services one can buy. **84**

recession   A period when aggregate output is declining. **7**

recognition lag   The time it takes for policymakers to be sure of what the data are signalling about the future course of the economy. **615**

redeposits   Transfers of government deposits from the Bank of Canada to direct clearers. **406**

Regulation Q   The regulation under which the Federal Reserve System had the power to set maximum interest rates that banks can pay on time deposits. **257**

regulatory arbitrage   A process in which banks keep on their books assets that have the same risk-based capital requirement but are relatively risky, such as a loan to a company with a very low credit rating, while taking off their books low-risk assets, such as a loan to a company with a very high credit rating. **228**

repo   See *special Purchase and Resale Agreements*. **404**

repurchase agreement (repo)   An arrangement whereby the central bank, or another party, purchases securities with the understanding that the seller will repurchase them in a short period of time, usually less than a week. **205**

reserve currency   A currency, such as the U.S. dollar, that is used by other countries to denominate the assets they hold as international reserves. **490**

reserves   Banks' settlement balances with the Bank of Canada plus currency that is physically held by banks (vault cash). **285, 367**

residual claimant   The right as a shareholder to receive whatever remains after all other claims against the firm's assets have been satisfied. **148**

restrictive covenants   Provisions that restrict and specify certain activities that a borrower can engage in. **173**

return   The payments to the owner of a security plus the change in the security's value, expressed as a fraction of its purchase price. More precisely called the rate of return. **79**

return on assets (ROA)   Net profit after taxes per dollar of assets. **296**

return on equity (ROE)   Net profit after taxes per dollar of equity capital. **296**

revaluation   Resetting of the fixed value of a currency at a higher level. **492**

reverse repo   See *Sale and Repurchase Agreements*. **404**

reverse transactions   Purchase or sale of eligible assets by the central bank under repurchase agreements or credit operations against eligible assets as collateral that are reversed within two weeks. **425**

reverses   Banks' holdings of deposits in accounts with the central bank plus currency that is physically held by banks (vault cash). **404**

risk   The degree of uncertainty associated with the return on an asset. **36**

risk of default   See *default*. **120**

risk premium   The spread between the interest rate on bonds with default risk and the interest rate on default-free bonds. **121**

risk sharing   The process of creating and selling assets with risk characteristics that people are comfortable with and then using the funds acquired by selling these assets to purchase other assets that may have far more risk. **36**

risk structure of interest rates   The relationship among the interest rates on various bonds with the same term to maturity. **120**

rules   Binding plans that specify how policy will respond (or not respond) to particular data such as unemployment and inflation. **636**

Sale and Repurchase Agreements (SRAs)   The Bank of Canada's sale of government securities to primary dealers with an agreement to repurchase them one business day later. **404**

sarbanes-oxley act   Passed by U.S. Congress in 2002, Sarbanes-Oxley aims to strengthen the integrity of the auditing process and the quality of information provided in corporate financial statements. **232**

Schedule I banks   Comprised of the Big Six, together with the Laurentian Bank of Canada, the Canadian Western Bank, and another 14 domestic banks. **261**

Schedule II banks   Comprised of 55 banks, including a number of domestic Schedule II banks and foreign bank subsidiaries. **261**

Schedule III banks   Foreign banks allowed to branch directly into Canada, under certain restrictions. **261**

secondary market   A financial market in which securities that have previously been issued (and are thus secondhand) can be resold. **25**

secondary reserves   Short-term government securities held by banks. **286**

secured debt   Debt guaranteed by collateral. **173**

securitization   The process of transforming illiquid financial assets into marketable capital market instruments. **255**

security   A claim on the borrower's future income that is sold by the borrower to the lender. Also called a *financial instrument*. **3**

segmented markets theory   A theory of term structure that sees markets for different-maturity bonds as completely separated and segmented such that the interest rate for bonds of a given maturity is determined solely by supply of and demand for bonds of that maturity. **132**

seigniorage   The revenue a government receives by issuing money. **249, 507**

self-correcting mechanism   A characteristic of the economy that causes output to return eventually to the natural rate level regardless of where it is initially. **581**

settlement balances   Deposits held by directly clearing members of the Canadian Payments Association at the Bank of Canada. They are also known as *clearing balances.* **285, 367**

shadow banking system   A system in which bank lending is replaced by lending via the securities market. **251**

short in a call   Sale of a call option. **324**

short in a put   Sale of a put option. **325**

short position   A contractual obligation to deliver an underlying financial instrument. **312**

short sales   Borrowing stock from brokers and then selling the stock in the market, with the hope that a profit will be earned by buying the stock back again ("covering the short") after it has fallen in price. **164**

short-term   With reference to a debt instrument, having a maturity of one year or less. **25**

simple deposit multiplier   The multiple increase in deposits generated from an increase in the banking system's reserves in a simple model in which the behaviour of depositors and banks plays no role. **375**

simple loan   A credit market instrument providing the borrower with an amount of funds that must be repaid to the lender at the maturity date along with an additional payment (interest). **69**

smart card   A stored-value card that contains a computer chip that lets it be loaded with digital cash from the owner's bank account whenever needed. **56**

sovereign loans   Loans to foreign governments and their agencies in the less developed countries. **273**

sovereign wealth fund   A state-owned investment fund that invests in foreign assets. **284**

special Purchase and Resale Agreements (sPRAs)   The Bank of Canada's purchase of government securities from primary dealers with an agreement to resell them one business day later. **404**

specials   See *term Purchase and Resale Agreements (PRAs)* and *Sale and Repurchase Agreements (SRAs).* **404**

speculative attack   A situation in which speculators engage in massive sales of a currency. **492**

spot exchange rate   The exchange rate for a spot transaction. **461**

spot rate   The interest rate at a given moment. **140**

spot transaction   The predominant type of exchange rate transaction, involving the immediate exchange of bank deposits denominated in different currencies. **461**

stagflation   A situation of rising inflation but a falling level of aggregate output. **586**

standing lending facility   A lending facility in which healthy banks are allowed to borrow all they want from a central bank. **410**

standing liquidity facilities   Refers to the Bank of Canada standing ready to lend to or borrow from a participant to bring their settlement balances to zero at the end of the banking day. **395**

state banks   State-chartered banks in the United States. **247**

state-owned banks   Banks that are owned by governments. **189**

sterilized foreign exchange intervention   A foreign exchange intervention with an offsetting open market operation that leaves the monetary base unchanged. **486**

stock   A security that is a claim on the earnings and assets of a company. **3**

stockholders   Those who hold stock in a corporation, own an interest in the corporation. **147** equal to the percentage of outstanding shares they own.

stock market risk   The risk associated with fluctuations in stock prices. **322**

stock option   An option on an individual stock. **324**

store of value   A repository of purchasing power over time. **53**

stress tests   Tests of financial institutions that calculate losses and the need for more capital under dire scenarios. **231**

structured credit products   Securities that are derived from cash flows of underlying assets and are tailored to have particular risk characteristics that appeal to investors with different preferences. **201**

subprime mortgages   Mortgages for borrowers with less than stellar credit records. **256**

supply curve   A curve depicting the relationship between quantity supplied and price when all other economic variables are held constant. **93**

supply shock   Any change in technology or the supply of raw materials that can shift the aggregate supply curve. **572**

swap   A financial contract that obligates one party to exchange (swap) a set of payments it owns for a set of payments owned by another party. **332**

sweep account   An arrangement in which any balances above a certain amount in a corporation's chequing account at the end of a business day are "swept out" of the account and invested in overnight repos that pay the corporation interest. **259**

systemic risk   The risk to the entire payments system due to the inability of one financial institution to fulfill its payment obligations in a timely fashion. **391**

systemically important financial institutions (SIFIs)   Firms designated as systemically important that are subject to additional oversight and regulation. **215**

T-account   A simplified balance sheet with lines in the form of a T that lists only the changes that occur in balance sheet items starting from some initial balance sheet position. **287**

target financing rate   The European Central Bank's target for the overnight cash rate, the interest rate for very-short-term interbank loans in the euro area. **425**

tariffs   Taxes on imported goods. **466**

Taylor principle   The principle that the monetary authorities should raise nominal interest rates by more than the increase in the inflation rate. **452, 551**

Taylor rule   Economist John Taylor's monetary policy rule that explains how the federal funds rate target is set. **452**

term Purchase and Resale Agreements (PRAs)   The Bank of Canada's purchase of government securities from primary dealers with an agreement to resell then at a specified future date. **414**

term repo   See *term Purchase and Resale Agreements (PRAs).* **414**

term structure of interest rates   The relationship among interest rates on bonds with different terms to maturity. **120**

theory of efficient capital markets   See efficient market hypothesis. **155**

theory of portfolio choice   A theory of how much of an asset people want to hold in their portfolio, with the amounts determined by wealth, expected returns, risk, and liquidity. **91**

theory of purchasing power parity (PPP)   The theory that exchange rates between any two currencies will adjust to reflect changes in the price levels of the two countries. **464**

time-inconsistency problem   The problem that occurs when monetary policymakers conduct monetary policy in a discretionary way and pursue expansionary policies that are attractive in the short run but lead to bad long-run outcomes. **431**

too-big-to-fail problem   It refers to certain financial institutions that must be supported by government when they face potential failure, because their failure will create big problems for the entire financial system. **225**

trade balance   The difference between merchandise exports and imports. **488**

trading at par   See *at the money option.* **325**

transaction costs   The time and money spent trying to exchange financial assets, goods, or services. **36**

transmission mechanisms of monetary policy   The channels through which the money supply affects economic activity. **653**

Troubled Asset Relief Plan (TARP) Provision of the Bush administration's Economic Recovery Act of 2008 that authorized the Treasury to spend $700 billion to purchase subprime mortgage assets from troubled financial institutions or to inject capital into these institutions. **209**

trustee The representative of a person or corporation. **268**

underwriting Purchasing securities from a corporation at a predetermined price and then reselling them in the market. **25, 42**

unemployment rate The percentage of the labour force not working. **7**

unexploited profit opportunity A situation in which an investor can earn a higher than normal return. **157**

unit of account Anything used to measure value in an economy. **52**

unsecured debt Debt not guaranteed by collateral. **173**

unsterilized foreign exchange intervention A foreign exchange intervention in which a central bank allows the purchase or sale of domestic currency to affect the monetary base. **485**

value at risk (VaR) Calculations that measure the size of the loss on a trading portfolio that might happen 1% of the time over a short period—say two weeks. **231**

venture capital firm A financial intermediary that pools the resources of its partners and uses the funds to help entrepreneurs start up new businesses. **183**

vault cash Currency that is physically held by banks and stored in vaults overnight. **285**

velocity of money The rate of turnover of money; the average number of times per year that a dollar is spent in buying the total amount of final goods and services produced in the economy. **514**

virtual bank A bank that has no building but rather exists only in cyberspace. **254**

wealth All resources owned by an individual, including all assets. **51**

World Bank The International Bank for Reconstruction and Development, an international organization that provides long-term loans to assist developing countries in building dams, roads, and other physical capital that would contribute to their economic development. **490**

World Trade Organization (WTO) An organization headquartered in Geneva, Switzerland, that monitors rules for the conduct of trade between countries (tariffs and quotas). **490**

yield curve A plot of the interest rates for particular types of bonds with different terms to maturity. **127**

yield to maturity The interest rate that equates the present value of payments received from a credit market instrument with its value today. **72**

zero-coupon bond See *discount bond.* **72**

zero-lower-bound problem The liquidity trap a central bank faces when the short-term nominal interest rate is zero or near zero. **413**

INDEX

Note: Page numbers followed by, *b*, *f*, or *t* represent boxes, figures, or tables, respectively.

A

Abe, Shinzo, 628
Abenomics program, 628–629
Accountability, 439
Accounting, mark-to-market, 232
Activists, 615–616
Act of Parliament, 230, 250, 277
Adaptive expectations, 153, 604
Adjustable-rate mortgages, 252
Adjusted forward-rate forecast, 141
Advances, 285
Adverse selection, 17, 23–24, 175, 196*f*, 197–198, 200–202, 659–660
  asymmetric information problems of, 289
  collateral and, 180
  financial institutions and, 302
  financial intermediaries and, 178–180
  in financial markets, 37
  government regulation and, 177–178
  government safety net and, 225
  influence on financial structure, 175–181
  in loan markets, 299
  private production and, 177
  sale of information and, 177
  tools for solving, 176–180, 187*t*
After-tax real interest rate formula, 85
Afxentiou, Panos, 353*b*
Agency theory, 175, 194
Aggregate Canadian Market Capitalization, 30
Aggregate demand, 401–402, 497
  components of, 531–536
  consumption expenditure and, 531–532
  curve, 567–571, 567*f*
  deriving, 566–567
  government purchases and, 531, 535
  net exports and, 531, 534–535
  planned expenditure and, 530–531

  planned investment spending and, 531–534
  taxes and, 535–536
Aggregate demand—aggregate supply (AD/AS) model, 530
  distinction between shifts in MP curve *vs* movements along MP curve, 554
  of foreign business cycle episodes, 591–595
  zero lower bound, 626
Aggregate demand and supply analysis
  adjustment to long-run equilibrium in, 579, 580*f*
  self-correcting mechanism, 581
  short-run equilibrium, 578–581
Aggregate demand curves, 565
  algebraically, 557
  deriving, 555–557, 556*f*, 557, 557*b*, 566–567
  factors that shift, 557–558, 560*f*, 567–571, 567*f*, 570*f*
  graphical representation os, 555–557, 556*f*, 558*f*
  positive demand shock, 581*f*
  vs shifts in *IS* curve, 557–558, 559*f*
  vs shifts in *MP* curve, 558, 560*f*
  with zero lower bound, 621–623, 622*f*
Aggregate demand shocks, 610, 615
  Bank of Canada Disinflation, 1981–1985, 582–583, 583*f*
  changes in equilibrium and, 581
  credibility and, 640–643, 642*f*
  effects of a rightward shift in curve, 583*f*
  inflation shocks and, 584–591
  negative, 641–643
  Negative Demand Shocks in the United States, 2001–2004, 584
  positive, 641
Aggregate income, 19
Aggregate output, 7, 566
  unemployment and, 566*b*
Aggregate price level, 8, 20
Aggregate supply curve
  expected inflation and, 571
  long-run, 571, 572*f*

  shifts in, 573–577
  short-run, 571–573, 572*f*
Aggregate supply shocks, 610, 615
  credibility and, 643–644
  negative supply shocks, 1973–1975 and 1978–1980, 587
  permanent negative supply shock, 587–590
  positive supply shocks, 1995–1999, 590–591
  temporary supply shocks, 584–587
AIG (American International Group), 197, 203, 208–209, 212, 215, 224, 226, 336–337
Alberta Treasury Branches (ATB) Financial, 271
American options, 323
American Recovery and Reinvestment Act of 2009 (U.S.), 616*b*
Anchor country, 501–504, 506–507, 649
Anchor currency, 489, 491, 494–495
Animal spirits, 533, 539
Annual percentage rate (APR), 232
Annuities, 41, 60*f*, 61
Anti-inflation program, 647*b*
Appreciation, 12, 462
Arbitrage, 157
Asset-backed commercial paper (ABCP) market, 210, 211*b*
Asset demand, determinants of, 89–91
Asset holdings, restriction on, 226–227
Asset-liability management (ALM) committee, 294
Asset management, 290, 293–294
Asset market approach, 95
Asset-price boom and bust, 197
Asset-price bubbles, 197
  credit-driven, 444–445
  driven by irrational exuberance, 445
  leaning against asset-price bubbles *vs* cleaning up, 445–446
  tech-stock bubble, 445
Asset prices, 7, 14, 95
Assets, 3
  cash item in process of collection, 286
  deposits, 286
  loans, 286–287
  physical capital, 287
  reserves, 285–286
  securities, 286

Asset transformation, 17, 37, 287
Asymmetric information, 37–38, 175
    in banking industry, 234b
    financial intermediaries and, 37–38
    government safety net and,
        222–226
    problems and tools to solve them,
        187t
At the money, 325, 327
Audits, 43t, 178, 232, 246f
Automated banking machine (ABM),
    254
Automated Clearing Settlement System
    (ACSS), 277, 392
Automated teller machine (ATM), 253,
    265–266
Autonomous consumption, 543
Autonomous consumption
    expenditure, 531, 559, 569
Autonomous easing of monetary policy,
    553f, 554, 555f, 561, 581, 614f
Autonomous investment, 533,
    543–544, 570
Autonomous investment spending,
    543–544
Autonomous monetary policy, 553f,
    560f, 567–569, 611f
Autonomous net exports, 534–535,
    544–545, 569
Autonomous spending, 543
Autonomous tightening of monetary
    policy, 553, 567f, 582, 611f,
    613f

B

Backup credit lines, 306
Balance of payments, 488–489
Balance-of-payments crises, 494
Balance sheet channel, 658–659
Bank Act, 1881–1913, 249–250
Bank Act of 1936, 235t
Bank Act of 1946, 361
Bank Act of 1954, 235t
Bank Act of 1967, 235t
Bank Act of 1981, 235t
Bank Act of 1992, 236t
Bank Act of 1997, 236t
Bank Act Reform, 2001, 262,
    275–278
    bank holding companies,
        275–276
    Canadian Payments Association Act
        to Canadian Payments Act
        (CP Act), 277

merger review policy, 277–278
ownership rules, 276–277
permitted investment regime, 276
Bank Act Reform of 2001, 236t
Bank balance sheet
    of all banks in Canada, 2014, 284t
    assets, 285–287
    liabilities, 283–285
Bank capital, 285
    prevention of bank failure, role in,
        295–296
    requirements, 297
    returns to equity holders and,
        296–297
    strategies for managing, 297–298
Bank credit cards, 253
Bank deposits, 6, 257, 265
Banker's risk, 286
Bank failure, 222
Bank for International Settlements
    (BIS), 227, 308, 358b, 391
Bank holding companies, 265,
    275–276
Banking, 287–289
    crisis, 197–198
    decline of traditional banking
        business, 259–261
    largest banks in world, 274t
    loss of income advantages due to
        financial innovations, 260
Bank lending channel, 658
Bank loans, 170, 171f
Bank management, general principles
    of asset management, 293–294
    capital adequacy management,
        295–297
    liability management, 294–295
    liquidity management, 290–293
    reserves, 290–293
Bank of America, 208, 254,
    264t, 268b
Bank of Canada, 11, 43t, 44,
    108, 224
    ability to control the monetary base,
        372
    accountability and transparency, 351
    approach to monetary policy,
        399–403
    argument for and against
        independence of, 352–354
    assets, 367
    balance sheet, 366–367
    bank rate, 292
    Board of Directors, 343–344

ceiling on the overnight interest
        rate, 411f
    central role in Canada's national
        payments system, 346
    changing face of, 349–351
    commitments to future policy
        actions, 419
    communications activities, 350
    controllability of short-term interest
        rates, 451
    controlling inflation and stabilizing
        real output, 452
    daily drawdowns, 406
    degree of independence of, 347–349
    deposits in an account at, 285–286
    disinflation, 582–583, 583f
    drawdown/redeposit mechanism,
        406
    evolution of monetary policy frame-
        work, 349–351
    financial system of, 345–346
    foreign exchange interventions by,
        484–486
    functions of, 344–346
    funds management, 345
    goal of low inflation, 346
    Governing Council of, 344
    government deposits at, 371
    governors, 344b
    holdings of securities, 367
    implementation of operating band
        for overnight interest rate,
        395–396
    internal organization of, 344
    level of monetary conditions and,
        401
    loans to financial institutions, 370–371
    managing rate of inflation,
        401f–402f
    monetary aggregates, 58, 59t
    monetary liabilities (currency in
        circulation and reserves),
        366–367, 371
    monetary policy and, 346, 392,
        395–396, 399–403, 550–551
    open market operations, 368–369,
        404–406
    open market sale operations, 369
    operating procedures limit fluctua-
        tions in the overnight interest rate,
        398, 399f
    operation of standing lending facility,
        410–412
    origins, 342–343

policy rate, 392
political environment and, 344*b*
preamble to legislation governing, 350
in preservation of integrity and safety of Canadian currency, 345
reserves, 367
role as federal government's "fiscal agent," 345
role as lender of last resort, 410–411
shift from deposits to currency, 370
standing liquidity facilities, 395
structure of, 343–344
system of "joint responsibility," 346
use of the Taylor Rule, 454*b*
victory over inflation, 648
watchers, 454*b*
Bank of Canada Act (1934), 235*t*
Bank of Canada Act (1992), 257
Bank of Canada Act, Amended, 1967, 349
Bank of Credit and Commerce International (BCCI), 234*b*
Bank of England, 234b, 344, 355, 361–362
inflation targeting, 438
Bank of Japan (Nippon Ginko), 361–362, 441, 628–629
Bank of Montreal, 29, 246, 271, 273, 277
Bank of New Brunswick, 246–247
Bank of Nova Scotia, 261, 262*t*, 271
Bank of Upper Canada, 197, 246, 248
Bank panics, 199, 223
form of government safety net and, 224
need for deposit insurance and, 222–224
Bank rate, 292, 367, 402
Banks, 6
holdings of securities, 286
lending to, 425
Barings Bank, 306
Barings collapse, 307*b*
Barter economy, 51
Basel Accord, 227, 229*b*
Basel Committee on Banking Supervision, 227, 229*b*
Base money, 346
Basic gap analysis, 303
Basis points, 125
BBB credit rating, 335
BBB-treasury spread in U.S., 124–125

Bearer deposit notes, 28
Bear Stearns, 7, 197, 208, 224, 226, 268*b*
Behavioural finance, 163–164
Bent, Bruce, 258, 258*b*
Bernanke, Ben, 202b, 205b, 205*b*, 418, 440, 626, 640, 655
Bitcoin, 58
"Black Monday," 4, 163, 412
Blanchard, Olivier, 610
Board of Directors of Bank of Canada, 343–344
Board of Governors of the Federal Reserve System, 355
Bolivia, 647*b*
Bolivian hyperinflation, 647*b*
Bond, 3, 23
Bond market, 3
demand curve, 92–93
lemons problem in, 176
market equilibrium, 94–95
supply and demand in, 92–95
supply curve, 93–94
Bond ratings
by DBRS, Moody's, Standard & Poor's, and Fitch, 123*t*
Bonds, 170, 171*f*
Borrowed reserves, 367, 372, 378
Borrowings, 285
Branches, bank, 247, 250, 254*b*
Brazil, 273, 431, 436, 460
"Breaking the buck" situation, 258*b*
Bretton Woods system, 490, 497
British-style universal banking system, 267
Brokerage firms, 211*b*, 232, 266
Brokers, 26
Brown, Gordon, 361
Brown, Henry, 258
Bubbles, 162
Budget deficits, 11–12, 11*f*, 352
government, 100–101
inflation and, 519–521
Budget surplus, 11
Bundesbank, 493–494, 500
Bundler, 256
Bureaucratic behavior theory, 354–355
Bush, George H. W., 358
Bush, George W., 358
Business cycles
interest rate and, 103–104, 104*f*
response to, 103*f*
Business expectations, 533

C
Caisses populaires, 6, 61, 245, 263, 266, 268–270, 277, 287
Call option, 324
Call (or redemption), 31
Call premium, 324
Call reports, 230
CAMELS rating, 228, 231
Canada
Canadian exchange rate, 1974–2014, 462*f*
central bank of, 343*b*
disintermediation process, 261
foreign banks in, 273–274
inflation rates and inflation targets, 1980–2014, 400*f*
inflation targeting in, 436–438, 437*f*
Large Value Transfer System (LVTS), 391
liquidity provision in, 414
purchasing power parity (PPP), 466*f*
reserve requirements, 257
Canada bond futures, 328–330
Canada bonds, 71, 124–125
yield curves for, 139*f*
Canada Deposit Insurance Corporation Act (1967), 235*t*
Canada Deposit Insurance Corporation (CDIC), 43*t*, 45, 223, 228, 237–241, 258, 411
banking regulations, 241
differential premiums, 237–238
Opting-Out By-law, 238
prompt corrective action provisions of, 239–240
provisions, 240
reductions of scope of deposit insurance by limiting insurance, 239
risk-based premiums, 240
Canada Mortgage and Housing Corporation (CMHC), 31, 224
Canada Premium Bonds (CPBs), 12
Canadas, 32
Canada's asset-backed commercial paper crisis, 211*b*
Canada Savings Bonds (CSBs), 31–32
Canadian banking system
Bank Act Reform, 2001, 275–278
bank holding companies, 265, 275–276
bank ownership laws, 263
branching restrictions, 264–266
Canadian banking overseas, 273

Canadian banking system (*Cont.*)
Canadian Payments Association Act to Canadian Payments Act (CP Act), 277
chartered banking industry, 261–263
cooperatives, 269–270
credit unions, 269–270
financial innovations, 251–261
four-pillar approach to, 266–268
free banking, concept of, 247–248
government savings institutions, 271
growth in international banking, 271–274
historical development, 246–250
insured commercial banks, 264*t*
list of banks, 262*t*
loan companies, 269
merger review policy, 277–278
ownership rules, 276–277
permitted investment regime, 276
separation of banking and other financial services, 267–268
shadow banking system, 251–261
trustees, 268–269
vs United States, 263–266
Canadian Commercial Bank, 413*b*
Canadian Derivatives Clearing Corporation (CDCC), 324
Canadian government Treasury bill, 91
Canadian Life and Health Insurance Compensation Corporation (CompCorp), 43*t*
Canadian Mint account, 366
Canadian Payments Association Act to Canadian Payments Act (CP Act), 277
Canadian Payments Association (CPA), 277, 392
Canadian Tire, 263
Capital, 24
Capital account, 488
Capital adequacy management, 290, 295–297
bank capital and returns to equity holders, 296–297
bank capital requirements, 297
prevention of bank failure, 295–296
trade-off between safety and returns to equity holders, 297
Capital controls, 496
on inflows, 498–499
on outflows, 498
Capital market, 26–27

Capital market instruments, 29–32
Canada Savings Bonds (CSBs), 31–32
consumers and bank commercial loans, 32
corporate bonds, 31
government agency securities, 32
Government of Canada Bonds, 31
mortgages and mortgage-backed securities, 30–31
municipal bonds or municipals, 32
provincial bonds or provincials, 32
stocks, 30
Capital requirements, as financial regulation, 227–228
Carney, Mark, 361
Cash flows, 68, 148
Cash items, 286
Cashless society, 57*b*
Central banks, 11, 247
asset-price bubbles, role in controlling, 445–448
Bank of England, 361–362
Bank of Japan (Nippon Ginko), 361–362
bureaucratic behaviour, 354–355
credibility, 648–650
European Central Bank (ECB), 359–362
Federal Reserve System, 355–359
independence of, 352–354
inflation targeting and, 439–440
macroeconomic performance and, 354
policy instruments, 448–451
structure and independence of, 355–362
transparency and accountability of, 439–440
worldwide, 343*b*
Certificate of deposit (CD), 28–29
Ceteris paribus, 92, 108
Channel/corridor system
quantitative easing in, 416*b*
for setting the overnight interest rate, 393, 396–398, 409–410
Chartered bank, 230
Chartered banking industry, 261–263
Chartered banks, 40–41
Chartering financial institutions, 228–230
Chequable deposit, 284
Cheques, 55–56

China
accumulation of $4 trillion of international reserves, 496
2007–2009 financial crisis and, 593–595, 595*f*
state of financial development in, 189–190
Clinton, Bill, 358
Coinsurance, 239
Collateral, 173, 180, 184–185
requirements for loans, 301–302
Treasury bills as, 29
tyranny of, 188*b*
Collateralized debt obligations (CDOs), 202, 202*b*, 205
Commercial paper, 29
Commercial paper market, 255
Commitments to future policy actions, 419
Commodity Futures Trading Commission (CFTC), 324
Commodity money, 54–55
Common stock, 3
Common stock, price of
models, 147–150
monetary policy and, 152
role of markets in setting, 150–151
Compensating balances, 301–302
Competition, restrictions on, 232
Conflicts of interest
financial intermediaries and, 38–39
"Conservative" central banker, 649–650
Consols, 77
Constant-money-growth-rate rule, 637
Constrained discretion, 639–640
Consumer durable expenditure, 654
Consumer expenditure, 657
Consumer Financial Protection Bureau, 215
Consumer price index (CPI), 400, 566, 566*b*
Consumer Protection Act of 2010, 214–215
Consumer protection regulation, 232
Consumers and bank commercial loans, 32
Consumption, 657
Consumption expenditure, 531–532, 565
Consumption function, 531–532
Contagion effect, 223

Contractual savings institutions, 41–42
Convergence, 266–267
Convertible bonds, 31
Cooperative Credit Associations Act (1992), 236t
Cooperatives, 269–270
Corporate bonds, 31, 71, 125
  default risk on, 122f
  purchase by contractual savings institutions, 41
Correspondent banking, 286
Costly state verification, 182
Cost-push inflation, 618–619, 619f, 621
Cost-push shocks, 572
Coupon bond, 71
  bond price for, 75
  yield to maturity on, 74–77
Coupon rate, 71
Covenants, monitoring and enforcement of restrictive, 300
Coyne, James, 348–349
Coyne Affair, 349
Credibility, 640
  aggregate demand shocks and, 640–643, 642f
  aggregate supply shocks and, 643–644
  anti-inflation policy and, 646–648, 646f
  Bank of Canada's victory over inflation and, 648
  central bank, 648–650
Credible nominal anchor, 640
Credit boom, 195
Credit default swap, 203, 215, 336–337
Credit derivatives
  credit-linked notes, 336
  credit options, 335
  credit swaps, 336
Credit-driven bubbles, 444–445
  bursting of, 446
Credit easing, 416–418
Credit-linked notes, 336
Credit market instruments
  coupon bond, 71
  discount bond, 72
  fixed-payment loan, 71
  simple loan, 71
Credit options, 335
Credit-rating agencies, 123, 124b

Credit rationing, 302
Credit risk, 290
  collateral requirements and, 301–302
  compensating balances and, 301–302
  loan commitments, 301
  long-term customer relationships, 300–301
  management of, 298–302
  screening and monitoring, 299–300
Credit spread, 200, 534
Credit swaps, 336
Credit Union Central of Canada (CUCC), 270
Credit unions, 277, 287
Credit Unions and Caisses Populaires (CUCPs), 41
Credit view of transmission mechanisms, 655, 658–661
Currency, 50
Currency board, 505–506
  of Argentine, 506b
Currency swaps, 332
Current account, 488
Current yield, 78

D

Daily drawdowns, 406
Data lag, 615
Dealers, 26
Debt contracts, 173
  moral hazard and, 183
Debt deflation, 198
Debt market, 25
Debt ratings, 124b
Default-free bonds, 121
Default risk, 120–124
Deflation, 441
Deleveraging, 195
Demand and supply curves for reserves, 396
Demand curve for bond, 92–93
  liquidity preference framework and, 105–107
  shifts in, 96–99, 96f
Demand curve for domestic assets, 467–468
Demand curve for money, 106
Demand curve for reserves, 396–397, 397f
Demand deposits, 284

Demand for money, 515
  empirical evidence for, 524–525
  factors influencing, 523–524, 524t
  interest rates and, 525
  Keynesian theories of, 521–522
  liquidity of assets and, 524, 524t
  portfolio theories of, 523–524
  risk and, 523–524, 524t
  stability of, 525
  wealth and, 523, 524t
Demand-pull inflation, 619–621, 620f, 621
Deposit facility, 425
Depository institutions, 40–41
Deposit outflows, 290–294
Deposit rate ceilings, 257
Deposits, 286
Depreciation, 462
Derivatives, 215
Desired reserve ratio, 286, 367
Desired reserves, 286, 367, 378–379
Devaluation, 491
Direct clearers, 392
Direct finance, 23
Dirty float, 489
Disclosure requirements, 231–232
Discount bond, 72
  yield to maturity on, 78–79
Discount factor, 148
Discount rate, 419
Discount window lending, 419
Discretion, 636
  case for, 638–639
  constrained, 639–640
Disintermediation, 257
Disintermediation process, 259
Disposable income, 531
Distributor, 256
Diversification, 37
Dividends, 25, 148
Divine coincidence, 610
Dodd-Frank bill, 214–215
Dollarization, 507
Domestic assets
  demand curve for, 467–468
  shifts in the demand for, 469–472, 473t
  supply curve for, 467
Domestic interest rate, 469–470, 470f
  inflation and, 475f
Dominated assets, 523
Dominion Bond Rating Service (DBRS), 123
Dominion Notes Act, 1870, 248–249

Dow Jones Industrial Average (New York), 34
DRs (Deposit Receipts), 29
Dual banking system of United States, 247*b*
Dual mandate, 435
Duration analysis, 303–304

E

E-cash, 56
"Econometric Policy Evaluation: A Critique" (Lucas), 635
Economies of scale, 36
Economies of scope, 267
   financial intermediaries and, 38–39
Effectiveness lag, 616
Efficient market hypothesis, 155–162
   "buy and hold" strategy, 161–162
   changes in stock prices, 161
   efficiency of, 162
   efficient market condition, 158
   expectations of future prices, 156
   expected return on a security, 157
   hot tips, 161
   optimal forecast of the return, 156
   random-walk stock prices, case of, 158–159
   rationale of, 157–158
   reports of investment advisers, 159–160
E-finance, 6
Electoral business cycles, 353
Electronic money (or e-money), 56–57
Electronic payment, 56
Emergency lending assistance, 413*b*
Emerging market countries, 498
Emerging-market countries
   dollarization, 507
   exchange-rate targeting, 505
Employment Act of 1946, 618
Enron collapse, 178*b*
Equation of exchange, 514
Equilibrium exchange rate, 474–475
Equilibrium interest rate, 94–105
   demand for money and, 108
   Fisher effect, 101–102
   liquidity preference framework and, 105–107
   supply and demand framework, 95–105
   supply of money and, 108, 109*t*

Equity capital, 180
Equity market, 25
Equity multiplier (EM), 296
Eurobond, 33–34
Eurocurrencies, 33–34
Eurocurrencies market, 271–272
Eurodollar market, 272*b*
Eurodollars, 33–34
European Central Bank
   monetary policy tools of, 425–426
   reserve requirements, 426
European Central Bank (ECB), 359–362
   degree of independence, 360–361
   Governing Council, 360
   monetary policy strategy, 438*b*
   monetary policy tools of, 419, 425–426
   open market operations, 425
   reserve requirements, 426
European Monetary System (EMS), 491
European options, 324
European Sovereign Debt Crisis, 207*b*
European System of Central Banks (ESCB), 359, 434
   vs Federal Reserve System, 359–360
Eurosystem, 359
Eurozone, 495
Ex ante real interest rate, 83
Excess demand, 94
Excess reserves, 367, 379
   ratio and currency ratio, 2007–2014, 385*f*
Excess supply, 94
Exchange Fund Account of the Department of Finance, 345
Exchange rate, 536
Exchange rate mechanism (ERM), 491
Exchange-rate peg, 501
Exchange rates, 461
   asset-market approach to, 476
   barriers to free trade and, 465–466
   Bretton Woods system, 490–491
   Canadian, 1974–2014, 462*f*
   effects of changes in interest rates on equilibrium, 474–475
   expected future exchange rate, 471–472, 472*f*
   factors affecting, 465–467, 466*t*
   fixed exchange rate regime, 491–492
   floating exchange rate regime, 489
   gold standard, 490

   importance of, 463–464
   in international financial system, 489–493
   in the long run, 463–467
   managed float regime, 489, 497–498
   preferences for foreign goods and, 466
   productivity and, 466–467
   relative price levels and, 465
   supply and demand approaches to, 467–469
   volatility of, 476
Exchange-rate targeting, 501–505
   advantages, 502
   disadvantages, 502–504
   in emerging market (including transition) countries, 505
   in industrialized countries, 504–505
Exchanges, 26
Exercise price, 323–327, 329, 331
Exogenous expenditure, 531
Expectations theory, 128–132
Expected future exchange rate, 471–472, 472*f*
Expected inflation, 97*t*, 100, 571
   interest rate and, 1953-2014, 101–102, 102*f*
   management of, 627, 628*f*
   response to a change in, 101*f*
Expected-inflation effects, 113
Expected interest rate, 97*t*
Expected profitability of investment opportunities, 100
Expected returns, 90
Ex post real interest rate, 83
External funds, source of, 171, 171*f*

F

Face value or par value, 71
Fair-value accounting, 232
Fallen angels, 124, 255
Federal Deposit Insurance Corporation (FDIC), 234*b*
Federal funds rate, 357, 419
Federal Open Market Committee (FOMC), 355, 357, 419
Federal Reserve
   balance sheet, 2007–2014, 415*f*
   of depository institutions in the United States (in billions), 417*f*
   discount lending and, 422–424
   equilibrium, 420*f*

large-scale asset purchases, 414–415
monetary policy tools of, 419–421
open market operations and, 421–422
required reserve ratio, 423–424
response to a change in interest rate on, 424, 424f
Federal Reserve Bank of New York, 358b
Federal Reserve Banks, 355–356, 357f
Federal Reserve System, 355–359
 Board of Governors, 355
 degree of independence, 357–359
 Federal Reserve banks, 355–356, 357f
 structure and responsibility for policy tools in, 356f
Fiat money, 55
Finance Act of 1914, 250
Finance companies, 42
Finance paper, 29
Financial consolidation process, 267
Financial crises, 7
 of 2007–2009, 201–210
 asset-price boom and bust, 197
 banking crisis, 197–198
 bank panics, 199
 Canada's asset-backed commercial paper crisis, 211b
 continuing decline in stock prices, 200–201
 credit boom and bust, 195–197
 credit crunch during the global financial crisis, 298
 debt deflation, 198, 201
 defined, 195
 demise of large, free-standing investment banks, 268b
 dynamics of, 195–201
 events in advanced economies, 196f
 financial conditions of global financial crisis and Canada's banks, 212–213
 Great Depression, 199, 199f–200f
 international dimensions, 201
 lessons from, 336–337
 mark-to-market accounting and, 233b
 response of financial regulation and, 213–215
 stock market crash, 199
 subprime mortgage crisis in Canada, 210–213

too-big-to-fail problem and, 216–217
Financial derivatives, 203, 252
 dangers with, 336–337
 risk management with, 312–314
Financial engineering, 251
Financial frictions, 195, 534, 570
Financial futures
 advantage over forward markets, 320
 globalization of, 318–319
 interest-rate futures, 315–316
 organization of trading with, 317–318
 success of, 319–320
Financial futures options, 324
Financial innovations, 6, 195
 bank credit, 253
 commercial paper market, 255
 credit cards, 253
 decline of traditional banking and, 259–261
 electronic banking, 253–254
 home banking, 253–254
 information technology, role of, 252–255, 262–263
 junk bonds, 255
 of money market mutual funds, 258–259
 regulations, 257–258
 shadow banking system, 251–261
 of sweep accounts, 259
Financial Institutions and Deposit Insurance System Amendment Act (1987), 236t
Financial instruments, 23
Financial intermediaries, 5–6, 172, 267
 adverse selection and, 37, 178–180
 asymmetric information and, 37–38
 conflicts of interest and, 38–39
 contractual savings institutions, 41–42
 depository institutions, 40–41
 economies of scope and, 38–39
 function of, 35–39
 in interest-rate swaps, 334–335
 investment intermediaries, 42
 liquidity services, 38
 moral hazard and, 38
 primary assets and liabilities of, 39t
 process of indirect financing using, 35
 relative sizes of financial institutions and pension plans, 40t

relative to securities markets, 35
 risk sharing and, 36–37
 transaction costs and, 36
 types of, 39–42
Financial liberalization, 195
Financial markets, 403
 allocation of capital, 24
 debt and equity markets, 25
 exchanges and over-the-counter markets, 26
 framework for studying, 14–15
 function of, 22–24
 instruments, 27–32
 internationalization of, 32–34
 money and capital markets, 26–27
 need to study, 2–5
 primary and secondary markets, 25–26
 promoting economic efficiency, role in, 24
 rational expectations in, 156–162
 structure of, 25–27
 well-being of consumers and, 24
Financial panic, 44
Financial regulation
 assessment of risk management, 230–231
 asymmetric information and, 43–44
 on branching, 264–265
 Canada reserve requirements, 257
 capital requirements, 227–228
 chartering and examination, 228–230
 compensation and, 217
 consumer protection, 232
 credit-rating agencies and, 217
 differences between Canadian and abroad, 45
 disclosure requirements, 231–232
 disclosure requirements and, 44
 financial intermediary soundness and, 44–45
 government-sponsored enterprises (GSEs) and, 217
 higher capital requirements and, 216
 information availability and, 44
 international, 234b
 issues for future regulation, 217
 prompt corrective action, 228
 response to 2007–2009 financial crisis, 213–215

Financial regulation (*Cont.*)
  restrictions on asset holdings, 226–227
  restrictions on assets and activities, 44
  restrictions on competition, 232
  restrictions on competition among financial intermediaries, 45
  restrictions on entry, 44
  restrictions on interest paid on deposits, 257–258
  supervision and, 234
  systemically important financial institutions (SIFIs) and, 215–216
  too-big-to-fail problem and, 216–217
Financial supervision, 228
Financial system
  access to securities markets, 172
  collateral, 173
  debt contracts, 173
  of developing and transition countries, 187–189
  direct finance *vs* indirect finance, 172
  flows of funds through, 23*f*
  marketable debt and equity securities, 172
  regulation of, 43–45
  source of external financing for businesses, 171
  structure of, 5–7, 170–173
Financial System Review Act (FSRA) of March 29, 2012, 236*t*
Financial Times Stock Exchange (FTSE) 100-Share Index (London), 34
Fire sales of assets, 198
First Bank Act, 1871, 249
Fiscal policy, monetary policy *vs*, 11–12
Fiscal stimulus package of 2009, 543
Fisher, Irving, 102
Fisher effect, 101–102
Fisher equation, 83, 474
Fitch Ratings, 123
Fixed exchange rate regime, 489, 491–492
Fixed investment, 532
Fixed-payment loan, 71–72
  yearly payment, 74
  yield to maturity on, 73–74
Fixed-term deposits, 284–285
Fleming, Donald, 349
Float, 371

Floating exchange rate regime, 489
Ford Motor Credit Company, 42
Foreign bonds, 32
Foreign exchange crisis of September 1992, 493–494, 503
Foreign exchange interventions, 492*f*
  money supply and, 484–486
  sterilized, 486–488
  unsterilized, 485–486, 487*f*
Foreign exchange market, 12, 460–464
  equilibrium in, 468–469, 468*f*
  trades in, 464
Foreign exchange rate, 12
  for Canadian Dollar, 1971–2014, 13*f*
  direct effects on Canadian consumers, 12
  random-walk behaviour of, 159*b*
  volatility of, 476
Foreign exchange risk, hedging with, 320–322
Foreign interest rate, 470–471, 471*f*
Foreign Stock Market Indexes, 14*b*
Forward contracts, 313
  interest-rate, 313–314
  pros and cons of, 314
Forward exchange rate, 462
Forward guidance, 418–419
Forward rate, 140–142
Forward transactions, 462
Free banking, concept of, 247–248
Free Banking Act, 1850, 247
Free capital mobility, 495
Free-rider problem, 177
Friedman, Milton
  on inflation, 617
  A Monetary History of the United States, 637
  on Phillips curve, 348
Fully amortized loan, 71
Fundamental economic values, 197
Futures contracts, 252
  profits and losses on options *vs*, 328*f*
Futures options, 324, 327–332
  hedging with, 329–330

G

Gap analysis, 303–304
GDP deflator, 566, 566*b*
General Agreement on Tariffs and Trade (GATT), 490

General equilibrium, 578
Generalized dividend valuation model, 149
Generalized multi-period formula for stock valuation, 149
Generally Accepted Accounting Principles (GAAP) (Canada), 233*b*
Generally Accepted Accounting Principles (GAAP) (U.S.), 233*b*
Germany, 362
  central bank of, 343*b*
  European Central Bank, 359
  foreign exchange crisis of September 1992, 493–494, 503
  insurance companies in, 278
  real-time settlement systems, 391
  universal banking in, 267
GICs (Guaranteed Investment Certificates), 29
GIRs (Guaranteed Investment Receipts), 29
Glass-Steagall, 268*b*
Global financial crisis, 124*b*
  stock market and, 152
Global financial crisis of 2007–2009
  asymmetric information, role of, 203
  autonomous monetary easing on, 554
  causes of, 201–203
  credit-rating agencies, role of, 203
  credit spreads and, 209*f*
  decline in asset prices in stock market, 206
  deterioration of financial institutions' balance sheets, 205
  effects of, 203–208
  Eurozone and, 497*b*
  financial innovation in mortgage markets and, 201–202
  financial markets and, 207
  government intervention and recovery, 208–209
  height of, 208
  housing price bubble, 203–205, 204*f*, 205*b*
  money multiplier and, 382*b*
  principal—agent problem in mortgage markets, 202–203
  rising defaults on mortgages, 206
  run on the shadow banking system and, 205–206
  stock prices in the United States and, 206*f*

subprime mortgage crisis in Canada, 210–212

U.S. dollar and, 476–477

worldwide government bailouts during, 210*b*

Goal independence, 347

Gold standard, 249, 490

Goods market equilibrium

IS curve derivation and, 537

solving for, 536–537

Gordon growth model, 149–150

Governing Council of Bank of Canada, 344

Government agency securities, 32

Government budget constraint, 519–520

Government budget deficits, 100–101

Government deposit insurance, 224*b*

Government of Canada Bonds, 31

Government of Canada securities, 286

Government of Canada Treasury bills, 28–29, 404

Government purchases, 531, 535, 566, 569

Government safety net

adverse selection and, 225

asymmetric information and, 222–226

for depositors, 223

financial consolidation and, 226

forms of, 224

moral hazard and, 225

too-big-to-fail problem and, 225–226

Great Depression, 7, 199, 199*f*, 403

consumers' balance sheets and, 660*b*

credit channel importance and, 661

credit spreads, 200*f*

Great Moderation, 442

Great recession, 661–662

Greenspan, Alan, 358, 445–446

Gross domestic product (GDP), 12

aggregate price level, 20

government budget surplus or deficit as a percentage of, 1961–2014, 11*f*

growth rate, 21

inflation rate, 21

real *vs* nominal magnitudes, 19–20

Growth rate, 21

GTCs (Guaranteed Trust Certificates), 29

H

Haircuts, 205

Hedge, 252, 312

Hedge funds, 42

Hedging, 312–313

basic principle of, 312

foreign exchange risk with forward contracts, 321

foreign exchange risk with futures contracts, 321–322

with futures options, 329–330

with interest-rate forward contracts, 313–314

with interest-rate futures, 316–317

with interest-rate swaps, 333

with stock index futures, 323

Hierarchical mandates, 434

High-powered money, 368

Humphrey-Hawkins Act of 1978, 618

Hyperinflation, 54

Hyperinflations, 520

I

ICE Futures Canada, 26

Implementation lag, 616

Impossible trinity, 495

Incentive-compatible debt contract, 185

Income, 51

changes in, 109, 110*f*

Income effect, 108

Income tax considerations, 125–126

Indebtedness, 273

Inflation

activist stabilization policy and, 618–621

annual Canadian Inflation and money growth rates, 1971–2014, 518*f*

average inflation rate *vs* average rate of money growth for selected countries, 2003–2013, 9*f*

Bank of Canada's role in managing, 401*f*–402*f*

budget deficits and, 519–521

cost-push, 618–619, 619*f*, 621

demand-pull, 619–621, 620*f*

growth rate of the money supply and, 8–10

money growth and, 517*f*

quantity theory of money and, 516

unemployment and, 1970–2014, 645*f*

Inflationary monetary policy, 617–618

causes, 617–621

Inflation gap, 607

Inflation hedges, 524

Inflation rate, 8, 21

Inflation-rate targeting, 399*b*

Inflation target, 607

Inflation targeting, 435–441

advantages of, 439–440

in Canada, 436–438, 437*f*

consistency with democratic principles, 440

disadvantages of, 440–441

elements in, 435–436

flexible, 440, 443–444

implications for, 443–444

level of, 443

in New Zealand, 436, 437*f*

performance and, 440

transparency and accountability aspects, 439–440

in United Kingdom, 437*f*, 438

Information technology, role in financial innovations, 252–255, 262–263

Instrument independence, 347

Insurance Companies Act (1992), 236*t*

Interest-rate forward contracts, 313

Interest-rate futures, 315–317

hedging with, 316–317

Interest-rate risk, 82, 252, 290

duration analysis and, 303–304

gap analysis and, 303–304

management of, 302–305

Interest rates, 3

bond market and, 3

business cycles and, 103–104, 104*f*

defined, 68

demand for money and, 525

distinction between returns and, 79–83

equilibrium, 94–107

ex ante real, 83

expected, 97*t*

expected inflation and, 1953–2014, 102*f*

ex post real, 83

forecasts, 139–141

Government of Canada Treasury bills, 29

Japanese, 104–105

liquidity preference framework and, 105–107

on long-term Canada bonds, 10*f*

Interest rates, (*Cont.*)
  on long-term corporate bonds, 3
  maturity and volatility of bond
    returns, 82
  measuring, 68–79
  money (money supply) and, 10
  nominal, 83–85, 85*f*
  one-year returns on different-maturity
    10%-coupon-rate bonds for
    different, 81*t*
  overnight, 29
  real, 83–85, 85*f*
  risk structure of, 120–126
  term structure equation of, 635–636
  term structure of, 126–142
  yield curves, interpreting,
    1986–2014, 138–139
Interest-rate swaps, 332–335
  advantages of, 334
  disadvantages of, 334
  financial intermediaries in, 334–335
  hedging with, 333
Interest-rate targets, 450*f*
  supply and demand analysis, 450
Interest-rate volatility, 251–252
Intermediate target, 448
Intermediate-term debt instrument, 25
International Accounting Standards
    Board (IASB), 233*b*
International finance, 12–13
International financial regulation, 234*b*
International Financial Reporting
    Standards (IFRS), 233*b*
International financial system, 13
Internationalization of financial
    markets, 34
International Monetary Fund (IMF), 490
  as an international lender, 499–500
International reserves, 484
In the money, 325, 327
Intrinsic value, 325
Inventory investment, 532–533
Inverted yield curve, 127
Investment, meaning of, 532*b*
Investment banks, 25, 42
Investment function, 533–534
Investment intermediaries, 42
IS curve, 538*f*
  autonomous spending changes on,
    543–545
  derivation of, 537
  equilibrium and, 539
  factors that shift, 539–545, 544*t*
  financial frictions on, 545

  goods market equilibrium and, 537
  government purchases and,
    539–540, 540*f*
  intuition behind, 537
  numerical example, 537–538
  tax changes on, 541–542, 542*f*

J

Japanese banking systems, 268
Japanese monetary policy
  in 2013, 628–630, 629*f*
  lessons learnt, 664
Junk bonds, 124, 255, 260

K

Kane, Edward, 257
Keynes, John Maynard, 521, 533
Keynesians, 615
Keynesian theories of money demand,
    521–522
  precautionary motive, 521
  speculative motive, 522
  transactions motive, 521
Keynesian transmission mechanism,
    403

L

Large-denomination time deposits
    (CDs), 285
Large-scale asset purchases, 414–415
Large Value Transfer System (LVTS),
    277, 367, 391–392
  Bank of Canada's standing liquidity
    facilities and, 395
  multilateral netting and, 392
  participants, 391
  settlement of payment obligations,
    391–392
Law of one price, 463–464
Leeson, Nick, 307*b*
Legislative lag, 615
Lehman Brothers, failure of, 258*b*
Lemons problem, 176
Lender of last resort, 250, 410–411
Lending, 300
Leverage cycle, 214
Leverage ratio, 227
Liabilities, 23, 283–285
  bank capital, 285
  borrowings, 285
  demand deposits, 284
  fixed-term deposits, 284–285
  notice deposits, 284
Liability management, 290, 294–295

Libor rate, 28*b*
Life insurance companies, 41
Liquidity, 26, 54, 91, 98–99, 125
  of bonds, 97*t*
  effect, 113
  money growth and, 113
Liquidity management, 290, 294–295
Liquidity preference framework,
    105–107
Liquidity preference theory, 521, 523
Liquidity Premium (Preferred Habitat)
    Theory, 137*f*
Liquidity premium theory, 133–135,
    134*f*
Liquidity services, 36
Liquidity trap, 525
Loan commitments, 301
Loan companies, 41, 269
Loan originator, 256
Loans, 286–287
Longer-term refinancing operations,
    425
Long in a call, 324
Long in a put, 325
Long position, 312
Long-run aggregate supply curve
    (*LRAS*), 571, 572*f*, 579
  shifts in, 573–574, 574*f*
Long-term bond yields, 1978–2014,
    121*f*
Long-term customer relationships,
    300–301
Long-term debt instrument, 25
  interest-rate risk, 82
Loophole mining, 257
Losses in call option, 324–325

M

M1+, 59, 60*f*
M1++, 59, 60*f*
M2, 60*f*, 61, 63*f*
M2+, 60*f*, 61, 63*f*
M2++, 60*f*, 61, 63*f*
M3, 61–62
Maastricht Treaty, 359–361, 434
MacKay, Harold, 241
MacKay Task Force, 241
Macroeconometric models, 634
Macro hedge, 317
Macroprudential policies, 447
Macroprudential regulation, 447
Macroprudential supervision, 213–214,
    447–448
Main refinancing operations, 425

Managed float regime, 489, 497–498
Management of expectations, 418
Marginal lending facility, 425
Marginal lending rate, 425
Marginal propensity to consume, 532
Margin requirement, 320
Marked-to-market contracts, 320
Market-clearing interest rate, 94
Market-clearing price, 94
Market equilibrium, 94–95
Market for money, equilibrium in, 107*f*
Market fundamentals, 162
Mark-to-market accounting, 232, 233*b*
Maturity buckets, 303
Maturity of a debt instrument, 25
McCallum, Bennett, 637
McFadden Act of 1927, 264–265
Medium of exchange, 51–52
Meltzer, Alan, 637
Merger review policy, 277–278
Micro hedge, 317
Microprudential supervision, 213–214
Modernized Standards By-law, 240
Modigliani, Franco, 657
Monetarists, 637
Monetary aggregates, 58, 59*t*
Monetary base
    Bank of Canada's ability to control, 371
    changes in, 370
    control of, 368–370
    factors affecting, 371
    float and, 371
    government deposits and, 371
    nonborrowed, 371, 378
    open market operations and, 368–369
    shifts from deposits into currency and, 370
Monetary base, 346, 366
Monetary conditions, 401
Monetary (or currency) union, 497
Monetary policy
    autonomous easing of, 554
    balance-of-payments considerations and, 501
    Bank of Canada and, 346, 392, 395–396, 399–403, 550–551. *See also* Bank of Canada
    channel/corridor system for setting the overnight interest rate, 393, 396–398, 409–410

conduct of, 11
conventional, 403–409
demand and supply curves for reserves and, 396–398, 397*f*
effect on economy, 400–402
effects of foreign exchange market on, 500
exchange rate considerations and, 501
financial stability goal of, 433
fiscal policy *vs*, 11–12
foreign exchange market stability as goal of, 434
framework for, 390–396
Global Financial Crisis and, 442–444
high employment and output stability goal of, 432–433
implementation in the LVTS environment, 394*b*, 406
inflation targeting goal of, 435–441
interest-rate stability goal of, 433–434
lessons from, 662–663
market equilibrium and, 398
market for settlement balances and, 396–398
nominal interest rates and, 402–403
nonconventional tools, 413–426
non-Large Value Transfer System and, 392
open markets operations and, 404–406
overnight interest rate and, 393
price stability goal of, 430–432
risk-taking channel of, 447
settlement balances management and, 406–409
steady economic growth goal of, 433
stock prices and, 152
at the zero lower bound, 621–624
Monetary policy (*MP*) curve, 551, 552*f*
    autonomous monetary easing on, 554
    movements along *vs* shifts in, 554–555
    shifts in, 553–554, 553*f*
    Taylor principle, 551–552
Monetary policy theory
    aggregate demand shock, response to, 608–610

    lags and policy implementation, 615–616
    permanent supply shock, response to, 610–611
    stabilization of economic activity and inflation, 615–616
    temporary supply shock, response to, 612–614
Monetary targeting in Switzerland, 639*b*
Monetary theory, 7
    quantity, 513–519
Monetizing the debt, 520
Money
    cheques, 55–56
    commodity, 54–55
    demand for, 515
    electronic (or e-money), 56–57
    electronic payment, 56
    factors that shift demand for and supply of, 109*t*
    fiat, 55
    functions of, 51–54
    growth rates of M2, M1++, and M2++, 1969–2014, 63*f*
    interest rate and, 111–112
    meaning of, 50–51
    measuring, 57–63
    as a medium of exchange, 51–52
    need in society, 52
    payments system and, 54–57
    in a Prisoner-of-War Camp and Modern Prisons, 52*b*
    smart card, 56
    as store of value, 53–54
    as unit of account, 52–53
    velocity of, 513–515
    as a weighted aggregate, 62–63
Money centre banks, 294
Money Growth (M2++ (Gross) Annual Rate), 1976–2014, 10*f*
Money market, 26–27
    interest rates, 28*b*, 30*b*
Money market instruments, 27–29
    certificate of deposit (CD), 28–29
    commercial paper, 29
    Government of Canada Treasury bills, 28–29
    overnight funds, 29
    repurchase agreements, or repos, 29
Money market mutual funds, 42, 258
    panic of 2008, 258*b*

Money (money supply)
    aggregate price level and, in Canada,
        1968–2014, 9f
    business cycles and, 7, 8f
    defined, 7
    inflation and, 8–10
    interest rates and, 10
Money multiplier
    2007–2009 financial crisis and,
        383b
    intuition behind, 382–383
    method to derive, 380–382
    resulting value of, 382
    values for currency ratio c and excess
        reserves ratio e, 382, 384–385, 385f
Money supply, 379t
    changes in, 110–111
    currency holdings and, 379
    definitions, 60f
    factors determining, 378–379
    global financial crisis, 2007–2014
        and, 384–385, 384f
    growth, 1968–2014, 115f
    major players in, 365
    players of, 379–380
    process, 379–380
    rate of growth and, 113–115
    related to desired reserve ratio,
        379
    related to excess reserves, 379
    related to level of borrowed reserves,
        379
    related to nonborrowed monetary
        base, 378
    response over time to an increase
        in, 114f
    response to changes in factors,
        383–384
Montreal Exchange (ME), 26
Moody's Investor Service, 123
Moral hazard, 175
    collateral and, 184–185
    debt contracts and, 183
    in equity contracts, 181–182
    financial intermediaries and, 183,
        186
    government regulation and,
        182–183
    government safety net and, 225
    influence in debt markets,
        184–190
    monitoring process and, 182,
        185–186
    restrictive covenants and, 185–186

tools for solving, 187t
    tools to solve, 182–183
Moral hazard in financial markets, 38
Mortgages and mortgage-backed secu-
    rities, 30–31
Multilateral netting, 392
Multiple deposit creation, 375t
    banking system and, 374–376
    critique of model for, 378
    derivation of formula for, 376–378
    single bank and, 372–374
Municipal bonds or municipals, 32
Mutual funds, 42

N

National banks, 247b
National Financial Services OmbudSer-
    vice (NFSO), 278
Natural rate of output, 571
Natural rate of unemployment, 571
Negative aggregate demand shock,
    641–643
Negative demand shocks, 2001–2004,
    585f
Negative supply shocks, 1973–1975
    and 1978–1980, 587, 588f
Negotiable CDs, 294–295
Net export function, 535
Net exports, 531, 534–535, 566
Net stable funding ratio (NSFR), 214
Net worth, 180, 184–185
Nikkei 300 Average (Tokyo), 34
NINJA loan, 232
Nixon, Richard, 638b
Nominal anchor, 431
Nominal GDP, 19–20
Nominal GDP targeting, 649
Nominal interest rate, 83–85, 85f
    effect of changes in short-term, 403
Nonaccelerating inflation rate of unem-
    ployment (NAIRU), 453
Nonactivists, 615
Nonbank loans, 170, 171f
Nonborrowed monetary base, 372, 378
Nonborrowed reserves, 449f
Nonconventional monetary policy
    asset purchases, 626–627
    liquidity provision, 625–626
    management of expectations, 627
Nonconventional monetary policy
    tools, 413–426
    discount lending, 422–424
    forward guidance, 418–419
    large-scale asset purchases, 414–415

liquidity provision, 414
    open market operations, 421–422
    quantitative easing, 416–418
    reserve ratio, 423–424
Non-LVTS (ACSS) transactions, 392
Non-mortgage loans, 287
No policy response, 608f, 609,
    611–613, 612f
Northland Bank, 413b
Note issuance facilities (NIFs), 306
Notice deposits, 284
Notional principal, 332

O

Off-balance-sheet activities, 227
    generation of income from fees,
        305–306
    loan sales, 305
    trading activities and risk
        management techniques, 306–308
Office of the Superintendent of Finan-
    cial Institutions Act (1987), 235t
Office of the Superintendent of
    Financial Institutions Canada
    (OSFI), 43t
Official reserve transactions balance,
    488
Oil price shocks, 644
One-period valuation model, 148–149
Ontario Securities Commission
    (OSC), 44
Open interest, 318
Open market buyback operations, 346
Open market operations, 368, 425
Open market purchase, 368
Open market sale, 368
Open markets operations, 404–406
Operating band for the overnight
    interest rate, 393, 393f, 402
Operating instrument, 448–451
Opportunity cost, 106
Optimal forecast, 153
Opting-Out By-law, 238
Options, 323–332
    call, 324–325, 325f
    factors affecting prices of premiums,
        331–332
    futures, 327–332
    put, 325–326, 326f
    stock, 324–326
Originate-to-distribute business model,
    256
Out of the money, 325
Output gap, 572

Overdraft loans, 285
Overdraft privileges, 306
Overnight cash rate, 425
Overnight funds, 29
Overnight interest rate, 28*b*, 29, 392
    Bank of Canada and, 395–396, 398,
        399*f*, 411*f*
    channel/corridor system and, 393
    inflation rate, 2007–2014 and, 555*f*
    monetary policy and, 393
    operating band for, 395–396
    operating procedures limit
        fluctuations in, 398, 399*f*
    targeting on, 450*f*
    Taylor rule, 1991–2014, 453*f*
Overnight rate, 390
Over-the-counter markets, 26

P

Paper loss, 81
Partisan business cycles, 353
Payments system
    cheques, 55–56
    commodity money, 54–55
    electronic money (or e-money),
        56–57
    electronic payment, 56, 521
    fiat money, 55
    smart card, 56
Payment technology, 521
Payoff method, 223
P&C Insurance Compensation
    Corporation (PACIC), 43*t*
Pension funds, 41–42
Perfect capital mobility, 492
Permanent supply shocks, 587–590,
    589*f*
Perpetuity, 77
Perpetuity, yield to maturity on,
    77–78
Phillips, A. W., 348
Phillips curve, 348
Phillips curve theory, 453
Physical capital, 287
Plain vanilla swaps, 332
Planned expenditure, 530
Planned investment spending,
    531–534, 565
    business expectations and, 533
    real interest rate for investments as
        determinant, 533
Policy instrument, 448–451
    controllability of, 451
    criteria for choosing, 451

observability and accurate
    measurement of, 451
    predictable effect on a goal, 451
Policy rate, 392
Policy trilemma, 494–496, 495*f*
Political business cycle, 352, 638,
    638*b*
Politico-institutional approaches to
    theory of economic policy, 353*b*
Portfolio, 37
Portfolio theory of demand for money,
    523–524
Positive aggregate demand
    shock, 641
Positive supply shocks, 1995–1999,
    590, 590*f*
Potential output, 571
Preferred habitat theory, 134
Premium, 323
Prescott, Edward, 588
Present value (or present discounted
    value), 69–70
    simple, 70
    worth of a jackpot in a lottery, 71
Price level
    changes in, 110, 110*f*
    quantity theory of money and,
        515–516
Price-level effect, 108
Price-level targeting, 399*b*
Price shocks, 572
Price stability, 361, 403
    Bank of Canada and, 350
    Bank of Japan and, 361
    European Central Bank (ECB) and,
        360–361
    hierarchical *vs* dual mandates,
        433–434
    as monetary policy goal, 350,
        430–432, 434–435
    nominal anchor and, 431
    time-inconsistency problem and,
        431–432
Primary dealers, 404
Primary market, 25–26
Prime rate, 28*b*, 400
Principal-agent problem, 181–182, 306
    tools for solving, 187*t*
    tools to solve, 182–183
Printing money, 520
Private pension funds, 41–42
Producer price index (PPI), 566*b*
Profitability of a call option, 324–325,
    325*f*

Property and Casualty (P&C)
    Insurance Companies, 41
Provincial bonds or provincials, 32
Provincial Notes Act, 1866, 248
Provincial securities and exchange
    commissions, 43*t*
Prudential supervision, 228
Public interest impact assessment
    (PIIA), 277
Public interest view, 354
Purchase and assumption method, 223
Put option, 325–326
    maturity of, 326
    payoff function from, 326
    profitability of, 325–326, 326*f*
Put premium, 325

Q

Quantitative easing, 384–385,
    416–418
    asset purchases and, 626–627
    in channel/corridor system, 416*b*,
        417*f*
    nonconventional monetary policy
        and, 624–628
Quantity theory of money
    demand for money and, 515
    equation of exchange, 514
    equation of exchange to, 515
    inflation and, 516
    in long run, 516–518
    price level and, 515–516
    in short run, 518–519
    testing of, 516–519
    velocity of money and, 513–515
Québec Deposit Insurance Board
    (QDIB), 43*t*, 237
Quotas, 466

R

Random-walk stock prices, case of,
    158–159
Rate of capital gain, 80
Rate of return, 79
Rational expectations, 153
    in financial markets, 156–162
Rational expectations revolution, 634
Rational expectations theory, Lucas
    and, 635
Reagan, Ronald, 358
Real business cycle theory, 588
Real exchange rate, 465
    net exports and, 536–537
Real GDP, 19–20

Real interest rate, 83–85, 85*f*
Real money balances, 522
Real terms, 84
Receiver general auctions,
    407–408
Recessions, 7
Recognition lag, 615
Redeposits, 406
Reference rate, 392
Registered bonds, 31
Regulation Q, 257
Regulatory agencies of the Canadian
    financial system, 43*t*
Regulatory arbitrage, 228
Repurchase agreements, or repos, 29,
    205
Required reserve ratio, 423–424
Reserve currency, 490
Reserves, 285–286
Residual claimant, 25, 148
Resolution authority, 215
Restrictive covenants, 173
Retirement funds, 41
Returns, 79
    on assets (ROA), 296
    on a bond, 80
    demand curve for bond, 92
    distinction between interest rate and,
        79–83
    on equity (ROE), 296
    expected, 98
    maturity and volatility of bond, 82
    uncertainty of an asset's, 90
Revaluation, 492
Reverse repos, 404
Reverses, 404
Reverse transactions, 425
Revolving underwriting facilities
    (RUFs), 306
Risk, 36, 90–91, 98
    of bonds, 97*t*
    default, 120–124
Risk-averse person, 91
Risk lover, 91
Risk management, assessment of,
    230–231
Risk management techniques,
    306–308
Risk of default, 120–124
Risk preferrer, 91
Risk premium, 121, 125
Risk sharing, 36–37
Rogoff, Kenneth, 649
Rules, 636

case for, 637–638
constant-money-growth-rate rule,
    637

S

Sale and Repurchase Agreements
    (SRAs), 404–406
    advantages of, 406
Sarbanes-Oxley Act, 232
Savings and Credit Union Act of the
    Province of Québec (1988), 236*t*
Schedule I, Schedule II and Schedule III
    banks, 261–262, 274
Schwartz, Anna, *A Monetary History of
    the United States*, 637
Secondary market, 25–26
Secondary reserves, 286
Secured debt, 173
Securities, 286
Securities and Exchange Commission
    (SEC), 324
Securitization, 255–257, 261
Security, 3
Segmented markets theory,
    132–133
Seigniorage, 249
Seignorage, 507
Self-correcting mechanism, 581
    at zero lower bound, 623–624, 624*f*
Settlement balances, 285, 367
Settlement balances management,
    406–409
    drawdown/redeposit mechanism,
        406
    receiver general auctions, 407–408
    target level of settlement balances,
        408–409
Shadow banking system, 251–261
    securitization and, 255–257
    working of, 256
Shiller, Robert, 163
Shirakawa, Masaaki, 628
Short in a call, 324
Short in a put, 325
Short position, 312
Short-run aggregate supply curve,
    571–573, 572*f*, 576*t*
    cost-push shocks, 572
    expected inflation, 571, 575, 575*f*
    inflation-shock, 575–577, 575*f*
    output gap, 572, 576–577, 577*f*
    price shocks, 572
    price stickiness and, 573
    supply shocks, 572

Short-run inflation stabilization,
    609–610, 609*f*, 613–614, 613*f*
Short-run output stabilization, 614,
    614*f*
Short sales/short selling, 164
Short-term debt instrument, 25
Simple deposit multiplier, 376
Simple loan, 71–72
    yield to maturity on, 72–73
Small-denomination time
    deposits, 285
Smart card, 56
Sovereign loans, 273
Special Purchase and Resale
    Agreements (special PRAs or
    SPRAs), 404
    advantages of, 406
    mechanics of, 405*f*
Special purpose vehicle (SPV), 202*b*
Speculative attack on a currency,
    492–493
Spot exchange rate, 462
Spot rates, 140
Spot transactions, 462
Stagflation, 586
Standardized gap analysis, 304
Standard & Poor's Corporation
    (S&P), 123
Standing lending facility, 410
Standing liquidity facilities, 395
State banks, 247*b*
State-owned banks, 189
Sterilized foreign exchange
    intervention, 486–488
Stock, 170, 171*f*
Stockholders, 147
Stock index futures contracts, 322
    hedging with, 323
Stock market, 3–5
    lemons problem in, 176
    S&P/TSX Composite Index,
        1956–2014, 5*f*
Stock market crashes, 163
Stock market risk, 322
Stock options, 324–326
Stocks, 30
Stock valuation models
    generalized dividend valuation
        model, 149
    Gordon growth model,
        149–150
    one-period valuation model,
        148–149
"Stop-go" policy, 501

Stored-value card, 56
Stress testing, 308
Stress tests, 231
Strike price, 323, 331
Structured credit products, 201
Subprime mortgage crisis in United
    States and Canada, 210–213, 232
Subprime mortgage market, 256–257
Super senior tranches, 202b
Supply curve for bond, 93–94
Supply curve for bonds, shifts in,
    99–101, 100f
Supply curve for domestic assets, 467
Supply of reserves, 397–398
Supply shocks, 572
Swaps
    credit, 336
    credit default, 336–337
    currency, 332
    with the exchange fund account,
        408
    interest-rate, 332–335
    plain vanilla, 332
Swaptions, 332
Sweep account, 259
Systemically important financial
    institutions (SIFIs), 215–216

T

T-account, 287–289, 368, 370,
    372–377
Target financing rate, 425
Tariffs, 466
Taxable bond, 126
Taxes, 535–536, 569
    changes on *IS* curve, 541–542,
        542f
Tax-exempt bond, 126
Taylor, John, 452
Taylor principle, 452
Taylor rule, 452–454
Tech-stock bubble, 445
Temporary supply shocks, 584–587,
    586f
Term deposit receipts (term notes), 28
Term Purchase and Resale Agreements
    (term PRAs), 414
Term repos, 414
Term securities lending, 414
Term structure of interest rates,
    126–142
    evidence on, 136–137
    expectations theory, 128–132
    interest-rate forecasts and, 139–141

liquidity premium theory, 133–135,
    134f
segmented markets theory, 132–133
Theory of bureaucratic behaviour,
    354–355
Theory of efficient capital markets, 155
Theory of portfolio choice, 91
Theory of purchasing power parity
    (PPP), 465–466
Theory of rational expectations,
    152–155
    adaptive expectations, 153
    forecast errors of expectations, 155
    formal statement of, 154
    implications of, 155
    optimal forecast, 153
    rationale for, 154–155
Time deposits, 285
Time-inconsistency problem, 431–432,
    435, 636–637
    inflation targeting and, 439
Tobin, James, 522
Too-big-to-fail problem
    financial regulation and, 216–217
    government safety net and, 225–226
Toronto Stock Exchange (TSX), 25–26
Towers, Graham, 348
Trade balance, 488
Trade-off between safety and returns to
    equity holders, 297
Trading activities, management of,
    306–308
Trading at par, 325
Tranches, 202b
Transaction costs, 36, 51
    economies of scale and, 174
    expertise and, 174
    financial intermediaries and, 174
    influence on financial structure,
        173–174
Transmission mechanisms of monetary
    policy
    balance sheet channel and, 658–659
    bank lending channel and, 658
    cash flow channel and, 659
    exchange rate effects on net exports
        and, 655
    household liquidity effects and,
        660–661
    interest-rate channels and, 654–655
    Tobin's *q* theory and, 655–657
    unanticipated price level channel
        and, 659–660
    wealth effect and, 657–658

Transparency, 439
Treasury bill rate, 28b
Treasury bills, 3
Troubled Asset Relief Program (TARP),
    209
Trust, 41
Trust and Loan Companies Act (1992),
    236t
Trust and Mortgage Loan Companies
    (TMLs), 45
Trustees, 268–269
TSX Venture Exchange, 25

U

U.K. Financial Crisis, 2007–2009, 593,
    594f
Uncertainty, financial crises and, 197
Uncertainty of an asset's returns, 90
Underwrite, 42
Underwriting securities, 25
Unemployment
    aggregate output and, 566b
    inflation and, 1970–2014, 645f
    natural rate of, 571
    rate, 7
Unexploited profit opportunities, 157
United States
    adoption of an inflation targeting
        approach to monetary policy, 403
    vs Canadian banking system,
        263–266
    central bank of, 343b
    current account deficit, 489b
    disintermediation process, 261
    Employment Act of 1946, 618
    Financial Crisis, 2007–2009 and,
        591–593
    financial crisis of 2007–2009 and
        money multiplier, 382b
    financial futures contracts in, 318t,
        319
    Humphrey-Hawkins Act of 1978,
        618
    insurance companies in, 278
    largest banks, 264t
    market for reserves in, 420–421
    negative supply and demand shocks
        in Financial Crisis, 2007–2009,
        592f
    Obama fiscal stimulus package,
        616b
    purchasing power parity (PPP), 466f
    separation of banking and other
        financial services, 267–268

Unit of account, 52–53
Universal banking, 267
Unsecured debt, 173
Unsterilized foreign exchange
        intervention, 485–486, 487*f*
U.S. Capital Markets, 33*b*
U.S. Generally Accepted Accounting
        Principles (GAAP), 233*b*
U.S. Treasury bills, real and nominal
        interest rates on, 84, 85*f*

V

Value-at-risk (VaR) calculations, 231
Vault cash, 285, 288
Velocity of money, 513–515
Venture capital firm, 183
Vietnam War Buildup, 1964–1969,
        540–541, 541*f*
Virtual banks ("clicks"), 254, 254*b*
Volcker, Paul, 215
Volcker rule, 215

W

Wealth, 51, 90, 96–98, 97*t*
Wells Fargo, 277
Western Financial Group, 263
Wheaton Group, 263
World Bank, 490
World stock markets, 34
World Trade Organization (WTO), 490
World War I, 54, 271, 490
World War II, 52, 198, 201, 208, 582,
        653

Y

Yield curves, 127, 128*b*
        as a forecasting tool for inflation and
                the business cycle, 138*b*
        interpreting, 1986–2014, 138–139
        liquidity premium theory and,
                133–135, 134*f*
        market's expectations of future
                short-term interest rates and, 137*f*

Yield to maturity, 72
        calculated for several bond
                prices, 76
        on coupon bond, 74–77
        on a 10%-coupon-rate bond
                maturing in 10 years, 76*t*
        on discount bond, 78–79
        on fixed-payment loan, 73–74
        on a perpetuity, 77–78
        on simple loan, 72–73

Z

Zero-coupon bond, 72, 82
Zero lower bound
        aggregate demand curves with,
                621–623, 622*f*
        monetary policy at, 621–624
        self-correcting mechanism at,
                623–624, 624*f*
Zero-lower-bound problem, 413
Zimbabwean hyperinflation, 520–521